MARKETING
An Introduction

sixth edition

GARY ARMSTRONG
University of North Carolina

PHILIP KOTLER
Northwestern University

Prentice Hall
Upper Saddle River, New Jersey 07458

Library of Congress Cataloging-in-Publication Data

Armstrong, Gary.
   Marketing: an introduction / Gary Armstrong, Philip Kotler.--6th ed.
     p. cm.
   Includes bibliographical references and index.
   ISBN 0-13-035133-4
   1. Marketing.   I. Kotler, Philip.   II. Title.
HF5415.K625 2002
658.8--dc21
2001050074

Senior Editor: Bruce Kaplan
Editor-in-Chief: Jeff Shelstad
Assistant Editor: Melissa Pellerano
Editorial Assistant: Danielle Serra
Media Project Manager: Anthony Palmiotto
Marketing Manager: Michelle O'Brien
Marketing Assistant: Christine Genneken
Managing Editor (Production): Judy Leale
Production Editor: Keri Jean
Production Assistant: Dianne Falcone
Permissions Coordinator: Suzanne Grappi
Associate Director, Manufacturing: Vincent Scelta
Production Manager: Arnold Vila
Manufacturing Buyer: Arnold Vila
Design Manager: Pat Smythe
Designer: Mike Fruhbeis
Cover Photo: Steve Lewis
Manager, Print Production: Christy Mahon
Composition: Progressive Information Technologies
Full-Service Project Management: Colleen Franciscus
Printer/Binder: R. R. Donnelley

Credits and acknowledgments borrowed from other sources and reproduced, with permission, in this textbook appear on page CR1.

Pearson Education LTD.
Pearson Education Australia PTY, Limited
Pearson Education Singapore, Pte. Ltd
Pearson Education North Asia Ltd
Pearson Education, Canada, Ltd
Pearson Educación de Mexico, S.A. de C.V.
Pearson Education–Japan
Pearson Education Malaysia, Pte. Ltd

10 9 8 7 6 5 4
ISBN 0-13-035133-4

To Kathy, K.C., and Mandy;
Nancy, Amy, Melissa, and Jessica

Brief Contents

Contents

About the Authors

As a team, Gary Armstrong and Philip Kotler provide a blend of skills uniquely suited to writing an introductory marketing text. Professor Armstrong is an award-winning teacher of undergraduate business students. Professor Kotler is one of the world's leading authorities on marketing. Together they make the complex world of marketing practical, approachable, and enjoyable.

Gary Armstrong is Crist W. Blackwell Distinguished Professor of Undergraduate Education in the Kenan-Flagler Business School at the University of North Carolina at Chapel Hill. He holds undergraduate and masters degrees in business from Wayne State University in Detroit, and he received his Ph.D. in marketing from Northwestern University. Dr. Armstrong has contributed numerous articles to leading business journals. As a consultant and researcher, he has worked with many companies on marketing research, sales management, and marketing strategy. But Professor Armstrong's first love is teaching. His Blackwell Distinguished Professorship is the only permanent endowed professor-  ship for distinguished undergraduate teaching at the University of North Carolina at Chapel Hill. He has been very active in the teaching and administration of Kenan-Flagler's undergraduate program. His administrative posts include Chair of the Marketing Faculty, Associate Director of the Undergraduate Business Program, Director of the Business Honors Program, and others. He works closely with business student groups and has received several campus-wide and Business School teaching awards. He is the only repeat recipient of school's highly regarded Award for Excellence in Undergraduate Teaching, which he has received three times.

Philip Kotler is S. C. Johnson & Son Distinguished Professor of International Marketing at the Kellogg Graduate School of Management, Northwestern University. He received his master's degree at the University of Chicago and his Ph.D. at M.I.T., both in economics. Dr. Kotler is author of *Marketing Management: Analysis, Planning, Implementation, and Control* (Prentice Hall), now in its eleventh edition and the world's most widely used marketing textbook in graduate schools of business. He has authored seventeen other successful books and has written over 100 articles in leading journals. He is the only three-time winner of the coveted

Alpha Kappa Psi award for the best annual article in the *Journal of Marketing*. Dr. Kotler's numerous major honors include the *Paul D. Converse Award* given by the American Marketing Association to honor "outstanding contributions to science in marketing" and the *Stuart Henderson Britt Award* as Marketer of the Year. He was named the first recipient of two major awards: the *Distinguished Marketing Educator of the Year Award* given by the American Marketing Association and the *Philip Kotler Award for Excellence in Health Care Marketing* presented by the Academy for Health Care Services Marketing. He has also received the *Charles Coolidge Parlin Award*, which each year honors an outstanding leader in the field of marketing. In 1995, he received the *Marketing Educator of the Year Award* from Sales and Marketing Executives International. Dr. Kotler has served as chairman of the College on Marketing of the Institute of Management Sciences (TIMS) and a director of the American Marketing Association. He has received honorary doctoral degrees from Stockholm University, the University of Zurich, Athens University of Economics and Business, DePaul University, the Cracow School of Business and Economics, Groupe H.E.C. in Paris, and the University of Economics and Business Administration in Vienna. He has consulted with many major U.S. and foreign companies in the areas of marketing strategy and planning, marketing organization, and international marketing. He has traveled extensively throughout Europe, Asia, and South America, advising and lecturing companies about global marketing opportunities.

Preface

Marketing: An Introduction, Sixth Edition, guides new marketing students down the intriguing, discovery-laden road to learning marketing. Its goal is to help students master the basic concepts and practices of modern marketing in an enjoyable and practical way. Achieving this goal involves a constant search for the best balance among the "three pillars" that support the text—theories and concepts, practices and applications, and pedagogy. *Marketing: An Introduction* provides the most authoritative and up-to-date coverage of marketing theory and concepts, brings the theory to life with real examples of marketing practices, and presents both theory and practice in a way that makes them easy and enjoyable to learn.

In the sixth edition of *Marketing: An Introduction,* we continue to shift the balance between theory, practice, and pedagogy more towards pedagogy—towards providing an effective *teaching and learning tool.* This exciting teaching and learning thrust comes to life through a short, lively design that features a set of 'Road to Marketing" learning aids that begins students on their marketing journey. To help students learn, link, and apply important marketing concepts more effectively, *Marketing: An Introduction,* is filled with "road map" learning tools throughout each chapter. These pedagogical guides help students by:

◆ challenging them to stop and think at important junctures in their journey
◆ previewing chapter material
◆ reviewing and linking key chapter concepts
◆ providing practical Internet and marketing-application exercises through which students apply newly-learned marketing concepts in realistic situations.

The result is an enhanced learning experience for the student.

Starting Down the Road to Marketing

Marketing is the business function that identifies customer needs and wants; determines which target markets the organization can serve best; and designs appropriate products, services, and programs to serve these markets. However, marketing is much more than just an isolated business function—it is a philosophy that guides the

→ 94 PART II ASSESSING OPPORTUNITIES IN A DYNAMIC MARKETING ENVIRONMENT

Like many other dot-coms, Pets.com never did figure out how to make money on the Web. Following the "dot-com meltdown," the once-bold e-tailer retired its popular Sock Puppet spokesdog and quietly closed its cyberdoors.

entire organization. The goal of marketing is to create customer satisfaction profitably by building value-laden relationships with important customers. The marketing department cannot accomplish this goal by itself. To provide superior value to customers, it must team up closely with other departments in the company and partner with other organizations throughout its entire value-delivery system. Thus, marketing calls upon everyone

Table 1-1 Marketing Connections in Transition	
The Old Marketing Thinking	The New Marketing Thinking
Connections with Customers	
Be sales and product centered	Be market and customer centered
Practice mass marketing	Target selected market segments or individuals
Focus on products and sales	Focus on customer satisfaction and value
Make sales to customers	Develop customer relationships
Get new customers	Keep old customers
Grow share of market	Grow share of customer
Serve any customer	Serve profitable customers, "fire" losing ones
Communicate through mass media	Connect with customers directly
Make standardized products	Develop customized products
Connections with Marketing Partners	
Leave customer satisfaction and value to sales and marketing	Enlist all departments in the cause of customer satisfaction and value
Go it alone	Partner with other firms
Connections with the World Around Us	

in the organization to "think customer" and to do all they can to help create and deliver superior customer value and satisfaction.

Marketing is all around us, and we all need to know something about it. Marketing is used not only by manufacturing companies, wholesalers, and retailers, but by all kinds of individuals and organizations. Lawyers, accountants, and doctors use marketing to manage demand for their services. So do hospitals, museums, and performing arts groups. No politician can get the needed votes, and no resort the needed tourists, without developing and carrying out marketing plans.

People throughout these organizations need to know how to define and segment a market and how to position themselves strongly by developing need satisfying products and services for chosen target segments. They must know how to price their offerings to make them attractive and affordable, and how to choose and manage intermediaries to make their products available to customers. They need to know how to advertise and promote products so customers will know about them and want them. Clearly, marketers need a broad range of skills in order to sense, serve, and satisfy consumer needs.

Students also need to know marketing in their roles as consumers and citizens. Someone is always trying to sell us something, so we need to recognize the methods they use. And when students enter the job market, they must do "marketing research" to find the best opportunities and the best ways to "market themselves" to prospective employers. Many will start their careers with marketing jobs in sales, retail, advertisement, research, or one of a dozen other marketing areas.

Marketing: An Introduction—*A New Learning Approach*

Our goal with the sixth edition of *Marketing: An Introduction* is to create an even more effective teaching and learning environment. Most students learning marketing want a broad picture of marketing's basics. They want to know about important marketing principles and concepts and how these concepts are applied in actual marketing management practice. However, they don't want to drown in a sea of details, or to be overwhelmed by marketing's nuances and complexities. Instead, they want a text that guides them effectively and efficiently down the road to learning marketing in an easy to grasp, lively, and enjoyable way.

Marketing: An Introduction, Sixth Edition, serves all of these important needs of beginning marketing students. The book is complete, covering all of the important principles and concepts that the marketer and consumer need to know. Moreover, it takes a practical, marketing-management approach—concepts are applied through countless examples of situations in which well known and little known companies assess and solve their marketing problems.

More than ever before, however, the sixth edition of *Marketing: An Introduction* makes the teaching and learning of marketing easier, more effective, and more enjoyable. The "Road to Marketing" aids help students to learn, link, and apply important concepts. The Sixth Edition's length makes it more manageable for beginning marketing students to cover the subject during a given quarter or semester. Its approachable writing style and level are well suited to the beginning marketing student. A livelier design, the abundant use of illustrations, and new Marketing at Work exhibits and video cases help bring life to the marketing journey.

Marketing: An Introduction, Sixth Edition, tells the stories that reveal the drama of modern marketing:

- ◆ **Ritz-Carlton's** zeal for taking care of customers
- ◆ **Home Depot's** penchant for taking care of those who take care of customers
- ◆ **Amazon.com's** pioneering struggle to become the Wal-Mart of the Internet
- ◆ **Charles Schwab Corporation's** transformation from a traditional "brick-and-mortar" marketer to a full-fledged, industry-leading "click-and-mortar" marketer
- ◆ **Harley-Davison's** success in selling to "Rubbies" (rich urban bikers) rather than rebels
- ◆ **Caterpillar's** and its dealers' promise to customers of "buy the iron, get the company"
- ◆ **Microsoft's** passion for innovation and its quest for "the Next Big Thing"
- ◆ **Dell Computer's** stunning direct selling formula, which has made Michael Dell one of the world's richest people
- ◆ **General Electric's** massive e-purchasing network which links more that 100,000 trading partners in 58 countries, generating $1 trillion worth of goods and services purchases annually
- ◆ **Coca-Cola's** international marketing prowess, which has made Coke not only as American as baseball and apple pie but also as English as Big Ben and afternoon tea, as Chinese as ping pong and the Great Wall, as Japanese as Sumo and sushi, and as German as bratwurst and beer.

These and dozens of other examples and illustrations throughout each chapter reinforce key concepts and bring marketing to life.

Changes in the Sixth Edition

The sixth edition of *Marketing: An Introduction* offers important improvements in content, organization, style, and pedagogy.

Content and Organization

As we enter the twenty-first century, the major marketing developments can be summed up in a single theme: *connectedness*. Rapidly changing computer, information, communication, and transportation technologies are making the world a smaller place. Now, more than ever before, we are all connected to each other and to things near and far in the world around us. Moreover, we are connecting in new and different ways. The sixth edition of *Marketing: An Introduction* has been thoroughly revised to reflect the major trends and forces that are impacting marketing in this new, connected millennium. It offers important new thinking and expanded coverage on:

Customers: connecting more selectively, more directly, and for life:

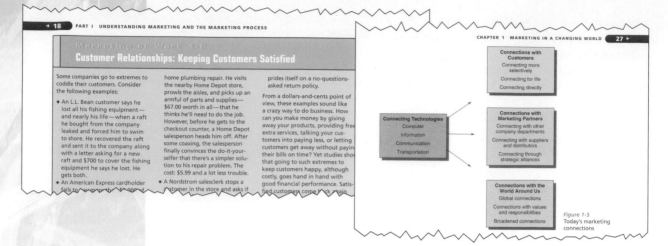

Marketing at Work 1-3

Customer Relationships: Keeping Customers Satisfied

Some companies go to extremes to coddle their customers. Consider the following examples:

♦ An L.L. Bean customer says he lost all his fishing equipment—and nearly his life—when a raft he bought from the company leaked and forced him to swim to shore. He recovered the raft and sent it to the company along with a letter asking for a new raft and $700 to cover the fishing equipment he says he lost. He gets both.

♦ An American Express cardholder fails to~~~~~~~~~~~~~~~~~~

home plumbing repair. He visits the nearby Home Depot store, prowls the aisles, and picks up an armful of parts and supplies—$67.00 worth in all—that he thinks he'll need to do the job. However, before he gets to the checkout counter, a Home Depot salesperson heads him off. After some coaxing, the salesperson finally convinces the do-it-your-selfer that there's a simpler solution to his repair problem. The cost: $5.99 and a lot less trouble.

♦ A Nordstrom salesclerk stops a customer in the store and asks if

prides itself on a no-questions-asked return policy.

From a dollars-and-cents point of view, these examples sound like a crazy way to do business. How can you make money by giving away your products, providing free extra services, talking your customers into paying less, or letting customers get away without paying their bills on time? Yet studies show that going to such extremes to keep customers happy, although costly, goes hand in hand with good financial performance. Satisfied customers come back again

Figure 1-5
Today's marketing connections

♦ **Relationship marketing**—developing *profitable customers* and capturing customer lifetime value by building value-laden customer relationships.

♦ **Delivering superior customer value, satisfaction, and quality**—attracting, keeping, and growing customers by developing market-centered strategies and "taking care of the customer."

♦ **Connecting technologies**—employing the Internet and other information, computer, communications, and transportation technologies to connect directly with customers and to shape marketing offers tailored to their needs.

Marketing partners: connecting inside and outside the company to jointly bring more value to customers:

♦ **The company value chain**—connecting inside the company to create cross-functional, customer-focused teamwork, and integrated action.

♦ **Value-delivery networks**—connecting with partners outside the company to create effective supply chains.

The world around us:

♦ **Global marketing**—connecting globally with customers and marketing partners. The sixth edition offers integrated chapter-by-chapter coverage plus a full chapter focusing on global marketing considerations.

♦ **Marketing ethics, environmentalism, and social responsibility**—reexamining connections with social values and responsibilities. This edition offers integrated chapter-by-chapter coverage plus a full chapter on social responsibility and marketing ethics.

♦ **Broadened connections**—the increasing adoption of marketing by nonprofit and government organizations.

A substantially revised Chapter 1 introduces and integrates these important themes to set the stage at the beginning of the course. The chapter concludes with an innovative new section on the challenges and opportunities marketers will face in the new, connected millennium. A new Chapter 3, Marketing in the Internet Age, assesses the impact of the Internet and other technologies on marketing. Recent technological advances, including the explosion of the Internet, have created an Internet age, which is having a dramatic impact on both buyers and the marketers who serve them. To thrive in this new Internet age—even to survive—marketers must rethink their strategies and practices. This new chapter introduces marketing in the Internet age and the exciting new strategies and tactics that firms are applying in order to prosper in today's high-tech environment. The chapter explores major forces shaping the Internet age; major e-commerce and e-marketing developments in B2C, B2B, C2C, and C2B domains; and strategies and tactics for setting up a successful e-commerce presence.

Additionally, each chapter of the sixth edition of *Marketing: An Introduction* provides fresh new material on everything from Internet research and the virtual reality displays that test new products to the high-tech approaches of the e-commerce marketers who sell them. Students will learn about the wonders of new marketing technologies, from the Internet, database marketing, customer relationship marketing, and Web-based marketing research to mass customization, Internet business-to-business purchasing networks, Web-based personal selling, and technological advances in marketing logistics. New and revised Traveling the Net sections at the end of each chapter provide exercises that guide students through the fascinating world of marketing and the Internet.

Click-and-mortar: Staples' Web site now supplements its brick-and-mortar operations. After two years on the Net, Staples captured online sales of more than $500 million.

Additional new material has been added on a wide range of subjects, including customer management and assessing customer value, brand equity and brand management, value propositions and positioning, experiences marketing, the new direct marketing model, "markets-of-one" marketing, internal and online marketing databases, Internet and online marketing research, cross-functional partnering and supply chain management, business-to-business marketing on the Internet, value pricing, integrated marketing communications, diversity, environmental sustainability, international marketing strategy, and much more.

The Sixth Edition contains many other important changes. New chapter-opening examples and Marketing at Work exhibits illustrate important new concepts with actual business applications. Countless new examples have been added within the running text. All tables, figures, examples, and references throughout the text have been thoroughly updated. The sixth edition of *Marketing: An Introduction* contains numerous new photos and advertisements that illustrate key points and make the text more effective and appealing. The new video cases that accompany the text help to bring the real world directly into the classroom.

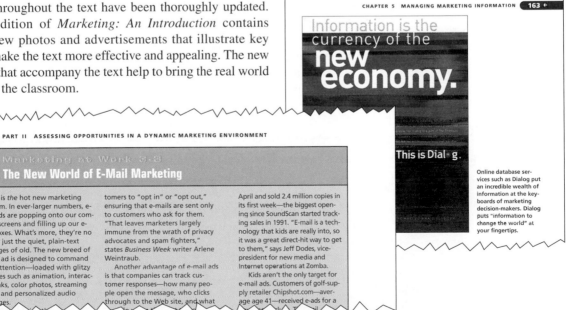

Information is the currency of the **new economy.**

This is Dial g.

Online database services such as Dialog put an incredible wealth of information at the keyboards of marketing decision-makers. Dialog puts "information to change the world" at your fingertips.

Marketing at Work 5-3
The New World of E-Mail Marketing

E-mail is *the* hot new marketing medium. In ever-larger numbers, e-mail ads are popping onto our computer screens and filling up our e-mailboxes. What's more, they're no longer just the quiet, plain-text messages of old. The new breed of e-mail ad is designed to command your attention—loaded with glitzy features such as animation, interactive links, color photos, streaming video, and personalized audio messages.

tomers to "opt in" or "opt out," ensuring that e-mails are sent only to customers who ask for them. "That leaves marketers largely immune from the wrath of privacy advocates and spam fighters," states *Business Week* writer Arlene Weintraub.

Another advantage of e-mail ads is that companies can track customer responses—how many people open the message, who clicks through to the Web site, and what

April and sold 2.4 million copies in its first week—the biggest opening since SoundScan started tracking sales in 1991. "E-mail is a technology that kids are really into, so it was a great direct-hit way to get to them," says Jeff Dodes, vice-president for new media and Internet operations at Zomba.

Kids aren't the only target for e-mail ads. Customers of golf-supply retailer Chipshot.com—average age 41—received e-ads for a

Learning Aids

The following "Road to Marketing" learning devices dispersed at critical points throughout the chapter help students to learn, link, and apply major concepts as they progress through their journey toward learning marketing.

Road Map

Previewing the Concepts: A section at the beginning of each chapter briefly previews chapter concepts, links them with previous chapter concepts, outlines chapter learning objectives, and introduces the chapter-opening vignette.

> **ROAD MAP:**
> **Previewing the Concepts**
>
> In the last chapter, you learned about the complex and changing marketing environment. In this chapter, we'll look at how companies develop and manage information about important elements of the environment—about their customers, competitors, products, and marketing programs. We'll examine marketing information systems designed to give managers the right information, in the right form, at the right time to help them make better marketing decisions. We'll also take a close look at the marketing research process and at some special marketing research considerations. To succeed in today's marketplace, companies must know how to manage mountains of marketing information effectively.
>
> ▶ After reading this chapter, you should be able to
>
> 1. explain the importance of information to the company
> 2. define the marketing information system and discuss its parts
> 3. outline the steps in the marketing research process
> 4. explain how companies analyze and distribute marketing information

larger market for companies such as Peapod (www.peapod.com), which teams up with large supermarket chains in many heavily populated areas to offer online grocery shopping and home delivery. They also represent a growing market for travel, sports, and other leisure-oriented products and services (see Marketing at Work 4-2).[25]

Speed Bump

Linking the Concepts: "Concept checks" inserted at key points in each chapter as "speed bumps" slow students down to be certain they are grasping and applying key concepts and linkages. Each speed bump consists of a brief statement and a few concept and application questions.

> ### Linking the Concepts
>
> Pull over here for a moment and think about how deeply these demographic factors impact all of us and, as a result, marketers' strategies.
>
> ◆ Apply these demographic developments to your own life. Think of some specific examples of how the changing demographic factors affect you and your buying behavior.
> ◆ Identify a specific company that has done a good job of reacting to the shifting demographic environment—generational segments (baby boomers, GenXers, or Generation Y), the changing American family, and increased diversity. Compare this company to one that's done a poor job.

Economic Environment

Rest Stop

Reviewing the Concepts: A summary of key concepts at the end of each chapter reviews chapter concepts and the chapter objectives.

> **STOP** **Rest Stop: Reviewing the Concepts**
>
> In the last chapter, this chapter, and the next two chapters, you'll examine the environments of marketing and how companies analyze these environments to discover opportunities and create effective marketing strategies. Companies must constantly watch and adapt to the *marketing environment* in order to seek opportunities and ward off threats. The marketing environment comprises all the actors and forces influencing the company's ability to transact business effectively with its target market.
>
> **1. Describe the environmental forces that affect the**
>
> combination of good quality and service at a fair price. The distribution of income also is shifting. The rich have grown richer, the middle class has shrunk, and the poor have remained poor, leading to a two-tiered market. Many companies now tailor their marketing offers to two different markets—the affluent and the less affluent.
>
> **3. Identify the major trends in the firm's natural and technological environments.**
>
> The *natural environment* shows three major trends: shortages of certain raw materials, higher pollution levels, and

3. It has been said that the single most important demographic trend in the United States is the changing age structure of the population. Characterize the differences between Baby Boomers, Generation X, and Generation Y. Using a personal computer for your example, indicate how this product should be sold to someone in each of the three aforementioned generations. Lastly, let us call the next generation on the horizon Generation D (the

ment perspective take positive proactive stances when confronted with problems rather than merely reacting to adversity. After reading about the controversies presented in Marketing at Work 4-4, assume your company is under attack by Mr. Richard Hatch. What would you do to meet the situation with proactive measures? What could you do to minimize negative publicity and consumer response? Explain your plan.

Mastering Marketing

The multimedia tool that means business. This technologically innovative CD-ROM uses video and interactive exercises to actively engage students in learning core marketing concepts.

> **[marketing]** **Mastering Marketing**
>
> Understanding one's environment is critical for any marketing manager. An environmental management perspective can literally make or break a company. Examine each of the environments and their respective publics faced by CanGo. List the critical factors in each of these environ- ments that must be proactively met by its marketing plan to be implemented ments examined, which one do you to the firm's long-term success? Ex

CD-ROM INCLUDED

sites engage consumers in an interaction that will move them closer to a direct purchase or other marketing outcome. Beyond simply setting up a site, companies must

Despite these challenges, most companies are rapidly integrating online marketing into their marketing strategies and mixes.

 ## Navigating the Key Terms

For a detailed analysis of the meaning and importance of each of the following key terms, visit our Web page at www.prenhall.com/kotler.

B2B (business-to-business) e-commerce
B2C (business-to-business) e-commerce
C2B (consumer-to-business)
Demography

C2C (consumer-to-consumer) e-commerce
Click-and-mortar companies
Click-only companies
Corporate Web site
Customerization
E-business
E-commerce
E-marketing
Extranet
Marketing environment

Intranet
Marketing Web site
Online advertising
Open trading networks
Private trading networks
Viral marketing
Web communities
Webcasting

Navigating the Key Terms
A list of the chapter's key terms and an accompanying Web site provide a detailed analysis of the meaning and importance of each term.

 ## Travel Log

The following concept checks and discussion questions will help you to keep track of and apply the concepts you've studied in this chapter.

Concept Checks
Fill in the blanks, then look for the correct answers.
1. A company's _____ consists of the actors and forces outside marketing that affect marketing management's ability to develop and maintain successful relationships with its target customers.

5. One distinguishing characteristic of Generation Y is their utter fluency and comfort with computer, digital, and Internet technology. For this reason, this generation has also been called _____.
6. One of _____ laws is that as family income rises, the percentage spent on food declines.
7. Marketers should be aware of several trends in the natural environment. Chief among these are the _____, _____, and _____.

Travel Log
Concept checks and discussion questions help students to keep trackof and apply what they've studied in the chapter.

 ## Traveling on the Net

Point of Interest. Placing Ads and Promotions Online
Move over Barnes and Noble, a new (yet old) player is about to take some of your bookselling business away. Borders (www.borders.com) booksellers is tired of finishing last when it comes to innovations on the Web. The Borders team is betting that its HTML-based e-mail campaign will be just what the doctor ordered to cure its many ills. With only $27 million in Internet sales last year, Borders certainly has room for improvement. However, its new tactic of adorning HTML-based e-mail messages with colorful graphics, images, and Web links means that Borders is delivering a message that looks and acts like a Web page. Ad...

Campus Books (www.campusbooks.com), Books-a-million (www.bamm.com), eCampus (www.ecampus.com), and Half Price (www.halfpricebooks.com) sites?
2. What online advertising techniques described in the chapter were used on the Borders Web site? On the competitive Web sites?
3. Considering the challenges facing e-marketing in the future, what do you think of using the "cookie" technique to collect data on customers? Under what circumstances would the approach be acceptable to you? When would it be unacceptable?
4. If the Borders approach is successful in getting con-

Traveling the Net
Application exercises and questions guide students through the fascinating real world of marketing and the Internet.

 ## MAP—Marketing Applications

MAP Stop 3
One of the oldest forms of marketing and promotion is word-of-mouth. In the new Internet age, word-of-mouth has become known as viral marketing. Viral marketing is really quite simple—tell a friend to tell a friend that something is hot and worth noticing. This has worked successfully with the Doom video game, *The Blair Witch Project* movie, Harry Potter books, Razor scooters, and Chrysler's PT Cruiser automobile, to name only a few. To create "buzz," the viral marketer targets a group of carefully chosen trend leaders in a community who are likely to use phone or Internet communication to spread the

viral marketers have learned it is this: start consumers talking and you will start selling.

Thinking Like a Marketing Manger
1. What applications can you think of for viral or buzz marketing on the Internet?
2. List three products that you have heard about from friends. Describe what you were told, how this matched ad claims, what action you took because of the information, and how likely you were to buy the products.
3. Assume you are the marketing manager for a new

MAP—Marketing Applications
Interesting case histories, real-life situations, and timely descriptions of business situations put students in the place of a marketing manager so they can make real marketing decisions.

Additional Learning Aids

Chapter-Opening Vignettes

Each chapter starts with a dramatic marketing story that introduces the chapter material and arouses student interest.

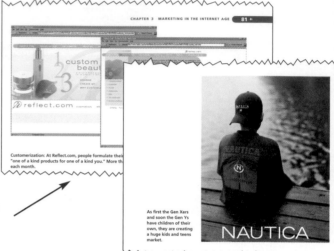

Full color figures...
vivid photographs, advertisements, and illustrations.
Throughout every chapter, key concepts and applications are illustrated with strong, full-color visual materials.

Marketing at Work Exhibits

Additional examples and important information are highlighted in Marketing at Work exhibits throughout the text.

Video Cases

Every chapter is supplemented with a written case that also has a video component that brings the material to life.

Glossary

At the end of the book, an extensive glossary provides quick reference to the key terms found in the book.

Appendixes

Two appendixes, "Marketing Arithmetic" and "Careers in Marketing," provide additional, practical information for students.

Indexes

Author, company and subject indexes reference all information and examples in the book.

A Total Teaching and Learning Package

A successful marketing course requires more than a well written book. Today's classroom requires a dedicated teacher and a fully-integrated teaching system. A total package of teaching and learning supplements extends this edition's emphasis on effective teaching and learning. The following aids support *Marketing: An Introduction.*

For the Instructor

- ◆ *On Location—Custom Case Videos for Marketing.* A new set of custom videos accompanies the sixth edition, together with new video cases. The new video cases include companies such as Exclusively Weddings (segmentation and targeting), Clarins (distribution), and American Standard (integrated marketing communications).

- ◆ *Instructor's Resource Manual.* This teaching guide contains chapter-by-chapter teaching outlines and answers to end-of-chapter problems and applications. Throughout, this guide places special emphasis on media supplements such as PowerPoint slides and Web resources. Then guide also includes Internet exercises and class projects.

- ◆ *Test Item File.* Acclaimed by users, this test bank has been carefully revised and tested. The test bank includes up to 85 multiple choice and true/false questions per chapter, together with essay and application questions. All questions are graded for difficulty and include section references.

- ◆ *Windows Test Manager.* The PH Test Manager offers electronic test generation and answer keys. All questions can be edited and scrambled to create fully customized tests.

- ◆ *Color Transparencies.* PowerPoint slides and text figures are available as acetate transparencies and as electronic files on disk.

- ◆ *PowerPoint Slides.* Up to 25 slides per chapter, this set of lecture aids follows the chapter outline and also offers additional material from outside the text. These files are also included on the CW Web site.

- ◆ *Instructor's Resource CD.* This handy resource provides one source for all your supplement needs. The CD contains the entire Instructor's Resource Manual, Test Item File, and PowerPoint Slides.

- ◆ *CW (Prentice Hall's Learning on the Internet Partnership).* This Web resource provides professors with a customized course Web site that features a complete array of teaching material including downloadable versions of the Instructor's Resource Manual and PowerPoint slides, plus great resources such as current events and Internet exercises. Also included is an interactive and exciting online Student Study Guide. Try the syllabus builder to plan your course. Go to www.prenhall.com/kotler to preview this resource.

For the Student

Marketing: An Introduction, Sixth Edition, can be packaged with any of the following student media supplements:

◆ **Mastering Marketing CD-ROM from the Mastering Business Series.** Included with every copy of this text. This technologically innovative CD-ROM uses video and interactive exercises to actively engage students in learning core marketing concepts. *Mastering Marketing* is tied directly to the text through sections at the end of every chapter.

◆ **Marketing Plan Pro CD-ROM.** Available at a modest extra charge in a package, this highly-acclaimed program enables students to build a marketing plan from scratch. Marketing Plan Pro also includes sample marketing plans. It is the best commercially available marketing plan software.

Acknowledgements

No book is the work only of its authors. We owe much to the pioneers of marketing who first identified its major issues and developed its concepts and techniques. Our thanks also go to our colleagues at the Kenan-Flagler Business School, University of North Carolina at Chapel Hill, and at the J. L. Kellogg Graduate School of Management, Northwestern University, for ideas and suggestions. We owe special thanks to Martha McEnally of the University of North Carolina, Greensboro for her valuable work in preparing high-quality video cases. We thank John R. Brooks, Jr. for his innovative and tireless work in preparing the Instructor's Resource Manual and the Test Bank, and to Kelley Brooks for preparing the PowerPoint slides. Finally, we thank Mandy Armstrong for able research assistance.

Many reviewers at other colleges and universities provided valuable comments and suggestions for this edition. We are indebted to the following colleagues who provided careful reviews for this edition:

Ron Lennon, *Barry University*

Alan Brokaw, *Michigan Technological University*

Mernoush Banton, *University of Miami*

Gordon Snider, *California Poly-Technical School of San Luis Obispo*

Karen Stone, *Southern New Hampshire University*

Martha Leham, *Diablo Valley College*

Thomas Drake, *University of Miami*

Rebecca Ratner, *University of North Carolina, Chapel Hill*

Steve Hoeffler, *University of North Carolina, Chapel Hill*

We also want to thank the people who so carefully reviewed previous editions:

Gemmy Allen, *Mountain View College*

Abi Almeer, *Nova University*

Arvid Anderson, *University of North Carolina, Wilmington*

Arnold Bornfriend, *Worcester State College*

Donald Boyer, *Jefferson College*

Alejandro Camacho, *University of Georgia*

William Carner, *University of Texas, Austin*

Gerald Cavallo, *Fairfield University*

Lucette Comer, *Florida International University*
Ron Cooley, *South Suburban College*
Michael Conard, *Teikyo Post University*
June Cotte, *University of Connecticut*
Ronald Cutter, *Southwest Missouri State University*
John de Young, *Cumberland County College*
Lee Dickson, *Florida International University*
Mike Dotson, *Appalachian State University*
Peter Doukas, *Westchester Community College*
David Forlani, *University of North Florida*
Jack Forrest, *Middle Tennessee State University*
John Gauthier, *Gateway Technical Institute*
Eugene Gilbert, *California State University, Sacramento*
Diana Grewel, *University of Miami*
Esther Headley, *Wichita State University*
Sandra Heusinkveld, *Normandale Community College*
James Jeck, *North Carolina State University*
Eileen Keller, *Kent State University*
James Kennedy, *Navarro College*
Eric Kulp, *Middlesex County College*
Ed Laube, *Macomb Community College*
Gregory Lincoln, *Westchester Community College*
John Lloyd, *Monroe Community College*
Dorothy Maas, *Delaware County Community College*
Ajay Manrai, *University of Delaware*
Lalita Manrai, *University of Delaware*
James McAlexander, *Oregon State University*
Donald McBane, *Clemson University*
Debbora Meflin-Bullock, *California State Polytechnic University*
Randall Mertz, *Mesa Community College*
Herbert Miller, *University of Texas, Austin*
Veronica Miller, *Mt. St. Mary's College*
Joan Mizis, *St. Louis Community College*
Melissa Moore, *University of Connecticut*
Robert Moore, *University of Connecticut*
William Morgenroth, *University of South Carolina, Columbia*
Linda Moroble, *Dallas County Community College*
Sandra Moulton, *Technical College of Alamance*
Jim Muney, *Valdosta State*
Lee Neuman, *Bucks County Community College*
Dave Olsen, *North Hennepin Community College*
Thomas Packzkowski, *Cayuga Community College*
George Paltz, *Erie Community College*
Tammy Pappas, *Eastern Michigan University*
Alison Pittman, *Brevard Community College*

Lana Podolak, *Community College of Beaver County*
Joel Porrish, *Springfield College*
Robert L. Powell, *Gloucester County College*
Eric Pratt, *New Mexico State University*
Robert Ross, *Wichita State University*
Andre San Augustine, *University of Arizona*
Dwight Scherban, *Central Connecticut College*
Eberhard Scheuing, *St. John's University*
Pamela Schindler, *Wittenberg University*
Raymond Schwartz, *Montclair State College*
Raj Sethuraman, *University of Iowa*
Reshima H. Shah, *University of Pittsburgh*
Jack Sheeks, *Broward Community College*
Herbert Sherman, *Long Island University, Southhampton*
Dee Smith, *Lansing Community College*
Jim Spiers, *Arizona State University*
Peter Stone, *Spartanburg Technical College*
Ira Teich, *Long Island University*
Donna Tillman, *California State Polytechnic University*
Andrea Weeks, *Fashion Institute of Design and Merchandising*
Summer White, *Massachusetts Bay Community College*
Bill Worley, *Allan Hancock College.*

We also owe a great deal to the people at Prentice Hall who helped develop this book.
Marketing Editor Bruce Kaplan provided caring and valuable advice and assistance
through several phases of this revision. We also owe much thanks to Whitney Blake, who
supplied many good ideas and substantial support and encouragement on this and previous
editions. Anthony Palmiotto was instrumental in setting up the Web site, Melissa Pellerano
helped organize and coordinate the supplements effort, and Michelle OBrien developed a
strong marketing program. Keri Jean, Suzanne Grappi, Judy Leale, Mike Fruhbeis, and
Arnold Vila helped shepherd the project smoothly through production.

Finally, we owe many thanks to our families—Kathy, K.C., and Mandy Armstrong;
and Nancy, Amy, Melissa, and Jessica Kotler—for their constant support and encouragement. To them, we dedicate this book.

Gary Armstrong
Philip Kotler

Marketing in a Changing World: Creating Customer Value and Satisfaction

ROAD MAP:
Previewing the Concepts

Fasten your seat belt! You're about to begin an exciting journey toward learning about marketing. To start you off in the right direction, we'll first define marketing and its key concepts. Then, you'll visit the various philosophies that guide marketing management and the challenges marketing faces as we move into the new millennium. The goal of marketing is to create profitable customer relationships by delivering superior value to customers. Understanding these basic concepts, and forming your own ideas about what they really mean to you, will give you a solid foundation for all that follows.

▶ **After studying this chapter, you should be able to**

1. **define what marketing is and discuss its core concepts**
2. **explain the relationships between customer value, satisfaction, and quality**
3. **define marketing management and understand how marketers manage demand and build profitable customer relationships**
4. **compare the five marketing management philosophies**
5. **analyze the major challenges facing marketers heading into the new "connected" millennium**

Our first stop: Amazon.com. In only a few years, Amazon.com has blossomed from an obscure dot-com upstart into one of the best-known names on the Internet. In the process, it has forever changed the practice of marketing. It pioneered the use of Web technology to build strong, one-to-one customer relationships based on creating genuine customer value. The only problem: Amazon has yet to prove that it can turn a long-term profit. As you read on, ask yourself: Will Amazon.com eventually become the Wal-Mart of the Internet? Or will it become just another dot-com has-been?

Chances are, when you think of shopping on the Web, you think first of Amazon.com. Amazon.com first opened its virtual doors in mid-July 1995, selling books out of founder Jeff Bezos's garage in suburban Seattle. It still sells books—by the millions. But it now sells products in a dozen other categories as well: from music, videos, consumer electronics, and computers to tools and hardware, kitchen and housewares, and toys and baby products. "We have the Earth's Biggest Selection," declares the company's Web site.

In only a few short years, upstart Amazon.com has become the best-known name on the Net. In the process, it is also rewriting the rules of marketing. "Amazon.com is blazing a trail in the world of commerce where no merchant has gone before," asserts business analyst Robert Hof. "By pioneering—and darn near perfecting—the art of selling online, . . . [Amazon.com has caused] a wrenching shift to a new way of doing business." Its most ardent fans view Amazon.com as *the* model for New Economy businesses of the twenty-first century. If any dot-com can make it, they believe, Amazon.com will.

But not everything is clicking smoothly for Amazon.com. If you believe the skeptics, the company may already be out of business by the time you read this story. Attracting customers and sales hasn't been a problem. In just the past two years, Amazon.com's customer base has grown more than sevenfold to 32 million customers in more than 160 countries. Sales have rocketed from a modest $15 million in 1996 to more than $2.8 billion today. So, what's the problem? Profits—or a lack thereof. Amazon.com's losses have mounted almost as fast as its sales, reaching more than $1.1 billion in 2000, or 40 percent of sales. Amazon.com turned its first profits in 2002. However, doubters say that Amazon.com's Web-only model can never be truly profitable. Supporters, on the other hand, attribute initial losses to high start-up costs. After all, they note, the company has started what amounts to several new businesses within only a few years.

No matter what your view on its future, there's little doubt that Amazon.com is an outstanding marketing company. To its core, the company is relentlessly customer-driven. "The thing that drives everything is creating genuine value for customers," says founder Jeff Bezos. "Nothing happens without that." A few years back, when asked when Amazon.com would start putting profits first rather than growth, Bezos replied, "Customers come first. If you focus on what customers want and build a relationship, they will allow you to make money."

The relationship with customers is the key to the company's future. Anyone at Amazon.com will tell you that the company wants to do much more than just sell books or DVDs or digital cameras. It wants to deliver a special *experience* to every customer. "The customer experience really matters," says Bezos. "We've focused on just having a better store, where it's easier to shop, where you can learn more about the products, where you have a bigger selection, and where you have the lowest prices. You combine all of that stuff together and people say, 'Hey, these guys really get it.'"

And they do get it. Most Amazon.com regulars feel a surprisingly strong and personal relationship with the company, especially given the almost complete lack of actual human interaction. Analyst Geoffrey Colvin comments:

I travel a lot and talk with all kinds of people, and I'm struck by how many of them speak passionately about their retail experience with Amazon.com. . . . How can people get so cranked up about an experience in which they don't see, touch, or hear another soul? The answer is that Amazon.com creates a more human relationship than most people realize. . . . The experience has been crafted so carefully that most of us actually enjoy it. It results from many people at headquarters obsessing over what customers want in a fundamentally new kind of relationship, the online experience.

Amazon.com really does obsess over making each customer's experience uniquely personal. For example, the site's "Recommendations" feature prepares personalized product recommendations, and its "New for You" feature links customers through to their own personalized home pages. Amazon.com was first to use "collaborative filtering" technology, which sifts through each customer's past purchases and the purchasing patterns of customers with similar profiles to come up with personalized site content. "We want Amazon.com to be the right store for you as an individual," says Bezos. "If we have 30 million customers, we should have 30 million stores."

Visitors to Amazon.com's Web site receive a unique blend of benefits: huge selection, good value, convenience, and what Amazon.com vice president Jason Kilar calls "discovery." In books alone, for example, Amazon.com offers an easily searchable virtual selection of more than 3 million titles, 15 times more than any physical bookstore. Good value comes in the form of reasonable prices, with everyday discounts off suggested retail. And at Amazon.com, it's irresistibly convenient to buy. With Amazon.com's one-click checkout feature, you can log on, find what you want, and order with a single mouse click, all in less time than it takes to find a parking space at the local mall.

But it's the "discovery" factor that makes the Amazon.com experience really special. Once on the Web site, you're compelled to stay for a while—looking, learning, and discovering. Amazon.com has become a kind of online *community,* in which customers can browse for products, research purchase alternatives, share opinions and reviews with other visitors, and chat online with authors and experts.

In addition to the ability to develop personalized relationships with millions of customers, selling on the Internet gives Amazon.com some real advantages over brick-and-mortar rivals. By selling direct, Amazon.com reaps significant cost advantages. It avoids the huge costs of building and operating stores and carrying large inventories. And whereas traditional retailers must continually build new stores to grow revenues, Amazon.com can boost sales by simply attracting more customers to its single existing Web store.

Selling on the Web also presents serious challenges. Although it doesn't face store costs, Amazon.com has had to make large initial investments in such things as computer systems, distribution centers, and customer acquisition. Perhaps more important, many people still like shopping in a real store, where they can rub elbows with other shoppers, touch and try out the merchandise, buy goods on the spot, and easily return purchases that don't work out.

Many experts predict that the future will belong to retailers who offer *both* "clicks" and "bricks." In fact, almost 60 percent of consumer online revenues are now captured by companies that sell both online and through traditional stores. In response to these new realities, Amazon.com is already partnering with real-world retailers. It recently teamed up with Toys 'R' Us to create a co-branded toys and games Web site. Toys 'R' Us handles purchasing and inventory; Amazon.com oversees the customer experience—maintaining the Web site, filling orders, and managing customer service. Amazon.com is also exploring a similar partnership with brick-and-mortar giant Wal-Mart.

So, what do you think? Does Amazon.com really create superior value for customers? Will it eventually become the Wal-Mart of the Web? Or will it end up as just another dot-com has-been? Here's one analyst's conclusion:

I'm betting on Amazon.com. . . . In the old days, only small outfits could keep track of customers: your local tailor, the local barber, the butcher at the grocery store. [Lately,] we've bemoaned the loss of that personal touch. The Net can bring it back. Amazon.com [understands] that the real opportunity is in using the technology to build long-term relationships. . . . What Amazon.com has done is invent and implement a model for interacting with millions of customers, one at a time. Old-line companies can't do that. . . . Amazon.com's technology gives me exactly what I want, in an extraordinarily responsive way.

Whatever its fate, Amazon.com has forever changed the face of marketing. "No matter what becomes of Amazon," says the analyst, "it has taught us something new."[1]

Today's successful companies at all levels have one thing in common: Like Amazon.com, they are strongly customer focused and heavily committed to marketing. These companies share an absolute dedication to understanding and satisfying the needs of customers in well-defined target markets. They motivate everyone in the organization to produce superior value for their customers, leading to high levels of customer satisfaction. As cofounder Bernie Marcus of Home Depot asserts, "All of our people understand what the Holy Grail is. It's not the bottom line. It's an almost blind, passionate commitment to taking care of customers."

What Is Marketing?

Marketing, more than any other business function, deals with customers. Creating customer value and satisfaction is at the very heart of modern marketing thinking and practice. Although we will explore more detailed definitions of marketing later in this chapter, perhaps the simplest definition is this one: Marketing is the delivery of customer satisfaction at a profit. The twofold goal of marketing is to attract new customers by promising superior value and to keep and grow current customers by delivering satisfaction.

Wal-Mart has become the world's largest retailer by delivering on its promise, "Always low prices—always." Dell leads the personal computer industry by consistently making good on its promise to "be direct," making it easy for customers to custom design their own computers and have them delivered quickly to their doorsteps or desktops. Ritz-Carlton promises—and delivers—truly "memorable experiences" for its hotel guests. AT&T says, "It's all within your reach—one connection: across town, across the country, across the world." And Coca-Cola, long the world's leading soft drink, delivers on the simple but enduring promise that with Coca-Cola, "life tastes good." These and other highly successful companies know that if they take care of their customers, market share and profits will follow.

Sound marketing is critical to the success of every organization—large or small, for-profit or not-for-profit, domestic or global. Large for-profit firms such as Microsoft, Sony, Wal-Mart, IBM, Charles Schwab, and Marriott use marketing. But so do not-for-profit organizations such as colleges, hospitals, museums, symphony orchestras, and even churches. Moreover, marketing is practiced not only in the United States but also in the rest of the world. Most countries in North and South America, Western Europe, and Asia have well-developed marketing systems. Even in Eastern Europe and other parts of the world where marketing long had a bad name, dramatic political and social changes have created new opportunities for marketing. Business and government leaders in most of these nations are eager to learn everything they can about modern marketing practices.

You already know a lot about marketing—it's all around you. You see the results of marketing in the abundance of products in your nearby shopping mall. You see marketing in the advertisements that fill your TV, spice up your magazines, stuff your mailbox, or enliven your Web pages. At home, at school, where you work, and where you play, you are exposed to marketing in almost everything you do. Yet, there is much more to marketing than meets the consumer's casual eye. Behind it all is a massive network of people and activities competing for your attention and purchasing dollars.

This book will give you a more complete and formal introduction to the basic concepts and practices of today's marketing. In this chapter, we begin by defining marketing and its core concepts, describing the major philosophies of marketing thinking and practice, and discussing some of the major new challenges that marketers face as we whirl into the new millennium.

Marketing Defined

What does the term *marketing* mean? Many people think of marketing only as selling and advertising. And no wonder—every day we are bombarded with television commercials, newspaper ads, direct-mail campaigns, sales calls, and Internet pitches. However, selling and advertising are only the tip of the marketing iceberg. Although they are important, they are only two of many marketing functions and are often not the most important ones.

Today, marketing must be understood not in the old sense of making a sale—"telling and selling"—but in the new sense of *satisfying customer needs.* If the marketer does a good job of understanding consumer needs; develops products that provide superior value; and prices, distributes, and promotes them effectively, these products will sell very easily. Thus, selling and advertising are only part of a larger "marketing mix"—a set of marketing tools that work together to affect the marketplace.

We define **marketing** as a social and managerial process whereby individuals and groups obtain what they need and want through creating and exchanging products and value with others.[2] To explain this definition, we will examine the following important terms: *needs, wants,* and *demands; products, services,* and *experiences; value, satisfaction,* and *quality; exchange, transactions,* and *relationships;* and *markets.* Figure 1-1 shows that these core marketing concepts are linked, with each concept building on the one before it.

Marketing
A social and managerial process by which individuals and groups obtain what they need and want through creating and exchanging products and values with others.

Needs, Wants, and Demands

The most basic concept underlying marketing is that of human needs. Human **needs** are states of felt deprivation. They include basic *physical* needs for food, clothing, warmth, and safety; *social* needs for belonging and affection; and *individual* needs for knowledge and self-expression. These needs were not invented by marketers; they are a basic part of the human makeup.

Need
A state of felt deprivation.

Wants are the form human needs take as they are shaped by culture and individual personality. An American *needs* food but *wants* a hamburger, French fries, and a soft drink. A person in Mauritius *needs* food but *wants* a mango, rice, lentils, and beans. Wants are shaped by one's society and are described in terms of objects that will satisfy needs.

Want
The form taken by a human need as shaped by culture and individual personality.

People have almost unlimited wants but limited resources. Thus, they want to choose products that provide the most value and satisfaction for their money. When backed by buying power, wants become **demands.** Consumers view products as bundles of benefits and choose products that give them the best bundle for their money. A Honda Civic means basic transportation, affordable price, and fuel economy; a Lexus means comfort, luxury, and status. Given their wants and resources, people demand products with the benefits that add up to the most satisfaction.

Demands
Human wants that are backed by buying power.

Outstanding marketing companies go to great lengths to learn about and understand their customers' needs, wants, and demands. They conduct consumer research about consumer likes and dislikes. They analyze customer inquiry, warranty, and service data. They

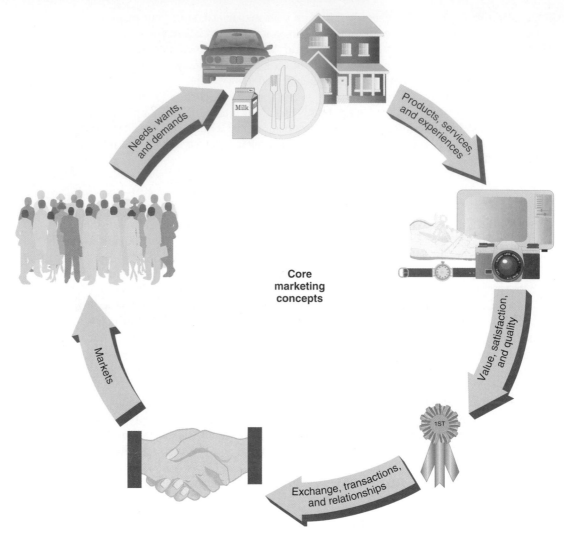

Figure 1-1
Core marketing concepts

observe customers using their own and competing products and train salespeople to be on the lookout for unfulfilled customer needs.

In these outstanding companies, people at all levels—including top management—stay close to customers. For example, top executives from Wal-Mart spend two days each week visiting stores and mingling with customers. At Disney World, at least once in his or her career, each manager spends a day touring the park in a Mickey, Minnie, Goofy, or other character costume. Moreover, all Disney World managers spend a week each year on the front line—taking tickets, selling popcorn, or loading and unloading rides. For years, Home Depot's Bernie Marcus spent 25 percent of his time out in the stores "pawing and pressing the flesh," meeting with customers and trying to understand them better. And at Marriott, to stay in touch with customers, Chairman of the Board and President Bill Marriott personally reads some 10 percent of the 8,000 letters and 2 percent of the 750,000 guest comment cards submitted by customers each year. Understanding customer needs, wants, and demands in detail provides important input for designing marketing strategies.

Products, Services, and Experiences

People satisfy their needs and wants with products and services. A **product** is anything that can be offered to a market to satisfy a need or want. The concept of *product* is not limited to physical objects—anything capable of satisfying a need can be called a product. In addition to tangible goods, products include **services,** which are activities or benefits offered for sale that are essentially intangible and do not result in the ownership of anything. Examples include banking, airline, hotel, tax preparation, and home repair services.

More broadly defined, products also include other entities such as *experiences, persons, places, organizations, information,* and *ideas.* For example, by orchestrating several services and goods, companies can create, stage, and market brand experiences. Disneyland is an experience; so is a ride on a Harley-Davidson, a visit to NikeTown or Barnes & Noble, or surfing Sony's playstation.com Web site. In fact, as products and services increasingly become commodities, experiences have emerged for many firms as the next step in differentiating the company's offer. "What consumers really want is products, communications, and marketing campaigns that dazzle their senses, touch their hearts, and

Product
Anything that can be offered to a market for attention, acquisition, use, or consumption that might satisfy a want or need. It includes physical objects, services, persons, places, organizations, and ideas.

Service
Any activity or benefit that one party can offer to another that is essentially intangible and does not result in the ownership of anything.

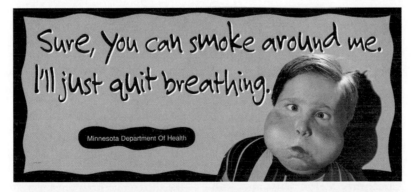

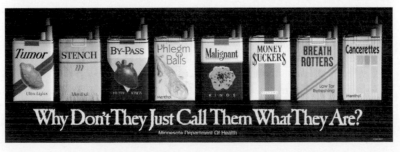

Products do not have to be physical objects. Here, the "product" is an idea: "Smoking bothers others."

stimulate their minds," declares one expert. "They want products, communications, and marketing campaigns to deliver an experience."[3]

In recent years, for example, a rash of theme stores and restaurants have burst onto the scene offering much more than just merchandise or food:

> Stores such as Niketown, Cabella's, and Recreational Equipment Incorporated draw consumers in by offering fun activities, fascinating displays, and promotional events (sometimes labeled "shoppertainment" or "entertailing"). At theme restaurants such as the Hard Rock Cafe, Planet Hollywood, or the House of Blues, the food is just a prop for what's known as "eatertainment." [One] entrepreneur in Israel has entered the experience economy with the opening of Cafe Ke'ilu, which roughly translates as "Cafe Make Believe." Manager Nir Caspi told a reporter that people come to cafes to be seen and to meet people, not for the food; Cafe Ke'ilu pursues that observation to its logical conclusion. The establishment serves its customers empty plates and mugs and charges guests $3 during the week and $6 on weekends for the social experience.[4]

Thus, the term *product* includes more than just the physical properties of a good or service. It also includes a brand's *meaning* to consumers. Coca-Cola means much more to consumers than just something to drink—it has become an American icon with a rich tradition and meaning. Nike is more than just shoes, it's what the shoes do for you and where they take you. The familiar Nike swoosh stands for high sports performance, famous athletes, and a "Just Do It!" attitude (see Marketing at Work 1-1).

The term *product* also includes more than just goods or services. Consumers decide which events to experience, which entertainers to watch on television, which places to visit on vacation, which organizations to support through contributions, and which ideas to adopt. To the consumer, these are all products. If at times the term *product* does not seem to fit, we could substitute other terms such as *satisfier, resource,* or *marketing offer.*

Many sellers make the mistake of paying more attention to the specific products they offer than to the benefits produced by these products. They see themselves as selling a product rather than providing a solution to a need. A manufacturer of quarter-inch drill bits may think that the customer needs a drill bit, but what the customer *really* needs is a quarter-inch hole. These sellers may suffer from "marketing myopia"—they are so taken with their products that they focus only on existing wants and lose sight of underlying customer needs.[5] They forget that a product is only a tool to solve a consumer problem. These sellers will have trouble if a new product comes along that serves the customer's need better or less expensively. The customer with the same *need* will *want* the new product.

Value, Satisfaction, and Quality

Consumers usually face a broad array of products and services that might satisfy a given need. How do they choose among these many products and services? Consumers make buying choices based on their perceptions of the value that various products and services deliver.

Customer value
The difference between the values the customer gains from owning and using a product and the costs of obtaining the product.

Customer Value **Customer value** is the difference between the values the customer gains from owning and using a product and the costs of obtaining the product. For example, FedEx customers gain a number of benefits. The most obvious are fast and reliable package delivery. However, when using FedEx, customers also may receive some status and image values. Using FedEx usually makes both the package sender and the receiver feel more important. When deciding whether to send a package via FedEx, customers will weigh these and other values against the money, effort, and psychic costs of using the service. Moreover, they will compare the value of using FedEx against the value of using other shippers—UPS, Airborne, the U.S. Postal Service—and select the one that gives them the greatest delivered value.

Marketing at Work 1-1

Nike: It's Not So Much the Shoes But Where They Take You!

The "swoosh"—it's everywhere! Just for fun, try counting the swooshes whenever you pick up the sports pages or watch a pickup basketball game or tune into a televised golf match. Nike has built the ubiquitous swoosh into one of the best-known brand symbols on the planet. And the swoosh has come to stand for all of the things that Nike means to those who wear it all around the world.

The power of its brand and logo speaks loudly of Nike's superb marketing skills. The company's strategy of building superior products around popular athletes and its classic "Just Do It!" ad campaign have forever changed the face of sports marketing. Nike spends hundreds of millions of dollars each year on big-name endorsements, splashy promotional events, and lots of attention-getting ads. Over the years, Nike has associated itself with some of the biggest names in sports, from Michael Jordan, Tiger Woods, Pete Sampras, and Mike Schmidt to Mia Hamm, Lance Armstrong, and Ronaldo. No matter what your sport, chances are good that one of your favorite athletes wears the Nike swoosh.

Nike knows, however, that good marketing is more than promotional hype and promises—it means consistently building strong relationships with customers based on real value. Nike's initial success resulted from the technical superiority of its running and basketball shoes, pitched to serious athletes who were frustrated by the lack of innovation in athletic equipment. To this day, Nike leads the industry in research and development spending.

But Nike gives its customers more than just good athletic gear. As the company notes on its Web page (www.nike.com), "Nike has always known the truth—it's not so much the shoes but where they take you." Beyond shoes, apparel, and equipment, Nike markets a way of life, a sports culture, a "just do it" attitude. That's the real meaning of Nike to its customers. Says Phil Knight, Nike's founder and chief executive, "Basically, our culture and our style is to be a rebel." The company was built on a genuine passion for sports, a maverick disregard for convention, hard work, and serious sports performance. Anyone at Nike will tell you, Nike is athletes, athletes are sports, *Nike is sports*.

The strong relationships between customers and its brand paid off handsomely for Nike. Over the decade ending in 1997, Nike's revenues grew at an incredible annual rate of 21 percent; annual return to investors averaged 47 percent. In the mid-1990s, Nike leveraged its brand strength, moving aggressively into new product categories, sports, and regions of the world. Its sports apparel business grew explosively; the company slapped its familiar swoosh logo on everything from sunglasses and soccer balls to batting gloves and hockey sticks. Nike invaded a dozen new sports, including baseball, golf, ice and street hockey, in-line skating, wall climbing, and hiking.

In the late 1990s, however, Nike stumbled and its sales slipped. Many factors contributed to the company's sales woes. The whole industry suffered a setback, as "brown shoe" craze for hiking and outdoor shoe styles ate into the athletic sneaker business. Competition improved: A revitalized Adidas saw its U.S. sales surge as Nike's sales declined. To make matters worse, college students on many

The power of the Nike swoosh speaks loudly of Nike's superb marketing skills. The ever-present symbol has come to stand for all that Nike means to those who wear it all around the world.

campuses protested against Nike for its alleged exploitation of child labor in Asia and its commercialization of sports.

But Nike's biggest obstacle may be its own incredible success—it may have overswooshed America. The brand appeared to suffer from big-brand backlash, and the swoosh become too common to be cool. According to one analyst, "When Tiger Woods made his debut in Nike gear, there were so many logos on him that he looked as if he'd got caught in an embroidering machine." A Nike executive admits, "There has been a little bit of backlash about the number of swooshes that are out there." Moreover, with sales of more than $9 billion, Nike has moved from maverick to mainstream. Today, rooting for Nike is like rooting for Microsoft.

To address these problems, Nike has returned to the basics—focusing on innovation, developing new product lines, creating subbrands, and focusing once again on product performance. The sports giant is also trimming its costs, including substantial cuts in its formerly lavish advertising budget.

Despite the recent ups and downs, Nike still flat out dominates the athletic shoe market. It captures a 42 percent market share in the United States and more than 25 percent abroad. Competitors can hope that Nike's slump will continue, but few are counting on it. Most can only sit back and marvel at Nike's marketing prowess. One market analyst comments, "Nike remains one of the great American brands, as well known around the world as Coke or McDonald's."

Still, to stay on top, Nike will have to find new ways to deliver the kind of quality, innovation, and value that built the brand so powerfully in the past. No longer the rebellious, anti-establishment upstart, huge Nike must continually reassess and rekindle its meaning to customers. Says Knight, "Now that we've [grown so large], there's a fine line between being a rebel and being a bully. [To our customers,] we have to be beautiful as well as big."

Sources: Quotes from Bill Saporito, "Can Nike Get Unstuck?" *Time,* March 30, 1998, pp. 48–53; Jolie Solomon, "When Cool Goes Cold," *Newsweek,* March 30, 1998, pp. 36–37; Jerry Edgerton, "Can Nike Still Play Above the Rim?" *Money,* May 1999, p. 48; and Louise Lee, "Can Nike Still Do It?" *Business Week,* February 21, 2000, pp. 121–128. Also see "Four Athletes to Be Honored as Nike World Headquarters Expansion Nears Completion of Second Phase," Nike press release, accessed online at www.nikebiz.com, June 12, 2001; and Douglas Robson, "Just Do . . . Something," *Business Week,* July 2, 2001, pp. 70–71.

Customers often do not judge product values and costs accurately or objectively. They act on *perceived* value. For example, does FedEx really provide faster, more reliable delivery? If so, is this better service worth the higher prices FedEx charges? The U.S. Postal Service argues that its express service is comparable, and its prices are much lower. However, judging by market share, most consumers perceive otherwise. Each day, they entrust FedEx with 50 percent more next-day air packages than they give to nearest competitor UPS. The Postal Service's challenge is to change these customer value perceptions.[6]

Customer satisfaction
The extent to which a product's perceived performance in delivering value matches a buyer's expectations.

Customer Satisfaction Customer satisfaction depends on a product's perceived performance in delivering value relative to a buyer's expectations. If the product's performance falls short of the customer's expectations, the buyer is dissatisfied. If performance matches expectations, the buyer is satisfied. If performance exceeds expectations, the buyer is delighted. Outstanding marketing companies go out of their way to keep their customers satisfied. Satisfied customers make repeat purchases, and they tell others about their good experiences with the product. The key is to match customer expectations with company performance. Smart companies aim to *delight* customers by promising only what they can deliver, then delivering *more* than they promise.[7]

Customer expectations are based on past buying experiences, the opinions of friends, and marketer and competitor information and promises. Marketers must be careful to set the right level of expectations. If they set expectations too low, they may satisfy those who buy but fail to attract enough buyers. If they raise expectations too high, buyers will be disappointed.

The American Customer Satisfaction Index, which tracks customer satisfaction in more than two dozen U.S. manufacturing and service industries, shows that overall customer satisfaction has been declining slightly in recent years.[8] It is unclear whether this has resulted from a decrease in product and service quality or from an increase in customer expectations. In either case, it presents an opportunity for companies that can deliver superior customer value and satisfaction.

Today's most successful companies are raising expectations—and delivering performance to match. These companies embrace *total customer satisfaction*. For example, Honda claims "One reason our customers are so satisfied is that we aren't." And Cigna vows "100% Satisfaction. 100% of the Time." Such companies track their customers' expectations, perceived company performance, and customer satisfaction.

However, although the customer-centered firm seeks to deliver high customer satisfaction relative to competitors, it does not attempt to *maximize* customer satisfaction. A company can always increase customer satisfaction by lowering its price or increasing its services, but this may result in lower profits. Thus, the purpose of marketing is to generate customer value profitably. This requires a very delicate balance: The marketer must continue to generate more customer value and satisfaction but not "give away the house."

Quality Quality has a direct impact on product or service performance. Thus, it is closely linked to customer value and satisfaction. In the narrowest sense, quality can be defined as "freedom from defects." But most customer-centered companies go beyond this narrow definition of quality. Instead, they define quality in terms of customer satisfaction. For example, the vice president of quality at Motorola, a company that pioneered total quality efforts in the United States, says that "quality has to do something for the customer. . . . Our definition of a defect is 'if the customer doesn't like it, it's a defect.'"[9] Similarly, the American Society for Quality defines quality as the characteristics of a product or service that bear on its ability to *satisfy stated or implied customer needs*.[10] These customer-focused definitions suggest that quality begins with customer needs and ends with customer satisfaction. The fundamental aim of today's *total quality* movement has become *total customer satisfaction*.

Total quality management (TQM) is an approach in which all the company's people are involved in constantly improving the quality of products, services, and business processes. TQM swept the corporate boardrooms of the 1980s. Companies ranging from giants such as AT&T, Xerox, and FedEx to smaller businesses such as the Granite Rock Company of Watsonville, California, credited TQM with greatly improving their market shares and profits. However, many companies adopted the language of TQM but not the substance, or viewed TQM as a cure-all for all the company's problems. Still others became obsessed with narrowly defined TQM principles and lost sight of broader concerns for customer value and satisfaction. As a result, many TQM programs begun in the 1980s failed, causing a backlash against TQM.

When applied in the context of creating customer satisfaction, however, *total quality* principles remain a requirement for success. Although many firms don't use the TQM label anymore, for most top companies customer-driven quality has become a way of doing business. Most customers will no longer tolerate even average quality. Companies today have no choice but to adopt quality concepts if they want to stay in the race, let alone be profitable. Thus, the task of improving product and service quality should be a company's top priority. However, quality programs must be designed to produce measurable results. Many companies now apply the notion of "return on quality (ROQ)." They make certain that the quality they offer is the quality that customers want. This quality, in turn, yields returns in the form of improved sales and profits.

Marketers have two major responsibilities in a quality-centered company. First, they must participate in forming strategies that will help the company win through total quality excellence. They must be the customer's watchdog or guardian, complaining loudly for the customer when the product or the service is not right. Second, marketers must deliver marketing quality as well as production quality. They must perform each marketing activity—marketing research, sales training, advertising, customer service, and others—to high standards.

Exchange, Transactions, and Relationships

Exchange
The act of obtaining a desired object from someone by offering something in return.

Marketing occurs when people decide to satisfy needs and wants through exchange. **Exchange** is the act of obtaining a desired object from someone by offering something in return. Exchange is only one of many ways that people can obtain a desired object. For example, hungry people could find food by hunting, fishing, or gathering fruit. They could beg for food or take food from someone else. Or they could offer money, another good, or a service in return for food.

As a means of satisfying needs, exchange has much in its favor. People do not have to prey on others or depend on donations, nor must they possess the skills to produce every necessity for themselves. They can concentrate on making things that they are good at making and trade them for needed items made by others. Thus, exchange allows a society to produce much more than it would with any alternative system.

Transaction
A trade between two parties that involves at least two things of value, agreed-upon conditions, a time of agreement, and a place of agreement.

Whereas exchange is the core concept of marketing, a transaction, in turn, is marketing's unit of measurement. A **transaction** consists of a trade of values between two parties: One party gives X to another party and gets Y in return. For example, you pay Sears $350 for a television set. This is a classic *monetary transaction,* but not all transactions involve money. In a *barter transaction,* you might trade your old refrigerator in return for a neighbor's secondhand television set.

In the broadest sense, the marketer tries to bring about a response to some offer. The response may be more than simply buying or trading goods and services. A political candidate, for instance, wants votes, a church wants membership, and a social action group wants idea acceptance. Marketing consists of actions taken to obtain a desired response from a target audience toward some product, service, idea, or other object.

Relationship marketing
The process of creating, maintaining, and enhancing strong, value-laden relationships with customers and other stakeholders.

Transaction marketing is part of the larger idea of **relationship marketing.** Beyond creating short-term transactions, marketers need to build long-term relationships with valued customers, distributors, dealers, and suppliers. They want to build strong economic and social connections by promising and consistently delivering high-quality products, good service, and fair prices. Beyond simply attracting new customers and creating transactions, the goal is to retain customers and grow their business with the company. Good relationships with customers begin with delivering superior value.

Increasingly, marketing is shifting from trying to maximize the profit on each individual transaction to building mutually beneficial relationships with consumers and other parties. In fact, ultimately, a company wants to build a unique company asset called a *marketing network.* A marketing network consists of the company and all its supporting stakeholders: customers, employees, suppliers, distributors, retailers, ad agencies, and others with whom it has built mutually profitable business relationships. Increasingly, competition is not between companies but rather between whole networks, with the prize going to the company that builds the better network. The operating principle is simple: Build a good network of relationships with key stakeholders and profits will follow.

Relationship marketing is oriented more toward the long term. The goal is to deliver long-term value to customers, and the measures of success are long-term customer satisfaction and retention. Beyond offering consistently high value and satisfaction, marketers can use a number of specific marketing tools to develop stronger bonds with consumers. First, a company might build value and satisfaction by adding *financial benefits* to the customer relationship. For example, airlines offer frequent-flyer programs, hotels give room upgrades to their frequent guests, and supermarkets give preferred-customer discounts.

A second approach is to add *social benefits* as well as financial benefits. Here, the company works to increase its social bonds with customers by learning individual customers' needs and wants and then personalizing its products and services. For example, Ritz-Carlton Hotels employees treat customers as individuals, not as nameless, faceless members of a mass market. Whenever possible, they refer to guests by name and give each guest a warm welcome every day. They record specific guest preferences in the company's customer database, which holds more than 500,000 individual customer preferences, accessible by all hotels in the worldwide Ritz chain. A guest who requests a foam pillow at the Ritz in Montreal will be delighted to find one waiting in the room when he or she checks into the Atlanta Ritz months later.[11]

To build better relationships with its customers, in the summer of 1994 and again in 1999 Saturn invited all of its owners to a "Saturn Homecoming" at its manufacturing facility in Spring Hill, Tennessee. The two-day affair included family events, plant tours, entertainment, music concerts, and physical challenge activities designed to build trust and a team spirit. Says Saturn's manager of corporate communications, "The Homecoming party is another way of building . . . relationships, and it shows that we treat our customers differently than any other car company." More than 60,000 people attended the most recent homecoming, traveling from as far as Alaska and Taiwan, with another 150,000 celebrating the occasion at the dealerships where they bought their cars.[12]

A third approach to building customer relationships is to add *structural ties* as well as financial and social benefits. For example, a business marketer might supply customers with special equipment or computer linkages that help them manage their orders or customer service. Dell Computer, for instance, creates personalized Web sites for its large commercial customers—called Premier Pages—that provide all of the information and support the customer would want in an interaction. The company's purchasing managers, information technology people, or individual employees can log into the company's Premier Page, build their own computers within preset specifications, receive price quotes based on prenegotiated pricing agreements, place an order, and have network-ready machines delivered within days. The site also supplies tailored technical support, diagnostic tools, and other features to suit the customer's special needs. Many larger customers set up multiple Dell Premier Pages, reflecting different purchasing agreements in different divisions. To date, Dell has set up roughly 15,000 such Web pages.[13]

We're about to reveal a Saturn trade secret. But first, raise your right hand and repeat after us, "I promise that what I'm about to hear will stay with me for the rest of my life." Promise? Okay, here goes: Treat people the same way you would like to be treated.

Which got us to thinking one day, what would a service area be without pinups?

Not *those* pinups, but rather pictures of Saturn owners. That way, when people brought their cars in for an oil change or something, we'd be able to place a name with a face.

Think about it. *Hey you* is not exactly the most endearing greeting, especially to someone who took the time to shop at your place and who spent their hard-earned money on one of your cars. *Hi, Yvonne* or *Hi, Steve* doesn't seem like it would be asking too much. It's certainly how we would like to be greeted if we were bringing in our car. Of course, it would go even further if our name were Steve, but hopefully you get the point.

A DIFFERENT KIND of COMPANY. A DIFFERENT KIND of CAR.

Relationship marketing: Saturn builds lasting relationships with customers. Many dealers post "pinups" of customers in their service areas to help employees place customer faces with cars. "'Hey you' is not exactly the most endearing greeting, especially to someone who took the time to shop at your place and who spent hard-earned money on one of your cars."

Relationship marketing means that marketers must focus on managing their customers as well as their products. At the same time, they don't want relationships with every customer. In fact, there are undesirable customers for every company. The objective is to determine which customers the company can serve most effectively relative to competitors. In some cases, companies may even want to "fire" customers that are too unreasonable or that cost more to serve than they are worth. Ultimately, marketing is the art of attracting, keeping, and growing *profitable customers*.

Markets

Market
The set of all actual and potential buyers of a product or service.

The concepts of exchange and relationships lead to the concept of a market. A **market** is the set of actual and potential buyers of a product. These buyers share a particular need or want that can be satisfied through exchanges and relationships. Thus, the size of a market depends on the number of people who exhibit the need, have resources to engage in exchange, and are willing to offer these resources in exchange for what they want.

Originally the term *market* stood for the place where buyers and sellers gathered to exchange their goods, such as a village square. Economists use the term *market* to refer to a collection of buyers and sellers who transact in a particular product class, as in the housing market or the grain market. Marketers, however, see the sellers as constituting an industry and the buyers as constituting a market.

Modern economies operate on the principle of division of labor, whereby each person specializes in producing something, receives payment, and buys needed things with this money. Thus, modern economies abound in markets. Producers go to resource markets (raw material markets, labor markets, money markets), buy resources, turn them into goods and services, and sell them to intermediaries, who sell them to consumers. The consumers sell their labor, for which they receive income to pay for the goods and services that they buy. The government is another market that plays several roles. It buys goods from resource, producer, and intermediary markets; it pays them; it taxes these markets (including consumer markets); and it returns needed public services. Thus, each nation's economy and the whole world economy consist of complex, interacting sets of markets that are linked through exchange processes.

Marketers are keenly interested in markets. Their goal is to understand the needs and wants of specific markets and to select the markets that they can serve best. In turn, they can develop products and services that will create value and satisfaction for customers in these markets, resulting in sales and profits for the company.

Marketing

The concept of markets finally brings us full circle to the concept of marketing. Marketing means managing markets to bring about exchanges and relationships for the purpose of creating value and satisfying needs and wants. Thus, we return to our definition of marketing as a process by which individuals and groups obtain what they need and want by creating and exchanging products and value with others.

Exchange processes involve work. Sellers must search for buyers, identify their needs, design good products and services, set prices for them, promote them, and store and deliver them. Activities such as product development, research, communication, distribution, pricing, and service are core marketing activities. Although we normally think of marketing as being carried on by sellers, buyers also carry on marketing activities. Consumers do marketing when they search for the goods they need at prices they can afford. Company purchasing agents do marketing when they track down sellers and bargain for good terms.

Figure 1-2 shows the main elements in a modern marketing system. In the usual situation, marketing involves serving a market of end users in the face of competitors. The

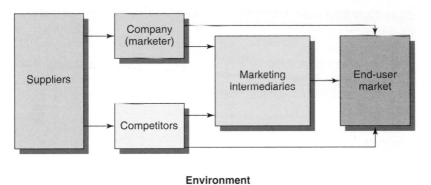

Figure 1-2
Main actors and forces in a modern marketing system

company and the competitors send their respective products and messages to consumers either directly or through marketing intermediaries to end users. All of the actors in the system are affected by major environmental forces (demographic, economic, physical, technological, political–legal, social–cultural).

Each party in the system adds value for the next level. Thus, a company's success depends not only on its own actions but also on how well the entire system serves the needs of final consumers. Wal-Mart cannot fulfill its promise of low prices unless its suppliers provide merchandise at low costs. And Ford cannot deliver high quality to car buyers unless its dealers provide outstanding service.

Linking the Concepts

Stop here for a moment and stretch your legs. What have you learned so far about marketing? For the moment, set aside the more formal definitions we've examined and try to develop your own understanding of marketing.

◆ In *your own words,* what *is* marketing? Write down *your* definition. Does your definition include such key concepts as customer value and relationships?
◆ What does marketing *mean* to you? How does it affect your life on a daily basis?
◆ What brand of athletic shoes did you purchase last? Describe your relationship with Nike, Reebok, Adidas, or whatever company made the shoes you purchased.

Marketing Management

We define **marketing management** as the analysis, planning, implementation, and control of programs designed to create, build, and maintain beneficial exchanges with target buyers for the purpose of achieving organizational objectives. Thus, marketing management involves managing demand, which in turn involves managing customer relationships.

Demand Management

Some people think of marketing management as finding enough customers for the company's current output, but this view is too limited. The organization has a desired level of demand for its products. At any point in time, there may be no demand, adequate demand, irregular demand, or too much demand, and marketing management must find ways to deal

Marketing management
The analysis, planning, implementation, and control of programs designed to create, build, and maintain beneficial exchanges with target buyers for the purpose of achieving organizational objectives.

Demarketing: To reduce demand for space on already congested expressways in Washington, DC, the Metropolitan Washington Council of Governments has set up a Web site encouraging commuters to carpool or use mass transit.

Demarketing
Marketing to reduce demand temporarily or permanently— the aim is not to destroy demand but only to reduce or shift it.

with these different demand states. Marketing management is concerned not only with finding and increasing demand but also with changing or even reducing it.

For example, the Golden Gate Bridge sometimes carries an unsafe level of traffic, and Yosemite National Park is badly overcrowded in the summer. Power companies sometimes have trouble meeting demand during peak usage periods. Expressways in big cities are clogged with traffic during rush hours. In these and other cases of excess demand, **demarketing** may be required to reduce demand temporarily or permanently. The aim of demarketing is not to destroy demand but only to reduce or shift it.[14] Thus, marketing management seeks to affect the level, timing, and nature of demand in a way that helps the organization achieve its objectives. Simply put, marketing management is *demand management*.

Building Profitable Customer Relationships

Managing demand means managing customers. A company's demand comes from two groups: new customers and repeat customers. Traditional marketing theory and practice have focused on attracting new customers and making the sale. Today, however, the emphasis is shifting. Beyond designing strategies to *attract* new customers and create *transactions* with them, companies now are going all out to *retain* current customers and build lasting customer *relationships*.

Why the new emphasis on keeping customers? In the past, companies facing an expanding economy and rapidly growing markets could practice the "leaky-bucket" approach to marketing. Growing markets meant a plentiful supply of new customers. Companies could keep filling the marketing bucket with new customers without worrying about losing old customers through holes in the bottom of the bucket. However, companies today are facing some new marketing realities. Changing demographics, a slow-growth economy, more sophisticated competitors, and overcapacity in many industries—all of these factors mean that there are fewer new customers to go around. Many companies now are fighting for shares of flat or fading markets. Thus, the costs of attracting new customers are rising. In fact, it costs five times as much to attract a new customer as it does to keep a current customer satisfied.[15]

Companies have also discovered that losing a customer means losing not only a single sale but also a lifetime's worth of purchases and referrals. For example, the *customer lifetime value* of a Taco Bell customer exceeds $12,000. For Lexus, one satisfied customer is worth $600,000 in lifetime purchases. Thus, working to keep profitable customers makes good economic sense.[16] The key to customer retention is superior customer value and satisfaction. With this in mind, many companies are going to extremes to keep their customers satisfied. (See Marketing at Work 1-2.)

Marketing Management Practice

All kinds of organizations use marketing, and they practice it in widely varying ways. Many large firms apply standard marketing practices in a formalized way. However, other companies use marketing in a less formal and orderly fashion. A recent book, *Radical Marketing,* praises companies such as Harley-Davidson, Virgin Atlantic Airways, and Boston Beer for succeeding by breaking many of the rules of marketing.[17] Instead of commissioning expensive marketing research, spending huge sums on mass advertising, and operating large marketing departments, these companies stretched their limited resources, lived close to their customers, and created more satisfying solutions to customer needs. They formed buyers' clubs, used creative public relations, and focused on delivering high product quality and winning long-term customer loyalty. It seems that not all marketing must follow in the footsteps of marketing giants such as Procter & Gamble.

In fact, marketing practice often passes through three stages: entrepreneurial marketing, formulated marketing, and intrepreneurial marketing.

◆ *Entrepreneurial marketing:* Most companies are started by individuals who live by their wits. They visualize an opportunity and knock on every door to gain attention. Jim Koch, founder of Boston Beer Company, whose Samuel Adams beer has become a top-selling "craft" beer, started out in 1984 carrying bottles of Samuel Adams beer from bar to bar to persuade bartenders to carry it. He would coax them into adding Samuel Adams beer to their menus. For 10 years, he couldn't afford advertising; he sold his beer through direct selling and grassroots public relations. Today, however, his business pulls in $210 million, making it the leader in the craft beer market.

◆ *Formulated marketing:* As small companies achieve success, they inevitably move toward more formulated marketing. Boston Beer recently opted to spend more than $15 million on television advertising in selected markets. The company now employs more than 175 salespeople and has a marketing department that carries out market research. Although Boston Beer is far less sophisticated than its archcompetitor, Anheuser-Busch, it has adopted some of the tools used in professionally run marketing companies.

◆ *Intrepreneurial marketing:* Many large and mature companies get stuck in formulated marketing, poring over the latest Nielsen numbers, scanning market research reports, and trying to fine-tune dealer relations and advertising messages. These companies sometimes lose the marketing creativity and passion that they had at the start. They now need to reestablish within their companies the entrepreneurial spirit and actions that made them successful in the first place. They need to encourage more initiative and "intrepreneurship" at the local level. Their brand and product managers need to get out of the office, start living with their customers, and visualize new and creative ways to add value to their customers' lives.

The bottom line is that effective marketing can take many forms. There will be a constant tension between the formulated side of marketing and the creative side. It is easier to learn the formulated side of marketing, which will occupy most of our attention in this book. But we will also see how real marketing creativity and passion operate in many companies—whether small or large, new or mature—to build and retain success in the marketplace.

Marketing at Work 1-2

Customer Relationships: Keeping Customers Satisfied

Some companies go to extremes to coddle their customers. Consider the following examples:

◆ An L.L. Bean customer says he lost all his fishing equipment—and nearly his life—when a raft he bought from the company leaked and forced him to swim to shore. He recovered the raft and sent it to the company along with a letter asking for a new raft and $700 to cover the fishing equipment he says he lost. He gets both.

◆ An American Express cardholder fails to pay more than $5,000 of his September bill. He explains that during the summer he'd purchased expensive rugs in Turkey. When he got home, appraisals showed that the rugs were worth half of what he'd paid. Rather than asking suspicious questions or demanding payment, the American Express representative notes the dispute, asks for a letter summarizing the appraisers' estimates, and offers to help solve the problem. Until the conflict is resolved, American Express doesn't ask for payment.

◆ Under the sultry summer sun, a Southwest Airlines flight attendant pulls shut the door and the Boeing 737 pushes away. Meanwhile, a ticketholder, sweat streaming from her face, races down the jetway, only to find that she's arrived too late. However, the Southwest pilot spies the anguished passenger and returns to the gate to pick her up. Says Southwest's executive vice president for customers, "It broke every rule in the book, but we congratulated the pilot on a job well done."

◆ A frustrated homeowner faces a difficult and potentially costly home plumbing repair. He visits the nearby Home Depot store, prowls the aisles, and picks up an armful of parts and supplies—$67.00 worth in all—that he thinks he'll need to do the job. However, before he gets to the checkout counter, a Home Depot salesperson heads him off. After some coaxing, the salesperson finally convinces the do-it-yourselfer that there's a simpler solution to his repair problem. The cost: $5.99 and a lot less trouble.

◆ A Nordstrom salesclerk stops a customer in the store and asks if the shoes she's wearing had been bought there. When the customer says yes, the clerk insists on replacing them on the spot because "they have not worn as well as they should." In another case, a salesclerk gives a customer a refund on a tire—Nordstrom doesn't carry tires, but the store prides itself on a no-questions-asked return policy.

From a dollars-and-cents point of view, these examples sound like a crazy way to do business. How can you make money by giving away your products, providing free extra services, talking your customers into paying less, or letting customers get away without paying their bills on time? Yet studies show that going to such extremes to keep customers happy, although costly, goes hand in hand with good financial performance. Satisfied customers come back again and again. Thus, in today's highly competitive marketplace, companies can well afford to lose money on one transaction if it helps to cement a profitable long-term customer relationship.

Keeping customers satisfied involves more than simply opening a complaint department, smiling a

Delighted customers come back again and again. American Express loves to tell stories about how its people have rescued customers from disasters ranging from civil wars to earthquakes, no matter what the cost.

lot, and being nice. Companies that do the best job of taking care of customers set high customer service standards and often make seemingly outlandish efforts to achieve them. At these companies, exceptional value and service are more than a set of policies or actions—they are a companywide attitude, an important part of the overall company culture.

American Express loves to tell stories about how its people have rescued customers from disasters ranging from civil wars to earthquakes, no matter what the cost. The company gives cash rewards of up to $1,000 to "Great Performers," such as Barbara Weber, who moved mountains of U.S. State Department and Treasury Department bureaucracy to refund $980 in stolen traveler's checks to a customer stranded in Cuba. Four Sea-

sons Hotels, long known for its outstanding service, tells its employees the story of Ron Dyment, a doorman in Toronto, who forgot to load a departing guest's briefcase into his taxi. The doorman called the guest, a lawyer in Washington, DC, and learned that he desperately needed the briefcase for a meeting the following morning. Without first asking for approval from management, Dyment hopped on a plane and returned the briefcase. The company named Dyment Employee of the Year. Similarly, the Nordstrom department store chain thrives on stories about its service heroics, such as employees dropping off orders at customers' homes or warming up cars while customers spend a little more time shopping. There's even a story about a man whose wife, a loyal Nordstrom cus-

tomer, died with her Nordstrom account $1,000 in arrears. Not only did Nordstrom settle the account, it also sent flowers to the funeral.

There's no simple formula for taking care of customers, but neither is it a mystery. According to the president of L.L. Bean, "A lot of people have fancy things to say about customer service . . . but it's just a day-in, day-out, ongoing, never-ending, unremitting, persevering, compassionate type of activity." For the companies that do it well, it's also very rewarding.

Sources: Bill Kelley, "Five Companies that Do It Right—and Make It Pay," *Sales and Marketing Management*, April 1988, pp. 57–64; Patricia Sellers, "Companies That Serve You Best," *Fortune*, May 31, 1993, pp. 74–88; Rahul Jacob, "Why Some Customers Are More Equal than Others," *Fortune*, September 19, 1994, pp. 215–224; Brian Silverman, "Shopping for Loyal Customers," *Sales and Marketing Management*, March 1995, pp. 96–97; and Howard E. Butz Jr. and Leonard Goodstein, "Measuring Customer Value: Gaining the Strategic Advantage," *Organizational Dynamics*, Winter 1996, pp. 63–77.

Marketing Management Philosophies

We describe marketing management as carrying out tasks to achieve desired exchanges with target markets. What *philosophy* should guide these marketing efforts? What weight should be given to the interests of the organization, customers, and society? Very often these interests conflict.

There are five alternative concepts under which organizations conduct their marketing activities: the *production, product, selling, marketing,* and *societal marketing concepts.*

The Production Concept

The **production concept** holds that consumers will favor products that are available and highly affordable. Therefore, management should focus on improving production and distribution efficiency. This concept is one of the oldest philosophies that guides sellers.

The production concept is still a useful philosophy in two types of situations. The first occurs when the demand for a product exceeds the supply. Here, management should look for ways to increase production. The second situation occurs when the product's cost is too high and improved productivity is needed to bring it down. For example, Henry Ford's whole philosophy was to perfect the production of the Model T so that its cost could be reduced and more people could afford it. He joked about offering people a car of any color as long as it was black.

Production concept
The philosophy that consumers will favor products that are available and highly affordable and that management should therefore focus on improving production and distribution efficiency.

For many years, Texas Instruments (TI) followed a philosophy of increased production and lower costs in order to bring down prices. It won a major share of the American handheld calculator market using this approach. However, companies operating under a production philosophy run a major risk of focusing too narrowly on their own operations. For example, when TI used this strategy in the digital watch market, it failed. Although TI's watches were priced low, customers did not find them very attractive. In its drive to bring down prices, TI lost sight of something else that its customers wanted—namely, affordable, *attractive* digital watches.

The Product Concept

Product concept
The idea that consumers will favor products that offer the most quality, performance, and features and that the organization should therefore devote its energy to making continuous product improvements.

Another major concept guiding sellers, the **product concept,** holds that consumers will favor products that offer the most in quality, performance, and innovative features. Thus, an organization should devote energy to making continuous product improvements. Some manufacturers believe that if they can build a better mousetrap, the world will beat a path to their door.[18] But they are often rudely shocked. Buyers may well be looking for a better solution to a mouse problem but not necessarily for a better mousetrap. The solution might be a chemical spray, an exterminating service, or something that works better than a mousetrap. Furthermore, a better mousetrap will not sell unless the manufacturer designs, packages, and prices it attractively; places it in convenient distribution channels; brings it to the attention of people who need it; and convinces buyers that it is a better product.

The product concept also can lead to marketing myopia. For instance, railroad management once thought that users wanted *trains* rather than *transportation* and overlooked the growing challenge of airlines, buses, trucks, and automobiles. Many colleges have assumed that high school graduates want a liberal arts education and have thus overlooked the increasing challenge of vocational schools.

The Selling Concept

Selling concept
The idea that consumers will not buy enough of the organization's products unless the organization undertakes a large-scale selling and promotion effort.

Many organizations follow the **selling concept,** which holds that consumers will not buy enough of the organization's products unless it undertakes a large-scale selling and promotion effort. The concept is typically practiced with unsought goods—those that buyers do not normally think of buying, such as encyclopedias or insurance. These industries must be good at tracking down prospects and selling them on product benefits.

Most firms practice the selling concept when they have overcapacity. Their aim is to sell what they make rather than make what the market wants. Such marketing carries high risks. It focuses on creating sales transactions rather than on building long-term, profitable relationships with customers. It assumes that customers who are coaxed into buying the product will like it. Or, if they don't like it, they will possibly forget their disappointment and buy it again later. These are usually poor assumptions to make about buyers. Most studies show that dissatisfied customers do not buy again. Worse yet, whereas the average satisfied customer tells three others about good experiences, the average dissatisfied customer tells ten others about his or her bad experiences.[19]

The Marketing Concept

Marketing concept
The marketing management philosophy that holds that achieving organizational goals depends on determining the needs and wants of target markets and delivering the desired satisfactions more effectively and efficiently than competitors do.

The **marketing concept** holds that achieving organizational goals depends on determining the needs and wants of target markets and delivering the desired satisfactions more effectively and efficiently than competitors do. The marketing concept has been stated in colorful ways, such as "We make it happen for you" (Marriott); "To fly, to serve" (British Airways); "We're not satisfied until you are" (GE); and "Let us exceed your expectations" (Celebrity Cruise Lines).

Figure 1-3
The selling and marketing concepts contrasted

The selling concept and the marketing concept are sometimes confused. Figure 1-3 compares the two concepts. The selling concept takes an *inside-out* perspective. It starts with the factory, focuses on the company's existing products, and calls for heavy selling and promotion to obtain profitable sales. It focuses primarily on customer conquest—getting short-term sales with little concern about who buys or why.

In contrast, the marketing concept takes an *outside-in* perspective. As Herb Kelleher, Southwest Airlines's colorful CEO, puts it, "We don't have a Marketing Department; we have a Customer Department." The marketing concept starts with a well-defined market, focuses on customer needs, coordinates all the marketing activities affecting customers, and makes profits by creating long-term customer relationships based on customer value and satisfaction. Thus, under the marketing concept, customer focus and value are the *paths* to sales and profits. In the words of one Ford executive, "If we're not customer driven, our cars won't be either."

Many successful and well-known companies have adopted the marketing concept. Procter & Gamble, Disney, Wal-Mart, Marriott, Nordstrom, Dell Computer, and Southwest Airlines follow it faithfully. The goal is to build customer satisfaction into the very fabric of the firm. L.L. Bean, the highly successful catalog retailer, was founded on the marketing concept. In 1912, in his first circulars, L.L. Bean included the following notice: "I do not consider a sale complete until goods are worn out and the customer still is satisfied. We will thank anyone to return goods that are not perfectly satisfactory. . . . Above all things we wish to avoid having a dissatisfied customer."

Today, L.L. Bean dedicates itself to giving perfect satisfaction in every way. To inspire its employees to practice the marketing concept, L.L. Bean has for decades displayed posters around its offices that proclaim the following:

> What is a customer? A customer is the most important person ever in this company—in person or by mail. A customer is not dependent on us, we are dependent on him. A customer is not an interruption of our work, he is the purpose of it. We are not doing a favor by serving him, he is doing us a favor by giving us the opportunity to do so. A customer is not someone to argue or match wits with—nobody ever won an argument with a customer. A customer is a person who brings us his wants—it is our job to handle them profitably to him and to ourselves.

In contrast, many companies claim to practice the marketing concept but do not. They have the *forms* of marketing, such as a marketing vice president, product managers, marketing plans, and marketing research, but this does not mean that they are market-focused and customer-driven companies. The question is whether they are finely tuned to changing customer needs and competitor strategies. Formerly great companies—General Motors, Sears, Zenith—all lost substantial market share because they failed to adjust their marketing strategies to the changing marketplace.

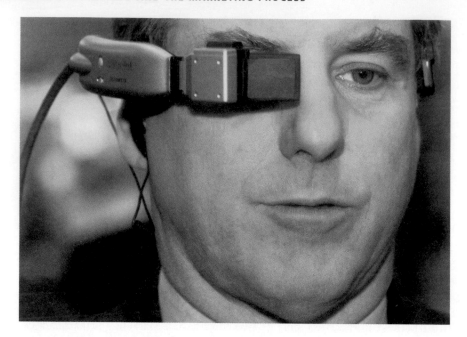

Customer-driving marketing: In many cases, customers don't know what they want or even what is possible. How many of us would have thought to ask IBM for a "wearable PC"?

Implementing the marketing concept often means more than simply responding to customers' stated desires and obvious needs. *Customer-driven* companies research current customers to learn about their desires, gather new product and service ideas, and test proposed product improvements. Such customer-driven marketing usually works well when a clear need exists and when customers know what they want. In many cases, however, customers *don't* know what they want or even what is possible. For example, 20 years ago, how many consumers would have thought to ask for cellular telephones, fax machines, home copiers, 24-hour Internet brokerage accounts, DVD players, or handheld global satellite positioning systems?

Such situations call for *customer-driving* marketing—understanding customer needs even better than customers themselves do, and creating products and services that will meet existing and latent needs now and in the future. As Sony's visionary leader, Akio Morita, puts it: "Our plan is to lead the public with new products rather than ask them what kinds of products they want. The public does not know what is possible, but we do." And according to an executive at 3M, a company known for its customer-driving innovativeness, "Our goal is to lead customers where they want to go before *they* know where they want to go."[20]

The Societal Marketing Concept

Societal marketing concept
The idea that the organization should determine the needs, wants, and interests of target markets and deliver the desired satisfactions more effectively and efficiently than do competitors in a way that maintains or improves the consumer's and society's well-being.

The **societal marketing concept** holds that the organization should determine the needs, wants, and interests of target markets. It should then deliver superior value to customers in a way that maintains or improves the consumer's *and the society's* well-being. The societal marketing concept is the newest of the five marketing management philosophies.

The societal marketing concept questions whether the pure marketing concept is adequate in an age of environmental problems, resource shortages, rapid population growth, worldwide economic problems, and neglected social services. It asks if the firm that senses, serves, and satisfies individual short-term wants is always doing what's best for consumers and society in the long run. According to the societal marketing concept, the

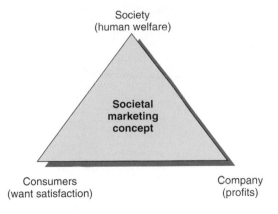

Figure 1-4
Three considerations underlying the societal marketing concept

pure marketing concept overlooks possible conflicts between consumer *short-run wants* and consumer *long-run welfare.*

Consider the fast-food industry. Most people see today's giant fast-food chains as offering tasty and convenient food at reasonable prices. Yet many consumer and environmental groups have voiced concerns. Critics point out that hamburgers, fried chicken, French fries, and most other foods sold by fast-food restaurants are high in fat and salt. The products are wrapped in convenient packaging, but this leads to waste and pollution. Thus, in satisfying consumer wants, the highly successful fast-food chains may be harming consumer health and causing environmental problems.

Such concerns and conflicts led to the societal marketing concept. As Figure 1-4 shows, the societal marketing concept calls on marketers to balance three considerations in setting their marketing policies: company profits, consumer wants, *and* society's interests. Originally, most companies based their marketing decisions largely on short-run company profit. Eventually, they began to recognize the long-run importance of satisfying consumer wants, and the marketing concept emerged. Now many companies are beginning to think of society's interests when making their marketing decisions.

One such company is Johnson & Johnson, rated each year in a *Fortune* magazine poll as one of America's most admired companies, especially for its community and environmental responsibility. Johnson & Johnson's concern for societal interests is summarized in a company document called "Our Credo," which stresses honesty, integrity, and putting people before profits. Under this credo, Johnson & Johnson would rather take a big loss than ship a bad batch of one of its products. And the company supports many community and employee programs that benefit its consumers and workers and the environment. Johnson & Johnson's chief executive puts it this way: "If we keep trying to do what's right, at the end of the day we believe the marketplace will reward us."[21]

The company backs these words with actions. Consider the tragic tampering case in which eight people died from swallowing cyanide-laced capsules of Tylenol, a Johnson & Johnson brand. Although Johnson & Johnson believed that the pills had been altered in only a few stores, not in the factory, it quickly recalled all of its product. The recall cost the company $240 million in earnings. In the long run, however, the company's swift recall of Tylenol strengthened consumer confidence and loyalty, and Tylenol remains the nation's leading brand of pain reliever. In this and other cases, Johnson & Johnson management has found that doing what's right benefits both consumers and the company. Says the chief executive, "The Credo should not be viewed as some kind of social welfare program . . . it's just plain good business."[22] Thus, over the years, Johnson & Johnson's dedication to consumers and community service has made it one of America's most-admired companies *and* one of the most profitable.

Our Credo

We believe our first responsibility is to the doctors, nurses and patients,
to mothers and fathers and all others who use our products and services.
In meeting their needs everything we do must be of high quality.
We must constantly strive to reduce our costs
in order to maintain reasonable prices.
Customers' orders must be serviced promptly and accurately.
Our suppliers and distributors must have an opportunity
to make a fair profit.

We are responsible to our employees,
the men and women who work with us throughout the world.
Everyone must be considered as an individual.
We must respect their dignity and recognize their merit.
They must have a sense of security in their jobs.
Compensation must be fair and adequate,
and working conditions clean, orderly and safe.
We must be mindful of ways to help our employees fulfill
their family responsibilities.
Employees must feel free to make suggestions and complaints.
There must be equal opportunity for employment, development
and advancement for those qualified.
We must provide competent management,
and their actions must be just and ethical.

We are responsible to the communities in which we live and work
and to the world community as well.
We must be good citizens — support good works and charities
and bear our fair share of taxes.
We must encourage civic improvements and better health and education.
We must maintain in good order
the property we are privileged to use,
protecting the environment and natural resources.

Our final responsibility is to our stockholders.
Business must make a sound profit.
We must experiment with new ideas.
Research must be carried on, innovative programs developed
and mistakes paid for.
New equipment must be purchased, new facilities provided
and new products launched.
Reserves must be created to provide for adverse times.
When we operate according to these principles,
the stockholders should realize a fair return.

Johnson & Johnson

Johnson & Johnson's concern for society is summarized in its credo and in the company's actions over the years.

Linking the Concepts

We've covered a lot of territory. Again, slow down for a moment and develop *your own* thoughts about marketing and marketing management.

◆ In *your own words,* what *is* marketing management and what does it seek to accomplish?
◆ What marketing management philosophy appears to guide Nike? How does this compare with the marketing philosophy that guides Johnson & Johnson? Can you think of another company guided by a very different philosophy? Is there one marketing management philosophy that's best for all companies?

Marketing Challenges in the New "Connected" Millennium

As the world spins into the first decade of the twenty-first century, dramatic changes are occurring in the marketing arena. Richard Love of Hewlett-Packard observes, "The pace of change is so rapid that the ability to change has now become a competitive advantage." Yogi Berra, the legendary New York Yankees catcher, summed it up more simply when he said, "The future ain't what it used to be." Technological advances, rapid globalization, and continuing social and economic shifts—all are causing profound changes in the market-place. As the marketplace changes, so must those who serve it.

The major marketing developments as we enter the new millennium can be summed up in a single theme: *connectedness*. Now, more than ever before, we are all connected to each other and to things near and far in the world around us. Moreover, we are connecting in new and different ways. Where it once took weeks or months to travel across the United States, we can now travel around the globe in only hours or days. Where it once took days or even weeks to receive news about important world events, we now see them as they are occurring through live satellite broadcasts. Where it once took days or weeks to correspond with others in distant places, they are now only moments away by phone or the Internet.

In this section, we examine the major trends and forces that are changing the marketing landscape and challenging marketing strategy in this new, connected millennium. As shown in Figure 1-5 and discussed in the following pages, sweeping changes in connecting technologies are causing marketers to redefine how they connect with the marketplace—with their customers, with marketing partners inside and outside the company, and with the world around them. We first look at the dramatic changes that are occurring in the connecting technologies. Then, we examine how these changes are affecting marketing connections.

Technologies for Connecting

The major force behind the new connectedness is technology. Explosive advances in computer, telecommunications, information, transportation, and other connecting technologies have created a New Economy. The technology boom has created exciting new ways to learn about and track customers, create products and services tailored to meet customer needs, distribute products more efficiently and effectively, and communicate with customers in large groups or one-to-one. For example, through videoconferencing, marketing researchers at a company's headquarters in New York can look in on focus groups in Chicago or Paris without ever stepping onto a plane. With only a few clicks of a mouse button, a direct marketer can tap into online data services to learn anything from what car you drive to what you read to what flavor of ice cream you prefer.

Using today's vastly more powerful computers, marketers create detailed databases and use them to target individual customers with offers designed to meet their specific needs and buying patterns. With a new wave of communication and advertising tools—ranging from cell phones, fax machines, CD-ROM, and interactive TV to video kiosks at airports and shopping malls—marketers can zero in on selected customers with carefully targeted messages. Through electronic commerce, customers can design, order, and pay

Explosive advances in connecting technologies have created exciting new ways to learn about customers and to create tailored products, distribute them more effectively, and communicate with customers in large groups or one-to-one.

for products and services—without ever leaving home. Then, through the marvels of express delivery, they can receive their purchases in less than 24 hours. From virtual reality displays that test new products to online virtual stores that sell them, the technology boom is affecting every aspect of marketing.

Internet

A vast public web of computer networks that connects users of all types all around the world to each other and to an amazingly large "information repository." The Internet makes up one big "information highway" that can dispatch bits at incredible speeds from one location to another.

The Internet   Perhaps the most dramatic new technology driving the connected age is the **Internet.** The Internet is a vast and burgeoning global web of computer networks with no central management or ownership. Today, the Internet links individuals and businesses of all types to each other and to information all around the world.

The Internet has been hailed as the technology behind a New Economy. It allows anytime, anywhere connections to information, entertainment, and communication. Companies are using the Internet to build closer relationships with customers and marketing partners and to sell and distribute their products more efficiently and effectively. Beyond competing in traditional marketplaces, they now have access to exciting new market*spaces.*

Internet usage surged in the 1990s with the development of the user-friendly World Wide Web. Entering the new millennium, Internet penetration in the United States has reached close to 60 percent, with some 160 million people accessing the Web in any given month. The Internet is truly a global phenomenon—the number of Internet users worldwide is expected to approach 1 billion by 2004.[23] This growing and diverse Internet population means that all kinds of people are now going to the Web for information and to buy products and services. Notes one analyst, "In just [a few short years], the Net has gone from a playground for nerds into a vast communications and trading center where . . . people swap information and do deals around the world. . . . [More and more] companies have hung www.shingle.com atop their digital doorways with the notion that being anywhere on the Net means selling virtually everywhere."[24]

Companies of all types are now attempting to snare new customers on the Web. Many traditional "brick-and-mortar" companies have now become "click-and-mortar" companies, venturing online in an effort to attract new customers and build stronger relationships with existing ones. The Internet also spawned an entirely new breed of "click-only" companies—the so-called "dot-coms." During the Web frenzy of the late 1990s, dot-coms popped up everywhere, selling everything from books, toys, and CDs to furniture, home mortgages, and 100-pound bags of dog food via the Internet. The frenzy cooled during the "dot-com meltdown" of 2000, when many poorly conceived e-tailers and other Web start-ups went out of business. Today, despite its turbulent start, online consumer buying is growing at a healthy rate, and many of the dot-com survivors face promising futures.[25]

If consumer e-commerce looks promising, business-to-business e-commerce is just plain booming. Business-to-business transactions online are expected to reach $3.6 trillion in 2003, compared with only $107 billion in consumer purchases. By 2005, more than 500,000 businesses will engage in e-commerce as buyers, sellers, or both. It seems that almost every major business has set up shop on the Web. Giants such as GE, IBM, Dell, Cisco Systems, Enron, Microsoft, and many others have moved quickly to exploit the power of the Internet.[26]

Thus, changes in connecting technologies are providing exciting new opportunities for marketers. We will explore the impact of the New Economy in more detail in Chapter 3. Here, we look at the ways these technological changes are affecting how companies connect with their customers, marketing partners, and the world around us (see Figure 1-5).

Connections with Customers

The most profound new developments in marketing involve the ways in which today's companies are connecting with their customers. Yesterday's companies focused on mass marketing to all comers at arm's length. Today's companies are selecting their customers

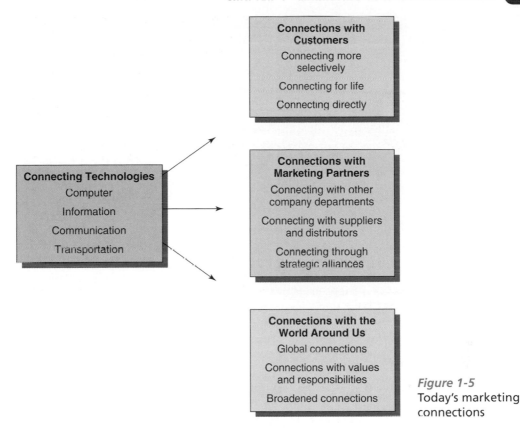

Figure 1-5
Today's marketing connections

more carefully and building more lasting and direct relationships with these carefully targeted customers.

Connecting with More Carefully Selected Customers Few firms today still practice true mass marketing—selling in a standardized way to any customer who comes along. Today, most marketers realize that they don't want to connect with just *any* customers. Instead, most are targeting fewer, more profitable customers.

The United States—in fact, the world—has become more of a "salad bowl" of diverse ethnic, cultural, social, and locational groups. Although these diverse groups have mixed together, they maintain diversity by keeping and valuing important differences. Moreover, customers themselves are connecting in new ways to form "consumer communities," in which buyers connect with each other by common interests, situations, and activities.

The greater diversity and new consumer connections have meant greater market fragmentation. In response, most firms have moved from mass marketing to segmented marketing, in which they target carefully chosen submarkets or even individual buyers. "One-to-one marketing" has become the order of the day for some marketers. They build extensive customer databases containing rich information on individual customer preferences and purchases. Then, they mine these databases to gain insights by which they can "mass-customize" their offerings to deliver greater value to individual buyers.

At the same time that companies are finding new ways to deliver more value *to* customers, they are also beginning to assess carefully the value *of* customers to the firm. They want to connect only with customers that they can serve *profitably*. Once they identify profitable customers, firms can create attractive offers and special handling to capture these customers and earn their loyalty (see Marketing at Work 1-3).

Wanted: Profitable Customers Only

All customers are created equal—right? Wrong! Whereas traditional marketing has involved casting a wide net to lure as many customers as possible, today's smart companies now focus on keeping and growing only the most profitable customers they already have. "They are aggressively mining their vast databases to weed out losers, or at least to charge them more, and to target the best customers for pampering," says Rick Brooks of the *Wall Street Journal.* Some industries have long favored "good" customers over lesser ones. For example, airlines, credit card companies, and hotels throw loads of special services at their "premier" or "platinum" customers. However, recent advances in technology now allow companies to assess the value of every customer more precisely, then weed out the less profitable ones.

Here are some examples of how companies are using customer profitability analysis to weed out losing customers and target the winning ones for pampering.

◆ Two years ago, shipping giant FedEx began analyzing the returns on its business for about 30 large customers that generate about 10 percent of its total volume. It found that certain customers, including some requiring lots of residential deliveries, weren't bringing in as much revenue as they had promised when they first negotiated discounted rates. So FedEx went on the offensive, demanding that some customers pay higher rates and imposing double-digit increases in a handful of instances. A couple of big customers who refused to budge were told they could

take their shipping business elsewhere. "We were willing to risk a point or two of market share to correct the problem," says a spokesman for FedEx. "You have to be willing to suck it up and walk away."

◆ At Thomas Cook Travel, differentiating between best and worst customers required a huge

change in the company's culture. Agents had always been coached to deliver top-level service to everyone. Realizing that such an attitude just isn't profitable anymore, the agency divided its customers into As (those who bring in $750 or more in annual revenues), Bs (those bringing in $250–$749), and Cs (those who

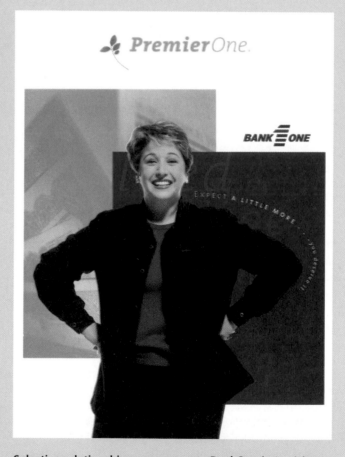

Selective relationship management: BankOne in Louisiana lets its "Premier One" customers know that they are "special, exclusive, privileged, and valued." For example, after presenting a special gold card to the "concierge" near the front door, they are whisked away to a special teller window with no line or to the desk of a specially trained bank officer.

bring in less than $250). It found that 80 percent of its customers were Cs. "It's not that you don't want them, it's just that you differentiate," says Wendy White, marketing manager for Thomas Cook Travel Canada. You still deliver professional service, she observes, but not every client requires—or deserves—two hours' worth of service to purchase an airline ticket. The travel agents at Thomas Cook now know which customers deserve the full treatment and which ones don't. When C clients demand time-consuming services—for example, asking an agent to research a trip they're not positive they want to take—they are now asked for a $25 deposit. Clients who are serious pay up; the fee simply goes toward their booking cost. And if they're not serious and don't pay, it frees up agents to deal with more profitable A and B clients. Agents also receive a quarterly printout from a database that lists the company's top 500 clients and the revenue each generates. It helps agents look for missed sales opportunities and "get a handle on the target and their needs," White adds. The change in focus has been lucrative for Thomas Cook Travel, resulting in 20 percent growth in the company's A and B level clients.

♦ The banking industry has led the way in assessing customer profitability. Take First Union as an example. After decades of casting a wide net to lure as many customers as possible, many banks are now mining their vast databases to identify winning customers and weed out losing ones. Fielding phone calls at First Union's huge customer service center [in Charlotte, NC], Amy Hathcock is

surrounded by reminders to deliver the personal touch. Televisions hang from the ceiling so she can glance at the Weather Channel to see if her latest caller just came in from the rain; a bumper sticker in her cubicle encourages, "Practice random kindness and senseless acts of beauty." But when it comes to answering yes or no to a customer who wants a lower credit card interest rate or to escape the bank's $28 bounced check fee, there is nothing random about it. The service all depends on the color of a tiny square—green, yellow, or red—that pops up on Ms. Hathcock's computer screen next to the customer's name. For customers who get a red pop-up, Ms. Hathcock rarely budges; these are the ones whose accounts lose money for the bank. Green means the customers generate hefty profits for First Union and should be granted waivers. Yellow is for in between customers: There's a chance to negotiate. The bank's computer system, called "Einstein," takes just 15 seconds to pull up the ranking on a customer, using a formula that calculates [customer value based on the account's] minimum balances, account activity, branch visits, and other variables. "Everyone isn't all the same anymore," says Steven G. Boehm, general manager of First Union's customer-information center.

This sorting out process, of course, has many risks. For one, future profits are hard to predict. A high school student on his or her way to a Harvard MBA and a plum job on Wall Street might be unprofitable now but worth courting for the future. So might an unprofitable customer who suddenly inherits

a lot of money and wants to plunk it in CDs or other products. "That shabby-looking guy might actually be or become an eccentric billionaire. But as a result of using this technology, do you give him the bum's rush?" asks one analyst. Still, most banks believe that the benefits outweigh the risks. For example, after First Chicago imposed a $3 teller fee in 1995 on some of its money-losing customers, 30,000 of them—or close to 3 percent of the bank's total customers—closed their accounts. Many marginal customers became profitable by boosting their account balances high enough to avoid the fee or by visiting ATMs instead of tellers. On balance, imposing the fee improved the profitability of the bank's customer base.

Thus, today's marketers are looking closely at the profitability of their customers. Analyst Erika Rasmusson summarizes: "All men may be created equal, but increasingly, all customers are not. . . . Learning where your customers rank in terms of profitability is the future of business, and companies that are doing it now have a distinct advantage over their competitors. Call it *selective* relationship management—companies need to pick wisely which customers they're going to have relationships with—and what kind of relationships."

Sources: Examples adapted from Rick Brooks, "Unequal Treatment: Alienating Customers Isn't Always a Bad Idea, Many Firms Discover," *Wall Street Journal*, January 7, 1999, p. A1; and Erika Rasmusson, "Wanted: Profitable Customers," *Sales and Marketing Management*, May 1999, pp. 28–34. Also see Peter Cockburn, "CRM for Profit," *Telecommunications*, December 2000, pp. 89–93; Joseph A. Ness, Michael J. Schrobeck, Rick A. Letendre, and Willmar J. Douglas, "The Role of ABM in Measuring Customer Value," *Strategic Finance*, March 2001, pp. 32–37; and Ness, Schrobeck, Letendre, and Douglas, "The Role of ABM in Measuring Customer Value—Part 2," *Strategic Finance*, April 2001, pp. 44–49.

Connecting for a Customer's Lifetime Just as companies are being more selective about which customers they choose to serve, they are serving those they choose in a deeper, more lasting way. In the past, many companies have focused on finding *new customers* for their products and closing *sales* with them. In recent years, this focus has shifted toward keeping *current customers* and building lasting customer *relationships*. Increasingly, the goal is shifting from making a profit on each sale to making long-term profits by managing the lifetime value of a customer.

In turn, as businesses do a better and better job of keeping old customers, competitors find it increasingly difficult to acquire new customers. As a result, marketers now spend less time figuring out how to increase "share of market" and more time trying to grow "share of customer." They offer greater variety to current customers and train employees to cross-sell and up-sell in order to market more products and services to existing customers. For example, Amazon.com began as an online bookseller, but now offers music, videos, gifts, toys, consumer electronics, home improvement items, and an online auction. In addition, based on each customer's purchase history, the company recommends related books, CDs, or videos that might be of interest. In this way, Amazon.com captures a greater share of each customer's leisure and entertainment budget.

Connecting Directly Beyond connecting more deeply with their customers, many companies are also connecting more *directly*. In fact, direct marketing is booming. Virtually all products are now available without going to a store—by telephone, mail-order catalogs, kiosks, and e-commerce. For example, customers surfing the Web can view pictures of almost any product, read the specs, shop among online vendors for the best prices and terms, speak with online vendors' shopping consultants, and place and pay for their orders—all with only a few mouse clicks. Business-to-business purchasing over the Internet has increased even faster than online consumer buying. Business purchasing agents routinely shop on the Web for items ranging from standard office supplies to high-priced, high-tech computer equipment.

Some companies sell *only* via direct channels—firms such as Dell Computer, Lands' End, 1-800-Flowers, and Amazon.com, to name only a few. Other companies use direct connections to supplement their other communications and distribution channels. For example, Procter & Gamble sells Pampers disposable diapers through retailers, supported by millions of dollars of mass-media advertising. However, P&G uses its www.Pampers.com Web site to build relationships with young parents by providing information and advice on diapering, baby care, and even child development. Similarly, you can't buy crayons from the Crayola Web site (www.crayola.com). However, you can find out how to remove crayon marks from your new carpeting or freshly painted walls.

Direct marketing is redefining the buyer's role in connecting with sellers. Instead of being the targets of a company's one-way marketing efforts, customers have now become active participants in shaping the marketing offer and process. Many companies now let customers design their own desired products online. For example, shoppers at the Lands' End site (www.LandsEnd.com) can build a "virtual model" with their own hair color, height, and shape. They then visit an online dressing room, where they can try clothes on the model to see how they would look in them. The site also gives buyers tips on how best to dress given their individual body styles.

Some marketers have hailed direct marketing as the "marketing model of the next millennium." They envision a day when all buying and selling will involve direct connections between companies and their customers. Others, although agreeing that direct marketing will play a growing and important role, see it as just one more way to approach the marketplace. We will take a closer look at the world of direct marketing in Chapter 14.

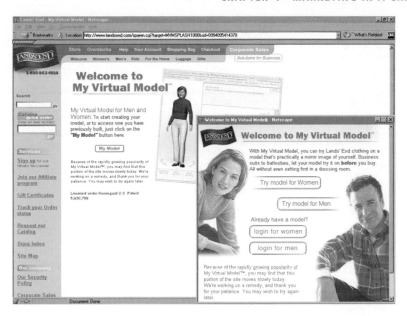

New customer connections: The Lands' End Web site lets shoppers build a "virtual model," then visit an online dressing room where they can try on clothes.

Connections with Marketing Partners

In these ever more connected times, major changes are occurring in how marketers connect with others inside and outside the company to jointly bring greater value to customers.

Connecting Inside the Company Traditionally, marketers have been charged with understanding customer needs and representing the customer to different company departments, which then acted upon these needs. The old thinking was that marketing is done only by marketing, sales, and customer support people. However, in today's connected world, every functional area can interact with customers, especially electronically. Marketing no longer has sole ownership of customer interactions. The new thinking is that every employee must be customer focused. David Packard, cofounder of Hewlett-Packard, wisely said: "Marketing is far too important to be left only to the marketing department."[27]

Today's forward-looking companies are reorganizing to align better with customer needs. Rather than letting each department go its own way, firms are linking all departments in the cause of creating customer value. Rather than assigning only sales and marketing people to customers, they are forming cross-functional customer teams. For example, Procter & Gamble assigns "customer development teams" to each of its major retailer accounts. These teams—consisting of sales and marketing people, operations and logistics specialists, market and financial analysts, and others—coordinate the efforts of many P&G departments toward helping the retailer be more successful.

Connecting with Outside Partners Rapid changes are also occurring in how marketers connect with their suppliers, channel partners, and even competitors. Most companies today are networked companies, relying heavily on partnerships with other firms.

SUPPLY CHAIN MANAGEMENT. Marketing channels consist of distributors, retailers, and others who connect the company to its buyers. The *supply chain* describes a longer channel, stretching from raw materials to components to final products that are carried to final buyers. For example, the supply chain for personal computers consists of suppliers of computer chips and other components, the computer manufacturer, and the distributors, retailers, and others who sell the computers to businesses and final customers. Each member of the supply chain creates and captures only a portion of the total value generated by the supply chain.

Through *supply chain management,* many companies today are strengthening their connections with partners all along the supply chain. They know that their fortunes rest not only on how well they perform. Success also rests on how well their entire supply chain performs against competitors' supply chains. Rather than treating suppliers as vendors and distributors as customers, a company treats both as partners in delivering consumer value. For example, Wal-Mart works with suppliers such as Procter & Gamble, Rubbermaid, and Black & Decker to streamline logistics and reduce joint distribution costs, resulting in lower prices to consumers. Saturn, on the one hand, works closely with carefully selected suppliers to improve quality and operations efficiency. On the other hand, it works with its franchise dealers to provide top-grade sales and service support that will bring customers in the door and keep them coming back.

STRATEGIC ALLIANCES.   Beyond managing the supply chain, today's companies are also discovering that they need *strategic* partners if they hope to be effective. In the new, more competitive global environment, going it alone is going out of style. *Strategic alliances* are booming across the entire spectrum of industries and services. For example, Dell Computer recently ran advertisements telling how it partners with Microsoft and Intel to provide customized e-business solutions. The ads ask: "Why do many corporations choose Windows 2000 running on Dell PowerEdge servers with Intel Pentium III Xeon processors to power their e-business solutions?" The answer: "At Dell, Microsoft, and Intel, we specialize in solving the impossible."

Companies need to give careful thought to finding partners who might complement their strengths and offset their weaknesses. Well-managed alliances can have a huge impact on sales and profits. A recent study found that one in every four dollars earned by the top 1,000 U.S. companies flows from alliances, double the rate in the early 1990s. As Jim Kelly, CEO at UPS, puts it, "The old adage 'If you can't beat 'em, join 'em,' is being replaced by 'Join 'em and you can't be beat.'"[28]

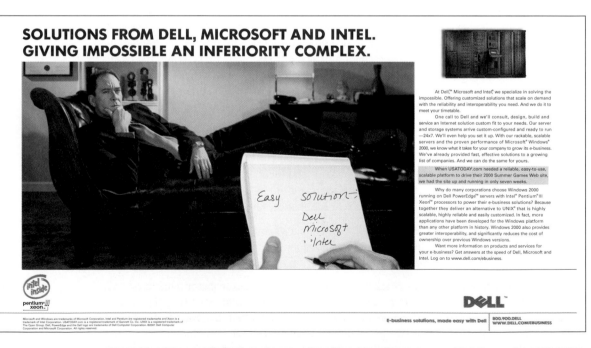

Strategic alliances: Dell recently ran ads telling how it partners with Microsoft and Intel to provide customized e-business solutions. "At Dell, Microsoft, and Intel, we specialize in solving the impossible."

Connections with the World Around Us

As they are redefining their relationships with customers and partners, marketers are also taking a fresh look at the ways in which they connect with the broader world around them. Here we look at trends toward increasing globalization, more concern for social and environmental responsibility, and greater use of marketing by nonprofit and public-sector organizations.

Global Connections In an increasingly smaller world, many marketers are now connected *globally* with their customers and marketing partners. The world economy has undergone radical change during the past two decades. Geographical and cultural distances have shrunk with the advent of jet planes, fax machines, world satellite television broadcasts, global Internet hookups, and other technical advances. This has allowed companies to greatly expand their geographical market coverage, purchasing, and manufacturing. The result is a vastly more complex marketing environment for both companies and consumers.

Today, almost every company, large or small, is touched in some way by global competition—from the neighborhood florist that buys its flowers from Mexican nurseries to the U.S. electronics manufacturer that competes in its home markets with giant Japanese rivals; from the fledgling Internet retailer that finds itself receiving orders from all over the world to the large American consumer goods producer that introduces new products into emerging markets abroad.

American firms have been challenged at home by the skillful marketing of European and Asian multinationals. Companies such as Toyota, Seimens, Nestlé, Sony, and Samsung have often outperformed their U.S. competitors in American markets. Similarly, U.S. companies in a wide range of industries have found new opportunities abroad. Coca-Cola, General Motors, ExxonMobil, IBM, General Electric, DuPont, Motorola, and dozens of other American companies have developed truly global operations, making and selling their products worldwide.

Today, companies are not only trying to sell more of their locally produced goods in international markets, they also are buying more supplies and components abroad. For example, Bill Blass, one of America's top fashion designers, may choose cloth woven from Australian wool with designs printed in Italy. He will design a dress and e-mail the drawing to a Hong Kong agent, who will place the order with a Chinese factory. Finished dresses will be air-freighted to New York, where they will be redistributed to department and specialty stores around the country.

Thus, managers in countries around the world are increasingly taking a global, not just local, view of the company's industry, competitors, and opportunities. They are asking: What is global marketing? How does it differ from domestic marketing? How do global competitors and forces affect our business? To what extent should we "go global"? Many companies are forming strategic alliances with foreign companies, even competitors, who serve as suppliers or marketing partners. Winning companies in the next century may well be those that have built the best global networks.

Connections with Our Values and Social Responsibilities Marketers are reexamining their connections with social values and responsibilities and with the very Earth that sustains us. As the worldwide consumerism and environmentalism movements mature, today's marketers are being called upon to take greater responsibility for the social and environmental impact of their actions. Corporate ethics and social responsibility have become hot topics in almost every business arena, from the corporate boardroom to the business school classroom. And few companies can ignore the renewed and very demanding environmental movement.

The social responsibility and environmental movements will place even stricter demands on companies in the future. Some companies resist these movements, budging only when forced by legislation or consumer outcries. More forward-looking companies, however, readily accept their responsibilities to the world around them. They view socially responsible actions as an opportunity to do well by doing good — to profit by serving the best long-run interests of their customers and communities. Some companies — such as Ben & Jerry's, Saturn, The Body Shop, and others — are practicing "caring capitalism" and distinguishing themselves by being more civic-minded and caring. They are building social responsibility and action into their company value and mission statements. For example, Ben & Jerry's mission statement challenges all employees, from top management to ice cream scoopers in each store, to include concern for individual and community welfare in their day-to-day decisions.[29]

Broadening Connections   Many different kinds of organizations are using marketing to connect with customers and other important constituencies. In the past, marketing has been most widely applied in the for-profit business sector. In recent years, however, marketing also has become a major part of the strategies of many nonprofit organizations, such as colleges, hospitals, museums, symphony orchestras, and even churches. Consider the following examples:

Siskin Hospital, a rehabilitation facility in the southeastern United States, has developed a marketing Web site — www.siskinrehab.org — which positions the hospital as a leader in rehabilitation. The site provides information and education to the hospital's 14 distinct target audiences, ranging from current and potential patients to health care professionals, hospital staff, job seekers, and the general public. Visitors can browse through an online newsletter to learn more about physical rehabilitation and Suskin's programs; review case histories of past patients and their successes; ask questions of the hospital's doctors, nurses, and therapists; and link to other information sources on the Web or in the hospital's "Patient's Library." Siskin regularly markets the Web site through events, specialty advertising items imprinted with the Web site address, and high-impact direct-mail pieces sent to key prospective users. How has the effort paid off? The site receives more than 400 hits per day and averages 10 to 15 inquiries weekly from potential employees or individuals seeking information on specific rehabilitation-related conditions or treatment programs.[30]

At the Sausalito Presbyterian Church, an affluent congregation just across the Golden Gate Bridge from San Francisco, worshipers who'd rather watch football or go to the beach on Sunday morning do church on Saturday evening at a rock and gospel music service called "Saturday Night Alive." What's particularly revealing about this gathering is the way it's advertised on the church's Web site, www.SausalitoPresbyterian.com. Saturday night worship, it seems, is very user-friendly. "Following the service," the Web page reads, "there is plenty of time to go to dinner, the movies, attend a party or other activities." It's a small but significant disclaimer, revealing how worship must now be marketed as just another diversion in the busy lives of folks in northern California. Church leaders across the nation are using computerized demographic studies and other sophisticated marketing techniques to fill their pews. "Mainline churches don't have to die," says church marketing consultant Richard Southern. "Anyone can learn these marketing and outreach techniques." Southern encourages "an essential . . . shift in the way church is done," putting the needs of potential "customers" before the needs of the institutional church. "Baby boomers think of churches like they think of supermarkets," Southern observes. "They want options, choices, and convenience. Imagine if

Safeway was only open one hour a week, had only one product, and didn't explain it in English."[31]

Similarly, private colleges, facing declining enrollments and rising costs, are using marketing to compete for students and funds. They are defining target markets, improving their communication and promotion, and responding better to student needs and wants. Many performing arts groups—even the Lyric Opera Company of Chicago, which has seasonal sellouts—face huge operating deficits that they must cover by more aggressive donor marketing. Finally, many long-standing nonprofit organizations—the YMCA, the Salvation Army, the Girl Scouts—have lost members and are now modernizing their missions and "products" to attract more members and donors.[32]

Government agencies have also shown an increased interest in marketing. For example, the U.S. Army has a marketing plan to attract recruits, and various government agencies are now designing *social marketing campaigns* to encourage energy conservation and concern for the environment or to discourage smoking, excessive drinking, and drug use. Even the once-stodgy U.S. Postal Service has developed innovative marketing to sell commemorative stamps, promote its priority mail services against those of its competitors, and lift its image. It has invested heavily in its "Fly Like an Eagle" image advertising campaign. Roxanne Symko, the USPS's manager of advertising and promotion, comments, "We want to position ourselves in a new light, as innovative and looking forward."[33]

Thus, it seems that every type of organization can connect through marketing. The continued growth of nonprofit and public-sector marketing presents new and exciting challenges for marketing managers.

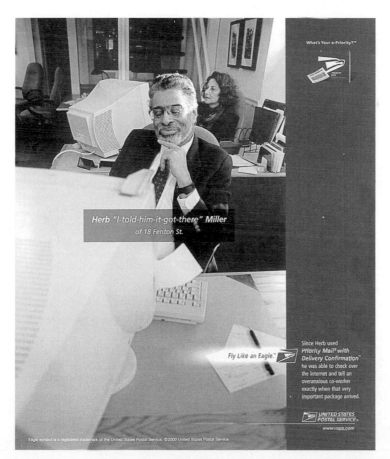

Broadening Connections: The once stodgy U.S. Postal Service has invested millions in its innovative "Fly Like an Eagle" image advertising campaign.

The New Connected World of Marketing

So, today, smart marketers of all kinds are taking advantage of new opportunities for connecting with their customers, their marketing partners, and the world around them. Table 1-1 compares the old marketing thinking to the new. The old marketing thinking saw marketing as little more than selling or advertising. It viewed marketing as customer acquisition rather than customer care. It emphasized trying to make a profit on each sale rather than trying to profit by managing customer lifetime value. And it concerned itself with trying to sell products rather than to understand, create, communicate, and deliver real value to customers.

Fortunately, this old marketing thinking is now giving way to newer ways of thinking. Today's smart marketing companies are improving their customer knowledge and customer connections. They are targeting profitable customers, then finding innovative ways to capture and keep these customers. They are forming more direct connections with customers and building lasting customer relationships. Using more targeted media and integrating their marketing communications, they are delivering meaningful and consistent messages through every customer contact. They are employing more technologies such as videoconferencing, sales automation software, and the Internet, intranets, and extranets. They view their suppliers and distributors as partners, not adversaries. In sum, today's companies are forming new kinds of connections for delivering superior value to their customers.

We will explore all of these developments in more detail in future pages. For now, we must recognize that marketing will continue to change dramatically as we move into the twenty-first century. The new millennium offers many exciting opportunities for forward-thinking marketers.

Table 1-1 Marketing Connections in Transition	
The Old Marketing Thinking	**The New Marketing Thinking**
Connections with Customers	
Be sales and product centered	Be market and customer centered
Practice mass marketing	Target selected market segments or individuals
Focus on products and sales	Focus on customer satisfaction and value
Make sales to customers	Develop customer relationships
Get new customers	Keep old customers
Grow share of market	Grow share of customer
Serve any customer	Serve profitable customers, "fire" losing ones
Communicate through mass media	Connect with customers directly
Make standardized products	Develop customized products
Connections with Marketing Partners	
Leave customer satisfaction and value to sales and marketing	Enlist all departments in the cause of customer satisfaction and value
Go it alone	Partner with other firms
Connections with the World Around Us	
Market locally	Market locally *and* globally
Assume profit responsibility	Assume social and environmental responsibility
Marketing for profits	Marketing for nonprofits
Conduct commerce in market*places*	Conduct e-commerce in market*spaces*

STOP *Rest Stop: Reviewing the Concepts*

Now that you've completed the first leg of your marketing journey, let's review what you've seen. So far, we've examined the basics of what marketing is, the philosophies that guide it, and the challenges it faces in the new connected millennium.

Today's successful companies—whether large or small, for-profit or nonprofit, domestic or global—share a strong customer focus and a heavy commitment to marketing. Many people think of marketing as only selling or advertising. But marketing combines many activities—marketing research, product development, distribution, pricing, advertising, personal selling, and others—designed to sense, serve, and satisfy consumer needs while meeting the organization's goals. Marketing seeks to attract new customers by promising superior value and to keep and grow current customers by delivering satisfaction.

Marketing operates within a dynamic global environment. Rapid changes can quickly make yesterday's winning strategies obsolete. In the next century, marketers will face many new challenges and opportunities. To be successful, companies will have to be strongly market focused.

1. Define what marketing is and discuss its core concepts.

Marketing is a social and managerial process whereby individuals and groups obtain what they need and want through creating and exchanging products and value with others. The core concepts of marketing are *needs, wants,* and *demands; products, services,* and *experiences; value, satisfaction,* and *quality; exchange, transactions,* and *relationships;* and *markets. Wants* are the form assumed by human needs when shaped by culture and individual personality. When backed by buying power, wants become *demands.* People satisfy their needs, wants, and demands with products and services. A *product* is anything that can be offered to a market to satisfy a need, want, or demand. Products also include *services* and other entities such as *experiences, persons, places, organizations, information,* and *ideas.*

2. Explain the relationships between customer value, satisfaction, and quality.

In deciding which products and services to buy, consumers rely on their perception of relative value. *Customer value* is the difference between the values the customer gains from owning and using a product and the costs of obtaining and using the product. *Customer satisfaction* depends on a product's perceived performance in delivering value relative to a buyer's expectations. Customer satisfaction is closely linked to *quality,* leading many companies to adopt *total quality* practices. Marketing occurs when people satisfy their needs, wants, and demands through *exchange.* Beyond creating short-term transactions, marketers need to build long-term relationships with valued customers, distributors, dealers, and suppliers.

3. Define marketing management and understand how marketers manage demand and build profitable customer relationships.

Marketing management is the analysis, planning, implementation, and control of programs designed to create, build, and maintain beneficial exchanges with target buyers for the purpose of achieving organizational objectives. It involves more than simply finding enough customers for the company's current output. Marketing is at times also concerned with changing or even reducing demand. Managing demand means managing customers. Beyond designing strategies to *attract* new customers and create *transactions* with them, today's companies are focusing on *retaining* current customers and building lasting relationships through offering superior customer value and satisfaction.

4. Compare the five marketing management philosophies.

Marketing management can be guided by five different philosophies. The *production concept* holds that consumers favor products that are available and highly affordable; management's task is to improve production efficiency and bring down prices. The *product concept* holds that consumers favor products that offer the most in quality, performance, and innovative features; thus, little promotional effort is required. The *selling concept* holds that consumers will not buy enough of the organization's products unless it undertakes a large-scale selling and promotion effort. The *marketing concept* holds that achieving organizational goals depends on determining the needs and wants of target markets and delivering the desired satisfactions more effectively and efficiently than competitors do. The *societal marketing concept* holds that generating customer satisfaction *and* long-run societal well-being are the keys to both achieving the company's goals and fulfilling its responsibilities.

5. Analyze the major challenges facing marketers heading into the new "connected" millennium.

As we head into the next millennium, dramatic changes in the marketplace are creating many marketing opportunities and challenges. Major marketing developments can be summed up in a single theme: *connections*. The explosive growth in connecting technologies—computer, information, telecommunications, and transportation technologies—has created an exciting New Economy, filled with new ways for marketers to learn about and serve consumers, in large groups or one-to-one. Marketers are rapidly redefining how they connect with their customers, with their marketing partners, and with the world around them. They are choosing their customers more carefully and developing closer, more direct, and more lasting connections with them. Realizing that going it alone is going out of style, they are connecting more closely with other company departments and with other firms in an integrated effort to bring more value to customers. They are taking a fresh look at the ways in which they connect with the broader world, resulting in increased globalization, growing attention to social and environmental responsibilities, and greater use of marketing by nonprofit and public-sector organizations. The new, connected millennium offers exciting possibilities for forward-thinking marketers.

Navigating the Key Terms

For a detailed analysis of the meaning and importance of each of the following key terms, visit our Web page at www.prenhall.com/kotler.

Customer
  satisfaction
Customer value
Demands

Demarketing
Exchange
Internet
Market
Marketing
Marketing concept
Marketing management
Need
Product

Product concept
Production concept
Relationship marketing
Selling concept
Service
Societal marketing
  concept
Transaction
Want

Travel Log

The following concept checks and discussion questions will help you to keep track of and apply the concepts you've studied in this chapter.

Concept Checks

Fill in the blanks, then see next page for the correct answers.

1. _____ is a social and managerial process whereby individuals and groups obtain what they need and want through creating and exchanging products and value with others.

2. Today, marketing must be understood not in the old sense of making a sale—"telling and selling"—but in the new sense of _____.

3. The concept of _____ is not limited to physical objects—anything capable of satisfying a need can be called a _____.

4. _____ is the difference between the values the customer gains from owning and using a product and the costs of obtaining the product.

5. Smart companies aim to _____ customers by promising only what they can deliver, then delivering more than they promise.

6. Many companies today apply the notion of "_____" when they make certain that the quality they offer is the quality that customers want.

7. The goal of _____ is to deliver long-term value to customers, and the measures of success are long-term customer satisfaction and retention.

8. A _____ is the set of actual and potential buyers of a product.

9. Most companies are started by individuals who live by their wits. This would be an example of _____ marketing.

10. There are five alternative concepts under which organizations conduct their marketing activities: they are the _____, _____, _____, _____, and _____ concepts.

11. "We make it happen for you," "To fly, to serve," "We're not satisfied until you are," and "Let us exceed your expectations" are all colorful illustrations of the _____ concept.

12. The major force behind the new connectedness in the "Connected" millennium is _____.

Concept Checks Answers: 1. Marketing; 2. satisfying customer needs; 3. product; product; 4. Customer value; 5. delight; 6. return on quality (ROQ); 7. relationship marketing; 8. market; 9. entrepreneurial; 10. production; product; selling; marketing; societal marketing; 11. marketing; 12. technology.

Discussing the Issues

1. Answer the question, "What is marketing?"

2. Discuss the concept of customer value and its importance to successful marketing. How are the concepts of customer value and relationship marketing linked?

3. Identify the single biggest difference between the marketing concept and the production, product, and selling concepts. Discuss which concepts are easier to apply in the short-run. Which concept offers the best long-run success potential? Why?

4. According to economist Milton Friedman, "Few trends could so thoroughly undermine the very foundations of our free society as the acceptance by corporate officials of a social responsibility other than to make as much money for their stockholders as possible." Do you agree or disagree with Friedman's statement? What are some of the drawbacks of the societal marketing concept?

5. The major marketing developments as we enter the new millennium can be summed up in a single theme: *connectedness*. Explain what "connectedness" is and how marketers can apply it to customers, marketing partners, and the world around us.

Mastering Marketing

Beyond creating short-term transactions, marketers need to build long-term relationships with valued customers, distributors, dealers, and suppliers. Cite three examples from CanGo of relationship marketing with customers, distributors, dealers, or suppliers. Be specific in your comments.

Traveling on the Net

Point of Interest: The Marketing Concept

Companies can demonstrate the marketing concept on their Web sites by including features that are important to customers and prospects. Web users want to know about product benefits and where they can purchase the firm's products. However, sites that give users something of interest beyond product descriptions create additional value for the customer. Many sites attempt to target customer segments by language, gender, degree of technical understanding, and age. Finally, an important sign of customer orientation is having a web address that is easy to remember, use, and communicate to the consumer. Evaluate the following Web site based on its perceived attention to the marketing concept: www.dell.com.

For Discussion

1. What do you think is the most important customer benefit stressed on this site?

2. What new products did you find?

3. To what extent does this site employ the marketing concept? Support your answer.

4. How does Dell attempt to build relationships with its customers? What evidence of enhanced customer value do you see?

5. Is there anything missing from the site? How could Dell improve the site to enhance the marketing of its products?

Application Thinking

Go to **www.compaq.com**, **www.apple.com**, and **www.ibm.com** and compare these sites to the **www.dell.com** site in terms of how well they apply the marketing concept. Develop a list of important site characteristics and construct a grid in which you compare the sites on these characteristics. Present your findings in class.

MAP—Marketing Applications

Using the MAP Feature

The best way to become a good marketing decision maker is to practice marketing decision making. In MAP (marketing application) stops at the end of each chapter, you will find interesting case histories, real-life situations, or timely descriptions from business articles which illustrate specific chapter subjects. At each MAP stop, you will be asked to make marketing decisions as if you were the marketing manager of the company in question. Here's your first MAP Stop—have fun on your journey!

MAP Stop 1

One of the most loyal but yet hard to reach markets among Gen Y teens is the skateboarder market. Of all the clothing and tennis shoe manufacturers, only California-based Vans, Inc. has really been successful. Vans has figured out that skateboarding has come a long way from the days when a kid made a board by nailing a pair of roller-skates to the bottom of a wooden plank. By pioneering thick-soled, slip-on sneakers which were able to absorb the shock of three- to five-foot leaps, Vans has remained "cool" with the skateboard crowd. Problem— how to grow your market when your target audience is part of an outlaw culture that has been banned from most modern malls and shopping centers. Vans believes that branching out into elaborate skateboard parks (eight have opened at the very malls that have banned skateboarders), designing clothing lines, and manufacturing snowboard boots will be the strategies that will serve them well in the next decade. Using its 140 retail stores (as well as a number of independents), Vans has carved out a one to two percent share of the giant sneakers market. Though

not exactly a Nike (that owns over fifty percent of this lucrative market), Vans is betting its future on a plan that will position them in the growing number of X-treme sports. However, one area that Vans is avoiding is inline skating since most Vans loyalists and skateboard enthusiasts consider this sport to be for wimps. Therefore, it appears that the number one guiding principle for Vans' strategic positioning in the future will be to remain authentic and loyal to their roots. Cawabungah!

Thinking Like a Marketing Manager

1. What elements of the marketing concept does Vans appear to be applying with their strategies?
2. Go to a retail outlet that carries Vans, or go online to **www.vans.com**, and review their product lines. What seem to be the advantages and the disadvantages of products they carry? After considering Vans' target market and its outlaw image, what do you think would be the best way to reach this target market? What "connections" is Vans attempting to make with its current promotions?
3. It has been reported that Vans is now attempting to reach the female market with its clothing line. Present three relationship- or value-oriented strategies that you believe might help them to accomplish this goal.
4. Keeping in mind the marketing concept, relationship marketing, and customer value, design a strategy to help Vans enter the snowboard market with its new line of snowboard boots. How will industry leader Burton Snowboards (**www.burton.com**) likely react to your entry and strategy? How would you deal with this reaction? Present your strategy and ideas to the class.

chapter 2

Strategic Planning and the Marketing Process

ROAD MAP:
Previewing the Concepts

Ready to travel on? In the first chapter, you learned the core concepts and philosophies of marketing. In this leg of your journey, we'll dig more deeply into marketing's role in the broader organization and into the specifics of the marketing process. First, marketing urges a whole-company philosophy that puts customers at the center. Then, marketers work with other company functions to design strategies for delivering value to carefully targeted customers and to develop "marketing mixes"—consisting of product, price, distribution, and promotion tactics—to carry out these strategies profitably. These first two chapters will give you a full introduction to the basics of marketing, the decisions marketing managers make, and where marketing fits into an organization. After that, we'll take a look at the environments in which marketing operates.

▶ After studying this chapter, you should be able to

1. explain companywide strategic planning and its four steps
2. discuss how to design business portfolios and develop growth strategies
3. explain functional planning strategies and assess marketing's role in strategic planning
4. describe the marketing process and the forces that influence it
5. list the marketing management functions, including the elements of a marketing plan

First stop: Intel, a company that flat-out dominates its industry. As you read about Intel, ask yourself: Just what *is* it about this company's marketing strategy that has generated 35 percent average annual sales growth and even more impressive returns to investors over the past decade? What is Intel doing so right? How will the company have to adapt its marketing strategy in future years to stay on top in its fast-changing high-tech marketplace?

For more than 30 years, Intel has dominated the microprocessor market for personal computers. How's this for eye-popping market performance: In the 20 years or so since IBM introduced its first PCs based on Intel's 8088 microprocessor, the chip giant's sales have jumped 25-fold to more than $33 billion. During the decade of the 1990s, Intel's share of the microprocessor market topped 90 percent, gross margins hovered above 60 percent, and annual return to investors averaged an astounding 38 percent.

Intel's stunning success has resulted from strong strategic planning and its relentless dedication to a simple marketing strategy: delivering superior value to customers by creating a continuous stream of leading-edge products. The company invests heavily to develop state-of-the-art products and bring them quickly to market—last year alone it spent a whopping $7.5 billion on R&D and capital spending. The result has been a rapid succession of better and better chips that no competitor can match.

Intel's microprocessors are true wonders of modern technology. Early PC users were dazzled by Intel's i386 chips, which contained one-quarter million transistors and ran at clock speeds approaching 20 megahertz. Just a dozen years later, current buyers yawn over Intel's Pentium 4 microprocessors, which contain more than 42 million transistors and run at speeds exceeding 1.5 *giga*hertz (1,500 megahertz). Incredibly, the Intel microprocessors of 2009 will pack a cool *one billion* transistors and will blaze along at clock speeds of 300 gigahertz. In fact, Intel has innovated at such a torrid pace that its microprocessors have sometimes outpaced market needs and capabilities. To help things along, Intel has invested heavily in market development, creating new PC applications that can take full advantage of the latest Intel-powered PCs.

Intel's marketing strategy goes far beyond innovative products and market development. It also includes innovative advertising. In mid-1991, Intel launched its groundbreaking "Intel Inside" advertising campaign to build relationships with final computer buyers—Intel's customers' customers. Traditionally, chip companies like Intel had marketed only to the manufacturers who buy chips directly. But as long as microprocessors remained anonymous little lumps hidden inside a user's computer, Intel remained at the mercy of the clone makers and other competitors. The brand-awareness ads create brand personality and convince PC buyers that Intel microprocessors really are superior. Intel also subsidizes ads by computer manufacturers that include the "Intel Inside" logo. Over the years, the hundreds of millions of dollars invested by Intel and its partners in the "Intel Inside" campaign have created strong brand preference for Intel chips among final buyers, in turn making Intel's chips more attractive to computer manufacturers.

Intel's strategy of innovation has brought it amazing success. However, no company can afford to rest on its laurels. Even the best marketing strategy requires constant adaptation and refinement—sometimes even radical transformation. During the past two decades, Intel's incredible success has gone hand in hand with the explosive growth of personal computer sales. Entering the twenty-first century, as the personal computer industry matured, Intel faced some difficult challenges. After two decades of 35 percent average annual growth, sales in 2001 grew only 5 percent and earnings declined for the first time in a decade. "The biggest culprit in Intel's slowdown was a changing PC landscape," explains an industry analyst. "PCs were losing some of their luster. Instead of clamoring for more power to run fatter software programs, many customers just wanted cheap PCs to get online. Low-cost PCs meant low-cost chips." Falling PC prices, coupled with stronger competition from new rivals, cut into Intel's sales, market share, and profit margins.

To meet this challenge, Intel has had to adapt its strategy and find new ways to grow. Of course, microprocessors are still the heart of Intel's business. To cement its dominance and sell more chips in the increasingly competitive PC market, Intel continues to invest heavily to develop the expected stream of new microprocessors needed to run the next-generation applications. But given the falloff in PC sales growth, Intel knows that it must move in new directions if it is to achieve the 20 percent annual growth it seeks. For starters, Intel has introduced a bevy of new non-PC microprocessors, including chips for everything from mobile phones to consumer electronics products.

But Intel's strategy is undergoing a far more sweeping transformation. The company is taking its passion for innovation in an exciting new direction—the Internet. "The PC was the dominant force in the last decade," says Intel president and CEO Craig Barrett. "The Internet is clearly the dominant force in the forthcoming decade. So we're hitching to that star and riding it as fast as we can." Our mission "for years was to be the building-block supplier to the computer industry," he says. Now, Intel must become "an integral part of the hearts and brains of the new Internet economy."

Intel really does believe in the promise of this new economy. Consider what happened at the company's recent developers' conference.

As 3,200 digit heads crammed into a ballroom at the . . . convention center, giant video screens flashed to life and the unmistakable riff of Steppenwolf's "Born To Be Wild" blared into the hall—only it had new lyrics: "Get your modem running, head out on the I-way. Looking for e-ventures, and whatever comes our way. Born to be wired." It was the warm-up for a speech by [former Intel CEO] Andy Grove. . . . Now, instead of being just the leading purveyor of PC technology, Grove says, Intel aims to make the building blocks for the entire Net Economy.

This new Internet mission takes Intel in some dramatically different directions. It's pushing rapidly into areas such as business networking, wireless communications, Web hosting services, and even running Web sites for other companies. Such new ventures are putting some strain on management and a culture that have long focused on a single product. When it comes to these new businesses, notes an industry analyst, "Intel is a gawky adolescent." But the new strategy is already producing results. Although such new initiatives now bring in only about 20 percent of Intel's business, they are growing at an impressive 50 percent annually.

Most experts agree that Intel has the skills, clout, and resources to build or buy its way into these new markets quickly. To speed the transformation, for example, Intel is spending lavishly to acquire existing technology companies. Over the past few years, it's spent billions to snap up companies such as Dialogic, which makes Internet telephony hardware; Ipivot, an e-commerce system vendor; and DSP Communications, a developer of mobile wireless chip technology. Intel also established an investment fund, called Intel Capital, which last year invested $1.2 billion in small technology start-up firms from which the company can draw insights and energy. "Our goal is to expose the company to every facet of the Internet economy," says the fund's manager. "It has already led to an opening of minds."

Looking ahead, Intel must plan its marketing strategy carefully. The driving force remains constant—innovate or fall by the wayside. To stay ahead of the pack, it must constantly adapt its marketing strategy to changing market needs and circumstances. Intel's top executives don't foresee any slowing of the pace. Says Barrett, "We picture ourselves going down the road at 120 miles an hour. Somewhere there's going to be a brick wall, . . . but our view is that it's better to run into the wall than to anticipate it and fall short."[1]

All companies must look ahead and develop long-term strategies to meet the changing conditions in their industries. Each company must find the game plan that makes the most sense given its specific situation, opportunities, objectives, and resources. The hard task of selecting an overall company strategy for long-run survival and growth is called *strategic planning.*

In this chapter, we look first at the organization's overall strategic planning. Next, we discuss marketing's role in the organization as defined by the overall strategic plan. Finally, we explain the marketing management process—the process that marketers undertake to carry out their role in the organization.

Strategic Planning

Many companies operate without formal plans. In new companies, managers are sometimes so busy they have no time for planning. In small companies, managers sometimes think that only large corporations need formal planning. In mature companies, many managers argue that they have done well without formal planning and that therefore it cannot be too important. They may resist taking the time to prepare a written plan. They may argue that the marketplace changes too quickly for a plan to be useful, that it would end up collecting dust.

Granted, planning is not much fun, and it takes time away from doing. Yet companies must plan. As someone said, "If you fail to plan, you are planning to fail."[2] Formal planning can yield many benefits for all types of companies, large and small, new and mature.

The process of planning may be as important as the plans that emerge. Planning encourages management to think systematically about what has happened, what is happening, and what might happen. It forces the company to sharpen its objectives and policies, leads to better coordination of company efforts, and provides clearer performance standards for control. The argument that planning is less useful in a fast-changing environment makes little sense. In fact, the opposite is true: Sound planning helps the company to anticipate and respond quickly to changes, and to prepare better for sudden developments.

Strategic planning
The process of developing and maintaining a strategic fit between the organization's goals and capabilities and its changing marketing opportunities. It involves defining a clear company mission, setting supporting objectives, designing a sound business portfolio, and coordinating functional strategies.

Companies usually prepare annual plans, long-range plans, and strategic plans. The annual and long-range plans deal with the company's current businesses and how to keep them going. In contrast, the strategic plan involves adapting the firm to take advantage of opportunities in its constantly changing environment. We define **strategic planning** as the process of developing and maintaining a strategic fit between the organization's goals and capabilities and its changing marketing opportunities.

Strategic planning sets the stage for the rest of the planning in the firm. It relies on defining a clear company mission, setting supporting company objectives, designing a sound business portfolio, and coordinating functional strategies (see Figure 2-1). At the corporate level, the company first defines its overall purpose and mission. This mission

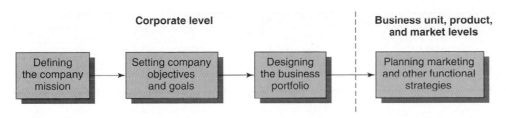

Corporate level | Business unit, product, and market levels

| Defining the company mission | → | Setting company objectives and goals | → | Designing the business portfolio | ⋮ → | Planning marketing and other functional strategies |

Figure 2-1
Steps in strategic planning

then is turned into detailed supporting objectives that guide the whole company. Next, headquarters decides what portfolio of businesses and products is best for the company and how much support to give each one. In turn, each business and product unit must develop detailed marketing and other departmental plans that support the companywide plan. Thus, marketing planning occurs at the business unit, product, and market levels. It supports company strategic planning with more detailed planning for specific marketing opportunities.[3]

Defining the Company's Business and Mission

An organization exists to accomplish something. At first, it has a clear purpose or mission, but over time its mission may become unclear as the organization grows, adds new products and markets, or faces new conditions in the environment. When management senses that the organization is drifting, it must renew its search for purpose. It is time to ask: What is our business? Who is the customer? What do consumers value? What should our business be? These simple-sounding questions are among the most difficult the company will ever have to answer. Successful companies continuously raise these questions and answer them carefully and completely.

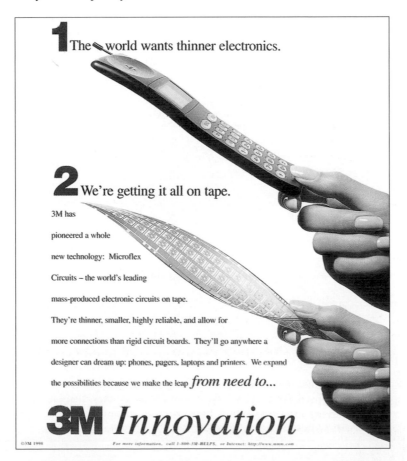

Company mission: 3M does more than just make adhesives, scientific equipment, health care, and communications products. It solves people's problems by putting innovation to work for them.

Marketing at Work 2-1

IBM: Big Blue Dinosaur or E-Business Animal?

Only a decade ago, if you'd asked top managers at IBM what business they were in, they might well have answered, "We sell computer hardware and software." Laboring under a pretty bad case of marketing myopia, a heavily product-focused IBM lost sight of its customers' needs. As a result, as customer needs changed, IBM didn't, and its fortunes slipped accordingly. By the early 1990s, "Big Blue's" market share and stock price were falling rapidly.

Since those sadly blue days, however, IBM has undergone a remarkable transformation. The turnaround started in 1993, when new CEO Lou Gerstner brought a renewed customer focus to IBM. As one of his first acts, Gerstner asked all top IBM managers to meet face to face with important customers—what he called "bear-hugging customers"—and report back concerning their problems and priorities. Gerstner and his managers learned that corporate computing is getting more and more confusing for customers. In this new high-tech, connected age, companies must master a dizzying array of information technologies to serve not only their customers but also suppliers, distributors, and employees.

Gerstner realized that in this more complex computing world, customers are buying much more from IBM than just computer hardware and software. They are buying solutions to ever-more-bewildering information technology (IT) problems. This realization led to a fundamental redefinition of IBM's business. Now, if you ask almost any IBM manager to define the business, he or she will tell you, "We deliver *solutions* to customers' information technology problems." In the words of the IBM ad slogan, IBM delivers "solutions for a small planet."

The fact is that most customers don't really care whose hardware or software they buy. For example, Pat Zilvitis, chief information officer at Gillette in Boston and a big IBM customer, claims that it's not IBM's PCs, servers, mainframes, or software that attracts him. "I often don't know if I need hardware or software or services, and I don't care," he says. What draws him to IBM is that Big Blue employs an unmatched breadth of products, people, and services to deliver an IT system that works. "I don't view IBM as a hardware vendor anymore," he says. "I think of them as an information technology [part-ner] that can help me in a number of different ways."

The new customer solutions focus has greatly promoted the role of services relative to hardware and software in the IBM mix. The company now offers an expanded set of IT consulting, total systems management, strategic outsourcing, and e-business services that can help customers with everything from assessing, planning, designing, implementing, and running their IT systems to bringing them up to speed on e-commerce. Some companies, such as AT&T, Eastman Kodak, and Hertz, have outsourced their entire IT systems to IBM. In such deals, IBM runs the whole IT show—the customer's IT employees work for IBM, and IBM owns the customer's computers, which it then manages. Services are now IBM's hottest

IBM defines its business as delivering solutions to customers' e-business problems. It asks, "Who do you need?" The answer: "People like Steve Joern, who can move easily between concepts of technology and concepts of business. People who get it. People who get it done."

growth area, accounting for 40 percent of the company's more than $88 billion in sales and 48 percent of its profits. Analysts predict that services will generate almost 46 percent of IBM's revenues by 2005. As one IBM watcher comments, "IBM—International Business Machines—is becoming IBS, where 'S' is for services, software, and solutions."

Still, few people realize that IBM is the world's largest supplier of IT services. To help close this perceptual gap, IBM launched a $75 million global services ad campaign with the tag line "People Who Think. People Who Do. People Who Get It." To counter the out-of-date notion that IBM provides only computer hardware, the campaign profiled specific IBM people—the "strategists, problem solvers, implementers . . . who make sure that the solution you want is the solution you get." One ad showcased Nick Simicich, an IBM ethical hacker (unofficial title: "paid professional paranoid") who purposely invaded customers' critical information systems to see if they're safe from hostile hackers. Another featured Patrick McMahon, who helped Prudential reengineer its sales processes, doubling the number of policies sold and raising commissions 153 percent in the pilot program. Patrick's mission: "To work with clients to ensure that IT solutions run smoothly and support their business objectives." According to an executive at IBM's advertising agency, the message is simple: "IBM has people who [can help you] excel in e-business and consulting, business recovery, and network systems management."

In the latest phase of its cus-tomer-solutions makeover, IBM is positioning itself as the "e-business solutions company." (It coined e-business as a catch-all term for Internet, Intranet, and e-commerce applications.) As more and more companies use the Internet as their primary connecting technology, e-business is growing explosively. IBM wants to be the company to turn to for e-business strategies and solutions.

At the heart of this e-business strategy is a division called Business Innovation Strategies. This group includes all of the company's e-business and Web-related initiatives, along with consulting services that help clients to take advantage of the Internet. In just the past two years, IBM has introduced 20 new e-business services, including customer relationship management, business intelligence, supply chain management, and business process management services. Big Blue claims to have 10,000 e-business customers. For some, this means little more than having IBM host their Web sites on one of its servers. For others, however, it means having IBM create and implement a totally new business–customer connection. For example, Federated Department Stores selected IBM to remake its rudimentary Macy's Web site into a full e-commerce enterprise. The results were dazzling. In only six months, IBM converted Macys.com from a site selling only 5,000 products to one that now features 250,000 products, along with software "wizards" that help visitors find the products they seek. IBM now serves as consultant and hosts the site.

E-business appears to be an ideal setting for IBM's soup-to-nuts menu of IT solutions. More than one-quarter of IBM's revenues now come from e-business products and services. Moreover, IBM appears to be capturing the minds of e-business customers as well as their purchases. As a result of both its e-business deeds and millions of dollars spent on worldwide advertising proclaiming its e-business prowess, IBM appears to own a major portion of the e-business position. A recent IBM survey of IT managers in 27 countries found that 8 out of 10 understood the meaning of "e-business" as defined by IBM.

Thus, in a remarkably short time, IBM has transformed itself from a company that "sells computer hardware and software" to one that "delivers customer IT solutions." It's not the old IBM anymore and the marketplace has responded strongly. Over the past four years, IBM has experienced steady sales growth, rapidly improving profits, and a fivefold increase in its stock price. By defining itself in terms of the customer needs it serves rather that the products it sells, IBM has been transformed "from a big blue dinosaur to an e-business animal."

Sources: See David Kirkpatrick, "IBM: From Big Blue Dinosaur to E-Business Animal," Fortune, April 26, 1999, pp. 116–125; Laura Loro, "IBM Touts Position as No. 1 in IT Services," Advertising Age's Business Marketing, April 1999, p. 41; David Rocks, "IBM's Hottest Product Isn't a Product," Business Week, October 2, 2000, pp. 118–120; Gary Hamel, "Waking Up IBM," Harvard Business Review, July–August 2000, pp. 137–146; John Dodge, "IBM," MC Technology Marketing Intelligence, January 2001, pp. 42–43; and Peter Burroughs and Andrew Park, "Can Compaq Escape from Hardware Hell?" Business Week, July 9, 2001, pp. 38–39.

Mission statement
A statement of the organization's purpose—what it wants to accomplish in the larger environment.

Many organizations develop formal mission statements that answer these questions. A **mission statement** is a statement of the organization's purpose—what it wants to accomplish in the larger environment. A clear mission statement acts as an "invisible hand" that guides people in the organization.

Traditionally companies have defined their businesses in product terms ("We manufacture furniture") or in technological terms ("We are a chemical-processing firm"). But mission statements should be *market oriented* (see Marketing at Work 2-1). Products and technologies eventually become outdated, but basic market needs may last forever. A market-oriented mission statement defines the business in terms of satisfying basic customer needs. For example, 3M does more than just make adhesives, scientific equipment, and health care products. It solves people's problems by putting innovation to work for them. Charles Schwab isn't just a brokerage firm—it sees itself as "guardians of our customers' financial dreams." Southwest Airlines sees itself as providing not only air travel but also total customer service. Its mission: "The mission of Southwest Airlines is dedication to the highest quality of customer service delivered with a sense of warmth, friendliness, individual pride, and company spirit." Likewise, eBay's mission isn't simply to hold online auctions. Instead, it connects individual buyers and sellers in "the world's online marketplace," a unique Web community in which they can shop around, have fun, and get to know each other, for example, by chatting at the eBay Cafe.[4] Table 2-1 provides several other examples of product-oriented versus market-oriented business definitions.

Management should avoid making its mission too narrow or too broad. A pencil manufacturer that says it is in the communication equipment business is stating its mission too broadly. Missions should be *realistic*. Singapore Airlines would be deluding itself if it adopted the mission to become the world's largest airline. Missions should also be *specific*. Many mission statements are written for public relations purposes and lack specific, workable guidelines. Too often, companies develop mission statements that look much like this tongue-and-cheek version:

> We are committed to serving the quality of life of cultures and communities everywhere, regardless of sex, age, sexual preference, religion, or disability, whether they be customers, suppliers, employees, or shareholders—we serve the planet—to the highest ethical standards of integrity, best practice, and sustainability, through policies of openness and transparency vetted by our participation in the International Quality Business Global Audit forum, to ensure measurable outcomes worldwide. . . .[5]

Such generic statements sound good but provide little real guidance or inspiration. In contrast, Celestial Seasonings' mission statement is very specific: "Our mission is to grow and dominate the U.S. specialty tea market by exceeding consumer expectations with: The best tasting, 100 percent natural hot and iced teas, packaged with Celestial art and philosophy, creating the most valued tea experience. . . "[6]

Missions should fit the *market environment*. The Girl Scouts of America would not recruit successfully in today's environment with its former mission: "to prepare young girls for motherhood and wifely duties." The organization should base its mission on its *distinctive competencies*. McDonald's could probably enter the solar energy business, but that would not take advantage of its core competence—providing low-cost food and fast service to large groups of customers.

Finally, mission statements should be *motivating*. A company's mission should not be stated as making more sales or profits—profits are only a reward for undertaking a useful activity. A company's employees need to feel that their work is significant and that it contributes to people's lives. One study found that "visionary companies" set a purpose beyond making money. For example, Walt Disney Company's aim is "making people happy." But even though profits may not be part of these companies' mission statements, they are the inevitable result. The study showed that 18 visionary companies outperformed other companies in the stock market by more than 6 to 1 over the period from 1926 to 1990.[7]

Table 2-1   Market-Oriented Business Definitions

Company	Product-Oriented Definition	Market-Oriented Definition
Amazon.com	We sell books, videos, CDs, toys, consumer electronics, hardware, housewares, and other products.	We make the Internet buying experience fast, easy, and enjoyable—we're the place where you can find and discover anything you want to buy online.
America Online	We provide online services.	We create customer connectivity, anytime, anywhere.
Disney	We run theme parks.	We create fantasies—a place where America still works the way it's supposed to.
eBay	We hold online auctions.	We connect individual buyers and sellers in the world's online marketplace, a unique Web community in which they can shop around, have fun, and get to know each other.
Home Depot	We sell tools and home repair and improvement items.	We provide advice and solutions that transform ham-handed homeowners into Mr. and Mrs. Fixits.
Revlon	We make cosmetics.	We sell lifestyle and self-expression; success and status; memories, hopes, and dreams.
Ritz-Carlton Hotels	We rent rooms.	We create the Ritz-Carlton experience—one that enlivens the senses, instills well-being, and fulfills even the unexpressed wishes and needs of our guests.
Wal-Mart	We run discount stores.	We deliver low prices, every day.

Setting Company Objectives and Goals

The company's mission needs to be turned into detailed supporting objectives for each level of management. Each manager should have objectives and be responsible for reaching them. For example, Monsanto operates in many businesses, including agriculture, pharmaceuticals, and food products. The company defines its mission as one of helping to feed the world's exploding population while at the same time sustaining the environment. This mission leads to a hierarchy of objectives, including business objectives and marketing objectives. Monsanto's overall objective is to create environmentally better products and get them to market faster at lower costs. For its part, the agricultural division's objective is to increase agricultural productivity and reduce chemical pollution by researching new pest- and disease-resistant crops that produce higher yields without chemical spraying. But research is expensive and requires improved profits to plow back into research programs. So improving profits becomes another major business objective. Profits can be improved by increasing sales or reducing costs. Sales can be increased by improving the company's share of the U.S. market, by entering new foreign markets, or both. These goals then become the company's current marketing objectives.

Marketing strategies must be developed to support these marketing objectives. To increase its U.S. market share, Monsanto might increase its products' availability and

Monsanto defines its mission as one of "food, hope, health"— of helping to feed the world's exploding population while at the same time sustaining the environment. This mission leads to specific business and marketing objectives.

promotion. To enter new foreign markets, the company may cut prices and target large farms abroad. These are its broad marketing strategies. Each broad marketing strategy must then be defined in greater detail. For example, increasing the product's promotion may require more salespeople and more advertising; if so, both requirements will have to be spelled out. In this way, the firm's mission is translated into a set of objectives for the current period. The objectives should be as specific as possible. The objective to "increase our market share" is not as useful as the objective to "increase our market share to 15 percent by the end of the second year."

Designing the Business Portfolio

Business portfolio
The collection of businesses and products that make up the company.

Guided by the company's mission statement and objectives, management now must plan its **business portfolio**—the collection of businesses and products that make up the company. The best business portfolio is the one that best fits the company's strengths and weaknesses to opportunities in the environment. The company must (1) analyze its *current* business portfolio and decide which businesses should receive more, less, or no investment, and (2) develop growth strategies for adding *new* products or businesses to the portfolio.

Analyzing the Current Business Portfolio

Portfolio analysis
A tool by which management identifies and evaluates the various businesses making up the company.

The major activity in strategic planning is business **portfolio analysis,** whereby management evaluates the businesses making up the company. The company will want to put strong resources into its more profitable businesses and phase down or drop its weaker ones. An excellent example is General Electric. Through skillful management of its portfolio of businesses, General Electric has grown to be one of the world's largest and most profitable companies. Over the past two decades, GE has shed many low-performing businesses, such as air-conditioning and housewares. It kept only those businesses that could be number one or number two in their industries. At the same time, it has acquired

The business portfolio: Through skillful management of its portfolio of businesses, General Electric has grown to be one of the world's largest and most profitable companies.

profitable businesses in broadcasting (NBC Television), financial services (Kidder, Peabody investment bank), and several other industries. GE now operates 49 business units selling an incredible variety of products and services—from consumer electronics, financial services, and television broadcasting to aircraft engines, plastics, industrial power, and a global Internet trading network. Superb management of this diverse portfolio has earned GE shareholders a 29 percent average annual return over the past 10 years.[8]

Management's first step is to identify the key businesses making up the company. These can be called the strategic business units. A **strategic business unit** (SBU) is a unit of the company that has a separate mission and objectives and that can be planned independently from other company businesses. An SBU can be a company division, a product line within a division, or sometimes a single product or brand.

The next step in business portfolio analysis calls for management to assess the attractiveness of its various SBUs and decide how much support each deserves. In some companies, this is done informally. Management looks at the company's collection of businesses or products and uses judgment to decide how much each SBU should contribute and receive. Other companies use formal portfolio-planning methods.

The purpose of strategic planning is to find ways in which the company can best use its strengths to take advantage of attractive opportunities in the environment. So most standard portfolio-analysis methods evaluate SBUs on two important dimensions—the attractiveness of the SBU's market or industry and the strength of the SBU's position in that market or industry. The best-known portfolio-planning method was developed by the Boston Consulting Group, a leading management consulting firm.

The Boston Consulting Group Approach Using the Boston Consulting Group (BCG) approach, a company classifies all its SBUs according to the **growth-share matrix** shown in Figure 2-2. On the vertical axis, *market growth rate* provides a measure of market attractiveness. On the horizontal axis, *relative market share* serves as a measure of company strength in the market. By dividing the growth-share matrix as indicated, four types of SBUs can be distinguished:

Stars. Stars are high-growth, high-share businesses or products. They often need heavy investment to finance their rapid growth. Eventually their growth will slow down, and they will turn into cash cows.

Strategic business unit (SBU)
A unit of the company that has a separate mission and objectives and that can be planned independently from other company businesses.

Growth-share matrix
A portfolio-planning method that evaluates a company's strategic business units in terms of their market growth rate and relative market share. SBUs are classified as stars, cash cows, question marks, or dogs.

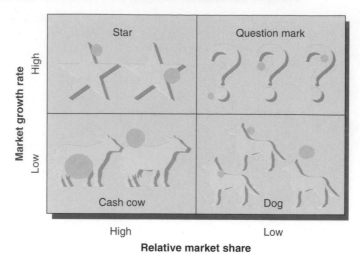

Figure 2-2
The BCG growth-share matrix

Cash cows. Cash cows are low-growth, high-share businesses or products. These established and successful SBUs need less investment to hold their market share. Thus, they produce a lot of cash that the company uses to pay its bills and to support other SBUs that need investment.

Question marks. Question marks are low-share business units in high-growth markets. They require a lot of cash to hold their share, let alone increase it. Management has to think hard about which question marks it should try to build into stars and which should be phased out.

Dogs. Dogs are low-growth, low-share businesses and products. They may generate enough cash to maintain themselves but do not promise to be large sources of cash.

The ten circles in the growth-share matrix represent a company's ten current SBUs. The company has two stars, two cash cows, three question marks, and three dogs. The areas of the circles are proportional to the SBU's dollar sales. This company is in fair shape, although not in good shape. It wants to invest in the more promising question marks to make them stars and to maintain the stars so that they will become cash cows as their markets mature. Fortunately, it has two good-sized cash cows whose income helps finance the company's question marks, stars, and dogs. The company should take some decisive action concerning its dogs and its question marks. The picture would be worse if the company had no stars, if it had too many dogs, or if it had only one weak cash cow.

Once it has classified its SBUs, the company must determine what role each will play in the future. One of four strategies can be pursued for each SBU. The company can invest more in the business unit in order to *build* its share. Or it can invest just enough to *hold* the SBU's share at the current level. It can *harvest* the SBU, milking its short-term cash flow regardless of the long-term effect. Finally, the company can *divest* the SBU by selling it or phasing it out and using the resources elsewhere.

As time passes, SBUs change their positions in the growth-share matrix. Each SBU has a life cycle. Many SBUs start out as question marks and move into the star category if they succeed. They later become cash cows as market growth falls, then finally die off or turn into dogs toward the end of their life cycle. The company needs to add new products and units continuously so that some of them will become stars and, eventually, cash cows that will help finance other SBUs.

Problems with Matrix Approaches The BCG and other formal methods revolutionized strategic planning. However, such approaches have limitations. They can be difficult, time-consuming, and costly to implement. Management may find it difficult to define

SBUs and measure market share and growth. In addition, these approaches focus on classifying *current* businesses but provide little advice for *future* planning. Management must still rely on its own judgment to set the business objectives for each SBU, to determine what resources each will be given, and to figure out which new businesses should be added.

Formal planning approaches can also lead the company to place too much emphasis on market-share growth or growth through entry into attractive new markets. Using these approaches, many companies plunged into unrelated and new high-growth businesses that they did not know how to manage—with very bad results. At the same time, these companies were often too quick to abandon, sell, or milk to death their healthy mature businesses. As a result, many companies that diversified too broadly in the past now are narrowing their focus and getting back to the basics of serving one or a few industries that they know best.

Despite such problems, and although many companies have dropped formal matrix methods in favor of more customized approaches that are better suited to their situations, most companies remain firmly committed to strategic planning. However, unlike former strategic-planning efforts, which rested mostly in the hands of senior managers, today's strategic planning has been decentralized. Increasingly, companies are moving responsibility for strategic planning out of company headquarters and placing it in the hands of cross-functional teams of line and staff managers who are close to their markets. Some teams even include customers and suppliers in their strategic-planning processes.[9]

Such analysis is no cure-all for finding the best strategy. But it can help management to understand the company's overall situation, to see how each business or product contributes, to assign resources to its businesses, and to orient the company for future success. When used properly, strategic planning is just one important aspect of overall strategic management, a way of thinking about how to manage a business.

Developing Growth Strategies in the Age of Connectedness

Beyond evaluating current businesses, designing the business portfolio involves finding businesses and products the company should consider in the future. Companies need growth if they are to compete more effectively, satisfy their stakeholders, and attract top talent. "Growth is pure oxygen," states one executive. "It creates a vital, enthusiastic corporation where people see genuine opportunity. . . . In that way, growth is more than our single most important financial driver; it's an essential part of our corporate culture." At the same time, a firm must be careful not to make growth itself an objective. The company's objective must be "profitable growth."

Marketing has the main responsibility for achieving profitable growth for the company. Marketing must identify, evaluate, and select market opportunities and lay down strategies for capturing them. One useful device for identifying growth opportunities is the **product/market expansion grid,**[10] shown in Figure 2-3. We apply it here to Starbucks (see Marketing at Work 2-2).

Product/market expansion grid
A portfolio-planning tool for identifying company growth opportunities through market penetration, market development, product development, or diversification.

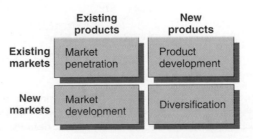

Figure 2-3
The product/market expansion grid

Marketing at Work 2-2

Starbucks Coffee: Where Things Are Really Perking

Back in 1983, Howard Schultz hit on the idea of bringing a European-style coffeehouse to America. People needed to slow down, he believed—to "smell the coffee" and enjoy life a little more. The result was Starbucks, the coffeehouse chain that started the trend in America of enjoying coffee to its fullest. Starbucks doesn't sell just coffee, it sells an experience. Says Howard Behar, Starbucks's international president, "We're not in the business of filling bellies, we're in the business of filling souls."

Starbucks is now a powerhouse premium brand in a category in which only cheaper commodity products existed just a decade ago. As the brand has perked, Starbucks's sales and profits have risen like steam off a mug of hot java. Twenty million customers visit the company's more than 4,000 stores worldwide each week—10 percent of them drop by twice a day. During the past five years, Starbucks's total sales have grown at an average of more than 36 percent annually; profits have grown at 22 percent a year.

Starbucks's success, however, has drawn a full litter of copycats, ranging from direct competitors such as Caribou Coffee to fast-food merchants. These days it seems that everyone is peddling its own brand of premium coffee. "Pull up to a Mobil gas station and the convenience store has certified organic coffee supplied by Green Mountain Coffee Co.," observes one analyst. "In the Pacific Northwest, McDonald's pours a blend from Seattle Coffee Co." To maintain its phenomenal growth in an increasingly overcaffeinated marketplace, Starbucks has brewed up an ambitious, multipronged growth strategy. Let's examine the key elements of this strategy:

◆ *More store growth:* More than 85 percent of Starbucks's sales come

from its stores. So, not surprisingly, Starbucks is opening new stores at a breakneck pace. It is currently opening new stores at a rate of almost 25 stores a week, 52 weeks a year. Five years ago, Starbucks had a total of just 1,015 stores, or 185 fewer than it will build this year alone. Although it may seem that there aren't many places left without a Starbucks, there's still plenty of room to expand. For example, Kansas City has only two Starbucks; the entire state of Indiana has only one; and the states of Alabama, Arkansas, Mississippi, and Tennessee have none at all. Even in crowded markets, such as New York City or San Francisco, the company seems unconcerned about store saturation. "Three years ago, when I said we were going to have 100 stores in New York, people thought it was crazy," says Schultz. "Well, now we have 70, and we're going to 200." He points to Vancouver, Canada, where competing Starbucks stores are located directly across the street

from one another. Both stores generate more than $1 million in annual sales, each well above the sales of a typical Starbucks. One three-block stretch in Chicago contains six of the trendy coffee bars.

Beyond opening new shops, Starbucks is expanding each store's food offerings, testing everything from Krispy Kreme doughnuts in New York City to Fresh Fields gourmet sandwiches in Washington, DC. Currently, beverages account for 80 percent of Starbucks's sales. However, more than 400 Starbucks are now serving lunch items, such as turkey sandwiches, Greek pasta salads, and assorted chips. By offering a beefed-up menu, the company hopes to increase the average customer sales ticket while also boosting lunch and dinner traffic.

◆ *New retail channels:* The vast majority of coffee in America is bought in stores and sipped at home. To capture this demand, Starbucks is also pushing into

To maintain its phenomenal growth in an increasingly overcaffeinated marketplace, Starbucks has brewed up an ambitious, multipronged growth strategy.

America's supermarket aisles. However, rather than going head-to-head with giants such as Procter & Gamble (Folgers) and Kraft (Maxwell House, Sanka), Starbucks struck a co-branding deal with Kraft. Under this deal, Starbucks will continue to roast and package its coffee while Kraft will market and distribute it. Both companies benefit: Starbucks gains quick entry into 25,000 U.S. supermarkets, supported by the marketing muscle of 3,500 Kraft salespeople. Kraft tops off its coffee line with the best-known premium brand and gains quick entry into the fast-growing premium coffee segment.

Beyond supermarkets, Starbucks has forged an impressive set of new ways to bring its brand to market. Some examples: Host Marriott operates Starbucks kiosks in more than 30 U.S. airports, and several airlines serve Starbucks coffee to their passengers. Westin and Sheraton hotels offer packets of Starbucks brew in their rooms. Barnes & Noble serves Starbucks coffee in all of the 375 cafes in its bookstores, making it one of the nation's largest retailers of both books and specialty coffees. Starbucks also sells gourmet coffee, tea, gifts, and related goods through business and consumer catalogs. And it has opened its own Web site, Starbucks.com, a kind of "lifestyle portal" on which it sells coffee, tea, coffeemaking equipment, compact discs, gifts, and collectibles. Starbucks customers' demographics are ideal for e-commerce—about 70 percent of customers are already on the Web and their typical household income approaches $75,000.

◆ *New products and store concepts:* Starbucks has partnered with several firms to extend its brand into new categories. For example, it joined with PepsiCo to stamp the Starbucks brand on bottled Frap-

puccino drinks. Starbucks ice cream, marketed in a joint venture with Breyer's, is now the leading brand of coffee ice cream. Moreover, at the same time it's trying to squeeze more business out of its regular coffee shops, Starbucks is also examining new store concepts. In Seattle, it's testing Café Starbucks, a European-style family bistro with a menu featuring everything from huckleberry pancakes to oven-roasted seared sirloin and Mediterranean chicken breast on focaccia. Whereas Starbucks's traditional coffeehouses ring up about half their sales before 11 A.M., Café Starbucks is designed to generate sales evenly throughout the day. Starbucks is also testing Circadia in San Francisco—a kind of bohemian coffeehouse concept with tattered rugs, high-speed Internet access, and live music as well as coffee specialties.

◆ *International growth:* Finally, Starbucks has taken its American-brewed concept global, especially in Asia. It plans to have 800 stores in the Pacific Rim by 2003, with 500 in Japan alone. Long lines are already common at Japanese Starbucks stores, and the company recently opened its first three locations in China. It is expanding rapidly in Taiwan, Thailand, Malaysia, Singapore, South Korea, and the Philippines. Starbucks also operates 80 stores in the United Kingdom and invaded mainland Europe in mid-2001.

Although Starbucks's growth strategy so far has met with great success, some analysts express strong concerns. What's wrong with Starbucks's rapid expansion? Some critics worry that the company may be overextending the Starbucks brand name. "People pay up to $3.15 for a caffe latte because it's supposed to be a premium product," asserts one

such critic. "When you see the Starbucks name on what an airline is pouring, you wonder." Others fear that, by pursuing such a broad-based growth strategy, Starbucks will stretch its resources too thin or lose its focus. According to one account: "All this sounds properly ambitious and aggressive, but to some . . . it has an ominous ring. The late 1990s are littered with the wreckage of restaurant chains that expanded too fast for their market and eventually collapsed. [A few years ago,] Planet Hollywood, with high profile backers like Bruce Willis and Arnold Schwarzenegger, was an investor darling. The stock hit $25 a share; today it trades for just over $1." Then there's Boston Market, the once high-flying chain that ended up declaring bankruptcy before being bought out by McDonald's.

Others, however, remain true believers. Some even see similarities between Starbucks and a young McDonald's, which rode the humble hamburger to such incredible success. "The similar focus on one product, the overseas opportunities, the rapid emergence as the dominant player in a new niche," says Goldman Sachs analyst Steve Kent, "this all applies to Starbucks, too." Only time will tell whether Starbucks turns out to be the next McDonald's or the next Boston Market. It all depends on how well the company manages growth. For now, things are really perking, but Starbucks has to be careful that it doesn't boil over.

Sources: Quotes from Nelson D. Schwartz, "Still Perking After All These Years," *Fortune,* May 24, 1999, pp. 203–210; Janice Matsumoto, "More than Mocha—Café Starbucks," *Restaurants and Institutions,* October 1, 1998, p. 21; Kelly Barron, "The Cappuccino Conundrum," *Forbes,* February 22, 1999, pp. 54–55; and Stephane Fitch, "Latte Grande, Extra Froth," *Forbes,* March 19, 2001, p. 58. Also see Louise Lee, "Now Starbucks Uses Its Bean," *Business Week,* February 14, 2000, pp. 92–94; Richard Papiernik, "Starbucks Still Taking Bows in Long-Running Coffeehouse Show," *Nation's Restaurant News,* February 12, 2001, pp. 11, 78; and "Starbucks Reports Second Quarter Results; 38% Increase in Net Earnings," Starbucks press release, accessed online at www.starbucks.com, April 26, 2001.

Market penetration
A strategy for company growth by increasing sales of current products to current market segments without changing the product.

First, Starbucks management might consider whether the company can achieve deeper **market penetration**—making more sales to current customers without changing its products. It might add new stores in current market areas to make it easier for more customers to visit. In fact, Starbucks plans to triple its store count by 2003. Improvements in advertising, prices, service, menu selection, or store design might encourage customers to stop by more often or to buy more during each visit. For example, Starbucks recently began adapting its menu to local tastes around the country.

> In the South, where customers tend to come later in the day and linger for a bit, [such tailoring] meant adding more appealing dessert offerings, as well as designing larger, more comfortable locations. [In Atlanta, Starbucks] opened bigger stores with such amenities as couches and outdoor tables, so that people would feel comfortable hanging out, especially in the evening. . . . Building on its Atlanta experience, Starbucks is tailoring its stores to local tastes around the country. That's why you find café au lait as well as toasted items in New Orleans, neither of which is available elsewhere in the country. (Bagel sales in New Orleans tripled once Starbucks began toasting them.) Or why coffee cake is featured in the Northeast, where it's more popular.[11]

Basically, Starbucks would like to increase patronage by current customers and attract competitors' customers to Starbucks shops.

Market development
A strategy for company growth by identifying and developing new market segments for current company products.

Second, Starbucks management might consider possibilities for **market development**—identifying and developing new markets for its current products. For instance, managers could review new *demographic markets*—such as senior consumers or ethnic groups—to see if new groups could be encouraged to visit Starbucks coffee shops for the first time or to buy more from them. Managers also could review new *geographical markets.* Starbucks is now expanding swiftly into new U.S. markets, especially in the Southeast and Southwest. It is also developing its international markets, with stores popping up rapidly in Asia, Europe, and Australia.

Product development
A strategy for company growth by offering modified or new products to current market segments.

Third, management could consider **product development**—offering modified or new products to current markets. For example, Starbucks is increasing its food offerings in an effort to bring customers into its stores during the lunch and dinner hours and to increase the amount of the average customer's sales ticket. The company is also partnering with other firms to sell coffee in supermarkets and to extend its brand to new products, such as coffee ice cream (with Breyer's) and bottled Frappuccino drinks (with PepsiCo).

Diversification
A strategy for company growth through starting up or acquiring businesses outside the company's current products and markets.

Fourth, Starbucks might consider **diversification.** It could start up or buy businesses outside of its current products and markets. For example, Starbucks is testing two new restaurant concepts—Café Starbucks and Circadia—in an effort to offer new formats to related but new markets. In a more extreme diversification, Starbucks might consider leveraging its strong brand name by making and marketing a line of branded casual clothing consistent with the "Starbucks experience." However, this would probably be unwise. Companies that diversify too broadly into unfamiliar products or industries can lose their market focus, something that some critics are already concerned about with Starbucks.

Planning Cross-Functional Strategies

The company's strategic plan establishes what kinds of businesses the company will be in and its objectives for each. Then, within each business unit more detailed planning must take place. The major functional departments in each unit—marketing, finance, accounting, purchasing, manufacturing, information systems, human resources, and others—must work together to accomplish strategic objectives.

Marketing's Role in Strategic Planning There is much overlap between overall company strategy and marketing strategy. Marketing looks at consumer needs and the company's ability to satisfy them; these same factors guide the company's overall mission and objectives.

Marketing plays a key role in the company's strategic planning in several ways. First, marketing provides a guiding *philosophy*—the marketing concept—that suggests company strategy should revolve around serving the needs of important consumer groups. Second, marketing provides *inputs* to strategic planners by helping to identify attractive market opportunities and by assessing the firm's potential to take advantage of them. Finally, within individual business units, marketing designs *strategies* for reaching the unit's objectives. Once the unit's objectives are set, marketing's task is to carry them out profitably.

Marketing and the Other Business Functions Customer value and satisfaction are important ingredients in the marketer's formula for success. However, as we noted in Chapter 1, marketing alone cannot produce superior value for customers. *All* departments must work together in this important task. Each company department can be thought of as a link in the company's **value chain**.[12] That is, each department carries out value-creating activities to design, produce, market, deliver, and support the firm's products. The firm's success depends not only on how well each department performs its work but also on how well the activities of various departments are coordinated.

For example, Wal-Mart's goal is to create customer value and satisfaction by providing shoppers with the products they want at the lowest possible prices. Marketers at Wal-Mart play an important role. They learn what customers need and want and stock the store's shelves with the desired products at unbeatable low prices. They prepare advertising and merchandising programs and assist shoppers with customer service. Through these and other activities, Wal-Mart's marketers help deliver value to customers. However, the marketing department needs help from the company's other departments. For example, Wal-Mart's ability to offer the right products at low prices depends on the purchasing department's skill in tracking down the needed suppliers and buying from them at low cost. Similarly, Wal-Mart's information systems department must provide fast and accurate information about which products are selling in each store. And its operations people must provide effective, low-cost merchandise handling.

A company's value chain is only as strong as its weakest link. Thus, success depends on how well each department performs its work of adding value for customers and on how well the activities of various departments are coordinated. At Wal-Mart, if purchasing can't wring the lowest prices from suppliers or if operations can't distribute merchandise at the lowest costs, then marketing can't deliver on its promise of lowest prices.

Ideally, then, a company's different functions should work in harmony to produce value for consumers. But, in practice, departmental relations are full of conflicts and misunderstandings. The marketing department takes the consumer's point of view. But when marketing tries to develop customer satisfaction, it can cause other departments to do a poorer job *in their terms*. Marketing department actions can increase purchasing costs, disrupt production schedules, increase inventories, and create budget headaches. Thus, the other departments may resist the marketing department's efforts.

Yet marketers must find ways to get all departments to "think consumer" and to develop a smoothly functioning value chain.

Creating value for buyers is much more than a "marketing function"; rather, [it's] analogous to a symphony orchestra in which the contribution of each subgroup

Value chain
The series of departments which carry out value-creating activities to design, produce, market, deliver, and support a firm's products.

 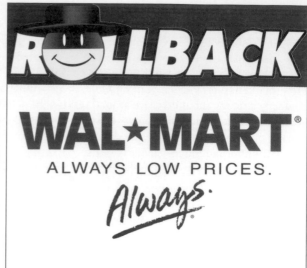

The value chain: Wal-Mart's ability to offer the right products at low prices depends on the contributions from people in all of the company's departments—marketing, purchasing, information systems, and operations.

is tailored and integrated by a conductor—with a synergistic effect. A seller must draw upon and integrate effectively . . . its entire human and other capital resources. . . . [Creating superior value for buyers] is the proper focus of the entire business and not merely of a single department in it.[13]

Marketing management can best gain support for its goal of customer satisfaction by working to understand the company's other departments. Marketing managers need to work closely with managers of other functions to develop a system of functional plans under which the different departments can work together to accomplish the company's overall strategic objectives.

Jack Welch, General Electric's highly regarded former CEO, told his employees: "Companies can't give job security. Only customers can!" He emphasized that all General Electric people, regardless of their department, have an impact on customer satisfaction and retention. His message: "If you are not thinking customer, you are not thinking."[14]

Marketing and Its Partners in the Marketing System In its search for competitive advantage, the firm needs to look beyond its own value chain and into the value chains of its suppliers, distributors, and, ultimately, customers. More companies today are "partnering" with the other members of the marketing system to improve the performance of the entire customer **value delivery network.** For example, Honda has designed a program for working closely with its suppliers to help them reduce their costs and improve quality. When Honda chose Donnelly Corporation to supply all of the mirrors for its U.S.-made cars, it sent engineers swarming over Donnelly's plants, looking for ways to improve its products and operations. This helped Donnelly reduce its costs by 2 percent in the first year. As a result of its improved performance, Donnelly's sales to Honda have grown from $5 million annually to more than $60 million in less than 10 years. In turn, Honda has gained an efficient, low-cost supplier of

Value delivery network
The network made up of the company, suppliers, distributors, and ultimately customers who "partner" with each other to improve the performance of the entire system.

quality components. And as a result of its partnerships with Donnelly and other suppliers, Honda can offer greater value to customers in the form of lower-cost, higher-quality cars.[15]

Increasingly in today's marketplace, competition no longer takes place between individual competitors. Rather, it takes place between the entire value delivery networks created by these competitors. Thus, Honda's performance against another automaker—say Toyota—depends on the quality of Honda's overall value delivery network versus Toyota's. Companies no longer compete—their entire marketing networks do.

Strategic Planning and Small Businesses

Many discussions of strategic planning focus on large corporations with many divisions and products. However, small businesses can also benefit from sound strategic planning. Whereas most small ventures start out with extensive business and marketing plans used to attract potential investors, strategic planning often falls by the wayside once the business gets going. Entrepreneurs and presidents of small companies are more likely to spend their time "putting out fires" than planning. But what does a small firm do when it finds that it has taken on too much debt, when its growth is exceeding production capacity, or when it's losing market share to a competitor with lower prices? Strategic planning can help small business managers to anticipate such situations and determine how to prevent or handle them.

King's Medical Company of Hudson, Ohio, provides an example of how one small company has used very simple strategic-planning tools to chart its course every three years. King's Medical owns and manages magnetic-resonance-imaging (MRI) equipment—million-dollar-plus machines that produce X-ray-type pictures. Several years ago, Dr. William Patton, Ph.D., then a consultant and the company's "planning guru," pointed to strategic planning as the key to this small company's very rapid growth and high profit margins. Patton claimed, "A lot of literature says there are three critical issues to a small company: cash flow, cash flow, cash flow. I agree those issues are critical, but so are three more: planning, planning, planning." King's Medical's planning process, which hinges on an assessment of the company, its place in the market, and its goals, includes the following steps.[16]

1. Identify the major elements of the business environment in which the organization has operated over the past few years.
2. Describe the mission of the organization in terms of its nature and function for the next two years.
3. Explain the internal and external forces that will impact the mission of the organization.
4. Identify the basic driving force that will direct the organization in the future.
5. Develop a set of long-term objectives that will identify what the organization will become in the future.
6. Outline a general plan of action that defines the logistical, financial, and personnel factors needed to integrate the long-term objectives into the total organization.

Clearly, strategic planning is crucial to a small company's future. Thom Wellington, president of Wellington Environmental Consulting and Construction, Inc., says that it's important to do strategic planning at a site away from the office. An off-site location offers psychologically neutral ground where employees can be "much more candid," and it takes entrepreneurs away from the scene of the fires they spend so much time stamping out.[17]

Linking the Concepts

Here's a good place to pause for a moment to think about and apply what you've read in the first part of this chapter.

◆ Why are we talking about companywide strategic planning so early in a marketing text? What *does* strategic planning have to do with marketing?

◆ What are IBM's mission and strategy? What role does marketing play in helping IBM to accomplish this mission and strategy?

◆ What roles do other functional departments play, and how can IBM marketers work more effectively with these other functions to maximize overall customer value?

The Marketing Process

Marketing process
The process of (1) analyzing marketing opportunities;
(2) selecting target markets;
(3) developing the marketing mix; and (4) managing the marketing effort.

The strategic plan defines the company's overall mission and objectives. Within each business unit, marketing plays a role in helping to accomplish the overall strategic objectives. Marketing's role and activities in the organization are shown in Figure 2-4, which summarizes the entire **marketing process** and the forces influencing company marketing strategy.

Target consumers stand in the center. The goal is to build strong and profitable connections with these consumers. The company first identifies the total market, then divides it into smaller segments, selects the most promising segments, and focuses on serving and

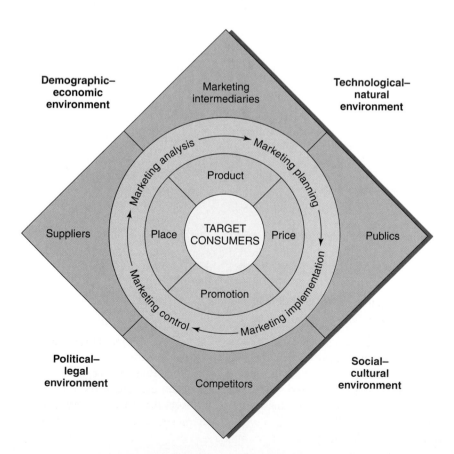

Figure 2-4
Factors influencing company marketing strategy

satisfying these segments. It designs a marketing mix made up of factors under its control—product, price, place, and promotion. To find the best marketing mix and put it into action, the company engages in marketing analysis, planning, implementation, and control. Through these activities, the company watches and adapts to the actors and forces in the marketing environment. We will now look briefly at each element in the marketing process. In later chapters, we will discuss each element in more depth.

Connecting with Consumers

To succeed in today's competitive marketplace, companies must be customer centered, winning customers from competitors, then keeping and growing them by delivering greater value. But before it can satisfy consumers, a company must first understand their needs and wants. Thus, sound marketing requires a careful analysis of consumers. Companies know that they cannot connect profitably with all consumers in a given market—at least not all consumers in the same way. There are too many different kinds of consumers with too many different kinds of needs. And some companies are in a better position to serve certain segments of the market. Thus, each company must divide up the total market, choose the best segments, and design strategies for profitably serving chosen segments better than its competitors do. This process involves three steps: *market segmentation, market targeting,* and *market positioning.*

Market Segmentation The market consists of many types of customers, products, and needs, and the marketer has to determine which segments offer the best opportunity for achieving company objectives. Consumers can be grouped and served in various ways based on geographic, demographic, psychographic, and behavioral factors. The process of dividing a market into distinct groups of buyers with different needs, characteristics, or behavior who might require separate products or marketing mixes is called **market segmentation.**

Every market has segments, but not all ways of segmenting a market are equally useful. For example, Tylenol would gain little by distinguishing between male and female users of pain relievers if both respond the same way to marketing efforts. A **market segment** consists of consumers who respond in a similar way to a given set of marketing efforts. In the car market, for example, consumers who choose the biggest, most comfortable car regardless of price make up one market segment. Another segment would be customers who care mainly about price and operating economy. It would be difficult to make one model of car that was the first choice of every consumer. Companies are wise to focus their efforts on meeting the distinct needs of one or more market segments.

Market Targeting After a company has defined market segments, it can enter one or many segments of a given market. **Market targeting** involves evaluating each market segment's attractiveness and selecting one or more segments to enter. A company should target segments in which it can profitably generate the greatest customer value and sustain it over time. A company with limited resources might decide to serve only one or a few special segments or "market niches." This strategy limits sales but can be very profitable. Or a company might choose to serve several related segments—perhaps those with different kinds of customers but with the same basic wants. Or a large company might decide to offer a complete range of products to serve all market segments.

Most companies enter a new market by serving a single segment, and if this proves successful, they add segments. Large companies eventually seek full market coverage. They want to be the General Motors of their industry. GM says that it makes a car for every "person, purse, and personality." The leading company normally has different products designed to meet the special needs of each segment.

Market segmentation
Dividing a market into distinct groups with distinct needs, characteristics, or behavior who might require separate products or marketing mixes.

Market segment
A group of consumers who respond in a similar way to a given set of marketing efforts.

Market targeting
The process of evaluating each market segment's attractiveness and selecting one or more segments to enter.

Positioning: Bentley promises "18 handcrafted feet of shameless luxury." In contrast, Toyota promises, "At 41 miles per gallon . . . it's not you. It's the car." Such deceptively simple statements form the backbone of a product's marketing strategy.

Market Positioning After a company has decided which market segments to enter, it must decide what positions it wants to occupy in those segments. A product's *position* is the place the product occupies relative to competitors in consumers' minds. If a product is perceived to be exactly like another product on the market, consumers would have no reason to buy it.

Market positioning is arranging for a product to occupy a clear, distinctive, and desirable place relative to competing products in the minds of target consumers. Thus, marketers plan positions that distinguish their products from competing brands and give them the greatest strategic advantage in their target markets. For example, the Ford Taurus is "built to last"; Chevy Blazer is "like a rock"; Toyota's economical Echo states, "It's not you. It's the car"; and Saturn is "a different kind of company, different kind of car." Lexus avows "the passionate pursuit of excellence," Jaguar is positioned as "the art of performance," and Mercedes says, "In a perfect world, everyone would drive a Mercedes." The luxurious Bentley promises "18 handcrafted feet of shameless luxury." Such deceptively simple statements form the backbone of a product's marketing strategy.

In positioning its product, the company first identifies possible competitive advantages on which to build the position. To gain competitive advantage, the company must offer greater value to chosen target segments, either by charging lower prices than competitors do or by offering more benefits to justify higher prices. But if the company positions the product as *offering* greater value, it must then *deliver* that greater value. Thus, effective positioning begins with actually *differentiating* the company's marketing offer so that it gives consumers more value than they are offered by the competition. Once the company has chosen a desired position, it must take strong steps to deliver and communicate that position to target consumers. The company's entire marketing program should support the chosen positioning strategy.

Market positioning
Arranging for a product to occupy a clear, distinctive, and desirable place relative to competing products in the minds of target consumers.

Developing the Marketing Mix

Once the company has decided on its overall competitive marketing strategy, it is ready to begin planning the details of the marketing mix, one of the major concepts in modern marketing. We define **marketing mix** as the set of controllable, tactical marketing tools that the firm blends to produce the response it wants in the target market. The marketing mix consists of everything the firm can do to influence the demand for its product. The many possibilities can be collected into four groups of variables known as the "four Ps": *product, price, place,* and *promotion.*[18] Figure 2-5 shows the particular marketing tools under each P.

Product means the goods-and-services combination the company offers to the target market. Thus, a Ford Taurus product consists of nuts and bolts, spark plugs, pistons, headlights, and thousands of other parts. Ford offers several Taurus styles and dozens of optional features. The car comes fully serviced and with a comprehensive warranty that is as much a part of the product as the tailpipe.

Price is the amount of money customers have to pay to obtain the product. Ford calculates suggested retail prices that its dealers might charge for each Taurus. But Ford dealers rarely charge the full sticker price. Instead, they negotiate the price with each customer, offering discounts, trade-in allowances, and credit terms to adjust for the current competitive situation and to bring the price into line with the buyer's perception of the car's value.

Place includes company activities that make the product available to target consumers. Ford maintains a large body of independently owned dealerships that sell the company's many different models. Ford selects its dealers carefully and supports them strongly. The dealers keep an inventory of Ford automobiles, demonstrate them to potential buyers, negotiate prices, close sales, and service the cars after the sale.

Promotion means activities that communicate the merits of the product and persuade target customers to buy it. Ford spends more than $1.6 billion each year on advertising to tell consumers about the company and its many products.[19] Dealership salespeople assist potential buyers and persuade them that Ford is the best car for them. Ford and its dealers offer special promotions—sales, cash rebates, low financing rates—as added purchase incentives.

An effective marketing program blends all of the marketing mix elements into a coordinated program designed to achieve the company's marketing objectives by delivering

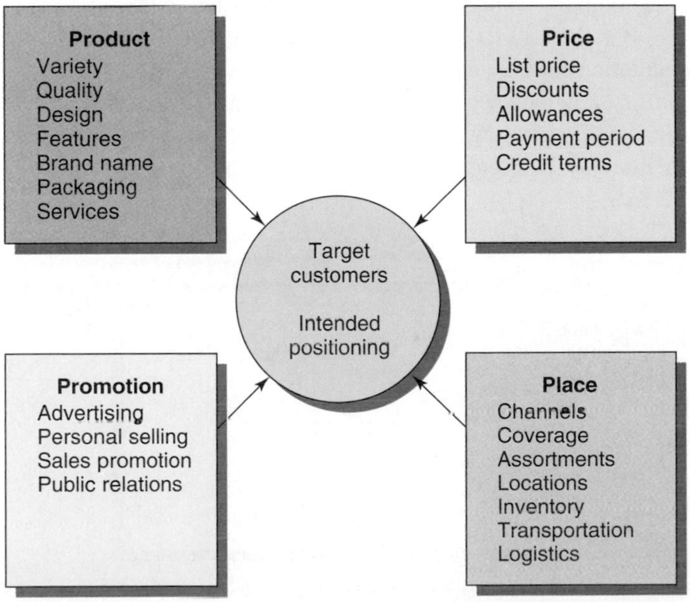

Marketing mix
The set of controllable tactical marketing tools—product, price, place, and promotion—that the firm blends to produce the response it wants in the target market.

Figure 2-5
The four Ps of the marketing mix

value to consumers. The marketing mix constitutes the company's tactical tool kit for establishing strong positioning in target markets.

Some critics feel that the four Ps may omit or underemphasize certain important activities. For example, they ask, "Where are services?" Just because they don't start with a P doesn't justify omitting them. The answer is that services, such as banking, airline, and retailing services, are products too. We might call them *service products*. "Where is packaging?" the critics might ask. Marketers would answer that they include packaging as just one of many product decisions. All said, as Figure 2-5 suggests, many marketing activities that might appear to be left out of the marketing mix are subsumed under one of the four Ps. The issue is not whether there should be four, six, or ten Ps so much as what framework is most helpful in designing marketing programs.

There is another concern, however, that is valid. It holds that the four Ps concept takes the seller's view of the market, not the buyer's view. From the buyer's viewpoint, in this age of connectedness, the four Ps might be better described as the four Cs:[20]

4Ps	4Cs
Product	Customer solution
Price	Customer cost
Place	Convenience
Promotion	Communication

Thus while marketers see themselves as selling products, customers see themselves as buying value or solutions to their problems. And customers are interested in more than just the price; they are interested in the total costs of obtaining, using, and disposing of a product. Customers want the product and service to be as conveniently available as possible. Finally, they want two-way communication. Marketers would do well to first think through the four Cs and then build the four Ps on that platform.

Managing the Marketing Effort

The company wants to design and put into action the marketing mix that will best achieve its objectives in its target markets. Figure 2-6 shows the relationship between the four marketing management functions—*analysis, planning, implementation,* and *control.* The company first develops overall strategic plans, then translates these companywide strategic plans into marketing and other plans for each division, product, and brand. Through implementation, the company turns the plans into actions. Control consists of measuring and

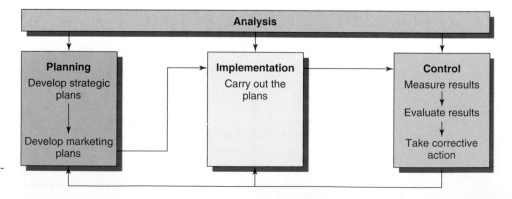

Figure 2-6
The relationship between analysis, planning, implementation, and control

Marketers must continually plan their analysis, implementation, and control of activities.

evaluating the results of marketing activities and taking corrective action where needed. Finally, marketing analysis provides information and evaluations needed for all of the other marketing activities.

Marketing Analysis

Managing the marketing function begins with a complete analysis of the company's situation. The company must analyze its markets and marketing environment to find attractive opportunities and to avoid environmental threats. It must analyze company strengths and weaknesses as well as current and possible marketing actions to determine which opportunities it can best pursue. Marketing provides input to each of the other marketing management functions. We discuss marketing analysis more fully in Chapter 5.

Marketing Planning

Through strategic planning, the company decides what it wants to do with each business unit. Marketing planning involves deciding on marketing strategies that will help the company attain its overall strategic objectives. A detailed marketing plan is needed for each business, product, or brand. What does a marketing plan look like? Our discussion focuses on product or brand plans.

Table 2-2 outlines the major sections of a typical product or brand plan. The plan begins with an executive summary, which quickly overviews major assessments, goals, and recommendations. The main section of the plan presents a detailed analysis of the current marketing situation as well as potential threats and opportunities. It next states major objectives for the brand and outlines the specifics of a marketing strategy for achieving them.

A **marketing strategy** is the marketing logic whereby the company hopes to achieve its marketing objectives. It consists of specific strategies for target markets, positioning, the marketing mix, and marketing expenditure levels. In this section, the planner explains how each strategy responds to the threats, opportunities, and critical issues spelled out earlier in the plan. Additional sections of the marketing plan lay out an action program for implementing the marketing strategy along with the details of a supporting *marketing budget*. The last section outlines the controls that will be used to monitor progress and take corrective action.

Marketing strategy
The marketing logic by which the business unit hopes to achieve its marketing objectives.

Table 2-2   Contents of a Marketing Plan

Section	Purpose
Executive summary	Presents a brief summary of the main goals and recommendations of the plan for management review, helping top management to find the plan's major points quickly. A table of contents should follow the executive summary.
Current marketing situation	Describes the target market and the company's position in it, including information about the market, product performance, competition, and distribution. This section includes: • A *market description* that defines the market and major segments, then reviews customer needs and factors in the marketing environment that may affect customer purchasing • A *product review* that shows sales, prices, and gross margins of the major products in the product line • A review of *competition,* which identifies major competitors and assesses their market positions and strategies for product quality, pricing, distribution, and promotion • A review of *distribution* that evaluates recent sales trends and other developments in major distribution channels.
Threats and opportunities analysis	Assesses major threats and opportunities that the product might face, helping management to anticipate important positive or negative developments that might have an impact on the firm and its strategies.
Objectives and issues	States the marketing objectives that the company would like to attain during the plan's term and discusses key issues that will affect their attainment. For example, if the goal is to achieve a 15 percent market share, this poses a key issue: How can market share be increased?
Marketing strategy	Outlines the broad marketing logic by which the business unit hopes to achieve its marketing objectives and the specifics of target markets, positioning, and marketing expenditure levels. It outlines specific strategies for each marketing mix element and explains how each responds to the threats, opportunities, and critical issues spelled out earlier in the plan.
Action programs	Spells out how marketing strategies will be turned into specific action programs that answer the following questions: *What* will be done? *When* will it be done? *Who* is responsible for doing it? And *how much* will it cost?
Budgets	Details a supporting marketing budget that is essentially a projected profit-and-loss statement. It shows expected revenues (forecasted number of units sold and the average net price) and expected costs (of production, distribution, and marketing). The difference is the projected profit. Once approved by higher management, the budget is the basis for materials buying, production scheduling, personnel planning, and marketing operations.
Controls	Outlines the controls that will be used to monitor progress and allow higher management to review implementation results and spot products that are not meeting their goals.

Marketing Implementation

Marketing implementation
The process that turns marketing strategies and plans into marketing actions in order to accomplish strategic marketing objectives.

Planning good strategies is only a start toward successful marketing. A brilliant marketing strategy counts for little if the company fails to implement it properly. **Marketing implementation** is the process that turns marketing *plans* into marketing *actions* in order to accomplish strategic marketing objectives. Implementation involves day-to-day, month-to-month activities that effectively put the marketing plan to work. Whereas marketing planning addresses the *what* and *why* of marketing activities, implementation addresses the *who, where, when,* and *how.*

Many managers think that "doing things right" (implementation) is as important as, or even more important than, "doing the right things" (strategy). The fact is that both are critical to success.[21] However, companies can gain competitive advantages through effective implementation. One firm can have essentially the same strategy as another yet win in the marketplace through faster or better execution. Still, implementation is difficult—it is often easier to think up good marketing strategies than it is to carry them out.

In an increasingly connected world, people at all levels of the marketing system must work together to implement marketing plans and strategies. At Black & Decker, for example, marketing implementation for the company's power tool products requires day-to-day decisions and actions by thousands of people both inside and outside the organization. Marketing managers make decisions about target segments, branding, packaging, pricing, promoting, and distributing. They connect with people elsewhere in the company to get support for their products and programs. They talk with engineering about product design, with manufacturing about production and inventory levels, and with finance about funding and cash flows. They also connect with outside people, such as advertising agencies to plan ad campaigns and the media to obtain publicity support. The sales force urges Home Depot, Wal-Mart, and other retailers to advertise Black & Decker products, provide ample shelf space, and use company displays.

Successful marketing implementation depends on how well the company blends its people, organizational structure, decision and reward systems, and company culture into a cohesive action program that supports its strategies. At all levels, the company must be staffed by people who have the needed skills, motivation, and personal characteristics. The company's formal organization structure plays an important role in implementing marketing strategy; so do its decision and reward systems. For example, if a company's compensation system rewards managers for short-run profit results, they will have little incentive to work toward long-run market-building objectives.

Finally, to be successfully implemented, the firm's marketing strategies must fit with its company culture, the system of values and beliefs shared by people in the organization. A study of America's most successful companies found that these companies have almost cultlike cultures built around strong, market-oriented missions. At companies such as Wal-Mart, Microsoft, Nordstrom, Citicorp, Procter & Gamble, Walt Disney, and Hewlett-Packard, "employees share such a strong vision that they know in their hearts what's right for their company."[22]

Marketing Department Organization

The company must design a marketing department that can carry out marketing strategies and plans. If the company is very small, one person might do all of the marketing work—research, selling, advertising, customer service, and other activities. As the company expands, a marketing department organization emerges to plan and carry out marketing activities. In large companies, this department contains many specialists. Thus, Black & Decker has product and market managers, sales managers and salespeople, market researchers, advertising experts, and other specialists.

Modern marketing departments can be arranged in several ways. The most common form of marketing organization is the *functional organization* in which different marketing activities are headed by a functional specialist—a sales manager, advertising manager, marketing research manager, customer service manager, new-product manager. A company that sells across the country or internationally often uses a *geographic organization* in which its sales and marketing people are assigned to specific countries, regions, and districts. Geographic organization allows salespeople to settle into a territory, get to know their customers, and work with a minimum of travel time and cost.

Companies with many very different products or brands often create a *product management organization*. Using this approach, a product manager develops and implements a complete strategy and marketing program for a specific product or brand. Product management first appeared at Procter & Gamble in 1929. A new company soap, Camay, was not doing well, and a young P&G executive was assigned to give his exclusive attention to developing and promoting this product. He was successful, and the company soon added other product managers.[23] Since then, many firms, especially consumer products companies, have set up product management organizations. However, recent changes in the marketing environment have caused many companies to rethink the role of the product manager. Many companies are finding that today's marketing environment calls for less brand focus and more customer focus. They are shifting toward *customer equity management*—moving away from managing just product profitability and toward managing *customer profitability*.[24]

For companies that sell one product line to many different types of markets and customers that have different needs and preferences, a *market or customer management organization* might be best. A market management organization is similar to the product management organization. Market managers are responsible for developing marketing strategies and plans for their specific markets or customers. This system's main advantage is that the company is organized around the needs of specific customer segments.

Large companies that produce many different products flowing into many different geographic and customer markets usually employ some *combination* of the functional, geographic, product, and market organization forms. This ensures that each function, product, and market receives its share of management attention. However, it can also add costly layers of management and reduce organizational flexibility. Still, the benefits of organizational specialization usually outweigh the drawbacks.

Marketing Control

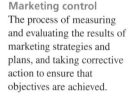

Marketing control
The process of measuring and evaluating the results of marketing strategies and plans, and taking corrective action to ensure that objectives are achieved.

Because many surprises occur during the implementation of marketing plans, the marketing department must practice constant marketing control. **Marketing control** involves evaluating the results of marketing strategies and plans and taking corrective action to ensure that objectives are attained. Figure 2-7 shows that marketing control involves four steps. Management first sets specific marketing goals. It then measures its performance in the marketplace and evaluates the causes of any differences between expected and actual performance. Finally, management takes corrective action to close the gaps between its goals and its performance. This may require changing the action programs or even changing the goals.

Operating control involves checking ongoing performance against the annual plan and taking corrective action when necessary. Its purpose is to ensure that the company achieves the sales, profits, and other goals set out in its annual plan. It also involves determining the profitability of different products, territories, markets, and channels.

Strategic control involves looking at whether the company's basic strategies are well matched to its opportunities. Marketing strategies and programs can quickly become

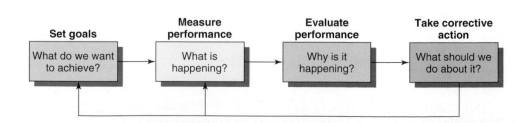

Figure 2-7
The control process

outdated, and each company should periodically reassess its overall approach to the marketplace. A major tool for such strategic control is a **marketing audit.** The marketing audit is a comprehensive, systematic, independent, and periodic examination of a company's environment, objectives, strategies, and activities to determine problem areas and opportunities. The audit provides good input for a plan of action to improve the company's marketing performance.[25]

The marketing audit covers *all* major marketing areas of a business, not just a few trouble spots. It assesses the marketing environment, marketing strategy, marketing organization, marketing systems, marketing mix, and marketing productivity and profitability. The audit is normally conducted by an objective and experienced outside party. The findings may come as a surprise—and sometimes as a shock—to management. Management then decides which actions make sense and how and when to implement them.

Marketing audit
A comprehensive, systematic, independent, and periodic examination of a company's environment, objectives, strategies, and activities to determine problem areas and opportunities and to recommend a plan of action to improve the company's marketing performance.

The Marketing Environment

Managing the marketing function would be hard enough if the marketer had to deal only with the controllable marketing mix variables. But the company operates in a complex marketing environment, consisting of uncontrollable forces to which the company must adapt. The environment produces both threats and opportunities. The company must carefully analyze its environment so that it can avoid the threats and take advantage of the opportunities.

The company's marketing environment includes forces close to the company that affect its ability to serve consumers, such as other company departments, channel members, suppliers, competitors, and publics. It also includes broader demographic and economic forces, political and legal forces, technological and ecological forces, and social and cultural forces. In order to connect effectively with consumers, others in the company, external partners, and the world around them, marketers need to consider all of these forces when developing and positioning its offer to the target market. The marketing environment is discussed more fully in Chapter 4.

 STOP *Rest Stop: Reviewing the Concepts*

What have you learned so far on your journey through marketing? So far, we've defined marketing and its core concepts and philosophies, examined marketing's role under overall company strategy, overviewed the key elements of the marketing process, and outlined the major marketing management functions. So you've had a pretty good overview of the fundamentals of marketing. In future chapters, we'll expand on these fundamentals.

Strategic planning sets the stage for the rest of the company's planning. Marketing contributes to strategic planning, and the overall plan defines marketing's role in the company. Although formal planning offers a variety of benefits to companies, not all companies use it or use it well. Although many discussions of strategic planning focus on large corporations, small business also can benefit greatly from sound strategic planning.

1. Explain companywide strategic planning and its four steps.

Strategic planning involves developing a strategy for long-run survival and growth. It consists of four steps: defining the company mission, setting objectives and goals, designing a business portfolio, and developing functional plans. *Defining a clear company mission* begins with drafting a formal mission statement, which should be market oriented, realistic, specific, motivating, and consistent with the market environment. The mission is then transformed into detailed *supporting goals and objectives* to guide the entire company. Based on those goals and objectives, headquarters designs a *business portfolio,* deciding which businesses and products should receive more or fewer resources. In turn, each business and product unit must develop detailed marketing plans in line with the companywide plan. Comprehensive and sound marketing plans support company strategic planning by detailing specific opportunities.

2. Discuss how to design business portfolios and develop growth strategies.

Guided by the company's mission statement and objectives, management plans its *business portfolio,* or the collection of businesses and products that make up the company. To produce a business portfolio that best fits the company's strengths and weaknesses to opportunities in the environment, the company must analyze and adjust its *current* business portfolio and develop growth strategies for adding *new* products or businesses to the portfolio. The company might use a formal portfolio-planning method like the *BCG growth-share matrix.* But many companies are now designing more customized portfolio-planning approaches that better suit their unique situations. The *product/market expansion grid* suggests four possible growth paths: market penetration, market development, product development, and diversification.

3. Explain functional planning strategies and marketing's role in strategic planning.

Once strategic objectives have been defined, management within each business must prepare a set of *functional plans* that coordinates the activities of the marketing, finance, operations, and other departments. A company's success depends on how well each department performs its customer value-adding activities and on how well the departments work together to serve the customer. Each department has a different idea about which objectives and activities are most important. The marketing department stresses the consumer's point of view, whereas the operations department may be more concerned with reducing production costs. In order to best accomplish the firm's overall strategic objectives, marketing managers must understand other functional managers' points of view.

Marketing plays an important role throughout the strategic planning process. It provides *inputs* to strategic planning concerning attractive market possibilities, and

marketing's customer focus serves as a guiding *philosophy* for planning. Marketers design *strategies* to help meet strategic objectives and prepare programs to carry them out profitably. Marketing also plays an integrative role to help ensure that departments work together toward the goal of delivering superior customer value and satisfaction.

4. Describe the marketing process and the forces that influence it.

The *marketing process* matches consumer needs with the company's capabilities and objectives. Consumers are at the center of the marketing process. The company divides the total market into smaller segments, selecting the segments it can best serve. It then designs a *marketing mix* to differentiate its marketing offer and position this offer in selected target segments. The marketing mix consists of product, price, place, and promotion decisions.

5. List the marketing management functions, including the elements of a marketing plan.

To find the best mix and put it into action, the company engages in marketing analysis, planning, implementation, and control. The main components of a *marketing plan* are the executive summary, current marketing situation, threats and opportunities, objectives and issues, marketing strategies, action programs, budgets, and controls. To plan good strategies is often easier than to carry them out. To be successful, companies must also be effective at *implementation*—turning marketing strategies into marketing actions.

Much of the responsibility for implementation goes to the company's marketing department. Modern marketing departments can be organized in one or a combination of ways: *functional marketing organization, geographic organization, product management organization,* or *market management organization.* Marketing organizations carry out *marketing control,* both operating control and strategic control. They use *marketing audits* to determine marketing opportunities and problems and to recommend short-run and long-run actions to improve overall marketing performance. Through these activities, the company watches and adapts to the marketing environment.

Navigating the Key Terms

For a detailed analysis of the meaning and importance of each of the following key terms, visit our Web page at www.prenhall.com/kotler.

Business portfolio
Diversification
Growth-share matrix
Market development

Market penetration
Market positioning
Market segment
Market segmentation

Market targeting
Marketing audit
Marketing control
Marketing implementation
Marketing mix

Marketing process
Marketing strategy
Mission statement
Portfolio analysis
Product development

Product/market expansion grid
Strategic business unit (SBU)
Strategic planning
Value chain
Value delivery network

Travel Log

The following concept checks and discussion questions will help you to keep track of and apply the concepts you've studied in this chapter.

Concept Checks

Fill in the blanks, then look for the correct answers.

1. _____ is the process of developing and maintaining a strategic fit between the organization's goals and capabilities and its changing marketing opportunities.

2. A _____ is a statement of the organization's purpose—what it wants to accomplish in the larger environment.

3. Management should avoid making its mission too narrow or too broad. According to this section of the text, missions should be _____, _____, fit the _____, be based on its _____, and be _____.

4. A business portfolio is the collection of businesses and products that make up the company. The best business portfolio is the one that _____ _____.

5. A company can classify all its SBUs according to a growth-share matrix. Four types of SBUs can usually be identified. The _____ are low-growth, high-share businesses or products. They produce a lot of cash that is used to support other SBUs.

6. Once a company has classified its SBUs, the company must determine what role each will play in the future. The company may choose one of four strategies. These strategies are to _____, _____, _____, or _____ the SBU.

7. When the marketing manager considers growth strategies, _____ would be chosen if the goal of the company was to make more sales to current customers without changing products.

8. When each department within a firm carries out value-creating activities to design, produce, market, deliver, and support the firm's products, the department can be thought of as a link in the company's _____.

9. _____ is the process of dividing a market into distinct groups of buyers with different needs, characteristics, or behavior who might require separate products or marketing mixes.

10. The "four Ps" of the marketing mix are _____, _____, _____, and _____.

11. The four marketing management functions are _____, _____, _____, and _____.

12. A _____ is the marketing logic whereby the company hopes to achieve its marketing objectives.

Concept Checks Answers: 1. Strategic planning; 2. mission statement; 3. realistic, specific, market environment, distinctive competencies, and motivating; 4. best fits the company's strengths and weaknesses to opportunities in the environment; 5. cash cows; 6. build, hold, harvest, or divest; 7. market penetration; 8. value chain; 9. Market segmentation; 10. product, price, place, and promotion; 11. analysis, planning, implementation, and control; 12. marketing strategy.

Discussing the Issues

1. Define strategic planning. List and briefly describe the four steps of the strategic-planning process.

2. In a series of job interviews, you ask three recruiters to describe the missions of their companies. One says, "To make profits." Another says, "To create customers." The third says, "To fight world hunger." Analyze and discuss what these mission statements

tell you about each of the companies. Which appears to be more *market oriented?* Explain and justify.

3. An electronics manufacturer obtains the semiconductors it uses in production from a company-owned subsidiary that also sells to other manufacturers. The subsidiary is smaller and less profitable than competing producers, and its growth rate has been below the industry average during the past five years.

Define which cell of the BCG growth-share matrix this strategic business unit would fall into. Explain your choice. What should the parent company do with this SBU?

4. Beyond evaluating current businesses, designing the business portfolio involves finding businesses and products the company should consider in the future. Using the product/market expansion grid, illustrate the process that a company can use to evaluate a portfolio. Pick an example for your demonstration

that is different from the one used in the text. Be sure your example covers all cells.

5. To succeed in today's marketplace, companies must be customer centered. Explain how (a) State Farm Insurance, (b) the Seattle Mariners, or (c) Ben & Jerry's Ice Cream can use the processes of market segmentation, marketing targeting, and marketing positioning to become more customer centered. Suggest a "new" position for each organization and explain and justify the position you have suggested.

Mastering Marketing

Building strategy is one of the most important tasks to be undertaken by the marketing manager. Using the product/market expansion grid shown in Figure 2-3, show how the products currently being produced by CanGo

might fit this grid. Next, suggest future product expansion using the grid cells. Justify your expansion alternative(s). Be specific in your comments.

Traveling on the Net

Point of Interest: Strategic Planning

Selling computers via the Internet is big business. Gateway 2000, Inc. has proven that ordering via the mail, telephone, or the Internet can be very profitable. This computer company was able to accomplish their successful marketing effort through careful strategic planning and marketing skill. As a future marketing manager you can learn some of Gateway's secrets by going to their Web site (www.gateway.com). The history of the company is very interesting and will allow you to trace some of the decisions that have allowed the company to grow at a fantastic rate. Evaluate this company's Web site as instructed below.

For Discussion

1. What appears to be the company's mission statement? How did you determine this?

2. Who are Gateway's target customers? What leads you to believe this? What new customer groups should Gateway consider? Why?

3. What market position does Gateway appear to be seeking?

4. What can you determine about Gateway's product strategy?

5. What can you determine about Gateway's pricing strategy?

6. What new distribution tactics has Gateway recently followed? Do they appear to be successful? How did you evaluate the successfulness of their distribution strategy?

7. What do you perceive Gateway's chief strategic advantage to be? Chief disadvantage?

Application Thinking

Assume that you are one of Gateway's competitors. Identify the strengths and weaknesses of their strategy. Design a strategic plan that will allow your company to effectively compete against Gateway in the future. Be sure to consider which target market you wish to pursue and how you might build a Web site that would rival that of Gateway's. Use any of the following three Web sites to help you in the construction of your strategy: (a) American Demographics and Marketing Tools (www.demographics.com)—provides information for strategic planners seeking to refine their demographic segments, (b) CNET (www.news.com)—focuses on the latest news in Internet and computer industries (good current events and background material), and (c) Dell Computers (www.dell.com)—shows how an online competitor uses the Internet to market its products and services.

MAP—Marketing Applications

MAP Stop 2

Using his "Nothing but Net" philosophy, Oracle Corp. founder and CEO Larry Ellison has just about owned the Internet database management and corporate software business since its inception. However, change may be in the air. Even though his verbal wars with longtime nemesis Microsoft are famous and have grabbed the most headlines, his toughest war is about to be fought and his toughest competitor is knocking on Oracle's door. Who is this new rival? Big Blue—IBM! This sleeping giant has suddenly awakened and is hungry. If one is to believe industry analysts, Oracle's corner on the very lucrative business market (estimated to be $50 billion) seems ripe for the taking. With stakes such as these, both of these industry giants are gearing up for battle. Each is using a different set of strategic tools. Oracle's strategy is to offer customers a complete and tightly integrated package of software that will fill all management needs. Using an almost reverse approach, IBM is backing what they call a "best-of-breed" approach in which they stitch together a quilt of business software programs from various companies, including themselves. Minor competitors are anxiously watching to see which approach industry seems to favor. If IBM wins, there would seem to be more business and applications for all. Oracle's turnkey operation closes some of those doors. At present IBM seems to be exploiting an Oracle weakness—it competes against many of its own partners in the database business. IBM presents itself as a neutral, noncompeting alternative. Even though Oracle is ahead at this point in time, IBM seems to have momentum on its side. To offset this momentum, Oracle has speeded up introduction of new products and applications and is raising doubt about IBM's credibility and intentions as a neutral, noncompeting partner. So as both of these fierce competitors raise their battle flags, a similar battle cry seems to be coming from both camps—Charge!

Thinking Like a Marketing Manager

1. After visiting the Web sites for both IBM (www.ibm.com) and Oracle (www.oracle.com), write out what you perceive to be the mission, goals, or objectives for both organizations. How do these missions, goals, or objectives match their recent competitive moves?

2. After reading about the new products being offered by both companies in the business software and database management markets, construct a product/market expansion grid to indicate the direction each company seems to be taking.

3. Use outside sources to explore the personalities and careers of IBM's CEO Louis V. Gerstner, Jr. and Oracle's Lawrence J. Ellison. What insight does this give you on the strategies being used in this corporate struggle? What vulnerabilities seem to be present? How could these be exploited by either party?

4. Pick one of the two combatants. Write a marketing strategy for your chosen company that will carry the firm toward 2010. Be sure to use the steps found in Figure 2-1 and the factors shown in Figure 2-4 in constructing your strategy. Report your ideas in class.

chapter 3

Marketing in the Internet Age

ROAD MAP:
Previewing the Concepts

It's time to shift gears. In the first two chapters, you learned about the basic concepts of marketing, marketing strategies, and the marketing process for bringing value and satisfaction to targeted consumers. However, marketing strategy and practice have undergone dramatic change during the past decade. Major technological advances, including the explosion of the Internet, have had a major impact on buyers and the marketers who serve them. To thrive in this new Internet age—even to survive—marketers must rethink their strategies and adapt them to today's new Internet environment.

▶ **After studying this chapter, you should be able to**

1. identify the major forces shaping the new Internet age
2. explain how companies have responded to the Internet and other powerful new technologies with e-business strategies, and how these strategies have resulted in benefits to both buyers and sellers
3. describe the four major e-commerce domains
4. discuss how companies go about conducting e-commerce to profitably deliver more value to customers
5. overview the promise and challenges that e-commerce presents for the future

As a tune-up, consider Charles Schwab Corporation. After at first resisting the Internet, Charles Schwab has transformed itself from a traditional "brick-and-mortar" marketer to a full-fledged "click-and-mortar" marketer. This transformation has propelled the company to leadership in the swiftly changing brokerage industry, richly rewarding shareholders along the way. For example, how much do you think founder Charles R. Schwab's 20 percent stake in the company is worth today? Roll on.

Charles Schwab Corporation began in 1976 as the nation's first discount brokerage. Over the next two decades, Schwab grew and prospered, showing an uncanny ability to adapt to the swiftly changing financial services market. However, when the World Wide Web took off in 1995, several fledgling Web-based brokerages—some offering unlimited trades for a low monthly fee—threatened to beat Schwab at its own value-pricing game. The company faced a difficult decision: Should it stay with the traditional "brick-and-mortar" operations that had made it so successful, or should it embrace the new Internet technology?

Looking back, the decision seems like a no-brainer. Surging Internet usage marked the dawning of a new Internet age, to which firms must quickly adapt or risk obsolescence. At the time, however, the idea of offering brokerage services online was downright revolutionary. Tradition dictated that investors needed lots of personal advice and hand-holding—things offered aplenty in Schwab's bustling branches and by its efficient phone

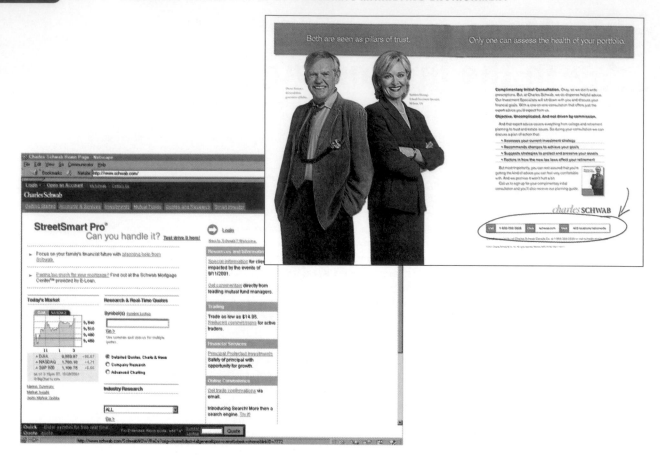

reps, but things not readily delivered via the Web. Moreover, by going online, Schwab would cannibalize its existing business. It would be swapping higher commissions on transactions conducted in branches or by phone for much lower online commissions. Further, going online would put Schwab in direct conflict with its large and profitable network of independent financial advisers and its corps of in-house investment specialists.

Staying offline, however, was perhaps even riskier than going online. Americans were rapidly discovering the wonders of the Web, and Internet trading offered real price and convenience advantages for customers. If Schwab didn't take advantage of these New Economy opportunities, some competitor would. The company decided that it was better to lead now than follow later. In late 1995, Schwab became the first major U.S. brokerage to go online. It set up a separate division called e.Schwab.

Under the new two-tiered system, Schwab customers had to be either online or offline. E.Schwab offered online customers cheap transactions—$29.95 per trade—but few services. Regular customers continued to place orders over the phone or at a branch, receiving more services but paying about twice the commissions. E.Schwab was a smashing success. By mid-1997, it was claiming an almost 50 percent share of all U.S. online brokerage accounts.

But as e.Schwab sales grew—so did customers' frustrations. Offline customers resented the lower prices given to Web-only customers. At the same time, e.Schwab users wanted access to the same investment advice and other services offered to regular traders. Customers didn't want *either/or*—they wanted *both*. So, once again, Schwab faced a difficult decision: Should it keep e.Schwab separate or merge it back into the company's mainstream services? Integrating the Web services would mean offering everyone the low

$29.95 trades, cutting Schwab's average commission in half and costing the firm an estimate $125 million in lost revenues.

Schwab didn't hesitate. In early 1998, putting customers' interests ahead of its own short-run profit concerns, Schwab integrated e.Schwab, offering low online rates and full offline services to all customers. "There were huge risks," says Charles R. Schwab, the company's founder and co-CEO, "but we thought [it] was better for customers." David Pottruck, Schwab's president and co-CEO adds, "We needed to focus on our clients and what we wanted to do for them; to make a difference in their lives."

At first, as predicted, sales and profits dropped, and so did Schwab's stock prices. Within a year, however, the gamble was paying off. The lower prices attracted hordes of new customers and ignited trading volume. At the same time, switching transactions to the Web created big productivity gains and reduced costs. For example, by the end of 1998, Schwab was handling five times as many trades on the Web as at its phone centers, producing some $100 million per year in savings. Schwab used the savings to expand investor services and draw even more clients. The results surprised even the most optimistic insiders. By early 1999, only three years after going to the Web, Schwab was capturing more than half of its trading volume online. Its 30 percent Web market share equaled that of its next three online competitors combined.

In melding the Net and non-Net worlds, Schwab created a powerful new "click-and-mortar" model of full-service brokerage—a robust one-stop shop for people's finances. The model recognizes that, most of the time, customers can handle their finances independently, and that they like the convenience and low prices afforded by the Web. Ultimately, however, many want some human contact. "For the vast majority of stock transactions that are fairly straightforward, the Net is a perfect medium," says Pottruck. "But what if you want advice on the right allocation for your portfolio? Then you're dealing with people's trust, and a mouse-click isn't enough."

Schwab's click-and-mortar model lets customers design the specific blend of high-tech independence and high-touch service they need. They can log onto Schwab.com, do their own account analysis, conduct investment research, and make trades. At Schwab.com's free online Learning Center, they can hear live audio feeds of lectures or take interactive courses on everything from "Investing Fundamentals" and "How to Place a Stock Order" to "Demystifying the Stock Market" and "The Basics of Bond Investing." Schwab.com also offers more advanced features. A "Portfolio Checkup" helps customers do online asset-allocation planning based on their tolerance for risk. A "Sell Analyzer" lets customers evaluate which securities to sell for tax losses, and a "Portfolio Tracker" allows them to assess their portfolios against standard indexes.

Customers who want more personal service or advice can call one of Schwab's round-the-clock call centers or stop by one of Schwab's 365 brick-and-mortar branches, staffed by an army of 7,000 investment advisers. Schwab has installed Web kiosks at its branches so that customers can go online to check their accounts or make a trade while at the same time getting personal help from a service rep on the spot. Branches also provide "Portfolio Consultation" services—for $400 investors can get their existing portfolios analyzed by a broker who offers advice about which stocks or funds to buy or which to drop.

This powerful combination of clicks and bricks presents a menu of options that Schwab's click-only or brick-only competitors simply can't match. Schwab's success with the merged model has competitors on both sides scrambling to catch up. Traditional brick-and-mortar competitors, such as Fidelity and Merrill-Lynch, are now clicking along with Web sites of their own. The once arrogant click-only brokerages, such as E*Trade, Datek, and WebStreet, are now building offline shops. Because of the tighter economy, brokerages these days must fight harder than ever to get every possible dollar from their customers. Thus, industry focus is shifting toward customer retention and cross-selling. Than means more services and hand-holding, which in turn mean a return to the good old bricks and mortar. An example of one Web-only firm trying to reinvent itself as a combination of clicks and mortar is E*Trade, which in 2000 began placing branded E*Trade Zone locations inside Target stores.

Just how successful has Schwab been with its click-and-mortar model? By any measure, the company's decision to put customers first has met with stunning success. Schwab now runs the world's largest e-commerce site. From nothing five years ago, Schwab now executes 85 percent of its trades online—some 300,000 trades per day—accounting for nearly one out of every four online trades in the industry. By 2000, Schwab had already passed its 2005 target of $1 trillion in assets under management—a more-than-threefold increase in just five years. Today, Schwab manages a staggering 42 percent of all online assets—handling more than twice the volume of its nearest competitor. Stockholders have shared richly in this success. Charles Schwab stock has soared 22,000 percent since a low point just after the 1987 crash. Founder Charles R. Schwab hasn't done badly either. His 20 percent stake in the company is now worth $7.5 billion.[1]

· ·

In Chapter 1, we discussed sweeping changes in the marketing landscape that are affecting marketing thinking and practice. Recent technological advances, including the widespread use of the Internet, have created what some call a New Economy. Although there has been widespread debate in recent years about the nature of—even the existence of—such a new economy, few would disagree that the Internet and other powerful new connecting technologies are having a dramatic impact on marketers and buyers. Many standard marketing strategies and practices of the past—mass marketing, product standardization, media advertising, store retailing, and others—were well suited to the so-called Old Economy. These strategies and practices will continue to be important in the New Economy. However, marketers will also have to develop new strategies and practices better suited to today's new environment.

In this chapter, we first describe the key forces shaping the new Internet age. Then we examine how marketing strategy and practice are changing to meet the requirements of this new age.

Major Forces Shaping the Internet Age

Many forces are playing a major role in reshaping the world economy, including technology, globalization, environmentalism, and others. Here we discuss four specific forces that underlie the new Internet age (see Figure 3-1): digitalization and connectivity, the Internet explosion, new types of intermediaries, and customization and customerization.

Digitalization and Connectivity

Many appliances and systems in the past—ranging from telephone systems, wristwatches, and musical recordings to industrial gauges and controls—operated on analog information. Analog information is continuously variable in response to physical stimuli. Today a growing number of appliances and systems operate on *digital information,* which comes as streams of zeros and ones, or *bits*. Text, data, sound, and images can be converted into *bitstreams.* A laptop computer manipulates bits in its thousands of applications. Software consists of digital content for operating systems, games, information storage, and other applications.

For bits to flow from one appliance or location to another requires *connectivity*, a telecommunications network. Much of the world's business today is carried out over

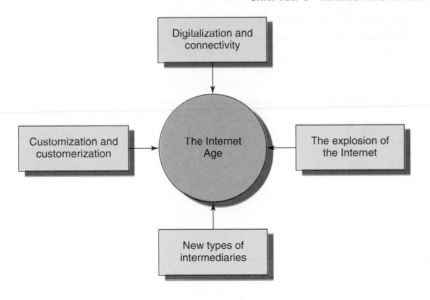

Figure 3-1
Forces shaping the
Internet age

networks that connect people and companies. **Intranets** are networks that connect people within a company to each other and to the company network. **Extranets** connect a company with its suppliers and distributors. And the **Internet**, a vast public web of computer networks, connects users of all types all around the world to each other and to an amazingly large "information repository." The Internet makes up one big "information highway" that can dispatch bits at incredible speeds from one location to another.

The Internet Explosion

With the creation of the World Wide Web and Web browsers in the 1990s, the Internet was transformed from a mere communication tool into a certifiably revolutionary technology. During the final decade of the twentieth century, the number of Internet users worldwide grew to almost 400 million. By early 2001, Internet penetration in the United States had reached close to 60 percent. Although the dot-com crash in 2000 led to cutbacks in technology spending, research suggests that the growth of Internet access among the world's citizens will continue to explode. The number of Web surfers worldwide is expected to approach 1 billion by 2004.

This explosive worldwide growth in Internet usage forms the heart of the so-called New Economy. The Internet has been *the* revolutionary technology of the new millennium, empowering consumers and businesses alike with blessings of connectivity. For nearly every New Economy innovation to emerge during the past decade, the Internet has played a starring—or at the very least a "best supporting"—role. The Internet enables consumers and companies to access and share unprecedented amounts of information with just a few mouse clicks. To be competitive in today's new marketplace, companies must adopt Internet technology or risk being left behind.

New Types of Intermediaries

New technologies have led thousands of entrepreneurs to launch Internet companies—the so-called dot-coms—in hopes of striking gold. The amazing success of early Internet-only companies, such as AOL, Amazon.com, Yahoo!, eBay, E*Trade, and dozens of others,

Intranet
A network that connects people within a company to each other and to the company network.

Extranet
A network that connects a company with its suppliers and distributors.

Internet
A vast public web of computer networks that connects users of all types all around the world to each other and to an amazingly large "information repository." The Internet makes up one big "information highway" that can dispatch bits at incredible speeds from one location to another.

struck terror in the hearts of many established manufacturers and retailers. For example, Compaq Computer, which sold its computers only through retailers, worried when Dell Computer grew faster by selling online. Toys 'R' Us worried when eToys lured toy buyers to the Web. Established store-based retailers of all kinds—from bookstores, music stores, and florists to travel agents, stockbrokers, and car dealers—began to doubt their futures as competitors sprung up selling their products and services via the Internet. They feared, and rightly so, being *disintermediated* by the new e-tailers—being cut out by this new type of intermediary.

The formation of new types of intermediaries and new forms of channel relationships caused existing firms to reexamine how they served their markets. At first, the established *brick-and-mortar* firms—such as Compaq, Barnes & Noble, and Merrill Lynch—dragged their feet hoping that the assaulting *click-only* firms would falter or disappear. Then they wised up and started their own online sales channels, becoming *click-and-mortar* competitors. Ironically, many click-and-mortar competitors have become stronger than the click-only competitors that pushed them reluctantly onto the Internet. Charles Schwab is a good example. In fact, although some click-only competitors are surviving and even prospering in today's marketplace, many once-formidable dot-coms—such as eToys, Pets.com, Garden.com, and Mothernature.com—have failed in recent years in the face of poor profitability and plunging stock values.

Customization and Customerization

The Old Economy revolved around *manufacturing companies* that mainly focused on standardizing their production, products, and business processes. They invested large sums in brand building to tout the advantages of their standardized market offerings. Through standardization and branding, manufacturers hoped to grow demand and take advantage of economies of scale. As a key to managing their assets, they set up command-and-control systems that would run their businesses like machines.

In contrast, the New Economy revolves around *information businesses*. Information has the advantages of being easy to differentiate, customize, personalize, and dispatch at incredible speeds over networks. With rapid advances in Internet and other connecting technologies, companies have grown skilled in gathering information about individual customers and business partners (suppliers, distributors, retailers). In turn, they have become more adept at individualizing their products and services, messages, and media. Dell Computer, for example, lets customers specify exactly what they want in their computers and delivers customer-designed units in only a few days. On its Reflect.com Web site, Procter & Gamble allows people to reflect their needs for, say, a shampoo by answering a set of questions. It then formulates a unique shampoo for each person. Similarly, Levi Strauss can now produce customized jeans based on a person's individual measurements.

Customization differs from *customerization*. Customization involves taking the initiative to customize the market offering. For example, a Levi-Strauss salesperson takes the person's measurements and the company customizes the jeans at the factory. Or a restaurant waiter takes a customer's order for a salad with more broccoli, no cheese, and dressing on the side and the restaurant *customizes* the salad for the customer. In **customerization**, the company leaves it to individual customers to design the offering. For example, jeans customers may take their own measurements and add specific features that they may want in their jeans, such as colorful patches. Restaurant customers go to a salad bar and *customerize* their salads by choosing the exact salad ingredients they want. Such companies have become facilitators and their customers have moved from being consumers to being *prosumers*.[2]

Customerization
Leaving it to individual customers to design the marketing offering—allowing customers to be *prosumers* rather than only consumers.

Customerization: At Reflect.com, people formulate their own beauty products—it offers "one of a kind products for one of a kind you." More than 650,000 people visit the site each month.

Marketing Strategy in the New Internet Age

Conducting business in the new Internet age will call for a new model for marketing strategy and practice. According to one strategist: "Sparked by new technologies, particularly the Internet, the corporation is undergoing a radical transformation that is nothing less than a new industrial revolution. . . . To survive and thrive in this century, managers will need to hard-wire a new set of rules into their brains. The 21st century corporation must adapt itself to management via the Web."[3] Suggests another, the Internet is "revolutionizing the way we think about . . . how to construct relationships with suppliers and customers, how to create value for them, and how to make money in the process; in other words, [it's] revolutionizing marketing."[4]

Some strategists envision a day when all buying and selling will involve direct electronic connections between companies and their customers. The new model will fundamentally change customers' notions of convenience, speed, price, product information, and service. This new consumer thinking will affect every business. Comparing the adoption of the Internet and other new marketing technologies to the early days of the airplane, Amazon.com CEO Jeff Bezos says, "It's the Kitty Hawk era of electronic commerce." Even those offering more cautious predictions agree that the Internet and e-business will have a tremendous impact on future business strategies.

The fact is that today's economy requires a mixture of Old Economy and New Economy thinking and action. Companies need to retain most of the skills and practices that have worked in the past. But they will also need to add major new competencies and practices if they hope to grow and prosper in the new environment. Marketing should play the *lead role* in shaping new company strategy.

E-Business, E-Commerce, and E-Marketing in the Internet Age

E-business
The use of electronic platforms—intranets, extranets, and the Internet—to conduct a company's business.

E-business involves the use of electronic platforms—intranets, extranets, and the Internet—to conduct a company's business. The Internet and other information and computer technologies have greatly increased the ability of companies to carry on their business faster, more accurately, and over a wider range of time and space. Countless companies have set up Web sites to inform about and promote their products and services. They have created intranets to help employees communicate with each other and access information found in the company's computers. They have set up extranets with their major suppliers and distributors to facilitate information exchange, orders, transactions, and payments. Companies such as Cisco, Microsoft, and Oracle run almost entirely as e-businesses, in which memos, invoices, engineering drawings, sales and marketing information—virtually everything—happen over the Internet instead of on paper.[5]

E-commerce
Buying and selling processes supported by electronic means, primarily the Internet.

E-commerce is more specific than e-business. Whereas e-business includes all electronics-based information exchanges within or between companies and customers, e-commerce involves buying and selling processes supported by electronic means, primarily the Internet. *E-markets* are "market*spaces*," rather than physical "market*places*," in which sellers offer their products and services online, and buyers search for information, identify what they want, and place orders using credit or other means of electronic payment.

E-marketing
The "e-selling" side of e-commerce—company efforts to communicate about, promote, and sell products and services over the Internet.

E-commerce includes *e-marketing* and *e-purchasing* (*e-procurement*). **E-marketing** is the "e-selling" side of e-commerce. It consists of company efforts to communicate about, promote, and sell products and services over the Internet. Thus, Amazon.com, Schwab.com, and Dell.com conduct e-marketing at their Web sites. The flip side of e-marketing is e-purchasing, the "e-buying" side of e-commerce. It consists of companies purchasing goods, services, and information from online suppliers. In business-to-business buying, e-marketers and e-purchasers come together in huge e-commerce networks. For example, GE Global eXchange Services (GXS) operates one of the world's largest business-to-business e-commerce networks (www.gegxs.com). More than 100,000 trading partners in 58 countries—including giants such as 3M, DaimlerChrysler, Target, JCPenney, Sara Lee, and Kodak—use the GXS network to complete some 1 billion transactions each year, accounting for $1 trillion worth of goods and services.[6]

E-commerce and the Internet bring many benefits to both buyers and sellers. Let's review some of these major benefits.

Benefits to Buyers

Internet buying benefits both final buyers and business buyers in many ways. It can be *convenient*: Customers don't have to battle traffic, find parking spaces, and trek through stores and aisles to find and examine products. They can do comparative shopping by browsing through mail catalogs or surfing Web sites. Direct marketers never close their doors. Buying is *easy* and *private*: Customers encounter fewer buying hassles and don't have to face salespeople or open themselves up to persuasion and emotional pitches. Business buyers can learn about and buy products and services without waiting for and tying up time with salespeople.

In addition, the Internet often provides buyers with greater *product access and selection*. For example, the world's the limit for the Web. Unrestrained by physical boundaries, cybersellers can offer an almost unlimited selection. Compare the incredible selections offered by Web merchants such as Amazon.com or eVineyard to the more meager assortments of their counterparts in the brick-and-mortar world.

Beyond a broader selection of sellers and products, e-commerce channels also give buyers access to a wealth of comparative *information*, information about companies, products, and competitors. Good sites often provide more information in more useful forms

Internet buying is easy and private: Final consumers can shop the world from home with few hassles; business buyers can learn about and obtain products and information without tying up time with salespeople.

than even the most solicitous salesperson can. For example, Amazon.com offers top-10 product lists, extensive product descriptions, expert and user product reviews, and recommendations based on customers' previous purchases.

Finally, online buying is *interactive* and *immediate*. Buyers often can interact with the seller's site to create exactly the configuration of information, products, or services they desire, then order or download them on the spot. Moreover, the Internet gives consumers a greater measure of control. "The Internet will empower consumers like nothing else ever has," notes one analyst. "Think about this: Already 16 percent of car buyers shop online before showing up at a dealership, and they aren't comparing paint jobs—they're arming themselves with information on dealer costs. . . . The new reality is consumer control."[7]

Benefits to Sellers

E-commerce also yields many benefits to sellers. First, the Internet is a powerful tool for *customer relationship building*. Because of its one-to-one, interactive nature, the Internet is an especially potent marketing tool. Companies can interact online with customers to learn more about specific needs and wants. In turn, online customers can ask questions and volunteer feedback. Based on this ongoing interaction, companies can increase customer value and satisfaction through product and service refinements. One expert concludes: "Contrary to the common view that Web customers are fickle by nature and will flock to the next new idea, the Web is actually a very sticky space in both business-to-consumer and business-to-business spheres. Most of today's online customers exhibit a clear [tendency] toward loyalty."[8]

The Internet and other electronic channels yield additional advantages, such as *reducing costs* and *increasing speed and efficiency*. E-marketers avoid the expense of maintaining a store and the accompanying costs of rent, insurance, and utilities. E-tailers such as Amazon.com reap the advantage of a negative operating cycle: Amazon.com receives cash from credit card companies just one day after customers place an order. Then it can hold on to the money for 46 days until it pays suppliers, the book distributors and publishers.

By using the Internet to link directly to suppliers, factories, distributors, and customers, businesses such as Dell Computer and General Electric are wringing waste out of the system and passing savings on to customers. Because customers deal directly with sellers, e-marketing often results in lower costs and improved efficiencies for channel and logistics functions such as order processing, inventory handling, delivery, and trade promotion. Finally, communicating electronically often costs less than communicating on paper through the mail. For instance, a company can produce digital catalogs for much less than the cost of printing and mailing paper ones.

E-marketing also offers greater *flexibility*, allowing the marketer to make ongoing adjustments to its offers and programs. For example, once a paper catalog is mailed to final consumer or business customers, the products, prices, and other catalog features are fixed until the next catalog is sent. However, an online catalog can be adjusted daily or even hourly, adapting product assortments, prices, and promotions to match changing market conditions.

Finally, the Internet is a truly *global* medium that allows buyers and sellers to click from one country to another in seconds. GE's GXS network provides business buyers with immediate access to suppliers in 58 countries, ranging from the United States and the United Kingdom to Hong Kong and the Philippines. A Web surfer from Paris or Istanbul can access an online Lands' End catalog as easily as someone living on 1 Lands' End Lane in Dodgeville, Wisconsin, the direct retailer's hometown. Thus, even small e-marketers find that they have ready access to global markets.

Linking the Concepts

Pull over here for a minute and think about this new Internet age. What, specifically, does the Internet age mean in *your* life?

◆ Look back through the major forces shaping the Internet Age and write down some specific ways that these forces have affected your everyday life.
◆ How often and in what ways do you use the Internet to research and buy products? How has the Internet changed what and how you buy?
◆ Go to the Web, visit SonyStyle.com, and have a look around. How does such a site benefit consumers like you? How does it benefit Sony?

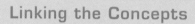

E-Commerce Domains

The four major Internet domains are shown in Figure 3-2 and discussed below. They include B2C (business to consumer), B2B (business to business), C2C (consumer to consumer), and C2B (consumer to business).

B2C (Business to Consumer)

B2C (business-to-consumer) e-commerce
The online selling of goods and services to final consumers.

The popular press has paid the most attention to **B2C (business-to-consumer) e-commerce**—the online selling of goods and services to final consumers. Despite some gloomy predictions, online consumer buying continues to grow at a healthy rate. Jupiter Research estimates that consumers will spend $130 billion online by 2006, up from $34 billion in 2001. The largest categories of consumer online spending include travel services, clothing, computer hardware and software, consumer electronics, books, music and video, health and beauty, home and garden, flowers and gifts, sports and fitness equipment, and toys.[9]

Online Consumers   When people envision the typical Internet user, some still mistakenly envision a pasty-faced computer nerd or "cyberhead." Others envision a young, techy, upscale male professional. Such stereotypes are sadly outdated. As more and more people

	Targeted to consumers	Targeted to businesses
Initiated by business	B2C (business to consumer)	B2B (business to business)
Initiated by consumer	C2C (consumer to consumer)	C2B (consumer to business)

Figure 3-2
E-Marketing domains

find their way onto the Internet, the cyberspace population is becoming more mainstream and diverse. "The Internet was, at first, an elitist country club reserved only for individuals with select financial abilities and technical skills," says an e-commerce analyst. "Now, nearly every socioeconomic group is aggressively adopting the Web."[10] (See Marketing at Work 3-1.)

Thus, increasingly, the Internet provides e-marketers with access to a broad range of demographic segments. For example, home Internet access for blue-collar workers is growing faster than for any other occupational group, surging 52 percent in just the past year. One study of Internet "newbies"—those who started using the Internet in the past year—found that 71 percent had no college degree, 65 percent earn less than $50,000 a year, and only 25 percent were younger than 30.

These days, everybody's logging on. . . . Doral Main, a 51-year-old mother of two and office manager of a low-income property company in Oakland, CA, saves precious time by shopping the Internet for greeting cards and getaways. Her Net-newbie father, Charles, 73, goes online to buy supplies for his wood-carving hobby. Even niece Katrina, 11, finds excitement on the Web, picking gifts she wants from the Disney.com site. "It's addictive," Main says of the Internet. [Indeed,] the Web isn't mostly a hangout for techno-nerds anymore.[11]

Growing Internet diversity continues to open new e-commerce targeting opportunities for marketers. For example, the Web now reaches consumers in all age groups. The populations of almost 12 million "Net kids" and more than 18 million teens have attracted a host of e-marketers. America Online offers a Kids Only area featuring homework help and online magazines along with the usual games, software, and chat rooms. The Microsoft Network site carries Disney's Daily Blast, which offers kids games, stories, comic strips with old and new Disney characters, and current events tailored to preteens. Nickelodeon (www.nick.com) offers a full slate of games based on favorite Nickelodeon characters.

Although Internet users are still younger on average than the population as a whole, consumers aged 50 and older make up almost 20 percent of the online population. Whereas younger groups are more likely to use the Internet for entertainment and socializing, older Internet surfers go online for more serious matters. For example, 24 percent of people in this age group use the Internet for investment purposes, compared with only 3 percent of those 25 to 29. Thus, older Netizens make an attractive market for Web businesses, ranging from florists and automotive retailers to financial services providers.[12]

To help online marketers to better target their customers, Internet research companies now segment the increasingly diverse Web population by needs and interests. For example, Harris Interactive has tabbed a segment it calls Cyberchondriacs, the roughly 100 million Americans who go online for health care information. Slightly older than the general population, typically they or someone else in their family has a medical condition. They view the Internet as a kind of mobile medical library and log on to dig out the latest research and treatments for a specific malady. Pharmaceutical firms such as Pfizer and Johnson & Johnson have launched Web sites to market their prescription drugs directly to

Marketing at Work 3-1

Online America: A Movable Feast for E-Marketers

Just a few years ago, when Forrester Research first began classifying North Americans into "technographic" types according to their affinity for technology, the vast majority of Internet users fell predictably into the same group. They were overwhelmingly male, overwhelmingly young, overwhelmingly college educated, and overwhelmingly high-techy. How times have changed. Today, Internet users are found in all of Forrester's segments, even those with downscale, late-adopting, technology-challenged families.

For marketers, the Internet now presents a movable feast of different kinds of people seeking different types of online experiences.

Now, in any given month, almost 60 percent of the U.S. population, more than 160 million people, are accessing the Internet, a 30 percent increase over a year earlier. Their average age—39 years and rising. Their average education—38 percent hold a college degree—is falling. Likewise, their socioeconomic status is sinking, thanks to the fastest-growing segment of Web newbies: Americans over 55 years old with working-class incomes and middlebrow tastes. In a final blow to the old stereotypes, the number of women online surpassed that of men for the first time in mid-2001.

This mixed portrait is a far cry from the old image of Net users as

geeky white guys (GWGs), technophiles who enjoyed hacking their way through chat rooms and bulletin boards. Since those early days, the Web community has exploded. A detailed analysis of wired America reveals an audience of Netizens nearly as diverse—and quirky—as consumers offline. Men and women, rich and poor, old and young—all go their separate ways on the Web.

For example, people from different socioeconomic levels use the Web differently. One study that classified Web users into PRIZM types (a geodemographic segmentation system that segments consumers into lifestyle niches) came up with some surprising results.

For marketers, the Internet now presents a moveable feast of different kinds of people seeking different types of online experiences.

True, the clusters with the greatest access to the Internet are still those containing early adopting, upscale Americans. But the clusters whose surfers spend the most time online at home left some analysts agog: Mid-City Mix, Norma Raeville, and Back Country Folks, characterized by people with lower incomes, modest educations, and blue-collar jobs who like to chat, exchange e-mail, and hang out at entertainment and sweepstakes sites.

Of course, spending more time on the Web doesn't necessarily equate with spending more money there. A kind of e-havioral divide is emerging in how different kinds of Americans use the Internet. The time-pressed consumers, from upscale PRIZM clusters such as Money & Brains (sophisticated urban-fringe couples) and Country Squires (elite exurban families), tend to view the Web as a transactional arena—a place to gather information or buy big ticket items. They visit news, travel, and financial sites, such as Schwab.com, smartmoney.com, and americanexpress.com. To them, the Internet is just one more tool to help them get information or buy things.

By contrast, Americans at the lower end of the socioeconomic ladder are more likely to view the Internet as a kind of home entertainment center for fun and games. In clusters such as Red, White & Blues (small-town, middle-class families) and Blue Highways (working-class farm families), residents are more likely to surf a variety of entertainment and sweepstakes sites, including icq.com, youwinit.com, and gamesville.com. "Lower-income Americans look to the Internet as a replacement for television," says one analyst.

Along with the socioeconomic differences, many researchers report a growing gender gap on the Internet. Although men and women engage in many activities at roughly equal rates—such as banking and downloading music—the sexes then part company. Men are more likely to go online to buy stocks, get news, compare and buy products, bid at auctions, and visit government Web sites. Women are more likely to send e-mail, play games, score coupons, and get information on health, jobs, and religion. This online gender gap forms early. A study of teenagers by Jupiter Media Metrix found that boys are much more likely to download software and play games online. Girls, by contrast, are more interested in reading online magazines, doing homework, and staying in touch with their e-buddies. Their parents would probably be shocked to find that American teenagers actually spend about 30 percent less time on the Web than adults.

For both sexes, Web behavior shifts with age. For example, women in their twenties and thirties patronize sites offering relationship and parenting information relevant to that life stage. In their forties, they shift to hobby and leisure sites featuring gardening and cooking content. Women in their fifties, meanwhile, turn to Web sites offering advice on financial investments and health care. "It's like holding a mirror to a woman's life," says a measurement analyst. "At every stage, her online preferences provide a readable map of her offline interests."

Despite studies showing the Internet gap shrinking between ethnic groups and the general population, differences remain. Asian Americans have been more prevalent online for years and are more likely to invest their money, make purchases, and research products over the Internet than is the general population. Although Hispanics and African Americans have yet to reach the usage levels of other groups online, blacks already top whites in conducting school research, getting sports news, and looking for a job. "African Americans tend to do serious things on the Internet," says one analyst. "Adults see it as an investment for themselves and their children."

In many ways, people behave online much like they do in real life—a pattern that's contrary to early predictions that Web use would be categorically different from day-to-day life. Futurists once maintained that Internet users would form virtual communities to the exclusion of real-world relationships. Well, it hasn't quite turned out that way. Although early research claimed that the Internet contributed to the social isolation of enthusiasts, more recent studies suggest that the opposite might be true. One recent survey found that social relationships are actually strengthened by online use. In another survey, 48 percent of people said that they communicate with their friends and family more often because of the Internet, compared with only 3 percent who said that their contact decreased.

Analysts estimate that the Internet population will reach between 75 percent and 85 percent of all Americans during the next decade. Internet researchers differ in their predictions on how long it will take for the Internet audience to reach its saturation point in the United States. However, they're in remarkable agreement on one point: Say farewell to the geeky white guys. The latest generation of connected Americans looks a lot more like the folks who cruise your local Wal-Mart.

Source: Adapted with permission from Michael J. Weiss, "Online America," *American Demographics*, March 2001, pp. 53–60.

The "mother of all customizers": Pfizer uses the Internet to serve the roughly 100 million Americans who go online for healthcare information relating to their specific needs.

these Cyberchondriacs, hoping to spur them to ask their doctors for the medication by brand name. "The Internet is the mother of all customizers," observes a Harris executive. "You can customize a product to a 36-year-old . . . diabetic with red hair. And you can do it in a way that you could never do with traditional media."[13]

Internet consumers differ from traditional offline consumers in their approaches to buying and in their responses to marketing. The exchange process in the Internet age has become more customer initiated and customer controlled. People who use the Internet place greater value on information and tend to respond negatively to messages aimed only at selling. Whereas traditional marketing targets a somewhat passive audience, e-marketing targets people who actively select which Web sites they will visit and what marketing information they will receive about which products and services and under what conditions. Marketers and their representatives are held at bay until customers invite them to participate in the exchange. Even after marketers enter the exchange process, customers define what information they need, what offerings they are interested in, and what prices they are willing to pay. Thus, the new world of e-commerce requires new marketing approaches.

B2C Web Sites Consumers can find a Web site for buying almost anything. The Internet is most useful for products and services when the shopper seeks greater ordering convenience or lower costs. The Internet also provides great value to buyers looking for information about differences in product features and value. However, consumers find the Internet less useful when buying products that must be touched or examined in advance. Still, even here there are exceptions. For example, who would have thought that people would order expensive computers from Dell or Gateway without seeing and trying them first? People now go online to order a wide range of goods—clothing from Gap or Lands' End, books or electronics from Amazon.com, furniture from Ethan Allen, major appliances from Sears, flowers from Calyx and Corolla, or even home mortgages from Quicken Loans.

◆ Calyx and Corolla, "The Flower Lover's Flower Company," sells fresh flowers directly to consumers. Customers can order bouquets or plants from a color catalog by phoning 1-800-877-0998 or place orders at the C&C Web site at www.calyxandcorolla.com.

Orders go immediately to one of 25 growers in the C&C network, who pick and package the flowers and ship orders via FedEx. When the flowers arrive, they are fresher and last about 10 days longer than flowers ordered from store-based retailers. Calyx and Corolla credits its success to a sophisticated information system and strong alliances with FedEx and the growers.

◆ At Quicken Loans (www.quickenloans.quicken.com), prospective borrowers receive a high-tech, high-touch, one-stop mortgage shopping experience. At the site, customers can research a wide variety of home financing and refinancing options, apply for a mortgage, and receive quick loan approval—all without leaving the comfort and security of their homes. The site provides useful interactive tools that help borrowers decide how much house they can afford, whether to rent or buy, whether to refinance a current mortgage, the economics of fixing up their current homes rather than moving, and much more. Customers can receive advice by phone or by chatting online with one of 400 loan consultants and sign up for later e-mail rate updates. Quicken Loans originated nearly $3.5 billion in mortgage loans last year.[14]

B2B (Business to Business)

Although the popular press has given the most attention to business-to-consumer (B2C) Web sites, consumer goods sales via the Web are dwarfed by **B2B (business-to-business) e-commerce**. Gartner Group, a major research firm on online commerce, estimates that B2B e-commerce will reach $3.6 trillion in 2003, compared with just $107 billion in B2C transactions. Gartner also estimates that by 2005, more than 500,000 enterprises will participate in e-commerce as buyers, sellers, or both.[15] These firms are using B2B trading networks, auction sites, spot exchanges, online product catalogs, barter sites, and other online resources to reach new customers, serve current customers more effectively, and obtain buying efficiencies and better prices.

> **B2B (business-to-business) e-commerce**
> Using B2B trading networks, auction sites, spot exchanges, online product catalogs, barter sites, and other online resources to reach new customers, serve current customers more effectively, and obtain buying efficiencies and better prices.

Most major business-to-business marketers now offer product information, customer purchasing, and customer support services online. For example, corporate buyers can visit Sun Microsystems' Web site (www.sun.com), select detailed descriptions of Sun's products and solutions, request sales and service information, and interact with staff members. The Sun site also offers background information on Sun and links visitors to articles on topics of interest to key customer segments. The site features real-time online discussions of hot topics, along with on-demand Webcasts of previous discussions. At the site, customers can also subscribe to free e-mail newsletters that provide a regular flow of the latest news, information, and technology from Sun. Some major companies conduct almost all of their business on the Web. For example, networking equipment and software maker Cisco Systems takes more than 80 percent of its orders over the Internet.

Much B2B e-commerce takes place in **open trading networks**—huge e-marketspaces in which buyers and sellers find each other online, share information, and complete transactions efficiently. Here are examples of B2B trading network sites:

> **Open trading networks**
> Huge e-marketspaces in which B2B buyers and sellers find each other online, share information, and complete transactions efficiently.

◆ PlasticsNet.com is an Internet marketplace for the plastic products industry, connecting more than 90,000 monthly visitors with more than 200 suppliers. In addition to facilitating online transactions, the site provides a supplier directory, material data sheets, an industry publication, a list of educational programs, and books and seminars relevant to the plastics industry.

◆ The Medical EquipNet serves as a medical equipment e-marketplace in which companies, doctors' offices, and hospitals can buy, sell, or auction off new, used, refurbished, or surplus medical equipment. Members can place classifieds or want ads, place or receive auction bids, or access medical equipment financing, shipping, repair, or installation services. To date, the site has attracted more than 4.5 million visits.

B2B e-commerce: Corporate buyers can visit Sun Microsystems' Web site, learn in detail about Sun's products, request sales and service information, and interact with staff members.

Private trading networks (PTNs)
B2B trading networks that link a particular seller with its own trading partners.

Despite the increasing popularity of such e-marketspaces, one Internet research firm estimates that 93 percent of all B2B e-commerce is conducted through private sites. Increasingly, online sellers are setting up their own **private trading networks (PTNs).** Whereas open trading networks such as PlasticsNet.com facilitate transactions between a wide range of online buyers and sellers, private trading networks link a particular seller with its own trading partners. Rather than simply completing transactions, PTNs give sellers greater control over product presentation and allow them to build deeper relationships with buyers and sellers by providing value-added services. As an example, take Trane Company, a maker of air-conditioning and heating systems:

Since last autumn, Trane . . . has been red-hot with the business-to-business Internet crowd. Each of the horde of B2B [open trading] exchanges targeting the construction industry wants Trane to join. "Construction.com, MyPlant.com, MyFacility.com—we get up to five calls a week," says James A. Bierkamp, head of Trane's e-business unit. But after some consideration, Bierkamp did not see what any of those [third-party] e-marketplaces could offer that his company couldn't do itself. So in May, Trane rolled out its own private exchange, which allows its 5,000 dealers to browse, buy equipment, schedule deliveries, and process warranties. The site lets Trane operate with greater efficiency and trim processing costs—without losing control of the presentation of its brand name or running the risks of rubbing elbows with competitors in an open exchange. "Why let another party get between us and our customers?'" asks Bierkamp.[17]

C2C (Consumer to Consumer)

Much **C2C (consumer-to-consumer) e-commerce** and communication occurs on the Web between interested parties over a wide range of products and subjects. In some cases, the Internet provides an excellent means by which consumers can buy or exchange goods or information directly with one another. For example, eBay, Amazon.com Auctions, and other auction sites offer popular marketspaces for displaying and selling almost anything, from art and antiques, coins and stamps, and jewelry to computers and consumer electronics. EBay's C2C online trading community of more than 30 million registered users transacted more than $5 billion in trades last year. The company's Web site hosts more than 2 million auctions each month for items in more than 1,000 categories. EBay also maintains auction sites in several foreign countries, including Japan, the United Kingdom, and Germany.

Such C2C sites give people access to much larger audiences than the local flea market or newspaper classifieds (which, by the way, are now also going online). Ask Barbara Dreschsler, a systems engineer in Roanoke, Texas, who has been buying and selling Beanie Babies via Internet auction sites such as eBay.com and Amazon.com for more than a year. What started out as a family hobby has rapidly morphed into a part-time business. In the first two months of this year, Dreschsler received 102 orders for Beanie Babies and other toys priced at $10 to $200. "We still call it a hobby, but we would love to do it full time," she says.[18]

In other cases, C2C involves interchanges of information through forums and Internet newsgroups that appeal to specific special-interest groups. Such activities may be organized for commercial or noncommercial purposes. *Forums* are discussion groups located on commercial online services such as AOL and CompuServe. A forum may take the form of a library, a "chat room" for real-time message exchanges, and even a classified ad directory. For example, America Online boasts some 14,000 chat rooms, which account for a third of its members' online time. It also provides "buddy lists," which alert members when friends are online, allowing them to exchange instant messages.

C2C (consumer-to-consumer) e-commerce Online exchanges of goods and information between final consumers.

C2C e-commerce: Last year, eBay's 30 million members transacted more than $5 billion in trades.

Newsgroups are the Internet version of forums. However, such groups are limited to people posting and reading messages on a specified topic, rather than managing libraries or conferencing. Internet users can participate in newsgroups without subscribing. There are tens of thousands of newsgroups dealing with every imaginable topic, from healthful eating and caring for your Bonsai tree to collecting antique cars or exchanging views on the latest soap opera happenings.

C2C means that online visitors don't just consume product information—increasingly, they create it. They join Internet interest groups to share information, with the result that "word of Web" is joining "word of mouth" as an important buying influence. Word about good companies and products travels fast. Word about bad companies and products travels even faster.

C2B (Consumer to Business)

C2B (consumer-to-business) e-commerce
Online exchanges in which consumers search out sellers, learn about their offers, and initiate purchases, sometimes even driving transaction terms.

The final e-commerce domain is **C2B (consumer-to-business) e-commerce**. Thanks to the Internet, today's consumers are finding it easier to contact and communicate with companies. Most companies now invite prospects and customers to send in suggestions and questions via company Web sites. Beyond this, rather than waiting for companies to send catalogs or other information, consumers can search out sellers on the Web, learn about their offers, and initiate purchases.

Using the Web, consumers can even drive transactions with businesses, rather than the other way around. For example, using Priceline.com, would-be buyers bid for airline tickets, hotel rooms, rental cars, and even home mortgages, leaving the sellers to decide whether to accept their offers.

Conducting E-Commerce

Companies of all types are now engaged in e-commerce. In this section, we first discuss different types of e-marketers shown in Figure 3-3. Then, we examine how companies go about conducting marketing online.

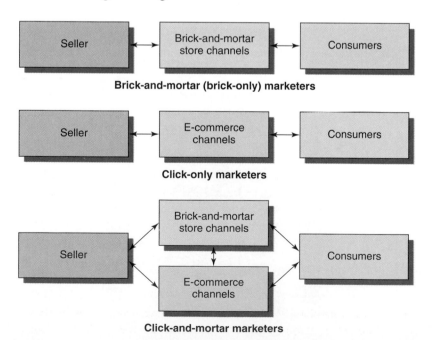

Figure 3-3
Types of e-marketers

Click-Only versus Click-and-Mortar E-Marketers

The Internet gave birth to a new species of e-marketers—the *click-only* dot-coms—which operate only online without any brick-and-mortar market presence. In addition, most traditional brick-and-mortar companies have now added e-marketing operations, transforming themselves into *click-and-mortar* competitors.

Click-Only Companies **Click-only companies** come in many shapes and sizes. They include *e-tailers*, dot-coms that sell products and services directly to final buyers via the Internet. Familiar e-tailers include Amazon.com, CDNow, and eVineyards. The click-only group also includes s*earch engines* and *portals* such as Yahoo!, Excite, and Go, which began as search engines and later added services such as news, weather, stock reports, entertainment, and storefronts, hoping to become the first port of entry to the Internet. *Internet service providers (ISPs)* such as AOL, CompuServe, and Earthlink are click-only companies that provide Internet and e-mail connections for a fee. *Transaction sites,* such as auction site eBay, take commissions for transactions conducted on their sites. Various *content sites*, such as *New York Times* on the Web (www.nytimes.com), ESPN.com, and Encyclopedia Britannica Online, provide financial, research, and other information. Finally, *enabler sites* provide the hardware and software that enable Internet communication and commerce.

> **Click-only companies**
> The so-called dot-coms, which operate only online without any brick-and-mortar market presence.

The hype surrounding such click-only Web businesses reached astronomical levels during the "dot-com gold rush" of the late 1990s, when avid investors drove dot-com stock prices to dizzying heights. However, the investing frenzy collapsed in the year 2000 and many high-flying, overvalued dot-coms came crashing back to earth. Even some of the strongest and most attractive e-tailers—eToys.com, Pets.com, Furniture.com, Motherna-ture.com, Garden.com, Eve.com, Living.com, ValueAmerica.com—filed for bankruptcy. Survivors such as Amazon.com and Priceline.com saw their stock values plunge. Notes one analyst, "Once teeming with thousands of vibrant new ideas, the consumer Net is beginning to look like the mall at midnight."[19]

Dot-coms failed for a variety of reasons. Many rushed into the market without proper research or planning, often with the primary goal of simply launching an initial public offering (IPO) while the market was hot. Many relied too heavily on spin and hype instead of developing sound marketing strategies. Flush with investors' cash, the dot-coms spent lavishly offline on mass marketing in an effort to establish brand identities and attract customers to their sites. For example, during the fourth quarter of 1999, the average e-tailer spent an astounding 109 percent of sales on marketing and advertising.[20] As one industry watcher concludes, many dot-coms failed because they "had dumb-as-dirt business models, not because the Internet lacks the power to enchant and delight customers in ways hitherto unimaginable."[21]

The dot-coms tended to devote too much effort to acquiring new customers instead of building loyalty and purchase frequency among current customers. In their rush to cash in, many dot-coms went to market with poorly designed Web sites that were complex, hard to navigate, and unreliable. When orders did arrive, some dot-coms found that they lacked the well-designed distribution systems needed to ship products on time and handle customer inquiries and problems. Finally, the ease with which competitors could enter the Web, and the ease with which customers could switch to Web sites offering better prices, forced many dot-coms to sell at margin-killing low prices.

Pets.com, the now defunct online pet store, provides a good example of how many dot-coms failed to understand their marketplaces.

From the start, Pets.com tried to force its way to online success with unbeatable low prices and heavy marketing hype. In the end, however, neither worked. During its first year of operation, Pets.com lost $61.8 million on a meager $5.8 million

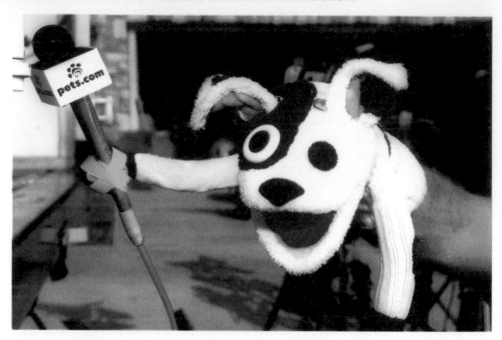

Like many other dot-coms, Pets.com never did figure out how to make money on the Web. Following the "dot-com meltdown," the once-bold e-tailer retired its popular Sock Puppet spokesdog and quietly closed its cyberdoors.

in sales. During that time, it paid $13.4 million for the goods it sold for just $5.8 million. Thus, for every dollar that Pets.com paid suppliers such as Ralston Purina for dog food and United Parcel Service for shipping, it collected only 43 cents from its customers. Moreover, by early spring of 1999, Pets.com had burned through more than $21 million on marketing and advertising to create an identity and entice pet owners to its site. Its branding campaign centered on the wildly popular Sock Puppet character, a white dog with black patches. Sock Puppet even made an appearance in Macy's Thanksgiving Day Parade in New York as a 36-foot-high balloon. The singing mascot was also featured in Super Bowl ads that cost Pets.com more than $2 million. At first, investors bought into Pets.com's "landgrab" strategy—investing heavily to stake out an early share, then finding ways later to make a profit. However, even though it attracted 570,000 customers, Pets.com never did figure out how to make money in a low-margin business with high shipping costs. Its stock price slid from a February 1999 high of $14 to a dismal 22 cents by the end of 2000. In early 2001, the once-bold e-tailer retired Sock Puppet and quietly closed its cyberdoors.[22]

At the same time, many click-only dot-coms are surviving and even prospering in today's marketspace. Others are showing losses today but promising profits tomorrow. Consider Earthlink.com:

Earthlink.com is an Internet service provider (ISP) that sells Internet and email connection time for a $20 monthly fee. Customer maintenance expenses amount to only $9 a month, leaving an $11 contribution margin. On average, it costs Earthlink $100 to acquire a new customer. Therefore, it takes 11 months before the company breaks even on a new customer. Fortunately, Earthlink keeps its customers for an average of 31 months. This leaves Earthlink with 20 months of net income from the average customer. At a $9 monthly contribution margin, Earthlink makes $180 (20 months × $9) on the average customer. When Sky Dayton, Earthlink's founder, was asked why Earthlink is still losing money, he answered that Earthlink is acquiring so many new customers that it will take a while for the inflow of contribution margin to cover the $100 customer acquisition.

Thus, for many dot-coms, including Internet giants such as Amazon.com, the Web is still not a moneymaking proposition. Companies engaging in e-commerce need to describe to their investors how they will eventually make profits. They need to define a *revenue and profit model*. Table 3-1 shows that a dot-com's revenues may come from any of several sources.

Click-and-Mortar Companies Many established companies moved quickly to open Web sites providing information about their companies and products. However, most resisted adding e-commerce to their sites. They felt that this would produce *channel conflict*, in that selling their products or services online would be competing with their offline retailers and agents. For example, Compaq Computer feared that its retailers would drop Compaq's computers if the company sold the same computers directly online. Merrill-Lynch hesitated to introduce online stock trading to compete with E*Trade, Charles Schwab, and other online brokerages, fearing that its own brokers would rebel. Even store-based bookseller Barnes & Noble delayed opening its online site to challenge Amazon.com.

These companies struggled with the question of how to conduct online sales without cannibalizing the sales of their own stores, resellers, or agents. However, they soon came to realize that the risks of losing business to online competitors were even greater than the

Table 3-1	Sources of E-Commerce Revenue
Product and service sales income	Many e-commerce companies draw a good portion of their revenues from markups on goods and services they sell online.
Advertising income	Sales of online ad space can provide a major source of revenue. At one point, Buy.com received so much advertising revenue that it was able to sell products at cost.
Sponsorship income	A dot-com can solicit sponsors for some of its content and collect sponsorship fees to help cover its costs.
Alliance income	Online companies can invite business partners to share costs in setting up a Web site and offer them free advertising on the site.
Membership and subscription income	Web marketers can charge subscription fees for use of their site. Many online newspapers (*Wall Street Journal* and *Financial Times*) require subscription fees for their online services. Auto-By-Tel receives income from selling subscriptions to auto dealers who want to receive hot car buyer leads.
Profile income	Web sites that have built databases containing the profiles of particular target groups may be able to sell these profiles if they get permission first. However, ethical and legal codes govern the use and sale of such customer information.
Transaction commissions and fees	Some dot-coms charge commission fees on transactions between other parties who exchanges goods on their Web sites. For example, eBay puts buyers in touch with sellers and takes from a 1.25 percent to a 5 percent commission on each transaction.
Market research and information fees	Companies can charge for special market information or intelligence. For example, NewsLibrary charges a dollar or two to download copies of archived news stories. LifeQuote provides insurance buyers with price comparisons from approximately 50 different life insurance companies, then collects a commission of 50 percent of the first year's premium from the company chosen by the consumer.
Referral income	Companies can collect revenue by referring customers to others. Edmunds receives a "finder's fee" every time a customer fills out an Auto-By-Tel form at its Edmunds.com Web site, regardless of whether a deal is completed.

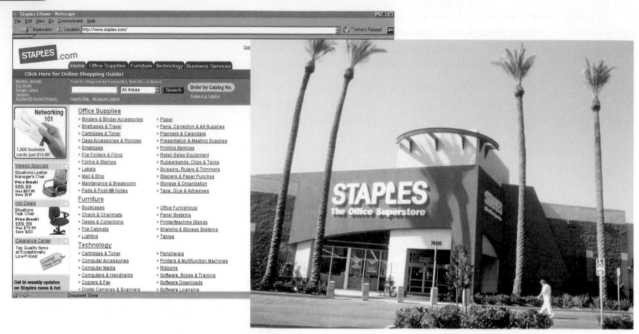

Click-and-mortar: Staples' Web site now supplements its brick-and-mortar operations. After two years on the Net, Staples captured online sales of more than $500 million.

Click-and-mortar companies
Traditional brick-and-mortar companies that have added e-marketing to their operations.

risks of angering channel partners. If they didn't cannibalize these sales, online competitors soon would. Thus, many established brick-and-mortar companies are now prospering as **click-and-mortar companies**. Consider Staples, the $10.7 billion office-supply retailer. After just two years on the Net, Staples captured annual online sales of $512 million last year. However, it's not robbing from store sales in the process. The average yearly spending of small business customers jumps from $600 when they shop in stores to $2,800 when they shop online. As a result, Staples is slowing new store openings to a trickle this year; it plans to spend $50 million on expanding its Net presence. "We're still going whole hog," says CEO Thomas Stemberg. "The payoffs are just very high."[23]

Most click-and-mortar marketers have found ways to resolve the resulting channel conflicts.[24] For example, Gibson Guitars found that although its dealers were outraged when it tried to sell guitars directly to consumers, the dealers didn't object to direct sales of accessories such as guitar strings and parts. Liberty Mutual asks its online customers whether they prefer to buy directly or through a financial adviser. It then refers interested customers and information about their needs to advisers, providing them with a good source of new business. Avon worried that direct online sales might cannibalize the business of its Avon ladies, who had developed close relationships with their customers. Fortunately, Avon's research showed little overlap between existing customers and potential Web customers. Avon shared this finding with the reps and then moved into e-marketing. As an added bonus for the reps, Avon also offered to help them set up their own Web sites. Finally, rather than only competing with its own stores, JCPenney uses its Web site to boost store sales by offering online coupons that can be printed and redeemed at stores. Moreover, it sells some offerings online that would not be profitable to sell through its stores.

Despite potential channel conflict issues, many click-and-mortar companies are now having more online success than their click-only competitors. In fact, in a recent study of the top 50 retail sites, ranked by the number of unique visitors, 56 percent were click-and-mortar retailers, whereas 44 percent were Internet-only retailers.[25]

What gives the click-and-mortar companies an advantage? Established companies such as Charles Schwab, Wal-Mart, Staples, or Gap have known and trusted brand names and greater financial resources. They have large customer bases, deeper industry knowledge and experience, and good relationships with key suppliers. By combining e-marketing and established brick-and-mortar operations, they can offer customers more options. For example, consumers can choose the convenience and assortment of 24-hour-a-day online shopping, the more personal and hands-on experience of in-store shopping, or both. Customers can buy merchandise online then easily return unwanted goods to a nearby store. For example, those wanting to do business with Fidelity Investments can call a Fidelity agent on the phone, go online to the company's Web site, or visit the local Fidelity branch office. Thus, in its advertising, Fidelity can issue a powerful invitation to "call, click, or visit Fidelity Investments."

Linking the Concepts

Pause here and cool your engine for a bit. Think about the relative advantages and disadvantages of *click-only*, *brick-and-mortar only*, and *click-and-mortar* retailers.

◆ Visit the Amazon.com Web site. Search for a specific book or DVD—perhaps one that's not too well known—and go through the buying process.
◆ Now visit www.bn.com and shop for the same book or video. Then visit a Barnes & Noble store and shop for the item there.
◆ What advantages does Amazon.com have over Barnes & Noble? What disadvantages? How does your local independent bookstore, with its store-only operations, fare against these two competitors?

Setting Up an E-Marketing Presence

Clearly all companies need to consider moving into e-marketing. Companies can conduct e-marketing in any of the four ways shown in Figure 3-4: creating a Web site, placing ads online, setting up or participating in Web communities, or using online e-mail or Webcasting.

Creating a Web Site For most companies, the first step in conducting e-marketing is to create a Web site. However, beyond simply creating a Web site, marketers must design attractive sites and find ways to get consumers to visit the site, stay around, and come back often.

TYPES OF WEB SITES. Web sites vary greatly in purpose and content. The most basic type is a **corporate Web site.** These sites are designed to build customer goodwill and to supplement other sales channels, rather than to sell the company's products directly. For example, you can't buy ice cream at benjerrys.com, but you can learn all about Ben & Jerry's

Corporate Web site
A Web site designed to build customer goodwill and to supplement other sales channels, rather than to sell the company's products directly.

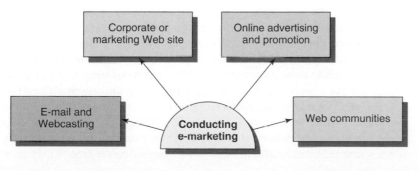

Figure 3-4
Setting up for e-marketing

Marketing Web site:
Visitors to
SonyStyle.com can
search for products,
check out the latest hot
deals, and place orders
online, all with a few
clicks of the mouse
button.

company philosophy, products, and locations; send a free e-card to a friend or subscribe to the Chunk Mail newsletter; and while away time in the Fun Stuff area, playing Scooper Challenge or Virtual Checkers.

Corporate Web sites typically offer a rich variety of information and other features in an effort to answer customer questions, build closer customer relationships, and generate excitement about the company. They generally provide information about the company's history, its mission and philosophy, and the products and services that it offers. They might also tell about current events, company personnel, financial performance, and employment opportunities. Most corporate Web sites also provide entertainment features to attract and hold visitors. Finally, the site might also provide opportunities for customers to ask questions or make comments through e-mail before leaving the site.

Marketing Web site
A Web site that engages consumers in interactions that will move them closer to a direct purchase or other marketing outcome.

Other companies create a **marketing Web site**. These sites engage consumers in an interaction that will move them closer to a direct purchase or other marketing outcome. Such sites might include a catalog, shopping tips, and promotional features such as coupons, sales events, or contests. For example, visitors to SonyStyle.com can search through dozens of categories of Sony products, review detailed features and specifications lists for specific items, read expert product reviews, and check out the latest hot deals. They can place an order for the desired Sony products online and pay by credit card, all with a few clicks of the mouse button. Companies aggressively promote their marketing Web sites in offline print and broadcast advertising and through "banner-to-site" ads that pop up on other Web sites.

Toyota operates a marketing Web site at www.toyota.com. Once a potential customer clicks in, the car maker wastes no time trying to turn the inquiry into a sale. The site offers plenty of useful information and a garage full of interactive selling features, such as detailed descriptions of current Toyota models and information on dealer locations and services, complete with maps and dealer Web links. Visitors who want to go further can use the Shop@Toyota feature to choose a Toyota, select equipment, and price it, then contact a dealer and even apply for credit. Or they fill out an online order form (supplying name, address, phone number, and e-mail address) for brochures and a free, interactive CD-ROM that shows off the features of Toyota models. The chances are good that before the CD-ROM arrives, a local dealer will call to invite the prospect in for a test drive. Toyota's Web site has now replaced its 800 number as the number-one source of customer leads.

B2B marketers also make good use of marketing Web sites. For example, customers visiting GE Plastics' Web site can draw on more than 1,500 pages of information to get answers about the company's products anytime and from anywhere in the world. FedEx's Web site (www.fedex.com) allows customers to schedule their own shipments, request package pickup, and track their packages in transit.

DESIGNING ATTRACTIVE WEB SITES. Creating a Web site is one thing; getting people to *visit* the site is another. The key is to create enough value and excitement to get consumers to come to the site, stick around, and come back again. This means that companies must constantly update their sites to keep them current, fresh, and exciting. Doing so involves time and expense, but the expense is necessary if the e-marketer wishes to cut through the increasing online clutter. In addition, many online marketers spend heavily on good old-fashioned advertising and other offline marketing avenues to attract visitors to their sites. Says one analyst, "The reality today is you can't build a brand simply on the Internet. You have to go offline."[26]

For some types of products, attracting visitors is easy. Consumers buying new cars, computers, or financial services will be open to information and marketing initiatives from sellers. Marketers of lower-involvement products, however, may face a difficult challenge in attracting Web site visitors. As one veteran notes, "If you're shopping for a computer and you see a banner that says, 'We've ranked the top 12 computers to purchase,' you're going to click on the banner. [But] what kind of banner could encourage any consumer to visit dentalfloss.com?"[27]

For such low-interest products, the company can create a corporate Web site to answer customer questions, build goodwill and excitement, supplement selling efforts through other channels, and collect customer feedback. For example, although Nabisco's LifeSavers Candystand Web site doesn't sell candy, it does generate a great deal of consumer excitement and sales support:

Nabisco's highly entertaining LifeSavers Candystand.com Web site, teeming with free videogames, endless sweepstakes, and sampling offers, has cast a fresh face on a brand that kid consumers once perceived as a stodgy adult confection. The Web site grabs 2.5 million visitors per month, mostly children and teenagers, and these surfers are not just passing through. They're clicking the mouse for an average 27-minute stay playing Foul Shot Shootout, Waterpark Pinball, and dozens of other arcade-style games, all while soaking in a LifeSavers aura swirling with information about products. "Our philosophy is to create an exciting online experience that reflects the fun and quality associated with the LifeSavers brands," says Silvio Bonvini, senior manager of new media at LifeSavers Company. "For the production cost of about two television spots we have a marketing vehicle that lives 24 hours a day, seven days a week, 365 days a year." While Candystand.com has not directly sold a single roll of candy, the buzz generated by the site makes it an ideal vehicle for offering consumers their first glimpse of a new product, usually with an offer to get free samples by mail. In addition, LifeSavers reps use the site as sales leverage to help seal distribution deals when they talk with retailers. And the site offers LifeSavers an efficient channel for gathering customer feedback. Its "What Do You Think?" feature has generated 180,000 responses since the site launched in March 1997. "It's instant communication that we pass along directly to our brand people," Bonvini says. "It's not filtered by an agency or edited in any way." Comments collected from the Web site have resulted in improved packaging of one LifeSavers product and the resurrection of the abandoned flavor of another.[28]

A key challenge is designing a Web site that is attractive on first view and interesting enough to encourage repeat visits. The early text-based Web sites have largely been replaced in recent years by graphically sophisticated Web sites that provide text, sound, and animation (for examples, see www.sonystyle.com or www.nike.com). To attract new visitors and to encourage revisits, suggests one expert, e-marketers should pay close attention to the 7Cs of effective Web site design:[29]

◆ *Context:* site's layout and design
◆ *Content:* text, pictures, sound, and video that the Web site contains
◆ *Community:* the ways that the site enables user-to-user communication
◆ *Customization:* site's ability to tailor itself to different users or to allow users to personalize the site
◆ *Communication:* the ways the site enables site-to-user, user-to-site, or two-way communication
◆ *Connection:* degree that the site is linked to other sites
◆ *Commerce:* site's capabilities to enable commercial transactions

In all, a Web site should be easy to use and physically attractive. Beyond this, however, Web sites must also be interesting, useful, and challenging. Ultimately, it's the value of the site's *content* that will attract visitors, get them to stay longer, and bring them back for more.

Effective Web sites contain deep and useful information, interactive tools that help buyers find and evaluate products of interest, links to other related sites, changing promotional offers, and entertaining features that lend relevant excitement. For example, in addition to convenient online purchasing, Clinique.com offers in-depth information about cosmetics, a library of beauty tips, a computer for determining the buyer's skin type, advice from visiting experts, a bulletin board, a bridal guide, a directory of new products, and pricing information. Burpee.com provides aspiring gardeners with everything they need to make this year's garden the best ever. Besides selling seeds and plants by the thousands, the site offers an incredible wealth of information resources, including a Garden Wizard (to help new gardeners pick the best plants for specific sun and soil conditions), the Burpee Garden School (online classes about plants and plant care), an archive of relevant service articles, and a chance to subscribe to an e-mail newsletter containing timely tips and gardening secrets.

Effective Web sites contain useful information, helpful tools, and entertaining features that lend excitement. Burpee.com provides aspiring gardeners with a wealth of resources, including the Burpee Garden School and a Garden Wizard to help them pick the best plants for specific conditions.

From time to time, a company needs to reassess its Web site's attractiveness and usefulness. One way is to invite the opinion of site design experts. But a better way is to have users themselves evaluate what they like and dislike about the site and offer suggestions for improving it. For example, Otis Elevator Company's Web site serves 20,000 registered customers, among them architects, general contractors, building managers, and others interested in elevators. The site, offered in 52 countries and 26 languages, provides a wealth of helpful information, from modernization, maintenance, and safety information to drawings of various Otis models. Otis uses two sources of information to gauge satisfaction with its complex site. First, in an effort to detect potential problems, it tracks hits, time spent on the site, frequently visited pages, and the sequence of pages the customer visits. Second, it conducts quarterly phone surveys with 200 customers each in half the countries in which Otis does business. Such customer satisfaction tracking has resulted in numerous site improvements. For example, Otis found that customers in other countries were having trouble linking to the page that would let them buy an elevator online; now, the link is easier to find. Some customers were finding it hard to locate a local Otis office, so the company added an Office Locator feature.[30]

Placing Ads and Promotions Online E-marketers can use **online advertising** to build their Internet brands or to attract visitors to their Web sites. Here, we discuss forms of online advertising promotion and their future.

Online advertising
Advertising that appears while consumers are surfing the Web, including banner and ticker ads, interstitials, skyscrapers, and other forms.

FORMS OF ONLINE ADVERTISING AND PROMOTION. Online ads pop up while Internet users are surfing online. Such ads include *banner ads* and *tickers* (banners that move across the screen). For example, a Web user or America Online subscriber who is looking up airline schedules or fares might find a flashing banner on the screen exclaiming, "Rent a car from Alamo and get up to 2 days free!" To attract visitors to its own Web site, Toyota sponsors Web banner ads on other sites, ranging from ESPN SportsZone (www.espn.com) to Parent Soup (www.parentsoup.com). New online ad formats include *skyscrapers* (tall, skinny ads at the side of a Web page and *rectangles* (boxes that are much larger than a banner).

Interstitials are online ads that pop up between changes on a Web site. Visitors to www.msnbc.com who visit the site's sports area might suddenly be viewing a separate window hawking wireless video cameras. Ads for Johnson & Johnson's Tylenol headache reliever pop up on brokers' Web sites whenever the stock market falls by 100 points or more. Sponsors of *browser ads* pay viewers to watch them. For example, Alladvantage.com downloads a view bar to users where ads are displayed to targeted users. Viewers earn 20 cents to $1 per hour in return.

Content sponsorships are another form of Internet promotion. Many companies gain name exposure on the Internet by sponsoring special content on various Web sites, such as news or financial information. For example, Advil sponsors ESPN SportsZone's Injury Report and Oldsmobile sponsors AOL's Celebrity Circle. The sponsor pays for showing the content and, in turn, receives recognition as the provider of the particular service on the Web site. Sponsorships are best placed in carefully targeted sites where they can offer relevant information or service to the audience.

E-marketers can also go online with *microsites,* limited areas on the Web managed and paid for by an external company. For example, an insurance company might create a microsite on a car-buying site, offering insurance advice for car buyers and at the same time offering good insurance deals. Internet companies can also develop alliances and affiliate programs in which they work with other online companies to "advertise" each other. For example, AOL has created many successful alliances with other companies and mentions their names on its site. Amazon.com has more than 350,000 affiliates who post Amazon.com banners on their Web sites.

Viral marketing
The Internet version of word-of-mouth marketing—e-mail messages or other marketing events that are so infectious that customers will want to pass them along to friends.

Finally, e-marketers can use **viral marketing**, the Internet version of word-of-mouth marketing. Viral marketing involves creating an e-mail message or other marketing event that is so infectious that customers will want to pass it along to their friends. Because customers pass the message or promotion along to others, viral marketing can be very inexpensive. And when the information comes from a friend, the recipient is much more likely to open and read it.

Viral marketing can be very effective. For example, e-mail provider Hotmail grew to 12 million users in 18 months by offering free e-mail—every e-mail message sent contained a Hotmail ad and tag line at the bottom. Viral marketing can also work well for B2B marketers. For example, to improve customer relationships, Hewlett-Packard recently sent tailored e-mail newsletters to customers who registered online. The newsletters contained information about optimizing the performance of H-P products and services. Now that was good, but here's the best part: The newsletters also featured a button that let customers forward the newsletters to friends or colleagues. By clicking the button, customers entered a Web site where they could type in the friend's e-mail address and a comment, then hit send. The system inserted the message above the newsletter and e-mailed the whole thing to the friend. New recipients were then asked if they'd like to receive future H-P newsletters themselves. In this textbook case of viral marketing, Hewlett-Packard inexpensively met its goal of driving consumers to its Web site and ultimately increasing sales. "For those on our original e-mail list, the click-through rate was ten to fifteen percent," says an H-P executive. "For those who received it from a friend or colleague, it was between twenty-five and forty percent."[31]

THE FUTURE OF ONLINE ADVERTISING.   Although online advertising serves a useful purpose, the Internet will not soon rival the major television and print media. Many marketers still question the value of Internet advertising as an effective tool. Costs are reasonable compared with those of other advertising media but Web surfers can easily ignore such advertising and often do. Although many firms are experimenting with Web advertising, it plays only a minor role in most promotion mixes.

As a result, online advertising expenditures still represent only a small fraction of overall advertising media expenditures. Moreover, in spite of its early promise, the growth of online advertising spending has slowed recently. According to one account:

> The Internet was supposed to be the ultimate ad medium, the killer app that would eclipse newspapers, magazines, even television. But it's become increasingly clear that the online ad boom was largely a mirage, one created by the unfettered spending of the dot-coms themselves. Flush with venture funding . . . , Internet companies had been only too happy to ring one another's Web sites with flashing banners. Those days are over: After growing at a compound annual rate of 103 percent to an estimated $8 billion last year, online ad spending [this year] is expected to be completely flat.[32]

The drop-off in Web advertising has caused hard times for companies that rely on it for profits. Companies such as DoubleClick and 24/7 Media that sell ads for large groups of Web sites are struggling. Many ad-dependent sites, such as AngryMan.com and Pseudo.com, have gone out of business entirely. The nation's most heavily trafficked Web site, Yahoo!, which relies on Web advertising for 90 percent of its revenue, has seen its stock price plunge from more than $250 at its peak to little more than $30 today. Facing these new realities, companies are now seeking more effective forms and uses of Web advertising and marketing (see Marketing at Work 3-2).

Online Advertising: For the Survivors, There Still Will Be Gold in Webland

Advertising was supposed to be the gold paving the Internet's busy streets. Consumers would eagerly surf, chat, and shop, and ads would pay Web companies for providing all those cool sites. In return, marketers would flash brightly colored banners at viewers, entice them to click through to their own sites, and get lots of business. But it didn't happen that way. Today, banner ad click-through rates have plummeted to a tiny 0.1 percent, ad rates may be heading from $33 per thousand-page-requests a year ago into the single digits, and ad volumes are falling. The blowout is pushing even the best-known sites down financial black holes.

What went wrong? It turns out that the Internet opened up brand-new worlds for advertisers, only they didn't see it. They tried to do what they always did—post their names in big letters, build their brands in two dimensions. But they didn't seize on the Net's potential or exploit its unique characteristics, such as the ability to target individual preferences and engage customers in interactivity. "This is the true value of what the Internet provides marketers," says Christopher Todd, analyst at Jupiter Media Metrix.

Web operators that based their businesses entirely on the expected free flow of ad dollars are learning that the hard way. "No longer can anyone in this space rely on only one revenue stream," warns John Fullmer, CEO of Internet direct marketer MyPoints.com. But those whose broader approach has kept them alive may yet reap benefits as marketers get smarter about the Net. For starters, advertising hasn't all dried up. Much of the current ad decline is due to the flameout of

dot-coms that spent wildly online to build their new brands. "The kindling has been burned through," says Tim McHale, chief media officer of Tribal DDB Worldwide, whose clients include Anheuser-Busch, McDonald's, and Volkswagen. Traditional marketers may be cutting back, but they're not bailing out. A few, like IBM, are even ratcheting up their Internet ad budgets.

But this time, it will be different. It's now clear that folks are getting as good at screening out online banner ads as they are at tuning out TV commercials or flipping past glossies in a magazine. So companies are finding ways to reach eyeballs without glazing them over.

Some advertisers are ditching banner ads totally, instead using old-fashioned TV spots to drive traffic directly to their Web sites, rather than through intermediaries like

portals. Other companies are signing up with sites that essentially pay consumers to engage with a mall full of marketers. At MyPoints.com, for example, surfers collect points and prizes for agreeing to visit companies' sites, read their e-mail, or buy their products online. Another tack: bidding for prime spots on search engines. By paying to top the list of results for users who search for, say, "banking" on GoTo.com, a marketer such as Citicorp ensures it is reaching live prospects. A study by researcher NPD Group Inc. shows that a top position is three times more effective than a banner ad in building brand awareness on a search-engine site.

And even though they're taking the biggest hit right now, banner ads aren't going away—just as roadside billboards didn't disappear

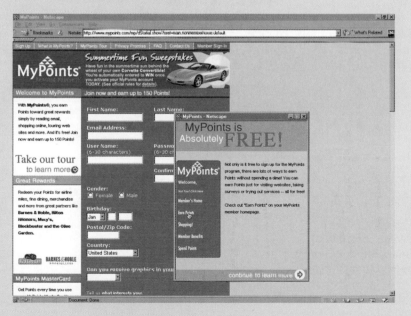

To reach eyeballs without glazing them over, MyPoints.com offers surfers points and prizes for agreeing to visit companies' sites, read their ads and e-mail, or buy their products online.

once such alternatives as TV arrived. Web sites are now willing to offer advertisers more shapes and sizes to play with, pop-up ads are developing a following, and the rollout of broadband will bring streaming videos with grabbier messages. And while banner ads could capture some data about clickers before, agencies are helping marketers track customer profiles more minutely. Avenue A Inc., for example, is working with client BestBuy.com Inc. to identify whether a visitor directed to its site by a banner ad has ever visited the site before, has visited but not purchased anything, or has purchased goods there many times.

Still, plenty of pain is in store for ad buyers and sellers groping their way around this new medium. "We keep turning up evidence that this works, but we need to get through the slowdown," says Avenue A CEO Brian P. McAndrews. For the survivors, there still will be gold in Webland.

Source: Reprinted with permission from Gerry Khermouch and Tom Lowry, "The Future of Advertising," *Business Week*, March 26, 2001, p. 138.

Despite the recent setbacks, some industry insiders remain optimistic about the future of online advertising. "The reports of online advertising's death are not just exaggerated," says one such optimist, "they are stupendously wrong. The online advertising business has grown from next to nothing in 1994 to $8.2 billion in 2000—a new-media trajectory unmatched in the annals of advertising. Web advertising has already blown past the venerable outdoor category, which had revenues of $5 billion last year. It is breathing down the tailpipes of the cable-TV ad business."[33]

Creating or Participating in Web Communities The popularity of forums and newsgroups has resulted in a rash of commercially sponsored Web sites called **Web communities**, which take advantage of the C2C properties of the Internet. Such sites allow members to congregate online and exchange views on issues of common interest. They are the cyberspace equivalent to a Starbucks coffeehouse, a place where everybody knows your e-mail address.

For example, iVillage.com is a Web community in which women can exchange views and obtain information, support, and solutions on families, food, fitness, relationships, relaxation, home and garden, news and issues, or just about any other topic. The site

Web communities
Web sites upon which members can congregate online and exchange views on issues of common interest.

Web communities: iVillage.com, a Web community for women, draws 214 million page views per month. The site provides an ideal environment for Web ads of companies such as Procter & Gamble, Kimberly Clark, Avon, Hallmark, and others.

draws 214 million page views per month, putting it in a league with magazines such as *Cosmopolitan*, *Glamour*, and *Vogue*. Another example is MyFamily.com, which aspires to be the largest and most active online community in the world for families. It provides free, private family Web sites upon which family members can connect online to hold family discussions, share family news, create online family photo albums, maintain a calendar of family events, share family history information, jointly build family trees, and buy gifts for family members quickly and easily. "People talk about forming communities on the Internet," says cofounder Paul Allen. "Well, the oldest community is the family."[34]

Visitors to these Internet neighborhoods develop a strong sense of community. Such communities are attractive to advertisers because they draw consumers with common interests and well-defined demographics. Moreover, cyberhood consumers visit frequently and stay online longer, increasing the chance of meaningful exposure to the advertiser's message. For example, iVillage provides an ideal environment for the Web ads of companies such as Procter & Gamble, Kimberly Clark, Avon, Hallmark, and others who target women consumers. And MyFamily.com hosts The Shops@MyFamily, in which such companies as Disney, Kodak, Hallmark, Compaq, Hewlett-Packard, and Microsoft advertise and sell their family-oriented products.

Web communities can be either social or work related. One successful work-related community is @griculture Online. This site offers commodity prices, recent farm news, and chat rooms of all types. Rural surfers can visit the Electronic Coffee Shop and pick up the latest down-on-the-farm joke or join a hot discussion on controlling soybean cyst nematodes. @griculture Online has been highly successful, attracting as many as 5 million hits per month.[35]

Using E-Mail and Webcasting   E-mail has exploded onto the scene as an important e-marketing tool. Jupiter Media Metrix estimates that companies will be spending $7.3 billion annually on e-mail marketing by 2005, up from just $164 million in 1999.[36] To compete effectively in this ever more cluttered e-mail environment, marketers are designing "enriched" e-mail messages—animated, interactive, and personalized messages full of streaming audio and video. Then they are targeting these attention-grabbers more carefully to those who want them and will act upon them. (See Marketing at Work 3-3.)

E-mail is becoming a mainstay for both B2C and B2B marketers. 3Com Corporation, a B2B marketer of high-tech computer hardware, made good use of e-mail to generate and qualify customer leads for its network interface cards. The company used targeted e-mail and banner ads on 18 different computer-related Web sites to attract potential buyers to its own Web site featuring a "3Com Classic" sweepstakes, where by filling out the entry form, visitors could register to win a 1959 Corvette. The campaign generated 22,000 leads, which were further qualified using e-mail and telemarketing. "Hot" leads were passed along to 3Com's inside sales force. "[Sales reps] were very skeptical," says a 3Com marketing manager, "but they were blown away by how well the contest did." Of the 482 leads given to reps, 71 turned into actual sales that totaled $2.5 million. What's more, states the manager, "Now I've got 22,000 names in my e-mail database that I can go back and market to."[37]

Companies can also sign on with any of a number of "**Webcasting**" services, which automatically download customized information to recipients' PCs. An example is Internet Financial Network's Infogate, which sends up-to-date financial news, market data, and real-time stock quotes to subscribers in the financial services industry for a fee. Infogate frames the top and bottom inch of subscribers' computer screens with personalized news and other information tailored to their specific interests. Rather than spending hours scouring the Internet, subscribers can sit back while Infogate automatically delivers information of interest to their desktops.[38] The major commercial online services also offer Webcasting to their members. For example, America Online offers a feature called Driveway that will

Webcasting
The automatic downloading of customized information of interest to recipients' PCs, affording an attractive channel for delivering Internet advertising or other information content.

Marketing at Work 3.3

The New World of E-Mail Marketing

E-mail is *the* hot new marketing medium. In ever-larger numbers, e-mail ads are popping onto our computer screens and filling up our e-mailboxes. What's more, they're no longer just the quiet, plain-text messages of old. The new breed of e-mail ad is designed to command your attention—loaded with glitzy features such as animation, interactive links, color photos, streaming video, and personalized audio messages.

But if you think that you're already getting too much e-mail, hang onto your mouse. Jupiter Media Metrix predicts that the number of commercial e-mail messages sent per year will increase from an already daunting 43 billion in 2000 to an inbox-busting 375 billion by 2005. And no wonder. E-mail allows marketers to send tailored messages to targeted consumers who actually want to receive them, at a cost of only a few cents per contact. Even better, they can target audiences in any country and get responses within 24 hours.

As in any other direct-marketing effort, e-mail success depends on a good customer database. Companies can obtain e-mail addresses from outside list brokers. However, the best way to build an e-mail database easily is simply to ask customers for their e-mail addresses at every point of contact. Marketers can ask for e-mail addresses on their Web sites, in their brick-and-mortar stores, via response cards sent with catalogs, during customer service calls, or even in print ads. Some marketers sponsor sign-up promotions, offering sweepstakes or prizes as incentives for customers who fork over their e-mail addresses. All of these are permission-based methods that allow cus-

tomers to "opt in" or "opt out," ensuring that e-mails are sent only to customers who ask for them. "That leaves marketers largely immune from the wrath of privacy advocates and spam fighters," states *Business Week* writer Arlene Weintraub.

Another advantage of e-mail ads is that companies can track customer responses—how many people open the message, who clicks through to the Web site, and what they do when they get there. And well-designed e-mail ads really do command attention and get customers to act. ITM Strategies, a sales and marketing research firm, estimates that permission e-mail campaigns typically achieve 10 percent to 15 percent click-through rates. That's pretty good when compared with the .5 percent to 2 percent average response rates for traditional direct mail.

E-mail success stories abound. *Business Week* offers these:

• •
Zomba Recording, corporate parent of teen band 'N Sync's label Jive Records, cooked up an e-campaign that made other marketers drool. In March, 200,000 fans received a video message about the album *No Strings Attached* that allowed them to hear band members speak and to listen to a snippet of the song "Bye Bye Bye." Fans went wild: 34 percent of the e-mail recipients, whose names had been collected from the 'N Sync Web site, downloaded the video. Of those, 88 percent clicked on one of the links. Thousands forwarded the e-mail to friends. In the world of direct marketing, where a 1 percent response rate is considered acceptable, the numbers were extraordinary. *No Strings Attached* had its debut in

April and sold 2.4 million copies in its first week—the biggest opening since SoundScan started tracking sales in 1991. "E-mail is a technology that kids are really into, so it was a great direct-hit way to get to them," says Jeff Dodes, vice-president for new media and Internet operations at Zomba.

Kids aren't the only target for e-mail ads. Customers of golf-supply retailer Chipshot.com—average age 41—received e-ads for a new line of clubs. The mail included streaming video and an audio message that greeted recipients by their first names. Of those who received it, 14.7 percent clicked through to the site, and 11.6 percent of them bought the clubs. "The multimedia message with animated graphics looked very attractive," says Nick Mehta, Chipshot's vice-president for interactive marketing. "We saw 98 percent more revenue per customer among people who received that message vs. those who got just a standard e-mail."

• •
Still, even permission-based e-mail can be very annoying. "Even among consumers who opt in to the e-mail barrage, there's a fine line between legitimate marketing and spam," says Weintraub. "As more companies glom onto the trend, there is strong potential for a backlash." Companies crossing that fine line will quickly learn that "opting out" is only a click away for disgruntled customers. According to Weintraub, marketers are aware of the potential for irritation and are taking steps to head it off:

• •
Petopia.com, which mails monthly e-newsletters and personalized pet birthday messages, has set its computer system to automatically limit

the number of e-mails any one customer receives in a month. Handheld-computer maker Palm Inc. has been experimenting with the length of its e-ads, and recently found that a 150-word message produced a better click-through rate than 300 words did. IKEA took an even more drastic step. In April, the furniture retailer promoted its new San Francisco store by e-mailing customers and inviting them to send virtual postcards to friends through its site. A mind-boggling 70,000 postcards were sent in 10 days. But when a handful of recipients cried "spam!," IKEA pulled the campaign. "We only want to communicate with customers in ways that they think are appropriate," says Rich D'Amico, IKEA's manager of new business development.

• •

Still, marketing history is full of examples of effective tactics that were taken too far, and some experts see little reason to expect that e-mail advertising will be any different. "It will be overdone," predicts the president of a firm which creates e-mail campaigns. "Brace your e-mail box for the results," adds Weintraub.

Sources: Quotes and extracts from Arlene Weintraub, "When e-Mail Ads Aren't Spam," *Business Week*, October 16, 2000, pp. 112–114. Also see Chad Kaydo, "As Good As It Gets," *Sales and Marketing Management*, March 2000, pp. 55–60; Eileen P. Gunn, Marketers Are Keen on Enriched E-Mail," *Advertising Age*, October 16, 2000, p. S12; Dana James, "Addresses (Are) the Issue," *Marketing News*, October 9, 2000, p. 19; and Stephen J. Eustace, "The World Is Your Cybermarket," *Target Marketing*, April 2001, pp. 54–56

fetch information, Web pages, and e-mail-based articles on members' preferences and automatically deliver it to their PCs.

Also known as "push" programming, Webcasting affords an attractive channel through which online marketers can deliver their Internet advertising or other information content. For example, via Infogate, advertisers can market their products and services using highly targeted messages to a desirable segment of at-work Internet users.

As with other types of online marketing, companies must be careful that they don't cause resentment among Internet users who are already overloaded with "junk e-mail." Warns one analyst, "There's a fine line between adding value and the consumer feeling that you're being intrusive."[39] Companies must beware of irritating consumers by sending unwanted e-mail to promote their products. Netiquette, the unwritten rules that guide Internet etiquette, suggests that marketers should ask customers for permission to e-mail marketing pitches—and tell recipients how to "opt in" or "opt out" of e-mail promotions at any time. This approach, known as permission-based marketing, has become a standard model for e-mail marketing.

The Promise and Challenges of E-Commerce

E-commerce continues to offer great promise for the future. Its most ardent apostles still envision a time when the Internet and e-commerce will replace magazines, newspapers, and even stores as sources for information and buying. However, such "dot-com fever" has cooled recently and a more realistic view has emerged. "It's time for Act II in the Internet revolution," suggests one analyst. "The first act belonged to dot-coms with big visions and small bank accounts. Now the stage will be taken by big companies that move their factories, warehouses, and customers onto the Web."[40]

To be sure, online marketing will become a successful business model for some companies—Internet firms such as Amazon.com, eBay, Yahoo, and Netscape and direct-marketing companies such as Charles Schwab and Dell Computer. Michael Dell's goal is one day ". . . to have *all* customers conduct *all* transactions on the Internet, globally." And e-business will continue to boom for many B2B marketers, companies such as Cisco Systems, General Electric and Hewlett-Packard.

However, for most companies, online marketing will remain just one important approach to the marketplace that works alongside other approaches in a fully integrated marketing mix. Eventually, the "e" will fall away from e-business or e-marketing as companies become more adept at integrating e-commerce with their everyday strategy and tactics. "The key question is not whether to deploy Internet technology—companies have no choice if they want to stay competitive—but how to deploy it," says business strategist Michael Porter. He continues: "We need to move away from the rhetoric about 'Internet industries,' 'e-business strategies,' and a 'new economy,' and see the Internet for what it is: . . . a powerful set of tools that can be used, wisely or unwisely, in almost any industry and as part of almost any strategy."[41]

Along with its considerable promise, e-commerce faces many challenges. Here are just some of the challenges that online marketers face:

◆ *Limited consumer exposure and buying:* Although expanding rapidly, online marketing still reaches only a limited marketspace. Moreover, in most product categories, many Web users still do more window browsing and product research than actual buying.

◆ *Skewed user demographics and psychographics:* Although the Web audience is becoming more mainstream, online users still tend to be somewhat more upscale and more technology oriented than the general population. This makes online marketing ideal for marketing computer hardware and software, consumer electronics, financial services, and certain other classes of products. However, it makes online marketing less effective for selling mainstream products.

◆ *Chaos and clutter:* The Internet offers millions of Web sites and a staggering volume of information. Thus, navigating the Internet can be frustrating, confusing, and time-consuming for consumers. In this chaotic and cluttered environment, many Web ads and sites go unnoticed or unopened. Even when noticed, marketers will find it difficult to hold consumer attention. One study found that a site must capture Web surfers' attention within eight seconds or lose them to another site. That leaves very little time for marketers to promote and sell their goods.

◆ *Security:* Some consumers still worry that unscrupulous snoopers will eavesdrop on their online transactions or intercept their credit card numbers and make unauthorized purchases. In turn, companies doing business online fear that others will use the Internet to invade their computer systems for the purposes of commercial espionage or even sabotage. Online marketers are developing solutions to such security problems, and this has relieved buyer fears greatly in recent years. However, there appears to be an ongoing competition between the technology of Internet security systems and the sophistication of those seeking to break them.

◆ *Ethical concerns:* Privacy is a primary concern. Marketers can easily track Web site visitors, and many consumers who participate in Web site activities provide extensive personal information. This may leave consumers open to information abuse if companies make unauthorized use of the information in marketing their products or exchanging electronic lists with other companies. There are also concerns about segmentation and discrimination. The Internet currently serves upscale consumers well. However, poorer consumers still have less access to the Internet, leaving them increasingly less informed about products, services, and prices.[42]

Despite these challenges, companies large and small are quickly integrating online marketing into their marketing strategies and mixes. As it continues to grow, online marketing will prove to be a powerful tool for building customer relationships, improving sales, communicating company and product information, and delivering products and services more efficiently and effectively.

STOP Rest Stop: Reviewing the Concepts

In the first two chapters, you discovered the fundamentals of marketing and marketing strategy. In this chapter, you learned about some major changes in the marketing landscape that are having an impact on marketing practice. Recent technological advances have created a new Internet age. To thrive in this new environment, marketers will have to add some Internet thinking to their strategies and tactics. This chapter introduces the forces shaping the new Internet environment and how marketers are adapting. In the next chapter, we'll take a look at other forces and actors affecting the complex and changing marketing environment.

1. Identify the major forces shaping the Internet age.

Four major forces underlie the Internet age: digitalization and connectivity, the explosion of the Internet, new types of intermediaries, and customization and customerization. Much of today's business operates on digital information, which flows through connected networks. Intranets, extranets, and the Internet now connect people and companies with each other and with important information. The Internet has grown explosively to become *the* revolutionary technology of the new millennium, empowering consumers and businesses alike with the blessings of connectivity.

The Internet and other new technologies have changed the ways that companies serve their markets. New Internet marketers and channel relationships have arisen to replace some types of traditional marketers. The new technologies are also helping marketers to tailor their offers effectively to targeted customers or even to help customers customerize their own marketing offers. Finally, the New Economy technologies are blurring the boundaries between industries, allowing companies to pursue opportunities that lie at the convergence of two or more industries.

2. Explain how companies have responded to the Internet and other powerful new technologies with e-business strategies, and how these strategies have resulted in benefits to both buyers and sellers.

Conducting business in the New Economy will call for a new model of marketing strategy and practice. Companies need to retain most of the skills and practices that have worked in the past. However, they must also add

major new competencies and practices if they hope to grow and prosper in the New Economy. E-business is the use of electronic platforms to conduct a company's business. E-commerce involves buying and selling processes supported by electronic means, primarily the Internet. It includes e-marketing (the selling side of e-commerce) and e-purchasing (the buying side of e-commerce).

E-commerce benefits both buyers and sellers. For buyers, e-commerce makes buying convenient and private, provides greater product access and selection, and makes available a wealth of product and buying information. It is interactive and immediate and gives the consumer a greater measure of control over the buying process. For sellers, e-commerce is a powerful tool for building customer relationships. It also increases the sellers' speed and efficiency, helping to reduce selling costs. E-commerce also offers great flexibility and better access to global markets.

3. Describe the four major e-commerce domains.

Companies can practice e-commerce in any or all of four domains. B2C (business-to-consumer) e-commerce is initiated by businesses and targets final consumers. Despite recent setbacks following the "dot-com gold rush" of the late 1990s, B2C e-commerce continues to grow at a healthy rate. Although online consumers are still somewhat higher in income and more technology oriented than traditional buyers, the cyberspace population is becoming much more mainstream and diverse. This growing diversity opens up new e-commerce targeting opportunities for marketers. Today, consumers can buy almost anything on the Web.

B2B (business-to-business) e-commerce dwarfs B2C e-commerce. Most businesses today operate Web sites or use B2B trading networks, auction sites, spot exchanges, online product catalogs, barter sites, or other online resources to reach new customers, serve current customers more effectively, and obtain buying efficiencies and better prices. Business buyers and sellers meet in huge marketspaces—or open trading networks—to share information and complete transactions efficiently. Or, they set up private trading networks that link them with their own trading partners.

Through C2C (consumer-to-consumer) e-commerce, consumers can buy or exchange goods and information directly from or with one another. Examples include online auction sites, forums, and Internet newsgroups. Finally, through C2B (consumer-to-business) e-commerce, consumers are now finding it easier to search out sellers on the Web, learn about their products and services, and initiate purchases. Using the Web, customers can even drive transactions with business, rather than the other way around.

4. Discuss how companies can go about conducting e-commerce to profitably deliver more value to customers.

Companies of all types are now engaged in e-commerce. The Internet gave birth to the *click-only* dotcoms, which operate only online. In addition, many traditional brick-and-mortar companies have now added e-marketing operations, transforming themselves into *click-and-mortar* competitors. Many click-and-mortar companies are now having more online success than their click-only competitors.

Companies can conduct e-marketing in any of the four ways: creating a Web site, placing ads and promotions online, setting up or participating in Web communities, or using online e-mail or Webcasting. The first step typically is to set up a Web site. Corporate Web sites are designed to build customer goodwill and to supplement other sales channels, rather than to sell the company's products directly. Marketing Web sites engage consumers in an interaction that will move them closer to a direct purchase or other marketing outcome. Beyond simply setting up a site, companies must make their sites engaging, easy to use, and useful in order to attract visitors, hold them, and bring them back again.

E-marketers can use various forms of online advertising to build their Internet brands or to attract visitors to their Web sites. Beyond online advertising, other forms of online marketing include content sponsorships, microsites, and viral marketing, the Internet version of word-of-mouth marketing. Online marketers can also participate in Web communities, which take advantage of the C2C properties of the Web. Finally, e-mail marketing has become a hot new e-marketing tool for both B2C and B2B marketers.

5. Overview the promise and challenges that e-commerce presents for the future.

E-commerce continues to offer great promise for the future. For most companies, online marketing will become an important part of a fully integrated marketing mix. For others, it will be the major means by which they serve the market. Eventually, the "e" will fall away from e-business or e-marketing as companies become more adept at integrating e-commerce with their everyday strategy and tactics. However, e-commerce also faces many challenges. Among these are limited consumer exposure and buying, skewed user profiles, chaos and clutter, security, and ethical concerns. Despite these challenges, most companies are rapidly integrating online marketing into their marketing strategies and mixes.

Navigating the Key Terms

For a detailed analysis of the meaning and importance of each of the following key terms, visit our Web page at **www.prenhall.com/kotler**.

B2B (business-to-business) e-commerce
B2C (business-to-consumer) e-commerce
C2B (consumer-to-business) e-commerce

C2C (consumer-to-consumer) e-commerce
Click-and-mortar companies
Click-only companies
Corporate Web site
Customerization
E-business
E-commerce
E-marketing
Extranet
Internet

Intranet
Marketing Web site
Online advertising
Open trading networks
Private trading networks
Viral marketing
Web communities
Webcasting

Travel Log

The following concept checks and discussion questions will help you to keep track of and apply the concepts you've studied in this chapter.

Concept Checks
Fill in the blanks, then look for the correct answers.

1. Four specific forces that underlie the New Economy are _____ and _____, the explosion of the Internet, new types of intermediaries, and _____ and _____.

2. _____ connect a company with its suppliers and distributors.

3. If a new e-tailer cuts out a traditional intermediary in a channel relationship, then the traditional intermediary has been _____.

4. In _____, the company leaves it to individual customers to design the product or service offering.

5. Internet buying benefits both final buyers and sellers in many ways. It is _____; buying is _____ and _____; buyers have greater _____ and _____; channels give comparative information; and online buying is interactive and immediate.

6. _____ networks are huge e-marketspaces in which buyers and sellers find each other online, share information, and complete transactions efficiently.

7. When buyers use Priceline.com to bid for airline tickets and hotel rooms, they are conducting _____ e-commerce.

8. According to Figure 3-3, the three types of e-marketers are _____, _____, and _____.

9. The 7Cs of effective Web site design are _____, _____, _____, _____, communication, connection, and commerce.

10. _____ marketing involves creating an e-mail message or other marketing event that is so infectious that customers will want to pass it along to their friends.

11. _____ services automatically download customized information to a recipient's PC.

12. Online users tend to be somewhat more upscale and more technology oriented than the general population. This would be an example of the _____ challenge that online marketers face.

Concept Checks Answers: 1. digitalization and connectivity; customization and customerization; 2. Extranets; 3. disintermediated; 4. customerization; 5. convenient; easy and private; product access and selection; 6. Open trading; 7. C2B (consumer-to-business); 8. click-only; brick-and-mortar only; click-and-mortar; 9. context, content, community, customization; 10. Viral; 11. Webcasting; 12. skewed user demographics and psychographics.

Discussing the Issues

1. Discuss how a traditional retailer or wholesaler can be *disintermediated* by the new e-tailer. Give an example to illustrate.

2. Customization differs from customerization. Explain and illustrate.

3. E-commerce and the Internet bring many benefits to both buyers and sellers. Describe and illustrate these benefits.

4. The statement has been made that all companies need to consider moving into e-marketing. List and discuss the four generally accepted ways that a company can conduct e-marketing. Pick a local retailer or service provider that has not yet moved into e-marketing and suggest how they might do this. Be specific.

5. Pick a favorite Web site and write a brief analysis of how the site rates on the 7Cs of effective Web site design. What forms of online advertising and promotion does your chosen Web site seem to be using to its advantage? How can the site be improved? Be specific.

Mastering Marketing

Having an effective e-marketing presence is of primary importance in today's competitive marketplace. Explain how CanGo has or should use marketing in the wired world. Critique the organization's efforts by using the evaluation and analysis options suggested in this chapter. How effective have their efforts been to date? What suggestions would you offer at this point to the company? Explain.

Traveling on the Net

Point of Interest: Placing Ads and Promotions Online

Move over Barnes and Noble, a new (yet old) player is about to take some of your bookselling business away. Borders (www.borders.com) booksellers is tired of finishing last when it comes to innovations on the Web. The Borders team is betting that its HTML-based e-mail campaign will be just what the doctor ordered to cure its many ills. With only $27 million in Internet sales last year, Borders certainly has room for improvement. However, its new tactic of adorning HTML-based e-mail messages with colorful graphics, images, and Web links means that Borders is delivering a message that looks and acts like a Web page. Additionally, using the "cookie" technique, Borders can capture recipients' e-mail and Internet addresses when one of it ads is opened. Tracking what consumers do while reading an e-mail message or visiting one of the suggested sites has obvious advantages. With a reported 20 percent click-through rate, Borders is achieving popularity with customers that it has not seen in years. In the question of graphics versus privacy, graphics seems to be winning in the customer response vote column. Finally, Borders' recent strategic alliance with Amazon.com will likely increase orders and traffic. Aligning with competitors is not an uncommon strategy in the new world of e-commerce. However, it remains to be seen whether the partnership with Amazon.com will be beneficial to Borders or not. Evaluate the Borders Web site with special attention to the questions found below.

For Discussion

1. What is your impression of the Borders Web site versus those of Barnes and Noble (www.bn.com), Campus Books (www.campusbooks.com), Books-a-million (www.bamm.com), eCampus (www.ecampus.com), and Half Price Books (www.halfpricebooks.com) sites?

2. What online advertising techniques described in the chapter were used on the Borders Web site? On the competitive Web sites?

3. Considering the challenges facing e-marketing in the future, what do you think of using the "cookie" technique to collect data on customers? Under what circumstances would the approach be acceptable to you? When would it be unacceptable?

4. If the Borders approach is successful in getting consumers to visit its Web site more frequently, what would be the advantages and disadvantages of this increased visitation by consumers?

5. What would you suggest that Borders do to improve their competitiveness against their major rivals? How does the partnership between Borders and Amazon.com affect your suggestion? What problems might this relationship cause?

Application Thinking

Assume that your marketing team has been asked to design a new HTML-based e-mail message for Borders to attract college freshmen interested in purchasing their text books for the upcoming semester. What would the message say? How would you reach this particular group of customers? What types of graphics, images, or Web links would be best for your message?

MAP—Marketing Applications

MAP Stop 3

One of the oldest forms of marketing and promotion is word-of-mouth. In the new Internet age, word-of-mouth has become known as viral marketing. Viral marketing is really quite simple—tell a friend to tell a friend that something is hot and worth noticing. This has worked successfully with the Doom video game, *The Blair Witch Project* movie, Harry Potter books, Razor scooters, and Chrysler's PT Cruiser automobile, to name only a few. To create "buzz," the viral marketer targets a group of carefully chosen trend leaders in a community who are likely to use phone or Internet communication to spread the word about the product, event, or service. Think about it. Who do you believe most—your friends or an ad? The friends win hands down. This form of messaging can also revive brands that have seen better days. Lucky Strike cigarettes, Lee dungarees, and even Vespa scooters have seen increases in sales and interest as a result of such "new buzz" tactics. However, buzz-building in this technologically savvy marketplace is no easy task. In fact, it can become a public relations nightmare if the selected communicators choose to "trash" your product. Effective viral marketing requires following a few simple rules to get just the right "buzz" about your product or service: (a) Identify trendsetters quickly and let them spread your message; (b) Withhold supply early to simulate scarcity—everyone wants what they cannot have; (c) Be authentic—no one wants a fake or to be tricked; and (d) Be prepared to change quickly—every good firefighter always knows when to retreat. If there is one thing that all viral marketers have learned it is this: start consumers talking and you will start selling.

Thinking Like a Marketing Manger

1. What applications can you think of for viral or buzz marketing on the Internet?

2. List three products that you have heard about from friends. Describe what you were told, how this matched ad claims, what action you took because of the information, and how likely you were to buy the products.

3. Assume you are the marketing manager for a new product to be sold primarily to consumers in your generation using the Internet. Describe how you would use viral marketing to accomplish this. Be specific in the descriptive steps of your plan.

4. Choose an actual product and start a positive buzz about it using one of the communication methods suggested in the chapter. Keep a record of what you communicated and how you communicated the information. What were the results of your communication? What could you do to increase the effectiveness of the communication? How were "connections" made? How could an e-marketer make the same "connections"?

5. Consider the ethics of viral marketing. What could be the potential problems with the method? What cautions should be taken by an e-marketer wishing to use this technique?

The Marketing Environment

ROAD MAP:
Previewing the Concepts

Now that you've seen how the New Economy has affected marketing strategy and practice, your marketing journey continues with a look into analyzing marketing opportunities. In this chapter, you'll discover that marketing does not operate in a vacuum, but rather in a complex and changing environment. Other *actors* in this environment—suppliers, intermediaries, customers, competitors, publics, and others—may work with or against the company. Major environmental *forces*—demographic, economic, natural, technological, political, and cultural—shape marketing opportunities, pose threats, and affect the company's ability to serve customers and develop lasting relationships with them. To understand marketing, and to develop effective marketing strategies, you must first understand the context in which marketing operates.

▶ After studying this chapter, you should be able to
1. describe the environmental forces that affect the company's ability to serve its customers
2. explain how changes in the demographic and economic environments affect marketing decisions
3. identify the major trends in the firm's natural and technological environments
4. explain the key changes in the political and cultural environments
5. discuss how companies can react to the marketing environment

At our first stop, we'll check out a major development in the marketing environment, millennial fever, and the nostalgia boom that it has produced. Volkswagen responded with the introduction of a born-again New Beetle. As you read on, ask yourself: What makes this little car so right for the times?

As we hurtle into the new millennium, social experts are busier than ever assessing the impact of a host of environmental forces on consumers and the marketers who serve them. "An old year turns into a new one," observes one such expert, "and the world itself, at least for a moment, seems to turn also. Images of death and re-birth, things ending and beginning, populate . . . and haunt the mind. Multiply this a thousand-fold, and you get 'millennial fever' . . . driving consumer behavior in all sorts of interesting ways."

Such millennial fever has hit the nation's baby boomers, the most commercially influential demographic group in history, especially hard. The oldest boomers, now in their mid-fifties, are resisting the aging process with the vigor they once reserved for antiwar protests. Other factors are also at work. Today, people of all ages seem to feel a bit over-worked, overstimulated, and overloaded. "Americans are overwhelmed . . . by the breath-taking onrush of the Information Age, with its high-speed modems, cell phones, and

pagers," suggests the expert. "While we hail the benefits of these wired [times], at the same time we are buffeted by the rapid pace of change."

The result of this "millennial fever" is a yearning to turn back the clock, to return to simpler times. This yearning has in turn produced a massive nostalgia wave. "We are creating a new culture, and we don't know what's going to happen," explains a noted futurist. "So we need some warm fuzzies from our past." Marketers of all kinds have responded to these nostalgia pangs by recreating products and images that help take consumers back to "the good old days." Examples are plentiful: Kellogg has revived old Corn Flakes packaging and car makers have created retro roadsters such as the Porsche Boxter and Chrysler's PT Cruiser. A Pepsi commercial rocks to the Rolling Stones's "Brown Sugar," James Brown's "I Feel Good" helps sell Senokot laxatives, and Janis Joplin's raspy voice crows, "Oh Lord, won't you buy me a Mercedes-Benz?" Disney developed an entire town—Celebration, Florida—to recreate the look and feel of 1940s neighborhoods. Heinz reintroduced its classic glass ketchup bottle, supported by nostalgic "Heinz was there" ads showing two 1950s-era boys eating hot dogs at a ballpark. Master marketer Coca-Cola resurrected the old red button logo and its heritage contour bottle. According to a Coca-Cola marketing executive, when the company introduced a plastic version of its famous contour bottle in 1994, sales grew by double digits in some markets.

Perhaps no company has more riding on the nostalgia wave than Volkswagen. The original Volkswagen Beetle first sputtered into America in 1949. With its simple, buglike design, no-frills engineering, and economical operation, the Beetle was the antithesis of Detroit's chrome-laden gas guzzlers. Although most owners would readily admit that their Beetles were underpowered, noisy, cramped, and freezing in the winter, they saw these as endearing qualities. Overriding these minor inconveniences, the Beetle was cheap to buy and own, dependable, easy to fix, fun to drive, and anything but flashy.

During the 1960s, as young baby boomers by the thousands were buying their first cars, demand exploded and the Beetle blossomed into an unlikely icon. Bursting with personality, the understated Bug came to personify an era of rebellion against conventions. It became the most popular car in American history, with sales peaking at 423,000 in 1968. By the late 1970s, however, the boomers had moved on, Bug mania had faded, and Volkswagen had dropped Beetle production for the United States. Still, more than 20 years later, the mere mention of these chugging oddities evokes smiles and strong emotions. Almost everyone over the age of 25, it seems, has a "feel-good" Beetle story to tell.

In an attempt to surf the nostalgia wave, Volkswagen introduced a New Beetle in 1998. Outwardly, the reborn Beetle resembles the original, tapping the strong emotions and memories of times gone by. Beneath the skin, however, the New Beetle is packed with modern features. According to an industry expert, "The Beetle comeback is . . . based on a combination of romance and reason—wrapping up modern conveniences in an old-style package. Built into the dashboard is a bud vase perfect for a daisy plucked straight from the 1960s. But right next to it is a high-tech multi-speaker stereo—and options like power windows, cruise control, and a power sunroof make it a very different car than the rattly old Bug. The new version . . . comes with all the modern features car buyers demand, such as four air bags and power outlets for cell phones. But that's not why VW expects folks to buy it. With a familiar bubble shape that still makes people smile as it skitters by, the new Beetle offers a pull that is purely emotional."

Initial advertising for the New Beetle played strongly on the nostalgia theme, while at the same time refreshing the old Beetle heritage. "If you sold your soul in the '80s," tweaked one ad, "here's your chance to buy it back." Other ads read, "Less flower, more power," and "Comes with wonderful new features. Like heat." Still another ad declared "0 to 60? Yes." The car's Web page (www3.vw.com/cars/newbeetle/main.html) summarizes: "The New Beetle has what any Beetle always had. Originality. Honesty. A point of view. It's an exhaustive and zealous rejection of banality. Isn't the world ready for that kind of car again?"

Volkswagen invested $560 million to bring the New Beetle to market. However, this investment has paid big dividends as demand quickly outstripped supply. Even before the first cars reached VW showrooms, dealers across the country had long waiting lists of people who'd paid for the car without ever seeing it, let alone driving it. One California dealer claimed that the New Beetle was such a traffic magnet that he had to remove it from his showroom floor every afternoon at 2 P.M. to discourage gawkers and let his salespeople work with serious prospects. The dealer encountered similar problems when he took to the streets in the new car. "You can't change lanes," said the dealer. "People drive up beside you to look."

Volkswagen's initial first-year sales projections of 50,000 New Beetles in North America proved pessimistic. After only nine months, the company had sold more than 64,000 of the new Bugs in the United States and Canada. The smart little car also garnered numerous distinguished awards, including *Motor Trend*'s 1999 Import Car of the Year, *Time* magazine's The Best of 1998 Design, *Business Week*'s Best New Products, and 1999 North American Car of the Year, awarded by an independent panel of top journalists who cover the auto industry. And sales are still sizzling—the New Beetle now accounts for more than a quarter of Volkswagen's U.S. sales and has helped win VW a fivefold increase in sales since 1993. The car was selected a *Money Magazine*'s Best Car of 2001. To follow up, Volkswagen plans to introduce a reincarnation of its old cult-classic flower-power Microbus in 2003.

The New Beetle has been a cross-generational hit, appealing to more than the stereotyped core demographic target of Woodstock-recovered baby boomers. Even kids too young to remember the original Bug appear to love this new one. "It's like you have a rock star here and everybody wants an autograph," states a VW sales manager. "I've never seen a car that had such a wide range of interest, from 16-year-olds to 65-year-olds." One wait-listed customer confirms the car's broad appeal. "In 1967, my Dad got me a VW. I loved it. I'm sure the new one will take me back," says the customer. "I'm getting the New Beetle as a surprise for my daughter, but I'm sure I'm going to be stealing it from her all the time."

"Millennial fever" results from the convergence of a wide range of forces in the marketing environment—from technological, economic, and demographic forces to cultural, social, and political ones. Most trend analysts believe that the nostalgia craze will only grow as the baby boomers continue to mature. If so, the New Beetle, so full of the past, has a very bright future. "The Beetle is not just empty nostalgia," says Gerald Celente, publisher of *Trend Journal.* "It is a practical car that is also tied closely to the emotions of a generation." Says another trend analyst, the New Beetle "is our romantic past, reinvented for our hectic here-and-now. Different, yet deeply familiar—a car for the times."[1]

As noted in Chapter 1, marketers operate in an increasing connected world. Today's marketers must connect effectively with customers, others in the company, and external partners in the face of major environmental forces that buffet all of these actors. A company's **marketing environment** consists of the actors and forces outside marketing that affect marketing management's ability to develop and maintain successful relationships with its target customers. The marketing environment offers both opportunities and threats. Successful companies know the vital importance of constantly watching and adapting to the changing environment.

As we move into the new millennium, both consumers and marketers wonder what the future will bring. The environment continues to change at a rapid pace. For example, think about how you buy groceries today. How will your grocery buying change during the next few decades? What challenges will these changes present for marketers? Here's what two leading futurists envision for the year 2025.[2]

We won't be shopping in 21-aisle supermarkets in 2025, predicts Gary Wright, corporate demographer for Procter & Gamble in Cincinnati. The growth of e-commerce and the rapid speed of the Internet will lead to online ordering of lower-priced, nonperishable products—everything from peanut butter to coffee filters. Retailers will become "bundlers," combining these orders into large packages of goods for each household and delivering them efficiently to their doorsteps. As a result, we'll see mergers between retailing and home-delivery giants—think Wal-MartExpress, a powerful combo of Wal-Mart and Federal Express. Consumers won't waste precious time searching for the best-priced bundle. Online information agents will do it for them, comparing prices among competitors.

Smart information agents also play a role in the world imagined by Ryan Mathews, futurist at First Matter LLC in Detroit. By 2025, computers will essentially be as smart as humans, he contends, and consumers will use them to exchange information with on-screen electronic agents that ferret out the best deals online. Thanks to embedded-chip technology in the pantry, products on a CHR (continuous household replenishment) list—such as paper towels and pet food—will sense when they're running low and reorder themselves automatically. If the information agent finds a comparable but cheaper substitute for a CHR product, the item will be switched instantly.

Such pictures of the future give marketers plenty to think about. A company's marketers take the major responsibility for identifying and predicting significant changes in the environment. More than any other group in the company, marketers must be the trend trackers and opportunity seekers. Although every manager in an organization needs to observe the outside environment, marketers have two special aptitudes. They have disciplined methods—marketing intelligence and marketing research—for collecting information about the marketing environment. They also spend more time in the customer and competitor environment. By conducting systematic environmental scanning, marketers can revise and adapt marketing strategies to meet new challenges and opportunities in the marketplace.

The marketing environment is made up of a *microenvironment* and a *macroenvironment*. The **microenvironment** consists of the forces close to the company that affect its ability to serve its customers—the company, suppliers, marketing channel firms, customer markets, competitors, and publics. The **macroenvironment** consists of the larger societal forces that affect the microenvironment—demographic, economic, natural, technological, political, and cultural forces. We look first at the company's microenvironment.

Marketing environment
The actors and forces outside marketing that affect marketing management's ability to develop and maintain successful transactions with its target customers.

Microenvironment
The forces close to the company that affect its ability to serve its customers—the company, suppliers, marketing channel firms, customer markets, competitors, and publics.

Macroenvironment
The larger societal forces that affect the microenvironment—demographic, economic, natural, technological, political, and cultural forces.

The Company's Microenvironment

Marketing management's job is to attract and build relationships with customers by creating customer value and satisfaction. However, marketing managers cannot accomplish this task alone. Their success will depend on other actors in the company's microenvironment—other company departments, suppliers, marketing intermediaries, customers, competitors, and various publics, which combine to make up the company's value delivery network.

The Company

In designing marketing plans, marketing management takes other company groups into account —groups such as top management, finance, research and development (R&D), purchasing, manufacturing, and accounting. All these interrelated groups form the internal environment (see Figure 4-1). Top management sets the company's mission, objectives, broad strategies, and policies. Marketing managers make decisions within the plans made by top management, and marketing plans must be approved by top management before they can be implemented.

Marketing managers must also work closely with other company departments. Finance is concerned with finding and using funds to carry out the marketing plan. The R&D department focuses on designing safe and attractive products. Purchasing worries about getting supplies and materials, whereas manufacturing is responsible for producing the desired quality and quantity of products. Accounting has to measure revenues and costs to help marketing know how well it is achieving its objectives. Together, all of these departments have an impact on the marketing department's plans and actions. Under the marketing concept, all of these functions must "think consumer," and they should work in harmony to provide superior customer value and satisfaction.

Suppliers

Suppliers are an important link in the company's overall customer value delivery system. They provide the resources needed by the company to produce its goods and services. Supplier problems can seriously affect marketing. Marketing managers must watch supply availability—supply shortages or delays, labor strikes, and other events can cost sales in the short run and damage customer satisfaction in the long run. Marketing managers also monitor the price trends of their key inputs. Rising supply costs may force price increases that can harm the company's sales volume.

Figure 4-1
The company's internal environment

Marketing Intermediaries

Marketing intermediaries
Firms that help the company to promote, sell, and distribute its goods to final buyers; they include resellers, physical distribution firms, marketing service agencies, and financial intermediaries.

Marketing intermediaries help the company to promote, sell, and distribute its goods to final buyers. They include *resellers, physical distribution firms, marketing services agencies,* and *financial intermediaries. Resellers* are distribution channel firms that help the company find customers or make sales to them. These include wholesalers and retailers, who buy and resell merchandise. Selecting and working with resellers is not easy. No longer do manufacturers have many small, independent resellers from which to choose. They now face large and growing reseller organizations. These organizations frequently have enough power to dictate terms or even shut the manufacturer out of large markets.

Physical distribution firms help the company to stock and move goods from their points of origin to their destinations. Working with warehouse and transportation firms, a company must determine the best ways to store and ship goods, balancing factors such as cost, delivery, speed, and safety. *Marketing services agencies* are the marketing research firms, advertising agencies, media firms, and marketing consulting firms that help the company target and promote its products to the right markets. When the company decides to use one of these agencies, it must choose carefully because these firms vary in creativity, quality, service, and price. *Financial intermediaries* include banks, credit companies, insurance companies, and other businesses that help finance transactions or ensure against the risks associated with the buying and selling of goods. Most firms and customers depend on financial intermediaries to finance their transactions.

Like suppliers, marketing intermediaries form an important component of the company's overall value delivery system. In its quest to create satisfying customer relationships, the company must do more than just optimize its own performance. It must partner effectively with marketing intermediaries to optimize the performance of the entire system.

Customers

The company needs to study its customer markets closely. Figure 4-2 shows five types of customer markets. *Consumer markets* consist of individuals and households that buy goods and services for personal consumption. *Business markets* buy goods and services for further processing or for use in their production process, whereas *reseller markets* buy goods and services to resell at a profit. *Government markets* are made up of government agencies that buy goods and services to produce public services or transfer the goods and services to others who need them. Finally, *international markets* consist of these buyers in other countries, including consumers, producers, resellers, and governments. Each market type has special characteristics that call for careful study by the seller.

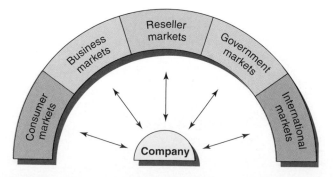

Figure 4-2
Types of customer markets

Competitors

The marketing concept states that to be successful, a company must provide greater customer value and satisfaction than its competitors do. Thus, marketers must do more than simply adapt to the needs of target consumers. They also must gain strategic advantage by positioning their offerings strongly against competitors' offerings in the minds of consumers.

No single competitive marketing strategy is best for all companies. Each firm should consider its own size and industry position compared to those of its competitors. Large firms with dominant positions in an industry can use certain strategies that smaller firms cannot afford. But being large is not enough. There are winning strategies for large firms, but there are also losing ones. And small firms can develop strategies that give them better rates of return than large firms enjoy.

Publics

The company's marketing environment also includes various publics. A **public** is any group that has an actual or potential interest in or impact on an organization's ability to achieve its objectives. Figure 4-3 shows seven types of publics.

◆ *Financial publics* influence the company's ability to obtain funds. Banks, investment houses, and stockholders are the major financial publics.
◆ *Media publics* carry news, features, and editorial opinion. They include newspapers, magazines, and radio and television stations.

Public
Any group that has an actual or potential interest in or impact on an organization's ability to achieve its objectives.

Publics: In this ad Wal-Mart recognizes the importance of both its local and employee publics. Its Competitive Edge scholarship program "is just one of the reasons Wal-Mart associates (such as Tiffany) in Mississippi, and all over the country, are proud to get involved in the communities they serve."

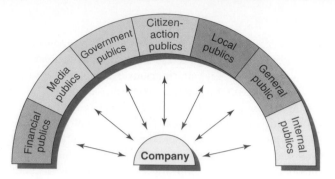

Figure 4-3
Types of publics

♦ *Government publics.* Management must take government developments into account. Marketers must often consult the company's lawyers on issues of product safety, truth in advertising, and other matters.

♦ *Citizen-action publics.* A company's marketing decisions may be questioned by consumer organizations, environmental groups, minority groups, and others. Its public relations department can help it stay in touch with consumer and citizen groups.

♦ *Local publics* include neighborhood residents and community organizations. Large companies usually appoint a community relations officer to deal with the community, attend meetings, answer questions, and contribute to worthwhile causes.

♦ *General public.* A company needs to be concerned about the general public's attitude toward its products and activities. The public's image of the company affects its buying.

♦ *Internal publics* include workers, managers, volunteers, and the board of directors. Large companies use newsletters and other means to inform and motivate their internal publics. When employees feel good about their company, this positive attitude spills over to external publics.

A company can prepare marketing plans for these major publics as well as for its customer markets. Suppose the company wants a specific response from a particular public, such as goodwill, favorable word of mouth, or donations of time or money. The company would have to design an offer to this public that is attractive enough to produce the desired response.

The Company's Macroenvironment

The company and all of the other actors operate in a larger macroenvironment of forces that shape opportunities and pose threats to the company. Figure 4-4 shows the six major forces in the company's macroenvironment. In the remaining sections of this chapter, we examine these forces and show how they affect marketing plans.

Demographic Environment

Demography
The study of human populations in terms of size, density, location, age, gender, race, occupation, and other statistics.

Demography is the study of human populations in terms of size, density, location, age, gender, race, occupation, and other statistics. The demographic environment is of major interest to marketers because it involves people, and people make up markets.

The world population is growing at an explosive rate. It now totals more than 6 billion and will exceed 7.9 billion by the year 2025.[3] The explosive world population growth has major implications for business. A growing population means growing human needs to satisfy. Depending on purchasing power, it may also mean growing market opportunities. For example, to curb its skyrocketing population, the Chinese

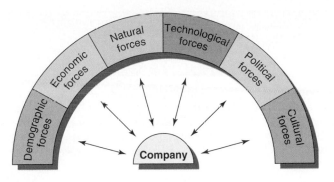

Figure 4-4
Major forces in the company's macro-environment

government has passed regulations limiting families to one child each. As a result, Chinese children are spoiled and fussed over as never before. Known in China as "little emperors and empresses," Chinese children are being showered with everything from candy to computers as a result of what's known as the "six-pocket syndrome." As many as six adults—including parents and two sets of doting grandparents—may be indulging the whims of each child. Parents in the average Beijing household now spend about 40 percent of their income on their cherished only child. This trend has encouraged toy companies such as Japan's Bandai Company (known for its Mighty Morphin Power Rangers), Denmark's Lego Group, and Mattel to enter the Chinese market. And McDonald's has triumphed in China in part because it has catered successfully to this pampered generation.[4]

The world's large and highly diverse population poses both opportunities and challenges (see Marketing at Work 4-1). Thus, marketers keep close track of demographic trends and developments in their markets, both at home and abroad. They track changing age and family structures, geographic population shifts, educational characteristics, and population diversity. Here, we discuss the most important demographic trends in the United States.

Changing Age Structure of the Population The U.S. population stood at more than 284 million in 2001 and may reach 340 million by the year 2025.[5] The single most important demographic trend in the United States is the changing age structure of the population. As shown in Figure 4-5, the U.S. population contains seven generational groups. Here, we discuss the three largest age groups—the baby boomers, Generation X, and Generation Y—and their impact on today's marketing strategies.

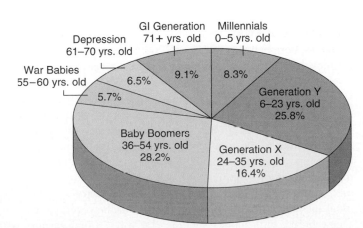

Figure 4-5
The seven U.S. generations

Source: Alison Stein Wellner, "Generational Divide," *American Demographics,* October 2000, pp. 53–58.

Marketing at Work 4-1
If the World Were a Village

Think for a few minutes about the world and your place in it. If we reduced the world to a village of 1,000 people representative of the world's population, this would be our reality:

◆ Our village would have 520 women and 480 men, 330 children and 60 people over age 65, 10 college graduates, and 335 illiterate adults.

◆ We'd have 52 North Americans, 55 Russians, 84 Latin Americans, 95 Europeans, 124 Africans, and 584 Asians.

◆ Communication would be difficult: 165 of us would speak Mandarin, 86 English, 83 Hindi, 64 Spanish, 58 Russian, and 37 Arabic. The other half of us would speak one of more than 200 other languages.

◆ Among us we'd have 329 Christians, 178 Moslems, 132 Hindus, 62 Buddhists, 3 Jews, 167 nonreligious, 45 atheists, and 84 others.

◆ About one-third of our people would have access to clean, safe drinking water. About half of our children would be immunized against infections.

◆ The woodlands in our village would be decreasing rapidly and wasteland would be growing. Forty percent of the village's crop

land, nourished by 83 percent of our fertilizer, would produce 72 percent of the food to feed its 270 well-fed owners. The remaining 60 percent of the land and 17 percent of the fertilizer would produce 28 percent of the food to feed the other 730 people. Five hundred people in the village would suffer from malnutrition.

◆ Only 200 of the 1,000 people would control 75 percent of our

village's wealth. Another 200 would receive only 2 percent of the wealth. Seventy people would own cars. One would have a computer, and that computer probably would not be connected to the Internet.

Source: The World Village Project, "Global Village," accessed online at www.cvu.cssd.k12.vt.us/ departments/science/environmental/writing/ globalvillage.html, June 21, 2001.

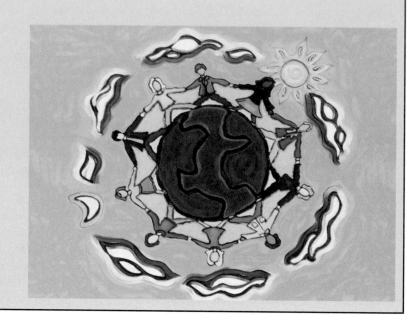

Baby boom

The major increase in the annual birthrate following World War II and lasting until the early 1960s. The "baby boomers," now moving into middle age, are a prime target for marketers.

THE BABY BOOMERS. The post–World War II baby boom produced 78 million **baby boomers,** born between 1946 and 1964. Since then, the baby boomers have become one of the most powerful forces shaping the marketing environment. The boomers have presented a moving target, creating new markets as they grew from infancy to their preadolescent, teenage, young adult, and now middle-age to mature years. Today's baby boomers account for about 28 percent of the population but earn more than half of all personal income.

Baby boomers cut across all walks of life. But marketers typically have paid the most attention to the smaller upper crust of the boomer generation—its more educated, mobile, and wealthy segments. These segments have gone by many names. In the 1980s, they were called "yuppies" (young urban professionals); "bumpies" (black upwardly mobile professionals); "yummies" (young upwardly mobile mommies), and "DINKs" (dual-income, no-kids couples). In the 1990s, however, yuppies and "DINKs" gave way to a new breed, with names such as "DEWKs" (dual-earners with kids) and "MOBYs" (mother older, baby younger). Now, to the chagrin of many in this generation, they are acquiring such titles as "WOOFs" (well-off older folks) or even "GRUMPIES" (just what the name suggests).

The youngest boomers are now in their late thirties; the oldest are in their mid-fifties. In fact, somewhere in America, seven boomers will turn 50 every minute from now until 2014. Thus, the boomers have evolved from the "youthquake generation" to the "backache generation." The maturing boomers are experiencing the pangs of midlife and rethinking the purpose and value of their work, responsibilities, and relationships. They are approaching life with a new stability and reasonableness in the way they live, think, eat, and spend. As they continue to age, they will create a large and important seniors market. By 2025, there will be 64 million baby boomers aged 61 to 79, a 90 percent increase in the size of this population from today.[6]

As they mature, the boomers are also reaching their peak earning and spending years. Thus, they constitute a lucrative market for new housing and home remodeling, financial services, travel and entertainment, eating out, health and fitness products, and high-priced cars and other luxuries. It would be a mistake to think of the boomers as aging and staid. Many boomers are rediscovering the excitement of life and have the means to play it out. For example, according to the Travel Industry Association of America, one-half of all U.S. adults took adventure vacations within the past five years. Some 56 percent of these travelers were boomers. And the median age of a Harley-Davidson buyer is 44.6 years old, squarely in the middle of the boomer age range.[7]

GENERATION X.   The baby boom was followed by a "birth dearth," creating another generation of 45 million people born between 1965 and 1976. Author Douglas Coupland calls them **Generation X,** because they lie in the shadow of the boomers and lack obvious distinguishing characteristics. Others call them the "baby busters," the "shadow generation," or the "yiffies"—young, individualistic, freedom-minded few.

Generation X
The group of people born between 1965 and 1976 during the "birth dearth."

The Generation Xers are defined as much by their shared experiences as by their age. Increasing divorce rates and higher employment for their mothers made them the first generation of latchkey kids. Whereas the boomers created a sexual revolution, the GenXers have lived in the age of AIDS. Having grown up during times of recession and corporate downsizing, they have developed a more cautious economic outlook. As a result, the GenXers are a more skeptical bunch, cynical of frivolous marketing pitches that promise easy success.

They buy lots of products, such as sweaters, boots, cosmetics, electronics, cars, fast food, computers, and mountain bikes. However, their cynicism makes them more savvy shoppers, and their financial pressures make them more value conscious. They like lower prices and a more functional look. The GenXers respond to honesty in advertising, and they like irreverence and sass and ads that mock the traditional advertising approach. For example, Miller Brewing Company ads appealing to this group have advised "It's time to embrace your inner idiot" and one featured images of a frenetic, sloppy hot-dog-eating contest.

GenXers share new cultural concerns. They care about the environment and respond favorably to socially responsible companies. Although they seek success, they are less materialistic; they prize experience, not acquisition. They are cautious romantics who want a better quality of life and are more interested in job satisfaction than in sacrificing personal happiness and growth for promotion.

Once labeled as "The MTV generation: Net surfing, nihilistic [body-piercing slackers] whining about McJobs," the GenXers are now growing up and beginning to take over. They do surf the Internet more than other groups, but with serious intent. The GenXers are poised to displace the lifestyles, culture, and materialistic values of the baby boomers. And they represent $125 billion in annual purchasing power. By the year 2010, they will have overtaken the baby boomers as a primary market for almost every product category.[8]

Generation Y (echo boom)
The 72 million children of the baby boomers, born between 1977 and 1994.

GENERATION Y. Both the baby boomers and GenXers will one day be passing the reins to the latest demographic group, **Generation Y** (or the echo boomers). Born between 1977 and 1994, these children of the baby boomers now number 72 million, dwarfing the GenXers and almost equal in size to the baby boomer segment. Ranging from preteens to early twenties, the echo boomer generation is still forming its buying preferences and behaviors.

The echo boom created large and growing kids and teens markets, spending some $600 billion a year.[9] After years of bust, markets for children's toys and games, clothes, furniture, and food have enjoyed a boom. For instance, in recent years, designers and retailers have created new lines, new products, and even new stores devoted to children and teens—Tommy Hilfiger, DKNY, Gap, Toys 'R' Us, Guess, Talbots, Pottery Barn, and Eddie Bauer, to name just a few. New media have appeared that cater specifically to this market: *Time, Sports Illustrated* and *People* have all started new editions for kids and teens. Banks offer banking and investment services for kids, including investment camps. Major advertising agencies have even opened new divisions—such as Saatchi & Saatchi Advertising's Kid Connection division and Grey Advertising's 18 & Under division—that specialize in helping their clients shape their appeals for young audiences.[10]

Generation Y oldsters are now graduating from college and beginning careers. Like the trailing edge of the Generation Xers ahead of them, one distinguishing characteristic of Generation Y is their utter fluency and comfort with computer, digital, and Internet technology. For this reason, one analyst has christened them the Net-Gens (or N-Gens). He observes:

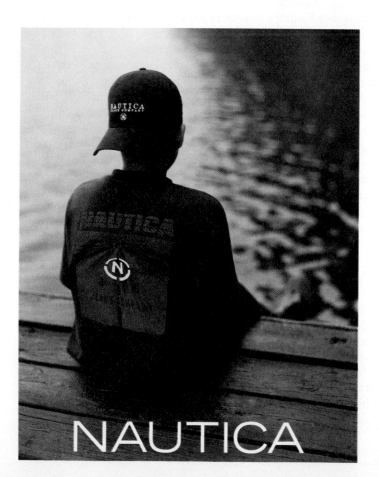

As first the Gen Xers and soon the Gen Ys have children of their own, they are creating a huge kids and teens market.

What makes this generation different . . . is not just its demographic muscle, but it is the first to grow up surrounded by digital media. Computers and other digital technologies, such as digital cameras, are commonplace to N-Gen members. They work with them at home, in school, and they use them for entertainment. Increasingly these technologies are connected to the Internet. . . . Constantly surrounded by technology, today's kids are accustomed to its strong presence in their lives. [They] are so bathed in bits that they are no more intimidated by digital technology than a VCR or a toaster. And it is through their use of the digital media that N-Gen will develop and superimpose its culture on the rest of society. Boomers stand back. Already these kids are learning, playing, communicating, working, and creating communities very differently than did their parents. They are a force for social transformation.[11]

Generation Y represents a complex target for marketers. Whereas Generation Y has grown up with the Internet, mobile communications, and video games, their baby boomer parents can still remember when digital technology was a futuristic notion. On average, Gen Ys have access to 62 TV channels, not to mention mobile phones, personal digital assistants (PDAs), and the Internet, offering broad media access. Studies have shown that Gen Y consumers are smart, aware, and fair-minded. They like to be entertained in ads directed at them but don't like ads that make fun of people. They love things that are "green" and they relate well to causes. Making connections now with Gen Ys will pay dividends to marketers beyond capturing their current spending. In future years, as they begin working and their buying power increases, this segment will more than rival the baby boomers in spending and market influence.[12]

GENERATIONAL MARKETING.   Do marketers have to create separate products and marketing programs for each generation? Some experts caution that each generation spans decades of time and many socioeconomic levels. For example, marketers often split the baby boomers into three smaller groups — leading boomers, core boomers, and trailing boomers — each with its own beliefs and behaviors. "These segments are so large they're meaningless as marketing targets," notes one expert. " 'Matures' range in age from 54 to 90; that isn't a target, it's a happening. Similarly, . . . boomers span almost twenty years." He suggests that marketers should form more precise age-specific segments within each group. More important, defining people by their birth date may be less effective than segmenting them by their lifestyle or life stage.

Others warn that marketers have to be careful about turning off one generation each time they craft a product or message that appeals effectively to another. "The idea is to try to be broadly inclusive and at the same time offer each generation something specifically designed for it. Tommy Hilfiger has big brand logos on his clothes for teenagers and little pocket polo logos on his shirts for baby boomers. It's a brand that has a more inclusive than exclusive strategy."[13]

The Changing American Family   The "traditional household" consists of a husband, wife, and children (and sometimes grandparents). Yet, the once American ideal of the two-child, two-car suburban family has lately been losing some of its luster. In the United States today, married couples with children now make up only about 35 percent of all U.S. households. A full 44 percent of today's households fall into the "diverse" or "nontraditional" category, including single live-alones, adult live-togethers of one or both sexes, single-parent families, childless married couples, or empty nesters.[14] More people are divorcing or separating, choosing not to marry, marrying later, or marrying without intending to have children. Marketers must increasingly consider the special needs of nontraditional households, because they are now growing more rapidly than traditional households. Each group has distinctive needs and buying habits. For example, people in the SSWD group (single, separated, widowed, divorced) need smaller apartments; inexpensive and smaller appliances, furniture, and furnishings; and food packaged in smaller sizes.

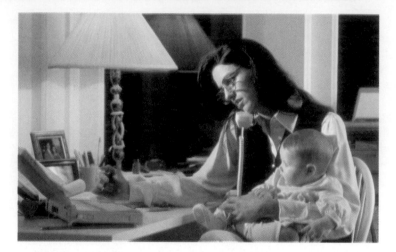

Changing American family: The increase in the number of working women has spawned many business opportunities.

The number of working women has also increased greatly, growing from under 30 percent of the U.S. workforce in 1950 to more than 46 percent by the late 1990s.[15] This trend has spawned the child day care business and increased consumption of convenience foods and services, career-oriented women's clothing, financial services, and many other business opportunities. For example, new niche malls feature customized mixes of specialty shops with extended hours for working women who can find time to shop only before or after work. Stores in these malls feature targeted promotions and phone-in shopping, by which busy shoppers can phone ahead with color choices and other preferences while store employees perform a "wardrobe consulting" service. At the same time, more and more workplaces and child-care centers are installing monitoring setups, such as "I See You" equipment from Simplex Knowledge. This system lets working parents see their children at different points throughout the day by viewing photos taken in the child-care center and posted on a secure Web site.[16]

Geographic Shifts in Population This is a period of great migratory movements between and within countries. Americans, for example, are a mobile people with about 16 percent of all U.S. residents moving each year.[17] Over the past two decades, the U.S. population has shifted toward the Sunbelt states. The West and South have grown while the Midwest and Northeast states have lost population. Such population shifts interest marketers because people in different regions buy differently. For example, research shows that people in Seattle buy more toothbrushes per capita than people in any other U.S. city; people in Salt Lake City eat more candy bars; people from New Orleans use more ketchup; and people in Miami drink more prune juice.

Also, for more than a century, Americans have been moving from rural to metropolitan areas. In the 1950s, they made a massive exit from the cities to the suburbs. Today, the migration to the suburbs continues, and demographers are noting another shift that they call "the rural rebound." Nonmetropolitan counties that lost population to cities for most of this century are now attracting large numbers of urban refugees. And more and more Americans are moving to "micropolitan areas," small cities located beyond congested metropolitan areas. These smaller micros offer many of the advantages of metro areas—jobs, restaurants, diversions, community organizations—but without the population crush, traffic jams, high crime rates, and high property taxes often associated with heavily urbanized areas.[18]

The shift in where people live has also caused a shift in where they work. For example, the migration toward micropolitan and rural areas has resulted in a rapid increase in the number of people who "telecommute"—work at home or in a remote office and conduct their business by phone, fax, modem, or the Internet. This trend, in turn, has created

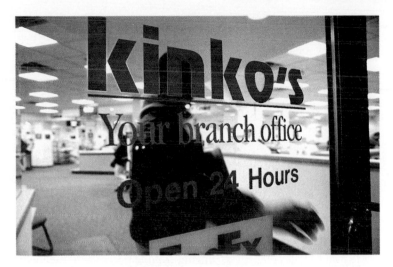

Geographic shifts: The shift in where people live has also caused a shift in where they work, creating a booming SOHO (small office/home office) market. Kinko's serves as "your branch office."

a booming SOHO (small office/home office) market. Nearly 40 million Americans are now working out of their homes with the help of electronic conveniences such as personal computers, cell phones, fax machines, and handheld organizers. Many marketers are actively courting the home office segment of this lucrative SOHO market. One example is Kinko's Copy Centers:

> Founded in the 1970s as a campus photocopying business, Kinko's is now reinventing itself as the well-appointed office outside the home. Where once there were copy machines, Kinko's 902 stores in this country and abroad now feature a uniform mixture of fax machines, ultrafast color printers, and networks of computers equipped with popular software programs and high-speed Internet connections. People can come to a Kinko's store to do all their office jobs: they can copy, send and receive faxes, use various programs on the computer, go on the Internet, order stationery and other printed supplies, and even teleconference. As more and more people join the work-at-home trend, Kinko's offers an escape from the isolation of the home office. Besides adding state-of-the-art equipment, the company is talking to Starbucks about opening up coffee shops adjacent to some Kinko's. The lettering on the Kinko's door sums up the $1 billion company's new business model: "Your branch office/Open 24 hours."[19]

A Better-Educated and More White-Collar Population The U.S. population is becoming better educated. For example, in 2000, 84 percent of the U.S. population over age 25 had completed high school and 26 percent had completed college, compared with 69 percent and 17 percent in 1980.[20] The rising number of educated people will increase the demand for quality products, books, magazines, travel, personal computers, and Internet services. It suggests a decline in television viewing because college-educated consumers watch less TV than does the population at large. The workforce also is becoming more white collar. Between 1950 and 1985, the proportion of white-collar workers rose from 41 percent to 54 percent, that of blue-collar workers declined from 47 percent to 33 percent, and that of service workers increased from 12 percent to 14 percent. These trends have continued into the new millennium.[21]

Increasing Diversity Countries vary in their ethnic and racial makeup. At one extreme is Japan, where almost everyone is ethnic Japanese. At the other extreme is the United States, with people from virtually all nations. The United States has often been called a melting pot in which diverse groups from many nations and cultures have melted into a single, more homogenous whole. Instead, the United States seems to have become more of a "salad bowl" in which various groups have mixed together but have maintained their diversity by retaining and valuing important ethnic and cultural differences.

Marketers are facing increasingly diverse markets, both at home and abroad, as their operations become more international in scope. In the United States alone, ethnic population growth is 12 times greater than the Caucasian growth rate, and ethnic consumers buy more than $600 billion of goods and services each year. The U.S. population is 71 percent white, with African Americans and Hispanics each making up another 12 percent. The U.S. Asian American population now totals about 4 percent of the population, with the remaining 1 percent made up of American Indian, Eskimo, and Aleut. These ethnic populations are expected to explode during the next 20 years. During that time, the number of African Americans will increase 25 percent, Hispanics about 64 percent, and Asian Americans almost 68 percent. Moreover, there are nearly 26 million people living in the United States—more than 9 percent of the population—who were born in another country.[22]

Many large companies, ranging from large retailers such as Sears and Wal-Mart to consumer products companies such as Levi Strauss, Procter & Gamble, and General Mills now target specially designed products and promotions to one or more of these groups. General Mills, for example, is targeting the African American market with four separate campaigns for its Big G cereals—Cheerios, Trix, Honey Nut Cheerios, and Cinnamon Toast Crunch. The campaigns consist of advertising, sponsorships, sampling, and community-based promotions that feature a strong family emphasis. For example, for the past several years, Honey Nut Cheerios has been the title sponsor of the Universal Circus, and for a "Soul Fest" music event that travels to 30 urban markets.[23]

Diversity goes beyond ethnic heritage. For example, many major companies have recently begun to explicitly target gay and lesbian consumers. A Simmons Research study of readers of the National Gay Newspaper Guild's 12 publications found that, compared to the average American, respondents are 12 times more likely to be in professional jobs, almost twice as likely to own a vacation home, 8 times more likely to own a notebook computer, and twice as likely to own individual stocks. They are twice as likely as the general population to have a household income between $60,000 and $250,000, making them a very attractive market segment.

Companies in several industries are now waking up to the needs and potential of the gay and lesbian segment. For example, ad spending to reach gay and lesbian consumers is booming. Gay.com, a Web site that attracts more than two million unique visitors each month, has also attracted a diverse set of well-known advertisers, from IBM, eBay, Quicken Mortgage, Saturn, and AT&T to American Airlines and Neiman Marcus. Here are two examples of gay and lesbian marketing efforts:[24]

American Express Financial Advisors launched print ads that depict same-sex couples planning their financial futures. The ads ran in *Out* and *The Advocate,* the two highest-circulation national gay publications. The company's director of segment marketing, Margaret Vergeyle, said: "We're targeting gay audiences with targeted ads and promotions that are relevant to them and say that we understand their specific needs. Often, gay couples are very concerned about issues like Social Security benefits and estate planning, since same-sex marriages often are not recognized under the law."

The British Tourist Authority teamed up with British Airways and the London Tourist Board to target the U.S. gay and lesbian travel market. The group worked with WinMark Concepts, a Washington marketing and advertising firm that specializes in advising mainstream companies on how to target the gay and lesbian market. "We wanted something that was gay-specific (and) fun, but also extremely tasteful," says WinMark's president. "These are educated, savvy consumers." One recent magazine ad shows five young to early-middle-aged men—the target age group is 35 to 50—posing in and around several of London's distinctive red phone booths. The headline reads: "One Call. A rainbow of choices." The campaign has been successful. "The magazine ads got the word out that Britain is gay- and lesbian-friendly and also generated a database of 40,000 names across the country. Now, it's time for a more targeted direct-mail and e-mail campaign to people we know are interested in our offer." Since BTA launched the campaign, both United Airlines and Virgin Airways have signed on to the program, as have the tourist boards of Manchester, Brighton, and Glasgow.

Another attractive segment is the more than 54 million people with disabilities in the United States—a market larger than African Americans or Hispanics—representing almost $800 billion in annual spending power. People with mobility challenges are an ideal target market for companies such as Peapod (www.peapod.com), which teams up with large supermarket chains in many heavily populated areas to offer online grocery shopping and home delivery. They also represent a growing market for travel, sports, and other leisure-oriented products and services (see Marketing at Work 4-2).[25]

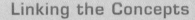

Linking the Concepts

Pull over here for a moment and think about how deeply these demographic factors impact all of us and, as a result, marketers' strategies.

◆ Apply these demographic developments to your own life. Think of some specific examples of how the changing demographic factors affect you and your buying behavior.

◆ Identify a specific company that has done a good job of reacting to the shifting demographic environment—generational segments (baby boomers, GenXers, or Generation Y), the changing American family, and increased diversity. Compare this company to one that's done a poor job.

Economic Environment

Markets require buying power as well as people. The **economic environment** consists of factors that affect consumer purchasing power and spending patterns. Nations vary greatly in their levels and distribution of income. Some countries have *subsistence economies*—they consume most of their own agricultural and industrial output. These countries offer few market opportunities. At the other extreme are *industrial economies,* which constitute rich markets for many different kinds of goods. Marketers must pay close attention to major trends and consumer spending patterns both across and within their world markets. Following are some of the major economic trends in the United States.

Economic environment
Factors that affect consumer buying power and spending patterns.

Changes in Income During the 1980s—tabbed the "roaring eighties" by some—American consumers fell into a consumption frenzy, fueled by income growth, federal tax reductions, rapid increases in housing values, and a boom in borrowing. They bought and bought, seemingly without caution, amassing record levels of debt. "It was fashionable to describe yourself as 'born to shop.' When the going gets tough, it was said, the tough go shopping."[26]

During the 1990s, the baby boom generation moved into its prime wage-earning years, and the number of small families headed by dual-career couples continued to increase. Thus, many consumers continued to demand quality products and better service, and they were able to pay for them. However, the free spending and high expectations of the 1980s were dashed by the recession in the early 1990s. In fact, the 1990s become the decade of the

Marketing at Work 4-2
Good Fun: Marketing Recreation to People with Disabilities

Julie Perez sees the difference when she goes to the Divi Hotels resort at Flamingo Beach on the Caribbean island of Bonaire. "It's famous for being totally accessible," she says. "The hotel brochures show the wheelchair access. The dive staff are trained and aware, and they really want to take disabled people diving. They're not afraid." Perez, 35, of Ventura, California, is an experienced scuba diver, a travel agent—and a quadriplegic. Before she had children, she made five trips a year to the Caribbean; these days, she gets there only once or twice a year.

People with disabilities are not only scuba diving, they are playing golf, riding horses, and whitewater rafting. They surf the Internet, work in their gardens, and read. Businesses are beginning to recognize the significance of this vast market of 54 million people who represent almost $1 trillion in spending

power. This spending power is likely to increase even more in the years ahead, as the wealthier, freer-spending baby boomers enter the "age of disabilities." As a result, new stores, services, products, and publications pop up all the time to serve the disabled.

The nonprofit American Association of People with Disabilities publishes *Enable,* a bimonthly magazine that hopes to attract advertising from mainstream corporations. According to *Enable* CEO Sandy Watson, the magazine "educates corporate America that these people exist. You have a target market." *Enable* features a Recreation and Leisure section that, in its inaugural issue, offered features on wheelchair athletes playing basketball, tennis, and rugby ("The hit ain't real till you bend some steel"), a guide to accessible summer camps, and a primer on San Francisco for

travelers with disabilities. Similarly, the Canadian Abilities Foundation provides a Web site (Enable*Link*) and magazine *(Abilities)* targeting people with disabilities.

Catalog shopping is convenient for everyone; those with mobility or other limitations are no exception. The adaptAbility Catalog from S&S Worldwide includes an extensive selection of "Leisure Time" products. These include large-face playing cards, automatic card shufflers, lightweight binoculars that double the size of television images, a pedal exerciser for use from a standard chair, and water dumbbells for low-impact water aerobics. Another S&S catalog features people in wheelchairs using special bowling ramps and bowling-ball pushers, taking shots on a minibasketball set, and playing beanbag horseshoes.

One in four Americans with disabilities is now on the Internet. Gimp

We build cars for people who love to drive. Some of them happen to use

wheelchairs. For these drivers, and for families who transport someone

in a wheelchair, we present the Volkswagen Mobility Access Program.

This is our way of lending a hand to anyone who needs to make a new

Volkswagen® more accessible. If you need to add hand controls, we'll

refund up to $500. If you need to add a lift, we'll refund up to $1000.

After all, when we say "Drivers wanted," we mean every one of them.

All drivers wanted.

Volkswagen targets people with disabilities who want to travel. It offers a Mobility Access Program and has even modified its catchy "Drivers Wanted" tag line to appeal to motorists with disabilities: "All Drivers Wanted."

on the Go (www.gimponthego.com) targets online travelers with disabilities. The Web site offers a searchable database of information on accessible hotels, restaurants, theaters, museums, and other attractions across the United States. Gimp on the Go also provides links to other travel resource sites and offers an online forum through which people with disabilities can exchange ideas and information they have gained through personal experience while traveling.

Volkswagen also targets people with disabilities who want to travel. For example, it recently launched a special marketing campaign for its EuroVan. The campaign touted the EuroVan's extra-wide doors, high ceilings, and overall roominess as features that accommodate most wheelchair lifts and make driving more fun for those traditionally ignored by mainstream automakers. To make the EuroVan even more accessible, Volkswagen offers its Mobility Access Program. Drivers with disabilities who purchase or lease any VW can take advantage of $1,500 in purchase assistance for modifications such as hand controls and wheelchair lifts. Volkswagen even modified its catchy tag line "Drivers Wanted" to appeal to motorists with disabilities, coining the new slogan "All Drivers Wanted."

To further encourage the disability community to get out on the road, Volkswagen cosponsored The Spirit of ADA Torch Relay with the American Association of People with Disabilities. The 24-city tour celebrated the tenth anniversary of the Americans with Disabilities Act. The relay coincided with a countrywide tour, which offered consumers a chance to check out a retrofitted EuroVan at a local dealer. The tour gave people with disabilities who require hand controls or lifts the opportunity for a test drive. The VW Web site sums up, "We build cars for people who love to drive. Some just happen to use wheelchairs."

People in the field, whether in business or as advocates for those with disabilities, have one simple piece of advice for those wanting to tap the disabled market: Make your product as accessible as possible. "Don't design for a disability," says ProMatura Group's Margaret Wylde. "Strive for universal design. A well-designed product is a benefit for lots and lots of people." Universal design means "products designed for the widest number of people," says Mary Lester, associate director of the Alliance for Technology Access, a group that works to make sure people with disabilities have access to the latest and greatest technology.

If a computer is made with built-in options for scanning, or a more wrist-friendly keyboard, "it's a better product," Lester says. Anyone can benefit. "A company can, if it spends time on design from top to bottom, from the packaging to plugging it into the wall, enhance and enlarge its market," says Wylde. For instance, says former alliance director Fred

Fiedler, people with disabilities led the move to "having the on-off button in front of the computer, instead of in the back where no one can reach." Vibrating pagers are another innovation, spurred by the hearing-impaired but now popular with the general population. Oxo kitchen utensils have excellent grips, says Wylde, appealing not only to people with arthritis, but to anyone who prepares food. Its carrot peeler "looks neat, very stylish. Nothing about it says 'disability.'" She also praises Rubbermaid for adding a tab to the lip of its lids. "It's easier to use. Period," Wylde says.

By the same token, make advertising inclusive. "Ads that feature people with disabilities appeal to everyone," says the Packaged Facts report. "Able-bodied persons are not put off by seeing attractive people with disabilities in advertising." Advertisers should keep images positive. "People with disabilities are very sensitive to being portrayed as dependent, vulnerable, or as objects of pity," says Packaged Facts. "Already well aware of the difficulties they face, they like to see images of themselves overcoming these difficulties, transcending their limits, and living life as other people do."

Sources: Adapted from Dan Frost, "The Fun Factor: Marketing Recreation to the Disabled," *American Demographics*, February 1998, pp. 54–58. Also see *Marketing to Americans with Disabilities*, Packaged Facts, New York, 1997; Michelle Wirth Fellman, "Selling IT Goods to Disabled End-Users," *Marketing News*, March 15, 1999, pp. 1, 17; Alison Stein Wellner, "The Internet's Nest Niche," *American Demographics*, September 2000, pp. 18–19; and information accessed online at Volkswagen's Web site (www.vw.com), June 2001.

"squeezed consumer." Along with rising incomes in some segments came increased financial burdens—repaying debts acquired during earlier spending splurges, facing increased household and family expenses, and saving ahead for college tuition payments and retirement. These financially squeezed consumers sobered up, pulled back, and adjusted to their changing financial situations. They spent more carefully and sought greater value in the products and services they bought. *Value marketing* became the watchword for many marketers.

As we move into the 2000s, despite many years of solid economic performance, consumers continue to spend carefully. Hence, the trend toward value marketing continues. Rather than offering high quality at a high price, or lesser quality at very low prices, marketers are looking for ways to offer today's more financially cautious buyers greater value—just the right combination of product quality and good service at a fair price.

Marketers should pay attention to *income distribution* as well as average income. Income distribution in the United States is still very skewed. At the top are *upper-class* consumers, whose spending patterns are not affected by current economic events and who are a major market for luxury goods. There is a comfortable *middle class* that is somewhat careful about its spending but can still afford the good life some of the time. The *working class* must stick close to the basics of food, clothing, and shelter and must try hard to save. Finally, the *underclass* (persons on welfare and many retirees) must count their pennies when making even the most basic purchases.

Over the past three decades, the rich have grown richer, the middle class has shrunk, and the poor have remained poor. In 1998, the top 5 percent of income-earning households in the United States captured more than 21 percent of aggregate income, up from 17.5 percent in 1967. Meanwhile, the share of income captured by the bottom 20 percent of income-earning households decreased from 4 percent to 3.6 percent.[27] This distribution of income has created a two-tiered market. Many companies are aggressively targeting the affluent:

> Driven by . . . low unemployment and inflation, and vast numbers of dual-income boomers in their prime earning years, . . . marketers have responded with a ceaseless array of pricey, upscale products aimed at satisfying wealthy Americans' appetite for "the very best": leather-lined SUVs as big as tanks, $1,300 sheets, restaurant-quality appliances, and vast cruise ships offering every form of luxurious coddling. . . . Huge increases in wealth among the very rich have fueled the sales of $17,500 Patek Philippe watches that are sold as family heirlooms (thus justifying the price tag), created the clamor for a $48,000 Lexus (options extra), and resulted in a two-year waiting list for $14,000 Hermes Kelly bags.[28]

Other companies are now tailoring their marketing offers to two different markets—the affluent and the less affluent. For example, Walt Disney Company markets two distinct Winnie-the-Pooh bears:

> The original line-drawn figure appears on fine china, pewter spoons, and pricey kids' stationery found in upscale specialty and department stores such as Nordstrom and Bloomingdale's. The plump, cartoonlike Pooh, clad in a red shirt and a goofy smile, adorns plastic key chains, polyester bed sheets, and animated videos. It sells in Wal-Mart stores and five-and-dime shops. Except at Disney's own stores, the two Poohs do not share the same retail shelf. [Thus, Disney offers both] upstairs and downstairs Poohs, hoping to land customers on both sides of the [income] divide.[29]

Changing Consumer Spending Patterns Table 4-1 shows the proportion of total expenditures made by U.S. households at different income levels for major categories of goods and services. Food, housing, and transportation use up most household income. However, consumers at different income levels have different spending patterns. Some of these differences were noted over a century ago by Ernst Engel, who studied how people shifted their spending as their income rose. He found that as family income rises, the percentage spent on food declines, the percentage spent on housing remains about constant (except for such utilities as gas, electricity, and public services, which decrease), and both the percentage spent on most other categories and that devoted to savings increase. **Engel's laws** generally have been supported by later studies.

Changes in major economic variables such as income, cost of living, interest rates, and savings and borrowing patterns have a large impact on the marketplace. Companies

Engel's laws
Differences noted over a century ago by Ernst Engel in how people shift their spending across food, housing, transportation, health care, and other goods and services categories as family income rises.

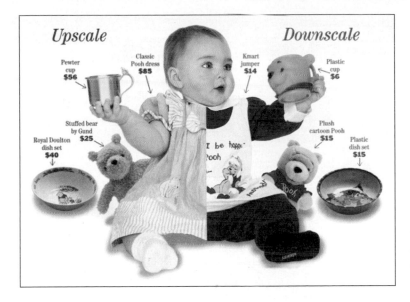

Income distribution: Walt Disney markets two distinct Pooh bears to match its two-tiered market.

watch these variables by using economic forecasting. Businesses do not have to be wiped out by an economic downturn or caught short in a boom. With adequate warning, they can take advantage of changes in the economic environment.

Natural Environment

The **natural environment** involves the natural resources that are needed as inputs by marketers or that are affected by marketing activities. Environmental concerns have grown steadily during the past three decades. Some trend analysts labeled the 1990s as the "Earth Decade," claiming that the natural environment is the major worldwide issue facing business and the public. The Earth Day movement turned 30 in the year 2000. In many cities around the world, air and water pollution have reached dangerous levels. World concern continues to mount about the depletion of the Earth's ozone layer and the resulting "greenhouse effect,"

Natural environment
Natural resources that are needed as inputs by marketers or that are affected by marketing activities.

Table 4-1 Consumer Spending at Different Income Levels			
	Percent of Spending at Different Income Levels		
Expenditure	**$10,000–$15,000**	**$30,000–$40,000**	**$70,000 and Over**
Food	14.8	14.5	11.4
Housing	26.8	24.4	25.6
Utilities	9.3	6.6	4.4
Clothing	4.5	5.4	4.7
Transportation	18.8	19.9	17.4
Health care	8.8	5.6	3.7
Entertainment	4.9	4.8	5.4
Contributions	2.6	3.0	4.3
Insurance	3.0	8.8	15.9

Source: Consumer Expenditure Survey, 1999, U.S. Department of Labor, Bureau of Labor Statistics, accessed online at http://stats.bis.gov/csxstnd.htm#1999, June 2001.

Enlightened companies have responded to concern for the natural environment. Dixon-Ticonderoga developed a crayon made from soybeans, a renewable resource, rather than paraffin wax, a byproduct of oil drilling.

a dangerous warming of the Earth. And many environmentalists fear that we soon will be buried in our own trash.

Marketers should be aware of several trends in the natural environment. The first involves growing *shortages of raw materials.* Air and water may seem to be infinite resources, but some groups see long-run dangers. Air pollution chokes many of the world's large cities, and water shortages are already a big problem in some parts of the United States and the world. Renewable resources, such as forests and food, also have to be used wisely. Nonrenewable resources, such as oil, coal, and various minerals, pose a serious problem. Firms making products that require these scarce resources face large cost increases, even if the materials do remain available.

A second environmental trend is *increased pollution.* Industry will almost always damage the quality of the natural environment. Consider the disposal of chemical and nuclear wastes; the dangerous mercury levels in the ocean; the quantity of chemical pollutants in the soil and food supply; and the littering of the environment with nonbiodegradable bottles, plastics, and other packaging materials.

A third trend is *increased government intervention* in natural resource management. The governments of different countries vary in their concern and efforts to promote a clean environment. Some, like the German government, vigorously pursue environmental quality. Others, especially many poorer nations, do little about pollution, largely because they lack the needed funds or political will. Even the richer nations lack the vast funds and political accord needed to mount a worldwide environmental effort. The general hope is that companies around the world will accept more social responsibility, and that less expensive devices can be found to control and reduce pollution.

In the United States, the Environmental Protection Agency (EPA) was created in 1970 to set and enforce pollution standards and to conduct pollution research. In the future, companies doing business in the United States can expect strong controls from government and pressure groups. Instead of opposing regulation, marketers should help develop solutions to the material and energy problems facing the world.

Concern for the natural environment has spawned the so-called green movement. Today, enlightened companies go beyond what government regulations dictate. They are developing *environmentally sustainable* strategies and practices in an effort to create a world economy that the planet can support indefinitely. They are responding to consumer demands with ecologically safer products, recyclable or biodegradable packaging, better pollution controls, and more energy-efficient operations. 3M runs a Pollution Prevention Pays program that has led to a substantial reduction in pollution and costs. AT&T uses a special software package to choose the least harmful materials, cut hazardous waste, reduce energy use, and improve product recycling in its operations. McDonald's eliminated polystyrene cartons and now uses smaller, recyclable paper wrappings and napkins. Dixon-Ticonderoga, the folks who developed the first pencil made in the United States, developed Prang crayons made from soybeans rather than paraffin wax, a by-product of oil drilling. Soybeans are a renewable resource and produce brighter, richer colors and a smoother texture. More and more, companies are recognizing the link between a healthy economy and a healthy ecology.[30]

Technological Environment

The **technological environment** is perhaps the most dramatic force now shaping our destiny. Technology has released such wonders as antibiotics, organ transplants, notebook computers, and the Internet. It also has released such horrors as nuclear missiles, chemical weapons, and assault rifles. It has released such mixed blessings as the automobile, television, and credit cards. Our attitude toward technology depends on whether we are more impressed with its wonders or its blunders.

> **Technological environment**
> Forces that create new technologies, in turn creating new product and market opportunities.

The technological environment changes rapidly. Think of all of today's common products that were not available 100 years ago or even 30 years ago. Abraham Lincoln did not know about automobiles, airplanes, radios, or the electric light. Woodrow Wilson did not know about television, aerosol cans, automatic dishwashers, room air conditioners, antibiotics, or computers. Franklin Delano Roosevelt did not know about xerography, synthetic detergents, tape recorders, birth control pills, or earth satellites. John F. Kennedy did not know about personal computers, CD players, or the World Wide Web.

New technologies create new markets and opportunities. However, every new technology replaces an older technology. Transistors hurt the vacuum-tube industry, xerography

Technological environment: Technology is perhaps the most dramatic force shaping the marketing environment. Here a Samburu warrior in northern Kenya makes a call on a cellular phone.

hurt the carbon-paper business, the auto hurt the railroads, and compact discs hurt phonograph records. When old industries fought or ignored new technologies, their businesses declined. Thus, marketers should watch the technological environment closely. Companies that do not keep up with technological change soon will find their products outdated. And they will miss new product and market opportunities.

The United States leads the world in research and development spending. Total U.S. R&D spending reached an estimated $277 billion in 2001. The federal government was the largest R&D spender at $72 billion.[31] Scientists today are researching a wide range of promising new products and services, ranging from practical solar energy, electric cars, and cancer cures to voice-controlled computers and genetically engineered food crops. Today's research usually is carried out by research teams rather than by lone inventors such as Thomas Edison, Samuel Morse, or Alexander Graham Bell. Many companies are adding marketing people to R&D teams to try to obtain a stronger marketing orientation. Scientists also speculate on fantasy products, such as flying cars, three-dimensional televisions, and space colonies. The challenge in each case is not only technical but also commercial—to make *practical, affordable* versions of these products.

As products and technology become more complex, the public needs to know that these are safe. Thus, government agencies investigate and ban potentially unsafe products. In the United States, the Federal Food and Drug Administration has set up complex regulations for testing new drugs. The Consumer Product Safety Commission sets safety standards for consumer products and penalizes companies that fail to meet them. Such regulations have resulted in much higher research costs and in longer times between new-product ideas and their introduction. Marketers should be aware of these regulations when applying new technologies and developing new products.

Political Environment

Marketing decisions are strongly affected by developments in the political environment. The **political environment** consists of laws, government agencies, and pressure groups that influence or limit various organizations and individuals in a given society.

Political environment
Laws, government agencies, and pressure groups that influence and limit various organizations and individuals in a given society.

Legislation Regulating Business Even the most liberal advocates of free-market economies agree that the system works best with at least some regulation. Well-conceived regulation can encourage competition and ensure fair markets for goods and services. Thus, governments develop *public policy* to guide commerce—sets of laws and regulations that limit business for the good of society as a whole. Almost every marketing activity is subject to a wide range of laws and regulations.

INCREASING LEGISLATION. Legislation affecting business around the world has increased steadily over the years. The United States has many laws covering issues such as competition, fair trade practices, environmental protection, product safety, truth in advertising, consumer privacy, packaging and labeling, pricing, and other important areas (see Table 4-2). The European Commission has been active in establishing a new framework of laws covering competitive behavior, product standards, product liability, and commercial transactions for the nations of the European Union. Several countries have gone farther than the United States in passing strong consumerism legislation. For example, Norway bans several forms of sales promotion—trading stamps, contests, premiums—as being inappropriate or unfair ways of promoting products. Thailand requires food processors selling national brands to market low-price brands also, so that low-income consumers can find economy brands on the shelves. In India, food companies must obtain special approval to launch brands that duplicate those already existing on the market, such as additional cola drinks or new brands of rice.

Table 4-2   Major U.S. Legislation Affecting Marketing

Legislation	Purpose
Sherman Antitrust Act (1890)	Prohibits monopolies and activities (price fixing, predatory pricing) that restrain trade or competition in interstate commerce.
Federal Food and Drug Act (1906)	Forbids the manufacture or sale of adulterated or fraudulently labeled foods and drugs. Created the Food and Drug Administration.
Clayton Act (1914)	Supplements the Sherman Act by prohibiting certain types of price discrimination, exclusive dealing, and tying clauses (which require a dealer to take additional products in a seller's line).
Federal Trade Commission Act (1914)	Establishes a commission to monitor and remedy unfair trade methods.
Robinson-Patman Act (1936)	Amends Clayton Act to define price discrimination as unlawful. Empowers FTC to establish limits on quantity discounts, forbid some brokerage allowances, and prohibit promotional allowances except when made available on proportionately equal terms.
Wheeler-Lea Act (1938)	Makes deceptive, misleading, and unfair practices illegal regardless of injury to competition. Places advertising of food and drugs under FTC jurisdiction.
Lanham Trademark Act (1946)	Protects and regulates distinctive brand names and trademarks.
National Traffic and Safety Act (1958)	Provides for the creation of compulsory safety standards for automobiles and tires.
Fair Packaging and Labeling Act (1966)	Provides for the regulation of packaging and labeling of consumer goods. Requires that manufacturers state what the package contains, who made it, and how much it contains.
Child Protection Act (1966)	Bans sale of hazardous toys and articles. Sets standards for child resistant packaging.
Federal Cigarette Labeling and Advertising Act (1967)	Requires that cigarette packages contain the following statement: "Warning: The Surgeon General Has Determined That Cigarette Smoking Is Dangerous To Your Health."
National Environmental Policy Act (1969)	Establishes a national policy on the environment. The 1970 Reorganization Plan established the Environmental Protection Agency.
Consumer Product Safety Act (1972)	Establishes the Consumer Product Safety Commission and authorizes it to set safety standards for consumer products as well as exact penalties for failure to uphold those standards.
Magnuson-Moss Warranty Act (1975)	Authorizes the FTC to determine rules and regulations for consumer warranties and provides consumer access to redress, such as the class-action suit.
Children's Television Act (1990)	Limits number of commercials aired during children's programs.
Nutrition Labeling and Education Act (1990)	Requires that food product labels provide detailed nutritional information.
Telephone Consumer Protection Act (1991)	Establishes procedures to avoid unwanted telephone solicitations. Limits marketers' use of automatic telephone dialing systems and artificial or prerecorded voices.

Table 4-2 Major U.S. Legislation Affecting Marketing *(contd.)*	
Legislation	Purpose
Americans with Disabilities Act (1991)	Makes discrimination against people with disabilities illegal in public accommodations, transportation, and telecommunications.
Children's Online Privacy Protection Act (2000)	Prohibits Web sites or online services operators from collecting personal information from children without obtaining consent from a parent and allowing parents to review information collected from their children.

Understanding the public policy implications of a particular marketing activity is not a simple matter. For example, in the United States, there are many laws created at the national, state, and local levels, and these regulations often overlap. Aspirins sold in Dallas are governed both by federal labeling laws and by Texas state advertising laws. Moreover, regulations are constantly changing—what was allowed last year may now be prohibited, and what was prohibited may now be allowed. Marketers must work hard to keep up with changes in regulations and their interpretations.

Business legislation has been enacted for a number of reasons. The first is to *protect companies* from each other. Although business executives may praise competition, they sometimes try to neutralize it when it threatens them. So laws are passed to define and prevent unfair competition. In the United States, such laws are enforced by the Federal Trade Commission and the Antitrust Division of the Attorney General's office.

The second purpose of government regulation is to *protect consumers* from unfair business practices. Some firms, if left alone, would make shoddy products, tell lies in their advertising, and deceive consumers through their packaging and pricing. Unfair business practices have been defined and are enforced by various agencies.

The third purpose of government regulation is to *protect the interests of society* against unrestrained business behavior. Profitable business activity does not always create a better quality of life. Regulation arises to ensure that firms take responsibility for the social costs of their production or products.

CHANGING GOVERNMENT AGENCY ENFORCEMENT. International marketers will encounter dozens, or even hundreds, of agencies set up to enforce trade policies and regulations. In the United States, Congress has established federal regulatory agencies such as the Federal Trade Commission, the Food and Drug Administration, the Interstate Commerce Commission, the Federal Communications Commission, the Federal Power Commission, the Civil Aeronautics Board, the Consumer Products Safety Commission, the Environmental Protection Agency, and the Office of Consumer Affairs. Because such government agencies have some discretion in enforcing the laws, they can have a major impact on a company's marketing performance. At times, the staffs of these agencies have appeared to be overly eager and unpredictable. Some of the agencies sometimes have been dominated by lawyers and economists who lacked a practical sense of how business and marketing work. In recent years, the Federal Trade Commission has added staff marketing experts, who can better understand complex business issues.

New laws and their enforcement will continue or increase. Business executives must watch these developments when planning their products and marketing programs. Marketers need to know about the major laws protecting competition, consumers, and society. They need to understand these laws at the local, state, national, and international levels.

Increased Emphasis on Ethics and Socially Responsible Actions Written regulations cannot possibly cover all potential marketing abuses, and existing laws are often difficult to enforce. However, beyond written laws and regulations, business is also governed by social codes and rules of professional ethics. Enlightened companies encourage their managers to look beyond what the regulatory system allows and simply "do the right thing." These socially responsible firms actively seek out ways to protect the long-run interests of their consumers and the environment. More companies are linking themselves to worthwhile causes and using public relations to build more positive images (see Marketing at Work 4-3).[32]

The recent rash of business scandals and increased concerns about the environment have created fresh interest in the issues of ethics and social responsibility. Almost every aspect of marketing involves such issues. Unfortunately, because these issues usually involve conflicting interests, well-meaning people can honestly disagree about the right course of action in a given situation. Thus, many industrial and professional trade associations have suggested codes of ethics, and many companies now are developing policies and guidelines to deal with complex social responsibility issues.

The boom in e-commerce and Internet marketing has created a new set of social and ethical issues. Privacy issues are the primary concern. For example, Web site visitors often provide extensive personal information that might leave them open to abuse by unscrupulous marketers. Moreover, both Intel and Microsoft have been accused of covert, high-tech computer chip and software invasions of customers' personal computers to obtain information for marketing purposes.

Another cyberspace concern is that of access by vulnerable or unauthorized groups. For example, marketers of adult-oriented materials have found it difficult to restrict access by minors. In a more specific example, sellers using eBay.com, the online auction Web site, recently found themselves the victims of a 13-year-old boy who'd bid on and purchased more than $3 million worth of high-priced antiques and rare artworks on the site. eBay has a strict policy against bidding by anyone under 18 but works largely on the honor system. Unfortunately, this honor system did little to prevent the teenager from taking a cyberspace joyride.[33]

Throughout the text, we present Marketing at Work exhibits that summarize the main public policy and social responsibility issues surrounding major marketing decisions. These exhibits discuss the legal issues that marketers should understand and the common ethical and societal concerns that marketers face. In Chapter 16, we discuss a broad range of societal marketing issues in greater depth.

Cultural Environment

The **cultural environment** is made up of institutions and other forces that affect a society's basic values, perceptions, preferences, and behaviors. People grow up in a particular society that shapes their basic beliefs and values. They absorb a worldview that defines their relationships with others. The following cultural characteristics can affect marketing decision making.

Cultural environment
Institutions and other forces that affect society's basic values, perceptions, preferences, and behaviors.

Persistence of Cultural Values People in a given society hold many beliefs and values. Their core beliefs and values have a high degree of persistence. For example, most Americans believe in working, getting married, giving to charity, and being honest. These beliefs shape more specific attitudes and behaviors found in everyday life. *Core* beliefs and values are passed on from parents to children and are reinforced by schools, churches, business, and government.

Secondary beliefs and values are more open to change. Believing in marriage is a core belief; believing that people should get married early in life is a secondary belief. Marketers have some chance of changing secondary values, but little chance of changing

Marketing at Work 4-3
Cause-Related Marketing: Doing Well by Doing Good

These days, every product seems to be tied to some cause. Buy Purina cat food and help the American Association of Zoological Parks and Aquariums save endangered big cat species. Drink Tang and earn money for Mothers Against Drunk Driving. Drive a Dollar rental car and help support the Special Olympics. Or if you want to help the Leukemia Society of America, buy Helping Hand trash bags or toilet paper. Pay for these purchases with the right charge card and you can support a local cultural arts group or help fight cancer or heart disease.

Cause-related marketing has become one of the hottest forms of corporate giving. It lets companies "do well by doing good" by linking purchases of the company's products or services with fund-raising for worthwhile causes or charitable organizations. Cause-related marketing has grown rapidly since the early 1980s, when American Express offered to donate 1 cent to the restoration of the Statue of Liberty for each use of its charge card. American Express ended up having to contribute $1.7 million, but the cause-related campaign produced a 28 percent increase in card usage.

Companies now sponsor dozens of cause-related marketing campaigns each year. Many are backed by large budgets and a full complement of marketing activities. Here are other examples:

Johnson & Johnson teamed with the Children's Hospital Medical Center and the National Safety Council to sponsor the National Safe Kids Campaign to reduce preventable children's injuries, the leading killer of children. The campaign offered consumers a free Safe Kids safety kit for children in exchange for proofs of purchase. Consumers could also buy a Child's Safety Video for $9.95. The video featured a game-show format that made learning about safety entertaining as well as educational. To promote the campaign, Johnson & Johnson distributed almost 50 million advertising inserts in daily newspapers and developed a special information kit for retailers containing posters, floor displays, and other in-store promotion materials. The National Safe Kids Campaign now has grown into an independent organization made up of 300 state and local coalitions across America. Johnson & Johnson continues to support the organization with millions of dollars in annual grants, public awareness campaigns, corporate advertising, and retail promotions.

Since 1993, American Express has joined with Share Our Strength (SOS), a hunger-relief organization, to sponsor its Charge Against Hunger program. Every time someone uses an American Express card between November 1 and December 31, the company donates 3 cents to SOS, up to a total of $5 million per year. In recent years, dozens of other corporations have "joined the charge," including Tyson's Foods, Evian, AOL, Yahoo!, Gallo, Barnes & Noble, Bloomingdale's, Macy's, Williams-Sonoma, Kraft Foods, and KitchenAid. The program has been highly successful. So far, SOS has raised more than $90 million. And American Express has found that the program has increased card transactions, merchant card acceptance, and cardholder support.

Avon, the world's largest direct seller of cosmetics and beauty items, has for years sponsored programs aimed at raising national

Cause-related marketing: As part of its Breast Cancer Awareness Crusade, Avon annually sponsors a series of dramatic fundraising walks called the Avon Breast Cancer 3-Day. Proceeds support programs that provide low-income, minority, and older women with education and early cancer screening services.

and global awareness of breast cancer, a problem afflicting its target audience—women. Avon's Breast Cancer Awareness Crusade in the United States raises money for programs that provide women—especially low-income, minority, and older women—with education and early cancer screening services. The company sells products featuring a pink ribbon (the international symbol of breast cancer) through its 450,000 sales representatives, then donates proceeds to nonprofit and university-based programs. Avon publicizes these efforts in its bimonthly sales brochures to 15 million U.S. customers and on its Web site. In addition, the company's famous in-person sales force is fully briefed on the company's efforts, putting a familiar face on the campaign. "The message in the United States and across all of the countries (where Avon does business) is the same: We're looking to position Avon as the company for women, whether that's the place to buy a product, to start your own business, where your health needs are addressed, (or) to function as an advocate on behalf of women's health," says Joanne Mazurki, Avon's director of global cause-related marketing.

Cause-related marketing has stirred some controversy. Critics are concerned that cause-related marketing might eventually undercut traditional "no-strings" corporate giving, as more and more companies grow to expect marketing benefits from their contributions. Critics also worry that cause-related marketing will cause a shift in corporate charitable support toward more visible, popular, and low-risk charities—those with more certain and substantial marketing appeal. For example, MasterCard's "Choose to Make a Difference" campaign raises money for six charities, each selected in part because of its popularity in a consumer poll. Finally, critics worry that cause-related marketing is more a strategy for selling than a strategy for giving, that "cause-related" marketing is really "cause-exploitative" marketing. Thus, companies using cause-related marketing might find themselves walking a fine line between increased sales and an improved image, and facing charges of exploitation.

However, if handled well, cause-related marketing can greatly benefit both the company and the cause. The company gains an effective marketing tool while building a more positive public image. One recent study found that 61 percent of consumers believe that cause-related marketing should be a standard practice. Some 83 percent say they have a more positive image of a company that supports a cause they care about and two-thirds say that if price and quality are equal, they are likely to switch to a civic-minded brand or retailer. Similarly, the charitable organization or cause gains greater visibility and important new sources of funding. This additional funding can be substantial. In total, such campaigns now contribute some $100 million annually to the coffers of charitable organizations, and surveys show that these cause-related contributions usually add to, rather than undercut, direct company contributions. Thus, when cause marketing works, everyone wins.

Sources: See Nancy Arnott, "Marketing with a Passion," *Sales and Marketing Management*, January 1994, pp. 64–71; Minette E. Drumwright, "Company Advertising with a Social Dimension: The Role of Noneconomic Criteria," *Journal of Marketing*, October 1996, pp. 71–87; Jerry C. Welsh, "Good Cause, Good Business," *Harvard Business Review*, September–October 1999, pp. 21–24; Mercedes M. Cardona, "Marketers Think Pink for Breast Cancer Awareness," *Advertising Age*, October 23, 2000, p. 18; and Michael Jay Polonsky and Greg Wood, "Can the Overcommercialization of Cause-Related Marketing Harm Society?" *Journal of Macromarketing*, June 2001, pp. 8, 15.

core values. For example, family-planning marketers could argue more effectively that people should get married later than that they should not get married at all.

Shifts in Secondary Cultural Values Although core values are fairly persistent, cultural swings do take place. Consider the impact of popular music groups, movie personalities, and other celebrities on young people's hairstyling, clothing, and sexual norms. Marketers want to predict cultural shifts in order to spot new opportunities or threats. Several firms offer "futures" forecasts in this connection, such as the Yankelovich Monitor, Market Facts' Brain-Waves Group, and the Trends Research Institute.

The Yankelovich Monitor has tracked consumer value trends for years. At the dawn of the twenty-first century, it looked back to capture lessons from the past decade that might offer insight into the 2000s. It identified the following eight major consumer themes:

1. *Paradox:* People agree that "Life is getting better and worse at the same time."
2. *Trust not:* Confidence in doctors, public schools, TV news, newspapers, federal government, and corporations drops sharply.
3. *Go it alone:* More people agree with the statement "I rely more on my own instincts than on experts."
4. *Smarts really count:* For example, fewer people agree with "It's risky to buy a brand you are not familiar with."
5. *No sacrifices:* For example, many people claim that looks are important but not at any price, that keeping house for show instead of comfort is over, and that giving up taste for nutrition is no longer acceptable.
6. *Stress hard to beat:* For example, more people claim that they are "concerned about getting enough rest."
7. *Reciprocity is the way to go:* More people agree that "Everybody should feel free to do his or her own thing."
8. *Me.2:* For example, people express the need to live in a world that is built by "me," not by you.

Yankelovich maintains that the decade drivers for the 2000s will primarily come from the baby boomers and Generation Xers. The baby boomers will be driven by four factors in the 2000s: "adventure" (fueled by a sense of youthfulness), "smarts" (fueled by a sense of empowerment and willingness to accept change), "intergenerational support" (caring for younger and older, often in nontraditional arrangements), and "retreading" (embracing early retirement with second career or phase of their work life). Gen Xers will be driven by three factors: "redefining the good life" (highly motivated to improve their economic well-being and remain in control), "new rituals" (returning to traditional values but with a tolerant mind-set and active lifestyle), and "cutting and pasting" (balancing work, play, sleep, family, and other aspects of their lives).

The major cultural values of a society are expressed in people's views of themselves and others, as well as in their views of organizations, society, nature, and the universe.

PEOPLE'S VIEWS OF THEMSELVES. People vary in their emphasis on serving themselves versus serving others. Some people seek personal pleasure, wanting fun, change, and escape. Others seek self-realization through religion, recreation, or the avid pursuit of careers or other life goals. People use products, brands, and services as a means of self-expression, and they buy products and services that match their views of themselves.

In the 1980s, personal ambition and materialism increased dramatically, with significant marketing implications. In a "me society," people buy their "dream cars" and take their "dream vacations." They tended to spend to the limit on self-indulgent goods and services. Today, in contrast, people are adopting more conservative behaviors and ambitions. Moving into the new millennium, materialism, flashy spending, and self-indulgence have been replaced by more sensible spending, saving, family concerns, and helping others. The maturing baby boomers are limiting their spending to products and services that improve their lives instead of boosting their images. This suggests a bright future for products and services that serve basic needs and provide real value rather than those relying on glitz and hype.

PEOPLE'S VIEWS OF OTHERS. Recently, observers have noted a shift from a "me society" to a "we society" in which more people want to be with and serve others. Notes one trend tracker, "People want to get out, especially those 48 million people working out of their home and feeling a little cooped-up [and] all those shut-ins who feel unfulfilled by the cyberstuff that was supposed to make them feel like never leaving home."[34] This trend suggests a greater demand for "social support" products and services that improve direct communication between people, such as health clubs and family vacations.

PEOPLE'S VIEWS OF ORGANIZATIONS. People vary in their attitudes toward corporations, government agencies, trade unions, universities, and other organizations. By and large, people are willing to work for major organizations and expect them, in turn, to carry out society's work. The late 1980s saw a sharp decrease in confidence in and loyalty toward America's business and political organizations and institutions. In the workplace, there has been an overall decline in organizational loyalty. During the 1990s, waves of company downsizings bred cynicism and distrust. Many people today see work not as a source of satisfaction but as a required chore to earn money to enjoy their nonwork hours. This trend suggests that organizations need to find new ways to win consumer and employee confidence.

PEOPLE'S VIEWS OF SOCIETY. People vary in their attitudes toward their society; patriots defend it, reformers want to change it, malcontents want to leave it. People's orientation to their society influences their consumption patterns, levels of savings, and attitudes toward the marketplace. The last two decades have seen an increase in consumer patriotism. For example, one study showed that more than 80 percent of those surveyed say, "Americans should always try to buy American"—up from 72 percent in 1972.[35] Many U.S. companies have responded with "made in America" themes and flag-waving promotions. For example, Black & Decker added a flaglike symbol to its tools. And for the past several years, the American textile industry has blitzed consumers with its "Crafted with Pride in the USA" advertising campaign, insisting that "made in the USA" matters.

PEOPLE'S VIEWS OF NATURE. People vary in their attitudes toward the natural world. Some feel ruled by it, others feel in harmony with it, and still others seek to master it. A long-term trend has been people's growing mastery over nature through technology and the belief that nature is bountiful. More recently, however, people have recognized that nature is finite and fragile, that it can be destroyed or spoiled by human activities.

Love of nature is leading to more camping, hiking, boating, fishing, and other outdoor activities. Business has responded by offering more products and services catering to these interests. Tour operators are offering more wilderness adventures, and retailers are offering more fitness gear and apparel. Marketing communicators are using appealing natural backgrounds in advertising their products. And food producers have found growing markets for natural and organic foods. Natural and organic products are now a $25 billion industry, growing at a rate of 20 percent annually. Niche marketers, such as Whole Foods Markets, have sprung up to serve this market, and traditional food chains such as Kroger and Safeway have added separate natural and organic food sections.[36]

PEOPLE'S VIEWS OF THE UNIVERSE. Finally, people vary in their beliefs about the origin of the universe and their place in it. Although most Americans practice religion, religious conviction and practice have been dropping off gradually through the years. Some futurists, however, have noted a renewed interest in spirituality, perhaps as a part of a broader search for a new inner purpose. People have been moving away from materialism and dog-eat-dog ambition to seek more permanent values—family, community, earth, faith—and a more certain grasp of right and wrong.

"Americans are on a spiritual journey," observes one expert, "increasingly concerned with the meaning of life and issues of the soul and spirit. The journey can encompass religion, but it is much more likely to take the form of . . . 'spiritual individualism.'" This new spiritualism affects consumers in everything from the television shows they watch and the books they read to the products and services they buy. "Since consumers don't park their beliefs and values on the bench outside the marketplace," adds the expert, "they are bringing this awareness to the brands they buy. Tapping into this heightened sensitivity presents a unique marketing opportunity for brands."[37]

Linking the Concepts

Slow down and cool your engine. You've now read about a large number of environmental forces. How are all of these environments *linked* with each other? With company marketing strategy?

◆ How are major demographic forces linked with economic changes? With major cultural trends? How are the natural and technological environments linked? Think of an example of a company that has recognized one of these links and turned it into a marketing opportunity.

◆ Is the marketing environment uncontrollable—something that the company can only prepare for and react to? Or can companies be proactive in changing environmental factors? Think of a good example that makes your point, then read on.

Responding to the Marketing Environment

Someone once observed, "There are three kinds of companies: those who make things happen; those who watch things happen; and those who wonder what's happened."[38] Many companies view the marketing environment as an uncontrollable element to which they must adapt. They passively accept the marketing environment and do not try to change it. They analyze the environmental forces and design strategies that will help the company avoid the threats and take advantage of the opportunities the environment provides.

Environmental management perspective
A management perspective in which the firm takes aggressive actions to affect the publics and forces in its marketing environment rather than simply watching and reacting to them.

Other companies take an **environmental management perspective.**[39] Rather than simply watching and reacting, these firms take aggressive actions to affect the publics and forces in their marketing environment. Such companies hire lobbyists to influence legislation affecting their industries and stage media events to gain favorable press coverage. They run advertorials (ads expressing editorial points of view) to shape public opinion. They press lawsuits and file complaints with regulators to keep competitors in line, and they form contractual agreements to better control their distribution channels.

Often, companies can find positive ways to overcome seemingly uncontrollable environmental constraints. For example:

> Cathay Pacific Airlines . . . determined that many travelers were avoiding Hong Kong because of lengthy delays at immigration. Rather than assuming that this was a problem they could not solve, Cathay's senior staff asked the Hong Kong government how to avoid these immigration delays. After lengthy discussions, the airline agreed to make an annual grant-in-aid to the government to hire more immigration inspectors—but these reinforcements would service primarily the Cathay Pacific gates. The reduced waiting period increased customer value and thus strengthened [Cathay's competitive advantage]. [40]

Marketing management cannot always control environmental forces. In many cases, it must settle for simply watching and reacting to the environment. For example, a company would have little success trying to influence geographic population shifts, the economic environment, or major cultural values. But whenever possible, smart marketing managers will take a *proactive* rather than *reactive* approach to the marketing environment (see Marketing at Work 4-4).

Marketing at Work 4-4
YourCompanySucks.com

Richard Hatch is one of the few people in this world with a passion for both Harley-Davidson motorcycles and collecting dolls and cute little toys. One day in 1997, the tattooed, 210-pound Hatch got into a shouting match with an employee in his local Wal-Mart and was banned from the store. Hatch claims that his actions didn't warrant his ouster. He says he'd complained to store managers for months that employees were snapping up the best Hot Wheels and NASCAR collectible toy cars before they hit the shelves.

Wal-Mart didn't budge and the angry Hatch retaliated. He hired a Web designer and created the Wal-Mart Sucks Web site (www.walmartsucks.com). In only a few years, according to one

account, the Web site "sprouted beyond Hatch's wildest dreams of revenge. [Thousands] of customers have written in to attack rude store managers, complain about alleged insects in the aisles, offer shoplifting tips, and, from time to time, write romantic odes to cashiers." Hatch, who has amassed some 5,000 Beanie Babies, also had a dispute with employees at his local Toys 'R' Us store about similar complaints. He was banished from there as well. His response? You guessed it: another sucks.com Web site (www.toysrussucks.com).

An extreme event? Not anymore. As more and more well-intentioned grassroots organizations, consumer watchdog groups, or just plain angry consumers take their gripes to the Web, such "sucks.com" sites

are becoming almost commonplace. A recent Google.com search for the words *ihate* and *sucks* yielded dozens of pages of hits. According to one source, more than half of the Fortune 1000 companies have encountered some type of Web site critical of their businesses. The sites target some highly respected companies with some highly *dis*respectful labels: Microsucks; Gapsucks.org; NonAmazon; Starbucked; BestBuy-sucks; The I Hate McDonald's Page; Just Do Not Do It (Nike); America Offline; Untied Airlines: The Most Unfriendly Skies; The Unofficial BMW Lemon Site; AllStateInsurancesucks ("Their hands in your pockets") ; and Dunkindonuts.org (featuring "unhappy tales about coffee, crullers, and cinnamon buns"); to

Environmental management: The best strategy for dealing with consumer hate sites is to address complaints directly. "If a company solves my problem, why would I keep up the Web site?"

name only a few. Some of these attack sites are little more than a nuisance. Others, however, can draw serious attention and create real headaches. "The same people who used to stand on [the] corner and rail against things to 20 people now can put up a Web site and rail in front of 2 million people," says William Comcowich, whose firm helps companies monitor what's said about them on the Internet.

How should companies react to these attack sites? The real quandary for targeted companies is figuring out how far they can go to protect their image without fueling the fire already raging at the sites. One point upon which all experts seem to agree: Don't try to retaliate in kind. "Avoid 'testosterosis'—or the urge to hit someone in the face because they are doing something you don't like," advises one consultant. "It's a free country, and the Web is completely unregulated. Don't get angry and think about doing foolish things."

Some companies have tried to silence the critics through lawsuits but few have succeeded. For example, McDonald's sued one such site for libel; it spent $16 million on the case and won the suit but received only $94,000 in damages. Wal-Mart's attorneys threatened Hatch with legal action unless he shut down his Wal-Mart sucks Web site. However, Hatch stood up to the $215 billion retailer, and Wal-Mart eventually backed down. As it turns out, a company has legal recourse only when the unauthorized use of its trademarks, brand names, or other intellectual property is apt to be confusing to the public. And no reasonable person is likely to be confused that Wal-Mart maintains and supports a site

tagged Walmartsucks.com. Beyond the finer legal points, Wal-Mart also feared that a lawsuit would draw only more attention to the consumer hate site. An industry analyst comments: "Those who operate hate sites adore posting cease-and-desist letters they receive from corporate attorneys. Such letters also validate their fight for the cause, whatever they perceive that to be, and they can use them to cast yet another negative spotlight on the company. They revel in the attention."

Given the difficulties of trying to sue consumer hate sites out of existence, some companies have tried other strategies. For example, most big companies now routinely buy up Web addresses for their firm names preceded by the words "Ihate" or followed by "sucks.com." In general, however, attempts to block, counterattack, or shut down consumer hate sites may be shortsighted. Such sites are often based on real consumer concerns. Hence, the best strategy might be to proactively monitor these sites and respond positively to the concerns they express.

Some targeted companies actively listen to concerns posted on hate sites and develop Web presentations to tell their own side of the story. For example, Nike is the target of at least eight different attack sites, mostly criticizing it for alleged unfair labor practices in Southeast Asia. In response, Nike commissioned an independent investigation of labor practices in its Indonesian factories and presented the results on its own Web site (www.Nikebiz.com/social/labor). Monitoring consumer hate sites can yield additional benefits. For example, some sites can actually provide

the targeted company with useful information. Walmartsucks.com posts customers' ratings of local stores for cleanliness, prices, and customer service, information that would be costly for Wal-Mart to develop on its own.

According to James Alexander, president of EWatch, an Internet monitoring service, the best strategy for dealing with consumer hate sites is to address their complaints directly. "If a company solves my problem," he says, "why would I keep up the Web site?" Take Dunkin' Donuts, for example:

After a disgruntled customer established dunkindonuts.org, an attack site that appeared on many Internet search engines ahead of the company's own Web page, the company contacted about 25 people who had written in with complaints and offered them coupons for free donuts. "If this was where customers were going to post their comments, we thought it was important for us to go ahead and address them," says spokesperson Jennifer Rosenberg. Now, the company is in negotiations to buy the site from its founder, 25-year-old David Felton, who says he'll sell because "they have been taking complaints and responding."

By proactively responding to a seemingly uncontrollable event in its environment, Dunkin' Donuts has been able to turn a negative into a positive. At Dunkin', sucks.com is now all smiles.com.

Sources: Quotes and excerpts from Leslie Goff, "[YourCompanyNameHere].sucks.com," *Computerworld*, July 20, 1998, pp. 57–58; and Mike France, "A Site for Soreheads," *Business Week*, April 12, 1999, pp. 86–90. Also see Oscar S. Cisneros, "Legal Tips for Your 'Sucks' Site," accessed online at www.wired.com, August 14, 2000 and Ronald F. Lopez, "Corporate Strategies for Addressing Internet "Complaint" Sites," accessed online at www.constructionweblinks.com, June 25, 2001.

STOP   *Rest Stop: Reviewing the Concepts*

In the last chapter, this chapter, and the next two chapters, you'll examine the environments of marketing and how companies analyze these environments to discover opportunities and create effective marketing strategies. Companies must constantly watch and adapt to the *marketing environment* in order to seek opportunities and ward off threats. The marketing environment comprises all the actors and forces influencing the company's ability to transact business effectively with its target market.

1. Describe the environmental forces that affect the company's ability to serve its customers.

The company's *microenvironment* consists of other actors close to the company that combine to form the company's value delivery network or that affect its ability to serve its customers. It includes the company's *internal environment*—its several departments and management levels—as it influences marketing decision making. *Marketing channel firms*—suppliers and marketing intermediaries, including resellers, physical distribution firms, marketing services agencies, and financial intermediaries—cooperate to create customer value. Five types of customer *markets* include consumer, business, reseller, government, and international markets. *Competitors* vie with the company in an effort to serve customers better. Finally, various *publics* have an actual or potential interest in or impact on the company's ability to meet its objectives.

The *macroenvironment* consists of larger societal forces that affect the entire microenvironment. The six forces making up the company's macroenvironment include demographic, economic, natural, technological, political, and cultural forces. These forces shape opportunities and pose threats to the company.

2. Explain how changes in the demographic and economic environments affect marketing decisions.

Demography is the study of the characteristics of human populations. Today's *demographic environment* shows a changing age structure, shifting family profiles, geographic population shifts, a better-educated and more white-collar population, and increasing diversity. The *economic environment* consists of factors that affect buying power and patterns. The economic environment is characterized by more consumer concern for value and shifting consumer spending patterns. Today's squeezed consumers are seeking greater value—just the right

combination of good quality and service at a fair price. The distribution of income also is shifting. The rich have grown richer, the middle class has shrunk, and the poor have remained poor, leading to a two-tiered market. Many companies now tailor their marketing offers to two different markets—the affluent and the less affluent.

3. Identify the major trends in the firm's natural and technological environments.

The *natural environment* shows three major trends: shortages of certain raw materials, higher pollution levels, and more government intervention in natural resource management. Environmental concerns create marketing opportunities for alert companies. The marketer should watch for four major trends in the *technological environment:* the rapid pace of technological change, high R&D budgets, the concentration by companies on minor product improvements, and increased government regulation. Companies that fail to keep up with technological change will miss out on new product and marketing opportunities.

4. Explain the key changes in the political and cultural environments.

The *political environment* consists of laws, agencies, and groups that influence or limit marketing actions. The political environment has undergone three changes that affect marketing worldwide: increasing legislation regulating business, strong government agency enforcement, and greater emphasis on ethics and socially responsible actions. The *cultural environment* is made up of institutions and forces that affect a society's values, perceptions, preferences, and behaviors. The environment shows long-term trends toward a "we society," a lessening trust of institutions, increasing patriotism, greater appreciation for nature, a new spiritualism, and the search for more meaningful and enduring values.

5. Discuss how companies can react to the marketing environment.

Companies can passively accept the marketing environment as an uncontrollable element to which they must adapt, avoiding threats and taking advantage of opportunities as they arise. Or they can take an *environmental management perspective*, proactively working to change the environment rather than simply reacting to it. Whenever possible, companies should try to be proactive rather than reactive.

Navigating the Key Terms

For a detailed analysis of the meaning and importance of each of the following key terms, visit our Web page at www.prenhall.com/kotler.

Baby boomers
Cultural environment
Demography

Economic environment
Engel's laws
Environmental management
  perspective
Generation X
Generation Y
Macroenvironment
Marketing environment

Marketing intermediaries
Microenvironment
Natural environment
Political environment
Public
Technological environment

Travel Log

The following concept checks and discussion questions will help you to keep track of and apply the concepts you've studied in this chapter.

Concept Checks

Fill in the blanks, then look for the correct answers.

1. A company's _____ consists of the actors and forces outside marketing that affect marketing management's ability to develop and maintain successful relationships with its target customers.

2. The _____ consists of the forces close to the company that affect its ability to serve its customers—the company, marketing channel firms, customer markets, competitors, and publics.

3. _____ (such as resellers, physical distribution firms, marketing services agencies, and financial intermediaries) help the company to promote, sell, and distribute its goods to final buyers.

4. The company's marketing environment includes various publics. If a company's marketing decisions were questioned by residents of a neighborhood or a community organization, then the company would need to develop strategies to respond to these _____ publics.

5. One distinguishing characteristic of Generation Y is their utter fluency and comfort with computer, digital, and Internet technology. For this reason, this generation has also been called _____ _____.

6. One of _____ laws is that as family income rises, the percentage spent on food declines.

7. Marketers should be aware of several trends in the natural environment. Chief among these are the _____ , _____ , and _____ .

8. Business legislation has been enacted for a number of reasons. Chief among these are: to protect _____ _____ , to protect _____ _____ , and to protect _____ .

9. The major cultural values of a society are expressed in people's views of themselves and others. Recent studies suggest that consumers are interested in getting out more, in family concerns, and in helping others. This is evidence that our society is moving more towards a "____-society."

10. Companies that take an _____ _____ take aggressive actions to affect the publics and forces in their marketing environment rather than simply watching and reacting to them.

Concept Checks Answers: 1. marketing environment; 2. microenvironment; 3. Marketing intermediaries; 4. local; 5. net-gens (or n-gens); 6. Engel's; 7. growing shortages of raw materials, increased pollution, and increased government intervention in natural resource management; 8. companies from each other, consumers from unfair business practices, and the interests of society against unrestrained business behavior; 9. we; 10. environmental management perspective.

Discussing the Issues

1. In the 1930s, President Franklin Roosevelt used his cigarette holder as a personal "trademark." Would a president be seen smoking today? Discuss how the cultural environment has changed. Considering the rash of recent court rulings and settlements concerning the tobacco industry, how might a cigarette manufacturer market its products differently to meet this new environment? What do you think are the long-term prospects for the industry?

2. Describe what "millennial fever" is and cite several examples. How can marketers use this phenomenon in designing their marketing strategies? What products are you nostalgic about?

3. It has been said that the single most important demographic trend in the United States is the changing age structure of the population. Characterize the differences between Baby Boomers, Generation X, and Generation Y. Using a personal computer for your example, indicate how this product should be sold to someone in each of the three aforementioned generations. Lastly, let us call the next generation on the horizon Generation D (the digital generation). What would you forecast for the preferences and buying patterns of this generation? Explain.

4. There is increasing pressure for businesses to be more ethically and socially responsible for their actions. One area where this has become increasingly important is e-commerce on the Internet. What do you think online businesses can do to be more ethical and socially responsible? Give an illustration. Next, give an illustration of an organization that does not seem be behaving in an ethical or socially responsible manner. What would you propose to correct their failure in this area?

5. Companies that maintain an environmental management perspective take positive proactive stances when confronted with problems rather than merely reacting to adversity. After reading about the controversies presented in Marketing at Work 4-4, assume your company is under attack by Mr. Richard Hatch. What would you do to meet the situation with proactive measures? What could you do to minimize negative publicity and consumer response? Explain your plan.

 ## Mastering Marketing

Understanding one's environment is critical for any marketing manager. An environmental management perspective can literally make or break a company. Examine each of the environments and their respective publics faced by CanGo. List the critical factors in each of these environments that must be proactively met by the company for its marketing plan to be implemented. Of the environments examined, which one do you think is most critical to the firm's long-term success? Explain.

 ## Traveling on the Net

Point of Interest: Product Appeals to Increasing Diversity

What do Levi Strauss, Procter & Gamble, General Mills, and M&Ms all have in common? If you said that they are all capitalizing on the trend toward more cultural diversity in the American marketplace by producing products that are aimed at ethnic and racial groups, you are correct. Mars Candy, makers of those lovable M&Ms, is the latest company to have discovered the potential gold mine that awaits those that pursue diversity policies and strategies. A new flavor of M&Ms is just hitting the retail shelves called Dulce de Leche-Carmel Candy. The five premiere markets for the new flavor that is specifically targeted to the growing Hispanic population are Miami, Los Angeles, San Diego, San Antonio, and McAllen-Brownsville, Texas. These cities have the largest concentrations of Hispanics in the U.S. Mars believes that the 35+ million Hispanics in the U.S. (with a purchasing power of $325 billion) are a market that is just too good to pass up. Dulce de Leche (caramelized sweetened condensed milk) is a flavor that has long been popular in Latin America. No matter which Hispanic culture you come from, Dulce de Leche is the "it" flavor to answer one's sweet tooth call. This new M&M flavor will be the sixth flavor extension for the popular brand. A distinctive red and yellow package will be used to showcase the new product. Will it ever replace the old standby dark brown M&Ms package ? Most chocolate lovers say "no way." However, Hispanics are expected to give Dulce de Leche an overwhelming vote of approval.

For Discussion

1. Given the universal appeal of milk chocolate M&Ms, why would Mars consider a new strategy of making a special product aimed at an ethnic group? Provide additional facts to support your answer.
2. What other examples can you provide that demonstrate the popularity of diversity approaches in marketing? Be specific with your answers.
3. After going to the M&Ms Web site (www.m-ms.com), analyze the M&M Network material provided. In what

target markets does the company show the most interest? How does the company attempt to capture your attention? What new facts did you learn about the company and its products?

4. Are there dangers in pursuing market segmentation and new product development based on diversity? If so, explain what these might be.

Application Thinking

Assume that your marketing team has been assigned the task of following up on the success of the Dulce de Leche product for M&Ms. With an eye towards generational and diversity marketing, what new flavors, candy colors, or product line extensions would you suggest to your marketing team? Explain your choices and how you would investigate the feasibility of such options.

 ## MAP—Marketing Applications

MAP Stop 4

When Stanford University graduate students Jerry Yang and David Filo developed Yahoo, they had little idea how far their revolutionary concept would go. Their original concept was to make "wasting time on the Internet" easier. Commercial applications came later. Today, more Internet users recognize the name Yahoo than Microsoft. One of the reasons for the search engine's popularity is its ability to focus on people's tastes rather than just delivering information or access to every Web site possible. Yahoo has become a full-blown package of information and services specifically focusing on the sub-topics of health, real estate, search, news, personalization, travel, and shopping. The challenge facing Yahoo today (as it has been in the past) is how to convince Corporate America that it can get a big bang for its bucks by advertising online with Yahoo's search engine service. However, this may not be an easy task, as recent events have shown. Huge challenges to Yahoo's traditional market base have been issued by AOL/Time-Warner and Microsoft. With badly decaying revenues, Yahoo released long-time CEO Timothy Koogle and brought in former Warner Bros. co-CEO Terry Semel to diversify the company. One of Semel's first tasks was to consider the competitive and market environment faced by Yahoo and then find new sources of revenue. Selling entertainment to customers, shoring up advertising revenues, and expanding its custom-made Web site business has to be Job #1 for Semel. If

the company can capitalize quickly on changing Net opportunities, shareholders may once again be singing "Yahoo!"

Thinking Like a Marketing Manager

1. How will a search engine like Yahoo affect a marketing company's technological environment? What makes Yahoo unique?
2. Pick a product or service category of your choice. Go to Yahoo at www.yahoo.com and review other sites for competing products or services in your chosen category. Think about how your product or service could be marketed via a Web site. What could Yahoo do to enhance the ability of your product or service site to be an "instant" success? What type of ads would you consider investing in on Yahoo?
3. Find out how much an ad costs on Yahoo. Evaluate whether this is a good deal or not. Explain your evaluation.
4. Keeping in mind how rapidly the Internet environment is changing and what you have just read about Yahoo, how do you think Yahoo will fare in the future? What critical issues or strategies must the company face or design? If you were the marketing manager of Yahoo, what future strategic alliances would you begin to investigate?
5. AOL/Time-Warner specializes in entertainment content. What should Yahoo do to offset this advantage? Explain.

chapter 5

Managing Marketing Information

ROAD MAP:
Previewing the Concepts

In the last chapter, you learned about the complex and changing marketing environment. In this chapter, we'll look at how companies develop and manage information about important elements of the environment—about their customers, competitors, products, and marketing programs. We'll examine marketing information systems designed to give managers the right information, in the right form, at the right time to help them make better marketing decisions. We'll also take a close look at the marketing research process and at some special marketing research considerations. To succeed in today's marketplace, companies must know how to manage mountains of marketing information effectively.

▶ After reading this chapter, you should be able to

1. explain the importance of information to the company
2. define the marketing information system and discuss its parts
3. outline the steps In the marketing research process
4. explain how companies analyze and distribute marketing information
5. discuss the special issues some marketing researchers face, including public policy and ethics issues

We'll start the chapter with a look at a classic marketing blunder—Coca-Cola's ill-considered decision some years ago to introduce New Coke. The company based its decision on substantial marketing research, yet the new product fizzled badly. As you read on, ask yourself how a large and resourceful marketing company such as Coca-Cola could make such a huge research mistake. The moral: If it can happen to Coca-Cola, it can happen to any company.

In 1985, in what has now become an all-time classic marketing tale, the Coca-Cola Company made a major marketing blunder. After 99 successful years, it set aside its long-standing rule—"Don't mess with Mother Coke"—and dropped its original formula Coke! In its place came *New* Coke with a sweeter, smoother taste.

At first, amid the introductory flurry of advertising and publicity, New Coke sold well. But sales soon went flat, as a stunned public reacted. Coke began receiving sacks of mail and more than 1,500 phone calls each day from angry consumers. A group called "Old Cola Drinkers" staged protests, handed out T-shirts, and threatened a class-action suit unless Coca-Cola brought back the old formula. After only three months, the Coca-Cola Company brought old Coke back. Now called "Coke Classic," it sold side-by-side with New Coke on supermarket shelves. The company said that New Coke would remain its flagship brand, but consumers had a different idea. By the end of that year, Classic was outselling New Coke in supermarkets by two to one.

Quick reaction saved the company from potential disaster. It stepped up efforts for Coke Classic and slotted New Coke into a supporting role. Coke Classic again became the company's main brand and the country's leading soft drink. New Coke became the company's "attack brand"—its Pepsi stopper—and ads boldly compared New Coke's taste with Pepsi's. Still, New Coke managed only a 2 percent market share. In the spring of 1990, the company repackaged New Coke and relaunched it as a brand extension with a new name, Coke II. Today, Coke Classic captures more than 20 percent of the U.S. soft drink market; Coke II has quietly disappeared.

Why was New Coke introduced in the first place? What went wrong? Many analysts blame the blunder on poor marketing research.

In the early 1980s, although Coke was still the leading soft drink, it was slowly losing market share to Pepsi. For years, Pepsi had successfully mounted the "Pepsi Challenge," a series of televised taste tests showing that consumers preferred the sweeter taste of Pepsi. By early 1985, although Coke led in the overall market, Pepsi led in share of supermarket sales by 2 percent. (That doesn't sound like much, but 2 percent of today's huge U.S. soft drink market amounts to more than $1.2 billion in retail sales!) Coca-Cola had to do something to stop the loss of its market share, and the solution appeared to be a change in Coke's taste.

Coca-Cola began the largest new-product research project in the company's history. It spent more than two years and $4 million on research before settling on a new formula. It conducted some 200,000 taste tests—30,000 on the final formula alone. In blind tests, 60 percent of consumers chose the new Coke over the old, and 52 percent chose it over Pepsi. Research showed that New Coke would be a winner, and the company introduced it with confidence. So what happened?

Looking back, we can see that Coke defined its marketing research problem too narrowly. The research looked only at taste; it did not explore consumers' feelings about dropping the old Coke and replacing it with a new version. It took no account of the *intangibles*—Coke's name, history, packaging, cultural heritage, and image. However, to many people, Coke stands alongside baseball, hot dogs, and apple pie as an American institution; it represents the very fabric of America. Coke's symbolic meaning turned out to be more important to many consumers than its taste. Research addressing a broader set of issues would have detected these strong emotions.

Coke's managers may also have used poor judgment in interpreting the research and planning strategies around it. For example, they took the finding that 60 percent of consumers preferred New Coke's taste to mean that the new product would win in the marketplace, as when a political candidate wins with 60 percent of the vote. But it also meant that 40 percent still liked the original formula. By dropping the old Coke, the company trampled the taste buds of the large core of loyal Coke drinkers who didn't want a change. The company might have been wiser to leave the old Coke alone and introduce New Coke as a brand extension, as it later did successfully with Cherry Coke.

The Coca-Cola Company has one of the largest, best-managed, and most advanced marketing research operations in America. Good marketing research has kept the company atop the rough-and-tumble soft drink market for decades. But marketing research is far from an exact science. Consumers are full of surprises and figuring them out can be awfully tough. If Coca-Cola can make a large marketing research mistake, any company can.[1]

• •

In order to produce superior value and satisfaction for customers, companies need information at almost every turn. As the New Coke story highlights, good products and marketing programs begin with a thorough understanding of consumer needs and wants. Companies also need an abundance of information on competitors, resellers, and other actors and forces in the marketplace.

Increasingly, marketers are viewing information not only as an input for making better decisions but also as an important strategic asset and marketing tool. A company's information may prove to be its chief competitive advantage. Competitors can copy each other's equipment, products, and procedures, but they cannot duplicate the company's information and intellectual capital. Several companies have recently recognized this by appointing vice presidents of knowledge, learning, or intellectual capital.[2]

Information overload: "In this oh so overwhelming Information age, it's all too easy to be buried, burdened, and burned out by data overload."

In today's more rapidly changing environments, managers need up-to-date information to make timely, high-quality decisions. In turn, with the recent explosion of information technologies, companies can now generate information in great quantities. In fact, today's managers often receive too much information. One study found that with all the companies offering data, and with all the information now available through supermarket scanners, a packaged-goods brand manager is bombarded with one million to one *billion* new numbers each week. Another study found that, on average, American office workers spend 60 percent of their time processing information; a typical manager reads about a million words a week. Thus, running out of information is not a problem but seeing through the "data smog" is. "In this oh so overwhelming Information Age," comments one observer, "it's all too easy to be buried, burdened, and burned out by data overload.[3]

Despite this data glut, marketers frequently complain that they lack enough information of the *right* kind. A recent survey of managers found that although half the respondents said they couldn't cope with the volume of information coming at them, two-thirds wanted even more. The researcher concluded that, "despite the volume, they're still not getting what they want."[4] Thus, most marketing managers don't need *more* information, they need *better* information. Companies must design effective marketing information systems that give managers the right information, in the right form, at the right time to help them make better marketing decisions.

Marketing information system (MIS)

People, equipment, and procedures to gather, sort, analyze, evaluate, and distribute needed, timely, and accurate information to marketing decision makers.

A **marketing information system (MIS)** consists of people, equipment, and procedures to gather, sort, analyze, evaluate, and distribute needed, timely, and accurate information to marketing decision makers. Figure 5-1 shows that the MIS begins and ends with information users—marketing managers, internal and external partners, and others who need marketing information. First, it interacts with these information users to assess *information needs*. Next, it *develops needed information* from internal company databases, marketing intelligence activities, and marketing research. Then it helps users to analyze information to put it in the

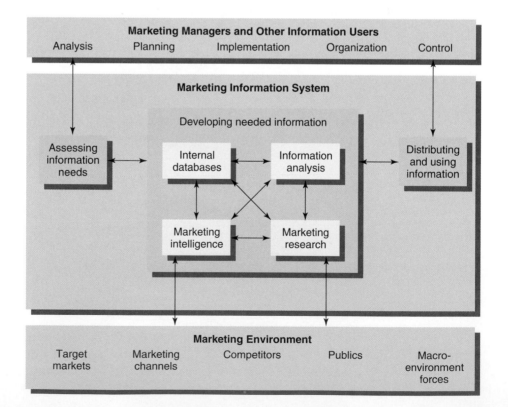

Figure 5-1
The marketing information system

right form for making marketing decisions and managing customer relationships. Finally, the MIS *distributes* the marketing information and helps managers *use* it in their decision making.

Assessing Marketing Information Needs

The marketing information system primarily serves the company's marketing and other managers. However, it may also provide information to external partners, such as suppliers or marketing services agencies. For example, Wal-Mart might give Procter & Gamble and other key suppliers access to information on customer buying patterns and inventory levels. In addition, important customers may be given limited access to the information system. Dell Computer creates tailored Premium Pages for large customers, giving them access to product design, order status, and product support and service information. FedEx lets customers into its information system to schedule and track shipments. In designing an information system, the company must consider the needs of all of these users.

A good marketing information system balances the information users would *like* to have against what they really *need* and what is *feasible* to offer. The company begins by interviewing managers to find out what information they would like. Some managers will ask for whatever information they can get without thinking carefully about what they really need. Too much information can be as harmful as too little. Other managers may omit things they ought to know or may not know to ask for some types of information they should have. For example, managers might need to know that a competitor plans to introduce a new product during the coming year. Because they do not know about the new product, they do not think to ask about it. The MIS must monitor the marketing environment in order to provide decision makers with information they should have to make key marketing decisions.

Sometimes the company cannot provide the needed information, either because it is not available or because of MIS limitations. For example, a brand manager might want to know how competitors will change their advertising budgets next year and how these changes will affect industry market shares. The information on planned budgets probably is not available. Even if it is, the company's MIS may not be advanced enough to forecast resulting changes in market shares.

Finally, the costs of obtaining, processing, storing, and delivering information can mount quickly. The company must decide whether the benefits of having additional information are worth the costs of providing it, and both value and cost are often hard to assess. By itself, information has no worth; its value comes from its *use*. In many cases, additional information will do little to change or improve a manager's decision, or the costs of the information may exceed the returns from the improved decision. Marketers should not assume that additional information will always be worth obtaining. Rather, they should weigh carefully the costs of additional information against the benefits resulting from it.

Developing Marketing Information

Marketers can obtain the needed information from *internal data, marketing intelligence,* and *marketing research*.

Internal Data

Many companies build extensive **internal databases**, electronic collections of information obtained from data sources within the company. Marketing managers can readily access

Internal databases
Electronic collections of information obtained from data sources within the company.

and work with information in the database to identify marketing opportunities and problems, plan programs, and evaluate performance.

Information in the database can come from many sources. The accounting department prepares financial statements and keeps detailed records of sales, costs, and cash flows. Manufacturing reports on production schedules, shipments, and inventories. The sales force reports on reseller reactions and competitor activities. The marketing department furnishes information on customer demographics, psychographics, and buying behavior, and the customer service department keeps records of customer satisfaction or service problems. Research studies done for one department may provide useful information for several others.

Here is an example of how one company uses its internal database to make better marketing decisions:

> USAA, which provides financial services to U.S. military personnel and their families, maintains a customer database built from customer purchasing histories and from information collected directly from customers. To keep the database fresh, the organization regularly surveys its 4.3 million customers worldwide to learn such things as whether they have children (and if so, how old they are), if they have moved recently, and when they plan to retire. USAA uses the database to tailor marketing offers to the specific needs of individual customers. For example, if the family has college-age children, the USAA sends those children information on how to manage their credit cards. If the family has younger children, it sends booklets on things like financing a child's education. Or, for customers looking toward retirement, it sends information on estate planning. Through skillful use of its database, USAA serves each customer uniquely, resulting in high levels of customer loyalty — the roughly $8.6 billion company retains 97 percent of its customers.[5]

Internal databases usually can be accessed more quickly and cheaply than other information sources, but they also present some problems. Because internal information was collected for other purposes, it may be incomplete or in the wrong form for making marketing decisions. For example, sales and cost data used by the accounting department for preparing financial statements must be adapted for use in evaluating product, sales force, or channel performance. Data ages quickly; keeping the database current requires a major effort. In addition, a large company produces mountains of information, and keeping track of it all is difficult. The database information must be well integrated and readily accessible through user-friendly interfaces so that managers can find it easily and use it effectively.

Marketing Intelligence

Marketing intelligence
The systematic collection and analysis of publicly available information about competitors and developments in the marketing environment.

Marketing intelligence is systematic collection and analysis of publicly available information about competitors and developments in the marketing environment. The goal of marketing intelligence is to improve strategic decision making, assess and track competitors' actions, and provide early warning of opportunities and threats.

Competitive intelligence gathering has grown dramatically as more and more companies are now busily snooping on their competitors. Techniques range from quizzing the company's own employees and benchmarking competitors' products to researching the Internet, lurking around industry trade shows, and rooting through rivals' trash bins.

Much intelligence can be collected from people inside the company — executives, engineers and scientists, purchasing agents, and the sales force. Consider this example:

> While talking with a Kodak copier salesperson, a Xerox technician learned that the salesperson was being trained to service Xerox products. The Xerox employee reported back to his boss, who in turn passed the news to Xerox's intelligence unit.

Using such clues as a classified ad Kodak placed seeking new people with Xerox product experience, Xerox verified Kodak's plan—code-named Ulysses—to service Xerox copiers. To protect its profitable service business, Xerox designed a Total Satisfaction Guarantee, which allowed copier returns for any reason as long as *Xerox* did the servicing. By the time Kodak launched Ulysses, *Xerox* had been promoting its new program for three months.[6]

The company can also obtain important intelligence information from suppliers, resellers, and key customers. Or it can get good information by observing competitors. It can buy and analyze competitors' products, monitor their sales, check for new patents, and examine various types of physical evidence. For example, one company regularly checks out competitors' parking lots—full lots might indicate plenty of work and prosperity; half-full lots might suggest hard times.[7] Some companies have even rifled their competitors' garbage, which is legally considered abandoned property once it leaves the premises. In one garbage snatching incident, Avon hired private detectives to paw through the dumpster of rival Mary Kay Cosmetics to search for revealing documents. An outraged Mary Kay sued to get its garbage back, but the dumpster had been located in a public parking lot and Avon had videotapes to prove it.[8]

Competitors may reveal intelligence information through their annual reports, business publications, trade show exhibits, press releases, advertisements, and Web pages. The Internet is proving to be a vast new source of competitor-supplied information. Most companies now place volumes of information on their Web sites, providing details to attract customers, partners, suppliers, or franchisees. For example, Allied Signal's Web site provides revenue goals and reveals the company's production-defect rate along with its plans to improve it. Mail Boxes Etc., a chain of mailing services, provides data on its average franchise, including square footage, number of employees, operating hours, and more—all valuable insights for a competitor.

"In today's information age, companies are leaving a paper trail of information online," says an online intelligence expert. Today's managers "don't have to simply rely on old news or intuition when making investment and business decisions."[9] Using Internet search engines, marketers can search specific competitor names, events, or trends and see what turns up. Intelligence seekers can also pore through any of thousands of online databases. Some are free. For example, the U.S. Security and Exchange Commission's database provides a huge stockpile of financial information on public competitors, and the U.S. Patent Office database reveals patents competitors have filed. And for a fee, companies can subscribe to any of more than 3,000 online databases and information search services such as Dialog, DataStar, Lexis-Nexis, Dow Jones News Retrieval, UMI ProQuest, and Dun & Bradstreet's Online Access.

The growing use of marketing intelligence raises a number of ethical issues. Although most of the preceding techniques are legal, and some are considered to be shrewdly competitive, some may involve questionable ethics. Clearly, companies should take advantage of publicly available information. However, they should not stoop to snoop. With all the legitimate intelligence sources now available, a company does not have to break the law or accepted codes of ethics to get good intelligence.[10]

Marketing Research

In addition to information about competitor and environmental happenings, marketers often need formal studies of specific situations. For example, Bayer wants to know what appeals will be most effective in advertising for its Aleve pain reliever. Or Toshiba wants to know how many and what kinds of people or companies will buy its new superfast notebook computer. In such situations, marketing intelligence will not provide the detailed information needed. Managers will need marketing research.

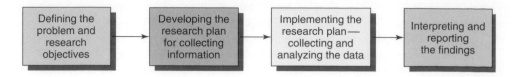

Figure 5-2
The marketing
research process

| Defining the problem and research objectives | → | Developing the research plan for collecting information | → | Implementing the research plan— collecting and analyzing the data | → | Interpreting and reporting the findings |

Marketing research
The systematic design,
collection, analysis, and
reporting of data relevant to a
specific marketing situation
facing an organization.

Marketing research is the systematic design, collection, analysis, and reporting of data relevant to a specific marketing situation facing an organization. Companies use marketing research in a wide variety of situations. For example, marketing research can help marketers assess market potential and market share; understand customer satisfaction and purchase behavior; and measure the effectiveness of pricing, product, distribution, and promotion activities.

Some large companies have their own research departments that work with marketing managers on marketing research projects. This is how Kraft, Citigroup, and many other corporate giants handle marketing research. In addition, these companies—like their smaller counterparts—frequently hire outside research specialists to consult with management on specific marketing problems and conduct marketing research studies. Sometimes firms simply purchase data collected by outside firms to aid in their decision making.

The marketing research process (see Figure 5-2) has four steps: *defining the problem and research objectives, developing the research plan, implementing the research plan,* and *interpreting and reporting the findings.*

Defining the Problem and Research Objectives

Marketing managers and researchers must work closely together to define the problem and agree on the research objectives. The manager best understands the decision for which information is needed; the researcher best understands marketing research and how to obtain the information.

Defining the problem and research objectives is often the hardest step in the research process. The manager may know that something is wrong, without knowing the specific causes. For example, in the classic New Coke case, Coca-Cola defined its research problem too narrowly, with disastrous results. In another example, managers of a large discount retail store chain hastily decided that falling sales were caused by poor advertising, and they ordered research to test the company's advertising. When this research showed that current advertising was reaching the right people with the right message, the managers were puzzled. It turned out that the real problem was that the chain was not delivering the prices, products, and service promised in the advertising. Careful problem definition would have avoided the cost and delay of doing advertising research.

Exploratory research
Marketing research to gather
preliminary information that
will help define problems and
suggest hypotheses.

After the problem has been defined carefully, the manager and researcher must set the research objectives. A marketing research project might have one of three types of objectives. The objective of **exploratory research** is to gather preliminary information that will help define the problem and suggest hypotheses. The objective of **descriptive research** is to describe things, such as the market potential for a product or the demographics and attitudes of consumers who buy the product. The objective of **causal research** is to test hypotheses about cause-and-effect relationships. For example, would a 10 percent decrease in tuition at a private college result in an enrollment increase sufficient to offset the reduced tuition? Managers often start with exploratory research and later follow with descriptive or causal research.

Descriptive research
Marketing research to better
describe marketing problems,
situations, or markets, such as
the market potential for a
product or the demographics
and attitudes of consumers.

The statement of the problem and research objectives guides the entire research process. The manager and researcher should put the statement in writing to be certain that they agree on the purpose and expected results of the research.

Causal research
Marketing research to test
hypotheses about cause-
and-effect relationships.

Developing the Research Plan

Once the research problems and objectives have been defined, researchers must determine the exact information needed, develop a plan for gathering it efficiently, and present the plan to management. The research plan outlines sources of existing data and spells out the specific research approaches, contact methods, sampling plans, and instruments that researchers will use to gather new data.

Research objectives must be translated into specific information needs. For example, suppose Campbell decides to conduct research on how consumers would react to the introduction of new bowl-shaped plastic containers that it has used successfully for a number of its other products. The containers would cost more but would allow consumers to heat the soup in a microwave oven without adding water or milk and to eat it without using dishes. This research might call for the following specific information:

◆ The demographic, economic, and lifestyle characteristics of current soup users (Busy working couples might find the convenience of the new packaging worth the price; families with children might want to pay less and wash the pan and bowls.)

◆ Consumer-usage patterns for soup: how much soup they eat, where, and when (The new packaging might be ideal for adults eating lunch on the go, but less convenient for parents feeding lunch to several children.)

◆ Retailer reactions to the new packaging (Failure to get retailer support could hurt sales of the new package.)

◆ Consumer attitudes toward the new packaging (The red-and-white Campbell can has become an American institution—will consumers accept the new packaging?)

◆ Forecasts of sales of both new and current packages (Will the new packaging increase Campbell's profits?)

Campbell managers will need these and many other types of information to decide whether to introduce the new packaging.

The research plan should be presented in a *written proposal*. A written proposal is especially important when the research project is large and complex or when an outside firm carries it out. The proposal should cover the management problems addressed and the research objectives, the information to be obtained, and the way the results will help management decision making. The proposal also should include research costs.

To meet the manager's information needs, the research plan can call for gathering secondary data, primary data, or both. **Secondary data** consist of information that already exists somewhere, having been collected for another purpose. **Primary data** consist of information collected for the specific purpose at hand.

Secondary data
Information that already exists somewhere, having been collected for another purpose.

Primary data
Information collected for the specific purpose at hand.

Gathering Secondary Data Researchers usually start by gathering secondary data. The company's internal database provides a good starting point. However, the company can also tap a wide assortment of external information sources, including commercial data services and government sources (see Table 5-1).

Companies can buy secondary data reports from outside suppliers.[11] For example, Information Resources, Inc. sells supermarket scanner purchase data from a panel of 55,000 households nationally, with measures of trial and repeat purchasing, brand loyalty, and buyer demographics. The *Monitor* service by Yankelovich and Partners sells information on important social and lifestyle trends. These and other firms supply high-quality data to suit a wide variety of marketing information needs.

Using commercial **online databases**, marketing researchers can conduct their own searches of secondary data sources. General database services such as CompuServe, Dialog, and LEXIS-NEXIS put an incredible wealth of information at the keyboards of marketing decision makers. Beyond commercial Web sites offering information for a fee, almost every industry association, government agency, business publication, and news medium offers free information to those tenacious enough to find their Web sites. There are so many Web sites offering data that finding the right ones can become an almost overwhelming task.

Online databases
Computerized collections of information available from online commercial sources or via the Internet.

Table 5-1   Selected External Information Sources

For business data:

AC Nielsen Corporation (www.acnielsen.com) provides supermarket scanner data on sales, market share, and retail prices; data on household purchasing; and data on television audiences.

Information Resources, Inc. (www.infores.com) provides supermarket scanner data for tracking grocery product movement and new product purchasing data.

Arbitron (www.arbitron.com) provides local-market and Internet radio audience and advertising expenditure information, among other media and ad spending data.

NDC Health Information Services (www.simatics.com/index.htm) reports on the movement of drugs, laboratory supplies, animal health products, and personal care products.

Simmons Market Research Bureau (www.smrb.com) provides detailed analysis of consumer patterns in 400 product categories in selected markets.

Dun & Bradstreet (www.dnb.com) maintains a database containing information on more than 50 million individual companies around the globe.

Media Metrix (www.mediametrix.com) provides audience measurement and geodemographic analysis of Internet and digital media users around the world.

Dialog (http://library.dialog.com) offers access to ABI/INFORM, a database of articles from 800+ publications and to reports, newsletters, and directories covering dozens of industries.

LEXIS-NEXIS (www.lexis-nexis.com) features articles from business, consumer, and marketing publications plus tracking of firms, industries, trends, and promotion techniques.

CompuServe (www.compuserve.com) provides access to databases of business and consumer demographics, government reports, and patent records, plus articles from newspapers, newsletters, and research reports.

Dow Jones Interactive (http://bis.dowjones.com) specializes in in-depth financial, historical, and operational information on public and private companies.

Hoovers Online (www.hoovers.com) provides business descriptions, financial overviews, and news about major companies around the world.

CNN (www.cnn.com) reports U.S. and global news and covers the markets and news-making companies in detail.

American Demographics (www.americandemographics.com) reports on demographic trends and their significance for businesses.

For government data:

Securities and Exchange Commission Edgar database (www.sec.gov) provides financial data on U.S. public corporations

Small Business Administration (www.sbaonline.gov) features information and links for small business owners.

Federal Trade Commission (www.ftc.gov) shows regulations and decisions related to consumer protection and antitrust laws.

Stat-USA (www.stat-usa.gov), a Department of Commerce site, highlights statistics on U.S. business and international trade.

U.S. Census (www.census.gov) provides detailed statistics and trends about the U.S. population.

U.S. Patent and Trademark Office (www.uspto.gov) allows searches to determine who has filed for trademarks and patents.

For Internet data:

CyberAtlas (http://cyberatlas.internet.com) brings together a wealth of information about the Internet and its users, from consumers to e-commerce.

Internet Advertising Bureau (www.iab.net) covers statistics about advertising on the Internet.

Media Metrix (www.mediametrix.com) monitors Web traffic and ranks the most popular sites.

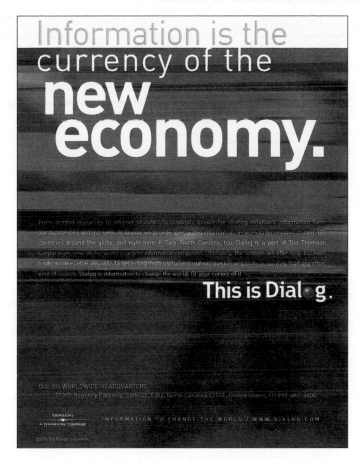

Online database ser-
vices such as Dialog put
an incredible wealth of
information at the key-
boards of marketing
decision-makers. Dialog
puts "information to
change the world" at
your fingertips.

Secondary data can usually be obtained more quickly and at a lower cost than primary data. For example, an Internet or online database search might provide all the information Campbell needs on soup usage, quickly and at low cost. A study to collect primary
information might take weeks or months and cost thousands of dollars. Also, secondary
sources sometimes can provide data an individual company cannot collect on its own—
information that either is not directly available or would be too expensive to collect. For
example, it would be too expensive for Campbell to conduct a continuing retail store audit
to find out about the market shares, prices, and displays of competitors' brands. But it can
buy the InfoScan service from Information Resources, Inc., which provides this information from thousands of scanner-equipped supermarkets in dozens of U.S. markets.

Secondary data can also present problems. The needed information may not exist—
researchers can rarely obtain all the data they need from secondary sources. For example,
Campbell will not find existing information about consumer reactions to new packaging
that it has not yet placed on the market. Even when data can be found, they might not be
very usable. The researcher must evaluate secondary information carefully to make certain
it is *relevant* (fits research project needs), *accurate* (reliably collected and reported),
current (up-to-date enough for current decisions), and *impartial* (objectively collected and
reported).

Primary Data Collection Secondary data provide a good starting point for research and
often help to define problems and research objectives. In most cases, however, the company must also collect primary data. Just as researchers must carefully evaluate the quality
of secondary information, they also must take great care when collecting primary data to

Table 5-2 Planning Primary Data Collection			
Research Approaches	Contact Methods	Sampling Plan	Research Instruments
Observation	Mail	Sampling unit	Questionnaire
Survey	Telephone	Sample size	Mechanical instruments
Experiment	Personal	Sampling procedure	
	Online		

make sure that it will be relevant, accurate, current, and unbiased. Table 5-2 shows that designing a plan for primary data collection calls for a number of decisions on *research approaches, contact methods, sampling plan,* and *research instruments.*

RESEARCH APPROACHES. Research approaches for gathering primary data include observation, surveys, and experiments. **Observational research** involves gathering primary data by observing relevant people, actions, and situations. For example, a consumer packaged-goods marketer might visit supermarkets and observe shoppers as they browse the store, pick up products and examine packages, and make actual buying decisions. Or a bank might evaluate possible new branch locations by checking traffic patterns, neighborhood conditions, and the location of competing branches. A wide range of companies now use *ethnographic research*—which combines intensive observation with customer interviews—to gain deep insights into how customers buy and live with their products (see Marketing at Work 5-1).

B2B marketers also employ observation in their marketing research. For example, Steelcase used it to help design new office furniture for use by work teams.

> To learn firsthand how teams actually operate, it set up video cameras at various companies and studied the tapes, looking for motions and behavior patterns that customers themselves might not even notice. It found that teams work best when they can do some work together and some privately. So Steelcase designed highly successful modular office units called Personal Harbor. These units are "rather like telephone booths in size and shape." They can be arranged around a common space where a team works, letting people work together but also alone when necessary. Says a Steelcase executive, "Market data wouldn't necessarily have pointed us that way. It was more important to know how people actually work."[12]

Observational research
The gathering of primary data by observing relevant people, actions, and situations.

Observational research: Steelcase set up video cameras at various companies to study motions and behavior patterns that customers themselves might not even notice. The result was the highly successful Personal Harbor modular office units.

Marketing At Work 5-1

Ethnographic Research: Keeping a Close Eye on Consumers

What do customers *really* think about your product and what do they say about it to their friends? How do they *really* use it? Will they tell you? *Can* they tell you? These are difficult questions for most marketers. And too often, traditional research simply can't provide accurate answers. To get better insights, many companies are now turning to an increasingly popular research approach—ethnographic or observational research.

Ethnographic research involves sending trained observers to watch consumers in their "natural environment"—to observe up close the subtleties of how consumers use and feel about products and services.

The 60-ish woman caught on the grainy videotape is sitting on her hotel bed, addressing her husband after a long day spent on the road. "Good job!" she exults. "We beat the s——out of the front desk and got a terrific room." No, this wasn't an FBI sting operation. Instead, the couple was part of [an ethnographic study in which Best Western International] paid 25 over 55 couples to tape themselves on cross-country journeys. The effort convinced the hotel chain that it didn't need to boost its standard 10 percent senior citizen discount. The tapes showed that seniors who talked the hotel clerk into a better deal didn't need the lower price to afford the room; they were after the thrill of the deal. Instead of attracting new customers, bigger discounts would simply allow the old customers to trade up to a fancier dinner down the street somewhere, doing absolutely nothing for Best Western. . . . Best Western captured such a wealth of customer behavior on tape that it has delayed its marketing plan in order to weave the insights into its core strategy. Unfortunately for

seniors, that means the rooms won't be getting any cheaper.

In today's intensely competitive marketplace, holding onto customers requires more than a superficial understanding of customers' interactions with a product. "You can run a marketing campaign that might make people pick up your product the first time, but if they live with it under different conditions than the advertised benefits, it's not likely that they're going to pick it up a second time," notes an ethnographic researcher. To keep customers coming back, companies must have a deep understanding of how they feel about and interact with products and adjust their marketing offers and programs accordingly. Ethnographic research helps provide such an understanding. It combines intense observation with customer interviews to get an up-close and personal view of how people actually live with prod-

ucts—how they buy and use them in their everyday lives. Here's another example:

A woman in suburban Baltimore is shopping for her family's meals for the week. She cruises past the poultry section, stopping only momentarily to drop a couple of packages of boneless chicken breasts into her cart. Then, the dreaded sea of red meat looms before her. Tentatively, she picks up a package of beef. "This cut looks good, not too fatty," she says, juggling her two-year-old on her hip. "But I don't know what it is. And I don't know how to cook it," she confesses. She trades it for a small package of sirloin and her regular order of ground beef. Scenes like this play out daily in supermarkets across the country. But this time, it's being captured on videotape, part of a recent ethnographic study of beef consumers for the National Cattlemen's Beef Association (NCBA) and major grocery retailers.

Using ethnographic research, companies observe consumers in their "natural environment." In one Best Western study, over-55 couples taped themselves on cross-country journeys, providing a wealth of consumer behavior insights.

Knowing what consumers actually do with beef is vital to the NCBA. Even though sales of ground beef have risen in recent years, other beef products have lost ground. To get a firsthand understanding of what really goes on in consumers' minds as they shop the meat case, NCBA researchers videotaped not only consumers' store behavior but also their preparation habits at home. And they interviewed consumers at each step, asking what they thought about beef, why they did or didn't select particular cuts, their thoughts on meat department layouts, how they prepared the family meal, and the availability of recipes.

The conclusion? Confusion. Although the typical shopper would initially say that she wasn't confused about buying beef, "when we went deeper, we found that she wasn't confused because she always buys the same cuts—ground beef, boneless chicken breast, maybe one steak," says Kevin Yost, NCBA's director of consumer marketing. "When you start to broaden the range [of meat selections], she has no idea what you're talking about." All of this was a revelation to the beef industry. "The first time I showed [the tapes] to a group of major retail-

ers, they started laughing," Yost says. The retailers couldn't believe how little consumers knew about something that seemed so familiar to them. The result? Many grocers' meat cases are now being rearranged to display beef by cooking method, rather than by cuts of meat. Simple, three step cooking instructions will soon be printed on the packages.

Ethnographic research often yields the kinds of intimate details that just don't emerge from traditional focus groups. For example, focus groups told Best Western that it's the men who decide when to stop for the night and where to stay. The videotapes showed it was usually the women. And by videotaping consumers in the shower, plumbing fixture maker Moen uncovered safety risks that consumers didn't recognize—such as the habit of some women while shaving their legs of holding onto one unit's temperature control. Moen would find it almost impossible to discover such design flaws simply by asking questions.

Bugle Boy found that traditional focus groups fail miserably in getting the scoop on teens and Gen Xers. These often-cynical young people are skeptical of sales pitches

and just won't speak up in a conference room with two-way mirrors. So Bugle Boy turned to ethnographic research. It plucked four young men out of obscurity, handed each of them a camcorder, and told them to document their lives. The young amateurs were given only broad categories to work with: school, home, closet, and shopping. Bugle Boy then used the videos to prompt discussions of product and lifestyle issues in "free-form" focus groups held in unconventional locations, such as restaurants. Says one Bugle Boy ad manager, "I think this really helped us to get a handle on what these kids do. It let us see what their lives are all about, their awareness of the Bugle Boy brand, and how they perceive the brand."

So, more and more, marketers are keeping a close eye on consumers. "Knowing the individual consumer on an intimate basis has become a necessity," says a research industry consultant, "and ethnography is the intimate connection to the consumer."

Sources: Excerpts from Kendra Parker, "How Do You Like Your Beef?" *American Demographics,* January 2000, pp. 35–37; and Gerry Khermouch, "Consumers in the Mist," *Business Week,* February 26, 2001, pp. 92–94.

Many companies collect data through *mechanical* observation via machine or computer. For example, Nielsen Media Research attaches *people meters* to television sets in selected homes to record who watches which programs. Other companies use *checkout scanners* to record shoppers' purchases so that manufacturers and retailers can assess product sales and store performance. And DoubleClick, among other Internet companies, places a *cookie*—a bit of information—on consumers' hard drives to monitor their Web surfing patterns. Similarly, MediaMetrix places special software on consumers' PCs to monitor Web surfing patterns and produce ratings for top Web sites.

Observational research can obtain information that people are unwilling or unable to provide. In some cases, observation may be the only way to obtain the needed information. In contrast, some things simply cannot be observed, such as feelings, attitudes and motives, or private behavior. Long-term or infrequent behavior is also difficult to observe. Because of these limitations, researchers often use observation along with other data collection methods.

Survey research, the most widely used method for primary data collection, is the approach best suited for gathering *descriptive* information. A company that wants to know

Survey research
The gathering of primary data by asking people questions about their knowledge, attitudes, preferences, and buying behavior.

about people's knowledge, attitudes, preferences, or buying behavior can often find out by asking them directly.

Some firms provide marketers with a more comprehensive look at buying patterns through **single-source data systems.** These systems combine surveys of huge consumer panels—carefully selected groups of consumers who agree to participate in ongoing research—and electronic monitoring of respondents' purchases and exposure to various marketing activities in an effort to better understand the link between consumer characteristics, attitudes, and purchase behavior.

The major advantage of survey research is its flexibility—it can be used to obtain many different kinds of information in many different situations. However, survey research also presents some problems. Sometimes people are unable to answer survey questions because they cannot remember or have never thought about what they do and why. People may be unwilling to respond to unknown interviewers or about things they consider private. Respondents may answer survey questions even when they do not know the answer in order to appear smarter or more informed. Or they may try to help the interviewer by giving pleasing answers. Finally, busy people may not take the time, or they might resent the intrusion into their privacy.

Whereas observation is best suited for exploratory research and surveys for descriptive research, **experimental research** is best suited for gathering *causal* information. Experiments involve selecting matched groups of subjects, giving them different treatments, controlling unrelated factors, and checking for differences in group responses. Thus, experimental research tries to explain cause-and-effect relationships.

For example, before adding a new sandwich to its menu, McDonald's might use experiments to test the effects on sales of two different prices it might charge. It could introduce the new sandwich at one price in one city and at another price in another city. If the cities are similar, and if all other marketing efforts for the sandwich are the same, then differences in sales in the two cities could be related to the price charged.

CONTACT METHODS. Information can be collected by mail, telephone, personal interview, or online. Table 5-3 shows the strengths and weaknesses of each of these contact methods.

Mail questionnaires can be used to collect large amounts of information at a low cost per respondent. Respondents may give more honest answers to more personal questions on a mail questionnaire than to an unknown interviewer in person or over the phone. Also, no

Single-source data systems
Electronic monitoring systems that link consumers' exposure to television advertising and promotion (measured using television meters) with what they buy in stores (measured using store checkout scanners).

Experimental research
The gathering of primary data by selecting matched groups of subjects, giving them different treatments, controlling related factors, and checking for differences in group responses.

Table 5-3 Strengths and Weaknesses of Contact Methods				
	Mail	Telephone	Personal	Online
Flexibility	Poor	Good	Excellent	Good
Quantity of data that can be collected	Good	Fair	Excellent	Good
Control of interviewer effects	Excellent	Fair	Poor	Fair
Control of sample	Fair	Excellent	Fair	Poor
Speed of data collection	Poor	Excellent	Good	Excellent
Response rate	Fair	Good	Good	Good
Cost	Good	Fair	Poor	Excellent

Source: Adapted with permission of Macmillan Publishing Company from *Marketing Research: Measurement and Method,* 7th ed., by Donald S. Tuli and Del I. Hawkins. Copyright 1993 by Macmillan Publishing Company.

interviewer is involved to bias the respondent's answers. However, mail questionnaires are not very flexible—all respondents answer the same questions in a fixed order. Mail surveys usually take longer to complete, and the response rate—the number of people returning completed questionnaires—is often very low. Finally, the researcher often has little control over the mail questionnaire sample. Even with a good mailing list, it is hard to control *who* at the mailing address fills out the questionnaire.

Telephone interviewing is the one of the best methods for gathering information quickly, and it provides greater flexibility than mail questionnaires. Interviewers can explain difficult questions and, depending on the answers they receive, skip some questions or probe on others. Response rates tend to be higher than with mail questionnaires, and interviewers can ask to speak to respondents with the desired characteristics or even by name.

However, with telephone interviewing, the cost per respondent is higher than with mail questionnaires. Also, people may not want to discuss personal questions with an interviewer. The method also introduces interviewer bias—the way interviewers talk, how they ask questions, and other differences may affect respondents' answers. Finally, different interviewers may interpret and record responses differently, and under time pressures some interviewers might even cheat by recording answers without asking questions.

Personal interviewing takes two forms—individual and group interviewing. *Individual interviewing* involves talking with people in their homes or offices, on the street, or in shopping malls. Such interviewing is flexible. Trained interviewers can guide interviews, explain difficult questions, and explore issues as the situation requires. They can show subjects actual products, advertisements, or packages and observe reactions and behavior. However, individual personal interviews may cost three to four times as much as telephone interviews.

Group interviewing consists of inviting six to ten people to talk with a trained moderator about a product, service, or organization. Participants normally are paid a small sum for attending. The moderator encourages free and easy discussion, hoping that group interactions will bring out actual feelings and thoughts. At the same time, the moderator "focuses" the discussion—hence the name **focus group interviewing.** The comments are recorded in writing or on videotape for later study.

Focus group interviewing has become one of the major marketing research tools for gaining insight into consumer thoughts and feelings. However, focus group studies usually employ small sample sizes to keep time and costs down, and it may be hard to generalize from the results. Because interviewers have more freedom in personal interviews, the problem of interviewer bias is greater.

Today, modern communications technology is changing the way that focus groups are conducted:

> Videoconferencing links, television monitors, remote-control cameras, and digital transmission are boosting the amount of focus group research done over long-distance lines. [In a typical videoconferencing system,] two cameras focused on the group are controlled by clients who hold a remote keypad. Executives in a far-off boardroom can zoom in on faces and pan the focus group at will. . . . A two-way sound system connects remote viewers to the backroom, focus group room, and directly to the monitor's earpiece. [Recently,] while testing new product names in one focus group, the [client's] creative director . . . had an idea and contacted the moderator, who tested the new name on the spot.[13]

Another form of interviewing is *computer-assisted interviewing,* a contact method in which respondents sit at computers, read questions on the screen, and type in their own answers while an interviewer is present. The computers might be located at a research center, trade show, shopping mall, or retail location.

Focus group interviewing
Personal interviewing that involves inviting six to ten people to gather for a few hours with a trained interviewer to talk about a product, service, or organization. The interviewer "focuses" the group discussion on important issues.

Online focus groups offer many advantages, including convenience and low cost. Says ActiveGroup about its online research: "No traveling, no scheduling, no problems."

The latest technology to hit marketing research is the Internet. Increasingly, marketing researchers are collecting primary data through **online (Internet) marketing research**—*Internet surveys, experiments,* and *online focus groups.* Online focus groups offer advantages over traditional methods:

> Janice Gjersten, director of marketing for an online entertainment company, wanted to . . . gauge reaction to a new Web site. [She] contacted Cyber Dialogue, which provided focus group respondents drawn from its 10,000-person database. The focus group was held in an online chat room, which Gjersten "looked in on" from her office computer. Gjersten could interrupt the moderator at any time with flash e-mails unseen by the respondents. Although the online focus group lacked voice and body cues, Gjersten says she will never conduct a traditional focus group again. Not only were respondents more honest, but the cost for the online group was one third that of a traditional focus group and a full report came to her in one day, compared to four weeks.[14]

Although online research offers much promise, and some analysts predict that the Internet will soon be the primary marketing research tool, others are more cautious. Marketing at Work 5-2 summarizes the advantages, drawbacks, and prospects for conducting marketing research on the Internet.

SAMPLING PLAN. Marketing researchers usually draw conclusions about large groups of consumers by studying a small sample of the total consumer population. A **sample** is a segment of the population selected to represent the population as a whole. Ideally, the sample should be representative so that the researcher can make accurate estimates of the thoughts and behaviors of the larger population.

Designing the sample requires three decisions. First, *who* is to be surveyed (what *sampling unit*)? The answer to this question is not always obvious. For example, to study the decision-making process for a family automobile purchase, should the researcher interview

Online (Internet) marketing research
Collecting primary data through Internet surveys and online focus groups.

Sample
A segment of the population selected for marketing research to represent the population as a whole.

Marketing At Work 6-2

Online Marketing Research

As more and more consumers connect with the Internet, an increasing number of marketers are moving their research onto the Web. Although online research currently makes up only about 2 percent of all marketing research spending, industry insiders predict phenomenal growth. In five years, some say, it could account for 50 percent of all research spending.

Web research offers some real advantages over traditional surveys and focus groups. The most obvious advantages are speed and cost-effectiveness. Online focus groups require some advance scheduling, but results are practically instantaneous. Survey researchers routinely complete their online studies in only a matter of days. For example, youth marketing consultancy Fusion 5 recently conducted an online survey to test teenager opinions of new packaging ideas for a soft drink company. The company's research firm designed a 10- to 15-minute Internet survey, which included dozens of questions along with 765 different images of labels, bottle shapes, and such. Some 600 teenagers participated over a three- to four-day period. Detailed analysis from the survey was available just five days after all the responses had come in—lightning quick compared to offline efforts.

Internet research is also relatively inexpensive. Participants can dial in for a focus group from anywhere in the world, eliminating travel, lodging, and facility costs. For surveys, the Internet eliminates most of the postage, phone, labor, and printing costs associated with other approaches. "The cost [of Web research] can be anywhere from 10 percent to 80 percent less," says Tod Johnson, head of NPD Group, a firm that conducts online research. Moreover, sample size has little influence

on costs. "There's not a huge difference between 10 and 10,000 on the Web," says Johnson.

Online surveys and focus groups are also excellent for reaching the hard-to-reach—the often elusive teen, single, affluent, and well-educated audiences. "It's very solid for reaching . . . doctors, lawyers, professionals—people you might have difficulty reaching because they are not interested in taking part in surveys," says Paul Jacobson, an executive of Greenfield

Online. "It's also a good medium for reaching working mothers and others who lead busy lives. They can do it in their own space and at their own convenience." The Internet also works well for bringing together people from different parts of the country, especially those in higher-income groups who can't spare the time to travel to a central site. For example, one virtual focus group convened by NFO Interactive to discuss the airline industry was made up of individuals with incomes of

Brand manager eliminates pilot costs, becomes hero

Testing new package designs online with rotating 3-D images not only saved the client expensive tooling costs but also saved time. Now manufacturers can design today and test tomorrow. Eliminating pilot costs and shortening "time to market" are just some of the many ways that Greenfield Online quantitative research beats the old-fashioned kind.
Put our expert consultants and advanced technology to work for you.
www.greenfield.com
888.291.9997

Greenfield Online
Leading the Research Revolution®

- Quantitative Studies
- Qualitative Studies
- Media Research
- Self-Directed Research
- Syndicated Studies
- Website Evaluations

HERO

©2000 Greenfield Online, Inc.

More and more companies are moving their research onto the Web. According to this Greenfield Online ad, in many ways, it "beats the old-fashioned kind."

$150,000 per year. "You just can't get these kinds of people to come into your office," says NFO's president, "but we can get them online."

However, using the Internet to conduct marketing research does have some drawbacks. For one, many consumers still don't have access to the Internet. Although the Web now attracts a more diverse audience, some segments haven't connected to the Web as quickly as the rest of the population. That makes it difficult to construct research samples that represent a broad cross section of Americans. Still, as Internet usage broadens, many mainstream marketers are now using Web research. General Mills, for example, conducts 60 percent of its consumer research online, reducing costs by 50 percent. And UPS uses online research extensively. "Between 40 percent and 50 percent of our customers are online, so it makes sense," says John Gilbert, UPS marketing research manager. He finds no difference in the results of traditional and online studies, and the online studies are much cheaper and faster to execute.

Another major problem of online research is controlling who's in the sample. Tom Greenbaum, president of Groups Plus, recalls a cartoon in *The New Yorker* in which two dogs are seated at a computer: "On the Internet, nobody knows you are a dog," one says to the other. "If you can't see a person with whom you are communicating, how do you know who they really are?" he says. Moreover, trying to draw conclusions from a "self-selected" sample of online users, those who clicked through to a questionnaire or accidentally landed in a chat room, can be troublesome.

To overcome such sample and response problems, many online research firms use opt-in communi-

ties and respondent panels. DMS, for example, recruits participants from America Online's 19 million subscribers, sending e-mail invitations to those who have agreed to participate. Greenfield Online maintains a 1.3 million–member Internet-based respondent panel, recruited through cooperative marketing arrangements with other sites. Because such respondents opt in and can answer questions whenever they are ready, they yield high response rates. Whereas response rates for telephone surveys have plummeted to less than 14 percent in recent years, online response rates typically reach 40 percent or higher.

Even when you reach the right respondents, online surveys and focus groups can lack the dynamics of more personal approaches. "You're missing all of the key things that make a focus group a viable method," says Greenbaum. "You may get people online to talk to each other and play off each other, but it's very different to watch people get excited about a concept." The online world is devoid of the eye contact, body language, and direct personal interactions found in traditional focus group research. And the Internet format—running, typed commentary and online "emoticons" (punctuation marks that express emotion, such as :-) to signify happiness)—greatly restricts respondent expressiveness.

Increasingly, however, advances in technology—such as the integration of animation, streaming audio and video, and virtual environments—will help to overcome these limitations. "In the online survey of the not-so-distant future," notes an online researcher, "respondents will be able to rotate, zoom in on and manipulate (like change the color or size of) three-dimensional products. They'll be able to peruse virtual stores, take items off shelves, and see how they function."

Just as the impersonal nature of the Web hinders two-way interactions, it can also provide anonymity. This often yields less guarded, more honest responses, especially when discussing topics such as income, medical conditions, lifestyle, or other sensitive issues. "People hiding behind a keyboard get pretty brave," says one researcher. Adds another:

From those questions that may simply make you squirm a little ("How much money did you lose in the stock market last month?"), to those you most probably don't want to answer to another human being, even if you don't know the person on the other end of the line ("How often do you have sex each week?"), Internet-based surveys tend to draw more honest responses. I once conducted the same survey in a mall and via the Internet. The question was, "How often do you bathe or shower each week?" The average answer, via the mall interview, was 6.2 times per week. The average via the Internet interview was 4.8 times per week, probably a more logical—and honest—response.

Perhaps the most explosive issue facing online researchers concerns consumer privacy. "The issue of privacy is going to be huge, huge—bigger than anybody imagines," says Rudy Nadilo, CEO of Greenfield Online. Critics worry that online researchers will spam our e-mail boxes with unsolicited e-mails to recruit respondents. They fear that unethical researchers will use the e-mail addresses and confidential responses gathered through surveys to sell products after the research is completed. They are concerned about the use of electronic agents (called Spambots or Spiders) that collect personal information without the respondents' consent. Failure to address such privacy issues could result in angry, less cooperative consumers and increased government intervention. Recognizing this fact, the research industry is setting tough standards for privacy protection and developing online research codes of ethics.

Although most researchers agree that online research will never completely replace traditional research, some are wildly optimistic about its prospects. Others, however, are more cautious. "Ten years from now, national telephone surveys will be the subject of research methodology folklore," proclaims one expert. "That's a little too soon," cautions another. "But in 20 years, yes."

Sources: Ian P. Murphy, "Interactive Research," *Marketing News*, January 20, 1997, pp. 1, 17; "NFO Executive Sees Most Research Going to Internet," *Advertising Age*, May 19, 1997, p. 50; Kate Maddox, "Virtual Panels Add Real Insight for Marketers," *Advertising Age*, June 29, 1998, pp. 34, 40; "Online or Off Target?" *American Demographics*, November 1998, pp. 20–21; Jon Rubin, "Online Marketing Research Comes of Age," *Brandweek*, October 30, 2000, pp. 26–28; Dana James, "The Future of Online Research," *Marketing News*, January 3, 2000, pp. 1, 11; "Web Smart," *Business Week*, May 14, 2001, p. EB56; and Noah Shachtman, "Web Enhanced Market Research," *Advertising Age*, June 18, 2001, p. T18.

the husband, wife, other family members, dealership salespeople, or all of these? The researcher must determine what information is needed and who is most likely to have it.

Second, *how many* people should be surveyed (what *sample size*)? Large samples give more reliable results than small samples. It is not necessary to sample the entire target market or even a large portion to get reliable results, however. If well chosen, samples of less than 1 percent of a population can often give good reliability.

Third, *how* should the people in the sample be *chosen* (what *sampling procedure*)? Table 5-4 describes different kinds of samples. Using *probability samples,* each population member has a known chance of being included in the sample, and researchers can calculate confidence limits for sampling error. But when probability sampling costs too much or takes too much time, marketing researchers often take *nonprobability samples,* even though their sampling error cannot be measured. These varied ways of drawing samples have different costs and time limitations as well as different accuracy and statistical properties. Which method is best depends on the needs of the research project.

RESEARCH INSTRUMENTS.   In collecting primary data, marketing researchers have a choice of two main research instruments—the *questionnaire* and *mechanical devices.* The *questionnaire* is by far the most common instrument, whether administered in person, by phone, or online.

Table 5-4 Types of Samples	
Probability Sample	
Sample random sample	Every member of the population has a known and equal chance of selection.
Stratified random sample	The population is divided into mutually exclusive groups (such as age groups), and random samples are drawn from each group.
Cluster (area) sample	The population is divided into mutually exclusive groups (such as blocks), and the researcher draws a sample of the groups to interview.
Nonprobability Sample	
Convenience sample	The researcher selects the easiest population members from which to obtain information.
Judgment sample	The researcher uses his or her judgment to select population members who are good prospects for accurate information.
Quota sample	The researcher finds and interviews a prescribed number of people in each of several categories.

Questionnaires are very flexible—there are many ways to ask questions. *Closed-end questions* include all the possible answers, and subjects make choices among them. Examples include multiple-choice questions and scale questions. *Open-end questions* allow respondents to answer in their own words. In a survey of airline users, Delta might simply ask, "What is your opinion of Delta Airlines?" Or it might ask people to complete a sentence: "When I choose an airline, the most important consideration is. . . ." These and other kinds of open-end questions often reveal more than closed-end questions because respondents are not limited in their answers. Open-end questions are especially useful in exploratory research, when the researcher is trying to find out *what* people think but not measuring *how many* people think in a certain way. Closed-end questions, on the other hand, provide answers that are easier to interpret and tabulate.

Researchers should also use care in the *wording* and *ordering* of questions. They should use simple, direct, unbiased wording. Questions should be arranged in a logical order. The first question should create interest if possible, and difficult or personal questions should be asked last so that respondents do not become defensive. A carelessly prepared questionnaire usually contains many errors (see Table 5-5).

Although questionnaires are the most common research instrument, *mechanical instruments* such as people meters and supermarket scanners are also used. Another group of mechanical devices measures subjects' physical responses. For example, a galvanometer measures the strength of interest or emotions aroused by a subject's exposure to different stimuli, such as an ad or picture. The galvanometer detects the minute degree of sweating that accompanies emotional arousal. Eye cameras are used to study respondents' eye movements to determine at what points their eyes focus first and how long they linger on a given item.

Implementing the Research Plan The researcher next puts the marketing research plan into action. This involves collecting, processing, and analyzing the information. Data collection can be carried out by the company's marketing research staff or by outside

---

Table 5-5   A "Questionable Questionnaire"

Suppose that a summer camp director had prepared the following questionnaire to use in interviewing the parents of prospective campers. How would you assess each question?

1. What is your income to the nearest hundred dollars? *People don't usually know their income to the nearest hundred dollars nor do they want to reveal their income that closely. Moreover, a researcher should never open a questionnaire with such a personal question.*
2. Are you a strong or weak supporter of overnight summer camping for your children? *What do strong and weak mean?*
3. Do your children behave themselves well at a summer camp? Yes ( ) no ( ) *Behave is a relative term. Furthermore, are yes and no the best response options for this question? Besides, will people answer this honestly and objectively? Why ask the question in the first place?*
4. How many camps mailed literature to you last year? This year? *Who can remember this?*
5. What are the most salient and determinant attributes in your evaluation of summer camps? *What are salient and determinant attributes? Don't use big words on me!*
6. Do you think it is right to deprive your child of the opportunity to grow into a mature person through the experience of summer camping? *A loaded question. Given the bias, how can any parent answer yes?*

 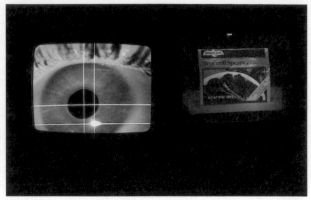

Mechanical research instruments: Eye cameras determine where eyes land and how long they linger on a given item.

firms. The data collection phase of the marketing research process is generally the most expensive and the most subject to error. The researcher should watch closely to make sure that the plan is implemented correctly and to guard against problems with contacting respondents, with respondents who refuse to cooperate or who give biased answers, and with interviewers who make mistakes or take shortcuts.

Researchers must process and analyze the collected data to isolate important information and findings. They need to check data for accuracy and completeness and code it for analysis. The researchers then tabulate the results and compute averages and other statistical measures.

Interpreting and Reporting the Findings   The market researcher must now interpret the findings, draw conclusions, and report them to management. The researcher should not try to overwhelm managers with numbers and fancy statistical techniques. Rather, the researcher should present important findings that are useful in the major decisions faced by management.

However, interpretation should not be left only to the researchers. They are often experts in research design and statistics, but the marketing manager knows more about the problem and the decisions that must be made. The best research is meaningless if the manager blindly accepts faulty interpretations from the researcher. Similarly, managers may be biased—they might tend to accept research results that show what they expected and to reject those that they did not expect or hope for. In many cases, findings can be interpreted in different ways, and discussions between researchers and managers will help point to the best interpretations. Thus, managers and researchers must work together closely when interpreting research results, and both must share responsibility for the research process and resulting decisions.

Analyzing Marketing Information

Information gathered in internal databases and through marketing intelligence and marketing research usually requires more analysis. And managers may need help to apply the information to their marketing problems and decisions. This help may include advanced statistical analysis to learn more about both the relationships within a set of data and their statistical reliability. Such analysis allows managers to go beyond means and standard deviations in the data and to answer questions about markets, marketing activities, and outcomes.

Information analysis might also involve a collection of analytical models that will help marketers make better decisions. Each model represents some real system, process, or outcome. These models can help answer the questions of *what if* and *which is best*. Marketing scientists have developed numerous models to help marketing managers make better marketing mix decisions, design sales territories and sales call plans, select sites for retail outlets, develop optimal advertising mixes, and forecast new-product sales.

Customer Relationship Management (CRM)

The question of how best to analyze and use individual customer data presents special problems. In recent years, many companies have acquired or developed special software and analysis techniques—called **customer relationship management (CRM)**—for integrating and applying the mountains of individual customer data contained in their databases. Customer relationship management (CRM) consists of sophisticated software and analytical tools that integrate customer information from all sources, analyze it in depth, and apply the results to build stronger customer relationships.

Most companies are awash in information about their customers. In fact, smart companies capture information at every possible customer *touch point*. These touch points include customer purchases, sales force contacts, service and support calls, Web site visits, satisfaction surveys, credit and payment interactions, market research studies—every contact between the customer and the company.

The trouble is that this information is usually scattered widely across the organization. It is buried deep in the separate databases, plans, and records of many different

Customer relationship management
Special software and analysis techniques for integrating and applying the individual customer data contained in databases.

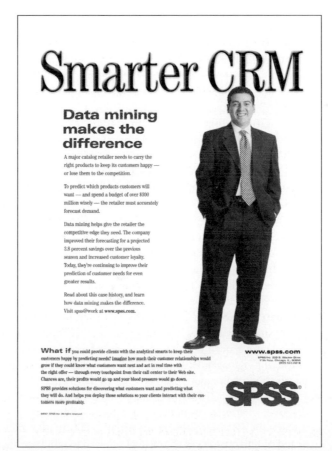

SPSS's CRM software integrates individual customer data from every touch point—from a company's call center to its Web site—to provide a 360-degree view of the customer relationship.

company functions and departments. CRM integrates everything that a company's sales, service, and marketing teams know about individual customers to provide a 360-degree view of the customer relationship. It pulls together, analyzes, and provides easy access to customer information from all of the various touch points. Companies use CRM analysis to assess the value of individual customers, identify the best ones to target, and customize their products and interactions to each customer.

CRM analysts develop *data warehouses* and use sophisticated *data mining* techniques to unearth the riches hidden in customer data. A data warehouse is a company-wide electronic storehouse of customer information—a centralized database of finely detailed customer data that needs to be sifted through for gems. The purpose of a data warehouse is not to gather information—many companies have already amassed endless stores of information about their customers. Rather, the purpose is to allow managers to integrate the information the company already has. Then, once the data warehouse brings the data together for analysis, the company uses high-powered data mining techniques to sift through the mounds of data and dig out interesting relationships and findings about customers.

Companies can gain many benefits from customer relationship management. By understanding customers better, they can provide higher levels of customer service and develop deeper customer relationships. They can use CRM to pinpoint high-value customers, target them more effectively, cross-sell their company's products, and create offers tailored to specific customer requirements. Consider the following examples:[15]

◆ FedEx recently launched a multimillion-dollar CRM initiative in an effort to cut costs, improve its customer support, and use its existing customer data to cross-sell and up-sell services to potential or existing customers. Using CRM software from Clarify Inc., the new system gives every member of FedEx's 3,300-person sales force a comprehensive view of every customer, detailing each one's needs and suggesting services that might meet those needs. For instance, if a customer who does a lot of international shipping calls to arrange a delivery, a sales rep will see a detailed customer history on his or her computer screen, assess the customer's needs, and determine the most appropriate offering on the spot. Beleaguered sales reps can use such high-tech help. FedEx offers 220 different services—from logistics to transportation to customs brokerage—often making it difficult for salespeople to identify the best fit for customers. The new CRM system will also help FedEx conduct promotions and qualify potential sales leads. The Clarify software will analyze market segments, point out market "sweet spots," and calculate how profitable those segments will be to the company and to individual salespeople.

◆ Ping, the golf equipment manufacturer, has used CRM successfully for about two years. Its data warehouse contains customer-specific data about every golf club it has manufactured and sold for the past fifteen years. The database, which includes grip size and special assembly instructions, helps Ping design and build golf clubs specifically for each of its customers and allows for easy replacement. If a golfer needs a new nine iron, for example, he can call in the serial number and Ping will ship an exact club to him within two days of receiving the order—a process that used to take two to three weeks. . . . This faster processing of data has given Ping a competitive edge in a market saturated with new products. "We've been up; the golf market has been down," says Steve Bostwick, Ping's marketing manager. Bostwick estimates the golf market to be down about 15 percent, but he says Ping has experienced double-digit growth.

◆ Lands' End invited IBM to mine its data on more than 2 million customers and help it discover customer groupings. Instead of coming up with the usual 5 segments, or 50 niches, the IBM researchers identified 5,000 market cells. One cell, for example, consisted of 850 customers who had purchased a light blue shirt and a red tie. Reasoning that these buyers might be more interested than the average customer in buying, say, a navy blue jacket, Lands' End might send a special offer for such a jacket to just these 850 customers. If the company is correct, the response rate in this market cell could be as high as 10 percent.

Most experts believe that good customer data, by itself, can give companies a substantial competitive advantage. Just ask American Express. At a secret location in Phoenix, security guards watch over American Express's 500 billion bytes of data on how customers have used its 35 million green, gold, and platinum charge cards. Amex uses the database to design carefully targeted offers in its monthly mailing of millions of customer bills.

CRM benefits don't come without cost or risk, not only in collecting the original customer data but also in maintaining and mining it. U.S. companies will spend an estimated $10 billion to $20 billion this year on CRM software alone from companies such as Siebel Systems and Oracle.[16] And as many as half of all CRM efforts fail to meet their objectives. The most common cause of CRM failures is that companies fail to clearly define their CRM goals or that they rely too heavily on the technology alone, rather than being truly customer-centered.

But when it works, the benefits of CRM usually outweigh the costs and risks. Based on regular polls of its customers, Siebel Systems claims that customers using its CRM software report an average 16 percent increase in revenues and 21 percent increase in customer loyalty and staff efficiency.[17]

During the past few years, CRM has exploded onto the corporate research scene. "No question that companies are getting tremendous value out of this," says one CRM consultant. "Companies [are] looking for ways to bring disparate sources of customer information together, then get it to all the customer touch points." Adds another consultant, these powerful new CRM techniques can unearth "a wealth of information to target that customer, to hit their hot button."[18]

Distributing and Using Marketing Information

Marketing information has no value until it is used to make better marketing decisions. Thus, the marketing information system must make the information available to the managers and others who make marketing decisions or deal with customers on a day-to-day basis. In some cases, this means providing managers with regular performance reports, intelligence updates, and reports on the results of research studies.

But marketing managers may also need nonroutine information for special situations and on-the-spot decisions. For example, a sales manager having trouble with a large customer may want a summary of the account's sales and profitability over the past year. Or a retail store manager who has run out of a best-selling product may want to know the current inventory levels in the chain's other stores. Increasingly, therefore, information distribution involves entering information into databases and making these available in a user-friendly and timely way.

Many firms use a company *intranet* to facilitate this process. The intranet provides ready access to research information, stored reports and articles, shared work documents, contact information for employees and other stakeholders, and more. For example, iGo, a catalog and Web retailer, integrates incoming customer service calls with up-to-date database information about customers' Web purchases and e-mail inquiries. By accessing this information on the intranet while speaking with the customer, iGo's service representatives can get a well-rounded picture of each customer's purchasing history and previous contacts with the company.

In addition, companies are increasingly allowing key customers and value-network members to access account and product information and other data on demand on *extranets*. Suppliers, customers, and select other network members may access a company's extranet to update their accounts, arrange purchases, and check orders against inventories to improve customer service. For example, one insurance firm allows its 200 independent agents access to a Web-based database of claim information covering 1 million customers. This allows the agents to avoid high-risk customers and to compare claim data with their own customer databases.[19]

Thanks to modern technology, today's marketing managers can gain direct access to the information system at any time and from virtually any location. While working at a home office, in a hotel room, on an airplane—anyplace where they can turn on a laptop computer and phone in—managers can obtain information from company databases or outside information services, analyze the information using statistical packages and models, prepare reports using word processing and presentation software, and communicate with others in the network through electronic communications. Such systems allow managers to get the information they need directly and quickly and to tailor it to their own needs.

Other Marketing Information Considerations

This section discusses marketing information in two special contexts: marketing research in small businesses and nonprofit organizations, and international marketing research. Finally, we look at public policy and ethics issues in marketing research.

Marketing Research in Small Businesses and Nonprofit Organizations

Just like their larger counterparts, small organizations need market information. Start-up businesses need information about their industries, competitors, potential customers, and reactions to new market offers. Existing small businesses must track changes in customer needs and wants, reactions to new products, and changes in the competitive environment.

Managers of small businesses and nonprofit organizations often think that marketing research can be done only by experts in large companies with big research budgets. Although large-scale research studies are beyond the budgets of most small businesses, many of the marketing research techniques discussed in this chapter also can be used by smaller organizations in a less formal manner and at little or no expense.

Managers of small businesses and nonprofit organizations can obtain good marketing information simply by observing things around them. For example, retailers can evaluate new locations by *observing* vehicle and pedestrian traffic. They can monitor competitor advertising by collecting ads from local media. They can evaluate their customer mix by recording how many and what kinds of customers shop in the store at different times. In addition, many small business managers routinely visit their rivals and socialize with competitors to gain insights. Tom Coohill, a chef who owns two Atlanta restaurants, gives managers a food allowance to dine out and bring back ideas. Atlanta jeweler Frank Maier Jr., who often visits out-of-town rivals, spotted and copied a dramatic way of lighting displays.[20]

Managers can conduct informal *surveys* using small convenience samples. The director of an art museum can learn what patrons think about new exhibits by conducting informal focus groups—inviting small groups to lunch and having discussions on topics of interest. Retail salespeople can talk with customers visiting the store; hospital officials can interview patients. Restaurant managers might make random phone calls during slack hours to interview consumers about where they eat out and what they think of various restaurants in the area.

Managers also can conduct their own simple *experiments*. For example, by changing the themes in regular fund-raising mailings and watching the results, a nonprofit manager can find out much about which marketing strategies work best. By varying newspaper advertisements, a store manager can learn the effects of things such as ad size and position, price coupons, and media used.

Small organizations can obtain most of the secondary data available to large businesses. In addition, many associations, local media, chambers of commerce, and government agencies provide special help to small organizations. The U.S. Small Business Administration offers dozens of free publications and a Web site (www.sbaonline.sba.gov) that give advice on topics ranging from starting, financing, and expanding a small business to ordering business cards. Other excellent Web resources for small businesses include the U.S. Census Bureau (www.census.gov) and the Bureau of Economic Analysis (www. bea.doc.gov).

The business sections at local libraries can also be a good source of information. They often provide access to resources such as *Standard & Poor's, Hoover's Handbooks, The Statistical Abstract of the United States, Dun & Bradstreet, Woods & Poole Economics, Sourcebook America, Claritas, Market Statistics,* and many business periodicals. Local newspapers often provide information on local shoppers and their buying patterns. Finally, small businesses can collect a considerable amount of information at very little cost on the Internet. They can scour competitor and customer Web sites and use Internet search engines to research specific companies and issues.

In summary, secondary data collection, observation, surveys, and experiments can all be used effectively by small organizations with small budgets. Although these informal research methods are less complex and less costly, they still must be conducted carefully. Managers must think carefully about the objectives of the research, formulate questions in advance, recognize the biases introduced by smaller samples and less skilled researchers, and conduct the research systematically.[21]

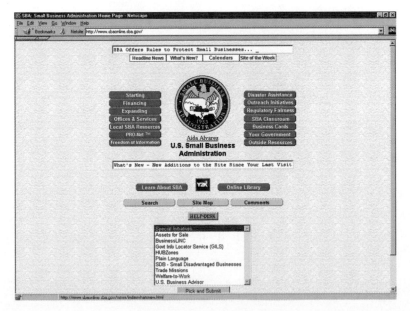

Many associations, media, and government agencies provide special help to small organizations. Here, the U.S. Small Business Administration offers a Web site that gives advice on topics ranging from starting, financing, and expanding a small business to ordering business cards.

International Marketing Research

International marketing researchers follow the same steps as domestic researchers, from defining the research problem and developing a research plan to interpreting and reporting the results. However, these researchers often face more and different problems. Whereas domestic researchers deal with fairly homogenous markets within a single country, international researchers deal with differing markets in many different countries. These markets often vary greatly in their levels of economic development, cultures and customs, and buying patterns.

In many foreign markets, the international researcher sometimes has a difficult time finding good secondary data. Whereas U.S. marketing researchers can obtain reliable secondary data from dozens of domestic research services, many countries have almost no research services at all. Some of the largest international research services do operate in many countries. For example, AC Nielsen Corporation, the world's largest marketing research company, has offices in more than 100 countries. And 47 percent of the revenues of the world's 25 largest marketing research firms come from outside their own countries.[22] However, most research firms operate in only a relative handful of countries. Thus, even when secondary information is available, it usually must be obtained from many different sources on a country-by-country basis, making the information difficult to combine or compare.

Because of the scarcity of good secondary data, international researchers often must collect their own primary data. Here again, researchers face problems not found domestically. For example, they may find it difficult simply to develop good samples. U.S.

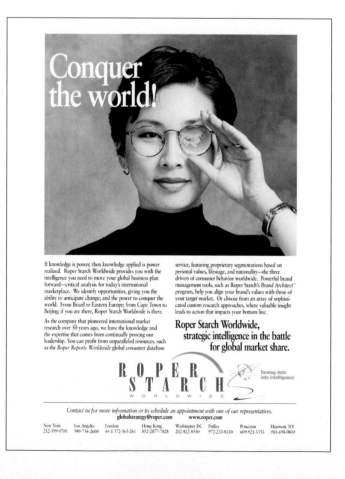

Some of the largest research services operate in many countries: Roper Starch Worldwide provides companies with information resources "from Brazil to Eastern Europe; from Cape Town to Beijing—if you are there, Roper Starch Worldwide is there."

researchers can use current telephone directories, census tract data, and any of several sources of socioeconomic data to construct samples. However, such information is largely lacking in many countries.

Once the sample is drawn, the U.S. researcher usually can reach most respondents easily by telephone, by mail, on the Internet, or in person. Reaching respondents is often not so easy in other parts of the world. Researchers in Mexico cannot rely on telephone and mail data collection—most data collection is door to door and concentrated in three or four of the largest cities. In some countries, few people have phones; for example, there are only thirty-two phones per thousand people in Argentina. In other countries, the postal system is notoriously unreliable. In Brazil, for instance, an estimated 30 percent of the mail is never delivered. In many developing countries, poor roads and transportation systems make certain areas hard to reach, making personal interviews difficult and expensive. Finally, few people in developing countries are connected to the Internet.[23]

Cultural differences from country to country cause additional problems for international researchers. Language is the most obvious obstacle. For example, questionnaires must be prepared in one language and then translated into the languages of each country researched. Responses then must be translated back into the original language for analysis and interpretation. This adds to research costs and increases the risks of error.

Translating a questionnaire from one language to another is anything but easy. Many idioms, phrases, and statements mean different things in different cultures. For example, a Danish executive noted, "Check this out by having a different translator put back into English what you've translated from English. You'll get the shock of your life. I remember [an example in which] 'out of sight, out of mind' had become 'invisible things are insane.'"[24]

Consumers in different countries also vary in their attitudes toward marketing research. People in one country may be very willing to respond; in other countries, nonresponse can be a major problem. Customs in some countries may prohibit people from talking with strangers. In certain cultures, research questions often are considered too personal. For example, in many Latin American countries, people may feel embarrassed to talk with researchers about their choices of shampoo, deodorant, or other personal care products.

Even when respondents are *willing* to respond, they may not be *able* to because of high functional illiteracy rates. And middle-class people in developing countries often make false claims in order to appear well-off. For example, in a study of tea consumption in India, over 70 percent of middle-income respondents claimed that they used one of several national brands. However, the researchers had good reason to doubt these results—more than 60 percent of the tea sold in India is unbranded generic tea.

Despite these problems, the recent growth of international marketing has resulted in a rapid increase in the use of international marketing research. Global companies have little choice but to conduct such research. Although the costs and problems associated with international research may be high, the costs of not doing it—in terms of missed opportunities and mistakes—might be even higher. Once recognized, many of the problems associated with international marketing research can be overcome or avoided.

Public Policy and Ethics in Marketing Research

Most marketing research benefits both the sponsoring company and its consumers. Through marketing research, companies learn more about consumers' needs, resulting in more satisfying products and services. However, the misuse of marketing research can also harm or annoy consumers. Two major public policy and ethics issues in marketing research are intrusions on consumer privacy and the misuse of research findings.

Intrusions on Consumer Privacy Many consumers feel positively about marketing research and believe that it serves a useful purpose. Some actually enjoy being interviewed and giving their opinions. However, others strongly resent or even mistrust marketing research. A few consumers fear that researchers might use sophisticated techniques to probe our deepest feelings and then use this knowledge to manipulate our buying. Or they worry that marketers are building huge databases full of personal information about customers. For example, DoubleClick has profiles on 100 million Web users, identified by cookies rather than by name. Privacy groups worry that such huge profiling databases could be merged with offline databases and threaten individual privacy. In fact, DoubleClick recently won a court case allowing it to integrate online data with that collected by a consumer panel firm.[25]

Others consumers may have been taken in by previous "research surveys" that actually turned out to be attempts to sell them something. Still other consumers confuse legitimate marketing research studies with telemarketing efforts and say "no" before the interviewer can even begin. Most, however, simply resent the intrusion. They dislike mail or telephone surveys that are too long or too personal or that interrupt them at inconvenient times.

Increasing consumer resentment has become a major problem for the research industry. One recent poll found that 82 percent of Americans worry that they lack control over how businesses use their personal information, and 41 percent said that business had invaded their privacy. These concerns have led to lower survey response rates in recent years. One study found that 38 percent of Americans now refuse to be interviewed in an average survey, up dramatically from a decade ago. Another study found that 59 percent of consumers had refused to give information to a company because they thought it was not really needed or too personal, up from 42 percent just five years earlier.[26]

The research industry is considering several options for responding to this problem. One is to expand its "Your Opinion Counts" program to educate consumers about the benefits of marketing research and to distinguish it from telephone selling and database building. Another option is to provide a toll-free number that people can call to verify that a survey is legitimate. The industry also has considered adopting broad standards, perhaps based on Europe's International Code of Marketing and Social Research Practice. This code outlines researchers' responsibilities to respondents and to the general public. For example, it says that researchers should make their names and addresses available to participants, and it bans companies from representing activities such as database compilation or sales and promotional pitches as research.

Many companies—including IBM, AT&T, American Express, DoubleClick, and Microsoft—are now appointing a "chief privacy officer," whose job is to safeguard the privacy of consumers who do business with the company. At least 100 U.S. companies now employ such privacy chiefs and the number is expected to grow rapidly. The chief privacy officer for Microsoft says that his job is to come up with data policies for the company to follow, make certain that every program the company creates enhances customer privacy, and inform and educate company employees about privacy issues and concerns.[27]

According to Sally Cowan, who runs the privacy operations of American Express, any business that deals with consumers' information has to take privacy issues seriously. "Privacy is not the new hot issue at American Express," she says. The company developed a set of formal privacy principles in 1991, and in 1998 it became one of the first companies to post privacy policies on its Web site. This penchant for customer privacy led American Express to introduce new services that protect consumers' privacy when they use an American Express card to buy items online. American Express views privacy as a way to gain competitive advantage—as something that leads consumers to choose one company over another.[28]

In the end, if researchers provide value in exchange for information, customers will gladly provide it. For example, Amazon.com's customers do not mind if the firm builds a database of products they buy in order to provide future product recommendations. This saves time and provides value. Similarly, Bizrate users gladly complete surveys rating e-tail sites because they can view the overall ratings of others when making purchase decisions. The best approach is for researchers to ask only for the information they need, to use it responsibly to provide value, and to avoid sharing information without the customer's permission.

Misuse of Research Findings Research studies can be powerful persuasion tools; companies often use study results as claims in their advertising and promotion. Today, however, many research studies appear to be little more than vehicles for pitching the sponsor's products. In fact, in some cases, the research surveys appear to have been designed just to produce the intended effect. Few advertisers openly rig their research designs or blatantly misrepresent the findings; most abuses tend to be subtle "stretches." Consider the following examples:[29]

A study by Chrysler contends that Americans overwhelmingly prefer Chrysler to Toyota after test-driving both. However, the study included just 100 people in each of two tests. More importantly, none of the people surveyed owned a foreign car, so they appear to be favorably predisposed to U.S. cars.

A Black Flag survey asked: "A roach disk . . . poisons a roach slowly. The dying roach returns to the nest and after it dies is eaten by other roaches. In turn these roaches become poisoned and die. How effective do you think this type of product would be in killing roaches?" Not surprisingly, 79 percent said effective.

A poll sponsored by the disposable diaper industry asked: "It is estimated that disposable diapers account for less than 2 percent of the trash in today's landfills. In contrast, beverage containers, third-class mail, and yard waste are estimated to account for about 21 percent of the trash in landfills. Given this, in your opinion, would it be fair to ban disposable diapers?" Again, not surprisingly, 84 percent said no.

Thus, subtle manipulations of the study's sample or the choice or wording of questions can greatly affect the conclusions reached.

In others cases, so-called independent research studies actually are paid for by companies with an interest in the outcome. Small changes in study assumptions or in how results are interpreted can subtly affect the direction of the results. For example, at least four widely quoted studies compare the environmental effects of using disposable diapers to those of using cloth diapers. The two studies sponsored by the cloth diaper industry conclude that cloth diapers are more environmentally friendly. Not surprisingly, the other two studies, sponsored by the paper diaper industry, conclude just the opposite. Yet both appear to be correct *given* the underlying assumptions used.

Recognizing that surveys can be abused, several associations—including the American Marketing Association, the Council of American Survey Research Organizations, and the Marketing Research Association—have developed codes of research ethics and standards of conduct.[30] In the end, however, unethical or inappropriate actions cannot simply be regulated away. Each company must accept responsibility for policing the conduct and reporting of its own marketing research to protect consumers' best interests and its own.

STOP *Rest Stop: Reviewing the Concepts*

In the previous chapter, we discussed the marketing environment. In this chapter, you've studied tools used to gather and manage information that marketing managers and others can use to assess opportunities in the environment and the impact of a firm's marketing efforts. After this brief pause for rest and reflection, we'll head out again in the next chapter to take a closer look at the object of all of this activity—consumers and their buying behavior.

In today's complex and rapidly changing environment, marketing managers need more and better information to make effective and timely decisions. This greater need for information has been matched by the explosion of information technologies for supplying information. Using today's new technologies, companies can now handle great quantities of information, sometimes even too much. Yet marketers often complain that they lack enough of the *right* kind of information or have an excess of the *wrong* kind. In response, many companies are now studying their managers' information needs, and designing information systems that help managers develop and manage market and customer information.

1. Explain the importance of information to the company.

Good products and marketing programs start with a complete understanding of consumer needs and wants. Thus, the company needs sound information in order to produce superior value and satisfaction for customers. The company also requires information on competitors, resellers, and other actors and forces in the marketplace. Increasingly, marketers are viewing information not only as an input for making better decisions but also as an important strategic asset and marketing tool.

2. Define the marketing information system and discuss its parts.

The *marketing information system (MIS)* consists of people, equipment, and procedures to gather, sort, analyze, evaluate, and distribute needed, timely, and accurate information to marketing decision makers. A well-designed information system begins and ends with users. The MIS first *assesses information needs,* then *develops information* from internal databases, marketing intelligence activities, and marketing research. *Internal databases* provide information on the company's own sales, costs, inventories, cash flows, and accounts receivable and payable. Such data can be obtained quickly and cheaply but often needs to be adapted for marketing decisions. *Marketing intelligence* activities supply everyday information about developments in the external marketing environment. *Market research* consists of collecting information relevant to a specific marketing problem faced by the company. Lastly, the MIS *distributes information* gathered from these sources to the right managers in the right form and at the right time to help them make better marketing decisions.

3. Outline the steps in the marketing research process.

The first step in the marketing research process involves *defining the problem and setting the research objectives,* which may be exploratory, descriptive, or causal research. The second step consists of *developing a research plan* for collecting data from primary and secondary sources. The third step calls for *implementing the marketing research plan* by gathering, processing, and analyzing the information. The fourth step consists of *interpreting and reporting the findings.* Additional information analysis helps marketing managers apply the information and provides them with sophisticated statistical procedures and models from which to develop more rigorous findings.

Both *internal* and *external* secondary data sources often provide information more quickly and at a lower cost than primary data sources, and they can sometimes yield information that a company cannot collect by itself. However, needed information might not exist in secondary sources, and even if data can be found, they might be largely unusable. Researchers must also evaluate secondary information to ensure that it is *relevant, accurate, current,* and *impartial.* Primary research must also be evaluated for these features. Each primary data collection method—*observational, survey,* and *experiment*—has its own advantages and disadvantages. Each of the various primary research contact methods—mail, telephone, personal interview, and online—also has its own advantages and drawbacks. Similarly, each contact method has its pluses and minuses.

4. Explain how companies analyze and distribute marketing information.

Information gathered in internal databases and through marketing intelligence and marketing research usually requires more analysis. This may include advanced statistical analysis or the application of analytical models that will help marketers make better decisions. In recent years, marketers have paid special attention to the analysis of individual customer data. Many companies have now acquired or developed special software and analysis techniques—called *customer relationship management (CRM)*—that integrate, analyze, and apply the mountains of individual customer data contained in their databases.

Marketing information has no value until it is used to make better marketing decisions. Thus, the marketing information system must make the information available to the managers and others who make marketing decisions or deal with customers. In some cases, this means providing regular reports and updates; in other cases it means making nonroutine information available for special situations and on-the-spot decisions. Many firms use company intranets and extranets to facilitate this process. Thanks to modern technology, today's marketing managers can gain direct access to the information system at any time and from virtually any location.

5. Discuss the special issues some marketing researchers face, including public policy and ethics issues.

Some marketers face special marketing research situations, such as those conducting research in small business, nonprofit, or international situations. Marketing research can be conducted effectively by small busi-

nesses and nonprofit organizations with limited budgets. International marketing researchers follow the same steps as domestic researchers but often face more and different problems. All organizations need to respond responsibly to major public policy and ethical issues surrounding marketing research, including issues of intrusions on consumer privacy and misuse of research findings.

Navigating the Key Terms

For a detailed analysis of the meaning and importance of each of the following key terms, visit our Web page at www.prenhall.com/kotler.

Causal research
Customer relationship management (CRM)
Descriptive research

Experimental research
Exploratory research
Focus group interviewing
Internal databases
Marketing information system (MIS)
Marketing intelligence
Marketing research
Observational research

Online databases
Online (Internet) marketing research
Primary data
Sample
Secondary data
Single-source data systems
Survey research

Travel Log

The following concept checks and discussion questions will help you to keep track of and apply the concepts you've studied in this chapter.

Concept Checks

Fill in the blanks, then look for the correct answers.

1. A _____ consists of people, equipment, and procedures to gather, sort, analyze, evaluate, and distribute needed, timely, and accurate information to marketing decision makers.

2. The information needed by marketing managers can be obtained from _____, _____, and _____.

3. _____ is a systematic collection and analysis of publicly available information about competitors and developments in the marketing environment.

4. _____ can be defined as the systematic design, collection, analysis, and reporting of data relevant to a specific marketing situation facing an organization.

5. The marketing research process has four steps: _____, _____, _____, and _____.

6. A marketing research project might have any one of three types of objectives. If the objective were to gather preliminary information that would help define the problem and suggest hypotheses, the researcher would use _____ research.

7. _____ data consist of information collected for the specific purpose at hand.

8. A wide range of companies now use _____ research—which combines intensive observation with customer interviews—to gain deep insights into how consumers buy and live with their products.

9. _____ research is the approach best suited for gathering descriptive information.

10. Of the four research contact methods discussed, _____ is the only one rated as "excellent" with respect to low cost.

11. A researcher is using a _____ sample when he or she selects the easiest population members from which to obtain information.

12. _____ consists of sophisticated software and analytical tools that integrate customer information from all sources, analyze it in depth, and apply the results to build stronger customer relationships.

Concept Checks Answers: 1. Marketing information system (MIS); 2. internal data, marketing intelligence, and marketing research; 3. Marketing intelligence; 4. Marketing research; 5. defining the problem and research objectives, developing the research plan, implementing the research plan, and interpreting and reporting the findings; 6. exploratory; 7. Primary; 8. ethnographic; 9. Survey; 10. online; 11. convenience; 12. Customer relationship management (CRM).

Discussing the Issues

1. Many companies build extensive internal databases so marketing managers can readily access and work with information in the database to identify marketing opportunities and problems, plan programs, and evaluate performance. If you were the marketing manager for a large computer software manufacturer, what type of information would you like to have available in your internal database? Explain.

2. Marketing intelligence has become increasingly important to marketing managers because of its ability to aid them in improving strategic decision making. What other benefits are attributed to a marketing intelligence function? Assuming that you have been hired as a consultant to a company that is developing a new highly-caffeinated energy drink, what type of intelligence sleuthing tips would you offer the firm?

3. Name the type of research that would be appropriate in the following situations, and explain why:
   a. Kellogg wants to investigate the impact of young children on their parent's decisions to buy breakfast foods.
   b. Your college bookstore wants to get some insights into how students feel about the store's merchandise, prices, and service.
   c. McDonald's is considering where to locate a new outlet in a fast-growing suburb.
   d. Gillette wants to determine whether a new line of deodorant for children will be profitable.

4. Focus group interviewing is both a widely used and widely criticized research technique in marketing. List the advantages and disadvantages of focus groups. Suggest some kinds of questions that are suitable for exploration by using focus groups. How could focus group research be done via the Internet?

5. Increasingly, companies are turning to customer relationship management (CRM) as a means for integrating and applying the mountains of customer data contained in their databases. Two techniques that analysts use to aid them in applying CRM are data warehousing and data mining. Explain each term and how each is used to improve relationships and "connections." Next, assume that your local grocery store has implemented a store service card. This card allows you to receive special patronage discounts and to cash personal checks. Beginning with the registration process for the card through its final usage at the checkout stand, discuss all the types of data that could be collected on customers and how this data could eventually be used to build relationships.

 **Mastering Marketing**

Using marketing information systems, marketing intelligence, marketing research, and customer relationship management is vital to today's competitive marketing organization. Take one of the above areas and demonstrate how CanGo has used the area to better understand its competitive environment and relate to its customers. Provide examples to illustrate your conclusions.

 Traveling on the Net

Point of Interest: Researching Young Women

Many marketing research endeavors examine changes in the marketing environment. This often means that marketers must meet new consumer needs that may be quite different—even directly opposite—from those in the past. An example would be investigations done by Mattel. Mattel's *Barbie* dolls began as high fashion playthings for little girls. In those days it was assumed that all little girls would be homemakers and high fashion fantasy was an acceptable dream. Today, Mattel sees a different role and relationship with young women. See Mattel's *Barbie* Web site at www.barbie.com. Mattel seeks to appreciate lifestyle changes taking place with young women. Issues such as diversity and individuality are considered by the company. By examining the history of the *Barbie* line, you can track changes in the marketing environment and among customers by examining how the company has modified its products.

For Discussion

1. Make a list of the ways *Barbie* has changed to meet the needs of the contemporary young woman. How do these changes affect female image, self-confidence, and prestige? What kind of research would Mattel use to discover these changes? Give examples.

2. Take your list and apply it to other gender-related Web sites such as www.delias.com, www.women.com, and www.ivillage.com. Do you see any similarities in the trends with respect to basic appeals to females? If so, what are they?

3. The *Barbie* web site allows a young female to custom design her own *Barbie* doll. Go to the Fashion Fun section and attempt to do this. What type of information has Mattel just collected about your demographics and preferences? How could this information be used to build "connections" with young women?

Application Thinking

Assume that you are the marketing manager for a proposed new lifestyle doll line for Mattel. Design a research plan that would yield information on what type of doll should be created by the company. Be sure to specify the forms of research you would suggest, the markets and preferences to be analyzed, and how (if possible) to use the Internet in your research endeavor. Present your recommendations to the class.

MAP—Marketing Applications

MAP Stop 5

The American consumer is one of the most researched subjects in the world. Millions of dollars are spent annually to find out what you want, when you want it, and how much you will pay for it. Becoming intimate with one's consumer is not a luxury, it is a necessity. The desire to become a closer companion to the customer has spurred interest in ethnographic research—which combines intensive observation with customer interviews (see *Marketing At Work 5-1* for more details). However, this form of research can often be an expensive pursuit for a company. Is there a lower cost alternative? Some in marketing believe that one of the oldest forms of research—the consumer poll—is the answer. At one time polling was expensive and often seriously inaccurate. What if the researcher could, however, get the advantages of participatory information results combined with low cost. If this were possible, it would be of great interest. Well, hold your questionnaires, the Internet has provided the answer—the online poll. While often not scientifically accurate, the online poll has become a great way to get large amounts of preferential information from an interested audience at a low cost. Trends do reveal themselves and, unlike normal polling, those who participate can be re-contacted by an interested marketer because a trail is left on the Internet. Ask someone a question in a shopping mall and then he or she is gone. On the Internet this same consumer can be re-contacted at a later date with a variety of messages. In fact, many do not mind the re-contact at all—it is a "connection" they actually desire. Have you been polled lately? If you want to participate in our society and marketplace, isn't it about time that you were?

Thinking Like a Marketing Manager

Interested in participating in a research process yourself? Go to the following Web sites: www.pollingreport.com, www.gallup.com, and www.cnn.com and answer questions 1–4 below.

1. Which of the polls or questionnaires seemed the most interesting to you?

2. Which of the polls were easiest to answer?

3. Which of the polls could be tied most easily to marketing research? Why?

4. Under what circumstances are you willing to supply information to an online researcher? To a Web site? Explain.

5. The American Consumer Opinion Web site (www.acop.com) maintains a panel of Internet users who agree to complete online surveys. Sign up and see how it works.

6. Assume that you are a marketing researcher that has just been hired to establish an online marketing poll for a product or service of your choice (your choice should not currently have an online polling mechanism). Using the product or service's Web site, construct an online poll for the company. Specify research objectives, questions for your poll, who the poll will be intended for, what you will learn from your poll, how the poll results will be fed back to those polled (if they will), and how the poll results or the poll itself will aid you in gaining data on and making "connections" with your customers or viewers. Report your results to the class.

chapter 6

Consumer and Business Buyer Behavior

ROAD MAP:
Previewing the Concepts

In the previous chapter, you studied how marketers obtain, analyze, and use information to identify marketing opportunities and to assess marketing programs. In this chapter, you'll continue your marketing journey with a closer look at the most important element of the marketing environment—customers. The aim of marketing is to somehow affect how customers think about and behave toward the organization and its marketing offers. To affect the whats, whens, and hows of buying behavior, marketers must first understand the *whys*. We look first at *final consumer* buying influences and processes and then at the buying behavior of *business customers*. You'll see that understanding buying behavior is an essential but very difficult task.

▶ After studying this chapter, you should be able to

1. understand the consumer market and the major factors that influence consumer buyer behavior
2. identify and discuss the stages in the buyer decision process
3. describe the adoption and diffusion process for new products
4. define the business market and identify the major factors that influence business buyer behavior
5. list and define the steps in the business buying decision process

Our first point of interest: Harley-Davidson, maker of the nation's top-selling heavyweight motorcycles. Who rides these big Harley "Hogs"? What moves them to tattoo their bodies with the Harley emblem, abandon home and hearth for the open road, and flock to Harley rallies by the hundreds of thousands? *You* might be surprised, but Harley-Davidson knows *very* well.

Few brands engender such intense loyalty as that found in the hearts of Harley-Davidson owners. "The Harley audience is granitelike" in its devotion, laments the vice president of sales for competitor Yamaha. Observes the publisher of *American Iron,* an industry publication, "You don't see people tattooing Yamaha on their bodies." And according to the president of a motorcycle research company, "For a lot of people, it's not that they want a motorcycle; it's that they want a Harley—the brand is that strong." Each year, in early March, more than 400,000 Harley bikers rumble through the streets of Daytona Beach, Florida, to attend Harley-Davidson's Bike Week celebration. Bikers from across the nation lounge on their low-slung Harleys, swap biker tales, and sport T-shirts proclaiming "I'd rather push a Harley than drive a Honda."

Riding such intense emotions, Harley-Davidson has rumbled its way to the top of the fast-growing heavyweight motorcycle market. Harley's "Hogs" capture more than one-fifth of all U.S. bike sales and more than half of the heavyweight segment. Both the segment and

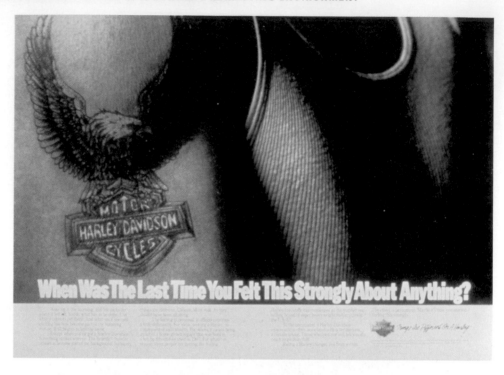

When Was The Last Time You Felt This Strongly About Anything?

Harley's sales are growing rapidly. In fact, for several years running, sales have far outstripped supply, with customer waiting lists of up to three years for popular models and street prices running well above suggested list prices. "We've seen people buy a new Harley and then sell it in the parking lot for $4,000 to $5,000 more," says one dealer. Since its initial public stock offering in 1986, by the year 2000, Harley-Davidson shares had split four times and were up more than 7,100 percent.

Harley-Davidson's marketers spend a great deal of time thinking about customers and their buying behavior. They want to know who their customers are, what they think and how they feel, and why they buy a Harley rather than a Yamaha or a Kawasaki or a big Honda American Classic. What is it that makes Harley buyers so fiercely loyal? These are difficult questions; even Harley owners themselves don't know exactly what motivates their buying. But Harley management puts top priority on understanding customers and what makes them tick.

Who rides a Harley? You might be surprised. It's no longer the Hell's Angels crowd—the burly, black-leather-jacketed rebels and biker chicks who once made up Harley's core clientele. Motorcycles are attracting a new breed of riders—older, more affluent, and better educated. Harley now appeals more to "rubbies" (rich urban bikers) than to rebels. The average Harley customer is a 46-year-old husband with a median household income of $73,800. Harley's big, comfortable cruisers give these new consumers the easy ride, prestige, and twist-of-the-wrist power they want and can afford.

Harley-Davidson makes good bikes, and to keep up with its shifting market, the company has upgraded its showrooms and sales approaches. But Harley customers are buying a lot more than just a quality bike and a smooth sales pitch. To gain a better understanding of customers' deeper motivations, Harley-Davidson conducted focus groups in which it invited bikers to make cut-and-paste collages of pictures that expressed their feelings about Harley-Davidsons. (Can't you just see a bunch of hard-core bikers doing this?) It then mailed out 16,000 surveys containing a typical battery of psychological, sociological, and demographic questions as well as subjective questions such as "Is Harley more typified by a brown bear or a lion?" The research revealed seven core customer types:

adventure-loving traditionalists, sensitive pragmatists, stylish status seekers, laid-back campers, classy capitalists, cool-headed loners, and cocky misfits. However, all owners appreciated their Harleys for the same basic reasons. "It didn't matter if you were the guy who swept the floors of the factory or if you were the CEO at that factory, the attraction to Harley was very similar," says a Harley executive. "Independence, freedom, and power were the universal Harley appeals."

These studies confirm that Harley customers are doing more than just buying motorcycles. They're making a lifestyle statement and displaying an attitude. As one analyst suggests, owning a Harley makes you "the toughest, baddest guy on the block. Never mind that [you're] a dentist or an accountant. You [feel] wicked astride all that power." Your Harley renews your spirits and announces your independence. As the Harley Web site's home page announces, "Thumbing the starter of a Harley-Davidson does a lot more than fire the engine. It fires the imagination." Adds a Harley dealer: "We sell a dream here. Our customers lead hardworking professional or computer-oriented lives. Owning a Harley removes barriers to meeting people on a casual basis, and it gives you maximum self-expression in your own space."

The classic look, the throaty sound, the very idea of a Harley—all contribute to its mystique. Owning this "American legend" makes you a part of something bigger, a member of the Harley family. The fact that you have to wait to get a Harley makes it all that much more satisfying to have one. In fact, the company deliberately restricts its output. "Our goal is to eventually run production at a level that's always one motorcycle short of demand," says Harley-Davidson's chief executive.

Such strong emotions and motivations are captured in a classic Harley-Davidson advertisement. The ad shows a close-up of an arm, the bicep adorned with a Harley-Davidson tattoo. The headline asks, "When was the last time you felt this strongly about anything?" The ad copy outlines the problem and suggests a solution: "Wake up in the morning and life picks up where it left off. You do what has to be done. Use what it takes to get there. And what once seemed exciting has now become part of the numbing routine. It all begins to feel the same. Except when you've got a Harley-Davidson. Something strikes a nerve. The heartfelt thunder rises up, refusing to become part of the background. Suddenly things are different. Clearer. More real. As they should have been all along. The feeling is personal. For some, owning a Harley is a statement of individuality. For others, owning a Harley means being a part of a home-grown legacy that was born in a tiny Milwaukee shed in 1903. . . . To the uninitiated, a Harley-Davidson motorcycle is associated with a certain look, a certain sound. Anyone who owns one will tell you it's much more than that. Riding a Harley changes you from within. The effect is permanent. Maybe it's time you started feeling this strongly. Things are different on a Harley."[1]

The Harley-Davidson example shows that many different factors affect consumer buying behavior. Buying behavior is never simple, yet understanding it is the essential task of marketing management. First, we explore the dynamics of final-consumer markets and consumer buyer behavior. We then examine business markets and the business buying process.

Consumer Markets and Consumer Buyer Behavior

Consumer buyer behavior refers to the buying behavior of final consumers, individuals and households who buy goods and services for personal consumption. All of these final consumers combine to make up the **consumer market.** The American consumer market consists of more than 284 million people who consume many trillions of dollars' worth of

Consumer buyer behavior
The buying behavior of final consumers—individuals and households who buy goods and services for personal consumption.

Consumer market
All the individuals and households who buy or acquire goods and services for personal consumption.

goods and services each year, making it one of the most attractive consumer markets in the world. The world consumer market consists of more than 6 *billion* people.[2]

Consumers around the world vary tremendously in age, income, education level, and tastes. They also buy an incredible variety of goods and services. How these diverse consumers connect with each other and with other elements of the world around them impacts their choices among various products, services, and companies. Here we examine the fascinating array of factors that affect consumer behavior.

Model of Consumer Behavior

Consumers make many buying decisions every day. Most large companies research consumer buying decisions in great detail to answer questions about what consumers buy, where they buy, how and how much they buy, when they buy, and why they buy. Marketers can study actual consumer purchases to find out what they buy, where, and how much. But learning about the *whys* of consumer buying behavior is not so easy—the answers are often locked deep within the consumer's head.

The central question for marketers is: How do consumers respond to various marketing efforts the company might use? The starting point is the stimulus–response model of buyer behavior shown in Figure 6-1. This figure shows that marketing and other stimuli enter the consumer's "black box" and produce certain responses. Marketing stimuli consist of the four Ps: product, price, place, and promotion. Other stimuli include major forces and events in the buyer's environment: economic, technological, political, and cultural. All these inputs enter the buyer's black box, where they are turned into a set of observable buyer responses: product choice, brand choice, dealer choice, purchase timing, and purchase amount.

The marketer wants to understand how the stimuli are changed into responses inside the consumer's black box, which has two parts. First, the buyer's characteristics influence how he or she perceives and reacts to the stimuli. Second, the buyer's decision process itself affects the buyer's behavior. We look first at buyer characteristics as they affect buying behavior and then discuss the buyer decision process.

Characteristics Affecting Consumer Behavior

Consumer purchases are influenced strongly by cultural, social, personal, and psychological characteristics, shown in Figure 6-2. For the most part, marketers cannot control such factors, but they must take them into account. We illustrate these characteristics for the case of a hypothetical consumer named Anna Flores. Anna is a married college graduate who works as a brand manager in a leading consumer packaged-goods company. She wants to find a new leisure-time activity that will provide some contrast to her working day. This need has led her to consider buying a camera and taking up photography. Many characteristics in her background will affect the way she evaluates cameras and chooses a brand.

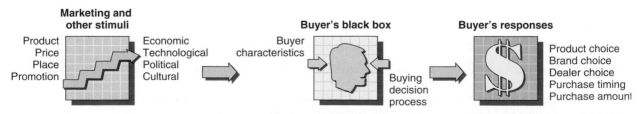

Figure 6-1
Model of buyer behavior

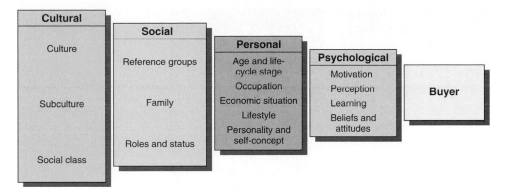

Figure 6-2
Factors influencing
consumer behavior

Cultural Factors   Cultural factors exert a broad and deep influence on consumer behavior. The marketer needs to understand the role played by the buyer's *culture, subculture,* and *social class.*

CULTURE.   Culture is the most basic cause of a person's wants and behavior. Human behavior is largely learned. Growing up in a society, a child learns basic values, perceptions, wants, and behaviors from the family and other important institutions. A child in the United States normally learns or is exposed to the following values: achievement and success, activity and involvement, efficiency and practicality, progress, material comfort, individualism, freedom, humanitarianism, youthfulness, and fitness and health. Every group or society has a culture, and cultural influences on buying behavior may vary greatly from country to country. Failure to adjust to these differences can result in ineffective marketing or embarrassing mistakes.

Culture
The set of basic values, perceptions, wants, and behaviors learned by a member of society from family and other important institutions.

Anna Flores's cultural background will affect her camera buying decision. Anna's desire to own a camera may result from her being raised in a modern society that has developed camera technology and a whole set of consumer learnings and values.

Marketers are always trying to spot *cultural shifts* in order to discover new products that might be wanted. For example, the cultural shift toward greater concern about health and fitness has created a huge industry for health and fitness services, exercise equipment and clothing, and lower-fat and more natural foods. The shift toward informality has resulted in more demand for casual clothing and simpler home furnishings.

SUBCULTURE.   Each culture contains smaller **subcultures,** or groups of people with shared value systems based on common life experiences and situations. Subcultures include nationalities, religions, racial groups, and geographic regions. Many subcultures make up important market segments, and marketers often design products and marketing programs tailored to their needs. Examples of four such important subculture groups include Hispanic, African American, Asian, and mature consumers. As we discuss them, it is important to note that each major subculture is, in turn, made of many smaller subcultures, each with its own preferences and behaviors.

Subculture
A group of people with shared value systems based on common life experiences and situations.

The U.S. *Hispanic market*—Americans of Cuban, Mexican, Central American, South American, and Puerto Rican descent—consists of 35 million consumers who buy nearly $400 billion worth of goods and services each year. Expected to grow in number by 64 percent during the next 20 years, Hispanics are easy to reach through the growing selection of Spanish-language broadcast and print media that cater to them.[3]

Hispanics have long been a target for marketers of food, beverages, and household care products. Most marketers now produce products tailored to the Hispanic market and promote them using Spanish-language ads and media. For example, General Mills offers a line of Para su Familia (for your family) cereals for Hispanics and Colgate's Suavitel

Targeting important subcultures: General Mills targets Hispanics with its Para su Familia cereals.

fabric softener is the number-two brand in the Hispanic segment.[4] But as the segment's buying power increases, Hispanics are now emerging as an attractive market for pricier products such as computers, financial services, photography equipment, large appliances, life insurance, and automobiles. Hispanic consumers tend to buy more branded, higher-quality products—generics don't sell well to Hispanics. Perhaps more important, Hispanics are very brand loyal, and they favor companies who show special interest in them.

Sears makes a special effort to market to Hispanic American consumers, especially for the 20 percent of its stores that are located in heavily Hispanic neighborhoods

Sears currently markets heavily to the attractive Hispanic segment. Last year, it spent some $25 million on advertising to Hispanics—more than any other retailer—and it recently launched a Spanish-language Web site. Sears neighborhoods receive regular visits from a Fiesta Mobile, a colorful Winnebago that plays music, gives out prizes, and promotes the Sears credit card. Sears also sponsors major Hispanic cultural festivals and concerts. One of its most successful marketing efforts is its magazine *Nuestra Gente*—which means Our People—the nation's largest Spanish-language magazine. The magazine features articles about Hispanic celebrities alongside glossy spreads of Sears fashions. Using a list culled from its database, Sears has built up a controlled circulation of about 700,000. The magazine is free, but subscriptions are available only by request. As a result of this careful cultivation of Hispanic consumers, although Sears has lost sales in recent years to discount retailers, the Hispanic segment has remained steadfastly loyal.[5]

If the U.S. population of *African Americans* were a separate nation, its buying power of $500 billion annually would rank twelfth in the free world.[6] The black population in the United States is growing in affluence and sophistication. Although more price conscious than other segments, blacks are also strongly motivated by quality and selection. They place more importance on brand names, are more brand loyal, and do less "shopping around."

In recent years, many companies have developed special products and services, packaging, and appeals to meet the needs of African Americans. Hallmark launched its Afrocentric brand, Mahogany, with only 16 cards in 1987; it offers 800 cards today. Other companies are moving away from creating separate products for African Americans. Instead, they are offering more inclusive product lines within the same brand that goes out to the general market. For example, Sara Lee discontinued its separate Color-Me-Natural

Discount broker Charles Schwab goes all out to court the large and particularly lucrative Chinese American market. It has opened 14 Chinese-language offices and its Chinese-language Web site now racks up more than five million hits per month.

line of L'eggs pantyhose for black women and now offers shades and sheer styles popular among black women as half of the company's general-focus subbrands.[7]

A wide variety of magazines, television channels, and other media now target African American consumers. Marketers are also reaching out to the African American virtual community. Per capita, black consumers spend twice as much as white consumers for online services. African Americans are increasingly turning to Web sites such as The Black World Today (www.tbwt.com), a black *USA Today* on the Internet, that address black culture in ways that network and cable TV rarely do. Other popular sites include Urban Sports Network, Net Noir, Afronet, and Black Voices.[8]

Asian Americans, the fastest-growing and most affluent U.S. demographic segment, now number more than 10 million with disposable income of $229 billion annually. Chinese Americans constitute the largest group, followed by Filipinos, Japanese Americans, Asian Indians, and Korean Americans. The U.S. Asian American population is estimated to reach 30 million by 2050.[9] Financial services marketers have long targeted Asian American consumers:

> Discount broker Charles Schwab goes all out to court the large and particularly lucrative Chinese American market. Schwab estimates that the U.S. Chinese community holds as much as $150 billion in investable assets. Schwab has opened 14 Chinese-language offices in such places as New York's and San Francisco's Chinatowns and plans to add many more. Its Chinese-language Web site, launched in 1998, now racks up more than five million hits per month. Schwab recently added an online Chinese-language news service, where customers can check market activity, news headlines, and earnings estimates. Although relatively small in number, Chinese Americans have plenty of money. The median Chinese-American household income is $65,000 a year, compared with $40,000 for Americans in general. Even more appealing to brokers is that Chinese American investors pour money into

stocks—they trade two and three times as much as other investors, generating a lot of commissions.[10]

Until recently, packaged-goods firms, automobile companies, retailers, and fast-food chains have lagged in this segment. Language and cultural traditions appear to be the biggest barriers. For example, 66 percent of Asian Americans are foreign born, and 56 percent of those five years and older do not speak English fluently. Still, because of the segment's rapidly growing buying power, many firms are now looking seriously at this market.[11]

As the U.S. population ages, *mature consumers* are becoming a very attractive market. Now 75 million strong, the 50 and older population will swell to 115 million in the next 25 years. The 65 and over crowd, alone, numbers 35 million and will swell to 70 million by 2030. Mature consumers are better off financially than are younger consumer groups—the 50-plus group controls 50 percent of all discretionary income and the median net worth of 65-plussers is more than double that of the national average.[12] Because mature consumers have more time and money, they are an ideal market for exotic travel, restaurants, high-tech home entertainment products, leisure goods and services, designer furniture and fashions, financial services, and health care services.

Their desire to look as young as they feel also makes more mature consumers good candidates for cosmetics and personal care products, health foods, fitness products, and other items that combat the effects of aging. The best strategy is to appeal to their active, multidimensional lives. For example, a recent Nike commercial features a senior weight lifter who proudly proclaims, "I'm not strong for my age. I'm strong!" Similarly, Kellogg aired a TV spot for All-Bran cereal in which individuals ranging in age from 53 to 81 are featured playing ice hockey, water skiing, running hurdles, and playing baseball, all to the tune of "Wild Thing." And an Aetna commercial portrays a senior who, after retiring from a career as a lawyer, fulfills a lifelong dream to become an archeologist.[13]

Social classes
Relatively permanent and ordered divisions in a society whose members share similar values, interests, and behaviors.

SOCIAL CLASS. Almost every society has some form of social class structure. **Social classes** are society's relatively permanent and ordered divisions whose members share similar values, interests, and behaviors. Social scientists have identified the seven American social classes (see Table 6-1).

Social class is not determined by a single factor, such as income, but is measured as a combination of occupation, income, education, wealth, and other variables. In some social systems, members of different classes are reared for certain roles and cannot change their social positions. In the United States, however, the lines between social classes are not fixed and rigid; people can move to a higher social class or drop into a lower one. Marketers are interested in social class because people within a given social class tend to exhibit similar buying behavior.[14]

Social classes show distinct product and brand preferences in areas such as clothing, home furnishings, leisure activity, and automobiles. Anna Flores's social class may affect her camera decision. If she comes from a higher social class background, her family probably owned an expensive camera and she may have dabbled in photography.

Social Factors A consumer's behavior also is influenced by social factors, such as the consumer's *small groups, family,* and *social roles* and *status.*

Group
Two or more people who interact to accomplish individual or mutual goals.

GROUPS. A person's behavior is influenced by many small **groups.** Groups that have a direct influence and to which a person belongs are called *membership groups.* In contrast, *reference groups* serve as direct (face-to-face) or indirect points of comparison or reference in forming a person's attitudes or behavior. People often are influenced by reference groups to which they do not belong. For example, an *aspirational group* is one to which the individual wishes to belong, as when a teenage basketball player hopes to play someday for the

Table 6-1   Characteristics of Seven Major American Social Classes
Upper uppers (less than 1 percent)
Upper uppers are the social elite who live on inherited wealth and have well-established family backgrounds. They give large sums to charity, own more than one home, and send their children to the finest schools. They are accustomed to wealth and often buy and dress conservatively rather than showing off their wealth.
Lower uppers (about 2 percent)
Lower uppers have earned high income or wealth through exceptional ability in the professions or business. They usually begin in the middle class. They tend to be active in social and civic affairs and buy for them- selves and their children the symbols of status, such as expensive homes, educations, and automobiles. They want to be accepted in the upper-upper stratum, a status more likely to be achieved by their children than by themselves.
Upper middles (12 percent)
Upper middles possess neither family status nor unusual wealth. They have attained positions as profession- als, independent businesspersons, and corporate managers. They have a keen interest in attaining the "bet- ter things in life." They believe in education and want their children to develop professional or administra- tive skills. They are joiners and highly civic-minded.
Middle class (32 percent)
The middle class is made up of average-pay white- and blue-collar workers who live on the "the better side of town" and try to "do the proper things." To keep up with the trends, they often buy products that are popular. Most are concerned with fashion, seeking the better brand names. Better living means owning a nice home in a nice neighborhood with good schools.
Working class (38 percent)
The working class consists of those who lead a "working-class lifestyle," whatever their income, school background, or job. They depend heavily on relatives for economic and emotional support, for advice on purchases, and for assistance in times of trouble.
Upper lowers (9 percent)
Upper lowers are working (are not on welfare), although their living standard is just above poverty. Although they strive toward a higher class, they often lack education and perform unskilled work for poor pay.
Lower lowers (7 percent)
Lower lowers are visibly poor. They are often poorly educated and work as unskilled laborers. However, they are often out of work and some depend on public assistance. They tend to live a day-to-day existence.
Sources: See Richard P. Coleman, "The Continuing Significance of Social Class to Marketing," *Journal of Consumer Research,* December 1983, pp. 265–280. ©Journal of Consumer Research, Inc., 1983. Also see Leon G. Shiffman and Leslie Lazar Kanuk, *Consumer Behavior,* 6th ed. (Upper Saddle River, NJ: Prentice Hall, 1997), p. 388; and Linda P. Morton, "Segmenting Publics by Social Class," *Public Relations Quarterly,* Summer 1999, pp. 45–46.

Los Angeles Lakers. Marketers try to identify the reference groups of their target markets. Reference groups expose a person to new behaviors and lifestyles, influence the person's attitudes and self-concept, and create pressures to conform that may affect the person's product and brand choices.

The importance of group influence varies across products and brands. It tends to be strongest when the product is visible to others whom the buyer respects. Manufacturers of products and brands subjected to strong group influence must figure out how to reach **opinion leaders**—people within a reference group who, because of special skills, knowl- edge, personality, or other characteristics, exert influence on others.

Opinion leader
Person within a reference group who, because of special skills, knowledge, personality, or other charac- teristics, exerts influence on others.

Many marketers try to identify opinion leaders for their products and direct marketing efforts toward them. In other cases, advertisements can simulate opinion leadership, thereby reducing the need for consumers to seek advice from others. For example, the hottest trends in teenage music, language, and fashion start in America's inner cities, then quickly spread to more mainstream youth in the suburbs. Thus, clothing companies who hope to appeal to these fickle and fashion-conscious youth often make a concerted effort to monitor urban opinion leaders' style and behavior.

FAMILY. Family members can strongly influence buyer behavior. The family is the most important consumer buying organization in society, and it has been researched extensively. Marketers are interested in the roles and influence of the husband, wife, and children on the purchase of different products and services.

Husband–wife involvement varies widely by product category and by stage in the buying process. Buying roles change with evolving consumer lifestyles. In the United States, the wife traditionally has been the main purchasing agent for the family, especially in the areas of food, household products, and clothing. But with 70 percent of women holding jobs outside the home and the willingness of husbands to do more of the family's purchasing, all this is changing. For example, women now make or influence up to 80 percent of car-buying decisions and men account for about 40 percent of food-shopping dollars.[15]

Such changes suggest that marketers who've typically sold their products to only women or only men are now courting the opposite sex. For example, with research revealing that women now account for nearly half of all hardware store purchases, home improvement retailers such as Home Depot and Builders Square have turned what once were intimidating warehouses into female-friendly retail outlets. The new Builders Square II outlets feature decorator design centers at the front of the store. To attract more women, Builders Square runs ads targeting women in *Home, House Beautiful, Woman's Day,* and *Better Homes and Gardens.* Home Depot even offers bridal registries.

Children may also have a strong influence on family buying decisions. Chevrolet recognizes these influences in marketing its Chevy Venture minivan. For example, it runs

Family buying influences: Children can exert a strong influence on family buying decisions. Chevrolet actively woos these "back-seat consumers" with carefully targeted advertising and a Chevy Venture Warner Bros. Edition, complete with a DVD player.

ads to woo these "back-seat consumers" in *Sports Illustrated for Kids,* which attracts mostly 8- to 14-year-old boys. "We're kidding ourselves when we think kids aren't aware of brands," says Venture's brand manager, adding that even she was surprised at how often parents told her that kids played a tie-breaking role in deciding which car to buy.[16]

ROLES AND STATUS. A person belongs to many groups—family, clubs, organizations. The person's position in each group can be defined in terms of both role and status. With her parents, Anna Flores plays the role of daughter; in her family, she plays the role of wife; in her company, she plays the role of brand manager. A *role* consists of the activities people are expected to perform according to the persons around them. Each of Anna's roles will influence some of her buying behavior. Each role carries a *status* reflecting the general esteem given to it by society. People often choose products that show their status in society. For example, the role of brand manager has more status in our society than does the role of daughter. As a brand manager, Anna will buy the kind of clothing that reflects her role and status.

Personal Factors A buyer's decisions also are influenced by personal characteristics such as the buyer's *age* and *life-cycle stage, occupation, economic situation, lifestyle,* and *personality* and *self-concept.*

AGE AND LIFE-CYCLE STAGE. People change the goods and services they buy over their lifetimes. Tastes in food, clothes, furniture, and recreation are often age related. Buying is also shaped by the stage of the *family life cycle*—the stages through which families might pass as they mature over time. Marketers often define their target markets in terms of life-cycle stage and develop appropriate products and marketing plans for each stage. Traditional family life-cycle stages include young singles and married couples with children. Today, however, marketers are increasingly catering to a growing number of alternative, nontraditional stages such as unmarried couples, singles marrying later in life, childless couples, same-sex couples, single parents, extended parents (those with young adult children returning home), and others.

OCCUPATION. A person's occupation affects the goods and services bought. Blue-collar workers tend to buy more rugged work clothes, whereas executives buy more business suits. Marketers try to identify the occupational groups that have an above-average interest in their products and services. A company can even specialize in making products needed by a given occupational group. Thus, computer software companies will design different products for brand managers, accountants, engineers, lawyers, and doctors.

ECONOMIC SITUATION. A person's economic situation will affect product choice. Anna Flores can consider buying an expensive Nikon if she has enough spendable income, savings, or borrowing power. Marketers of income-sensitive goods watch trends in personal income, savings, and interest rates. If economic indicators point to a recession, marketers can take steps to redesign, reposition, and reprice their products closely.

LIFESTYLE. People coming from the same subculture, social class, and occupation may have quite different lifestyles. **Lifestyle** is a person's pattern of living as expressed in his or her *psychographics.* It involves measuring consumers' major *AIO dimensions—activities* (work, hobbies, shopping, sports, social events), *interests* (food, fashion, family, recreation), and *opinions* (about themselves, social issues, business, products). Lifestyle captures something more than the person's social class or personality. It profiles a person's whole pattern of acting and interacting in the world.

    Several research firms have developed lifestyle classifications. The most widely used is SRI Consulting's *Values and Lifestyles (VALS)* typology. VALS classifies people

Lifestyle
A person's pattern of living as expressed in his or her activities, interests, and opinions.

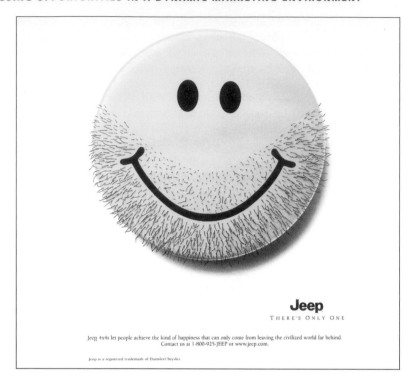

Jeep
THERE'S ONLY ONE

Jeep 4x4s let people achieve the kind of happiness that can only come from leaving the civilized world far behind.
Contact us at 1-800-925-JEEP or www.jeep.com.

Jeep is a registered trademark of DaimlerChrysler.

Lifestyles: Jeep targets people who want to "leave the civilized world behind."

according to how they spend their time and money. It divides consumers into eight groups based on two major dimensions: self-orientation and resources. *Self-orientation* groups include *principle-oriented* consumers who buy based on their views of the world; *status-oriented* buyers who base their purchases on the actions and opinions of others; and *action-oriented* buyers who are driven by their desire for activity, variety, and risk taking. Consumers within each orientation are further classified into those with *abundant resources* and those with *minimal resources,* depending on whether they have high or low levels of income, education, health, self-confidence, energy, and other factors. Consumers with either very high or very low levels of resources are classified without regard to their self-orientations (actualizers, strugglers). Actualizers are people with so many resources that they can indulge in any or all self-orientations. In contrast, strugglers are people with too few resources to be included in any consumer orientation.

Iron City beer, a well-known brand in Pittsburgh, used VALS to update its image and improve sales. Iron City was losing sales—its aging core users were drinking less beer, and younger men weren't buying the brand. According to VALS research, experiencers drink the most beer, followed by strivers. To assess Iron City's image problems, the company interviewed men in these categories. It gave the men stacks of pictures of different kinds of people and asked them to identify first Iron City brand users and then people most like themselves. The men pictured Iron City drinkers as blue-collar steelworkers stopping off at the local bar. However, they saw themselves as more modern, hardworking, and fun loving. They strongly rejected the outmoded, heavy-industry image of Pittsburgh. Based on this research, Iron City created ads linking its beer to the new self-image of target consumers. The ads mingled images of the old Pittsburgh with those of the new, dynamic city and scenes of young experiencers and strivers having fun and working hard. Within just one month of the start of the campaign, Iron City sales shot up by 26 percent.[17]

Lifestyle segmentation can also be used to understand Internet behavior. Forrester developed its "Technographics" scheme, which segments consumers according to motivation, desire, and ability to invest in technology.[18] The framework splits people into 10 categories, such as

◆ *Fast Forwards:* The biggest spenders on computer technology. Fast Forwards are early adopters of new technology for home, office, and personal use.
◆ *New Age Nurturers:* Also big spenders but focused on technology for home uses, such as a family PC.
◆ *Mouse Potatoes:* Consumers who are dedicated to interactive entertainment and willing to spend for the latest in "technotainment."
◆ *Techno-Strivers:* Consumers who use technology primarily to gain a career edge.
◆ *Handshakers:* Older consumers, typically managers, who don't touch computers at work and leave that to younger assistants.

Delta Airlines used Technographics to better target online ticket sales. It created marketing campaigns for time-strapped "Fast Forwards" and "New Age Nurturers," and eliminated "technology pessimists" from its list of targets.

When used carefully, the lifestyle concept can help the marketer understand changing consumer values and how they affect buying behavior. Anna Flores, for example, can choose to live the role of a capable homemaker, a career woman, or a free spirit—or all three. She plays several roles, and the way she blends them expresses her lifestyle. If she becomes a professional photographer, this would change her lifestyle, in turn changing what and how she buys.

PERSONALITY AND SELF-CONCEPT. Each person's distinct personality influences his or her buying behavior. *Personality* refers to the unique psychological characteristics that lead to relatively consistent and lasting responses to one's own environment. Personality is usually described in terms of traits such as self-confidence, dominance, sociability, autonomy, defensiveness, adaptability, and aggressiveness. Personality can be useful in analyzing consumer behavior for certain product or brand choices. For example, coffee marketers have discovered that heavy coffee drinkers tend to be high on sociability. Thus, to attract customers, Starbucks and other coffeehouses create environments in which people can relax and socialize over a cup of steaming coffee.

Many marketers use a concept related to personality—a person's *self-concept* (also called *self-image*). The basic self-concept premise is that people's possessions contribute to and reflect their identities; that is, "we are what we have." Thus, in order to understand

Heavy coffee drinkers tend to be high on sociability, so to attract customers, Starbucks and other coffeehouses create environments in which people can relax and socialize over a cup of steaming coffee.

consumer behavior, the marketer must first understand the relationship between consumer self-concept and possessions. For example, the founder and chief executive of Barnes & Noble, the nation's leading bookseller, notes that people buy books to support their self-images:

> People have the mistaken notion that the thing you do with books is read them. Wrong . . . People buy books for what the purchase says about them—their taste, their cultivation, their trendiness. Their aim . . . is to connect themselves, or those to whom they give the books as gifts, with all the other refined owners of Edgar Allan Poe collections or sensitive owners of Virginia Woolf collections. . . . [The result is that] you can sell books as consumer products, with seductive displays, flashy posters, an emphasis on the glamour of the book, and the fashionableness of the bestseller and the trendy author.[19]

Psychological Factors   A person's buying choices are further influenced by four major psychological factors: *motivation, perception, learning,* and *beliefs and attitudes.*

MOTIVATION.   We know that Anna Flores became interested in buying a camera. Why? What is she *really* seeking? What *needs* is she trying to satisfy? A person has many needs at any given time. Some are *biological,* arising from states of tension such as hunger, thirst, or discomfort. Others are *psychological,* arising from the need for recognition, esteem, or belonging. A need becomes a *motive* when it is aroused to a sufficient level of intensity. A **motive** (or *drive*) is a need that is sufficiently pressing to direct the person to seek satisfaction. Psychologists have developed theories of human motivation. Two of the most popular—the theories of Sigmund Freud and Abraham Maslow—have quite different meanings for consumer analysis and marketing.

Sigmund Freud assumed that people are largely unconscious about the real psychological forces shaping their behavior. He saw the person as growing up and repressing many urges. These urges are never eliminated or under perfect control; they emerge in dreams, in slips of the tongue, in neurotic and obsessive behavior, or ultimately in psychoses. Thus, Freud suggested that a person does not fully understand his or her motivation. If Anna Flores wants to purchase an expensive camera, she may describe her motive as wanting a hobby or career. At a deeper level, she may be purchasing the camera to impress others with her creative talent. At a still deeper level, she may be buying the camera to feel young and independent again. Motivation researchers collect in-depth information from small samples of consumers to uncover the deeper motives for their product choices (see Marketing at Work 6-1).

Abraham Maslow sought to explain why people are driven by particular needs at particular times. Why does one person spend much time and energy on personal safety and another on gaining the esteem of others? Maslow's answer is that human needs are arranged in a hierarchy, as shown in Figure 6-3, from the most pressing at the bottom to the least pressing at the top. They include *physiological* needs, *safety* needs, *social* needs, *esteem* needs, and *self-actualization* needs. A person tries to satisfy the most important need first. When that need is satisfied, it will stop being a motivator and the person will then try to satisfy the next most important need. For example, starving people (physiological need) will not take an interest in the latest happenings in the art world (self-actualization needs), nor in how they are seen or esteemed by others (social or esteem needs), nor even in whether they are breathing clean air (safety needs). But as each important need is satisfied, the next most important need will come into play.

What light does Maslow's theory throw on Anna Flores's interest in buying a camera? We can guess that Anna has satisfied her physiological, safety, and social needs; they

Motive (drive)
A need that is sufficiently pressing to direct the person to seek satisfaction of the need.

"Touchy-Feely" Research into Consumer Motivations

The term *motivation research* refers to qualitative research designed to probe consumers' hidden, subconscious motivations. Consumers often don't know or can't describe just why they act as they do. Thus, motivation researchers use a variety of nondirective and projective techniques to uncover underlying emotions and attitudes toward brands and buying situations that will help them to form deeper, stronger connections with consumers. The techniques range from sentence completion, word association, and inkblot or cartoon interpretation tests, to having consumers describe typical brand users or form daydreams and fantasies about brands or buying situations. Some of these techniques verge on the bizarre. One writer offers the following tongue-in-cheek summary of a motivation research session:

Good morning, ladies and gentlemen. We've called you here today for a little consumer research. Now, lie down on the couch, toss your inhibitions out the window, and let's try a little free association. First, think about brands as if they were your *friends*. Imagine you could talk to your TV dinner. What would he say? And what would you say to him? . . . Now, think of your shampoo as an animal. Go on, don't be shy. Would it be a panda or a lion? A snake or a wooly worm? For our final exercise, let's all sit up and pull out our magic markers. Draw a picture of a typical cake-mix user. Would she wear an apron or a negligee? A business suit or a can-can dress?

Such projective techniques seem pretty goofy. But more and more, marketers are turning to these touchy-feely approaches to probe consumer psyches and develop better marketing strategies.

Many advertising agencies employ teams of psychologists, anthropologists, and other social scientists to carry out motivation research. One agency routinely conducts one-on-one, therapy-like interviews to delve into the inner workings of consumers. Another agency asks consumers to describe their favorite brands as animals or cars (say, Cadillacs versus Chevrolets) in order to assess the prestige associated with various brands. Still another agency has consumers draw figures of typical brand users:

In one instance, the agency asked 50 interviewees to sketch likely buyers of two different brands of cake mixes. Consistently, the group portrayed Pillsbury customers as apron-clad, grandmotherly types, whereas they pictured Duncan Hines purchasers as svelte, contemporary women.

Some motivation research studies employ more basic techniques, such as simply mingling with or watching consumers to find out what makes them tick (refer back to Marketing at Work 5-1). For example, in the appliance industry, consumer brand loyalties have been built up over decades and passed on from generation to generation. To shake up entrenched market share and tap into consumers' often unexpressed needs, appliance giant Whirlpool Corporation hired an anthropologist who went to people's homes, observed how they used their appliances, and talked with all the household members. Whirlpool found that in busy families these days, women aren't the only ones doing the laundry. Armed with this knowledge, company engineers came up with color-coded washer and dryer controls to make it easier for kids and men to pitch in.

Similarly, researchers at Sega of America's ad agency have learned a lot about video game buying behavior by hanging around with 150 kids in their bedrooms and by shopping with them in malls. Above all else, they learned, do everything fast. As a result, in Sega's most recent 15-second commercials, some images fly by so quickly that adults

Motivation research: When asked to sketch figures of typical cake-mix users, subjects portrayed Pillsbury customers as grandmotherly types and Duncan Hines buyers as svelte and contemporary.

cannot recall seeing them, even after repeated showings. The kids, weaned on MTV, recollect them keenly.

Some marketers dismiss such motivation research as mumbo jumbo. And these approaches do present some problems: They use small samples and researcher interpretations of results are often highly subjective, sometimes leading to rather exotic explanations of

otherwise ordinary buying behavior. However, others believe strongly that these approaches can provide interesting nuggets of insight into the relationships between consumers and the brands they buy. To marketers who use them, motivation research techniques provide a flexible and varied means of gaining insights into deeply held and often mysterious motivations behind consumer buying behavior.

Sources: See Annetta Miller and Dody Tsiantar, "Psyching Out Consumers," *Newsweek,* February 27, 1989, pp. 46–47; "They Understand Your Kids," *Fortune,* special issue, Autumn–Winter 1993, pp. 29–30; Ronald B. Lieber, "Storytelling: A New Way to Get Close to Your Customer," *Fortune,* February 3, 1997, pp. 102–108; Jerry W. Thomas, "Finding Unspoken Reasons for Consumers' Choices," *Marketing News,* June 8, 1998, pp. 10–11; Michele Marchetti, "Marketing's Weird Science," *Sales and Marketing Management,* May 1999, p. 87; Gerry Khermouch, "Consumers in the Mist," *Business Week,* February 26, 2001, pp. 92–94; and Alison Stein Wellner, "Research on a Shoestring," *American Demographics,* April 2001, pp. 38–39.

do not motivate her interest in cameras. Her camera interest might come from a strong need for more esteem. Or it might come from a need for self-actualization—she might want to be a creative person and express herself through photography.

PERCEPTION.   A motivated person is ready to act. How the person acts is influenced by his or her own perception of the situation. All of us learn by the flow of information through our five senses: sight, hearing, smell, touch, and taste. However, each of us receives, organizes, and interprets this sensory information in an individual way. **Perception** is the process by which people select, organize, and interpret information to form a meaningful picture of the world.

People can form different perceptions of the same stimulus because of three perceptual processes: selective attention, selective distortion, and selective retention. People are exposed to a great amount of stimuli every day. For example, the average person may be exposed to more than 1,500 ads in a single day. It is impossible for a person to pay attention to all these stimuli. *Selective attention*—the tendency for people to screen out most of the information to which they are exposed—means that marketers have to work especially hard to attract the consumer's attention.

Even noted stimuli do not always come across in the intended way. Each person fits incoming information into an existing mind-set. *Selective distortion* describes the tendency of people to interpret information in a way that will support what they already

Perception
The process by which people select, organize, and interpret information to form a meaningful picture of the world.

Figure 6-3
Maslow's hierarchy of needs

Sources: From *Motivation and Personality* by Abraham H. Maslow. Copyright © 1970 by Abraham H. Maslow. Copyright 1954, 1987 by Harper & Row Publishers, Inc. Reprinted by permission of Addison Wesley Educational Publishers Inc. Also see Barbara Marx Hubbard, "Seeking Our Future Potentials," *The Futurist,* May 1998, pp. 29–32.

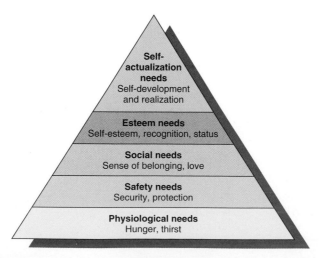

believe. Anna Flores may hear a salesperson mention some good and bad points about a competing camera brand. Because she already has a strong leaning toward Nikon, she is likely to distort those points in order to conclude that Nikon is the better camera. Selective distortion means that marketers must try to understand the mind-sets of consumers and how these will affect interpretations of advertising and sales information.

People also will forget much that they learn. They tend to retain information that supports their attitudes and beliefs. Because of *selective retention,* Anna is likely to remember good points made about the Nikon and to forget good points made about competing cameras. Because of selective exposure, distortion, and retention, marketers have to work hard to get their messages through. This fact explains why marketers use so much drama and repetition in sending messages to their market.

Interestingly, although most marketers worry about whether their offers will be perceived at all, some consumers worry that they will be affected by marketing messages without even knowing it—through *subliminal advertising.* In 1957, a researcher announced that he had flashed the phrases "Eat popcorn" and "Drink Coca-Cola" on a screen in a New Jersey movie theater every five seconds for 1/300th of a second. He reported that although viewers did not consciously recognize these messages, they absorbed them subconsciously and bought 58 percent more popcorn and 18 percent more Coke. Suddenly advertisers and consumer-protection groups became intensely interested in subliminal perception. People voiced fears of being brainwashed, and California and Canada declared the practice illegal. Although the researcher later admitted to making up the data, the issue has not died. Some consumers still fear that they are being manipulated by subliminal messages.

Numerous studies by psychologists and consumer researchers have found no link between subliminal messages and consumer behavior. It appears that subliminal advertising simply doesn't have the power attributed to it by its critics. Most advertisers scoff at the notion of an industry conspiracy to manipulate consumers through "invisible" messages.

LEARNING. When people act, they learn. **Learning** describes changes in an individual's behavior arising from experience. Learning theorists say that most human behavior is learned. Learning occurs through the interplay of *drives, stimuli, cues, responses,* and *reinforcement.*

We saw that Anna Flores has a drive for self-actualization. A *drive* is a strong internal stimulus that calls for action. Her drive becomes a motive when it is directed toward a particular *stimulus object,* in this case a camera. Anna's response to the idea of buying a camera is conditioned by the surrounding cues. *Cues* are minor stimuli that determine when, where, and how the person responds. Seeing cameras in a shop window, hearing of a special sale price, and receiving her husband's support are all cues that can influence Anna's *response* to her interest in buying a camera.

Suppose Anna buys the Nikon. If the experience is rewarding, she will probably use the camera more and more. Her response to cameras will be *reinforced.* Then the next time she shops for a camera, binoculars, or some similar product, the probability is greater that she will buy a Nikon product. The practical significance of learning theory for marketers is that they can build up demand for a product by associating it with strong drives, using motivating cues, and providing positive reinforcement.

BELIEFS AND ATTITUDES. Through doing and learning, people acquire beliefs and attitudes. These, in turn, influence their buying behavior. A **belief** is a descriptive thought that a person has about something. Anna Flores may believe that a Nikon camera takes great pictures, stands up well under hard use, and costs $450. These beliefs may be based on real knowledge, opinion, or faith, and may or may not carry an emotional charge. For

Learning
Changes in an individual's behavior arising from experience.

Belief
A descriptive thought that a person holds about something.

example, Anna Flores's belief that a Nikon camera is heavy may or may not matter to her decision.

Marketers are interested in the beliefs that people formulate about specific products and services, because these beliefs make up product and brand images that affect buying behavior. If some of the beliefs are wrong and prevent purchase, the marketer will want to launch a campaign to correct them.

People have attitudes regarding religion, politics, clothes, music, food, and almost everything else. **Attitude** describes a person's relatively consistent evaluations, feelings, and tendencies toward an object or idea. Attitudes put people into a frame of mind of liking or disliking things, of moving toward or away from them. Thus, Anna Flores may hold attitudes such as "Buy the best," "The Japanese make the best products in the world," and "Creativity and self-expression are among the most important things in life." If so, the Nikon camera would fit well into Anna's existing attitudes.

Attitudes are difficult to change. A person's attitudes fit into a pattern, and to change one attitude may require difficult adjustments in many others. Thus, a company should usually try to fit its products into existing attitudes rather than attempt to change attitudes. Of course, there are exceptions in which the great cost of trying to change attitudes may pay off handsomely:

> By 1994, milk consumption had been in decline for 20 years. The general perception was that milk was unhealthy, outdated, just for kids, or good only with cookies and cake. Beginning in 1994, the National Fluid Milk Processors Education Program (MilkPEP) began a $55 million print ad campaign featuring milk

Attitude
A person's consistently favorable or unfavorable evaluations, feelings, and tendencies toward an object or idea.

Attitudes are difficult to change, but the National Fluid Milk Processors' wildly popular milk mustache campaign succeeded in changing attitudes toward milk.

be-mustached celebrities like Cindy Crawford, Danny DeVito, Patrick Ewing, and Ivana Trump with the tag line "Milk: Where's your mustache?" The campaign has not only been wildly popular, it has been successful as well—not only did it stop the decline, milk consumption actually increased. The campaign was still running and MilkPEP had upped spending on it to more than $100 million a year. Although initially the target market was women in their twenties, the campaign has been expanded to other target markets and has gained cult status with teens, much to their parents' delight. Teens collect the print ads featuring celebrities ranging from music stars Hanson and Leann Rimes, supermodel Tyra Banks, Kermit the Frog, and Garfield to sports idols such as Mark McGuire, Jeff Gordon, Pete Sampras, Mia Hamm, Gabriela Sabatini, and Dennis Rodman. (Says Dennis, "Three glasses a day give the average man all the calcium he needs. Maybe I should drink six.") "Milking" the success of the print ads, milk producers set up Club Milk on a Web site (www.whymilk.com) where they limit membership only to those who pledge they will drink three glasses of the white fluid a day.[20]

We can now appreciate the many forces acting on consumer behavior. The consumer's choice results from the complex interplay of cultural, social, personal, and psychological factors.

The Buyer Decision Process

Now that we have looked at the influences that affect buyers, we are ready to look at how consumers make buying decisions. Figure 6-4 shows that the buyer decision process consists of five stages: *need recognition, information search, evaluation of alternatives, purchase decision,* and *postpurchase behavior.* Clearly, the buying process starts long before actual purchase and continues long after. Marketers need to focus on the entire buying process rather than on just the purchase decision.

The figure implies that consumers pass through all five stages with every purchase. But in more routine purchases, consumers often skip or reverse some of these stages. A woman buying her regular brand of toothpaste would recognize the need and go right to the purchase decision, skipping information search and evaluation. However, we use the model in Figure 6-4 because it shows all the considerations that arise when a consumer faces a new and complex purchase situation.

Need Recognition   The buying process starts with need recognition—the buyer recognizes a problem or need. The need can be triggered by *internal stimuli* when one of the person's normal needs—hunger, thirst, sex—rises to a level high enough to become a drive. A need can also be triggered by *external stimuli.* Anna Flores might feel the need for a new hobby when her busy season at work slowed down, and she thought of cameras after talking to a friend about photography or seeing a camera ad. At this stage, the marketer should research consumers to find out what kinds of needs or problems arise, what brought them about, and how they led the consumer to this particular product.

Information Search   An interested consumer may or may not search for more information. If the consumer's drive is strong and a satisfying product is near at hand, the consumer is likely to buy it then. If not, the consumer may store the need in memory or undertake an information search related to the need. At the least, Anna Flores will

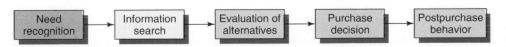

Figure 6-4
Buyer decision process

Need recognition can be triggered by advertising. This ad asks an arresting question that alerts parents to the need for a high-quality bike helmet.

probably pay more attention to camera ads, cameras used by friends, and camera conversations. Or Anna may actively look for reading material, phone friends, and gather information in other ways. The amount of searching she does will depend on the strength of her drive, the amount of information she starts with, the ease of obtaining more information, the value she places on additional information, and the satisfaction she gets from searching.

The consumer can obtain information from any of several sources. These include *personal sources* (family, friends, neighbors, acquaintances), *commercial sources* (advertising, salespeople, dealers, packaging, displays), *public sources* (mass media, consumer-rating organizations), and *experiential sources* (handling, examining, using the product). The relative influence of these information sources varies with the product and the buyer. Generally, the consumer receives the most information about a product from commercial sources—those controlled by the marketer. The most effective sources, however, tend to be personal. Commercial sources normally *inform* the buyer, but personal sources *legitimize* or *evaluate* products for the buyer.

As more information is obtained, the consumer's awareness and knowledge of the available brands and features increase. In her information search, Anna Flores learned about the many camera brands available. The information also helped her drop certain brands from consideration. A company must design its marketing mix to make prospects aware of and knowledgeable about its brand. It should carefully identify consumers' sources of information and the importance of each source.

Evaluation of Alternatives We have seen how the consumer uses information to arrive at a set of final brand choices. How does the consumer choose among the alternative brands? The marketer needs to know about alternative evaluation—that is, how the consumer processes information to arrive at brand choices. Unfortunately, consumers do not use a simple and single evaluation process in all buying situations. Instead, several evaluation processes are at work.

The consumer arrives at attitudes toward different brands through some evaluation procedure. How consumers go about evaluating purchase alternatives depends on the individual consumer and the specific buying situation. In some cases, consumers use careful calculations and logical thinking. At other times, the same consumers do little or no evaluating; instead they buy on impulse and rely on intuition. Sometimes consumers make buying decisions on their own; sometimes they turn to friends, consumer guides, or salespeople for buying advice.

Suppose Anna Flores has narrowed her choices to four cameras. And suppose that she is primarily interested in four attributes—picture quality, ease of use, camera size, and price. Anna has formed beliefs about how each brand rates on each attribute. Clearly, if one camera rated best on all the attributes, we could predict that Anna would choose it. However, the brands vary in appeal. Anna might base her buying decision on only one attribute, and her choice would be easy to predict. If she wants picture quality above everything, she will buy the camera that she thinks has the best picture quality. But most buyers consider several attributes, each with different importance. If we knew the importance weights that Anna assigns to each of the four attributes, we could predict her camera choice more reliably.

Marketers should study buyers to find out how they actually evaluate brand alternatives. If they know what evaluative processes go on, marketers can take steps to influence the buyer's decision.

Purchase Decision In the evaluation stage, the consumer ranks brands and forms purchase intentions. Generally, the consumer's purchase decision will be to buy the most preferred brand, but two factors can come between the purchase *intention* and the purchase *decision*. The first factor is the *attitudes of others.* If Anna Flores's husband feels strongly that Anna should buy the lowest-priced camera, then the chances of Anna's buying a more expensive camera will be reduced.

The second factor is *unexpected situational factors.* The consumer may form a purchase intention based on factors such as expected income, expected price, and expected product benefits. However, unexpected events may change the purchase intention. Anna Flores may lose her job, some other purchase may become more urgent, or a friend may report being disappointed in her preferred camera. Or a close competitor may drop its price. Thus, preferences and even purchase intentions do not always result in actual purchase choice.

Postpurchase Behavior The marketer's job does not end when the product is bought. After purchasing the product, the consumer will be satisfied or dissatisfied and will engage in postpurchase behavior of interest to the marketer. What determines whether the buyer is satisfied or dissatisfied with a purchase? The answer lies in the relationship between the *consumer's expectations* and the product's *perceived performance.* If the product falls short of expectations, the consumer is disappointed; if it meets expectations, the consumer is satisfied; if it exceeds expectations, the consumer is delighted.

The larger the gap between expectations and performance, the greater the consumer's dissatisfaction. This suggests that sellers should make product claims that faithfully represent the product's performance so that buyers are satisfied. Some sellers might even understate performance levels to boost consumer satisfaction with the product. For example, Boeing's salespeople tend to be conservative when they estimate the potential benefits of their aircraft. They almost always underestimate fuel efficiency—they promise a 5 percent savings that turns out to be 8 percent. Customers are delighted with better-than-expected performance; they buy again and tell other potential customers that Boeing lives up to its promises.

Almost all major purchases result in **cognitive dissonance,** or discomfort caused by postpurchase conflict. After the purchase, consumers are satisfied with the benefits of the chosen brand and are glad to avoid the drawbacks of the brands not bought. However, every purchase involves compromise. Consumers feel uneasy about acquiring the drawbacks of the chosen brand and about losing the benefits of the brands not purchased. Thus, consumers feel at least some postpurchase dissonance for every purchase.[21]

Cognitive dissonance
Buyer discomfort caused by postpurchase conflict.

Why is it so important to satisfy the customer? Such satisfaction is important because a company's sales come from two basic groups—*new customers* and *retained customers.* It usually costs more to attract new customers than to retain current ones, and the best way to retain current customers is to keep them satisfied. Customer satisfaction is a key to making lasting connections with consumers—to keeping and growing consumers and reaping their customer lifetime value. Satisfied customers buy a product again, talk favorably to others about the product, pay less attention to competing brands and advertising, and buy other products from the company. Many marketers go beyond merely *meeting* the expectations of customers—they aim to *delight* the customer.

A dissatisfied consumer responds differently. Whereas, on average, a satisfied customer tells three people about a good product experience, a dissatisfied customer gripes to 11 people. In fact, one study showed that 13 percent of the people who had a problem with an organization complained about the company to more than 20 people.[22] Clearly, bad word of mouth travels farther and faster than good word of mouth and can quickly damage consumer attitudes about a company and its products.

Therefore, a company would be wise to measure customer satisfaction regularly. It cannot simply rely on dissatisfied customers to volunteer their complaints when they are dissatisfied. Some 96 percent of unhappy customers never tell the company about their problem. Companies should set up systems that *encourage* customers to complain (see Marketing at Work 6-2). In this way, the company can learn how well it is doing and how it can improve. The 3M company claims that over two-thirds of its new-product ideas come from listening to customer complaints. But listening is not enough—the company also must respond constructively to the complaints it receives.

By studying the overall buyer decision, marketers may be able to find ways to help consumers move through it. For example, if consumers are not buying a new product because they do not perceive a need for it, marketing might launch advertising messages that trigger the need and show how the product solves customers' problems. If customers know about the product but are not buying because they hold unfavorable attitudes toward it, the marketer must find ways to either change the product or change consumer perceptions.

The Buyer Decision Process for New Products

We have looked at the stages buyers go through in trying to satisfy a need. Buyers may pass quickly or slowly through these stages, and some of the stages may even be reversed. Much depends on the nature of the buyer, the product, and the buying situation.

New product
A good, service, or idea that is perceived by some potential customers as new.

Adoption process
The mental process through which an individual passes from first hearing about an innovation to final adoption.

We now look at how buyers approach the purchase of new products. A **new product** is a good, service, or idea that is perceived by some potential customers as new. It may have been around for a while, but our interest is in how consumers learn about products for the first time and make decisions on whether to adopt them. We define the **adoption process** as "the mental process through which an individual passes from first learning about an innovation to final adoption," and *adoption* as the decision by an individual to become a regular user of the product.[23]

Stages in the Adoption Process Consumers go through five stages in the process of adopting a new product:

◆ *Awareness:* The consumer becomes aware of the new product, but lacks information about it.
◆ *Interest:* The consumer seeks information about the new product.
◆ *Evaluation:* The consumer considers whether trying the new product makes sense.
◆ *Trial:* The consumer tries the new product on a small scale to improve his or her estimate of its value.
◆ *Adoption:* The consumer decides to make full and regular use of the new product.

Got a Problem? Just Phone, Fax, E-Mail, or Web-Chat with Us!

What should companies do about dissatisfied customers? Everything they can! Unhappy customers not only stop buying but also can quickly damage the company's image by spreading bad word of mouth. Enlightened companies don't try to hide from dissatisfied customers. They go out of their way to *encourage* customers to complain, then bend over backward to make disgruntled buyers happy again.

At a minimum, most companies offer toll-free numbers to handle complaints, inquiries, and orders. For example, over the past two decades, the Gerber help line (1-800-4-GERBER) has received more than 5 million calls. Help line staffers, most of them mothers or grandmothers themselves, handle customer concerns and provide baby care advice 24 hours a day, 365 days a year to more than 2,400 callers a day. The help line is staffed by English-, French-, and Spanish-speaking operators, and interpreters are available for most other languages. Callers include new parents, day care providers, and even health professionals. They ask a wide variety of questions, from when to feed a baby specific foods to how to babyproof a home. One in five calls to the help line comes from men.

General Electric's Answer Center may be the most extensive 800-number system in the nation. It handles more than 3 million calls a year, only 5 percent of them complaints. At the heart of the system is a giant database that provides the center's service reps with instant access to more than 1 million answers concerning 8,500 models in 120 product lines. The center receives some unusual calls, as when a submarine off the Connecticut coast requested help

fixing a motor. Still, according to GF, its people resolve 90 percent of complaints or inquiries on the first call, and complainers often become even more loyal customers. GE has now set up two answer centers online (www.ge.oac and www.geappliances.com/geac/) that help customers obtain product and service information, troubleshoot product problems, locate dealers, and even schedule service appointments.

Companies such as Famous Smoke Shop view their call centers as a tool not just for handling complaints but also for making the most out of each and every customer interaction. For example, whenever cigar enthusiast Cara Biden has called Famous Smoke Shops in search of highly coveted Short Stories cigars, they've been

out of stock. Yet, this hasn't stopped Biden from staying loyal. Every time Biden phones Famous, a system known as an ACD (automatic call distributor) immediately kicks in to answer the call and route it to the appropriate contact person. Biden has been impressed with how fast the ACD funnels her to a customer service representative. She also enjoys chatting with the highly knowledgeable rep about alternatives to the tough-to-find cigars. The rep is knowledgeable not only about cigars but also about Biden—whenever she calls, her sales history and previous queries pop up on his computer screen.

Most call centers today are much more than just a bank of phones that receives complaints. They are

Web-enabled customer *contact* centers: Customers can initiate a chat session with a 1-800-Flowers service representative who answers questions and "pushes" pages to their browsers. In the future, interactive voice and image technology will even let customers see and talk with reps on their computer screens.

high-tech, Web-enabled *contact* centers that employ a sophisticated mix of phone, e-mail, fax, and interactive voice and data technologies. Consider the following scenario:

It's February 14, and you've just remembered that it's Valentine's Day. There's no time for florist shops, so you jump online to www.1800FLOWERS.com. Then you pause. Red roses? Boxed or in a vase? One dozen or two? Just as your head starts to pound, you notice a button on the Web site. Click on it, and you're connected to a customer service rep at the call center who can help sniff out your options. A chat page opens on your screen, allowing a real-time dialog with the agent. The service rep even "pushes" pages to your browser so you can see different floral arrangements and how much they cost. In minutes, you have placed your order online, with a little hand-holding. Fiction? Not really. Several e-marketers, including 1-800-Flowers, are testing or already offer live interaction with service reps. Some feature real-time chat sessions, others voice-over-Web capabilities. In the future, a "call cam" may even let consumers see an agent on their computer screen.

The idea is to make customers' interactions with companies seamless and uniform, no matter which form of communication they choose. Integrate the telephone with Web technology and you have an extremely powerful means of handling customer questions and concerns. This technology lets a customer browse a Web site on a PC at the same time that a customer service agent browses the site. The two can talk over a separate telephone line or an Internet connection to discuss problems or compare products. For example, Logistix, a California technology company, uses technology that allows it to synchronize Web screens viewed by the company's agents and customers as they talk. The technology even lets either party draw circles around words or pictures for both to see. This may not seem like a big deal, but when discussing a complex technological device, it really helps if customer and agent are viewing a common diagram. Using the technology, Logistix has turned its call center into a central point of customer contact.

Of course, the best way to keep customers happy is to provide good products and services in the first place. Short of that, however, a company must develop a good system for ferreting out problems and connecting with customers. Such a system is much more than just a necessary evil—customer happiness usually shows up on the company's bottom line. One recent study found that dollars invested in complaint-handling and customer contact systems yield an average return of between 100 percent and 200 percent. Maryanne Rasmussen, vice president of worldwide quality at American Express, offers this formula: "Better complaint handling equals higher customer satisfaction equals higher brand loyalty equals higher performance."

Sources: Quotes from *PR Newswire*, Ziff Communications, "On Mother's Day, Advice Goes a Long Way," May 2, 1995; Alessandra Bianchi, "Lines of Fire," *Inc. Technology*, 1998, pp. 36–48; Matt Hamblen, "Call Centers and Web Sites Cozy Up," *Computerworld*, March 2, 1998, p. 1; and Ellen Jovin and Jennifer Lach, "Online with the Operator," *American Demographics*, February 1999, pp. 36–39. Also see Marcia Stepanek, "You'll Wanna Hold Their Hands," *Business Week*, March 22, 1999, pp. EB30–EB31; and Bob Wallace and George V. Hulme, "The Modern Call Center," *Informationweek*, April 9, 2001, pp. 38–46.

This model suggests that the new-product marketer should think about how to help consumers move through these stages. A manufacturer of large-screen televisions may discover that many consumers in the interest stage do not move to the trial stage because of uncertainty and the large investment. If these same consumers were willing to use a large-screen television on a trial basis for a small fee, the manufacturer should consider offering a trial-use plan with an option to buy.

Individual Differences in Innovativeness People differ greatly in their readiness to try new products. In each product area, there are "consumption pioneers" and early adopters. Other individuals adopt new products much later. People can be classified into the adopter categories shown in Figure 6-5. After a slow start, an increasing number of people adopt the new product. The number of adopters reaches a peak and then drops off as fewer nonadopters remain. Innovators are defined as the first 2.5 percent of the buyers to adopt a new idea (those beyond two standard deviations from mean adoption time); the early adopters are the next 13.5 percent (between one and two standard deviations); and so forth.

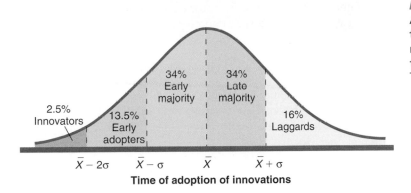

Figure 6-5
Adopter categorization on the basis of relative time of adoption of innovations

Source: Reprinted with the permission of The Free Press, a Division of Simon & Schuster, from *Diffusion of Innovations,* Fourth Edition, by Everett M. Rogers. Copyright © 1962, 1971, 1983 by The Free Press.

The five adopter groups have differing values. *Innovators* are venturesome—they try new ideas at some risk. *Early adopters* are guided by respect—they are opinion leaders in their communities and adopt new ideas early but carefully. The *early majority* are deliberate—although they rarely are leaders, they adopt new ideas before the average person. The *late majority* are skeptical—they adopt an innovation only after a majority of people have tried it. Finally, *laggards* are tradition bound—they are suspicious of changes and adopt the innovation only when it has become something of a tradition itself.

This adopter classification suggests that an innovating firm should research the characteristics of innovators and early adopters and should direct marketing efforts toward them. In general, innovators tend to be relatively younger, better educated, and higher in income than later adopters and nonadopters. They are more receptive to unfamiliar things, rely more on their own values and judgment, and are more willing to take risks. They are less brand loyal and more likely to take advantage of special promotions such as discounts, coupons, and samples.

Influence of Product Characteristics on Rate of Adoption The characteristics of the new product affect its rate of adoption. Some products catch on almost overnight (Beanie Babies), whereas others take a long time to gain acceptance (high-definition television, HDTV). Five characteristics are especially important in influencing an innovation's rate of adoption. For example, consider the characteristics of HDTV in relation to the rate of adoption:

◆ *Relative advantage:* The degree to which the innovation appears superior to existing products. The greater the perceived relative advantage of using HDTV—say, in picture quality and ease of viewing—the sooner such HDTVs will be adopted.

◆ *Compatibility:* The degree to which the innovation fits the values and experiences of potential consumers. HDTV, for example, is highly compatible with the lifestyles found in upper-middle-class homes. However, it is not very compatible with the programming and broadcasting systems currently available to consumers.

◆ *Complexity:* The degree to which the innovation is difficult to understand or use. HDTVs are not very complex and, therefore, once programming is available and prices come down, will take less time to penetrate U.S. homes than more complex innovations.

◆ *Divisibility:* The degree to which the innovation may be tried on a limited basis. HDTVs are still very expensive. To the extent that people can lease them with an option to buy, their rate of adoption will increase.

◆ *Communicability:* The degree to which the results of using the innovation can be observed or described to others. Because HDTV lends itself to demonstration and description, its use will spread faster among consumers.

Other characteristics influence the rate of adoption, such as initial and ongoing costs, risk and uncertainty, and social approval. The new-product marketer has to research all these factors when developing the new product and its marketing program.

Consumer Behavior Across International Borders

Understanding consumer behavior is difficult enough for companies marketing within the borders of a single country. For companies operating in many countries, however, understanding and serving the needs of consumers can be daunting. Although consumers in different countries may have some things in common, their values, attitudes, and behaviors often vary greatly. International marketers must understand such differences and adjust their products and marketing programs accordingly.

Sometimes the differences are obvious. For example, in the United States, where most people eat cereal regularly for breakfast, Kellogg focuses its marketing on persuading consumers to select a Kellogg brand rather than a competitor's brand. In France, however, where most people prefer croissants and coffee or no breakfast at all, Kellogg advertising simply attempts to convince people that they should eat cereal for breakfast. Its packaging includes step-by-step instructions on how to prepare cereal. In India, where many consumers eat heavy, fried breakfasts and many consumers skip the meal altogether, Kellogg's advertising attempts to convince buyers to switch to a lighter, more nutritious breakfast diet.

Often, differences across international markets are more subtle. They may result from physical differences in consumers and their environments. For example, Remington makes smaller electric shavers to fit the smaller hands of Japanese consumers and battery-powered shavers for the British market, where few bathrooms have electrical outlets. Other differences result from varying customs. In Japan, for example, where humility and deference are considered great virtues, pushy, hard-hitting sales approaches are considered offensive. Failing to understand such differences in customs and behaviors from one country to another can spell disaster for a marketer's international products and programs.

Marketers must decide on the degree to which they will adapt their products and marketing programs to meet the unique cultures and needs of consumers in various markets. On the one hand, they want to standardize their offerings in order to simplify operations and take advantage of cost economies. On the other hand, adapting marketing efforts within each country results in products and programs that better satisfy the needs of local consumers. The question of whether to adapt or standardize the marketing mix across international markets has created a lively debate in recent years.

Linking the Concepts

Here's a good place to pull over and apply the concepts you've examined in the first part of this chapter.

◆ Think about a specific major purchase you've made recently. What buying process did you follow? What major factors influenced your decision?

◆ Pick a company that we've discussed in a previous chapter—Nike, Coca-Cola, Starbucks, Wal-Mart, Volkswagen, Amazon.com, or another. Does the company you chose understand its customers and their buying behavior?

◆ Think about Intel (from Chapter 2), which sells its products to computer makers and other businesses rather than to final consumers. How would Intel's marketing to business customers differ from Nike's marketing to final consumers? The second part of the chapter deals with this issue.

Business Markets and Business Buyer Behavior

In one way or another, most large companies sell to other organizations. Many companies, such as DuPont, Boeing, Cisco Systems, Motorola, and countless other firms, sell *most* of their products to other businesses. Even large consumer-products companies, which make products used by final consumers, must first sell their products to other businesses. For example, General Mills makes many familiar consumer products—Cheerios, Betty Crocker cake mixes, Gold Medal flour, and others. But to sell these products to consumers, General Mills must first sell them to the wholesalers and retailers that serve the consumer market.

Business buyer behavior refers to the buying behavior of all the organizations that buy goods and services for use in the production of other products and services that are sold, rented, or supplied to others. It also includes retailing and wholesaling firms that acquire goods for the purpose of reselling or renting them to others at a profit.

Business buyer behavior
The buying behavior of organizations that buy goods and services for use in the production of other products and services that are sold, rented, or supplied to others.

Business Markets

The business market is *huge.* In fact, business markets involve far more dollars and items than do consumer markets. For example, think about the large number of business transactions involved in the production and sale of a single set of Goodyear tires. Various suppliers sell Goodyear the rubber, steel, equipment, and other goods that it needs to produce the tires. Goodyear then sells the finished tires to retailers, who in turn sell them to consumers. Thus, many sets of *business* purchases were made for only one set of *consumer* purchases. In addition, Goodyear sells tires as original equipment to manufacturers who install them on new vehicles, and as replacement tires to companies that maintain their own fleets of company cars, trucks, buses, or other vehicles.

In some ways, business markets are similar to consumer markets. Both involve people who assume buying roles and make purchase decisions to satisfy needs. However, business markets differ in many ways from consumer markets. The main differences are in *market structure and demand,* the *nature of the buying unit,* and the *types of decisions and the decision process* involved.

Market Structure and Demand The business marketer normally deals with *far fewer but far larger buyers* than the consumer marketer does. For example, when Goodyear sells replacement tires to final consumers, its potential market includes the owners of the millions of cars currently in use in the United States. But Goodyear's fate in the business market depends on getting orders from one of only a few large automakers. Even in large business markets, a few buyers normally account for most of the purchasing.

Business markets are also *more geographically concentrated.* More than half the nation's business buyers are concentrated in eight states: California, New York, Ohio, Illinois, Michigan, Texas, Pennsylvania, and New Jersey. Further, business demand is **derived demand**—it ultimately derives from the demand for consumer goods. General Motors buys steel because consumers buy cars. If consumer demand for cars drops, so will the demand for steel and all the other products used to make cars. Therefore, business marketers sometimes promote their products directly to final consumers to increase business demand. For example, Intel's long-running "Intel Inside" advertising campaign sells personal computer buyers on the virtues of Intel microprocessors. The increased demand for Intel chips boosts demand for the PCs containing them, and both Intel and its business partners win.

Derived demand
Business demand that ultimately comes from (derives from) the demand for consumer goods.

Nature of the Buying Unit Compared with consumer purchases, a business purchase usually involves *more decision participants* and a *more professional purchasing effort.*

Derived demand: Intel's long-running "Intel Inside" logo advertising campaign boosts demand for Intel chips and for the PCs containing them. Now, most computer makers feature a logo like this one in their ads.

Often, business buying is done by trained purchasing agents who spend their working lives learning how to buy better. The more complex the purchase, the more likely that several people will participate in the decision-making process. Buying committees made up of technical experts and top management are common in the buying of major goods. As one observer notes, "It's a scary thought: Your customers may know more about your company and products than you do. . . . Companies are putting their best and brightest people on procurement patrol."[24] Therefore, business marketers must have well-trained salespeople to deal with well-trained buyers.

Types of Decisions and the Decision Process Business buyers usually face *more complex* buying decisions than do consumer buyers. Purchases often involve large sums of money, complex technical and economic considerations, and interactions among many people at many levels of the buyer's organization. Because the purchases are more complex, business buyers may take longer to make their decisions.

The business buying process tends to be *more formalized* than the consumer buying process. Large business purchases usually call for detailed product specifications, written purchase orders, careful supplier searches, and formal approval. Finally, in the business buying process, buyer and seller are often much *more dependent* on each other. Consumer marketers are often at a distance from their customers. In contrast, business marketers may roll up their sleeves and work closely with their customers during all stages of the buying process—from helping customers define problems, to finding solutions, to supporting after-sale operation. In the long run, business marketers keep a customer's sales by meeting current needs *and* by working with customers to help them succeed with their own customers.

Business Buyer Behavior

At the most basic level, marketers want to know how business buyers will respond to various marketing stimuli. Figure 6-6 shows a model of business buyer behavior. In this model, marketing and other stimuli affect the buying organization and produce certain buyer responses. As with consumer buying, the marketing stimuli for business buying consist of the four Ps: product, price, place, and promotion. Other stimuli include major forces in the environment: economic, technological, political, cultural, and competitive. These stimuli enter the organization and are turned into buyer responses: product or service choice; supplier choice; order quantities; and delivery, service, and payment terms. In order to design good marketing mix strategies, the marketer must understand what happens within the organization to turn stimuli into purchase responses.

Within the organization, buying activity consists of two major parts: the buying center, made up of all the people involved in the buying decision, and the buying decision process. The model shows that the buying center and the buying decision process are influenced by internal organizational, interpersonal, and individual factors as well as by external environmental factors.

The model in Figure 6-6 suggests four questions about business buyer behavior: What buying decisions do business buyers make? Who participates in the buying process? What are the major influences on buyers? How do business buyers make their buying decisions?

Major Types of Buying Situations   There are three major types of buying situations.[25] At one extreme is the *straight rebuy,* which is a fairly routine decision. At the other extreme is the *new task,* which may call for thorough research. In the middle is the *modified rebuy,* which requires some research.

In a **straight rebuy,** the buyer reorders something without any modifications. It is usually handled on a routine basis by the purchasing department. Based on past buying satisfaction, the buyer simply chooses from the various suppliers on its list. "In" suppliers try to maintain product and service quality. They often propose automatic reordering systems so that the purchasing agent will save reordering time. "Out" suppliers try to offer something new or exploit dissatisfaction so that the buyer will consider them.

In a **modified rebuy,** the buyer wants to modify product specifications, prices, terms, or suppliers. The modified rebuy usually involves more decision participants than does the straight rebuy. The in suppliers may become nervous and feel pressured to put their best foot forward to protect an account. Out suppliers may see the modified rebuy situation as an opportunity to make a better offer and gain new business.

A company buying a product or service for the first time faces a **new-task** situation. In such cases, the greater the cost or risk, the larger the number of decision participants and the greater their efforts to collect information will be. The new-task situation is the marketer's greatest opportunity and challenge. The marketer not only tries to reach as many key buying influences as possible but also provides help and information.

Straight rebuy
A business buying situation in which the buyer routinely reorders something without any modifications.

Modified rebuy
A business buying situation in which the buyer wants to modify product specifications, prices, terms, or suppliers.

New task
A business buying situation in which the buyer purchases a product or service for the first time.

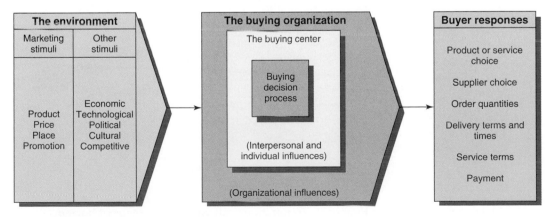

Figure 6-6
A model of business buyer behavior

Systems selling
Buying a packaged solution to a problem from a single seller, thus avoiding all the separate decisions involved in a complex buying situation.

Many business buyers prefer to buy a packaged solution to a problem from a single seller. Instead of buying and putting all the components together, the buyer may ask sellers to supply the components *and* assemble the package or system. The sale often goes to the firm that provides the most complete system meeting the customer's needs. Thus, **systems selling** is often a key business marketing strategy for winning and holding accounts.

For example, the Indonesian government requested bids to build a cement factory near Jakarta. An American firm's proposal included choosing the site, designing the cement factory, hiring the construction crews, assembling the materials and equipment, and turning the finished factory over to the Indonesian government. A Japanese firm's proposal included all of these services, plus hiring and training workers to run the factory, exporting the cement through their trading companies, and using the cement to build some needed roads and new office buildings in Jakarta. Although the Japanese firm's proposal cost more, it won the contract. Clearly, the Japanese viewed the problem not as just building a cement factory (the narrow view of systems selling) but of running it in a way that would contribute to the country's economy. They took the broadest view of the customer's needs. This is true systems selling.

Participants in the Business Buying Process Who does the buying of the trillions of dollars' worth of goods and services needed by business organizations? The decision-making unit of a buying organization is called its **buying center:** all the individuals and units that participate in the business decision-making process. The buying center includes all members of the organization who play a role in the purchase decision process. This group includes the actual users of the product or service, those who make the buying decision, those who influence the buying decision, those who do the actual buying, and those who control buying information.

Buying center
All the individuals and units that participate in the business buying-decision process.

The buying center is not a fixed and formally identified unit within the buying organization. It is a set of buying roles assumed by different people for different purchases.

Buying center: Allegiance Healthcare Corporation deals with a wide range of buying influences, from purchasing executives and hospital administrators to the surgeons who actually use its products.

Within the organization, the size and makeup of the buying center will vary for different products and for different buying situations. For some routine purchases, one person—say a purchasing agent—may assume all the buying center roles and serve as the only person involved in the buying decision. For more complex purchases, the buying center may include 20 or 30 people from different levels and departments in the organization.

The buying center concept presents a major marketing challenge. The business marketer must learn who participates in the decision, each participant's relative influence, and what evaluation criteria each decision participant uses. For example, Allegiance Healthcare Corporation, the large health care products and services company, sells disposable surgical gowns to hospitals. It identifies the hospital personnel involved in this buying decision as the vice president of purchasing, the operating room administrator, and the surgeons. Each participant plays a different role. The vice president of purchasing analyzes whether the hospital should buy disposable gowns or reusable gowns. If analysis favors disposable gowns, then the operating room administrator compares competing products and prices and makes a choice. This administrator considers the gown's absorbency, antiseptic quality, design, and cost, and normally buys the brand that meets requirements at the lowest cost. Finally, surgeons affect the decision later by reporting their satisfaction or dissatisfaction with the brand.

The buying center usually includes some obvious participants who are involved formally in the buying decision. For example, the decision to buy a corporate jet will probably involve the company's CEO, chief pilot, a purchasing agent, some legal staff, a member of top management, and others formally charged with the buying decision. It may also involve less obvious, informal participants, some of whom may actually make or strongly affect the buying decision. Sometimes, even the people in the buying center are not aware of all the buying participants. For example, Gulfstream has found that the decision about which corporate jet to buy may be influenced by some not-so-obvious participants:

> Although many people inside the customer company can be influential, the most important influence may turn out to be the CEO's spouse. The typical buyer spends about $4 million to outfit the plane's interior. This covers top-of-the-line stereo sound and video systems, a lavish galley, and a bewildering array of custom-made furnishings. To help with such decisions, many CEOs hire designers and bring their spouses along to planning sessions. As one salesperson notes, "Wives are behind the CEO's decisions on a lot of things, not just airplanes. . . . A crucial moment in a deal comes when the CEO's wife takes off her shoes and starts decorating the plane."[27]

Major Influences on Business Buyers Business buyers are subject to many influences when they make their buying decisions. Some marketers assume that the major influences are economic. They think buyers will favor the supplier who offers the lowest price or the best product or the most service. They concentrate on offering strong economic benefits to buyers. However, business buyers actually respond to both economic and personal factors. Far from being cold, calculating, and impersonal, business buyers are human and social as well. They react to both reason and emotion.

Today, most business-to-business marketers recognize that emotion plays an important role in business buying decisions. For example, you might expect that an advertisement promoting large trucks to corporate truck fleet buyers would stress objective technical, performance, and economic factors. However, a recent ad for Volvo heavy-duty trucks shows two drivers arm wrestling and claims "It solves all your fleet problems. Except who gets to drive." It turns out that, in the face an industrywide driver shortage, the type of truck a fleet provides can help it to attract qualified drivers. The Volvo ad stresses the raw beauty of the truck and its comfort and roominess, features that make it more

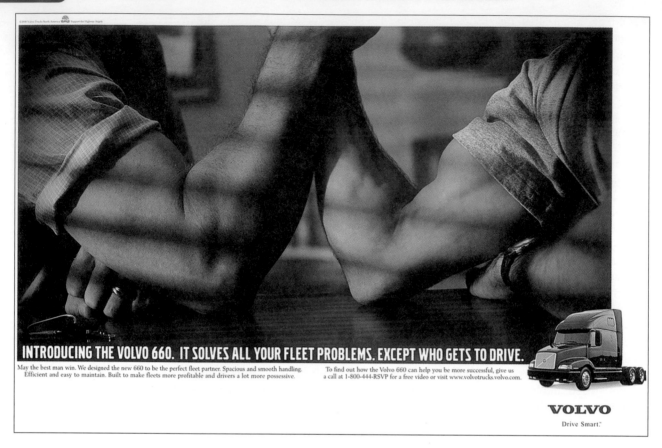

Emotions play an important role in business buying: This Volvo truck ad mentions objective factors, such as efficiency and ease of maintenance. But it stresses more emotional factors such as the raw beauty of the truck and its comfort and roominess, features that make "drivers a lot more possessive."

appealing to drivers. The ad concludes that Volvo trucks are "built to make fleets more profitable and drivers a lot more possessive."

Figure 6-7 lists various groups of influences on business buyers—environmental, organizational, interpersonal, and individual.[28] *Environmental factors* play a major role. For example, buyer behavior can be heavily influenced by factors in the current and expected economic environment, such as the level of primary demand, the economic

Figure 6-7
Major influences on business buyer behavior

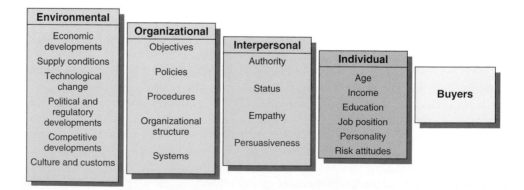

Environmental
Economic developments
Supply conditions
Technological change
Political and regulatory developments
Competitive developments
Culture and customs

Organizational
Objectives
Policies
Procedures
Organizational structure
Systems

Interpersonal
Authority
Status
Empathy
Persuasiveness

Individual
Age
Income
Education
Job position
Personality
Risk attitudes

Buyers

outlook, and the cost of money. Another environmental factor is shortages in key materials. Many companies now are more willing to buy and hold larger inventories of scarce materials to ensure adequate supply. Business buyers also are affected by technological, political, and competitive developments in the environment. Finally, culture and customs can strongly influence business buyer reactions to the marketer's behavior and strategies, especially in the international marketing environment (see Marketing at Work 6-3).

Business buyer behavior is also influenced strongly by *organizational factors*. Each buying organization has its own objectives, policies, procedures, structure, and systems, and the business marketer must understand these factors well. Questions such as these arise: How many people are involved in the buying decision? Who are they? What are their evaluative criteria? What are the company's policies and limits on its buyers?

The buying center usually includes many participants who influence each other, so *interpersonal factors* also influence the business buying process. However, it is often difficult to assess such interpersonal factors and group dynamics. As one writer notes, "Managers do not wear tags that say 'decision maker' or 'unimportant person.' The powerful are often invisible, at least to vendor representatives."[29] Nor does the buying center participant with the highest rank always have the most influence. Participants may influence the buying decision because they control rewards and punishments, are well liked, have special expertise, or have a special relationship with other important participants. Interpersonal factors are often very subtle. Whenever possible, business marketers must try to understand these factors and design strategies that take them into account.

Finally, business buyers are influenced by *individual factors*. Each participant in the business buying decision process brings in personal motives, perceptions, and preferences. These individual factors are affected by personal characteristics such as age, income, education, professional identification, personality, and attitudes toward risk. Also, buyers have different buying styles. Some may be technical types who make in-depth analyses of competitive proposals before choosing a supplier. Other buyers may be intuitive negotiators who are adept at pitting the sellers against one another for the best deal.

The Business Buying Process Figure 6-8 lists the eight stages of the business buying process.[30] Buyers who face a new-task buying situation usually go through all stages of the buying process. Buyers making modified or straight rebuys may skip some of the stages. We will examine these steps for the typical new-task buying situation.

PROBLEM RECOGNITION. The buying process begins when someone in the company recognizes a problem or need that can be met by acquiring a specific product or service. Problem recognition can result from internal or external stimuli. Internally, the company may decide to launch a new product that requires new production equipment and materials. Or a machine may break down and need new parts. Perhaps a purchasing manager is unhappy with a current supplier's product quality, service, or prices. Externally, the buyer may get some new ideas at a trade show, see an ad, or receive a call from a salesperson

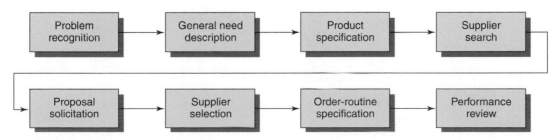

Figure 6-8
Stages of the business buying process

Marketing at Work 6-3

International Marketing Manners: When in Rome, Do as the Romans Do

Picture this: Consolidated Amalgamation, Inc. thinks it's time that the rest of the world enjoyed the same fine products it has offered American consumers for two generations. It dispatches Vice President Harry E. Slicksmile to Europe to explore the territory. Mr. Slicksmile stops first in London, where he makes short work of some bankers—he rings them up on the phone. He handles Parisians with similar ease: After securing a table at La Tour d'Argent, he greets his luncheon guest, the director of an industrial engineering firm, with the words, "Just call me Harry, Jacques."

In Germany, Mr. Slicksmile is a powerhouse. Whisking through a lavish, state-of-the-art marketing presentation, complete with the flip charts and audiovisuals, he shows 'em that this Georgia boy *knows* how to make a buck. Heading on to Milan, Harry strikes up a conversation with the Japanese businessman sitting next to him on the plane. He flips his card onto the guy's tray and, when the two say good-bye, shakes hands warmly and clasps the man's right arm. Later, for his appointment with the owner of an Italian packaging design firm, our hero wears his comfy corduroy sport coat, khaki pants, and Topsiders. Everybody knows Italians are zany and laid back, right?

Wrong. Six months later, Consolidated Amalgamation has nothing to show for the trip but a pile of bills. In Europe, they weren't wild about Harry.

This hypothetical case has been exaggerated for emphasis. Americans are seldom such dolts. But experts say success in international business has a lot to do with knowing the territory and its people. By learning English and extending themselves in other ways, the world's business leaders have met Americans more than halfway. In contrast, Americans too often do little except assume that others will march to their music. "We want things to be 'American' when we travel. Fast. Convenient. Easy. So we become 'ugly Americans' by demanding that others change," says one American world trade expert. "I think more business would be done if we tried harder."

Poor Harry tried, all right, but in all the wrong ways. The British do not, as a rule, make deals over the phone as much as Americans do. It's not so much a "cultural" difference as a difference in approach. A proper Frenchman neither likes instant familiarity—questions about family, church, or alma mater—nor refers to strangers by their first names. "That poor fellow, Jacques, probably wouldn't show anything, but he'd recoil. He'd *not* be pleased," explains an expert on French business practices. "It's con-sidered poor taste," he continues. "Even after months of business dealings, I'd wait for him or her to make the invitation [to use first names]. . . . You are always right, in Europe, to say 'Mister.'"

Harry's flashy presentation would likely have been a flop with the Germans, who dislike overstatement and ostentatiousness. According to one German expert, however, German businessmen have become accustomed to dealing with Americans. Although differences in body language and customs remain, the past 20 years have softened them. "I hugged an American woman at a business meeting last night," he said. "That would be normal in France, but [older] Germans still have difficulty [with the custom]." He says that calling secretaries by their first names would still be considered rude: "They have a right to be called by the surname. You'd certainly ask—and get—permission first." In Germany, people address each other formally and correctly—

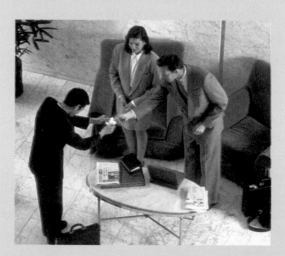

American companies must help their managers understand international needs, customers, and cultures. For example, Japanese people revere the business card as an extension of self—they do not hand it to people, they present it.

someone with two doctorates (which is fairly common) must be referred to as "Herr Doktor Doktor."

When Harry Slicksmile grabbed his new Japanese acquaintance by the arm, the executive probably considered him disrespectful and presumptuous. Japan, like many Asian countries, is a "no-contact culture" in which even shaking hands is a strange experience. Harry made matters worse by tossing his business card. Japanese people revere the business card as an extension of self and as an indicator of rank. They do not *hand* it to people, they *present* it—with both hands. In addition, the Japanese are sticklers

about rank. Unlike Americans, they don't heap praise on subordinates in a room; they will praise only the highest-ranking official present.

Hapless Harry's last gaffe was assuming that Italians are like Hollywood's stereotypes of them. The flair for design and style that has characterized Italian culture for centuries is embodied in the businesspeople of Milan and Rome. They dress beautifully and admire flair, but they blanch at garishness or impropriety in others' attire.

Thus, to compete successfully in global markets, or even to deal effectively with international firms in their home markets, companies

must help their managers to understand the needs, customs, and cultures of international business buyers. The old advice is still good advice: When in Rome, do as the Romans do.

Sources: Adapted from Susan Harte, "When in Rome, You Should Learn to Do What the Romans Do," *The Atlanta Journal-Constitution*, January 22, 1990, pp. D1, D6. Also see Terri Morrison, Wayne A. Conway, and George A. Borden, *Kiss, Bow, or Shake Hands: How to Do Business in 60 Countries* (Adams Media Corporation, 1994); Cynthia Kemper, "Global Sales Success Depends on Cultural Insight," *World Trade*, May 1998, pp. S2–S4; Ann Marie Sabath, *International Business Etiquette Europe: What You Need to Know to Conduct Business Abroad with Charm and Savvy* (Career Press, 1999); and Terri Morrison, Wayne A. Conway, and Joseph J. Douress, *Dun & Bradstreet's Guide to Doing Business Around the World* (Upper Saddle River, NJ: Prentice Hall, 2000).

who offers a better product or a lower price. In fact, in their advertising, business marketers often alert customers to potential problems and then show how their products provide solutions.

GENERAL NEED DESCRIPTION. Having recognized a need, the buyer next prepares a general need description that describes the characteristics and quantity of the needed item. For standard items, this process presents few problems. For complex items, however, the buyer may have to work with others—engineers, users, consultants—to define the item. The team may want to rank the importance of reliability, durability, price, and other attributes desired in the item. In this phase, the alert business marketer can help the buyers define their needs and provide information about the value of different product characteristics.

PRODUCT SPECIFICATION. The buying organization next develops the item's technical product specifications, often with the help of a value analysis engineering team. **Value analysis** is an approach to cost reduction in which components are studied carefully to determine if they can be redesigned, standardized, or made by less costly methods of production. The team decides on the best product characteristics and specifies them accordingly. Sellers, too, can use value analysis as a tool to help secure a new account. By showing buyers a better way to make an object, outside sellers can turn straight rebuy situations into new-task situations that give them a chance to obtain new business.

Value analysis
An approach to cost reduction in which components are studied carefully to determine if they can be redesigned, standardized, or made by less costly methods of production.

SUPPLIER SEARCH. The buyer now conducts a supplier search to find the best vendors. The buyer can compile a small list of qualified suppliers by reviewing trade directories, doing a computer search, or phoning other companies for recommendations. Today, more and more companies are turning to the Internet to find suppliers. For marketers, this has leveled the playing field—smaller suppliers have the same advantages as larger ones and can be listed in the same online catalogs for a nominal fee:

Worldwide Internet Solutions Network, better known as WIZnet (www. wiznet.net) has built an "interactive virtual library of business-to-business catalogs" that is global in coverage. At last report, its database included complete specifications for more than 10 million products and services from 90,000 manufacturers, distributors, and industrial service providers. For purchasing managers, who routinely receive a foot-high stack of mail each day, much of it catalogs, this kind of one-stop shopping will be an incredible time saver (and price saver, because it allows easier comparison shopping). When told by a management consultant, "Do a search for 3.5-inch platinum ball valves available from a Michigan source," WIZnet found six Michigan sources for buying the exact product in about 15 seconds. More than just electronic Yellow Pages, such as the Thomas Register or Industry.net, WIZnet includes all specifications for the products right in the system and offers secure e-mail to communicate directly with vendors to ask for requests for bids or to place an order. More than 10,000 product specs are added to WIZnet per week, and its database includes catalogs from Germany, Taiwan, the Czech Republic, and other countries.[31]

The newer the buying task, and the more complex and costly the item, the greater the amount of time the buyer will spend searching for suppliers. The supplier's task is to get listed in major directories and build a good reputation in the marketplace. Salespeople should watch for companies in the process of searching for suppliers and make certain that their firm is considered.

PROPOSAL SOLICITATION. In the proposal solicitation stage of the business buying process, the buyer invites qualified suppliers to submit proposals. In response, some suppliers will send only a catalog or a salesperson. However, when the item is complex or expensive, the buyer will usually require detailed written proposals or formal presentations from each potential supplier.

Business marketers must be skilled in researching, writing, and presenting proposals in response to buyer proposal solicitations. Proposals should be marketing documents, not just technical documents. Presentations should inspire confidence and should make the marketer's company stand out from the competition.

SUPPLIER SELECTION. The members of the buying center now review the proposals and select a supplier or suppliers. During supplier selection, the buying center often will draw up a list of the desired supplier attributes and their relative importance. In one survey, purchasing executives listed the following attributes as most important in influencing the relationship between supplier and customer: quality products and services, on-time delivery, ethical corporate behavior, honest communication, and competitive prices. Other important factors include repair and servicing capabilities, technical aid and advice, geographic location, performance history, and reputation. The members of the buying center will rate suppliers against these attributes and identify the best suppliers.

Buyers may attempt to negotiate with preferred suppliers for better prices and terms before making the final selections. In the end, they may select a single supplier or a few suppliers. Many buyers prefer multiple sources of supplies to avoid being totally dependent on one supplier and to allow comparisons of prices and performance of several suppliers over time.

ORDER-ROUTINE SPECIFICATION. The buyer now prepares an order-routine specification. It includes the final order with the chosen supplier or suppliers and lists items such as technical specifications, quantity needed, expected time of delivery, return policies, and warranties. In the case of maintenance, repair, and operating items, buyers may use *blanket contracts* rather than periodic purchase orders. A blanket contract creates a long-term relationship in which the supplier promises to resupply the buyer as needed at agreed prices for a set time period. A blanket order eliminates the expensive process of renegotiating a purchase each time that stock is required. It also allows buyers to write more, but smaller, purchase orders, resulting in lower inventory levels and carrying costs. Blanket contracting leads to more single-source buying and to buying more items from that source. This practice locks the supplier in tighter with the buyer and makes it difficult for other suppliers to break in unless the buyer becomes dissatisfied with prices or service.

PERFORMANCE REVIEW. In this stage, the buyer reviews supplier performance. The buyer may contact users and ask them to rate their satisfaction. The performance review may lead the buyer to continue, modify, or drop the arrangement. The seller's job is to monitor the same factors used by the buyer to make sure that the seller is giving the expected satisfaction.

We have described the stages that typically would occur in a new-task buying situation. The eight-stage model provides a simple view of the business buying decision process. The actual process is usually much more complex. In the modified rebuy or straight rebuy situation, some of these stages would be compressed or bypassed. Each organization buys in its own way, and each buying situation has unique requirements. Different buying center participants may be involved at different stages of the process. Although certain buying process steps usually do occur, buyers do not always follow them in the same order, and they may add other steps. Often, buyers will repeat certain stages of the process. Finally, a customer relationship might involve many different types of purchases ongoing at a given time, all in different stages of the buying process. The seller must manage the total customer relationship, not just individual purchases.

Business Buying on the Internet

During the past few years, advances in information technology have changed the face of the business-to-business marketing process. Increasingly, business buyers are purchasing all kinds of products and services electronically, either through electronic data interchange links (EDI) or on the Internet. Such "e-procurement" gives buyers access to new suppliers, lowers purchasing costs, and hastens order processing and delivery. In turn, business marketers are connecting with customers online to share marketing information, sell products and services, provide customer support services, and maintain ongoing customer relationships. In addition to their own Web pages on the Internet, they are establishing extranets that link a company's communications and data with its regular suppliers and distributors.

So far, most of the products bought by businesses through Internet and extranet connections are MRO materials—maintenance, repair, and operations. For instance, Los Angeles County purchases everything from chickens to lightbulbs over the Internet. National Semiconductor has automated almost all of the company's 3,500 monthly requisitions to buy materials ranging from the sterile booties worn in its fabrication plants to state-of-the-art software. The actual dollar amount spent on these types of MRO materials pales in comparison to the amount spent for items such as airplane parts, computer systems, and steel tubing. Yet, MRO materials make up 80 percent of all business orders and the transaction costs for order processing are high. Thus, companies have much to gain by streamlining the MRO buying process on the Web.

General Electric, one of the world's biggest purchasers, plans to be buying a substantial portion of its general operating and industrial supplies online within the next few years. Such electronic purchasing has given GE buyers access to new suppliers, lower purchasing costs, and faster order processing. GE's Global eXchange Services (GXS) division is now developing a public exchange network by which non-GE companies can purchase supplies online (see Marketing at Work 6-4).

The rapid-growth business-to-business e-procurement yields many benefits.[32] First, it shaves transaction costs and results in more efficient purchasing for both buyers and

Marketing at Work 6.4

General Electric's Global Business-to-Business Cyberbazaar

To most consumers, all the buzz about Internet buying has focused on B2C Web sites selling computers, software, clothing, books, flowers, or other retail goods. However, consumer goods sales via the Web are dwarfed by the Internet sales of business goods. In fact, B2B e-procurement now accounts for a lion's share of the dollar value of all e-commerce transactions.

General Electric is among the pioneers in electronic and Internet purchasing. In 1999, GE launched its GE Global Supplier Network that allows buyers in GE's many divisions to purchase industrial products online. This Web site lets GE buyers snap out requests for bids to thousands of suppliers, who can then respond over the Internet. Such electronic purchasing has saved GE's many divisions money, time, and piles of paperwork. Here's an example of how it can work:

Last month the machinery at a GE Lighting factory in Cleveland broke down. GE Lighting needed custom replacement parts, fast. In the past GE would have asked for bids from just four domestic suppliers. There was just too much hassle getting the paperwork and production-line blueprints together and sent out to [a long list of] suppliers. But this time it posted the specifications and "requests for quotes" on GE's Web site—and drew seven other bidders. The winner was a Hungarian [vendor] . . . that would not [even] have been contacted in the days of paper purchasing forms. The Hungarian firm's replacement parts arrived quicker, and GE Lighting paid just $320,000, a 20 percent savings.

Within little more than a year, GE's Internet purchasing system had logged more than $350 million worth of purchases by GE divisions, at a 10 percent to 15 percent savings in costs and a five-day reduction in average order time. By 2000, GE was purchasing $5 billion worth of materials via the Internet.

Based on its own huge success with electronic and Internet buying, GE's GXS division is now developing a public exchange network called Express Marketplace, by which non-GE companies can buy online. Express Marketplace lets member buyers prepare bids, select suppliers, and post orders to its Web site. Users can select items they wish to

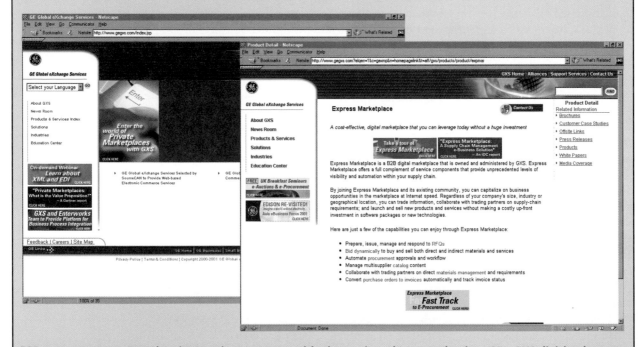

B2B e-procurement: Based on its own huge success with electronic and Internet buying, GE's GXS division is now developing a public exchange network called Express Marketplace, by which non-GE companies can buy online.

buy and use a purchasing card for payment. Once the order is placed, Express Marketplace sends a purchase order to a selected supplier or asks for bids from several qualified suppliers. GE's head start gives it a substantial advantage over rivals like IBM and CommerceOne, which are building competing networks.

Beyond its Internet buying system, GE's GXS division operates a vast electronic data interchange (EDI) e-procurement network linking both GE and non-GE companies. This e-purchasing system has now grown to become one of the largest B2B e-commerce networks in the world, with more than 100,000 trading partners in 58 countries. The network's 1 billion annual transactions account for $1 trillion in goods and services purchases.

Electronic purchasing via the Internet promises to change greatly the business buying process, and hence the business-to-business marketing process. Jupiter Research predicts that by 2005, 42 percent of all B2B buying will be conducted online and that more than a third of that online trade will be conducted through trading networks like GXS's.

As one expert suggests, "Internet presence is becoming as common as business cards and faxes." To stay in the game, B2B marketers will need a well-thought-out Internet marketing strategy to support their other business marketing efforts.

Sources: Scott Woolley, "Double Click for Resin," *Forbes,* March 10, 1997, p. 132; John Evan Frook, "Buying Behemoth—By Shifting $5B in Spending to Extranets, GE Could Ignite a Development Frenzy," *Internetweek,* August 17, 1998, p. 1; "Net Markets Surge," *Sales and Marketing Management,* January 2001, p. 32; and "GXS Overview," accessed online at www.gegxs.com, July 2001.

---

suppliers. A Web-powered purchasing program eliminates the paperwork associated with traditional requisition and ordering procedures. At National Semiconductor, for example, the $75 to $250 cost of processing each paper-based requisition has been cut to just $3 per electronic order. A more efficient centralized purchasing platform also saves time and money. One key motivation for GE's massive move to online purchasing has been a desire to get rid of overlapping purchasing systems across its many divisions.

E-procurement reduces the time between order and delivery. Time savings are particularly dramatic for companies with many overseas suppliers. Adaptec, a leading supplier of computer storage, used an extranet to tie all of its Taiwanese chip suppliers together in a kind of virtual family. Now messages from Adaptec flow in seconds from its headquarters to its Asian partners, and Adaptec has reduced the time between the order and delivery of its chips from as long as 16 weeks to just 55 days—the same turnaround time for companies that build their own chips.

The rapidly expanding use of e-purchasing, however, also presents some problems. For example, it cuts purchasing jobs for millions of clerks and order processors. National Semiconductor reduced its purchasing staff by more than half when it took its purchasing activities online. On the other hand, for many purchasing professionals, going online means reducing drudgery and paperwork and spending more time managing inventory and working creatively with suppliers.

More important, at the same time that the Web makes it possible for suppliers and customers to share business data and even collaborate on product design, it can also erode decades-old customer–supplier relationships. Many firms are using the Web to search for better suppliers. Japan Airlines (JAL) has used the Internet to post orders for in-flight materials such as plastic cups. On its Web site it posts drawings and specifications that will attract proposals from any firm that comes across the site, rather than from just the usual Japanese suppliers.

Finally, e-purchasing can create potential security disasters. More than 80 percent of companies say security is the leading barrier to expanding electronic links with customers and partners. Although e-mail and home banking transactions can be protected through basic encryption, the secure environment that businesses need to carry out confidential interactions is still lacking. Companies are spending millions for research on defensive strategies to keep hackers at bay. Cisco Systems, for example, specifies the types of routers, firewalls, and security procedures that its partners must use to safeguard extranet connections. In fact, the company goes even further—it sends its own security engineers to examine a partner's defenses and holds the partner liable for any security breach that originates from its computer.

STOP *Reviewing the Concepts*

This chapter is the last of four chapters on analyzing marketing opportunities by looking closely at consumers and their buying behavior. The American consumer market consists of more than 284 million people who consume many trillions of dollars' worth of goods and services each year. The business market involves far more dollars and items than the consumer market. Final consumers and business buyers vary greatly in their characteristics and circumstances. Understanding *consumer* and *business buyer behavior* is one of the biggest challenges marketers face.

1. Understand the consumer market and the major factors that influence consumer buyer behavior.

The *consumer market* consists of all the individuals and households who buy or acquire goods and services for personal consumption. A simple stimulus–response model of consumer behavior suggests that marketing stimuli and other major forces enter the consumer's "black box." This black box has two parts: buyer characteristics and the buyer's decision process. Once in the black box, the inputs result in observable buyer responses, such as product choice, brand choice, dealer choice, purchase timing, and purchase amount.

 Consumer buyer behavior is influenced by four key sets of buyer characteristics: cultural, social, personal, and psychological. Understanding these factors can help marketers to identify interested buyers and to shape products and appeals to serve consumer needs better. *Culture* is the most basic determinant of a person's wants and behavior. People in different cultural, subcultural, and social class groups have different product and brand preferences. *Social factors*—such as small group and family influences—strongly affect product and brand choices, as do *personal characteristics,* such as age, life-cycle stage, occupation, economic circumstances, lifestyle, and personality. Finally, consumer buying behavior is influenced by four major sets of *psychological factors*—motivation, perception, learning, and beliefs and attitudes. Each of these factors provides a different perspective for understanding the workings of the buyer's black box.

2. Identify and discuss the stages in the buyer decision process.

When making a purchase, the buyer goes through a decision process consisting of need recognition, information search, evaluation of alternatives, purchase decision, and postpurchase behavior. During *need recognition,* the consumer recognizes a problem or need that could be satisfied by a product or service. Once the need is recognized, the consumer moves into the *information search* stage. With information in hand, the consumer proceeds to *alternative evaluation* and assesses brands in the choice set. From there, the consumer makes a *purchase decision* and actually buys the product. In the final stage of the buyer decision process, *postpurchase behavior,* the consumer takes action based on satisfaction or dissatisfaction. The marketer's job is to understand the buyer's behavior at each stage and the influences that are operating.

3. Describe the adoption and diffusion process for new products.

The product *adoption process* is comprised of five stages: awareness, interest, evaluation, trial, and adoption. New-product marketers must think about how to help consumers move through these stages. With regard to the *diffusion process* for new products, consumers respond at different rates, depending on consumer and product characteristics. Consumers may be innovators, early adopters, early majority, late majority, or laggards. Each group may require different marketing approaches. Marketers often try to bring their new products to the attention of potential early adopters, especially those who are opinion leaders.

4. Define the business market and identify the major factors that influence business buyer behavior.

The *business market* comprises all organizations that buy goods and services for use in the production of other products and services or for the purpose of reselling or renting them to others at a profit. As compared to consumer markets, business markets usually have fewer, larger buyers who are more geographically concentrated. Business demand is derived demand, and the business buying decision usually involves more, and more professional, buyers.

Business buyers make decisions that vary with the three types of *buying situations:* straight rebuys, modified rebuys, and new tasks. The decision-making unit of a buying organization—the *buying center*—can consist of many different persons playing many different roles. The business marketer needs to know the following: Who are the major buying center participants? In what decisions do they exercise influence and to what degree? What evaluation criteria does each decision participant use? The business marketer also needs to understand the major environmental, organizational, interpersonal, and individual influences on the buying process.

5. List and define the steps in the business buying decision process.

The *business buying decision process* itself can be quite involved, with eight basic stages: problem recognition, general need description, product specification,

supplier search, proposal solicitation, supplier selection, order-routine specification, and performance review. Buyers who face a new-task buying situation usually go through all stages of the buying process. Buyers making modified or straight rebuys may skip some of the stages. Companies must manage the overall customer relationship, which often includes many different buying decisions in various stages of the buying decisions process.

Recent advances in information technology have given birth to "e-purchasing," by which business buyers are purchasing all kinds of products and services electronically, either through electronic data interchange links (EDI) or on the Internet. Such cyberbuying gives buyers access to new suppliers, lowers purchasing costs, and hastens order processing and delivery. However, it can also erode customer–supplier relationships and create potential security problems. Still, business marketers are increasingly connecting with customers online to share marketing information, sell products and services, provide customer support services, and maintain ongoing customer relationships.

Navigating the Key Terms

For a detailed analysis of the meaning and importance of each of the following key terms, visit our Web page at **www.prenhall.com/kotler**.

Adoption process
Attitude
Belief
Business buyer
   behavior

Buying center
Cognitive dissonance
Consumer buyer behavior
Consumer market
Culture
Derived demand
Groups
Learning
Lifestyle
Modified rebuy

Motive (or drive)
New product
New task
Opinion leaders
Perception
Social class
Straight rebuy
Subculture
Systems selling
Value analysis

Travel Log

The following concept checks and discussion questions will help you to keep track of and apply the concepts you've studied in this chapter.

Concept Checks

Fill in the blanks, then look for the correct answers.

1. _____ refers to the buying behavior of final consumers —individuals and

households who buy goods and services for personal consumption.

2. _____ is the most basic cause of a person's wants and behavior.

3. _____ are society's relatively permanent and ordered divisions whose members share similar values, interests, and behaviors.

4. People within a reference group who, because of special skills, knowledge, personality, or other characteristics, exert influence on others are called _____.

5. Lifestyle is a person's pattern of living as expressed in his or her psychographics. It involves measuring consumer's major *AIO* dimensions, where A = _____, I = _____, and O = _____.

6. Abraham Maslow sought to explain why people are driven by particular needs at particular times. He identified five primary need categories, which include: _____ needs, _____ needs, _____ needs, _____ needs, and _____ needs.

7. The buyer decision process consists of five stages: _____, _____, _____, _____, and _____.

8. Consumers go through five stages in the process of adopting a new product: _____, _____, _____, _____, and _____.

9. Five characteristics are especially important in influencing an innovation's rate of adoption. _____ is the degree to which the innovation appears superior to existing products.

10. With respect to business buying situations, there are three major types: _____, _____, and _____.

11. The decision-making unit of a buying organization is called its _____ and it includes all individuals and units that participate in the business decision-making process.

12. The eight stages of the business buying process include problem recognition, general need description, product specification, _____, _____, _____, _____, and performance review.

Concept Checks Answers: 1. Consumer buyer behavior; 2. Culture; 3. Social classes; 4. opinion leaders: 5. activities, interests, and opinions; 6. physiological, safety, social, esteem, and self-actualization; 7. need recognition, information search, evaluation of alternatives, purchase decision, and postpurchase behavior; 8. awareness, interest, evaluation, trial, and adoption; 9. relative advantage; 10. straight rebuy, modified rebuy, and new-task; 11. buying center; 12. suppliers search, proposal solicitation, supplier selection, and order-routine specification.

Discussing the Issues

1. List several factors that you could add to the model shown in Figure 6-1 to make it a more complete description of consumer behavior. Explain your ideas and reasoning.

2. In designing the advertising for a soft drink, which would you find more helpful, information about consumer demographics or information about consumer lifestyles? Select a new soft drink on the market and give examples of how you would use each type of information.

3. Using Figure 6-4, trace a recent purchase you have made. Examine each of the five stages of the buyer decision process and detail your experiences in each stage. What could the seller have done to make your buying experience better? Did you experience any cognitive dissonance? Explain.

4. Which of the major types of business buying situations is represented by each of the following? (a) Chrysler's purchase of computers that go in cars and adjust engine performance to changing driving conditions. (b) Volkswagen's purchase of spark plugs for its line of vans. (c) Honda's purchase of light bulbs for a new Acura model.

5. Increasingly, business buyers are purchasing all kinds of products and services electronically, either through electronic data interchange links (EDI) or on the Internet. List the benefits of "cyberpurchasing" and "e-procurement." Illustrate your view with an example from the Internet.

 *Mastering Marketing*

Using the information from either Figure 6-1 or Figure 6-8, demonstrate how CanGo or its consumers are required to make buying decisions. Do you see any problems or opportunities? Discuss and explain.

Traveling on the Net

Point of Interest: Adapting Products to Consumer Lifestyles

When H. J. Heinz needed a boost for sagging ketchup sales, it turned to an old formula for an answer—match consumer lifestyles with a bold innovation and consumers will beat a path to your door. Heinz and competitors have for years assumed that ketchup was for grownups. Wrong! Ketchup is also for kids. This realization gave Heinz a whole new avenue for growth. Today's kids were brought up on Nickelodeon's green slime and like stuff that most adults would find to be gross—things like gummy worms, slime pops, and weird versions of candy and soft drinks. How could Heinz set off a kid's gross-o-meter? With Blastin' Green Ketchup! Although it tastes the same as regular ketchup, this new version comes in a striped bottle shaped for a kid's hands and has a new nozzle that is perfect for writing and drawing with ketchup. As a result, kids are taking the ketchup out of the refrigerator more often, using it for more cool stuff, and participating in the buying process as never before. The new green stuff has boosted Heinz's sales by 5 per cent and market share by 4 percent. So what is next? Beginning in the Fall of 2001, Heinz has introduced another kid-friendly ketchup called Funky Purple. The company is betting that when you construct your French fry fort or burger castle you will decorate it with red, green, and purple ketchup. Sounds gross—that's just what this market ordered!

For Discussion

1. List the ways in which Heinz has adapted its new products to the lifestyles of kids. How has Heinz persuaded adults to buy the product for their kids?
2. After examining the buyer decision process shown in Figure 6-1, discuss how this new product can be adapted to the process. How could Heinz overcome difficulties with an adult market?
3. How can Heinz use the packaging features to its advantage? How can Heinz turn the short-term sales and market share gain into a long-term advantage? What does the company need to know about lifestyles in its various markets to increase sales in the future?
4. Would you buy green or purple ketchup? Why or why not? If you answered "no," construct a strategy that might change your mind. Consider the sections in the text on attitudes and beliefs as you construct your strategy.

Application Thinking

Assume that you have been hired by Heinz to recommend the next color change for its new line of ketchup. After visiting the EZ Squirt Web site (see **www.ezsquirt.com**), describe how you would conduct research to determine this new color alternative. Who would you research? What would you ask? How would you measure lifestyles? Finally, pick a color and justify your pick. Present your idea to the class.

MAP—Marketing Applications

MAP Stop 6

Performance review is one of the most critical stages in a business buying process. Perhaps nowhere is this more important than in the highly competitive aircraft manufacturing business. Whether the planes are large or small, once a purchase is made, the buyer is tied to the manufacturer for a long time for service and parts requirements. "Air Wars" are currently being fought between Europe's Airbus Industrie and America's Boeing. To a lesser extent the same competitive conflict exists in the smaller personal and corporate aircraft market between Cessna and Lear Jet. Who will eventually win these dramatic competitive struggles is literally "up in the air." Note: for additional information, see **www.airbus.com**, **www.boeing.com**, **www.cessna.textron.com**, and **www.learjet.com**.

Thinking Like a Marketing Manager

1. Apply either of the above two competitive situations to Figure 6-6 and demonstrate the critical factors that might be present in a business buying situation.
2. How would performance review be conducted in either of the above two situations? Who might be responsible for such a performance review?

3. If the review was negative, how might the selling organization overcome this difficulty?
   a. Examine Figure 6-7. Which specific components might be involved in a performance review of aircraft safety?

   b. Find a recent example of "Air Wars" competitiveness and bring the example to class for discussion. How does your example relate to business-to-business marketing and business buying?

chapter 7

Market Segmentation, Targeting, and Positioning for Competitive Advantage

ROAD MAP:
Previewing the Concepts

So far in your marketing journey, you've learned what marketing is and about the complex environments in which it operates. With that as background, you're now ready to travel more deeply into marketing strategy and tactics. This chapter looks further into key marketing strategy decisions—how to divide up markets into meaningful customer groups (market segmentation), choose which customer groups to serve (market targeting), and create marketing offers that best serve targeted customers (positioning). Then, the chapters that follow explore in depth the tactical marketing tools—the 4Ps—through which marketers bring these strategies to life.

▶ After studying this chapter, you should be able to

1. define the three steps of target marketing: market segmentation, market targeting, and market positioning
2. list and discuss the major levels of market segmentation and bases for segmenting consumer and business markets
3. explain how companies identify attractive market segments and choose a market-coverage strategy
4. discuss how companies position their products for maximum competitive advantage in the marketplace

Next stop: Procter & Gamble, one of the world's premier consumer goods companies. Some 99 percent of all U.S. households use at least one P&G brand, and the typical household regularly buys and uses from one to two *dozen* P&G brands. How many P&G products can you name? Why does this superb marketer compete with itself on supermarket shelves by marketing eight different brands of laundry detergent? The P&G story provides a great example of how smart marketers use segmentation, targeting, and positioning.

Procter & Gamble (P&G) sells eight brands of laundry detergent in the United States (Tide, Cheer, Bold, Gain, Era, Dreft, Febreze, and Ivory Snow). It also sells five brands each of hand soap (Ivory, Safeguard, Camay, Olay, and Zest) and shampoo (Pantene, Head & Shoulders, Pert Plus, Physique, and Vidal Sassoon); four brands of dishwashing detergent (Dawn, Ivory, Joy, and Cascade); three brands each of tissues and towels (Charmin, Bounty, Puffs), floor cleaners (Spic & Span, Top Job, and Mr. Clean), deodorant (Secret, Sure, and Old Spice), cosmetics (Cover Girl, Max Factor, and Olay), and skin care potions (Oil of Olay, Noxema, and Clearasil); and two brands each of fabric softener (Downy and Bounce) and disposable diapers (Pampers and Luvs). Moreover, P&G has many additional brands in each category for different international markets. For example, it sells sixteen different laundry product brands in Latin America and nineteen in Europe, the Middle

East, and Africa. (See Procter & Gamble's Web site at www.pg.com for a full glimpse of the company's impressive lineup of familiar brands.)

These P&G brands compete with one another on the same supermarket shelves. But why would P&G introduce several brands in one category instead of concentrating its resources on a single leading brand? The answer lies in the fact that different people want different *mixes of benefits* from the products they buy. Take laundry detergents as an example. People use laundry detergents to get their clothes clean. But they also want other things from their detergents—such as economy, bleaching power, fabric softening, fresh smell, strength or mildness, and lots of suds or only a few. We all want *some* of every one of these benefits from our detergent, but we may have different *priorities* for each benefit. To some people, cleaning and bleaching power are most important; to others, fabric softening matters most; still others want a mild, fresh-scented detergent. Thus, there are groups—or segments—of laundry detergent buyers, and each segment seeks a special combination of benefits.

Procter & Gamble has identified at least eight important laundry detergent segments, along with numerous subsegments, and has developed a different brand designed to meet the special needs of each. The eight P&G brands are positioned for different segments as follows:

◆ *Tide* "helps keep clothes looking like new." It's the all-purpose family detergent that is "tough on greasy stains." *Tide with Bleach* is "so powerful, it whitens down to the fiber."

◆ *Cheer with Triple Color Guard* is the "color expert." It guards against fading, color transfer, and fuzzy buildup. *Cheer Free* is "dermatologist tested . . . contains no irritating perfume or dye."

◆ *Bold* is the detergent with built-in fabric softener. It's "for clean, soft, fresh-smelling clothes." *Bold* liquid adds "the fresh fabric softener scent."

◆ *Gain*, originally P&G's "enzyme" detergent, was repositioned as the detergent that gives you clean, fresh-smelling clothes. It "cleans and freshens like sunshine. It's not just plain clean, it's Gain clean."

◆ *Era* has "built-in stain removers." It's "the power tool for stains."

◆ *Dreft* also "helps remove tough baby stains . . . for a clean you can trust." It's "pediatrician recommended and the first choice of mothers." It "doesn't remove the flame resistance of children's sleepwear."

◆ *Febreze Clean Wash* "doesn't just cover up odors, it truly eliminates worked in, driven in, cooked-in odors in just one wash." It's "the Cleaner Clean for where you live."

◆ *Ivory Snow* is "Ninety-nine and forty-four one hundredths percent pure." It "gently cleans fine washables and baby clothes . . . leaving them feeling soft."

Within each segment, Procter & Gamble has identified even *narrower* niches. For example, you can buy regular Tide (in powder or liquid form) or any of several formulations:

◆ *Tide with Bleach* helps to "keep your whites white and your colors bright," "kills 99.9 percent of bacteria."

◆ *Tide Clean Rinse* "goes beyond stain removal to prevent dingy buildup on clothes."

◆ *Tide Mountain Spring* lets you "bring the fresh clean scent of the great outdoors inside—the scent of crisp mountain air and fresh wildflowers."

◆ *Tide High Efficiency* is "formulated for high efficiency top-loading machines"—it prevents oversudsing.

◆ *Tide Free* "provides all the stain removal benefits without any dyes or perfumes."

◆ *Tide WearCare* "prevents damage to cotton clothes so they last longer."

◆ *Tide Rapid Action Tablets* are portable and powerful. It's Tide "all concentrated into a little blue and white tablet that fits into your pocket."

By segmenting the market and having several detergent brands, Procter & Gamble has an attractive offering for consumers in all important preference groups. As a result, P&G is really cleaning up in the $4.3 billion U.S. laundry detergent market. Tide, by itself, captures a whopping 38 percent market share. All P&G brands combined take a 57 percent share of the market—two and one-half times that of nearest rival Unilever and much more than any single brand could obtain by itself.[1]

• •

Companies today recognize that they cannot appeal to all buyers in the marketplace, or at least not to all buyers in the same way. Buyers are too numerous, too widely scattered, and too varied in their needs and buying practices. Moreover, the companies themselves vary widely in their abilities to serve different segments of the market. Rather than trying to compete in an entire market, sometimes against superior competitors, each company must identify the parts of the market that it can serve best and most profitably.

Thus, most companies are being more choosy about the customers with whom they wish to connect. Most have moved away from mass marketing and toward *market segmentation and targeting*—identifying market segments, selecting one or more of them, and developing products and marketing programs tailored to each. Instead of scattering their marketing efforts (the "shotgun" approach), firms are focusing on the buyers who have greater interest in the values they create best (the "rifle" approach).

Figure 7-1 shows the three major steps in target marketing. The first is **market segmentation**—dividing a market into smaller groups of buyers with distinct needs, characteristics, or behaviors who might require separate products or marketing mixes. The company identifies different ways to segment the market and develops profiles of the resulting market segments. The second step is **market targeting**—evaluating each market segment's attractiveness and selecting one or more of the market segments to enter. The third step is **market positioning**—setting the competitive positioning for the product and creating a detailed marketing mix. We discuss each of these steps in turn.

Market segmentation
Dividing a market into smaller groups of buyers with distinct needs, characteristics, or behaviors who might require separate products or marketing mixes.

Market targeting
The process of evaluating each market segment's attractiveness and selecting one or more segments to enter.

Market positioning
Arranging for a product to occupy a clear, distinctive, and desirable place relative to competing products in the minds of target consumers.

Figure 7-1
Steps in market segmentation, targeting, and positioning

Market Segmentation

Markets consist of buyers, and buyers differ in one or more ways. They may differ in their wants, resources, locations, buying attitudes, and buying practices. Through market segmentation, companies divide large, heterogeneous markets into smaller segments that can be reached more efficiently and effectively with products and services that match their unique needs. In this section, we discuss five important segmentation topics: levels of market segmentation, segmenting consumer markets, segmenting business markets, segmenting international markets, and requirements for effective segmentation.

Levels of Market Segmentation

Because buyers have unique needs and wants, each buyer is potentially a separate market. Ideally, then, a seller might design a separate marketing program for each buyer. However, although some companies attempt to serve buyers individually, many others face larger numbers of smaller buyers and do not find complete segmentation worthwhile. Instead, they look for broader classes of buyers who differ in their product needs or buying responses. Thus, market segmentation can be carried out at several different levels. Figure 7-2 shows that companies can practice no segmentation (mass marketing), complete segmentation (micromarketing), or something in between (segment marketing or niche marketing).

Mass Marketing Companies have not always practiced target marketing. For most of the past century, major consumer products companies held fast to *mass marketing*—mass producing, mass distributing, and mass promoting about the same product in about the same way to all consumers. Henry Ford epitomized this marketing strategy when he offered the Model T Ford to all buyers; they could have the car "in any color as long as it is black." Similarly, Coca-Cola at one time produced only one drink for the whole market, hoping it would appeal to everyone.

The traditional argument for mass marketing is that it creates the largest potential market, which leads to the lowest costs, which in turn can translate into either lower prices or higher margins. However, many factors now make mass marketing more difficult. For example, the world's mass markets have slowly splintered into a profusion of smaller segments—the baby boomers here, the Gen Xers there; here the Hispanic segment, there the African American segment; here working women, there single parents; here the Sun Belt, there the Rust Belt. Today, marketers find it very hard to create a single product or program that appeals to all of these diverse groups.

The proliferation of distribution channels and advertising media has also made it difficult to practice "one-size-fits-all" marketing. Today's consumers can shop at megamalls, superstores, or specialty shops; through mail catalogs or virtual stores on the Internet. They are bombarded with messages delivered via media ranging from old standards such as television, radio, magazines, newspapers, and telephone to newcomers such as Web banners, fax, and

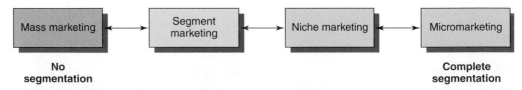

Figure 7-2
Levels of marketing segmentation

e-mail. No wonder some have claimed that mass marketing is dying. Not surprisingly, many companies are retreating from mass marketing and turning to segmented marketing.

Segment Marketing A company that practices **segment marketing** isolates broad segments that make up a market and adapts its offers to more closely match the needs of one or more segments. Thus, Marriott markets to a variety of segments—business travelers, families, and others—with packages adapted to their varying needs. GM has designed specific models for different income and age groups. In fact, it sells models for segments with varied *combinations* of age and income. For instance, GM designed its Buick Park Avenue for older, higher-income consumers.

Segment marketing offers several benefits over mass marketing. The company can market more *efficiently,* targeting its products or services, channels, and communications programs toward only consumers that it can serve best and most profitably. The company can also market more *effectively* by fine-tuning its products, prices, and programs to the needs of carefully defined segments. And the company may face fewer competitors if fewer competitors are focusing on this market segment.

Niche Marketing Market segments are normally large, identifiable groups within a market—for example, luxury car buyers, performance car buyers, utility car buyers, and economy car buyers. **Niche marketing** focuses on subgroups within these segments. A *niche* is a more narrowly defined group, usually identified by dividing a segment into subsegments or by defining a group with a distinctive set of traits that may seek a special combination of benefits. For example, the utility vehicles segment might include light-duty pickup trucks and sport utility vehicles (SUVs). The sport utility vehicles subsegment might be further divided into standard SUV (as served by Ford and Chevrolet) and luxury SUV (as served by Lincoln and Lexus) niches.

Whereas segments are fairly large and normally attract several competitors, niches are smaller and normally attract only one or a few competitors. Niche marketers presumably understand their niches' needs so well that their customers willingly pay a price premium. For example, the luxurious Bentley gets a high price for its cars because its loyal buyers feel that no other automobile comes close to offering the product-service-membership benefits that Bentley does.

Niching offers smaller companies an opportunity to compete by focusing their limited resources on serving niches that may be unimportant to or overlooked by larger competitors. For example, tiny Vans Inc. specializes in making thick-soled, slip-on sneakers for skateboarders that can absorb the shock of a five-foot leap on wheels. Although it captures only a point or two of market share in the overall athletic shoe market, Vans' small but intensely loyal customer base has made the company more profitable than many of its larger competitors.[2]

Large companies also serve niche markets. For example, American Express offers not only its traditional green cards but also gold cards, corporate cards, and even a black card, called the Centurian, with a $1,000 annual fee aimed at a niche of "superpremium customers."[3] And Nike makes athletic gear for basketball, running, and soccer but also for smaller niches such as biking and street hockey.

In many markets today, niches are the norm. As an advertising agency executive observed, "There will be no market for products that everybody likes a little, only for products that somebody likes a lot." Other experts assert that companies will have to "niche or be niched."[4]

Micromarketing Segment and niche marketers tailor their offers and marketing programs to meet the needs of various market segments. At the same time, however, they do not customize their offers to each individual customer. Thus, segment marketing and niche marketing fall between the extremes of mass marketing and micromarketing.

Segment marketing
Isolating broad segments that make up a market and adapting the marketing offer to match the needs of one or more segments.

Niche marketing
Focusing on subsegments or niches with distinctive traits that may seek a special combination of benefits.

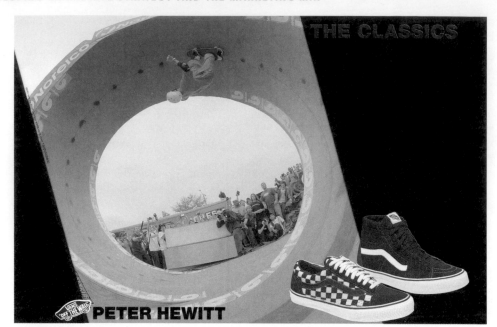

Niche marketing: Tiny Vans Inc. specializes in making thick-soled, slip-on sneakers for skateboarders that can absorb the shock of a five-foot leap on wheels.

Micromarketing
The practice of tailoring products and marketing programs to the needs and wants of specific individuals and local customer groups—includes *local marketing* and *individual marketing.*

Local marketing
Tailoring brands and promotions to the needs and wants of local customer groups—cities, neighborhoods, and even specific stores.

Micromarketing is the practice of tailoring products and marketing programs to suit the tastes of specific individuals and locations. Micromarketing includes *local marketing* and *individual marketing.*

LOCAL MARKETING. **Local marketing** involves tailoring brands and promotions to the needs and wants of local customer groups—cities, neighborhoods, and even specific stores. Retailers such as Sears and Wal-Mart routinely customize each store's merchandise and promotions to match its specific clientele. Citibank provides different mixes of banking services in its branches depending on neighborhood demographics. Kraft helps supermarket chains identify the specific cheese assortments and shelf positioning that will optimize cheese sales in low-income, middle-income, and high-income stores and in different ethnic communities.

Local marketing has some drawbacks. It can drive up manufacturing and marketing costs by reducing economies of scale. It can also create logistics problems as companies try to meet the varied requirements of different regional and local markets. Further, a brand's overall image might be diluted if the product and message vary too much in different localities. Still, as companies face increasingly fragmented markets, and as new supporting technologies develop, the advantages of local marketing often outweigh the drawbacks. Local marketing helps a company to market more effectively in the face of pronounced regional and local differences in demographics and lifestyles. It also meets the needs of the company's first-line customers—retailers—who prefer more fine-tuned product assortments for their neighborhoods.

Individual marketing
Tailoring products and marketing programs to the needs and preferences of individual customers.

INDIVIDUAL MARKETING. In the extreme, micromarketing becomes **individual marketing**—tailoring products and marketing programs to the needs and preferences of individual customers. Individual marketing has also been labeled *one-to-one marketing, customized marketing,* and *markets-of-one marketing.*[5]

The widespread use of mass marketing has obscured the fact that for centuries consumers were served as individuals: The tailor custom-made the suit, the cobbler designed shoes for the individual, the cabinetmaker made furniture to order. Today, however, new technologies are permitting many companies to return to customized marketing. More powerful computers, detailed databases, robotic production and flexible manufacturing, and immediate and interactive communication media such as e-mail, fax, and the Internet—all have combined to foster "mass customization." *Mass customization* is the process through which firms interact one-to-one with masses of customers to create customer-unique value by designing products and services tailor-made to individual needs (see Marketing at Work 7-1).

Thus, Dell Computer delivers computers to individual customers loaded with customer-specified hardware and software. Peapod, the online grocery shopping and delivery service, lets customers create the virtual supermarket that best fits their individual needs. And Ritz-Carlton Hotels creates custom-designed experiences for its delighted guests:

> Check into any Ritz-Carlton hotel around the world, and you'll be amazed at how well the hotel's employees anticipate your slightest need. Without ever asking, they seem to know that you want a nonsmoking room with a king-size bed, a non-allergenic pillow, and breakfast with decaffeinated coffee in your room. How does Ritz-Carlton work this magic? The hotel employs a system that combines information technology and flexible operations to customize the hotel experience. At the heart of the system is a huge customer database, which contains information about guests gathered through the observations of hotel employees. Each day, hotel staffers—from those at the front desk to those in maintenance and housekeeping—discreetly record the unique habits, likes, and dislikes of each guest on small "guest preference pads." These observations are then transferred to a corporatewide "guest preference database." Every morning, a "guest historian" at each hotel reviews the files of all new arrivals who have previously stayed at a Ritz-Carlton and prepares a list of suggested extra touches that might delight each guest. Guests have responded strongly to such markets-of-one service. Since inaugurating the guest-history system in 1992, Ritz-Carlton has boosted guest retention by 23 percent. An amazing 95 percent of departing guests report that their stay has been a truly memorable experience.

Business-to-business marketers are also finding new ways to customize their offerings. For example, Becton-Dickinson, a major medical supplier, offers to customize almost anything for its hospital customers. It offers custom-designed labeling, individual packaging, customized quality control, customized computer software, and customized billing. Motorola salespeople use a handheld computer to custom-design pagers following individual business customer wishes. The design data are transmitted to the Motorola factory and production starts within seventeen minutes. The customized pagers are ready for shipment within two hours. And John Deere manufactures seeding equipment that can be configured in more than two million versions to individual customer specifications. The seeders are produced one at a time, in any sequence, on a single production line.[6]

The move toward individual marketing mirrors the trend in consumer *self-marketing*. Increasingly, individual customers are taking more responsibility for determining which products and brands to buy. Consider two business buyers with two different purchasing styles. The first sees several salespeople, each trying to persuade him to buy his or her product. The second sees no salespeople but rather logs onto the Internet; searches for information on available products; interacts electronically with various suppliers, users, and product analysts; and then makes up her own mind about the best offer. The second purchasing agent has taken more responsibility for the buying process, and the marketer has had less influence over her buying decision.

As the trend toward more interactive dialogue and less advertising monologue continues, self-marketing will grow in importance. As more buyers look up consumer reports, join Internet product discussion forums, and place orders via phone or online, marketers will have to influence the buying process in new ways. They will need to involve customers more in all phases of the product development and buying processes, increasing opportunities for buyers to practice self-marketing.

Marketing at Work 7.1

Markets of One: "Anything You can Digitize, You can Customize"

Imagine walking into a booth that bathes your body in patterns of white light and, in a matter of seconds, captures your exact three-dimensional form. The digitized data are then imprinted on a credit card, which you use to order customized clothing. No, this isn't a scene from the next Star Wars sequel; it's a peek ahead at how you will be able to buy clothing in the not-so-distant future. A consortium of over 100 apparel companies, including Levi Strauss, has banded together to develop body scanning technology in the hope of making mass customization commonplace.

Although body scanning technology and smart cards carrying customer measurements are still in development, many companies are now using existing technologies to tailor products to individual customers. Dell creates custom-configured computers, Reflect.com formulates customized beauty products, Ford lets buyers "build a vehicle" from a palette of options, and Golf to Fit crafts custom clubs based on consumer measurements and preferences. Here are some other examples of companies in the forefront of the mass customization economy:

Levi Strauss. In 1994, Levi began making measure-to-fit women's jeans under its in-store Personal Pair program. Consumer response was so positive that Levi developed an expanded in-store customization concept called Original Spin, which works a lot like the futuristic sizing scenario described above. Customers—both men and women—enter a booth in which a 3-D Body Scanner creates personalized measurements against a backdrop of

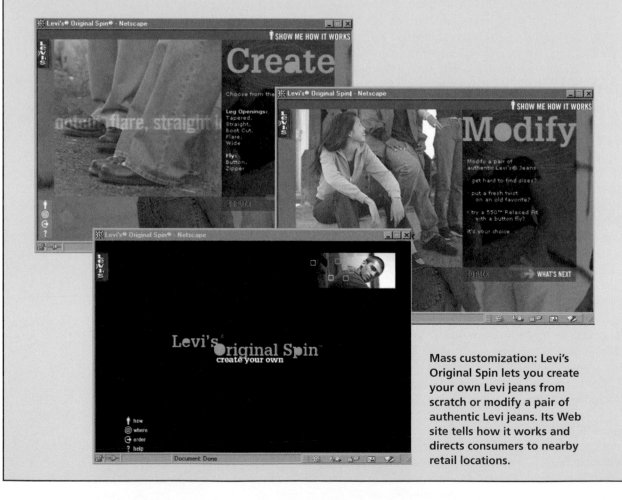

Mass customization: Levi's Original Spin lets you create your own Levi jeans from scratch or modify a pair of authentic Levi jeans. Its Web site tells how it works and directs consumers to nearby retail locations.

strobe lights and space-age music. Using the Original Spin terminals, customers can then choose from a range of cuts and styles that represent hundreds of different pairs of jeans available for purchase. Whereas a fully stocked Levi's store carries 130 pairs of ready-to-wear jeans for a given waist and inseam, with Original Spin the number jumps to 750.

Mattel. Since 1998, girls have been able to log onto the "My Design" page of the Barbie Web site (www.barbie.com) and create their very own "friend of Barbie" doll. They choose the doll's skin tone, eye color, hairstyle and hair color, clothes, accessories, and name. They even fill out a questionnaire detailing their doll's likes and dislikes. When Barbie's special friend arrives in the mail, the girls find the doll's name on the packaging along with a computer-generated paragraph about her personality.

Nike ID. This Nike Web site (www.NikeID.com) lets customers design their own athletic shoes online. The site leads buyers through a set of questions about their preferences for shoe style, base and accent colors, shoe construction, and even personalized IDs of up to 16 characters to be printed on the sole of each shoe. When the customers submit the final design, Nike transmits the order to a specially equipped plant in China or Korea, where the information is fed into a production line that pumps out the customized shoes. Customers pay only an extra $10 for this service.

Consumer goods marketers aren't the only ones going one-to-one. B2B marketers also provide customers with tailor-made goods, often more cheaply and quickly than it used to take to make standardized ones. Particularly for small

companies, mass customization provides a way to stand out against larger competitors:

ChemStation. This small industrial-detergent company offers individually concocted soap formulas to its industrial customers, which range from car washes to the U.S. Air Force. What cleans a car won't work to clean an airplane or equipment in a mine shaft. ChemStation salespeople collect information about a specific customer's cleaning needs and enter it into a customer database called the Tank Management System (TMS). Next, a company chemist develops a special "detergent recipe" for the customer. The recipe is fed into a computer-controlled machine, which mixes up a batch of the special brew. ChemStation delivers the custom-made mixture to a tank installed at the customer's site. It then monitors usage and automatically refills the tank when supplies run low. Because the customization system gives customers exactly what they need, it helps ChemStation to lock out competitors. No one—not even the customer—knows what goes into each formula, making it hard for a customer to jump to competitors. "We tell [customers] it's a secret," says founder and CEO George Homan. "We're not as protective [about our formulas] as Coca-Cola, but we're close."

Lear Corporation. Think of a dashboard that looks like Swiss cheese, with spaces to plug in different dials and gauges in any range of combinations. The car radio can have knobs, slide handles, or old-fashioned dials. The interior fabric that lines the roof might match a family tartan or be turned into a giant speaker. If Lear, the world's largest automotive-interiors supplier, has its way, customers can even tell automakers to make their dashboard translucent orange. All

this is made possible by the "Common Architecture Strategy," recently unveiled by Lear. People would get this level of customization at close to the same price and about the same delivery time as a regular upgraded automobile. If the automakers buy the idea, it could be ready for 2002 car models.

Two trends underlie the growth in one-to-one marketing. One is the ever-increasing emphasis on customer value and satisfaction. Today's consumers have very high expectations—they expect products and services that meet their individual needs. Yet, it would be prohibitively expensive or downright impossible to meet these individual demands if it weren't for another trend: rapid advances in technology. Data warehouses allow companies to store trillions of bytes of customer information. Computer-controlled factory equipment and industrial robots can now quickly readjust assembly lines. Bar code scanners make it possible to track parts and products. Most important, the Internet ties it all together and makes it easy for a company to interact with customers, learn about their preferences, and respond. Indeed, the Internet appears to be the ultimate one-to-one medium.

The notion of personal relationships on the Internet might seem like an oxymoron. But unlike mass production, which eliminates the need for human interaction, mass customization has made relationships with customers more important than ever. For instance, when Levi's sells made-to-order jeans, the company not only captures consumer data in digitized form but also becomes the customer's "jeans adviser." Through its customization program, ChemStation becomes a trusted partner to its clients—95 percent of customers never leave because teaching another company their cleansing needs is not worth the effort. And Mattel is building a database of information from all the customers who purchase My Design dolls so it can start long-term, one-to-one relationships with each customer.

Just as mass production was the marketing principle of the last century, mass customization is becoming the marketing principle for the twenty-first century. The world appears to be coming full circle—from the good old days when customers were treated as individuals, to mass marketing when nobody knew your name, and back again. As Joseph Pine, author of *Mass Customization*, concludes, "Anything you can digitize, you can customize."

Sources: Erick Schonfeld, "The Customized, Digitized, Have-It-Your-Way Economy," *Fortune*, September 28, 1998, pp. 115–124; Ronald Alsop, "A Special Report on Trends in Industry and Finance," *Wall Street Journal*, April 29, 1999, p. A1; James H. Gilmore and B. Joseph Pine, *Markets of One: Creating Customer-Unique Value through Mass Customization* (Boston: Harvard Business School Press, 2001); Diane Brady, "Customizing for the Masses," *Business Week*, March 20, 2000, pp. 130B–130F; Paul Zipkin, "The Limits of Mass Customization," *MIT Sloan Management Review*, Spring 2001; and information accessed online at www.Barbie.com, www.NikeID.com, and www.chemstation.com, July 2001.

Segmenting Consumer Markets

There is no single way to segment a market. A marketer has to try different segmentation variables, alone and in combination, to find the best way to view the market structure. Table 7-1 outlines the major variables that might be used in segmenting consumer markets. Here we look at the major *geographic, demographic, psychographic,* and *behavioral variables.*

Geographic segmentation
Dividing a market into different geographical units such as nations, states, regions, counties, cities, or neighborhoods.

Geographic Segmentation **Geographic segmentation** calls for dividing the market into different geographical units such as nations, regions, states, counties, cities, or neighborhoods. A company may decide to operate in one or a few geographical areas, or to operate in all areas but pay attention to geographical differences in needs and wants.

Many companies today are localizing their products, advertising, promotion, and sales efforts to fit the needs of individual regions, cities, and even neighborhoods. For example, Campbell sells Cajun gumbo soup in Louisiana and Mississippi and makes its nacho cheese soup spicier in Texas and California. Starbucks offers more desserts and larger, more comfortable coffee shops in the South, where customers tend to arrive later in

Geographic segmentation: Parker Brothers offers localized versions of its popular Monopoly game for several major cities. Here are two Red Sox baseball players enjoying the Boston Red Sox Collectors Edition.

Table 7-1   Major Segmentation Variables for Consumer Markets

Geographic	
World region or country	North America, Western Europe, Middle East, Pacific Rim, China, India, Canada, Mexico
Country region	Pacific, Mountain, West North Central, West South Central, East North Central, East South Central, South Atlantic, Middle Atlantic, New England
City or metro size	Under 5,000; 5,000–20,000, 20,000–50,000, 50,000–100,000; 100,000–250,000; 250,000–500,000; 500,000–1,000,000; 1,000,000–4,000,000; 4,000,000 or over
Density	Urban, suburban, rural
Climate	Northern, southern
Demographic	
Age	Under 6, 6–11, 12–19, 20–34, 35–49, 50–64, 65+
Gender	Male, female
Family size	1–2, 3–4, 5+
Family life-cycle	Young, single; young, married, no children; young, married with children; older, married with children; older, married, no children under 18; older, single; other
Income	Under $10,000; $10,000–$20,000; $20,000–$30,000; $30,000–$50,000; $50,000–$100,000; $100,000 and over
Occupation	Professional and technical; managers, officials, and proprietors; clerical; sales; craftspeople; supervisors; operatives; farmers; retired; students; homemakers; unemployed
Education	Grade school or less; some high school; high school graduate; some college; college graduate
Religion	Catholic, Protestant, Jewish, Muslim, Hindu, other
Race	Asian, Hispanic, black, white
Generation	Baby boomer, Generation X, Generation Y
Nationality	North American, South American, British, French, German, Italian, Japanese
Psychographic	
Social class	Lower lowers, upper lowers, working class, middle class, upper middles, lower uppers, upper uppers
Lifestyle	Achievers, strivers, strugglers
Personality	Compulsive, gregarious, authoritarian, ambitious
Behavioral	
Occasions	Regular occasion; special occasion
Benefits	Quality, service, economy, convenience, speed
User status	Nonuser, ex-user, potential user, first-time user, regular user
User rates	Light user, medium user, heavy user
Loyalty status	None, medium, strong, absolute
Readiness stage	Unaware, aware, informed, interested, desirous, intending to buy
Attitude toward product	Enthusiastic, positive, indifferent, negative, hostile

the day and stay longer. And Parker Brothers offers localized versions of its popular Monopoly game for several major cities, including Chicago, New York, San Francisco, St. Louis, and Las Vegas. The Las Vegas version features a black board with The Strip rather than Boardwalk, hotel casinos, red Vegas dice, and custom pewter tokens including black-jack cards, a wedding chapel, and a roulette wheel.[7]

Other companies are seeking to cultivate as-yet untapped geographic territory. For example, many large companies are fleeing the fiercely competitive major cities and suburbs to set up shop in small-town America. Hampton Inns has opened a chain of smaller-format motels in towns too small for its standard-size units. For example, Townsend, Tennessee, with a population of only 329, is small even by small town standards. But looks can be deceiving. Situated on a heavily traveled and picturesque route between Knoxville and the Smoky Mountains, the village serves both business and vacation travelers. Hampton Inns opened a unit in Townsend and plans to open 100 more in small towns. It costs less to operate in these towns, and the company builds smaller units to match lower volume. The Townsend Hampton Inn, for example, has 54 rooms instead of the usual 135. Retailers from Home Depot to Saks Fifth Avenue are following suit. For example, Home Depot is testing four pint-sized Villager's Hardware stores in New Jersey. Saks is implementing a new "Main Street" strategy, opening smaller stores in affluent suburbs and small towns that cannot support full-line Saks stores. Its new store in Greenwich, Connecticut, is less than one-third the size of regular stores found in malls and big cities.[8]

Demographic segmentation
Dividing the market into groups based on demographic variables such as age, sex, family size, family life-cycle, income, occupation, education, religion, race, and nationality.

Demographic Segmentation **Demographic segmentation** divides the market into groups based on variables such as age, gender, family size, family life-cycle, income, occupation, education, religion, race, generation, and nationality. Demographic factors are the most popular bases for segmenting customer groups. One reason is that consumer needs, wants, and usage rates often vary closely with demographic variables. Another is that demographic variables are easier to measure than most other types of variables. Even when market segments are first defined using other bases, such as benefits sought or behavior, their demographic characteristics must be known in order to assess the size of the target market and to reach it efficiently.

Age and life-cycle segmentation
Dividing a market into different age and life-cycle groups.

AGE AND LIFE-CYCLE STAGE. Consumer needs and wants change with age. Some companies use **age and life-cycle segmentation,** offering different products or using different marketing approaches for different age and life-cycle groups. For example, McDonald's targets different age groups—from children and teens to adults and seniors—with different ads and media. Its ads to teens feature dance-beat music, adventure, and fast-paced cutting from scene to scene; ads to seniors are softer and more sentimental. Procter & Gamble boldly targets its Oil of Olay ProVital Series subbrand at women over 50 years of age—it's "specially designed to meet the increased moisturization needs of more mature skin."[9] And Gap has branched out to target people at different life stages. In addition to its standard line of clothing, the retailer now offers Baby Gap, Gap Kids, and Gap Maternity.

Sega, the computer games giant, which has typically focused on the teen market, is now targeting older customers. According to a Sega licensing executive, Sega's core market of 10- to 18-year-olds "sit in their bedrooms playing games for hours." Then, however, "they turn 18 and discover girls . . . and the computer gets locked away." To retain these young customers as they move into new life-cycle stages, Sega is launching a range of products for adults under its Sega Sports brand, including clothing, shoes, watches, and sports equipment such as Sega Sports–branded footballs and basketballs.[10]

Marketers must be careful to guard against stereotypes when using age and life-cycle segmentation. For example, although some 70-year-olds require wheelchairs, others play tennis. Similarly, whereas some 40-year-old couples are sending their children off to college, others are just beginning new families. Thus, age is often a poor predictor of a person's life-cycle, health, work or family status, needs, and buying power. Companies marketing to mature consumers usually employ positive images and appeals. For example, ads for Olay ProVital feature attractive older spokeswomen and uplifting messages. "Many women 50 and older have told us that as they age, they feel more confident, wiser, and freer than ever before," observes Olay's marketing director. "These women are redefining beauty."[11]

GENDER. **Gender segmentation** has long been used in clothing, cosmetics, toiletries, and magazines. For example, Procter & Gamble was among the first with Secret, a brand specially formulated for a woman's chemistry, packaged and advertised to reinforce the female image. Recently, other marketers have noticed opportunities for gender segmentation. Merrill Lynch offers a *Financial Handbook for Women Investors* who want to "shape up their finances." Owens-Corning consciously aimed a major advertising campaign for home insulation at women after its study on women's roles in home improvement showed that two-thirds were involved in materials installation, with 13 percent doing it themselves. Half the women surveyed compared themselves to Bob Vila, whereas less than half compared themselves to Martha Stewart. Similarly, after its research showed that women make 90 percent of all home improvement decisions, home improvement retailer Lowe's recently launched a family-oriented advertising campaign that reaches out to women buyers.[12]

The automobile industry also uses gender segmentation extensively. Women buy half of all new cars sold in the United States and influence 80 percent of all new-car

Gender segmentation
Dividing a market into different groups based on sex.

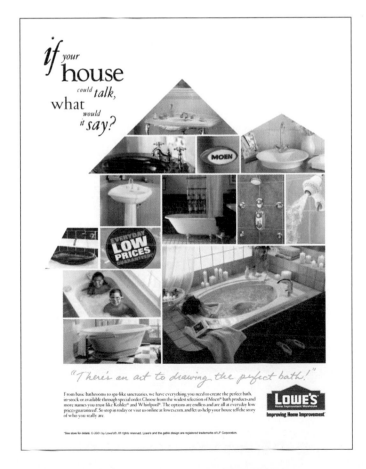

Gender segmentation: After research showed that women make 90 percent of all home improvement decisions, Lowe's recently launched a family oriented advertising campaign that reaches out to women buyers.

purchasing decisions. "Selling to women should be no different than selling to men," notes one analyst. "But there are subtleties that make a difference." Women have different frames, less upper-body strength, and greater safety concerns. To address these issues, automakers are designing cars with hoods and trunks that are easier to open, seat belts that fit women better, and an increased emphasis on safety features. Male car designers at Cadillac now go about their work with paper clips on their fingers to simulate what it feels like to operate buttons, knobs, and other interior features with longer fingernails. Under the hood, yellow markings highlight where fluid fills go.[13]

A growing number of Web sites also target women. For example, Oxygen Media's Girls On Web site (www.girlson.com) appeals to 18- to 34-year-old women with fresh and hip, twenty-somethings film, television, and book reviews and features. After only two years, this site has 100,000 members and averages 5 million page views per month. The leading women's online community, iVillage (www.iVillage.com), offers "real solutions for real women" and entreats visitors to "Join our community of smart, compassionate, real women." Various iVillage channels cover topics ranging from babies, food, fitness, pets, and relationships to careers, finance, and travel. The site now attracts 5.7 million unique visitors each month.[14]

Income segmentation
Dividing a market into different income groups.

INCOME. Income segmentation has long been used by the marketers of products and services such as automobiles, boats, clothing, cosmetics, financial services, and travel. Many companies target affluent consumers with luxury goods and convenience services. Stores such as Neiman Marcus pitch everything from expensive jewelry and fine fashions to glazed Australian apricots priced at $20 a pound. To cater to its best customers, Neiman Marcus created its InCircle Rewards program. InCircle members, who must spend $3,000 a year using their Neiman Marcus credit cards to be eligible, earn points with each purchase—one point for each dollar spent. They then cash in points for anything from a snakeskin-patterned Nokia phone cover (10,000 points) or a trip to Los Angeles for a movie premiere with *Instyle* (100,000 points) to a photo shoot with celebrity photographer Annie Leibovitz (1 million points). Car fanatics can trade points for one of six automobiles, from 500,000 points for a Volkswagen Blue Dog Beetle up to 5 million points for

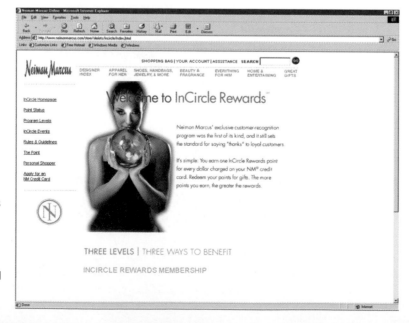

Income segmentation: To cater to its best customers, Neiman Marcus created its InCircle Rewards program. InCircle members have an average household income of $568,373 and an average net worth of almost $2.4 million.

a BMW Z8 convertible. InCircle members have an average household income of $568,373 and an average net worth of almost $2.4 million.[15]

However, not all companies that use income segmentation target the affluent. Despite their lower spending power, the nearly one-third of the nation's households that earn less that $25,000 per year offer an attractive market. For example, Greyhound Lines, with its inexpensive nationwide bus network, targets lower-income consumers. Almost half of its revenues come from people with annual incomes under $15,000. Many retailers also target this group, including chains such as Dollar General, Family Dollar, and Dollar Tree stores. When Family Dollar real estate experts scout locations for new stores, they look for lower-middle-class neighborhoods where people wear less expensive shoes and drive old cars that drip a lot of oil. The typical Family Dollar customer's household earns about $25,000 a year, and the average customer spends only about $8 per trip to the store. Similarly, half of Dollar General's customers earn less than $20,000 a year, and about half of its target shoppers do not work. Yet both stores' low-income strategy has put them among the most profitable discount chains in the country.[16]

Psychographic Segmentation **Psychographic segmentation** divides buyers into different groups based on social class, lifestyle, or personality characteristics. People in the same demographic group can have very different psychographic makeups.

In Chapter 6, we discussed how the products people buy reflect their *lifestyles*. As a result, marketers often segment their markets by consumer lifestyles. For example, Duck Head apparel targets a casual student lifestyle, claiming, "You can't get them old until you get them new." One forward-looking grocery store found that segmenting its self-service meat products by lifestyle had a big payoff:

> Walk by the refrigerated self-service meat cases of most grocery stores and you'll usually find the offering grouped by type of meat. Pork is in one case, lamb is in another, and chicken is in a third. However, a Nashville, Tennessee, Kroger super-market decided to experiment and offer groupings of different meats by lifestyle. For instance, the store had a section called "Meals in Minutes," one called "Cookin' Lite," another, filled with prepared products like hot dogs and ready-made ham-burger patties, called "Kids Love This Stuff," and one called "I Like to Cook." By focusing on lifestyle needs and not on protein categories, Kroger's test store encour-aged habitual beef and pork buyers to consider lamb and veal as well. As a result, the 16-foot service case has seen a substantial improvement in both sales and profits.[17]

Marketers also have used *personality* variables to segment markets. For example, the marketing campaign for Honda's Helix and Elite motor scooters *appears* to target hip and trendy 22-year-olds. But it is *actually* aimed at a much broader personality group. One ad, for example, shows a delighted child bouncing up and down on his bed while the announcer says, "You've been trying to get there all your life." The ad reminds viewers of the euphoric feelings they got when they broke away from authority and did things their parents told them not to do. It suggests that they can feel that way again by riding a Honda scooter. Thus, Honda is appealing to the rebellious kid in all of us. As Honda notes on its Web page, "Fresh air, freedom, and flair—on a Honda scooter, every day is independence day!" In fact, more than half of Honda's scooter sales are to young professionals and older buyers—15 percent are purchased by the over-50 group. Aging baby boomers, now thrill-seeking middle-agers, caused a 26 percent jump in scooter sales last year.[18]

Behavioral Segmentation **Behavioral segmentation** divides buyers into groups based on their knowledge, attitudes, uses, or responses to a product. Many marketers believe that behavior variables are the best starting point for building market segments.

Psychographic segmentation
Dividing a market into different groups based on social class, lifestyle, or personality characteristics.

Behavioral segmentation
Dividing a market into groups based on consumer knowledge, attitude, use, or response to a product.

Occasion segmentation
Dividing the market into groups according to occasions when buyers get the idea to buy, actually make their purchase, or use the purchased item.

OCCASIONS.   Buyers can be grouped according to occasions when they get the idea to buy, actually make their purchase, or use the purchased item. **Occasion segmentation** can help firms build up product usage. For example, orange juice is most often consumed at break-fast, but orange growers have promoted drinking orange juice as a cool and refreshing drink at other times of the day. In contrast, Coca-Cola's "Coke in the Morning" advertising campaign attempts to increase Coke consumption by promoting the beverage as an early morning pick-me-up. Some holidays, such as Mother's Day and Father's Day, were origi-nally promoted partly to increase the sale of candy, flowers, cards, and other gifts. And many food marketers prepare special offers and ads for holiday occasions. For example, Beatrice Foods runs special Thanksgiving and Christmas ads for Reddi-wip during Novem-ber and December, months that account for 30 percent of all whipped cream sales.

Kodak, Konica, Fuji, and other camera makers use occasion segmentation in design-ing and marketing their single-use cameras. By mixing lenses, film speeds, and accessories, they have developed special disposable cameras for about any picture-taking occasion, from underwater photography to taking baby pictures.

Standing on the edge of the Grand Canyon? Try Konica's Panoramic, which features a 17 mm lens that takes in nearly 100 degrees horizontally. Going rafting, skiing, or snorkeling? You need Kodak's Max Sport, a rugged camera that can be used underwater to 14 feet. It has big knobs and buttons that let you use it with gloves. Want some pictures of the baby? Kodak offers a model equipped with a short focal-length lens and fast film requiring less light for parents who would like to take snapshots of their darlings without the disturbing flash. Need to check out your golf swing? Just point and shoot the QuickSnap Golf disposable camera, which snaps off

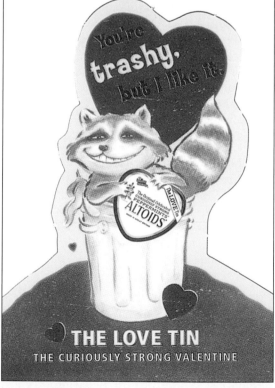

Occasion segmentation: Altoids created a special "Love Tin"—a "curiously strong valentine."

eight frames per click showing how your body and club do during the swing. In one Japanese catalog aimed at young women, Kodak sells a package of five pastel-colored cameras, including a version with a fish-eye lens to create a rosy, romantic glow. To make certain that the right cameras are available in the right places, Kodak is rolling out climate-controlled, Internet-connected vending machines in as many as 10,000 locations, including zoos, stadiums, parks, hotels, and resorts.[19]

BENEFITS SOUGHT. A powerful form of segmentation is to group buyers according to the different *benefits* that they seek from the product. **Benefit segmentation** requires finding the major benefits people look for in the product class, the kinds of people who look for each benefit, and the major brands that deliver each benefit. For example, one study of the benefits derived from travel uncovered three major market segments: those who travel to get away and be with family, those who travel for adventure or educational purposes, and people who enjoy the "gambling" and "fun" aspects of travel.[20] Airlines, hotels, and travel agents would market differently to each benefit group.

> **Benefit segmentation**
> Dividing the market into groups according to the different benefits that consumers seek from the product.

The Champion athletic wear division of Sara Lee Corporation segments its markets according to benefits that different consumers seek from their activewear. For example, "fit and polish" consumers seek a balance between function and style—they exercise for results but want to look good doing it. "Serious sports competitors" exercise heavily and live in and love their activewear—they seek performance and function. By contrast, "value seeking moms" have low sports interest and low activewear involvement—they buy for the family and seek durability and value. Thus, each segment seeks a different mix of benefits. Champion must target the benefit segment or segments that it can serve best and most profitably using appeals that match each segment's benefit preferences.

USER STATUS. Markets can be segmented into groups of nonusers, ex-users, potential users, first-time users, and regular users of a product. For example, one study found that blood donors are low in self-esteem, low risk takers, and more highly concerned about their health; nondonors tend to be the opposite on all three dimensions. This suggests that social agencies should use different marketing approaches for keeping current donors and attracting new ones. A company's market position also influences its focus. Market share leaders focus on attracting potential users, whereas smaller firms focus on attracting current users away from the market leader.

USAGE RATE. Markets can also be segmented into light, medium, and heavy product users. Heavy users are often a small percentage of the market but account for a high percentage of total consumption. Marketers usually prefer to attract one heavy user to their product or service rather than several light users. For example, a study of U.S.-branded ice cream buyers showed that heavy users make up only 18 percent of all buyers but consume 55 percent of all the ice cream sold. On average, these heavy users pack away 13 gallons of ice cream per year versus only 2.4 gallons for light users.

Similarly, in the fast-food industry, heavy users make up only 20 percent of patrons but eat up about 60 percent of all the food served. A single heavy user, typically a single male who doesn't know how to cook, might spend as much as $40 in a day at fast-food restaurants and visit them more than 20 times a month. Heavy users "come more often, they spend more money, and that's what makes the cash registers ring," says a Burger King marketing executive. Interestingly, although fast-food companies such as Burger King, McDonald's, and KFC depend a lot on heavy users and do all they can to keep them satisfied with every visit, these companies often target light users with their ads and promotions. The heavy users "are in our restaurants already," says the Burger King marketer. The company's marketing dollars are more often spent trying to convince light users that they want a burger in the first place.[21]

LOYALTY STATUS.   A market can also be segmented by consumer loyalty. Consumers can be loyal to brands (Tide), stores (Wal-Mart), and companies (Ford). Buyers can be divided into groups according to their degree of loyalty. Some consumers are completely loyal—they buy one brand all the time. Othsers are somewhat loyal—they are loyal to two or three brands of a given product or favor one brand while sometimes buying others. Still other buyers show no loyalty to any brand. They either want something different each time they buy or they buy whatever's on sale.

A company can learn a lot by analyzing loyalty patterns in its market. It should start by studying its own loyal customers. For example, to better understand the needs and behavior of its core soft drink consumers, Pepsi observed them in places where its products are consumed—in homes, in stores, in movie theaters, at sporting events, and at the beach. "We learned that there's a surprising amount of loyalty and passion for Pepsi's products," says Pepsi's director of consumer insights. "One fellow had four or five cases of Pepsi in his basement and he felt he was low on Pepsi and had to go replenish." The company used these and other study findings to pinpoint the Pepsi target market and develop marketing appeals.[22]

By studying its less loyal buyers, the company can detect which brands are most competitive with its own. If many Pepsi buyers also buy Coke, Pepsi can attempt to improve its positioning against Coke, possibly by using direct-comparison advertising. By looking at customers who are shifting away from its brand, the company can learn about its marketing weaknesses. As for nonloyals, the company may attract them by putting its brand on sale.

Using Multiple Segmentation Bases   Marketers rarely limit their segmentation analysis to only one or a few variables. Rather, they are increasingly using multiple segmentation bases in an effort to identify smaller, better-defined target groups. Thus, a bank may not only identify a group of wealthy retired adults but also, within that group, distinguish several segments depending on their current income, assets, savings and risk preferences, and lifestyles. Companies often begin by segmenting their markets using a single base, then expand using other bases.

One good example of multivariable segmentation is "geodemographic" segmentation. Several business information services have arisen to help marketing planners link U.S. Census data with lifestyle patterns to better segment their markets down to Zip codes, neighborhoods, and even city blocks. One of the leading lifestyle segmentation systems is PRIZM by Claritas, Inc. (see Marketing at Work 7-2).

Segmenting Business Markets

Consumer and business marketers use many of the same variables to segment their markets. Business buyers can be segmented geographically, demographically (industry, company size), or by benefits sought, user status, usage rate, and loyalty status. Yet, business marketers also use some additional variables, such as customer *operating characteristics, purchasing approaches, situational factors,* and *personal characteristics.*

By going after segments instead of the whole market, companies have a much better chance to deliver value to consumers and to receive maximum rewards for close attention to consumer needs. Thus, Hewlett-Packard's Computer Systems Division targets specific industries that promise the best growth prospects, such as telecommunications and financial services. Its "red team" sales force specializes in developing and serving major customers in these targeted industries.[23] Within the chosen industry, a company can further segment by *customer size* or *geographic location.* For example, Hewlett-Packard's "blue team" telemarkets to smaller accounts and to those that don't fit neatly into the strategically targeted industries on which HP focuses.

A company might also set up separate systems for dealing with larger or multiple-location customers. For example, Steelcase, a major producer of office furniture, first

Marketing at Work 7.2

Blue Blood Estates to Shotguns & Pickups: Segmenting America's Neighborhoods

Using a host of demographic and socioeconomic factors drawn from the U.S. Census data, Claritas, Inc.'s PRIZM system has classified every one of the more than 260,000 U.S. neighborhoods into one of 62 clusters.

You're 35 years old. The price tag on your suits shows that you're a success. You drive a Volvo. You know your way around the olive oil section of the store, buy fresh-ground coffee, and go on scuba-diving trips. You're living out your own, individual version of the good life in the suburbs. You're unique—not some demographic cliche. Right? Wrong. You're a prime example of [PRIZM's] "Kids & Cul-de-Sacs." . . . If you consume, you can't hide from Zip code seer Claritas.

The "Kids & Cul-de-Sacs" cluster points to a new migration to the suburbs. Other PRIZM clusters include "Blue Blood Estates," "Money & Brains," "Young Literati," "Shotguns & Pickups," "American Dreams," "New Eco-topias," "Mobility Blues," and "Gray Power." The clusters were formed by manipulating characteristics such as education, income, occupation, family life-cycle, housing, ethnicity, and urbanization. For example, "Blue Blood Estates" neighborhoods are suburban areas populated mostly by active, college-educated, successful managers and professionals. They include some of America's wealthiest neighborhoods, areas characterized by low household density, highly homogenous residents, a heavy family orientation, and mostly single-unit housing. In contrast, the "Shotguns & Pickups" cluster includes the blue-collar neighborhoods found in the Northeast, Southeast, Great Lakes,

and Piedmont industrial regions of America. "American Dreams" reflects new waves of American immigrants, "Young Literati" taps Generation X, and "New Ecotopia" focuses on the country's aging hippies. Each of the other clusters has a unique combination of characteristics.

Companies can combine these geodemographic PRIZM clusters with other data on product and service usage, media usage, and lifestyles to get a better picture of specific market areas. For example, the "Shotguns & Pickups" cluster is populated by lower-middle-class, blue-collar consumers who use chain saws and snuff and buy more canning jars, dried soups, and powdered soft drinks, The "Hispanic Mix" cluster prefers high-quality dresses, nonfilter cigarettes, and lip gloss. People in this cluster are

highly brand conscious, quality conscious, and brand loyal. They have a strong family and home orientation.

Such geodemographic segmentation provides a powerful tool for segmenting markets, refining demand estimates, selecting target markets, and shaping promotion messages. For example, in marketing its Suave shampoo, Unilever's Helene Curtis division uses PRIZM to identify neighborhoods with high concentrations of working women. Such women respond best to advertising messages that Suave is inexpensive yet will make their hair "look like a million." Bookseller Barnes & Noble locates its stores where there are concentrations of "Money & Brains" consumers because they buy lots of books.

Ohio's Lakewood Public Library used PRIZM to address a low

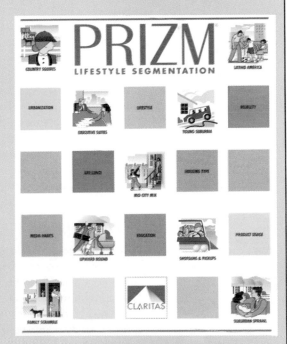

Using a host of demographic and socioeconomic factors drawn from the U.S. Census data, the PRIZM system has classified every one of the more than 260,000 U.S. neighborhood markets in one of 62 clusters.

patronage problem. The PRIZM analysis revealed that one of Lakewood's biggest subsets of residents was hardly using the library.

"Many people had a perception of Lakewood as being a city of families and senior citizens," said John Guscott, Lakewood Public Library's manager of electronic services. "Our experiences at the library over the past few years suggested otherwise—that it was fast becoming a city dominated by young, professional singles." PRIZM proved Guscott right. The largest single PRIZM cluster was Urban Achievers, which comprised nearly 26 percent of area residents. These Urban Achievers were characterized as "behaving like middle-class sophisticates" and gravitating toward "specialty shops, ethnic markets, family restaurants, delis, sushi bars, taco joints, Nordstrom, jazz music, Kias, Volkswagens, and Nissans." Their interests also included "multiculturalism, intellectually challenging pursuits, theater, adult education, libraries, public broadcasting, and alterna-

tive health." The Lakewood Public Library offered very little of interest to this Gen Xer group. Based on the analysis, the library revamped its collections to cater to its newly discovered target consumers. Today, Lakewood has no problem attracting patrons. The Gen Xer crowd flocks to the library to sample the rich array of programs and the diverse book and CD collections designed just for them. "Our circulation for audio CDs has just flown off the charts," says Guscott.

One large packaged-goods company used a similar system, Claritas' ClusterPLUS, in combination with Nielsen television ratings and data from Simmons Market Research Bureau to more effectively market an ingredient used in baking cakes and cookies. The company first identified the clusters most likely to contain consumers who regularly bake from scratch. According to Simmons data, the top-ranking cluster is "Low-Mobility Rural Families"; 39 percent of this group bake heavily from scratch, far greater than the 17 percent national average.

Merging the 10 highest-ranking clusters, the company identified the best prospects as older, rural, and blue-collar consumers in the South and Midwest.

Next, using Nielsen ratings, the company examined the television viewing habits of the ten best clusters. It turns out that the from-scratch bakers watch many highly rated programs, but some generally less popular programs are also popular with this group. The packaged-goods company improved its efficiency by running ads only on programs reaching large concentrations of from-scratch bakers, regardless of the size of the total audience. Thus, the ClusterPLUS–Simmons-Nielsen connection resulted in a basic shift in the company's television advertising, from a mass-media, "shotgun" approach to a more highly targeted one.

Sources: Extracts from Christina Del Valle, "They Know Where You Live—And How You Buy," *Business Week*, February 7, 1994, p. 89; and Evan St. Lifer, "Tapping into the Zen of Marketing," *Library Journal*, May 1, 2001, pp. 44–46. Also see Philip Kotler, *Kotler on Marketing* (Upper Saddle River, NJ: Prentice Hall, 1999), pp. 78–79; Michael J. Weiss, *The Clustered World* (New York: Little, Brown, 2000); and www.claritas.com, December, 2001.

segments customers into ten industries, including banking, insurance, and electronics. Next, company salespeople work with independent Steelcase dealers to handle smaller, local, or regional Steelcase customers in each segment. But many national, multiple-location customers, such as ExxonMobile or IBM, have special needs that may reach beyond the scope of individual dealers. So Steelcase uses national accounts managers to help its dealer networks handle its national accounts.

Within a given target industry and customer size, the company can segment by purchase approaches and criteria. As in consumer segmentation, many marketers believe that *buying behavior* and *benefits* provide the best basis for segmenting business markets.[24]

Segmenting International Markets

Few companies have either the resources or the will to operate in all, or even most, of the countries that dot the globe. Although some large companies, such as Coca-Cola or Sony, sell products in more than 200 countries, most international firms focus on a smaller set. Operating in many countries presents new challenges. Different countries, even those that are close together, can vary greatly in their economic, cultural, and political makeup. Thus, just as they do within their domestic markets, international firms need to group their world markets into segments with distinct buying needs and behaviors.

Intermarket segmentation: MTV targets teens around the world by appealing to what they have in common.

Companies can segment international markets using one or a combination of several variables. They can segment by *geographic location*, grouping countries by regions such as Western Europe, the Pacific Rim, the Middle East, or Africa. Geographic segmentation assumes that nations close to one another will have many common traits and behaviors. Although this is often the case, there are many exceptions. For example, although the United States and Canada have much in common, both differ culturally and economically from neighboring Mexico. Even within a region, consumers can differ widely. For example, many U.S. marketers think that all Central and South American countries are the same, including their 400 million inhabitants. However, the Dominican Republic is no more like Brazil than Italy is like Sweden. Many Latin Americans don't speak Spanish, including 140 million Portuguese-speaking Brazilians and the millions in other countries who speak a variety of Indian dialects.

World markets can also be segmented on the basis of *economic factors*. For example, countries might be grouped by population income levels or by their overall level of economic development. Some countries, such as the United States, Britain, France, Germany, Japan, Canada, Italy, and Russia, have established, highly industrialized economies. Other countries have newly industrialized or developing economies (Singapore, Taiwan, Korea, Brazil, Mexico). Still others are less developed (China, India). A company's economic structure shapes its population's product and service needs and, therefore, the marketing opportunities it offers.

Countries can be segmented by *political and legal factors* such as the type and stability of government, receptivity to foreign firms, monetary regulations, and the amount of bureaucracy. Such factors can play a crucial role in a company's choice of which countries to enter and how. *Cultural factors* can also be used, grouping markets according to common languages, religions, values and attitudes, customs, and behavioral patterns.

Segmenting international markets on the basis of geographic, economic, political, cultural, and other factors assumes that segments should consist of clusters of countries. However, many companies use a different approach called **intermarket segmentation.** Using this approach, they form segments of consumers who have similar needs and buying behavior even though they are located in different countries. For example, Mercedes-Benz targets the world's well-to-do, regardless of their country. MTV targets the world's

Intermarket segmentation
Forming segments of consumers who have similar needs and buying behavior even though they are located in different countries.

teenagers. One study of more than 6,500 teenagers from 26 countries showed that teens around the world live surprisingly parallel lives. As one expert notes, "From Rio to Rochester, teens can be found enmeshed in much the same regimen: . . . drinking Coke, . . . dining on Big Macs, and surfin' the Net on their computers."[25] The world's teens have a lot in common: They study, shop, and sleep. They are exposed to many of the same major issues: love, crime, homelessness, ecology, and working parents. In many ways, they have more in common with each other than with their parents. MTV bridges the gap between cultures, appealing to what teens around the world have in common.[26]

Requirements for Effective Segmentation

Clearly, there are many ways to segment a market, but not all segmentations are effective. For example, buyers of table salt could be divided into blond and brunette customers. But hair color obviously does not affect the purchase of salt. Furthermore, if all salt buyers bought the same amount of salt each month, believed that all salt is the same, and wanted to pay the same price, the company would not benefit from segmenting this market.

To be useful, market segments must be:

◆ *Measurable:* The size, purchasing power, and profiles of the segments can be measured. Certain segmentation variables are difficult to measure. For example, there are 32.5 million left-handed people in the United States—almost equaling the entire population of Canada. Yet few products are targeted toward this left-handed segment. The major problem may be that the segment is hard to identify and measure. There are no data on the demographics of lefties, and the U.S. Census Bureau does not keep track of left-handedness in its surveys. Private data companies keep reams of statistics on other demographic segments but not on left-handers.

◆ *Accessible:* The market segments can be effectively reached and served. Suppose a fragrance company finds that heavy users of its brand are single men and women who stay out late and socialize a lot. Unless this group lives or shops at certain places and is exposed to certain media, its members will be difficult to reach.

◆ *Substantial:* The market segments are large or profitable enough to serve. A segment should be the largest possible homogenous group worth pursuing with a tailored marketing program. It would not pay, for example, for an automobile manufacturer to develop cars especially for people whose height is less than four feet.

◆ *Differentiable:* The segments are conceptually distinguishable and respond differently to different marketing mix elements and programs. If married and unmarried women respond similarly to a sale on perfume, they do not constitute separate segments.

◆ *Actionable:* Effective programs can be designed for attracting and serving the segments. For example, although one small airline identified seven market segments, its staff was too small to develop separate marketing programs for each segment.

Linking the Concepts

Slow down a bit and smell the roses. How do the companies you do business with employ the segmentation concepts you're reading about here?

◆ Take another look at Figure 7-2. Can you identify specific companies, other than the examples already discussed, that practice each level of segmentation?
◆ Using the segmentation bases you've just read about, segment the U.S. footwear market. Describe each of the major segments and subsegments. Keep these segments in mind as you read the next section on market targeting.

Market Targeting

Market segmentation reveals the firm's market segment opportunities. The firm now has to evaluate the various segments and decide how many and which ones to target. We now look at how companies evaluate and select target segments.

Evaluating Market Segments

In evaluating different market segments, a firm must look at three factors: segment size and growth, segment structural attractiveness, and company objectives and resources. The company must first collect and analyze data on current segment sales, growth rates, and expected profitability for various segments. It will be interested in segments that have the right size and growth characteristics. But "right size and growth" is a relative matter. The largest, fastest-growing segments are not always the most attractive ones for every company. Smaller companies may lack the skills and resources needed to serve the larger segments or may find these segments too competitive. Such companies may select segments that are smaller and less attractive, in an absolute sense, but that are potentially more profitable for them.

The company also needs to examine major structural factors that affect long-run segment attractiveness.[27] For example, a segment is less attractive if it already contains many strong and aggressive *competitors*. The existence of many actual or potential *substitute products* may limit prices and the profits that can be earned in a segment. The relative *power of buyers* also affects segment attractiveness. Buyers with strong bargaining power relative to sellers will try to force prices down, demand more services, and set competitors against one another—all at the expense of seller profitability. Finally, a segment may be less attractive if it contains *powerful suppliers* who can control prices or reduce the quality or quantity of ordered goods and services.

Even if a segment has the right size and growth and is structurally attractive, the company must consider its own objectives and resources in relation to that segment. Some attractive segments could be dismissed quickly because they do not mesh with the company's long-run objectives. Even if a segment fits the company's objectives, the company must consider whether it possesses the skills and resources it needs to succeed in that segment. If the company lacks the strengths needed to compete successfully in a segment and cannot readily obtain them, it should not enter the segment. Even if the company possesses the *required* strengths, it needs to employ skills and resources *superior* to those of the competition in order to really win in a market segment. The company should enter only segments in which it can offer superior value and gain advantages over competitors.

Selecting Market Segments

After evaluating different segments, the company must now decide which and how many segments to serve. This is the problem of *target market selection*. A **target market** consists of a set of buyers who share common needs or characteristics that the company decides to serve. Figure 7-3 shows that the firm can adopt one of three market-coverage strategies: *undifferentiated marketing, differentiated marketing,* and *concentrated marketing.*

Undifferentiated Marketing   Using an **undifferentiated marketing** (or mass-marketing) strategy, a firm might decide to ignore market segment differences and go after the whole market with one offer. This mass-marketing strategy focuses on what is *common* in the needs of consumers rather than on what is *different*. The company designs a product and a marketing program that will appeal to the largest number of buyers. It relies on mass

Target market
A set of buyers sharing common needs or characteristics that the company decides to serve.

Undifferentiated marketing
A market-coverage strategy in which a firm decides to ignore market segment differences and go after the whole market with one offer.

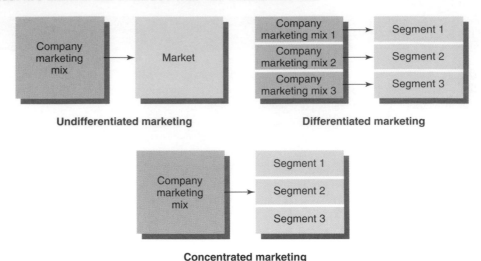

Figure 7-3
Three alternative
market-coverage
strategies

distribution and mass advertising, and it aims to give the product a superior image in people's minds. As noted earlier in the chapter, most modern marketers have strong doubts about this strategy. Difficulties arise in developing a product or brand that will satisfy all consumers. Moreover, mass marketers often have trouble competing with more focused firms that do a better job of satisfying the needs of specific segments and niches.

Differentiated marketing
A market-coverage strategy in which a firm decides to target several market segments and designs separate offers for each.

Differentiated Marketings Using a **differentiated marketing** strategy, a firm decides to target several market segments or niches and designs separate offers for each. General Motors tries to produce a car for every "purse, purpose, and personality." Nike offers athletic shoes for a dozen or more different sports, from running, fencing, and aerobics to bicycling and baseball. Estée Lauder offers dozens of different products aimed at carefully defined niches:

> The four best-selling prestige perfumes in the United States belong to Estée Lauder. So do seven of the top ten prestige makeup products and eight of the ten best-selling prestige skin care products. Estée Lauder is an expert in creating differentiated brands that serve the tastes of different market segments. There's the original Estée Lauder brand, which appeals to older, junior league types. Then there's Clinique, perfect for the middle-aged mom with a GMC Suburban and no time to waste. For the youthful hipster, there's the hip M.A.C. line. And, for the New Age type, there's upscale Aveda, with its aromatherapy line, and earthy Origins, which the company expects will become a $1 billion brand. The company even offers downscale brands, such as Jane by Sassaby, for teens at Wal-Mart and Rite Aid.[28]

By offering product and marketing variations, these companies hope for higher sales and a stronger position within each market segment. Developing a stronger position within several segments creates more total sales than undifferentiated marketing across all segments. Procter & Gamble gets more total market share with eight brands of laundry detergent than it could with only one.

But differentiated marketing also increases the costs of doing business. A firm usually finds it more expensive to develop and produce, say, 10 units of 10 different products than 100 units of one product. Developing separate marketing plans for the separate segments requires extra marketing research, forecasting, sales analysis, promotion planning, and channel management. And trying to reach different market segments with different

Concentrated marketing: Oshkosh Truck has found its niche as the world's largest producer of airport rescue trucks and front-loading concrete mixers.

advertising increases promotion costs. Thus, the company must weigh increased sales against increased costs when deciding on a differentiated marketing strategy.

Concentrated Marketing A third market-coverage strategy, **concentrated marketing,** is especially appealing when company resources are limited. Instead of going after a small share of a large market, the firm goes after a large share of one or a few segments or niches. For example, Oshkosh Truck is the world's largest producer of airport rescue trucks and front-loading concrete mixers. Tetra sells 80 percent of the world's tropical fish food, and Steiner Optical captures 80 percent of the world's military binoculars market.

> **Concentrated marketing**
> A market-coverage strategy in which a firm goes after a large share of one or a few sub-markets.

Today, the low cost of setting up shop on the Internet makes it even more profitable to serve seemingly minuscule niches. Small businesses, in particular, are realizing riches from serving small niches on the Web. Here is a "Webpreneur" who achieved astonishing results:[29]

> Whereas Internet giants like Amazon.com have yet to even realize a profit, Steve Warrington is earning a six-figure income online selling ostriches—and every product derived from them—online (www.ostrichesonline.com). Launched for next to nothing on the Web in 1996, *Ostrichesonline.com.* now boasts that it sends newsletters to 27,000 subscribers and sells 17,500 ostrich products to more than 8,000 satisfied clients worldwide. The site tells visitors everything they ever wanted to know about ostriches and much, much more—it supplies ostrich facts, ostrich pictures, an ostrich farm index, and a huge ostrich database and reference index. Visitors to the site can buy ostrich meat, feathers, leather jackets, videos, eggshells, and skin care products derived from ostrich body oil.

Concentrated marketing provides an excellent way for small new businesses to get a foothold against larger, more resourceful competitors. For example, Southwest Airlines began by concentrating on serving intrastate, no-frills commuters. Wal-Mart got its start by bringing everyday low prices to small towns and rural areas.

Through concentrated marketing, the firm achieves a strong market position because of its greater knowledge of consumer needs in the segments or niches it serves and the special reputation it acquires. It also enjoys many operating economies because of specialization in production, distribution, and promotion. If the segment is well chosen, the firm can earn a high rate of return on its investment.

At the same time, concentrated marketing involves higher-than-normal risks. The particular market segment can turn sour. Or larger competitors may decide to enter the same segment. For example, California Cooler's success in the wine cooler segment attracted many large competitors, causing the original owners to sell to a larger company that had more marketing resources. For these reasons, many companies prefer to diversify in several market segments.

Choosing a Market-Coverage Strategy Companies need to consider many factors when choosing a market-coverage strategy. Which strategy is best depends on *company resources.* When the firm's resources are limited, concentrated marketing makes the most sense. The best strategy also depends on the degree of *product variability.* Undifferentiated marketing is more suited for uniform products such as grapefruit or steel. Products that can vary in design, such as cameras and automobiles, are more suited to differentiation or concentration. The *product's life-cycle stage* also must be considered.

When a firm introduces a new product, it may be practical to launch only one version, and undifferentiated marketing or concentrated marketing may make the most sense. In the mature stage of the product life-cycle, however, differentiated marketing begins to make more sense. Another factor is *market variability.* If most buyers have the same tastes, buy the same amounts, and react the same way to marketing efforts, undifferentiated marketing is appropriate. Finally, *competitors' marketing strategies* are important. When competitors use differentiated or concentrated marketing, undifferentiated marketing can be suicidal. Conversely, when competitors use undifferentiated marketing, a firm can gain an advantage by using differentiated or concentrated marketing.

Socially Responsible Target Marketing

Smart targeting helps companies to be more efficient and effective by focusing on the segments that they can satisfy best and most profitably. Targeting also benefits consumers—companies reach specific groups of consumers with offers carefully tailored to satisfy their needs. However, target marketing sometimes generates controversy and concern. Issues usually involve the targeting of vulnerable or disadvantaged consumers with controversial or potentially harmful products.

For example, over the years, the cereal industry has been heavily criticized for its marketing efforts directed toward children. Critics worry that premium offers and high-powered advertising appeals presented through the mouths of lovable animated characters will overwhelm children's defenses. The marketers of toys and other children's products have been similarly battered, often with good justification.

Other problems arise when the marketing of adult products spills over into the kid segment—intentionally or unintentionally. For example, the Federal Trade Commission and citizen action groups have accused tobacco companies of targeting underage smokers. And a recent FTC study found that 80 percent of R-rated movies and 70 percent of video games with a mature rating were targeted to children under 17.[30] Some critics have even called for a complete ban on advertising to children. To encourage responsible advertising to children, the Children's Advertising Review Unit, the advertising industry's self-regulatory agency, has published extensive children's advertising guidelines that recognize the special needs of child audiences.

Cigarette, beer, and fast-food marketers have also generated much controversy in recent years by their attempts to target inner-city minority consumers. For example, McDonald's and other chains have drawn criticism for pitching their high-fat, salt-laden fare to low-income, inner-city residents who are much more likely than are suburbanites to be heavy consumers. R.J. Reynolds took heavy flak in the early 1990s when it announced plans to market Uptown, a menthol cigarette targeted toward low-income blacks. It quickly dropped the brand in the face of a loud public outcry and heavy pressure from black leaders. G. Heileman Brewing made a similar mistake with PowerMaster, a potent malt liquor. Because malt liquor had become the drink of choice among many in the inner city, Heileman focused its

Socially responsible targeting: Golden Ribbon Playthings developed a highly acclaimed "Huggy Bean" doll. Huggy comes with books and toys that connect her with her African heritage.

marketing efforts for PowerMaster on inner-city consumers. However, this group suffers disproportionately from liver diseases brought on by alcohol, and the inner city is already plagued by alcohol-related problems such as crime and violence. Thus, Heileman's targeting decision drew substantial criticism.[31]

The meteoric growth of the Internet and other carefully targeted direct media has raised fresh concerns about potential targeting abuses. The Internet allows increasing refinement of audiences and, in turn, more precise targeting. This might help makers of questionable products or deceptive advertisers to more readily victimize the most vulnerable audiences. As one expert observes, "In theory, an audience member could have tailor-made deceptive messages sent directly to his or her computer screen."[32]

Not all attempts to target children, minorities, or other special segments draw such criticism. In fact, most provide benefits to targeted consumers. For example, Colgate-Palmolive's Colgate Junior toothpaste has special features designed to get children to brush longer and more often—it's less foamy, has a milder taste, contains sparkles, and exits the tube in a star-shaped column.

Golden Ribbon Playthings developed a highly acclaimed and very successful black character doll named "Huggy Bean" targeted toward minority consumers. Huggy comes with books and toys that connect her with her African heritage. Many cosmetics companies have responded to the special needs of minority segments by adding products specifically designed for African American, Hispanic, or Asian women. Black-owned ICE theaters noticed that although moviegoing by blacks has surged, there are few inner-city theaters. The chain has opened a theater in Chicago's South Side as well as two other Chicago theaters, and it plans to open in four more cities this year. ICE partners with the black communities in which it operates theaters, using local radio stations to promote films and featuring favorite food items at concession stands.

Thus, in market targeting, the issue is not really *who* is targeted but rather *how* and for *what*. Controversies arise when marketers attempt to profit at the expense of targeted segments—when they unfairly target vulnerable segments or target them with questionable products or tactics. Socially responsible marketing calls for segmentation and targeting that serve not only the interests of the company but also the interests of those targeted.

Linking the Concepts

Time to coast for a bit and take stock.

◆ At the last speed bump, you segmented the U.S. footwear market. Now, pick two companies that serve this market and describe their segmentation and targeting strategies. Can you come up with one that targets many different segments versus another that focuses on only one or a few segments?

◆ How does each company you chose differentiate its marketing offer and image? Has each done a good job of establishing this differentiation in the minds of targeted consumers? The final section in this chapter deals with such positioning issues.

Positioning for Competitive Advantage

Product position
The way the product is defined by consumers on important attributes—the place the product occupies in consumers' minds relative to competing products.

Beyond deciding which segments of the market it will enter, the company must decide what positions it wants to occupy in those segments. A **product's position** is the way the product is *defined by consumers* on important attributes—the place the product occupies in consumers' minds relative to competing products. Positioning involves implanting the brand's unique benefits and differentiation in customers' minds. Tide is positioned as a powerful, all-purpose family detergent; Ivory Snow is positioned as the gentle detergent for fine washables and baby clothes. In the automobile market, Toyota Tercel and Subaru are positioned on economy, Mercedes and Cadillac on luxury, and Porsche and BMW on performance. Volvo positions powerfully on safety.

Consumers are overloaded with information about products and services. They cannot reevaluate products every time they make a buying decision. To simplify the buying process, consumers organize products into categories—they "position" products, services, and companies in their minds. A product's position is the complex set of perceptions, impressions, and feelings that consumers have for the product compared with competing products.

Consumers position products with or without the help of marketers. But marketers do not want to leave their products' positions to chance. They must *plan* positions that will give their products the greatest advantage in selected target markets, and they must design marketing mixes to create these planned positions.

Choosing a Positioning Strategy

Some firms find it easy to choose their positioning strategy. For example, a firm well known for quality in certain segments will go for this position in a new segment if there are enough buyers seeking quality. But in many cases, two or more firms will go after the same position. Then, each will have to find other ways to set itself apart. Each firm must differentiate its offer by building a unique bundle of benefits that appeals to a substantial group within the segment.

The positioning task consists of three steps: identifying a set of possible competitive advantages upon which to build a position, choosing the right competitive advantages, and selecting an overall positioning strategy. The company must then effectively communicate and deliver the chosen position to the market.

Identifying Possible Competitive Advantages

The key to winning and keeping customers is to understand their needs and buying processes better than competitors do and to deliver more value. To the extent that a

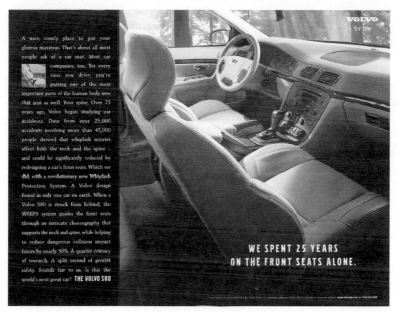

WE SPENT 25 YEARS
ON THE FRONT SEATS ALONE.

Competitive advantages: Volvo positions powerfully on safety: All most people want from a car seat is "a nice, comfy place to put your "gluteus maximus." However, when a Volvo is struck from behind, a sophisticated system "guides the front seats through an intricate choreography that supports the neck and spine while helping to reduce dangerous collision impact forces."

company can position itself as providing superior value to selected target markets, it gains **competitive advantage.** But solid positions cannot be built on empty promises. If a company positions its product as *offering* the best quality and service, it must then *deliver* the promised quality and service. Thus, positioning begins with actually *differentiating* the company's marketing offer so that it will give consumers more value than competitors' offers do.

To find points of differentiation, marketers must think through the customer's entire experience with the company's product or service. An alert company can find ways to differentiate itself at every point where it comes in contact with customers.[33] In what specific ways can a company differentiate its offer from those of competitors? A company or market offer can be differentiated along the lines of *product, services, channels, people,* or *image.*

Product differentiation takes place along a continuum. At one extreme we find physical products that allow little variation: chicken, steel, aspirin. Yet even here some meaningful differentiation is possible. For example, Perdue claims that its branded chickens are better — fresher and more tender — and gets a 10 percent price premium based on this differentiation. At the other extreme are products that can be highly differentiated, such as automobiles, commercial machinery, and furniture. Such products can be differentiated on features, performance, or style and design. Thus, Volvo provides new and better safety features; Whirlpool designs its dishwasher to run more quietly; Bose positions its speakers on their striking design characteristics. Similarly, companies can differentiate their products on such attributes as *consistency, durability, reliability,* or *repairability.*

Beyond differentiating its physical product, a firm can also differentiate the services that accompany the product. Some companies gain *services differentiation* through speedy, convenient, or careful *delivery.* For example, BankOne has opened full-service branches in supermarkets to provide location convenience along with Saturday, Sunday, and weekday-evening hours. *Installation* can also differentiate one company from another, as can *repair* services. Many an automobile buyer will gladly pay a little more and travel a little farther to buy a car from a dealer that provides top-notch repair service. Some companies differentiate their offers by providing *customer training service* or *consulting services* — data, information systems, and advising services that buyers need. McKesson Corporation,

Competitive advantage
An advantage over competitors gained by offering consumers greater value, either through lower prices or by providing more benefits that justify higher prices.

a major drug wholesaler, consults with its 12,000 independent pharmacists to help them set up accounting, inventory, and computerized ordering systems. By helping its customers compete better, McKesson gains greater customer loyalty and sales.

Firms that practice *channel differentiation* gain competitive advantage through the way they design their channel's coverage, expertise, and performance. Caterpillar's success in the construction-equipment industry is based on superior channels. Its dealers worldwide are renowned for their first-rate service. Dell Computer and Avon distinguish themselves by their high-quality direct channels. And Iams pet food achieved success by going against tradition, distributing its products only through veterinarians and pet stores.

Companies can gain a strong competitive advantage through *people differentiation*—hiring and training better people than their competitors do. Thus, Disney people are known to be friendly and upbeat. Singapore Airlines enjoys an excellent reputation largely because of the grace of its flight attendants. IBM offers people who make sure that the solution customers want is the solution they get: "People Who Think. People Who Do. People Who Get It." People differentiation requires that a company select its customer-contact people carefully and train them well. For example, Disney trains its theme park people thoroughly to ensure that they are competent, courteous, and friendly. From the hotel check-in agents, to the monorail drivers, to the ride attendants, to the people who sweep Main Street USA, each employee understands the importance of understanding customers, communicating with them clearly and cheerfully, and responding quickly to their requests and problems. Each is carefully trained to "make a dream come true."

Even when competing offers look the same, buyers may perceive a difference based on company or brand *image differentiation*. A company or brand image should convey the product's distinctive benefits and positioning. Developing a strong and distinctive image calls for creativity and hard work. A company cannot plant an image in the public's mind overnight using only a few advertisements. If Ritz-Carlton means quality, this image must be supported by everything the company says and does. *Symbols*—such as the McDonald's golden arches, the Prudential rock, the Nike swoosh, the Intel Inside logo, or the Pillsbury doughboy—can provide strong company or brand recognition and image differentiation. The company might build a brand around a famous person, as Nike did with its Air Jordan basketball shoes. Some companies even become associated with colors, such as IBM (blue), Campbell (red and white), or Kodak (red and yellow). The chosen symbols, characters, and other image elements must be communicated through advertising that conveys the company's or brand's personality.

Choosing the Right Competitive Advantages Suppose a company is fortunate enough to discover several potential competitive advantages. It now must choose the ones on which it will build its positioning strategy. It must decide *how many* differences to promote and *which ones.*

HOW MANY DIFFERENCES TO PROMOTE? Many marketers think that companies should aggressively promote only one benefit to the target market. Ad man Rosser Reeves, for example, said a company should develop a *unique selling proposition* (*USP*) for each brand and stick to it. Each brand should pick an attribute and tout itself as "number one" on that attribute. Buyers tend to remember number one better, especially in an overcommunicated society. Thus, Crest toothpaste consistently promotes its anticavity protection and Volvo promotes safety. A company that hammers away at one of these positions and consistently delivers on it probably will become best known and remembered for it.

Other marketers think that companies should position themselves on more than one differentiating factor. This may be necessary if two or more firms are claiming to be best on the same attribute. Today, in a time when the mass market is fragmenting into many small segments, companies are trying to broaden their positioning strategies to appeal to more segments. For example, Unilever introduced the first 3-in-1 bar soap—Lever 2000—offering cleansing, deodorizing, *and* moisturizing benefits. Clearly, many buyers want all three benefits, and the challenge was to convince them that one brand can deliver all three. Judging from Lever 2000's outstanding success, Unilever easily met the challenge. However, as companies increase the number of claims for their brands, they risk disbelief and a loss of clear positioning.

In general, a company needs to avoid three major positioning errors. The first is *underpositioning*—failing ever to really position the company at all. Some companies discover that buyers have only a vague idea of the company or that they do not really know anything special about it. The second error is *overpositioning*—giving buyers too narrow a picture of the company. Thus, a consumer might think that the Steuben glass company makes only fine art glass costing $1,000 and up, when in fact it makes affordable fine glass starting at around $50. Finally, companies must avoid *confused positioning*—leaving buyers with a confused image of a company. For example, over the past two decades, Burger King has fielded a dozen separate advertising campaigns, with themes ranging from "Herb the nerd doesn't eat here" to "Sometimes you've got to break the rules," "BK Tee Vee," and "Got the Urge?" This barrage of positioning statements has left consumers confused and Burger King with poor sales and profits.

WHICH DIFFERENCES TO PROMOTE? Not all brand differences are meaningful or worthwhile; not every difference makes a good differentiator. Each difference has the potential to create company costs as well as customer benefits. Therefore, the company must carefully select the ways in which it will distinguish itself from competitors. A difference is worth establishing to the extent that it satisfies the following criteria:

◆ *Important:* The difference delivers a highly valued benefit to target buyers.
◆ *Distinctive:* Competitors do not offer the difference, or the company can offer it in a more distinctive way.
◆ *Superior:* The difference is superior to other ways that customers might obtain the same benefit.
◆ *Communicable:* The difference is communicable and visible to buyers.
◆ *Preemptive:* Competitors cannot easily copy the difference.
◆ *Affordable:* Buyers can afford to pay for the difference.
◆ *Profitable:* The company can introduce the difference profitably.

Many companies have introduced differentiations that failed one or more of these tests. The Westin Stamford hotel in Singapore advertises that it is the world's tallest hotel, a distinction that is not important to most tourists—in fact, it turns many off. Polaroid's Polarvision, which produced instantly developed home movies, bombed too. Although Polarvision was distinctive and even preemptive, it was inferior to another way of capturing motion, namely, camcorders. When Pepsi introduced clear Crystal Pepsi some years ago, customers were unimpressed. Although the new drink was distinctive, consumers didn't see "clarity" as an important benefit in a soft drink. Thus, choosing competitive advantages upon which to position a product or service can be difficult, yet such choices may be crucial to success.

Selecting an Overall Positioning Strategy Consumers typically choose products and services that give them the greatest value. Thus, marketers want to position their brands on the key benefits that they offer relative to competing brands. The full positioning of a brand is called the brand's **value proposition**—the full mix of benefits upon which the brand is positioned. It is the answer to the customer's question "Why should

Value proposition
The full positioning of a brand—the full mix of benefits upon which it is positioned.

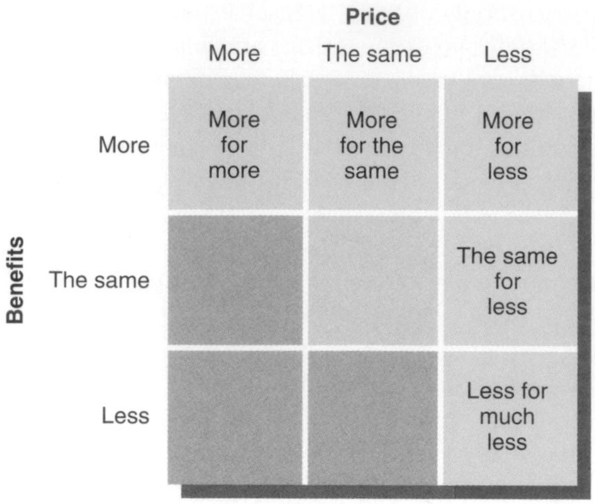

Price

	More	The same	Less
More	More for more	More for the same	More for less
The same			The same for less
Less			Less for much less

(Benefits on the vertical axis)

Figure 7-4
Possible value propositions

I buy your brand?" Volvo's value proposition hinges on safety but also includes reliability, roominess, and styling, all for a price that is higher than average but seems fair for this mix of benefits.

Figure 7-4 shows possible value propositions upon which a company might position its products. In the figure, the five green cells represent winning value propositions—positioning that gives the company competitive advantage. The orange cells, however, represent losing value propositions, and the center yellow cell represents at best a marginal proposition. In the following sections, we discuss the five winning value propositions upon which companies can position their products: more for more, more for the same, the same for less, less for much less, and more for less.[34]

MORE FOR MORE. "More for more" positioning involves providing the most upscale product or service and charging a higher price to cover the higher costs. Ritz-Carlton Hotels, Mont Blanc writing instruments, Mercedes-Benz automobiles—each claims superior quality, craftsmanship, durability, performance, or style and charges a price to match. Not only is the marketing offer high in quality, it also offers prestige to the buyer. It symbolizes status and a loftier lifestyle. Often, the price difference exceeds the actual increment in quality.

Sellers offering "only the best" can be found in every product and service category, from hotels, restaurants, food, and fashion to cars and kitchen appliances. Consumers are sometimes surprised, even delighted, when a new competitor enters a category with an unusually high-priced brand. Starbucks coffee entered as a very expensive brand in a largely commodity category; Häagen-Dazs came in as a premium ice cream brand at a price never before charged.

In general, companies should be on the lookout for opportunities to introduce a "much more for much more" brand in any underdeveloped product or service category. Yet "more for more" brands can be vulnerable. They often invite imitators who claim the same quality but at a lower price. Luxury goods that sell well during good times may be at risk during economic downturns when buyers become more cautious in their spending.

MORE FOR THE SAME. Companies can attack a competitor's more for more positioning by introducing a brand offering comparable quality but at a lower price. For example, Toyota introduced its Lexus line with a "more for the same" value proposition. Its headline read: "Perhaps the first time in history that trading a $72,000 car for a $36,000 car could be considered trading up." It communicated the high quality of its new Lexus through rave reviews in car magazines, through a widely distributed videotape showing side-by-side

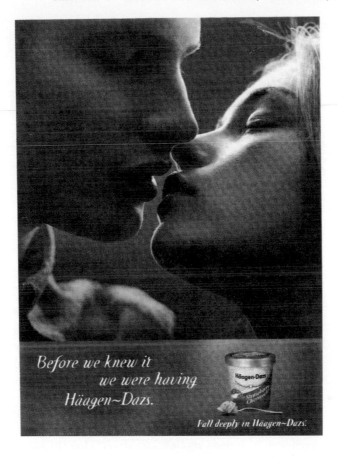

"Much more for much more" value proposition: Häagen-Dazs offers its superpremium ice cream at a price never before charged.

comparisons of Lexus and Mercedes-Benz automobiles, and through surveys showing that Lexus dealers were providing customers with better sales and service experiences than were Mercedes dealerships. Many Mercedes-Benz owners switched to Lexus, and the Lexus repurchase rate has been 60 percent, twice the industry average.

THE SAME FOR LESS. Offering "the same for less" can be a powerful value proposition—everyone likes a good deal. For example, Amazon.com sells the same book titles as its brick-and-mortar competitors but at lower prices, and Dell Computer offers equivalent quality at a better "price for performance." Discount stores such as Wal-Mart and "category killers" such as Best Buy, Circuit City, and Sportmart also use this positioning. They don't claim to offer different or better products. Instead, they offer many of the same brands as department stores and specialty stores but at deep discounts based on superior purchasing power and lower-cost operations.

Other companies develop imitative but lower-priced brands in an effort to lure customers away from the market leader. For example, Advanced Micro Devices (AMD) makes less expensive versions of Intel's market-leading microprocessor chips. Many personal computer companies make "IBM clones" and claim to offer the same performance at lower prices.

LESS FOR MUCH LESS. A market almost always exists for products that offer less and therefore cost less. Few people need, want, or can afford "the very best" in everything they buy. In many cases, consumers will gladly settle for less than optimal performance or give up some of the bells and whistles in exchange for a lower price. For example, many travelers seeking lodgings prefer not to pay for what they consider unnecessary extras, such as a pool, attached restaurant, or mints on the pillow. Motel chains such as Motel 6 suspend some of these amenities and charge less accordingly.

"Less for much less" positioning involves meeting consumers' lower performance or quality requirements at a much lower price. For example, Family Dollar and Dollar General stores offer more affordable goods at very low prices. Sam's Club warehouse stores offer less merchandise selection and consistency, and much lower levels of service; as a result, they charge rock-bottom prices. Southwest Airlines, the nation's most profitable air carrier, also practices less for much less positioning. It charges incredibly low prices by not serving food, not assigning seats, and not using travel agents.

MORE FOR LESS. Of course, the winning value proposition would be to offer "more for less." Many companies claim to do this. For example, Dell Computer claims to have better products *and* lower prices for a given level of performance. Procter & Gamble claims that its laundry detergents provide the best cleaning *and* everyday low prices. In the short run, some companies can actually achieve such lofty positions. For example, when it first opened for business, Home Depot had arguably the best product selection and service *and* the lowest prices compared to local hardware stores and other home improvement chains.

Yet in the long run, companies will find it very difficult to sustain such best-of-both positioning. Offering more usually costs more, making it difficult to deliver on the "for less" promise. Companies that try to deliver both may lose out to more focused competitors. For example, facing determined competition from Lowe's stores, Home Depot must now decide whether it wants to compete primarily on superior service or on lower prices.

All said, each brand must adopt a positioning strategy designed to serve the needs and wants of its target markets. "More for more" will draw one target market, "less for much less" will draw another, and so on. Thus, in any market, there is usually room for many different companies, each successfully occupying different positions (see Marketing at Work 7-3).

The important thing is that each company must develop its own winning positioning strategy, one that makes it special to its target consumers. Offering only "the same for the same" provides no competitive advantage, leaving the firm in the middle of the pack. Companies offering one of the three losing value propositions—"the same for more," "less for more," and "less for the same"—will inevitably fail. Here, customers soon realize that they've been underserved, tell others, and abandon the brand.

Communicating and Delivering the Chosen Position

Once it has chosen a position, the company must take strong steps to deliver and communicate the desired position to target consumers. All the company's marketing mix efforts must support the positioning strategy. Positioning the company calls for concrete action, not just talk. If the company decides to build a position on better quality and service, it must first *deliver* that position. Designing the marketing mix—product, price, place, and promotion—involves working out the tactical details of the positioning strategy. Thus, a firm that seizes on a "more for more" position knows that it must produce high-quality products, charge a high price, distribute through high-quality dealers, and advertise in high-quality media. It must hire and train more service people, find retailers who have a good reputation for service, and develop sales and advertising messages that broadcast its superior service. This is the only way to build a consistent and believable more for more position.

Companies often find it easier to come up with a good positioning strategy than to implement it. Establishing a position or changing one usually takes a long time. In

Marketing at Work 7-3

Airline Positioning: "More for More" or "Less for Much Less"?

Southwest Airlines and Midwest Express Airlines couldn't be more different in their positioning. Southwest offers a classic "less for much less" value proposition. In contrast, Midwest Express offers "more for a tad more." What they have in common, however, is that both have consistently soared above their competitors. In an industry often plagued by huge losses, Southwest has experienced 28 straight years of profits; Midwest Express has turned a profit for 14 years in a row. Both owe their success to strong and clear positioning that serves a well-defined target segment. Here, we compare the alternative positions that have made these airlines so successful.

Southwest Airlines

Southwest Airlines knows its niche. From the start, it has positioned itself firmly as *the* short-haul, no-frills, low-price airline. Its average flight time is just one hour; its average one way fare just $85. Southwest's passengers have learned to fly without the amenities. For example, the airline provides no meals—just peanuts. It also offers no first-class section, only three-across seating in all of its planes. There's no such thing as a reserved seat on a Southwest flight. Passengers receive numbered boarding passes—first come, first served—and are herded onto the plane in groups of 30. "Southwest will get you and your luggage where you're going," comments an industry analyst, "but we don't call their planes cattle cars for nothing. It's a mercy that Southwest is a short-haul airline, because you can get pretzelated on their planes p.d.q."

Why, then, do so many passengers love Southwest? Perhaps most importantly, Southwest excels at the basics of getting passengers where they want to go and on time. In 1992, Southwest received the U.S. Department of Transportation's first-ever Triple Crown Award for best on-time service, best baggage handling, *and* best customer service, a feat it repeated for the next five straight years. For more than a decade, Southwest has been an industry leader in on-time performance.

Beyond these basics, however, there are two key elements to Southwest's strong positioning. The analyst sums up Southwest's positioning this way: "It is not luxurious, . . . but it's cheap and it's fun." Southwest is a model of efficiency and low-cost operations. As a result, its prices are shockingly low. In fact, prices are so low that when Southwest enters a new market, it actually increases total air traffic by attracting customers who might otherwise travel by car or bus. For example, when Southwest began its Louisville–Chicago flight at a one-way rate of $49 versus competitors' $250, total weekly air passenger traffic between the two cities increased from 8,000 to 26,000.

No frills and low prices, however, don't mean drudgery. To lighten things up, Southwest adds another key positioning ingredient—lots of good, clean fun. With its happy-go-lucky CEO, Herb Kelleher, leading the charge, Southwest refuses to take itself seriously. Cheerful employees go out of their way to amuse, surprise, or somehow entertain passengers. According to one account:

> Southwest employees are apt to dress as leprechauns on St. Patrick's Day, rabbits on Easter, and almost anything on Halloween. I have heard flight attendants sing the safety lecture as country music, blues, and rap; I have heard them compare the pilot to Rocky Raccoon and insist that passengers introduce themselves to one another, then hug, then kiss, then propose marriage.

> Kelleher himself has been known to dress up as Elvis Presley to greet passengers.

Southwest offers a classic "less for much less" value proposition, with lots of zany fun (here, happy-go-lucky CEO Herb Kelleher impersonates Elvis)...

During delays at the gate, ticket agents will award prizes to the passenger with the largest hole in his or her sock. Flight attendants have been known to hide in overhead luggage bins and then pop out when passengers start filing onboard. Veteran Southwest fliers have learned to listen up to announcements over the intercom. On a recent flight, the pilot suggested, "Flight attendants will please prepare their hair for departure." Later in the flight, he announced, "Good morning, ladies and gentlemen. Those of you who wish to smoke will please file out to our lounge on the wing, where you can enjoy our feature film, *Gone with the Wind.*" Safety instructions from the flight attendant included the advice, "In the event of a water landing, please remember to paddle, kick, kick, paddle, kick, kick, all the way back."

As a result of its strong positioning, Southwest has grown to become the nation's fourth-largest domestic carrier. The company has successfully beaten off determined challenges from several major competitors who have tried to copy its winning formula, including Continental Lite, Delta Express, and Shuttle by United. Over the past 10 years, Southwest has expanded to serve 56 cities, its revenues have grown 388 percent, its net earnings have soared 1,490 percent, and its stock has yielded an average annual return to investors of 35 percent.

Midwest Express Airlines

Midwest Express Airlines' positioning stands in stark contrast to Southwest's. Whereas Southwest offers no frills, low prices, and zany fun, Midwest Express provides all the creature comforts and calm, refined service at higher but still competitive prices. It targets older, more affluent business travelers—thirty-five percent of Midwest

Express fliers earn more than $100,000 per year and a majority are between the ages of 35 and 54. These fliers want more service and Midwest Express delivers it to them.

Flying Midwest Express is a special experience:

You slip into your leather seat. You don't tussle for the armrest with some sweaty stranger in the middle, because there is no middle; everyone sits two by two with loads of legroom. . . . On breakfast flights, the chilled champagne is free. At lunch and dinner, you can choose a quality merlot or Chardonnay poured from bottles with actual

corks. Next comes the hot food on real china. Yes, food—not pretzels or a deli bag, but lobster or salmon, served by certifiably cordial airline employees. You can cover your shirt with a linen napkin. And, in a burst of true genius, the glass you're drinking from is made of . . . glass! This isn't a frequent flier's fantasy; it's a real utopia on a shockingly civilized airline called Midwest Express.

Consistent with its motto, "The Best Care in the Air," Midwest Express provides high-quality, near-first-class service to all passengers. All seats are leather and a full 21 inches wide, compared to the 17-

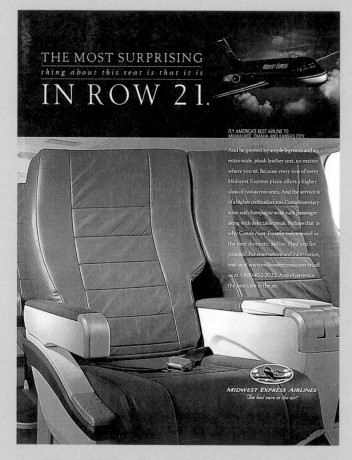

. . . Midwest Express offers a "more for a tad more" value proposition—it's calm, refined service provides "the best care in the air."

to 18-inch-wide seats of competitors. There are no more than 4 seats per row, eliminating the dreaded middle seat. Congenial but reserved flight attendants serve hot and elegant meals with complimentary wine or champagne, followed by a helping of the airline's signature chocolate chip cookies, sinfully gooey from being baked right on board. Midwest Express spends about $10 per passenger meal—twice the industry average (Southwest boasts that its average food cost per passenger is about 20¢). In a recent survey rating airline comfort, Midwest Express rated 98 on a scale 100 versus 67 to 74 for the major airlines.

Midwest Express is still a pretty small operation compared with Southwest and other major airlines. Unless you live in Milwaukee, Kansas City, or Omaha, Midwest's primary cities, you've probably never heard of it. Yet the classy little airline has developed a devout following. Sales are growing steadily and the airline recently posted its fourteenth consecutive year of profitability. Last year, Midwest's revenues were up 13 percent, income increased by 44 percent, and the airline flew a record 2 million passengers. Adding additional luster, three national travel magazines named it the best U.S. airline.

Midwest Express passengers pay more for its first-rate service. The airline's prices are a tad higher than those of competitors and the company sells very few economy seats. But to those who choose Midwest Express, the extras are well worth the additional costs. As for the future, Midwest Express is constantly on the lookout for new ways to please its already highly satisfied passengers. Says Tim Hoeksema, Midwest's president, "We're already looking for tomorrow's cookie—whatever makes somebody climb aboard [next year] and say, 'Wow.'"

Sources: Quotes from Molly Ivins, "From Texas, with Love and Peanuts," *New York Times,* March 14, 1999, p. 11; Daniel Pedersen, "Cookies and Champagne," *Newsweek,* April 27, 1998, p. 60; and Wendy Zellner, "Southwest: After Kelleher, More Blue Skies," *Business Week,* April 2, 2001, p. 45. Also see Ellen Jovin, "Buckling Up the Business Traveler," *American Demographics,* December 1998, pp. 48–51; Tania D. Panczyk, "Midwest Express Shifts to Spots Touting Service," *Adweek,* April 23, 2001, p. 3; "How Herb Keeps Southwest Hopping," *Money,* June 1999, pp. 61–62; Katrina Brooker, "The Chairman of the Board Looks Back," *Fortune,* May 28, 2001, pp. 63–74; *Southwest Airlines Fact Sheet—June 2001* at www.southwest.com; and information accessed online at www.midwestexpress.com, July 2001.

contrast, positions that have taken years to build can quickly be lost. Once a company has built the desired position, it must take care to maintain the position through consistent performance and communication. It must closely monitor and adapt the position over time to match changes in consumer needs and competitors' strategies. However, the company should avoid abrupt changes that might confuse consumers. Instead, a product's position should evolve gradually as it adapts to the ever-changing marketing environment.

STOP   *Rest Stop: Reviewing the Concepts*

Time to stop and stretch your legs. In this chapter, you've learned about the major elements of marketing strategy: segmentation, targeting, and positioning. Marketers know that they cannot appeal to all buyers in their markets, or at least not to all buyers in the same way. Buyers are too numerous, too widely scattered, and too varied in their needs and buying practices. Therefore, most companies today are moving away from mass marketing. Instead, they practice *target marketing*—identifying market segments, selecting one or more of them, and developing products and marketing mixes tailored to each. In this way, sellers can develop the right product for each target market and adjust their prices, distribution channels, and advertising to reach the target market efficiently.

1. Define the three steps of target marketing: market segmentation, market targeting, and market positioning.

Market segmentation is the act of dividing a market into distinct groups of buyers with different needs, characteristics, or behaviors who might require separate products or marketing mixes. Once the groups have been identified, *market targeting* evaluates each market segment's attractiveness and suggests one or more segments to enter. *Market positioning* consists of setting the competitive positioning for the product and creating a detailed marketing plan.

2. List and discuss the major levels of market segmentation and bases for segmenting consumer and business markets.

Market segmentation can be carried out at several different levels, including no segmentation (mass marketing), complete segmentation (micromarketing), or something in between (segment marketing or niche marketing). *Mass marketing* involves mass producing, mass distributing, and mass promoting about the same product in about the same way to all consumers. Using *segmented marketing,* the company tries to isolate broad segments that make up a market and adapt its offers to more closely match the needs of one or more segments. *Niche marketing* focuses on more narrowly defined subgroups within these segments, groups with distinctive sets of traits that may seek a special combination of benefits. *Micromarketing* is the practice of tailoring products and marketing programs to suit the tastes of specific individuals and locations. Micromarketing includes *local marketing* and *individual marketing.*

There is no single way to segment a market. Therefore, the marketer tries different variables to see which give the best segmentation opportunities. For consumer marketing, the major segmentation variables are geographic, demographic, psychographic, and behavioral. In *geographic segmentation,* the market is divided into different geographical units such as nations, regions, states, counties, cities, or neighborhoods. In *demographic segmentation,* the market is divided into groups based on demographic variables, including age, gender, family size, family life-cycle, income, occupation, education, religion, race, generation, and nationality. In *psychographic segmentation,* the market is divided into different groups based on social class, lifestyle, or personality characteristics. In *behavioral segmentation,* the market is divided into groups based on consumers' knowledge, attitudes, uses, or responses to a product.

Business marketers use many of the same variables to segment their markets. But business markets also can be segmented by business consumer *demographics* (industry, company size), *operating characteristics, purchasing approaches, situational factors,* and *personal characteristics.* The effectiveness of segmentation analysis depends on finding segments that are *measurable, accessible, substantial, differentiable,* and *actionable.*

3. Explain how companies identify attractive market segments and choose a market-coverage strategy.

To target the best market segments, the company first evaluates each segment's size and growth characteristics, structural attractiveness, and compatibility with company objectives and resources. It then chooses one of three market-coverage strategies. The seller can ignore segment differences (*undifferentiated marketing*), develop different market offers for several segments (*differentiated marketing*), or go after one or a few market segments (*concentrated marketing*). Much depends on company resources, product variability, product life-cycle stage, market viability, and competitive marketing strategies.

4. Discuss how companies can position their products for maximum competitive advantage in the marketplace.

Once a company has decided which segments to enter, it must decide on its *market positioning* strategy—on which positions to occupy in its chosen segments. The positioning task consists of three steps: identifying a set of possible competitive advantages upon which to build a position, choosing the right competitive advantages, and selecting an overall positioning strategy. The brand's full positioning is called its *value proposition*—the full mix of benefits upon which the brand is positioned. In general, companies can choose from one of five winning value propositions upon which to position their products: more for more, more for the same, the same for less, less for much less, or more for less. They must then effectively communicate and deliver the chosen position to the market.

Navigating the Key Terms

For a detailed analysis of the meaning and importance of each of the following key terms, visit our Web page at **www.prenhall.com/kotler**.

Age and life-cycle segmentation
Behavioral segmentation
Benefit segmentation
Competitive advantage

Concentrated marketing
Demographic segmentation
Differentiated marketing
Gender segmentation

Geographic segmentation
Income segmentation
Individual marketing
Intermarket segmentation
Local marketing
Market positioning

Market segmentation
Market targeting
Micromarketing
Niche marketing
Occasion segmentation
Product position

Psychographic segmentation
Segment marketing
Target market
Undifferentiated marketing
Value proposition

Travel Log

The following concept checks and discussion questions will help you to keep track of and apply the concepts you've studied in this chapter.

Concept Checks

Fill in the blanks, then look for the correct answers.

1. The first step in target marketing is _____—dividing a market into smaller groups of buyers with distinct needs, characteristics, or behaviors who might require separate products or marketing mixes.

2. According to this chapter, the three major steps in target marketing are market segmentation, _____ _____, and _____.

3. The following statements symbolize which levels of market segmentation: (a) Henry Ford offered Model Ts to customers "in any color as long as it was black." This market segmentation level equals _____; (b) GM has designed specific models of cars for different income and age groups. This market segmentation level equals _____; (c) An auto insurance company sells "nonstandard" auto insurance to high-risk drivers with a record of auto accidents or drunkenness. This market segmentation level equals _____; (d) A microbrewery tailors its products and marketing programs to suit the tastes of specific individuals and/or locations. This market segmentation level equals _____.

4. The major variables that might be used in segmenting consumer markets include: _____, _____, _____, and _____ _____ variables.

5. _____ segmentation divides the market into groups based on variables such as age, gender, family size, family life-cycle, income, occupation, education, religion, race, and nationality.

6. Proctor & Gamble was practicing _____ segmentation when they designed Secret deodorant, a brand specially formulated for a woman's chemistry, packaged and advertised to reinforce the female image.

7. There are several requirements for effective segmentation. To be useful, market segments must be _____, _____, _____ _____, _____, and _____.

8. A _____ consists of a set of buyers who share common needs or characteristics that the company decides to serve.

9. Nike is using a _____ marketing strategy when it offers athletic shoes for a dozen or more different sports, from running, fencing, and aerobics to bicycling and baseball.

10. In general, a company needs to avoid three major positioning errors: _____ positioning, _____ positioning, and _____ positioning.

11. In considering which differences to promote, a difference is worth establishing to the extent that it satisfies the following criteria: important, distinctive, _____, _____, _____ _____, _____, and profitable.

12. The full positioning of a brand is called the brand's _____—the full mix of benefits upon which the brand is positioned.

Concept Checks Answers: 1. market segmentation; 2. market targeting, and market positioning; 3. mass marketing, segment marketing, niche marketing, and micromarketing; 4. geographic, demographic, psychographic, and behavioral; 5. Demographic; 6. gender; 7. measurable, accessible, substantial, differentiable, actionable; 8. target market; 9. differentiated; 10. under, over, confused; 11. superior, communicable, preemptive, affordable; 12. value proposition.

Discussing the Issues

1. Describe how the Ford Motor Company has moved from mass marketing to segment marketing. Do

you think the company will be able to move toward niche marketing or micromarketing? If so, how? How is the company using the Internet (see www.ford.com) to change its marketing segmentation approach?

2. Several years ago Samuel Adams Brewery led a charge of "microbreweries" in an attack on the established brewers' domestic beers. What is "micromarketing" and how might it have been used by these "microbreweries"? Do you see evidence that breweries such as Samuel Adams have moved to "local" or "individual" marketing? Evaluate the "micromarketing" strategies used by this industry. (For more information see www.samadams.com.)

3. There are many ways to segment a market. Using the four segmentation variables shown in Table 7-1, discuss which variables would be *most important* for segmenting (a) Internet users, (b) drivers of a proposed new sports car, and (c) the adult student who returns to college to get an undergraduate degree. Explain your choices. What assumptions did you make? In each case, where would you find the information needed to segment the markets? Be creative with your research thoughts.

4. Need help with your financial planning? Software maker Intuit (see www.intuit.com) probably has a product just for you. The company's Quicken (financial planning software) and TurboTax (the #1 income tax preparation software) have given Intuit a strong position in the rapidly growing financial planning and services market. Assuming that the company would like to expand, which of the market-coverage strategies shown in Figure 7-3 would you suggest? Explain how the strategy you've chosen would help the company to meet strong competitive challenges from Microsoft and other software makers.

5. Collect advertisements that demonstrate the positioning of different automobile brands. Sort the various brands into categories of brands with similar positions. Using Figure 7-4, state the *value proposition* for each of the brands you surveyed. Do the advertised positions match your perceptions of where each brand belongs?

Mastering Marketing

Using the information from Figure 7-3, identify the market-coverage strategy being used by CanGo. Critique and comment on this strategy. Should a change be made? Explain. Next, using the information found in Figure 7-4,

state the value proposition of CanGo's primary product line. Critique this proposition and comment. Should a change be made? Explain.

Traveling on the Net

Point of Interest: Attracting Market Segments

Tweens–youths aged 8–14—face pressures to grow up quickly. Research shows that Tweens are among today's most targeted consumer groups. They spend some $12 million annually to surround themselves with computers, electronic gadgets, music, clothing, magazines, and other gear that express their lifestyles. Figuring out how to reach this market segment is a challenge to many marketers. Two companies that seem to have found success with Tweens are Mountain Dew (Pepsi) and Sprite (Coca-Cola). By reorganizing their Web sites and revamping their marketing efforts, these two popular soft drinks have struck the right chord with youth. To reach this demanding segment, the Mountain Dew Web site uses links to popular music, NASCAR, pirate radio, TV ad clips, wakeboard and skateboard stars, and computer geeks (a computer

virus "Code Red" was even named after the Code Red Mountain Dew product). In contrast, the Sprite Web site appeals to a slightly different audience with "hip" music, concerts, music group sponsorship, cell phone give-aways, music code games, and Rocket cash (credits that can be used for merchandise). The two companies seem to be dividing the Tweens into "X-tremes and geeks" versus "Hip Hop and Rappers." Which is the best segment to pursue? Mountain Dew and Sprite believe that both hold real promise. To learn more about marketing to Tweens, visit the following Web sites: a) Mountain Dew: www.mountaindew.com; b) Sprite: www.sprite.com; c) Gap:www.gap.com; d) Tommy Hilfiger:www.tommy.com; e) the Limited Too: www.limitedtoo.com; and f) Nintendo: www.nintendo. com.

For Discussion

1. Using other data sources, profile the Tweens market segment.
2. How do companies seem to be marketing toward this age segment? Indicate strategies and competitive positions.
3. What strategies seem to be most popular with the Web sites mentioned above?
4. Choose a company that currently markets to older youth and young adults. Explain how this company might attract Tweens to its products.
5. What types of social responsibility issues might be encountered by a company targeting this group? Explain.

Application Thinking

Assume that you have been hired by Red Bull (an energy drink) to devise a strategy for cracking the market dominance of Mountain Dew and Sprite in the Tween market. After reviewing the Red Bull Web site (see www.redbull.com), describe how you would attract the Tween market. Would you further subdivide the market segment? What positioning strategy would be best? What difficulties would you have to overcome? Present your strategy to the class.

Map—Marketing Applications

Map Stop 7

Recent events suggest that marketers are increasingly moving beyond demographics in their segmentation efforts. Demographics have not been replaced but have instead been merged with psychographic and behavioral variables. For example, many companies today appear to be tailoring their products, promotions, and strategies to two tiers of American consumers. Some call this the "Tiffany/Wal-Mart" approach. In automobiles, several General Motors divisions are selling record numbers of new SUVs to "upscale" consumers (those seeking more features at higher prices). At the same time, GM's Saturn division is selling record numbers of pre-owned cars to "downscale" consumers (those seeking value and low cost). In clothing, Gap's Banana Republic stores sell "upscale" jeans for $50 or more, whereas its Old Navy stores sell "value" jeans for $20 or less. During the past decade, marketers have seen the wealthiest 5 percent of consumers grow richer while the average American's income has remained relatively stagnant.

Thinking Like a Marketing Manager

1. What other examples of two-tier marketing can you find?

2. How does a two-tier (upscale versus downscale) consumer economy affect a marketing manager's marketing strategy?
3. What geographic, demographic, psychographic, or behavioral variables would be most important in designing appeals for the "upscale" and "downscale" markets found in a two-tier economy?
4. One organization that carefully tracks changing income and spending levels is the American Association of Retired Persons (AARP). Visit the AARP Web site (see www.aarp.org and its magazine *Modern Maturity*—www.modernmaturity.org) for additional data. What effect does a two-tier market have on seniors? Give an example of a company that seems to be approaching seniors with a two-tier market strategy.
5. Assume that you are the marketing manager for (a) a Wal-Mart store, (b) a Barnes and Noble bookseller store, and (c) a Sears department store. Design a marketing strategy for attracting (a) "upscale" consumers, (b) "downscale" consumers, or (c) both to your store. Can strategies for these two distinctly different markets coexist for each of these stores? Use Figure 7-4 for aid and additional information.

chapter 8

Product and Services Strategy

ROAD MAP:
Previewing the Concepts

Now that you've had a good look at marketing strategy, we'll journey on into the marketing mix—the tactical tools that marketers use to implement their strategies. In this and the next chapter, we'll study how companies develop and manage products. Then, in the chapters that follow, we'll look at pricing, distribution, and marketing communication tools. The product is usually the first and most basic marketing consideration. How well firms manage their individual brands and their overall product and service offerings has a major impact on their success in the marketplace. We'll start with a seemingly simple question: What *is* a product? As it turns out, however, the answer is not so simple.

▶ After studying this chapter, you should be able to:

1. define *product* and the major classifications of products and services
2. describe the roles of product and service branding, packaging, labeling, and product support services
3. explain the decisions companies make when developing product lines and mixes
4. identify the four characteristics that affect the marketing of a service
5. discuss the additional marketing considerations that services require

First stop on this leg of the journey: cosmetics marketing. Remember that seemingly simple question—what is a product? The cosmetics industry example shows why there is no easy answer. What, really, *are* cosmetics? Cosmetics makers like Aveda know that when a woman buys cosmetics, she buys much, much more than scented ingredients in fancy bottles.

Each year, cosmetics companies sell billions of dollars' worth of potions, lotions, and fragrances to consumers around the world. In one sense, these products are no more than careful mixtures of oils and chemicals that have nice scents and soothing properties. But the cosmetics companies know that they sell much more than just mixtures of ingredients—they sell the promise of what these concoctions will do for the people who use them.

Of course, in the cosmetics business, like anywhere else, quality and performance contribute to success or failure. For example, perfume marketers agree, "No smell; no sell." However, $180-an-ounce perfume may cost no more than $10 to produce. Thus, to perfume consumers, many things beyond the scent and a few dollars' worth of ingredients add to a perfume's allure. For instance, a perfume's packaging is an important product attribute—the package and bottle are the most real symbols of the perfume and its image. The *name* is also important—fragrance names such as Obsession, Passion, Gossip,

Wildheart, Opium, Joy, White Linen, Youth Dew, Eternity, and Love suggest that the perfumes will do something more than just make you smell better.

What *is* the promise of cosmetics? The following account by a *New York Times* reporter suggests the extent to which cosmetics take on meaning far beyond their physical makeup.

Last week I bathed in purple water (*I Trust* bubble bath, made by Philosophy) and powdered up with pink powder (*Rebirth,* by 5S, "to renew the spirit and recharge the soul"). My moisturizer was *Bliss* (Chakra VII by Aveda, for "the joyful enlightenment and soaring of the spirit"); my nail polish was *Spiritual* (by Tony and Tina, "to aid connection with the higher self"). My teeth were clean, my heart was open—however, my bathroom was so crowded with bottles and brochures, the latest tools and totems from the human potential movement, that I could hardly find my third eye. Still, my "Hope in a Jar" package (from Philosophy) pretty well summed it up: "Where there is hope there can be faith. Where there is faith miracles can occur."

If you are looking for enlightenment in all the wrong places, cosmetics companies are eager to help. Because today, feeling good is the new religion. And cosmetics companies are the newest of the new prophets, turning the old notion of hope in a jar on its head.

"Cosmetics are our satellite to the divine!" This is what you'll hear from Tony and Tina, for example. Tony and Tina (Anthony Gillis and Cristina Bornstein) are nice young artists. He's from London, she grew up in New York. Chakra nail polish, which they invented for an installation at the Gershwin Gallery in Manhattan two years ago, was intended as an ironic commentary on the beauty business. But then a friend suggested they get into the beauty business, and now Tony and Tina have a $2 million cosmetics company with a mission statement: "To aid in the evolution of human consciousness." Their products include nail polishes (Vibrational Remedies) in colors meant to do nice things to your chakras, as well as body glitter and hair mascara, lipstick and eyeshadow. You can buy them at Fred

hope in a jar®
for all skin types

philosophy®: where there is hope there can be faith. where there is faith miracles can occur.

2 oz. - 56.7 g

Segal, Nordstrom, and Bloomingdale's, where last month they outsold Hard Candy and Urban Decay. "We think color therapy is going to be the new medicine," said Tony.

Rainbows are proliferating as rapidly in the New Age as angels once did. Philosophy, a three-year-old Arizona company, makes a sort of head/heart kit—"a self-help program," the company insists—called the *Rainbow Connection.* You pay $45 for seven bottles of colored bubble bath in a metal box. "Choose your colored bath according to the area of your emotional life that needs attention, i.e., self-love, self-worth," the brochure reads. "My role as I see it," said Christina Carlino, Philosophy's founder, "is to help you stay on your destiny path. It's not about what you look like. Beauty is defined by your deeds."

5S, a new sprout of the Japanese cosmetics company Shiseido, offers a regimen that plays, the company says, on the "fundamental and mythical significance of 5" (Five Pillars of Islam, Five Classics of Confucianism, and so on), and which is organized into emotional rather than physical categories. At the 5S store in SoHo, you don't buy things for dry skin, you buy things that are "energizing" or "nurturing" or "adoring." The company also believes in color therapy. Hence, *Rebirth,* products tinted "nouveau pink" (the color of bubble gum). A customer can achieve rebirth with 5S pink soap, pink powder, and pink toner.

Here are products that are not intended to make you look better, but to make you act better, feel better, and be a better person. You don't need a month's visit to India to find your higher self; you need only buy this bubble bath, that lipstick, this night cream. The beauty business's old come-on (trap your man!) has been swept away in favor of a new pitch. I don't have wrinkles anymore. I've got a chakra blockage.

Of course, who knew about chakras before Aveda? In 1989, the plant-based, eco-friendly cosmetics company Aveda trademarked Chakras I through VII to use as titles for moisturizers and scents. Chakra products were perhaps a little ahead of their time back then. However, the purchase of Aveda [a while] ago by the Estée Lauder Companies, the General Motors of the cosmetics world, suggests that the pendulum of history has finally caught up. "Aveda isn't a marketing idea," says Jeanette Wagner, the vice chairman of Estée Lauder. "It is a passionately held belief." Estée Lauder plans to extend the Aveda concept through "lifestyle" stores built with sustainable woods and nontoxic elements, selling "beauty, health, lifestyle, you name it." "From my point of view," Wagner says, "the appeal is first the spirituality, and then the products."

All this might sound like only so much flimflam, but the underlying point is legitimate. The success of such brands affirms that products really are more than just the physical entities. When a woman buys cosmetics, she really does buy much, much more than just oils, chemicals, and fragrances. The cosmetic's image, its promises and positioning, its ingredients, its name and package, the company that makes it, the stores that sell it—all become a part of the total cosmetic product. When Aveda, Philosophy, and 5S sell cosmetics, they sell more than just tangible goods. They sell lifestyle, self-expression, exclusivity, and spirituality; achievement, success, and status; romance, passion, and fantasy; memories, hopes, and dreams.[1]

●●

Clearly, cosmetics are more than just cosmetics when Aveda sells them. This chapter begins with a deceptively simple question: *What is a product?* After answering this question, we look at ways to classify products in consumer and business markets. Then we discuss the important decisions that marketers make regarding individual products, product lines, and product mixes. Finally, we examine the characteristics and marketing requirements of a special form of product—services.

What Is a Product?

Product
Anything that can be offered to a market for attention, acquisition, use, or consumption that might satisfy a want or need.

Service
Any activity or benefit that one party can offer to another that is essentially intangible and does not result in the ownership of anything.

A Sony DVD player, a Ford Taurus, a Costa Rican vacation, a Caffé Mocha at Starbucks, Charles Schwab online investment services, and advice from your family doctor—all are products. We define a **product** as anything that can be offered to a market for attention, acquisition, use, or consumption and that might satisfy a want or need. Products include more than just tangible goods. Broadly defined, products include physical objects, services, events, persons, places, organizations, ideas, or mixes of these entities. Thus, throughout this text, we use the term *product* broadly to include any or all of these entities.

Because of their importance in the world economy, we give special attention to services. **Services** are a form of product that consists of activities, benefits, or satisfactions offered for sale that are essentially intangible and do not result in the ownership of anything. Examples are banking, hotel, tax preparation, and home repair services. We will look at services more closely in a section at the end of this chapter.

Products, Services, and Experiences

A company's offer to the marketplace often includes both tangible goods and services. Each component can be a minor or a major part of the total offer. At one extreme, the offer may consist of a *pure tangible good,* such as soap, toothpaste, or salt—no services accompany the product. At the other extreme are *pure services,* for which the offer consists primarily of a service. Examples include a doctor's exam or financial services. Between these two extremes, however, many goods and services combinations are possible.

For example, a company's offer may consist of a *tangible good with accompanying services.* Ford offers more than just automobiles. Its offer also includes repair and maintenance services, warranty fulfillment, showrooms and waiting areas, and a host of other support services. A *hybrid offer* consists of equal parts of goods and services. For instance, people patronize restaurants for both their food and their service. A *service with accompanying minor goods* consists of a major service along with supporting goods. For example, American Airlines passengers primarily buy transportation service, but the trip also includes some tangibles, such as food, drinks, and an airline magazine. The service also requires a capital-intensive good—an airplane—for its delivery, but the primary offer is a service.

Today, as products and services become more and more commoditized, many companies are moving to a new level in creating value for their customers. To differentiate their offers, they are developing and delivering total customer *experiences.* Whereas products are tangible and services are intangible, experiences are memorable. Whereas products and services are external, experiences are personal and take place in the minds of individual consumers. Companies that market experiences realize that customers are really buying much more than just products and services. They are buying what those offers will *do* for them—the experiences they gain in purchasing and consuming these products and services (see Marketing at Work 8-1).[2]

Levels of Product

Product planners need to think about products and services on three levels. The most basic level is the *core product,* which addresses the question *What is the buyer really buying?* As Figure 8-1 illustrates, the core product stands at the center of the total product. It consists of the core, problem-solving benefits that consumers seek when they buy a product or service. A woman buying lipstick buys more than lip color. Charles Revson of Revlon saw this early: "In the factory, we make cosmetics; in the store, we sell hope." And

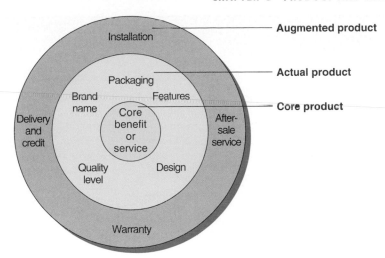

Augmented product

Actual product

Core product

Figure 8-1
Three levels of
product

Ritz-Carlton Hotels knows that it offers its guests more than simply rooms for rent—it provides "memorable travel experiences." And Charles Schwab does more than sell financial services—it promises the fulfillment of customers' "financial dreams." Thus, when designing products, marketers must first define the core of *benefits* the product will provide to consumers. They must understand the total customer *experience* that surrounds the purchase and use of the product.

Core, actual, and
augmented product:
Consumers perceive
this Sony camcorder
as a complex bundle of
tangible and intangible
features and services
that deliver a core
benefit—a convenient,
high-quality way to
capture important
moments.

Beyond Products and Services: Welcome to the Experience Economy

In their book, *The Experience Economy,* Joseph Pine and James Gilmore argue that, as products and services become less and less differentiated, companies are moving to a new level in creating value for customers. As the next step in differentiating their offers, beyond simply making products and delivering services, companies are staging, marketing, and delivering memorable experiences. Consider the evolution of the birthday cake:

[In an] *agrarian* economy, mothers made birthday cakes from scratch, mixing farm commodities (flour, sugar, butter, and eggs) that together cost mere dimes. As the *goods-based* industrial economy advanced, moms paid a dollar or two to Betty Crocker for premixed ingredients. Later, when the *service* economy took hold, busy parents ordered cakes from the bakery or grocery store, which, at $10 or $15, cost ten times as much as the packaged ingredients. Now, . . . time-starved parents neither make the birthday cake nor even throw the party. Instead, they spend $100 or more to "outsource" the entire event to Chuck E. Cheese's, the Discovery Zone, the Mining Company, or some other business that stages a memorable event for the kids—and often throws in the cake for free. Welcome to the emerging *experience* economy. . . . From now on, leading-edge companies—whether they sell to consumers or businesses—will find that the next competitive battleground lies in staging experiences.

Experiences are sometimes confused with services, but experiences are as distinct from services as services are distinct from goods. Whereas products and services are external, experiences exist only in the mind of the individual. They are rich with emotional, physical, intellectual, or spiritual sensations created within the consumer. According to Pine and Gilmore:

An experience occurs when a company intentionally uses services as the stage, and goods as props, to engage individual customers in a way that creates a memorable event. . . . To appreciate the difference between services and experiences, recall the episode of the old television show *Taxi* in which Iggy, a usually atrocious (but fun-loving) cab driver, decided to become the best taxi driver in the world. He served sandwiches and drinks, conducted tours of the city, and even sang Frank Sinatra tunes. By engaging passengers in a way that turned an ordinary cab ride into a memorable event, Iggy created something else entirely—a distinct economic offering. The experience of riding in his cab was more valuable to his customers than the service of being transported by the cab—and in the TV show, at least, Iggy's customers happily responded by giving bigger tips. By asking to go around the block again, one patron even paid more for poorer service just to prolong his enjoyment. The service Iggy provided—taxi transportation— was simply the stage for the experience that he was really selling.

Experiences have always been important in the entertainment industry—Disney has long manufactured memories through its movies and theme parks. Today, however, all kinds of firms are recasting their traditional goods and services to create experiences. For example, restaurants create value well beyond the food they serve. Starbucks patrons are paying for more than just coffee. "Customers at Starbucks are paying for staged experiences," comments one analyst. "The company treats patrons to poetry on its wallpaper and tabletops, jaunty apron-clad performers behind the espresso machine, and an interior ambience that's both cozy and slick, marked by earth tones, brushed steel, and retro music (also for sale). Few people leave without feeling a little more affluent, sophisticated, or jazzed."

Many retailers also stage experiences. Niketown stores create "shoppertainment" by offering interactive displays, engaging activities, and promotional events in a stimulating shopping environment. At stores such as Sharper Image and Brookstone, "people play with the gadgets, listen to miniaturized stereo equipment, sit in massage chairs, and then leave without paying for what they valued, namely, the experience."

In San Francisco, Sony of America has developed Metreon, an "interactive entertainment experience," where visitors can shop, eat, drink, play, or simply soak up the experiences (check it out at www.metreon.com). The huge Metreon complex features nineteen theaters, including a Sony-IMAX Theater, eight restaurants, and several interactive attractions, such as *Where the Wild Things Are* (an interactive playspace inspired by Maurice Sendak's popular children's book) and Moebius' Airtight Garage (an adventure zone featuring original interactive games based on the work of French graphic novelist Jean Giraud). Visitors can also experience any of nine interactive stores, including the flagship Discovery Channel Store: Destination San Francisco (featuring interactive educational exhibits inspired by programming from the Discovery Channel, TLC, and Animal Planet cable networks), Sony Style (a high-touch boutique

Marketing experiences: Sony's Metreon markets an "interactive entertainment experience: four floors and 350,000 square feet jam-packed with ways to entertain and escape into a whole new reality."

of Sony products), and microsoftSF (where shoppers can play with the latest computer software and hardware). In all, Metreon offers a dazzling experience that far transcends the goods and services assortment it contains. Sony sums up the experience this way:

Use your eyes, ears, hands, and brain . . . sensory overload to a phenomenal degree. . . . Four floors and 350,000 square feet jam-packed with ways to entertain and escape into a whole new reality. Dazzle a date. Bring wonder to your kids. Shop in amazement. Have fun with your friends. Whenever you want real entertainment, head to Metreon.

The experience economy goes beyond the entertainment and retailing businesses. All companies stage experiences whenever they engage customers in a personal, memorable way:

In the travel business, former British Airways chairman Sir Colin Marshall has noted that the "commodity mind-set" is to "think that a business is merely performing a function—in our case, transporting

people from point A to point B on time and at the lowest possible price." What British Airways does, according to Sir Colin, is "to go beyond the function and compete on the basis of providing an experience." The company uses its base service (the travel itself) as the stage for a distinctive en route experience—one that attempts to transform air travel into a respite from the traveler's normally frenetic life.

Business-to-business marketers also stage experiences for their customers. For example, one Minneapolis computer installation and repair company has found a way to turn its otherwise humdrum service into a memorable encounter. Calling itself the Geek Squad, it sends "special agents" dressed in white shirts with thin black ties and pocket protectors, carrying badges, and driving old cars. Similarly, Silicon Graphics creates an experience as elaborate as any Disney attraction:

[Its] Visionarium Reality Center at corporate headquarters in Mountain View, California, brings customers and engineers together in an envi-

ronment where they can interact with real-time, three-dimensional product visualizations. Customers can view, hear, and touch—as well as drive, walk, or fly—through myriad product possibilities. [According to one Silicon Graphics executive,] "This is experiential computing at its ultimate, where our customers can know what their products will look like, sound like, and feel like before manufacturing."

Thus, as we move into the new millennium, marketers seeking new ways to bring value to customers must look beyond the goods and services they make and sell. They must find ways to turn their offers into total customer experiences. As the experience economy grows, Pine and Gilmore caution, it "threatens to render irrelevant those who relegate themselves to the diminishing world of goods and services."

Sources: Excerpts and quotes from "Welcome to the Experience Economy," *Harvard Business Review,* July–August 1998, pp. 97–105; Wade Roush, "Now Playing: Your Business," *Technology Review,* May–June 1999, p. 96; and Sony's Metreon Web site, www.metreon.com, December 2001. Also see B. Joseph Pine and James H. Gilmore, *The Experience Economy* (New York: Free Press, 1999); and Scott Mac Stravic, "Make Impressions Last: Focus on Value," *Marketing News,* October 23, 2000, pp. 44–45.

The product planner must next build an *actual product* around the core product. Actual products may have as many as five characteristics: a quality level, features, design, a brand name, and packaging. For example, a Sony camcorder is an actual product. Its name, parts, styling, features, packaging, and other attributes have all been combined carefully to deliver the core benefit—a convenient, high-quality way to capture important moments.

Finally, the product planner must build an *augmented product* around the core and actual products by offering additional consumer services and benefits. Sony must offer more than just a camcorder. It must provide consumers with a complete solution to their picture-taking problems. Thus, when consumers buy a Sony camcorder, Sony and its dealers also might give buyers a warranty on parts and workmanship, instructions on how to use the camcorder, quick repair services when needed, and a toll-free telephone number to call if they have problems or questions.

Therefore, a product is more than a simple set of tangible features. Consumers tend to see products as complex bundles of benefits that satisfy their needs. When developing products, marketers first must identify the *core* consumer needs the product will satisfy. They must then design the *actual* product and find ways to *augment* it in order to create the bundle of benefits that will provide the most satisfying customer experience.

Product Classifications

Products and services fall into two broad classes based on the types of consumers that use them—*consumer products* and *industrial products*. Broadly defined, products also include other marketable entities such as experiences, organizations, persons, places, and ideas.

Consumer Products

Consumer product
Product bought by final consumer for personal consumption.

Convenience product
Consumer product that the customer usually buys frequently, immediately, and with a minimum of comparison and buying effort.

Shopping product
Consumer good that the customer, in the process of selection and purchase, characteristically compares on such bases as suitability, quality, price, and style.

Specialty product
Consumer product with unique characteristics or brand identification for which a significant group of buyers is willing to make a special purchase effort.

Consumer products are those bought by final consumers for personal consumption. Marketers usually classify these goods further based on how consumers go about buying them. Consumer products include *convenience products, shopping products, specialty products,* and *unsought products*. These products differ in the ways consumers buy them and therefore in how they are marketed (see Table 8-1).

Convenience products are consumer products and services that the customer usually buys frequently, immediately, and with a minimum of comparison and buying effort. Examples include soap, candy, newspapers, and fast food. Convenience products are usually low priced, and marketers place them in many locations to make them readily available when customers need them.

Shopping products are less frequently purchased consumer products and services that customers compare carefully on suitability, quality, price, and style. When buying shopping products and services, consumers spend much time and effort in gathering information and making comparisons. Examples include furniture, clothing, used cars, major appliances, and hotel and motel services. Shopping products marketers usually distribute their products through fewer outlets but provide deeper sales support to help customers in their comparison efforts.

Specialty products are consumer products and services with unique characteristics or brand identification for which a significant group of buyers is willing to make a special purchase effort. Examples include specific brands and types of cars, high-priced photographic equipment, designer clothes, and the services of medical or legal specialists. A Lamborghini automobile, for example, is a specialty product because buyers are usually willing to travel great distances to buy one. Buyers normally do not compare

Table 8-1   Marketing Considerations for Consumer Products

Marketing Considerations	Type of Consumer Product			
	Convenience	Shopping	Specialty	Unsought
Customer buying behavior	Frequent purchase, little planning, little comparison or shopping effort, low customer involvement	Less frequent purchase, much planning and shopping effort, comparison of brands on price, quality, style	Strong brand preference and loyalty, special purchase effort, little comparison of brands, low price sensitivity	Little product awareness, knowledge, or, if aware, little interest (or negative interest)
Price	Low price	Higher price	High price	Varies
Distribution	Widespread distribution, convenient locations	Selective distribution in fewer outlets	Exclusive distribution in only one or a few outlets per market area	Varies
Promotion	Mass advertising and sales promotion by the producer	Advertising and personal selling by producer and resellers	More carefully targeted promotion by producer and resellers	Aggressive advertising and personal selling by producer and resellers
Examples	Toothpaste, magazines, laundry detergent	Major appliances, televisions, furniture, clothing	Luxury goods, such as Rolex watches or fine crystal	Life insurance, Red Cross blood donations

specialty products. They invest only the time needed to reach dealers carrying the wanted products.

Unsought products are consumer products that the consumer either does not know about or knows about but does not normally think of buying. Most major new innovations are unsought until the consumer becomes aware of them through advertising. Classic examples of known but unsought products and services are life insurance and blood donations to the Red Cross. By their very nature, unsought products require a lot of advertising, personal selling, and other marketing efforts.

Unsought product
Consumer product that the consumer either does not know about or knows about but does not normally think of buying.

Industrial Products

Industrial products are those purchased for further processing or for use in conducting a business. Thus, the distinction between a consumer product and an industrial product is based on the *purpose* for which the product is bought. If a consumer buys a lawn mower for use around home, the lawn mower is a consumer product. If the same consumer buys the same lawn mower for use in a landscaping business, the lawn mower is an industrial product.

The three groups of industrial products and services include materials and parts, capital items, and supplies and services. *Materials and parts* include raw materials and manufactured materials and parts. Raw materials consist of farm products (wheat, cotton, livestock, fruits, vegetables) and natural products (fish, lumber, crude petroleum, iron ore). Manufactured materials and parts consist of component materials (iron, yarn, cement, wires) and component parts (small motors, tires, castings). Most manufactured materials and parts are sold directly to industrial users. Price and service are the major marketing factors; branding and advertising tend to be less important.

Industrial product
Product bought by individuals and organizations for further processing or for use in conducting a business.

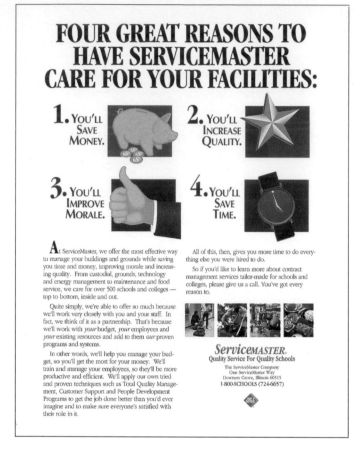

Business services: ServiceMaster supplies business services for a wide range of organizations. This advertisement to schools and colleges offers services ranging from custodial, grounds, technology, and energy management services to maintenance and food services.

Capital items are industrial products that aid in the buyer's production or operations, including installations and accessory equipment. Installations consist of major purchases such as buildings (factories, offices) and fixed equipment (generators, drill presses, large computer systems, elevators). Accessory equipment includes portable factory equipment and tools (hand tools, lift trucks) and office equipment (fax machines, desks). They have a shorter life than installations and simply aid in the production process.

The final group of business products is *supplies and services.* Supplies include operating supplies (lubricants, coal, paper, pencils) and repair and maintenance items (paint, nails, brooms). Supplies are the convenience products of the industrial field because they are usually purchased with a minimum of effort or comparison. Business services include maintenance and repair services (window cleaning, computer repair) and business advisory services (legal, management consulting, advertising). Such services are usually supplied under contract.

Organizations, Persons, Places, and Ideas

In addition to tangible products and services, in recent years marketers have broadened the concept of a product to include other "marketable entities"—organizations, persons, places, and ideas.

Organizations often carry out activities to "sell" the organization itself. *Organization marketing* consists of activities undertaken to create, maintain, or change the attitudes and behavior of target consumers toward an organization. Both profit and nonprofit organizations practice organization marketing. Business firms sponsor public relations or corporate advertising campaigns to polish their images. *Corporate image advertising* is a major tool companies use to market themselves to various publics. For example, Lucent puts out ads with the tag line "We make the things that make communications work." IBM wants to establish itself as the company to turn to for "e-Business Solutions." And Ford Motor Company has "Better Ideas." Similarly, nonprofit organizations, such as churches, colleges, charities, museums, and performing arts groups, market their organizations in order to raise funds and attract members or patrons.

People can also be thought of as products. *Person marketing* consists of activities undertaken to create, maintain, or change attitudes or behavior toward particular people. All kinds of people and organizations practice person marketing. Presidents must be skillful in marketing themselves, their parties, and their platforms to get needed votes and program support. Entertainers and sports figures use marketing to promote their careers and improve their impact and incomes. Professionals such as doctors, lawyers, accountants, and architects market themselves in order to build their reputations and increase business. Business leaders use person marketing as a strategic tool to develop their companies' fortunes as well as their own. Businesses, charities, sports teams, fine arts groups, religious groups, and other organizations also use person marketing. Creating or associating with well-known personalities often helps these organizations achieve their goals better. That's why 12 different companies—including Nike, Buick, American Express, Disney, and Titleist—pay a combined $54 million a year to link themselves with golf superstar Tiger Woods.[3]

Place marketing involves activities undertaken to create, maintain, or change attitudes or behavior toward particular places. Cities, states, regions, and even entire nations compete to attract tourists, new residents, conventions, and company offices and factories. Today, almost every city, state, and country markets its tourist attractions. Texas advertises "It's Like a Whole Other Country," Michigan touts "Great Lakes, Great Times," and New York State shouts "I Love New York!"[4] Stratford, Ontario, in Canada was a little-known town with one big marketing asset—its name and a river called Avon. This became the basis for an annual Shakespeare festival, now the Stratford Festival of Canada, which put Stratford on the tourist map. Most states and nations also operate industrial development offices that try to sell companies on the advantages of locating new plants in them. For example, Ireland is an outstanding place marketer. The Irish Development Agency has attracted over 1,100 companies to locate their plants in Ireland. At the same time, the Irish Tourist Board has built a flourishing tourism business by advertising "over 11,000 places to stay and 14,000 things to do." And the Irish Export Board has created attractive markets for Irish exports.[5]

Ideas can also be marketed. In one sense, all marketing is the marketing of an idea, whether it be the general idea of brushing your teeth or the specific idea that Crest toothpastes "create smiles every day" through effective tartar control and decay prevention. Here, however, we narrow our focus to the marketing of *social ideas,* such as public health campaigns to reduce smoking, alcoholism, drug abuse, and overeating; environmental campaigns to promote wilderness protection, clean air, and conservation; and other campaigns such as family planning, human rights, and racial equality. This area has been called **social marketing,** defined by the Social Marketing Institute as the use of commercial marketing concepts and tools in programs designed to influence individuals' behavior to improve their well-being and that of society.[6] It includes the creation and implementation of programs seeking to increase the acceptability of a social idea, cause, or practice within targeted groups.

The Ad Council of America has developed dozens of social advertising campaigns, including classics such as "Smokey the Bear," "Keep America Beautiful," "Friends Don't Let Friends Drive Drunk," "Say No to Drugs," and "A Mind Is a Terrible Thing to Waste." It now represents 40 causes in issues areas such as improving the quality of life for

Social marketing
The design, implementation, and control of programs seeking to increase the acceptability of a social idea, cause, or practice among a target group.

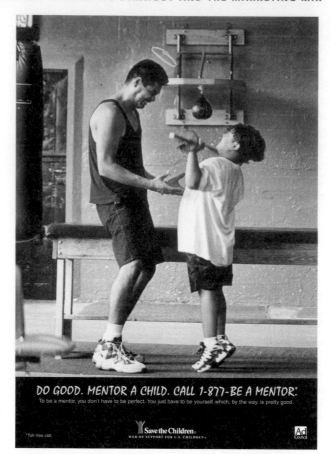

Social marketing: The Ad Council has developed dozens of social marketing campaigns. This one urges adults to mentor a child: "You don't have to be perfect. You just have to be yourself which, by the way, is pretty good."

children, preventive health, education, community well-being, environmental preservation, and strengthening families (see www.adcouncil.org). But social marketing involves much more than just advertising. Many public marketing campaigns fail because they assign advertising the primary role and fail to develop and use all the marketing mix tools. The Social Marketing Institute encourages the use of a broad range of marketing tools. "Social marketing goes well beyond the promotional '*P*' of the marketing mix to include every other element to achieve its social change objectives," says the SMI's executive director.[7]

Individual Product Decisions

Figure 8-2 shows the important decisions in the development and marketing of individual products and services. We will focus on decisions about *product attributes, branding, packaging, labeling,* and *product support services.*

Figure 8-2
Individual product decisions

Product attributes → Branding → Packaging → Labeling → Product support services

Product Attributes

Developing a product or service involves defining the benefits that it will offer. These benefits are communicated and delivered by product attributes such as *quality, features,* and *style and design.*

Product Quality   Quality is one of the marketer's major positioning tools. **Product quality** has two dimensions—level and consistency. In developing a product, the marketer must first choose a *quality level* that will support the product's position in the target market. Here, product quality means *performance quality*—the ability of a product to perform its functions. For example, a Rolls-Royce provides higher performance quality than a Chevrolet: It has a smoother ride, handles better, and lasts longer. Companies rarely try to offer the highest possible performance quality level—few customers want or can afford the high levels of quality offered in products such as a Rolls-Royce automobile, a Sub Zero refrigerator, or a Rolex watch. Instead, companies choose a quality level that matches target market needs and the quality levels of competing products.

Beyond quality level, high quality also can mean high levels of quality *consistency.* Here, product quality means *conformance quality*—freedom from defects and *consistency* in delivering a targeted level of performance. All companies should strive for high levels of conformance quality. In this sense, a Chevrolet can have just as much quality as a Rolls-Royce. Although a Chevy doesn't perform as well as a Rolls, it can as consistently deliver the quality that customers pay for and expect.

During the past two decades, a renewed emphasis on quality has spawned a global quality movement. Most firms implemented "total quality management" (TQM) programs, efforts to improve product and process quality constantly in every phase of their operations. Recently, however, the total quality management movement has drawn criticism. Too many companies viewed TQM as a magic cure-all and created token total quality programs that applied quality principles only superficially. Today, companies are taking a "return on quality" approach, viewing quality as an investment and holding quality efforts accountable for bottom-line results.[8]

Beyond simply reducing product defects, the ultimate goal of total quality is to improve customer satisfaction and value. For example, when Motorola first began its total quality program in the early 1980s, its goal was to drastically reduce manufacturing defects. Later, however, Motorola's quality concept evolved into one of *customer-defined quality* and *total customer satisfaction.* "Quality," noted Motorola's vice president of quality, "has to do something for the customer. . . . Our definition of a defect is 'if the customer doesn't like it, it's a defect.'" Similarly, Siemans defines quality this way: "Quality is when our customers come back and our products don't."[9] As more and more companies have moved toward such customer-driven definitions of quality, their TQM programs are evolving into customer satisfaction and customer retention programs.

Thus, many companies today have turned customer-driven quality into a potent strategic weapon. They create customer satisfaction and value by consistently and profitably meeting customers' needs and preferences for quality. In fact, quality has now become a competitive necessity—in the twenty-first century, only companies with the best quality will thrive.

Product Features   A product can be offered with varying features. A stripped-down model, one without any extras, is the starting point. The company can create higher-level models by adding more features. Features are a competitive tool for differentiating the company's product from competitors' products. Being the first producer to introduce a needed and valued new feature is one of the most effective ways to compete.

How can a company identify new features and decide which ones to add to its product? The company should periodically survey buyers who have used the product and ask these questions: How do you like the product? Which specific features of the product do you like

Product quality
The ability of a product to perform its functions; it includes the product's overall durability, reliability, precision, ease of operation and repair, and other valued attributes.

most? Which features could we add to improve the product? The answers provide the company with a rich list of feature ideas. The company can then assess each feature's *value* to customers versus its *cost* to the company. Features that customers value little in relation to costs should be dropped; those that customers value highly in relation to costs should be added.

Product Style and Design Another way to add customer value is through distinctive *product style and design.* Some companies have reputations for outstanding style and design, such as Black & Decker in cordless appliances and tools, Steelcase in office furniture and systems, Bose in audio equipment, and Ciba Corning in medical equipment. Design can be one of the most powerful competitive weapons in a company's marketing arsenal.

Design is a larger concept than style. *Style* simply describes the appearance of a product. Styles can be eye-catching or yawn producing. A sensational style may grab attention and produce pleasing aesthetics, but it does not necessarily make the product *perform* better. Unlike style, *design* is more than skin deep—it goes to the very heart of a product. Good design contributes to a product's usefulness as well as to its looks.

Good style and design can attract attention, improve product performance, cut production costs, and give the product a strong competitive advantage in the target market. For example, consider Apple's iMac personal computer:

> Who said that computers have to be beige and boxy? Apple's iMac is anything but. The iMac—which features a sleek, egg-shaped monitor and hard drive, all in one unit, in a futuristic translucent turquoise casing—redefined the look and feel of the personal computer. There's no clunky tower or desktop hard drive to clutter up your office area. There's also no floppy drive—with more and more software being distributed via CDs or the Internet, Apple thinks the floppy is on the verge of extinction. Featuring one-button Internet access, this is a machine designed specifically for cruising the Internet (that's what the "i" in "iMac" stands for). The dramatic iMac won raves for design and lured buyers in droves. Only one month after the iMac hit the stores, it was the number-two best-selling computer. Within a year, it had sold more than a million units, marking Apple's reemergence as a legitimate contender in the personal computer industry.[10]

Brand
A name, term, sign, symbol, design, or combination of these, intended to identify the goods or services of one seller or group of sellers and to differentiate them from those of competitors.

Branding

Perhaps the most distinctive skill of professional marketers is their ability to create, maintain, protect, and enhance brands of their products and services. A **brand** is a name, term,

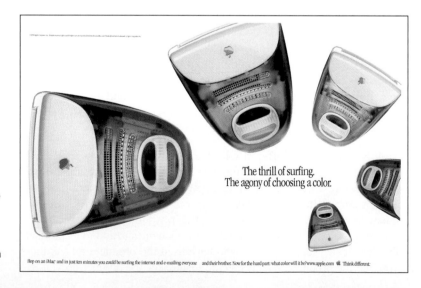

The dramatic iMac— with its sleek, egg-shaped, single-unit monitor and hard drive in a futuristic translucent casing—helped reestablish Apple as a legitimate contender in the PC industry.

The thrill of surfing.
The agony of choosing a color.

sign, symbol, or design, or a combination of these, that identifies the maker or seller of a product or service. Consumers view a brand as an important part of a product, and branding can add value to a product. For example, most consumers would perceive a bottle of White Linen perfume as a high-quality, expensive product. But the same perfume in an unmarked bottle would likely be viewed as lower in quality, even if the fragrance were identical.

Branding has become so strong that today hardly anything goes unbranded. Salt is packaged in branded containers, common nuts and bolts are packaged with a distributor's label, and automobile parts—spark plugs, tires, filters—bear brand names that differ from those of the automakers. Even fruits, vegetables, and poultry are branded—Sunkist oranges, Dole pineapples, Chiquita bananas, Fresh Express salad greens, and Perdue chickens.

Branding helps buyers in many ways. Brand names help consumers identify products that might benefit them. Brands also tell the buyer something about product quality. Buyers who always buy the same brand know that they will get the same features, benefits, and quality each time they buy. Branding also gives the seller several advantages. The brand name becomes the basis on which a whole story can be built about a product's special qualities. The seller's brand name and trademark provide legal protection for unique product features that otherwise might be copied by competitors. And branding helps the seller to segment markets. For example, General Mills can offer Cheerios, Wheaties, Total, Kix, Lucky Charms, Trix, and many other cereal brands, not just one general product for all consumers.

Brand Equity Brands vary in the amount of power and value they have in the marketplace. A powerful brand has high **brand equity.** Brands have higher brand equity to the extent that they have higher brand loyalty, name awareness, perceived quality, strong brand associations, and other assets such as patents, trademarks, and channel relationships.

A brand with strong brand equity is a very valuable asset. Measuring the actual equity of a brand name is difficult. However, according to one estimate, the brand equity of Coca-Cola is $69 billion, Microsoft is $65 billion, and IBM is $53 billion. Other brands rating among the world's most valuable include General Electric, Nokia, Intel, Disney, Ford, McDonald's, and AT&T.[11] "Brand equity has emerged over the past few years as a key strategic asset," observes a brand consultant. "CEOs in many industries now see their brands as a source of control and a way to build stronger relationships with customers."[12]

Brand equity
The value of a brand, based on the extent to which it has high brand loyalty, name awareness, perceived quality, strong brand associations, and other assets such as patents, trademarks, and channel relationships.

Branding has become so strong that hardly anything goes unbranded, even fruits and vegetables.

A strong brand is a valuable asset—the brand equity of Coca-Cola is estimated at $69 billion. How many familiar brands and brand symbols can you find in this picture?

Although we normally think of brand equity as something accruing to products, service companies also prize it. As Wall Street competition intensifies, financial service companies are spending millions on their brand names in order to attract investors. Just as Coke wants you to reach for its soda when you're thirsty, Merrill Lynch and Charles Schwab want you to call them when you need financial know-how. Hence, brand-building advertising by financial services companies has soared in recent years.

High brand equity provides a company with many competitive advantages. A powerful brand enjoys a high level of consumer brand awareness and loyalty. Because consumers expect stores to carry the brand, the company has more leverage in bargaining with resellers. Because the brand name carries high credibility, the company can more easily launch line and brand extensions, as when Coca-Cola leveraged its well-known brand to introduce Diet Coke or when Procter & Gamble introduced Ivory dishwashing detergent. Above all, a powerful brand offers the company some defense against fierce price competition.

Some analysts see brands as *the* major enduring asset of a company, outlasting the company's specific products and facilities. Yet every powerful brand really represents a set of loyal customers. Therefore, the fundamental asset underlying brand equity is *customer equity.* This suggests that the proper focus of marketing planning is that of extending *loyal customer lifetime value,* with brand management serving as a major marketing tool.[13]

Branding poses challenging decisions to the marketer. Figure 8-3 shows the key branding decisions.

Brand Name Selection   A good name can add greatly to a product's success. However, finding the best brand name is a difficult task. It begins with a careful review of the product and its benefits, the target market, and proposed marketing strategies.

Desirable qualities for a brand name include the following: (1) It should suggest something about the product's benefits and qualities. Examples: DieHard, Easy-Off, Craftsman, Sunkist, Snuggles, Merrie Maids, and OFF! bug spray. (2) It should be easy to pronounce,

Figure 8-3
Major branding decisions

recognize, and remember. Short names help. Examples: Tide, Aim, Puffs. But longer ones are sometimes effective. Examples: "Love My Carpet" carpet cleaner, "I Can't Believe It's Not Butter" margarine, Better Business Bureau. (3) The brand name should be distinctive. Examples: Taurus, Kodak, Exxon, Oracle. (4) It should be extendable: Amazon.com began as an online bookseller but chose a name that would allow expansion into other categories. (5) The name should translate easily into foreign languages. Before spending $100 million to change its name to Exxon, Standard Oil of New Jersey tested several names in 54 languages in more than 150 foreign markets. It found that the name Enco referred to a stalled engine when pronounced in Japanese. (6) It should be capable of registration and legal protection. A brand name cannot be registered if it infringes on existing brand names.

Once chosen, the brand name must be protected. Many firms try to build a brand name that will eventually become identified with the product category. Brand names such as Kleenex, Levi's, Jell-O, Scotch Tape, Formica, Zip-loc, and Fiberglas have succeeded in this way. However, their very success may threaten the company's rights to the name. Many originally protected brand names—such as cellophane, aspirin, nylon, kerosene, linoleum, yo-yo, trampoline, escalator, thermos, and shredded wheat—are now generic names that any seller can use.

Brand Sponsor A manufacturer has four sponsorship options. The product may be launched as a *manufacturer's brand* (or national brand), as when Kellogg and IBM sell their output under their own manufacturer's brand names. Or the manufacturer may sell to resellers who give it a *private brand* (also called a *store brand* or *distributor brand*). Although most manufacturers create their own brand names, others market *licensed brands*. Finally, two companies can join forces and *co-brand* a product.

MANUFACTURERS' BRANDS VERSUS PRIVATE BRANDS. Manufacturers' brands have long dominated the retail scene. In recent times, however, an increasing number of retailers and wholesalers have created their own **private brands** (or *store brands*). For example, Sears has created several names—DieHard batteries, Craftsman tools, Kenmore appliances, Weatherbeater paints. Wal-Mart offers Sam's Choice beverages and food products, Spring Valley nutritional products, Ol' Roy dog food (named for Sam Walton's Irish setter), and White Cloud brand toilet tissue, diapers, detergent, and fabric softener to compete against major national brands. Private brands can be hard to establish and costly to stock and promote. However, they also yield higher profit margins for the reseller, and they give resellers exclusive products that cannot be bought from competitors, resulting in greater store traffic and loyalty.

In the so-called *battle of the brands* between manufacturers' and private brands, retailers have many advantages. They control what products they stock, where they go on the shelf, and which ones they will feature in local circulars. Retailers price their store brands lower than comparable manufacturers' brands, thereby appealing to budget-conscious shoppers, especially in difficult economic times. And most shoppers believe that store brands are often made by one of the larger manufacturers anyway. Most retailers also charge manufacturers **slotting fees**—payments demanded by retailers before they will accept new products and find "slots" for them on the shelves. Slotting fees have recently received much scrutiny from the Federal Trade Commission, which worries that they might dampen competition by restricting retail shelf access for smaller manufacturers who can't afford the fees.[14]

Private brand (or store brand)
A brand created and owned by a reseller of a product or service.

Slotting fees
Payments demanded by retailers before they will accept new products and place them on shelves.

As store brands improve in quality and as consumers gain confidence in their store chains, store brands are posing a strong challenge to manufacturers' brands. Consider the case of Loblaws, the Canadian supermarket chain. Its President's Choice Decadent Chocolate Chip Cookies brand is now the leading cookie brand in Canada. Loblaws' private label President's Choice cola racks up 50 percent of Loblaws' canned cola sales. Based on this success, the private label powerhouse has expanded into a wide range of food categories. For example, it now offers more than 2,500 items under the President's Choice label, ranging from frozen desserts to paper, prepared foods, and boxed meats. The brand has become so popular that Loblaws now licenses it to retailers across the United States and eight other countries where Loblaws has no stores of its own. President's Choice Decadent Chocolate Chip Cookies are now sold by Jewel Food Stores in Chicago, where they are the number-one seller, beating out even Nabisco's Chips Ahoy brand. The company also offers a Web site where consumers can purchase its branded products directly.[15]

In U.S. supermarkets, taken as a single brand, private-label products are the number-one, -two, or -three brand in over 40 percent of all grocery product categories. In all, they capture more than a 20 percent share of U.S. supermarket sales. Private labels are even more prominent in Europe, accounting for as much as 36 percent of supermarket sales in Britain and 24 percent in France. French retail giant Carrefour sells more than 3,000 in-house brands, ranging from cooking oil to car batteries. To fend off private brands, leading brand marketers will have to invest in R&D to bring out new brands, new features, and continuous quality improvements. They must design strong advertising programs to maintain high awareness and preference. They must find ways to "partner" with major distributors in a search for distribution economies and improved joint performance.[16]

LICENSING. Most manufacturers take years and spend millions to create their own brand names. However, some companies license names or symbols previously created by other manufacturers, names of well-known celebrities, characters from popular movies and books—for a fee, any of these can provide an instant and proven brand name. Apparel and accessories sellers pay large royalties to adorn their products—from blouses to ties, and linens to luggage—with the names or initials of well-known fashion innovators such as Calvin Klein,

Store brands: Loblaws' President's Choice brand has become so popular that the company now licenses it to retailers across the United States and eight other countries where Loblaws has no stores of its own.

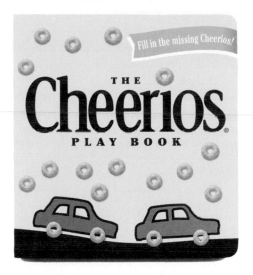

Brand licensing: Snack-brand children's books have exploded onto the scene in recent years.

Tommy Hilfiger, Gucci, or Armani. Sellers of children's products attach an almost endless list of character names to clothing, toys, school supplies, linens, dolls, lunch boxes, cereals, and other items. Licensed character names range from classics such as *Sesame Street,* Disney, Peanuts, Winnie the Pooh, the Muppets, Scooby Doo, and Dr. Seuss characters to the more recent Teletubbies, Pokeman, Powerpuff Girls, Rugrats, Blue's Clues, and Harry Potter characters. Almost half of all retail toy sales come from products based on television shows and movies such as *The Rugrats, Scooby Doo, The Lion King, Batman, Star Trek, Star Wars, Men in Black,* or *Jurassic Park.*[17]

There's even value in everyday food brand names:

> As the host of the "Bring Your Own Baby" reading group at the Enchanted Forest bookstore in Dallas, Susan Minshall meets plenty of parents anxious to start their toddlers reading—and to make them sit still. So she recommends the "Kellogg's Froot Loops! Counting Fun Book," which invites toddlers to insert the sugary cereal in cut-out holes in its cardboard pages. Parents and teachers can choose from a sudden proliferation of books starring brand-name candies and snacks like Froot Loops, Cheerios, M&M's, Pepperidge Farm Goldfish, Reese's Pieces, Skittles, Hershey's chocolates, Sun-Maid raisins, and Oreo cookies. Introduced six years ago by a Massachusetts nursery school teacher, snack-brand children's books have exploded onto the scene in the last two years as more publishers have jumped into the field. Millions of copies have been sold, with a full shelf of new titles on the way. Both the publishers and the food companies benefit from such licensing agreements. The publishers get instant brand familiarity for their books. In turn, the food companies receive a licensing fee and gai---n a novel opportunity to market to toddlers. "It is a great way to get the Froot Loops brand equity into a different place, where normally you don't get exposure—taking it from the cereal aisle and into another area like learning," said Meghan Parkhurst, a spokeswoman for Kellogg, adding that the company also provides Froot Loops book covers to schools.[18]

Name and character licensing has grown rapidly in recent years. Annual retail sales of licensed products in the United States and Canada have grown from only $4 billion in 1977 to $55 billion in 1987 and more than $71 billion today. The fastest-growing licensing category is corporate brand licensing, as more and more for-profit and nonprofit organizations are licensing their names to generate additional revenues and brand recognition (see Marketing at Work 8-2).

Marketing at Work 8.2

From Harley-Davidson Armchairs to Coca-Cola Fishing Lures: The Rise of Corporate Branding

When BMW bought the Rolls-Royce name—nothing else, just the *name*—for $60 million, it confirmed what savvy investors have always known: A strong brand name is one of the most valuable assets a company has. Now companies are realizing that they shouldn't confine such assets only to their showrooms, stationery, business cards, or the company's core product. Instead, companies from the Fortune 500 to the not-for-profit sector, are licensing their names to generate additional brand recognition and revenues. That's why we're suddenly seeing products such as Pillsbury doughboy potholders, Coca-Cola Picnic Barbie, Crayola house paints, Jeep bicycles, Royal Doulton perfume, and Harley-Davidson armchairs and baby clothes.

Last year, retail sales of all licensed products totaled $71 billion in the United States and Canada, more than $132 billion worldwide. Corporate brand licensing, the fastest-growing category, claimed 22 percent of that total, the same amount earned from entertainment property licensing. According to a licensing industry executive, at a recent international licensing show, "The showroom floor [read] like a Fortune 500 directory, packed with such high-profile corporate brands as Coca-Cola, Jeep, Chrysler, Anheuser-Busch, Pillsbury, Texaco, Popsicle, Harley-Davidson, Schwinn, McDonald's, Taco Bell, and many more."

When it comes to corporate brand licensing, few companies can equal Coca-Cola, whose extraordinary success has inspired hundreds of companies to follow suit. Yet few people know that Coca-Cola's entry into licensing was purely defensive. In the early 1980s, lawyers advised the company that if it didn't enter the Coca-Cola T-shirt market, others legally could. Coca-Cola responded by setting up a licensing program, which started modestly but now consists of a large department overseeing some 320 licensees in 57 countries producing more than 10,000 products, ranging from baby clothes and boxer shorts to earrings, a Coca-Cola Barbie Doll, and even a fishing lure shaped like a tiny Coke can. Last year, licensees sold more than $1 billion worth of licensed Coca-Cola products.

Although most companies have long sold promotional merchandise bearing their names and logos to dealers and distributors, full-scale retail merchandising is a real shift. Companies are making this shift both to capitalize on brand awareness in current markets and to extend their brands into new markets. For example, Caterpillar and John Deere, both companies with narrow markets, are now licensing a wide range of products aimed at generating additional sales among those already hooked on their brands. Caterpillar has set up licensing agreements with apparel and footwear companies to make Caterpillar work clothes and work boots. The "Cat" work boot is now Wolverine World Wide's (of Hush Puppies fame) hottest product. Visitors to the online John Deere Mall (mall.deere.com) will discover an array of licensed "Deere Gear" that includes everything from logo hats, shirts, jackets, mugs, watches, and license plate frames to John Deere versions of Canon calculators, Victorinox penknives, Ellipse sunglasses, Mini Mag-Lite flashlights, and hand-rubbed rosewood pens.

Sometimes companies get into licensing as a way to extend the brand to a new target market. Although a Harley-Davidson armchair seems like an unlikely product, it's the motorcycle company's way of reaching out to women, who make up only 9 percent of the company's market. Harley also licenses toys, including a Barbie dressed in a "very feminine outfit" to appeal to future generations of Harley purchasers. The ultimate goal is to sell more bikes to buyers who are not part of the core market. Similarly, Caterpillar is teaming up with Mattel to create a line of toys based on its construction equipment.

At the same time that corporate brand licensing lets companies reap some of the value they've built up in their brands, it also provides an additional tool for building even more brand value. For example, Unilever has invested heavily in advertising to create positioning and personality for its Snuggle fabric softener brand and for the cute little Snuggle Bear that appears on the label. Now licensing the Snuggle Bear for use on other carefully selected products, says a Unilever brand manager, "will be another way to . . . help Snuggle leave lasting impressions long after our thirty-second commercial is over."

What's in corporate licensing for the licensees, the manufacturers who pay large sums for the right to use corporate brand names or trademarks on their products? Compared to celebrity and entertainment names, corporate brands are much less risky. For example, what happens to a product brandishing a sports celebrity's name when that celebrity is busted for drugs? Or what can a manufacturer do with all its Godzilla backpacks after the *Godzilla* movie flops (as it did)? Corporate brands are much safer bets. Many have been around for decades and have a proven, surprisingly strong appeal for customers. There are powerful forces behind the impulse to buy a Coke beach towel, a Good Humor die-cast truck, Harley-Davidson boots, or Doulton perfume. Says Seth Siegel, cochairman of the Beanstalk Group, which manages licensing for Coca-Cola and Harley-Davidson, "We live in a . . . society [where] people still love to surround themselves with icons that move them."

Sources: Quotes and other information from Constance L. Hays, "Licensing of Names Adds to Image and Profit," *New York Times*, June 12, 1998, p. D1; Laura Petrecca, "'Corporate Brands' Put Licensing in the Spotlight," *Advertising Age*, June 14, 1999, p. 1; "Licensing Industry Sets Trends for the Future at LICENSING 99 International," International Licensing Industry Merchandisers' Association press release, accessed online at www.licensing.org, June 8, 1999; and Bob Vavra, "The Game of the Name," *Supermarket Business*, March 15, 2001, pp. 45-46, http://merchandise.cat.com/caterpillar, December 2001; and http://mall.deere.com, December 2001.

Even the Vatican engages in licensing: Heavenly images from its art collection, architecture, frescoes, and manuscripts are now imprinted on such earthly objects as T-shirts, ties, glassware, candles, and ornaments.[19]

Many companies have mastered the art of peddling their established brands and characters. For example, through savvy marketing, Warner Brothers has turned Bugs Bunny, Daffy Duck, Foghorn Leghorn, and its more than 100 other *Looney Tunes* characters into the world's favorite cartoon brand. The *Looney Tunes* license, arguably the most sought-after nonsports license in the industry, generates $4 billion in annual retail sales by more than 225 licensees. Warner Brothers has yet to tap the full potential of many of its secondary characters. The Tazmanian Devil, for example, initially appeared in only five cartoons. But through cross-licensing agreements with organizations such as Harley-Davidson and the NFL, Taz has become something of a pop icon. Warner Brothers sees similar potential for Michigan Frog or Speedy Gonzales for the Hispanic market. The company recently inked an agreement with Bravo Foods to offer Looney Tunes milk in five flavors: Vanilla, featuring Bugs Bunny; Strawberry, featuring Bugs Bunny and Lola Bunny; Banana, featuring Tweety; Chocolate, featuring the Tasmanian Devil; and Orange Creme, featuring Wylie Coyote and the Roadrunner.[20]

CO-BRANDING. Although companies have been **co-branding** products for many years, there has been a recent resurgence in co-branded products. Co-branding occurs when two established brand names of different companies are used on the same product. For example, Nabisco joined with Pillsbury to create Pillsbury Oreo Bars baking mix and with Kraft Foods' Post cereal division to create Oreo O's cereal. Kellogg joined forces with ConAgra to co-brand Healthy Choice from Kellogg's cereals. Ford and Eddie Bauer co-branded a sport utility vehicle—the Ford Explorer, Eddie Bauer edition. General Electric worked with Culligan to develop its Water by Culligan Profile Performance refrigerator with a built-in Culligan water filtration system. Mattel teamed with Coca-Cola to market Soda Fountain Sweetheart Barbie. In most co-branding situations, one company licenses another company's well-known brand to use in combination with its own.

Co-branding
The practice of using the established brand names of two different companies on the same product.

Co-branding offers many advantages. Because each brand dominates in a different category, the combined brands create broader consumer appeal and greater brand equity. Co-branding also allows a company to expand its existing brand into a category it might otherwise have difficulty entering alone. For example, by licensing its Healthy Choice brand to Kellogg, ConAgra entered the breakfast segment with a solid product. In return, Kellogg could leverage the broad awareness of the Healthy Choice name in the cereal category.

Co-branding also has limitations. Such relationships usually involve complex legal contracts and licenses. Co-branding partners must carefully coordinate their advertising, sales promotion, and other marketing efforts. Finally, when co-branding, each partner must trust the other will take good care of its brand. As one Nabisco manager puts it, "Giving away your brand is a lot like giving away your child—you want to make sure everything is perfect."[21]

PRODUCT CATEGORY

	Existing	New
Existing	Line extension	Brand extension
New	Multibrands	New brands

BRAND NAME

Figure 8-4
Four brand strategies

Brand Strategy A company has four choices when it comes to brand strategy (see Figure 8-4). It can introduce *line extensions* (existing brand names extended to new forms, sizes, and flavors of an existing product category), *brand extensions* (existing brand names extended to new product categories), *multibrands* (new brand names introduced in the same product category), or *new brands* (new brand names in new product categories).

Line extension
Using a successful brand name to introduce additional items in a given product category under the same brand name, such as new flavors, forms, colors, added ingredients, or package sizes.

LINE EXTENSIONS. **Line extensions** occur when a company introduces additional items in a given product category under the same brand name, such as new flavors, forms, colors, ingredients, or package sizes. Thus, Dannon introduced several line extensions, including seven new yogurt flavors, a fat-free yogurt, and a large, economy-size yogurt. The vast majority of all new-product activity consists of line extensions.

A company might introduce line extensions as a low-cost, low-risk way to introduce new products in order to meet consumer desires for variety, to utilize excess capacity, or simply to command more shelf space from resellers. However, line extensions involve some risks. An overextended brand name might lose its specific meaning or heavily extended brands can cause consumer confusion or frustration. For example, a consumer buying cereal at the local supermarket will be confronted by more than 150 brands—up to 30 different brands, flavors, and sizes of oatmeal alone. By itself, Quaker offers its original Quaker Oats, several flavors of Quaker instant oatmeal, and several dry cereals such as Oatmeal Squares, Toasted Oatmeal, and Toasted Oatmeal–Honey Nut. Another risk is that sales of an extension may come at the expense of other items in the line. A line extension works best when it takes sales away from competing brands, not when it "cannibalizes" the company's other items.

Line extensions: Heavily extended brands can also cause consumer confusion or frustration. A consumer buying cereal at the local supermarket will be confronted by up to 30 different brands, flavors, and sizes of oatmeal alone.

BRAND EXTENSIONS. A **brand extension** involves the use of a successful brand name to launch new or modified products in a new category. Mattel has extended its incredibly popular and enduring Barbie Doll brand into new categories ranging from Barbie home furnishings, Barbie cosmetics, and Barbie electronics to Barbie books, Barbie sporting goods, and even a Barbie band—Beyond Pink. Honda uses its company name to cover different products such as its automobiles, motorcycles, snowblowers, lawn mowers, marine engines, and snowmobiles. This allows Honda to advertise that it can fit "six Hondas in a two-car garage." Swiss Army brand sunglasses, Disney Cruise Lines, Cosmopolitan low-fat dairy products, Century 21 Home Improvements, and Brinks home security systems—all are brand extensions.

A brand extension gives a new product instant recognition and faster acceptance. It also saves the high advertising costs usually required to build a new brand name. At the same time, a brand extension strategy involves some risk. Brand extensions such as Bic pantyhose, Heinz pet food, Life Savers gum, and Clorox laundry detergent met early deaths. The extension may confuse the image of the main brand. For example, when clothing retailer Gap saw competitors targeting its value-conscious customers with Gap-like fashions at lower prices, it began testing Gap Warehouse, which sold merchandise at a cut below Gap quality and price. However, the connection confused customers and eroded Gap image. As a result, the company renamed the stores Old Navy Clothing Company, a brand that has become enormously successful.[22]

If a brand extension fails, it may harm consumer attitudes toward the other products carrying the same brand name. Further, a brand name may not be appropriate to a particular new product, even if it is well made and satisfying—would you consider buying Texaco milk or Alpo chili? A brand name may lose its special positioning in the consumer's mind through overuse. Companies that are tempted to transfer a brand name must research how well the brand's associations fit the new product.[23]

MULTIBRANDS. Companies often introduce additional brands in the same category. Thus, P&G markets many different brands in each of its product categories. *Multibranding* offers a way to establish different features and appeal to different buying motives. It also allows a company to lock up more reseller shelf space. Or the company may want to protect its major brand by setting up *flanker* or *fighter brands*. Seiko uses different brand names for its higher-priced watches (Seiko Lasalle) and lower-priced watches (Pulsar) to protect the flanks of its mainstream Seiko brand. Finally, companies may develop separate brand names for different regions or countries, perhaps to suit different cultures or languages. Procter & Gamble dominates the U.S. laundry detergent market with Tide, which in all its forms captures more than a 40 percent market share. Outside North America, however, P&G leads the detergent category with its Ariel brand, now Europe's number-two packaged-goods brand behind Coca-Cola. In the United States, P&G targets Ariel to Hispanic markets.

A major drawback of multibranding is that each brand might obtain only a small market share, and none may be very profitable. The company may end up spreading its resources over many brands instead of building a few brands to a highly profitable level. These companies should reduce the number of brands they sell in a given category and set up tighter screening procedures for new brands.

NEW BRANDS. A company may create a new brand name when it enters a new product category for which none of the company's current brand names is appropriate. For example, Japan's Matsushita uses separate names for its different families of products: Technics, Panasonic, National, and Quasar. Or, a company might believe that the power of its existing brand name is waning and a new brand name is needed. The company may obtain new brands in new categories through acquisitions. S.C. Johnson & Son, marketer of Pledge furniture polish, Glade air freshener, Raid insect spray, Edge shaving gel, and many other

---

Brand extension
Using a successful brand name to launch a new or modified product in a new category.

well-known brands, added several new powerhouse brands through its acquisition of Drackett Company, including Windex, Drano, and Vanish toilet bowl cleaner.

As with multibranding, offering too many new brands can result in a company spreading its resources too thin. And in some industries, such as consumer packaged goods, consumers and retailers have become concerned that there are already too many brands, with too few differences between them. Thus, Procter & Gamble, Frito-Lay, and other large consumer-product marketers are now pursuing *megabrand* strategies—weeding out weaker brands and focusing their marketing dollars only on brands that can achieve the number-one or -two market share positions in their categories.

Linking the Concepts

Building and maintaining strong brands is at the heart of successful marketing. Stop and think about all the familiar brands you encounter daily.

◆ List as many specific examples as you can find of each of the following: (1) brand licensing, (2) co-branding, (3) line extensions, and (4) brand extensions. Can you find a single brand that has done all of these?

◆ Pick and describe a familiar brand that has been widely extended. What are the benefits and dangers for this specific brand? Can you find some inappropriate brand extensions?

Packaging

Packaging
The activities of designing and producing the container or wrapper for a product.

Packaging involves designing and producing the container or wrapper for a product. The package may include the product's primary container (the tube holding Colgate Total toothpaste); a secondary package that is thrown away when the product is about to be used (the cardboard box containing the tube of Colgate); and the shipping package necessary to store, identify, and ship the product (a corrugated box carrying six dozen tubes of Colgate). Labeling, printed information appearing on or with the package, is also part of packaging.

Traditionally, the primary function of the package was to contain and protect the product. In recent times, however, numerous factors have made packaging an important marketing tool. Increased competition and clutter on retail store shelves means that packages must now perform many sales tasks—from attracting attention, to describing the product, to making the sale. Companies are realizing the power of good packaging to create instant consumer recognition of the company or brand. For example, in an average supermarket, which stocks 15,000 to 17,000 items, the typical shopper passes by some 300 items per minute, and 53 percent of all purchases are made on impulse. In this highly competitive environment, the package may be the seller's last chance to influence buyers. It becomes a "five-second commercial." The Campbell Soup Company estimates that the average shopper sees its familiar red-and-white can 76 times a year, creating the equivalent of $26 million worth of advertising. The package can also reinforce the product's positioning. Coca-Cola's familiar contour bottle speaks volumes about the product inside. "Even in a shadow, people know it's a Coke," observes a packaging expert. "It's a beautiful definition of how a package can influence the way a consumer perceives a product. People taste Coke differently from a contour bottle versus a generic package."[24]

Innovative packaging can give a company an advantage over competitors. Liquid Tide quickly attained a 10 percent share of the heavy-duty detergent market, partly because of the popularity of its container's innovative drip-proof spout and cap. In contrast, poorly designed packages can cause headaches for consumers and lost sales for the company (see Marketing at Work 8-3). For example, a few years ago, Planters Lifesavers Company

Marketing at Work 8-3
Those Frustrating, Not-So-Easy-to-Open Packages

Some things, it seems, will never change. This classic letter from an angry consumer to Robert D. Stuart, then chairman of Quaker Oats, beautifully expresses the utter frustration all of us have experienced in dealing with so-called easy-opening packages.

Dear Mr. Stuart:

I am an 86-year-old widow in fairly good health. (You may think of this as advanced age, but for me that description pertains to the years ahead. Nevertheless, if you decide to reply to this letter I wouldn't dawdle, actuarial tables being what they are.)

As I said, my health is fairly good. Feeble and elderly, as one understands these terms, I am not. My two Doberman Pinschers and I take a brisk 3-mile walk every day. They are two strong and energetic animals and it takes a bit of doing to keep "brisk" closer to a stroll than a mad dash. But I manage because as yet I don't lack the strength. You will shortly see why this fact is relevant.

I am writing to call your attention to the cruel, deceptive, and utterly [false] copy on your Aunt Jemima buttermilk complete pancake and waffle mix. The words on your package read, "to open —press here and pull back."

Mr. Stuart, though I push and press and groan and strive and writhe and curse and sweat and jab and push, poke and ram . . . whew!—I have never once been able to do what the package instructs—to "press here and pull back" the [blankety-blank]. It can't be done! Talk about failing strength! Have you ever tried and succeeded?

My late husband was a gun collector who among other lethal weapons kept a Thompson

machine gun in a locked cabinet. It was a good thing that the cabinet was locked. Oh, the number of times I was tempted to give your package a few short bursts.

That lock and a sense of ladylike delicacy kept me from pursuing that vengeful fantasy. Instead, I keep a small cleaver in my pantry for those occasions when I need to open a package of your delicious Aunt Jemima pancakes.

For many years that whacking away with my cleaver served a dual purpose. Not only to open the [blankety-blank] package but also to vent my fury at your sadists who willfully and maliciously did design that torture apparatus that passes for a package.

Sometimes just for the [blank] of it I let myself get carried away. I don't stop after I've lopped off the top. I whack away until the package is utterly destroyed in an outburst of rage, frustration, and vindictiveness. I wind up with a floorful of your delicious Aunt Jemima pancake mix. But that's a small price to

pay for blessed release. (Anyway, the Pinschers lap up the mess.)

So many ingenious, considerate (even compassionate) innovations in package closures have been designed since Aunt Jemima first donned her red bandana. Wouldn't you consider the introduction of a more humane package to replace the example of marketing malevolence to which you resolutely cling? Don't you care, Mr. Stuart?

I'm really writing this to be helpful and in that spirit I am sending a copy to Mr. Tucker, president of Container Corp. I'm sure their clever young designers could be of immeasurable help to you in this matter. At least I feel it's worth a try.

Really, Mr. Stuart, I hope you will not regard me as just another cranky old biddy. I am The Public, the source of your fortunes.

Ms. Roberta Pavloff
Malvern, Pa.

Source: This letter was reprinted in "Some Designs Should Just Be Torn Asunder," *Advertising Age,* January 17, 1983, p. M54.

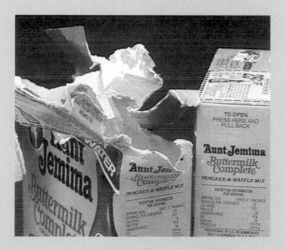

An easy-to-open package?

attempted to use innovative packaging to create an association between fresh-roasted peanuts and fresh-roasted coffee. It packaged its Fresh Roast Salted Peanuts in vacuum-packed "Brik-Pacs," similar to those used for ground coffee. Unfortunately, the coffeelike packaging worked too well: Consumers mistook the peanuts for a new brand of flavored coffee and ran them through supermarket coffee-grinding machines, creating a gooey mess, disappointed customers, and lots of irate store managers.[25]

Developing a good package for a new product requires making many decisions. First, the company must establish the *packaging concept,* which states what the package should *be* or *do* for the product. Should it mainly offer product protection, introduce a new dispensing method, suggest certain qualities about the product, or do something else? Decisions then must be made on specific elements of the package, such as size, shape, materials, color, text, and brand mark. These elements must work together to support the product's position and marketing strategy. The package must be consistent with the product's advertising, pricing, and distribution.

In recent years, product safety has also become a major packaging concern. We have all learned to deal with hard-to-open "childproof" packages. And after the rash of product tampering scares during the 1980s, most drug producers and food makers are now putting their products in tamper-resistant packages. In making packaging decisions, the company also must heed growing environmental concerns and make decisions that serve society's interests as well as immediate customer and company objectives. Shortages of paper, aluminum, and other materials suggest that marketers should try to reduce packaging. Many packages end up as broken bottles and crumpled cans littering the streets and countryside. All of this packaging creates a major problem in solid waste disposal, requiring huge amounts of labor and energy.

Fortunately, many companies have gone "green." For example, S.C. Johnson repackaged Agree Plus shampoo in a stand-up pouch using 80 percent less plastic. P&G eliminated outer cartons from its Secret and Sure deodorants, saving 3.4 million pounds of paperboard per year. Tetra Pak, a major Swedish multinational company, provides an example of the power of innovative packaging that takes environmental concerns into account.

> Tetra Pak invented an "aseptic" package that enables milk, fruit juice, and other perishable liquid foods to be distributed without refrigeration or preservatives. Not only is this packaging more environmentally responsible, it also provides economic and distribution advantages. Aseptic packaging allows companies to distribute liquid food products over a wider area without investing in refrigerated trucks and warehouses. Supermarkets can carry Tetra Pak packaged products on ordinary shelves, allowing them to save expensive refrigerator space. Tetra's motto is "a package should save more than it cost." Tetra Pak promotes the benefits of its packaging to consumers directly and even initiates recycling programs to save the environment.

Labeling

Labels may range from simple tags attached to products to complex graphics that are part of the package. They perform several functions. At the very least, the label *identifies* the product or brand, such as the name Sunkist stamped on oranges. The label might also *describe* several things about the product—who made it, where it was made, when it was made, its contents, how it is to be used, and how to use it safely. Finally, the label might *promote* the product through attractive graphics.

There has been a long history of legal concerns about packaging and labels. The Federal Trade Commission Act of 1914 held that false, misleading, or deceptive labels or packages constitute unfair competition. Labels can mislead customers, fail to describe important ingredients, or fail to include needed safety warnings. As a result, several federal and state laws regulate labeling. The most prominent is the Fair Packaging and Labeling Act of 1966,

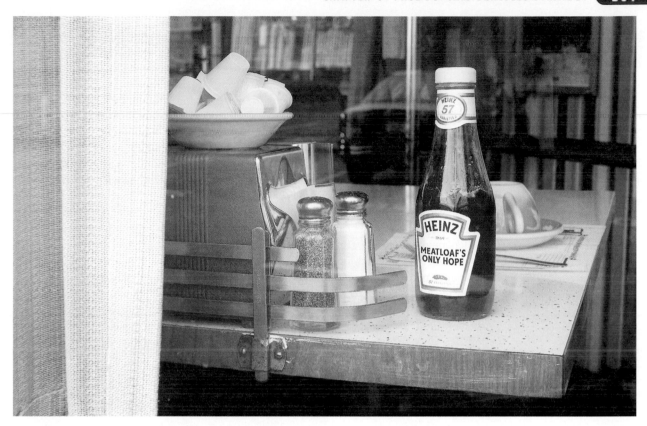

Innovative labeling can help to promote a product.

which set mandatory labeling requirements, encouraged voluntary industry packaging standards, and allowed federal agencies to set packaging regulations in specific industries.

Labeling has been affected in recent times by *unit pricing* (stating the price per unit of standard measure), *open dating* (stating the expected shelf life of the product), and *nutritional labeling* (stating the nutritional values in the product). The Nutritional Labeling and Educational Act of 1990 requires sellers to provide detailed nutritional information on food products, and recent sweeping actions by the Food and Drug Administration regulate the use of health-related terms such as *low-fat, light,* and *high-fiber.* Sellers must ensure that their labels contain all the required information.

Product Support Services

Customer service is another element of product strategy. A company's offer to the marketplace usually includes some services, which can be a minor or a major part of the total offer. Later in the chapter, we will discuss services as products in themselves. Here, we discuss *product support services*—services that augment actual products. More and more companies are using product support services as a major tool in gaining competitive advantage.

A company should design its product and support services to profitably meet the needs of target customers. The first step is to survey customers periodically to assess the value of current services and to obtain ideas for new ones. For example, Cadillac holds regular focus group interviews with owners and carefully watches complaints that come into its dealerships. From this careful monitoring, Cadillac has learned that buyers are very upset by repairs that are not done correctly the first time.

Once the company has assessed the value of various support services to customers, it must next assess the costs of providing these services. It can then develop a package of services that will both delight customers and yield profits to the company. Based on its consumer interviews, Cadillac has set up a system directly linking each dealership with a group of 10 engineers who can help walk mechanics through difficult repairs. Such actions helped Cadillac jump, in one year, from fourteenth to seventh in independent rankings of service.[26]

Many companies are now using the Internet and other modern technologies to provide support services that were not possible before. Using the Web, 24-hour telephone help lines, self-service kiosks, and other digital technologies, these companies are now empowering consumers to tailor their own service and support experiences. Schwab gives customers access to a wide variety of online services, helping them manage their own investment processes. Its "MySchwab" feature lets customers create personal Web pages that link them to whatever support services they might need, whenever needed. Similarly, Kaiser-Permanente, the nation's largest health maintenance organization (HMO), has rolled out a Web site that lets members register online for office visits and send e-mail questions to nurses and pharmacists (and get responses within 24 hours). Kaiser also plans to give members access to lab results and pharmaceutical refills online. And American Airlines provides a support Web site for its frequent-flyer members. Members can streamline the booking process by creating profiles of their home airports, usual routes, and seating and meal preferences for themselves and their families. Beyond using the site to book tickets, members can check the status of their frequent-flyer accounts and take advantage of special member fares. Moreover, using these profiles, American can, say, offer discounts on flights to Disney World for parents whose children's school vacations start in a few weeks.[27]

Product Decisions and Social Responsibility

Product decisions have attracted much public attention. Marketers should consider carefully a number of public policy issues and regulations involving acquiring or dropping products, patent protection, product quality and safety, and product warranties.

Regarding the addition of new products, the government may prevent companies from adding products through acquisitions if the effect threatens to lessen competition. Companies dropping products must be aware that they have legal obligations, written or implied, to their suppliers, dealers, and customers who have a stake in the discontinued product. Companies must also must obey U.S. patent laws when developing new products. A company cannot make its product illegally similar to another company's established product.

Manufacturers must comply with specific laws regarding product quality and safety. The Federal Food, Drug, and Cosmetic Act protects consumers from unsafe and adulterated food, drugs, and cosmetics. Various acts provide for the inspection of sanitary conditions in the meat- and poultry-processing industries. Safety legislation has been passed to regulate fabrics, chemical substances, automobiles, toys, and drugs and poisons. The Consumer Product Safety Act of 1972 established a Consumer Product Safety Commission, which has the authority to ban or seize potentially harmful products and set severe penalties for violation of the law.

If consumers have been injured by a product that has been designed defectively, they can sue manufacturers or dealers. Product liability suits are now occurring in federal and state courts at the rate of almost 110,000 per year, with a median jury award of $1.8 million and individual awards often running into the tens of millions of dollars.[28] This phenomenon has resulted in huge increases in product liability insurance premiums, causing big problems in some industries. Some companies pass these higher rates along to consumers by raising prices. Others are forced to discontinue high-risk product lines.

Many manufacturers offer written product warranties to convince customers of their products' quality. To protect consumers, Congress passed the Magnuson-Moss Warranty

Act in 1975. The act requires that full warranties meet certain minimum standards, including repair "within a reasonable time and without charge" or a replacement or full refund if the product does not work "after a reasonable number of attempts" at repair. Otherwise, the company must make it clear that it is offering only a limited warranty. The law has led several manufacturers to switch from full to limited warranties and others to drop warranties altogether as a marketing tool.

Product Line Decisions

We have looked at product strategy decisions such as branding, packaging, labeling, and support services for individual products and services. But product strategy also calls for building a product line. A **product line** is a group of products that are closely related because they function in a similar manner, are sold to the same customer groups, are marketed through the same types of outlets, or fall within given price ranges. For example, Nike produces several lines of athletic shoes, Nokia produces several lines of telecommunications products, and Charles Schwab produces several lines of financial services. In developing product line strategies, marketers face a number of tough decisions.

Product line
A group of products that are closely related because they function in a similar manner, are sold to the same customer groups, are marketed through the same types of outlets, or fall within given price ranges.

The major product line decision involves *product line length*—the number of items in the product line. The line is too short if the manager can increase profits by adding items; the line is too long if the manager can increase profits by dropping items. Product line length is influenced by company objectives and resources.

Product lines tend to lengthen over time. The sales force and distributors may pressure the product manager for a more complete line to satisfy their customers. Or, the manager may want to add items to the product line to create growth in sales and profits. However, as the manager adds items, several costs rise: design and engineering costs, inventory costs, manufacturing changeover costs, transportation costs, and promotional costs to introduce new items. Eventually top management calls a halt to the mushrooming product line. Unnecessary or unprofitable items will be pruned from the line in a major effort to increase overall profitability. This pattern of uncontrolled product line growth followed by heavy pruning is typical and may repeat itself many times.

The company must manage its product lines carefully. It can systematically increase the length of its product line in two ways: by *stretching* its line and by *filling* its line. *Product line stretching* occurs when a company lengthens its product line beyond its current range. The company can stretch its line downward, upward, or both ways.

Many companies initially locate at the upper end of the market and later stretch their lines *downward*. A company may stretch downward to plug a market hole that otherwise would attract a new competitor or to respond to a competitor's attack on the upper end. Or it may add low-end products because it finds faster growth taking place in the low-end segments. Mercedes-Benz stretched downward for all these reasons. Facing a slow-growth luxury car market and attacks by Japanese automakers on its high-end positioning, DaimlerChrysler successfully introduced its Mercedes C-Class cars at less than $30,000 without harming its ability to sell other Mercedes for $100,000 or more. And Rolex launched its Rolex Tudor watch retailing for about $1,000, compared with a Rolex Submariner, usually priced at $8,050.[29]

Companies at the lower end of the market may want to stretch their product lines *upward*. Sometimes, companies stretch upward in order to add prestige to their current products. They may be attracted by a faster growth rate or higher margins at the higher end, or they may simply want to position themselves as full-line manufacturers. Each of the leading Japanese auto companies introduced an upmarket automobile: Toyota launched Lexus; Nissan launched Infinity; and Honda launched Acura. They used entirely new names rather than their own names. Other companies have included their own names in

Stretching downward: Rolex launched its Rolex Tudor watch retailing for about $1,000, compared with a Rolex Submariner, usually priced at $8,050.

moving upmarket. For example, Gallo introduced Ernest and Julio Gallo Varietals and priced these wines at more than twice the price of its regular wines. General Electric introduced GE Profile brand appliances targeted at the select few households earning more than $100,000 per year and living in houses valued at more than $400,000.[30]

Companies in the middle range of the market may decide to stretch their lines in *both directions.* Marriott did this with its hotel product line. Along with regular Marriott hotels, it added the Marriott Marquis line to serve the upper end of the market and the Fairfield Inn line to serve the moderate and lower ends. Each branded hotel line is aimed at a different target market. Marriott Marquis aims to attract and please top executives; Marriotts, middle managers; Courtyards, salespeople and other "road warriors"; and Fairfield Inns, vacationers and business travelers on a tight travel budget. ExecuStay by Marriott provides corporate housing solutions for business travelers staying in a given location for 30 days or longer. Marriott's Residence Inn provides a home away from home for people who travel for a living, who are relocating, or who are on assignment and need inexpensive temporary lodging.[31] The major risk with this strategy is that some travelers will trade down after finding that the lower-price hotels in the Marriott chain give them pretty much everything they want. However, Marriott would rather capture its customers who move downward than lose them to competitors.

An alternative to product line stretching is *product line filling*—adding more items within the present range of the line. There are several reasons for product line filling: reaching for extra profits, satisfying dealers, using excess capacity, being the leading full-line company, and plugging holes to keep out competitors. Domino's introduced "Italian Originals," an upscale line of pizzas with toppings such as chicken and roasted vegetables. Sony filled its Walkman line by adding solar-powered and waterproof Walkmans, an ultra-light model that attaches to a sweatband for exercisers, the MiniDisc Walkman, the CD Walkman, and the Memory Stick Walkman, which enables users to download tracks straight from the Net. However, line filling is overdone if it results in cannibalization and customer confusion. The company should ensure that new items are noticeably different from existing ones.

Product Mix Decisions

An organization with several product lines has a product mix. A **product mix** (or **product assortment**) consists of all the product lines and items that a particular seller offers for sale. Avon's product mix consists of four major product lines: beauty, wellness products, jewelry and accessories, and "inspirational" products (gifts, books, music, and home accents). Each product line consists of several sublines. For example, the beauty line breaks down into makeup, skin care, bath and beauty, fragrance, and outdoor protection products. Each line and subline has many individual items. Altogether, Avon's product mix includes 1,300 items. In contrast, a typical Kmart stocks 15,000 items, 3M markets more than 60,000 products, and General Electric manufactures as many as 250,000 items.

A company's product mix has four important dimensions: width, length, depth, and consistency. Product mix *width* refers to the number of different product lines the company carries. Procter & Gamble markets a fairly wide product mix consisting of many product lines, including baby care, beauty care, fabric and home care, feminine care, food and beverage, health care, and tissues and towels products. Product mix *length* refers to the total number of items the company carries within its product lines. P&G typically carries many brands within each line. For example, it sells eight laundry detergents, five hand soaps, five shampoos, and four dishwashing detergents.

Product line *depth* refers to the number of versions offered of each product in the line. Thus, P&G's Crest toothpaste comes in eight varieties, from Crest Multicare, Crest Cavity Protection, and Crest Tartar Protection to Crest Sensitivity Protection, Crest Dual Action Whitening, and Crest Baking Soda & Peroxide Whitening formulations. (Talk about niche marketing! Remember our Chapter 7 discussion?). Finally, the *consistency* of the product mix refers to how closely related the various product lines are in end use, production requirements, distribution channels, or some other way. P&G's product lines are consistent insofar as they are consumer products that go through the same distribution channels. The lines are less consistent insofar as they perform different functions for buyers.

These product mix dimensions provide the handles for defining the company's product strategy. The company can increase its business in four ways. It can add new product lines, thus widening its product mix. In this way, its new lines build on the company's reputation in its other lines. The company can lengthen its existing product lines to become a more full-line company. Or it can add more versions of each product and thus deepen its product mix. Finally, the company can pursue more product line consistency — or less — depending on whether it wants to have a strong reputation in a single field or in several fields.

Product mix (or product assortment)
The set of all product lines and items that a particular seller offers for sale.

Linking the Concepts

Slow down for a minute. To get a better sense of how large and complex a company's product offering can become, investigate Procter & Gamble's product mix.

◆ Using P&G's Web site (www.pg.com), its annual report, or other sources, develop a list of all the company's product lines and individual products. What surprises you about this list of products?

◆ Is P&G's product mix consistent? What overall strategy or logic appears to have guided the development of this product mix?

Services Marketing

One of the major world trends in recent years has been the dramatic growth of services. As a result of rising affluence, more leisure time, and the growing complexity of products that require servicing, the United States has become the world's first service economy. Services now account for 74 percent of U.S. gross domestic product and nearly 60 percent of personal consumption expenditures. Whereas service jobs accounted for 55 percent of all U.S. jobs in 1970, by 1996 they accounted for 80 percent of total employment. Services are growing even faster in the world economy, making up a quarter of the value of all international trade. In fact, a variety of service industries—from banking, insurance, and communications to transportation, travel, and entertainment—now accounts for well over 60 percent of the economy in developed countries around the world.[32]

Service industries vary greatly. *Governments* offer services through courts, employment services, hospitals, loan agencies, military services, police and fire departments, postal service, regulatory agencies, and schools. *Private nonprofit organizations* offer services through museums, charities, churches, colleges, foundations, and hospitals. A large number of *business organizations* offer services—airlines, banks, hotels, insurance companies, consulting firms, medical and law practices, entertainment companies, real estate firms, advertising and research agencies, and retailers.

Nature and Characteristics of a Service

A company must consider four special service characteristics when designing marketing programs: *intangibility, inseparability, variability,* and *perishability.* These characteristics are summarized in Figure 8-5 and discussed in the following sections.

Service intangibility
A major characteristic of services—they cannot be seen, tasted, felt, heard, or smelled before they are bought.

Service inseparability
A major characteristic of services—they are produced and consumed at the same time and cannot be separated from their providers, whether the providers are people or machines.

Service intangibility means that services cannot be seen, tasted, felt, heard, or smelled before they are bought. For example, people undergoing cosmetic surgery cannot see the result before the purchase. Airline passengers have nothing but a ticket and the promise that they and their luggage will arrive safely at the intended destination, hopefully at the same time. To reduce uncertainty, buyers look for "signals" of service quality. They draw conclusions about quality from the place, people, price, equipment, and communications that they can see. Therefore, the service provider's task is to make the service tangible in one or more ways. Whereas product marketers try to add intangibles to their tangible offers, service marketers try to add tangibles to their intangible offers.

Physical goods are produced, then stored, later sold, and still later consumed. In contrast, services are first sold, then produced and consumed at the same time. **Service inseparability** means that services cannot be separated from their providers, whether the

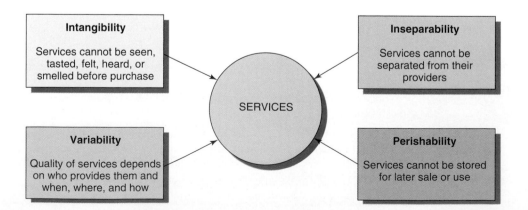

Figure 8-5
Four service characteristics

providers are people or machines. If a service employee provides the service, then the employee is a part of the service. Because the customer is also present as the service is produced, *provider–customer interaction* is a special feature of services marketing. Both the provider and the customer affect the service outcome.

Service variability means that the quality of services depends on who provides them as well as when, where, and how they are provided. For example, some hotels—say, Marriott—have reputations for providing better service than others. Still, within a given Marriott hotel, one registration-desk employee may be cheerful and efficient, whereas another standing just a few feet away may be unpleasant and slow. Even the quality of a single Marriott employee's service varies according to his or her energy and frame of mind at the time of each customer encounter.

Service perishability means that services cannot be stored for later sale or use. Some doctors charge patients for missed appointments because the service value existed only at that point and disappeared when the patient did not show up. The perishability of services is not a problem when demand is steady. However, when demand fluctuates, service firms often have difficult problems. For example, because of rush-hour demand, public transportation companies have to own much more equipment than they would if demand were even throughout the day. Thus, service firms often design strategies for producing a better match between demand and supply. Hotels and resorts charge lower prices in the off-season to attract more guests. And restaurants hire part-time employees to serve during peak periods.

> **Service variability**
> A major characteristic of services—their quality may vary greatly, depending on who provides them and when, where, and how.

> **Service perishability**
> A major characteristic of services—they cannot be stored for later sale or use.

Marketing Strategies for Service Firms

Just like manufacturing businesses, good service firms use marketing to position themselves strongly in chosen target markets. Southwest Airlines positions itself as a no-frills, short-haul airline charging very low fares. Ritz-Carlton Hotels positions itself as offering a memorable experience that "enlivens the senses, instills well-being, and fulfills even the unexpressed wishes and needs of our guests." These and other service firms establish their positions through traditional marketing mix activities.

However, because services differ from tangible products, they often require additional marketing approaches. In a product business, products are fairly standardized and can sit on shelves waiting for customers. But in a service business, the customer and front-line service employee *interact* to create the service. Thus, service providers must interact effectively with customers to create superior value during service encounters. Effective interaction, in turn, depends on the skills of front-line service employees and on the service production and support processes backing these employees.

The Service–Profit Chain Successful service companies focus their attention on *both* their customers and their employees. They understand the **service–profit chain,** which links service firm profits with employee and customer satisfaction. This chain consists of five links:[33]

> **Service–profit chain**
> The chain that links service firm profits with employee and customer satisfaction.

- ◆ *Internal service quality:* Superior employee selection and training, a quality work environment, and strong support for those dealing with customers, which results in . . .
- ◆ *Satisfied and productive service employees:* More satisfied, loyal, and hardworking employees, which results in . . .
- ◆ *Greater service value:* More effective and efficient customer value creation and service delivery, which results in . . .
- ◆ *Satisfied and loyal customers:* Satisfied customers who remain loyal, repeat purchases, and refer other customers, which results in . . .
- ◆ *Healthy service profits and growth:* Superior service firm performance

Therefore, reaching service profits and growth goals begins with taking care of those who take care of customers (see Marketing at Work 8-4).

Marketing at Work 8-4

Ritz-Carlton: Taking Care of Those Who Take Care of Customers

Ritz-Carlton, a chain of luxury hotels renowned for outstanding service, caters to the top 5 percent of corporate and leisure travelers. The company's Credo sets lofty customer service goals: "The Ritz-Carlton Hotel is a place where the genuine care and comfort of our guests is our highest mission. We pledge to provide the finest personal service and facilities for our guests who will always enjoy a warm, relaxed yet refined ambience. The Ritz-Carlton experience enlivens the senses, instills well-being, and fulfills even the unexpressed wishes and needs of our guests." The company's Web page concludes: "Here a calm settles over you. The world, so recently at your door, is now at your feet."

The Credo is more than just words on paper—Ritz-Carlton delivers on its promises. In surveys of departing guests, some 95 percent report that they've had a truly memorable experience. In fact, at Ritz-Carlton, exceptional service encounters have become almost commonplace. Take the experiences of Nancy and Harvey Heffner of Manhattan, who stayed at the Ritz-Carlton Naples, in Naples, Florida (recently rated the best hotel in the United States, fourth best in the world, by *Travel & Leisure* magazine). As reported in the *New York Times:*

"The hotel is elegant and beautiful," Mrs. Heffner said, "but more important is the beauty expressed by the staff. They can't do enough to please you." When the couple's son became sick last year in Naples, the hotel staff brought him hot tea with honey at all hours of the night, she said. When Mr. Heffner had to fly home on business for a day and his return flight was delayed, a driver for the hotel waited in the lobby most of the night.

Such personal, high-quality service has also made the Ritz-Carlton a favorite among conventioneers. Comments one convention planner, "They not only treat us like kings when we hold our top-level meetings in their hotels, but we just never get any complaints."

In 1992, Ritz-Carlton became the first hotel company to win the Malcolm Baldrige National Quality Award. Since its incorporation in 1983, the company has received virtually every major award that the hospitality industry bestows. More importantly, service quality has resulted in high customer retention: More than 90 percent of Ritz-Carlton customers return. And despite its hefty room rates, the chain enjoys a 70 percent occupancy rate, almost nine points above the industry average.

Most of the responsibility for keeping guests satisfied falls to Ritz-Carlton's customer-contact employees. Thus, the hotel chain takes great care in selecting its personnel. "We want only people who care about people," notes the company's vice president of quality. Once selected, employees are given intensive training in the art of coddling customers. New employees attend a two-day orientation, in which top management drums into them the "20 Ritz-Carlton Basics." Basic number one: "The Credo will be known, owned, and energized by all employees."

Employees are taught to do everything they can never to lose a guest. "There's no negotiating at Ritz-Carlton when it comes to solving customer problems," says the quality executive. Staff learn that *anyone* who receives a customer complaint *owns* that complaint until it's resolved (Ritz-Carlton Basic number eight). They are trained to drop whatever they're doing to

---

THE RITZ-CARLTON®

CREDO

The Ritz-Carlton Hotel is a place where the genuine care and comfort of our guests is our highest mission.

We pledge to provide the finest personal service and facilities for our guests who will always enjoy a warm, relaxed yet refined ambience.

The Ritz-Carlton experience enlivens the senses, instills well-being, and fulfills even the unexpressed wishes and needs of our guests.

THREE STEPS OF SERVICE

1
A warm and sincere greeting. Use the guest name, if and when possible.

2
Anticipation and compliance with guest needs.

3
Fond farewell. Give them a warm good-bye and use their name, if and when possible.

THE EMPLOYEE PROMISE

At The Ritz-Carlton, our Ladies and Gentlemen are the most important resource in our service commitment to our guests.

By applying the principles of trust, honesty, respect, integrity and commitment, we nurture and maximize talent to the benefit of each individual and the company.

The Ritz-Carlton fosters a work environment where diversity is valued, quality of life is enhanced, individual aspirations are fulfilled, and The Ritz-Carlton mystique is strengthened.

"We Are Ladies and Gentlemen Serving Ladies and Gentlemen"

The Credo and Employee Promise: Ritz-Carlton knows that to take care of customers, you must first take care of those who take care of customers.

help a customer—no matter what they're doing or what their department. Ritz-Carlton employees are empowered to handle problems on the spot, without consulting higher-ups. Each employee can spend up to $2,000 to redress a guest grievance, and each is allowed to break from his or her routine for as long as needed to make a guest happy. "We master customer satisfaction at the individual level," adds the executive. "This is our most sensitive listening post . . . our early warning system." Thus, while competitors are still reading guest comment cards to learn about customer problems, Ritz-Carlton has already resolved them.

Ritz-Carlton instills a sense of pride in its employees. "You serve," they are told, "but you are not servants." The company motto states, "We are ladies and gentlemen serving ladies and gentlemen." Employees understand their role in Ritz-Carlton's success. "We might not be able to afford a hotel like this," says employee Tammy Patton, "but we can make it so people who can afford it will want to keep coming here."

And so they do. When it comes to customer satisfaction, no detail is too small. Customer-contact people are taught to greet guests warmly and sincerely, using guest names when possible. They learn to use the proper language with guests— phrases such as *good morning, certainly, I'll be happy to, welcome back,* and *my pleasure,* never *hi* or *how's it going*? The Ritz-Carlton Basics urge employees to escort guests to another area of the hotel rather than pointing out directions, to answer the phone within three rings and with a "smile," and to take pride and care in their personal appearance. As the general manager of the Ritz-Carlton Naples, puts it, "When you invite guests to your house, you want everything to be perfect."

Ritz-Carlton recognizes and rewards employees who perform feats of outstanding service. Under its 5-Star Awards program, outstanding performers are nominated by peers and managers, and winners receive plaques at dinners celebrating their achievements. For on-the-spot recognition, managers award Gold Standard Coupons, redeemable for items in the gift shop and free

weekend stays at the hotel. Ritz-Carlton further rewards and motivates its employees with events such as Super Sports Day, an employee talent show, luncheons celebrating employee anniversaries, a family picnic, and special themes in employee dining rooms. As a result, Ritz-Carlton's employees appear to be just as satisfied as its customers. Employee turnover is less than 30 percent a year, compared with 45 percent at other luxury hotels.

Ritz-Carlton's success is based on a simple philosophy: To take care of customers, you must first take care of those who take care of customers. Satisfied employees deliver high service value, which then creates satisfied customers. Satisfied customers, in turn, create sales and profits for the company.

Sources: Quotes and other information from Edwin McDowell, "Ritz-Carlton's Keys to Good Service," *New York Times,* March 31, 1993, p. D1; Howard Schlossberg, "Measuring Customer Satisfaction Is Easy to Do—Until You Try," *Marketing News,* April 26, 1993, pp. 5, 8; Ginger Conlon, "True Romance," *Sales and Marketing Management,* May 1996, pp. 85–90; and information accessed at the Ritz-Carlton Web site at www.ritzcarlton.com, December 2001. Also see Larry Davis, "Individualism Powers Innovation," *Executive Excellence,* October 2000, p. 9; and Patricia Sheehan, "Back to Bed: Selling the Perfect Night's Sleep," *Lodging Hospitality,* March 15, 2001, pp. 22–24.

All of this suggests that service marketing requires more than just traditional external marketing using the four Ps. Figure 8-6 shows that service marketing also requires *internal marketing* and *interactive marketing*. **Internal marketing** means that the service firm must effectively train and motivate its customer-contact employees and all the supporting service people to work as a *team* to provide customer satisfaction. For the firm to deliver consistently high service quality, marketers must get everyone in the organization to practice a customer orientation. In fact, internal marketing must *precede* external marketing. Ritz-Carlton orients its employees carefully, instills in them a sense of pride, and motivates them by recognizing and rewarding outstanding service deeds.

Interactive marketing means that service quality depends heavily on the quality of the buyer–seller interaction during the service encounter. In product marketing, product quality often depends little on how the product is obtained. But in services marketing, service quality depends on both the service deliverer and the quality of the delivery. Service marketers cannot assume that they will satisfy the customer simply by providing good technical service. They have to master interactive marketing skills as well. Thus, Ritz-Carlton selects only "people who care about people" and instructs them carefully in the fine art of interacting with customers to satisfy their every need.

Internal marketing
Marketing by a service firm to train and effectively motivate its customer-contact employees and all the supporting service people to work as a team to provide customer satisfaction.

Interactive marketing
Marketing by a service firm that recognizes that perceived service quality depends heavily on the quality of buyer-seller interaction.

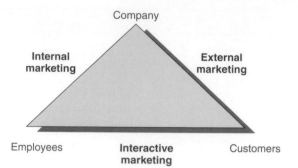

Figure 8-6
Three types of service marketing

Today, as competition and costs increase, and as productivity and quality decrease, more service marketing sophistication is needed. Service companies face three major marketing tasks: They want to increase their *competitive differentiation, service quality,* and *productivity.*

Managing Service Differentiation   In these days of intense price competition, service marketers often complain about the difficulty of differentiating their services from those of competitors. To the extent that customers view the services of different providers as similar, they care less about the provider than the price.

The solution to price competition is to develop a differentiated offer, delivery, and image. The *offer* can include innovative features that set one company's offer apart from competitors' offers. Some hotels offer car rental, banking, and business center services in their lobbies. Many airlines have introduced innovations such as in-flight movies, advance seating, air-to-ground telephone service, and frequent-flyer award programs to differentiate their offers. British Airways even offers international travelers beds and private "demi-cabins," hot showers, and cooked-to-order breakfasts.

Service companies can differentiate their service *delivery* by having more able and reliable customer-contact people, by developing a superior physical environment in which the service product is delivered, or by designing a superior delivery process. For example, many banks offer their customers Internet banking as a better way to access banking services than having to drive, park, and wait in line.

Finally, service companies also can work on differentiating their *images* through symbols and branding. The Harris Bank of Chicago adopted the lion as its symbol on its stationery, in its advertising, and even as stuffed animals offered to new depositors. The well-known Harris lion confers an image of strength on the bank. Other well-known service symbols include The Travelers' red umbrella, Merrill Lynch's bull, and Allstate's "good hands."

Managing Service Quality   One of the major ways a service firm can differentiate itself is by delivering consistently higher quality than its competitors do. Like manufacturers before them, most service industries have now joined the total quality movement. And like product marketers, service providers need to identify the expectations of target customers concerning service quality. Unfortunately, service quality is harder to define and judge than is product quality. For instance, it is harder to get agreement on the quality of a haircut than on the quality of a hair dryer. Customer retention is perhaps the best measure of quality—a service firm's ability to hang onto its customers depends on how consistently it delivers value to them.[34]

Service companies want to ensure that customers will receive consistently high-quality service in every service encounter. However, unlike product manufacturers who

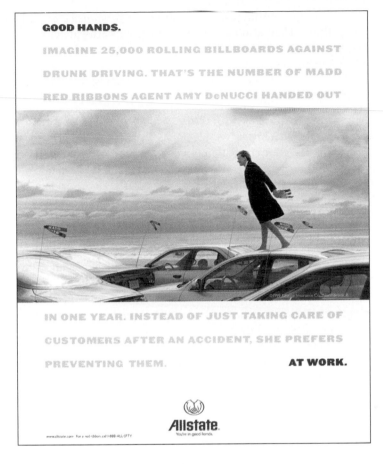

GOOD HANDS.

IMAGINE 25,000 ROLLING BILLBOARDS AGAINST

DRUNK DRIVING. THAT'S THE NUMBER OF MADD

RED RIBBONS AGENT AMY DeNUCCI HANDED OUT

IN ONE YEAR. INSTEAD OF JUST TAKING CARE OF

CUSTOMERS AFTER AN ACCIDENT, SHE PREFERS

PREVENTING THEM.   **AT WORK.**

Allstate
You're in good hands.

Service companies differentiate their images through symbols and branding. Note the now very familiar "Allstate: You're in good hands" brand and symbol at the bottom of this ad.

can adjust their machinery and inputs until everything is perfect, service quality will always vary, depending on the interactions between employees and customers. Problems will inevitably occur. As hard as they try, even the best companies will have an occasional late delivery, burned steak, or grumpy employee. However, although a company cannot always prevent service problems, it can learn to recover from them. And good *service recovery* can turn angry customers into loyal ones. In fact, good recovery can win more customer purchasing and loyalty than if things had gone well in the first place. Therefore, companies should take steps not only to provide good service every time but also to recover from service mistakes when they do occur.[35]

The first step is to *empower* front-line service employees—to give them the authority, responsibility, and incentives they need to recognize, care about, and tend to customer needs. At Marriott, for example, well-trained employees are given the authority to do whatever it takes, on the spot, to keep guests happy. They are also expected to help management ferret out the cause of guests' problems and to inform managers of ways to improve overall hotel service and guests' comfort.

Studies of well-managed service companies show that they share a number of common virtues regarding service quality. Top service companies are *customer obsessed* and set *high service quality standards*. They do not settle for merely good service; they aim for 100 percent defect-free service. A 98 percent performance standard may sound good but, using this standard, 64,000 FedEx packages would be lost each day, 10 words would be misspelled on each printed page, 400,000 prescriptions would be misfilled daily, and drinking water would be unsafe 8 days a year.[36]

Top service firms also *watch service performance closely,* both their own and that of competitors. They also communicate their concerns about service quality to employees and provide performance feedback. At FedEx, quality measurements are everywhere. When employees walk in the door in the morning, they see the previous week's on-time percentages. Then, the company's in-house television station gives them detailed breakdowns of what happened yesterday and any potential problems for the day ahead.

Managing Service Productivity   With their costs rising rapidly, service firms are under great pressure to increase service productivity. They can do so in several ways. The service providers can train current employees better or hire new ones who will work harder or more skillfully. Or the service providers can increase the quantity of their service by giving up some quality. The provider can "industrialize the service" by adding equipment and standardizing production, as in McDonald's assembly-line approach to fast-food retailing. Finally, the service provider can harness the power of technology. Although we often think of technology's power to save time and costs in manufacturing companies, it also has great—and often untapped—potential to make service workers more productive.

Similarly, a well-designed Web site can allow customers to obtain buying information, narrow their purchase options, or make a purchase directly, saving service provider time. For example, personal computer buyers can visit the Dell Web site (www.Dell.com), review the characteristics of various Dell models, check out prices, and organize their questions ahead of time. Even if they choose to call a Dell telesales representative rather than buying via the Web site, they are better informed and require less personal service.

However, companies must avoid pushing productivity so hard that doing so reduces quality. Attempts to industrialize a service or to cut costs can make a service company more efficient in the short run but reduce its longer-run ability to innovate, maintain service quality, or respond to consumer needs and desires. In some cases, service providers accept reduced productivity in order to create more service differentiation or quality.

International Product and Services Marketing

International product and service marketers face special challenges. First, they must figure out what products and services to introduce and in which countries. Then, they must decide how much to standardize or adapt their products and services for world markets. On the one hand, companies would like to standardize their offerings. Standardization helps a company to develop a consistent worldwide image. It also lowers manufacturing costs and eliminates duplication of research and development, advertising, and product design efforts. On the other hand, consumers around the world differ in their cultures, attitudes, and buying behaviors. And markets vary in their economic conditions, competition, legal requirements, and physical environments. Companies must usually respond to these differences by adapting their product offerings. Something as simple as an electrical outlet can create big product problems:

> Those who have traveled across Europe know the frustration of electrical plugs, different voltages, and other annoyances of international travel. . . . Philips, the electrical appliance manufacturer, has to produce 12 kinds of irons to serve just its European market. The problem is that Europe does not have a universal [electrical] standard. The ends of irons bristle with different plugs for different countries. Some have three prongs, others two; prongs protrude straight or angled, round or rectangular, fat, thin, and sometimes sheathed. There are circular plug faces, squares, pentagons, and hexagons. Some are perforated and some are notched. One French plug has a niche like a keyhole.[37]

Packaging also presents new challenges for international marketers. Packaging issues can be subtle. For example, names, labels, and colors may not translate easily from one country to another. A firm using yellow flowers in its logo might fare well in the United States but meet with disaster in Mexico, where a yellow flower symbolizes death or disrespect. Similarly, although Nature's Gift might be an appealing name for gourmet mushrooms in America, it would be deadly in Germany, where *gift* means poison. Packaging may also have to be tailored to meet the physical characteristics of consumers in various parts of the world. For instance, soft drinks are sold in smaller cans in Japan to fit the smaller Japanese hand better. Thus, although product and package standardization can produce benefits, companies must usually adapt their offerings to the unique needs of specific international markets.

Service marketers also face special challenges when going global. Some service industries have a long history of international operations. For example, the commercial banking industry was one of the first to grow internationally. Banks had to provide global services in order to meet the foreign exchange and credit needs of their home country clients wanting to sell overseas. In recent years, many banks have become truly global operations. Germany's Deutsche Bank, for example, has branches in 41 countries. Thus, for its clients around the world who wish to grow globally, Deutsche Bank can raise money not only in Frankfurt but also in Zurich, London, Paris, and Tokyo.

The travel industry also moved naturally into international operations. American hotel and airline companies grew quickly in Europe and Asia during the economic expansion that followed World War II. Credit card companies soon followed—the early worldwide presence of American Express has now been matched by Visa and MasterCard. Business travelers and vacationers like the convenience, and they have now come to expect that their credit cards will be honored wherever they go.

Professional and business services industries such as accounting, management consulting, and advertising have only recently globalized. The international growth of these firms followed the globalization of the manufacturing companies they serve. For example, as their client companies began to employ global marketing and advertising strategies, advertising agencies and other marketing services firms responded by globalizing their own operations. McCann-Erickson Worldwide, the largest U.S. advertising

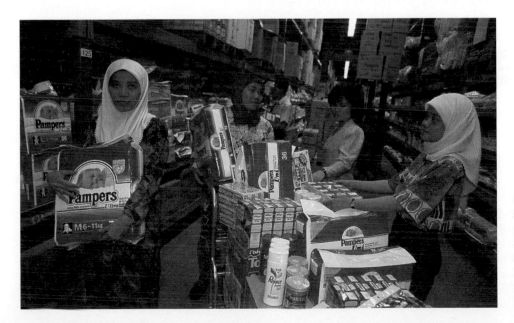

Retailers are among the latest service businesses to go global. Here, Asian shoppers buy American products in a Dutch-owned Makro store in Kuala Lumpur.

agency, operates in more than 130 countries, serving international clients such as Coca-Cola, Microsoft, Johnson & Johnson, and Unilever in markets ranging from the United States and Canada to Korea to Kazakhstan.

Retailers are among the latest service businesses to go global. As their home markets become saturated with stores, American retailers such as Wal-Mart, Kmart, Toys 'R' Us, Office Depot, Saks Fifth Avenue, and Disney are expanding into faster-growing markets abroad. For example, every year since 1995, Wal-Mart has entered a new country; its international division's sales grew 40 percent last year, skyrocketing to more than $32 billion. Foreign retailers are making similar moves. The Japanese retailer Yaohan now operates the largest shopping center in Asia, the 21-story Nextage Shanghai Tower in China, and Carrefour of France is the leading retailer in Brazil and Argentina. Asian shoppers now buy American products in Dutch-owned Makro stores, now Southeast Asia's biggest store group with sales in the region of more than $2 billion.[38]

Service companies wanting to operate in other countries are not always welcomed with open arms. Whereas manufacturers usually face straightforward tariff, quota, or currency restrictions when attempting to sell their products in another country, service providers are likely to face more subtle barriers. In some cases, rules and regulations affecting international service firms reflect the host country's traditions. In others, they appear to protect the country's own fledgling service industries from large global competitors with greater resources. In still other cases, however, the restrictions seem to have little purpose other than to make entry difficult for foreign service firms.

A Turkish law, for example, forbids international accounting firms from bringing capital into the country to set up offices and requires them to use the names of local partners in their marketing rather than their own internationally known company names. To audit the books of a multinational company's branch in Buenos Aires, an accountant must have the equivalent of a high school education in Argentinean geography and history. In New Delhi, India, international insurance companies are not allowed to sell property and casualty policies to the country's fast-growing business community or life insurance to its huge middle class.[39]

Despite such difficulties, the trend toward growth of global service companies will continue, especially in banking, airlines, telecommunications, and professional services. Today service firms are no longer simply following their manufacturing customers. Instead, they are taking the lead in international expansion.

STOP *Rest Stop: Reviewing the Concepts*

Time to kick back and reflect on the key concepts in this first marketing mix chapter on products and services. A product is more than a simple set of tangible features. In fact, many marketing offers consist of combinations of both tangible goods and services, ranging from *pure tangible goods* at one extreme to *pure services* at the other. Each product or service offered to customers can be viewed on three levels. The *core product* consists of the core problem-solving benefits that consumers seek when they buy a product. The *actual product* exists around the core and includes the quality level, features, design, brand name, and packaging. The *augmented product* is the actual product plus the various services and benefits offered with it, such as warranty, free delivery, installation, and maintenance.

1. Define *product* and the major classifications of products and services.

Broadly defined, a *product* is anything that can be offered to a market for attention, acquisition, use, or consumption that might satisfy a want or need. Products include physical objects, services, events, persons, places, organizations, ideas, or mixes of these entities. Services are products that consist of activities, benefits, or satisfactions offered for sale that are essentially intangible, such as banking, hotel, tax preparation, and home repair services.

Products and services fall into two broad classes based on the types of consumers that use them. *Consumer products*—those bought by final consumers—are usually classified according to consumer shopping habits (convenience products, shopping products, specialty products, and unsought products). *Industrial products*—purchased for further processing or for use in conducting a business—are classified according to their cost and the way they enter the production process (materials and parts, capital items, and supplies and services). Other marketable entities—such as organizations, persons, places, and ideas—can also be thought of as products.

2. Describe the roles of product and service branding, packaging, labeling, and product support services.

Companies develop strategies for items in their product lines by making decisions about product attributes, branding, packaging, labeling, and product support services. *Product attribute* decisions involve the product quality, features, and style and design the company will offer. *Branding* decisions include selecting a brand name, garnering brand sponsorship, and developing a brand strategy. *Packaging* provides many key benefits, such as protection, economy, convenience, and promotion. Package decisions often include designing *labels,* which identify, describe, and possibly promote the product. Companies also develop *product support services* that enhance customer service and satisfaction and safeguard against competitors.

3. Explain the decisions that companies make when developing product lines and mixes.

Most companies produce a product line rather than a single product. A *product line* is a group of products that are related in function, customer-purchase needs, or distribution channels. In developing a product line strategy, marketers face a number of tough decisions. *Line stretching* involves extending a line downward, upward, or in both

directions to occupy a gap that might otherwise by filled by a competitor. In contrast, *line filling* involves adding items within the present range of the line. The set of product lines and items offered to customers by a particular seller make up the *product mix.* The mix can be described by four dimensions: width, length, depth, and consistency. These dimensions are the tools for developing the company's product strategy.

4. Identify the four characteristics that affect the marketing of a service.

As we move toward a *world service economy,* marketers need to know more about marketing services. *Services* are characterized by four key characteristics. First, services are *intangible*—they cannot be seen, tasted, felt, heard, or smelled. Services are also *inseparable* from their service providers. Services are *variable* because their quality depends on the service provider as well as the environment surrounding the service delivery. Finally, services are *perishable.* As a result, they cannot be inventoried, built up, or back ordered. Each characteristic poses problems and marketing requirements. Marketers work to find ways to make the service more tangible, to increase the productivity of providers who are inseparable from their products, to standardize the quality in the face of variability, and to improve demand movements and supply capacities in the face of service perishability.

5. Discuss the additional marketing considerations that services require.

Good service companies focus attention on *both* customers and employees. They understand the *service–profit chain,* which links service firm profits with employee and customer satisfaction. Services marketing strategy calls not only for external marketing but also for *internal marketing* to motivate employees and *interactive marketing* to create service delivery skills among service providers. To succeed, service marketers must create *competitive differentiation,* offer high *service quality,* and find ways to increase *service productivity.*

Navigating the Key Terms

For a detailed analysis of the meaning and importance of each of the following key terms, visit our Web page at **www.prenhall.com/ kotler**.

Brand
Brand equity
Brand extension
Co-branding
Consumer product

Convenience product
Industrial product
Interactive marketing
Internal marketing
Line extension

Packaging
Private brand (or store brand)
Product
Product line
Product mix (or product assortment)
Product quality

Service
Service inseparability
Service intangibility
Service perishability
Service–profit chain
Service variability

Shopping product
Slotting fees
Social marketing
Specialty product
Unsought product

Travel Log

The following concept checks and discussion questions will help you to keep track of and apply the concepts you've studied in this chapter.

Concept Checks

Fill in the blanks, then look for the correct answers.

1. The text defines a _____ as anything that can be offered to a market for attention, acquisition, use, or consumption and that might satisfy a want or need.

2. _____ are a form of product that consist of activities, benefits, or satisfactions offered for sale that are essentially intangible and do not result in the ownership of anything.

3. Product planners need to think about products and services on three levels: the _____ product, the _____ product, and the _____ product.

4. _____ products are less frequently purchased consumer products and services that customers carefully compare on suitability, quality, price, and style.

5. Three groups of industrial products and services include _____ and parts, _____, and _____ and services.

6. "Smokey the Bear," "Keep America Beautiful," and "Join the Peace Corps" are all examples of advertising campaigns that were directed toward

_____ marketing efforts of the Advertising Council of America.

7. A _____ is a name, term, sign, symbol, or design, or a combination of these that identifies the maker or seller of a product or service.

8. Desirable qualities for a brand name include: (a) It should suggest something about the product's _____, and _____; (b) It should be easy to _____, _____, and _____; (c) The brand name should be _____; (d) It should be _____; and, (e) It should translate easily into foreign languages.

9. _____ occur when a company introduces additional items in a given category under the same brand name, such as new flavors, forms, colors, ingredients, or package sizes.

10. Product mix _____ refers to the number of different product lines the company carries.

11. A company must consider four special service characteristics when designing marketing programs: _____, _____, _____, and _____.

12. A company's service–profit chain consists of five links: Internal service quality; _____; _____; _____; and Healthy service profits and growth.

Concept Checks Answers: 1. product; 2. services; 3. core, actual, and augmented; 4. shopping; 5. materials, capital items, supplies; 6. social; 7. brand; 8. benefits and qualities; pronounce, recognize, and remember; distinctive; extendible; 9. line extensions; 10. width; 11. intangibility, inseparability, variability, and perishability; 12. satisfied and productive service employees; greater service value; satisfied and loyal customers.

Discussing the Issues

1. What are the primary differences between products and services? Give illustrations of the differences that you identify. Give an original example of a hybrid offer.

2. List and explain the core, actual, and augmented products for educational experiences that universities offer. How are these different (if there is a differ-

ence) from the products offered by junior colleges? Which of these experiences (products) could be moved online? How would these moves affect the educational institution's marketing effort?

3. The text identifies social marketing as the use of commercial marketing concepts and tools in programs designed to influence individuals' behavior in a way that improves their well being and that of

society. Take a recent social marketing effort, identify its intended target market, list the primary objectives of the campaign, suggest how effectiveness could be measured, and document the overall impact of the campaign. Critique the campaign and comment on what you would do to improve the effort.

4. For many years there was one type of Coca-Cola, one type of Tide, and one type of Crest (in mint and regular). Now we find Coke in six or more varieties; Tide in Ultra, Liquid, and Unscented versions; and Crest Gel with sparkles for kids. List some of the issues these brand extensions raise for the manufacturers, retailers, and consumers. Is more always better? How does co-branding impact the questioned brand extension? Suggest a co-branding opportunity that you believe would make good sense from a marketing perspective.

5. Illustrate how a movie theater can deal with the intangibility, inseparability, variability, and perishability of the services it provides. Give specific examples to illustrate your thoughts. How could the movie theater use internal and interactive marketing to enhance the service it provides?

Mastering Marketing

To explore the impact of products and services on the organization, you have two assignments. First, outline a brand extension plan for CanGo. Identify any co-branding opportunities that you perceive would be good long-term investments. Explain your choices. Second, outline the service–profit chain that seems to be in place for CanGo. What improvements would you suggest?

Traveling on the Net

Point of Interest: Matching Service Strategies

Whether it's partnering with the U.S. Postal Service or providing entertainment and supplies for Tom Hanks in *Castaway,* FedEx has been on top of the parcel delivery business for some time. However, United Parcel Service (UPS) has started a "ground war" whose aim is to overtake #1 FedEx. UPS doesn't plan to do this with cheaper rates, better trucks, faster computers, or more manpower. Plain and simple—the key is better service. UPS can move merchandise around the world in a mere 12 hours because its service–profit chain is better. UPS finds the cheapest way for a client to ship merchandise and bets that, in the long-run, relationships will yield more business and profits. For example, if a chipmaker in Singapore were to use a UPS competitor to ship a box of chips, they might be forced to use expensive overnight air express. Why? Because that method would be the most profitable for the shipping company. UPS, in contrast, would aid the chipmaker in designing its warehouse operation, propose a customized tracking system, counsel on its logistics, and find a shipping method that would be profitable for both itself and the client. When UPS integrates the client into its operations, both parties benefit financially in delivering goods and pleasing the ultimate consumer. For these reasons and others, UPS is rapidly overtaking FedEx both domestically and globally as the shipper of preference. In addition, the Web generation seems to prefer UPS for e-commerce. The company now handles 55 percent of all online purchases. The threat has not gone unnoticed by FedEx. Since FedEx was the pioneer of both overnight delivery of packages and the ability to track their journey via computers, the company is now planning new innovations in tracking, service, and accountability. Will it be too little, too late? The customer will eventually decide!

For Discussion

1. What are the common services that seem to be present in the majority of service strategies? Which of these services are present in the FedEx and UPS service options?

2. How is UPS using the service–profit chain to its advantage? Do either of these firms appear to employ interactive or integrated marketing? Explain.

3. Match the services provided by these two competitors to the characteristics shown in Figure 8-5. Where does UPS seem to have strengths? Weaknesses? Evaluate FedEx in a similar manner. Where do opportunities appear to exist for UPS?

4. If you were choosing one of these service providers to deliver a package for you, how would you make your choice? What factors would be important to you?

Application Thinking

Assume that you are the shipping manager for a company that grows and distributes perishable cut flowers. Your base of operation is in Peru. After examining the UPS (www.ups.com) and FedEx (www.fedex.com) Web sites, evaluate which might be the best company for your business. Describe how you would make your evaluation, the types of services you might need, and how the carrier could aid you in your business. Discuss your conclusions in class.

 MAP—Marketing Applications

MAP Stop 8

Which company has the world's strongest brand? To find the answer, what questions would you ask? Is brand strength determined by sales volume, a global presence, innovation, reputation, amount of advertising, success on the Internet, positive public relations, stock value, or all of these things? Marketing managers know that strong brand equity is the key to entering new markets and successfully penetrating old ones. Brand image also shapes corporate strategy, advertising campaigns, and overall marketing effort. Alliances are encouraged or dropped based on brand reputation and confidence. Strong brands can command premium prices. Hence, the brand is a company's most important asset and profit producer. In contrast, loss of confidence in a brand, such as the recent Ford and Firestone public relations nightmare, can affect not only the companies involved but also all of the distributors, service providers, and secondary publics that are affiliated with the industry. However, when a strong brand faces difficulty, its reputation can help earn it a second chance. So, what is the world's strongest brand? According to recent studies, the vote goes to Coca-Cola, followed by Microsoft, IBM, GE, and Nokia. Were these your picks? Do you buy products from these companies? Many, many in the world do.

Thinking Like a Marketing Manager

1. What makes a strong brand? How would you go about measuring brand equity?

2. What makes Coca-Cola the number one brand in the world? What characteristics do the company and its brand possess that competitors do not?

3. With all of its legal difficulties, how can Microsoft be considered the second strongest global brand? Does its status help it overcome public relations and legal problems? Explain.

4. Examine the Web sites for the listed brands (www.cocacola.com, www.ibm.com, www.ge.com, www.microsoft.com, and www.nokia.com). Based on your answers to question one above, construct a grid that evaluates each of these brands. How does your evaluation match the order suggested above?

5. Go to the Internet and examine another brand that you perceive to be a superior brand. Discuss the characteristics of the brand you value. How could its brand equity be improved?

6. Assuming that you were the marketing manager for a new dot-com startup, develop a branding strategy that would match the characteristics of "great" global brands to your enterprise. Discuss your proposal with the class.

New-Product Development and Product Life-Cycle Strategies

chapter **9**

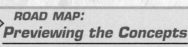

ROAD MAP:
Previewing the Concepts

In the previous chapter, you learned about decisions that marketers make in managing individual brands and entire product mixes. In this chapter, we'll cruise on into two additional product topics: developing new products and managing products through their life cycles. New products are the lifeblood of an organization. However, new-product development is risky, and many new products fail. So, the first part of this chapter lays out a process for finding and growing successful new products. Once introduced, marketers want their products to enjoy a long and happy life. In the second part of the chapter, you'll see that every product passes through several life-cycle stages and that each stage poses new challenges requiring different marketing strategies and tactics.

▶ **After studying this chapter, you should be able to**

1. explain how companies find and develop new-product ideas
2. list and define the steps in the new-product development process
3. describe the stages of the product life cycle
4. describe how marketing strategies change during the product's life cycle

First point of interest: Microsoft. The chances are good that you use several Microsoft products and services. Microsoft's Windows software owns a mind-boggling 97 percent share of the PC operating system market and its Office software captures a 90 percent share! However, this $25 billion company doesn't rest on past performance. As you'll see, it owes much of this success to a passion for innovation, abundant new-product development, and its quest for "the Next Big Thing."

No matter what brand of computer you're using or what you're doing on it, you're almost certain to be using some type of Microsoft product or service. In the world of computer and Internet software and technology, Microsoft dominates.

Microsoft's Windows operating system captures an astonishing 97 percent share of the PC market and a better than 40 percent share in the business server market. Microsoft Office, the company's largest moneymaker, grabs 90 percent of all office applications suite sales. The company's MSN Internet portal (msn.com) attracts more than 50 million surfers per month, second only to Yahoo! Its MSN Internet-access service, with 5 million subscribers, trails only America Online as the most popular way for consumers to get onto the Web. Microsoft's Hotmail is the world's most used free e-mail service, hosting more than 100 million accounts, and its instant messaging service has nearly 30 million users.

These and other successful products and services have made Microsoft incredibly profitable. During the first seven months of 2001, even as the stocks of other tech companies plunged, Microsoft's stock soared 62 percent. "Profits are pouring in so fast," writes

a *Fortune* magazine analyst, "that Microsoft's legendary cash hoard, already $30 billion, is growing by $1 billion a month." Over the long haul, an investment of $2,800 in 100 shares of Microsoft stock when the company went public 25 years ago would now have mushroomed into 14,400 shares worth a cool $1 million. All this has made Microsoft cofounder, Bill Gates (pictured above), the world's richest man, worth well over $50 billion.

A happy ending to a rags to riches fairy tale? Not quite. In Microsoft's fast-changing high-tech world, nothing lasts forever—or even for long. Beyond maintaining its core products and businesses, Microsoft knows that its future depends on its ability to conquer new markets with innovative new products.

Microsoft hasn't always been viewed as an innovator. In fact, it has long been regarded as "a big fat copycat." Gates bought the original MS/DOS operating system software upon which he built the company's initial success from a rival programmer for $50,000. Later, Microsoft was accused of copying the user-friendly Macintosh "look and feel." More recently, the company was accused of copying Netscape's Internet browser. It wasn't innovation that made Microsoft, critics claim, but rather its brute-force use of its PC operating system monopoly to crush competitors and muscle into markets. But no more. The technology giant is now innovating at a breakneck pace.

Thanks to its Windows and Office monopolies, Microsoft has plenty of cash to pump into new products and technologies. This year alone, it will spend $4.2 billion on R&D, more than competitors America Online, Sun Microsystems, and Oracle combined. Along with the cash, Microsoft has a strong, visionary leader in its efforts to innovate—no less than Bill Gates himself. Last year, Gates turned the CEO-ship of the company over to long-time number two, Steve Ballmer, and named himself "Chief Software Architect." He now spends most of his time and considerable talents happily attending to the details of Microsoft's new-product and technology development.

At the heart of Gates's innovation strategy is the Internet. "Gates sees a day when Microsoft software will . . . be at nearly every point a consumer or corporation touches the Web, . . . easily connecting people to the Internet wherever they happen to be," says *Business Week* analyst Jay Greene. In this new world, any software application on your computer—or on your cell phone or handheld device—will tap directly into Internet services that help you manage your work and your life. To prepare for such "anytime, anywhere" computing, Microsoft will transform itself from a software company into an Internet services company. As a part of its Web services, Microsoft will one day rent out the latest versions of its software programs via the Net. "Once that happens," says Greene, "Microsoft hopes to deliver software like a steady flow of electricity, collecting monthly or annual usage fees that will give it a lush, predictable revenue stream."

This vision drives two major Microsoft innovation initiatives—dubbed HailStorm and Dot.Net:

> HailStorm is the first of Microsoft's "personal Web services" and an opening [move] in its Dot.Net strategy to upgrade the Internet to be more versatile and inter-active. HailStorm's initial service, called Passport, provides an online repository for all sorts of personal information and privileges that you can tap into from any computer with a Web browser: contacts, credit card accounts, calendar, file space for documents,... an electronic ID card, and more. It will give you access to your important information from anywhere and also simplify online transactions such as purchasing merchandise or airline tickets. Because Passport knows you already, no matter which Web merchant you deal with, it promises to let you transact your business with far fewer clicks and much tighter security and privacy.

Passport members can subscribe to other HailStorm services, including everything from notifying them of specific events to automatically updating their calendars when they purchase tickets or make an appointment online.

Within this broad strategic framework, Microsoft is now unleashing its biggest-ever new-products assault. "We've never had a year with this many new products," crows Gates. Here are just a few of the new products and technologies that Microsoft has recently launched or will soon introduce (as described in recent *Business Week* and *Fortune* accounts):

- *Dot.Net Services:* Technology that lets unrelated Web sites talk with one another and with PC programs. One click can trigger a cascade of actions without the user having to open new programs or visit new Web sites.
- *Stinger:* Microsoft's latest software for cell phones. It will incorporate the functions of a PDA-address book, calendar, audio and video capabilities, and Internet connectivity to give access to HailStorm services, e-mail, and Web browsing.
- *Xbox:* Microsoft's bold leap into $20 billion game-console business. This game box will be three times more powerful than Sony's PlayStation 2 and Nintendo's Gamecube and will include Web browsing and e-mail applications.
- *Natural-language processing:* Software that will let computers respond to questions or commands in everyday language, not just computerese or a long series of mouse clicks. Combine that with speech recognition—another area in which Microsoft researchers are plugging away—and one day you'll be able to talk to your computer the same way you do to another person.
- *Face mapping:* Using a digital camera to scan a PC user's head into a 3D image. Software then adds a full range of emotions. The point? Microsoft thinks that gamers will want to use their own images in role-playing games.
- *Information agents:* Software agents that help you sort the deluge of electronic information. One day, an agent will study what types of messages you read first and know your schedule. Then it will sort e-mail and voice mail, interrupting you with only key messages.
- *Small business technologies:* Customer-relationship, human resources, and supply-chain software for small and medium-size businesses. Microsoft also offers bCentral, a Web site and e-commerce hosting service. For a monthly fee, it will host a Web site and provide e-mail services, as well as a shopping-cart setup for e-commerce transactions, credit card clearing, and customer management.

So, far from resting on its remarkable past successes, Microsoft is on a quest to discover tomorrow's exciting new technologies. "Even while its latest products are waiting on the launchpad, it continues to pour money into R&D in search of the Next Big Thing," comments Greene. Gates is jazzed about the future. "He gets wound up like a kid over stuff like creating a computer that watches your actions with a small video camera and determines if you're too busy to be interrupted with a phone call or e-mail," says Greene. An excited Gates shares the simple but enduring principle that guides innovation at Microsoft: "The whole idea of valuing the user's time, that's the Holy Grail," he says.[1]

A company has to be good at developing and managing new products. Every product seems to go through a life-cycle—it is born, goes through several phases, and eventually dies as newer products come along that better serve consumer needs. This product life-cycle presents two major challenges: First, because all products eventually decline, a firm must be good at developing new products to replace aging ones (the problem of *new-product development*). Second, the firm must be good at adapting its marketing strategies in the face of changing tastes, technologies, and competition as products pass through life-cycle stages (the problem of *product life-cycle strategies*). We first look at the problem of finding and developing new products and then at the problem of managing them successfully over their life-cycles.

New-Product Development Strategy

New-product development
The development of original products, product improvements, product modifications, and new brands through the firm's own R&D efforts.

Given the rapid changes in consumer tastes, technology, and competition, companies must develop a steady stream of new products and services. A firm can obtain new products in two ways. One is through *acquisition*—by buying a whole company, a patent, or a license to produce someone else's product. The other is through **new-product development** in the company's own research and development department. By *new products* we mean original products, product improvements, product modifications, and new brands that the firm develops through its own research and development efforts. In this chapter, we concentrate on new-product development.

Innovation can be very risky. Ford lost $350 million on its Edsel automobile; RCA lost $580 million on its SelectaVision videodisc player; and Texas Instruments lost a staggering $660 million before withdrawing from the home computer business. Other costly product failures from sophisticated companies include New Coke (Coca-Cola Company), Eagle Snacks (Anheuser-Busch), Zap Mail electronic mail (FedEx), Polarvision instant movies (Polaroid), Premier "smokeless" cigarettes (R.J. Reynolds), Clorox detergent (Clorox Company), and Arch Deluxe sandwiches (McDonald's).[2]

New products continue to fail at a disturbing rate. One source estimates that new consumer packaged goods (consisting mostly of line extensions) fail at a rate of 80 percent. Another study suggested that of the staggering 25,000 new consumer food, beverage, beauty, and health care products to hit the market each year, only 40 percent will be around five years later. Moreover, failure rates for new industrial products may be as high as 30 percent.[3] Why do so many new products fail? There are several reasons. Although an idea may be good, the market size may have been overestimated. Perhaps the actual product was not designed as well as it should have been. Or maybe it was incorrectly positioned in the market, priced too high, or advertised poorly. A high-level executive might push a favorite idea despite poor marketing research findings. Sometimes the costs of product development are higher than expected, and sometimes competitors fight back harder than expected.

Because so many new products fail, companies are anxious to learn how to improve their odds of new-product success. One way is to identify successful new products and find

Figure 9-1
Major stages in new-product development

out what they have in common. Another is to study new-product failures to see what lessons can be learned (see Marketing at Work 9-1). Various studies suggest that new-product success depends on developing a *unique superior product,* one with higher quality, new features, and higher value in use. Another key success factor is a *well-defined product concept* prior to development, in which the company carefully defines and assesses the target market, the product requirements, and the benefits before proceeding. Other success factors have also been suggested—senior management commitment, relentless innovation, and a smoothly functioning new-product development process. In all, to create successful new products, a company must understand its consumers, markets, and competitors and develop products that deliver superior value to customers.

So companies face a problem—they must develop new products, but the odds weigh heavily against success. The solution lies in strong new-product planning and in setting up a systematic *new-product development process* for finding and growing new products. Figure 9-1 shows the eight major steps in this process.

Idea Generation

New-product development starts with **idea generation**—the systematic search for new-product ideas. A company typically has to generate many ideas in order to find a few good ones. According to one well-known management consultant, "For every 1,000 ideas, only 100 will have enough commercial promise to merit a small-scale experiment, only ten of those will warrant substantial financial commitment, and of those, only a couple will turn out to be unqualified successes."[4] His conclusion? "If you want to find a few ideas with the power to enthrall customers, foil competitors, and thrill investors, you must first generate hundreds and potentially thousands of unconventional strategic ideas."

Major sources of new-product ideas include internal sources, customers, competitors, distributors and suppliers, and others. Using *internal sources,* the company can find new ideas through formal research and development. It can pick the brains of its executives, scientists, engineers, manufacturing, and salespeople. Some companies have developed successful "intrapreneurial" programs that encourage employees to think up and develop new-product ideas. For example, 3M's well-known "15 percent rule" allows employees to spend 15 percent of their time "bootlegging"—working on projects of personal interest whether those projects directly benefit the company. The spectacularly successful Post-it notes evolved out of this program. Similarly, Texas Instruments's IDEA program provides funds for employees who pursue their own ideas. Among the successful new products to come out of the IDEA program

Idea generation
The systematic search for new-product ideas.

Marketing at Work 9.1

Mr. Failure's Lessons for Sweet Success

Strolling the aisles at Robert McMath's New Product Showcase and Learning Center is like finding yourself in some nightmare version of a supermarket. There's Gerber food for adults (pureed sweet-and-sour pork and chicken Madeira), Hot Scoop microwaveable ice cream sundaes, Ben-Gay aspirin, Premier smokeless cigarettes, and Miller Clear Beer. How about Richard Simmons Dijon Vinaigrette Salad Spray, Look of Buttermilk shampoo, or garlic cake in a jar, parsnip chips, and aerosol mustard? Most of the 80,000 products on display were abject flops. Behind each of them are squandered dollars and hopes, but McMath, the genial curator of this Smithsonian of consumerism, believes that even failure—or perhaps *especially* failure—offers valuable lessons.

The New Product Showcase and Learning Center is a place where product developers pay hundreds of dollars an hour to visit and learn

from others' mistakes. McMath's unusual showcase represents $4 billion in product investment. From it he has distilled dozens of lessons for an industry that, by its own admission, has a very short memory. McMath "draws large audiences and commands a hefty speaking fee by decrying the convoluted thought processes of marketers, package designers, and consumer-opinion pundits who brought these and thousands of other duds-in-the-making to market," comments one analyst. "He gets laughs when he asks, 'What were they thinking?'" For those who can't make the trip to the center or pay a steep consulting fee, McMath has now put his unique insights into a book by that same name, *What Were They Thinking?* Here are a few of the marketing lessons McMath espouses:

◆ *Offer real value.* Many classic flops failed to deliver what customers really wanted. New Coke flopped

when Coca-Cola failed to see the real value of the Coke brand to customers—tradition as well as taste. Ford pitched its Edsel as revolutionary; consumers saw it as merely revolting. And consumers quickly snuffed out R.J. Reynolds's Premier smokeless cigarettes. It seemed like a good idea at the time—who could argue against a healthier, nonpolluting cigarette? But Premier didn't deliver what smokers really wanted—smoke. In the first place, in the words of RJR's CEO, the cigarettes "tasted like [expletive]!" Moreover, what is a cigarette without smoke? "It took them a while to figure out that smokers actually like the smoke part of smoking," McMath notes. "The only people who loved the product were nonsmokers, and they somehow aren't the market RJR was trying to reach." Looking back, what was RJR thinking?

◆ *Cherish thy brand!* The value of a brand is its good name, which it

The New Product Showcase and Learning Center is like finding yourself in some nightmare version of a supermarket. Each product failure represents squandered dollars and hopes.

earns over time. People become loyal to it. They trust it to deliver a consistent set of attributes. Don't squander this trust by attaching your good name to something totally out of character. Louis Sherry No Sugar Added Gorgonzola Cheese Dressing was everything that Louis Sherry, known for its rich candies and ice cream, shouldn't be: sugarless, cheese, and salad dressing. Similarly, when you hear the name Ben-Gay, you immediately think of the way that Ben-Gay cream sears and stimulates your skin? Can you imagine swallowing Ben-Gay aspirin? Or how would you feel about quaffing a can of Exxon fruit punch or Kodak quencher? Cracker Jack cereal, Smucker's premium ketchup, and Fruit of the Loom laundry detergent were other misbegotten attempts to stretch a good name. What *were* they thinking?

◆ *Be different.* Me-too marketing is the number-one killer of new products. Most such attempts fail. The ones that succeed usually require resources and persistence beyond the capabilities of most marketers. Pepsi-Cola led a very precarious existence for decades before establishing itself as the major competitor to Coca-Cola. More to the point, though, Pepsi is one of the few survivors among

dozens of other brands that have challenged Coke for more than a century. Ever hear of Toca-Cola? Coco-Cola? Yum Yum cola? French Wine of Cola? How about King-Cola, "the royal drink"? More recently, Afri Cola failed to attract African American soda drinkers and Cajun Cola pretty well flopped in the land of gumbo. All things equal, an established product has a distinct advantage over any new product that is not notably different.

◆ *But don't be too different.* Some products are notably different from the products, services, or experiences that consumers normally purchase. *Too* different. They fail because consumers don't relate to them. You can tell that some innovative products are doomed as soon as you hear their names: Toaster Eggs. Cucumber antiperspirant spray. Health-Sea sea sausage. Look of Buttermilk shampoo. Other innovative ideas have been victims of a brand's past success. For example, Nabisco's Oreo Little Fudgies, a confectionery product with a chocolate coating meant to compete with candy, sounds like a natural. But for many years Nabisco has encouraged people to pull apart Oreo cookies and lick out the filling. However, it's very messy to open an Oreo with

a chocolate coating. What was *Nabisco* thinking?

◆ *Accentuate the positive.* Don't be fooled by the success of all the *Dummy's Guide to . . .* books. People usually don't buy products that remind them of their shortcomings. Gillette's For Oily Hair Only shampoo wavered because people did not want to confess that they had greasy hair. People will use products that discreetly say "for oily hair" or "for sensitive skin" in small print on containers that are otherwise identical to the regular product. But they don't want to be hit over the head with reminders that they are overweight, have bad breath, sweat too much, or are elderly. Nor do they wish to advertise their faults and foibles to other people by carrying such products in their grocery carts. Really, what were they thinking?

Sources: Quotes from Gary Slack, "Innovations and Idiocities," *Beverage World,* November 15, 1998, p. 122; and Cliff Edwards, "Where Have All the Edsels Gone?" *Greensboro News Record,* May 24, 1999, p. B6. Bulleted points based on information found in Robert M. McMath and Thom Forbes, *What Were They Thinking? Money-Saving, Time-Saving, Face-Saving Marketing Lessons You Can Learn from Products That Flopped* (New York: Times Business, 1999), various pages. Also see Paul Lukas, "The Ghastliest Product Launches," *Fortune,* March 16, 1996, p. 44; Jan Alexander, "Failure Inc.," *Worldbusiness,* May–June 1996, p. 46; Ted Anthony, "Where's Farrah Shampoo? Next to the Salsa Ketchup," *Marketing News,* May 6, 1996, p. 13; and Melissa Master, "Spectacular Failures," *Across the Board,* March–April 2001, p. 24.

was TI's Speak 'n' Spell, the first children's toy to contain a microchip. Many other speaking toys followed, ultimately generating several hundred million dollars for TI.[5]

Good new-product ideas also come from watching and listening to *customers.* The company can analyze customer questions and complaints to find new products that better solve consumer problems. Company engineers or salespeople can meet with and work alongside customers to get suggestions and ideas. The company can conduct surveys or focus groups to learn about consumer needs and wants. Heinz did just that when its researchers approached children, who consume more than half of the ketchup sold, to find out what would make ketchup more appealing to them. "When we asked them what would make the product more fun," says a Heinz spokesperson, "changing the color was among the top responses." Change the color. So, Heinz developed and launched EZ Squirt, green ketchup that comes in a soft, squeezable bottle targeted at kids. The bottle's special nozzle

"Intrapreneurial" programs encourage employees to think up and develop new product ideas. 3M's spectacularly successful Post-it notes evolved out of such a program.

also emits a thin ketchup stream, "so tykes can autograph their burgers (or squirt someone across the table, though Heinz neglects to mention that)."[6]

Finally, consumers often create new products and uses on their own, and companies can benefit by finding these products and putting them on the market. Customers can also be a good source of ideas for new product uses that can expand the market for and extend the life of current products. For example, Avon capitalized on new uses discovered by consumers for its Skin-So-Soft bath oil and moisturizer. For years, customers have been spreading the word that Skin-So-Soft bath oil is also a terrific bug repellent. Whereas some consumers were content simply to bathe in water scented with the fragrant oil, others carried it in their backpacks to mosquito-infested campsites or kept a bottle on the deck of their beach houses. Now, Avon offers a complete line of Skin-So-Soft Bug Guard products, including Bug Guard Mosquito Repellent Moisturizing Towelettes and Bug Guard Plus, a combination moisturizer, insect repellent, and sunscreen.[7]

Competitors are another good source of new-product ideas. Companies watch competitors' ads and other communications to get clues about their new products. They buy competing new products, take them apart to see how they work, analyze their sales, and decide whether they should bring out a new product of their own. Finally, *distributors and suppliers* contribute many good new-product ideas. Resellers are close to the market and can pass along information about consumer problems and new-product possibilities. Suppliers can tell the company about new concepts, techniques, and materials that can be used to develop new products. Other idea sources include trade magazines, shows, and seminars; government agencies; new-product consultants; advertising agencies; marketing research firms; university and commercial laboratories; and inventors.

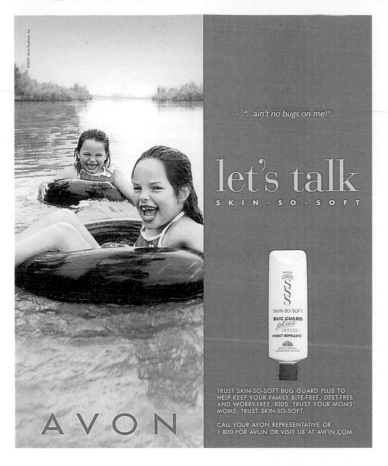

Avon capitalized on new uses discovered by consumers for its Skin-So-Soft bath oil and moisturizer by developing a complete line of Skin-So-Soft Bug Guard products.

The search for new-product ideas should be systematic rather than haphazard. Otherwise, few new ideas will surface and many good ideas will sputter and die. Top management can avoid these problems by installing an *idea management system* that directs the flow of new ideas to a central point where they can be collected, reviewed, and evaluated. In setting up such a system, the company can do any or all of the following:[8]

◆ Appoint a respected senior person to be the company's idea manager.
◆ Create a multidisciplinary idea management committee consisting of people from R&D, engineering, purchasing, operations, finance, and sales and marketing to meet regularly and evaluate proposed new product and service ideas.
◆ Set up a toll-free number for anyone who wants to send a new idea to the idea manager.
◆ Encourage all company stakeholders—employees, suppliers, distributors, dealers—to send their ideas to the idea manager.
◆ Set up formal recognition programs to reward those who contribute the best new ideas.

The idea manager approach yields two favorable outcomes. First, it helps create an innovation-oriented company culture. It shows that top management supports, encourages, and rewards innovation. Second, it will yield a larger number of ideas among which will be found some especially good ones. As the system matures, ideas will flow more freely. No longer will good ideas wither for the lack of a sounding board or a senior product advocate.

Idea Screening

Idea screening
Screening new-product ideas
in order to spot good ideas
and drop poor ones as soon
as possible.

The purpose of idea generation is to create a large number of ideas. The purpose of the succeeding stages is to *reduce* that number. The first idea-reducing stage is **idea screening,** which helps spot good ideas and drop poor ones as soon as possible. Product development costs rise greatly in later stages, so the company wants to go ahead only with the product ideas that will turn into profitable products. As one marketing executive suggests, "Three executives sitting in a room can get 40 good ideas ricocheting off the wall in minutes. The challenge is getting a steady stream of good ideas out of the labs and creativity campfires, through marketing and manufacturing, and all the way to consumers."[9]

Many companies require their executives to write up new-product ideas on a standard form that can be reviewed by a new-product committee. The write-up describes the product, the target market, and the competition. It makes some rough estimates of market size, product price, development time and costs, manufacturing costs, and rate of return. The committee then evaluates the idea against a set of general criteria. For example, at Kao Company, the large Japanese consumer-products company, the committee asks questions such as these: Is the product truly useful to consumers and society? Is it good for our particular company? Does it mesh well with the company's objectives and strategies? Do we have the people, skills, and resources to make it succeed? Does it deliver more value to customers than do competing products? Is it easy to advertise and distribute? Many companies have well-designed systems for rating and screening new-product ideas.

Concept Development and Testing

Product concept
The idea that consumers will favor products that offer the most quality, performance, and features and that the organization should therefore devote its energy to making continuous product improvements.

An attractive idea must be developed into a **product concept.** It is important to distinguish between a product idea, a product concept, and a product image. A *product idea* is an idea for a possible product that the company can see itself offering to the market. A *product concept* is a detailed version of the idea stated in meaningful consumer terms. A *product image* is the way consumers perceive an actual or potential product.

Concept Development DaimlerChrysler is getting ready to commercialize its experimental fuel-cell-powered electric car. This car's nonpolluting fuel-cell system runs directly off liquid hydrogen, producing only water as a byproduct. It is highly fuel efficient (75 percent more efficient than gasoline engines) and gives the new car an environmental advantage over standard internal combustion engine cars or even today's super efficient gasoline–electric hybrid cars. DaimlerChrysler is currently road testing its NECAR 5 (New Electric Car) subcompact prototype and plans to deliver the first fuel-cell cars to customers in 2004. Based on the tiny Mercedes A-Class, the car accelerates quickly, reaches speeds of 90 miles per hour, and has a 280-mile driving range, giving it a huge edge over battery-powered electric cars that travel only about 80 miles before needing 3 to 12 hours of recharging.[10]

DaimlerChrysler's task is to develop this new product into alternative product concepts, find out how attractive each concept is to customers, and choose the best one. It might create the following product concepts for the fuel-cell electric car:

Concept 1   A moderately priced subcompact designed as a second family car to be used around town. The car is ideal for running errands and visiting friends.

Concept 2   A medium-cost sporty compact appealing to young people.

Concept 3   An inexpensive subcompact "green" car appealing to environmentally conscious people who want practical transportation and low pollution.

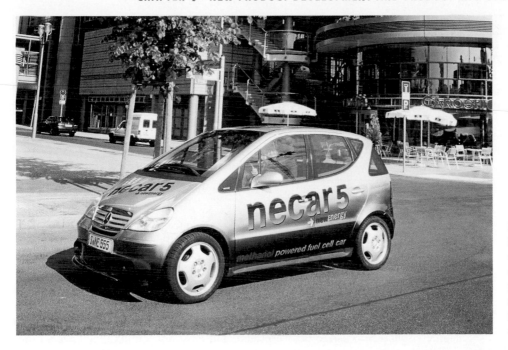

DaimlerChrysler's task is to develop its fuel-cell-powered electric car into alternative product concepts, find out how attractive each is to customers, and choose the best one.

Concept 4   A high-end SUV appealing to those who love the space SUVs provide but lament the poor gas mileage.

Concept Testing   **Concept testing** calls for testing new-product concepts with groups of target consumers. The concepts may be presented to consumers symbolically or physically. Here, in words, is concept 3:

> An efficient, fun-to-drive, fuel-cell-powered electric subcompact car that seats four. This high-tech wonder runs on liquid hydrogen, providing practical and reliable transportation with virtually no pollution. It goes up to 90 miles per hour and, unlike battery-powered electric cars, it never needs recharging. It's priced, fully equipped, at $20,000.

For some concept tests, a word or picture description might be sufficient. However, a more concrete and physical presentation of the concept will increase the reliability of the concept test. Today, some marketers are finding innovative ways to make product concepts more real to consumer subjects. For example, some are using virtual reality to test product concepts. Virtual reality programs use computers and sensory devices (such as gloves or goggles) to simulate reality. A designer of kitchen cabinets can use a virtual reality program to help a customer "see" how his or her kitchen would look and work if remodeled with the company's products. Hairdressers have used virtual reality for years to show consumers how they might look with a new style. Although virtual reality is still in its infancy, its applications are increasing daily.[11]

After being exposed to the concept, consumers then may be asked to react to it by answering questions such as those in Table 9-1. The answers will help the company decide which concept has the strongest appeal. For example, the last question asks about the consumer's intention to buy. Suppose 10 percent of the consumers said they "definitely" would buy and another 5 percent said "probably." The company could project these figures to the full population in this target group to estimate sales volume. Even then, the estimate is uncertain because people do not always carry out their stated intentions.

Many firms routinely test new-product concepts with consumers before attempting to turn them into actual new products. For example, each month Richard Saunders,

Concept testing
Testing new-product concepts with a group of target consumers to find out if the concepts have strong consumer appeal.

Table 9-1   Questions for Fuel-Cell Electric Car Concept Test
1. Do you understand the concept of a fuel-cell-powered electric car?
2. Do you believe the claims about the car's performance?
3. What are the major benefits of the fuel-cell-powered electric car compared with a conventional car?
4. What are its advantages compared with a battery-powered electric car?
5. What improvements in the car's features would you suggest?
6. For what uses would you prefer a fuel-cell-powered electric car to a conventional car?
7. What would be a reasonable price to charge for the car?
8. Who would be involved in your decision to buy such a car? Who would drive it?
9. Would you buy such a car? (definitely, probably, probably not, definitely not)

Inc.'s Acu-Poll research system tests 35 new-product concepts in person on 100 nationally representative grocery store shoppers, rating them as "Pure Gold" or "Fool's Gold" concepts. In recent polls, Nabisco's Oreo Chocolate Cones concept received a rare A+ rating, meaning that consumers think it is an outstanding concept that they would try and buy. Glad Ovenware, Reach Whitening Tape dental floss, and Lender's Bake at Home Bagels were also big hits. Other product concepts didn't fare so well. Nubrush Anti-Bacterial Toothbrush Spray disinfectant, from Applied Microdontics, received an F. Consumers found Nubrush to be overpriced, and most don't think they have a problem with "infected" toothbrushes. Nor did consumers think much of Excedrin Tension Headache Cooling Pads and Moist Mates premoistened toilet tissues. Another concept that fared poorly was Chef Williams 5 Minute Marinade, which comes with a syringe customers use to inject the marinade into meats. "I can't see that on grocery shelves," comments an Acu-Poll executive. Some consumers might find the thought of injecting something into meat a bit repulsive, and "it's just so politically incorrect to have this syringe on there."[12]

Marketing Strategy Development

Marketing strategy development
Designing an initial marketing strategy for a new product based on the product concept.

Suppose DaimlerChrysler finds that concept 3 for the fuel-cell-powered electric car tests best. The next step is **marketing strategy development,** designing an initial marketing strategy for introducing this car to the market.

The *marketing strategy statement* consists of three parts. The first part describes the target market; the planned product positioning; and the sales, market share, and profit goals for the first few years. Thus:

> The target market is younger, well-educated, moderate-to-high-income individuals, couples, or small families seeking practical, environmentally responsible transportation. The car will be positioned as more economical to operate, more fun to drive, and less polluting than today's internal combustion engine or hybrid cars, and as less restricting than battery-powered electric cars, which must be recharged regularly. The company will aim to sell 100,000 cars in the first year, at a loss of not more than $15 million. In the second year, the company will aim for sales of 120,000 cars and a profit of $25 million.

The second part of the marketing strategy statement outlines the product's planned price, distribution, and marketing budget for the first year:

> The fuel-cell-powered electric car will be offered in three colors—red, white, and blue—and will have optional air-conditioning and power-drive features. It will sell at a retail price of $20,000—with 15 percent off the list price to dealers. Dealers who sell more than 10 cars per month will get an additional discount of

5 percent on each car sold that month. An advertising budget of $20 million will be split 50–50 between national and local advertising. Advertising will emphasize the car's fun spirit and low emissions. During the first year, $100,000 will be spent on marketing research to find out who is buying the car and their satisfaction levels.

The third part of the marketing strategy statement describes the planned long-run sales, profit goals, and marketing mix strategy:

DaimlerChrysler intends to capture a 3 percent long-run share of the total auto market and realize an after-tax return on investment of 15 percent. To achieve this, product quality will start high and be improved over time. Price will be raised in the second and third years if competition permits. The total advertising budget will be raised each year by about 10 percent. Marketing research will be reduced to $60,000 per year after the first year.

Business Analysis

Once management has decided on its product concept and marketing strategy, it can evaluate the business attractiveness of the proposal. **Business analysis** involves a review of the sales, costs, and profit projections for a new product to find out whether they satisfy the company's objectives. If they do, the product can move to the product development stage.

To estimate sales, the company might look at the sales history of similar products and conduct surveys of market opinion. It can then estimate minimum and maximum sales to assess the range of risk. After preparing the sales forecast, management can estimate the expected costs and profits for the product, including marketing, R&D, operations, accounting, and finance costs. The company then uses the sales and costs figures to analyze the new product's financial attractiveness.

Business analysis
A review of the sales, costs, and profit projections for a new product to find out whether these factors satisfy the company's objectives.

Product Development

So far, for many new-product concepts, the product may have existed only as a word description, a drawing, or perhaps a crude mock-up. If the product concept passes the business test, it moves into **product development.** Here, R&D or engineering develops the product concept into a physical product. The product development step, however, now calls for a large jump in investment. It will show whether the product idea can be turned into a workable product.

The R&D department will develop and test one or more physical versions of the product concept. R&D hopes to design a prototype that will satisfy and excite consumers and that can be produced quickly and at budgeted costs. Developing a successful prototype can take days, weeks, months, or even years. Often, products undergo rigorous functional tests to make sure that they perform safely and effectively. Here are some examples of such functional tests:[13]

Product development
Developing the product concept into a physical product in order to ensure that the product idea can be turned into a workable product.

A scuba-diving Barbie doll must swim and kick for 15 straight hours to satisfy Mattel that she will last at least one year. But because Barbie may find her feet in small owners' mouths rather than in the bathtub, Mattel has devised another, more torturous test: Barbie's feet are clamped by two steel jaws to make sure that her skin doesn't crack—and choke—potential owners.

At Shaw Industries, temps are paid $5 an hour to pace up and down 5 long rows of sample carpets for up to 8 hours a day, logging an average of 14 miles each. One regular reads 3 mysteries a week while pacing and shed 40 pounds in 2 years. Shaw Industries counts walkers' steps and figures that 20,000 steps equal several years of average carpet wear.

Product testing: Shaw Industries pays temps to pace up and down five long rows of sample carpets for up to eight hours a day, logging an average of 14 miles each.

Acting on behalf of manufacturers, the Buyers Laboratory in Hackensack, New Jersey, an independent office products testing lab, tests the writing quality of ballpoint, felt-tip, and roller-ball pens. Its 50-pound "pen rig" measures a pen's life span. The range fluctuates, but a medium-tip, made-in-the-U.S.A. ballpoint might last for 7,775 feet. In general, pens that blob, skip, and dot receive low ratings. Which pens fail the test altogether? "Some points are so fine they cut through the paper," says one supervisor, "and some felt-tips wear down long before the ink runs out."

The prototype must have the required functional features and also convey the intended psychological characteristics. The electric car, for example, should strike consumers as being well built, comfortable, and safe. Management must learn what makes consumers decide that a car is well built. To some consumers, this means that the car has "solid-sounding" doors. To others, it means that the car is able to withstand heavy impact in crash tests. Consumer tests are conducted in which consumers test-drive the car and rate its attributes.

Test Marketing

Test marketing
The stage of new-product development in which the product and marketing program are tested in more realistic market settings.

If the product passes functional and consumer tests, the next step is **test marketing,** the stage at which the product and marketing program are introduced into more realistic market settings. Test marketing gives the marketer experience with marketing the product before going to the great expense of full introduction. It lets the company test the product and its entire marketing program—positioning strategy, advertising, distribution, pricing, branding and packaging, and budget levels.

The amount of test marketing needed varies with each new product. Test marketing costs can be enormous, and it takes time that may allow competitors to gain advantages. When the costs of developing and introducing the product are low, or when management is already confident about the new product, the company may do little or no test marketing. Companies often do not test-market simple line extensions or copies of successful competitor products. For example, Procter & Gamble introduced its Folger's decaffeinated coffee crystals without test marketing, and Pillsbury rolled out Chewy granola bars and chocolate-covered Granola Dipps with no standard test market. However, when introducing a new product requires a big investment, or when management is not sure of the product or marketing program, a company may do a lot of test marketing. For instance, Lever USA spent two years testing its highly successful Lever 2000 bar soap in Atlanta before introducing it internationally. Frito-Lay did eighteen months of testing in three markets on at least five formulations before introducing its Baked Lays line of low-fat snacks. And both Procter & Gamble and Unilever have spent many months testing their new Juvian and MyHome valet laundry and home fabric care services.[14]

The costs of test marketing can be high, but they are often small when compared with the costs of making a major mistake. For example, Nabisco's launch of one new product without testing had disastrous—and soggy—results:[15]

Nabisco hit a marketing homerun with its Teddy Grahams, teddy-bear-shaped graham crackers in several different flavors. So, the company decided to extend Teddy Grahams into a new area. In 1989, it introduced chocolate, cinnamon, and honey versions of Breakfast Bears Graham Cereal. When the product came out, however, consumers didn't like the taste enough, so the product developers went back to the kitchen and modified the formula. But they didn't test it. The result was a disaster. Although the cereal may have tasted better, it no longer stayed crunchy in milk, as the advertising on the box promised. Instead, it left a gooey mess of graham mush on the bottom of cereal bowls. Supermarket managers soon refused to restock the cereal, and Nabisco executives decided it was too late to reformulate the product again. So a promising new product was killed through haste to get it to market.

Recently, some marketers have begun to use interesting new high-tech approaches to test-market research, such as virtual reality and the Internet (see Marketing at Work 9-2).

Commercialization

Test marketing gives management the information needed to make a final decision about whether to launch the new product. If the company goes ahead with **commercialization**—introducing the new product into the market—it will face high costs. The company will have to build or rent a manufacturing facility. And it may have to spend, in the case of a new consumer packaged good, between $10 million and $200 million for advertising, sales promotion, and other marketing efforts in the first year.

The company launching a new product must first decide on introduction *timing*. If DaimlerChrysler's new fuel-cell electric car will eat into the sales of the company's other cars, its introduction may be delayed. If the car can be improved further, or if the economy is down, the company may wait until the following year to launch it.

Next, the company must decide *where* to launch the new product—in a single location, a region, the national market, or the international market. Few companies have the confidence, capital, and capacity to launch new products into full national or international distribution. They will develop a planned *market rollout* over time. In particular, small companies may enter attractive cities or regions one at a time. Larger companies, however, may quickly introduce new models into several regions or into the full national market.

Companies with international distribution systems may introduce new products through global rollouts. Colgate-Palmolive used to follow a "lead-country" strategy. For example, it launched its Palmolive Optima shampoo and conditioner first in Australia, the Philippines, Hong Kong, and Mexico, then rapidly rolled it out into Europe, Asia, Latin America, and Africa. However, most international companies now introduce their new

Commercialization
Introducing a new product into the market.

Marketing at Work 9-2
Virtual Reality Test Marketing: The Future Is Now

It's a steamy summer Saturday after-noon. Imagine that you're stopping off at the local supermarket to pick up some icy bottles of your favorite sports drink before heading to the tennis courts. You park the car, cross the parking lot, and walk through the store's automatic doors. You head for aisle 5, passing several dis-plays along the way, and locate your usual sports drink brand. You pick it up, check the price, and take it to the checkout counter. Sounds like a pretty typical shopping experience, doesn't it? But in this case, the entire experience took place on your computer screen, not at the supermarket.

You've just experienced virtual reality—the wave of the future for test marketing and concept-testing research—courtesy of Gadd Inter-national Research. Gadd has devel-oped a research tool called Simul-Shop, a virtual reality approach that recreates shopping situations in which researchers can test con-sumers' reactions to factors such as product positioning, store layouts, and package designs.

For example, suppose General Mills wants to test reactions to a new Cheerios package design and store shelf positioning. Using Simul-Shop on a standard desktop PC, test shoppers begin their shopping spree with a screen showing the outside of a grocery store. They click to enter the virtual store and are guided to the appropriate store section. Once there, they can scan the shelf, pick up various cereal packages, rotate them, study the labels—even look around to see

what is on the shelf behind them. About the only thing they can't do is open the box and taste the cereal.

The virtual shopping trip includes full sound and video, along with a guide who directs users through the experience and answers their questions. Explains a Gadd's research director, "Once [users] move toward the item we want to test, [they] can look at dif-ferent packaging, shelf layouts, and package colors. Depending on the activity, we can even ask users why they did what they did."

Virtual reality testing can take any of several forms. For example, Elumens has created a virtual reality amphitheater called the Vision-Dome. The Dome offers 360 by 160 degrees of film projection, allowing

Virtual reality: The wave of the future for marketing-testing and concept-testing research. Elumens' VisionDome allows as many as 45 people at a time to participate in a virtual reality experience.

as many as 45 people at one time to participate in a virtual reality experience. The VisionDome is like an IMAX theater, but with one big difference—it's interactive. "When you use a computer to generate an image, . . . you have the advantage of making that image interactive," comments an Elumens executive. When conducting research on a car, he suggests, "We can go into a VisionDome, see that car in three dimensions, look at it from every angle, take it out for a test drive, and allow the customer to configure that car exactly the way he wants it." Caterpillar sees enormous potential for the Dome. "We can put one of our tractors in a VisionDome and actually have a customer sit in it and test it under whatever conditions they would use it for," says a Caterpillar design engineer. "The ability to immerse people in the product makes it a phenomenal [research and sales] tool."

Virtual reality as a research tool offers several advantages. For one, it's relatively inexpensive. For example, a firm can conduct a Simul-Shop study for only about $25,000, including initial programming and the actual research on 75 to 100 people. This makes virtual reality research accessible to firms that can't afford full market-testing campaigns or the expense of creating actual mock-ups for each different product color, shape, or size. Another advantage is flexibility. A virtual reality store can display an almost infinite variety of

products, sizes, styles, and flavors in response to consumers' desires and needs. Research can be conducted in almost any simulated surroundings, ranging from food store interiors and new car showrooms to farm fields or the open road. The technique also offers great interactivity, allowing marketers and consumers to work together via computer on designs of new products and marketing programs.

Finally, virtual reality has great potential for international research, which has often been difficult for marketers to conduct. With virtual reality, researchers can use a single standardized approach to evaluate products and programs worldwide. Consider the following example:

One multinational company has begun to conduct virtual-shopping studies in North and South America, Europe, Asia, and Australia. Researchers create virtual stores in each country and region using the appropriate local products, shelf layouts, and currencies. Once the stores are online, a product concept can be quickly tested across locations. When the studies are completed, the results are communicated to headquarters electronically. The analysis reveals which markets offer the greatest opportunity for a successful launch.

Virtual reality research also has its limitations. The biggest problem: Simulated shopping situations never quite match the real thing.

Observes one expert, "Just because it's technically [feasible], that doesn't mean that when you put [people] behind a computer you're going to get true responses. Anytime you simulate an experience you're not getting the experience itself. It's still a simulation."

So what's ahead for virtual reality in marketing? Some pioneers are extremely enthusiastic about the technology—not only as a research tool but also as a place where even real buying and selling can occur. They predict that the virtual store may become a major channel for personal and direct interactions with consumers, interactions that encompass not only research but sales and service as well. They see great potential for conducting this type of research over the Internet, and virtual stores have become a reality on the Web. As one observer notes, "This is what I read about in science fiction books when I was growing up. It's the thing of the future." For many marketers, that future is already a virtual reality.

Sources: Quotes and extracts from Raymond R. Burke, "Virtual Shopping: Breakthrough in Marketing Research," *Harvard Business Review,* March–April, 1996, pp. 120–131; Tom Dellacave Jr., "Curing Market Research Headaches," *Sales and Marketing Management,* July 1996, pp. 84–85; Brian Silverman, "Get Em While They're Hot," *Sales and Marketing Management,* February 1997, pp. 47–48, 52; and Mike Hoffman, "Virtual Shopping," *Inc.,* July 1998, p. 88. Also see Sara Sellar, "The Perfect Trade Show Rep," *Sales and Marketing Management,* April 1999, p. 11; Christopher Ryan, "Virtual Reality in Marketing," *Direct Marketing,* April 2001, pp. 57–62; and information accessed online at www.elumens.com/products/visiondome.htm, December 2001.

products in swift global assaults. Last year, in its fastest new-product rollout ever, Colgate introduced its Actibrush battery-powered toothbrush into 50 countries in a year, generating $115 million in sales. Such rapid worldwide expansion solidified the brand's market position before foreign competitors could react.[16]

Speeding Up New-Product Development

Many companies organize their new-product development process into the orderly sequence of steps shown in Figure 9-1, starting with idea generation and ending with

Sequential product development
A new-product development approach in which one company department works to complete its stage of the process before passing the new product along to the next department and stage.

Simultaneous (or team-based) product development
An approach to developing new products in which various company departments work closely together, overlapping the steps in the product-development process to save time and increase effectiveness.

commercialization. Under this **sequential product development** approach, one company department works individually to complete its stage of the process before passing the new product along to the next department and stage. This orderly, step-by-step process can help bring control to complex and risky projects. But it also can be dangerously slow. In fast-changing, highly competitive markets, such slow-but-sure product development can result in product failures, lost sales and profits, and crumbling market positions. "Speed to market" and reducing new-product development cycle time have become pressing concerns to companies in all industries.

In order to get their new products to market more quickly, many companies are adopting a faster team-oriented approach called **simultaneous product development** (or teamed-based or collaborative product development). Under this approach, company departments work closely together through cross-functional teams, overlapping the steps in the product development process to save time and increase effectiveness. Instead of passing the new product from department to department, the company assembles a team of people from various departments that stays with the new product from start to finish. Such teams usually include people from the marketing, finance, design, manufacturing, and legal departments, and even supplier and customer companies.

Top management gives the product development team general strategic direction but no clear-cut product idea or work plan. It challenges the team with stiff and seemingly contradictory goals—"turn out carefully planned and superior new products, but do it quickly"—and then gives the team whatever freedom and resources it needs to meet the challenge. In the sequential process, a bottleneck at one phase can seriously slow the entire project. In the simultaneous approach, if one functional area hits snags, it works to resolve them while the team moves on.

The Allen-Bradley Company, a maker of industrial controls, realized tremendous benefits by using simultaneous development. Under its old sequential approach, the company's marketing department handed off a new-product idea to designers, who worked in isolation to prepare concepts that they then passed along to product engineers. The engineers, also working by themselves, developed expensive prototypes and handed them off to manufacturing, which tried to find a way to build the new product. Finally, after many years and dozens of costly design compromises and delays, marketing was asked to sell the new product, which it often found to be too high priced or sadly out of date. Now, all of Allen-Bradley's departments work together to develop new products. The results have been astonishing. For example, the company recently developed a new electrical control in just two years; under the old system, it would have taken six years.

The simultaneous team-based approach does have some limitations. Superfast product development can be riskier and more costly than the slower, more orderly sequential approach. Moreover, it often creates increased organizational tension and confusion. And the company must take care that rushing a product to market doesn't adversely affect its quality—the objective is not only to create products faster, but to create them *better* and faster. Despite these drawbacks, in rapidly changing industries facing increasingly shorter product life-cycles, the rewards of fast and flexible product development far exceed the risks. Companies that get new and improved products to the market faster than competitors often gain a dramatic competitive edge. They can respond more quickly to emerging consumer tastes and charge higher prices for more advanced designs. As one auto industry executive states, "What we want to do is get the new car approved, built, and in the consumer's hands in the shortest time possible. . . . Whoever gets there first gets all the marbles."[17]

Linking the Concepts

Take a break. Think about new products and how companies find and develop them.

◆ Suppose that you're on a panel to nominate the "best new products of the year." What products would you nominate and why? See what you can learn about the new-product development process for one of these products.

◆ Applying the new-product development process you've just studied, develop an idea for an innovative new snack food product and sketch out a brief plan for bringing it to market. Loosen up and have some fun with this.

Product Life-Cycle Strategies

After launching the new product, management wants the product to enjoy a long and happy life. Although it does not expect the product to sell forever, the company wants to earn a decent profit to cover all the effort and risk that went into launching it. Management is aware that each product will have a life-cycle, although its exact shape and length is not known in advance.

Figure 9-2 shows a typical **product life-cycle (PLC),** the course that a product's sales and profits take over its lifetime. The product life-cycle has five distinct stages:

Product life-cycle (PLC)
The course of a product's sales and profits over its lifetime. It involves five distinct stages: product development, introduction, growth, maturity, and decline.

1. *Product development* begins when the company finds and develops a new-product idea. During product development, sales are zero and the company's investment costs mount.
2. *Introduction* is a period of slow sales growth as the product is introduced in the market. Profits are nonexistent in this stage because of the heavy expenses of product introduction.
3. *Growth* is a period of rapid market acceptance and increasing profits.
4. *Maturity* is a period of slowdown in sales growth because the product has achieved acceptance by most potential buyers. Profits level off or decline because of increased marketing outlays to defend the product against competition.
5. *Decline* is the period when sales fall off and profits drop.

Not all products follow this product life-cycle. Some products are introduced and die quickly; others stay in the mature stage for a long, long time. Some enter the decline stage and are then cycled back into the growth stage through strong promotion or repositioning.

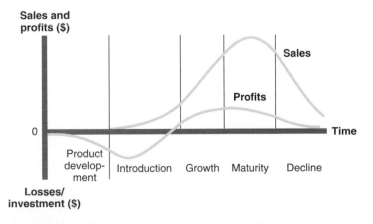

Figure 9-2
Sales and profits over the product's life from inception to demise

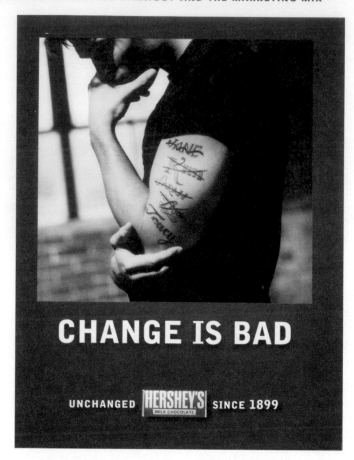

Product life-cycle: Companies want their products to enjoy long and happy life-cycles. Hershey's chocolate bars have been "unchanged since 1899."

The PLC concept can describe a *product class* (gasoline-powered automobiles), a *product form* (minivans), or a *brand* (the Ford Taurus). The PLC concept applies differently in each case. Product classes have the longest life-cycles—the sales of many product classes stay in the mature stage for a long time. Product forms, in contrast, tend to have the standard PLC shape. Product forms such as "cream deodorants," "dial telephones," and "phonograph records" passed through a regular history of introduction, rapid growth, maturity, and decline. A specific brand's life-cycle can change quickly because of changing competitive attacks and responses. For example, although laundry soaps (product class) and powdered detergents (product form) have enjoyed fairly long life-cycles, the life-cycles of specific brands have tended to be much shorter. Today's leading brands of powdered laundry soap are Tide and Cheer; the leading brands 75 years ago were Fels Naptha, Octagon, and Kirkman.[18]

The PLC concept also can be applied to what are known as styles, fashions, and fads. Their special life-cycles are shown in Figure 9-3. A **style** is a basic and distinctive mode of expression. For example, styles appear in homes (colonial, ranch, transitional), clothing (formal, casual), and art (realist, surrealist, abstract). Once a style is invented, it may last for generations, passing in and out of vogue. A style has a cycle showing several periods of renewed interest. A **fashion** is a currently accepted or popular style in a given field. For example, the more formal "business attire" look of corporate dress of the 1980s and early 1990s has now given way to the "business casual" look of today. Fashions tend to grow slowly, remain popular for a while, then decline slowly.

Fads are fashions that enter quickly, are adopted with great zeal, peak early, and decline very quickly. They last only a short time and tend to attract only a limited following.

Style
A basic and distinctive mode of expression.

Fashion
A currently accepted or popular style in a given field.

Fads
Fashions that enter quickly, are adopted with great zeal, peak early, and decline very quickly.

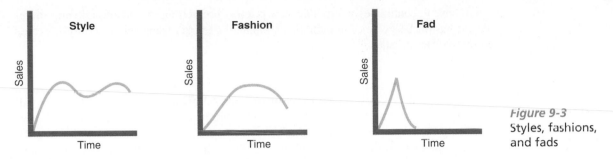

Figure 9-3
Styles, fashions, and fads

"Pet rocks" are a classic example of a fad. Upon hearing his friends complain about how expensive it was to care for their dogs, advertising copywriter Gary Dahl joked about his pet rock and was soon writing a spoof of a dog-training manual for it. Soon Dahl was selling some 1.5 million ordinary beach pebbles at $4 a pop. Yet the fad, which broke in October 1975, had sunk like a stone by the next February. Dahl's advice to those who want to succeed with a fad: "Enjoy it while it lasts." Other examples of fads include Rubik's Cubes, lava lamps, CB radios, and scooters. Most fads do not survive for long because they normally do not satisfy a strong need or satisfy it well.[19]

The PLC concept can be applied by marketers as a useful framework for describing how products and markets work. But using the PLC concept for forecasting product performance or for developing marketing strategies presents some practical problems. For example, managers may have trouble identifying which stage of the PLC the product is in, pinpointing when the product moves into the next stage, and determining the factors that affect the product's movement through the stages. In practice, it is difficult to forecast the sales level at each PLC stage, the length of each stage, and the shape of the PLC curve.

Using the PLC concept to develop marketing strategy also can be difficult because strategy is both a cause and a result of the product's life-cycle. The product's current PLC position suggests the best marketing strategies, and the resulting marketing strategies affect product performance in later life-cycle stages. Yet, when used carefully, the PLC concept can help in developing good marketing strategies for different stages of the product life-cycle.

We looked at the product development stage of the product life-cycle in the first part of the chapter. We now look at strategies for each of the other life-cycle stages.

Introduction Stage

The **introduction stage** starts when the new product is first launched. Introduction takes time, and sales growth is apt to be slow. Well-known products such as instant coffee, frozen orange juice, and powdered coffee creamers lingered for many years before they entered a stage of rapid growth.

In this stage, as compared to other stages, profits are negative or low because of the low sales and high distribution and promotion expenses. Much money is needed to attract distributors and build their inventories. Promotion spending is relatively high to inform consumers of the new product and get them to try it. Because the market is not generally ready for product refinements at this stage, the company and its few competitors produce basic versions of the product. These firms focus their selling on those buyers who are the most ready to buy.

A company, especially the *market pioneer,* must choose a launch strategy that is consistent with the intended product positioning. It should realize that the initial strategy is just the first step in a grander marketing plan for the product's entire life-cycle. If the pioneer chooses its launch strategy to make a "killing," it will be sacrificing long-run revenue for the sake of short-run gain. As the pioneer moves through later stages of the life-cycle,

Introduction stage
The product life-cycle stage in which the new product is first distributed and made available for purchase.

it will have to continuously formulate new pricing, promotion, and other marketing strategies. It has the best chance of building and retaining market leadership if it plays its cards correctly from the start.[20]

Growth Stage

Growth stage
The product life-cycle stage in which a product's sales start climbing quickly.

If the new product satisfies the market, it will enter a **growth stage,** in which sales will start climbing quickly. The early adopters will continue to buy, and later buyers will start following their lead, especially if they hear favorable word of mouth. Attracted by the opportunities for profit, new competitors will enter the market. They will introduce new product features, and the market will expand. The increase in competitors leads to an increase in the number of distribution outlets, and sales jump just to build reseller inventories. Prices remain where they are or fall only slightly. Companies keep their promotion spending at the same or a slightly higher level. Educating the market remains a goal, but now the company must also meet the competition.

Profits increase during the growth stage, as promotion costs are spread over a large volume and as unit manufacturing costs fall. The firm uses several strategies to sustain rapid market growth as long as possible. It improves product quality and adds new product features and models. It enters new market segments and new distribution channels. It shifts some advertising from building product awareness to building product conviction and purchase, and it lowers prices at the right time to attract more buyers.

In the growth stage, the firm faces a trade-off between high market share and high current profit. By spending a lot of money on product improvement, promotion, and distribution, the company can capture a dominant position. In doing so, however, it gives up maximum current profit, which it hopes to make up in the next stage.

Maturity Stage

Maturity stage
The stage in the product life-cycle in which sales growth slows or levels off.

At some point, a product's sales growth will slow down, and the product will enter a **maturity stage.** This maturity stage normally lasts longer than the previous stages, and it poses strong challenges to marketing management. Most products are in the maturity stage of the life-cycle, and therefore most of marketing management deals with the mature product.

The slowdown in sales growth results in many producers with many products to sell. In turn, this overcapacity leads to greater competition. Competitors begin marking down prices, increasing their advertising and sales promotions, and upping their R&D budgets to find better versions of the product. These steps lead to a drop in profit. Some of the weaker competitors start dropping out, and the industry eventually contains only well-established competitors.

Although many products in the mature stage appear to remain unchanged for long periods, most successful ones are actually evolving to meet changing consumer needs (see Marketing at Work 9-3). Product managers should do more than simply ride along with or defend their mature products—a good offense is the best defense. They should consider modifying the market, product, and marketing mix.

In *modifying the market,* the company tries to increase the consumption of the current product. It looks for new users and market segments, as when Johnson & Johnson targeted the adult market with its baby powder and shampoo. The manager also looks for ways to increase usage among present customers. Campbell does this by offering recipes and convincing consumers that "soup is good food." Or the company may want to reposition the brand to appeal to a larger or faster-growing segment, as Arrow did when it introduced its new line of casual shirts and announced, "We're loosening our collars."

The company might also try *modifying the product*—changing characteristics such as quality, features, or style to attract new users and to inspire more usage. It might improve the product's quality and performance—its durability, reliability, speed, taste. It can improve

Marketing at Work 9.3

Age-Defying Products or Just Skillful PLC Management?

Some products are born and die quickly. Others, however, seem to defy the product life-cycle, enduring for decades or even generations with little or no apparent change in their makeup or marketing. Look deeper, however, and you'll find that such products are far from unchanging. Rather, skillful product life-cycle management keeps them fresh, relevant, and appealing to customers. Here are examples of three products that might have been only fads but instead were turned into long-term market winners with plenty of staying power.

Beanie Babies

When Ty Inc. unleashed Beanie Babies on the market in 1993, most experts saw them as just a passing fad. Priced under $5, the tiny bean-filled creatures were designed as a back-to-basics toy that kids could buy with their own allowance money. Soon, however, adults began compulsively collecting the floppy little animals, and the company couldn't get them onto store shelves fast enough.

Yet Ty quickly realized that scarcity would be the key to keeping the Beanie Babies craze going—and going and going. The company became adept at maintaining consumer demand by limiting distribution and keeping the character lineup fresh. Ty adds to the hype by regularly retiring old characters and replacing them with many new ones. Retired models fetch as much as $1,000 from hard-core collectors. In early 2000, Ty stunned collectors when it announced its intention to stop making Beanie Babies altogether. After receiving stacks of letters from children, teachers, hospitals, clinics, and charities around the world, Ty reconsidered. It conducted a worldwide vote by telephone and

the Internet to let consumers decide whether it should continue to make the little animals. More than 200,000 people responded; 91 percent favored continued production. Skeptics suspected that Ty had planned all along to continue Beanie Babies—at the time of the announcement, it had recently expanded its factories and held several trademarks for new Beanies. Whatever the explanation, long after the experts would have predicted the demise of these cute little critters, avid collectors are still lining up to get their hands on new styles.

Barbie

Talk about age-defying products. Although Mattel's Barbie turned 43 this year, Mattel has kept Barbie both timeless and trendy. Since her creation in 1959, Barbie has mirrored girls' dreams of what they'd like to be when they grow up. As such, Barbie has changed as girls' dreams have changed. Her aspira-

tions have evolved from jobs such as stewardess, fashion model, and nurse to astronaut, rock singer, surgeon, and presidential candidate. These days, Barbie hardly notices her age—she's too busy being a WNBA basketball player, Olympic skater, and NASCAR race car driver.

Pursuing its mission to "engage, enchant, and empower girls," Mattel introduces new Barbie dolls every year in order to keep up with the latest definitions of achievement, glamour, romance, adventure, and nurturing. Barbie also reflects America's diverse and changing population. Mattel has produced African American Barbie dolls since 1968 and has since introduced Hispanic and Asian dolls as well. In recent years, Mattel has introduced Crystal Barbie (a gorgeous glamour doll), Puerto Rican Barbie (part of its "dolls of the world" collection), Great Shape Barbie (to tie into the fitness craze), Flight Time Barbie (a pilot), Soccer Barbie (to tie in with the recent boom in girls' soccer), and

Some products seem to defy the product life-cycle: Although Mattel's Barbie is well into her 40s, she hardly notices her age—she's too busy being a WNBA basketball star, a NASCAR race car driver, a soccer player, and a pilot.

Children's Doctor Barbie (the first in the "I Can Be" Career Series Barbies). Barbie herself has received several makeovers. The most recent one gave her a wider face, her first belly button, slightly less prominent breasts, and a more athletic body.

As a result of Mattel's adept product life-cycle handling, Barbie has kept her market allure as well as her youth. Available in 150 countries, Barbie now sells at a rate of two each second worldwide and racks up sales of more than $1.5 billion a year. If you placed head to foot every doll ever sold, Barbie and her friends would circle the globe 72 times.

Crayola Crayons

Over the past 100 years or so, Binney & Smith's Crayola crayons have become a household staple in more than 60 countries around the world. Few people can forget their first pack of "64s"—64 beauties neatly arranged in the familiar green and yellow flip-top box with a sharpener on the back. The aroma of a freshly opened Crayola box still drives kids into a frenzy and takes members of the older generation back to some of their fondest childhood memories.

In some ways, Crayola crayons haven't changed much since 1903, when they were sold in an eight-pack for a nickel. But a closer look reveals that Binney & Smith has made many adjustments to keep the brand out of decline. The company has added a steady stream of new colors, shapes, sizes, and pack-ages. It has gradually increased the number of colors from the original eight in 1903 (red, yellow, blue, green, orange, black, brown, and white) to 120 in 2001. In 1962, as a result of the civil rights movement, it changed its crayon color "flesh" to "peach"; and in 1992, it added multicultural skin tones by which "children are able to build a positive sense of self and respect for cultural diversity." Binney & Smith has also extended the Crayola brand to new markets such as Crayola Markers, watercolor paints, themed stamps and stickers, and stencils. Crayola now offers washable markers, as well as washable crayons for the kids who love to color on walls. The company has licensed the Crayola brand for use on everything from lunch boxes and children's apparel to house paints. Finally, the company has added several programs and services to help strengthen its relationships with Crayola customers. Its *Crayola Kids* magazine and Crayola Web site offer features for children along with interactive art and craft suggestions for parents and educators on helping develop reading skills and creativity.

Not all of Binney & Smith's life-cycle adjustments have been greeted favorably by consumers. For example, in 1990, to make room for more modern colors, it retired 8 colors from the time-honored box of 64—raw umber, lemon yellow, maize, blue grey, orange yellow, orange red, green blue, and violet blue—into the Crayola Hall of Fame. The move unleashed a groundswell of protest from loyal Crayola users, who formed such organizations as the RUMPS—the Raw Umber and Maize Preservation Society—and the National Committee to Save Lemon Yellow. Company executives were flabbergasted—"We were aware of the loyalty and nostalgia surrounding Crayola crayons," a spokesperson says, "but we didn't know we [would] hit such a nerve." The company reissued the old standards in a special collector's tin—it sold all of the 2.5 million tins made.

Thus, Crayola continues its long and colorful life-cycle. Through smart product life-cycle management, Binney & Smith, now a subsidiary of Hallmark, has dominated the crayon market for almost a century. The company now makes nearly 3 billion crayons a year, enough to circle the world six times. Sixty-five percent of all American children between the ages of two and seven pick up a crayon at least once a day and color for an average of 28 minutes. Nearly 80 percent of the time, they pick up a Crayola crayon.

Sources: See Carole Schmidt and Lynn Kaladjian, "Ty Connects Hot-Property Dots," *Brandweek,* June 16, 1997, p. 26; "Consumers Vote for More Beanie Babies," *New York Times,* January 3, 2000, p. C2; information accessed online at www.ty.com, December 2001; Alice Cuneo and Laura Petrecca, "Barbie Has to Work Harder to Help Out Sagging Mattel," *Advertising Age,* March 6, 2000, p. 4; Christopher Palmeri, "Mattel: Up the Hill Minus Jill," *Business Week,* April 9, 2001, pp. 53–54; and information accessed at www.barbie.com, December 2001; "Hue and Cry Over Crayola May Revive Old Colors," *Wall Street Journal,* June 14, 1991, p. B1; Margaret O. Kirk, "Coloring Our Children's World Since '03," *Chicago Tribune,* October 29, 1986, sec. 5, p. 1; "Crayon Maker Announces Color Census Results," Crayola press release, accessed online at www.crayola.com, January 31, 2001.

the product's styling and attractiveness. Thus, car manufacturers restyle their cars to attract buyers who want a new look. The makers of consumer food and household products introduce new flavors, colors, ingredients, or packages to revitalize consumer buying. Or the company might add new features that expand the product's usefulness, safety, or convenience. For example, Sony keeps adding new styles and features to its Walkman and Discman lines, and Volvo adds new safety features to its cars. Kimberly-Clark is adding a new twist to revitalize the product life-cycle of an old standby, toilet tissue:

Almost without exception, every American family knows what the paper roll next to the toilet is for, knows how to use it, and purchases it faithfully. Selling an omnipresent household item requires a vital brand that stands out at the supermarket, but how do you make toilet tissue new and exciting? Kimberly-Clark, the maker of Cottonelle and Kleenex, has the answer with an unprecedented innovation: a premoistened toilet paper called Rollwipes. Like baby wipes on a roll, the product is designed to complement traditional toilet tissue. "In this category, your growth has to come from significant product innovations," says a marketing director for Cottonelle. Another marketing executive agrees: "Without new products, old brands become older brands. In categories where there's basic satisfactions with the products, you still have to provide new benefits . . . to build brand share."[21]

Finally, the company can try *modifying the marketing mix*—improving sales by changing one or more marketing mix elements. It can cut prices to attract new users and competitors' customers. It can launch a better advertising campaign or use aggressive sales promotions—trade deals, cents-off, premiums, and contests. The company can also move into larger market channels, using mass merchandisers, if these channels are growing. Finally, the company can offer new or improved services to buyers.

Linking the Concepts

Pause for a moment and think about some products that, like Crayola Crayons, have been around for a long time.

◆ Ask a grandparent or someone else who shaved back then to compare a 1940s or 1950s Gillette razor to the most current model. Is Gillette's latest razor really a new product or just a "retread" of the previous version? What do you conclude about product life-cycles?

◆ The Monopoly board game has been around for decades. How has Parker Brothers protected Monopoly from old age and decline (check out www.monopoly.com)?

Decline Stage

The sales of most product forms and brands eventually dip. The decline may be slow, as in the case of oatmeal cereal, or rapid, as in the case of phonograph records. Sales may plunge to zero, or they may drop to a low level where they continue for many years. This is the **decline stage.**

Sales decline for many reasons, including technological advances, shifts in consumer tastes, and increased competition. As sales and profits decline, some firms withdraw from the market. Those remaining may prune their product offerings. They may drop smaller market segments and marginal trade channels, or they may cut the promotion budget and reduce their prices further.

Carrying a weak product can be very costly to a firm, and not just in profit terms. There are many hidden costs. A weak product may take up too much of management's time. It often requires frequent price and inventory adjustments. It requires advertising and sales force attention that might be better used to make "healthy" products more profitable. A product's failing reputation can cause customer concerns about the company and its other products. The biggest cost may well lie in the future. Keeping weak products delays the search for replacements, creates a lopsided product mix, hurts current profits, and weakens the company's foothold on the future.

For these reasons, companies need to pay more attention to their aging products. The firm's first task is to identify those products in the decline stage by regularly reviewing

Decline stage
The product life-cycle stage in which a product's sales decline.

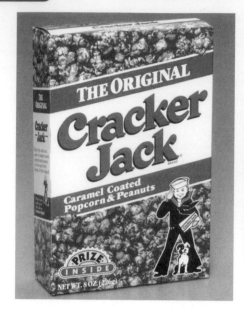

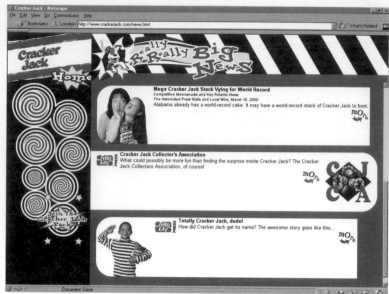

Back into the growth stage: When this timeless brand was running out of time, Frito-Lay reconnected it with a new generation of kids. Sales more than doubled during the two years following the acquisition.

sales, market shares, costs, and profit trends. Then, management must decide whether to maintain, harvest, or drop each of these declining products.

Management may decide to *maintain* its brand without change in the hope that competitors will leave the industry. For example, Procter & Gamble made good profits by remaining in the declining liquid soap business as others withdrew. Or management may decide to reposition or reformulate the brand in hopes of moving it back into the growth stage of the product life-cycle. Frito-Lay did this with the classic Cracker Jack brand:

When Cracker Jack passed the 100-year-old mark, it seemed that the timeless brand was running out of time. By the time Frito-Lay acquired the classic snack-food brand from Borden Foods in 1997, sales and profits had been declining for five straight years. Frito-Lay set out to reconnect the box of candy-coated popcorn, peanuts, and a prize with a new generation of kids. "We made the popcorn bigger and fluffier with more peanuts and bigger prizes, and we put it in bags, as well as boxes," says Chris Neugent, VP-marketing for wholesome snacks for Frito-Lay. New promotional programs shared a connection with baseball and fun for kids, featuring baseball star Mark McGwire, Rawlings Sporting Goods trading cards, F.A.O. Schwarz, and Pokemon and Scooby Doo characters. The revitalized marketing pulled Cracker Jack out of decline. Sales more than doubled during the two years following the acquisition and the brand has posted double-digit increases each year since.[22]

Management may decide to *harvest* the product, which means reducing various costs (plant and equipment, maintenance, R&D, advertising, sales force) and hoping that sales hold up. If successful, harvesting will increase the company's profits in the short run. Or management may decide to *drop* the product from the line. It can sell it to another firm or simply liquidate it at salvage value. If the company plans to find a buyer, it will not want to run down the product through harvesting.

Table 9-2 summarizes the key characteristics of each stage of the product life-cycle. The table also lists the marketing objectives and strategies for each stage.[23]

Table 9-2   Summary of Product Life-Cycle Characteristics, Objectives, and Strategies

	Introduction	Growth	Maturity	Decline
Characteristics				
Sales	Low sales	Rapidly rising sales	Peak sales	Declining sales
Costs	High cost per customer	Average cost per customer	Low cost per customer	Low cost per customer
Profits	Negative	Rising profits	High profits	Declining profits
Customers	Innovators	Early adopters	Middle majority	Laggards
Competitors	Few	Growing number	Stable number beginning to decline	Declining number
Marketing Objectives	Create product and trial	Maximize market share	Maximize profit while defending market share	Reduce expenditure and milk the brand
Strategies				
Product	Offer a basic product	Offer product extensions, service, warranty	Diversify brand and models	Phase out weak items
Price	Use cost-plus formula	Price to penetrate market	Price to match or best competitors	Cut price
Distribution	Build selective distribution	Build intensive distribution	Build more intensive distribution	Go selective: Phase out unprofitable outlets
Advertising	Build product awareness among early adopters and dealers	Build awareness and interest in the mass market	Stress brand differences and benefits	Reduce to level needed to retain hard-core loyals
Sales promotion	Use heavy sales promotion to entice trial	Reduce to take advantage of heavy consumer demand	Increase to encourage brand switching	Reduce to minimal level

Source: Philip Kotler, *Marketing Management: Analysis, Planning, Implementation, and Control,* 11th ed. (Upper Saddle River, NJ: Prentice Hall, 2003), Chap. 10.

 STOP *Rest Stop: Reviewing the Concepts*

Well, there's one more travel sticker on your marketing bumper. Before we move on to the next marketing mix destination, let's review the important new product and product life-cycle concepts. A company's current products face limited life spans and must be replaced by newer products. But new products can fail—the risks of innovation are as great as the rewards. The key to successful innovation lies in a total-company effort, strong planning, and a systematic *new-product development* process.

1. Explain how companies find and develop new-product ideas.

Companies find and develop new-product ideas from a variety of sources. Many new-product ideas stem from *internal sources.* Companies conduct formal research and development, pick the brains of their employees, and brainstorm at executive meetings. By conducting surveys and focus groups and analyzing *customer* questions and complaints, companies can generate new-product ideas that will meet specific consumer needs. Companies track *competitors'* offerings and inspect new products, dismantling them, analyzing their performance, and deciding whether to introduce a similar or improved product. *Distributors and suppliers* are close to the market and can pass along information about consumer problems and new-product possibilities.

2. List and define the steps in the new-product development process.

The new-product development process consists of eight sequential stages. The process starts with *idea generation.* Next comes *idea screening,* which reduces the number of ideas based on the company's own criteria. Ideas that pass the screening stage continue through *product concept development,* in which a detailed version of the new-product idea is stated in meaningful consumer terms. In the next stage, *concept testing,* new-product concepts are tested with a group of target consumers to determine whether the concepts have strong consumer appeal. Strong concepts proceed to *marketing strategy development,* in which an initial marketing strategy for the new product is developed from the product concept. In the *business analysis* stage, a review of the sales, costs, and profit projections for a new product is conducted to determine whether the new product is likely to satisfy the company's objectives. With positive results here, the ideas become more concrete through *product development* and *test marketing* and finally are launched during *commercialization.*

3. Describe the stages of the product life-cycle.

Each product has a *life-cycle* marked by a changing set of problems and opportunities. The sales of the typical product follow an S-shaped curve made up of five stages. The cycle begins with the *product development stage* when the company finds and develops a new-product idea. The *introduction stage* is marked by slow growth and low profits as the product is distributed to the market. If successful, the product enters a *growth stage,* which offers rapid sales growth and increasing profits. Next comes a *maturity stage* when sales growth slows down and profits stabilize. Finally, the product enters a *decline stage* in which sales and profits dwindle. The company's task during this stage is to recognize the decline and to decide whether it should maintain, harvest, or drop the product.

4. Explain how marketing strategies change during the product's life-cycle.

In the *introduction stage,* the company must choose a launch strategy consistent with its intended product positioning. Much money is needed to attract distributors and build their inventories and to inform consumers of the new product and achieve trial. In the *growth stage,* companies continue to educate potential consumers and distributors. In addition, the company works to stay ahead of the competition and sustain rapid market growth by improving product quality, adding new product features and models, entering new market segments and distribution channels, shifting advertising from building product awareness to building product conviction and purchase, and lowering prices at the right time to attract new buyers. In the *maturity stage,* companies continue to invest in maturing products and consider modifying the market, the product, and the marketing mix. When *modifying the market,* the company attempts to increase the consumption of the current product. When *modifying the product,* the company changes some of the product's characteristics—such as quality, features, or style—to attract new users or inspire more usage. When *modifying the marketing mix,* the company works to improve sales by changing one or more of the marketing mix elements. Once the company recognizes that a product has entered the *decline stage,* management must decide whether to *maintain* the brand without change, hoping that competitors will drop out of the market; *harvest* the product, reducing costs and trying to maintain sales; or *drop* the product, selling it to another firm or liquidating it at salvage value.

 ## *Navigating the Key Terms*

For a detailed analysis of the meaning and importance of each of the following key terms, visit our Web page at www.prenhall.com/kotler.

Business analysis
Commercialization
Concept testing
Decline stage
Fad

Fashion
Growth stage
Idea generation
Idea screening
Introduction stage

Marketing strategy development
Maturity stage
New-product development
Product concept

Product development
Product life-cycle (PLC)
Sequential product
 development

Simultaneous (or team-based)
 product development
Style
Test marketing

Travel Log

The following concept checks and discussion questions will help you to keep track of and apply the concepts you've studied in this chapter.

Concept Checks

Fill in the blanks, then look for the correct answers.

1. Original products, product improvements, product modifications, and new brands that the firm develops through it own research and development efforts can all be called _____.

2. The eight steps in the new-product development process are idea generation, _____, concept development and testing, _____, business analysis, _____, test marketing, and _____.

3. Major sources of new product ideas include _____, _____, _____, and distributors and suppliers.

4. A _____ is a detailed version of the idea stated in meaningful consumer terms.

5. A marketing strategy statement consists of three parts. Part one describes the target market, the planned product positioning, and the sales, market share, and profit goals for the first few years. Part two outlines the product's planned price, distribution, and marketing budget for the first year. Part

three describes _____, _____, and _____.

6. _____ gives the marketer experience with marketing the product before going to the great expense of full introduction.

7. Under _____ product development, one company department works individually to complete its stage of the process before passing the new product along to the next department and stage.

8. The five stages of the product life-cycle (PLC) include _____, _____, _____, _____, and _____.

9. The _____ stage is a period of rapid market acceptance and increasing profits.

10. Most products are in the _____ stage of the life-cycle and, therefore, most marketing management deals with this type of product.

11. In the maturity stage, "the best offense is a good defense." The marketer can consider modifying the _____, _____, or _____.

12. As compared with other stages in Table 9-2, the _____ stage is characterized as having profits that are negative because of low sales and high cost per customer.

Concept Checks Answers: 1. new products; 2. idea screening, marketing strategy, product development, commercialization; 3. internal sources, customers, competitors; 4. product concept; 5. the planned long-run sales, profit goals, marketing mix strategy; 6. Test marketing; 7. sequential; 8. product development, introduction, growth, maturity, decline; 9. growth; 10. maturity; 11. market, product, marketing mix; 12. introduction.

Discussing the Issues

1. Pick a familiar company and assume you are responsible for generating new-product ideas. How you would structure your new-product development process? What sources of new ideas would be most valuable? How would you stimulate the new idea development process in the organization?

2. One of the challenges faced by today's new-product development manager is how to use the Internet to get new ideas from customers and competitors. Propose three ways to form relationships with con-

sumers to encourage and get new ideas. Next, propose three ways to observe competitors to gain insight into what they are thinking and doing in the new-product arena.

3. General Mills' latest entry in the highly competitive $2 billion-a-year yogurt market—a tubular yogurt called Go-Gurt—seems to be a hit with the lunch-box set. Why tubular yogurt? Children like yogurt but are not impressed with it. Some believe yogurt is "old people food." Not so with Go-Gurt (see **www.go-gurt.com**). With flavors like Chill Out

Cherry and Rad Raspberry, Go-Gurt can be eaten like regular yogurt, frozen like a frozen pop, or carried in a shirt pocket. Can this product be expanded to an adult market? Devise a plan for test marketing Go-Gurt to 25- to 45-year-old adults. What factors would be critical to your test? What types of test subjects would you want for your test? Using procedures and ideas presented in the text, evaluate the chances for success of this new adult product. Would a name change be necessary? Explain.

4. Pick a soft drink, car, fashion, food product, or electronic appliance and trace the product's life-cycle.

Do appropriate research to make your timeline and application as accurate as possible. Explain how you separated the stages of the product's development. Project when the product might enter a decline stage.

5. Which product life-cycle stage do you think is the most important? Which stage has the highest risk? Which stage seems to hold the greatest profit potential? Which stage needs the greatest amount of "hands-on" management? Explain your thinking behind each of your answers.

Mastering Marketing

Examine the new product development process for CanGo. Carry the company through the new product development process for an existing product. Next, propose an innovative product for the company to consider. After reviewing the first several phases of the development process to ensure that the innovative idea has merit, propose how the product concept could be tested. What markets would be best for this testing? Explain your thinking.

Traveling the Net

Point of Interest: Life-cycle for a New Product

"Danger Will Robinson! Danger!" might be one of the most memorable phrases ever uttered by a robot. However, today the phrase would more likely be "Buy Me! Take Me Home!" Who will offer the first practical, affordable home robot? NASA? Intel? Sony? Lego? Did you say "Lego?" Yes, the same little company that developed those great plastic building blocks has now developed several models of home robots (such as the R2D2 model from *Star Wars*) that sell for as little as $220. These model kits contain Lego pieces, light sensors, touch sensors, gears, and a minicomputer brick that forms the core of the system. The small, efficient robots already perform many hard-to-believe tasks (without complaining), and Lego is making daily upgrades. Copycat competitors have already begun a modification frenzy that will one day produce an awesome personal assistant. See **www.lego.com**, **www.legomindstorms. com**, **www.lugnet.com**, and **www.crynwr.com/ lego-robotics** for more information.

For Discussion

1. Who might be the first customers for a Lego robot? Explain.
2. Project the life-cycle for this new product. Explain your thinking.
3. Outline a strategy for positioning this product away from the toy category and into the "personal-device" category. What would be the key to your strategy?
4. What headline would you select for a first Lego robot ad appearing in *USA Today?* In *Business Week?*
5. What other new products has Lego produced to complement its robot line? What suggestions can you offer to extend its robot concept?

Application Thinking

Assume that you are the new product development manager for Lego. Devise a quick test market study for the Lego robot that would be administered at the annual computer and software convention (COMDEX) in Las Vegas, Nevada. Explain your thinking.

MAP—Marketing Applications

MAP Stop 9

What is the hottest new trend in shoes for teens? Would it be Air Jordans, soccer shoes, combat boots, or old tennis shoes? If you answered "none of the above" you were correct. The newest fad to hit teen footwear are Heelys. Heelys look like thick-soled sneakers, but they have a wheel embedded in each heel that allows them to switch (morph) from walking to skating shoes by simply shifting one's balance and weight. Texas-based Heelying Sports, Ltd., which produces these unique shoes, has venture capitalists lined up at its door. Why? Because teens are lined up in the outlets that carry the shoe. Heelying has avoided putting its product in big-box stores such as Target and has focused instead on skate, surf shops, and mall chains such as Gadzooks. All of these outlets target teens and offer higher price margins. Early test marketing for the Heelys took place around malls, skate parks, college campuses, and amusement parks. The shoes seem to be hottest in the Southwestern states and Heelying expects to ship more than a million pairs by the end of the year. Watch closely and you may soon see someone "heeling" by.

Thinking Like a Marketing Manager

1. After visiting the Heelys Web site at www.heelys.com, comment on the strategy devised by the company to reach its target market. What improvements are needed?

2. What stage of the product life-cycle does the product currently occupy? Using the information found in Table 9-2, comment on what the company must do to move forward to the next stage. How can Heelying Sports turn its fad into a long-term trend?

3. How has the company used the Internet to expand sales? Comment.

4. What other target markets should the company be considering? What other distribution outlets should be contacted? How could the company expand into new markets and outlets but still remain true to its core following?

5. As the new product development manager for Heelying Sports, Ltd., what new product would you advise for next year's shoe market? Explain your thinking and outline a plan for accomplishing development, testing, and introduction.

chapter 10

Pricing Products: Pricing Considerations and Strategies

ROAD MAP:
Previewing the Concepts

We continue your marketing journey with a look at a second major marketing mix tool—pricing. According to one pricing expert, "If effective product development, promotion, and distribution sow the seeds of business success, effective pricing is the harvest."[1] Firms successful at the other marketing mix activities, he continues, "can still fail unless they can capture some of the value they create in the prices they earn." Yet, despite its importance, many firms do not handle pricing well. In this chapter, we'll examine factors that affect pricing decisions, general pricing approaches, and specific pricing strategies.

▶ After studying this chapter, you should be able to

1. **identify and explain the external and internal factors affecting a firm's pricing decisions**
2. **contrast the three general approaches to setting prices**
3. **describe the major strategies for pricing imitative and new products**
4. **explain how companies find a set of prices that maximizes the profits from the total product mix**
5. **discuss how companies adjust their prices to take into account different types of customers and situations**
6. **discuss the key issues related to initiating and responding to price changes**

First stop on the pricing tour: Kellogg. For decades, Kellogg dazzled Wall Street with its impressive market performance. As time passed, however, Kellogg began boosting profits by steadily raising its prices without adding real value for customers. Consumers paid the price in the short run, but guess who paid in the end?

For decades preceding 1995, Kellogg was beloved on Wall Street—it was a virtual money machine. The cereal giant's 1995 sales of $7 billion represented its fifty-first straight year of rising revenues. Over the previous 30 years, Kellogg's sales had grown at one and a half times the industry growth rate, and its share of the U.S. cereal market had consistently exceeded 40 percent. Over the preceding decade, annual returns to shareholders had averaged 19 percent, with gross margins running as high as 55 percent. In 1995, Kellogg held a 42 percent worldwide market share, with a 48 percent share in Asia and Europe and a mind-blowing 69 percent share in Latin America. Things, it seemed, could only get better for Kellogg.

Behind these dazzling numbers, however, Kellogg's cereal empire had begun to lose its luster. Much of its recent success, it now appears, had come at the expense of cereal customers. Kellogg's recent gains—and those of major competitors General Mills, Post, and Quaker—had come not from innovative new products, creative marketing programs, and

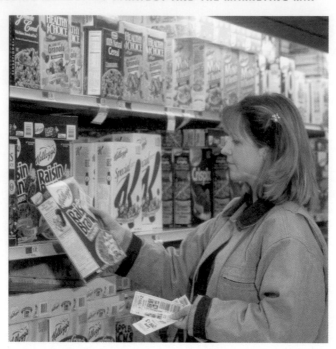

operational improvements that added value for customers. Instead, these gains had come almost entirely from price increases that padded the sales and profits of the cereal makers.

Throughout most of the 1980s and early 1990s, Kellogg had boosted profit margins by steadily raising prices on its Rice Krispies, Special K, Raisin Bran, and Frosted Flakes—often twice a year. For example, by early 1996, a 14-ounce box of Raisin Bran that had sold for $2.39 in 1985 was going for as much as $4.00 to $5.00, but with little or no change in the costs of the materials making up the cereal or its packaging. Since World War II, no food category had had more price increases than cereal. The price increases were very profitable for Kellogg and the other cereal companies—on average, the cereal makers were reaping more than twice the operating margins of the food industry as a whole. However, the relentless higher-priced cereal became increasingly difficult for customers to swallow.

So, not surprisingly, in 1994 the cereal industry's pricing policies began to backfire as frustrated consumers retaliated with a quiet fury. Cereal buyers began shifting away from branded cereal toward cheaper private-label brands; by 1995, private labels were devouring 10 percent of the American cereal market, up from a little more than 5 percent only five years earlier. Worse, many Americans switched to less expensive, more portable handheld breakfast foods, such as bagels, muffins, and breakfast bars. As a result, total American cereal sales began falling off by 3 to 4 percent a year. Kellogg's sales and profits sagged and its U.S. market share dropped to 36 percent. By early 1996, after what most industry analysts viewed as years of outrageous and self-serving pricing policies, Kellogg and the other cereal makers faced a full-blown crisis.

Post Cereal was the first competitor to break away. Belated research showed that exorbitant pricing was indeed the cause of the industry's doldrums. "Every statistic, every survey we took only showed that our customers were becoming more and more dissatisfied," said Mark Leckie, then general manager of Post Cereal. "You can see them walking down cereal aisles, clutching fistfuls of coupons and looking all over the shelves, trying to match them with a specific brand." To boost its soggy sales, in April 1996 Post slashed the prices on its 22 cereal brands an average of 20 percent—a surprise move that rocked the industry.

At first, Kellogg, General Mills, and Quaker held stubbornly to their premium prices. However, cereal buyers began switching in droves to Post's lower-priced brands—Post quickly stole 4 points from Kellogg's market share alone. Kellogg and the others had little choice but to follow Post's lead. Kellogg announced price cuts averaging 19 percent on two-thirds of all brands sold in the United States, marking the start of what would become a long and costly industry price war. In recanting their previous pricing excesses, the cereal makers swung wildly in the opposite direction, caught up in layoffs, plant closings, and other cost-cutting measures and fresh rounds of price-cutting. "It reminds me of one of those World War I battles where there's all this firing but when the smoke clears you can't tell who won," noted an industry analyst. In fact, it appears that nobody won, as the fortunes of all competitors suffered.

Kellogg was perhaps the hardest hit of the major competitors. Post Cereal's parent company, consumer-foods powerhouse Philip Morris, derived only about 2 percent of its sales and profits from cereal and could easily offset the losses elsewhere. However, Kellogg, which counted on domestic cereal sales for 42 percent of its revenues and 43 percent of its operating profits, suffered enormously. Its operating margins were halved, and even after lowering its prices, Kellogg's revenues and profits continued to decline.

Now, several years after the initial price rollbacks, Kellogg and the cereal industry are still feeling the aftershocks. Entering the new millennium, the total American cereal market is growing at a meager 1 percent a year, private brands now capture an impressive 18 percent market share, and alternative breakfast foods continue their strong growth. Kellogg's market share has slumped to 32 percent, down from 42 percent in 1988, and its sales and profits are flat. During the past several years, Kellogg has watched its stock price languish, and in 2001 it fell to number two in the industry behind General Mills.

Recently, Kellogg and the other cereal titans have quietly begun pushing ahead with modest price increases. The increases are needed, they argue, to fund the product innovation and marketing support necessary to stimulate growth in the stagnant cereal category. But there's an obvious risk. Consumers have long memories, and if the new products and programs aren't exciting enough, the higher prices may well push consumers further toward less expensive private-label cereal and alternative breakfast foods. "It's almost a no-win situation," says another analyst.

Despite its problems, the Kellogg brand name is still one of the world's best known and most respected. And Kellogg's recent initiatives to cut costs, get reacquainted with its customers, and develop innovative new products and marketing programs—all of which promise to add value for customers rather than simply cutting prices—has Wall Street cautiously optimistic about Kellogg's future. But events of the past several years teach an important lesson. When setting prices, as when making any other marketing decisions, a company can't afford to focus on its own costs and profits. Instead, it must focus on customers' needs and the value they receive from the company's total marketing offer. If a company doesn't give customers full value for the price they're paying, they'll go elsewhere. In this case, Kellogg stole profits by steadily raising prices without also increasing customer value. Customers paid the price in the short run—but Kellogg is paying the price in the long run.[2]

All profit organizations and many nonprofit organizations must set prices on their products or services. In the narrowest sense, **price** is the amount of money charged for a product or service. More broadly, price is the sum of all the values that consumers exchange for the benefits of having or using the product or service. Throughout most of history, prices were set by negotiation between buyers and sellers. *Fixed-price* policies—setting one price for all buyers—is a relatively modern idea that arose with the development of large-scale retailing at the end of the nineteenth century.

Price
The amount of money charged for a product or service, or the sum of the values that consumers exchange for the benefits of having or using the product or service.

Dynamic pricing
The practice of charging different prices depending on individual customers and situations.

Now, some one hundred years later, the Internet promises to reverse the fixed pricing trend and take us back to an era of **dynamic pricing**—charging different prices depending on individual customers and situations (see Marketing at Work 10-1). The Internet, corporate networks, and wireless communications are connecting sellers and buyers as never before. Web sites such as CompareNet and PriceSCAN allow buyers to compare products and prices quickly and easily. Online auction sites such as eBay.com and Amazon.com Auctions make it easy for buyers and sellers to negotiate prices on thousands of items—from refurbished computers to antique tin trains. At the same time, new technologies allow sellers to collect detailed data about customers' buying habits, preferences—even spending limits—so they can tailor their products and prices.[3]

Price is the only element in the marketing mix that produces revenue; all other elements represent costs. Price is also one of the most flexible elements of the marketing mix. Unlike product features and channel commitments, price can be changed quickly. At the same time, pricing and price competition is the number-one problem facing many marketing executives. Yet, as the chapter-opening Kellogg example illustrates, many companies do not handle pricing well. The most common mistakes are pricing that is too cost oriented rather than customer-value oriented; prices that are not revised often enough to reflect market changes; pricing that does not take the rest of the marketing mix into account; and prices that are not varied enough for different products, market segments, and purchase occasions.

In this chapter, we focus on the process of setting prices. We look first at the factors marketers must consider when setting prices and at general pricing approaches. Then, we examine pricing strategies for new-product pricing, product mix pricing, price adjustments for buyer and situational factors, and price changes.

Factors to Consider When Setting Prices

A company's pricing decisions are affected by both internal company factors and external environmental factors (see Figure 10-1).[4]

Internal Factors Affecting Pricing Decisions

Internal factors affecting pricing include the company's marketing objectives, marketing mix strategy, costs, and organizational considerations.

Marketing Objectives Before setting price, the company must decide on its strategy for the product. If the company has selected its target market and positioning carefully, then its marketing mix strategy, including price, will be fairly straightforward. For example, if General Motors decides to produce a new sports car to compete with European sports cars in the high-income segment, this suggests charging a high price. Motel 6, Econo Lodge, and Red Roof Inn have positioned themselves as motels that provide economical rooms for

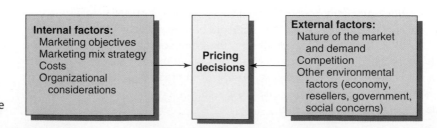

Figure 10-1
Factors affecting price decisions

Marketing at Work 10-1

Back to the Future: Dynamic Pricing on the Web

The Internet is more than simply a new "marketspace"—it's actually changing the rules of commerce. Take pricing, for example. From the mostly fixed pricing practices of the past century, the Web seems now to be taking us back—into a new age of fluid pricing. "Potentially, [the Internet] could push aside sticker prices and usher in an era of dynamic pricing," says *Business Week* writer Robert Hof, "in which a wide range of goods would be priced according to what the market will bear—instantly, constantly." Here's how the Internet is changing the rules of pricing for both sellers and buyers.

Sellers Can . . .

CHARGE LOWER PRICES AND REAP HIGHER MARGINS. Web buying and selling can result in drastically lower costs, allowing online sellers to charge lower prices and still make higher margins. "Thanks to their Internet connections, buyers and sellers around the world can connect at almost no cost—making instant bargaining [economically feasible]," observes Hof. Reduced inventory and distribution costs add to the savings. For example, by selling made-to-order computers online, Dell Computer greatly reduces inventory costs and eliminates retail markups. It shares the savings with buyers in the form of the "lowest price per performance."

MONITOR CUSTOMER BEHAVIOR AND TAILOR OFFERS TO INDIVIDUALS. With the help of new technologies, Web merchants can now target special prices to specific customers. For example, Internet sellers such as Amazon.com can mine their databases to gauge a specific shopper's desires, measure his or her means, instantaneously tailor products to that shopper's behavior, and price products accordingly. However, companies must be careful in how they apply dynamic pricing. When it recently came to light that Amazon.com had been charging different prices to different customers for the same DVDs, many customers were angry. Amazon.com claims that the pricing variations were a "pure and simple price test" and stopped the practice as soon as complaints began coming in.

CHANGE PRICES ON THE FLY ACCORDING TO CHANGES IN DEMAND OR COSTS. Just ask online catalog retailers such as Lands' End, Spiegel, or Fingerhut. With printed catalogs, a price is a price, at least until the next catalog is printed. Online sellers, however, can change prices for specific items on a day-by-day or even hour-by-hour basis, adjusting quickly to changing costs and merchandise movement. Many B2B marketers monitor inventories, costs, and demand at any given moment and adjust prices instantly. For example, IBM automatically adjusts prices on its servers based on customer demand and product life-cycle factors. As a result, customers will find that prices change dynamically when they visit the IBM Web site on any given day. Dell also uses dynamic online pricing. "If the price of memory or processors decreases, we pass those savings along to the customer almost in real time," says a Dell spokesperson.

Both Sellers and Buyers Can . . .

NEGOTIATE PRICES IN ONLINE AUCTIONS AND EXCHANGES. Suddenly the centuries-old art of haggling is

The Internet is ushering in a new era of fluid pricing. MySimon is an independent site that provides product comparisons and guides and searches all merchant sites for the best prices.

back in vogue. Want to sell that antique pickle jar that's been collecting dust for generations? Post it on eBay, the world's biggest online flea market. Want to purchase vintage baseball cards at a bargain price? Go to Boekhout's Collectibles Mall at www.azww.com/mall/. Want to dump that excess inventory? Try adding an auction feature to your own Web site—Sharper Image claims it's getting 40 percent of retail for excess goods sold via its online auction site, compared with only 20 percent from liquidators.

Of the dozens of Internet auction sites, eBay and Amazon.com Auctions are the largest. eBay, which began when its owner used the Web to find a market for his girlfriend's vintage Pez dispenser collection, hosts more than 2 million auctions each month for items in more than 1,000 categories, generating more than $5 billion in trades annually. Buyers like auctions because, quite simply, they like the bargains they find. Sellers like auctions because, over the Internet, the cost per transaction drops dramatically. Thus, it becomes practical—even profitable—to auction an item for mere dollars rather than thousands of dollars. For example, the seller can program its computers to accept the 3,000 best bids higher than $2.10 for 3,000 pieces of costume jewelry. Business marketers, whose transactions account for 68 percent of online auction sales, also use auctions to offer time-sensitive deals and gauge interest on possible price points for new products.

Buyers Can . . .

GET INSTANT PRICE COMPARISONS FROM THOUSANDS OF VENDORS.
The Internet gives consumers access to reams of data about products and prices. Online comparison guides—such as CompareNet and Price-SCAN—give product and price comparisons at the click of a mouse. Other sites offer intelligent shopping agents—such as MySimon—that seek out products, prices, and reviews. MySimon (www.mySimon.com), for instance, takes a buyer's criteria for a PC, camcorder, or collectible Barbie, then roots through top sellers' sites to find the best match at the best price.

FIND AND NEGOTIATE LOWER PRICES.
With market information and access come buyer power. In addition to simply finding the vendor with the best price, customers armed with price information can often negotiate lower prices. Here are examples of both consumers and industrial buyers exercising this newfound power:

In search of the best possible deal on a Palm organizer, Stephen Manes first checked PriceSCAN.com, where he learned that buy.com had the high-tech gadget for only $358. buy.com, however, was "out of stock," as was the second lowest-priced vendor, mcglen.com. Undaunted, Stephen skipped to the other end of the list were he found that PC Zone was offering the device for $449, and it was in stock. "Time to haggle," said Stephen. "I picked up the phone. In seconds, an eager salesperson quoted me the official price. 'I saw it at buy.com

for $358,' I said, omitting mention of the word[s 'out of stock']. 'I don't know if I can match buy.com,' came the response. 'But we can do it for $375.'" Stephen snapped up the offer, saving himself a bundle off the store price. Business buyers have also learned the price advantages of shopping the Web. For example, hoping to save some money, United Technologies Corporation tried something new last year. Instead of the usual haggling with dozens of individual vendors to secure printed circuit boards for various subsidiaries worldwide, UTC put the contract out on FreeMarkets, an online marketplace for industrial goods. To the company's delight, bids poured in from 39 suppliers, saving UTC a cool $10 million off its initial $24 million estimate. Says a UTC executive, "The technology drives the lowest price in a hurry."

Will dynamic pricing sweep the marketing world? "Not entirely," says Hof. "It takes a lot of work to haggle—which is why fixed prices happened in the first place." However, he continues, "Pandora's E-box is now open, and pricing will never be the same. For many . . . products, millions of buyers figure a little haggling is a small price to pay for a sweet deal."

Sources: Quotes and extracts from Robert D. Hof, "Going, Going, Gone," *Business Week,* April 12, 1999, pp. 30–32; Hof, "The Buyer Always Wins," *Business Week,* March 22, 1999, pp. EB26–EB28; Stephen Manes, "Off-Web Dickering," Forbes, April 5, 1999, p. 134; and Michael Vizard, Ed Scannell, and Dan Neel, "Suppliers Toy with Dynamic Pricing," *InfoWorld,* May 14, 2001, p. 28. Also see David Streitfield, "On the Web, Price Tags Blur", *Washington Post,* September 27, 2000, p. A1; and Walter Baker, Mike Marn, and Craig Zawada, "Price Smarter on the Net," *Harvard Business Review,* February 2001, pp. 122–127.

budget-minded travelers; this position requires charging a low price. Thus, pricing strategy is largely determined by decisions on market positioning.

At the same time, the company may seek additional objectives. Common objectives include *survival, current profit maximization, market share leadership,* and *product quality leadership.* Companies set *survival* as their major objective if they are troubled by too much capacity, heavy competition, or changing consumer wants. To keep a plant going, a company may set a low price, hoping to increase demand. In the long run, however, the firm must learn how to add value that consumers will pay for or face extinction.

Many companies use *current profit maximization* as their pricing goal. They estimate what demand and costs will be at different prices and choose the price that will produce the maximum current profit, cash flow, or return on investment. Other companies want to obtain *market share leadership*. To become the market share leader, these firms set prices as low as possible.

A company might decide that it wants to achieve *product quality leadership*. This normally calls for charging a high price to cover higher performance quality and the high cost of R&D. For example, Caterpillar charges 20 percent to 30 percent more than competitors for its heavy construction equipment based on superior product and service quality. Gillette's product superiority lets it price its Mach3 razor cartridges at a 50 percent premium over its own SensorExcel and competitors' cartridges. Maytag has long built high-quality washing machines and priced them higher. Its ads use the long-running Maytag slogan "Built to last longer" and feature the Lonely Maytag Repairman (who's lonely because no one ever calls him for service). The ads point out that washers are custodians of what is often a $300 to $400 load of clothes, making them worth the higher price tag. For instance, at $1,099, Maytag's Neptune, a front-loading washer without an agitator, sells for double what most other washers cost because the company's marketers claim that it uses less water and electricity and prolongs the life of clothing by being less abrasive.[5]

A company might also use price to attain other, more specific objectives. It can set prices low to prevent competition from entering the market or set prices at competitors'

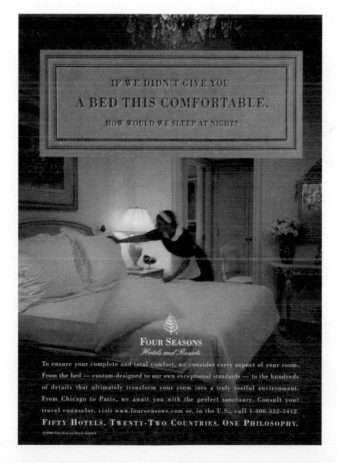

Product quality leadership: Four Seasons starts with very high-quality service, then charges a price to match.

levels to stabilize the market. Prices can be set to keep the loyalty and support of resellers or to avoid government intervention. Prices can be reduced temporarily to create excitement for a product or to draw more customers into a retail store. One product may be priced to help the sales of other products in the company's line. Thus, pricing may play an important role in helping to accomplish the company's objectives at many levels.

Marketing Mix Strategy Price is only one of the marketing mix tools that a company uses to achieve its marketing objectives. Price decisions must be coordinated with product design, distribution, and promotion decisions to form a consistent and effective marketing program. Decisions made for other marketing mix variables may affect pricing decisions. For example, producers using many resellers who are expected to support and promote their products may have to build larger reseller margins into their prices. The decision to position the product on high-performance quality will mean that the seller must charge a higher price to cover higher costs.

Companies often position their products on price and then base other marketing mix decisions on the prices they want to charge. Here, price is a crucial product-positioning factor that defines the product's market, competition, and design. Many firms support such price-positioning strategies with a technique called **target costing,** a potent strategic weapon. Target costing reverses the usual process of first designing a new product, determining its cost, and then asking, "Can we sell it for that?" Instead, it starts with an ideal selling price based on customer considerations, then targets costs that will ensure that the price is met.

The original Swatch watch provides a good example of target costing. Rather than starting with its own costs, Swatch surveyed the market and identified an unserved segment of watch buyers who wanted "a low-cost fashion accessory that also keeps time." Swatch set out to give consumers in this segment the watch they wanted at a price they

Target costing
Pricing that starts with an ideal selling price, then targets costs that will ensure that the price is met.

Target costing: By managing costs carefully, Swatch was able to create a watch that offered just the right blend of fashion and function at a price consumers were willing to pay.

were willing to pay, and it managed the new product's costs accordingly. Like most watch buyers, targeted consumers were concerned about precision, reliability, and durability. However, they were also concerned about fashion and affordability. To keep costs down, Swatch designed fashionably simpler watches that contained fewer parts and that were constructed from high-tech but less expensive materials. It then developed a revolutionary automated process for mass producing the new watches and exercised strict cost controls throughout the manufacturing process. By managing costs carefully, Swatch created a watch that offered just the right blend of fashion and function at a price consumers were willing to pay. As a result of its initial major success, consumers have placed increasing value on Swatch products, allowing the company to introduce successively higher-priced designs.[6]

Other companies deemphasize price and use other marketing mix tools to create *nonprice* positions. Often, the best strategy is not to charge the lowest price, but rather to differentiate the marketing offer to make it worth a higher price. For example, for years Johnson Controls, a producer of climate-control systems for office buildings, used initial price as its primary competitive tool. However, research showed that customers were more concerned about the total cost of installing and maintaining a system than about its initial price. Repairing broken systems was expensive, time-consuming, and risky. Customers had to shut down the heat or air-conditioning in the whole building, disconnect a lot of wires, and face the dangers of electrocution. So Johnson designed an entirely new system called "Metasys." To repair the new system, customers need only pull out an old plastic module and slip in a new one—no tools required. Metasys costs more to make than the old system, and customers pay a higher initial price, but it costs less to install and maintain. Despite its higher asking price, the new Metasys system brought in $500 million in revenues in its first year.[7]

Thus, marketers must consider the total marketing mix when setting prices. If the product is positioned on nonprice factors, then decisions about quality, promotion, and distribution will strongly affect price. If price is a crucial positioning factor, then price will strongly affect decisions made about the other marketing mix elements. But even when featuring price, marketers need to remember that customers rarely buy on price alone. Instead, they seek products that give them the best value in terms of benefits received for the price paid.

Costs   Costs set the floor for the price that the company can charge for its product. The company wants to charge a price that both covers all its costs for producing, distributing, and selling the product and delivers a fair rate of return for its effort and risk. A company's costs may be an important element in its pricing strategy. Many companies work to become the "low-cost producers" in their industries. Companies with lower costs can set lower prices that result in greater sales and profits.

A company's costs take two forms, fixed and variable. *Fixed costs* (also known as overhead) are costs that do not vary with production or sales level. For example, a company must pay each month's bills for rent, heat, interest, and executive salaries, whatever the company's output. *Variable costs* vary directly with the level of production. Each personal computer produced by Compaq involves a cost of computer chips, wires, plastic, packaging, and other inputs. These costs tend to be the same for each unit produced. They are called variable because their total varies with the number of units produced. *Total costs* are the sum of the fixed and variable costs for any given level of production. Management wants to charge a price that will at least cover the total production costs at a given level of production.

The company must watch its costs carefully. If it costs the company more than its competitors to produce and sell its product, the company will have to charge a higher price or make less profit, putting it at a competitive disadvantage.

Organizational Considerations Management must decide who within the organization should set prices. Companies handle pricing in a variety of ways. In small companies, prices are often set by top management rather than by the marketing or sales departments. In large companies, pricing is typically handled by divisional or product line managers. In industrial markets, salespeople may be allowed to negotiate with customers within certain price ranges. Even so, top management sets the pricing objectives and policies, and it often approves the prices proposed by lower-level management or salespeople. In industries in which pricing is a key factor (aerospace, steel, railroads, oil companies), companies often have a pricing department to set the best prices or help others in setting them. This department reports to the marketing department or top management. Others who have an influence on pricing include sales managers, production managers, finance managers, and accountants.

External Factors Affecting Pricing Decisions

External factors that affect pricing decisions include the nature of the market and demand, competition, and other environmental elements.

The Market and Demand Whereas costs set the lower limit of prices, the market and demand set the upper limit. Both consumer and industrial buyers balance the price of a product or service against the benefits of owning it. Thus, before setting prices, the marketer must understand the relationship between price and demand for its product. In this section, we explain how the price–demand relationship varies for different types of markets and how buyer perceptions of price affect the pricing decision. We then discuss methods for measuring the price–demand relationship.

PRICING IN DIFFERENT TYPES OF MARKETS. The seller's pricing freedom varies with different types of markets. Economists recognize four types of markets, each presenting a different pricing challenge.

Under *pure competition,* the market consists of many buyers and sellers trading in a uniform commodity such as wheat, copper, or financial securities. No single buyer or seller has much effect on the going market price. A seller cannot charge more than the going price because buyers can obtain as much as they need at the going price. Nor would sellers charge less than the market price because they can sell all they want at this price. If price and profits rise, new sellers can easily enter the market. In a purely competitive market, marketing research, product development, pricing, advertising, and sales promotion play little or no role. Thus, sellers in these markets do not spend much time on marketing strategy.

Under *monopolistic competition,* the market consists of many buyers and sellers who trade over a range of prices rather than a single market price. A range of prices occurs because sellers can differentiate their offers to buyers. Either the physical product can be varied in quality, features, or style, or the accompanying services can be varied. Buyers see differences in sellers' products and will pay different prices for them. Sellers try to develop differentiated offers for different customer segments and, in addition to price, freely use branding, advertising, and personal selling to set their offers apart. Because there are many competitors in such markets, each firm is less affected by competitors' marketing strategies than in oligopolistic markets.

Under *oligopolistic competition,* the market consists of a few sellers who are highly sensitive to each other's pricing and marketing strategies. The product can be uniform (steel, aluminum) or nonuniform (cars, computers). There are few sellers because it is difficult for new sellers to enter the market. Each seller is alert to competitors' strategies and moves. If a steel company slashes its price by 10 percent, buyers will quickly switch to this supplier. The other steelmakers must respond by lowering their prices or increasing their

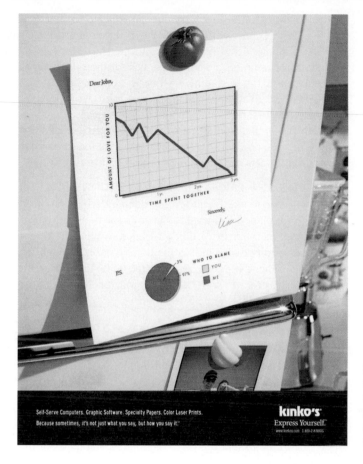

Monopolistic competition: Kinko's differentiates its offer through strong branding and advertising, reducing the impact of pricing.

services. An oligopolist is never sure that it will gain anything permanent through a price cut. In contrast, if an oligopolist raises its price, its competitors might not follow this lead. The oligopolist then would have to retract its price increase or risk losing customers to competitors.

In a *pure monopoly,* the market consists of one seller. The seller may be a government monopoly (the U.S. Postal Service), a private regulated monopoly (a power company), or a private nonregulated monopoly (DuPont when it introduced nylon). Pricing is handled differently in each case. A government monopoly can pursue a variety of pricing objectives. It might set a price below cost because the product is important to buyers who cannot afford to pay full cost. Or the price might be set either to cover costs or to produce good revenue. It can even be set quite high to slow down consumption. In a regulated monopoly, the government permits the company to set rates that will yield a "fair return," one that will let the company maintain and expand its operations as needed. Nonregulated monopolies are free to price at what the market will bear. However, they do not always charge the full price for a number of reasons: a desire not to attract competition, a desire to penetrate the market faster with a low price, or a fear of government regulation.

CONSUMER PERCEPTIONS OF PRICE AND VALUE. In the end, the consumer will decide whether a product's price is right. Pricing decisions, like other marketing mix decisions, must be buyer oriented. When consumers buy a product, they exchange something of value (the price) to get something of value (the benefits of having or using the product). Effective, buyer-oriented pricing involves understanding how much value consumers place on the benefits they receive from the product and setting a price that fits this value.

A company often finds it hard to measure the values customers will attach to its product. For example, calculating the cost of ingredients in a meal at a fancy restaurant is relatively easy. But assigning a value to other satisfactions such as taste, environment, relaxation, conversation, and status is very hard. And these values will vary both for different consumers and different situations. Still, consumers will use these values to evaluate a product's price. If customers perceive that the price is greater than the product's value, they will not buy the product. If consumers perceive that the price is below the product's value, they will buy it, but the seller loses profit opportunities.

ANALYZING THE PRICE–DEMAND RELATIONSHIP. Each price the company might charge will lead to a different level of demand. The relationship between the price charged and the resulting demand level is shown in the **demand curve** in Figure 10-2. The demand curve shows the number of units the market will buy in a given time period at different prices that might be charged. In the normal case, demand and price are inversely related; that is, the higher the price, the lower the demand. Thus, the company would sell less if it raised its price from P_1 to P_2. In short, consumers with limited budgets probably will buy less of something if its price is too high.

In the case of prestige goods, the demand curve sometimes slopes upward. Consumers think that higher prices mean more quality. For example, Gibson Guitar Corporation recently toyed with the idea of lowering its prices to compete more effectively with Japanese rivals such as Yamaha and Ibanez. To its surprise, Gibson found that its instruments didn't sell as well at lower prices. "We had an inverse [price–demand relationship]," noted Gibson's chief executive officer. "The more we charged, the more product we sold." Gibson's slogan promises: "The world's finest musical instruments." It turns out that low prices simply aren't consistent with "Gibson's century old tradition of creating investment-quality instruments that represent the highest standards of imaginative design and masterful craftsmanship."[8] Still, if the company charges too high a price, the level of demand will be lower.

Most companies try to measure their demand curves by estimating demand at different prices. The type of market makes a difference. In a monopoly, the demand curve shows the total market demand resulting from different prices. If the company faces competition, its demand at different prices will depend on whether competitors' prices stay constant or change with the company's own prices.

In measuring the price–demand relationship, the market researcher must not allow other factors affecting demand to vary. For example, if Sony increased its advertising at the same time that it lowered its television prices, we would not know how much of the increased demand was due to the lower prices and how much was due to the increased advertising. The same problem arises if a holiday weekend occurs when the lower price is

Demand curve

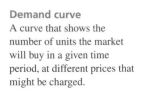

A curve that shows the number of units the market will buy in a given time period, at different prices that might be charged.

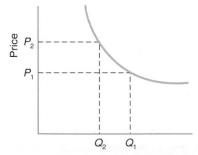

Figure 10-2
Demand curve

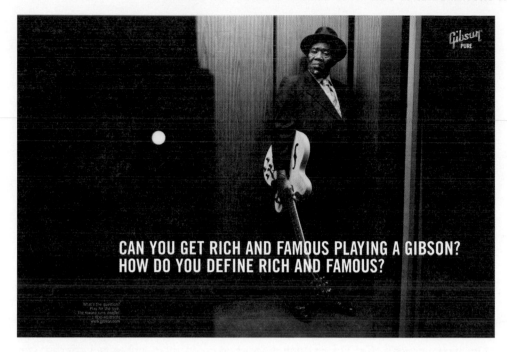

CAN YOU GET RICH AND FAMOUS PLAYING A GIBSON?
HOW DO YOU DEFINE RICH AND FAMOUS?

The demand curve sometimes slopes upward: Gibson was surprised to learn that its high-quality instruments didn't sell as well at lower prices.

set—more gift giving over the holidays causes people to buy more televisions. Economists show the impact of nonprice factors on demand through shifts in the demand curve rather than movements along it.

PRICE ELASTICITY OF DEMAND. Marketers also need to know **price elasticity**—how responsive demand will be to a change in price. If demand hardly changes with a small change in price, we say the demand is *inelastic*. If demand changes greatly, we say the demand is *elastic*.

> **Price elasticity**
> A measure of the sensitivity of demand to changes in price.

What determines the price elasticity of demand? Buyers are less price sensitive when the product they are buying is unique or when it is high in quality, prestige, or exclusiveness. They are also less price sensitive when substitute products are hard to find or when they cannot easily compare the quality of substitutes. Finally, buyers are less price sensitive when the total expenditure for a product is low relative to their income or when the cost is shared by another party.[9]

If demand is elastic rather than inelastic, sellers will consider lowering their price. A lower price will produce more total revenue. This practice makes sense as long as the extra costs of producing and selling more do not exceed the extra revenue. At the same time, most firms want to avoid pricing that turns their products into commodities. In recent years, forces such as deregulation and the instant price comparisons afforded by the Internet and other technologies have increased consumer price sensitivity, turning products ranging from telephones and computers to new automobiles into commodities in consumers' eyes. Marketers need to work harder than ever to differentiate their offerings when a dozen competitors are selling virtually the same product at a comparable or lower price. More than ever, companies need to understand the price sensitivity of their customers and prospects and the trade-offs people are willing to make between price and product characteristics. In the words of marketing consultant Kevin Clancy, those who target only the price sensitive are "leaving money on the table."

Even in the energy marketplace, where you would think that a kilowatt is a kilowatt is a kilowatt, some utility companies are beginning to wake up to this fact. They are differentiating their power, branding it, marketing it, and providing unique services to customers, even if it means higher prices. For example, Green Mountain Power (GMP), a small Vermont utility, is approaching the deregulated consumer energy marketplace with the firm belief that even kilowatt hours can be differentiated. GMP conducted extensive marketing research and uncovered a large segment of prospects who not only were concerned with the environment but also were willing to support their attitudes with dollars. Because GMP is a "green" power provider—a large percentage of its power is hydroelectric—customers had an opportunity to ease the environmental burden by purchasing GMP power. GMP has already participated in two residential power-selling pilot projects in Massachusetts and New Hampshire, successfully competing against "cheaper" brands that focused on more price-sensitive consumers.[10]

Competitors' Costs, Prices, and Offers   Another external factor affecting the company's pricing decisions is competitors' costs and prices and possible competitor reactions to the company's own pricing moves. A consumer who is considering the purchase of a Canon camera will evaluate Canon's price and value against the prices and values of comparable products made by Nikon, Minolta, Pentax, and others. In addition, the company's pricing strategy may affect the nature of the competition it faces. If Canon follows a high-price, high-margin strategy, it may attract competition. A low-price, low-margin strategy, however, may stop competitors or drive them out of the market.

Canon needs to benchmark its costs against its competitors' costs to learn whether it is operating at a cost advantage or disadvantage. It also needs to learn the price and quality of each competitor's offer. Once Canon is aware of competitors' prices and offers, it can use them as a starting point for its own pricing. If Canon's cameras are similar to Nikon's, it will have to price close to Nikon or lose sales. If Canon's cameras are not as good as Nikon's, the firm will not be able to charge as much. If Canon's products are better than Nikon's, it can charge more. Basically, Canon will use price to position its offer relative to the competition.

Other External Factors   When setting prices, the company also must consider other factors in its external environment. *Economic conditions* can have a strong impact on the firm's pricing strategies. Economic factors such as boom or recession, inflation, and interest rates affect pricing decisions because they affect both the costs of producing a product and consumer perceptions of the product's price and value. The company must also consider what impact its prices will have on other parties in its environment. How will *resellers* react to various prices? The company should set prices that give resellers a fair profit, encourage their support, and help them to sell the product effectively. The *government* is another important external influence on pricing decisions. Finally, *social concerns* may have to be taken into account. In setting prices, a company's short-term sales, market share, and profit goals may have to be tempered by broader societal considerations.

General Pricing Approaches

The price the company charges will be somewhere between one that is too low to produce a profit and one that is too high to produce any demand. Figure 10-3 summarizes the major considerations in setting price. Product costs set a floor to the price; consumer perceptions of the product's value set the ceiling. The company must consider competitors' prices and other external and internal factors to find the best price between these two extremes.

Companies set prices by selecting a general pricing approach that includes one or more of these three sets of factors. We will examine the following approaches: the *cost-based approach* (cost-plus pricing, break-even analysis, and target profit pricing), the

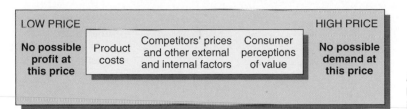

Figure 10-3
Major considerations
in setting price

buyer-based approach (value-based pricing), and the *competition-based approach* (going-rate and sealed-bid pricing).

Cost-Based Pricing

The simplest pricing method is **cost-plus pricing**—adding a standard markup to the cost of the product. For example, an appliance retailer might pay a manufacturer $20 for a toaster and mark it up to sell at $30, a 50 percent markup on cost. The retailer's gross margin is $10. If the store's operating costs amount to $8 per toaster sold, the retailer's profit margin will be $2.

> **Cost-plus pricing**
> Adding a standard markup to the cost of the product.

The manufacturer that made the toaster probably used cost-plus pricing. If the manufacturer's standard cost of producing the toaster was $16, it might have added a 25 percent markup, setting the price to the retailers at $20. Similarly, construction companies submit job bids by estimating the total project cost and adding a standard markup for profit. Lawyers, accountants, and other professionals typically price by adding a standard markup to their costs. Some sellers tell their customers they will charge cost plus a specified markup; for example, aerospace companies price this way to the government.

Does using standard markups to set prices make sense? Generally, no. Any pricing method that ignores demand and competitor prices is not likely to lead to the best price. Steel manufacturer Nucor Corporation successfully uses cost-based pricing. Notes the company's general manager, "We base the price on what it costs to run the mill to capacity twenty-four hours a day." However, Nucor's very low costs allow it to charge very low prices relative to competitors. In contrast, the retail graveyard is full of merchants who insisted on using standard markups after their competitors had gone to discount pricing.[11]

Still, markup pricing remains popular for many reasons. First, sellers are more certain about costs than about demand. By tying the price to cost, sellers simplify pricing—they do not have to make frequent adjustments as demand changes. Second, when all firms in the industry use this pricing method, prices tend to be similar and price competition is thus minimized. Third, many people feel that cost-plus pricing is fairer to both buyers and sellers. Sellers earn a fair return on their investment but do not take advantage of buyers when buyers' demand becomes great.

Another cost-oriented pricing approach is **break-even pricing,** or a variation called *target profit pricing.* The firm tries to determine the price at which it will break even or make the target profit it is seeking. Target pricing is used by General Motors, which prices its automobiles to achieve a 15 to 20 percent profit on its investment. This pricing method is also used by public utilities, which are constrained to make a fair return on their investment.

> **Break-even pricing (target profit pricing)**
> Setting price to break even on the costs of making and marketing a product; or setting price to make a target profit.

Target pricing uses the concept of a *break-even chart,* which shows the total cost and total revenue expected at different sales volume levels. Figure 10-4 shows a hypothetical break-even chart. Here, fixed costs are $6 million regardless of sales volume, and variable costs are $5 per unit. Variable costs are added to fixed costs to form total costs, which rise with each unit sold. The slope of the total revenue curve reflects the price. Here, the price is $15 (for example, the company's revenue is $12 million on 800,000 units, or $15 per unit).

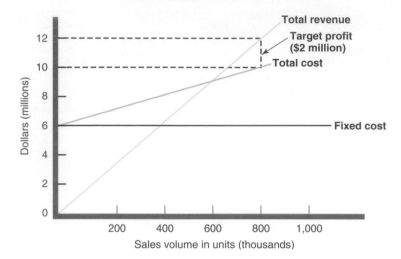

Figure 10-4
Break-even chart for determining target price

At the $15 price, the company must sell at least 600,000 units to *break even*—that is, at this level, total revenues will equal total costs of $9 million. If the company wants a target profit of $2 million, it must sell at least 800,000 units to obtain the $12 million of total revenue needed to cover the costs of $10 million plus the $2 million of target profits. In contrast, if the company charges a higher price, say $20 million, it will not need to sell as many units to break even or to achieve its target profit. In fact, the higher the price, the lower the company's break-even point will be.

However, as the *price* increases, *demand* decreases, and the market may not buy even the lower volume needed to break even at the higher price. Much depends on the relationship between price and demand. For example, suppose the company calculates that given its current fixed and variable costs, it must charge a price of $30 for the product in order to earn its desired target profit. But marketing research shows that few consumers will pay more than $25. In this case, the company will have to trim its costs in order to lower the break-even point so that it can charge the lower price consumers expect.

Thus, although break-even analysis and target profit pricing can help the company to determine minimum prices needed to cover expected costs and profits, they do not take the price–demand relationship into account. When using this method, the company must also consider the impact of price on sales volume needed to realize target profits and the likelihood that the needed volume will be achieved at each possible price.

Value-Based Pricing

An increasing number of companies are basing their prices on the product's perceived value. **Value-based pricing** uses buyers' perceptions of value, not the seller's cost, as the key to pricing. Value-based pricing means that the marketer cannot design a product and marketing program and then set the price. Price is considered along with the other marketing mix variables *before* the marketing program is set.

Value-based pricing
Setting price based on buyers' perceptions of value rather than on the seller's cost.

Figure 10-5 compares cost-based pricing with value-based pricing. Cost-based pricing is product driven. The company designs what it considers to be a good product, totals the costs of making the product, and sets a price that covers costs plus a target profit. Marketing must then convince buyers that the product's value at that price justifies its purchase. If the price turns out to be too high, the company must settle for lower markups or lower sales, both resulting in disappointing profits.

Value-based pricing reverses this process. The company sets its target price based on customer perceptions of the product value. The targeted value and price then drive

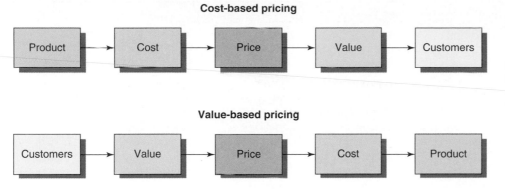

Figure 10-5
Cost-based versus value-based pricing

Source: Thomas T. Nagle and Reed K. Holden, *The Strategy and Tactics of Pricing,* 2nd ed. (Upper Saddle River, NJ: Prentice Hall, 1995), p. 5.

decisions about product design and what costs can be incurred. As a result, pricing begins with analyzing consumer needs and value perceptions, and price is set to match consumers' perceived value.

A company using value-based pricing must find out what value buyers assign to different competitive offers. However, measuring perceived value can be difficult. Sometimes, consumers are asked how much they would pay for a basic product and for each benefit added to the offer. Or a company might conduct experiments to test the perceived value of different product offers. If the seller charges more than the buyers' perceived value, the company's sales will suffer. Many companies overprice their products, and their products sell poorly. Other companies underprice. Underpriced products sell very well, but they produce less revenue than they would have if price were raised to the perceived-value level.

During the past decade, marketers have noted a fundamental shift in consumer attitudes toward price and quality. Many companies have changed their pricing approaches to bring them into line with changing economic conditions and consumer price perceptions. According to Jack Welch, former CEO of General Electric, "The value decade is upon us. If you can't sell a top-quality product at the world's best price, you're going to be out of the game. . . . The best way to hold your customers is to constantly figure out how to give them more for less."[12]

Thus, more and more, marketers have adopted **value pricing** strategies—offering just the right combination of quality and good service at a fair price. In many cases, this has involved the introduction of less expensive versions of established, brand name products. Campbell introduced its Great Starts Budget frozen-food line, Holiday Inn opened several Holiday Express budget hotels, Revlon's Charles of the Ritz offered the Express Bar collection of affordable cosmetics, and fast-food restaurants such as Taco Bell and McDonald's offered "value menus." In other cases, value pricing has involved redesigning existing brands in order to offer more quality for a given price or the same quality for less.

In many business-to-business marketing situations, the pricing challenge is to find ways to maintain the company's *pricing power*—its power to maintain or even raise prices without losing market share. To retain pricing power—to escape price competition and to justify higher prices and margins—a firm must retain or build the value of its marketing offer. This is especially true for suppliers of commodity products, which are characterized by little differentiation and intense price competition. In such cases, many companies adopt *value-added* strategies. Rather than cutting prices to match competitors, they attach value-added services to differentiate their offers and thus support higher margins (see Marketing at Work 10-2).[13]

An important type of value pricing at the retail level is *everyday low pricing (EDLP)*. EDLP involves charging a constant, everyday low price with few or no temporary price

Value pricing
Offering just the right combination of quality and good service at a fair price.

Marketing at Work 10.2

Pricing Power: The Value of Value Added

When a company finds its major competitors offering a similar product at a lower price, the natural tendency is to try to match or beat that price. Although the idea of undercutting competitors' prices and watching customers flock to you is tempting, there are dangers. Successive rounds of price-cutting can lead to price wars that erode the profit margins of all competitors in an industry. Or worse, discounting a product can cheapen it in the minds of customers, greatly reducing the seller's power to maintain profitable prices in the long term. "It ends up being a losing battle," notes one marketing executive. "You focus away from quality, service, prestige—the things brands are all about."

So, how can a company keep its pricing power when a competitor undercuts its price? Often, the best strategy is not to price below the competitor, but rather to price above and convince customers that the product is worth it. The company should ask, "What is the value of the product to the customer?" then stand up for what the product is worth. In this way, the company shifts the focus from price to value.

But what if the company is operating in a "commodity" business, in which the products of all competitors seem pretty much alike? In such cases, the company must find ways to "decommoditize" its products— to create superior value for customers. It can do this by developing value-added features and services that differentiate its offer and justify higher prices and margins. Here are some examples of how suppliers are using value-added features and services to give them a competitive edge:

◆ *Caterpillar:* Caterpillar is a master at charging premium prices for its heavy construction and mining equipment and convincing customers that its products and service justify every additional cent— or, rather, the extra tens of thousands of dollars. Caterpillar typically reaps a 20 to 30 percent price premium over competitors—that can amount to an extra $200,000 or more on one of those huge yellow million-dollar dump trucks. When a large potential customer says, "I can get it for less from a competitor," rather than discounting the price, the Caterpillar dealer explains that, even at the higher price, Cat offers the best value. Caterpillar equipment is designed with modular componentry that can be removed and repaired quickly, minimizing machine downtime. Caterpillar dealers carry an extensive parts inventory and guarantee delivery within 48 hours anywhere in the world, again minimizing downtime. Cat's products are designed to be rebuilt, providing a "second life" that competitors cannot match. As a result, Caterpillar used-equipment prices are often 20 percent to 30 percent higher. In all, the dealer explains, even at the higher initial price, Caterpillar equipment delivers the lowest total cost per cubic yard of earth moved, ton of coal uncovered, or mile of road graded over the life of the product—guaranteed! Most customers seem to agree with Caterpillar's value proposition—the company dominates its markets with a more than 40 percent worldwide market share.

◆ *Pioneer Hi-Bred International:* A major supplier of corn seed and other agricultural products often thought of as commodities, DuPont subsidiary Pioneer

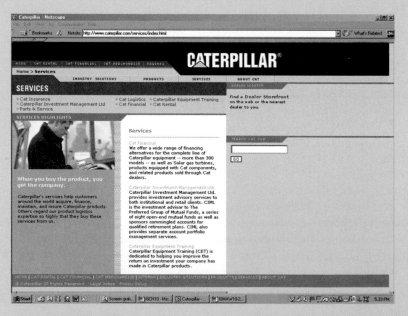

Value added: Caterpillar offers its dealers a wide range of value-added services—from guaranteed parts delivery to investment management advice and equipment training. Such added value supports a higher price.

Hi-Bred hardly acts like a commodity supplier. Its patented hybrid seeds yield 10 percent more corn than competitors' seeds. Beyond producing a superior product, Pioneer Hi-Bred provides a bundle of value-added services. For example, it equips its sales representatives with notebook computers that allow them to provide farmers with customized information and advice. The rep can plug in the type of hybrid that a farmer is using, along with information about pricing, acreage, and yield characteristics, then advise the farmer on how to do a better job of farm management. The reps can also supply farmers with everything from agricultural research reports to assistance in comparison shopping. Pioneer Hi-Bred also offers farmers crop insurance, financing, and marketing services. Its superior products and value-added services give Pioneer Hi-Bred plenty of pricing power. Despite charging a significant price premium—or perhaps because of it—the company's share of the North American corn market has grown from 35 percent during the mid-1980s to its current level of 44 percent.

◆ *Jefferson Smurfit Corporation:* When General Electric expanded a no-frost refrigerator line in 1990, it needed more shipping boxes, and fast. Jefferson Smurfit Corporation, a $4.5 billion packaging supplier, assigned a coordinator to juggle production from three of its plants—and sometimes even divert product intended for other customers—to keep GE's Decatur plant humming. This kind of value-added hustling helped Jefferson Smurfit win the GE appliance unit's "Distinguished Supplier Award." It has also sheltered Smurfit from the bruising struggle of competing only on price. "Today, it's not just getting the best price but getting the best value—and there are a lot of pieces to value," says a vice president for procurement at Emerson Electric Company, a major Smurfit customer that has cut its supplier count by 65 percent.

◆ *Microsystems Engineering Company:* "The way we sell on value is by differentiating ourselves," says Mark Beckman, director of sales for Microsystems, a software company. "My product is twice as much as my nearest competitor's, but we sell as much—if not more than—our competition." Rather than getting into price wars, Microsystems adds value to its products by adding new components and services. "[Customers] get more for their money," says Beckman. "We get the price because we understand what people want." When customers see the extra value, price becomes secondary. Ultimately, Beckman asserts, "Let the customer decide whether the price you're charging is worth all the things they're getting." What if the answer is no? Beckman would suggest that dropping price is the last thing you want to do. Instead, look to the value of value added.

Sources: Jim Morgan, "Value Added: From Cliché to the Real Thing," *Purchasing,* April 3, 1997, pp. 59–61; James E. Ellis, "There's Even a Science to Selling Boxes," *Business Week,* August 3, 1992, pp. 51–52; John Jesitus, "Close Connections," *Industry Week,* October 6, 1997, pp. 28–34; James C. Anderson and James A. Narus, "Business Marketing: Understand What Customers Value," *Harvard Business Review,* November–December 1998, pp. 53–65; Tom Nagle, "How to Pull It Off," *Across the Board,* March 1999, pp. 53–56; Robert B. Tucker, "Adding Value Profitably," *The American Salesman,* April 2001, pp. 17–20; and information accessed online at www.pioneer.com, December 2001.

discounts. In contrast, *high–low pricing* involves charging higher prices on an everyday basis but running frequent promotions to lower prices temporarily on selected items below the EDLP level. In recent years, high–low pricing has given way to EDLP in retail settings ranging from Saturn car dealerships to upscale department stores such as Nordstrom. Retailers adopt EDLP for many reasons, the most important of which is that constant sales and promotions are costly and have eroded consumer confidence in the credibility of everyday shelf prices. Consumers also have less time and patience for such time-honored traditions as watching for supermarket specials and clipping coupons.

The king of EDLP is Wal-Mart, which practically defined the concept.[14] Except for a few sale items every month, Wal-Mart promises everyday low prices on everything it sells. In contrast, Sears's attempts at EDLP in 1989 failed. To offer everyday low prices, a company must first have everyday low costs. Wal-Mart's EDLP strategy works well because its expenses are only 15 percent of sales. Sears, however, was spending 29 percent of sales to cover administrative and other overhead costs. As a result, Sears now offers everyday *fair* pricing, under which it tries to offer customers differentiated products at a consistent, fair price with fewer markdowns.

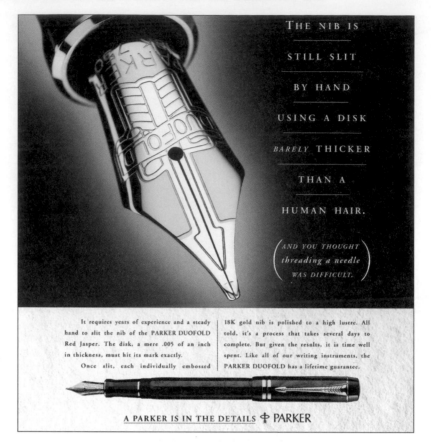

THE NIB IS

STILL SLIT

BY HAND

USING A DISK

BARELY THICKER

THAN A

HUMAN HAIR.

(AND YOU THOUGHT threading a needle WAS DIFFICULT.)

It requires years of experience and a steady hand to slit the nib of the PARKER DUOFOLD Red Jasper. The disk, a mere .005 of an inch in thickness, must hit its mark exactly.

Once slit, each individually embossed

18K gold nib is polished to a high lustre. All told, it's a process that takes several days to complete. But given the results, it is time well spent. Like all of our writing instruments, the PARKER DUOFOLD has a lifetime guarantee.

A PARKER IS IN THE DETAILS ✦ PARKER

Perceived value: A less-expensive pen might write as well, but some consumers will pay much more for the intangibles. This Parker model runs $185. Others are priced as high as $3,500.

Linking the Concepts

The concept of value is critical to good pricing and to successful marketing in general. Slow down for a minute and be certain that you appreciate what value really means.

◆ A few years ago, Buick pitched its top-of-the-line Park Avenue model as "America's best car value." Does this fit with your idea of value?

◆ Pick two competing brands from a familiar product category (watches, perfume, consumer electronics, restaurants)—one low priced and the other high priced. Which, if either, offers the greatest value?

◆ Does "value" mean the same thing as "low price"? How do these concepts differ?

Competition-Based Pricing

Competition-based pricing
Setting prices based on the prices that competitors charge for similar products.

Consumers will base their judgments of a product's value on the prices that competitors charge for similar products. One form of **competition-based pricing** is *going-rate pricing,* in which a firm bases its price largely on competitors' prices, with less attention paid to its own costs or to demand. The firm might charge the same as, more than, or less than its major competitors. In oligopolistic industries that sell a commodity such as steel, paper, or fertilizer, firms normally charge the same price. The smaller firms follow the leader: They change their prices when the market leader's prices change, rather than when their own demand or costs change. Some firms may charge a bit more or less, but they hold the amount of difference constant. Thus, minor gasoline retailers usually charge a few cents less than the major oil companies, without letting the difference increase or decrease.

Going-rate pricing is quite popular. When demand elasticity is hard to measure, firms feel that the going price represents the collective wisdom of the industry concerning the price that will yield a fair return. They also feel that holding to the going price will prevent harmful price wars.

Competition-based pricing is also used when firms *bid* for jobs. Using *sealed-bid pricing,* a firm bases its price on how it thinks competitors will price rather than on its own costs or on the demand. The firm wants to win a contract, and winning the contract requires pricing less than other firms. Yet the firm cannot set its price below a certain level. It cannot price below cost without harming its position. In contrast, the higher the company sets its price above its costs, the lower its chance of getting the contract.

New-Product Pricing Strategies

Pricing decisions are subject to an incredibly complex array of environmental and competitive forces. A company sets not a single price, but rather a *pricing structure* that covers different items in its line. This pricing structure changes over time as products move through their life cycles. The company adjusts product prices to reflect changes in costs and demand and to account for variations in buyers and situations. As the competitive environment changes, the company considers when to initiate price changes and when to respond to them.

We now examine the major dynamic pricing strategies available to management. In turn, we look at *new-product pricing strategies* for products in the introductory stage of the product life cycle, *product mix pricing strategies* for related products in the product mix, *price-adjustment strategies* that account for customer differences and changing situations, and strategies for initiating and responding to *price changes.*[15]

Pricing strategies usually change as the product passes through its life cycle. The introductory stage is especially challenging. Companies bringing out a new product face the challenge of setting prices for the first time. They can choose between two broad strategies: *market-skimming pricing* and *market-penetration pricing.*

Market-Skimming Pricing

Many companies that invent new products initially set high prices to "skim" revenues layer by layer from the market. Intel is a prime user of this strategy, called **market-skimming pricing.** When Intel first introduces a new computer chip, it charges a premium price—a price that makes it *just* worthwhile for some segments of the market to adopt computers containing the chip. The new chips power top-of-the-line PCs and servers purchased by customers who just can't wait. As initial sales slow down, and as competitors threaten to introduce similar chips, Intel lowers the price to draw in the next price-sensitive layer of customers. Prices eventually bottom out at a level that makes the chip a hot mass-market processor. In this way, Intel skims a maximum amount of revenue from the various segments of the market.[16]

Market skimming makes sense only under certain conditions. First, the product's quality and image must support its higher price, and enough buyers must want the product at that price. Second, the costs of producing a smaller volume cannot be so high that they

Market-skimming pricing
Setting a high price for a new product to skim maximum revenues layer by layer from the segments willing to pay the high price; the company makes fewer but more profitable sales.

cancel the advantage of charging more. Finally, competitors should not be able to enter the market easily and undercut the high price.

Market-Penetration Pricing

Market-penetration pricing

Setting a low price for a new product in order to attract a large number of buyers and a large market share.

Rather than setting a high initial price to *skim* off small but profitable market segments, some companies use **market-penetration pricing.** They set a low initial price in order to *penetrate* the market quickly and deeply—to attract a large number of buyers quickly and win a large market share. The high sales volume results in falling costs, allowing the company to cut its price even further. For example, Dell used penetration pricing to enter the personal computer market, selling high-quality computer products through lower-cost direct channels. Its sales soared when IBM, Compaq, Apple, and other competitors selling through retail stores could not match its prices. Wal-Mart and other discount retailers also use penetration pricing.

Several conditions must be met for this low-price strategy to work. First, the market must be highly price sensitive so that a low price produces more market growth. Second, production and distribution costs must fall as sales volume increases. Finally, the low price must help keep out the competition, and the penetration pricer must maintain its low-price position—otherwise, the price advantage may be only temporary. For example, Dell faced difficult times when IBM and Compaq established their own direct distribution channels. However, through its dedication to low production and distribution costs, Dell has retained its price advantage and established itself as the industry's fastest-growing computer maker and number two in personal computers behind Compaq.

Market penetration: Dell used penetration pricing to enter the personal computer market, selling high-quality computer products through lower-cost direct channels.

Product Mix Pricing Strategies

The strategy for setting a product's price often has to be changed when the product is part of a product mix. In this case, the firm looks for a set of prices that maximizes the profits on the total product mix. Pricing is difficult because the various products have related demand and costs and face different degrees of competition. We now take a closer look at five product mix pricing situations: *product line pricing, optional-product pricing, captive-product pricing, by-product pricing,* and *product bundle pricing.*

Product Line Pricing

Companies usually develop product lines rather than single products. For example, Snapper makes many different lawn mowers, ranging from simple walk-behind versions priced at $259.95, $299.95, and $399.95, to elaborate riding mowers priced at $1,000 or more. Each successive lawn mower in the line offers more features. Kodak offers not just one type of film, but an assortment, including regular Kodak film, higher-priced Kodak Royal Gold film for special occasions, and still higher-priced Advantix APS film for Advanced Photo System cameras. It offers each of these brands in a variety of sizes and film speeds. In **product line pricing,** management must decide on the price steps to set between the various products in a line.

> **Product line pricing**
> Setting the price steps between various products in a product line based on cost differences between the products, customer evaluations of different features, and competitors' prices.

The price steps should take into account cost differences between the products in the line, customer evaluations of their different features, and competitors' prices. In many industries, sellers use well-established *price points* for the products in their line. Thus, men's clothing stores might carry men's suits at three price levels: $185, $325, and $495. The customer will probably associate low-, average-, and high-quality suits with the three price points. Even if the three prices are raised a little, men normally will buy suits at their own preferred price points. The seller's task is to establish perceived quality differences that support the price differences.

Optional-Product Pricing

Many companies use **optional-product pricing**—offering to sell optional or accessory products along with their main product. For example, a car buyer may choose to order power windows, cruise control, and a CD changer. Pricing these options is a sticky problem. Automobile companies have to decide which items to include in the base price and which to offer as options. Until recent years, General Motors' normal pricing strategy was to advertise a stripped-down model at a base price to pull people into showrooms and then devote most of the showroom space to showing option-loaded cars at higher prices. The economy model was stripped of so many comforts and conveniences that most buyers rejected it. More recently, however, GM and other U.S. car makers have followed the example of the Japanese and German automakers and included in the sticker price many useful items previously sold only as options. The advertised price now often represents a well-equipped car.

> **Optional-product pricing**
> The pricing of optional or accessory products along with a main product.

Captive-Product Pricing

Companies that make products that must be used along with a main product are using **captive-product pricing.** Examples of captive products are razor blades, camera film, video games, and computer software. Producers of the main products (razors, cameras, video game consoles, and computers) often price them low and set high markups on the supplies. Thus, Polaroid prices its cameras low because it makes its money on the film

> **Captive-product pricing**
> Setting a price for products that must be used along with a main product, such as blades for a razor and film for a camera.

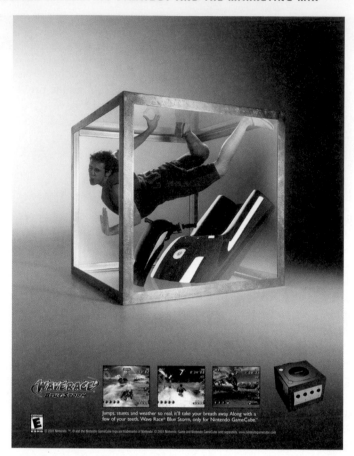

Captive-product pricing: Nintendo sells game consoles at reasonable prices and makes money on video game titles.

it sells. Gillette sells low-priced razors but makes money on the replacement cartridges. U-Haul rents out trucks at low rates but commands high margins on accessories such as boxes, pads, insurance, and storage space rental. Nintendo sells its game consoles at low prices and makes money on video game titles. In fact, whereas Nintendo's margins on its consoles run a mere 1 percent to 5 percent, margins on its game cartridges run close to 45 percent. Video game sales contribute more than half the company's profits.[17]

In the case of services, this strategy is called *two-part pricing.* The price of the service is broken into a *fixed fee* plus a *variable usage rate.* Thus, a telephone company charges a monthly rate—the fixed fee—plus charges for calls beyond some minimum number—the variable usage rate. Amusement parks charge admission plus fees for food, midway attractions, and rides over a minimum. Theaters charge admission, then generate additional revenues from concessions. The service firm must decide how much to charge for the basic service and how much for the variable usage. The fixed amount should be low enough to induce usage of the service; profit can be made on the variable fees.

By-Product Pricing

By-product pricing
Setting a price for by-products in order to make the main product's price more competitive.

In producing processed meats, petroleum products, chemicals, and other products, there are often by-products. If the by-products have no value and if getting rid of them is costly, this will affect the pricing of the main product. Using **by-product pricing,** the manufacturer will seek a market for these by-products and should accept any price that covers more than the cost of storing and delivering them. This practice allows the seller to reduce the main product's price to make it more competitive. By-products can even turn out to be profitable. For example, many lumber mills have begun to sell bark chips and sawdust profitably as decorative mulch for home and commercial landscaping.

Sometimes, companies don't realize how valuable their by-products are. For example, most zoos don't realize that one of their by-products—their occupants' manure—can be an excellent source of additional revenue. But the Zoo Doo Compost Company has helped many zoos understand the costs and opportunities involved with these by-products. Zoo Doo licenses its name to zoos and receives royalties on manure sales. "Many zoos don't even know how much manure they are producing or the cost of disposing of it," explains president and founder Pierce Ledbetter. Zoos are often so pleased with any savings they can find on disposal that they don't think to move into active by-product sales. However, sales of the fragrant by-product can be substantial. So far, novelty sales have been the largest, with tiny containers of Zoo Doo (and even "Love, Love Me Doo" valentines) available in 160 zoo stores and 700 additional retail outlets. You can also buy Zoo Doo products online ("the easiest way to buy our crap," says Zoo Doo) or even send a friend (or perhaps a foe) a free Poopy Greeting via e-mail. For the long-term market, Zoo Doo looks to organic gardeners who buy 15 to 70 pounds of manure at a time. Zoo Doo is already planning a "Dung of the Month" club to reach this lucrative by-products market.[18]

Product Bundle Pricing

Using **product bundle pricing,** sellers often combine several of their products and offer the bundle at a reduced price. Thus, theaters and sports teams sell season tickets at less than the cost of single tickets; hotels sell specially priced packages that include room, meals, and entertainment; computer makers include attractive software packages with their personal computers. Price bundling can promote the sales of products consumers might not otherwise buy, but the combined price must be low enough to get them to buy the bundle.[19]

Product bundle pricing
Combining several products and offering the bundle at a reduced price.

Price-Adjustment Strategies

Companies usually adjust their basic prices to account for various customer differences and changing situations. Here we examine six price-adjustment strategies: *discount and allowance pricing, segmented pricing, psychological pricing, promotional pricing, geographical pricing,* and *international pricing.*

Discount and Allowance Pricing

Most companies adjust their basic price to reward customers for certain responses, such as early payment of bills, volume purchases, and off-season buying. These price adjustments—called *discounts* and *allowances*—can take many forms.

The many forms of **discounts** include a *cash discount,* a price reduction to buyers who pay their bills promptly. A typical example is "2/10, net 30," which means that although payment is due within 30 days, the buyer can deduct 2 percent if the bill is paid within 10 days. The discount must be granted to all buyers meeting these terms. Such discounts are customary in many industries and help to improve the sellers' cash situation and reduce bad debts and credit-collection costs.

A *quantity discount* is a price reduction to buyers who buy large volumes. A typical example might be "$10 per unit for less than 100 units, $9 per unit for 100 or more

Discount
A straight reduction in price on purchases during a stated period of time.

units." By law, quantity discounts must be offered equally to all customers and must not exceed the seller's cost savings associated with selling large quantities. These savings include lower selling, inventory, and transportation expenses. Discounts provide an incentive to the customer to buy more from one given seller, rather than from many different sources.

A *functional discount* (also called a *trade discount*) is offered by the seller to trade channel members who perform certain functions, such as selling, storing, and record keeping. Manufacturers may offer different functional discounts to different trade channels because of the varying services they perform, but manufacturers must offer the same functional discounts within each trade channel.

A *seasonal discount* is a price reduction to buyers who buy merchandise or services out of season. For example, lawn and garden equipment manufacturers offer seasonal discounts to retailers during the fall and winter months to encourage early ordering in anticipation of the heavy spring and summer selling seasons. Hotels, motels, and airlines will offer seasonal discounts in their slower selling periods. Seasonal discounts allow the seller to keep production steady during an entire year.

Allowances are another type of reduction from the list price. For example, *trade-in allowances* are price reductions given for turning in an old item when buying a new one. Trade-in allowances are most common in the automobile industry but are also given for other durable goods. *Promotional allowances* are payments or price reductions to reward dealers for participating in advertising and sales support programs.

Allowance
Promotional money paid by manufacturers to retailers in return for an agreement to feature the manufacturer's products in some way.

Segmented Pricing

Segmented pricing
Selling a product or service at two or more prices, where the difference in prices is not based on differences in costs.

Companies will often adjust their basic prices to allow for differences in customers, products, and locations. In **segmented pricing,** the company sells a product or service at two or more prices, even though the difference in prices is not based on differences in costs (see Marketing at Work 10-3).

Segmented pricing takes several forms. Under *customer-segment* pricing, different customers pay different prices for the same product or service. Museums, for example, will charge a lower admission for students and senior citizens. Under *product-form pricing,* different versions of the product are priced differently but not according to differences in their costs. For instance, Black & Decker prices its most expensive iron at $54.98, which is $12.00 more than the price of its next most expensive iron. The top model has a self-cleaning feature, yet this extra feature costs only a few more dollars to make. Using *location pricing,* a company charges different prices for different locations, even though the cost of offering each location is the same. For instance, theaters vary their seat prices because of audience preferences for certain locations, and state universities charge higher tuition for out-of-state students. Finally, using *time pricing,* a firm varies its price by the season, the month, the day, and even the hour. Public utilities vary their prices to commercial users by time of day and weekend versus weekday. The telephone company offers lower off-peak charges, and resorts give seasonal discounts.

For segmented pricing to be an effective strategy, certain conditions must exist. The market must be segmentable, and the segments must show different degrees of demand. Members of the segment paying the lower price should not be able to turn around and resell the product to the segment paying the higher price. Competitors should not be able to undersell the firm in the segment being charged the higher price. Nor should the costs of segmenting and watching the market exceed the extra revenue obtained from the price difference. Of course, the segmented pricing must also be legal. Most importantly, segmented prices should reflect real differences in customers' perceived value. Otherwise, in the long run, the practice will lead to customer resentment and ill will.

Marketing at Work 10-3

Segmented Pricing: The Right Product to the Right Customer at the Right Time for the Right Price

Many companies would love to raise prices across the board—but fear losing business. When the Washington Opera Company, located in the nation's capital, was considering increasing ticket prices after a difficult season, Ticket Services Manager Jimmy Legarreta decided there had to be a better way. He found one after carefully reviewing opera economics. Legarreta knew—and his computer system confirmed—that the company routinely turned away people for Friday and Saturday night performances, particularly for prime seats. Meanwhile, midweek tickets went begging.

Legarreta also knew that not all seats were equal, even in the sought-after orchestra section. So the ticket manager and his staff sat in every one of the opera house's 2,200 seats and gave each a value according to the view and the acoustics. With his revenue goal in mind, Legarreta played with ticket prices until he arrived at nine levels, up from five. In the end, the opera raised prices for its most coveted seats by as much as 50 percent but also dropped the prices of some 600 seats. The gamble paid off in a 9 percent revenue increase during the next season.

Legarreta didn't have a name for it, but he was practicing "segmented pricing," an approach that also has many other labels. Airlines, hotels, and restaurants call it "yield management" and practice it religiously. The airlines, for example, routinely set prices on an hour-by-hour—even minute-by-minute—basis, depending on seat availability and demand. "A business traveler who shells out $1,700 for a coach seat bought at the last minute is well aware that the passenger in

the next seat might have paid $300 for a ticket booked weeks in advance while another passenger across the aisle may have scored a seat through a discount broker for, perhaps, $129," observes an industry analyst. Robert Cross, a longtime consultant to the airlines, calls it "revenue management." According to Cross, the practice ensures that "companies will sell the right product to the right consumer at the right time for the right price."

Segmented pricing and yield management aren't really new ideas. For instance, Marriott Corporation used seat-of-the-pants yield-management approaches long before it installed its current sophisticated system. Back when J. W. "Bill" Marriott was a young man working at the family's first hotel, the Twin Bridges in Washington, DC, he sold rooms from a drive-up window. As Bill tells it, the hotel

charged a flat rate for a single occupant, with an extra charge for each additional person staying in the room. When room availability got tight on some nights, Bill would lean out the drive-up window and assess the cars waiting in line. If some of the cars were filled with passengers, Bill would turn away vehicles with just a single passenger to sell his last rooms to those farther back in line who would be paying for multiple occupants. He might have accomplished the same result by charging a higher rate at peak times, regardless of the number of room occupants.

Cross's underlying premise: No two customers value a product or service exactly the same way. Furthermore, the perceived value of a product results from many variables that change over time. Some of Cross's clients use sophisticated yield-management simulation

Segmented pricing: Not all seats in an opera house are equal. After sitting in every one of the Washington Opera House's 2,200 seats, management arrived at nine pricing levels. The result: a 9 percent revenue increase.

models and high-powered computer systems to predict sales at different price levels. But the technique doesn't have to be rocket science. If you understand your customers' motivation for buying and you keep careful sales records, it's possible to adjust prices to remedy supply-and-demand imbalances. Legarreta, for example, ended his midweek slump by making opera affordable for more people, yet he accurately predicted that the Washington in-crowd would pay higher prices for the best weekend seats.

Probably the simplest form of segmented pricing is off-peak pricing, common in the entertainment and travel industries. Marc Epstein, owner of the Milk Street Cafe in Boston, discovered that technique more than 10 years ago, when he noticed he had lines out the door at noon but a near-empty restaurant around his 3 P.M. closing time. After some experimentation, Epstein settled on a 20 percent discount for the hours just before noon and

after 2 P.M.—and he's pleased with the results. "If we didn't offer this, our overall revenue would be less," he argues. Epstein did not feel he could simultaneously raise prices during the lunch rush; instead, he has expanded the corporate-catering side of his business, where he can charge more per sandwich because "the perceived value of a catered lunch is higher."

Many other companies could conceivably segment their prices to increase revenues and profits. Cross cites examples ranging from a one-chair barbershop, to an accounting firm, to a health center. But there are risks. When you establish a range of prices, customers who pay the higher ones may feel cheated. "It can't be a secret that you're charging different prices for the same service," Cross advises. "Customers must know, so they can choose when to use a service."

Even so, promotions designed to shift customer traffic to off-peak times can backfire. Rick Johnson,

owner of Madison Car Wash in Montgomery, Alabama, describes his experience with a "Wonderful Wednesday" special: "The incentive was too good. It took away from the rest of the week and made Wednesday a monster day; it was a horrible strain on my facility and my people. I played around with the discount, but it was still a problem. So I finally dropped it."

The moral of the story? You can never know too much about your customers and the different values they assign to your product or service. With that customer knowledge comes power—to make the best pricing decisions.

Source: Portions adapted with permission from Susan Greco, "Are Your Prices Right?" *Inc.,* January 1997, pp. 88–89. Copyright 1997 by Goldhirsh Group, Inc., 38 Commercial Wharf, Boston, MA 02110. Other information from Robert G. Cross, *Revenue Management: Hard-Core Tactics for Market Domination* (New York: Broadway Books, 1998); and Joe Sharkey, "Hotels Take a Lesson from Airline Pricing," *New York Times,* December 17, 2000, p. D3. Also see Ramarao Desiraju and Steven M. Shugan, "Strategic Service Pricing and Yield Management," *Journal of Marketing,* January 1999, pp. 44–56; and James Schembari, "More and More, We Get Less and . . . ," *New York Times,* January 14, 2001, p. D2.

Psychological Pricing

Price says something about the product. For example, many consumers use price to judge quality. A $100 bottle of perfume may contain only $3 worth of scent, but some people are willing to pay the $100 because this price indicates something special.

Psychological pricing
A pricing approach that considers the psychology of prices and not simply the economics; the price is used to say something about the product.

In using **psychological pricing,** sellers consider the psychology of prices and not simply the economics. For example, consumers usually perceive higher-priced products as having higher quality. When they can judge the quality of a product by examining it or by calling on past experience with it, they use price less to judge quality. But when they cannot judge quality because they lack the information or skill, price becomes an important quality signal:

Heublein produces Smirnoff, America's leading vodka brand. Some years ago, Smirnoff was attacked by another brand. Wolfschmidt, priced at one dollar less per bottle, claimed to have the same quality as Smirnoff. To hold on to market share, Heublein considered either lowering Smirnoff's price by one dollar or holding Smirnoff's price but increasing advertising and promotion expenditures. Either strategy would lead to lower profits and it seemed that Heublein faced a no-win situation. At this point, however, Heublein's marketers thought of a third strategy. They *raised* the price of Smirnoff by one dollar! Heublein then introduced a new brand, Relska, to compete with Wolfschmidt. Moreover, it

Psychological pricing: What do the prices marked on this tag suggest about the product and buying situation?

introduced yet another brand, Popov, priced even *lower* than Wolfschmidt. This clever strategy positioned Smirnoff as the elite brand and Wolfschmidt as an ordinary brand, producing a large increase in Heublein's overall profits. The irony is that Heublein's three brands are pretty much the same in taste and manufacturing costs. Heublein knew that a product's price signals its quality. Using price as a signal, Heublein sells roughly the same product at three different quality positions.

Another aspect of psychological pricing is **reference prices**—prices that buyers carry in their minds and refer to when looking at a given product. The reference price might be formed by noting current prices, remembering past prices, or assessing the buying situation. Sellers can influence or use these consumers' reference prices when setting price. For example, a company could display its product next to more expensive ones in order to imply that it belongs in the same class. Department stores often sell women's clothing in separate departments differentiated by price: Clothing found in the more expensive department is assumed to be of better quality. Companies can also influence consumers' reference prices by stating high manufacturer's suggested prices, by indicating that the product was originally priced much higher, or by pointing to a competitor's higher price.

Even small differences in price can suggest product differences. Consider a stereo priced at $300 compared to one priced at $299.95. The actual price difference is only 5 cents, but the psychological difference can be much greater. For example, some consumers will see the $299.95 as a price in the $200 range rather than the $300 range. The $299.95 will more likely be seen as a bargain price, whereas the $300 price suggests more quality. Some psychologists argue that each digit has symbolic and visual qualities that should be considered in pricing. Thus, 8 is round and even and creates a soothing effect, whereas 7 is angular and creates a jarring effect.[20]

Reference prices
Prices that buyers carry in their minds and refer to when they look at a given product.

Promotional Pricing

Promotional pricing
Temporarily pricing products below the list price, and sometimes even below cost, to increase short-run sales.

With **promotional pricing,** companies will temporarily price their products below list price and sometimes even below cost. Promotional pricing takes several forms. Supermarkets and department stores will price a few products as *loss leaders* to attract customers to the store in the hope that they will buy other items at normal markups. Sellers will also use *special-event pricing* in certain seasons to draw more customers. Thus, linens are promotionally priced every January to attract weary Christmas shoppers back into stores.

Manufacturers will sometimes offer *cash rebates* to consumers who buy the product from dealers within a specified time; the manufacturer sends the rebate directly to the customer. Rebates have been popular with automakers and producers of durable goods and small appliances, but they are also used with consumer packaged goods. Some manufacturers offer *low-interest financing, longer warranties,* or *free maintenance* to reduce the consumer's "price." This practice has recently become a favorite of the auto industry. Or, the seller may simply offer *discounts* from normal prices to increase sales and reduce inventories.

Promotional pricing, however, can have adverse effects. Used too frequently and copied by competitors, price promotions can create "deal-prone" customers who wait until brands go on sale before buying them. Or, constantly reduced prices can erode a brand's value in the eyes of customers. Marketers sometimes use price promotions as a quick fix instead of sweating through the difficult process of developing effective longer-term strategies for building their brands. In fact, one observer notes that price promotions can be downright addicting to both the company and the customer: "Price promotions are the brand equivalent of heroin: easy to get into but hard to get out of. Once the brand and its customers are addicted to the short-term high of a price cut it is hard to wean them away to real brand building. . . . But continue and the brand dies by 1000 cuts."[21]

Jack Trout, a well-known marketing author and consultant, cautions that some categories tend to self-destruct by always being on sale. Discount pricing has become routine for a surprising number of companies. Furniture, automobile tires, and many other categories of goods are rarely sold at anything near list price, and when automakers get rebate happy, the market just sits back and waits for a deal. Even Coca-Cola and Pepsi, two of the world's most popular brands, engage in regular price wars that ultimately tarnish their brand equity. Trout offers several "Commandments of Discounting," such as "Thou shalt not offer discounts because everyone else does," "Thou shalt be creative with your discounting," "Thou shalt put time limits on the deal," and "Thou shalt stop discounting as soon as you can."[22] The point is that promotional pricing can be an effective means of generating sales in certain circumstances but can be damaging if taken as a steady diet.

Linking the Concepts

Here's a good place to take a brief break. Think about some of the companies and industries you deal with that are "addicted" to promotional pricing.

◆ Many industries have created "deal-prone" consumers through the heavy use of promotional pricing—fast food, airlines, tires, furniture, and others. Pick a company in one of these industries and suggest ways that it might deal with this problem.

◆ How does the concept of value relate to promotional pricing? Does promotional pricing add to or detract from customer value?

Geographical Pricing

A company also must decide how to price its products for customers located in different parts of the country or world. Should the company risk losing the business of more distant customers by charging them higher prices to cover the higher shipping costs? Or should the company charge all customers the same prices regardless of location? We will look at five geographical pricing strategies for the following hypothetical situation:

> The Peerless Paper Company is located in Atlanta, Georgia, and sells paper products to customers all over the United States. The cost of freight is high and affects the companies from whom customers buy their paper. Peerless wants to establish a geographical pricing policy. It is trying to determine how to price a $100 order to three specific customers: Customer A (Atlanta), Customer B (Bloomington, Indiana), and Customer C (Compton, California).

One option is for Peerless to ask each customer to pay the shipping cost from the Atlanta factory to the customer's location. All three customers would pay the same factory price of $100, with Customer A paying, say, $10 for shipping; Customer B, $15; and Customer C, $25. Called *FOB-origin pricing,* this practice means that the goods are placed *free on board* (hence, *FOB*) a carrier. At that point the title and responsibility pass to the customer, who pays the freight from the factory to the destination. Because each customer picks up its own cost, supporters of FOB pricing feel that this is the fairest way to assess freight charges. The disadvantage, however, is that Peerless will be a high-cost firm to distant customers.

Uniform-delivered pricing is the opposite of FOB pricing. Here, the company charges the same price plus freight to all customers, regardless of their location. The freight charge is set at the average freight cost. Suppose this is $15. Uniform-delivered pricing therefore results in a higher charge to the Atlanta customer (who pays $15 freight instead of $10) and a lower charge to the Compton customer (who pays $15 instead of $25). Although the Atlanta customer would prefer to buy paper from another local paper company that uses FOB-origin pricing, Peerless has a better chance of winning over the California customer. Other advantages of uniform-delivered pricing are that it is fairly easy to administer and it lets the firm advertise its price nationally.

Zone pricing falls between FOB-origin pricing and uniform-delivered pricing. The company sets up two or more zones. All customers within a given zone pay a single total price; the more distant the zone, the higher the price. For example, Peerless might set up an East Zone and charge $10 freight to all customers in this zone, a Midwest Zone in which it charges $15, and a West Zone in which it charges $25. In this way, the customers within a given price zone receive no price advantage from the company. For example, customers in Atlanta and Boston pay the same total price to Peerless. The complaint, however, is that the Atlanta customer is paying part of the Boston customer's freight cost.

Using *basing-point pricing,* the seller selects a given city as a "basing point" and charges all customers the freight cost from that city to the customer location, regardless of the city from which the goods are actually shipped. For example, Peerless might set Chicago as the basing point and charge all customers $100 plus the freight from Chicago to their locations. This means that an Atlanta customer pays the freight cost from Chicago to Atlanta, even though the goods may be shipped from Atlanta. If all sellers used the same basing-point city, delivered prices would be the same for all customers and price competition would be eliminated. Industries such as sugar, cement, steel, and automobiles used basing-point pricing for years, but this method has become less popular today. Some companies set up multiple basing points to create more flexibility: They quote freight charges from the basing-point city nearest to the customer.

Finally, the seller who is anxious to do business with a certain customer or geographical area might use *freight-absorption pricing.* Using this strategy, the seller absorbs all or part of the actual freight charges in order to get the desired business. The seller might reason that if it can get more business, its average costs will fall and more than compensate for its extra freight cost. Freight-absorption pricing is used for market penetration and to hold on to increasingly competitive markets.

International Pricing

Companies that market their products internationally must decide what prices to charge in the different countries in which they operate. In some cases, a company can set a uniform worldwide price. For example, Boeing sells its jetliners at about the same price everywhere, whether in the United States, Europe, or a third world country. However, most companies adjust their prices to reflect local market conditions and cost considerations.

The price that a company should charge in a specific country depends on many factors, including economic conditions, competitive situations, laws and regulations, and development of the wholesaling and retailing system. Consumer perceptions and preferences also may vary from country to country, calling for different prices. Or the company may have different marketing objectives in various world markets, which require changes in pricing strategy. For example, Sony might introduce a new product into mature markets in highly developed countries with the goal of quickly gaining mass-market share—this would call for a penetration-pricing strategy. In contrast, it might enter a less developed market by targeting smaller, less price-sensitive segments; in this case, market-skimming pricing makes sense.

Costs play an important role in setting international prices. Travelers abroad are often surprised to find that goods that are relatively inexpensive at home may carry outrageously higher price tags in other countries. A pair of Levi's selling for $30 in the United States goes for about $63 in Tokyo and $88 in Paris. A McDonald's Big Mac selling for a modest $2.25 here costs $5.75 in Moscow, and an Oral-B toothbrush selling for $2.49 at

Companies that market products internationally must decide what prices to charge in the different countries.

home costs $10 in China. Conversely, a Gucci handbag going for only $60 in Milan, Italy, fetches $240 in the United States. In some cases, such *price escalation* may result from differences in selling strategies or market conditions. In most instances, however, it is simply a result of the higher costs of selling in another country—the additional costs of product modifications, shipping and insurance, import tariffs and taxes, exchange-rate fluctuations, and physical distribution.

For example, Campbell found that distribution in the United Kingdom cost 30 percent more than in the United States. U.S. retailers typically purchase soup in large quantities—48-can cases of a single soup by the dozens, hundreds, or carloads. In contrast, English grocers purchase soup in small quantities—typically in 24-can cases of *assorted* soups. Each case must be handpacked for shipment. To handle these small orders, Campbell had to add a costly extra wholesale level to its European channel. The smaller orders also mean that English retailers order two or three times as often as their U.S. counterparts, bumping up billing and order costs. These and other factors caused Campbell to charge much higher prices for its soups in the United Kingdom.[23]

Thus, international pricing presents some special problems and complexities. We discuss international pricing issues in more detail in Chapter 15.

Price Changes

After developing their pricing structures and strategies, companies often face situations in which they must initiate price changes or respond to price changes by competitors.

Initiating Price Changes

In some cases, the company may find it desirable to initiate either a price cut or a price increase. In both cases, it must anticipate possible buyer and competitor reactions.

Initiating Price Cuts Several situations may lead a firm to consider cutting its price. One such circumstance is excess capacity. In this case, the firm needs more business and cannot get it through increased sales effort, product improvement, or other measures. It may drop its "follow-the-leader pricing"—charging about the same price as its leading competitor—and aggressively cut prices to boost sales. But as the airline, construction equipment, fast-food, and other industries have learned in recent years, cutting prices in an industry loaded with excess capacity may lead to price wars as competitors try to hold on to market share.

Another situation leading to price changes is falling market share in the face of strong price competition. Several American industries—automobiles, consumer electronics, cameras, watches, and steel, for example—lost market share to Japanese competitors whose high-quality products carried lower prices than did their American counterparts. In response, American companies resorted to more aggressive pricing action. A company may also cut prices in a drive to dominate the market through lower costs. Either the company starts with lower costs than its competitors, or it cuts prices in the hope of gaining market share that will further cut costs through larger volume. Bausch & Lomb used an aggressive low-cost, low-price strategy to become an early leader in the competitive soft contact lens market.

Initiating Price Increases A successful price increase can greatly increase profits. For example, if the company's profit margin is 3 percent of sales, a 1 percent price increase will increase profits by 33 percent if sales volume is unaffected. A major factor in price increases is cost inflation. Rising costs squeeze profit margins and lead companies to pass cost increases along to customers. Another factor leading to price increases is overdemand: When a company cannot supply all its customers' needs, it can raise its prices, ration products to customers, or both.

Companies can increase their prices in a number of ways to keep up with rising costs. Prices can be raised almost invisibly by dropping discounts and adding higher-priced units to the line. Or prices can be pushed up openly. In passing price increases on to customers, the company must avoid being perceived as a price gouger. Companies also need to think of who will bear the brunt of increased prices. As the Kellogg example at the beginning of the chapter suggests, customer memories are long, and they will eventually turn away from companies or even whole industries that they perceive as charging excessive prices.

Wherever possible, the company should consider ways to meet higher costs or demand without raising prices. For example, it can consider more cost-effective ways to produce or distribute its products. It can shrink the product instead of raising the price, as candy bar manufacturers often do. It can substitute less expensive ingredients or remove certain product features, packaging, or services. Or it can "unbundle" its products and services, removing and separately pricing elements that were formerly part of the offer. IBM, for example, now offers training and consulting as separately priced services.

Buyer Reactions to Price Changes Whether the price is raised or lowered, the action will affect buyers, competitors, distributors, and suppliers and may interest government as well. Customers do not always interpret prices in a straightforward way. They may view a price *cut* in several ways. For example, what would you think if Sony were suddenly to cut its computer prices in half? You might think that these computers are about to be replaced by newer models or that they have some fault and are not selling well. You might think that Sony is abandoning the computer business and may not stay in this business long enough to supply future parts. You might believe that quality has been reduced. Or you might think that the price will come down even further and that it will pay to wait and see.

Similarly, a price *increase,* which would normally lower sales, may have some positive meanings for buyers. What would you think if Sony *raised* the price of its latest computer model? On the one hand, you might think that the item is very "hot" and may be

Buyer reactions to price changes? What would you think if the price of Joy was suddenly cut in half?

unobtainable unless you buy it soon. Or you might think that the computer is an unusually good value. On the other hand, you might think that Sony is greedy and charging what the traffic will bear.[24]

Competitor Reactions to Price Changes A firm considering a price change has to worry about the reactions of its competitors as well as those of its customers. Competitors are most likely to react when the number of firms involved is small, when the product is uniform, and when the buyers are well informed.

How can the firm anticipate the likely reactions of its competitors? If the firm faces one large competitor, and if the competitor tends to react in a set way to price changes, that reaction can be easily anticipated. But if the competitor treats each price change as a fresh challenge and reacts according to its self-interest, the company will have to figure out just what makes up the competitor's self-interest at the time.

The problem is complex because, like the customer, the competitor can interpret a company price cut in many ways. It might think the company is trying to grab a larger market share, that the company is doing poorly and trying to boost its sales, or that the company wants the whole industry to cut prices to increase total demand.

When there are several competitors, the company must guess each competitor's likely reaction. If all competitors behave alike, this amounts to analyzing only a typical competitor. In contrast, if the competitors do not behave alike—perhaps because of differences in size, market shares, or policies—then separate analyses are necessary. However, if some competitors will match the price change, there is good reason to expect that the rest will also match it.

Responding to Price Changes

Here we reverse the question and ask how a firm should respond to a price change by a competitor. The firm needs to consider several issues: Why did the competitor change the price? Was it to take more market share, to use excess capacity, to meet changing cost conditions, or to lead an industrywide price change? Is the price change temporary or permanent? What will happen to the company's market share and profits if it does not respond? Are other companies going to respond? And what are the competitor's and other firms' responses to each possible reaction likely to be?

Besides these issues, the company must make a broader analysis. It has to consider its own product's stage in the life cycle, the product's importance in the company's product mix, the intentions and resources of the competitor, and the possible consumer reactions to price changes. The company cannot always make an extended analysis of its alternatives at the time of a price change, however. The competitor may have spent much time preparing this decision, but the company may have to react within hours or days. About the only way to cut down reaction time is to plan ahead for both possible competitor's price changes and possible responses.

Figure 10-6 shows the ways a company might assess and respond to a competitor's price cut. Once the company has determined that the competitor has cut its price and that this price reduction is likely to harm company sales and profits, it might simply decide to hold its current price and profit margin. The company might believe that it will not lose too much market share, or that it would lose too much profit if it reduced its own price. It might decide that it should wait and respond when it has more information on the effects of the competitor's price change. For now, it might be willing to hold on to good customers, while giving up the poorer ones to the competitor. The argument against this holding strategy, however, is that the competitor may get stronger and more confident as its sales increase and that the company might wait too long to act.

If the company decides that effective action can and should be taken, it might make any of four responses. First, it could *reduce its price* to match the competitor's price. It

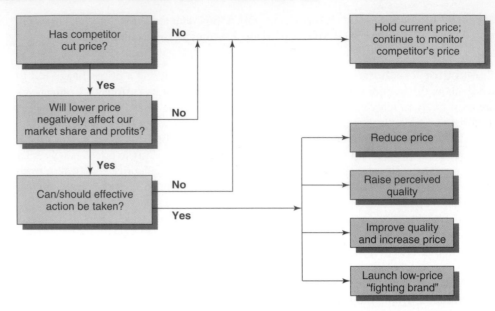

Figure 10-6
Assessing and responding to competitor price changes

may decide that the market is price sensitive and that it would lose too much market share to the lower-priced competitor. Or it might worry that recapturing lost market share later would be too hard. Cutting the price will reduce the company's profits in the short run. Some companies might also reduce their product quality, services, and marketing communications to retain profit margins, but this will ultimately hurt long-run market share. The company should try to maintain its quality as it cuts prices.

Alternatively, the company might maintain its price but *raise the perceived quality* of its offer. It could improve its communications, stressing the relative quality of its product over that of the lower-price competitor. The firm may find it cheaper to maintain price and spend money to improve its perceived value than to cut price and operate at a lower margin.

Or, the company might *improve quality and increase price,* moving its brand into a higher-price position. The higher quality justifies the higher price, which in turn preserves the company's higher margins. Or the company can hold price on the current product and introduce a new brand at a higher-price position.

Finally, the company might *launch a low-price "fighting brand"* —adding a lower-price item to the line or creating a separate lower-price brand. This is necessary if the particular market segment being lost is price sensitive and will not respond to arguments of higher quality. Thus, when challenged on price by store brands and other low-price entrants, Procter & Gamble turned a number of its brands into fighting brands, including Luvs disposable diapers, Joy dishwashing detergent, and Camay beauty soap. In turn, P&G competitor Kimberly-Clark offers its value-priced Scott Towels brand as "the Bounty killer." It scores well on customer satisfaction measures but sells for a lower price than P&G's Bounty brand.[25]

Public Policy and Pricing

Price competition is a core element of our free-market economy. In setting prices, companies are not usually free to charge whatever prices they wish. Many federal, state, and even local laws govern the rules of fair play in pricing. In addition, companies must consider

Fighting brands: Kimberly Clark offers its value-priced Scott Towels brand as "the Bounty killer." It scores well on customer satisfaction but sells for a lower price than P&G's Bounty.

broader societal pricing concerns. The most important pieces of legislation affecting pricing are the Sherman, Clayton, and Robinson-Patman acts, initially adopted to curb the formation of monopolies and to regulate business practices that might unfairly restrain trade. Because these federal statutes can be applied only to interstate commerce, some states have adopted similar provisions for companies that operate locally.

Figure 10-7 shows the major public policy issues in pricing. These include potentially damaging pricing practices within a given level of the channel (price-fixing and predatory pricing) and across levels of the channel (retail price maintenance, discriminatory pricing, and deceptive pricing).[26]

Pricing within Channel Levels

Federal legislation on *price-fixing* states that sellers must set prices without talking to competitors. Otherwise, price collusion is suspected. Price-fixing is illegal per se—that is, the government does not accept any excuses for price-fixing. Companies found guilty of such practices can receive heavy fines. For example, when the U.S. Justice Department found that Archer Daniels Midland Company and three of its competitors had met regularly in the early 1990s to illegally fix prices, the four companies paid more than $100 million to settle the charges. Recently, governments at the state and national levels have been aggressively enforcing price-fixing regulations in industries ranging from tobacco, gasoline, and newsprint to vitamins and compact discs.[27]

Even a simple conversation between competitors can have serious consequences. For example, during the early 1980s, American Airlines and Braniff were immersed in a price

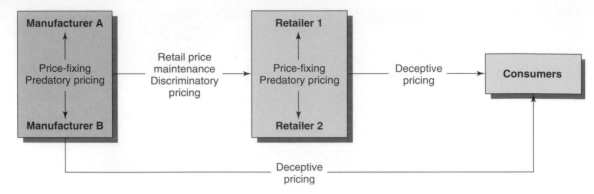

Figure 10-7
Public policy issues in pricing

war in the Texas market. In the heat of the battle, American's CEO, Robert Crandall, called the president of Braniff and said, "Raise your . . . fares 20 percent. I'll raise mine the next morning. You'll make more money and I will, too." Fortunately for Crandall, the Braniff president warned him off, saying, "We can't talk about pricing!" As it turns out, the phone conversation had been recorded, and the U.S. Justice Department began action against Crandall and American for price-fixing. The charges were eventually dropped—the courts ruled that because Braniff had rejected Crandall's proposal, no actual collusion had occurred and that a proposal to fix prices was not an actual violation of the law. Still, as part of the settlement, for two years Crandall was required to keep a detailed log of his conversations with fellow airline chiefs.[28] Such cases have made most executives very reluctant to discuss prices in any way with competitors.

Sellers are also prohibited from using *predatory pricing*—selling below cost with the intention of punishing a competitor or gaining higher long-run profits by putting competitors out of business. This protects small sellers from larger ones who might sell items below cost temporarily or in a specific locale to drive them out of business. The biggest problem is determining just what constitutes predatory pricing behavior. Selling below cost to sell off excess inventory is not considered predatory; selling below cost to drive out competitors is. Thus, the same action may or may not be predatory depending on intent, and intent can be very difficult to determine or prove.

In recent years, several large and powerful companies have been accused of this practice. For example, Wal-Mart has been sued by dozens of small competitors charging that it lowered prices in their specific areas to drive them out of business. In another recent case, the Justice Department sued American Airlines for allegedly using predatory pricing to muscle three small competitors—Vanguard Airlines, Sun Jet, and Western Pacific—out of its huge Dallas–Fort Worth hub. American prevailed by arguing that it was just being a tough competitor.[29] Giant Microsoft has also been a Justice Department target:

> When Microsoft targets a market for domination, it frequently wins over customers with an irresistible offer: free products. In 1996, Microsoft started giving away Internet Explorer, its Web browser—and in some cases arguably even "paid" people to use it by offering free software and marketing assistance. The strategy was crucial in wresting market dominance from Netscape Communications Corporation. Netscape constantly revised its pricing structure but "better than free" is not the most appealing sales pitch. Most of Microsoft's giveaways were offered as part of its effort to gain share in the interactive corporate computing market. For instance, the company offered free Web-server software to customers who purchase the Windows NT network operating system. Netscape was selling a higher-powered version of the

same software for $4,100. Although such pricing and promotion strategies might be viewed as shrewd marketing by some, competitors saw them as purely predatory. They noted that in the past, once Microsoft had used these tactics to gain a lion's share of the market, it had tended to raise prices *above* market levels. For example, the wholesale price it charged PC makers for its Windows operating system (in which is bundled the Internet Explorer) had doubled during the past seven years.[30]

Pricing across Channel Levels

The Robinson-Patman Act seeks to prevent unfair *price discrimination* by ensuring that sellers offer the same price terms to customers at a given level of trade. For example, every retailer is entitled to the same price terms from a given manufacturer, whether the retailer is Sears or the local bicycle shop. However, price discrimination is allowed if the seller can prove that its costs are different when selling to different retailers—for example, that it costs less per unit to sell a large volume of bicycles to Sears than to sell a few bicycles to a local dealer. Or the seller can discriminate in its pricing if the seller manufactures different qualities of the same product for different retailers. The seller has to prove that these differences are proportional. Price differentials may also be used to "match competition" in "good faith," provided the price discrimination is temporary, localized, and defensive rather than offensive.

Retail price maintenance is also prohibited—a manufacturer cannot require dealers to charge a specified retail price for its product. Although the seller can propose a manufacturer's *suggested* retail price to dealers, it cannot refuse to sell to a dealer who takes independent pricing action, nor can it punish the dealer by shipping late or denying advertising allowances. For example, in 1996 the Federal Trade Commission (FTC) charged that New Balance had engaged in fixing retail prices for its athletic shoes. Its agreements with retailers required that the retailers raise the price of New Balance products, maintain prices at levels set by New Balance, and not discount the products.

Deceptive pricing occurs when a seller states prices or price savings that mislead consumers or are not actually available to consumers. This might involve bogus reference or comparison prices, as when a retailer sets artificially high "regular" prices then announces "sale" prices close to its previous everyday prices. Such comparison pricing is widespread:

> Open any Sunday newspaper and find hundreds of such promotions being offered by a variety of retailers, such as supermarkets, office supply stores, furniture stores, computer stores, appliance stores, pharmacies and drugstores, car dealers, department stores, and others. Surf the Internet and see similar price promotions. Watch the shopping channels on television and find more of the same. It seems that, today, selling prices rarely stand alone. Instead retailers are using an advertised reference price (e.g., regular price, original price, manufacturer's suggested price) to suggest that buyers will save money if they take advantage of the "deal" being offered.[31]

Such claims are legal if they are truthful. However, the FTC's *Guides Against Deceptive Pricing* warns sellers not to advertise a price reduction unless it is a saving from the usual retail price, not to advertise "factory" or "wholesale" prices unless such prices are what they are claimed to be, and not to advertise comparable value prices on imperfect goods.

Other deceptive pricing issues include *scanner fraud* and price confusion. The widespread use of scanner-based computer checkouts has led to increasing complaints of retailers overcharging their customers. Most of these overcharges result from poor management—from a failure to enter current or sale prices into the system. Other cases, however, involve intentional overcharges. *Price confusion* results when firms employ pricing methods that make it difficult for consumers to understand just what price they are really paying. For example, consumers are sometimes misled regarding the real price of a home mortgage or car leasing agreement. In other cases, important pricing details may be buried in the "fine print."

Many federal and state statutes regulate against deceptive pricing practices. For example, the Automobile Information Disclosure Act requires automakers to attach a statement to new car windows stating the manufacturer's suggested retail price, the prices of optional equipment, and the dealer's transportation charges. However, reputable sellers go beyond what is required by law. Treating customers fairly and making certain that they fully understand prices and pricing terms is an important part of building strong and lasting customer relationships.[32]

STOP   *Rest Stop: Reviewing the Concepts*

Before you put pricing in the rearview mirror, let's review the important concepts. *Price* can be defined as the sum of the values that consumers exchange for the benefits of having and using the product or service. It is the only marketing mix element that produces revenue; all other elements represent costs. Even so, many companies are not good at handling pricing. Pricing decisions are subject to an incredibly complex array of environmental and competitive forces.

1. Identify and explain the external and internal factors affecting a firm's pricing decisions.

External factors that influence pricing decisions include the nature of the *market* and *demand; competitors' costs, prices, and offers;* and factors such as *the economy, reseller needs, government actions,* and *social concerns.* The seller's pricing freedom varies with different types of markets. Ultimately, the consumer decides whether the company has set the right price. The consumer weighs the price against the perceived values of using the product—if the price exceeds the sum of the values, consumers will not buy. Therefore, *demand* and *consumer value perceptions* set the ceiling for prices. Consumers also compare a product's price to the prices of *competitors'* products. As a result, a company must learn the price and quality of competitors' offers.

Many *internal factors* influence the company's pricing decisions, including the firm's *marketing objectives, marketing mix strategy, costs,* and *organization for pricing.* Common pricing objectives include survival, current profit maximization, market share leadership, and product quality leadership. The pricing strategy is largely determined by the company's *target market* and *position-*

ing objectives. Pricing decisions affect and are affected by product design, distribution, and promotion decisions and must be carefully coordinated with these other marketing mix variables. *Costs* set the floor for the company's price—the price must cover all the costs of making and selling the product, plus a fair rate of return. Finally, in order to coordinate pricing goals and decisions, management must decide who within the organization is responsible for setting price.

2. Contrast the three general approaches to setting prices.

A company can select one or a combination of three general pricing approaches: the *cost-based approach* (cost-plus pricing, break-even analysis, and target profit pricing); the *value-based approach;* and the *competition-based approach.* Cost-based pricing sets prices based on the seller's cost structure, whereas value-based pricing relies on consumer perceptions of value to drive pricing decisions. Competition-based pricing involves setting prices based on what competitors are charging or are expected to charge.

3. Describe the major strategies for pricing imitative and new products.

Pricing is a dynamic process. Companies design a *pricing structure* that covers all their products. They change this structure over time and adjust it to account for different customers and situations. Pricing strategies usually change as a product passes through its life cycle. The company can decide on one of several price quality strategies for introducing an imitative product, including premium pricing, economy pricing, good-value pricing, or overcharging. In pricing innovative new products, it can follow a *skimming policy* by initially setting high prices to "skim" the maximum amount of revenue from various segments of the market. Or it can use *penetration pricing* by setting a low initial price to penetrate the market deeply and win a large market share.

4. Explain how companies find a set of prices that maximizes the profits from the total product mix.

When the product is part of a product mix, the firm searches for a set of prices that will maximize the profits from the total mix. In *product line pricing,* the company decides on price steps for the entire set of products it offers. In addition, the company must set prices for *optional products* (optional or accessory products included with the main product), *captive products* (products that are required for use of the main product), *by-products* (waste or residual products produced when making the main product), and *product bundles* (combinations of products at a reduced price).

5. Discuss how companies adjust their prices to take into account different types of customers and situations.

Companies apply a variety of *price-adjustment strategies* to account for differences in consumer segments and situations. One is *discount and allowance pricing,* whereby the company establishes cash, quantity, functional, or seasonal discounts, or varying types of allowances. A second strategy is *segmented pricing,* whereby the company sells a product at two or more prices to accommodate different customers, product forms, locations, or times. Sometimes companies consider more than economics in their pricing decisions, using *psychological pricing* to better communicate a product's intended position. In *promotional pricing,* a company offers discounts or temporarily sells a product

below list price as a special event, sometimes even selling below cost as a loss leader. Another approach is *geographical pricing,* whereby the company decides how to price to near and distant customers. Finally, *international pricing* means that the company adjusts its price to meet conditions and expectations in different world markets.

6. Discuss the key issues related to initiating and responding to price changes.

When a firm considers initiating a *price change,* it must consider customers' and competitors' reactions. There are different implications to *initiating price cuts* and *initiating price increases.* Buyer reactions to price changes are influenced by the meaning customers see in the price change. Competitors' reactions flow from a set reaction policy or a fresh analysis of each situation. There are also many factors to consider in responding to a competitor's price changes. The company that faces a price change initiated by a competitor must try to understand the competitor's intent as well as the likely duration and impact of the change. If a swift reaction is desirable, the firm should preplan its reactions to different possible price actions by competitors. When facing a competitor's price change, the company might sit tight, reduce its own price, raise perceived quality, improve quality and raise price, or launch a fighting brand.

Companies are not usually free to charge whatever prices they wish. Many federal, state, and even local laws govern the rules of fair play in pricing. The major public policy issues in pricing include potentially damaging pricing practices within a given level of the channel (price-fixing and predatory pricing) and across levels of the channel (retail price maintenance, discriminatory pricing, and deceptive pricing).

Navigating the Key Terms

For a detailed analysis of the meaning and importance of each of the following key terms, visit our Web page at www.prenhall.com/kotler.

Allowance
Break-even pricing (target profit pricing)
By-product pricing

Captive-product pricing
Competition-based pricing
Cost-plus pricing
Demand curve
Discount
Dynamic pricing
Market-penetration pricing
Market-skimming pricing
Optional-product pricing
Price

Price elasticity
Product bundle pricing
Product line pricing
Promotional pricing
Psychological pricing
Reference prices
Segmented pricing
Target costing
Value pricing
Value-based pricing

Travel Log

The following concept checks and discussion questions will help you to keep track of and apply the concepts you've studied in this chapter.

Concept Checks

Fill in the blanks, then look for the correct answers.

1. With _____ pricing, different prices are charged, depending on individual customers and situations.
2. Common objectives with respect to pricing include survival, _____, _____, and _____.
3. Economists recognize four types of markets, each presenting a different pricing challenge: _____; _____; _____; and _____.
4. Price elasticity measures how responsive demand will be to a change in price. If demand changes greatly, we say the demand is _____.
5. The simplest pricing method is _____ where the marketer adds a standard markup to the cost of the product.
6. _____ pricing means that the marketer cannot design a product and marketing program and then set the price. Price is considered along with the other marketing-mix variables before the marketing program is set.
7. _____-based pricing is used when firms bid for jobs. A special version of this pricing form would be going-rate pricing and sealed-bid pricing.
8. If a company chooses to set a low initial price in order to go into the market quickly and deeply (to attract a large number of buyers quickly and win a large market share), the company would be using a _____ pricing strategy.
9. Examples of products that would use _____ pricing would include razor blades, camera film, video games, and computer software.
10. A typical example of a _____ discount is "2/10, net 30," which means that although payment is due within 30 days, the buyer can deduct 2 percent if the bill is paid within 10 days.
11. Consumers usually perceive higher-priced products as having higher quality. This would be a case where _____ pricing was used.
12. If a customer is asked to pay the entire cost of freight from the factory to the customer's destination (distant customers will have to pay more), the company is most likely using the _____ pricing form of geographical pricing.

Concept Checks Answers: 1. dynamic; 2. current profit maximization, market share leadership, product quality leadership; 3. pure competition, monopolistic competition, oligopolistic competition, and pure monopoly; 4. elastic; 5. cost-plus pricing; 6. Value-based; 7. Competition; 8. market-penetration; 9. captive-product; 10. cash; 11. psychological; 12. FOB-origin.

Discussing the Issues

1. Assume you are the vice-president for financial affairs at a major college or university. For the past three years, enrollments and revenues have declined steadily at a rate of about 10 percent per year. You are under great pressure to raise tuition to compensate for the falling revenues. However, you suspect that raising tuition might only make matters worse. What internal and external pricing factors should you consider before you make your decision? Explain.
2. Discuss the typical pricing objectives outlined in the chapter. Which of these objectives do you believe: (a) is the most commonly used; (b) is the most difficult to achieve; (c) has the greatest potential for long-term growth of the organization; and, (d) is most likely to be a pricing objective used by a dot-com e-commerce-oriented company? Explain.
3. After examining Figure 10-5, compare and contrast cost-based pricing and value-based pricing. What situations favor each pricing method?
4. Which pricing strategy—market skimming or market penetration—does each of the following companies use? (a) McDonald's, (b) Curtis Mathes (televisions and other home electronics), (c) Bic Corporation (pens, lighters, razors, and related products), and (d) IBM (personal computers). Are these the right strategies for these companies? Explain.
5. Formulate rules that might govern (a) initiating a price cut, (b) initiating a price increase, (c) a negative reaction on the part of buyers to a price change by your company, (d) a competitor's response to your price change, and (e) your response to a competitor's price change. State the assumptions underlying your proposed rules.

Mastering Marketing

Pricing is one of the most important and difficult decisions a firm must make. Choose a product from CanGo. (a) What pricing objective is the company using with respect to the product? Is this the correct objective? (b) Into which of the four types of economic markets does this product fit? (c) Which general pricing approach is the company using with respect to this product? Is this the best approach? (d) Would you favor market skimming or market penetration pricing for this product? Explain. (e) If a product-mix pricing strategy were to be used, which technique would be most appropriate? Explain. (f) Is a price change needed? Explain how this might be done and why the change might be necessary.

Traveling the Net

Point of Interest: Pricing in a Wired World

"Gallery Furniture Saves You Money!" is an advertising slogan heard many times a day in the Houston, Texas, market. This dynamic furniture outlet uses many types of advertising media to spread its consistent message to cost-conscious consumers. Gallery Furniture not only sells from its vast showroom and warehouse facility but also promotes its products nationwide via an elaborate Web site (see **www.galleryfurniture.com**). When visiting the Web site, consumers can see showroom furniture in "real time" via robotic cameras that have the ability to pan throughout the entire store. This feature allows customers to see what is currently on the showroom floor and how much the item costs (including specials of the day). This form of shopping saves time and money and avoids traffic in one of America's largest cities. By using the robotic-camera feature, Gallery Furniture can constantly update its prices without having to manually update its Web site. Locally, Gallery Furniture boasts, "Buy it today, receive it tonight!" As an extension of this pledge, the company recently declared that one of its new goals was to expand statewide (and eventually nationwide) with its aggressive pricing policies. Would you be willing to shop for furniture from Houston if it could be delivered promptly and at a cost comparable with local competitors? Gallery Furniture is exploring the possibility that you (and thousands of others) will.

For Discussion

1. Which general pricing strategy does Gallery Furniture use? Which pricing objective does it pursue? Are the strategy and objective consistent? Explain.
2. If Gallery Furniture expands into state and national markets, which geographical pricing method would you recommend?
3. What internal and external factors would affect Gallery Furniture's decision to expand?
4. Which product-mix pricing strategies could be beneficial to Gallery Furniture? Explain.
5. Would psychological pricing make sense for this organization? Explain.
6. What other features did you find on the organization's Web site that help to enhance the position of the firm?

Application Thinking

After visiting Gallery Furniture's Web site and familiarizing yourself with the organization's approach to pricing and selling furniture, assume that you are the marketing manager of a rival furniture organization (see **www.starfurniture.com**, **www.ikea.com**, or **www.bassettfurniture.com**). After carefully considering the information found in this chapter, outline a plan for attacking Gallery Furniture's pricing strategy. What role would your Web site play in this strategy?

Map—Marketing Applications

Map Stop 10

Conduct a pricing survey of several gasoline stations in your city. Check prices at stations near exit ramps on a major highway, at stations on your local commercial strip, at a convenience store, at smaller stations that are not located near other stations, and at a truck stop.

Record the brand of gasoline, prices of regular and premium grades, type of location, distance to the nearest competitor, whether the station is multi-purpose (includes a food store or fast food facility), and competitors' prices. (For additional information on gasoline, see www.amoco.com, www.chevron.com, www.mobil.com, or www.shell.com).

Thinking Like a Marketing Manager

1. What patterns do you detect for the pricing of gasoline at the various outlets?

2. Do these stations appear to be using cost-based, buyer-based, or competition-based pricing? What internal and external factors would be important to consider when choosing a pricing strategy in this industry?

3. Talk to several station operators. What factors do they think usually trigger a price war? How much control do the station operators have over pricing?

4. What did you learn about pricing strategy and tactics from this experience?

chapter
11

Marketing Channels and Supply Chain Management

ROAD MAP:
Previewing the Concepts

We now arrive at the third marketing mix tool—distribution. Firms rarely work alone in bringing value to customers. Instead, most are only a single link in a larger supply chain or distribution channel. As such, an individual firm's success depends not only on how well *it* performs but also on how well its *entire distribution channel* competes with competitors' channels. For example, Ford can make the world's best cars but still will not do well if its dealers perform poorly in sales and service against the dealers of Toyota, GM, Chrysler, or Honda. Ford must choose its channel partners carefully and work with them effectively. The first part of this chapter explores the nature of distribution channels and the marketer's channel design and management decisions. We then examine physical distribution—or logistics—an area that is growing dramatically in importance and sophistication. In the next chapter, we'll look more closely at two major channel intermediaries—retailers and wholesalers.

▶ After studying this chapter, you should be able to

1. explain why companies use distribution channels and discuss the functions these channels perform
2. discuss how channel members interact and how they organize to perform the work of the channel
3. identify the major channel alternatives open to a company
4. explain how companies select, motivate, and evaluate channel members
5. discuss the nature and importance of marketing logistics and integrated supply chain management

While your engine's warming up, we'll take a look at Caterpillar. You might think that Caterpillar's success, and its ability to charge premium prices, rests on the quality of the construction and mining equipment that it produces. But Caterpillar's former chairman and CEO sees things differently. The company's dominance, he claims, results from its unparalleled distribution and customer support system—from the strong and caring partnerships that it has built with independent Caterpillar dealers. Read on and see why.

For more than half a century, Caterpillar has dominated the world's markets for heavy construction and mining equipment. Its familiar yellow tractors, crawlers, loaders, and trucks are a common sight at any construction area. With sales of $20 billion, Caterpillar is half again as large as its nearest competitor. It now captures more than a 35 percent share of the world's heavy construction equipment market, selling more than 300 products in nearly 200 countries.

Many factors contribute to Caterpillar's enduring success—high-quality products, flexible and efficient manufacturing, a steady stream of innovative new products, and

a lean organization that is responsive to customer needs. Although Caterpillar charges premium prices for its equipment, its high-quality and trouble-free operation provide greater long-term value. Yet these are not the most important reasons for Caterpillar's dominance. Instead, Caterpillar credits its focus on customers and its corps of 211 outstanding dealers worldwide, who do a superb job of taking care of every customer need. According to former Caterpillar CEO Donald Fites:

> After the product leaves our door, the dealers take over. They are the ones on the front line. They're the ones who live with the product for its lifetime. They're the ones customers see. Although we offer financing and insurance, they arrange those deals for customers. They're out there making sure that when a machine is delivered, it's in the condition it's supposed to be in. They're out there training a customer's operators. They service a product frequently throughout its life, carefully monitoring a machine's health and scheduling repairs to prevent costly downtime. The customer . . . knows that there is a $20-billion-plus company called Caterpillar. But the dealers create the image of a company that doesn't just stand *behind* its products but *with* its products, anywhere in the world. Our dealers are the reason that our motto—Buy the Iron, Get the Company—is not an empty slogan.

Caterpillar's dealers build strong customer relationships in their communities. "Our independent dealer in Novi, Michigan, or in Bangkok, Thailand, knows so much more about the requirements of customers in those locations than a huge corporation like Caterpillar could," says Fites. Competitors often bypass their dealers and sell directly to big customers to cut costs or make more profits for themselves. However, Caterpillar wouldn't think of going around its dealers. "The knowledge of the local market and the close relations with customers that our dealers provide are worth every penny," he asserts with passion. "We'd rather cut off our right arm than sell directly to customers and bypass our dealers."

Caterpillar and its dealers work in close harmony to find better ways to bring value to customers. The entire system is linked by a single worldwide computer network. For example, working at their desktop computers, Caterpillar managers can check to see how many Cat machines in the world are waiting for parts. Closely linked dealers play a vital role in almost every aspect of Caterpillar's operations, from product design and delivery, to product service and support, to market intelligence and customer feedback.

In the heavy-equipment industry, in which equipment downtime can mean big losses, Caterpillar's exceptional service gives it a huge advantage in winning and keeping customers. Consider Freeport-McMoRan, a Cat customer that operates one of the world's largest copper and gold mines, 24 hours a day, 365 days a year. High in the mountains of Indonesia, the mine is accessible only by aerial cableway or helicopter. Freeport-McMoRan relies on more than 500 pieces of Caterpillar mining and construction equipment—worth several hundred million dollars—including loaders, tractors, and mammoth 240-ton, 2,000-plus-horsepower trucks. Many of these machines cost well over $1 million apiece. When equipment breaks down, Freeport-McMoRan loses money fast. Freeport-McMoRan gladly pays a premium price for machines and service it can count on. It knows that it can count on Caterpillar and its outstanding distribution network for superb support.

The close working relationship between Caterpillar and its dealers comes down to more than just formal contracts and business agreements. The powerful partnership rests on a handful of basic principles and practices:

- *Dealer profitability:* Caterpillar's rule: "Share the gain as well as the pain." When times are good, Caterpillar shares the bounty with its dealers rather than trying to grab all the riches for itself. When times are bad, Caterpillar protects its dealers. In the mid-1980s, facing a depressed global construction-equipment market and cutthroat competition, Caterpillar sheltered its dealers by absorbing much of the economic damage. It lost almost $1 billion dollars in just three years but didn't lose a single dealer. In contrast, competitors' dealers struggled and many failed. As a result, Caterpillar emerged with its distribution system intact and its competitive position stronger than ever.

- *Extraordinary dealer support:* Nowhere is this support more apparent than in the company's parts delivery system, the fastest and most reliable in the industry. Caterpillar maintains 36 distribution centers and 1,500 service facilities around the world, which stock 320,000 different parts and ship 84,000 items per day, every day of the year. In turn, dealers have made huge investments in inventory, warehouses, fleets of trucks, service bays, diagnostic and service equipment, and information technology. Together, Caterpillar and its dealers guarantee parts delivery within 48 hours anywhere in the world. The company ships 80 percent of parts orders immediately and 99 percent on the same day the order is received. In contrast, it's not unusual for competitors' customers to wait 4 or 5 days for a part.

- *Communications:* Caterpillar communicates with its dealers—fully, frequently, and honestly. According to Fites, "There are no secrets between us and our dealers. We have the financial statements and key operating data of every dealer in the world. . . . In addition, virtually all Caterpillar and dealer employees have real-time access to continually updated databases of service information, sales trends and forecasts, customer satisfaction surveys, and other critical data. . . . [Moreover,] virtually everyone from the youngest design engineer to the CEO now has direct contact with somebody in our dealer organizations."

- *Dealer performance:* Caterpillar does all it can to ensure that its dealerships are run well. It closely monitors each dealership's sales, market position, service capability, financial situation, and other performance measures. It genuinely wants each dealer to succeed, and when it sees a problem, it jumps in to help. As a result, Caterpillar dealerships, many of which are family businesses, tend to be stable and profitable. The average Caterpillar dealership has remained in the hands of the same family for more than 50 years. Some actually predate the 1925 merger that created Caterpillar.

- *Personal relationships:* In addition to more formal business ties, Cat forms close personal ties with its dealers in a kind of family relationship. Fites relates the following example: "When I see Chappy Chapman, a retired executive vice-president . . . , out on the golf course, he always asks about particular dealers or about their children, who may be running the business now. And every time I see those dealers, they inquire, 'How's Chappy?' That's the sort of relationship we have. . . . I consider the majority of dealers personal friends."

Thus, Caterpillar's superb distribution system serves as a major source of competitive advantage. The system is built on a firm base of mutual trust and shared dreams. Caterpillar and its dealers feel a deep pride in what they are accomplishing together. As Fites puts it, "There's a camaraderie among our dealers around the world that really makes it more than just a financial arrangement. They feel that what they're doing is good for the world because they are part of an organization that makes, sells, and tends to the machines that make the world work."[1]

Marketing channel decisions are among the most important decisions that management faces. A company's channel decisions are linked with every other marketing decision. The company's pricing depends on whether it uses mass merchandisers or high-quality specialty stores. The firm's sales force and advertising decisions depend on how much persuasion, training, motivation, and support the dealers need. Whether a company develops or acquires certain new products may depend on how well those products fit the capabilities of its channel members.

Companies often pay too little attention to their distribution channels, however, sometimes with damaging results. In contrast, many companies have used imaginative distribution systems to *gain* a competitive advantage. FedEx's creative and imposing distribution system made it the leader in the small-package delivery industry. General Electric gained a strong advantage in selling its major appliances by supporting its dealers with a sophisticated computerized order-processing and delivery system. Dell Computer revolutionized its industry by selling personal computers directly to consumers rather than through retail stores. And Charles Schwab & Company pioneered the delivery of financial services via the Internet.

Distribution channel decisions often involve long-term commitments to other firms. For example, companies such as Ford, IBM, or McDonald's can easily change their advertising, pricing, or promotion programs. They can scrap old products and introduce new ones as market tastes demand. But when they set up distribution channels through contracts with franchisees, independent dealers, or large retailers, they cannot readily replace these channels with company-owned stores or Web sites if conditions change. Therefore, management must design its channels carefully, with an eye on tomorrow's likely selling environment as well as today's.

This chapter examines four major questions concerning distribution channels: What is the nature of distribution channels? How do channel firms interact and organize to do the work of the channel? What problems do companies face in designing and managing their channels? What role do physical distribution and supply chain management play in attracting and satisfying customers? In Chapter 12, we will look at distribution channel issues from the viewpoint of retailers and wholesalers.

The Nature of Distribution Channels

Most producers use intermediaries to bring their products to market. They try to forge a **distribution channel**—a set of interdependent organizations involved in the process of making a product or service available for use or consumption by the consumer or business user.[2]

Why Are Marketing Intermediaries Used?

Why do producers give some of the selling job to intermediaries? After all, doing so means giving up some control over how and to whom the products are sold. The use of intermediaries results from their greater efficiency in making goods available to target markets. Through their contacts, experience, specialization, and scale of operation, intermediaries usually offer the firm more than it can achieve on its own.

Figure 11-1 shows how using intermediaries can provide economies. Figure 11-1A shows three manufacturers, each using direct marketing to reach three customers. This system requires nine different contacts. Figure 11-1B shows the three manufacturers working through one distributor, which contacts the three customers. This system requires only six contacts. In this way, intermediaries reduce the amount of work that must be done by both producers and consumers.

From the economic system's point of view, the role of marketing intermediaries is to transform the assortments of products made by producers into the assortments wanted by consumers. Producers make narrow assortments of products in large quantities, but consumers want broad assortments of products in small quantities. In the distribution channels, intermediaries buy large quantities from many producers and break them down into the smaller quantities and broader assortments wanted by consumers. Thus, intermediaries play an important role in matching supply and demand.

Distribution channel
A set of interdependent organizations involved in the process of making a product or service available for use or consumption by the consumer or business user.

Distribution Channel Functions

The distribution channel moves goods and services from producers to consumers. It overcomes the major time, place, and possession gaps that separate goods and services from those who would use them. Members of the marketing channel perform many key functions. Some help to complete transactions:

◆ *Information:* Gathering and distributing marketing research and intelligence information about actors and forces in the marketing environment needed for planning and aiding exchange.
◆ *Promotion:* Developing and spreading persuasive communications about an offer.
◆ *Contact:* Finding and communicating with prospective buyers.

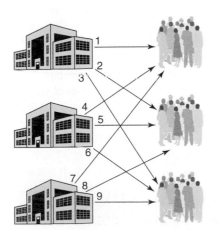

A. Number of contacts without a distributor
M × C = 3 × 3 = 9

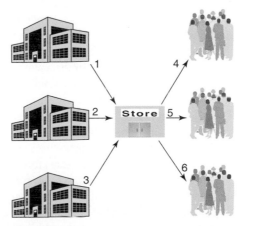

B. Number of contacts with a distributor
M + C = 3 + 3 = 6

 = Manufacturer    = Customer   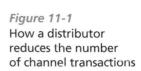 = Distributor

Figure 11-1
How a distributor reduces the number of channel transactions

◆ *Matching:* Shaping and fitting the offer to the buyers' needs, including activities such as manufacturing, grading, assembling, and packaging.
◆ *Negotiation:* Reaching an agreement on price and other terms of the offer so that ownership or possession can be transferred.

Others help to fulfill the completed transactions:

◆ *Physical distribution:* Transporting and storing goods.
◆ *Financing:* Acquiring and using funds to cover the costs of the channel work.
◆ *Risk taking:* Assuming the risks of carrying out the channel work.

The question is not *whether* these functions need to be performed—they must be—but rather *who* will perform them. To the extent that the manufacturer performs these functions, its costs go up and its prices have to be higher. When some of these functions are shifted to intermediaries, the producer's costs and prices may be lower, but the intermediaries must charge more to cover the costs of their work. In dividing the work of the channel, the various functions should be assigned to the channel members who can perform them most efficiently and effectively to provide satisfactory assortments of goods to target consumers.

Number of Channel Levels

Channel level
A layer of intermediaries that performs some work in bringing the product and its ownership closer to the final buyer.

Direct marketing channel
A marketing channel that has no intermediary levels.

Indirect marketing channel
Channel containing one or more intermediary levels.

Distribution channels can be described by the number of channel levels involved. Each layer of marketing intermediaries that performs some work in bringing the product and its ownership closer to the final buyer is a **channel level.** Because the producer and the final consumer both perform some work, they are part of every channel. We use the *number of intermediary levels* to indicate the *length* of a channel. Figure 11-2, part A, shows several consumer distribution channels of different lengths.

Channel 1, called a **direct marketing channel,** has no intermediary levels. It consists of a company selling directly to consumers. For example, Avon, Amway, and Tupperware sell their products door to door or through home and office sales parties; Singer sells its sewing machines through its own stores; and Dell sells computers direct through telephone selling and its Web site. The remaining channels in Figure 11-2A are **indirect marketing channels.** Channel 2 contains one intermediary level. In consumer markets, this level is typically a retailer. For example, the makers of televisions, cameras, tires, furniture, major appliances, and many other products sell their goods directly to large retailers such as Wal-Mart and Sears, which then sell the goods to final consumers. Channel 3 contains two intermediary levels, a wholesaler and a retailer. This channel is often used by small manufacturers of food, drugs, hardware, and other products. Channel 4 contains three intermediary levels. In the meatpacking industry, for example, jobbers buy from wholesalers and sell to smaller retailers who generally are not served by larger wholesalers. Distribution channels with even more levels are sometimes found, but less often. From the producer's point of view, a greater number of levels means less control and greater channel complexity.

Figure 11-2, part B, shows some common business distribution channels. The business marketer can use its own sales force to sell directly to business customers. It can also sell to industrial distributors, who in turn sell to business customers. It can sell through manufacturers' representatives or its own sales branches to business customers, or it can use these representatives and branches to sell through industrial distributors. Thus, business markets commonly include multilevel distribution channels.

All of the institutions in the channel are connected by several types of *flows.* These include the *physical flow* of products, the *flow of ownership,* the *payment flow,* the *information flow,* and the *promotion flow.* These flows can make even channels with only one or a few levels very complex.

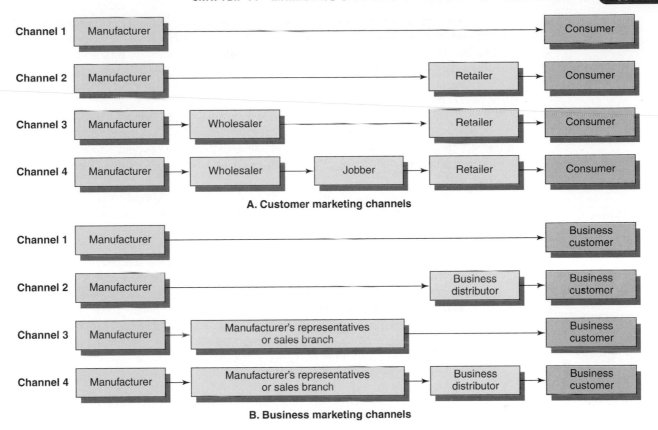

Figure 11-2
Consumer and business marketing channels

Channel Behavior and Organization

Distribution channels are more than simple collections of firms tied together by various flows. They are complex behavioral systems in which people and companies interact to accomplish individual, company, and channel goals. Some channel systems consist only of informal interactions among loosely organized firms; others consist of formal interactions guided by strong organizational structures. Moreover, channel systems do not stand still—new types of intermediaries emerge and whole new channel systems evolve. Here we look at channel behavior and at how members organize to do the work of the channel.

Channel Behavior

A distribution channel consists of firms that have banded together for their common good. Each channel member is dependent on the others. For example, a Ford dealer depends on the Ford Motor Company to design cars that meet consumer needs. In turn, Ford depends on the dealer to attract consumers, persuade them to buy Ford cars, and service cars after the sale. The Ford dealer also depends on other dealers to provide good sales and service that will uphold the reputation of Ford and its dealer body. In fact, the success of individual Ford dealers depends on how well the entire Ford distribution channel competes with the channels of other auto manufacturers.

Each channel member plays a role in the channel and specializes in performing one or more functions. For example, Compaq's role is to produce personal computers that consumers will like and to create demand through national advertising. Best Buy's role is to display these Compaq computers in convenient locations, to answer buyers' questions, and to close sales. The channel will be most effective when each member is assigned the tasks it can do best.

Ideally, because the success of individual channel members depends on overall channel success, all channel firms should work together smoothly. They should understand and accept their roles, coordinate their goals and activities, and cooperate to attain overall channel goals. By cooperating, they can more effectively sense, serve, and satisfy the target market.

However, individual channel members rarely take such a broad view. They are usually more concerned with their own short-run goals and their dealings with those firms closest to them in the channel. Cooperating to achieve overall channel goals sometimes means giving up individual company goals. Although channel members are dependent on one another, they often act alone in their own short-run best interests. They often disagree on the roles each should play—on who should do what and for what rewards. Such disagreements over goals and roles generate **channel conflict.**

Horizontal conflict occurs among firms at the same level of the channel. For instance, some Ford dealers in Chicago might complain about other dealers in the city who steal sales from them by being too aggressive in their pricing and advertising or by selling outside their assigned territories. Or Holiday Inn franchisees might complain about other Holiday Inn franchisees overcharging guests or giving poor service, hurting the overall Holiday Inn image.

Vertical conflict, conflicts between different levels of the same channel, is even more common. For example, McDonald's came into conflict with some of its California dealers when its aggressive expansion plans called for placing new stores in areas that took business from existing locations. Office furniture maker Herman Miller created conflict with its dealers when it opened an online store—www.hmstore.com—and began selling its products directly to customers. Although Herman Miller believed that the Web site was reaching only smaller customers who weren't being served by current channels, dealers complained loudly. To help resolve the conflict, Herman Miller embarked on a communication campaign to educate dealers on how the online efforts would help them rather than hurt them. It now sells more than $67 million worth of furniture a year via the Web to customers ranging from Fortune 1000 firms to lone eagles toiling in their home offices.[3]

Some conflict in the channel takes the form of healthy competition. Such competition can be good for the channel—without it, the channel could become passive and noninnovative.

> Anne Mulcahy enjoys the tension. As president of Xerox General Markets Operations (GMO), a $6 billion business with 6,000 employees worldwide, she has steered Xerox away from using only field salespeople and championed a model that also uses retailers, resellers, dealers, the Internet, and inside reps. "Those that don't aggressively embrace multiple channels for multiple products will get left behind," says Mulcahy. The inherent conflict in this business model, she freely admits, is not only a reality of business, it's a sign of a healthy company. "Channel conflict is just a cost of trying to extend coverage in the market," says marketing consultant Tim Furey. The upside: Competition turns resellers into smart partners that offer added value—not mere products—and forces field salespeople to work with those partners to provide customers with complete solutions.[4]

But if it gets out of hand, conflict can disrupt channel effectiveness and cause lasting harm to channel relationships. For the channel as a whole to perform well, each channel

Channel conflict
Disagreement among marketing channel members on goals and roles—who should do what and for what rewards.

member's role must be specified and channel conflict must be managed. Cooperation, role assignment, and conflict management in the channel are attained through strong channel leadership. The channel will perform better if it includes a firm, agency, or mechanism that has the power to assign roles and manage conflict.

Vertical Marketing Systems

Historically, distribution channels have been loose collections of independent companies, each showing little concern for overall channel performance. These *conventional distribution channels* have lacked strong leadership and have been troubled by damaging conflict and poor performance. One of the biggest channel developments has been the *vertical marketing systems* that have emerged over the years to challenge conventional marketing channels. Figure 11-3 contrasts the two types of channel arrangements.

A **conventional distribution channel** consists of one or more independent producers, wholesalers, and retailers. Each is a separate business seeking to maximize its own profits, even at the expense of profits for the system as a whole. No channel member has much control over the other members, and no formal means exists for assigning roles and resolving channel conflict. In contrast, a **vertical marketing system (VMS)** consists of producers, wholesalers, and retailers acting as a unified system. One channel member owns the others, has contracts with them, or wields so much power that they must all cooperate. The VMS can be dominated by the producer, wholesaler, or retailer. Vertical marketing systems came into being to control channel behavior and manage channel conflict.

We look now at three major types of VMSs: *corporate, contractual,* and *administered.* Each uses a different means for setting up leadership and power in the channel. We now take a closer look at each type of VMS.

Corporate VMS   A **corporate VMS** combines successive stages of production and distribution under single ownership. Coordination and conflict management are attained through regular organizational channels. For example, Sears obtains more than 50 percent of its goods from companies that it partly or wholly owns. Giant Food Stores operates an

Conventional distribution channel
A channel consisting of one or more independent producers, wholesalers, and retailers, each a separate business seeking to maximize its own profits even at the expense of profits for the system as a whole.

Vertical marketing system (VMS)
A distribution channel structure in which producers, wholesalers, and retailers act as a unified system. One channel member owns the others, has contracts with them, or has so much power that they all cooperate.

Corporate VMS
A vertical marketing system that combines successive stages of production and distribution under single ownership—channel leadership is established through common ownership.

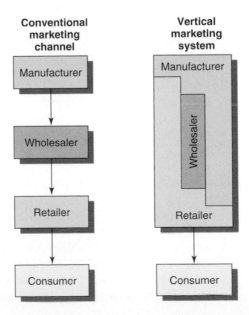

Figure 11-3
Comparison of conventional distribution channel with vertical marketing system

ice-making facility, a soft drink bottling operation, an ice cream plant, and a bakery that supplies Giant stores with everything from bagels to birthday cakes.

Controlling the entire distribution chain has turned Spanish clothing chain Zara into the world's fastest-growing fashion retailer.

The secret to Zara's success is its control over almost every aspect of the supply chain, from design and production to its own worldwide distribution network. Zara makes 40 percent of its own fabrics and produces more than half of its own clothes, rather than relying on a hodgepodge of slow-moving suppliers. New styles take shape in Zara's own design centers, supported by real-time sales data. New designs feed into Zara manufacturing centers, which ship finished products directly to 450 Zara stores in 30 countries, saving time, eliminating the need for warehouses, and keeping inventories low. Effective vertical integration makes Zara faster, more flexible, and more efficient than international competitors such as Gap, Benetton, and Sweden's H&M. Zara can make a new line from start to finish in just three weeks, so a look seen on MTV can be in Zara stores within a month, versus an industry average of nine months. And Zara's low costs let it offer midmarket chic at downmarket prices. The company's stylish but affordable offerings have attracted a cult following, and the company's sales have more than doubled to $2.3 billion in the past five years.[5]

Contractual VMS

A vertical marketing system in which independent firms at different levels of production and distribution join together through contracts to obtain more economies or sales impact than they could achieve alone.

Contractual VMS A **contractual VMS** consists of independent firms at different levels of production and distribution who join together through contracts to obtain more economies or sales impact than each could achieve alone. Coordination and conflict management are attained through contractual agreements among channel members. There are three types of contractual VMSs: wholesaler-sponsored voluntary chains, retailer cooperatives, and franchise organizations.

In *wholesaler-sponsored voluntary chains,* wholesalers organize voluntary chains of independent retailers to help them compete with large chain organizations. The wholesaler develops a program in which independent retailers standardize their selling practices and achieve buying economies that let the group compete effectively with chain organizations. Examples include the Independent Grocers Alliance (IGA), Western Auto, and Do it Best hardwares.

In *retailer cooperatives,* retailers organize a new, jointly owned business to carry on wholesaling and possibly production. Members buy most of their goods through the retailer co-op and plan their advertising jointly. Profits are passed back to members in proportion to their purchases. Examples include Certified Grocers, Associated Grocers, and Ace Hardware.

Franchise organization

A contractual vertical marketing system in which a channel member, called a franchiser, links several stages in the production-distribution process.

In **franchise organizations,** a channel member called a *franchiser* links several stages in the production-distribution process. An estimated 2,000 franchised U.S. companies with over 320,000 outlets account for some $1 trillion in annual sales.[6] Almost every kind of business has been franchised—from motels and fast-food restaurants to dental centers and dating services, from wedding consultants and maid services to funeral homes and fitness centers.

There are three forms of franchises. The first form is the *manufacturer-sponsored retailer franchise system,* as found in the automobile industry. Ford, for example, licenses dealers to sell its cars; the dealers are independent businesspeople who agree to meet various conditions of sales and service. The second type of franchise is the *manufacturer-sponsored wholesaler franchise system,* as found in the soft drink industry. Coca-Cola, for example, licenses bottlers (wholesalers) in various markets who buy Coca-Cola syrup concentrate and then carbonate, bottle, and sell the finished product to retailers in local markets. The third franchise form is the *service-firm-sponsored retailer franchise system,* in which a service firm licenses a system of retailers to bring its service to consumers.

Contractual VMS: An estimated 2,000 franchised U.S. companies with over 320,000 outlets account for some $1 trillion in annual sales.

Examples are found in the auto-rental business (Hertz, Avis), the fast-food service business (McDonald's, Burger King) and the motel business (Holiday Inn, Ramada Inn).

The fact that most consumers cannot tell the difference between contractual and corporate VMSs shows how successfully the contractual organizations compete with corporate chains. Chapter 12 presents a fuller discussion of the various contractual VMSs.

Administered VMS   An **administered VMS** coordinates successive stages of production and distribution, not through common ownership or contractual ties but through the size and power of one of the parties. In an *administered VMS,* leadership is assumed by one or a few dominant channel members. Manufacturers of a top brand can obtain strong trade cooperation and support from resellers. For example, General Electric, Procter & Gamble, and Kraft can command unusual cooperation from resellers regarding displays, shelf space, promotions, and price policies. Large retailers such as Wal-Mart and Barnes & Noble can exert strong influence on the manufacturers that supply the products they sell.

Administered VMS
A vertical marketing system that coordinates successive stages of production and distribution, not through common ownership or contractual ties, but through the size and power of one of the parties.

Horizontal Marketing Systems

Another channel development is the **horizontal marketing system,** in which two or more companies at one level join together to follow a new marketing opportunity. By working together, companies can combine their capital, production capabilities, or marketing resources to accomplish more than any one company could alone. Companies might join forces with competitors or noncompetitors. They might work with each other on a temporary or permanent basis, or they may create a separate company. For example, the Lamar Savings Bank of Texas arranged to locate its savings offices and automated teller machines in Safeway stores. Lamar gained quicker market entry at a low cost, and Safeway was able to offer in-store banking convenience to its customers. Similarly, McDonald's now places "express" versions of its restaurants in Wal-Mart stores. McDonald's benefits from Wal-Mart's considerable store traffic, while Wal-Mart keeps hungry shoppers from having to go elsewhere to eat.

Such channel arrangements also work well globally. For example, because of its excellent coverage of international markets, Nestlé jointly sells General Mills's cereal

Horizontal marketing system
A channel arrangement in which two or more companies at one level join together to follow a new marketing opportunity.

Horizontal marketing systems: Nestlé jointly sells General Mills cereal brands in markets outside North America.

brands in markets outside North America. Coca-Cola and Nestlé formed a joint venture to market ready-to-drink coffee and tea worldwide. Coke provides worldwide experience in marketing and distributing beverages, and Nestlé contributes two established brand names—Nescafé and Nestea. Similarly, Coca-Cola and Procter & Gamble have created distribution systems linking Coca-Cola soft drinks and Pringles potato crisps in global markets. Seiko Watch's distribution partner in Japan, K. Hattori, markets Schick's razors there, giving Schick the leading market share in Japan, despite Gillette's overall strength in many other markets.[7]

Hybrid Marketing Systems

Hybrid marketing channel
Multichannel distribution system in which a single firm sets up two or more marketing channels to reach one or more customer segments.

In the past, many companies used a single channel to sell to a single market or market segment. Today, with the proliferation of customer segments and channel possibilities, more and more companies have adopted *multichannel distribution systems*—often called **hybrid marketing channels.** Such multichannel marketing occurs when a single firm sets up two or more marketing channels to reach one or more customer segments. The use of hybrid channel systems has increased greatly in recent years.

Figure 11-4 shows a hybrid channel. In the figure, the producer sells directly to consumer segment 1 using direct-mail catalogs, telemarketing, and the Internet and reaches consumer segment 2 through retailers. It sells indirectly to business segment 1 through distributors and dealers and to business segment 2 through its own sales force.

IBM uses such a hybrid channel effectively. For years, IBM sold computers only through its own sales force, which sold its large systems to business customers. However, the market for computers and information technology has now exploded into a profusion of products and services for dozens of segments and niches, ranging from large corporate buyers to small businesses to home and home office buyers. As a result, IBM has dramatically had to rethink the way it goes to market. To serve the diverse needs of these many segments, IBM added 18 new channels in less than 10 years. For example, in addition to selling through the vaunted IBM sales force, IBM also sells through a comprehensive

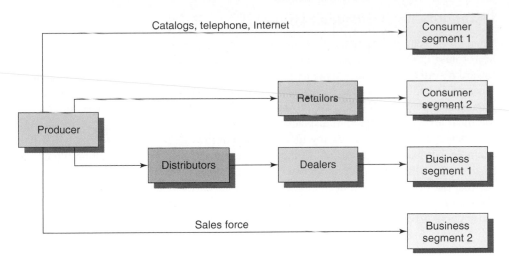

Figure 11-4
Hybrid marketing channel

network of distributors and value-added resellers, which sell IBM computers, systems, and services to a variety of special business segments. Final customers can buy IBM personal computers from specialty computer stores or any of several large retailers, including Wal-Mart, Circuit City, and Office Depot. IBM uses telemarketing to service the needs of small and medium-size business. And both business and final consumers can buy online from the company's ShopIBM Web site (www.ibm.com).

Hybrid channels offer many advantages to companies facing large and complex markets. With each new channel, the company expands its sales and market coverage and gains opportunities to tailor its products and services to the specific needs of diverse customer segments. But such hybrid channel systems are harder to control, and they generate conflict as more channels compete for customers and sales. For example, when IBM began selling directly to customers through catalogs, telemarketing, and its own Web site, many of its retail dealers cried "unfair competition" and threatened to drop the IBM line or to give it less emphasis. Many outside salespeople felt that they were being undercut by the new "inside channels."

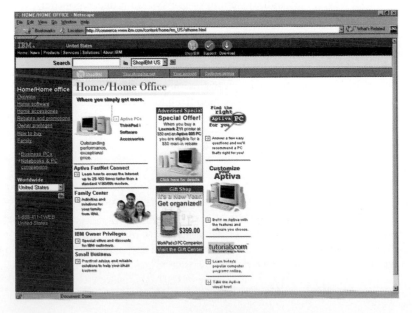

Hybrid channels: In addition to its sales force, IBM sells through distributors and value-added resellers, specialty computer stores and large retailers, telemarketing, and its ShopIBM Web site.

Changing Channel Organization

Disintermediation
The displacement of traditional resellers from a marketing channel by radical new types of intermediaries.

Changes in technology and the explosive growth of direct and online marketing are having a profound impact on the nature and design of marketing channels. One major trend is toward **disintermediation**—a big term with a clear message and important consequences. Disintermediation means that more and more, product and service producers are bypassing intermediaries and going directly to final buyers, or that radically new types of channel intermediaries are emerging to displace traditional ones.

Thus, in many industries, traditional intermediaries are dropping by the wayside. For example, companies such as Dell Computer and American Airlines are selling directly to final buyers, eliminating retailers from their marketing channels. E-commerce is growing rapidly, taking business from traditional brick-and-mortar retailers. Consumers can buy Flowers from 1-800-Flowers.com; books, videos, CDs, toys, consumer electronics, and other goods from Amazon.com; and clothes from landsend.com or gap.com, all without ever visiting a store.

Disintermediation presents problems and opportunities for both producers and intermediaries (see Marketing at Work 11-1). To avoid being swept aside, traditional intermediaries must find new ways to add value in the supply chain. To remain competitive, product and service producers must develop new channel opportunities, such as Internet and other direct channels. However, developing these new channels often brings them into direct competition with their established channels, resulting in conflict. To ease this problem, companies often look for ways to make going direct a plus for both the company and its channel partners:

> Going direct is rarely an all-or-nothing proposition. For example, to trim costs and add business, Hewlett-Packard opened three direct-sales Web sites—Shopping Village (for consumers), HP Commerce Center (for businesses buying from authorized resellers), and Electronic Solutions Now (for existing contract customers). However, to avoid conflicts with its established reseller channels, HP forwards all its Web orders to resellers, who complete the orders, ship the products, and get the commissions. In this way, HP gains the advantages of direct selling but also boosts business for resellers.

> However, although this compromise system reduces conflicts, it also creates inefficiencies. "That all sounds great and everyone's happy," says a distribution consultant, "but kicking the customer over to the reseller . . . is a lot more expensive than letting customers order directly from the manufacturer. HP is spending a fair chunk of change to set this up, plus the business partner still wants eight percent margins for getting the product to the customer."[8] To be truly efficient in the long run, HP eventually will have to find ways for its resellers to add value or drop them from the direct channel.

Linking the Concepts

Stop here for a moment and apply the distribution channel concepts we've discussed so far.

◆ Compare the Caterpillar and IBM channels. Draw a diagram that shows the types of intermediaries in each channel. What kind of channel system does each company use?

◆ What are the roles and responsibilities of the members in each channel? How well do these channel members work together toward overall channel success?

Disintermediation: A Fancy Word But a Clear Message

Belair/Empress Travel in Bowie, Maryland, typifies the kind of business most threatened by the advent of new marketing channels, particularly the surge in Internet selling. Like other traditional travel agencies, Belair/Empress faces some scary new competitors, giant online travel supersites such as Expedia or Travelocity, that let consumers surf the Web for rock-bottom ticket prices. To make matters worse, the airlines themselves have opened Web sites to sell seats. Last year American, Continental, United, Northwest, and Delta airlines joined forces to launch Orbitz.com, a Web site that offers "the most low airfares on the Internet, plus great values on rental cars, hotel rooms, and more."

These new channels give consumers more choices, but they threaten the very existence of Belair/Empress Travel and other traditional travel agents. During the 1990s, the number of U.S. travel agents dropped by 18 percent, and some studies suggest that another 25 percent will go out of business during the next few years.

Resellers in dozens of industries face similar situations as new channel forms threaten to make them obsolete. There's even a fancy 17-letter word to describe this phenomenon: *disintermediation*. Strictly speaking, disintermediation means the elimination of a layer of intermediaries from a marketing channel. For example, for years personal computer makers assumed that customers needed hands-on buying experience, with lots of point-of-sale inventory and hand-holding sales assistance from retailers. Then, along came Dell Computer with its direct model. By eliminating retailers, Dell eliminated many costs and inefficiencies

from the traditional computer supply chain.

More broadly, disintermediation includes not only the elimination of channel levels through direct marketing but also the displacement of traditional resellers by radically new types of intermediaries. For example, the publishing industry had for decades assumed that book buyers wanted to purchase their books from small, intimate neighborhood bookshops. Then, along came the book superstores—Barnes & Noble and Borders—with their huge inventories and low prices. Disintermediation occurred as the new intermediaries rapidly displaced traditional independent booksellers. Then, online bookseller Amazon.com emerged to threaten the category killers. Amazon.com doesn't eliminate the retail channel—it's actually a new type of retailer that increases consumers' channel choices rather than reducing them. Still, disintermediation has occurred as Amazon.com and the superstores' own Web sites are displacing traditional brick-and-mortar retailers.

Disintermediation is often associated with the surge in e-commerce and online selling. And, in fact, the Internet is a major disintermediating force. By facilitating direct contact between buyers and sellers, the Internet is displacing channels in industries ranging from books, apparel, and consumer electronics to travel, stock brokerage, and real estate services. However, disintermediation can involve almost any new form of channel competition. For example, Dell bypassed retailers through telephone and mail-order selling long before it took to the Internet.

Disintermediation works only when a new channel form succeeds

in bringing greater value to consumers. Thus, if Amazon.com weren't giving buyers greater convenience, selection, and value, it wouldn't be able to lure customers away from traditional retailers. If Dell's direct channel weren't more efficient and effective in serving the needs of computer buyers, traditional retail channels would have little to fear. However, the success of these new channels suggests that they *are* bringing greater value to significant segments of consumers.

From a producer's viewpoint, although eliminating unneeded intermediaries makes sense, disintermediation can be very difficult. One analyst summarizes it this way:

> You thought e-commerce would bring nothing but good news. Here at last, you reasoned, is a way to add customers, boost market share, and cut sales costs. All manufacturers have to do is set up an electronic conduit between themselves and their customers and voila, instant sales channel. There's just one little hitch. Those same thoughts terrify the retailers, distributors, and resellers that account for up to 90 percent of manufacturers' revenues. They fear that their role between company and customer will be rendered obsolete by the virtual marketplace. And that puts manufacturers in a bind. Either they surrender to the seductions of e-commerce and risk a mutiny from those valuable partners, or they do nothing and risk the wrath of [successful e-commerce competitors].

Thus, Dell had the advantage of starting from scratch in designing its direct channel. However, for Compaq, IBM, and other computer producers that are already locked into traditional retail channels, disintermediation presents real problems. To compete more effectively with Dell, both Compaq and IBM have now developed their own direct-sales operations. However, although the direct channel helps Compaq to compete better with Dell, it worries and displeases the established retail partners that Compaq counts on for the bulk of its sales.

Still, most producers know that when more effective channels come along, they have no choice but to change. There is a Dell at work or in waiting in every industry, and traditional producers can't afford to wait very long to get inefficiencies out of their distribution channels. Despite the risks, most companies are more afraid of being late to the party than of angering their channel partners. The major question often is not whether to move to a new, high-growth channel but how quickly and what to do with the established channel. One answer is to join forces with channel partners so that both benefit from new channel opportunities. For example, consider Maytag:

Appliance giant Maytag wanted to leverage its powerful brand name and great quality reputation by selling appliances on the Web. Maytag's goal was to sell to customers without forcing them to travel to a dealer, where they might be seduced by other brands. However, Maytag didn't want to damage its relationships with the

thousands of dealers around the country that sell the bulk of its appliances. The solution was to help *dealers* close sales online. The company created My Maytag, a feature on its main Web site, by which customers could learn about and purchase Maytag products. But rather than filling the orders directly, the company handed them off to dealers. With My Maytag, everyone wins: Online consumers get a convenient and seamless shopping experience, dealers get the sales, and Maytag avoids channel conflict and boosts its business.

What about traditional resellers? How can they avoid being "Amazoned"? The answer lies in continually looking for new ways to create real customer value. Blair/Express Travel plans to deemphasize airline ticket sales and become a market nicher specializing in specialty cruises. The owner plans to do what computers can't—get to know his customers so well that he can provide personal advice on the cruises he books. Many companies threatened by Internet competitors have themselves learned to leverage the Web to serve customers better. To maintain sales, some smaller booksellers, such as WordsWorth Books in Cambridge, Massachusetts, are going online but retaining their independent feel. WordsWorth designed its Web site to mirror its retail locations, focusing on good customer

service and tapping into customer loyalty.

Discount brokerage Charles Schwab also proves the value point. Facing a horde of price-cutting e-commerce competitors who got there first—including E*Trade and Ameritrade—Schwab jumped into the Internet with both feet (remember our Chapter 3 discussion?). However, instead of becoming just another no-frills Internet trading operation, Schwab did competitors one better. It plied customers with a wealth of tools and information for managing their accounts, assuming the role of an investment adviser. Rather than dragging its feet or fighting the change, Schwab embraced the new channel as a competitive opportunity.

Thus, disintermediation is a big word but the meaning is clear. Those who continually seek new ways to add real value for customers have little to fear. However, those who fall behind in adding value risk being swept aside by their customers and channel partners.

Sources: Quotes and extracts from Rochelle Garner, "Mad as Hell," *Sales and Marketing Management,* June 1999, pp. 55–61; Maricris G. Briones, "What Technology Wrought: Distribution Channel in Flux," *Marketing News,* February 1, 1999, pp. 3, 15; Barb Gomolski, "No Channel Conflict," *InfoWorld,* July 9, 2001, p. 10; and information accessed online at www.orbitz.com, August 2001. Also see James Champy, "How to Fire Your Dealers," *Forbes,* June 14, 1999, p. 141; Jeffery D. Zbar, "Familiarity Breeds Success in Web Retailing," *Advertising Age,* September 13, 1999; Tyler Maroney, "An Air Battle Comes to the Web," *Fortune,* June 26, 2000, pp. 315–318; and Timothy J. Mullaney, "Orbitz Doesn't Soar," *Business Week,* July 9, 2001, p. 8.

Channel Design Decisions

We now look at several channel decisions manufacturers face. In designing marketing channels, manufacturers struggle between what is ideal and what is practical. A new firm with limited capital usually starts by selling in a limited market area. Deciding on the *best* channels might not be a problem: The problem might simply be how to convince one or a few good intermediaries to handle the line.

If successful, the new firm might branch out to new markets through the existing intermediaries. In smaller markets, the firm might sell directly to retailers; in larger markets, it might sell through distributors. In one part of the country, it might grant exclusive franchises; in another, it might sell through all available outlets. Then, it might add a Web store that sells directly to hard-to-reach customers. In this way, channel systems often evolve to meet market opportunities and conditions. However, for maximum effectiveness, channel analysis and decision making should be more purposeful. Designing a channel system calls for analyzing consumer service needs, setting channel objectives and constraints, identifying major channel alternatives, and evaluating them.

Analyzing Consumer Service Needs

As noted previously, marketing channels can be thought of as *customer value delivery systems* in which each channel member adds value for the customer. Thus, designing the distribution channel starts with finding out what targeted consumers want from the channel. Do consumers want to buy from nearby locations or are they willing to travel to more distant centralized locations? Would they rather buy in person, over the phone, through the mail, or via the Internet? Do they value breadth of assortment or do they prefer specialization? Do consumers want many add-on services (delivery, credit, repairs, installation), or will they obtain these elsewhere? The faster the delivery, the greater the assortment provided, and the more add-on services supplied, the greater the channel's service level.

But providing the fastest delivery, greatest assortment, and most services may not be possible or practical. The company and its channel members may not have the resources or skills needed to provide all the desired services. Also, providing higher levels of service results in higher costs for the channel and higher prices for consumers. The company must balance consumer service needs not only against the feasibility and costs of meeting these needs but also against customer price preferences. The success of off-price and discount retailing shows that consumers are often willing to accept lower service levels if this means lower prices.

Setting Channel Objectives and Constraints

Channel objectives should be stated in terms of the desired service level of target consumers. Usually, a company can identify several segments wanting different levels of channel service. The company should decide which segments to serve and the best channels to use in each case. In each segment, the company wants to minimize the total channel cost of meeting customer service requirements.

The company's channel objectives are also influenced by the nature of the company, its products, its marketing intermediaries, its competitors, and the environment. For example, the company's size and financial situation determine which marketing functions it can handle itself and which it must give to intermediaries. Companies selling perishable products may require more direct marketing to avoid delays and too much handling. In some cases, a company may want to compete in or near the same outlets that carry competitors' products. In other cases, producers may avoid the channels used by competitors. Avon, for example, uses door-to-door selling rather than going head to head with other cosmetics makers for scarce positions in retail stores. And GEICO markets auto and homeowners insurance directly to consumers via the telephone rather than through agents. Finally, environmental factors such as economic conditions and legal constraints may affect channel objectives and design. For example, in a depressed economy, producers want to distribute their goods in the most economical way, using shorter channels and dropping unneeded services that add to the final price of the goods.

Product characteristics affect channel decisions: Fresh flowers must be delivered quickly with a minimum of handling.

Identifying Major Alternatives

When the company has defined its channel objectives, it should next identify its major channel alternatives in terms of *types* of intermediaries, the *number* of intermediaries, and the *responsibilities* of each channel member.

Types of Intermediaries   A firm should identify the types of channel members available to carry out its channel work. For example, suppose a manufacturer of test equipment has developed an audio device that detects poor mechanical connections in machines with moving parts. Company executives think this product would have a market in all industries in which electric, combustion, or steam engines are made or used. The company's current sales force is small, and the problem is how best to reach these different industries. The following channel alternatives might emerge from management discussion:

> *Company sales force:* Expand the company's direct sales force. Assign outside salespeople to territories and have them contact all prospects in the area or develop separate company sales forces for different industries. Or, add an inside telesales operation in which telephone salespeople handle small or midsize companies.

> *Manufacturer's agency:* Hire manufacturers' agents — independent firms whose sales forces handle related products from many companies — in different regions or industries to sell the new test equipment.

> *Industrial distributors:* Find distributors in the different regions or industries who will buy and carry the new line. Give them exclusive distribution, good margins, product training, and promotional support.

Number of Marketing Intermediaries   Companies must also determine the number of channel members to use at each level. Three strategies are available: intensive distribution, exclusive distribution, and selective distribution. Producers of convenience products and common raw materials typically seek **intensive distribution** — a strategy in which they stock their products in as many outlets as possible. These goods must be available

Intensive distribution
Stocking the product in as many outlets as possible.

where and when consumers want them. For example, toothpaste, candy, and other similar items are sold in millions of outlets to provide maximum brand exposure and consumer convenience. Kraft, Coca-Cola, Kimberly-Clark, and other consumer goods companies distribute their products in this way.

By contrast, some producers purposely limit the number of intermediaries handling their products. The extreme form of this practice is **exclusive distribution,** in which the producer gives only a limited number of dealers the exclusive right to distribute its products in their territories. Exclusive distribution is often found in the distribution of new automobiles and prestige women's clothing. For example, Rolls-Royce dealers are few and far between—even large cities may have only one or two dealers. By granting exclusive distribution, Rolls-Royce gains stronger distributor selling support and more control over dealer prices, promotion, credit, and services. Exclusive distribution also enhances the car's image and allows for higher markups.

Between intensive and exclusive distribution lies **selective distribution**—the use of more than one, but fewer than all, of the intermediaries who are willing to carry a company's products. Most television, furniture, and small-appliance brands are distributed in this manner. For example, Maytag, Whirlpool, and General Electric sell their major appliances through dealer networks and selected large retailers. By using selective distribution, they do not have to spread their efforts over many outlets, including many marginal ones. They can develop good working relationships with selected channel members and expect a better-than-average selling effort. Selective distribution gives producers good market coverage with more control and less cost than does intensive distribution.

Responsibilities of Channel Members The producer and intermediaries need to agree on the terms and responsibilities of each channel member. They should agree on price policies, conditions of sale, territorial rights, and specific services to be performed by each party. The producer should establish a list price and a fair set of discounts for intermediaries. It must define each channel member's territory, and it should be careful about where it places new resellers. Mutual services and duties need to be spelled out carefully, especially in franchise and exclusive distribution channels. For example, McDonald's provides franchisees with promotional support, a record-keeping system, training at Hamburger University, and general management assistance. In turn, franchisees must meet company standards for physical facilities, cooperate with new promotion programs, provide requested information, and buy specified food products.

Exclusive distribution
Giving a limited number of dealers the exclusive right to distribute the company's products in their territories.

Selective distribution
The use of more than one, but fewer than all, of the intermediaries who are willing to carry the company's products.

Exclusive distribution: Luxury car makers sell exclusively through a limited number of dealerships. Such limited distribution enhances the car's image and generates stronger dealership support.

Evaluating the Major Alternatives

Suppose a company has identified several channel alternatives and wants to select the one that will best satisfy its long-run objectives. Each alternative should be evaluated against economic, control, and adaptive criteria.

Using *economic criteria,* a company compares the likely profitability of different channel alternatives. It estimates the sales that each channel would produce and the costs of selling different volumes through each channel. The company must also consider *control issues.* Using intermediaries usually means giving them some control over the marketing of the product, and some intermediaries take more control than others. Other things being equal, the company prefers to keep as much control as possible. Finally, the company must apply *adaptive criteria.* Channels often involve long-term commitments to other firms, making it hard to adapt the channel to the changing marketing environment. The company wants to keep the channel as flexible as possible. Thus, to be considered, a channel involving long-term commitment should be greatly superior on economic and control grounds.

Designing International Distribution Channels

International marketers face many additional complexities in designing their channels. Each country has its own unique distribution system that has evolved over time and changes very slowly. These channel systems can vary widely from country to country. Thus, global marketers must usually adapt their channel strategies to the existing structures within each country. In some markets, the distribution system is complex and hard to penetrate, consisting of many layers and large numbers of intermediaries. Consider Japan:

> The Japanese distribution system stems from the early seventeenth century when cottage industries and a [quickly growing] urban population spawned a merchant class. . . . Despite Japan's economic achievements, the distribution system has remained remarkably faithful to its antique pattern. . . . [It] encompasses a wide range of wholesalers and other agents, brokers, and retailers, differing more in number than in function from their American counterparts. There are myriad tiny retail shops. An even greater number of wholesalers supplies goods to them, layered tier upon tier, many more than most U.S. executives would think necessary. For example, soap may move through three wholesalers plus a sales company after it leaves the manufacturer before it ever reaches the retail outlet. A steak goes from rancher to consumers in a process that often involves a dozen middle agents. . . . The distribution network . . . reflects the traditionally close ties among many Japanese companies . . . [and places] much greater emphasis on personal relationships with users. . . . Although [these channels appear] inefficient and cumbersome, they seem to serve the Japanese customer well. . . . Lacking much storage space in their small homes, most Japanese homemakers shop several times a week and prefer convenient [and more personal] neighborhood shops.[9]

Many Western firms have had great difficulty breaking into the closely knit, tradition-bound Japanese distribution network.

At the other extreme, distribution systems in developing countries may be scattered and inefficient, or altogether lacking. For example, China and India would appear to be huge markets, each with populations in the hundreds of millions. In reality, however, these markets are much smaller than the population numbers suggest. Because of inadequate distribution systems in both countries, most companies can profitably access only a small portion of the population located in each country's most affluent cities.[10]

The Japanese distribution system has remained remarkably traditional. A profusion of tiny retail shops are supplied by an even greater number of small wholesalers.

Thus, international marketers face a wide range of channel alternatives. Designing efficient and effective channel systems between and within various country markets poses a difficult challenge. We discuss international distribution decisions further in Chapter 15.

Channel Management Decisions

Once the company has reviewed its channel alternatives and decided on the best channel design, it must implement and manage the chosen channel. Channel management calls for selecting and motivating individual channel members and evaluating their performance over time.

Selecting Channel Members

Producers vary in their ability to attract qualified marketing intermediaries. Some producers have no trouble signing up channel members. For example, when Toyota first introduced its Lexus line in the United States, it had no trouble attracting new dealers. In fact, it had to turn down many would-be resellers. In some cases, the promise of exclusive or selective distribution for a desirable product will draw plenty of applicants.

At the other extreme are producers who have to work hard to line up enough qualified intermediaries. When Polaroid started, for example, it could not get photography stores to carry its new cameras, and it had to go to mass-merchandising outlets. Similarly, when the U.S. Time Company first tried to sell its inexpensive Timex watches through regular jewelry stores, most jewelry stores refused to carry them. The company then managed to get its watches into mass-merchandise outlets. This turned out to be a wise decision because of the rapid growth of mass merchandising.

When selecting intermediaries, the company should determine what characteristics distinguish the better ones. It will want to evaluate each channel member's years in business, other lines carried, growth and profit record, cooperativeness, and reputation. If the intermediaries are sales agents, the company will want to evaluate the number and character of other lines carried and the size and quality of the sales force. If the intermediary is a retail store that wants exclusive or selective distribution, the company will want to evaluate the store's customers, location, and future growth potential.

Motivating Channel Members

Once selected, channel members must be continuously motivated to do their best. The company must sell not only *through* the intermediaries but *to* them. Most companies see their intermediaries as first-line customers. Some use the carrot-and-stick approach: At times they offer *positive* motivators such as higher margins, special deals, premiums, cooperative advertising allowances, display allowances, and sales contests. At other times they use *negative* motivators, such as threatening to reduce margins, to slow down delivery, or to end the relationship altogether. A producer using this approach usually has not done a good job of studying the needs, problems, strengths, and weaknesses of its distributors.

More advanced companies try to forge long-term partnerships with their channel partners to create a marketing system that meets the needs of both the manufacturer *and* the partners. In managing its channels, a company must convince distributors that they can succeed better by working together as a part of a cohesive value delivery system.[11] Thus, Procter & Gamble and Wal-Mart work together to create superior value for final consumers. They jointly plan merchandising goals and strategies, inventory levels, and advertising and promotion plans. Similarly, GE Appliances works closely with its independent dealers to help them be successful in selling the company's products (see Marketing at Work 11-2).

Many companies are now developing *partner relationship management* (PRM) systems to coordinate their whole-channel marketing efforts. Here's how Hewlett-Packard does it:

> With more than 20,000 channel partners selling everything from pocket calculators to computer networks, Hewlett-Packard's small business group faces a staggering coordination challenge. Something as simple as distributing sales leads collected through various HP marketing campaigns—everything from business cards dropped in fish bowls at trade shows to requests for product information from HP's Internet site—can be a daunting task. To manage these tasks, HP set up an integrating partner relationship management (PRM) system, which links HP directly with its channel partners and helps coordinate channelwide marketing efforts. Using a secure Web site, HP channel partners can log on at any time to obtain leads that have been generated for them. They can also use the Web site to order literature and sales support materials, obtain product specifications and pricing information, and check their co-op funding. The PRM system not only provides strong support for channel partners, it improves their collective effectiveness and provides assessment feedback to HP. Under the old system, says an HP manager, "We would generate a mass-mailing campaign, send it off to who knows where, out it would go, and we'd hope it would work. Now we can generate a targeted campaign, see when the opportunities start coming back, and . . . the channel partner tells us what happened. . . . It's changing the way we do campaigns."[12]

Evaluating Channel Members

The producer must regularly check channel member performance against standards such as sales quotas, average inventory levels, customer delivery time, treatment of damaged and lost goods, cooperation in company promotion and training programs, and services to

Marketing at Work 11.2

GE Appliances Forges Strong Partnerships with Dealers

Before the late 1980s, General Electric's appliance division worked at selling *through* its dealers rather than *to* them or *with* them. GE Appliances operated a traditional system of trying to load up the channel with its appliances on the premise that "loaded dealers are loyal dealers." Loaded dealers would have less space to feature other brands and would recommend GE appliances to reduce their high inventories. To load its dealers, GE Appliances would offer the lowest price when the dealer ordered a full truckload of products.

GE Appliances eventually realized that this approach created many problems, especially for smaller, independent appliance dealers who could ill afford to carry a large stock. These dealers were hard-pressed to meet price competition from larger, multibrand dealers. Rethinking its strategy from the point of view of creating dealer satisfaction and profitability, GE Appliances created an alternative distribution system to serve its dealers—a system now called GE CustomerNet.

GE CustomerNet gives dealers instant online access to GE Appliances' distribution and order-processing system, 24 hours a day, 7 days a week. By logging onto the GE CustomerNet Web site, dealers can obtain product specifications, photos, feature lists, and side-by-side model comparisons for hundreds of GE appliance models. They can check on product availability and prices, place orders, and review order status. They can even create custom brochures, order point-of-purchase materials, or download "advertising slicks"—professionally prepared GE appliance ads ready for insertion in local media. Says GE Appliances' sales vice president, "With this system, we're putting all

our backroom capabilities right in the store with our [dealers]. We want [them] to get closer to us and have better access to our data."

GE CustomerNet yields substantial benefits to dealers. Instead of loading them up with big inventories, the system gives them a large "virtual inventory" from which to satisfy their customers' needs. GE promises next-day delivery on most appliance models, so dealers need carry only display models in their stores and can rely on the virtual inventory to fill orders. This greatly reduces inventory costs, making even small dealers more price competitive. GE CustomerNet also helps dealers to sell GE appliances more easily and effectively. A dealer can put a computer terminal on the showroom floor, where salespeople and customers together can use the

system to dig through detailed product specifications and check availability for GE's entire line of appliances. As one dealer states, "You can quickly tell customers whether or not a product is available, and you can print them a great looking picture with the click of a button."

GE Appliances also benefits from the new system. GE CustomerNet dramatically decreases the volume of costly and time-consuming phone inquiries and orders, and the electronic order-entry system saves the company substantial clerical costs. GE Appliances now knows the actual sales of its goods at the retail level, which helps it to schedule production more accurately. It now can produce in response to demand rather than to meet inventory replenishment rules. And GE has

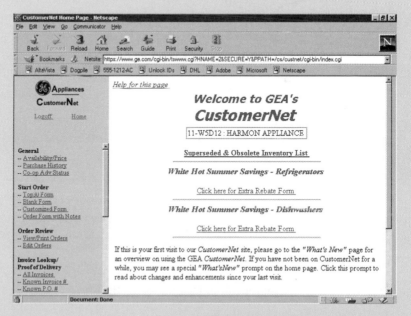

Creating dealer satisfaction and profitability: Using GE's CustomerNet system, dealers have instant online access to GE Appliances' distribution system, 24 hours a day, 7 days a week to check on product availability and prices, place orders, review order status, and even create custom brochures or order point-of-purchase materials.

been able to simplify its warehouse locations, so it can deliver appliances to 90 percent of the United States within 24 hours.

Perhaps the biggest benefit to GE Appliances, however, is that the system builds strong bonds between the company and its dealers and motivates dealers to put more push behind the company's products. Beyond its sales support features, GE CustomerNet contains an online feedback system that lets

dealers communicate promptly and regularly with GE Appliances about anything related to products, service, or the Web site. Notes the sales executive, "We want to make it simple and easy for [dealers] who have questions, complaints, and suggestions. This helps us constantly enhance relationships with our customers."

The GE CustomerNet system now serves more than 8,000 dealers and handles upward of 50,000 transac-

tions per week. Thus, with CustomerNet, GE Appliances has replaced the old "us-against-them" mentality with a passion for partnerships that benefits both the company and its dealers.

Sources: Cathy Ciccolella, "GE to Offer Online Dealer Support with CustomerNet," *Twice,* April 21, 1997, p. 88; Cathy Ciccolella, "GE Online Support Wins Dealers Over," *Twice,* February 9, 1998, p. 38; Mitch Betts, "GE Appliance Park Still an IT Innovator," *Computerworld,* January 29, 2001, pp. 20–21; and "What Is GE CustomerNet?" accessed online at www.geappliances.com/buildwithge/index_cnet.htm, December 2001.

the customer. The company should recognize and reward intermediaries who are performing well and adding good value for consumers. Those who are performing poorly should be assisted or, as a last resort, replaced. A company may periodically "requalify" its intermediaries and prune the weaker ones.

Finally, manufacturers need to be sensitive to their dealers. Those who treat their dealers poorly risk not only losing dealer support but also causing some legal problems. The next section describes various rights and duties pertaining to manufacturers and their channel members.

Linking the Concepts

Time for another break. This time, compare the Caterpillar and GE Appliances channel systems.

◆ Diagram the Caterpillar and GE Appliances systems. How do they compare in terms of channel levels, types of intermediaries, channel member roles and responsibilities, and other characteristics? How well is each system designed?
◆ Assess how well Caterpillar and GE Appliances have managed and supported their channels. With what results?

Public Policy and Distribution Decisions

For the most part, companies are legally free to develop whatever channel arrangements suit them. In fact, the laws affecting channels seek to prevent the exclusionary tactics of some companies that might keep another company from using a desired channel. Most channel law deals with the mutual rights and duties of the channel members once they have formed a relationship.

Many producers and wholesalers like to develop exclusive channels for their products. When the seller allows only certain outlets to carry its products, this strategy is called *exclusive distribution.* When the seller requires that these dealers not handle competitors' products, its strategy is called *exclusive dealing.* Both parties can benefit from exclusive arrangements: The seller obtains more loyal and dependable outlets, and the dealers obtain a steady source of supply and stronger seller support. But exclusive arrangements also exclude other producers from selling to these dealers. This situation brings exclusive dealing contracts under the scope of the Clayton Act of 1914. They are legal as long as they do not substantially lessen competition or tend to create a monopoly and as long as both parties enter into the agreement voluntarily.

Exclusive dealing often includes *exclusive territorial agreements*. The producer may agree not to sell to other dealers in a given area, or the buyer may agree to sell only in its own territory. The first practice is normal under franchise systems as a way to increase dealer enthusiasm and commitment. It is also perfectly legal—a seller has no legal obligation to sell through more outlets than it wishes. The second practice, whereby the producer tries to keep a dealer from selling outside its territory, has become a major legal issue.

Producers of a strong brand sometimes sell it to dealers only if the dealers will take some or all of the rest of the line. This is called full-line forcing. Such *tying agreements* are not necessarily illegal, but they do violate the Clayton Act if they tend to lessen competition substantially. The practice may prevent consumers from freely choosing among competing suppliers of these other brands.

Finally, producers are free to select their dealers, but their right to terminate dealers is somewhat restricted. In general, sellers can drop dealers "for cause." However, they cannot drop dealers if, for example, the dealers refuse to cooperate in a doubtful legal arrangement, such as exclusive dealing or tying agreements.[13]

Marketing Logistics and Supply Chain Management

In today's global marketplace, selling a product is sometimes easier than getting it to customers. Companies must decide on the best way to store, handle, and move their products and services so that they are available to customers in the right assortments, at the right time, and in the right place. Physical distribution and logistics effectiveness has a major impact on both customer satisfaction and company costs. Here we consider the *nature and importance of logistics management in the supply chain, goals of the logistics system, major logistics functions,* and the need for *integrated supply chain management.*

Nature and Importance of Marketing Logistics

To some managers, marketing logistics means only trucks and warehouses. But modern logistics is much more than this. **Marketing logistics**—also called **physical distribution**—involves planning, implementing, and controlling the physical flow of goods, services, and related information from points of origin to points of consumption to meet customer requirements at a profit. In short, it involves getting the right product to the right customer in the right place at the right time.

Traditional physical distribution typically started with products at the plant and then tried to find low-cost solutions to get them to customers. However, today's marketers prefer customer-centered logistics thinking, which starts with the marketplace and works backward to the factory, or even to sources of supply. Marketing logistics addresses not only *outbound distribution* (moving products from the factory to resellers and ultimately to customers) but also *inbound distribution* (moving products and materials from suppliers to the factory) and *reverse distribution* (moving broken, unwanted, or excess products returned by consumers or resellers). That is, it involves entire **supply chain management**—managing value-added flows of materials, final goods, and related information

Marketing logistics (physical distribution)
The tasks involved in planning, implementing, and controlling the physical flow of materials, final goods, and related information from points of origin to points of consumption to meet customer requirements at a profit.

Supply chain management
Managing value-added flows of materials, final goods, and related information between suppliers, the company, resellers, and final users.

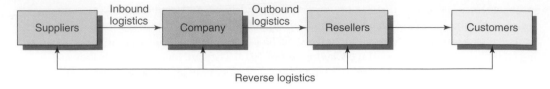

Figure 11-5
Supply chain management

between suppliers, the company, resellers, and final users, as shown in Figure 11-5. Thus, the logistics manager's task is to coordinate activities of suppliers, purchasing agents, marketers, channel members, and customers. These activities include forecasting, information systems, purchasing, production planning, order processing, inventory, warehousing, and transportation planning.

Companies today are placing greater emphasis on logistics for several reasons. First, companies can gain a powerful competitive advantage by using improved logistics to give customers better service or lower prices. Second, improved logistics can yield tremendous cost savings to both the company and its customers. About 15 percent of an average product's price is accounted for by shipping and transport alone. Last year, American companies spent more than $900 billion—close to 10 percent of gross domestic product—to wrap, bundle, load, unload, sort, reload, and transport goods. By itself, Ford has more than 500 million tons of finished vehicles, production parts, and aftermarket parts in transit at any given time, running up an annual logistics bill of around $4 billion.[14] Shaving off even a small fraction of these costs can mean substantial savings.

Third, the explosion in product variety has created a need for improved logistics management. For example, in 1911 the typical A&P grocery store carried only 270 items. The store manager could keep track of this inventory on about 10 pages of notebook paper stuffed in a shirt pocket. Today, the average A&P carries a bewildering stock of more than 16,700 items. Kmart stores carry more than 100,000 products, while Kmart's online arm, Bluelight.com, carries more than 220,000.[15] Ordering, shipping, stocking, and controlling such a variety of products presents a sizable logistics challenge.

Finally, improvements in information technology have created opportunities for major gains in distribution efficiency. Using sophisticated supply chain management software, Web-based logistics systems, point-of-sale scanners, uniform product codes, satellite tracking, and electronic transfer of order and payment data, companies can quickly and efficiently manage the flow of goods, information, and finances through the supply chain.

Goals of the Logistics System

Some companies state their logistics objective as providing maximum customer service at the least cost. Unfortunately, no logistics system can *both* maximize customer service *and* minimize distribution costs. Maximum customer service implies rapid delivery, large inventories, flexible assortments, liberal returns policies, and other services—all of which raise distribution costs. In contrast, minimum distribution costs imply slower delivery, smaller inventories, and larger shipping lots—which represent a lower level of overall customer service.

The goal of marketing logistics should be to provide a *targeted* level of customer service at the least cost. A company must first research the importance of various distribution services to customers and then set desired service levels for each segment. The objective is to maximize *profits,* not sales. Therefore, the company must weigh the benefits of providing higher levels of service against the costs. Some companies offer less service than their competitors and charge a lower price. Other companies offer more service and charge higher prices to cover higher costs.

Major Logistics Functions

Given a set of logistics objectives, the company is ready to design a logistics system that will minimize the cost of attaining these objectives. The major logistics functions include *order processing, warehousing, inventory management,* and *transportation.*

Order Processing Orders can be submitted in many ways—through salespeople, by mail or telephone, via the Internet, or through electronic data interchange (EDI), the electronic exchange of data between companies. The company wants to design a simple, accessible, fast, and accurate process for capturing and processing orders. Both the company and its customers benefit when order processing is carried out quickly and efficiently.

In some cases, suppliers might actually be asked to generate orders and arrange deliveries for their customers. Many large retailers—such as Wal-Mart and Home Depot—work closely with major suppliers such as Procter & Gamble or Black & Decker to set up *vendor-managed inventory* (VMI) systems (or Collaborative Planning, Forecasting, and Replenishment [CPFR] systems, if you're looking for an even fancier name).[16] Using VMI, the retailer shares real-time data on sales and current inventory levels with the supplier. The supplier then takes full responsibility for managing inventories and deliveries. Some retailers even go so far as to shift inventory and delivery costs to the supplier. Such systems require close cooperation between the buyer and seller.

Warehousing Production and consumption cycles rarely match. So most companies must store their tangible goods while they wait to be sold. For example, Snapper, Toro, and other lawn mower manufacturers run their factories all year long and store up products for the heavy spring and summer buying seasons. The storage function overcomes differences in needed quantities and timing, ensuring that products are available when customers are ready to buy them.

A company must decide on *how many* and *what types* of warehouses it needs and *where* they will be located. The company might use either *storage warehouses* or *distribution centers.* Storage warehouses store goods for moderate to long periods. **Distribution centers** are designed to move goods rather than just store them. They are large and highly automated warehouses designed to receive goods from various plants and suppliers, take orders, fill them efficiently, and deliver goods to customers as quickly as possible. For example, Wal-Mart operates a network of 62 huge U.S. distribution centers and another 37 around the globe. Almost 84 percent of the merchandise shipped to Wal-Mart stores is routed through one of its own distribution centers, giving Wal-Mart tremendous control over inventory management. One center, which serves the daily needs of 165 Wal-Mart stores, contains some 28 acres of space under a single roof. Laser scanners route as many as 190,000 cases of goods per day along 11 miles of conveyer belts, and the center's 1,000 workers load or unload 310 trucks daily.[17]

Like almost everything else these days, warehousing has seen dramatic changes in technology in recent years. Older, multistoried warehouses with outdated materials-handling methods are steadily being replaced by newer, single-storied *automated warehouses* with advanced, computer-controlled materials-handling systems requiring few employees. Computers and scanners read orders and direct lift trucks, electric hoists, or robots to gather goods, move them to loading docks, and issue invoices.

Distribution center
A large, highly automated warehouse designed to receive goods from various plants and suppliers, take orders, fill them efficiently, and deliver goods to customers as quickly as possible.

Inventory Management Inventory levels also affect customer satisfaction. Here, managers must maintain the delicate balance between carrying too much inventory and carrying too little. Carrying too much inventory results in higher-than-necessary inventory-carrying costs and stock obsolescence. Carrying too little risks stock outs, causing customer dissatisfaction and costly emergency shipments or production. Thus, when managing inventory, firms must balance the costs of carrying larger inventories against resulting sales and profits.

Many companies have greatly reduced their inventories and related costs through *just-in-time* logistics systems. Through such systems, producers and retailers carry only small inventories of parts or merchandise, often only enough for a few days of operations. For example, Dell Computer, a master just-in-time producer, carries just 5 days of inventory, whereas competitors might carry 40 days or even 60.[18] New stock arrives exactly when needed, rather than being stored in inventory until being used. Just-in-time systems require accurate forecasting along with fast, frequent, and flexible delivery so that new supplies will be available when needed. However, these systems result in substantial savings in inventory-carrying and handling costs.

Transportation Marketers need to take an interest in their company's *transportation* decisions. The choice of transportation carriers affects the pricing of products, delivery performance, and condition of the goods when they arrive—all of which will affect customer satisfaction. In shipping goods to its warehouses, dealers, and customers, the company can choose among five transportation modes: truck, rail, water, pipeline, and air.

Trucks have increased their share of transportation steadily and now account for 39 percent of total cargo ton-miles (more than 69 percent of actual tonnage).[19] They account for the largest portion of transportation *within* cities as opposed to *between* cities. Each year in the United States, trucks travel more than 600 billion miles—equal to nearly 1.3 million round trips to the moon—carrying 7.7 billion tons of freight. Trucks are highly flexible in their routing and time schedules, and they can usually offer faster service than railroads. They are efficient for short hauls of high-value merchandise. Trucking firms have added many services in recent years. For example, Roadway Express and most other major carriers now offer satellite tracking of shipments and sleeper tractors that move freight around the clock.

Railroads account for 38 percent of total cargo ton-miles moved. They are one of the most cost-effective modes for shipping large amounts of bulk products—coal, sand, minerals, farm and forest products—over long distances. In recent years, railroads have increased their customer services by designing new equipment to handle special categories of goods, providing flatcars for carrying truck trailers by rail (piggyback), and providing in-transit services such as the diversion of shipped goods to other destinations en route and the processing of goods en route.

Water carriers, which account for about 10 percent of cargo ton-miles, transport large amounts of goods by ships and barges on U.S. coastal and inland waterways. Although the cost of water transportation is very low for shipping bulky, low-value, nonperishable products such as sand, coal, grain, oil, and metallic ores, water transportation is the slowest mode and may be affected by the weather. *Pipelines* are a specialized means of shipping petroleum, natural gas, and chemicals from sources to markets. Most pipelines are used by their owners to ship their own products.

Although *air* carriers transport less than 1 percent of the nation's goods, they are an important transportation mode. Airfreight rates are much higher than rail or truck rates, but airfreight is ideal when speed is needed or distant markets have to be reached. Among the most frequently airfreighted products are perishables (fresh fish, cut flowers) and high-value, low-bulk items (technical instruments, jewelry). Companies find that airfreight also reduces inventory levels, packaging costs, and the number of warehouses needed.

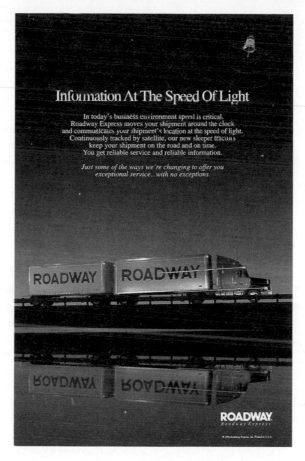

Roadway and other trucking firms have added many services in recent years, such as satellite tracking of shipments and sleeper tractors that keep freight moving around the clock.

Shippers increasingly are using **intermodal transportation**—combining two or more modes of transportation. *Piggyback* describes the use of rail and trucks; *fishyback,* water and trucks; *trainship,* water and rail; and *airtruck,* air and trucks. Combining modes provides advantages that no single mode can deliver. Each combination offers advantages to the shipper. For example, not only is piggyback cheaper than trucking alone but it also provides flexibility and convenience.

In choosing a transportation mode for a product, shippers must balance many considerations: speed, dependability, availability, cost, and others. Thus, if a shipper needs speed, air and truck are the prime choices. If the goal is low cost, then water or pipeline might be best.

Intermodal transportation
Combining two or more modes of transportation.

Integrated Supply Chain Management

Today, more and more companies are adopting the concept of **integrated supply chain management.** This concept recognizes that providing better customer service and trimming distribution costs requires *teamwork,* both inside the company and among all the marketing channel organizations. Inside, the company's various functional departments must work closely together to maximize the company's own logistics performance. Outside, the company must integrate its logistics system with those of its suppliers and customers to maximize the performance of the entire distribution system.

Cross-Functional Teamwork Inside the Company In most companies, responsibility for various logistics activities is assigned to many different functional units—marketing, sales, finance, manufacturing, purchasing. Too often, each function tries to optimize its own

Integrated supply chain management
The logistics concept that emphasizes teamwork, both inside the company and among all the marketing channel organizations, to maximize the performance of the entire distribution system.

logistics performance without regard for the activities of the other functions. However, transportation, inventory, warehousing, and order-processing activities interact, often in an inverse way. Lower inventory levels reduce inventory-carrying costs. But they may also reduce customer service and increase costs from stock outs, back orders, special production runs, and costly fast-freight shipments. Because distribution activities involve strong trade-offs, decisions by different functions must be coordinated to achieve superior overall logistics performance.

The goal of integrated supply chain management is to harmonize all of the company's logistics decisions. Close working relationships among functions can be achieved in several ways. Some companies have created permanent logistics committees made up of managers responsible for different physical distribution activities. Companies can also create management positions that link the logistics activities of functional areas. For example, Procter & Gamble has created supply managers, who manage all of the supply chain activities for each of its product categories. Many companies have a vice president of logistics with cross-functional authority. Finally, companies can employ sophisticated, systemwide supply chain management software, now available from Oracle and other software providers.[20] The important thing is that the company coordinate its logistics and marketing activities to create high market satisfaction at a reasonable cost.

Building Channel Partnerships Companies must do more than improve their own logistics. They must also work with other channel members to improve whole-channel distribution. The members of a distribution channel are linked closely in delivering customer satisfaction and value. One company's distribution system is another company's supply system. The success of each channel member depends on the performance of the entire supply chain. For example, Wal-Mart can charge the lowest prices at retail only if its entire supply chain—consisting of thousands of merchandise suppliers, transport companies, warehouses, and service providers—operates at maximum efficiency.

Smart companies coordinate their logistics strategies and forge strong partnerships with suppliers and customers to improve customer service and reduce channel costs. Many companies have created *cross-functional, cross-company teams.* For example, Procter & Gamble has a team of almost 100 people living in Bentonville, Arkansas, home of Wal-Mart. The P&Gers work jointly with their counterparts at Wal-Mart to find ways to squeeze costs out of their distribution system. Working together benefits not only P&G and Wal-Mart but also their final consumers. Haggar Apparel Company has a similar system called "multiple points of contact," in which a Haggar team works with JCPenney people at corporate, divisional, and store levels. Haggar ships the merchandise "floor ready"—hangered and pretagged—reducing the time it takes JCPenney to move the stock from receiving docks to the sales floor from four days to just one. [21]

Other companies partner through *shared projects.* For example, many larger retailers are working closely with suppliers on in-store programs. Home Depot allows key suppliers to use its stores as a testing ground for new merchandising programs. The suppliers spend time at Home Depot stores watching how their product sells and how customers relate to it. They then create programs specially tailored to Home Depot and its customers. Western Publishing Group, publisher of "Little Golden Books" for children, formed a similar partnership with Toys 'R' Us. Western and the giant toy retailer coordinated their marketing strategies to create minibookstore sections—called Books 'R' Us—within each Toys 'R' Us store. Toys 'R' Us provides the locations, space, and customers; Western serves as distributor, consolidator, and servicer for the Books 'R' Us program.[22] Clearly, both the supplier and the customer benefit from such partnerships.

Channel partnerships may also take the form of *information sharing* and *continuous inventory replenishment* systems. Companies manage their supply chains

Western Publishing Group partners with Toys 'R' Us to create mini-bookstore sections—called Books 'R' Us—within each store. Toys 'R' Us provides the space and customers; Western serves as distributor and servicer for the Books 'R' Us sections.

through information. Suppliers link up with customers to share information and coordinate their logistics decisions. Here is an example:

> The Branded Apparel division of giant Sara Lee Corporation says that retailer Dayton-Hudson's willingness to share information with suppliers separates this company from its competitors. Dayton's Global Merchandising System (GMS), its supply chain management system, consists of more than 60 applications, including forecasting, ordering, and trend analysis. A Dayton company, such as Target stores, can use GMS to order a certain number of sweatshirts from Sara Lee Branded Apparel without specifying more than style. As the delivery date draws near, Target analyzes trends for colors and sizes. Based on those forecasts, Sara Lee makes trial lots and Target starts to sell them. If customers buy more navy sweatshirts than initially predicted, Target adjusts its order. The result: Both Sara Lee and Target have fewer goods in inventory while at the same time doing a better job of meeting customer preferences, which in turn results in fewer markdowns.[23]

Third-Party Logistics Most businesses perform their own logistics functions. However, a growing number of firms now outsource some or all of their logistics to **third-party logistics (3PL) providers** such as Ryder Systems, UPS Worldwide Logistics, FedEx Logistics, Roadway Logistics Services, or Emery Global Logistics (see Marketing at Work 11-3). Such integrated logistics companies perform any or all of the functions required to get their clients' product to market. For example, Emery's Global Logistics unit provides clients with coordinated, single-source logistics services including supply

Third-party logistics (3PL) provider
An independent logistics provider that performs any or all of the functions required to get its clients' product to market.

Marketing at Work 11.3

Go Ryder, and Leave the Delivering to Us

Most big companies love to make and sell their products. But many loathe the associated logistics "grunt work"—the bundling, loading, unloading, sorting, storing, reloading, transporting, and tracking required to supply their factories and to get products out to customers. They hate it so much that 60 percent of the Fortune 500 now outsource some or all of these functions. Increasingly, companies are handing over their logistics to suppliers that specialize in helping them tighten up sluggish, overstuffed supply chains, slash inventories, and get products to customers more quickly and reliably. Below are some examples:

Saturn. Saturn's just-in-time production system allows for almost no parts inventory at the plant. Instead, it relies on a world-class logistics system to keep parts flowing into the factory at precisely the times they're needed. Saturn is so adroit in managing its supply chain that in four years it has had to halt production just once—for only 18 minutes—because the right part failed to arrive at the right time. Most of the credit, however, goes to Ryder Integrated Logistics, the nation's largest logistics management firm. Ryder, best known for renting trucks, manages Saturn's far-ranging supply chain, moving the automaker's materials, parts, and products efficiently and reliably from supplier to factory to dealer showroom.

To keep Saturn's assembly lines humming, Ryder transports thousands of preinspected and presorted parts—more than 2,200 receiving dock transactions every day—hitting delivery windows as narrow as five minutes. Ryder keeps its parts, people, and trucks in a nearly

constant blur of high-tech motion. For example, according to one account, when delivering service parts to Saturn dealerships, Ryder's long-haul drivers "plug a plastic key, loaded with electronic data, into an onboard computer. The screen tells them exactly where to go, which route to take, and how much time to spend getting there." Ryder's effective supply chain management results in lower costs, improved operations, more productive deal-

ers, and—in the end—more satisfied customers.

Cisco Systems. This vendor of computer networking equipment and network management software ships tons of routers to Europe daily. It needs to know where each box is at any given time and may have to reroute orders on short notice to fill urgent customer requests. Moreover, Cisco's customers need to know exactly when orders will arrive. When Cisco

When Friendlys needed to meet growing customer demand, they chose the first name in transportation: Cindy.

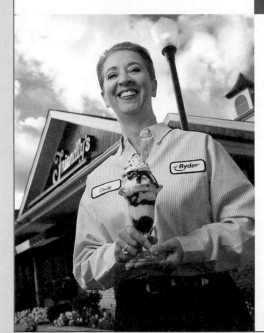

Cindy Carre specializes in transportation solutions at Ryder. With our Full Service Lease, Cindy and her team work with Friendly's to keep their refrigerated trailers on the road, and their products in the hands of a hungry marketplace. Thanks to Ryder, Friendly's doesn't have to worry about breakdowns. Or meltdowns.

At Ryder, you'll find lots of people like Cindy—people who help companies like Friendly's, Hewlett Packard, and Ace Hardware become more efficient and profitable.

Want to know more? Visit us at www.ryder.com or call 1 800 RYDER OK ext. 1012. It's time you got to know us on a first-name basis.

Cindy Carre
Service Team Leader

Ryder Transportation Services
1 800 RYDER OK
www.ryder.com

©1999 Ryder System, Inc.
Ryder is an equal opportunity employer.

Third-party logistics: Many companies are now outsourcing logistics to companies like Ryder Integrated Logistics. Here, Ryder describes a system designed to keep Friendly's refrigerated trucks on the road. "Thanks to Ryder, Friendly's doesn't have to worry about breakdowns. Or meltdowns."

handled its own logistics, deliveries took up to three weeks. Now, the company contracts its complex distribution process to UPS Worldwide Logistics. Leveraging its knowledge of international plane, train, and trucking schedules, UPS Worldwide can speed routers to European customers in less than four days. If its own planes or trucks can't make the fastest delivery, UPS subcontracts the job to Lufthansa, KLM, or Danzas, a European trucking firm. Such superfast delivery saves Cisco Systems a bundle on inventories. Soon, UPS Worldwide will begin installing custom software into Cisco's routers at its warehouse in the Netherlands, letting Cisco cut its inventories even more.

Cisco reaps some additional advantages from the logistics partnership. For example, UPS Worldwide has extensive knowledge of local customs laws and import duties. It recently arranged with Dutch customs to aggregate Cisco's import duties into a monthly bill, paid once customers receive shipments instead of each time the routers land at the airport. The result: even more savings in time and paperwork.

National Semiconductor. In the early 1990s, National Semiconductor—whose chips end up inside everything from cars and computers to telecommunications gear—faced a logistics nightmare. National produced and assembled chips at 13 plants located in the United States, Britain, Israel, and Southeast Asia. Finished products were then shipped to an array of large customers—IBM, Toshiba, Compaq, Ford, Siemens—each with factories scattered around the globe. On their way to customers, chips traveled any of 20,000 direct routes, mostly in the cargo holds of planes flown by 12 airlines, stopping along the way at 10 different warehouses. National's logistics per-

formance left much to be desired: Ninety-five percent of its products were delivered within 45 days of the order. The other 5 percent took as long as 90 days. Because customers never knew which 5 percent would be late, they demanded 90 days' worth of inventory in everything. "We had buffer stocks all along the line," comments a National executive. "The whole system was awash in inventory."

National's management set out to overhaul its global logistics network. It decided that all finished products would be transported to a central distribution center in Asia, where they would be sorted and airfreighted to customers. Although strategically sound, the plan created some big practical problems: National knew a lot about making chips but very little about airfreight. "To do that," says the executive, "we would have had to make our company into FedEx." Instead, National *hired* FedEx to handle its global distribution. FedEx Logistics now runs National's distribution center in Singapore, conducting all storage, sorting, and shipping activities. The results have been startling. Within two years, National's distribution costs fell 27 percent. At the same time, sales jumped by $584 million and delivery performance improved dramatically. National can now move products from the factory to customers in an average of four days or less, and it's well on its way toward its goal of a 72-hour turnaround. Thus, by outsourcing its distribution to a firm that specializes in efficient logistics, National Semiconductor has both cut its costs and improved its service to customers.

Sony. Sony knows logistics. In fact, the company considers logistics to be one of its competitive advantages. So you might wonder why an industry leader would outsource half of its distribution requirements

in Mexico to Redwood Systems, a third-party logistics (3PL) provider with headquarters in Atlanta. It turns out that even a logistics leader needs help some of the time. The reasons are growth and speed to market. "In Mexico, logistics is challenging because of a lack of infrastructure," says Carlos Rojas, logistics division manager for Sony Electronicas, Mexico. "Given those limitations, we couldn't take advantage of a growing market without a 3PL partner who could quickly expand our operations. By relying on Redwood to manage the day-to-day details of our Mexico-based distribution, we can concentrate on marketing and sales instead of logistics, and do it without adding to our head count." To service Sony's needs, Redwood created a direct [electronic] link between its . . . facility in Guadalajara and Sony's operations in Mexico City.

Today, Redwood manages over 500 different products and another 15,000 different parts for Sony. Product is received into the facility from all over the world, and in quantities ranging from parcel shipments to full containers. The 3PL supplier ships an estimated 200 orders per day, with an average of 10 line items per order. "They handle our orders as if we were handling them ourselves," Rojas says of his relationship with Redwood. "And they have adapted their management style to our processes. That's allowing us to achieve our goals."

Sources: Quotes and other information from Ronald Henkoff, "Delivering the Goods," *Fortune,* November 28, 1994, pp. 64–77; Lisa H. Harrington, "Special Report on Contract Logistics," *Transportation and Distribution,* September 1996, pp. A–N; Scott Woolley, "Replacing Inventory with Information," *Forbes,* March 24, 1997, pp. 54–58; Allen Allnoch, "Third-Party Logistics Industry Poised for Growth in U.S. and Abroad," *IIE Solutions,* January 1998, p. 10; Martha Celestino, "Choosing a Third-Party Logistics Provider," *World Trade,* July 1999, pp. 54–56; and "Even a Logistics Leader Needs Help Some of the Time," *Modern Materials Handling,* December 2000, p. S15.

chain management, customized information technology, inventory control, warehousing, transportation management, customer service and fulfillment, and freight auditing and control. "From sourcing raw materials to delivering finished products to stores," proclaims the Emery Web site, "our experts work with you to streamline and manage your entire supply chain and to keep you in control." Last year, U.S. manufacturers and distributors spent more than $45 billion on third-party logistics (also called *outsourced logistics* or *contract logistics*) services, and the market is expected to grow by at least 18 percent per year.[24]

Companies use third-party logistics providers for several reasons. First, because getting the product to market is their main focus, these providers can often do it more efficiently and at lower cost. According to one study, outsourcing typically results in 15 percent to 30 percent cost savings.[25] Second, outsourcing logistics frees a company to focus more intensely on its core business. Finally, integrated logistics companies understand increasingly complex logistics environments. This can be especially helpful to companies attempting to expand their global market coverage. For example, companies distributing their products across Europe face a bewildering array of environmental restrictions that affect logistics, including packaging standards, truck size and weight limits, and noise and emissions pollution controls. By outsourcing its logistics, a company can gain a complete pan-European distribution system without incurring the costs, delays, and risks associated with setting up its own system.

STOP *Rest Stop: Reviewing the Concepts*

So, what have you learned about distribution channels and integrated supply chain management? Marketing channel decisions are among the most important decisions that management faces. A company's channel decisions directly affect every other marketing decision. Each channel system creates a different level of revenues and costs and reaches a different segment of target consumers. Management must make channel decisions carefully, incorporating today's needs with tomorrow's likely selling environment. Some companies pay too little attention to their distribution channels, but others have used imaginative distribution systems to gain competitive advantage.

1. Explain why companies use distribution channels and discuss the functions these channels perform.

Most producers use intermediaries to bring their products to market. They try to forge a *distribution channel*—a set of interdependent organizations involved in the process of making a product or service available for use or consumption by the consumer or business user. Through their contacts, experience, specialization, and scale of operation, intermediaries usually offer the firm more than it can achieve on its own. Distribution channels perform many key functions. Some help *complete* transactions by gathering and distributing *information* needed for plan-

ning and aiding exchange; by developing and spreading persuasive *communications* about an offer; by performing *contact* work—finding and communicating with prospective buyers; by *matching*—shaping and fitting the offer to the buyer's needs; and by entering into *negotiation* to reach an agreement on price and other terms of the offer so that ownership can be transferred. Other functions help to *fulfill* the completed transactions by offering *physical distribution*—transporting and storing goods; *financing*—acquiring and using funds to cover the costs of the channel work; and *risk taking*—assuming the risks of carrying out the channel work.

2. Discuss how channel members interact and how they organize to perform the work of the channel.

The channel will be most effective when each member is assigned the tasks it can do best. Ideally, because the success of individual channel members depends on overall channel success, all channel firms should work together smoothly. They should understand and accept their roles, coordinate their goals and activities, and cooperate to attain overall channel goals. By cooperating, they can more effectively sense, serve, and satisfy the target market. In a large company, the formal organization structure assigns roles and provides needed leadership. But in a distribution channel made up of independent firms, leadership and power are not formally set. Traditionally, distribution channels have lacked the leadership needed to assign roles and manage conflict. In recent years, however, new types of channel organizations have appeared that provide stronger leadership and improved performance.

3. Identify the major channel alternatives open to a company.

Each firm identifies alternative ways to reach its market. Available means vary from direct selling to using one, two, three, or more intermediary *channel levels.* Marketing channels face continuous and sometimes dramatic change. Three of the most important trends are the growth of *vertical, horizontal,* and *hybrid marketing systems.* These trends affect channel cooperation, conflict, and competition. *Channel design* begins with assessing customer channel service needs and company channel objectives and constraints. The company then identifies the major channel alternatives in terms of the *types* of intermediaries, the *number* of intermediaries, and the *channel responsibilities* of each. Each channel alternative must be evaluated according to economic, control, and adaptive criteria. Channel management calls for selecting qualified intermediaries and motivating them. Individual channel members must be evaluated regularly.

4. Explain how companies select, motivate, and evaluate channel members.

Producers vary in their ability to attract qualified marketing intermediaries. Some producers have no trouble signing up channel members. Others have to work hard to line up enough qualified intermediaries. When selecting intermediaries, the company should evaluate each channel member's qualifications and select those who best fit its channel objectives. Once selected, channel members must be continuously motivated to do their best. The company must sell not only *through* the intermediaries but *to* them. It should work to forge long-term partner-ships with the channel partners to create a marketing system that meets the needs of both the manufacturer *and* the partners. The company must also regularly check channel member performance against established performance standards, rewarding intermediaries who are performing well and assisting or replacing weaker ones.

5. Discuss the nature and importance of marketing logistics and integrated supply chain management.

Just as firms are giving the marketing concept increased recognition, more business firms are paying attention to *marketing logistics* (or *physical distribution*). Logistics is an area of potentially high cost savings and improved customer satisfaction. Marketing logistics addresses not only *outbound distribution* but also *inbound distribution* and *reverse distribution.* That is, it involves entire *supply chain management*—managing value-added flows between suppliers, the company, resellers, and final users. No logistics system can both maximize customer service and minimize distribution costs. Instead, the goal of logistics management is to provide a *targeted* level of service at the least cost. The major logistics functions include *order processing, warehousing, inventory management,* and *transportation.*

The *integrated supply chain management concept* recognizes that improved logistics requires teamwork in the form of close working relationships across functional areas inside the company and across various organizations in the supply chain. Companies can achieve logistics harmony among functions by creating cross-functional logistics teams, integrative supply manager positions, and senior-level logistics executives with cross-functional authority. Channel partnerships can take the form of cross-company teams, shared projects, and information sharing systems. Today, some companies are outsourcing their logistics functions to third-party logistics providers to save costs, increase efficiency, and gain faster and more effective access to global markets.

Navigating the Key Terms

For a detailed analysis of the meaning and importance of each of the following key terms, visit our Web page at **www.prenhall.com/ kotler.**

Administered VMS
Channel conflict
Channel level
Contractual VMS
Conventional distribution channel

Corporate VMS
Direct marketing channel
Disintermediation
Distribution center
Distribution channel

Exclusive distribution
Franchise organization
Horizontal marketing system
Hybrid marketing channel
Indirect marketing channel
Integrated supply chain management

Intensive distribution
Intermodal transportation
Marketing logistics (or) physical
   distribution
Selective distribution
Supply chain management

Third-party logistics (3PL)
   provider
Vertical marketing system (VMS)

Travel Log

The following concept checks and discussion questions will help you to keep track of and apply the concepts you've studied in this chapter.

Concept Checks

Fill in the blanks, then look for the correct answers.

1. A _____ is a set of interdependent organizations involved in the process of making a product or service available for use or consumption by the consumer or business user.

2. Members of the marketing channel perform many key functions. Chief among these would be _____, _____, _____, _____, _____, physical distribution, financing, and risk taking.

3. A _____ marketing channel has no intermediary levels.

4. Disagreements over goals and roles generate channel conflict. McDonald's recently had a form of _____ conflict with some of its dealers when its aggressive expansion plans called for placing new stores in areas that took business from existing locations.

5. Three forms of vertical marketing systems (VMS) include _____, _____, and _____ VMS.

6. Changes in technology have caused traditional distribution to undergo changes such as _____,

where more and more product and service producers are bypassing intermediaries and going directly to final buyers, or where radically new types of channel intermediaries are emerging to displace traditional ones.

7. Companies must determine the number of channel members to use at each level. Producers of convenience products and common raw materials typically seek _____ distribution—a strategy in which they stock their products in as many outlets as possible.

8. Another term used to describe physical distribution is _____.

9. Managing value-added flows of materials, final goods, and related information between suppliers, the company, resellers, and final users is called _____ management.

10. The major logistics functions include _____, _____, _____, and _____.

11. With respect to common transportation modes, _____ are the nation's largest carriers, accounting for 39 percent of total cargo ton-miles moved (more than 69 percent of actual tonnage), and are highly flexible in their routing and time schedules.

12. Given the growing popularity of outsourcing, _____ logistics providers such as Ryder Systems, UPS Worldwide Logistics, and FedEx Logistics are providing more services for customers than ever before.

Concept check answers: 1. distribution channel; 2. information, promotion, contact, matching, negotiation; 3. direct; 4. vertical; 5. corporate, contractual, administered; 6. intensive; 7. intensive; 8. marketing logistics; 9. supply chain management; 10. order processing, warehousing, inventory management, transportation; 11. railroads; 12. third-party.

Discussing the Issues

1. List and briefly discuss the marketing channel functions that are involved in completing and fulfilling transactions. Which function applies most in each of the following situations? (a) A retailer puts in a rush reorder for a needed Christmas item that is in short supply. (b) An Internet marketer seeks ways to iden-

tify and contact its market. (c) A small retailer wants to expand its order size but does not currently have funds to pay for the expanded order. (d) A business buyer attends a large trade show wanting to buy higher quality products on a limited budget.

2. Give your own example of each of the three major forms of vertical marketing systems described in the

chapter. What advantages do such systems have over traditional channel organizations? Where could problems occur? Explain and illustrate.

3. What is "disintermediation?" Give an example other than those discussed in the chapter. What opportunities and problems does disintermediation present for traditional retailers? Explain.

4. Which distribution strategy—intensive, selective, or exclusive—is used for the following products, and why? (a) Piaget watches, (b) Acura automobiles, and (c) Snickers candy bars.

5. Regarding outsourcing: (a) Why would a company choose to outsource its distribution function? (b) What major factors contribute to a successful outsourcing relationship? What are the potential dangers of such a relationship? (c) Give an example of a company that could benefit from outsourcing its logistics and suggest some practical outsourcing alternatives for the company. (For additional information on outsourcing, see the Outsourcing Institute's Web site at **www.outsourcing.com**.)

Mastering Marketing

Examine the distribution arrangements available to CanGo and then answer the following questions: (a) How many intermediaries are used by the company? Are they all necessary? (b) Diagram a potential vertical marketing system that might make the company more effective and efficient. (c) Propose a new distribution network that might be beneficial for the company. (d) How could channel members be better motivated to increase effectiveness and efficiency? (e) Propose an integrated supply chain that would make the company and its distribution process more competitive. (f) How can the company integrate the Internet into its distribution process?

Traveling the Net

Point of Interest: Hybrid Marketing Systems

Marketers in many industries are constantly looking for new ways to put their products into the hands of consumers. They want to surround the consumer with alternatives. Such is the case in the music industry. Multichannel distribution alternatives include retail stores of many types (department stores, specialty stores, discount stores), catalog merchants, mail-order clubs, and Internet Web sites (both for the company and for those that carry the company's products). Music is one of the easiest items to buy on the Web, and purchasing music via the Web is gaining popularity. In fact, the Web has become a major channel choice for many younger buyers (the chief market for the industry). Buyers have learned that they can often obtain better prices from Web retailers than from record stores, even after paying shipping and handling. Examine the following Web sites for more information on purchasing music via the Web: (a) Amazon.com at **www.amazon.com**, (b) Music Boulevard at **www.musicblvd.com**, (c) Compact Disc Connection at **www.cdconnection.com**, and (d) Columbia House at **www.columbiahouse.com**.

For Discussion

1. What are the primary advantages of ordering music tapes or CDs via the Internet? The disadvantages?

2. How will Web music retailing affect the more traditional channels such as record stores and book-record combination stores?

3. In what ways can music producers handle the conflicts that are bound to arise when they use multichannel distribution alternatives?

4. After visiting each of the noted Web sites, compare marketing and distribution strategies for each of the distributors. (a) Prepare a grid that compares the sites on important attributes. (b) Which site do you find to be the most customer-friendly? Which seems to be the easiest to use? From which would you be most likely to order? Explain.

Application Thinking

What characteristics are most important in your choice of a place to purchase a tape or CD? How would you rank the importance of factors such as price, location, selection, personal service, atmosphere, guarantees, and being able to take your selection home immediately? Companies that sell through Web sites are betting that price and selection (especially for those hard-to-find titles) will rank higher than location (such as a mall) or immediate possession. Most online music sellers guarantee shipment of a top 100 title almost immediately and of most obscure titles within 4 to 10 days. These online companies have access to 200,000 or more titles and can almost always get and ship hard-to-find titles more quickly than music stores using traditional ordering processes. Moreover, they typically offer lower prices, lots of discounts, and bonuses on volume purchases.

Such price and access benefits, however, may be offset by membership requirements (as with Columbia House), an inability to give the consumer immediate purchase gratification, or complicated ordering and return processes. Assume that you are the marketing manager for an online music service. Construct policies and strategies that will make you competitive with other types of music resellers. Prepare a list of "musts" that your service will have to accomplish in order to attract consumer attention. Be sure to consider how you will deal with music download or share services. Evaluate your chances of success.

 Map—Marketing Applications

MAP Stop 11

You know about the Internet but have you ever heard of the "extranet"? An "extranet" occurs when a company opens its own internal network (or intranet) to selected business partners. Trusted suppliers, distributors, and other special users can then link into the company's network without having to go through traditional "red-tape." The connecting company can use the Internet or virtual private networks for communication. Once inside the company's intranet, the outside company (or partner) can view whatever data the company makes available. What types of data? A supplier might analyze a customer's inventory needs: Boeing booked $100 million in spare parts from airline customers in one year. Partners might swap customer lists for interrelated products and services or share purchasing systems to gain savings through more efficient purchasing: General Electric claims that $500 million can be saved in purchasing costs by using the "extranet" portion of the Internet. Imagine the strategic advantages that are created when "virtual" partners move information to one another in seconds about shifting supply and demand situations, customer requests and opportunities, and just-in-time inventory needs. Purchase

processing times can be reduced from weeks to minutes at enormous cost savings that can be passed along to consumers.

Thinking Like a Marketing Manager

1. What role might an extranet play in distribution decisions for (a) retailers, (b) wholesalers, and (c) manufacturers?
2. What are the potential dangers of an extranet system?
3. What areas of a marketing organization's intranet would be most interesting to a partner using the extranet?
4. Assume that you are the marketing manager of Cisco Systems (investigate this master of e-commerce and networking at **www.cisco.com**). How could an extranet help you to better assist resellers? How could costs be saved by using an extranet? How does an extranet work with an outsourcing concept (if at all)? After examining the advantages and disadvantages of using an extranet, write a short position paper that outlines your thoughts on the subject and its future in marketing commerce.

chapter 12

Retailing and Wholesaling

ROAD MAP:
Previewing the Concepts

In the previous chapter, you learned the basics of distribution channel design and management. Now, we'll look more deeply into the two major intermediary channel functions, retailing and wholesaling. You already know something about retailing—you're served every day by retailers of all shapes and sizes. However, you probably know much less about the hoard of wholesalers that work behind the scenes. In this chapter, we'll navigate through the characteristics of different kinds of retailers and wholesalers, the marketing decisions they make, and trends for the future. You'll see that the retailing and wholesaling landscapes are changing rapidly to match explosive changes in markets and technology.

▶ After studying this chapter, you should be able to

1. explain the roles of retailers and wholesalers in the distribution channel
2. describe the major types of retailers and give examples of each
3. identify the major types of wholesalers and give examples of each
4. explain the marketing decisions facing retailers and wholesalers

To start the tour, we'll look in on Home Depot, the highly successful home improvement retailer. This "category killer's" rapid growth has resulted not from a focus on sales but from an obsession with building customer relationships. However, to take care of customers, Home Depot must first take care of those who take care of customers.

Home Depot, the giant do-it-yourself home improvement retail chain, is one of the world's hottest retailers. It's one of a breed of retailers called *category killers*—giant retailers that offer a huge selection of merchandise in a single product category at such low prices that they destroy the competition. At first glance, a cavernous Home Depot store doesn't look like much. With its cement floors and drafty, warehouselike interior, the store offers all the atmosphere of an airplane hangar. But the chances are good that you'll find exactly what you're looking for, priced to make it a real value. Home Depot carries a huge assortment of some 40,000 to 50,000 items—anything and everything related to home improvement. Its prices run 20 to 30 percent below those of local hardware stores.

Home Depot provides more than the right products at the right prices, however. Perhaps the best part of shopping at Home Depot is the high quality of its customer service. Home Depot is more than just customer driven—it's customer *obsessed*. In the words of cofounder Bernie Marcus, "All of our people understand what the Holy Grail is. It's not the bottom line. It's an almost blind, passionate commitment to taking care of customers." Arthur Blank, Home Depot's joint cofounder, has offered all new store managers the following six pieces of advice: "Serve the customer, serve the customer, serve the customer, serve the customer, serve the customer. And number 6, kick [butt]."

Bernie Marcus and Arthur Blank founded Home Depot with the simple mission of helping customers solve their home improvement problems. Their goal: "To take ham-handed homeowners who lack the confidence to do more than screw in a light bulb and transform them into Mr. and Ms. Fixits." Accomplishing this mission takes more than simply peddling the store's products and taking the customers' money. It means building lasting customer relationships.

Bernie and Arthur understand the importance of customer satisfaction. They calculate that a satisfied customer is worth more than $25,000 in customer lifetime value ($38 per store visit, times 30 visits per year, times about 22 years of patronage). Customer satisfaction, in turn, results from interactions with well-trained, highly motivated employees who consistently provide good value and high-quality service. "The most important part of our formula," says Arthur, "is the quality of caring that takes place in our stores between the employee and the customer." Thus, at Home Depot, taking care of customers begins with taking care of employees.

Home Depot attracts the best salespeople by paying above-average salaries; then it trains them thoroughly. All employees take regular "product knowledge" classes to gain hands-on experience with problems customers will face. When it comes to creating customer value and satisfaction, Home Depot treats its employees as partners. All full-time employees receive at least seven percent of their annual salary in company stock. As a result, Home Depot employees take ownership in the business of serving customers. Each employee wears a bright orange apron labeled "Hello, I'm _____, a Home Depot stockholder. Let me help you."

Home Depot avoids the high-pressure sales techniques used by some retailers. Instead, it encourages salespeople to build long-term relationships with customers—to spend whatever time it takes, visit after visit, to solve customer problems. Home Depot pays employees a straight salary so that they can spend as much time as necessary with customers without worrying about making the sale. Bernie Marcus once declared, "The day I'm dead with an apple in my mouth is the day we'll pay commissions." In fact, rather than pushing customers to *overspend*, employees are trained to help customers spend *less* than they expected. "I love it when shoppers tell me they were prepared to spend $150 and our people showed them how to do the job for four or five bucks," says Bernie.

Home Depot has also extended its high-grade relationship-building efforts to the Internet. In addition to selling goods online, the company's Web site also offers plenty of how-to tips for household projects: how to fix it, build it, grow it, decorate it, or install it. It provides useful tools, such as calculators for figuring out how much paint or wallpaper is needed to cover a given amount of space. Home Depot also sends e-mail to regular site users alerting them to how-to workshops or other events at nearby stores.

Taking care of customers has made Home Depot one of today's most successful retailers. Founded in 1978, in less than 25 years it has grown explosively to become the world's largest do-it-yourself chain, with nearly 1,200 stores reaping more than $45 billion in sales. Home Depot sales have grown at more than 30 percent annually over the past decade, with 10-year average annual returns to shareholders of 32 percent. The company's stock price has rocketed up 28,000 percent—yes, 28,000 percent—since the company went public in 1981! In fact, a current problem in some stores is too many customers—some outlets are generating an astounding $600 of sales per square foot (compared with Wal-Mart at $250 and Kmart at $150). This has created problems with clogged aisles, stock outs, too few salespeople, and long checkout lines. Although many retailers would welcome this kind of problem, it bothers Bernie and Arthur greatly, and they've quickly taken corrective action. Continued success, they know, depends on the passionate pursuit of customer satisfaction. Bernie will tell you, "Every customer has to be treated like your mother, your father, your sister, or your brother." You certainly wouldn't want to keep your mother waiting in line.[1]

• •

The Home Depot's story provides many insights into the workings of one of today's most successful retailers. This chapter looks at *retailing* and *wholesaling*. In the first section, we look at the nature and importance of retailing, major types of store and nonstore retailers, the decisions retailers make, and the future of retailing. In the second section, we discuss these same topics as they relate to wholesalers.

Retailing

What is retailing? We all know that Wal-Mart, Sears, and Kmart are retailers, but so are Avon representatives, Amazon.com, the local Holiday Inn, and a doctor seeing patients. **Retailing** includes all the activities involved in selling goods or services directly to final consumers for their personal, nonbusiness use. Many institutions—manufacturers, wholesalers, and retailers—do retailing. But most retailing is done by **retailers:** businesses whose sales come *primarily* from retailing.

Although most retailing is done in retail stores, in recent years *nonstore retailing* has been growing much faster than has store retailing. Nonstore retailing includes selling to final consumers through direct mail, catalogs, telephone, TV home shopping shows, home and office parties, door-to-door contact, vending machines, the Internet, and other direct retailing approaches. We discuss such direct-marketing approaches in detail in Chapter 14. In this chapter, we focus on store retailing.

Retailing
All activities involved in selling goods or services directly to final consumers for their personal, nonbusiness use.

Retailer
A business whose sales come *primarily* from retailing.

Types of Retailers

Retail stores come in all shapes and sizes, and new retail types keep emerging. The most important types of retail stores are described in Table 12-1 and discussed in the following sections. They can be classified in terms of several characteristics, including the *amount of*

Table 12-1	Major Types of Retailers	
Type	Description	Examples
Specialty stores	Carry a narrow product line with a deep assortment within that line: apparel stores, sporting-goods stores, furniture stores, florists, and book stores. Specialty stores can be subclassified by the degree of narrowness in their product line. A clothing store would be a *single-line store;* a men's clothing store would be a *limited-line store;* and a men's custom-shirt store would be a *superspecialty* store.	Athlete's Foot, Tall Men, Gap, The Body Shop
Department stores	Carry several product lines—typically clothing, home furnishings, and household goods with each line operated as a separate department managed by specialist buyers or merchandisers.	Sears, Saks Fifth Avenue, Marshall Fields, May's, JCPenney, Nordstrom, Macy's
Supermarkets	Relatively large, low-cost, low-margin, high-volume, self-service operations designed to serve the consumer's total needs for food, laundry, and household maintenance products.	Safeway, Kroger, A&P, Winn-Dixie, Publix, Food Lion, Vons, Jewel
Convenience stores	Relatively small stores that are located near residential areas, open long hours seven days a week, and carry a limited line of high-turnover convenience products. Their long hours and their use by consumers mainly for "fill-in" purchases make them relatively high-price operations.	7-Eleven, Circle K, Stop-N-Go, White Hen Pantry, Wal-Mart Supercenter, Super Target, and Super Kmart Center;
Superstores	Larger stores that aim at meeting consumers' total needs for routinely purchased food and nonfood items. They include *supercenters,* combined supermarket and discount stores, which feature cross-merchandising. They also include so-called *category killers* that carry a very deep assortment of a particular line. Another superstore variation is *hypermarkets,* huge stores that combine supermarket, discount, and warehouse retailing to sell routinely purchased goods as well as furniture, large and small appliances, clothing, and many other items.	*Supercenters:* Wal-Mart Supercenter, SuperTarget, and Super Kmart Center; *Category killers:* Toys 'R' Us (toys), Petsmart (pet supplies), Staples (office supplies), Home Depot (home improvement), Best Buy (consumer electronics); *Hypermarkets:* Carrefour (France); Pyrca (Spain); Meijer's (Netherlands)
Discount stores	Sell standard merchandise at lower prices by accepting lower margins and selling higher volumes. A true discount store *regularly* sells its merchandise at lower prices, offering mostly national brands, not inferior goods. Discount retailers include both general merchandise and specialty merchandise stores.	*General discount stores:* Wal-Mart, Kmart, Target; *Specialty discount stores:* Circuit City (electronics), Crown Book (books)
Off-price retailers	Sell a changing and unstable collection of higher-quality merchandise, often leftover goods, over-runs, and irregulars obtained at reduced prices from manufacturers or other retailers. They buy at less than regular wholesale prices and charge consumers less than retail. They include three main types:	

Type	Description	Examples
Independent off-price retailers	Owned and run either by entrepreneurs or by divisions of large retail corporations.	T.J. Maxx, Filene's Basement, Value City, and Hit or Miss
Factory outlets	Owned and operated by manufacturers and normally carry the manufacturers' surplus, discontinued, or irregular goods. Such outlets increasingly group together in *factory outlet malls,* where dozens of outlet stores offer prices as much as 50 percent below retail on a broad range of items.	Mikasa (dinnerware), Dexter (shoes), Ralph Lauren and Liz Claiborne (upscale apparel).
Warehouse clubs (or wholesale clubs)	Sell a limited selection of brand name grocery items, appliances, clothing, and a hodgepodge of other goods at deep discounts to members who pay $25 to $50 annual membership fees. They serve small businesses and other club members out of huge, low-overhead, warehouselike facilities and offer few frills or services.	Wal-Mart-owned Sam's Club, Costco, BJ's Wholesale Club.

service they offer, the breadth and depth of their *product lines,* the *relative prices* they charge, and how they are *organized.*

Amount of Service Different products require different amounts of service, and customer service preferences vary. Retailers may offer one of three levels of service—self-service, limited service, and full service.

Self-service retailers serve customers who are willing to perform their own "locate-compare-select" process to save money. Self-service is the basis of all discount operations and is typically used by sellers of convenience goods (such as super-markets) and nationally branded, fast-moving shopping goods (such as Best Buy or Service Merchandise).

Limited-service retailers, such as Sears or JCPenney, provide more sales assistance because they carry more shopping goods about which customers need information. Their increased operating costs result in higher prices. In *full-service retailers,* such as specialty stores and first-class department stores, salespeople assist customers in every phase of the shopping process. Full-service stores usually carry more specialty goods for which customers like to be "waited on." They provide more services resulting in much higher operating costs, which are passed along to customers as higher prices.

Product Line Retailers also can be classified by the length and breadth of their product assortments. Some retailers, such as **specialty stores,** carry narrow product lines with deep assortments within those lines. Today, specialty stores are flourishing. The increasing use of market segmentation, market targeting, and product specialization has resulted in a greater need for stores that focus on specific products and segments.

In contrast, **department stores** carry a wide variety of product lines. In recent years, department stores have been squeezed between more focused and flexible specialty stores on the one hand, and more efficient, lower-priced discounters on the other. In response, many have added "bargain basements" and promotional events to meet the discount threat. Others have set up store brand programs, "boutiques" and "designer shops" (such as Tommy Hilfiger or Polo shops within department stores), and other store formats that compete with specialty stores. Still others are trying mail-order, telephone, and Web site

Specialty store
A retail store that carries a narrow product line with a deep assortment within that line.

Department store
A retail organization that carries a wide variety of product lines—typically clothing, home furnishings, and household goods; each line is operated as a separate department managed by specialist buyers or merchandisers.

selling. Service remains the key differentiating factor. Department stores such as Nordstrom, Saks, Neiman Marcus, and other high-end department stores are doing well by emphasizing high-quality service.

Supermarket
Large, low-cost, low-margin, high-volume, self-service store that carries a wide variety of food, laundry, and household products.

Supermarkets are the most frequently shopped type of retail store. Today, however, they are facing slow sales growth because of slower population growth and an increase in competition from convenience stores, discount food stores, and superstores. Supermarkets also have been hit hard by the rapid growth of out-of-home eating. Thus, most supermarkets are making improvements to attract more customers. In the battle for "share of stomachs," most large supermarkets have moved upscale, providing from-scratch bakeries, gourmet deli counters, and fresh seafood departments. Others are cutting costs, establishing more efficient operations, and lowering prices in order to compete more effectively with food discounters.

Convenience store
A small store, located near a residential area, that is open long hours seven days a week and carries a limited number of high-turnover convenience goods.

Convenience stores are small stores that carry a limited line of high-turnover convenience goods. Some 120,000 U.S. convenience stores posted sales last year of $269 billion. During the 1990s, the convenience store industry suffered from overcapacity as its primary market of young, blue-collar men shrunk. As a result, many chains are redesigning their stores with female customers in mind. They are shedding the image of a "truck stop" where men go to buy beer, cigarettes, and magazines, and instead offer fresh, prepared foods and cleaner, safer environments. Many convenience chains also are experimenting with micromarketing—tailoring each store's merchandise to the specific needs of its surrounding neighborhood. For example, a Stop-N-Go in an affluent neighborhood carries fresh produce, gourmet pasta sauces, chilled Evian water, and expensive wines. Stop-N-Go stores in Hispanic neighborhoods carry Spanish-language magazines and other goods catering to the specific needs of Hispanic consumers.[2]

Superstore
A store much larger than a regular supermarket that carries a large assortment of routinely purchased food and nonfood items and offers services such as dry cleaning, post offices, photo finishing, check cashing, bill paying, lunch counters, car care, and pet care.

Superstores are much larger than regular supermarkets and offer a large assortment of routinely purchased food products, nonfood items, and services. Examples include Safeway's Pak 'N Pay and Pathmark Super Centers. Wal-Mart, Kmart, Target and other discount retailers also offer *supercenters,* combination food and discount stores that emphasize cross-merchandising. For example, at a Super Kmart Center, toasters are above the fresh-baked bread, kitchen gadgets are across from produce, and infant centers carry everything from baby food to clothing. Supercenters are growing in the United States at an annual rate of 25 percent, compared with a supermarket industry growth rate of only 1 percent. Wal-Mart, which opened its first supercenter in 1988, now has more than 720, capturing almost two-thirds of all supercenter volume. By 2005, the retailing giant will likely more than double the number of supercenters to 1,900.[3]

Recent years have also seen the explosive growth of superstores that are actually giant specialty stores, the so-called **category killers.** They feature stores the size of airplane hangars that carry a very deep assortment of a particular line with a knowledgeable staff. Category killers are prevalent in a wide range of categories, including books, baby gear, toys, electronics, home improvement products, linens and towels, party goods, sporting goods, even pet supplies. Another superstore variation, *hypermarkets,* are huge superstores, perhaps as large as *six* football fields. Although hypermarkets have been very successful in Europe and other world markets, they have met with little success in the United States.

Category killer
Giant specialty store that carries a very deep assortment of a particular line and is staffed by knowledgeable employees.

Finally, for some retailers, the product line is actually a service. Service retailers include hotels and motels, banks, airlines, colleges, hospitals, movie theaters, tennis clubs, bowling alleys, restaurants, repair services, hair care shops, and dry cleaners. Service retailers in the United States are growing faster than product retailers.

Relative Prices Retailers can also be classified according to the prices they charge. Most retailers charge regular prices and offer normal-quality goods and customer service. Others offer higher-quality goods and service at higher prices. The retailers that feature low prices are discount stores and "off-price" retailers (see Table 12-1).

DISCOUNT STORES. A **discount store** sells standard merchandise at lower prices by accepting lower margins and selling higher volume. The early discount stores cut expenses by offering few services and operating in warehouselike facilities in low-rent, heavily traveled districts. In recent years, facing intense competition from other discounters and department stores, many discount retailers have "traded up." They have improved decor, added new lines and services, and opened suburban branches, which have led to higher costs and prices.

OFF-PRICE RETAILERS. When the major discount stores traded up, a new wave of **off-price retailers** moved in to fill the low-price, high-volume gap. Ordinary discounters buy at regular wholesale prices and accept lower margins to keep prices down. In contrast, off-price retailers buy at less-than-regular wholesale prices and charge consumers less than retail. Off-price retailers can be found in all areas, from food, clothing, and electronics to no-frills banking and discount brokerages.

The three main types of off-price retailers are *independents, factory outlets,* and *warehouse clubs.* **Independent off-price retailers** either are owned and run by entrepreneurs or are divisions of larger retail corporations. Although many off-price operations are run by smaller independents, most large off-price retailer operations are owned by bigger retail chains. Examples include store retailers such as T.J. Maxx, Filene's Basement, and Value City, and Web sellers such as RetailExchange.com, Redtag.com, and CloseOutNow.com.

Factory outlets—such as the Burlington Coat Factory Warehouse, Manhattan's Brand Name Fashion Outlet, and the factory outlets of Levi Strauss, Carters, and Ship 'n' Shore—sometimes group together in *factory outlet malls* and *value-retail centers,* where dozens of outlet stores offer prices as low as 50 percent below retail on a wide range of items. Whereas outlet malls consist primarily of manufacturers' outlets, value-retail centers combine manufacturers' outlets with off-price retail stores and department store clearance outlets. Factory outlet malls have become one of the hottest growth areas in retailing.

The malls now are moving upscale—and even dropping "factory" from their descriptions—narrowing the gap between factory outlet and more traditional forms of retailers. As the gap narrows, the discounts offered by outlets are getting smaller. However, a growing number of outlet malls now feature brands such as Coach, Esprit, Liz Claiborne, Polo Ralph Lauren, Calvin Klein, and Nike, causing department stores to protest to the manufacturers of these brands. Given their higher costs, the department stores have to charge more than the off-price outlets. Manufacturers counter that they send last year's merchandise and seconds to the factory outlet malls, not the new merchandise that they supply to the department stores. The malls are also located far from urban areas, making travel to them more difficult. Still, the department stores are concerned about the growing number of shoppers willing to make weekend trips to stock up on branded merchandise at substantial savings.[4]

Warehouse clubs (or *wholesale clubs* or *membership warehouses*), such as Sam's Club, Costco, and BJ's, operate in huge, drafty, warehouselike facilities and offer few frills. Customers themselves must wrestle furniture, heavy appliances, and other large items to the checkout line. Such clubs make no home deliveries and often accept no credit cards. However, they do offer ultralow prices and surprise deals on selected branded merchandise. Entering the new millennium, whereas a weakening economy slowed the growth of many traditional retailers, warehouse club sales have soared recently. These days, "Consumers are laser beam-focused on finding the best value," says an industry analyst, "and the absolute best value is at a club."[5]

Discount store
A retail institution that sells standard merchandise at lower prices by accepting lower margins and selling at higher volume.

Off-price retailer
Retailer that buys at less-than-regular wholesale prices and sells at less than retail. Examples are factory outlets, independents, and warehouse clubs.

Independent off-price retailer
Off-price retailer that is either owned and run by entrepreneurs or is a division of a larger retail corporation.

Factory outlet
Off-price retailing operation that is owned and operated by a manufacturer and that normally carries the manufacturer's surplus, discontinued, or irregular goods.

Warehouse club
Off-price retailer that sells a limited selection of brand name grocery items, appliances, clothing, and a hodgepodge of other goods at deep discounts to members who pay annual membership fees.

Category killers: Best Buy has stores the size of airplane hangars that carry a deep assortment of consumer electronics, personal computers, entertainment software, and appliances.

Retail Organizations Although many retail stores are independently owned, an increasing number are banding together under some form of corporate or contractual organization. The major types of retail organizations—*corporate chains, voluntary chains and retailer cooperatives, franchise organizations,* and *merchandising conglomerates*—are described in Table 12-2.

Table 12-2   Major Types of Retail Organizations

Type	Description	Examples
Corporate chain stores	Two or more outlets that are commonly owned and controlled, employ central buying and merchandising, and sell similar lines of merchandise. Corporate chains appear in all types of retailing, but they are strongest in department stores, variety stores, food stores, drugstores, shoe stores, and women's clothing stores.	Tower Records, Fayva (shoes), Pottery Barn (dinnerware and home furnishings)
Voluntary chains	Wholesaler-sponsored groups of independent retailers engaged in bulk buying and common merchandising.	Independent Grocers Alliance (IGA), Sentry Hardwares, Western Auto, True Value
Retailer cooperatives	Groups of independent retailers who set up a central buying organization and conduct joint promotion efforts.	Associated Grocers (groceries), ACE (hardware)
Franchise organizations	Contractual association between a *franchiser* (a manufacturer, wholesales, or service organization) and *franchisees* (Independent businesspeople who buy the right to own and operate one or more units in the franchise system). Franchise organizations are normally based on some unique product, service, or method of doing business, or on a trade name or patent, or on goodwill that the franchiser had developed.	McDonald's, Subway, Pizza Hut, Jiffy Lube, Meineke Mufflers, 7-Eleven.
Merchandising conglomerates	A free-form corporation that combines several diversified retailing lines and forms under central ownership, along with some integration of their distribution and management functions.	Dayton-Hudson

Chain stores are two or more outlets that are commonly owned and controlled. They have many advantages over independents. Their size allows them to buy in large quantities at lower prices. They can afford to hire corporate-level specialists to deal with areas such as pricing, promotion, merchandising, inventory control, and sales forecasting. And corporate chains gain promotional economies because their advertising costs are spread over many stores and over a large sales volume.

The great success of corporate chains caused many independents to band together in one of two forms of contractual associations. One is the *voluntary chain*—a wholesaler-sponsored group of independent retailers that engages in group buying and common merchandising—that we discussed in Chapter 11. Examples include Western Auto and Do it Best hardwares. The other form of contractual association is the *retailer cooperative*—a group of independent retailers that bands together to set up a jointly owned, central wholesale operation and conducts joint merchandising and promotion efforts. Examples are Associated Grocers and Ace Hardware. These organizations give independents the buying and promotion economies they need to meet the prices of corporate chains.

Another form of contractual retail organization is a **franchise.** The main difference between franchise organizations and other contractual systems (voluntary chains and retail cooperatives) is that franchise systems are normally based on some unique product or service; on a method of doing business; or on the trade name, goodwill, or patent that the franchiser has developed. Franchising has been prominent in fast foods, video stores, health or fitness centers, haircutting, auto rentals, motels, travel agencies, real estate, and dozens of other product and service areas. Franchising is described in detail in Marketing at Work 12-1.

Finally, *merchandising conglomerates* are corporations that combine several different retailing forms under central ownership. An example is Dayton-Hudson, which operates Target (upscale discount stores), Mervyn's (middle-market apparel and home soft goods), and three department stores—Dayton's, Hudson's, and Marshall Fields. Diversified retailing, which provides superior management systems and economies that benefit all the separate retail operations, is likely to continue to increase as the retailing industry continues to consolidate.

Chain stores
Two or more outlets that are owned and controlled in common, have central buying and merchandising, and sell similar lines of merchandise.

Franchise
A contractual association between a manufacturer, wholesaler, or service organization (a franchiser) and independent businesspeople (franchisees) who buy the right to own and operate one or more units in the franchise system.

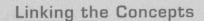

Linking the Concepts

Slow down and think about all the different kinds of retailers you deal with regularly, many of which overlap in the products they carry.

◆ Pick a familiar product: a camera, microwave oven, hand tool, or something else. Shop for this product at two very different store types, say a discount store or category killer on the one hand, and a department store or smaller specialty store on the other. Compare the stores on product assortment, services, and prices. If you were going to buy the product, where would you buy it and why?

◆ What does your shopping trip suggest about the futures of the competing store formats that you sampled?

Retailer Marketing Decisions

Retailers are searching for new marketing strategies to attract and hold customers. In the past, retailers attracted customers with unique products, more or better services than their competitors offered, or credit cards. Today, national-brand manufacturers, in their drive for volume, have placed their branded goods everywhere. Thus, stores offer more similar assortments—national brands are found not only in department stores but also in

Franchise Fever

Once considered upstarts among independent businesses, franchises now command 35 percent of all retail sales in the United States. These days, it's nearly impossible to stroll down a city block or drive on a suburban street without seeing a McDonald's, Subway, Jiffy Lube, or Holiday Inn. One of the best-known and most successful franchisers, McDonald's, now has 29,250 stores in 120 countries and racks up more than $40 billion in systemwide sales. More than 70 percent of McDonald's restaurants worldwide are owned and operated by franchisees. Gaining fast is Subway Sandwiches and Salads, one of the fastest-growing franchises, with more than 15,200 shops in 76 countries. Franchising is even moving into new areas such as education. For example, LearnRight Corporation franchises its methods for teaching students thinking skills.

How does a franchising system work? The individual franchises are a tightly knit group of enterprises whose systematic operations are planned, directed, and controlled by the operation's innovator, called a *franchiser*. Generally, franchises are distinguished by three characteristics:

1. *The franchiser owns a trade or service mark and licenses it to franchisees in return for royalty payments.*

2. *The franchisee is required to pay for the right to be part of the system.* Yet this initial fee is only a small part of the total amount that franchisees invest when they sign a franchising contract. Start-up costs include rental and lease of equipment and fixtures and sometimes a regular license fee. McDonald's franchisees may invest as much as $600,000 in initial start-up costs. The franchisee then pays McDonald's a service fee and a rental charge that equal 11.5 percent of the franchisee's sales volume. Subway's success is partly due to its low start-up cost average of just

Franchising fever: Most of us encounter dozens of franchised businesses each day, from familiar fast-food restaurants to franchised education systems such as LearnRight.

$100,000, which is lower than 70 percent of other franchise system start-up costs. However, Subway franchisees pay an 8 percent royalty on gross sales, highest in the food franchise industry, plus a 3.5 percent advertising fee. Hotel franchisees pay anywhere from 5 percent to 11 percent of room revenue—Holiday Inn franchisees pay 9.6 percent.

3. *The franchiser provides its franchisees with a marketing and operations system for doing business.* McDonald's requires franchisees to attend its "Hamburger University" in Oak Brook, Illinois, for three weeks to learn how to manage the business. Franchisees must also adhere to certain procedures in buying materials.

In the best cases, franchising is mutually beneficial to both franchiser and franchisee. Franchisers can cover a new territory in little more than the time it takes the franchisee to sign a contract. They can achieve enormous purchasing power (consider the purchase order that Holiday Inn is likely to make for bed linens, for instance). Franchisers also benefit from the franchisees' familiarity with local communities and conditions and from the motivation and hard work of employees who are entrepreneurs rather than "hired hands." Similarly, franchisees benefit from buying into a proven business with a well-known and accepted brand name. And they receive ongoing support in areas ranging from marketing and advertising to site selection, staffing, and financing.

As a result of the franchise explosion in recent years, many types of franchisers (such as fast-food franchisers) are facing worrisome market saturation. One indication is the number of franchisee complaints filed with the Federal Trade Commission against parent companies, which has been growing by more than 50 percent annually since 1990. The most common complaint: Franchisers "encroach" on existing franchisees' territory by bringing in another store. For example, McDonald's franchisees in California and other states recently complained when the company decided to open new company-owned stores in their areas.

Or franchisees may object to parent company marketing programs that may adversely affect their local operations. For instance, a few years ago, franchisees strongly resisted McDonald's "Campaign 55" promotion, in which the company reduced prices on Big Macs and Egg McMuffins to 55 cents in an effort to revive stagnant sales. Many franchisees believed that the promotion might cheapen McDonald's image and unnecessarily reduce their profit margins.

Another complaint is higher-than-advertised failure rates. Subway, in particular, has been criticized for misleading its franchisees by telling them that it has only a 2 percent failure rate when the reality is much different. In addition, some franchisees feel that they've been misled by exaggerated claims of support, only to feel abandoned after the contract is signed and $100,000 is invested.

There will *always* be a conflict between the franchisers, who seek systemwide growth, and the franchisees, who want to earn a good living from their individual franchises. Some new directions that may deliver both franchiser growth and franchisee earnings are:

◆ *Strategic alliances with major outside corporations:* An example is the alliance between film company Fuji USA and Moto Photo, a one-hour photo developer. Fuji gained instant market penetration through Moto Photo's 400 locations, and Moto Photo franchisees enjoyed Fuji's brand name recognition and advertising reach.

◆ *Expansion abroad:* Fast-food franchises have become very popular throughout the world. For example, Domino's has franchised operations in 64 countries. It entered Japan with master franchisee Ernest Higa, who owns 106 stores in Japan with combined sales of $140 million. Part of Higa's success can be attributed to adapting Domino's product to the Japanese market, where food presentation is everything. Higa carefully charted the placement of pizza toppings and made cut-mark perforations in the boxes for perfectly uniform slices.

◆ *Nontraditional site locations:* Franchises are opening in airports, convenience stores, truck stops, college campuses, sporting facilities, hospitals, military bases, gambling casinos, theme parks, convention halls, and even riverboats.

Thus, it appears, franchise fever will not cool down soon. Some experts predict that franchises will capture almost 50 percent of all U.S. retail sales within the decade.

Sources: Norman D. Axelrad and Robert E. Weigand, "Franchising—A Marriage of System Members," in Sidney Levy, George Frerichs, and Howard Gordon, eds., *Marketing Managers Handbook,* 3rd ed. (Chicago: Dartnell, 1994), pp. 919–934; Patrick J. Kaufmann and Sevgin Eroglu, "Standardization and Adaptation in Business Format Franchising," *Journal of Business Venturing,* January 1999, pp. 69–85; Jerry Wilkerson, "Annual Franchise Business Development Survey Predicts 13 Percent Growth for Franchising in 2001," *Franchising World,* March 2001, pp. 30–32; and information accessed online at www.mcdonalds.com and www.subway.com, December 2001.

Figure 12-1
Retailer marketing
decisions

mass-merchandise and off-price discount stores. As a result, stores are looking more and more alike.

Service differentiation among retailers has also eroded. Many department stores have trimmed their services, whereas discounters have increased theirs. Customers have become smarter and more price sensitive. They see no reason to pay more for identical brands, especially when service differences are shrinking. For all these reasons, many retailers today are rethinking their marketing strategies.

As shown in Figure 12-1, retailers face major marketing decisions about their *target market* and *positioning, product assortment and services, price, promotion,* and *place.*

Target Market and Positioning Decision Retailers first must define their target markets and then decide how they will position themselves in these markets. Should the store focus on upscale, midscale, or downscale shoppers? Do target shoppers want variety, depth of assortment, convenience, or low prices? Until they define and profile their markets, retailers cannot make consistent decisions about product assortment, services, pricing, advertising, store decor, or any of the other decisions that must support their positions.

Too many retailers fail to define their target markets and positions clearly. They try to have "something for everyone" and end up satisfying no market well. In contrast, successful retailers define their target markets well and position themselves strongly. For example, in 1963, Leslie H. Wexner borrowed $5,000 from his aunt to create *The Limited,* which started as a single store targeted to young, fashion-conscious women. All aspects of the store—clothing assortment, fixtures, music, colors, personnel—were orchestrated to match the target consumer. He continued to open more stores, but a decade later his original customers were no longer in the "young" group. To catch the new "youngs," he started Express. Over the years, he has started or acquired other highly targeted store chains, including Lane Bryant, Victoria's Secret, Lerner, Structure, Bath & Body Works, and others to reach new segments. Today The Limited, Inc. operates more than 5,100 stores in several different segments of the market, with sales of more than $10 billion.[6]

Even large stores such as Wal-Mart, Sears, Kmart, and Target must define their major target markets in order to design effective marketing strategies. In fact, in recent years, thanks to strong targeting and positioning, Wal-Mart has zoomed past Sears and Kmart to become the world's largest retailer (see Marketing at Work 12-2). How can any discounter hope to compete with the likes of huge and dominating Wal-Mart? Again, the answer is good targeting and positioning. For example, rather than facing Wal-Mart head-on, Target aims for a seemingly oxymoronic niche—the "upscale discount" segment.

Target—or Tar-*zhay* as many fans call it—has developed its own distinct targeting and positioning. "Going to Target is a cool experience, and everybody now considers it cool to save money," says one retailing consultant. "On the other hand,

Marketing at Work 12.2

Wal-Mart: The World's Largest Retailer

In 1962, Sam Walton and his brother opened the first Wal-Mart discount store in small-town Rogers, Arkansas. It was a big, flat, warehouse-like store that sold everything from apparel to automotive supplies to small appliances at very low prices. Experts gave the fledgling retailer little chance—conventional wisdom suggested that discount stores could succeed only in large cities.

Yet, from these modest beginnings, the chain exploded onto the national retailing scene. Incredibly, Wal-Mart's annual sales now exceed $200 billion—more than those of Sears, Kmart, JCPenney, Target, and French giant Carrefour combined—making it the world's second largest company. Each year in the United States, Wal-Mart sells one out of every four quarts of motor oil, one out of every five deodorants, and one out of every four replacement toilet seats. It sells a Timex watch every 7.4 seconds and a Barbie Doll every 2 seconds. One out of every 240 men, women, and children in the United States is a Wal-Mart associate.

Wal-Mart's phenomenal growth shows few signs of slowing. In recent years, the company has taken its winning formula into new growth areas. For example, the company is now well established in larger cities and is expanding rapidly into international markets. Within only a few years of entering the grocery business with its supercenters—and more recently with its smaller Neighborhood Market stores—Wal-Mart will soon become the nation's largest grocery retailer. And Wal-Mart is now flexing its cybermuscles (www.walmart.com). Many industry experts believe that Wal-Mart will soon dominate Internet marketspaces in the same way that it now dominates the physical marketplace. "At the end of the

next four years," predicts one retailing industry consultant, "Wal-Mart will be number one on land and online."

What are the secrets behind this spectacular success? Wal-Mart listens to and takes care of its customers, treats employees as partners, and keeps a tight rein on costs.

Listening to and Taking Care of Customers

Wal-Mart positioned itself strongly in a well-chosen target market. Initially, Sam Walton focused on value-conscious consumers in small-town America. The chain built a strong everyday low-price position long before it became fashionable in retailing. It grew rapidly by bringing the lowest possible prices to towns ignored by national discounters— towns such as Van Buren, Arkansas, and Idabel, Oklahoma.

Wal-Mart knows its customers and takes good care of them. As one analyst puts it, "The company gospel . . . is relatively simple: Be an agent for customers, find out what

A Wal-Mart people greeter lends a hand.

they want, and sell it to them for the lowest possible price." Thus, the company listens carefully—for example, each top Wal-Mart executive spends at least two days a week visiting stores, talking directly with customers and getting a firsthand look at operations. Then, Wal-Mart delivers what customers want: a broad selection of carefully selected goods at unbeatable prices. Concludes Wal-Mart's current president and chief executive, "We're obsessed with delivering value to customers."

But the right merchandise at the right price isn't the only key to Wal-Mart's success. Wal-Mart also provides the kind of service that keeps customers satisfied. A sign reading "Satisfaction Guaranteed" hangs prominently at each store's entrance. Another sign inside the store reads "At Wal-Mart, our goal is: You're always next in line!" Customers are often welcomed by "people greeters" eager to lend a helping hand or just to be friendly. And, sure enough, the store opens extra checkout counters to keep waiting lines short.

Treating Employees as Partners

Wal-Mart believes that, in the final accounting, the company's people are what really make it better. Thus, it works hard to show employees that it cares about them. Wal-Mart was first to call employees "associates," a practice now widely copied by competitors. The associates work as partners, become deeply involved in operations, and share rewards for good performance.

Everyone at Wal-Mart [is] an associate—from [the CEO] . . . to a cashier named Janet at the Wal-Mart on Highway 50 in Ocoee, Florida. "We," "us," and "our" are the operative words. Wal-Mart department heads, hourly associates

who look after one of more than 30-some departments ranging from sporting goods to electronics, see figures that many companies never show general managers: costs, freight charges, profit margins. The company sets a profit margin for each store, and if the store exceeds it, then the hourly associates share part of the additional profit.

The partnership concept is deeply rooted in the Wal-Mart corporate culture. Wal-Mart's concern for its employees translates into high employee satisfaction, which in turn translates into greater customer satisfaction.

Keeping a Tight Rein on Costs

Wal-Mart has the lowest cost structure in the industry. Thus, Wal-Mart can charge lower prices but still reap higher profits, allowing it to offer better service. Wal-Mart's lower prices and better service attract more shoppers, producing more sales, making the company more efficient, and enabling it to lower prices even more.

Wal-Mart's low costs result in part from superior management and more sophisticated technology. Its Bentonville, Arkansas, headquarters contains a computer communications system that the Defense Department would envy, giving managers around the country instant access to sales and operating information. And its huge, fully automated distribution centers employ the latest technology to supply stores efficiently. Wal-Mart also spends less than competitors on advertising—only 0.5 percent of sales, compared to 2.5 percent at Kmart and 3.8 percent at Sears. Because Wal-Mart has what customers want at the prices they'll pay, its reputation has spread rapidly by word of mouth. It has not needed more advertising.

Finally, Wal-Mart keeps costs down through good old "tough buying." Whereas the company is known for the warm way it treats customers, it is equally well known for the cold, calculated way it wrings low prices from suppliers. The following passage describes a visit to Wal-Mart's buying offices:

Don't expect a greeter and don't expect friendly. . . . Once you are ushered into one of the spartan little buyers' rooms, expect a steely eye across the table and be prepared to cut your price. "They are very, very focused people, and they use their buying power more forcefully than anyone else in America," says the marketing vice president of a major vendor. "All the normal mating rituals are [forbidden]. Their highest priority is making sure everyone at all times in all cases knows who's in charge, and it's Wal-Mart. They talk softly, but they have piranha hearts, and if you aren't totally prepared when you go in there, you'll have your [head] handed to you."

Some observers wonder whether Wal-Mart can be so big and still retain its focus and positioning. They wonder if an ever-larger Wal-Mart can stay close to its customers and employees. The company's managers are betting on it. No matter where it operates, Wal-Mart's announced policy is to take care of customers "one store at a time." Says one top executive: "We'll be fine as long as we never lose our responsiveness to the consumer."

Sources: Quotes and other material from Bill Saporito, "Is Wal-Mart Unstoppable?" *Fortune*, May 6, 1991, pp. 50–59; John Huey, "Wal-Mart: Will It Take Over the World?" *Fortune*, January 30, 1998, pp. 52–61; and Carol J. Loomis, "Sam Would Be Proud," *Fortune*, April 17, 2001, pp. 131–144. Also see Joe Ronning, "Understanding Wal-Mart," *Discount Merchandiser*, April 1999, pp. 48–50; Wendy Zellner, "Will Wal-Mart.com Get It Right This Time?" *Business Week*, November 6, 2000, pp. 104–112; Richard Turcsik and Jenny Summerour, "David vs. Goliath," *Progressive Grocer*, March 2001, p. 7; and *Wal-Mart Annual Report 2001*, accessed online at www.walmartstores.com.

is it cool to save at Kmart, at Wal-Mart? I don't think so." Target isn't Wal-Mart, the giant that wooed suburbia with its acres of guns and gummy bears. And it definitely isn't Kmart, which still seems downscale despite its Martha Stewart tea-towel sets. Target's aim is more subtle: Stick to low prices, of course, but rise above the discount fray with upmarket style and design and higher-grade service. Target's ability to position itself as an upscale alternative really separates it from its mass-merchant peers. "We have a very clear strategy and a very clear brand," says Target vice chairman Jerry Storch. And it's all based on a clearly defined customer. Target's "expect more, pay less" positioning appeals to more affluent consumers. Its average customer is typically female, 40, and college educated, with a household income approaching $50,000. On average, Target customers spend $40 a visit, almost twice that of other mass merchants. "The higher-income, better educated guest is in our stores," says Storch. "As your income rises, you love Target more and more." Target's upscale discount niche has helped insulate it from giant competitor Wal-Mart. "Wal-Mart is the greatest retailer that ever was," says Storch. "Very few have been able to compete with them and survive." Now 1,000 stores strong, more than survive, Target has thrived. "People used to say, 'Ooh, a Nordstrom's coming to town,'" says the consultant. "Those same people now say, 'Ooh, we're getting a Target!'" [7]

Product Assortment and Services Decision Retailers must decide on three major product variables: *product assortment, services mix,* and *store atmosphere.*

The retailer's *product assortment* should match target shoppers' expectations. In its quest to differentiate itself from competitors, a retailer can use any of several product-differentiation strategies. For one, it can offer merchandise that no other competitor carries—its own private brands or national brands on which it holds exclusives. For example, The Limited designs most of the clothes carried by its store and Saks gets exclusive rights to carry a well-known designer's labels. Second, the retailer can feature blockbuster merchandising events—Bloomingdale's is known for running spectacular shows featuring goods from a certain country, such as India or China. Or the retailer can offer surprise merchandise, as when Costco offers surprise assortments of seconds, overstocks, and closeouts. Finally, the retailer can differentiate itself by offering a highly targeted product assortment—Lane Bryant carries goods in larger sizes; Brookstone offers an unusual assortment of gadgets in what amounts to an adult toy store.

Retailers also must decide on a *services mix* to offer customers. The old mom-and-pop grocery stores offered home delivery, credit, and conversation—services that today's supermarkets ignore. The services mix is one of the key tools of nonprice competition for setting one store apart from another.

The *store's atmosphere* is another element in its product arsenal. Every store has a physical layout that makes moving around in it either hard or easy. Each store has a "feel"; one store is cluttered, another charming, a third plush, a fourth somber. The store must have a planned atmosphere that suits the target market and moves customers to buy.

Increasingly, retailers are turning their stores into theaters that transport customers into unusual, exciting shopping environments. For example, Barnes & Noble uses atmospherics to turn shopping for books into entertainment. It has found that "to consumers, shopping is a social activity. They do it to mingle with others in a prosperous-feeling crowd, to see what's new, to enjoy the theatrical dazzle of the display, to treat themselves to something interesting or unexpected." Thus, Barnes & Noble stores are designed with "enough woody, traditional, soft-colored library to please book lovers; enough sophisticated modern architecture and graphics, sweeping vistas, and stylish displays to satisfy fans of the theater of consumption. And for everyone, plenty of space, where they can meet other people and feel at home. . . . [Customers] settle in at heavy chairs and tables to browse through piles of books; they fill the cafes [designed] to increase the festivities. . . ." As one

Barnes & Noble executive notes: "The feel-good part of the store, the quality of life contribution, is a big part of the success."[8]

Perhaps the most dramatic conversion of stores into theater is the Mall of America near Minneapolis. Containing more than 520 specialty stores and 49 restaurants, the mall is a veritable playground. Under a single roof, it shelters a seven-acre Camp Snoopy amusement park featuring 25 rides and attractions, an ice-skating rink, an Underwater World featuring hundreds of marine specimens and a dolphin show, and a two-story miniature golf course. One of the stores, Oshman Supersports USA, features a basketball court, a boxing gym, a baseball batting cage, a 50-foot archery range, and a simulated ski slope.[9]

All of this confirms that retail stores are much more than simply assortments of goods. They are environments to be experienced by the people who shop in them. Store atmospheres offer a powerful tool by which retailers can differentiate their stores from those of competitors.

Price Decision A retailer's price policy is a crucial positioning factor and must be decided in relation to its target market, its product and service assortment, and its competition. All retailers would like to charge high markups and achieve high volume, but the two seldom go together. Most retailers seek *either* high markups on lower volume (most specialty stores) *or* low markups on higher volume (mass merchandisers and discount stores). Thus, Bijan's boutique on Rodeo Drive in Beverly Hills sells $375 silk ties and $19,000 ostrich-skin vests. Its "by appointment only" policy is designed to make its wealthy, high-profile clients comfortable with these prices. (Says Mr. Bijan, "If a man is going to spend $400,000 on his visit, don't you think it's only fair that he have my full attention?")[10] Bijan's sells a low volume but makes hefty profits on each sale. At the other extreme, T.J. Maxx sells brand name clothing at discount prices, settling for a lower margin on each sale but selling at a much higher volume.

Promotion Decision Retailers use the normal promotion tools—advertising, personal selling, sales promotion, public relations, and direct marketing—to reach consumers. They advertise in newspapers, magazines, radio, and television. Advertising may be supported by newspaper inserts and direct-mail pieces. Personal selling requires

Bijan's boutique on Rodeo Drive in Beverly Hills sells $375 silk ties and $19,000 ostrich-skin vests. Its "by appointment only" policy makes wealthy, high-profile clients comfortable with these prices.

careful training of salespeople in how to greet customers, meet their needs, and handle their complaints. Sales promotions may include in-store demonstrations, displays, contests, and visiting celebrities. Public relations activities, such as press conferences and speeches, store openings, special events, newsletters, magazines, and public service activities, are always available to retailers. Most retailers have also set up Web sites, offering customers information and other features and often selling merchandise directly.

Place Decision Retailers often cite three critical factors in retailing success: *location, location,* and *location!* A retailer's location is key to its ability to attract customers. And the costs of building or leasing facilities have a major impact on the retailer's profits. Thus, site-location decisions are among the most important the retailer makes. Small retailers may have to settle for whatever locations they can find or afford. Large retailers usually employ specialists who select locations using advanced methods. Two of the savviest location experts in recent years have been the off-price retailer T.J. Maxx and toy-store giant Toys 'R' Us. Both put the majority of their new locations in rapidly growing areas where the population closely matches their customer base. The undisputed winner in the "place race" has been Wal-Mart, whose strategy of being the first mass merchandiser to locate in small and rural markets was one of the key factors in its phenomenal early success.

Most stores today cluster together to increase their customer pulling power and to give consumers the convenience of one-stop shopping. *Central business districts* were the main form of retail cluster until the 1950s. Every large city and town had a central business district with department stores, specialty stores, banks, and movie theaters. When people began to move to the suburbs, however, these central business districts, with their traffic, parking, and crime problems, began to lose business. Downtown merchants opened branches in suburban shopping centers, and the decline of the central business districts continued. In recent years, many cities have joined with merchants to try to revive downtown shopping areas by building malls and providing underground parking.

A **shopping center** is a group of retail businesses planned, developed, owned, and managed as a unit. A *regional shopping center,* the largest and most dramatic shopping center, contains from 40 to over 200 stores. It is like a covered minidowntown and attracts customers from a wide area. A *community shopping center* contains between 15 and 40 retail stores. It normally contains a branch of a department store or variety store, a supermarket, specialty stores, professional offices, and sometimes a bank. Most shopping centers are *neighborhood shopping centers* or *strip malls* that generally contain between 5 and 15 stores. They are close and convenient for consumers. They usually contain a supermarket, perhaps a discount store, and several service stores—dry cleaner, self-service laundry, drugstore, video-rental outlet, barber or beauty shop, hardware store, or other stores.

Shopping center
A group of retail businesses planned, developed, owned, and managed as a unit.

Combined, all shopping centers now account for about one-third of all retail sales, but they may have reached their saturation point. Through the past decade, on average, consumers have been going to traditional malls less often, staying a shorter period of time, and visiting fewer stores. Why are people using shopping malls less? First, with more dual-income households, people have less time to shop. "You have two workers in every family and no one has time to go to the mall for four hours anymore," observes one industry analyst. "People who used to go to the mall 20 times a year now go two or three times."[11]

Second, shoppers appear to be tiring of traditional malls, which are too big, too crowded, and too much alike. Today's large malls offer great selection but are less comfortable and convenient. Finally, today's consumers have many alternatives to traditional malls, ranging from online shopping to so-called *power centers*. These huge unenclosed

Shopping centers: The spectacular Mall of America contains more than 520 specialty stores, 49 restaurants, a 7-acre indoor theme park, an Underwater World featuring hundreds of marine specimens and a dolphin show, and a two-story miniature golf course.

shopping centers consist of a long strip of retail stores, including large, free-standing anchors such as Wal-Mart, Home Depot, Best Buy, Michaels, OfficeMax, and Comp-USA. Each store has its own entrance with parking directly in front for shoppers who wish to visit only one store. Power centers have increased rapidly during the past few years to challenge traditional indoor malls. "Malls have been hit hard by competition from street shopping and from recent retail innovations—especially power centers," concludes the analyst. "And . . . malls in the same city may no longer be differentiated by their anchors; they seem to have the same stores. Add to all this the emergence of Internet shopping, and the concept of the traditional shopping mall is beginning to look dated."[12]

Thus, despite the recent development of many new "megamalls," such as the spectacular Mall of America, the current trend is toward value-oriented outlet malls and power centers on the one hand, and smaller malls on the other. Many shoppers now prefer to shop at "lifestyle centers," smaller malls with upscale stores, convenient locations, and expensive atmospheres. "Think of lifestyle centers as part Main Street and part Fifth Avenue," comments one industry observer. "The idea is to combine the hominess and community of an old-time village square with the cachet of fashionable urban stores; the smell and feel of a neighborhood park with the brute convenience of a strip center."[13]

The Future of Retailing

Retailers operate in a harsh and fast-changing environment, which offers threats as well as opportunities. For example, the industry suffers from chronic overcapacity, resulting in fierce competition for customer dollars. Consumer demographics, lifestyles, and shopping patterns are changing rapidly, as are retailing technologies. To be successful, then, retailers will have to choose target segments carefully and position themselves strongly. They will have to take the following retailing developments into account as they plan and execute their competitive strategies.

New Retail Forms and Shortening Retail Life Cycles New retail forms continue to emerge to meet new situations and consumer needs, but the life cycle of new retail forms is getting shorter. Department stores took about 100 years to reach the mature stage of the life cycle; more recent forms, such as warehouse stores, reached maturity in about 10 years. In such an environment, seemingly solid retail positions can crumble quickly. Of the top 10 discount retailers in 1962 (the year that Wal-Mart and Kmart began), not one still exists today.

Consider the Price Club, the original warehouse store chain. When Sol Price opened his first warehouse store outside San Diego in 1976, he launched a retailing revolution. Selling everything from tires and office supplies to five-pound tubs of peanut butter at superlow prices, his store chain was generating $2.6 billion a year in sales within 10 years. But Price refused to expand beyond its California base. And as the industry quickly matured, Price ran headlong into wholesale clubs run by such retail giants as Wal-Mart and Kmart. Only 17 years later, in a stunning reversal of fortune, a faltering Price sold out to competitor Costco. Price's rapid rise and fall "serves as a stark reminder to mass-market retailers that past success means little in a fiercely competitive and rapidly changing industry."[14] Thus, retailers can no longer sit back with a successful formula. To remain successful, they must keep adapting.

Many retailing innovations are partially explained by the **wheel of retailing concept**.[15] According to this concept, many new types of retailing forms begin as low-margin, low-price, low-status operations. They challenge established retailers that have become "fat" by letting their costs and margins increase. The new retailers' success leads them to upgrade their facilities and offer more services. In turn, their costs increase, forcing them to increase their prices. Eventually, the new retailers become like the conventional retailers they replaced. The cycle begins again when still newer types of retailers evolve with lower costs and prices. The wheel of retailing concept seems to explain the initial success and later troubles of department stores, supermarkets, and discount stores, and the recent success of off-price retailers.

Wheel of retailing concept
A concept of retailing that states that new types of retailers usually begin as low-margin, low-price, low-status operations but later evolve into higher-priced, higher-service operations, eventually becoming like the conventional retailers they replaced.

Growth of Nonstore Retailing Although most retailing still takes place the old-fashioned way across countertops in stores, consumers now have an array of alternatives, including mail order, television, phone, and online shopping (see Marketing at Work 12-3). "Some Americans never face a single crowd at holiday time; they do all of their gift shopping via phone or computer. A few may never even talk to a human being; they can punch in their order and credit card numbers on a Web site and have gifts delivered to recipients. This might remove some of the personal touch from the process, but it sure saves time."[16] Although such advances may threaten some traditional retailers, they offer exciting opportunities for others. Most store retailers are now actively developing direct retailing channels. In fact, more nonstore retailing is conducted by "click-and-brick" retailers than by "click-only" retailers. For example, office-supply retailer Office Depot is now the world's biggest online retailer after Amazon.com.[17]

Marketing at Work 12.3

E-Tailing: Still Alive, Well, and Growing

Most of us still make most of our purchases the old-fashioned way: We go to the store, find what we want, wait patiently in line to plunk down our cash or credit card, and bring home the goods. However, a growing number of retailers now provide an attractive alternative—one that lets us browse, select, order, and pay with little more effort than it takes to apply an index finger to a mouse button. They sell a rich variety of goods ranging from books, CDs, flowers, and food to stereo equipment, kitchen appliances, airplane tickets, auto parts, home mortgages, and bags of cement.

Only a few years ago, prospects for online retailing were soaring. Many experts predicted that—as more and more consumers flocked to the Web—a new breed of fast-moving e-tailers would quickly surpass stodgy "old economy" store retailers. Some even saw a day when we'd be doing almost all of our shopping via the Internet. However, the dot-com meltdown of 2000 dashed these overblown expectations, as many once-brash Web sellers such as eToys.com, Pets.com, Webvan.com, and Garden.com crashed and burned. In fact, after the shakeout of 2000, expectations reversed almost overnight. The experts now began to predict that no Web-only retailer could survive and that e-tailing was destined to be little more than a tag-on to in-store retailing.

Such doom-and-gloom scenarios, however, don't reflect the current state of Internet retailing. Although the pace has slowed and the playing ground is shifting, today's e-tailing is alive, well, and growing. Projected online retail sales of $34 billion in 2001 are expected to grow to $130 billion by 2006. "The bubble may have burst, but this hasn't stopped

millions of people from shopping online," says Toys 'R' Us executive Ray Arthur. Bill Bass of Landsend.com

often fields the same question from reporters, "How are you surviving the bloodbath?" He often retorts,

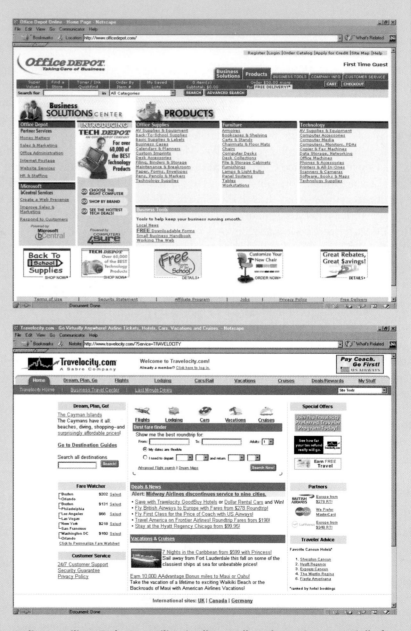

Online retailing: Today's e-tailing is alive, well, and growing, especially for click-and-brick competitors such as Office Depot. Last year, the company's Internet sales grew 143 percent, accounting for 14 percent of overall sales. Business is also booming for click-only e-tailers such as Travelocity.

"What bloodbath?" Sales on the Lands' End Web site have more than doubled during the past two years and now bring in 16 percent of the company's revenues.

Although the dramatic dot-com collapses have grabbed most of the headlines, some click-only retailers are now making it big on the Web. Heading this group is online auction site eBay, which has been consistently profitable since its inception—click-only competitors such as eBay and Amazon.com Auctions account for a lion's share of the online auctions business. Pure-play e-tailers account for a majority of online sales in several other categories as well, including books, music and video, foods and beverages, and collectibles. Business is also booming for online travel companies such as Travelocity.com and Expedia, which use the Web to sell airline tickets, hotel rooms, and discount travel packages to consumers. Thanks to these sites, online travel bookings grew 59 percent this year. In many ways, selling air travel on the Internet is a natural. Most air travel sold online uses e-tickets and e-confirmations, so no products need to be stored or shipped. "There are a bunch of businesses that don't make sense on the Internet," says a Wall Street analyst. "Travel is the quintessential one that does."

Still, much of the anticipated growth in online sales will go to multichannel retailers—the click-and-brick marketers who can successfully merge the virtual and physical worlds. Toys 'R' Us's Ray Arthur points out that Toysrus .com's initial online competitors,

click-only operations such as eToys.com and Toysmart.com, have now shuttered their cyberdoors. In their place is a new lineup of click-and-brick competitors such as Walmart.com, Kbkids.com, and Kmart's BlueLight.com. In other categories as well, the true winners these days appear to be established brick-and-mortar companies that have added Web selling. It seems that almost every established retailer is now hanging out a shingle in Webland. Examples include Charles Schwab and Fidelity Investments (financial services), Dell and IBM (computers), Lands' End and L.L. Bean (apparel), and Staples and Office Depot (office supplies), to name just a few.

Consider retailer Office Depot's burgeoning Web business:

Since the early 1990s, Bank of America executives have been letting employees order supplies from their desktop computers, but they were using an old-fashioned system that was expensive and difficult to operate. The bankers knew that there had to be a better way, but they couldn't figure it out on their own. That's when Monica Luechtefeld, Office Depot's chief of e-commerce, came calling. She explained how the office-supply retailer could easily plug its online store into Bank of America's internal network. Bank of America would be able to set it up to recognize who had clearance to buy an executive chair or a box of pencils. And Luechtefeld offered rebates for online purchases. It was a winning pitch. Today, Bank of America orders 85 percent of its supplies

online through Office Depot and is saving millions of dollars a year.

Now, 40 percent of Office Depot's major customers are using the online network to buy everything from paper clips to cherry conference-room tables. Office Depot's online unit booked $982 million in sales last year—nearly double that of the nearest competitor, Staples. That makes Office Depot the biggest online retailer after Amazon.com. Better yet, unlike Amazon, Office Depot says its online unit is profitable. . . . Last year, the company's Internet sales grew 143 percent, compared with a 12 percent increase in overall revenue. This year, the company expects its online sales to contribute 14 percent of overall sales. How has Office Depot succeeded online where so many dot-coms have failed? "Office Depot gets it," says an e-commerce consultant. "It used the Net to build deeper relationships with customers."

So, despite some serious setbacks and uncertainties, online retailing is anything but dead. Says one analyst about the recent successes of Travelocity.com and Expedia: "None of this guarantees that online travel won't crash someday like the rest of the dot-coms. But as the market takes off, these skies are looking downright friendly."

Sources: Based on information found in Dennis K. Berman and Heather Green, "Cliff-Hanger Christmas," *Business Week,* October 23, 2000, pp. EB30–EB38; Molly Prior, "E-Commerce Alive and Well in the New Economy," *Dsn Retailing Today,* June 4, 2001, p. 10; Wendy Zellner, "Where the Net Delivers: Travel," *Business Week,* June 11, 2001, pp. 142–144; Lewis Braham, "E-Tailers Are Clicking," *Business Week,* July 23, 2001, p. 73; and Charles Haddad, "Office Depot's E-Diva," *Business Week,* August 6, 2001, pp. EB22–EB24.

Increasing Intertype Competition   Today's retailers increasingly face competition from many different forms of retailers. For example, consumers can buy CDs at specialty music stores, discount music stores, electronics superstores, general merchandise discount stores, video-rental outlets, and through dozens of Web sites. They can buy books at stores ranging from independent local bookstores to discount stores such as Wal-Mart, superstores such as Barnes & Noble or Borders, or Web sites such as

Amazon.com. And when it comes to brand name appliances, department stores, discount stores, off-price retailers, or electronics superstores all compete for the same customers. Suggests one industry expert, "What we're seeing is cross-shopping—consumers buying one item at Neiman Marcus and another at Wal-Mart or General Dollar."[18]

The competition between chain superstores and smaller, independently owned stores has become particularly heated. Because of their bulk buying power and high sales volume, chains can buy at lower costs and thrive on smaller margins. The arrival of a superstore can quickly force nearby independents out of business. For example, the decision by electronics superstore Best Buy to sell CDs as loss leaders at rock-bottom prices pushed a number of specialty record store chains into bankruptcy. And Wal-Mart has been accused of destroying independents in countless small towns around the country. Yet the news is not all bad for smaller companies. Many small, independent retailers are thriving. Independents are finding that sheer size and marketing muscle are often no match for the personal touch small stores can provide or the specialty niches that small stores fill for a devoted customer base.

The Rise of Megaretailers The rise of huge mass merchandisers and specialty superstores, the formation of vertical marketing systems and buying alliances, and a rash of retail mergers and acquisitions have created a core of superpower megaretailers. Through their superior information systems and buying power, these giant retailers are able to offer better merchandise selections, good service, and strong price savings to consumers. As a result, they grow even larger by squeezing out their smaller, weaker competitors. The megaretailers also are shifting the balance of power between retailers and producers. A relative handful of retailers now controls access to enormous numbers of consumers, giving them the upper hand in their dealings with manufacturers. For example, in the United States, Wal-Mart's revenues are more than five times those of Procter & Gamble, and Wal-Mart generates more than 20 percent of P&G's revenues. Wal-Mart can, and often does, use this power to wring concessions from P&G and other suppliers.[19]

Growing Importance of Retail Technology Retail technologies are becoming critically important as competitive tools. Progressive retailers are using computers to produce better forecasts, control inventory costs, order electronically from suppliers, send e-mail between stores, and even sell to customers within stores. They are adopting checkout scanning systems, online transaction processing, electronic funds transfer, electronic data interchange, in-store television, and improved merchandise-handling systems.

Perhaps the most startling advances in retailing technology concern the ways in which today's retailers are connecting with customers:

> In the past, life was simple. Retailers connected with their customers through stores, through their salespeople, through the brands and packages they sold, and through direct mail and advertising in the mass media. But today, life is more complex. There are dozens of new ways to attract and engage consumers. . . . Indeed, even if one omits the obvious—the Web—retailers are still surrounded by technical innovations that promise to redefine the way they and manufacturers interact with customers. Consider, as just a sampling, touch screen kiosks, electronic shelf labels and signs, handheld shopping assistants, smart cards, self-scanning systems, virtual reality displays, and intelligent agents. So, if we ask the question, Will technology change the way [retailers] interface with customers in the future? the answer has got to be yes.[20]

Global Expansion of Major Retailers Retailers with unique formats and strong brand positioning are increasingly moving into other countries. Many are expanding internationally to escape mature and saturated home markets. Over the years, several giant U.S. retailers—McDonald's, Gap, Toys 'R' Us—have become globally prominent as a result of their great marketing prowess. Others, such as Wal-Mart and Kmart, are rapidly establishing a global presence. Wal-Mart, which now operates more than 1,000 stores in 9 countries abroad, sees exciting global potential. Its international division racked up fiscal 2001 sales of more than $32 billion, an increase of 41 percent over the previous year. Here's what happened when it opened two new stores in Shenzhen, China:[21]

> [Customers came] by the hundreds of thousands—up to 175,000 on Saturdays alone—to China's first Wal-Mart Supercenter and Sam's Club. They broke the display glass to snatch out chickens at one store and carted off all the big-screen TVs before the other store had been open an hour. The two outlets . . . were packed on Day One and have been bustling ever since.

However, U.S retailers are still significantly behind Europe and Asia when it comes to global expansion. Only 18 percent of the top U.S. retailers operate globally, compared to 40 percent of European retailers and 31 percent of Asian retailers. Among foreign retailers that have gone global are Britain's Marks and Spencer, Italy's Benetton, France's Carrefour hypermarkets, Sweden's IKEA home furnishings stores, and Japan's Yaohan supermarkets.[22]

Marks and Spencer, which started out as a penny bazaar in 1884, grew into a chain of variety stores over the decades and now has a thriving string of 150 franchised stores around the world, which sell mainly its private-label clothes, including Brooks Brothers. It also runs a major food business. IKEA's well-constructed but fairly inexpensive furniture has proven very popular in the United States, where shoppers often spend an entire day in an IKEA store. And Carrefour, the world's second largest retailer after Wal-Mart, has embarked on an aggressive mission to extend its role as a leading international retailer:

> Nowhere has that been more obvious than in its own backyards of France and Europe, where Carrefour operates 680 hypermarkets, 2,260 supermarkets, and 3,120 deep discount food stores. By purchasing or merging with a variety of retailers, Carrefour has accelerated its hold over the European market, where it now claims retail dominance in four leading markets: France, Spain, Belgium and Greece; it's the No. 2 retailer in Italy. But one of the retailer's greatest strengths is its market position outside of France and Europe. In South America, for instance, Carrefour is the market leader in Brazil and Argentina, where it operates more than 300 stores. By comparison, Wal-Mart has only 25 units in those two countries. In China, the land of more than a billion consumers, Carrefour operates 22 hypermarkets to Wal-Mart's five supercenters and one Sam's Club. In the Pacific rim, excluding China, Carrefour operates 33 hypermarkets in five countries to Wal-Mart's five units in South Korea alone. Carrefour is also on track to beat the competition into the Japanese market, the world's second largest nation in terms of consumption. In the all-important emerging markets of China, South America, and the Pacific rim, Carrefour outpaces Wal-Mart five-to-one in actual revenue. In short, Carrefour is bounding ahead of Wal-Mart in most markets outside North America. The only question: Can the French titan hold its lead? While no one retailer can rightly claim to be in the same league with Wal-Mart as an overall retail presence, Carrefour stands a better chance than most to dominate global retailing.[23]

Retailer communities: Sony's Playstation.com Web site builds community among its customers. The site's message boards are incredibly active, discussing techie topics but also lifestyle issues, such as music and personal taste.

Retail Stores as "Communities" or "Hangouts"   With the rise in the number of people living alone, working at home, or living in isolated and sprawling suburbs, there has been a resurgence of establishments that, regardless of the product or service they offer, also provide a place for people to get together. These places include cafes, tea shops, juice bars, bookshops, superstores, children's play spaces, brew pubs, and urban greenmarkets. Brew pubs such as New York's Zip City Brewing and Seattle's Trolleyman Pub (run by Red Hook Brewery) offer tastings and a place to pass the time. The Discovery Zone, a chain of children's play spaces, offers indoor spaces where kids can go wild without breaking anything and stressed-out parents can exchange stories. And today's bookstores have become part bookstore, part library, and part living room.

> Welcome to today's bookstore. The one featuring not only shelves and cash registers but also cushy chairs and coffee bars. It's where backpack-toting high school students come to do homework, where retirees thumb through the gardening books and parents read aloud to their toddlers. If no one actually buys books, that's just fine, say bookstore owners and managers. They're offering something grander than ink and paper, anyway. They're selling comfort, relaxation, community.[24]

Brick-and-mortar retailers are not the only ones creating community. Others have also built virtual communities on the Internet.

> Sony actively builds community among its Playstation customers. Its recent Playstation.com campaign created message boards where its game players could post messages to one another. The boards are incredibly active, discussing techie topics but also providing the opportunity for members, fiercely competitive and opinionated, to vote on lifestyle issues, such as music and personal taste, no matter how trivial. Although Sony is laissez-faire about the boards and does not feed them messages, the company sees the value in having its customers' adamant conversations occur directly on its site. "Our customers are our evangelists. They are a very vocal and loyal fan base," says a Sony spokesperson. "There are things we can learn from them."[25]

Linking the Concepts

Time out! So-called experts have long predicted that nonstore retailing eventually will replace store retailing as our primary way to shop. What do you think?

◆ Shop for a good book at the Barnes & Noble Web site (www.bn.com), taking time to browse the site and see what it has to offer. Next, shop at a nearby Barnes & Noble, Borders Books, or other book store. Compare the two shopping experiences. Where would you rather shop? On what occasions? Why?

◆ A Barnes & Noble store creates an ideal "community" where people can "hang out." How does its Web site compare on this dimension?

Wholesaling

Wholesaling includes all activities involved in selling goods and services to those buying for resale or business use. We call **wholesalers** those firms engaged *primarily* in wholesaling activity.

Wholesalers buy mostly from producers and sell mostly to retailers, industrial consumers, and other wholesalers. But why are wholesalers used at all? For example, why would a producer use wholesalers rather than selling directly to retailers or consumers? Quite simply, wholesalers are often better at performing one or more of the following channel functions:

◆ *Selling and promoting:* Wholesalers' sales forces help manufacturers reach many small customers at a low cost. The wholesaler has more contacts and is often more trusted by the buyer than the distant manufacturer.
◆ *Buying and assortment building:* Wholesalers can select items and build assortments needed by their customers, thereby saving the consumers much work.
◆ *Bulk breaking:* Wholesalers save their customers money by buying in carload lots and breaking bulk (breaking large lots into small quantities).
◆ *Warehousing:* Wholesalers hold inventories, thereby reducing the inventory costs and risks of suppliers and customers.
◆ *Transportation:* Wholesalers can provide quicker delivery to buyers because they are closer than the producers.
◆ *Financing:* Wholesalers finance their customers by giving credit, and they finance their suppliers by ordering early and paying bills on time.
◆ *Risk bearing:* Wholesalers absorb risk by taking title and bearing the cost of theft, damage, spoilage, and obsolescence.
◆ *Market information:* Wholesalers give information to suppliers and customers about competitors, new products, and price developments.
◆ *Management services and advice:* Wholesalers often help retailers train their salesclerks, improve store layouts and displays, and set up accounting and inventory control systems.

Types of Wholesalers

Wholesalers fall into three major groups (see Table 12-3): *merchant wholesalers, agents and brokers,* and *manufacturers' sales branches and offices.* **Merchant wholesalers** are the largest single group of wholesalers, accounting for roughly 50 percent of all

Wholesaling
All activities involved in selling goods and services to those buying for resale or business use.

Wholesaler
A firm engaged *primarily* in wholesaling activity.

Merchant wholesaler
An independently owned business that takes title to the merchandise it handles.

Table 12-3 Major Types of Wholesalers

Type	Description
Merchant wholesalers	Independently owned businesses that take title to the merchandise they handle. In different trades they are called *jobbers,* distributors *or mill supply houses.* Include full-service wholesalers and limited-service wholesalers:
Full-service wholesalers	Provide a full line of services: carrying stock, maintaining a sales force, offering credit, making deliveries and providing management assistance. There are two types:
Wholesale merchants	Sell primarily to retailers and provide a full range of services *General merchandise wholesalers* carry several merchandise lines, whereas *general line wholesalers* carry one or two lines in great depth. *Specialty wholesalers* specialize in carrying only part of a line. Examples: health food wholesalers, seafood wholesalers.
Industrial distributors	Sell to manufacturers rather than to retailers. Provide several services, such as carrying stock, offering credit, and providing delivery. May carry a broad range of merchandise, a general line, or a specialty line.
Limited-service wholesalers	Offer fewer services than full-service wholesalers. Limited-service wholesalers are of several types:
Cash-and-carry wholesalers	Carry a limited line of fast-moving goods and sell to small retailers for cash. Normally do not deliver. Example: A small fish store retailer may drive to a cash-and-carry fish wholesaler, buy fish for cash, and bring the merchandise back to the store.
Truck wholesalers (or truck jobbers)	Perform primarily a selling and delivery function. Carry limited line of semiperishable merchandise (such as milk, bread, snack foods), which they sell for cash as they make their rounds to supermarkets, small groceries, hospitals, restaurants, factory cafeterias, and hotels.
Drop shippers	Do not carry inventory or handle the product. On receiving an order, they select a manufacturer, who ships the merchandise directly to the customer. The drop shipper assumes title and risk from the time the order is accepted to its delivery to the customer. They operate in bulk industries, such as coal, lumber, and heavy equipment.
Rack jobbers	Serve grocery and drug retailers, mostly in nonfood items. They send delivery trucks to stores, where the delivery people set up toys, paperbacks, hardware items, health and beauty aids, or other items. They price the goods, keep them fresh, set up point-of-purchase displays, and keep inventory records. Rack jobbers retain title to the goods and bill the retailers only for the goods sold to consumers.
Producers' cooperatives	Owned by farmer members and assemble farm produce to sell in local markets. The co-op's profits are distributed to members at the end of the year. They often attempt to improve product quality and promote a co-op brand name, such as Sun Maid raisins, Sunkist oranges, or Diamond walnuts.
Mail-order wholesalers	Send catalogs to retail, industrial, and institutional customers featuring jewelry, cosmetics, specialty foods, and other small items. Maintain no outside sales force. Main customers are businesses in small outlying areas. Orders are filled and sent by mail, truck, or other transportation.
Brokers and agents	Do not take title to goods. Main function is to facilitate buying and selling, for which they earn a commission on the selling price. Generally specialize by product line or customer types.
Brokers	Chief function is bringing buyers and sellers together and assisting in negotiation. They are paid by the party who hired them and do not carry inventory,

Table 12-3 (continued)	
Type	**Description**
	get involved in financing, or assume risk. Examples: food brokers, real estate brokers, insurance brokers, and security brokers.
Agents	Represent either buyers or sellers on a more permanent basis than brokers do. There are several types:
Manufacturers' agents	Represent two or more manufacturers of complementary lines. A formal written agreement with each manufacturer covers pricing, territories, order-handling, delivery service and warranties, and commission rates. Often used in such lines as apparel, furniture and electrical goods. Most manufacturers' agents are small businesses, with only a few skilled salespeople as employees. They are hired by small manufacturers who cannot afford their own field sales forces and by large manufacturers who use agents to open new territories or to cover territories that cannot support full-time salespeople.
Selling agents	Have contractual authority to sell a manufacturer's entire output. The manufacturer either is not interested in the selling function or feels unqualified. The selling agent serves as a sales department and has significant influence over prices, terms, and conditions of sale. Found in product areas such as textiles, industrial machinery and equipment, coal and coke, chemicals, and metals.
Purchasing agents	Generally have a long-term relationship with buyers and make purchases for them, often receiving, inspecting, warehousing, and shipping the merchandise to the buyers. They provide helpful market information to clients and help them obtain the best goods and prices available.
Commission merchants	Take physical possession of products and negotiate sales. Normally, they are not employed on a long-term basis. Used most often in agricultural marketing by farmers who do not want to sell their own output and do not belong to producers' cooperatives. The commission merchant takes a truckload of commodities to a central market, sells it for the best price, deducts a commission and expenses, and remits the balance to the producers.
Manufacturers' and retailers' branches and offices	Wholesaling operations conducted by sellers or buyers themselves rather than through independent wholesalers. Separate branches and offices can be dedicated to either sales or purchasing.
Sales branches and offices	Set up by manufacturers to improve inventory control, selling, and promotion. *Sales branches* carry inventory and are found in industries such as lumber and automotive equipment and parts. *Sales offices* do not carry inventory and are most prominent in dry-goods and notions industries.
Purchasing offices	Perform a role similar to that of brokers or agents but are part of the buyer's organization. Many retailers set up purchasing offices in major market centers such as New York and Chicago.

wholesaling. Merchant wholesalers include two broad types: full-service wholesalers and limited-service wholesalers. *Full-service wholesalers* provide a full set of services, whereas the various *limited-service wholesalers* offer fewer services to their suppliers and customers. The several different types of limited-service wholesalers perform varied specialized functions in the distribution channel.

Brokers and *agents* differ from merchant wholesalers in two ways: They do not take title to goods, and they perform only a few functions. Like merchant wholesalers, they generally specialize by product line or customer type. A **broker** brings buyers and sellers

Broker
A wholesaler who does not take title to goods and whose function is to bring buyers and sellers together and assist in negotiation.

Merchant wholesalers: A typical Fleming Companies, Inc., wholesale food distribution center. The average Fleming warehouse contains 500,000 square feet of floor space (with a 30-foot-high ceiling), carries 16,000 different food items, and serves 150 to 200 retailers within a 500-mile radius.

Agent
A wholesaler who represents buyers or sellers on a relatively permanent basis, performs only a few functions, and does not take title to goods.

Manufacturers' sales branches and offices
Wholesaling by sellers or buyers themselves rather than through independent wholesalers.

together and assists in negotiation. **Agents** represent buyers or sellers on a more permanent basis. *Manufacturers' agents* (also called manufacturers' representatives) are the most common type of agent wholesaler. The third major type of wholesaling is that done in **manufacturers' sales branches and offices** by sellers or buyers themselves rather than through independent wholesalers.

Wholesaler Marketing Decisions

Wholesalers have experienced growing competitive pressures in recent years. They have faced new sources of competition, more demanding customers, new technologies, and more direct-buying programs on the part of large industrial, institutional, and retail buyers. As a result, they have had to improve their strategic decisions on target markets and positioning, and on the marketing mix—product assortments and services, price, promotion, and place (see Figure 12-2).

Target Market and Positioning Decision Like retailers, wholesalers must define their target markets and position themselves effectively—they cannot serve everyone. They can choose a target group by size of customer (only large retailers), type of customer (convenience stores only), need for service (customers who need credit), or other factors. Within the target group, they can identify the more profitable customers, design stronger offers, and build better relationships with them. They can propose automatic reordering systems, set up management-training and advising systems, or even sponsor a voluntary chain. They can discourage less profitable customers by requiring larger orders or adding service charges to smaller ones.

Marketing Mix Decisions Like retailers, wholesalers must decide on product assortment and services, prices, promotion, and place. The wholesaler's "product" is the assortment of *products and services* that it offers. Wholesalers are under great pressure to carry a full line and to stock enough for immediate delivery. But this practice can

Figure 12-2
Wholesaler marketing
decisions

damage profits. Wholesalers today are cutting down on the number of lines they carry, choosing to carry only the more profitable ones. Wholesalers are also rethinking which services count most in building strong customer relationships and which should be dropped or charged for. The key is to find the mix of services most valued by their target customers.

Price is also an important wholesaler decision. Wholesalers usually mark up the cost of goods by a standard percentage—say, 20 percent. Expenses may run 17 percent of the gross margin, leaving a profit margin of 3 percent. In grocery wholesaling, the average profit margin is often less than 2 percent. Wholesalers are trying new pricing approaches. They may cut their margin on some lines in order to win important new customers. They may ask suppliers for special price breaks when they can turn them into an increase in the supplier's sales.

Although *promotion* can be critical to wholesaler success, most wholesalers are not promotion minded. Their use of trade advertising, sales promotion, personal selling, and public relations is largely scattered and unplanned. Many are behind the times in personal selling—they still see selling as a single salesperson talking to a single customer instead of as a team effort to sell, build, and service major accounts. Wholesalers also need to adopt some of the nonpersonal promotion techniques used by retailers. They need to develop an overall promotion strategy and to make greater use of supplier promotion materials and programs.

Finally, *place* is important—wholesalers must choose their locations and facilities carefully. Wholesalers typically locate in low-rent, low-tax areas and tend to invest little money in their buildings, equipment, and systems. As a result, their materials-handling and order-processing systems are often outdated. In recent years, however, large and progressive wholesalers are reacting to rising costs by investing in automated warehouses and online ordering systems. Orders are fed from the retailer's system directly into the wholesaler's computer, and the items are picked up by mechanical devices and automatically taken to a shipping platform where they are assembled. Most large wholesalers use computers to carry out accounting, billing, inventory control, and forecasting. Modern wholesalers are adapting their services to the needs of target customers and finding cost-reducing methods of doing business.

Trends in Wholesaling

As the thriving wholesaling industry moves into the twenty-first century, it faces considerable challenges. The industry remains vulnerable to one of the most enduring trends of the last decade—fierce resistance to price increases and the winnowing out of suppliers based on cost and quality. Progressive wholesalers constantly watch for better ways to meet the changing needs of their suppliers and target customers. They recognize that, in the long run, their only reason for existence comes from adding value by increasing the efficiency

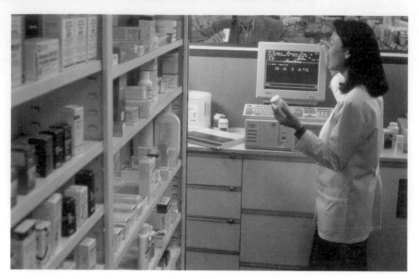

To improve efficiency and service, McKesson set up an extensive online supply management system by which customers can order, track, and manage their pharmaceutical and medical-surgical supplies. Retailers can even use the McKesson system to maintain medical profiles on their customers.

and effectiveness of the entire marketing channel. To achieve this goal, they must constantly improve their services and reduce their costs.

McKesson HBOC, the nation's leading wholesaler of pharmaceuticals, health and beauty care, and home health care products, provides an example of progressive wholesaling. To survive, McKesson HBOC has to remain more cost effective than manufacturers' sales branches. Thus, the company has built efficient automated warehouses, established direct computer links with drug manufacturers, designed a computerized accounts-receivable program for pharmacists, and set up an extensive online supply management system by which customers can order, track, and manage their pharmaceutical and medical-surgical supplies. Retailers can even use the McKesson system to maintain medical profiles on their customers. According to McKesson, it adds value in the channel by "delivering unique supply and information management solutions that reduce costs and improve quality for its health care customers."[26]

The distinction between large retailers and large wholesalers continues to blur. Many retailers now operate formats such as wholesale clubs and hypermarkets that perform many wholesale functions. In return, many large wholesalers are setting up their own retailing operations. SuperValu and Fleming, both leading food wholesalers, now operate their own retailing operations. For example, SuperValu, the nation's largest food wholesaling company, is also the country's tenth largest food retailer. Almost 40 percent of the company's $20 billion in sales comes from its Bigg's, Cub Foods, Farm Fresh, Hornbacher's, Laneco, Metro, Scott's Foods, Save-A-Lot, Shop 'n Save, and Shoppers Food Warehouse stores.[27]

Wholesalers will continue to increase the services they provide to retailers—retail pricing, cooperative advertising, marketing and management information reports, accounting services, online transactions, and others. Rising costs on the one hand, and the demand for increased services on the other, will put the squeeze on wholesaler profits. Wholesalers who do not find efficient ways to deliver value to their customers will soon drop by the wayside. However, the increased use of computerized, automated, and Web-based systems will help wholesalers to contain the costs of ordering, shipping, and inventory holding, boosting their productivity.

Finally, facing slow growth in their domestic markets and such developments as the North American Free Trade Agreement, many large wholesalers are now going global. For example, in 1991, McKesson bought out its Canadian partner, Provigo. The company now receives about 3 percent of its total revenues from Canada.

STOP   *Rest Stop: Reviewing the Concepts*

Pull in here and reflect back on this retailing and wholesaling chapter, the last of two chapters on distribution channels. In this chapter, we first looked at the nature and importance of retailing, major types of retailers, the decisions retailers make, and the future of retailing. We then examined these same topics for wholesalers. Although most retailing is conducted in retail stores, in recent years, nonstore retailing has increased rapidly. In addition, although many retail stores are independently owned, an increasing number are now banding together under some form of corporate or contractual organization. Wholesalers, too, have experienced recent environmental changes, most notably mounting competitive pressures. They have faced new sources of competition, more demanding customers, new technologies, and more direct-buying programs on the part of large industrial, institutional, and retail buyers.

1. Explain the roles of retailers and wholesalers in the distribution channel.

Retailing and wholesaling consist of many organizations bringing goods and services from the point of production to the point of use. *Retailing* includes all activities involved in selling goods or services directly to final consumers for their personal, nonbusiness use. *Wholesaling* includes all the activities involved in selling goods or services to those who are buying for the purpose of resale or for business use. Wholesalers perform many functions, including selling and promoting, buying and assortment building, bulk breaking, warehousing, transporting, financing, risk bearing, supplying market information, and providing management services and advice.

2. Describe the major types of retailers and give examples of each.

Retailers can be classified as *store retailers* and *nonstore retailers*. Although most goods and services are sold through stores, nonstore retailing has been growing much faster than has store retailing. Store retailers can be further classified by the *amount of service* they provide (self-service, limited service, or full service), *product line sold* (specialty stores, department stores, supermarkets, convenience stores, superstores, and service businesses), and *relative prices* (discount stores and off-price retailers). Today, many retailers are banding together in corporate and contractual *retail organizations* (corporate chains, voluntary chains and retailer cooperatives, franchise organizations, and merchandising conglomerates).

3. Identify the major types of wholesalers and give examples of each.

Wholesalers fall into three groups. First, *merchant wholesalers* take possession of the goods. They include *full-service wholesalers* (wholesale merchants, industrial distributors) and *limited-service wholesalers* (cash-and-carry wholesalers, truck wholesalers, drop shippers, rack jobbers, producers' cooperatives, and mail-order wholesalers). Second, *brokers* and *agents* do not take possession of the goods but are paid a commission for aiding buying and selling. Finally, *manufacturers' sales branches and offices* are wholesaling operations conducted by nonwholesalers to bypass the wholesalers.

4. Explain the marketing decisions facing retailers and wholesalers.

Each retailer must make decisions about its target markets and positioning, product assortment and services, price, promotion, and place. Retailers need to choose target markets carefully and position themselves strongly. Today, wholesaling is holding its own in the economy. Progressive wholesalers are adapting their services to the needs of target customers and are seeking cost-reducing methods of doing business. Faced with slow growth in their domestic markets and developments such as the North American Free Trade Agreement, many large wholesalers are also now going global.

Navigating the Key Terms

For a detailed analysis of the meaning and importance of each of the following key terms, visit our Web page at **www.prenhall.com/kotler**.

Agent
Broker
Category killer
Chain stores

Convenience store
Department store
Discount store
Factory outlets

Franchise
Independent off-price retailer
Manufacturers' sales branches
  and offices
Merchant wholesaler
Off-price retailer

Retailers
Retailing
Shopping center
Specialty store
Supermarket
Superstore

Warehouse club
Wheel of retailing concept
Wholesaling
Wholesaler

 Travel Log

The following concept checks and discussion questions will help you to keep track of and apply the concepts you've studied in this chapter.

Concept Checks

Fill in the blanks, then look for the correct answers.

1. _____ includes all the activities involved in selling goods or services directly to final consumers for their personal, nonbusiness use.

2. Retailers can be classified by the length and breadth of their product assortments. _____ stores carry narrow product lines with deep assortments within those lines.

3. Recent years have seen the explosive growth of superstores that are actually giant specialty stores called _____. They feature stores the size of airplane hangars that carry a very deep assortment of a particular line with a knowledgeable staff.

4. The major types of retail organizations include corporate chains, _____ chains and _____ cooperatives, _____, and _____.

5. When establishing themselves, retailers must decide on three major product variables:_____, _____, and _____.

6. Retailers often cite three critical factors in retailing success: _____, _____, and _____!

7. According to the _____ concept, many new types of retailing forms begin as low-margin, low-price, low-status operations.

8. With the rise in the number of people _____, _____, or living in isolated and sprawling suburbs, there has been a resurgence of retail establishments that provide a place for people to get together.

9. _____ includes all activities involved in selling goods and services to those buying for resale or business use.

10. Typical functions performed by wholesalers include: (a) Selling and promoting, (b) _____, (c) _____, (d) _____, (e) _____, (f) _____, (g) Risk bearing, (h) Market information, and (i) Management services and advice.

11. _____ wholesalers are the largest single group of wholesalers, accounting for roughly 50 percent of all wholesaling.

12. According to Table 12-3, _____ wholesalers carry a limited line of semiperishable merchandise (such as milk or bread), which they sell for cash to customers (such as grocery stores).

Concept Checks Answers: 1. Retailing; 2. Specialty; 3. category killers; 4. voluntary (chains) and retailer (cooperatives), franchise organizations, merchandising conglomerates; 5. product assortment, services mix, store atmosphere; 6. location, location, location; 7. wheel of retailing; 8. living alone, working at home; 9. Wholesaling; 10. buying and assortment building, bulk breaking, warehousing, transportation, financing; 11. Merchant; 12. truck (or truck jobbers);

Discussing the Issues

1. Giant superstores called category killers are an emerging trend. Answer the following questions: (a) How is a category killer different from other types of retailers? (b) Why has this form of retailing grown so rapidly? (c) What types of retailers are most threatened by category killers? Why? (d) How will online retailing affect category killers? Give an example of a category killer that has been affected by online marketing.

2. How has the growth of other types of large retailers affected the willingness of manufacturers to sell to off-price retailers at or below regular wholesale rates? What policy should Sony set for selling the following products to off-price retailers: (a) HDTV

televisions, (b) big screen televisions, (c) regular televisions, (d) Walkman cassette players. Explain.

3. Compare the basic marketing decisions made by retailers and wholesalers to those made by manufacturers. Give examples that show the similarities and differences in marketing decisions made by these groups.

4. Use the "wheel of retailing" concept to assess the emergence and evolution of outlet malls. What do you predict will be the future of outlet malls? Explain.

5. List and describe each of the channel functions that have been traditionally assigned to wholesalers. How will wholesalers have to change to meet the threat of increasing competition from large retailers? What type of wholesaler seems best equipped to meet competition and change in the next decade? Explain.

Mastering Marketing

Examine the retailing and wholesaling relationships available to CanGo. Which of these seem strong? Which seem weak? Which need to be changed? What would you recommend to improve the company's retailing and wholesaling arrangements? What is the greatest distribution challenge that the company will face in the next few years? How would you solve this challenge? Explain.

Traveling the Net

Point of Interest: Wal-Mart, King of Cybermarketing?

When Wal-Mart flexes its cybermuscles, everyone pays attention. Wal-Mart, after several years of careful study, has jumped into cyberspace in a big way. It has a new beefed-up Web site that is selling everything from toothpaste to apparel to consumer electronics. Long-range plans call for Wal-Mart's Web site to rival its brick-and-mortar stores. Through the cyberspace medium, everyone will have access to Wal-Mart and its thousands of products. These moves have caught the attention of other Web merchants such as Amazon.com. In fact, Wal-Mart and Amazon.com have explored partnering on the Web. Wal-Mart would handle purchasing and inventory; Amazon.com would maintain the Web site, fill orders, and manage customer service. Whatever approach it uses, Wal-Mart believes that customers have spoken, and they're saying, "Move to the Web." When the customer speaks, Wal-Mart listens.

For Discussion

1. Compare Wal-Mart's Web site (www.walmart.com) to those of competitors Kmart (www.kmart.com) and Target (www.targetstores.com). What are the strengths and weaknesses of each of the three sites?

2. What are the similarities and differences between the Amazon.com (www.amazon.com) and the Wal-Mart sites? Which seems to have the advantage in cybermarketing? Explain.

3. Are the markets for Wal-Mart's brick-and-mortar stores different from those of its cyberstore? How?

4. Would a Web partnership with Amazon.com be good for Wal-Mart? For Amazon.com?

5. What other opportunities do you see for Wal-Mart on the Web? What difficulties?

Application Thinking

Using the information found in Marketing at Work 12-2 and 12-3, construct a cybermarketing policy and strategy statement for Wal-Mart. Your statement should contain strengths and weaknesses, competitive challenges, cyber and marketing opportunities, and a prediction of success. How would your statement help Wal-Mart expand globally? What new partnerships might be in the organization's best interest? How can Wal-Mart's distribution expertise help its cyber effort? What do you foresee in the cyber future for this retailing giant?

MAP—Marketing Applications

MAP Stop 12

If people had told you a few years ago that you would willingly stand in line to pay $2 for a cup of coffee, you would have thought they were nuts. Not so any more. Consumers do it every day at the coffee counters of some 2,000 Starbucks locations across the country. Daily espresso has become an expensive must for millions of Americans. However, as with all retailing trends, success may be fleeting without constant change. Starbucks' success has drawn an explosion of competitors from "look-a-likes," to grocery stores (and their sophisticated coffee aisles), to ice cream distributors, and even restaurants. Starbucks is at a crossroads. How can it maintain its phenomenal 40 percent earnings growth rate? The company has decided on expansion as the best course of action. Current expansion strategies include new product development (juices, teas, and frozen drinks), expansion of past new product stars (Frappuccino—a cold-blended drink), joint ventures (partnering with PepsiCo for bottling Frappuccino and with Dreyers Grand Ice Cream to package coffee ice cream). Also in the works are expansions in traditional retail endeavors (such as more stores and more partnerships with retail giants such as Barnes & Noble) and moves into untested waters (opening several Cafe Starbucks and expansion into international markets).

Thinking Like a Marketing Manager

1. Assess Starbucks' retail strategy so far. Why has it been so successful? What appear to be its major strengths and weaknesses? (See www.starbucks.com for additional information.)

2. How dependent is Starbucks' growth on direct retail sales? Do you see any potential problems with the company's aggressive expansion plans? Will cannibalization among stores and formats be a problem?

3. How might other fast-growing franchises that offer coffee products (such as Krispy Kreme Doughnuts at www.krispykreme.com) be a threat to Starbucks? How should these challenges be met?

4. Assume that you are the marketing manager for Starbucks. Design a growth strategy for this company for the next two years. Look for new growth possibilities that will avoid cannibalism among existing outlets. What partnerships, alliances, and new product alternatives seem to be "naturals" for the company? What forms of new competition do you think will emerge? How are competitors and other distribution forms likely to react to your plan? What will you do about this?

Integrated Marketing Communications: Advertising, Sales Promotion, and Public Relations

ROAD MAP:
Previewing the Concepts

We'll forge ahead now into the last of the marketing mix tools—promotion. You'll find that promotion is not a single tool but rather a mix of several tools. Ideally, under the concept of *integrated marketing communications,* the company will carefully coordinate these promotion elements to deliver a clear, consistent, and compelling message about the organization and its products. We'll begin by introducing you to the various promotion mix tools and to the importance of integrated marketing communications. Then, we'll look more carefully at three of the tools—advertising, sales promotion, and public relations. In the next chapter, we'll visit personal selling and direct marketing.

▶ After reading this chapter, you should be able to

1. discuss the process and advantages of integrated marketing communications
2. define the five promotion tools and discuss the factors that must be considered in shaping the overall promotion mix
3. describe and discuss the major decisions involved in developing an advertising program
4. explain how sales promotion campaigns are developed and implemented
5. explain how companies use public relations to communicate with their publics

First stop: American Standard. Suppose you were a brand manager at American Standard and were assigned the task of preparing a promotion campaign for the company's line of toilets. That's right, toilets (somebody has to do it!). Not an exciting prospect? As it turns out, the assignment offers some very interesting possibilities. Read on.

You probably haven't thought much about your bathroom—it's not something that most of us get all that inspired about. But as it turns out, you probably have a relationship with your bathroom unlike that with any other room in your house. It's where you start and end your day, primp and preen and admire yourself, escape from the rigors of everyday life, and do some of your best thinking. The marketers at American Standard, the plumbing fixtures giant, understand this often-overlooked but special little room. A few years back they set out upon a mission to help people design bathrooms worthy of their finest moments.

Working with its ad agency, Carmichael Lynch, American Standard created a wonderfully warm and highly effective but not-so-standard integrated marketing campaign. The campaign, called "We want you to love your bathroom," targeted men and

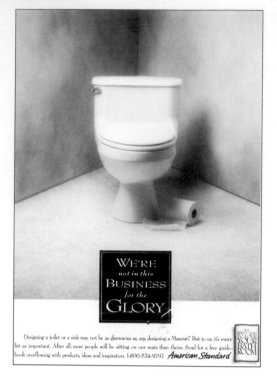

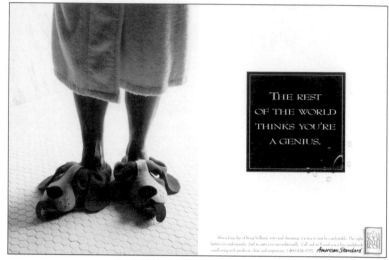

women aged 25 to 54 from households planning to remodel bathrooms or replace fixtures. The campaign employed a carefully integrated mix of brand-image and direct-response media ads, direct mailings, and personal contacts to create a customer database, generate sales leads, gently coax customers into its retail showrooms, and build sales and market share.

The campaign began with a series of humorous, soft-sell brand-image ads in home and shelter magazines such as *Home, House Beautiful,* and *Country Living,* which reach a high percentage of readers undertaking remodeling projects. Featuring simple but artistic shots of ordinary bathroom fixtures and scenes, the ads positioned American Standard as a company that understands the special relationships we have with our bathrooms. For example, one ad showed a white toilet and a partially unwound roll of toilet paper, artfully arranged in a corner against plain blue-gray walls. "We're not in this business for the glory," proclaimed the headline. "Designing a toilet or sink may not be as glamorous as, say, designing a Maserati. But to us, it's every bit as important. After all, more people will be sitting on our seats than theirs."

Another ad showed the feet of a man standing on a white tile bathroom floor wearing his goofy-looking floppy-eared-dog slippers. "The rest of the world thinks you're a genius," noted the ad. But "after a long day of being brilliant, witty, and charming, it's nice just to be comfortable. The right bathroom understands. And accepts you unconditionally." Each simple but engaging ad included a toll-free phone number and urged readers to call for a free guidebook "overflowing with products, ideas, and inspiration."

Whereas the brand-image ads positioned American Standard and its products, when it came to generating inquiries, the real workhorses were the one-third-page, couponlike direct-response ads that ran in the same magazines. One such ad noted, "You will spend seven years of your life in the bathroom. You will need a good book." Readers could obtain the free guidebook by mailing in the coupon or calling the toll-free number listed in the ad.

Consumers who responded found that they'd taken the first step in a carefully orchestrated relationship-building venture. First, they received the entertaining, highly informative, picture-filled 30-page guidebook *We Want You to Love Your Bathroom,* along with a folksy letter thanking them for their interest and noting the locations of nearby American Standard dealers. The guidebook's purpose was straightforward—"Walk into your bathroom, turn the knob and suddenly, for a moment or an hour, the world stops turning. You should love the place. If you don't, well, American Standard wants to further your relationship. Thumb through this book. In the bathroom, perhaps. . . ."

The guidebook was chock-full of helpful tips on bathroom design, starting with answers to some simple questions: What kind of lavatory—what color? The bathtub—how big; big enough for two? The toilet—sleek one-piece or familiar two-piece? The faucet? "You'll fumble for it every morning, so be particular about how it operates." To spice things up, the guidebook also contained loads of entertaining facts and trivia. An example: Did you know that "you will spend seven years in your bathroom . . . here's hoping your spouse doesn't sneak in first!" Another example: "During the Middle Ages, Christianity preached that to uncover your skin, even to bathe it, was an invitation to sin. Thank heavens for perfume. These days, we average about 4 baths or 7.5 showers a week." And, of course, the booklet contained plenty of information on American Standard products, along with a tear-out card that prospective customers could return to obtain more detailed guides and product catalogs.

In addition to the guidebook, customers received a carefully coordinated stream of communications from American Standard, starting with a series of "Bathroom Reading" bulletins, each containing information on specific bathroom design issues. For example, one issue contained information and tips on how to make a bathroom safer; another offered "10 neat ways to save water."

Meanwhile, information about prospective customers and their remodeling projects collected by the 1-800 operator or from the coupon went into American Standard's customer database. The database generated leads for salespeople at American Standard's showrooms around the country. The company marketed the program to key distributors and kitchen and bath dealers, motivating them to follow up on leads and training them how to do it effectively.

The key was to get customers who'd made inquiries to come into the showroom. Not long after making their inquiries, prospective customers typically received a handwritten postcard—or perhaps even a phone call—from a local dealer's showroom consultant, who extended a personal invitation to visit, see American Standard products firsthand, and discuss bathroom designs. Thus, the integrated direct-marketing program built relationships not just with buyers but with dealers as well.

American Standard's integrated direct-marketing campaign did wonders for the company's positioning and performance. After the campaign began, American Standard's plumbing division experienced steady increases in sales and earnings. The campaign generated tens of thousands of qualified leads for local showrooms—more than a half million qualified leads in the first two years.

Research has confirmed significant shifts in consumer perceptions of American Standard and its products—from "boring and institutional" to well designed and loaded with "personal spirit." According to Bob Srenaski, group vice president of marketing at American Standard, the campaign "totally repositioned our company and established a momentum and winning spirit that is extraordinary." Says Joe Summary, an account manager at Carmichael Lynch, "The campaign was incredible. It gave American Standard and its products a more personal face, one that's helped us to build closer relationships with customers and dealers. From the first ad to the last contact with our dealers, the campaign was designed to help customers create bathrooms they'd love."

•••

Modern marketing calls for more than just developing a good product, pricing it attractively, and making it available to target customers. Companies must also *communicate* with current and prospective customers, and what they communicate should not be left to chance.

The Marketing Communications Mix

Marketing communications mix (promotion mix)
The specific mix of advertising, personal selling, sales promotion, and public relations a company uses to pursue its advertising and marketing objectives.

Advertising
Any paid form of non-personal presentation and promotion of ideas, goods, or services by an identified sponsor.

Sales promotion
Short-term incentives to encourage the purchase or sale of a product or service.

Public relations
Building good relations with the company's various publics by obtaining favorable publicity, building up a good corporate image, and handling or heading off unfavorable rumors, stories, and events.

Personal selling
Personal presentation by the firm's sales force for the purpose of making sales and building customer relationships.

Direct marketing
Direct communications with carefully targeted individual consumers to obtain an immediate response.

A company's total **marketing communications mix**—also called its **promotion mix**—consists of the specific blend of advertising, sales promotion, public relations, personal selling, and direct-marketing tools that the company uses to pursue its advertising and marketing objectives. Definitions of the five major promotion tools follow:[1]

> **Advertising:** Any paid form of nonpersonal presentation and promotion of ideas, goods, or services by an identified sponsor.
> **Sales promotion:** Short-term incentives to encourage the purchase or sale of a product or service.
> **Public relations:** Building good relations with the company's various publics by obtaining favorable publicity, building up a good corporate image, and handling or heading off unfavorable rumors, stories, and events.
> **Personal selling:** Personal presentation by the firm's sales force for the purpose of making sales and building customer relationships.
> **Direct marketing:** Direct connections with carefully targeted individual consumers to both obtain an immediate response and cultivate lasting customer relationships—the use of telephone, mail, fax, e-mail, the Internet, and other tools to communicate directly with specific consumers.

Each category involves specific tools. For example, advertising includes print, broadcast, outdoor, and other forms. Sales promotion includes point-of-purchase displays, premiums, discounts, coupons, specialty advertising, and demonstrations. Public relations includes press releases and special events. Personal selling includes sales presentations, trade shows, and incentive programs. Direct marketing includes catalogs, telephone marketing, kiosks, the Internet, and more. Thanks to technological breakthroughs, people can now communicate through traditional media (newspapers, radio, telephone, television) as well as through newer media forms (fax, cell phones, and computers).

At the same time, communication goes beyond these specific promotion tools. The product's design, its price, the shape and color of its package, and the stores that sell it—*all* communicate something to buyers. Thus, although the promotion mix is the company's primary communication activity, the entire marketing mix—promotion *and* product, price, and place—must be coordinated for greatest communication impact.

In this chapter, we begin by examining the rapidly changing marketing communications environment and the concept of integrated marketing communications. Next, we discuss the factors that marketing communicators must consider in shaping an overall communication mix. Finally, we look at the first three promotion tools—advertising, sales promotion, and public relations. Chapter 14 examines the remaining promotion tools—personal selling and direct marketing.

Integrated Marketing Communications

During the past several decades, companies around the world have perfected the art of mass marketing—selling highly standardized products to masses of customers. In the process, they have developed effective mass-media advertising techniques to support their mass-marketing strategies. These companies routinely invest millions of dollars in the mass media, reaching tens of millions of customers with a single ad. However, as we move into the twenty-first century, marketing managers face some new marketing communications realities.

The Changing Communications Environment

Two major factors are changing the face of today's marketing communications. First, as mass markets have fragmented, marketers are shifting away from mass marketing. More and more, they are developing focused marketing programs designed to build closer relationships with customers in more narrowly defined micromarkets. Second, vast improvements in information technology are speeding the movement toward segmented marketing. Today's information technology helps marketers to keep closer track of customer needs—more information about consumers at the individual and household levels is available than ever before. New technologies also provide new communications avenues for reaching smaller customer segments with more tailored messages.

The shift from mass marketing to segmented marketing has had a dramatic impact on marketing communications. Just as mass marketing gave rise to a new generation of mass-media communications, the shift toward one-to-one marketing is spawning a new generation of more specialized and highly targeted communications efforts.

The new media environment: The relatively few mass magazines of past decades have been replaced today by thousands of magazines targeting special-interest audiences. Condé Nast Publications alone publishes 16 specialty magazines—ranging from *Vogue*, *Bride's*, and *Self* to *The New Yorker*, *Wired*, and *Bon Appétit*—not to mention a number of online magazines, such as Style.com.

Given this new communications environment, marketers must rethink the roles of various media and promotion mix tools. Mass-media advertising has long dominated the promotion mixes of consumer product companies. However, although television, magazines, and other mass media remain very important, their dominance is now declining. *Market* fragmentation has resulted in *media* fragmentation — in an explosion of more focused media that better match today's targeting strategies. Beyond the traditional mass-media channels, advertisers are making increased use of new, highly targeted media, ranging from highly focused specialty magazines and cable television channels, to CD catalogs and Web coupon promotions, to airport kiosks and floor decals in supermarket aisles. In all, companies are doing less *broadcasting* and more *narrowcasting*.

The Need for Integrated Marketing Communications

The shift from mass marketing to targeted marketing, and the corresponding use of a larger, richer mix of communication channels and promotion tools, poses a problem for marketers. Customers don't distinguish between message sources the way marketers do. In the consumer's mind, advertising messages from different media and different promotional approaches all become part of a single message about the company. Conflicting messages from these different sources can result in confused company images and brand positions.

All too often, companies fail to integrate their various communications channels. The result is a hodgepodge of communications to consumers. Mass-media advertisements say one thing, a price promotion sends a different signal, a product label creates still another message, company sales literature says something altogether different, and the company's Web site seems out of sync with everything else.

The problem is that these communications often come from different company sources. Advertising messages are planned and implemented by the advertising department or advertising agency. Personal selling communications are developed by sales management. Other functional specialists are responsible for public relations, sales promotion, direct marketing, online sites, and other forms of marketing communications. Recently, such functional separation has been a major problem for many companies and their Internet communications activities, which are often split off into separate organizational units. "These new, forward-looking, high-tech functional groups, whether they exist as part of an established organization or as a separate new business operation, commonly are located in separate space, apart from the traditional operation," observes one IMC expert. "They generally are populated by young, enthusiastic, technologically proficient people with a burning desire to 'change the world,'" he adds, but "the separation and the lack of cooperation and cohesion" can be a *dis*integrating force in marketing communications (see Marketing at Work 13-1).

In the past, no one person or department was responsible for thinking through the communication roles of the various promotion tools and coordinating the promotion mix. Today, however, more companies are adopting the concept of **integrated marketing communications (IMC).** Under this concept, as illustrated in Figure 13-1, the company carefully integrates and coordinates its many communications channels to deliver a clear, consistent, and compelling message about the organization and its products.[2] As one marketing executive puts it, "IMC builds a strong brand identity in the marketplace by tying together and reinforcing all your images and messages. IMC means that all your corporate messages, positioning and images, and identity are coordinated across all [marketing communications] venues. It means that your PR materials say the same thing as your direct mail campaign, and your advertising has the same 'look and feel' as your Web site."[3]

IMC calls for recognizing all contact points where the customer may encounter the company, its products, and its brands. Each *brand contact* will deliver a message, whether good, bad, or indifferent. The company must strive to deliver a consistent and positive message at all contact points.

Integrated marketing communications (IMC)
The concept under which a company carefully integrates and coordinates its many communications channels to deliver a clear, consistent, and compelling message about the organization and its products.

Marketing at Work 13-1

The Internet and IMC: *Dis*integrated Marketing Communications?

Ever had a day when you couldn't get a TV commercial out of your head? Or do ad lines and jingles from yesteryear sometimes stick in your cranium, such as "I'd like to buy the world a Coke," "Plop, plop, fizz, fizz. Oh what a relief it is," or "Whassssupppppp"? Or do long lost words such as "Two all beef patties, special sauce, lettuce, cheese, pickles, onions, on a sesame seed bun" suddenly and inexplicably burst from your mouth? If you're like most people, you sop up more than a fair share of TV advertising.

Now, try to remember the last ad you saw while surfing the Internet. Drawing a blank? That's not surprising. The Web's ineffectiveness as a major brand-building tool is one of the today's hottest marketing issues. The problem? According to integrated marketing communication guru Don Schultz, all the special attention this new medium has gotten may have resulted in *dis*integrated marketing communications. Says Schultz:

My mailbox has been filled with brochures, invitations, meetings, get-togethers, and debates all promising to explain interactivity, new media, e-commerce, and electronic media. Each . . . promises to give me the full picture of how to do the Internet, the Web, extranets, intranets, and all the other "nets" that are popping up everywhere. Not one has even suggested how all this new stuff might fit with, coordinate alongside, relate to, or be integrated with the existing media systems. Nothing on how to combine or bring together existing programs and existing customers with the brave new world of the 21st century.

Most troubling is that many firms have organized their new e-commu-

nications operations into separate groups or divisions, isolating them from mainstream marketing activities. "It is . . . the apartness that concerns me," Schultz observes. "We seem to be creating the same problems with new media, new marketing, and new commerce that we created years ago when we developed separate sales promotion groups, separate direct-marketing activities, separate public relations departments, separate events organizations, and so on. . . . In my view, we are well on the way to *dis*integrating our marketing and communication programs and processes all over again."

However, whereas companies appear to be compartmentalizing the new communications tools, customers won't. According to Schultz:

The truth is, most [consumers] won't compartmentalize their use of the new systems. They won't say, "Hey, I'm going off to do a bit of Net surfing. Burn my TV, throw out all my radios, cancel all my magazine subscriptions and, by the way, take out my telephone and don't deliver any mail anymore." It's not that kind of world for consumers, and it shouldn't be that kind of world for marketers either.

To be sure, the Internet promises exciting marketing communications potential. However, marketers trying to use the Web to build brands face many challenges. One limitation is that the Internet doesn't build mass brand awareness. Instead, it's like having millions of private conversations. The Web simply can't match the impact of the Super Bowl, where tens of millions of people see the same 30-second Nike or Hallmark ad at the same time. Using the Internet, it's hard to establish the universal meanings—such as "Just Do It!" or

"When you care enough to send the very best"—that are at the heart of brand recognition and brand value. And whereas some advocates claim that the Web's interactivity and high involvement make it superior to an increasingly fragmented and cluttered television medium, others disagree:

Some still think that the Web will replace TV as a major branding medium. I doubt it. Now, log on. Start clicking. Do you really believe that advertising-like solutions are going to work better on the Web than they do on CBS, ABC, NBC and the other 200 channels? There are millions—not hundreds—of places to go on the Web and everybody surfs with mouse in hand. Take a took at virtually any page—clutter galore: banners, icons, animated GIFs and Java applets are everywhere you look. [Thus,] the new collective wisdom—branding on the Web will be built through experience, not [advertising].

Another Internet limitation is format and quality constraints. Web ads are still low in quality and impact. Large advertisers have been pushing to get Internet publishers to allow larger, more complex types of ads with high-quality sound and full-motion video. So far, however, ads on the Internet are all too ignorable. Even if advertisers could put larger, richer ads on the Web, they would likely face a consumer backlash. In the digital world, consumers control ad exposure. Many consumers who've grown up with the Internet are skeptical of ads in general and resentful of Web ads in particular. Internet advertisers face an uphill battle in getting such consumers to click onto their ads. Facing such realities, most marketers opt for fuller promotion campaigns to build their brands. Even companies that rely primarily on e-commerce for sales are conducting most of their branding efforts offline. Business-to-business e-commerce star Cisco Systems spends ad money for full-page ads in the *Wall Street Journal* rather than on Web banners. Dell Computer, which now conducts 50 percent of all transactions online, is also one of the largest ad spenders in tech trade magazines and runs a $200 million–plus branding campaign almost entirely on TV.

Similarly, most traditional marketers have added the Web as an enhancement to their more traditional communication media. They wed the emotional pitch and impact of traditional brand marketing with the interactivity and real service offered online. For example, television ads for Saturn still offer the same old-fashioned humorous appeal. But now they point viewers to the company's Web site, which offers lots of help and very little hype. The site helps serious car buyers select a model, calculate payments, and find a dealer online. Even marketers that can't really sell their goods via the Web are using the Internet as an effective customer communication and relationship enhancer. For example, Procter & Gamble has turned Pampers.com into a one-stop center for addressing issues of concern to new or expectant parents. The site's research, learning, playing, and sharing centers offer information and advice on diapers and a whole lot more.

Thus, although the Internet offers good prospects for marketing communication, it can rarely stand alone as a brand-building tool. Moreover, if treated as a special case, it can disrupt an otherwise effective communications program. Instead, it must be carefully integrated into the broader marketing communications mix. Schultz makes this plea: "My cry is to integrate, not isolate. Yes, we need to explore and develop new media and new approaches, but we need to . . . integrate [them] with the old, melding e-commerce and across-the-counter commerce. There never has been a greater need for integration than there is today. Let's recognize and develop the new electronic forms on the basis of what they are—alternatives and perhaps enhancements for the existing approaches presently in place—and nothing more. Then again, they are nothing less, either."

Sources: Quotes and excerpts from Don E. Schultz, "New Media, Old Problem: Keep Marcom Integrated," *Marketing News,* March 29, 1999; and Robert C. Hacker, "The End of Brand Marketing on the Web?" *Target Marketing,* January 2000, pp. 42–44. Also see Al Ries and Laura Ries, *Immutable Laws of Internet Branding* (New York: HarperBusiness, 2000); Marc Braunstein, Ned Levine, and Edward H. Levine, *Deep Branding on the Internet: Applying Heat and Pressure Online to Ensure a Lasting Brand* (Roseville, CA: Prima Publishing, 2000); and Deborah Kania, *Branding.com: On-Line Branding for Marketing Success* (New York: NTC Publishing, 2001).

It's difficult to do major brand-building on the Web. Thus, e-commerce companies like Dell use off line promotion to build their online business.

A View of the Communication Process

Integrated marketing communications involve identifying the target audience and shaping a well-coordinated promotional program to elicit the desired audience response. Too often, marketing communications focus on overcoming immediate awareness, image, or

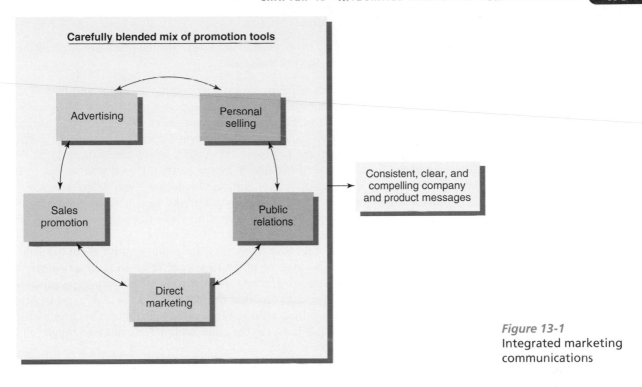

Figure 13-1
Integrated marketing
communications

preference problems in the target market. But this approach to communication is too short-sighted. Today, marketers are moving toward viewing communications as *managing the customer relationship over time,* during the preselling, selling, consuming, and post-consumption stages. Because customers differ, communications programs need to be developed for specific segments, niches, and even individuals. And, given the new interactive communications technologies, companies must ask not only, "How can we reach our customers?" but also, "How can we find ways to let our customers reach us?"

Thus, the communications process should start with an audit of all the potential contacts target customers may have with the company and its brands. For example, someone purchasing a new computer may talk to others, see television ads, read articles and ads in newspapers and magazines, visit various Web sites, and try out computers in one or more stores. The marketer needs to assess what influence each of these communications experiences will have at different stages of the buying process. This understanding will help marketers allocate their communication dollars more efficiently and effectively.

Setting the Overall Communication Mix

The concept of integrated marketing communications suggests that the company must blend the promotion tools carefully into a coordinated *promotion mix.* But how does the company determine what mix of promotion tools it will use? Companies within the same industry differ greatly in the design of their promotion mixes. For example, Avon spends most of its promotion funds on personal selling and direct marketing, whereas Revlon spends heavily on consumer advertising. Compaq Computer relies on advertising and promotion to retailers, whereas Dell Computer uses only direct marketing. We now look at factors that influence the marketer's choice of promotion tools.

The Nature of Each Promotion Tool

Each promotion tool has unique characteristics and costs. Marketers must understand these characteristics in selecting their mix of tools.

Advertising Advertising can reach masses of geographically dispersed buyers at a low cost per exposure, and it enables the seller to repeat a message many times. For example, television advertising can reach huge audiences. More than 131 million Americans tuned in to at least part of the most recent Super Bowl, some 72 million people watched at least part of the last Academy Awards broadcast, and nearly 52 million watched the final episode of the first *Survivor* series. "If you want to get to the mass audience," says a media services executive, "broadcast TV is where you have to be." He adds, "For anybody introducing anything who has to lasso audience in a hurry—a new product, a new campaign, a new movie—the networks are still the biggest show in town." [4]

Beyond its reach, large-scale advertising says something positive about the seller's size, popularity, and success. Because of advertising's public nature, consumers tend to view advertised products as more legitimate. Advertising is also very expressive—it allows the company to dramatize its products through the artful use of visuals, print, sound, and color. On the one hand, advertising can be used to build up a long-term image for a product (such as Coca-Cola ads). On the other hand, advertising can trigger quick sales (as when Sears advertises a weekend sale).

Advertising also has some shortcomings. Although it reaches many people quickly, advertising is impersonal and cannot be as directly persuasive as can company salespeople. For the most part, advertising can carry on only a one-way communication with the audience, and the audience does not feel that it has to pay attention or respond. In addition, advertising can be very costly. Although some advertising forms, such as newspaper and radio advertising, can be done on smaller budgets, other forms, such as network TV advertising, require very large budgets.

Personal Selling Personal selling is the most effective tool at certain stages of the buying process, particularly in building up buyers' preferences, convictions, and actions. It involves personal interaction between two or more people, so each person can observe the other's needs and characteristics and make quick adjustments. Personal selling also allows all kinds of relationships to spring up, ranging from a matter-of-fact selling relationship to personal friendship. The effective salesperson keeps the customer's interests at heart in order to build a long-term relationship. Finally, with personal selling the buyer usually feels a greater need to listen and respond, even if the response is a polite "no thank you."

These unique qualities come at a cost, however. A sales force requires a longer-term commitment than does advertising—advertising can be turned on and off, but sales force size is harder to change. Personal selling is also the company's most expensive promotion tool, costing companies $170 on average per sales call.[5] U.S. firms spend up to three times as much on personal selling as they do on advertising.

Sales Promotion Sales promotion includes a wide assortment of tools—coupons, contests, cents-off deals, premiums, and others—all of which have many unique qualities. They attract consumer attention, offer strong incentives to purchase, and can be used to dramatize product offers and to boost sagging sales. Sales promotions invite and reward quick response—whereas advertising says, "Buy our product," sales promotion says, "Buy it now." Sales promotion effects are often short lived, however, and often are not as effective as advertising or personal selling in building long-run brand preference.

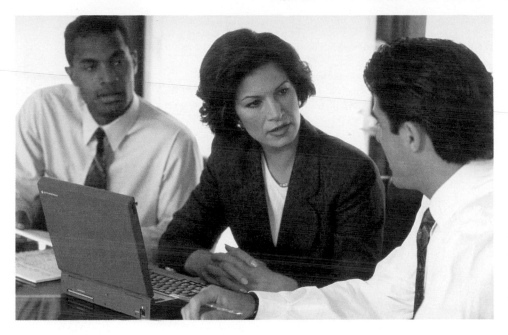

With personal selling, the customer feels a greater need to listen and respond, even if the response is a polite "no, thank you."

Public Relations Public relations is very believable—news stories, features, and events seem more real and believable to readers than ads do. Public relations can also reach many prospects who avoid salespeople and advertisements—the message gets to the buyers as "news" rather than as a sales-directed communication. And, as with advertising, public relations can dramatize a company or product. Marketers tend to underuse public relations or to use it as an afterthought. Yet a well-thought-out public relations campaign used with other promotion mix elements can be very effective and economical.

Direct Marketing Although there are many forms of direct marketing—telephone marketing, direct mail, online marketing, and others—they all share four distinctive characteristics. Direct marketing is *nonpublic:* The message is normally directed to a specific person. Direct marketing is *immediate* and *customized:* Messages can be prepared very quickly and can be tailored to appeal to specific consumers. Finally, direct marketing is *interactive:* It allows a dialogue between the marketing team and the consumer, and messages can be altered depending on the consumer's response. Thus, direct marketing is well suited to highly targeted marketing efforts and to building one-to-one customer relationships.

Promotion Mix Strategies

Marketers can choose from two basic promotion mix strategies—*push* promotion or *pull* promotion. Figure 13-2 contrasts the two strategies. The relative emphasis on the specific promotion tools differs for push and pull strategies. A **push strategy** involves "pushing" the product through distribution channels to final consumers. The producer directs its marketing activities (primarily personal selling and trade promotion) toward channel members to induce them to carry the product and to promote it to final consumers. Using a **pull strategy,** the producer directs its marketing activities (primarily advertising and consumer promotion) toward final consumers to induce them to buy the product. If the pull strategy is effective, consumers will then demand the product from channel members, who will in turn demand it from producers. Thus, under a pull strategy, consumer demand "pulls" the product through the channels.

Push strategy
A promotion strategy that calls for using the sales force and trade promotion to push the product through channels.

Pull strategy
A promotion strategy that calls for spending a lot on advertising and consumer promotion to build up consumer demand.

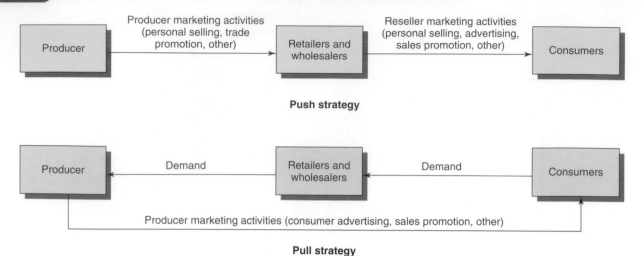

Figure 13-2
Push versus pull promotion strategy

Some industrial goods companies use only push strategies; some direct-marketing companies use only pull. However, most large companies use some combination of both. For example, Kraft uses mass-media advertising and consumer promotions to pull its products and a large sales force and trade promotions to push its products through the channels.

Companies consider many factors when designing their promotion mix strategies, including *type of product/market* and the *product life-cycle stage*. For example, the importance of different promotion tools varies between consumer and business markets. B2C companies usually "pull" more, putting more of their funds into advertising, followed by sales promotion, personal selling, and then public relations. In contrast, B2B marketers tend to "push" more, putting more of their funds into personal selling, followed by sales promotion, advertising, and public relations. In general, personal selling is used more heavily with expensive and risky goods and in markets with fewer and larger sellers.

Now that we've examined the concept of integrated marketing communications and the factors that firms consider when shaping their promotion mixes, let's look more closely at the specific marketing communications tools.

Advertising

Advertising can be traced back to the very beginnings of recorded history. Archaeologists working in the countries around the Mediterranean Sea have dug up signs announcing various events and offers. The Romans painted walls to announce gladiator fights, and the Phoenicians painted pictures promoting their wares on large rocks along parade routes. Modern advertising, however, is a far cry from these early efforts. U.S. advertisers now run up an estimated annual advertising bill of nearly $244 billion; worldwide ad spending exceeds $465 billion. General Motors, the nation's largest advertiser, last year spent more than $4 billion on advertising.[6]

Although advertising is used mostly by business firms, it also is used by a wide range of nonprofit organizations, professionals, and social agencies that advertise their causes to various target publics. In fact, the twenty-first largest advertising spender is a nonprofit organization—the U.S. government. Advertising is a good way to inform and persuade,

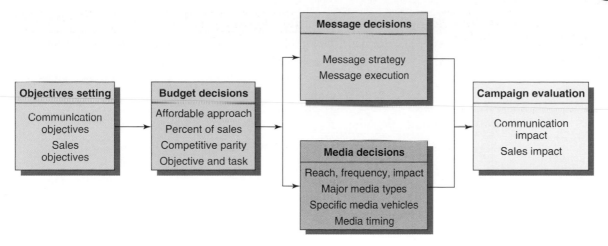

Figure 13-3
Major decisions in advertising

whether the purpose is to sell Coca-Cola worldwide or to get consumers in a developing nation to drink milk or use birth control.

Marketing management must make four important decisions when developing an advertising program (see Figure 13-3): *setting advertising objectives, setting the advertising budget, developing advertising strategy* (*message decisions* and *media decisions*), and *evaluating advertising campaigns.*

Setting Advertising Objectives

The first step is to set *advertising objectives.* These objectives should be based on past decisions about the target market, positioning, and marketing mix, which define the job that advertising must do in the total marketing program.

An **advertising objective** is a specific communication *task* to be accomplished with a specific *target* audience during a specific period of *time.* Advertising objectives can be classified by primary purpose—whether the aim is to *inform, persuade,* or *remind.* Table 13-1 lists examples of each of these objectives.

Informative advertising is used heavily when introducing a new product category. In this case, the objective is to build primary demand. Thus, producers of DVD players must first inform consumers of the image quality and convenience benefits of the new product. *Persuasive advertising* becomes more important as competition increases. Here, the company's objective is to build selective demand. For example, once DVD players are established, Sony begins trying to persuade consumers that *its* brand offers the best quality for their money.

Some persuasive advertising has become *comparative advertising,* in which a company directly or indirectly compares its brand with one or more other brands. Comparative advertising has been used for products ranging from soft drinks and computers to batteries, pain relievers, car rentals, and credit cards. For example, in its classic comparative campaign, Avis positioned itself against market-leading Hertz by claiming, "We're number two, so we try harder." More recently, in its long-running comparative campaign, VISA has advertised, "American Express is offering you a new credit card, but you don't have to accept it. Heck, 7 million merchants don't." American Express has responded with ads bashing Visa, noting that AmEx's cards offer benefits not available with Visa's regular card, such as rapid replacement of lost cards and higher credit limits. As often happens with comparative advertising, both sides complain that the other's ads are misleading.

Advertising objective
A specific communication *task* to be accomplished with a specific *target* audience during a specific period of *time.*

Table 13-1 Possible Advertising Objectives		
Informative advertising	Telling the market about a new product	Describing available services
	Suggesting new uses for a product	Correcting false impressions
	Informing the market of a price change	Reducing consumers' fears
	Explaining how the product works	Building a company image
Persuasive advertising	Building brand preference Encouraging switching to your brand	Persuading customer to purchase now
	Changing customer's perception of product attributes	Persuading customer to receive a sales call
Reminder advertising	Reminding consumer that the product may be needed in the near future	Keeping it in customer's mind during off-seasons
	Reminding consumer where to buy it	Maintaining its top-of-mind awareness

Reminder advertising is important for mature products—it keeps consumers thinking about the product. Expensive Coca-Cola television ads primarily remind people about Coca-Cola rather than informing or persuading them.

Setting the Advertising Budget

After determining its advertising objectives, the company next sets its *advertising budget* for each product and market. How does a company decide on its promotion budget? We look at four common methods used to set the total budget for advertising: the *affordable method,* the *percentage-of-sales method,* the *competitive-parity method,* and the *objective-and-task method.*

Affordable method

Setting the promotion budget at the level management thinks the company can afford.

Affordable Method Some companies use the **affordable method:** They set the promotion budget at the level they think the company can afford. Small businesses often use this method, reasoning that the company cannot spend more on advertising than it has. They start with total revenues, deduct operating expenses and capital outlays, and then devote some portion of the remaining funds to advertising.

Unfortunately, this method of setting budgets completely ignores the effects of promotion on sales. It tends to place advertising last among spending priorities, even in situations in which advertising is critical to the firm's success. It leads to an uncertain annual promotion budget, which makes long-range market planning difficult. Although the affordable method can result in overspending on advertising, it more often results in underspending.

Percentage-of-sales method

Setting the promotion budget at a certain percentage of current or forecasted sales or as a percentage of the unit sales price.

Percentage-of-Sales Method Other companies use the **percentage-of-sales method,** setting their promotion budget at a certain percentage of current or forecasted sales. Or they budget a percentage of the unit sales price. The percentage-of-sales method has advantages. It is simple to use and helps management think about the relationships between promotion spending, selling price, and profit per unit.

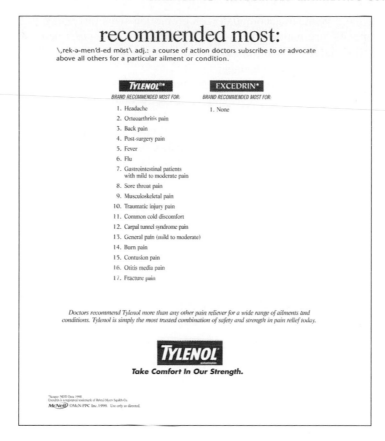

Comparative advertising: This ad compares Tylenol—very favorably—to Excedrin.

Despite these claimed advantages, however, the percentage-of-sales method has little to justify it. It wrongly views sales as the *cause* of promotion rather than as the *result*. Studies often show positive correlations between advertising expenditures on a brand and brand performance. However, these findings may represent "effect and cause" rather than "cause and effect." Brands with higher sales can afford bigger advertising investments. Thus, the percentage-of-sales budget is based on availability of funds rather than on opportunities. It may prevent the increased spending sometimes needed to turn around falling sales. Because the budget varies with year-to-year sales, long-range planning is difficult. Finally, the method does not provide any basis for choosing a *specific* percentage, except what has been done in the past or what competitors are doing.

Competitive-Parity Method Still other companies use the **competitive-parity method,** setting their promotion budgets to match competitors' outlays. They monitor competitors' advertising or get industry promotion spending estimates from publications or trade associations and then set their budgets based on the industry average.

Two arguments support this method. First, competitors' budgets represent the collective wisdom of the industry. Second, spending what competitors spend helps prevent promotion wars. Unfortunately, neither argument is valid. There are no grounds for believing that the competition has a better idea of what a company should be spending on promotion than does the company itself. Companies differ greatly, and each has its own special promotion needs. Finally, there is no evidence that budgets based on competitive parity prevent promotion wars.

Objective-and-Task Method The most logical budget-setting method is the **objective-and-task method,** whereby the company sets its promotion budget based on

Competitive-parity method
Setting the promotion budget to match competitors' outlays.

Objective-and-task method
Developing the promotion budget by (1) defining specific objectives; (2) determining the tasks that must be performed to achieve these objectives; and (3) estimating the costs of performing these tasks. The sum of these costs is the proposed promotion budget.

what it wants to accomplish with promotion. This budgeting method entails (1) defining specific promotion objectives, (2) determining the tasks needed to achieve these objectives, and (3) estimating the costs of performing these tasks. The sum of these costs is the proposed promotion budget.

The objective-and-task method forces management to spell out its assumptions about the relationship between dollars spent and promotion results. But it is also the most difficult method to use. Often, it is hard to figure out which specific tasks will achieve specific objectives. For example, suppose Sony wants 95 percent awareness for its latest DVD player during the six-month introductory period. What specific advertising messages and media schedules should Sony use to attain this objective? How much would these messages and media schedules cost? Sony management must consider such questions, even though they are hard to answer.

No matter what method is used, deciding how much to spend on advertising is one of the hardest marketing decisions facing a company. Measuring the results of advertising spending and "advertising return on investment" remains an inexact science. John Wanamaker, the department store magnate, once said, "I know that half of my advertising is wasted, but I don't know which half. I spent $2 million for advertising, and I don't know if that is half enough or twice too much." Thus, it is not surprising that companies vary widely in how much they spend on promotion. Even within a given industry, both low and high spenders can be found.[7]

Developing Advertising Strategy

Advertising strategy consists of two major elements: creating advertising *messages* and selecting advertising *media*. In the past, companies often viewed media planning as secondary to the message-creation process. The creative department first created good advertisements, then the media department selected the best media for carrying these advertisements to desired target audiences. This often caused friction between creatives and media planners.

Today, however, media fragmentation, soaring media costs, and more focused target marketing strategies have promoted the importance of the media-planning function. More and more, advertisers are orchestrating a closer harmony between their messages and the media that deliver them. In some cases, an advertising campaign might start with a great message idea, followed by the choice of appropriate media. In other cases, however, a campaign might begin with a good media opportunity, followed by advertisements designed to take advantage of that opportunity. Among the more noteworthy ad campaigns based on tight media-creative partnerships is the pioneering campaign for Absolut Vodka, marketed by Seagram.

The Absolut team and its ad agency meet once each year with a slew of magazines to set Absolut's media schedule. The schedule consists of up to 100 magazines, ranging from consumer and business magazines to theater playbills. The agency's creative department then creates media-specific ads. The result is a wonderful assortment of very creative ads for Absolut, tightly targeted to audiences of the media in which they appear. For example, an "Absolut Bravo" ad in playbills has roses adorning a clear bottle, while business magazines contain an "Absolut Merger" foldout. In New York-area magazines, "Absolut Manhattan" ads feature a satellite photo of Manhattan, with Central Park assuming the distinctive outline of an Absolut bottle. In Chicago, the Windy City, ads show an Absolut bottle with the letters on the label blown askew. An "Absolut Primary" ad run during the political season featured the well-known bottle spattered with mud. In some cases, the creatives even developed ads for magazines not yet on the schedule, such as a clever "Absolut Centerfold" ad for *Playboy* magazine. The ad portrayed a clear, unadorned playmate bottle ("11-inch bust, 11-inch waist, 11-inch hips"). In all, Absolut has developed more than 500 ads

Media planners for Absolut Vodka work with creatives to design ads targeting specific media audiences. "Absolut Bravo" appears in theater playbills. "Absolut Chicago" targets people in the Windy City.

for the almost two-decades-old campaign. At a time of soaring media costs and cluttered communication channels, a closer cooperation between creative and media people has paid off handsomely for Absolut. Largely as a result of its breakthrough advertising, Absolut now captures a 63 percent share of the imported vodka market.[8]

Creating the Advertising Message No matter how big the budget, advertising can succeed only if commercials gain attention and communicate well. Good advertising messages are especially important in today's costly and cluttered advertising environment. The average number of television channels beamed into U.S. homes has skyrocketed from 3 in 1950 to 47 today, and consumers have more than 17,800 magazines from which to choose.[9] Add the countless radio stations and a continuous barrage of catalogs, direct-mail and online ads, and out-of-home media, and consumers are being bombarded with ads at home, at work, and at all points in between.

If all this advertising clutter bothers some consumers, it also causes big problems for advertisers. Take the situation facing network television advertisers. They regularly pay $200,000 or more for 30 seconds of advertising time during a popular prime-time program, even more if it's an especially popular program such as *ER* ($620,000 per 30-second spot), *Friends* ($540,000), *Just Shoot Me* ($465,000 per spot), *Everybody Loves Raymond* ($460,000), or a mega-event such as the Super Bowl (more than $2 million!).[10] Then, their ads are sandwiched in with a clutter of some 60 other commercials, announcements, and network promotions per hour.

Until recently, television viewers were pretty much a captive audience for advertisers. Viewers had only a few channels from which to choose. But with the growth in cable and satellite TV, VCRs, and remote-control units, today's viewers have many more options. They can avoid ads by watching commercial-free cable channels. They can "zap" commercials by pushing the fast-forward button during taped programs. With remote control, they can instantly turn off the sound during a commercial or "zip" around the channels to see what else is on. A recent study found that half of all television viewers now switch channels when the commercial break starts. And the new wave of digital video recorders (DVRs) and personal television services—such as TiVo, ReplayTV, and Microsoft's UltimateTV—have armed viewers with an arsenal of new-age zipping and zapping weapons.[11]

Just to gain and hold attention, today's advertising messages must be better planned, more imaginative, more entertaining, and more rewarding to consumers. "Today we have to entertain and not just sell, because if you try to sell directly and come off as boring or obnoxious, people are going to press the remote on you," points out one advertising executive. "When most TV viewers are armed with remote channel switchers, a commercial has to cut through the clutter and seize the viewers in one to three seconds, or they're gone," comments another.[12] Some advertisers even create intentionally controversial ads to break through the clutter and gain attention for their products (see Marketing at Work 13-2).

MESSAGE STRATEGY.   The first step in creating effective advertising messages is to decide what general message will be communicated to consumers—to plan a *message strategy.* The purpose of advertising is to get consumers to think about or react to the product or company in a certain way. People will react only if they believe that they will benefit from doing so. Thus, developing an effective message strategy begins with identifying customer *benefits* that can be used as advertising appeals. Ideally, advertising message strategy will follow directly from the company's broader positioning strategy.

Message strategy statements tend to be plain, straightforward outlines of benefits and positioning points that the advertiser wants to stress. The advertiser must next develop a compelling *creative concept*—or *"big idea"*—that will bring the message strategy to life in a distinctive and memorable way. At this stage, simple message ideas become great ad campaigns. Usually, a copywriter and art director will team up to generate many creative concepts, hoping that one of these concepts will turn out to be the big idea. The creative concept may emerge as a visualization, a phrase, or a combination of the two.

The creative concept will guide the choice of specific appeals to be used in an advertising campaign. *Advertising appeals* should have three characteristics: First, they should be *meaningful,* pointing out benefits that make the product more desirable or interesting to consumers. Second, appeals must be *believable*—consumers must believe that the product or service will deliver the promised benefits. However, the most meaningful and believable benefits may not be the best ones to feature. Appeals should also be *distinctive*—they should tell how the product is better than the competing brands. For example, the most meaningful benefit of owning a wristwatch is that it keeps accurate time, yet few watch ads feature this benefit. Instead, based on the distinctive benefits they offer, watch advertisers might select any of a number of advertising themes. For years, Timex has been the affordable watch that "Takes a lickin' and keeps on tickin'." In contrast, Swatch has featured style and fashion, whereas Rolex stresses luxury and status.

MESSAGE EXECUTION.   The advertiser now has to turn the big idea into an actual ad execution that will capture the target market's attention and interest. The creative people must

Marketing at Work 13-2

Advertising on the Edge: You Either Hate 'Em or Love 'Em

You may remember the ad. It opens with a calm, deep-voiced announcer sitting comfortably in a leather chair in a library setting. The spot cuts to a concrete wall with "Outpost.com" emblazoned on it. "Hello," he intones, "we want you to remember our name—Outpost.com." To the shock of some viewers and to the surprised delight of others, he continues, "That's why we've decided to fire gerbils out of this cannon through the 'O' in Outpost." He gives a nod, and his assistant fires a nearby cannon. "Boom!" The cannon hurls a gerbil toward the hole. "Splat!" A near miss—the gerbil hits the wall, then falls to the ground and scurries away. "Cute little guy," says the announcer, smiling warmly. "Again," he instructs. "Boom!" This time, a gerbil sails high over the wall. "Boom!" "Splat!" "Boom!" "Splat!" "So close," affirms the announcer. Finally, the cannon blasts a gerbil cleanly through the "O," setting off a fanfare of sirens, buzzers, and flashing lights. The ad closes with an invitation to viewers to "Send complaints to Outpost.com—the cool place to buy computer stuff online."

It was all pretend, of course, but complain people did. These ads by Outpost.com—the Internet company that sells computer technology products and consumer electronics online—set off a flurry of controversy on Madison Avenue and among animal-protection groups. But the ads did draw attention—Outpost.com rocketed from near obscurity into the national spotlight in a matter of weeks.

Outpost.com's commercials were in the vanguard of a new genre of irreverent, cutting-edge advertising: commercials that intentionally create controversy, even if it means turning off some potential customers. In today's cluttered

SHRINKAGE MAY OCCUR
THE CURIOUSLY STRONG MINTS

CURIOUS?

WWW.TOOHOT.COM

To be truly cutting-edge, advertising must do more than just capture attention. Altoids' irreverent ads fit the brand's "curious, strong, original" positioning and appeal to its cutting-edge target consumers.

advertising environment, such ads go to extremes to get attention—you either love 'em or hate 'em. "It's the age-old question of breaking through the clutter," says the creative director of the ad agency that developed the Outpost.com ads. You turn to "anything you can to get noticed," he says.

Other controversial ads abound. While flipping through your favorite magazine you might encounter a Toyota ad targeting Gen Ys with the headline "Attention nose pickers. . . ." On the next page is a boundary-pushing ad from Candies, featuring company spokesmodel Jenny McCarthy sitting on a toilet with her pants around her calves, wearing little more than her bright orange Candies shoes. Next comes an Altoids ad in which a man peers down the front of his boxer shorts: "Shrinkage may occur," proclaims the ad's headline. "The curiously strong mints." Other Altoids ads feature a woman in a seductively devilish outfit, complete with horns, and headlines such as "Hot and bothered?" "Frigid?" and "Taste like hell!"

On television, a Fox Sports television ad shows an able-bodied young guy, engrossed in his Fox Sports Web site, casually ignoring an old man just a few feet away struggling to get a jar down from a shelf. An Orange Slice "twisted taste" commercial opens with the camera panning across a row of squeamish students in a science class, frog legs dangling from their dissection trays. As the teacher drones on about ruptured spleens and green discharges, one kid lunches on his lab project.

For pure gross-out value, few ads top the "Blind Date" spot from SmartBeep, the retail paging-services provider. The spot, which generated enormous response, was part of a wacky five-part campaign that contrasted smart versus not-so-smart behavior to promote SmartBeep's free pagers and low rates on paging services. In it, a woman climbs into the front seat of her blind date's car. While he's crossing around to the other side, thinking she is alone, she leans to one side and lets rip a frat-house blast of gas. When her date hops in the car, she hesitates then turns red with embarrassment as he introduces her to another couple in the backseat. "You guys meet? Gregg, Janice?" he asks, to which Janice in the backseat responds, "We sure did." The announcer concludes, "That was stupid. . . . This is smart. A beeper service for just $1.99 a month." The ad closes: "We've got chemistry here. You feel it?" says the blind-date guy. "I felt it!" says Janice from the backseat. The ad became an immediate Internet cult item.

Outpost.com's ads—three in all—themselves rated pretty high on the irreverence meter. The gerbils ad wasn't the only one to set fur flying. In a second ad, a tattoo artist attempted to make the Outpost.com name more memorable by inscribing it on the foreheads of six-year-old kids at a day-care center, reducing them to tears. In a third, a high school marching band spelling out the company's name on a football field is attacked by "a pack of ravenous wolves," who jump on band members, tearing at their limbs. "Ha, ha, ha," said the announcer, "That's good stuff."

Outpost.com's marketers knew that the ads would be controversial—that was the point. "Our intent was to create memorable ads that would force people to remember our name," said an Outpost.com spokesperson. The agency creative director adds, "We told the people at Outpost.com that we didn't know if these ads were good or bad. What we told

them was that they were memorable—they'll get people to your Web site."

Mission accomplished. Site traffic doubled and Outpost.com signed 15,000 new customers in the two weeks after the commercials first aired, 30,000 new customers by the end of the campaign. Moreover, as a testament to its cutting-edge creativity, the campaign amassed more than a dozen of the ad industry's highest awards and spawned many competitors.

However, although the outrageous ads grabbed attention and awards, they did little to position Outpost.com or to tell people what it had to sell. Although Outpost.com's name was all over the place, nobody knew *why* he or she should visit the site. The ads mentioned "computer stuff," laments the company's current CEO, but "the ads were so dominating that people missed that. They didn't know that we sold computers. They thought that we sold clothes or didn't sell anything. We had a lot of visitors—but no buyers."

A year after the first ads ran, Outpost.com shifted to a more serious campaign chock-full of information and positioning the company on its products and free overnight delivery policy. The new campaign resulted in a 40 percent increase in site visitors, and people who visited the site were also buying. However, it may have been too little, too late. Recently acquired by information technology firm PC Connections, Outpost.com is still struggling to turn its first profits.

So, it appears that to be truly cutting edge, advertising must do more than just capture attention. It must support and enhance the brand and its positioning. If used properly, cutting-edge humor can help do that, as proved by Altoids and its "Curiously Strong" campaign. In these ads, the irreverence fits the brand's "curious, strong, original" positioning. It also appeals to the tastes as well as the taste buds of Altoids' cutting-edge target consumers. As a result, in only two years, the small-budget but high-impact ad campaign has propelled Altoids past longtime strong-mint market leader Tic Tac. "Altoids is now—improbably—the boss of the mint world," says an analyst. What's the power behind this cheeky campaign? The analyst confirms that "Everything links back to [the brand's] 'curiously strong' and 'original' [positioning]."

Sources: Melanie Wells, "Wanted: Television Ad Complaints," *USA Today*, January 11, 1999, p. 4B; Dottie Enrico, "Creature Feature," *TV Guide*, January 23, 1999, p. 13; Hank Kim, "Creature Feature," *Adweek*, November 23, 1998, p. 20; Tom Kurtz, "Unsettling TV Commercials: And Now, a Gross-Out from Our Sponsor," *New York Times*, July 25, 1999, p. 7; Anne Marie Borrego, "Wild Ads Make Web Stars," *Inc*, February 2000, p. 66; Verne Gay, "Best Use of Out-of-Home: Stargate Worldwide," *Adweek*, June 19, 2000, pp. M6–M10; and "Business Brief—PC Connection Inc.: Cyberian Outpost Is to Be Acquired in a Stock Deal," *Wall Street Journal*, May 31, 2001 p. 1.

find the best style, tone, words, and format for executing the message. Any message can be presented in different *execution styles,* such as the following:

◆ *Slice of life:* This style shows one or more "typical" people using the product in a normal setting. For example, two mothers at a picnic discuss the nutritional benefits of Jif peanut butter.

◆ *Lifestyle:* This style shows how a product fits in with a particular lifestyle. For example, an ad for Mongoose mountain bikes shows a serious biker traversing remote and rugged but beautiful terrain and states, "There are places that are so awesome and so killer that you'd like to tell the whole world about them. But please, *don't.*"

◆ *Fantasy:* This style creates a fantasy around the product or its use. For instance, many ads are built around dream themes. Gap even introduced a perfume named Dream. Ads show a woman sleeping blissfully and suggests that the scent is "the stuff that clouds are made of."

◆ *Mood or image:* This style builds a mood or image around the product, such as beauty, love, or serenity. No claim is made about the product except through suggestion. Bermuda tourism ads create such moods.

◆ *Musical:* This style shows one or more people or cartoon characters singing about the product. For example, one of the most famous ads in history was a Coca-Cola ad built around the song "I'd Like to Teach the World to Sing."

◆ *Personality symbol:* This style creates a character that represents the product. The character might be *animated* (the Jolly Green Giant, Cap'n Crunch, Garfield the Cat) or *real* (the Marlboro man, Ol' Lonely the Maytag repairman, Joe Isuzu, Morris the 9-Lives Cat).

◆ *Technical expertise:* This style shows the company's expertise in making the product. Thus, Maxwell House shows one of its buyers carefully selecting coffee beans, and Gallo tells about its many years of wine-making experience.

◆ *Scientific evidence:* This style presents survey or scientific evidence that the brand is better or better liked than one or more other brands. For years, Crest toothpaste has used scientific evidence to convince buyers that Crest is better than other brands at fighting cavities.

◆ *Testimonial evidence or endorsement:* This style features a highly believable or likable source endorsing the product. It could be ordinary people saying how much they like a given product ("My doctor said Mylanta") or a celebrity presenting the product. Many companies use actors or sports celebrities as product endorsers.

The advertiser also must choose a *tone* for the ad. Procter & Gamble always uses a positive tone: Its ads say something very positive about its products. P&G usually avoids humor that might take attention away from the message. In contrast, many advertisers now use edgy humor to break through the commercial clutter.

The advertiser must use memorable and attention-getting *words* in the ad. For example, rather than claiming simply that "a BMW is a well-engineered automobile," BMW uses more creative and higher-impact phrasing: "The ultimate driving machine." Instead of stating

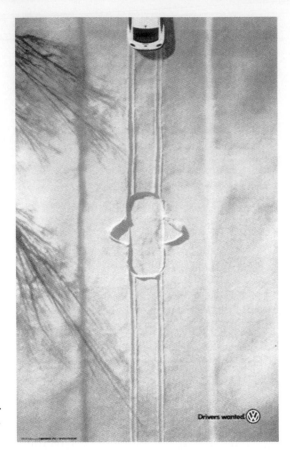

In an effective ad, like this award-winning Volkswagen ad, all of the elements work together to attract attention and communicate the brand's personality and positioning.

plainly that Hanes socks last longer than less expensive ones, Hanes suggests, "Buy cheap socks and you'll pay through the toes." It's not Häagen-Dazs is "a good-tasting luxury ice cream," it's "Our passport to indulgence: passion in a touch, perfection in a cup, summer in a spoon, one perfect moment."

Finally, *format* elements make a difference on an ad's impact as well as on its cost. A small change in ad design can make a big difference in its effect. The *illustration* is the first thing the reader notices—it must be strong enough to draw attention. Next, the *headline* must effectively entice the right people to read the copy. Finally, the *copy*—the main block of text in the ad—must be simple but strong and convincing. Moreover, these three elements must effectively work *together.*

Selecting Advertising Media   The major steps in media selection are (1) deciding on *reach, frequency,* and *impact;* (2) choosing among major *media types;* (3) selecting specific *media vehicles;* and (4) deciding on *media timing.*

DECIDING ON REACH, FREQUENCY, AND IMPACT.   To select media, the advertiser must decide what reach and frequency are needed to achieve advertising objectives. *Reach* is a measure of the *percentage* of people in the target market who are exposed to the ad campaign during a given period of time. For example, the advertiser might try to reach 70 percent of the target market during the first three months of the campaign. *Frequency* is a measure of how many *times* the average person in the target market is exposed to the message. For example, the advertiser might want an average exposure frequency of three. The advertiser also must decide on the desired *media impact*—the *qualitative value* of a message exposure through a given medium. For example, for products that need to be demonstrated, messages on television may have more impact than messages on radio because television uses sight *and* sound. The same message in one magazine (say, *Newsweek*) may be more believable than in another (say, *The National Enquirer*). In general, the more reach, frequency, and impact the advertiser seeks, the higher the advertising budget will have to be.

CHOOSING AMONG MAJOR MEDIA TYPES. The media planner has to know the reach, frequency, and impact of each of the major media types. As summarized in Table 13-2, the major media types are newspapers, television, direct mail, radio, magazines, outdoor, and the Internet. Each medium has advantages and limitations.

Media planners consider many factors when making their media choices. The *media habits of target consumers* will affect media choice—advertisers look for media that reach target consumers effectively. So will the *nature of the product*—for example, fashions are best advertised in color magazines, and automobile performance is best demonstrated on television. Different *types of messages* may require different media. A message announcing a major sale tomorrow will require radio or newspapers; a message with a lot of technical data might require magazines, direct mailings, or an online ad and Web site. *Cost* is another major factor in media choice. For example, network television is very expensive, whereas newspaper or radio advertising costs much less but also reaches fewer consumers. The media planner looks both at the total cost of using

Table 13-2 Profiles of Major Media Types		
Medium	Advantages	Limitations
Newspapers	Flexibility; timeliness; good local market coverage; broad acceptability; high believability	Short life; poor reproduction quality; small pass-along audience
Television	Good mass-market coverage; low cost per exposure; combines sight, sound, and motion; appealing to the senses	High absolute costs; high clutter; fleeting exposure; less audience selectivity
Direct mail	High audience selectivity; flexibility; no ad competition within the same medium; allows personalization	Relatively high cost per exposure; "junk mail" image
Radio	Good local acceptance; high geographic and demographic selectivity; low cost	Audio only; fleeting exposure; low attention ("the half-heard" medium) fragmented audiences
Magazines	High geographic and demographic selectivity; credibility and prestige; high-quality reproduction; long life and good pass-along readership	Long ad-purchase lead time; high cost; no guarantee of position
Outdoor	Flexibility; high repeat exposure; low cost; low message competition; good positional selectivity	Little audience selectivity; creative limitations
Online	High selectivity; low cost; immediacy; interactive capabilities	Small audience; relatively low impact; audience controls exposure

a medium and at the cost per thousand exposures—the cost of reaching 1,000 people using the medium.

Media impact and cost must be reexamined regularly. For a long time, television and magazines have dominated in the media mixes of national advertisers, with other media often neglected. Recently, however, the costs and clutter of these media have gone up, audiences have declined, and marketers are adopting strategies beamed at narrower segments. As a result, advertisers are increasingly turning to alternative media—ranging from cable TV and outdoor advertising to parking meters and elevators—that cost less and target more effectively (see Marketing at Work 13-3).

SELECTING SPECIFIC MEDIA VEHICLES. The media planner now must choose the best *media vehicles*—specific media within each general media type. For example, television vehicles include *ER* and *ABC World News Tonight.* Magazine vehicles include *Newsweek, People, In Style,* and *Sports Illustrated.*

Media planners must compute the cost per thousand persons reached by a vehicle. For example, if a full-page, four-color advertisement in *Time* costs $192,000 and *Time's* readership is 4.1 million people, the cost of reaching each group of 1,000 persons is about $47. The same advertisement in *Business Week* may cost only $92,500 but reach only 948,000 persons—at a cost per thousand of about $98. The media planner ranks each magazine by cost per thousand and favors those magazines with the lower cost per thousand for reaching target consumers.[13]

The media planner must also consider the costs of producing ads for different media. Whereas newspaper ads may cost very little to produce, flashy television ads may cost millions. On average, U.S. advertisers pay $343,000 to produce a single 30-second television commercial. A few years ago, Nike paid a cool $2 million to make a single ad called "The Wall."[14]

In selecting media vehicles, the media planner must balance media cost measures against several media impact factors. First, the planner should balance costs against the media vehicle's *audience quality.* For a baby lotion advertisement, for example, *New Parents* magazine would have a high-exposure value; *Gentlemen's Quarterly* would have a low-exposure value. Second, the media planner should consider *audience attention.* Readers of *Vogue,* for example, typically pay more attention to ads than do *Newsweek* readers. Third, the planner should assess the vehicle's *editorial quality*—*Time* and the *Wall Street Journal* are more believable and prestigious than *The National Enquirer.*

DECIDING ON MEDIA TIMING. The advertiser must also decide how to schedule the advertising over the course of a year. Suppose sales of a product peak in December and drop in March. The firm can vary its advertising to follow the seasonal pattern, to oppose the seasonal pattern, or to be the same all year. Most firms do some seasonal advertising. Some do *only* seasonal advertising: For example, Hallmark advertises its greeting cards only before major holidays.

Finally, the advertiser has to choose the pattern of the ads. *Continuity* means scheduling ads evenly within a given period. *Pulsing* means scheduling ads unevenly over a given time period. Thus, 52 ads could either be scheduled at one per week during the year or pulsed in several bursts. The idea is to advertise heavily for a short period to build awareness that carries over to the next advertising period. Those who favor pulsing feel that it can be used to achieve the same impact as a steady schedule but at a much lower cost. However, some media planners believe that although pulsing achieves minimal awareness, it sacrifices depth of advertising communications.

Recent advances in technology have had a substantial impact on the media planning and buying functions. Today, for example, computer software applications called

Advertisers Seek Alternative Media

As network television costs soar and audiences shrink, many advertisers are looking for new ways to reach consumers. The move toward micro-marketing strategies, focused more narrowly on specific consumer groups, has also fueled the search for alternative media to replace or supplement network television. Advertisers are shifting larger portions of their budgets to media that cost less and target more effectively.

Three media benefiting greatly from the shift are outdoor advertising, cable television, and digital satellite television systems. Billboards have undergone a resurgence in recent years. Gone are the ugly eyesores of the past; in their place we now see cleverly designed, colorful attention grabbers. Outdoor advertising provides an excellent way to reach important local consumer segments at a fraction of the cost per exposure of other major media. Cable television and digital satellite systems are also booming. Such systems allow narrow programming formats such as all sports, all news, nutrition, arts, gardening, cooking, travel, history, and others that target select groups. Advertisers can take advantage of such "narrowcasting" to "rifle in" on special market segments rather than use the "shotgun" approach offered by network broadcasting.

Outdoor, cable, and satellite media seem to make good sense. But, increasingly, ads are popping up in far less likely places. In their efforts to find less costly and more highly targeted ways to reach consumers, advertisers have discovered a dazzling collection of "alternative media." As consumers, we're used to ads on television, in magazines and newspapers, on the radio, and along the roadways. But

these days, no matter where you go or what you do, you probably will run into some new form of advertising.

Tiny billboards attached to shopping carts, ads on shopping bags, and even advertising decals on supermarket floors urge you to buy Jell-O Pudding Pops or Pampers. Signs atop parking meters hawk everything from Jeeps to Minolta cameras to Recipe dog food. A city bus rolls by, fully wrapped for Trix cereal. You escape to the ballpark, only to find billboard-size video screens running Budweiser ads while a blimp with an electronic message board circles lazily overhead. How about a quiet trip in the country? Sorry—you find an enterprising farmer using his milk cows as four-legged billboards mounted with ads for Ben & Jerry's ice cream.

You pay to see a movie at your local theater, but first you view a two minute science fiction fantasy that turns out to be an ad for General Electric portable stereo boxes. Then the movie itself is full of not-so-subtle promotional plugs for Pepsi, Domino's Pizza, MasterCard, Fritos, BMWs, Ray Ban sunglasses, or any of a dozen other products. You head home for a little TV to find your favorite sitcom full of "virtual placements" of Coca-Cola, Sony, or M&M/Mars products digitally inserted into the program.

At the local rail station, it's the Commuter Channel. At the airport you're treated to the CNN Airport Network while ads for Kenneth Cole baggage roll by on the luggage carousel conveyor belt. Boats cruise along public beaches flashing advertising messages for Sundown Sunscreen as sunbathers spread

Marketers have discovered a dazzling array of "alternative media."

their towels over ads for Snapple pressed into the sand. Even church bulletins carry ads for Campbell's soup.

These days, you're likely to find ads—well, anywhere. Ad space is being sold on video cases, parking-lot tickets, golf scorecards, delivery trucks, gas pumps, ATMs, and municipal garbage cans. The following accounts takes a humorous look ahead at what might be in store for the future:

Tomorrow your alarm clock will buzz at 6 A.M., as usual. Then the digital readout will morph into an ad for Burger King's breakfast special. Hungry for a Croissan'wich, you settle for a bagel that you plop into the toaster. The coils burn a Toastmaster brand onto the sides. Biting into your embossed bread, you

pour a cup of coffee as the familiar green-and-white Starbucks logo forms on the side. Sipping the brew, you slide on your Nikes to go grab the newspaper. The pressure sensitive shoes leave a temporary trail of swooshes behind them wherever you step. Walking outside, you pick up the Times and gaze at your lawn, where the fertilizer you put down last month time-releases ads for Scotts Turf Builder, Toro lawn-mowers, Weber grills. . . .

Even some of the current alternative media seem a bit far-fetched, and they sometimes irritate consumers who resent it all as "ad nauseam." But for many marketers, these media can save money and provide a way to hit selected consumers where they live, shop, work, and play. "We like to call it the

captive pause," says an executive or an alternative media firm, where consumers "really have nothing else to do but either look at the person in front of them or look at some engaging content as well as 15-second commercials"—the average person waits in line about 30 minutes a day. Of course, this may leave you wondering if there are any commercial-free havens remaining for ad-weary consumers. The back-seat of a taxi, perhaps, or public elevators, or stalls in a public restroom? Forget it! Each has already been invaded by innovative marketers.

Sources: See Cara Beardi, "From Elevators to Gas Stations, Ads Multiplying," *Advertising Age,* November 13, 2000, pp. 40–42; Charles Pappas, "Ad Nauseam," *Advertising Age,* July 10, 2000, pp. 16–18; Beardi, "Airport Powerhouses Make Connection," *Advertising Age,* October 2, 2000, p. 8; and Wayne Friedman, "Eagle-Eye Marketers Find Right Spot," *Advertising Age,* January 22, 2001, pp. S2–S3.

optimizers allow media planners to evaluate vast combinations of television programs and prices. Such programs help advertisers to make better decisions about which mix of networks, programs, and day parts will yield the highest reach per ad dollar.[15]

Evaluating Advertising

The advertising program should evaluate both the communication effects and the sales effects of advertising regularly. Measuring the *communication effects* of an ad—*copy testing*—tells whether the ad is communicating well. Copy testing can be done before or after an ad is printed or broadcast. Before the ad is placed, the advertiser can show it to consumers, ask how they like it, and measure recall or attitude changes resulting from it. After the ad is run, the advertiser can measure how the ad affected consumer recall or product awareness, knowledge, and preference.

But what *sales* are caused by an ad that increases brand awareness by 20 percent and brand preference by 10 percent? The *sales effects* of advertising are often harder to measure than the communication effects. Sales are affected by many factors besides advertising—such as product features, price, and availability.

One way to measure the sales effect of advertising is to compare past sales with past advertising expenditures. Another way is through experiments. For example, to test the effects of different advertising spending levels, Coca-Cola could vary the amount it spends on advertising in different market areas and measure the differences in the resulting sales levels. It could spend the normal amount in one market area, half the normal amount in another area, and twice the normal amount in a third area. If the three market areas are similar, and if all other marketing efforts in the area are the same, then differences in sales in the three areas could be related to advertising level. More complex experiments could be designed to include other variables, such as difference in the ads or media used.

Other Advertising Considerations

In developing advertising strategies and programs, the company must address two additional questions. First, how will the company organize its advertising function—who will perform which advertising tasks? Second, how will the company adapt its advertising strategies and programs to the complexities of international markets?

Organizing for Advertising Different companies organize in different ways to handle advertising. In small companies, advertising might be handled by someone in the sales department. Large companies set up advertising departments whose job it is to set the advertising budget, work with the ad agency, and handle other advertising not done by the agency. Most large companies use outside advertising agencies because they offer several advantages.

How does an **advertising agency** work? Advertising agencies were started in the mid-to-late 1800s by salespeople and brokers who worked for the media and received a commission for selling advertising space to companies. As time passed, the salespeople began to help customers prepare their ads. Eventually, they formed agencies and grew closer to the advertisers than to the media. Today's agencies employ specialists who can often perform advertising tasks better than can the company's own staff. Agencies also bring an outside point of view to solving the company's problems, along with lots of experience from working with different clients and situations. Thus, today, even companies with strong advertising departments of their own use advertising agencies.

Advertising agency
A marketing services firm that assists companies in planning, preparing, implementing, and evaluating all or portions of their advertising programs.

Some ad agencies are huge—the largest U.S. agency, McCann-Erickson Worldwide, has annual gross income of $1.8 billion on billings (the dollar amount of advertising placed for clients) of more than $17 billion. In recent years, many agencies have grown by gobbling up other agencies, thus creating huge agency holding companies. The largest of these agency "megagroups," WPP Group, includes several large advertising, public relations, and promotion agencies with combined worldwide gross income of $8 billion on billings exceeding $67 billion.[16] Most large advertising agencies have the staff and resources to handle all phases of an advertising campaign for their clients, from creating a marketing plan to developing ad campaigns and preparing, placing, and evaluating ads.

International Advertising Decisions International advertisers face many complexities not encountered by domestic advertisers. The most basic issue concerns the degree to which global advertising should be adapted to the unique characteristics of various country markets. Some large advertisers have attempted to support their global brands with highly standardized worldwide advertising, with campaigns that work as well in Bangkok as they do in Baltimore. For example, Jeep has created a worldwide brand image of ruggedness and reliability; Coca-Cola's Sprite brand uses standardized appeals to target the world's youth. Gillette's ads for its Sensor Excel for Women are almost identical worldwide, with only minor adjustments to suit the local culture. Ericsson, the Swedish telecommunications giant, spent $100 million on a standardized global television campaign with the tag line "make yourself heard," which features Agent 007, James Bond.

Standardization produces many benefits—lower advertising costs, greater global advertising coordination, and a more consistent worldwide image. But it also has drawbacks. Most importantly, it ignores the fact that country markets differ greatly in their cultures, demographics, and economic conditions. Thus, most international advertisers "think globally but act locally." They develop global advertising *strategies* that make their

DaimlerChrysler creates a worldwide brand image of ruggedness and reliability for its Jeep brand. Here, its Thai, German, and U.S. Web sites contain only minor adjustments in messages to suit local languages and cultures.

worldwide advertising efforts more efficient and consistent. Then they adapt their advertising *programs* to make them more responsive to consumer needs and expectations within local markets.

For example, Coca-Cola has a pool of different commercials that can be used in or adapted to several different international markets. Some can be used with only minor changes—such as language—in several different countries. Local and regional managers decide which commercials work best for which markets. Recently, in a reverse of the usual order, a series of Coca-Cola commercials developed for the Russian market, using a talking bear and a man who transforms into a wolf, was shown in the United States. "This approach fits perfectly with the global nature of Coca-Cola," says the president of Coca-Cola's Nordic division. "[It] offers people a special look into a culture that is different from their own."[17]

Global advertisers face several special problems. For instance, advertising media costs and availability differ vastly from country to country. Countries also differ in the extent to which they regulate advertising practices. Many countries have extensive systems of laws restricting how much a company can spend on advertising, the media used, the nature of advertising claims, and other aspects of the advertising program. Such restrictions often require advertisers to adapt their campaigns from country to country.

For example, alcoholic products cannot be advertised or sold in Muslim countries. In many countries, Norway and Sweden, for example, no TV ads may be directed at children under 12. Moreover, Sweden is lobbying to extend that ban to all European Union member countries. To play it safe, McDonald's advertises itself as a family restaurant in Sweden. Comparative ads, while acceptable and even common in the United States and Canada, are less commonly used in the United Kingdom, unacceptable in Japan, and illegal in India and Brazil. China has restrictive censorship rules for TV and radio advertising; for example, the words *the best* are banned, as are ads that "violate social customs" or present women in "improper ways." Coca-Cola's Indian subsidiary was forced to end a promotion that offered prizes, such as a trip to Hollywood, because it violated India's established trade practices by encouraging customers to buy in order to "gamble."[18]

Thus, although advertisers may develop global strategies to guide their overall advertising efforts, specific advertising programs must usually be adapted to meet local cultures and customs, media characteristics, and advertising regulations.

Linking the Concepts

Think about what goes on behind the scenes for the ads we all tend to take for granted.

◆ Pick a favorite print or television ad. Why do you like it? Do you think that it's effective? Can you think of an ad that people like that may not be effective?
◆ Dig a little deeper and learn about the campaign *behind* your ad. What are the campaign's objectives? What is its budget? Assess the campaign's message and media strategies. Looking beyond your own feelings about the ad, is the campaign likely to be effective?

Sales Promotion

Advertising and personal selling often work closely with another promotion tool, sales promotion. *Sales promotion* consists of short-term incentives to encourage purchase or sales of a product or service. Whereas advertising and personal selling offer reasons to buy a product or service, sales promotion offers reasons to buy *now*.

Examples of sales promotions are found everywhere. A freestanding insert in the Sunday newspaper contains a coupon offering $1 off Folgers coffee. An e-mail from Amazon.com offers free shipping on your next purchase over $35. The end-of-the-aisle display in the local supermarket tempts impulse buyers with a wall of Coke cartons. An executive who buys a new Compaq laptop gets a free carrying case, or a family buys a new Taurus and receives a rebate check for $500. A hardware store chain receives a 10 percent discount on selected Black & Decker portable power tools if it agrees to advertise them in local newspapers. Sales promotion includes a wide variety of promotion tools designed to stimulate earlier or stronger market response.

Rapid Growth of Sales Promotion

Sales promotion tools are used by most organizations, including manufacturers, distributors, retailers, trade associations, and nonprofit institutions. They are targeted toward final buyers (*consumer promotions*), retailers and wholesalers (*trade promotions*), business customers (*business promotions*), and members of the sales force (*sales force promotions*). Today, in the average consumer packaged-goods company, sales promotion accounts for 74 percent of all marketing expenditures.[19]

Several factors have contributed to the rapid growth of sales promotion, particularly in consumer markets. First, inside the company, product managers face greater pressures to increase their current sales, and promotion is viewed as an effective short-run sales tool. Second, externally, the company faces more competition and competing brands are less differentiated. Increasingly, competitors are using sales promotion to help differentiate their offers. Third, advertising efficiency has declined because of rising costs, media clutter, and legal restraints. Finally, consumers have become more deal oriented and ever-larger retailers are demanding more deals from manufacturers.

The growing use of sales promotion has resulted in *promotion clutter,* similar to advertising clutter. Consumers are increasingly tuning out promotions, weakening their ability to trigger immediate purchase. Manufacturers are now searching for ways to rise above the clutter, such as offering larger coupon values or creating more dramatic point-of-purchase displays.

In developing a sales promotion program, a company must first set sales promotion objectives and then select the best tools for accomplishing these objectives.

Sales Promotion Objectives

Sales promotion objectives vary widely. Sellers may use *consumer promotions* to increase short-term sales or to help build long-term market share. Objectives for *trade promotions* include getting retailers to carry new items and more inventory, getting them to advertise the product and give it more shelf space, and getting them to buy ahead. For the *sales force,* objectives include getting more sales force support for current or new products or getting salespeople to sign up new accounts. Sales promotions are usually used together with advertising, personal selling, or other promotion mix tools. Consumer promotions must usually be advertised and can add excitement and pulling power to ads. Trade and sales force promotions support the firm's personal selling process.

In general, rather than creating only short-term sales or temporary brand switching, sales promotions should help to reinforce the product's position and build long-term *customer relationships.* Increasingly, marketers are avoiding "quick fix," price-only promotions in favor of promotions designed to build brand equity. Even price promotions can be designed to help build customer relationships. Examples include all of the "frequency marketing programs" and clubs that have mushroomed in recent years. For example, Waldenbooks sponsors a Preferred Reader Program, which has attracted more than 4 million members, each paying $5 to receive mailings about new books, a 10 percent discount on book purchases, toll-free ordering, and many other services. American Express's Custom Extras program automatically awards customers deals and discounts based on frequency of purchases at participating retailers. Norwegian Cruise Lines sponsors a loyalty program called Latitudes, a co-branding effort with Visa. The program includes a two-for-one cruise offer and a Latitudes Visa card that rewards users with points redeemable for discounts on NCL cruises. If properly designed, every sales promotion tool has the potential to build consumer relationships.

Major Sales Promotion Tools

Many tools can be used to accomplish sales promotion objectives. Descriptions of the main consumer, trade, and business promotion tools follow.

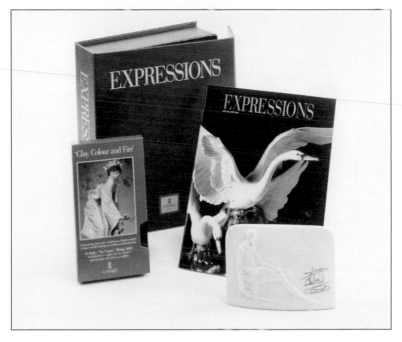

Customer relationship-building promotions: "Frequency marketing programs" and clubs have mushroomed in recent years. Lladro's Collectors Society members receive a subscription to Expressions magazine, a bisque plaque, free enrollment in the Lladro Museum of New York, and other relationship-building benefits.

Consumer Promotion Tools The main *consumer promotion tools* include samples, coupons, cash refunds, price packs, premiums, advertising specialties, patronage rewards, point-of-purchase displays and demonstrations, and contests, sweepstakes, and games.

Samples are offers of a trial amount of a product. Sampling is the most effective—but most expensive—way to introduce a new product. Some samples are free; for others, the company charges a small amount to offset its cost. The sample might be delivered door-to-door, sent by mail, handed out in a store, attached to another product, or featured in an ad. Sometimes, samples are combined into sample packs, which can then be used to promote other products and services. Procter & Gamble has even distributed samples via the Internet: [20]

When Procter & Gamble decided to relaunch Pert Plus shampoo, it extended its $20 million ad campaign by constructing a new Web site (www.pertplus.com). P&G had three objectives for the Web site: to create awareness for reformulated Pert Plus, get consumers to try the product, and gather data about Web users. The site's first page invites visitors to place their heads against the computer screen in a mock attempt to measure the cleanliness of their hair. After "tabulating the results," the site tells visitors that they "need immediate help." The solution: "How about a free sample of new Pert Plus?" Visitors obtain the sample by filling out a short demographic form. The site offers other interesting features as well. For example, clicking "get a friend in a lather" produces a template that will send an e-mail to a friend with an invitation to visit the site and receive a free sample. How did the sampling promotion work out? Even P&G was shocked by the turnout. Within just two months of launching the site, 170,000 people visited and 83,000 requested samples. More surprising, given that the site is only 10 pages deep, the average person visited the site 1.9 times and spent a total of 7.5 minutes each visit.

Coupons are certificates that give buyers a saving when they purchase specified products. Most consumers love coupons: They clip some 4.8 billion of them each year with

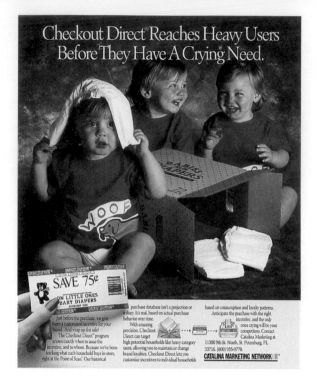

Point-of-sale couponing: Using Checkout Direct technology, marketers can dispense personalized coupons to carefully targeted buyers at the checkout counter. This avoids the waste of poorly targeted coupons delivered through FSIs (coupon pages inserted into newspapers).

an average face value of 70 cents, for a total savings of $3.4 billion.[21] Coupons can stimulate sales of a mature brand or promote early trial of a new brand. However, as a result of coupon clutter, redemption rates have been declining in recent years. Thus, most major consumer goods companies are issuing fewer coupons and targeting them more carefully. They are also cultivating new outlets for distributing coupons, such as supermarket shelf dispensers, electronic point-of-sale coupon printers, or "paperless coupon systems." An example is Catalina Marketing Network's Checkout Direct system, which dispenses personalized discounts to targeted buyers at the checkout counter in stores. Some companies also offer coupons on their Web sites or through online coupon services such as coolsavings.com, valupage.com, hotcoupons.com, and directcoupons.com.[22]

Cash refund offers (or *rebates*) are like coupons except that the price reduction occurs after the purchase rather than at the retail outlet. The consumer sends a "proof of purchase" to the manufacturer, who then refunds part of the purchase price by mail. For example, Toro ran a clever preseason promotion on some of its snowblower models, offering a rebate if the snowfall in the buyer's market area turned out to be below average. Competitors were not able to match this offer on such short notice, and the promotion was very successful.

Price packs (also called *cents-off deals*) offer consumers savings off the regular price of a product. The reduced prices are marked by the producer directly on the label or package. Price packs can be single packages sold at a reduced price (such as two for the price of one), or two related products banded together (such as a toothbrush and toothpaste). Price packs are very effective—even more so than coupons—in stimulating short-term sales.

Premiums are goods offered either free or at low cost as an incentive to buy a product, ranging from toys included with kids' products to phone cards and CDs. A premium may come inside the package (in-pack), outside the package (on-pack), or through the mail. In its "Treasure Hunt" promotion, for example, Quaker Oats inserted $5 million worth of gold and silver coins in Ken-L Ration dog food packages. In another premium promotion, Cutty Sark offered a brass tray with the purchase of one bottle of its scotch and a desk lamp with the purchase of two. United Airlines rewarded Chicago-area 75,000 Mileage Plus frequent-flyer club members with a custom CD. The 10-song, Chicago-themed compilation disk, entitled "Chicago—Our Kind of Town," was widely played on local radio stations. It became so popular that United ended up selling it at record stores. The airline plans similar custom-designed premiums for four other major cities it serves.[23]

Advertising specialties are useful articles imprinted with an advertiser's name given as gifts to consumers. Typical items include pens, calendars, key rings, matches, shopping bags, T-shirts, caps, nail files, and coffee mugs. Such items can be very effective. In a recent study, 63 percent of all consumers surveyed were either carrying or wearing an ad specialty item. More than three-quarters of those who had an item could recall the advertiser's name or message before showing the item to the interviewer.[24]

Patronage rewards are cash or other awards offered for the regular use of a certain company's products or services. For example, airlines offer frequent-flyer plans, awarding points for miles traveled that can be turned in for free airline trips. Hotels have adopted honored-guest plans that award points to users of their hotels. And supermarkets issue frequent shopper cards that dole out a wealth of discounts at the checkout. Baskin-Robbins offers frequent-purchase awards—for every 10 purchases, customers receive a free quart of ice cream.

Point-of-purchase (POP) promotions include displays and demonstrations that take place at the point of purchase or sale. An example is a five-foot-high cardboard display of Cap'n Crunch next to Cap'n Crunch cereal boxes. Unfortunately, many retailers do not like to handle the hundreds of displays, signs, and posters they receive from manufacturers each year. Manufacturers have responded by offering better POP materials, tying them in with television or print messages, and offering to set them up.

Contests, sweepstakes, and *games* give consumers the chance to win something, such as cash, trips, or goods, by luck or through extra effort. A *contest* calls for consumers to submit an entry—a jingle, guess, suggestion—to be judged by a panel that will select the best entries. A *sweepstakes* calls for consumers to submit their names for a drawing. A *game* presents consumers with something—bingo numbers, missing letters—every time they buy, which may or may not help them win a prize. A sales contest urges dealers or the sales force to increase their efforts, with prizes going to the top performers.

Trade Promotion Tools Manufacturers direct more sales promotion dollars toward retailers and wholesalers (68 percent) than to consumers (32 percent). Trade promotion can persuade resellers to carry a brand, give it shelf space, promote it in advertising, and push it to consumers. Shelf space is so scarce these days that manufacturers often have to offer price-offs, allowances, buy-back guarantees, or free goods to retailers and wholesalers to get products on the shelf and, once there, to stay on it.

Manufacturers use several trade promotion tools. Many of the tools used for consumer promotions—contests, premiums, displays—can also be used as trade promotions. Or the manufacturer may offer a straight *discount* off the list price on each case purchased during a stated period of time (also called a *price-off, off-invoice,* or *off-list*). Manufacturers also may offer an *allowance* (usually so much off per case) in return for the retailer's agreement to feature the manufacturer's products in some way. An *advertising allowance* compensates retailers for advertising the product. A *display allowance* compensates them for using special displays.

Manufacturers may offer *free goods,* which are extra cases of merchandise, to resellers who buy a certain quantity or who feature a certain flavor or size. They may offer *push money*—cash or gifts to dealers or their sales forces to "push" the manufacturer's goods. Manufacturers may give retailers free *specialty advertising items* that carry the company's name, such as pens, pencils, calendars, paperweights, matchbooks, memo pads, and yardsticks.

Business Promotion Tools Companies spend billions of dollars each year on promotion to industrial customers. These *business promotion tools* are used to generate business leads, stimulate purchases, reward customers, and motivate salespeople. Business promotion includes many of the same tools used for consumer or trade promotions. Here, we focus on two additional major business promotion tools—conventions and trade shows, and sales contests.

Many companies and trade associations organize *conventions and trade shows* to promote their products. Firms selling to the industry show their products at the trade show. More than 4,300 trade shows take place every year, drawing as many as 85 million people. Vendors receive many benefits, such as opportunities to find new sales leads, contact customers, introduce new products, meet new customers, sell more to present customers, and educate customers with publications and audiovisual materials. Trade shows also help companies reach many prospects not reached through their sales forces. About 90 percent of a trade show's visitors see a company's salespeople for the first time at the show. Business marketers may spend as much as 35 percent of their annual promotion budgets on trade shows.[25]

A *sales contest* is a contest for salespeople or dealers to motivate them to increase their sales performance over a given period. Sales contests motivate and recognize good company performers, who may receive trips, cash prizes, or other gifts. Some companies award points for performance, which the receiver can turn in for any of a variety of prizes. Sales contests work best when they are tied to measurable and achievable sales objectives (such as finding new accounts, reviving old accounts, or increasing account profitability).

More than 4,300 trade shows take place every year, drawing as many as 85 million people, giving sellers chances to introduce new products and meet new customers. At this consumer electronics trade show, 2,000 exhibitors attracted more than 91,000 professional visitors.

Developing the Sales Promotion Program

The marketer must make several other decisions in order to define the full sales promotion program. First, the marketer must decide on the *size of the incentive.* A certain minimum incentive is necessary if the promotion is to succeed; a larger incentive will produce more sales response. The marketer also must set *conditions for participation.* Incentives might be offered to everyone or only to select groups.

The marketer must then decide how to *promote and distribute the promotion* program itself. A 50-cents-off coupon could be given out in a package, at the store, by mail, or in an advertisement. Each distribution method involves a different level of reach and cost. Increasingly, marketers are blending several media into a total campaign concept. The *length of the promotion* is also important. If the sales promotion period is too short, many prospects (who may not be buying during that time) will miss it. If the promotion runs too long, the deal will lose some of its "act now" force.

Evaluation is also very important. Yet many companies fail to evaluate their sales promotion programs, and others evaluate them only superficially. The most common evaluation method is to compare sales before, during, and after a promotion. Suppose a company has a 6 percent market share before the promotion, which jumps to 10 percent during the promotion, falls to 5 percent right after, and rises to 7 percent later on. The promotion seems to have attracted new triers and more buying from current customers. After the promotion, sales fell as consumers used up their inventories. The long-run rise to 7 percent means that the company gained some new users. If the brand's share had returned to the old level, then the promotion would have changed only the *timing* of demand rather than the *total* demand.

Consumer research would also show the kinds of people who responded to the promotion and what they did after it ended. *Surveys* can provide information on how many consumers recall the promotion, what they thought of it, how many took advantage of it, and how it affected their buying. Sales promotions also can be evaluated through *experiments* that vary factors such as incentive value, length, and distribution method.

Clearly, sales promotion plays an important role in the total promotion mix. To use it well, the marketer must define the sales promotion objectives, select the best tools, design the sales promotion program, implement the program, and evaluate the results. Moreover, sales promotion must be coordinated carefully with other promotion mix elements within the integrated marketing communications program.

Public Relations

Another major mass-promotion tool is *public relations*—building good relations with the company's various publics by obtaining favorable publicity, building up a good corporate image, and handling or heading off unfavorable rumors, stories, and events. Public relations departments may perform any or all of the following functions:[26]

◆ *Press relations or press agentry:* Creating and placing newsworthy information in the news media to attract attention to a person, product, or service.
◆ *Product publicity:* Publicizing specific products.
◆ *Public affairs:* Building and maintaining national or local community relations.
◆ *Lobbying:* Building and maintaining relations with legislators and government officials to influence legislation and regulation.

- *Investor relations:* Maintaining relationships with shareholders and others in the financial community.
- *Development:* Public relations with donors or members of nonprofit organizations to gain financial or volunteer support.

Public relations is used to promote products, people, places, ideas, activities, organizations, and even nations. Trade associations have used public relations to rebuild interest in declining commodities such as eggs, apples, milk, and potatoes. New York City turned its image around when its "I ♥ New York!" campaign took root, bringing millions more tourists to the city. Johnson & Johnson's masterly use of public relations played a major role in saving Tylenol from extinction after its product-tampering scare. Nations have used public relations to attract more tourists, foreign investment, and international support.

Public relations can have a strong impact on public awareness at a much lower cost than advertising can. The company does not pay for the space or time in the media. Rather, it pays for a staff to develop and circulate information and to manage events. If the company develops an interesting story, it could be picked up by several different media, having the same effect as advertising that would cost millions of dollars. And it would have more credibility than advertising.

Public relations results can sometimes be spectacular. Here's how publisher Scholastic, Inc. used public relations to turn a simple new book introduction into a major international event, all on a very small budget:

> Secret codes. A fiercely guarded text. Huddled masses lined up in funny hats at the witching hour. Welcome to one of the biggest and oddest literary events in history. As the clock crept past midnight, kids worldwide rushed to buy the fourth installment of the Harry Potter series. It was the fastest-shrinking book pile in history—with nearly 3 million copies selling in 48 hours in the United States alone. The spellbinding plots, written by Scottish welfare-mom-turned-millionaire J. K. Rowling, captivated kids everywhere, but the hidden hand of [public relations] played a role, too. With contests, theme parties, and giveaways, conditions were hot for Harry. How do you whip up a consumer frenzy with a mere $1.8 million promotion budget? Scholastic mixed in-store promotions with a few carefully placed ads [and a heap of public relations hype] to create a sense of celebration. It heightened the tension by keeping the title and book jacket under wraps almost until the last minute, even forcing booksellers to sign secrecy agreements.[27]

Despite its potential strengths, public relations is often described as a marketing stepchild because of its limited and scattered use. The public relations department is usually located at corporate headquarters. Its staff is so busy dealing with various publics—stockholders, employees, legislators, city officials—that public relations programs to support product marketing objectives may be ignored. Marketing managers and public relations practitioners do not always talk the same language. Many public relations practitioners see their job as simply communicating. In contrast, marketing managers tend to be much more interested in how advertising and public relations affect sales and profits.

This situation is changing, however. Many companies now want their public relations departments to manage all of their activities with a view toward marketing the company and improving the bottom line. They know that good public relations can be a powerful brand-building tool. Two well-known marketing consultants provide the following advice, which points to the potential power of public relations as a first step in building brands:

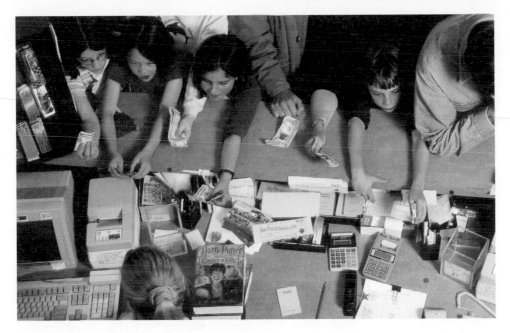

Public relations results can sometimes be spectacular. Scholastic sponsored low-cost sleepovers, games, and costume contests to whip up consumer frenzy for the fourth installment of its Harry Potter series.

Just because a heavy dose of advertising is associated with most major brands doesn't necessarily mean that advertising built the brands in the first place. The birth of a brand is usually accomplished with [public relations], not advertising. Our general rule is [PR] first, advertising second. [Public relations] is the nail, advertising the hammer. [PR] creates the credentials that provide the credibility for advertising. . . . Anita Roddick built the Body Shop into a major brand with no advertising at all. Instead, she traveled the world on a relentless quest for publicity. . . . Until recently Starbucks Coffee Co. didn't spend a hill of beans on advertising, either. In 10 years, the company spent less than $10 million on advertising, a trivial amount for a brand that delivers annual sales of $1.3 billion. Wal-Mart Stores became the world's largest retailer . . . with very little advertising. . . . In the toy field, Furby, Beanie Babies, and Tickle Me Elmo became highly successful . . . and on the Internet, Yahoo!, Amazon.com, and Excite became powerhouse brands, [all] with virtually no advertising.[28]

Thus, some companies are setting up special units called *marketing public relations* to support corporate and product promotion and image making directly. Many companies hire marketing public relations firms to handle their PR programs or to assist the company public relations team.

Major Public Relations Tools

Public relations professionals use several tools. One of the major tools is *news.* PR professionals find or create favorable news about the company and its products or people. Sometimes news stories occur naturally, and sometimes the PR person can suggest events or activities that would create news. *Speeches* can also create product and company publicity. Increasingly, company executives must field questions from the media or give talks at trade associations or sales meetings, and these events can either build or hurt the company's image.

Another common PR tool is *special events,* ranging from news conferences, press tours, grand openings, and fireworks displays to laser shows, hot air balloon releases, multimedia presentations and star-studded spectaculars, or educational programs designed to reach and interest target publics.

Public relations people also prepare *written materials* to reach and influence their target markets. These materials include annual reports, brochures, articles, and company newsletters and magazines. *Audiovisual materials,* such as films, slide-and-sound programs, and video- and audiocassettes, are being used increasingly as communication tools. *Corporate identity materials* can also help create a corporate identity that the public immediately recognizes. Logos, stationery, brochures, signs, business forms, business cards, buildings, uniforms, and company cars and trucks—all become marketing tools when they are attractive, distinctive, and memorable. Finally, companies can improve public goodwill by contributing money and time to *public service activities.*

A company's Web site can be a good public relations vehicle. Consumers and members of other publics can visit the site for information and entertainment. Such sites can be extremely popular. For example, Butterball's site (www.butterball.com), which features cooking and carving tips, received 550,000 visitors in one day during Thanksgiving week last year. Web sites can also be ideal for handling crisis situations. For example, when several bottles of Odwalla apple juice sold on the West Coast were found to contain E. coli bacteria, Odwalla initiated a massive product recall. Within only three hours, it set up a Web site laden with information about the crisis and Odwalla's response. Company staffers also combed the Internet looking for newsgroups discussing Odwalla and posted links to the site. In another example, American Home Products quickly set up a Web site to distribute accurate information and advice after a model died reportedly after inhaling its Primatene Mist. The Primatene site, up less than 12 hours after the crisis broke, remains in place today (www.primatene.com). In all, notes one analyst, "Today, public relations is reshaping the Internet and the Internet, in turn, is redefining the practice of public relations." Says another, "People look to the Net for information, not salesmanship, and that's the real opportunity for public relations." [29]

As with the other promotion tools, in considering when and how to use product public relations, management should set PR objectives, choose the PR messages and vehicles, implement the PR plan, and evaluate the results. The firm's public relations should be blended smoothly with other promotion activities within the company's overall integrated marketing communications effort.

A company's Web site can be a good public relations vehicle. Butterball's site, which features cooking and carving tips, received 550,000 visits in one day during Thanksgiving week last year.

STOP Rest Stop: Reviewing the Concepts

In this chapter, you've learned about the concept of integrated marketing communications (IMC), defined the major marketing communications tools, and overviewed the general promotion mix strategies. We've also explored three of the specific communications mix elements—advertising, sales promotion, and public relations—more deeply. Before moving on to other promotion tools, let's briefly review the important concepts.

Modern marketing calls for more than just developing a good product, pricing it attractively, and making it available to target customers. Companies also must *communicate* with current and prospective customers to inform them about product benefits and carefully position products in consumers' minds. To do this, they must blend five communication-mix tools, guided by a well designed and implemented integrated marketing communications strategy.

1. Discuss the process and advantages of integrated marketing communications.

Recent shifts toward targeted or one-to-one marketing, coupled with advances in information technology, have had a dramatic impact on marketing communications. As marketing communicators adopt richer but more fragmented media and promotion mixes to reach their diverse markets, they risk creating a communications hodgepodge for consumers. To prevent this, more companies are adopting the concept of *integrated marketing communications (IMC)*. Guided by an overall IMC strategy, the company works out the roles that the various promotional tools will play and the extent to which each will be used. It carefully coordinates the promotional activities and the timing of when major campaigns take place. Finally, to help implement its integrated marketing strategy, the company appoints a marketing communications director who has overall responsibility for the company's communications efforts.

2. Define the five promotion tools and discuss factors that must be considered in shaping the overall promotion mix.

A company's total *marketing communications mix*—also called its *promotion mix*—consists of the specific blend of *advertising, personal selling, sales promotion, public relations,* and *direct-marketing* tools that the company uses to pursue its advertising and marketing objectives. Advertising includes any paid form of nonpersonal presentation and promotion of ideas, goods, or services by an identified

sponsor. In contrast, public relations focuses on building good relations with the company's various publics by obtaining favorable unpaid publicity. Personal selling is any form of personal presentation by the firm's sales force for the purpose of making sales and building customer relationships. Firms use sales promotion to provide short-term incentives to encourage the purchase or sale of a product or service. Finally, firms seeking immediate response from targeted individual customers use nonpersonal direct-marketing tools to communicate with customers.

The company wants to create an integrated *promotion mix.* It can pursue a *push* or a *pull* promotional strategy, or a combination of the two. The best specific blend of promotion tools depends on the type of product/market and the product life-cycle stage. People at all levels of the organization must be aware of the many legal and ethical issues surrounding marketing communications.

3. Describe and discuss the major decisions involved in developing an advertising program.

Advertising—the use of paid media by a seller to inform, persuade, and remind about its products or organization—is a strong promotion tool that takes many forms and has many uses. *Advertising decision making* involves decisions about the objectives, the budget, the message, the media, and, finally, the evaluation of results. Advertisers should set clear *objectives* as to whether the advertising is supposed to inform, persuade, or remind buyers. The advertising *budget* can be based on what is affordable, on sales, on competitors' spending, or on the objectives and tasks. The *message decision* calls for planning a message strategy and executing it effectively. The *media decision* involves defining reach, frequency, and impact goals; choosing major media types; selecting media vehicles; and deciding on media timing. Message and media decisions must be closely coordinated for maximum campaign effectiveness. Finally, *evaluation* calls for evaluating the communication and sales effects of advertising before, during, and after the advertising is placed.

4. Explain how sales promotion campaigns are developed and implemented.

Sales promotion covers a wide variety of short-term incentive tools—coupons, premiums, contests, buying allowances—designed to stimulate final and business consumers, the trade, and the company's own sales force. Sales promotion spending has been growing faster than advertising spending in recent years. A sales promotion campaign first calls for setting sales promotion objectives (in general, sales promotions should be *consumer relationship building*). It then calls for developing and implementing the sales promotion program by using consumer promotion tools (*samples, coupons, cash refunds* or *rebates, price packs, premiums, advertising specialties, patronage rewards*, and others); trade promotion tools (*discounts, allowances, free goods, push money*); and business promotion tools (*conventions, trade shows, sales contests*). The sales promotion effort should be coordinated carefully with the firm's other promotion efforts.

5. Explain how companies use public relations to communicate with their publics.

Public relations involves building good relations with the company's various publics. Its functions include *press*

agentry, product publicity, public affairs, lobbying, investor relations, and *development.* Public relations can have a strong impact on public awareness at a much lower cost than advertising can, and public relations results can sometimes be spectacular. Despite its potential strengths, however, public relations sometimes sees only limited and scattered use. Public relations tools include *news, speeches, special events, written materials, audiovisual materials, corporate identity materials,* and *public service activities.* A company's Web site can be a good public relations vehicle. In considering when and how to use product public relations, management should set PR objectives, choose the PR messages and vehicles, implement the PR plan, and evaluate the results. Public relations should be blended smoothly with other promotion activities within the company's overall integrated marketing communications effort.

Navigating the Key Terms

For a detailed analysis of the meaning and importance of each of the following key terms, visit our Web page at www.prenhall.com/kotler.

Advertising
Advertising agency
Advertising objective

Affordable method
Competitive-parity method
Direct marketing
Integrated marketing
   communications (IMC)
Marketing communications mix
   (promotion mix)
Objective-and-task method

Percentage-of-sales method
Personal selling
Public relations
Pull strategy
Push strategy
Sales promotion

Travel Log

The following concept checks and discussion questions will help you to keep track of and apply the concepts you've studied in this chapter.

Concept Checks

Fill in the blanks, then look for the correct answers.

1. A company's marketing communications mix consists of a blend of _____, _____, _____, _____, and _____ tools.

2. _____ is any paid form of nonpersonal presentation and promotion of ideas, goods, or services by an identified sponsor.

3. _____ builds strong brand identity in the market-

place by tying together and reinforcing all your images and messages.

4. _____ can reach masses of geographically dispersed buyers at a low cost per exposure, and it enables the seller to repeat a message many times.

5. Using a _____ strategy, the producer directs its marketing activities (primarily advertising and consumer promotion) toward final consumers to induce them to buy the product.

6. Advertising objectives can be classified by primary purpose—whether the aim is to _____, _____, or _____.

7. There are four common methods used to set the total budget for advertising: the affordable method, the

_____ method, the _____ method, and the _____ method.

8. Advertising appeals should have three characteristics: (1) _____; (2) _____; and (3) _____.

9. _____ is a measure of how many times the average person in the target market is exposed to the message.

10. _____ consists of short-term incentives to encourage purchase or sales of a product or service.

11. The main consumer promotion tools include _____, _____, price packs, premiums, advertising specialties, patronage rewards, _____, and contests, sweepstakes, and _____.

12. Public relations departments perform many functions. Under the _____ function, the department conducts public relations with donors or members of nonprofit organizations to gain financial or volunteer support.

Concept Checks Answers: 1. advertising, personal selling, sales promotion, public relations, and direct-marketing; 2. Advertising; 3. Integrated marketing communications (IMC); 4. Advertising; 5. pull; 6. inform, persuade, or remind; 7. percentage-of-sales, competitive-parity, and objective-and-task; 8. meaningful, believable, distinctive; 9. Frequency; 10. Sales promotion; 11. samples, coupons, cash refunds, games; 12. development;

Discussing the Issues

1. The shift from mass marketing to targeted marketing, and the corresponding use of a richer mix of promotion tools and communication channels, poses problems for many marketers. Using all of the promotion-mix elements suggested in the chapter, propose a plan for integrating marketing communications for one of the following: (a) your university or college, (b) McDonald's, (c) Burton Snowboards, and (d) a local zoo, museum, theater, or civic event.

2. Advertising objectives can be classified by primary purpose: to inform, persuade, or remind. Using your local newspaper, find examples of ads that address each of these objectives. Using Table 13-1, discuss why your examples fit the chosen objective.

3. The chapter lists nine different execution styles that are often used by advertisers to meet advertising objectives. Which of these styles do you think is most commonly used? Explain. Pick any three styles and find an example of each. Critique each example selected on its content, effectiveness, and match to selected target market.

4. Which of the sales promotion tools described in the chapter would be best for stimulating sales of the following products or services: (a) a dry cleaner wishing to emphasize low prices on washed and pressed dress shirts, (b) Gummy Bears new Black Cherry flavor, (c) Procter & Gamble's efforts to bundle laundry detergent and fabric softener together in a combined marketing effort, (d) a company that wants its customers to aid in developing a new jingle, and (e) Outpost.com attempts to help consumers remember what it sells as well as its Web address.

5. The latest public relations frontier is the Internet. Cyber-travelers can now post their problems with goods and services on electronic bulletin boards and in company chat rooms, putting pressure on companies to respond. Customers regularly share their experiences with product design flaws, service difficulties, prices, warranties, and other problems. What kinds of special public relations problems and opportunities does the Internet present to today's companies? How should companies change their company policies and Web sites to deal with these problems and opportunities? Find an example of a company that uses its Web site as a proactive public relations tool.

 **Mastering Marketing**

After examining the communication and promotion function of CanGo, comment on the extent of the organization's ability to integrate these functions into an overall IMC effort. Comment on strengths and weaknesses. How can the weaknesses be corrected? Which of the promotional tools needs to be used more? Are current communication and promotion objectives sufficient? Comment, explain, and offer suggestions.

Traveling the Net

Point of Interest: Public Relations and Controversial Products

Philip Morris Company is the world's largest tobacco company. It is also one of the most controversial. Philip Morris is full of apparent contradictions. For example, it spent $100 million to persuade children not to smoke; it contributes $60 million in cash and $15 million in food each year to fight hunger, combat domestic violence, and support the arts; and it has paid billions of dollars to reimburse states for the costs of treating smoking-related illnesses. Even its employees give millions of dollars each year to charities. Such numbers are impressive by any standard. So why is Philip Morris on every social crusader's hit list? The answer: the tobacco culture that engulfs the organization. For years Philip Morris operated under a siege mentality, closing itself off from the questions and criticism coming from the outside world. Recently, however, this culture has slowly begun to change. This $80 billion company has for the last several years renewed its efforts to change its image and business values. However, being a responsible corporate citizen and changing the company's culture, products, and image will not be easy.

For Discussion

1. What public relations issues does Philip Morris face?

2. On its Web site (www.philipmorris.com), Philip Morris admits to the addictive nature of smoking cigarettes. What kinds of public relations advantages does this admission create? What problems?
3. Visit the Web sites of other Philip Morris companies. What public relations synergies do you see? What problems might these synergies create?
4. Outline a public relations program for gaining public trust and shareholder interest.

Application Thinking

Cigarette smoking and the use of tobacco products have been under attack in the United States for several decades. However, this is not always the case in other countries. Although health advocates point to the rising instance of smoking-related illnesses in Europe, Africa, and Asia (especially China and Japan), smoking is still a very popular and growing habit. Considering the social and public relations approaches being used by Philip Morris in the United States, outline a global public relations strategy for the company. What role would advertising, sales promotion, and use of the company's Web site play in such a strategy? Discuss your strategy with your class.

MAP—Marketing Applications

MAP Stop 13

Is online advertising a boom or a bust? Even most critics still believe that advertising on the Internet has a bright future as long as its unique features are expanded and exploited. You can't treat an online advertisement like it was just another television or magazine advertisement, they say, although in the beginning that's just what many advertisers did. Banners, pop-ups, sponsorships, vertical and horizontal space usage, and the ability to target unique (and interested) audiences will be strengths upon which new and dynamic communication strategies can be built. In fact, most large advertising agencies now have online advertising divisions to ensure that this media form is utilized effectively and correctly. How is the

medium doing? With about $7 billion in sales annually at the beginning of the 21st century, it has already surpassed outdoor advertising and is close behind many forms of cable-TV advertising. Even though Web-based advertising is not designed to broadcast messages to the masses in the same way television advertising does, it can focus directly on particular upscale markets that are interesting to many sellers. To counter the Internet advertising problems of the past, advertisers are now spending more carefully and employing more carefully targeted messages. The new challenge in online advertising will be to determine not only how many times a consumer views an ad but who views it. Although it may take a while, the medium may yet achieve superstar status.

Thinking Like a Marketing Manager

1. DoubleClick, one of the largest online advertising firms, specializes in targeted advertising. Visit the Web site at http://www.doubleclick.com. Look in the section targeted toward advertisers and describe how DoubleClick attempts to target ads using audience psychographics and buying behavior.

2. When compared to television and magazine advertising, what are the advantages and disadvantages of online advertising?

3. How does online advertising monitor consumers' behavior and capture data about them? Do other media forms do this? Comment.

4. Assume that you are the advertising manager for a large toy manufacturer that is considering a significant expenditure in online advertising for the upcoming Christmas season. Visit NetRatings (www.netratings.com) to examine the statistics on the top banner ads currently online. Then, design a banner ad which you think would be most effective for your company. Explain any assumptions you made about your company and its products when you designed your ad.

Integrated Marketing Communications: Personal Selling and Direct Marketing

chapter **14**

ROAD MAP:
Previewing the Concepts

In the previous chapter, you learned about integrated marketing communication (IMC) and three specific elements of the marketing communications mix—advertising, sales promotion, and publicity. In this chapter, we'll move on down the road to learn about the final two IMC elements—personal selling and direct marketing. Personal selling is the interpersonal arm of marketing communications in which the sales force interacts with customers and prospects to make sales and build relationships. Direct marketing consists of direct connections with carefully targeted consumers to both obtain an immediate response and cultivate lasting customer relationships. Actually, direct marketing can be viewed as more than just a communications tool. In many ways, it constitutes an overall marketing *approach*—a blend of communications and distribution channels all rolled into one. As you read on, remember that although this chapter examines personal selling and direct marketing as separate tools, they must be carefully coordinated with other elements of the marketing communication mix.

▶ **After studying this chapter, you should be able to**

1. **discuss the role of a company's salespeople in creating value for customers and building customer relationships**
2. **identify and explain the six major sales force management steps**
3. **discuss the personal selling process, distinguishing between transaction-oriented marketing and relationship marketing**
4. **define direct marketing and discuss its benefits to customers and companies**
5. **identify and discuss the major forms of direct marketing**

We'll begin this leg of the journey with a look at Lear Corporation's sales force. Although you may never have heard of Lear, the chances are good that you've spent lots of time in one or more of the car interiors that it supplies to the world's major automotive manufacturers. Before you read on, close your eyes for a moment and envision a typical salesperson. If what you see is a stereotypical glad-hander out to lighten your wallet or purse by selling you something that you don't really need, you might be in for a surprise.

W hen someone says "salesperson," what image comes to mind? Perhaps it's the stereotypical "traveling salesman"—the fast-talking, ever-smiling peddler who travels his territory foisting his wares on reluctant customers. Such stereotypes, however, are sadly out of date. Today, most professional salespeople are well-educated, well-trained men and women who work to build long-term, value-producing relationships with their customers. They succeed not by taking customers in but by helping them out—by assessing customer needs and solving customer problems.

511

Consider Lear Corporation, one of the largest, fastest-growing, and most successful automotive suppliers in the world. Each year, Lear produces more than $14 billion worth of automotive interiors—seat systems, instrument panels, door panels, floor and acoustic systems, overhead systems, and electronic and electrical distribution systems. Its customers include most of the world's leading automotive companies, from Ford, DaimlerChrysler, General Motors, Fiat, Toyota, and Volvo to BMW, Ferrari, Rolls-Royce, and more than a dozen others. Lear now operates more than 300 facilities in 32 countries around the globe. During the past few years, Lear has achieved record-breaking sales and earnings growth. Lear's sales during the past five years have more than doubled, and its "average content per car" in North America has increased more than fourfold since 1990. It owns about a 30 percent share of the North American interior components market.

Lear Corporation owes its success to many factors, including a strong customer orientation and a commitment to continuous improvement, teamwork, and customer value. But perhaps more than any other part of the organization, it's Lear's outstanding 145-person sales force that makes the company's credo, "Consumer driven. Customer focused," ring true. Lear's sales force was recently rated by *Sales and Marketing Management* magazine as one of "America's Best Sales Forces." What makes this an outstanding sales force? Lear knows that good selling these days takes much more than just a sales rep covering a territory and convincing customers to buy the product. It takes teamwork, relationship building, and doing what's best for the customer. Lear's sales force excels at these tasks.

Lear's sales depend completely on the success of its customers. If the automakers don't sell cars, Lear doesn't sell interiors. So the Lear sales force strives to create not just sales, but customer success. In fact, Lear salespeople aren't "sales reps," they're "account managers" who function more as consultants than as order getters. "Our salespeople don't really close deals," notes a senior marketing executive. "They consult and work with customers to learn exactly what's needed and when."

To more fully match up with customers' needs, Lear has diversified its product line to become a kind of "one-stop shopping" source. Until a few years ago, Lear supplied only seats; now it sells almost everything for a car's interior. Providing complete interior solutions for customers also benefits Lear. "It used to be that we'd build a partnership and then get only a limited amount of revenue from it," the executive says. "Now we can get as much as possible out of our customer relationships."

Lear is heavily customer focused, so much so that it's broken up into separate divisions dedicated to specific customers. For example, there's a Ford division and a General Motors division, and each operates as its own profit center. Within each division, high-level "platform teams"—made up of salespeople, engineers, and program managers—work closely with their customer counterparts. These platform teams are closely supported by divisional manufacturing, finance, quality, and advanced technology groups. Lear's limited customer base, consisting of only a few dozen customers in all, allows Lear's sales teams to get very close to their customers. "Our teams don't call on purchasers; they're linked to customer operations at all levels," the marketer notes. "We try to put a system in place that creates continuous contact with customers." In fact, Lear often locates its sales offices in customers' plants. For example, the team that handles GM's light truck division works at GM's truck operation campus. "We can't just be there to give quotes and ask for orders," says the marketing executive. "We need to be involved with customers every step of the way—from vehicle concept through launch."

Lear's largest customers are worth billions of dollars in annual sales to the company. Maintaining profitable relationships with such large customers takes much more than a nice smile and a firm handshake. And certainly there's no place for the "smoke and mirrors" or "flimflam" sometimes mistakenly associated with personal selling. Success in such a selling environment requires careful teamwork among well-trained, dedicated sales professionals who are bent on profitably taking care of their customers.[1]

In this chapter, we examine two more marketing communication and promotion tools—*personal selling* and *direct marketing*. Both involve direct connections with customers aimed toward building customer-unique value and lasting relationships.

Personal Selling

Robert Louis Stevenson once noted that "everyone lives by selling something." We are all familiar with the sales forces used by business organizations to sell products and services to customers around the world. But sales forces are also found in many other kinds of organizations. For example, colleges use recruiters to attract new students, and churches use membership committees to attract new members. Hospitals and museums use fund-raisers to contact donors and raise money. Even governments use sales forces. The U.S. Postal Service, for instance, uses a sales force to sell Express Mail and other services to corporate customers. In the first part of this chapter, we examine the role of personal selling in the organization, sales force management decisions, and the personal selling process.

The Nature of Personal Selling

Selling is one of the oldest professions in the world. The people who do the selling go by many names: *salespeople, sales representatives, account executives, sales consultants, sales engineers, agents, district managers, marketing representatives,* and *account development reps,* to name just a few.

People hold many stereotypes of salespeople—including some unfavorable ones. "Salesman" may bring to mind the image of Arthur Miller's pitiable Willy Loman in *Death of a Salesman.* Or you might think of Meredith Willson's cigar-smoking, backslapping, joke-telling Harold Hill in *The Music Man.* Both examples depict salespeople as loners, traveling their territories, trying to foist their wares on unsuspecting or unwilling buyers.

However, modern salespeople are a far cry from these unfortunate stereotypes. Today, most salespeople are well-educated, well-trained professionals who work to build

 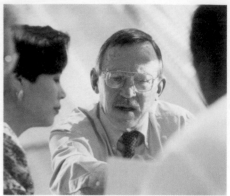

The term *salesperson* covers a wide range of positions, from the clerk selling in a retail store to the engineering salesperson who consults with client companies.

and maintain long-term customer relationships by listening to their customers, assessing customer needs, and organizing the company's efforts to solve customer problems. Consider Boeing, the aerospace giant competing in the rough and tumble worldwide commercial aircraft market. It takes more than a warm smile to sell expensive airplanes:

> Selling high-tech aircraft at $70 million or more a copy is complex and challenging. A single big sale can easily run into billions of dollars. Boeing salespeople head up an extensive team of company specialists—sales and service technicians, financial analysts, planners, engineers—all dedicated to finding ways to satisfy airline customer needs. The salespeople begin by becoming experts on the airlines, much like Wall Street analysts would. They find out where each airline wants to grow, when it wants to replace planes, and details of its financial situation. The team runs Boeing and competing planes through computer systems, simulating the airline's routes, cost per seat, and other factors to show that their planes are most efficient. Then the high-level negotiations begin. The selling process is nerve-rackingly slow—it can take two or three years from the first sales presentation to the day the sale is announced. Sometimes top executives from both the airline and Boeing are brought in to close the deal. After getting the order, salespeople then must stay in almost constant touch to keep track of the account's equipment needs and to make certain the customer stays satisfied. Success depends on building solid, long-term relationships with customers, based on performance and trust.[2]

Salesperson
An individual acting for a company by performing one or more of the following activities: prospecting, communicating, servicing, and information gathering.

The term **salesperson** covers a wide range of positions. At one extreme, a salesperson might be largely an *order taker,* such as the department store salesperson standing behind the counter. At the other extreme are *order getters,* whose positions demand the *creative selling* of products and services ranging from appliances, industrial equipment, or airplanes to insurance, advertising, or consulting services. Here, we focus on the more creative types of selling and on the process of building and managing an effective sales force.

The Role of the Sales Force

Personal selling is the interpersonal arm of the promotion mix. Advertising consists of one-way, nonpersonal communication with target consumer groups. In contrast, personal selling involves two-way, personal communication between salespeople and individual customers—whether face to face, by telephone, through video or Web conferences, or by other means. Personal selling can be more effective than advertising in more complex selling situations. Salespeople can probe customers to learn more about their problems, then adjust the marketing offer to fit the special needs of each customer and negotiate terms of sale. They can build long-term personal relationships with key decision makers.

The role of personal selling varies from company to company. Some firms have no salespeople at all—for example, companies that sell only through mail-order catalogs or companies that sell through manufacturers' reps, sales agents, or brokers. In most firms, however, the sales force plays a major role. In companies that sell business products and services, such as Xerox, Cisco Systems, or DuPont, the company's salespeople work directly with customers. In consumer product companies such as Procter & Gamble or Nike that sell through intermediaries, final consumers rarely meet salespeople or even know about them. Still, the sales force plays an important behind-the-scenes role. It works with wholesalers and retailers to gain their support and to help them be more effective in selling the company's products.

The sales force serves as a critical link between a company and its customers. In many cases, salespeople serve both masters—the seller and the buyer. First, they *represent the company to customers.* They find and develop new customers and communicate information about the company's products and services. They sell products by approaching customers, presenting their products, answering objections, negotiating prices and terms, and closing sales. In addition, salespeople provide customer service and carry out market research and intelligence work.

At the same time, salespeople *represent customers to the company,* acting inside the firm as "champions" of customers' interests and managing the buyer–seller relationship. Salespeople relay customer concerns about company products and actions back inside to those who can handle them. They learn about customer needs and work with other marketing and nonmarketing people in the company to develop greater customer value. The old view was that salespeople should worry about sales and the company should worry about profit. However, the current view holds that salespeople should be concerned with more than just producing *sales*—they should work with others in the company to produce *customer satisfaction* and *company profit.*

Managing the Sales Force

We define **sales force management** as the analysis, planning, implementation, and control of sales force activities. It includes designing sales force strategy and structure and recruiting, selecting, training, compensating, supervising, and evaluating the firm's salespeople. These major sales force management decisions are shown in Figure 14-1 and discussed in the following sections.

Sales force management
The analysis, planning, implementation, and control of sales force activities. It includes setting and designing sales force strategy; and recruiting, selecting, training, supervising, compensating, and evaluating the firm's salespeople.

Designing Sales Force Strategy and Structure

Marketing managers face several sales force strategy and design questions. How should salespeople and their tasks be structured? How big should the sales force be? Should

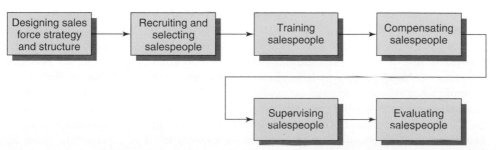

Figure 14-1
Major sales force management decisions

salespeople sell alone or work in teams with other people in the company? Should they sell in the field or by telephone? We address these issues below.

Sales Force Structure   A company can divide up sales responsibilities along any of several lines. The decision is simple if the company sells only one product line to one industry with customers in many locations. In that case the company would use a *territorial sales force structure.* However, if the company sells many products to many types of customers, it might need either a *product sales force structure,* a *customer sales force structure,* or a combination of the two.

Territorial sales force structure
A sales force organization that assigns each salesperson to an exclusive geographic territory in which that salesperson sells the company's full line.

TERRITORIAL SALES FORCE STRUCTURE.   In the **territorial sales force structure,** each salesperson is assigned to an exclusive geographic area and sells the company's full line of products or services to all customers in that territory. This organization clearly defines each salesperson's job and fixes accountability. It also increases the salesperson's desire to build local business relationships that, in turn, improve selling effectiveness. Finally, because each salesperson travels within a limited geographic area, travel expenses are relatively small.

A territorial sales organization is often supported by many levels of sales management positions. For example, Campbell Soup uses a territorial structure in which each salesperson is responsible for selling all Campbell Soup products. Starting at the bottom of the organization, *sales merchandisers* report to *sales representatives,* who report to *retail supervisors,* who report to *directors of retail sales operations,* who report to 1 of 22 *regional sales managers.* Regional sales managers, in turn, report to 1 of 4 *general sales managers* (West, Central, South, and East), who report to a *vice president* and *general sales manager.*

Product sales force structure
A sales force organization under which salespeople specialize in selling only a portion of the company's products or lines.

PRODUCT SALES FORCE STRUCTURE.   Salespeople must know their products—especially when the products are numerous and complex. This need, together with the growth of product management, has led many companies to adopt a **product sales force structure,** in which the sales force sells along product lines. For example, Kodak uses different sales forces for its film products than for its industrial products. The film products sales force deals with simple products that are distributed intensively, whereas the industrial products sales force deals with complex products that require technical understanding.

The product structure can lead to problems, however, if a single large customer buys many different company products. For example, Allegiance Healthcare Corporation, the large health care products and services company, has several product divisions, each with a separate sales force. Several Allegiance salespeople might end up calling on the same hospital on the same day. This means that they travel over the same routes and wait to see the same customer's purchasing agents. These extra costs must be compared with the benefits of better product knowledge and attention to individual products.

Customer sales force structure
A sales force organization under which salespeople specialize in selling only to certain customers or industries.

CUSTOMER SALES FORCE STRUCTURE.   More and more companies are now using a **customer sales force structure,** in which they organize the sales force along customer or industry lines. Separate sales forces may be set up for different industries, for serving current customers versus finding new ones, and for major accounts versus regular accounts.

Organizing the sales force around customers can help a company to become more customer focused and build closer relationships with important customers. For example, IBM shifted from a product-based structure to a customer-based one. Before the shift, droves of salespeople representing different IBM software, hardware, and services divisions might call on a single large client, creating confusion and frustration. Such large customers wanted a "single face," one point of contact for all of IBM's vast array of products and services. Following the restructuring, a single IBM "client executive" works with each large customer and manages a team of IBMers—product reps, systems engineers, consultants, and others—who work with the customer. The client executive becomes an expert in the customer's industry. Greg Buseman, a client executive in the distribution industry who spends most of his time working with a major consumer packaged-goods customer, describes his role this way: "I am the owner of the business relationship with the client. If the client has a problem, I'm the one who pulls together software or hardware specialists or consultants. At the customer I work most closely with, we usually have 15 to 20 projects going at once, and I have to manage them."[3] Such an intense focus on customers is widely credited for IBM's dramatic turnaround in recent years.

COMPLEX SALES FORCE STRUCTURES.   When a company sells a wide variety of products to many types of customers over a broad geographic area, it often combines several types of sales force structures. Salespeople can be specialized by customer and territory, by product and territory, by product and customer, or by territory, product, and customer. No single structure is best for all companies and situations. Each company should select a sales force structure that best serves the needs of its customers and fits its overall marketing strategy.

Sales Force Size   Once the company has set its structure, it is ready to consider *sales force size.* Salespeople constitute one of the company's most productive—and most expensive—assets. Therefore, increasing their number will increase both sales and costs.

Many companies use some form of *workload approach* to set sales force size. Using this approach, a company first groups accounts into different classes according to size, account status, or other factors related to the amount of effort required to maintain them. It then determines the number of salespeople needed to call on each class of accounts the desired number of times. The company might think as follows: Suppose we have 1,000 Type-A accounts and 2,000 Type-B accounts. Type-A accounts require 36 calls a year and Type-B accounts require 12 calls a year. In this case, the sales force's *workload*—the number of calls it must make per year—is 60,000 calls [$(1,000 \times 36) + (2,000 \times 12) = 36,000 + 24,000 = 60,000$]. Suppose our average salesperson can make 1,000 calls a year. Thus, the company needs 60 salespeople ($60,000 \div 1,000$).

Other Sales Force Strategy and Structure Issues   Sales management must also decide who will be involved in the selling effort and how various sales and sales support people will work together.

OUTSIDE AND INSIDE SALES FORCES.   The company may have an **outside sales force** (or *field sales force*), an **inside sales force,** or both. Outside salespeople travel to call on customers. Inside salespeople conduct business from their offices via telephone or visits from prospective buyers.

To reduce time demands on their outside sales forces, many companies have increased the size of their inside sales forces. Inside salespeople include technical support people, sales assistants, and telemarketers. *Technical support people* provide technical information and answers to customers' questions. *Sales assistants* provide clerical backup for outside salespeople. They call ahead and confirm appointments, conduct credit checks, follow up on deliveries, and answer customers' questions when outside salespeople cannot be reached. *Telemarketers* use the phone to find new leads and qualify prospects for the field sales force, or to sell and service accounts directly.

The inside sales force frees outside salespeople to spend more time selling to major accounts and finding major new prospects. Depending on the complexity of the product and customer, a telemarketer can make from 20 to 33 decision-maker contacts a day, compared to the average of 4 that an outside salesperson can make. And for many types of products and selling situations, telemarketing can be as effective as a personal call but much less expensive. Whereas the average personal sales call costs about $170, a routine industrial telemarketing call costs only about $5 and a complex call about $20.[4] Notes a DuPont telemarketer: "I'm more effective on the phone. [When you're in the field], if some guy's not in his office, you lose an hour. On the phone, you lose 15 seconds. . . . Through my phone

Outside sales force
(or *field sales force***)**
Outside salespeople who travel to call on customers.

Inside sales force
Inside salespeople who conduct business from their offices via telephone or visits from prospective buyers.

calls, I'm in the field as much as the rep is." There are other advantages. "Customers can't throw things at you," quips the rep, "and you don't have to outrun dogs."[5]

Telephone marketing can be used successfully by both large and small companies:

IBM's traditional image has long been symbolized by the salesman in the blue suit, crisp white shirt, and red tie—an imposing fellow far more comfortable in Corporate America's plush executive suites than in the cramped quarters of some fledgling entrepreneur. Small businesses were often ignored. Now, to sell its e-business solutions to small businesses, IBM is boosting emphasis on its telemarketing effort. Stroll through the IBM call center in suburban Atlanta, with its sea of cubicles, and a new image of the IBM salesperson emerges: men and women, many recent college grads, sporting golf shirts and khakis or—gasp!—blue jeans. They wear headsets and talk on the phone with customers they'll likely never meet in person. IBM's roughly 1,200 phone reps now generate 30 percent of IBM's revenues from small and midsize businesses. The reps focus on specific industries and each calls on as many as 300 accounts. They nurture client relationships, pitch IBM solutions, and, when needed, refer customers to product and service specialists within the call center or to resellers in their region.[6]

Climax Portable Machine Tools has proven that a small company can use telemarketing to save money and still lavish attention on buyers. Under the old system, Climax sales engineers spent one-third of their time on the road, training distributor salespeople and accompanying them on calls. They could make about 4 contacts a day. Now, each of 5 sales engineers on Climax's telemarketing team calls about 30 prospects a day, following up on leads generated by ads and direct mail. Because

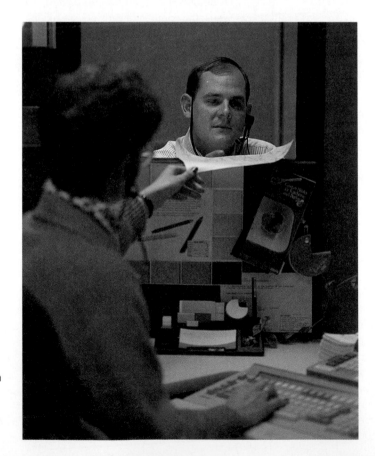

Experienced telemarketers sell complex chemical products by telephone at DuPont's Customer Telecontact Center. Quips one, "I'm more effective on the phone . . . and you don't have to outrun dogs."

it takes about 5 calls to close a sale, the sales engineers update a prospect's computer file after each contact, noting the degree of commitment, requirements, next call date, and personal comments. "If anyone mentions he's going on a fishing trip, our sales engineer enters that in the computer and uses it to personalize the next phone call," says Climax's president, noting that's just one way to build good relations. Another is that the first mailing to a prospect includes the sales engineer's business card with his picture on it. Of course, it takes more than friendliness to sell $15,000 machine tools over the phone (special orders may run $200,000), but the telemarketing approach is working well. When Climax customers were asked, "Do you see the sales engineer often enough?" the response was overwhelmingly positive. Obviously, many people didn't realize that the only contact they'd had with Climax had been on the phone.[7]

Just as telemarketing is changing the way that many companies go to market, the Internet offers explosive potential for restructuring sales forces and conducting sales operations. More and more companies are now using the Internet to support their personal selling efforts—not just for selling, but for everything from training salespeople to conducting sales meetings and servicing accounts (see Marketing at Work 14-1).

TEAM SELLING. As products become more complex, and as customers grow larger and more demanding, a single salesperson simply can't handle all of a large customer's needs. Instead, most companies now are using **team selling** to service large, complex accounts. Companies are finding that sales teams can unearth problems, solutions, and sales opportunities that no individual salesperson could. Such teams might include experts from any area or level of the selling firm—sales, marketing, technical and support services, R&D, engineering, operations, finance, and others. In team selling situations, the salesperson shifts from "soloist" to "orchestrator."

Team selling
Using teams of people from sales, marketing, engineering, finance, technical support, and even upper management to service large, complex accounts.

In many cases, the move to team selling mirrors similar changes in customers' buying organizations. According to a recent study by *Purchasing* magazine, nearly 70 percent of companies polled are using or are extremely interested in using multifunctional buying teams. Says the director of sales education at Dow Chemical, to sell effectively to such buying teams, "Our sellers . . . have to captain selling teams. There are no more lone wolves."[8]

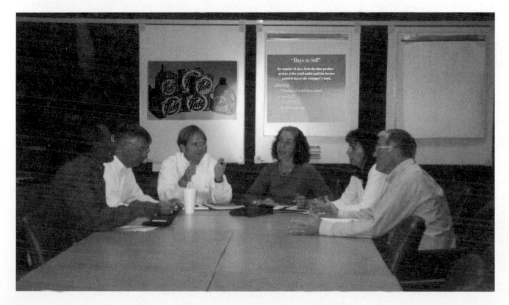

This Procter & Gamble "customer business development team" serves a major southeastern grocery retailer. It consists of a customer business development manager and five account executives (shown here), along with specialists from other functional areas.

Marketing as Work 14.1

Point, Click, and Sell: Welcome to the Web-Based Sales Force

There are few rules at Fisher Scientific International's sales training sessions. The chemical company's salespeople are allowed to show up for new workshops in their pajamas. And no one flinches if they stroll in at midnight for their first class, take a dozen breaks to call clients, or invite the family cat to sleep in their laps while they take an exam. Sound unorthodox? It would be if Fisher's salespeople were trained in a regular classroom. But for the past year and a half, the company has been using the Internet to teach the majority of its salespeople in the privacy of their homes, cars, hotel rooms, or wherever else they bring their laptops.

To get updates on Fisher's pricing or refresh themselves on one of the company's highly technical products, all salespeople have to do is log onto the Web site and select from the lengthy index. Any time of the day or night, they can get information on a new product, take an exam, or post messages for product experts—all without ever entering a corporate classroom. Welcome to the new world of the Web-based sales force.

In the past few years sales organizations around the world have begun saving money and time by using a host of new Web approaches to train reps, hold sales meetings, and even conduct live sales presentations. "Web-based technologies are becoming really hot in sales because they save salespeople's time," says technology consultant Tim Sloane. Web-based technologies help companies save time and travel costs while keeping reps up to speed on their company's new products and sales strategies. Fisher Scientific's reps can dial up the Web site at their leisure, and whereas newer reps might spend hours online going

through each session in order, more seasoned sellers might just log on for a quick refresher on a specific product before a sales call. "It allows them to manage their time better, because they're only getting training when they need it, in the doses they need it in," says John Pavlik, director of the company's training department. If salespeople are spending less time on training, Pavlik says, they're able to spend more time on what they do best: selling.

Training is only one of the ways sales organizations are using the Internet. Many companies are using the Web to make sales presentations and service accounts. For example, Digital Equipment Corporation's salespeople used to spend a great deal of time traveling to the offices of clients and prospects. But since 1997 the company (now a division of Compaq) has been delivering sales pitches by combining teleconferences with Web presentations.

For example, when Digital's account team in Connecticut needed to see what marketing manager Joe Batista and his team in Massachusetts had prepared for a client, Batista input his ideas into a PowerPoint presentation and uploaded it using Internet Conference Center, Web-based software provided by Contigo Software. The account team joined Batista via teleconference and used their own computers to log onto the Web site Batista specified.

Once everyone was logged on, Batista was able to take control of the browsers and lead the reps through the presentation in real time, highlighting and pointing out specific items as he went. The account reps added their comments, based on their more detailed knowledge of the client, and the revised presentation was then shown online to the client. The beauty of the whole process?

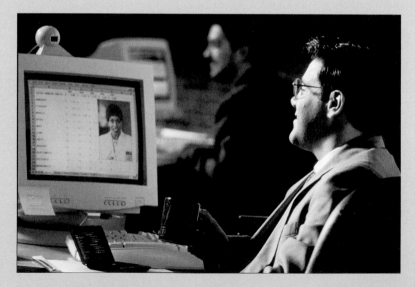

Internet selling support: Sales organizations around the world are now using a host of new Web approaches to train reps, hold sales meetings, and even conduct live sales presentations.

It's so fast. "The use of [the Web] clearly helps shorten our sales cycle," Batista says. Presentations are created and delivered in less time—sometimes weeks less than the process would take face-to-face—and salespeople are able to close deals more quickly.

Other companies are using Web-based sales presentations to find new prospects. Oracle Corporation, the $8 billion software and information technology services company, conducts online, live product seminars for prospective clients. Prospects can scan the high-tech company's Web site to see which seminars they might want to attend, then dial in via modem and telephone at the appropriate time (Oracle pays for the cost of the phone call). The seminars, which usually consist of a live lecture describing the product's applications followed by a question-and-answer session, average about 125 prospective clients apiece. Once a seminar is completed, prospects are directed to another part of Oracle's Web site, from which they can order products. "It costs our clients nothing but time," says Oracle's manager of Internet marketing programs, "and we're reaching a much wider audience than we would if we were doing in-person seminars."

The Internet can also be a handy way to hold sales strategy meetings. Consider Cisco Systems, which provides networking solutions for the Internet. Sales meetings used to take an enormous bite out of

Cisco's travel budget. Now the company saves about $1 million per month by conducting many of those sessions on the Web using Place-Ware virtual conference center software. Whenever Cisco introduces a new product, it holds a Web meeting to update salespeople, in groups of 100 or more, on the product's marketing and sales strategy.

Usually led by the product manager or a vice president of sales, the meetings typically begin with a 10-minute slide presentation that spells out the planned strategy. Then, salespeople spend the next 50 or so minutes asking questions via teleconference. The meeting's leader can direct attendees' browsers to competitors' Web sites or ask them to vote on certain issues by using the software's instant polling feature. "Our salespeople are actually meeting more online then they ever were face-to-face," says Mike Mitchell, Cisco's distance learning manager, adding that some salespeople who used to meet with other reps and managers only a few times a quarter are meeting online nearly every day. "That's very empowering for the sales force, because they're able to make suggestions at every step of the way about where we're going with our sales and marketing strategies."

Thus, Web-based technologies can produce big organizational benefits for sales forces. They help conserve salespeople's valuable time, save travel dollars, and give salespeople a new vehicle for sell-

ing and servicing accounts. But the technologies also have some drawbacks. For starters, they're not cheap. Setting up a Web-based system can cost up to several hundred thousand dollars. And such systems can intimidate low-tech salespeople or clients. "You must have a culture that is comfortable using computers," says one marketing communications manager. "As simple as it is, if your salespeople or clients aren't comfortable using the Web, you're wasting your money." Also, Web tools are susceptible to server crashes and other network difficulties, not a happy event when you're in the midst of an important sales meeting or presentation.

For these reasons, some high-tech experts recommend that sales executives use Web technologies for training, sales meetings, and preliminary client sales presentations, but resort to old-fashioned, face-to-face meetings when the time draws near to close the deal. "When push comes to shove, if you've got an account worth closing, you're still going to get on that plane and see the client in person," says sales consultant Sloane. "Your client is going to want to look you in the eye before buying anything from you, and that's still one thing you just can't do online."

Sources: Adapted from Melinda Ligos, "Point, Click, and Sell," *Sales and Marketing Management,* May 1999, pp. 51–55. Also see Chad Kaydo, "You've Got Sales," *Sales and Marketing Management,* October 1999, pp. 29–39; Ginger Conlon, "Ride the Wave," *Sales and Marketing Management,* December 2000, pp. 67–74; and Tom Reilly, "Technology and the Salesperson," *Industrial Distribution,* January 2001, p. 88.

Some companies, such as IBM, Xerox, and Procter & Gamble, have used teams for a long time. P&G sales reps are organized into "customer business development (CBD) teams." Each CBD team is assigned to a major P&G customer. Teams consist of a customer business development manager, several account executives (each responsible for a specific category of P&G products), and specialists in marketing strategy, operations, information systems, logistics, and finance. This organization places the focus on serving the complete needs of each important customer.

Other companies have only recently reorganized to adopt the team concept. For example, Cutler-Hammer, which supplies circuit breakers, motor starters, and other electrical equipment to heavy industrial manufacturers such as Ford, recently developed "pods" of salespeople that focus on a specific geographical region, industry, or market. Each pod member contributes unique expertise and knowledge about a product or service that salespeople can leverage when selling to increasingly sophisticated buying teams.[9]

Team selling does have some pitfalls. For example, selling teams can confuse or overwhelm customers who are used to working with only one salesperson. Salespeople who are used to having customers all to themselves may have trouble learning to work with and trust others on a team. Finally, difficulties in evaluating individual contributions to the team selling effort can create some sticky compensation issues.

Recruiting and Selecting Salespeople

At the heart of any successful sales force operation is the recruitment and selection of good salespeople. The performance difference between an average salesperson and a top salesperson can be substantial. In a typical sales force, the top 30 percent of the salespeople might bring in 60 percent of the sales. Thus, careful salesperson selection can greatly increase overall sales force performance. Beyond the differences in sales performance, poor selection results in costly turnover. When a salesperson quits, the costs of finding and training a new salesperson—plus the costs of lost sales—can run as high as $50,000 to $75,000. Also, a sales force with many new people is less productive.[10]

What traits spell surefire sales success? One survey suggests that good salespeople have a lot of enthusiasm, persistence, initiative, self-confidence, and job commitment. They are committed to sales as a way of life and have a strong customer orientation. Another study suggests that good salespeople are independent and self-motivated and are excellent listeners. Still another study advises that salespeople should be friends to the customers as well as persistent, enthusiastic, attentive, and—above all—honest. They must be internally motivated, disciplined, hardworking, and able to build strong relationships with customers. Finally, studies show that good salespeople are team players rather than loners (see Marketing at Work 14-2).[11]

When recruiting, companies should analyze the sales job itself and the characteristics of its most successful salespeople to identify the traits needed by a successful salesperson in their industry. Does the job require a lot of planning and paperwork? Does it call for much travel? Will the salesperson face a lot of rejections? Will the salesperson be working with high-level buyers? The successful salesperson should be suited to these duties.

After management has decided on needed traits, it must *recruit* salespeople. The human resources department looks for applicants by getting names from current salespeople, using employment agencies, placing classified ads, searching the Web, and contacting college students. Another source is to attract top salespeople from other companies. Proven salespeople need less training and can be immediately productive.

Recruiting will attract many applicants from whom the company must select the best. The selection procedure can vary from a single informal interview to lengthy testing and interviewing. Many companies give formal tests to sales applicants. Tests typically measure sales aptitude, analytical and organizational skills, personality traits, and other characteristics. Test results count heavily in companies such as IBM, Prudential, Procter & Gamble, and Gillette. Gillette claims that tests have reduced turnover by 42 percent and that test scores have correlated well with the later performance of new salespeople. But test scores provide only one piece of information in a set that includes personal characteristics, references, past employment history, and interviewer reactions.[12]

Marketing at Work 14.2

Great Salespeople: Drive, Discipline, and Relationship-Building Skills

What sets great salespeople apart from all the rest? What separates the masterful from the merely mediocre? In an effort to profile top sales performers, Gallup Management Consulting Group, a division of the well-known Gallup polling organization, has interviewed as many as half a million salespeople. Its research suggests that the best salespeople possess four key talents: intrinsic motivation, disciplined work style, the ability to close a sale, and perhaps most important, the ability to build relationships with customers.

Intrinsic Motivation

"Different things drive different people—pride, happiness, money, you name it," says one expert. "But all great salespeople have one thing in common: an unrelenting drive to excel." This strong, internal drive can be shaped and molded, but it can't be taught. The source of the motivation varies—some are driven by money, some by hunger for recognition, some by a yearning to build relationships.

The Gallup research revealed four general personality types, all high performers, but all with different sources of motivation. *Competitors* are people who not only want to win but also crave the satisfaction of beating specific rivals—other companies *and* their fellow salespeople. They'll come right out and say to a colleague, "With all due respect, I know you're salesperson of the year, but I'm going after your title." The *ego driven* are salespeople who just want to experience the glory of winning. They want to be recognized as being the best, regardless of the competition. *Achievers* are a rare breed who are almost completely self-motivated. They like accom-

plishment and routinely set goals that are higher than what is expected of them. They often make the best sales managers because they don't mind seeing other people succeed, as long as the organization's goals are met. Finally, *service-oriented* salespeople are those whose strength lies in their ability to build and cultivate relationships. They are generous, caring, and empathetic. "These people are golden," says the national training manager of Minolta Corporation's business equipment division. "We need salespeople who will take the time to follow up on the 10 questions a customer might have, salespeople who love to stay in touch."

No one is purely a competitor, an achiever, ego driven, or service driven. There's at least some of each

in most top performers. "A *competitor* with a strong sense of *service* will probably bring in a lot of business while doing a great job of taking care of customers," observes the managing director of the Gallup Management Consulting Group. "Who could ask for anything more?"

Disciplined Work Style

Whatever their motivation, if salespeople aren't organized and focused, and if they don't work hard, they can't meet the ever-increasing demands customers are making these days. Great salespeople are tenacious about laying out detailed, organized plans, then following through in a timely, disciplined way. There's no magic here, just solid organization and hard

Great salespeople: The best salespeople possess intrinsic motivation, disciplined work style, the ability to close a sale, and perhaps most important, the ability to build relationships with customers.

work. "Our best sales reps never let loose ends dangle," says the president of a small business equipment firm. "If they say they're going to make a follow-up call on a customer in six months, you can be sure that they'll be on the doorstep in six months." Top sellers rely on hard work, not luck or gimmicks. "Some people say it's all technique or luck," notes one sales trainer. "But luck happens to the best salespeople when they get up early, work late, stay up till two in the morning working on a proposal, or keep making calls when everyone is leaving at the end of the day."

The Ability to Close a Sale

Other skills mean little if a seller can't ask for the sale. No close, no sale. Period. So what makes for a great closer? For one thing, an unyielding persistence, say managers and sales consultants. Claims one, "Great closers are like great

athletes. They're not afraid to fail, and they don't give up until they close." Part of what makes the failure rate tolerable for top performers is their deep-seated belief in themselves and what they are selling. Great closers have a high level of self-confidence and believe that they are doing the right thing. And they've got a burning need to make the sale happen—to do whatever it takes within legal and ethical standards to get the business.

The Ability to Build Relationships

Perhaps most important in today's relationship-marketing environment, top salespeople are customer problem solvers and relationship builders. They have an instinctive understanding of their customers' needs. Talk to sales executives and they'll describe top performers in these terms: Empathetic. Patient. Caring. Responsive. Good listeners.

Even *honest.* Top sellers can put themselves on the buyer's side of the desk and see the world through their customers' eyes. Today, customers are looking for business partners, not golf partners. "At the root of it all," says a Dallas sales consultant, "is an integrity of intent. High performers don't just want to be liked, they want to add value." High-performing salespeople, he adds, are "always thinking about the big picture, where the customer's organization is going, and how they can help them get there."

Sources: Adapted from Geoffrey Brewer, "Mind Reading: What Drives Top Salespeople to Greatness?" *Sales and Marketing Management,* May 1994, pp. 82–88. Also see Roberta Maynard, "Finding the Essence of Good Salespeople," *Nation's Business,* February 1998, p. 10; Jeanie Casison, "Closest Thing to Cloning," *Incentive,* June 1999, p. 7; Erika Rasmusson, "The 10 Traits of Top Salespeople," *Sales and Marketing Management,* August 1999, pp. 34–37; Kevin Dobbs, Jack Gordon, Kim Kiser, and David Stamps, "The Seven Secrets of Great Salespeople," *Training,* January 2000, p. 14; and Andy Cohen, "The Traits of Great Sales Forces," *Sales and Marketing Management,* October 2000, pp. 67–72.

Training Salespeople

New salespeople may spend anywhere from a few weeks or months to a year or more in training. The average initial training period is four months. Then, most companies provide continuing sales training via seminars, sales meetings, and the Web throughout the salesperson's career. In all, U.S. companies spend more than $7 billion annually on training salespeople and devote more than 33 hours per year to the average salesperson.[13] Although training can be expensive, it can also yield dramatic returns on the training investment. For example, Nabisco did an extensive analysis of the return on investment of its two-day Professional Selling Program, which teaches sales reps how to plan for and make professional presentations to their retail customers. Although it cost about $1,000 to put each sales rep through the program, the training resulted in additional sales of more than $122,000 per rep and yielded almost $21,000 of additional profit per rep.[14]

Training programs have several goals. Salespeople need to know and identify with the company, so most training programs begin by describing the company's history and objectives, its organization, its financial structure and facilities, and its chief products and markets. Salespeople also need to know the company's products, so sales trainees are shown how products are produced and how they work. They also need to know customers' and competitors' characteristics, so the training program teaches them about competitors' strategies and about different types of customers and their needs, buying motives, and buying habits. Because salespeople must know how to make effective presentations, they are trained in the principles of selling. Finally, salespeople need to understand field procedures and responsibilities. They learn how to divide time between

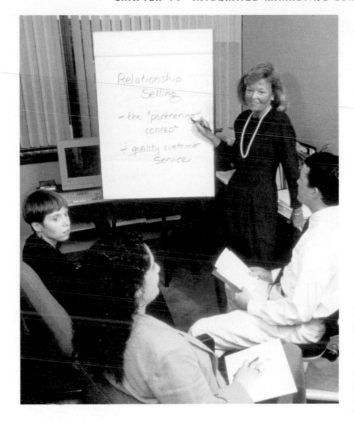

Sales training: U.S. companies spend more than $7 billion annually on training salespeople and devote more than 22 hours per year to the average salesperson.

active and potential accounts and how to use an expense account, prepare reports, and route communications effectively.

Today, many companies are adding Web-based training to their sales training programs. Such training may range from simple text-based product information to Internet-based sales exercises that build sales skills to sophisticated simulations that re-create the dynamics of real-life sales calls. IBM is learning that using the Internet to train salespeople offers many advantages.

> With some 300,000 sales associates scattered in various locales, IBM is using the Internet to supplement on-the-job and other sales training approaches. The computer services giant uses online workshops to deliver increments of training when salespeople need updates on new products or customers. Salespeople dig into such training as deeply as their needs dictate, getting just enough information, just in time to complete the project at hand. The trainees are then encouraged to share and expand on what they've learned in informal discussions with others. "We're seeking greater efficiency, greater productivity, greater advantage," says Milt Hearne, IBM's vice president of worldwide high-performance selling. IBM hopes to move at least 35 percent of its training online. It expects the move to reduce days spent on formal training by a third and save upwards of $200 million on travel and hotel costs, time away from work, instructor salaries, and other expenses associated with formal training.[15]

Compensating Salespeople

To attract salespeople, a company must have an appealing compensation plan. Compensation is made up of several elements—a fixed amount, a variable amount, expenses, and fringe benefits. The fixed amount, usually a salary, gives the salesperson some stable income. The

Table 14-1   The Relationship Between Overall Marketing Strategy and Sales Force Compensation

	Strategic Goal		
	To Rapidly Gain Market Share	To Solidify Market Leadership	To Maximize Profitability
Ideal salesperson	• An independent self-starter	• A competitive problem solver	• A team player • A relationship manager
Sales focus	• Deal making • Sustained high effort	• Consultative selling	• Account penetration
Compensation role	• To capture accounts • To reward high performance	• To reward new and existing sales	• To manage the product mix • To encourage team selling • To reward account management

Source: Adapted from Sam T. Johnson, "Sales Compensation: In Search of a Better Solution," *Compensation & Benefits Review,* November–December 1993, pp. 53–60.

variable amount, which might be commissions or bonuses based on sales performance, rewards the salesperson for greater effort. Expense allowances, which repay salespeople for job-related expenses, let salespeople undertake needed and desirable selling efforts. Fringe benefits, such as paid vacations, sickness or accident benefits, pensions, and life insurance, provide job security and satisfaction.

Management must decide what *mix* of these compensation elements makes the most sense for each sales job. Different combinations of fixed and variable compensation give rise to four basic types of compensation plans—straight salary, straight commission, salary plus bonus, and salary plus commission. A study of sales force compensation plans showed that 70 percent of all companies surveyed use a combination of base salary and incentives. The average plan consisted of about 60 percent salary and 40 percent incentive pay.[16]

The sales force compensation plan can both motivate salespeople and direct their activities. Compensation should direct the sales force toward activities that are consistent with overall marketing objectives. Table 14-1 illustrates how a company's compensation plan should reflect its overall marketing strategy. For example, if the strategy is to grow rapidly and gain market share, the compensation plan might include a larger commission component coupled with a new-account bonus to encourage high sales performance and new-account development. In contrast, if the goal is to maximize current account profitability, the compensation plan might contain a larger base-salary component with additional incentives for current account sales or customer satisfaction. In fact, more and more companies are moving away from high commission plans that may drive salespeople to make short-term grabs for business. Notes one sales force expert, "The last thing you want is to have someone ruin a customer relationship because they're pushing too hard to close a deal." Instead, companies are designing compensation plans that reward salespeople for building customer relationships and growing the long-run value of each customer.[17]

Supervising Salespeople

New salespeople need more than a territory, compensation, and training—they need *supervision.* Through supervision, the company *directs* and *motivates* the sales force to do a better job.

Companies vary in how closely they supervise their salespeople. Many help their salespeople in identifying customer targets and setting call norms. Some may also specify how much time the sales forces should spend prospecting for new accounts and set other time-management priorities. One tool is the *annual call plan* that shows which customers and prospects to call on in which months and which activities to carry out. Activities include taking part in trade shows, attending sales meetings, and carrying out marketing research. Another tool is *time-and-duty analysis.* In addition to time spent selling, the salesperson spends time traveling, waiting, eating, taking breaks, and doing administrative chores.

Figure 14-2 shows how salespeople spend their time. On average, actual face-to-face selling time accounts for less than 30 percent of total working time! If selling time could be raised from 30 percent to 40 percent, this would be a 33 percent increase in the time spent selling. Companies always are looking for ways to save time—using phones instead of traveling, simplifying record-keeping forms, finding better call and routing plans, and supplying more and better customer information.

Many firms have adopted *sales force automation systems,* computerized sales force operations for more efficient order-entry transactions, improved customer service, and better salesperson decision-making support. Salespeople use laptops, handheld computing devices, and Web technologies, coupled with customer-contact software and customer relationship management (CRM) software, to profile customers and prospects, analyze and forecast sales, manage account relationships, schedule sales calls, make presentations, enter orders, check inventories and order status, prepare sales and expense reports, process correspondence, and carry out many other activities. Sales force automation not only lowers sales force costs and improves productivity, it also improves the quality of sales management decisions. Here is an example of successful sales force automation:[18]

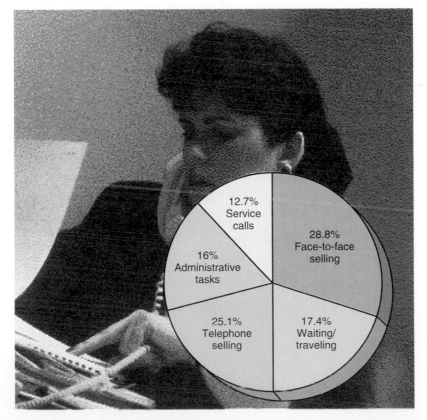

Figure 14-2
How salespeople spend their time

Source: Dartnell Corporation; *30th Sales Force Compensation Survey.* © 1998 Dartnell Corporation.

Owens-Corning has put its sales force online with FSA—its Field Sales Advantage system. FSA gives Owens-Corning salespeople a constant supply of information about their company and the people they're dealing with. Using laptop computers, each salesperson can access three types of programs. First, FSA gives them a set of *generic tools,* everything from word processing to fax and e-mail transmission to creating presentations online. Second, it provides *product information*—tech bulletins, customer specifications, pricing information, and other data that can help close a sale. Finally, it offers up a wealth of *customer information*—buying history, types of products ordered, and preferred payment terms. Before FSA, reps stored such information in loose-leaf books, calendars, and account cards. Now, FSA makes working directly with customers easier than ever. Salespeople can prime themselves on backgrounds of clients; call up prewritten sales letters; transmit orders and resolve customer-service issues on the spot during customer calls; and have samples, pamphlets, brochures, and other materials sent to clients with a few keystrokes. With FSA, "salespeople automatically become more empowered," says Charley Causey, regional general manager. "They become the real managers of their own business and their own territories."

Perhaps the fastest-growing sales force technology tool is the Internet. In a survey by Dartnell Corporation of 1,000 salespeople, 61 percent reported using the Internet regularly in their daily selling activities. The most common uses include gathering competitive information, monitoring customer Web sites, and researching industries and specific customers. As more and more companies provide their salespeople with Web access, experts expect continued growth in sales force Internet usage.[19]

Beyond directing salespeople, sales managers must also motivate them. Some salespeople will do their best without any special urging from management. To them, selling may be the most fascinating job in the world. But selling can also be frustrating. Salespeople often work alone and they must sometimes travel away from home. They may face aggressive competing salespeople and difficult customers. Therefore, salespeople often need special encouragement to do their best.

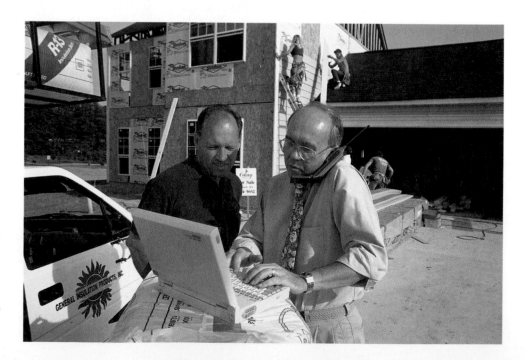

Owens-Corning's Field Sales Advantage system gives salespeople a constant supply of information about their company and the people with whom they're dealing.

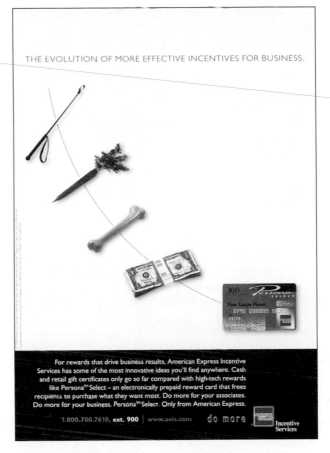

THE EVOLUTION OF MORE EFFECTIVE INCENTIVES FOR BUSINESS.

For rewards that drive business results, American Express Incentive Services has some of the most innovative ideas you'll find anywhere. Cash and retail gift certificates only go so far compared with high-tech rewards like Persona℠ Select – an electronically prepaid reward card that frees recipients to purchase what they want most. Do more for your associates. Do more for your business. Persona℠ Select. Only from American Express.

1.800.700.7610, **ext. 900** | www.aeis.com   **do more**   Incentive Services

Sales force incentives: Many companies offer cash, trips, or merchandise as incentives. American Express suggests that companies reward outstanding sales performers with high-tech Persona Select cards—electronically prepaid reward cards that allow recipients to purchase whatever they want most.

Management can boost sales force morale and performance through its organizational climate, sales quotas, and positive incentives. *Organizational climate* describes the feeling that salespeople have about their opportunities, value, and rewards for a good performance. Some companies treat salespeople as if they are not very important, and performance suffers accordingly. Other companies treat their salespeople as valued contributors and allow virtually unlimited opportunity for income and promotion. Not surprisingly, these companies enjoy higher sales force performance and less turnover.

Many companies motivate their salespeople by setting **sales quotas**—standards stating the amount they should sell and how sales should be divided among the company's products. Compensation is often related to how well salespeople meet their quotas. Companies also use various *positive incentives* to increase sales force effort. *Sales meetings* provide social occasions, breaks from routine, chances to meet and talk with "company brass," and opportunities to air feelings and to identify with a larger group. Companies also sponsor *sales contests* to spur the sales force to make a selling effort above what would normally be expected. Other incentives include honors, merchandise and cash awards, trips, and profit-sharing plans.

Sales quota
A standard that states the amount a salesperson should sell and how sales should be divided among the company's products.

Evaluating Salespeople

We have thus far described how management communicates what salespeople should be doing and how it motivates them to do it. This process requires good feedback. And good feedback means getting regular information about salespeople to evaluate their performance.

Management gets information about its salespeople in several ways. The most important source is *sales reports,* including weekly or monthly work plans and longer-term territory marketing plans. Salespeople also write up their completed activities on *call reports* and turn in *expense reports* for which they are partly or wholly repaid. Additional information comes from personal observation, customer surveys, and talks with other salespeople.

Using various sales force reports and other information, sales management evaluates members of the sales force. It evaluates salespeople on their ability to "plan their work and work their plan." Formal evaluation forces management to develop and communicate clear standards for judging performance. It also provides salespeople with constructive feedback and motivates them to perform well.

Linking the Concepts

Take a break and reexamine your thoughts about salespeople and sales management.

- As you did at the start of the chapter, close your eyes and envision a typical salesperson. Have your perceptions of salespeople changed after what you've just read? How? Be specific.
- Apply each of the steps in sales force management shown in Figure 14-1 to the chapter-opening Lear Corporation example.
- Find and talk with someone employed in professional sales. Ask about and report on how this salesperson's company designs its sales force and recruits, selects, trains, compensates, supervises, and evaluates its salespeople. Would you like to work as a salesperson for this company?

The Personal Selling Process

Selling process

The steps that the salesperson follows when selling, which include prospecting and qualifying, preapproach, approach, presentation and demonstration, handling objections, closing, and follow-up.

We now turn from designing and managing a sales force to the actual personal selling process. The **selling process** consists of several steps that the salesperson must master (see Figure 14-3). These steps focus on the goal of getting new customers and obtaining orders from them. However, most salespeople spend much of their time maintaining existing accounts and building long-term customer *relationships*. We discuss the relationship aspect of the personal selling process in a later section.

Prospecting and Qualifying The first step in the selling process is **prospecting**—identifying qualified potential customers. Approaching the right potential customers is crucial to selling success. As one expert puts it: "If the sales force starts chasing anyone who is breathing and seems to have a budget, you risk accumulating a roster of expensive-to-serve, hard-to-satisfy customers who never respond to whatever value proposition you

Figure 14-3
Major steps in
effective selling

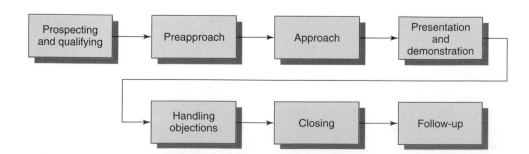

have." He continues, "The solution to this isn't rocket science. [You must] train salespeople to actively scout the right prospects. If necessary, create an incentive program to reward proper scouting."[20]

The salesperson must often approach many prospects to get just a few sales. Although the company supplies some leads, salespeople need skill in finding their own. They can ask current customers for referrals. They can cultivate referral sources, such as suppliers, dealers, noncompeting salespeople, and bankers. They can search for prospects in directories or on the Web and track down leads using the telephone and direct mail. Or they can drop in unannounced on various offices (a practice known as "cold calling").

Salespeople also need to know how to *qualify* leads—that is, how to identify the good ones and screen out the poor ones. Prospects can be qualified by looking at their financial ability, volume of business, special needs, location, and possibilities for growth.

Preapproach Before calling on a prospect, the salesperson should learn as much as possible about the organization (what it needs, who is involved in the buying) and its buyers (their characteristics and buying styles). This step is known as the **preapproach.** The salesperson can consult standard industry and online sources, acquaintances, and others to learn about the company. The salesperson should set *call objectives,* which may be to qualify the prospect, to gather information, or to make an immediate sale. Another task is to decide on the best approach, which might be a personal visit, a phone call, or a letter. The best timing should be considered carefully because many prospects are busiest at certain times. Finally, the salesperson should give thought to an overall sales strategy for the account.

Approach During the **approach** step, the salesperson should know how to meet and greet the buyer and get the relationship off to a good start. This step involves the salesperson's appearance, opening lines, and the follow-up remarks. The opening lines should be positive to build goodwill from the beginning of the relationship. This opening might be followed by some key questions to learn more about the customer's needs or by showing a display or sample to attract the buyer's attention and curiosity. As in all stages of the selling process, listening to the customer is crucial.

Presentation and Demonstration During the **presentation** step of the selling process, the salesperson tells the product "story" to the buyer, presenting customer benefits and showing how the product solves the customer's problems. The problem-solver salesperson fits better with today's marketing concept than does a hard-sell salesperson or the glad-handing extrovert. Buyers today want solutions, not smiles; results, not razzle-dazzle. They want salespeople who listen to their concerns, understand their needs, and respond with the right products and services.

This *need-satisfaction approach* calls for good listening and problem-solving skills. "I think of myself more as a . . . well, psychologist," notes one experienced salesperson. "I listen to customers. I listen to their wishes and needs and problems, and I try to figure out a solution. If you're not a good listener, you're not going to get the order." Another salesperson suggests, "It's no longer enough to have a good relationship with a client. You have to understand their problems. You have to feel their pain."[21] The qualities that buyers *dislike most* in salespeople include being pushy, late, deceitful, and unprepared or disorganized. The qualities they *value most* include empathy, good listening, honesty, dependability, thoroughness, and follow-through. Great salespeople know how to sell, but more importantly they know how to listen and to build strong customer relationships.[22]

Prospecting
The step in the selling process in which the salesperson identifies qualified potential customers.

Preapproach
The step in the selling process in which the salesperson learns as much as possible about a prospective customer before making a sales call.

Approach
The step in the selling process in which the salesperson meets the customer for the first time.

Presentation
The step in the selling process in which the salesperson tells the "product story" to the buyer, highlighting customer benefits.

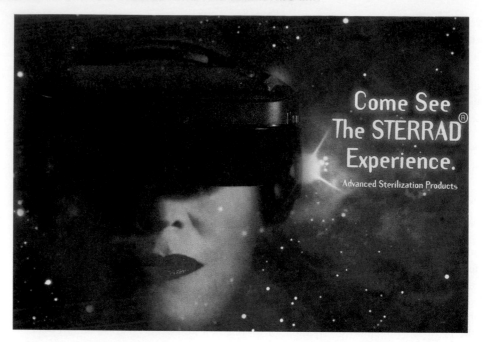

New sales presentation technologies: Advanced Sterilization Products, a Johnson & Johnson Company, provides its sales force with a presentation in which prospects don a helmet for a virtual reality tour of the inner workings of the sterilization system for medical devices and surgical instruments, known as STERRAD.

Today, advanced presentation technologies allow for full multimedia presentations to only one or a few people. Audio- and videocassettes, laptop computers with presentation software, and online presentation technologies have replaced the flip chart. Advanced Sterilization Products, a Johnson & Johnson company, even provides its sales force with a virtual reality presentation, called the STERRAD Experience. Originally designed for use at conferences, the presentation equipment has been redesigned for sales calls and consists of a small video player with five headsets, all easily transported in an ordinary-sized briefcase. Prospects don a helmet for a virtual reality tour of the inner workings of the Sterrad Sterilization System for medical devices and surgical instruments. The presentation provides more information in a more engaging way than could be done by displaying the actual machinery.[23]

Handling objections
The step in the selling process in which the salesperson seeks out, clarifies, and overcomes customer objections to buying.

Handling Objections Customers almost always have objections during the presentation or when asked to place an order. The problem can be either logical or psychological, and objections are often unspoken. In **handling objections,** the salesperson should use a positive approach, seek out hidden objections, ask the buyer to clarify any objections, take objections as opportunities to provide more information, and turn the objections into reasons for buying. Every salesperson needs training in the skills of handling objections.

Closing
The step in the selling process in which the salesperson asks the customer for an order.

Closing After handling the prospect's objections, the salesperson now tries to close the sale. Some salespeople do not get around to **closing** or do not handle it well. They may lack confidence, feel guilty about asking for the order, or fail to recognize the right moment to close the sale. Salespeople should know how to recognize closing signals from the buyer, including physical actions, comments, and questions. For example, the customer might sit forward and nod approvingly or ask about prices and credit terms. Salespeople can use one of several closing techniques. They can ask for the order, review points of agreement, offer to help write up the order, ask whether the buyer wants this model or that one, or note that the buyer will lose out if the order is not placed now. The salesperson may offer the buyer special reasons to close, such as a lower price or an extra quantity at no charge.

Follow-up The last step in the selling process—**follow-up**—is necessary if the salesperson wants to ensure customer satisfaction and repeat business. Right after closing, the salesperson should complete any details on delivery time, purchase terms, and other matters. The salesperson then should schedule a follow-up call when the initial order is received to make sure there is proper installation, instruction, and servicing. This visit would reveal any problems, assure the buyer of the salesperson's interest, and reduce any buyer concerns that might have arisen since the sale.

Follow-up
The last step in the selling process in which the salesperson follows up after the sale to ensure customer satisfaction and repeat business.

Relationship Marketing

The principles of personal selling as just described are *transaction oriented*—their aim is to help salespeople close a specific sale with a customer. But in many cases, the company is not seeking simply a sale: It has targeted a major customer that it would like to win and keep. The company would like to show that it has the capabilities to serve the customer over the long haul in a mutually profitable *relationship*. **Relationship marketing** emphasizes maintaining profitable long-term relationships with customers by creating superior customer value and satisfaction.

Today's large customers favor suppliers who can sell and deliver a coordinated set of products and services to many locations, and who can work closely with customer teams to improve products and processes. For these customers, the first sale is only the beginning of the relationship. Unfortunately, some companies ignore these new realities. They sell their products through separate sales forces, each working independently to close sales. Their technical people may not be willing to lend time to educate a customer. Their engineering, design, and manufacturing people may have the attitude that "it's our job to make good products and the salesperson's to sell them to customers." Other companies, however, recognize that winning and keeping accounts requires more than making good products and directing the sales force to close lots of sales. It requires a carefully coordinated whole-company effort to create value-laden, satisfying relationships with important customers.

Relationship marketing
The process of creating, maintaining, and enhancing strong, value-laden relationships with customers and other stakeholders.

Direct Marketing

Many of the marketing and promotion tools that we've examined in previous chapters were developed in the context of *mass marketing:* targeting broad markets with standardized messages and offers distributed through intermediaries. Today, however, with the trend toward more narrowly targeted or one-to-one marketing, many companies are adopting *direct marketing,* either as a primary marketing approach or as a supplement to other approaches. Increasingly, companies are using direct marketing to reach carefully targeted customers more efficiently and to build stronger, more personal, one-to-one relationships with them. In this section, we explore the exploding world of direct marketing.

Direct marketing consists of direct connections with carefully targeted individual consumers to both obtain an immediate response and cultivate lasting customer relationships. Direct marketers communicate directly with customers, often on a one-to-one, interactive basis. Using detailed databases, they tailor their marketing offers and communications to the needs of narrowly defined segments or even individual buyers. Beyond brand and image building, they usually seek a direct, immediate, and measurable consumer response. For example, Dell Computer interacts directly with customers, by telephone or through its Web site, to design built-to-order systems that meet customers' individual needs. Buyers order directly from Dell, and Dell quickly and efficiently delivers the new computers to their homes or offices.

Direct marketing
Direct connections with carefully targeted individual consumers to both obtain an immediate response and cultivate lasting customer relationships.

The New Direct-Marketing Model

Early direct marketers—catalog companies, direct mailers, and telemarketers—gathered customer names and sold goods mainly by mail and telephone. Today, however, fired by rapid advances in database technologies and new marketing media—especially the Internet—direct marketing has undergone a dramatic transformation.

In previous chapters, we've discussed direct marketing as direct distribution—as marketing channels that contain no intermediaries. We also include direct marketing as one element of the marketing communications mix—as an approach for communicating directly with consumers. In actuality, direct marketing is both these things.

Most companies still use direct marketing as a supplementary channel or medium for marketing their goods. Thus, Lexus markets mostly through mass-media advertising and its high-quality dealer network but also supplements these channels with direct marketing. Its direct marketing includes promotional videos and other materials mailed directly to prospective buyers and a Web page (www.lexus.com) that provides consumers with information about various models, competitive comparisons, financing, and dealer locations. Similarly, office-supply retailer Staples conducts most of its business through brick-and-mortar stores but also markets directly through its Web site. And most department stores sell the majority of their merchandise off their store shelves but also mail out catalogs.

However, for many companies today, direct marketing is more than just a supplementary channel or medium. For these companies, direct marketing—especially in its newest transformation, Internet marketing and e-commerce—constitutes a new and complete model for doing business. "The Internet is not just another marketing channel; it's not just another advertising medium; it's not just a way to speed up transactions," says one strategist. "The Internet is the foundation for a new industrial order. [It] will change the relationship between consumers and producers in ways more profound than you can yet imagine."[24] This new *direct model* is rapidly changing the way companies think about building relationships with customers.

Whereas most companies use direct marketing and the Internet as supplemental approaches, firms employing the direct model use it as the *only* approach. Some of these companies, such as Dell Computer, Amazon.com, and eBay, began as only direct marketers. Other companies—such as Cisco Systems, Charles Schwab, IBM, and many others—are rapidly transforming themselves into direct-marketing superstars. The company that perhaps best exemplifies this new direct-marketing model is Dell Computer (see Marketing at Work 14-3). Dell has built its entire approach to the marketplace around direct marketing. This direct model has proved highly successful, not just for Dell, but for the fast-growing number of other companies that employ it. Many strategists have hailed direct marketing as the new marketing model of the next millennium.

Benefits and Growth of Direct Marketing

Whether employed as a complete business model or as a supplement to a broader integrated marketing mix, direct marketing brings many benefits to both buyers and sellers. As a result, direct marketing is growing very rapidly.

For buyers, direct marketing is convenient, easy to use, and private. From the comfort of their homes or offices, they can browse mail catalogs or company Web sites at any time of the day or night. Direct marketing gives buyers ready access to a wealth of products and information, at home and around the globe. Finally, direct marketing is immediate and interactive—buyers can interact with sellers by phone or on the seller's Web site to create exactly the configuration of information, products, or services they desire, then order them on the spot.

Dell: Be Direct!

When 19-year-old Michael Dell began selling personal computers out of his college dorm room in 1984, competitors and industry insiders scoffed at the concept of mail-order computer marketing. PC buyers, they contended, needed the kind of advice and hand-holding that only full-service channels could provide. Yet young Michael Dell has proved the skeptics wrong—way wrong. In less than two decades, he has turned his dorm-room mail-order business into a burgeoning, $32 billion computer empire.

Dell Computer is now the world's largest direct marketer of computer systems and the number-one PC maker worldwide. In the United States, Dell is number-one in desktop PC sales, number-one in laptops, and number one in servers. Over the past five years, despite the recent tech slump, Dell's sales have grown at an average annual rate of over 40 percent and Dell's stock has delivered a dazzling 57 percent average annual return to shareholders. Dell's stock was the number-one performer of the 1990s, yielding an incredible 97 percent average annual return. Once-skeptical competitors are now scrambling to build their own direct-marketing systems.

What's the secret to Dell's stunning success? Anyone at Dell can tell you without hesitation: It's the company's radically different business model—the *direct model*. "We have a tremendously clear business model," says Michael Dell, the 36-year-old founder. "There's no confusion about what the value proposition is, what the company offers, and why it's great for customers. That's a very simple thing, but it has tremendous power and appeal."

Dell's direct-marketing approach delivers greater customer value through an unbeatable combination of product customization, low prices, fast delivery, and award-winning customer service. A customer can talk by phone with a Dell representative or log onto www.dell.com on Monday morning; order a fully customized, state-of-the-art PC to suit his or her special needs; and have the machine delivered to his or her doorstep or desktop by Wednesday—all at a price that's 10 to 15 percent below competitors' prices for a comparably performing PC. Dell backs its products with high-quality service and support. As a result, Dell consistently ranks among the industry leaders in product reliability and service, and its customers are routinely among the industry's most satisfied.

Dell customers get exactly the machines they need. Michael Dell's initial idea was to serve individual buyers by letting them customize machines with the special features they wanted at low prices. However, this one-to-one approach also appeals strongly to corporate buyers, because Dell can so easily preconfigure each computer to precise requirements. Dell routinely preloads machines with a company's own software and even undertakes tedious tasks such as pasting inventory tags onto each machine so that computers can be delivered directly to a given employee's desk. As a result, nearly two-thirds of Dell's sales now come from large corporate, government, and educational buyers.

Direct selling results in more efficient selling and lower costs, which translate into lower prices for customers. Because Dell builds machines to order, it carries barely any inventory—less than five days' worth by some accounts. Dealing one-to-one with customers helps the company react immediately to shifts in demand, so Dell doesn't get stuck with PCs no one wants. Finally, by selling directly, Dell has no dealers to pay. As a result,

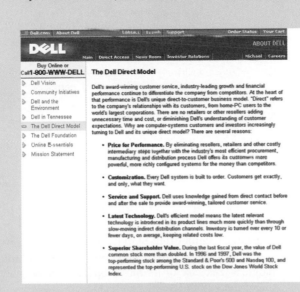

The Dell Direct Model: Dell's direct-marketing approach delivers greater customer value through an unbeatable combination of product customization, low prices, fast delivery, and award-winning customer service.

on average, Dell's costs are 12 percent lower than those of Compaq, its leading PC competitor.

Dell knows that time is money, and the company is obsessed with "speed." For example, Dell has long been a model of just-in-time manufacturing and efficient supply chain management. Dell has also mastered the intricacies of today's lightning-fast electronic commerce. According to one account, "Dell calls it 'velocity'—squeezing time out of every step in the process—from the moment an order is taken to collecting the cash. [By selling direct, manufacturing to order, and] tapping credit cards and electronic payment, Dell converts the average sale to cash in less than 24 hours. By contrast, Compaq Computer, which sells primarily through dealers, takes 35 days, and even mail-order rival Gateway 2000 takes 16.4 days."

Such blazing speed results in more satisfied customers and still lower costs. For example, customers are often delighted to find their new computers arriving within as few as 36 hours of placing an order. And because Dell doesn't order parts until an order is booked, it can take advantage of ever-falling component costs. On average, its parts are 60 days newer than those in competing machines, and, hence, 60 days farther down the price curve. This gives Dell a 6 percent profit advantage from parts costs alone. It also gives Dell what one analysts calls a "negative cash con-

version cycle." Says the analyst, "Because it keeps only five days of inventories, manages receivables to 30 days, and pushes payables out to 59 days, the Dell model will generate cash even if the company were to report no profit whatsoever."

The Internet is a perfect extension of Dell's direct-marketing model. Customers who are already comfortable buying direct from Dell now have an even more powerful way to do so. Now, by simply clicking the "Buy a Dell" icon at Dell's Web site (www.dell.com), customers can design and price customized computer systems electronically. Then, with a click on the "purchase" button, they can submit an order, choosing from online payment options that include a credit card, company purchase order, or corporate lease. Dell dashes out a digital confirmation to customers within five minutes of receiving the order. After receiving confirmation, customers can check the status of the order online at any time. "The Internet," says Michael Dell, "is the ultimate direct model. . . . [Customers] like the immediacy, convenience, savings, and personal touches that the [Internet] experience provides. Not only are some sales done online, but people who call on the phone after having visited Dell.com are twice as likely to buy."

The direct-marketing pioneer now sells more than $43 million worth of computers daily from its more than 50 country-specific Web

sites, accounting for more than 50 percent of revenues. Buyers range from individuals purchasing home computers to large business users buying high-end $30,000 servers. "The Internet is like a booster rocket on our sales and growth," proclaims Dell. "Our vision is to have *all* customers conduct *all* transactions on the Internet, globally."

As you might imagine, competitors are no longer scoffing at Michael Dell's vision of the future. In fact, competing and noncompeting companies alike are studying the Dell model closely. "Somehow Dell has been able to take flexibility and speed and build it into their DNA. It's almost like drinking water," says the CEO of another Fortune 500 company, who visited recently to absorb some of the Dell magic to apply to his own company. "I'm trying to drink as much water here as I can." It's hard to argue with success, and Michael Dell has been very successful. By following his hunches, at the tender age of 36 he has built one of the world's hottest companies. In the process, he's amassed a personal fortune exceeding $17 billion.

Sources: Quotes and Dell performance statistics from Gary McWilliams, "Whirlwind on the Web," *Business Week,* April 7, 1997, pp. 132–136; "The InternetWeek Interview—Michael Dell," *InternetWeek,* April 13, 1999, p. 8; Betsy Morris, "Can Michael Dell Escape the Box?" *Fortune,* October 16, 2000, pp. 93–110; "Surveys: Dell Tops Compaq Worldwide," *Computerworld,* April 23, 2001, p. 6; J. William Gurley, "Why Dell's World Isn't Dumb," *Fortune,* July 9, 2001, pp. 134–136; and information accessed online at www.dell.com/us/en/gen/corporate/vision_directmodel.htm, December 2001.

For sellers, direct marketing is a powerful tool for building customer relationships. Using database marketing, today's marketers can target small groups or individual consumers, tailor offers to individual needs, and promote these offers through personalized communications. Direct marketing can also be timed to reach prospects at just the right moment. Because of its one-to-one, interactive nature, the Internet is an especially potent direct-marketing tool. Direct marketing also gives sellers access to buyers that they could not reach through other channels. For example, the Internet provides access to *global* markets that might otherwise be out of reach.

Finally, direct marketing can offer sellers a low-cost, efficient alternative for reaching their markets. For example, direct marketing has grown rapidly in B2B marketing, partly in response to the ever-increasing costs of marketing through the sales force. When personal sales calls cost $170 per contact, they should be made only when necessary and to high-potential customers and prospects. Lower cost-per-contact media—such as telemarketing, direct mail, and company Web sites—often prove more cost effective in reaching and selling to more prospects and customers.

As a result of these advantages to both buyers and sellers, direct marketing has become the fastest growing form of marketing. Sales through traditional direct-marketing channels (telephone marketing, direct mail, catalogs, direct-response television, and others) have been growing rapidly. Whereas U.S. retail sales over the past five years have grown at about 6 percent annually, direct-marketing sales grew at about 10 percent annually. According to the Direct Marketing Association, total U.S. spending on direct marketing exceeded $190 billion in 2000, or more than 56 percent of total U.S. advertising expenditures.[25]

Customer Database and Direct Marketing

Effective direct marketing begins with a good customer database. A **customer database** is an organized collection of comprehensive data about individual customers or prospects, including geographic, demographic, psychographic, and behavioral data. The database can be used to locate good potential customers, tailor products and services to the special needs of targeted consumers, and maintain long-term customer relationships.

Many companies confuse a customer mailing list with a customer database. A customer mailing list is simply a set of names, addresses, and telephone numbers. A customer database contains much more information. In B2B marketing, the salesperson's customer profile might contain the products and services the customer has bought; past volumes and prices; key contacts (and their ages, birthdays, hobbies, and favorite foods); competitive suppliers; status of current contracts; estimated customer spending for the next few years; and assessments of competitive strengths and weaknesses in selling and servicing the account. In consumer marketing, the customer database might contain a customer's demographics (age, income, family members, birthdays), psychographics (activities, interests, and opinions), buying behavior (past purchases, buying preferences), and other relevant information. For example, the catalog company Fingerhut maintains a database containing some 3,000 pieces of information about each of 30 million households. Ritz-Carlton's database holds more than 500,000 individual customer preferences. Pizza Hut's database lets it track the purchases of more than 50 million customers. And Wal-Mart's database contains more than 100 terabytes of data—that's 100 trillion bytes, equivalent to 16,000 bytes for every one of the world's 6 billion people.[26]

Armed with the information in their databases, these companies can identify small groups of customers to receive fine-tuned marketing offers and communications. Kraft Foods has amassed a list of more than 30 million users of its products who have responded to coupons or other Kraft promotions. Based on their interests, the company sends these customers tips on issues such as nutrition and exercise, as well as recipes and coupons for specific Kraft brands. FedEx uses its sophisticated database to create 100 highly targeted, customized direct-mail and telemarketing campaigns each year to its nearly 5 million customers shipping to 212 countries. By analyzing customers carefully and reaching the right customers at the right time with the right promotions, FedEx achieves response rates of 20 to 25 percent and earns an 8-to-1 return on its direct-marketing dollars.[27]

Smaller companies can also make good use of database marketing:[28]

Over the last few years, nearly 9,000 grocery chains have introduced frequent-shopper programs. Now they're rifling through household shopping histories as fast as they can to tell cardholders what's running low in the pantry. Dick's Supermarkets, an eight-store chain in Wisconsin, uses transaction data from its loyalty-card

Customer database
An organized collection of comprehensive data about individual customers or prospects, including geographic, demographic, psychographic, and behavioral data.

NAME, ADDRESS, SOCIAL SECURITY NUMBER

LAST PURCHASE

NUMBER OF KIDS

HOUSEHOLD INCOME

PAYMENT HISTORY

BIRTHDATES OF FAMILY MEMBERS

SPANISH OR ENGLISH CATALOG

ACCEPTS TELEMARKETING CALLS

Effective direct marketing begins with a good customer database. Catalog company Fingerhut maintains a database containing some 3,000 pieces of information about each of 30 million households.

program to personalize shopping lists that it mails every two weeks to nearly 30,000 members. The shopping lists contain timed offers based on past purchases. A consumer who bought Tide several weeks ago, for example, may be offered a $1.50 coupon to restock. If that customer buys laundry detergent every week, he or she may be offered twice as much to purchase a larger size of Tide, or two packages of the size normally purchased. Customers who regularly purchase low fat salad dressing might be offered a free sample of a new brand of low fat salad mix.

Companies use their databases in many ways. They can use a database to identify prospects and generate sales leads by advertising products or offers. Or they can use the database to profile customers based on previous purchasing and to decide which customers should receive particular offers. Databases can help the company to deepen customer loyalty—companies can build customers' interest and enthusiasm by remembering buyer preferences and by sending appropriate information, gifts, or other materials.

For example, Mars, a market leader in pet food as well as candy, maintains an exhaustive pet database. In Germany, the company has compiled the names of virtually every German family that owns a cat. It has obtained these names by contacting veterinarians, via its Katzen-Online.de Web site, and by offering the public a free booklet titled "How to Take Care of Your Cat." People who request the booklet fill out a questionnaire, providing their cat's name, age, birthday, and other information. Mars then sends a birthday card to each cat in Germany each year, along with a new cat food sample and money-saving coupons for Mars brands. The result is a lasting relationship with the cat's owner.

The database can help a company make attractive offers of product replacements, upgrades, or complementary products, just when customers might be ready to act. For example, a General Electric appliance customer database contains each customer's demographic and psychographic characteristics along with an appliance purchasing history. Using this database, GE marketers assess how long specific customers have owned their current appliances and which past customers might be ready to purchase again. They can determine which customers need a new GE range, refrigerator, clothes washer, or something else to go with other recently purchased products. Or they can identify the best past GE purchasers and send them gift certificates or other promotions to apply against their next GE purchases. A rich customer database allows GE to build profitable new business by locating good prospects, anticipating customer needs, cross-selling products and services, and rewarding loyal customers.

Like many other marketing tools, database marketing requires a special investment. Companies must invest in computer hardware, database software, analytical programs, communication links, and skilled personnel. The database system must be user-friendly and available to various marketing groups, including those in product and brand management, new-product development, advertising and promotion, direct mail, telemarketing, Web marketing, field sales, order fulfillment, and customer service. A well-managed database should lead to sales gains that will more than cover its costs.

Forms of Direct Marketing

The major forms of direct marketing—as shown in Figure 14-4—include *personal selling, telephone marketing, direct-mail marketing, catalog marketing, direct-response television marketing, kiosk marketing,* and *online marketing.* We examined personal selling in depth earlier in this chapter and looked closely at online marketing in Chapter 3. Here, we examine the other direct-marketing forms.

Telephone Marketing **Telephone marketing**—using the telephone to sell directly to consumers—has become the major direct-marketing communication tool. Telephone marketing now accounts for more than 38 percent of all direct-marketing media expenditures and 36 percent of direct-marketing sales. We're all familiar with telephone marketing directed toward consumers, but B2B marketers also use telephone marketing extensively, accounting for 58 percent of all telephone marketing sales.[29]

Marketers use *outbound* telephone marketing to sell directly to consumers and businesses. *Inbound* toll-free 800 numbers are used to receive orders from television and radio ads, direct mail, or catalogs. The use of 800 numbers has taken off in recent years as more

Telephone marketing
Using the telephone to sell directly to customers.

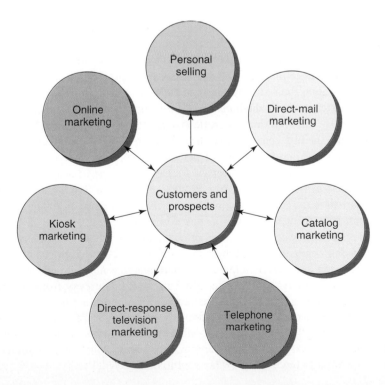

Figure 14-4
Forms of direct marketing

Telemarketing: Each call to 900-CALL-RMHC results in a $15 contribution charged to the caller's phone bill.

and more companies have begun using them, and as current users have added new features such as toll-free fax numbers. Residential use has also grown. To accommodate this rapid growth, new toll-free area codes (888, 877, 866) have been added. After the 800 area code was established in 1967, it took almost 30 years before its 8 million numbers were used up. In contrast, 888 area code numbers, established in 1996, were used up in only 2 years.[30]

Other marketers use 900 numbers to sell consumers information, entertainment, or the opportunity to voice an opinion on a pay-per-call basis. For example, for a charge, consumers can obtain weather forecasts from American Express (900-WEATHER—75 cents a minute); pet care information from Quaker Oats (900-990-PETS—95 cents a minute); advice on snoring and other sleep disorders from Somnus (900-USA-SLEEP—$2 for the first minute, then $1 a minute); golf lessons from *Golf Digest* (900-454-3288—95 cents a minute); or individual answers to nutrition questions from a registered dietician sponsored by the American Dietetic Association (900-CALL-AN-RD—$1.95 for the first minute, then 95 cents a minute). In addition to its 800 number and Internet site, Nintendo offers a 900 number, for $1.50 per minute, for game players wanting assistance with the company's video games. Ronald McDonald House Charities uses a 900 number to raise funds. Each call to 900-CALL-RMHC results in a $15.00 contribution, which is simply charged to the caller's local phone bill. Overall, the use of 900 numbers has grown by more than 10 percent a year over the past five years.[31]

Properly designed and targeted telemarketing provides many benefits, including purchasing convenience and increased product and service information. However, the recent explosion in unsolicited telephone marketing has annoyed many consumers who object to the almost daily "junk phone calls" that pull them away from the dinner table or fill the answering machine. Lawmakers around the country are responding with legislation ranging from banning unsolicited telemarketing calls during certain hours to letting households sign up for "Do not call" lists. Most telemarketers support some action against random and poorly targeted telemarketing. As a Direct Marketing Association executive notes, "We want to target people who want to be targeted."[32]

Direct-Mail Marketing **Direct-mail marketing** involves sending an offer, announcement, reminder, or other item to a person at a particular address. Using highly selective mailing lists, direct marketers send out millions of mail pieces each year—letters, ads, brochures, samples, video- and audiotapes, CDs, and other "salespeople with wings." Direct mail accounts for more than 23 percent of all direct-marketing media expenditures and 31 percent of direct-marketing sales. Together, telemarketing and direct-mail marketing account for more than 60 percent of direct-marketing expenditures and 66 percent of direct-marketing sales.[33]

Direct mail is well suited to direct, one-to-one communication. It permits high target-market selectivity, can be personalized, is flexible, and allows easy measurement of results. Although the cost per thousand people reached is higher than with mass media such as television or magazines, the people who are reached are much better prospects. Direct mail has proved successful in promoting all kinds of products, from books, magazine subscriptions, and insurance to gift items, clothing, gourmet foods, and industrial products. Direct mail is also used heavily by charities to raise billions of dollars each year.

The direct-mail industry constantly seeks new methods and approaches. For example, videotapes and CDs are now among the fastest-growing direct-mail media. For instance, to introduce its Donkey Kong Country video game, Nintendo of America created a 13-minute MTV-style video and sent 2 million copies to avid video game players. This direct-mail video helped Nintendo sell 6.1 million units of the game in only 45 days, making it the fastest-selling game in industry history. America Online has mailed out CDs by the hundreds of millions in one of the most successful direct-mail campaigns in history. Now other marketers, especially those in technology or e-commerce, are using CDs in their direct-mail offers. Used in conjunction with the Internet, CDs offer an affordable way to drive traffic to Web pages personalized for a specific market segment or a specific promotion. They can also be useful for demonstrations of computer-related products. For example, Sony recently sent out a CD that allowed PC users to demo its new VAIO portable notebook on their own computers.[34]

Until recently, all mail was paper based and handled by the U.S. Post Office or delivery services such as FedEx, DHL, or Airborne Express. Recently, however, three new forms of mail delivery have become popular:

- ◆ *Fax mail:* Marketers now routinely send fax mail announcing special offers, sales, and other events to prospects and customers with fax machines. Fax mail messages can be sent and received almost instantaneously. However, some prospects and customers resent receiving unsolicited fax mail, which ties up their machines and consumes their paper.
- ◆ *E-mail:* Many marketers now send sales announcements, offers, product information, and other messages to e-mail addresses—sometimes to a few individuals, sometimes to large groups. As discussed in Chapter 3, today's e-mail messages have moved far beyond the drab text-only messages of old. The new breed of e-mail ad uses glitzy features such as animation, interactive links, streaming video, and personalized audio messages to reach out and grab attention. However, as people receive more and more e-mail, they resent the intrusion of unrequested messages. Smart marketers are using permission-based programs, sending e-mail ads only to those who want to receive them.
- ◆ *Voice mail:* Voice mail is a system for receiving and storing oral messages at a telephone address. Some marketers have set up automated programs that exclusively target voice mail boxes and answering machines with prerecorded messages. These systems target homes between 10 A.M. and 4 P.M. and businesses between 7 P.M. and 9 P.M. when people are least likely to answer. If the automated dialer hears a live voice, it disconnects. Such systems thwart hang-ups by annoyed potential customers. However, they can also create substantial ill will.[35]

Direct-mail marketing
Direct marketing through single mailings that include letters, ads, samples, fold-outs, and other "salespeople with wings" sent to prospects on mailing lists.

These new forms deliver direct mail at incredible speeds compared to the post office's "snail mail" pace. Yet, much like mail delivered through traditional channels, it may be resented as "junk mail" if sent to people who have no interest in it. For this reason, marketers must carefully identify appropriate targets so as not waste their money and recipients' time (see Marketing at Work 14-4).

Catalog Marketing Advances in technology, along with the move toward personalized, one-to-one marketing, have resulted in exciting changes in **catalog marketing.** *Catalog Age* magazine used to define a *catalog* as "a printed, bound piece of at least eight pages, selling multiple products, and offering a direct ordering mechanism." Today, only a few years later, this definition is sadly out of date. With the stampede to the Internet, more and more catalogs are going electronic. Many traditional print catalogers have added Web-based catalogs to their marketing mixes and a variety of new Web-only catalogers have emerged. However, the Internet has not yet killed off printed catalogs—far from it. Printed catalogs remain the primary medium and many former Web-only companies have created printed catalogs to expand their business.

Catalog marketing has grown explosively during the past 25 years. Annual catalog sales (both print and electronic) are expected to grow from $68 billion in 2000 to more than $94 billion by 2002.[36] Some huge general-merchandise retailers—such as JCPenney and Spiegel—sell a full line of merchandise through catalogs. In recent years, these giants have been challenged by thousands of specialty catalogs that serve highly specialized market niches. According to one study, some 10,000 companies now produce 14,000 unique catalog titles in the United States.[37]

Catalog marketing
Direct marketing through print, video, or electronic catalogs that are mailed to select customers, made available in stores, or presented online.

Catalog marketing has grown explosively during the past 25 years. Some 10,000 companies now produce 14,000 unique catalog titles in the United States.

*Mis*directed Marketing: My Dead Dog May Already Be a Winner!

Poor database management and wrongly targeted direct marketing not only aggravates consumers, it costs companies millions of dollars each year and sometimes makes them look downright foolish. Take the following account, written by Lee Coppola, the bemused recipient of some of this misdirected mania:

Ever wonder what happens when a pet takes on a persona? Ashley could have told you, if he could have talked. Ashley was the family mutt, an SPCA special, part beagle and part spaniel. For years, most of them after he died, he also served as the family's representative in the local telephone book. He was picked for the role quite haphazardly one day when I tried to keep my number out of the book to avoid getting business calls at home. When I balked at the $60-a-year fee, the cheery telephone company representative suggested I list the number in one of my children's names.

I was munching on a sandwich at the time and Ashley followed me around the kitchen waiting for a crumb to fall. "Can I put the phone in any name?" I asked the rep as I sidestepped Ashley. "Certainly," she answered, and therein gave birth to 10 years of telephone calls and mail to a dog.

"A remarkable new book about the Coppolas since the Civil War is about to make history—and you, Ashley Coppola, are in it," touted one letter asking Ashley to send $10 right away for "this one-time offer." Ashley received hundreds of pieces of mail, the bulk soliciting his money.

The most ironic pitches for cash were from the SPCA and the Buffalo Zoo, a kind of animal-helping-animal scenario. And we wondered

how the chief executive of a local cemetery might react if he knew he was asking a canine to buy a plot to give his family "peace of mind." Or a local lawn service's thoughts about asking a dog who daily messed the grass, "Is your lawn as attractive as it could be?" Then there was the letter offering Ashley "reliable electronic security to protect your home." One of the kids asked if that wasn't Ashley's job.

The kids soon got into the swing of having their dog receive mail and telephone calls. "He's sleeping under the dining room table," one would tell telemarketers. "He's out in the backyard taking a whiz," was the favorite reply of another. My wife would have nothing of that frivolity, preferring to simply reply, "He's deceased."

But that tack backfired on her one day when our youngest child took an almost pleading call from a survey-company employee looking for Ashley. "I'm Ashley," the 17-year-old politely replied, taking pity on the caller. He dutifully gave his age and answered a few questions before he realized he was late for an appointment and hurriedly cut short the conversation. "Can I call you again?" the surveyor asked. "OK," our son said as he hung up.

Sure enough, the surveyor called again the next day and asked for Ashley. But this time Mom answered and gave her standard reply. "Oh, my God," exclaimed the caller. "I'm so, so sorry." The surveyor's horrified grief puzzled my wife until our son explained how he had been a healthy teenage Ashley the day before.

Sometimes we worried about our dog's fate. You see, he broke several chain letters urging him to copy and send 20 others or risk

some calamity. After all, Ashley was warned, didn't one person die nine days after throwing out the letter?

Did I mention credit cards? Ashley paid his bills on time, judging from the $5,000 lines-of-credit for which he "automatically" qualified. Made us wonder about the scrutiny of the nation's credit-card industry.

Of course, Ashley was no ordinary dog. He was an Italian dog. How else to explain the solicitation to Mr. Coppola Ashley that came all the way from Altamura, Italy, and sought donations to an orphanage? Then there was the offer to obtain his family's cherished crest, "fashioned hundreds of years ago in Italy," and purchase the Coppola family registry that listed him along with all the other Coppolas in America.

Is there some message to all this? Think of the saplings that were sacrificed to try to squeeze money from a canine. Or the time, energy, and money that were wasted each time a postage or bulk-mail stamp was affixed to an envelope being sent to a mutt. We did feel sheepish about the deception when the mail came from the self-employed trying to make a buck. We wondered if a local dentist really would have given Ashley a "complete initial consultation, exam, and bitewing X-rays for ONLY THREE DOLLARS." And what might have been the expression on the saleswoman's face if Ashley had shown up for his complimentary Mary Kay facial?

Ashley did appreciate, however, the coupon for dog food.

Sources: Lee Coppola, "My Dead Dog May Already Be a Winner!" *Newsweek,* July 5, 1999, p. 11. Also see Louella Miles, "Should DM Still Be Missing Its Mark?" *Marketing,* June 14, 2001, pp. 29–31.

Consumers can buy just about anything from a catalog. Sharper Image sells $2,400 jet-propelled surfboards. The Banana Republic Travel and Safari Clothing Company features everything you would need to go hiking in the Sahara or the rain forest. And each year Lillian Vernon sends out 33 editions of its catalogs with total circulation of 178 million copies to its 20-million person database, selling everything from shoes to decorative lawn birds and monogrammed oven mitts.[38] Specialty department stores, such as Neiman Marcus, Bloomingdale's, and Saks Fifth Avenue, use catalogs to cultivate upper-middle-class markets for high-priced, often exotic, merchandise. Several major corporations have also developed or acquired catalog divisions. For example, Avon now issues 10 women's fashion catalogs along with catalogs for children's and men's clothes. Walt Disney Company mails out over 6 million catalogs each year featuring videos, stuffed animals, and other Disney items.

More than three-quarters of all catalog companies now present merchandise and take orders over the Internet. For example, the Lands' End Web site, which debuted in 1995, greeted 28 million visitors last year. Its Web-based sales have more than doubled in the past two years, now accounting for 16 percent of total sales. During the hectic Christmas season, the site handled a record of 15,000 visitors in just one hour.[39] Here's another example that illustrates this dramatic shift in catalog marketing:

When novelty gifts marketer Archie McPhee launched its Web site in September 1995, response was underwhelming. But when the company added a shopping basket ordering feature in 1997, the site roared to life. According to Mark Pahlow, president of the catalog company, the site now has 35,000 unique visitors each month, generating 55 percent of the cataloger's total sales. The Web numbers are so positive that Archie McPhee has slashed circulation of its print catalog from 1 million to less than 300,000, and reduced the frequency from five issues a year to three. The Web site has saved the company more than 50 percent in the costs of producing, printing, and mailing its color catalog, which had been as high as $700,000 annually. The site can also offer interactive features, such as "The Nerd Test" and a fortune-telling ball, as well as much more merchandise. "A 48-page catalog would show fewer than 200 items, whereas the Web site offers more than 500," Pahlow notes. Another benefit is the site's real-time inventory feature. "The day a new product arrives, it is shown on the site. The moment we run out of an item, we pull it off. We are also able to show items we have small quantities of as Web-only specials."[40]

Along with the benefits, however, Web-based catalogs also present challenges. Whereas a print catalog is intrusive and creates its own attention, Web catalogs are passive and must be marketed. "Attracting new customers is much more difficult to do with a Web catalog," says an industry consultant. "You have to use advertising, linkage, and other means to drive traffic to it." Thus, even catalogers who are sold on the Web are not likely to abandon their print catalogs completely. For example, Archie McPhee relies on its print catalogs to promote its site. "I think we will always produce at least one catalog a year," Pahlow says.

Direct-Response Television Marketing **Direct-response television marketing** takes one of two major forms. The first is *direct-response advertising.* Direct marketers air television spots, often 60 or 120 seconds long, that persuasively describe a product and give customers a toll-free number for ordering. Television viewers often encounter 30-minute advertising programs, or *infomercials,* for a single product.

Some successful direct-response ads run for years and become classics. For example, Dial Media's ads for Ginsu knives ran for seven years and sold almost 3 million sets of knives worth more than $40 million in sales; its Armourcote cookware ads generated more than twice that much. And over the past 40 years, infomercial czar Ron Popeil's company,

Direct-response television marketing
Direct marketing via television, including *direct-response television advertising* or *infomercials* and *home shopping channels.*

The current infomercial champ? Direct-response TV ads helped George Foreman's Lean Mean Fat-Reducing Grilling Machines notch $400 million in sales last year.

Ronco, has sold more than $1 billion worth of TV-marketed gadgets, including the original Veg-O-Matic, The Pocket Fisherman, Mr. Microphone, the Giant Food Dehydrator and Beef Jerky Machine, and the Showtime Rotisserie & BBQ.[41] The current infomercial champ?

It's three o'clock in the morning. Plagued with insomnia, you grab the remote and flip around until a grinning blonde in an apron catches your attention: "I'm going to show you something you won't believe! Juicy meals in minutes! Something else you won't believe…George Foreman!" The studio roars, and boxing's elder statesman, in a red apron, shows off his Lean Mean Fat-Reducing Grilling Machine and highlights the grease caught in the pan below. "Eew!" the audience screams. It can be yours for three easy payments of $19.95 (plus shipping and handling). Don't laugh. Such infomercials helped the Foreman grills product line notch almost $400 million in sales last year.[42]

For years, infomercials have been associated with somewhat questionable pitches for juicers and other kitchen gadgets, get-rich-quick schemes, and nifty ways to stay in shape without working very hard at it. Recently, however, a number of large companies—GTE, Johnson & Johnson, MCA Universal, Sears, Procter & Gamble, Revlon, Apple Computer, Cadillac, Volvo, Land Rover, Anheuser-Busch, even the U.S. Navy—have begun using infomercials to sell their wares over the phone, refer customers to retailers, or send out coupons and product information.[43]

Home shopping channels, another form of direct-response television marketing, are television programs or entire channels dedicated to selling goods and services. Some home shopping channels, such as Home Shopping Network (HSN), the Quality Value Channel (QVC), and ValueVision, broadcast 24 hours a day. On HSN, the program's hosts offer bargain prices on products ranging from jewelry, lamps, collectible dolls, and clothing to power tools and consumer electronics—usually obtained by the home shopping channel at closeout prices. Viewers call a toll-free number to order goods. At the other end of the operation, 400 operators handle more than 1,200 incoming lines, entering orders directly into computer terminals.

With widespread distribution on cable and satellite television, the top three shopping networks combined now reach 248 million homes worldwide, selling more than $4 billion of goods each year. They are now combining direct-response television marketing with online selling. For example, QVC recently launched a feature called "61st Minute," in which QVC viewers are urged to go online immediately after a given product showcase. Once there, viewers find a Webcast continuation of the product pitch.[44]

Kiosk Marketing Some companies place information and ordering machines—called *kiosks* (in contrast to vending machines, which dispense actual products)—in stores, airports, and other locations. Hallmark and American Greetings use kiosks to help customers create and purchase personalized greeting cards. Tower Records has listening kiosks that let customers listen to the music before purchase. Kiosks in the do-it-yourself ceramics stores of California-based Color Me Mine Inc. contain clip-art images that customers can use to decorate the ceramics pieces they purchase in the store. At the local Disney Store, kiosk guests can buy merchandise online, purchase theme-park passes, and learn more about Disney vacations and entertainment products. At Car Max, the used-car superstore, customers use a kiosk with a touch-screen computer to get information about its vast inventory of as many as 1,000 cars and trucks. Customers can choose a handful and print out photos, prices, features, and location on the store's lot. The use of such kiosks is expected to increase fivefold during the next three years.[45]

Business marketers also use kiosks. For example, Dow Plastics places kiosks at trade shows to collect sales leads and to provide information on its 700 products. The kiosk system reads customer data from encoded registration badges and produces technical data sheets that can be printed at the kiosk or faxed or mailed to the customer. The system has resulted in a 400 percent increase in qualified sales leads.[46]

Like about everything else these days, kiosks are also going online, as many companies merge the powers of the real and virtual worlds. For example, in some Levi Strauss stores, you can plug your measurements into a Web kiosk and have custom-made jeans delivered to your home within two weeks. Gap has installed interactive kiosks, called Web lounges, in some of its stores that provide gift ideas or let customers match up outfits without trying them on in dressing rooms. Outdoor equipment retailer REI recently outfitted its stores with kiosks that provide customers with product information and let them place orders online.[47]

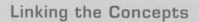

Linking the Concepts

Hold up a moment and think about the impact of direct marketing on your life.

◆ When was the last time that you *bought* something via direct marketing? What did you buy and why did you buy it direct? When was the last time that you *rejected* a direct-marketing offer? Why did you reject it? Based on these experiences, what advice would you give to direct marketers?

◆ For the next week, keep track of all the direct-marketing offers that come your way via direct mail and catalogs, telephone, and direct-response television. Then analyze the offers by type, source, and what you liked or disliked about each offer and the way it was delivered. Which offer best hit its target (you)? Which missed by the widest margin?

Integrated Direct Marketing

Too often, a company's individual direct-marketing efforts are not well integrated with one another or with other elements of its marketing and promotion mixes. For example, a firm's media advertising may be handled by the advertising department working with

Figure 14-5
An integrated direct-marketing campaign

a traditional advertising agency. Meanwhile, its direct-mail and catalog business may be handled by direct-marketing specialists while its Web site is developed and operated by an outside Internet firm. Even within a given direct-marketing campaign, too many companies use only a "one-shot" effort to reach and sell a prospect or a single vehicle in multiple stages to trigger purchases.

A more powerful approach is **integrated direct marketing,** which involves using carefully coordinated multiple-media, multiple-stage campaigns. Such campaigns can greatly improve response. Whereas a direct-mail piece alone might generate a 2 percent response, adding a Web site and toll-free phone number might raise the response rate by 50 percent. Then, a well-designed outbound telemarketing effort might lift response by an additional 500 percent. Suddenly, a 2 percent response has grown to 15 percent or more by adding interactive marketing channels to a regular mailing.

More elaborate integrated direct-marketing campaigns can be used. Consider the multimedia, multistage campaign shown in Figure 14-5. Here, the paid ad creates product awareness and stimulates inquiries. The company immediately sends direct mail to those who inquire. Within a few days, the company follows up with a phone call seeking an order. Some prospects will order by phone; others might request a face-to-face sales call. In such a campaign, the marketer seeks to improve response rates and profits by adding media and stages that contribute more to additional sales than to additional costs.

Integrated direct marketing
Direct-marketing campaigns that use multiple vehicles and multiple stages to improve response rates and profits.

Public Policy and Ethical Issues in Direct Marketing

Direct marketers and their customers usually enjoy mutually rewarding relationships. Occasionally, however, a darker side emerges. The aggressive and sometimes shady tactics of a few direct marketers can bother or harm consumers, giving the entire industry a black eye. Abuses range from simple excesses that irritate consumers to instances of unfair practices or even outright deception and fraud. The direct-marketing industry has also faced growing concerns about invasion-of-privacy issues.

Irritation, Unfairness, Deception, and Fraud Direct-marketing excesses sometimes annoy or offend consumers. Most of us dislike direct-response TV commercials that are too loud, too long, and too insistent. Especially bothersome are dinnertime or late-night phone calls. Beyond irritating consumers, some direct marketers have been accused of taking unfair advantage of impulsive or less sophisticated buyers. TV shopping shows and program-long "infomercials" seem to be the worst culprits. They feature smooth-talking hosts, elaborately staged demonstrations, claims of drastic price reductions, "while they last" time limitations, and unequaled ease of purchase to inflame buyers who have low sales resistance.

Worse yet, so-called heat merchants design mailers and write copy intended to mislead buyers. Even well-known direct mailers have been accused of deceiving consumers. Sweepstakes promoter Publishers Clearing House recently paid $52 million to settle accusations that its high-pressure mailings confused or misled consumers, especially the elderly, into believing that they had won prizes or would win if they bought the company's magazines.[48]

Other direct marketers pretend to be conducting research surveys when they are actually asking leading questions to screen or persuade consumers. Fraudulent schemes, such as investment scams or phony collections for charity, have also multiplied in recent years. Crooked direct marketers can be hard to catch: Direct-marketing customers often respond quickly, do not interact personally with the seller, and usually expect to wait for delivery. By the time buyers realize that they have been bilked, the thieves are usually somewhere else plotting new schemes.

Invasion of Privacy Invasion of privacy is perhaps the toughest public policy issue now confronting the direct-marketing industry. These days, it seems that almost every time consumers enter a sweepstakes, apply for a credit card, take out a magazine subscription, or order products by mail, telephone, or the Internet, their names are entered into some company's already bulging database. Using sophisticated computer technologies, direct marketers can use these databases to "microtarget" their selling efforts.

Consumers often benefit from such database marketing—they receive more offers that are closely matched to their interests. However, many critics worry that marketers may know *too* much about consumers' lives and that they may use this knowledge to take unfair advantage of consumers. At some point, they claim, the extensive use of databases intrudes on consumer privacy.

For example, they ask, should AT&T be allowed to sell marketers the names of customers who frequently call the 800 numbers of catalog companies? Should a company such as American Express be allowed to make data on its 175 million American cardholders available to merchants who accept AmEx cards? Is it right for credit bureaus to compile and sell lists of people who have recently applied for credit cards—people who are considered prime direct-marketing targets because of their spending behavior? Or is it right for states to sell the names and addresses of driver's license holders, along with height, weight, and gender information, allowing apparel retailers to target tall or overweight people with special clothing offers?

In their drives to build databases, companies sometimes get carried away. For example, when first introduced, Intel's Pentium III chip contained an embedded serial number that allowed the company to trace users' equipment. When privacy advocates screamed, Intel disabled the feature. Similarly, Microsoft caused substantial privacy concerns when it introduced its Windows 95 software. It used a "Registration Wizard," which allowed users to register their new software online. However, when users went online to register, without their knowledge, Microsoft "read" the configurations of their PCs to learn about the major software products running on each customer's system. When users learned of this invasion, they protested loudly and Microsoft abandoned the practice. Such actions have spawned a quiet but determined "privacy revolt" among consumers and public policy makers.[49]

In one survey of consumers, 79 percent of respondents said that they were concerned about threats to their personal privacy. In a survey of Internet users, 71 percent of respondents said there should be laws to protect Web privacy and a full 84 percent objected to firms selling information about users to other companies. In yet another survey, *Advertising Age* asked advertising industry executives how they felt about database marketing and the privacy issue. The responses of two executives show that even industry insiders have mixed feelings:[50]

> It doesn't bother me that people know I live in a suburb of Columbus, Ohio, and have X number of kids. It [does] bother me that these people know the names of my wife and kids and where my kids go to school. They . . . act like they know me when the bottom line is they're attempting to sell me something. I do feel that database marketing has allowed companies to cross the fine line of privacy. . . . [And] in a lot of cases, I think they know they have crossed it.

The direct-marketing industry is addressing issues of ethics and public policy. For example, in an effort to build consumer confidence in shopping direct, the Direct

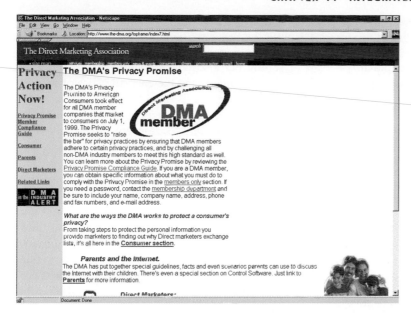

The DMA recently developed its "Privacy Promise to American Consumers," which attempts to build consumer confidence by requiring that all DMA members adhere to certain carefully developed consumer privacy rules.

Marketing Association (DMA)—the largest association for businesses interested in interactive and database marketing with more than 4,600 member companies—launched a "Privacy Promise to American Consumers." This initiative requires that all DMA members adhere to a carefully developed set of consumer privacy rules. The Privacy Promise requires that members notify customers when any personal information is rented, sold, or exchanged with others. DMA members must also honor consumer requests to "opt out" of information exchanges with other marketers or not to receive mail, telephone, or other solicitations again. Finally, they must abide by the DMA's Mail Preference Service (www.the-dma.org/consumers/offmailinglist.html) and Telephone Preference Service (www.the-dma.org/consumers/offtelephonelist.html), two national services to remove the names of consumers who wish not to receive mail or telephone offers at home.

Direct marketers know that, left untended, such problems will lead to increasingly negative consumer attitudes, lower response rates, and calls for more restrictive state and federal legislation. More importantly, most direct marketers want the same things that consumers want: honest and well-designed marketing offers targeted only toward consumers who will appreciate and respond to them. Direct marketing is just too expensive to waste on consumers who don't want it.

STOP *Rest Stop: Reviewing the Concepts*

Hit the brakes, pull over, and revisit this chapter's key concepts. The chapter is the second of two chapters covering the final marketing mix element—promotion. The previous chapter dealt with advertising, sales promotion, and public relations. This one investigates personal selling and direct marketing.

Personal selling and direct marketing are both direct tools for communicating with and persuading current and prospective customers. Selling is the interpersonal arm of the communications mix. To be successful in personal selling, a company must first build and then manage an effective sales force. Firms must also be good at direct marketing, the process of forming one-to-one connections with customers. Today, many companies are turning to direct marketing in an effort to reach carefully targeted customers more efficiently and to build stronger, more personal, one-to-one relationships with them.

1. Discuss the role of a company's salespeople in creating value for customers and building customer relationships.

Most companies use salespeople, and many companies assign them an important role in the marketing mix. For companies selling business products, the firm's salespeople work directly with customers. Often, the sales force is the customer's only direct contact with the company and therefore may be viewed by customers as representing the company itself. In contrast, for consumer product companies that sell through intermediaries, consumers usually do not meet salespeople or even know about them. The sales force works behind the scenes, dealing with wholesalers and retailers to obtain their support and helping them become effective in selling the firm's products.

As an element of the promotion mix, the sales force is very effective in achieving certain marketing objectives and carrying out such activities as prospecting, communicating, selling and servicing, and information gathering. But with companies becoming more market oriented, a market-focused sales force also works to produce both *customer satisfaction* and *company profit*. To accomplish these goals, the sales force needs skills in marketing analysis and planning in addition to the traditional selling skills.

2. Identify and explain the six major sales force management steps.

High sales force costs necessitate an effective *sales management process* consisting of six steps: *designing sales force strategy and structure, recruiting and selecting, training, compensating, supervising,* and *evaluating* salespeople.

In designing a sales force, sales management must address issues such as what type of sales force structure will work best (territorial, product, customer, or complex structure); how large the sales force should be; who will be involved in the selling effort; and how its various sales and sales support people will work together (inside or outside sales forces and team selling).

To hold down the high costs of hiring the wrong people, salespeople must be *recruited* and *selected* carefully. In recruiting salespeople, a company may look to job duties and the characteristics of its most successful salespeople to suggest the traits it wants in its salespeople and then look for applicants through recommendations of current salespeople, employment agencies, classified ads, and the Internet, and by contacting college students. In the selection process, the procedure can vary from

a single informal interview to lengthy testing and interviewing. After the selection process is complete, *training* programs familiarize new salespeople not only with the art of selling but also with the company's history, its products and policies, and the characteristics of its market and competitors.

The sales force *compensation* system helps to reward, motivate, and direct salespeople. In compensating salespeople, companies try to have an appealing plan, usually close to the going rate for the type of sales job and needed skills. In addition to compensation, all salespeople need *supervision,* and many need continuous encouragement because they must make many decisions and face many frustrations. Periodically, the company must *evaluate* their performance to help them do a better job. In evaluating salespeople, the company relies on getting regular information gathered through sales reports, personal observations, customers' letters and complaints, customer surveys, and conversations with other salespeople.

3. Discuss the personal selling process, distinguishing between transaction-oriented marketing and relationship marketing.

The art of selling involves a seven-step *selling process: prospecting and qualifying, preapproach, approach, presentation and demonstration, handling objections, closing,* and *follow-up.* These steps help marketers close a specific sale and as such are *transaction oriented.* However, a seller's dealings with customers should be guided by the larger concept of *relationship marketing.* The company's sales force should help to orchestrate a whole-company effort to develop profitable long-term relationships with key customers based on superior customer value and satisfaction.

4. Define direct marketing and discuss its benefits to customers and companies.

Direct marketing consists of direct connections with carefully targeted individual consumers to both obtain an immediate response and cultivate lasting customer relationships. Using detailed databases, direct marketers tailor their offers and communications to the needs of narrowly defined segments or even individual buyers.

For buyers, direct marketing is convenient, easy to use, and private. It gives them ready access to a wealth of products and information, at home and around the globe. Direct marketing is also immediate and interactive, allowing buyers to create exactly the configuration of information, products, or services they desire, then order them on the spot. For sellers, direct marketing is a powerful tool for building customer relationships. Using database marketing, today's marketers can target small groups or individual consumers, tailor offers to individual needs, and promote these offers through personalized communications. It also offers them a low-cost, efficient alternative for reaching their markets. As a result of these advantages to both buyers and sellers, direct marketing has become the fastest growing form of marketing.

5. Identify and discuss the major forms of direct marketing.

The main forms of direct marketing include *personal selling, telephone marketing, direct-mail marketing, catalog marketing, direct-response television marketing, kiosk marketing,* and *online marketing.* We discuss personal selling in the first part of this chapter and examined online marketing in detail in Chapter 3. *Telephone mar-* *keting* consists of using the telephone to sell directly to consumers. *Direct-mail marketing* consists of the company sending an offer, announcement, reminder, or other item to a person at a specific address. Recently, three new forms of mail delivery have become popular—*fax mail, e-mail,* and *voice mail.* Some marketers rely on *catalog marketing,* or selling through catalogs mailed to a select list of customers or made available in stores. *Direct-response television marketing* has two forms: *direct-response advertising* or *infomercials* and *home shopping channels. Kiosks* are information and ordering machines that direct marketers place in stores, airports, and other locations. *Online marketing,* discussed in Chapter 3, involves online channels and e-commerce, which electronically link consumers with sellers.

Navigating the Key Terms

For a detailed analysis of the meaning and importance of each of the following key terms, visit our Web page at www.prenhall.com/kotler.

Approach
Catalog marketing
Closing
Customer database
Customer sales force structure
Direct-mail marketing

Direct marketing
Direct-response television
  marketing
Follow-up
Handling objections
Inside sales force
Integrated direct marketing
Outside sales force
Preapproach
Presentation
Product sales force structure

Prospecting
Relationship marketing
Sales force management
Sales quotas
Salesperson
Selling process
Team selling
Telephone marketing
Territorial sales force structure

Travel Log

The following concept checks and discussion questions will help you to keep track of and apply the concepts you've studied in this chapter.

Concept Checks

Fill in the blanks, then look for the correct answers.

1. Robert Louis Stevenson once noted that "everyone lives by _____ something."
2. In the _____ structure, each salesperson is assigned to an exclusive geographic area and sells the company's full line of products or services to all customers in that geographic area.
3. Compensation of salespeople is made up of several elements—a _____ amount, a _____ amount, _____ , and _____ .

4. If the strategic goal were to maximize profitability, the ideal salesperson would be a _____ and a _____ manager.
5. According to Figure 14-3, the selling process consists of the following steps: _____ and qualifying, _____ , approach, presentation and demonstration, _____ , _____ , and follow-up.
6. Many companies today are moving away from _____ marketing with its emphasis on making a sale, and are moving toward _____ marketing, which emphasizes maintaining profitable long-term relationships with customers by creating superior customer value and satisfaction.
7. _____ consists of direct connections with carefully targeted individual consumers to

obtain an immediate response and cultivate lasting customer relationships.

8. A _____ is an organized collection of comprehensive data about individual customers or prospects, including geographic, demographic, psychographic, and behavioral data.

9. Companies use their databases in many ways: they can use a database to _____ and generate sales leads, profile customers based on previous purchasing, or deepen_____.

10. According to Figure 14-4, the major forms of direct marketing include: personal selling, _____

_____ , _____ , _____ , direct-response television marketing, _____ , and online marketing.

11. _____ marketing involves sending an offer, announcement, reminder, or other item to a person at a particular address.

12. In the past, too many companies used a "one-shot" effort to reach and sell a prospect. A more powerful approach is _____ marketing, which involves using carefully coordinated multiple-media, multiple-stage campaigns.

Concept Checks Answers: 1. selling; 2. territorial sales force; 3. fixed, variable, expenses, fringe benefits; 4. team player, relationship; 5. prospecting, preapproach, handling objections, closing; 6. transaction, relationship; 7. Direct marketing; 8. customer database; 9. identify prospects, customer loyalty; 10. telephone marketing, direct-mail marketing, catalog marketing, kiosk marketing; 11. Direct-mail; 12. integrated direct.

Discussing the Issues

1. What did Robert Louis Stevenson mean when he said that "everyone lives by selling something"? Describe all the various positions and roles the modern salesperson might be required to fill or play.

2. One of the most pressing issues that sales managers face is how to structure salespeople and their tasks. Evaluate the methods described in the text. For each method, provide (a) a brief description of its chief characteristics, (b) an example of how it's used, and (c) a critique of its effectiveness.

3. List and briefly describe the steps in the personal selling process. Which step do you think is the most difficult for the average salesperson? Which step is the most critical to successful selling? Which step do you think is usually done most correctly?

4. Explain the meaning of relationship marketing. Describe how relationship marketing might be used in (a) selling a personal computer to a final consumer, (b) selling a new car, (c) providing a student with a college education, and (d) selling season tickets for a local drama theater.

5. Contact one of the personal computer direct marketers (such as Dell Computer at **www.dell.com** or Gateway at **www.gateway.com**). (a) How does the company make it easy to order its products? (b) What differentiates this company from traditional retailers or manufacturers? (c) What are the company's chief advantages and disadvantages? (d) How does it provide security for customers (or not)? (e) Based this experience, what is your opinion of online marketers?

Mastering Marketing

After examining the sales function of CanGo, devise a plan where the company could alter its sales force strategy and structure to better serve the needs of present and future customers. Be specific with your comments. Next, devise a plan where CanGo could implement a program of direct marketing. Specify why this might be a good idea, how a customer database could be used, and what the anticipated results of this effort might be.

Traveling the Net

Point of Interest: Changing Sales Formats

Being a stock broker can be an exciting and challenging occupation. In years past, young broker trainees received extensive training on the technical workings of the stock market and characteristics of potential clients. One of the most difficult tasks for new brokers was finding and developing clients. This involved long and often discouraging hours spent on the telephone "prospecting" and "cold-calling" potential clients. Today, however, things are changing. The rapid expansion of investment and information alternatives have made the broker's job more challenging. Most major investment services brokerages are now online and brokers can now help information-hungry investors in ways that would have been unimaginable only a few years ago. Visit the following Web sites: E*TRADE (www.etrade.com), Fidelity Investments (www.fidelity.com), DLJ Direct (www.dljdirect.com), Sure Trade (www.suretrade.com), Charles Schwab (www.schwab.com), Datek (www.datek.com), and Waterhouse (www.waterhouse.com).

For Discussion

1. How have such sites changed the brokerage business? How is the selling function in the brokerage business changing?
2. How can online brokerage services help the average broker to be a more effective salesperson? What sales strategies appear to be most appropriate for the broker who wishes to use personal contact and online connections to do business?
3. Which Web site did you find to be the most "user friendly?" Why? Which of the sites would make it easiest for you to get in touch with a broker in your local area? How could a broker find out that you had been using his or her company's online service?

4. Prepare an analysis grid that compares the above sites with respect to sales stimulation, information services, cost, graphic design, responsiveness, security, and relationship marketing. Which site is best? Explain.

Application Thinking

Will online marketing eventually replace the human contact that has been an essential ingredient of sales relationships? Online stock and bond trading provides a good case in point. Online investment trading is different from ordering merchandise, designing custom clothing, or playing with computer design options. Quick response, security, expert advice and the latest information, trend analysis, and low cost per trade appear to be much more important than the normal services provided by the average online retailer. In the past, stockbrokers served as a link between the trader and the vast information services provided by the brokerage company. Online trading now appears to be altering this relationship. Assume that you are an online trader about to invest $20,000 in the stock market. (a) Which of the Web sites and the associated brokerage companies would you feel most comfortable with? Why? (b) If you used this site, what would be the nature of your relationship with the brokerage? Did personal selling associated with your chosen site influence your decision? (c) How could local brokers use their company's Web site to improve their selling function and skills?

 MAP—Marketing Applications

MAP Stop 14

Jonathan Ellermann was excited about his new job as a personal communication consultant for Nokia (www.nokia.com), the giant phone producer that captures a quarter of the global market and half the profits. Rivals such as Vodafone (www. vodaphone.com), Ericsson (www.ericsson.se), Panasonic (www.panasonic.com), and Motorola (www.motorola.com) have vowed to make things tougher for Nokia in the coming year. They've developed new designs, communications applications, and strategic alliances between hardware and software makers in an effort to lure fickle consumers away from Nokia.

Thinking Like a Marketing Manager

1. Ellermann is seeking to sell Nokia's latest model personal communication device to Shell Oil's Houston branch (approximately 5,000 phones). What sales strategy and plan should Ellermann recommend? In your answer, consider the advantages and disadvantages of Nokia's product.
2. Would you recommend that Nokia employ individual selling or team selling? Explain.
3. Which step of the sales process do you think will be most critical to Ellermann's success?
4. What could Ellermann do to establish a strong relationship with local Shell representatives?

chapter 15

The Global Marketplace

ROAD MAP: *Previewing the Concepts*

You've come a long way on your marketing journey. You've now learned the fundamentals of how companies develop marketing strategies and marketing mixes to build lasting customer relationships by creating superior customer value. In the final two chapters, we'll extend these fundamentals to two special areas—global marketing, and social responsibility and marketing ethics. Although we've visited these topics regularly in each previous chapter, because of their special importance, we will focus exclusively on them here at the end of your journey. We'll look first at special considerations in global marketing. As we move into the new millennium, advances in communication, transportation, and other technologies have made the world a much smaller place. Today, almost every firm, large or small, faces international marketing issues. In this chapter, we will examine six major decisions marketers make in going global.

► **After studying this chapter, you should be able to**

1. **discuss how the international trade system, economic, political–legal, and cultural environments affect a company's international marketing decisions**
2. **describe three key approaches to entering international markets**
3. **explain how companies adapt their marketing mixes for international markets**
4. **identify the three major forms of international marketing organization**

Buckle up and let's get going! Our first stop is Coca-Cola—America's soft drink. Or *is* it just America's brand? Read on and see how finding the right balance between global standardization and local adaptation has made Coca-Cola the number-one brand worldwide.

What could be more American than Coca-Cola—right? The brand is as American as baseball and apple pie. Coke got its start in an Atlanta pharmacy in 1893, where it sold for five cents a glass. From there, the company's first president, savvy businessman Asa Candler, set out to convince America that Coca-Cola really was "the pause that refreshes." He printed coupons offering complimentary first tastes of Coca-Cola and outfitted pharmacists who distributed the brand with clocks, calendars, scales, and trays bearing the now so-familiar red-and-white Coca-Cola logo. The beverage quickly became an all-American phenomenon; by 1895, the company had set up syrup plants in Chicago, Dallas, and Los Angeles.

But from the get-go, Coke was destined to be more than just America's soft drink. By 1900, Coca-Cola had already ventured beyond America's borders into numerous countries, including Cuba, Puerto Rico, and France. By the 1920s, Coca-Cola was slapping its logo on everything from dogsleds in Canada to the walls of bullfighting arenas in Spain. During World War II, Coca-Cola built bottling plants in Europe and Asia to supply American soldiers in the field.

As the years passed, Coca-Cola's persuasive and plentiful advertising cemented the brand at home as the "All-American" beverage. At the same time, strong marketing abroad fueled Coke's popularity throughout the world. In 1971, the company ran its legendary "I'd like to buy the world a Coke" television spot, in which a crowd of children sang the song from atop a hill in Italy. More recently, Coca-Cola's increased focus on emerging markets such as China, India, and Indonesia—home to 2.4 billion people, half the world's population—has bolstered the brand's global success. Coca-Cola is now arguably the best-known and most admired brand in the world.

Coca-Cola's worldwide success results from a skillful balancing of global standardization and brand building with local adaptation. For years, the company has adhered to the mantra, "think globally, act locally." Coca-Cola spends lavishly on global Coke advertising—some $900 million a year—to create a consistent overall positioning for the brand across the 200 countries it serves. In addition, Coke's taste and packaging are largely standardized around the world—the bottle of Coke you'd drink in New York or Philadelphia looks and tastes much the same as one you might order in Paris, Hong Kong, Moscow, Sidney, or Abu Dhabi. As one ad agency executive asserts, "There are about two products that lend themselves to global marketing—and one of them is Coca-Cola."

Although Coke's taste and positioning are fairly consistent worldwide, in other ways Coca-Cola's marketing is relentlessly local. The company carefully adapts its mix of brands and flavors, promotions, price, and distribution to local customs and preferences in each market. For example, beyond its core Coca-Cola brand, the company makes some 230 different beverage brands, created especially for the taste buds of local consumers. It sells a pear-flavored drink in Turkey, a berry-flavored Fanta for Germany, a honey-flavored green tea in China, and a sports drink called Aquarius in Belgium and the Netherlands.

Consistent with this local focus, within the framework of its broader global positioning, Coca-Cola adapts specific ads to individual country markets. For example, Coke's now classic "Mean Joe Green" TV ad from the United States—in which the weary football star reluctantly accepts a Coke from an admiring young fan and then tosses the awed kid his jersey in appreciation—was replicated in several different regions using the same format but substituting famous local athletes (ads in South America used Argentine soccer star, Maradona; those in Asia used Thai soccer star, Niat). More recently, a localized

Chinese New Year television ad featured a dragon in a holiday parade, adorned from head to tail with red Coke cans. The spot concluded, "For many centuries, the color red has been the color for good luck and prosperity. Who are we to argue with ancient wisdom?"

In India, Coca-Cola uses local promotions to aggressively cultivate a local image. It claimed official sponsorship for World Cup cricket, a favorite national sport, and used Indian cricket fans rather than actors to promote Coke products. Coca-Cola markets effectively in India to both retailers and imbibers. Observes one Coke watcher, "The company hosts massive gatherings of up to 15,000 retailers to showcase everything from the latest coolers and refrigerators, which Coke has for loan, to advertising displays. And its salespeople go house-to-house in their quest for new customers. In New Delhi alone, workers handed out more than 100,000 free bottles of Coke and Fanta last year."

Nothing better illustrates Coca-Cola's skill in balancing standardized global brand building with local adaptation than the explosive global growth of Sprite. Sprite's advertising uniformly targets the world's young people with the tag line "Image is nothing. Thirst is everything. Obey your thirst." The campaign taps into the rebellious side of teenagers and into their need to form individual identities. According to Sprite's director of brand marketing, "The meaning [of Sprite] and what we stand for is exactly the same globally. Teens tell us it's incredibly relevant in nearly every market we go into." However, as always, Coca-Cola tailors its message to local consumers. In China, for example, the campaign was given a softer edge: "You can't be irreverent in China, because it's not acceptable in that society. It's all about being relevant [to the specific audience]," notes the marketer. As a result of such smart targeting and powerful positioning, Sprite's worldwide sales surged 35 percent within three years of the start of the campaign, making it the world's number-four soft drink brand.

As a result of its international marketing prowess, Coca-Cola dominates the global soft drink market. More than 70 percent of the company's sales come from abroad. In the United States Coca-Cola captures an impressive 44 percent market share versus Pepsi's 31 percent. Overseas, however, it outsells Pepsi 2.5 to 1 and boasts 4 of the world's 6 leading soft drink brands: Coca-Cola, Diet Coke, Sprite, and Fanta.

Thus, Coca-Cola is truly an all-world brand. No matter where in the world you are, you'll find Coke "within an arm's length of desire." Yet, Coca-Cola also has a very personal meaning to consumers in different parts of the globe. Coca-Cola *is* as American as baseball and apple pie. But it's also as English as Big Ben and afternoon tea, as German as bratwurst and beer, as Japanese as sumo and sushi, and as Chinese as Ping-Pong and the Great Wall. Consumers in more than 200 countries think of Coke as *their* beverage. In Spain, Coke has been used as a mixer with wine; in Italy, Coke is served with meals in place of wine or cappuccino; in China, the beverage is served at special government occasions.

Coca-Cola's CEO recently asked that company managers go one step further in making Coca-Cola everyone's brand—to adopt a new mantra of "think local and act local." Says the company's Web site, "We need to listen to all the voices around the world asking for beverages that span the entire spectrum of tastes and occasions. . . . Whether you're a student in the United States enjoying a refreshing Coca-Cola, a woman in Italy taking a tea break, a child in Peru asking for a juice drink, or a couple in Korea buying bottled water after a run together, we're there for you. . . . It's a special thing to have billions of friends around the world, and we never forget it."[1]

· ·

In the past, U.S. companies paid little attention to international trade. If they could pick up some extra sales through exporting, that was fine. But the big market was at home, and it teemed with opportunities. The home market was also much safer. Managers did not need to learn other languages, deal with strange and changing currencies, face political and legal uncertainties, or adapt their products to different customer needs and expectations. Today, however, the situation is much different.

Global Marketing into the Twenty-First Century

The world is shrinking rapidly with the advent of faster communication, transportation, and financial flows. Products developed in one country—Gucci purses, Mont Blanc pens, McDonald's hamburgers, Japanese sushi, German BMWs—are finding enthusiastic acceptance in other countries. We would not be surprised to hear about a German businessman wearing an Italian suit meeting an English friend at a Japanese restaurant who later returns home to drink Russian vodka and watch *Frasier* on TV.

International trade is booming. Since 1969, the number of multinational corporations in the world's 14 richest countries has more than tripled, from 7,000 to 24,000. Imports of goods and services now account for 24 percent of gross domestic product worldwide, twice the level of 40 years ago. International trade now accounts for a quarter of the United States' GDP, and between 1996 and 2006, U.S. exports are expected to increase 51 percent.[2]

Many U.S. companies have long been successful at international marketing: Coca-Cola, McDonald's, IBM, Xerox, Corning, Gillette, Colgate, General Electric, Caterpillar, Ford, Kodak, 3M, Boeing, Motorola, and dozens of other American firms have made the world their market. And in the United States, names such as Sony, Toyota, Nestlé, Norelco,

Many American companies have made the world their market.

Nokia, Mercedes, Panasonic, and Prudential have become household words. Other products and services that appear to be American are in fact produced or owned by foreign companies: Bantam books, Baskin-Robbins ice cream, GE and RCA televisions, Carnation milk, Pillsbury food products, Universal Studios, and Motel 6, to name just a few. "Already two-thirds of all industry either operates globally or is in the process of doing so," notes one analyst. "Michelin, the oh-so-French tire manufacturer, now makes 35 percent of its money in the U.S., while Johnson & Johnson does 43 percent of its business abroad. . . . The scope of every manager is the world."[3]

But today global competition is intensifying. Foreign firms are expanding aggressively into new international markets, and home markets are no longer as rich in opportunity. Few industries are now safe from foreign competition. Although some companies would like to stem the tide of foreign imports through protectionism, in the long run this would only raise the cost of living and protect inefficient domestic firms. The better way for companies to compete is to continuously improve their products at home and expand into foreign markets.

Companies that delay taking steps toward internationalizing risk being shut out of growing markets in Western Europe, Eastern Europe, the Pacific Rim, and elsewhere. Firms that stay at home to play it safe not only might lose their chances to enter other markets but also risk losing their home markets. Domestic companies that never thought about foreign competitors suddenly find these competitors in their own backyards.

Ironically, although the need for companies to go abroad is greater today than in the past, so are the risks. Companies that go global confront several major problems. High debt, inflation, and unemployment in many countries have resulted in highly unstable governments and currencies, which limit trade and expose U.S. firms to many risks. Governments are placing more regulations on foreign firms, such as requiring joint ownership with domestic partners, mandating the hiring of nationals, and limiting profits that can be taken from the country. Moreover, foreign governments often impose high tariffs or trade barriers in order to protect their own industries. Finally, corruption is an increasing problem—officials in several countries often award business not to the best bidder but to the highest briber.

Still, companies selling in global industries have no choice but to internationalize their operations. A *global industry* is one in which the competitive positions of firms in given local or national markets are affected by their global positions. A **global firm** is one that, by operating in more than one country, gains marketing, production, R&D, and financial advantages that are not available to purely domestic competitors. The global company sees the world as one market. It minimizes the importance of national boundaries and raises capital, obtains materials and components, and manufactures and markets its goods wherever it can do the best job. For example, Ford's "world truck" sports a cab made in Europe and a chassis built in North America. It is assembled in Brazil and imported to the United States for sale. Otis Elevator gets its elevators' door systems from France, small geared parts from Spain, electronics from Germany, and special motor drives from Japan. It uses the United States only for systems integration. Thus, global firms gain advantages by planning, operating, and coordinating their activities on a worldwide basis.

This does not mean that small and medium-size firms must operate in a dozen countries to succeed. These firms can practice global niching. In fact, companies marketing on the Internet may find themselves going global whether they intend it or not (see Marketing at Work 15-1). But the world is becoming smaller, and every company operating in a global industry—whether large or small—must assess and establish its place in world markets.

The rapid move toward globalization means that all companies will have to answer some basic questions: What market position should we try to establish in our country, in

Global firm
A firm that, by operating in more than one country, gains R&D, production, marketing, and financial advantages in its costs and reputation that are not available to purely domestic competitors.

Marketing at Work 15-1

www.TheWorldIsYourOyster.com: The Ins and Outs of Global E-Commerce

Companies large and small are now taking advantage of cyberspace's vanishing national boundaries. Major marketers doing global e-commerce range from automakers (General Motors and Toyota) to computer makers (Dell and IBM) to direct-mail companies (L.L. Bean and Lands' End) to Internet superstars such as Amazon.com and Yahoo!

For some companies, global Web marketing has been a hit or miss affair. They put their Web site content in English for the American market, and if any international users stumble across it and end up buying something, so much the better. Such orders can be gravy for U.S.-focused marketers. For example, Hyperspace Cowgirls, a six-year-old developer of chil-

dren's multimedia software, has several European deals in the works even though it does no overseas marketing. "We don't advertise overseas at all," says Susan Shaw, president of the company, whose Web address is www.hyperspacegirls.com. "People just find you."

Other marketers have made a more strategic decision to dive into the global marketspace. They're using the Web and online services to reach new customers outside their home countries, support existing customers who live abroad, source from international suppliers, and build global brand awareness. Most international companies have adapted their Web sites to provide country-specific content and services to their best potential

international markets, often in the local language. Go to www.nike.com and Nike's home Web page first asks which site you want: North America, Europe, Asia Pacific, or Latin America. The European option lists five language choices, ranging from English, Deutsch, and Français to Espanol and Italiano. Similarly, Dell Computer offers dozens of country-specific, local-language Web sites for markets, from France, Germany, China, and Japan to Belgium and Brunei. And Texas Instruments uses tailored "TI & Me" sites to sell and support its signal processors, logic devices, and other chips in B2B markets across Europe, Asia, and South America.

Before expanding their Web presences internationally,

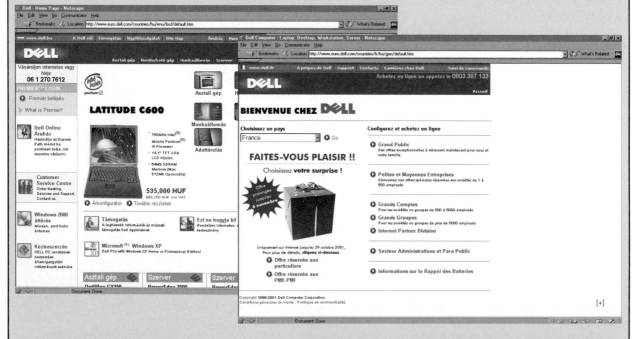

Many marketers are taking advantage of the Internet's global reach. For example, Dell Computer offers dozens of different Web site choices tailored to the languages and situations of specific countries, here Hungary and France.

companies need to find the countries or regions with the largest potential online populations. The biggest growth area today is the Asia-Pacific region. By 2004, the number of Asia-Pacific Internet users is expected to swell to 188 million, thanks to declines in Internet access costs, increases in local-language content, and infrastructure improvements. Europe is another hot spot for Internet growth. Europe has typically lagged about four years behind the United States but is now catching up quickly. European Internet penetration, which stood at 19 percent in 1999, is expected to rise to 33 percent by 2003. By then, the five countries with the highest penetration levels—Germany, France, the Netherlands, the United Kingdom, and Sweden—will have online populations totaling 60 million, up from 34 million in 1999.

Despite these encouraging global e-commerce developments in Asia and Europe, Internet marketers sometimes overstate global opportunities. Although developed countries offer many choices for Internet access—Hong Kong alone has more than 240 registered Internet service providers (ISPs)—less developed countries in Central and South America or Africa have fewer or none at all, forcing users to make international calls to go online. As of 2000, only 6 percent of the world's population had Internet access. Even with adequate phone lines and PC penetration, high connection costs sharply restrict Internet use. In Asia, ISP

subscriptions can run up to $60 a month, more than triple the average U.S. rate.

In addition, global marketers may run up against governmental or cultural restrictions. France, for instance, has laws against providing encrypted content. In Germany, a vendor can't accept payment via credit card until two weeks after an order has been sent. German law also prevents companies from using certain marketing techniques, such as unconditional lifetime guarantees. This affects companies with international Web sites, such as Lands' End, which prominently features its lifetime guarantee on its network of Web sites. On a wider scale, the issue of who pays sales taxes and duties on global e-commerce is murkier still.

Businesses need to realize that the Web does not offer complete solutions for transacting global business—and it probably never will. Most companies will always find it difficult to complete a big business-to-business deal via e-mail. The Internet will not surmount customs red tape or local regulations regarding import or export of certain goods. The Web also can't guarantee that goods will arrive in perfect condition.

What the Web can do is give companies access to markets they could never serve otherwise. The Web certainly has done that for Lands' End. The direct clothing retailer now has online stores in the United Kingdom, Ireland, France, Italy, Germany, and Japan—markets

it would have great difficulty developing through its traditional catalog channels. According to Sam Taylor, vice president of international operations at Lands' End:

The challenge in launching a catalog business is customer acquisition. When you're starting out, you have to rent lists of names, . . . it's so expensive to print and mail those catalogs, and the conversion rate is very low. So the cost to acquire customers is very high. Now, the Internet has changed all that. All of a sudden, we've got a French Web site. We do some PR, we do some limited online advertising, we get word of mouth, and the business starts to build. We're not overinvesting in upfront marketing. At some point in the future, once the business is big enough, we will launch a paper catalog [in France], but not before the business is ready. That's one of the good things about the Internet. It has totally turned businesses upside down and changed how we do business.

However, Lands' End is landing right-side up in the international arena. The company now ships products to 185 countries out of its Dodgeville, Wisconsin, warehouses. International Web sales now contribute about 14 percent of Lands' End's total revenues.

Sources: "One in Three Europeans Will Embrace a Digital Lifestyle by 2003, According to Forrester," *Business Wire,* December 6, 2000; Brandon Mitchener, "E-Commerce: Border Crossings," *Wall Street Journal,* November 22, 1999, p. R41; Janet Purdy Levaux, "Adapting Products and Services for Global E-Commerce," *World Trade,* January 2001, pp. 52–54; and Carol Sliwa, "Clothing Retailer Finds Worldwide Business on the Web," *Computerworld,* April 30, 2001, p. 40.

our economic region, and globally? Who will our global competitors be, and what are their strategies and resources? Where should we produce or source our products? What strategic alliances should we form with other firms around the world?

As shown in Figure 15-1, a company faces six major decisions in international marketing. Each decision will be discussed in detail in this chapter.

Figure 15-1
Major international
marketing decisions

Looking at the Global Marketing Environment

Before deciding whether to operate internationally, a company must thoroughly understand the international marketing environment. That environment has changed a great deal in the last two decades, creating both new opportunities and new problems. The world economy has globalized. World trade and investment have grown rapidly, with many attractive markets opening up in Western and Eastern Europe, China and the Pacific Rim, Russia, and elsewhere. There has been a growth of global brands in automobiles, food, clothing, electronics, computers and software, and many other categories. The number of global companies has grown dramatically.

The International Trade System

The U.S. company looking abroad must start by understanding the international *trade system.* When selling to another country, the U.S. firm faces various trade restrictions. The most common is the **tariff,** which is a tax levied by a foreign government against certain imported products. The tariff may be designed either to raise revenue or to protect domestic firms. The exporter also may face a **quota,** which sets limits on the amount of goods the importing country will accept in certain product categories. The purpose of the quota is to conserve on foreign exchange and to protect local industry and employment. An **embargo,** or boycott, which totally bans some kinds of imports, is the strongest form of quota.

American firms may face **exchange controls** that limit the amount of foreign exchange and the exchange rate against other currencies. The company also may face **nontariff trade barriers,** such as biases against U.S. company bids or restrictive product standards or other rules that go against American product features:

> One of the cleverest ways the Japanese have found to keep foreign manufacturers out of their domestic market is to plead "uniqueness." Japanese skin is different, the government argues, so foreign cosmetics companies must test their products in Japan before selling there. The Japanese say their stomachs are small and have room for only the *mikan,* the local tangerine, so imports of U.S. oranges are limited. Now the Japanese have come up with what may be the flakiest argument yet: Their snow is different, so ski equipment should be too.[4]

At the same time, certain forces *help* trade between nations. Examples include the General Agreement on Tariffs and Trade and various regional free trade agreements.

The World Trade Organization and GATT The General Agreement on Tariffs and Trade (GATT) is a 54-year-old treaty designed to promote world trade by reducing tariffs and other international trade barriers. Since the treaty's inception in 1948, member nations

Tariff
A tax levied by a government against certain imported products.

Quota
A limit on the amount of goods that an importing country will accept in certain product categories.

Embargo
A ban on the import of a certain product.

Exchange controls
Government limits on the amount of foreign exchange with other countries and on the exchange rate against other currencies.

Nontariff trade barriers
Nonmonetary barriers to foreign products, such as biases against a foreign company's bids or product standards that go against a foreign company's product features.

(currently numbering more than 140) have met in eight rounds of GATT negotiations to reassess trade barriers and set new rules for international trade. The first seven rounds of negotiations reduced the average worldwide tariffs on manufactured goods from 45 percent to just 5 percent.

The most recently completed GATT negotiations, dubbed the Uruguay Round, dragged on for seven long years before concluding in 1993. The benefits of the Uruguay Round will be felt for many years as the accord promotes long-term global trade growth. It reduced the world's remaining merchandise tariffs by 30 percent, boosting global merchandise trade by as much as 10 percent, or $270 billion in current dollars, by 2002. The new agreement also extended GATT to cover trade in agriculture and a wide range of services, and it toughened international protection of copyrights, patents, trademarks, and other intellectual property.[5]

Beyond reducing trade barriers and setting international standards for trade, the Uruguay Round established the World Trade Organization (WTO) to enforce GATT rules. One of the WTO's first major tasks was to host negotiations on the General Agreement on Trade in Services, which deals with worldwide trade in banking, securities, and insurance services. In general, the WTO acts as an umbrella organization, overseeing GATT, the General Agreement on Trade in Services, and a similar agreement governing intellectual property. In addition, the WTO mediates global disputes and imposes trade sanctions, authorities that the previous GATT organization never possessed. Top decision makers from the WTO meet once every two years to discuss matters pertaining to all WTO agreements. The most recent meetings took place in Doha, Qatar, in late 2001.

Regional Free Trade Zones   Certain countries have formed *free trade zones* or **economic communities**—groups of nations organized to work toward common goals in the regulation of international trade. One such community is the *European Union (EU)*. Formed in 1957, the European Union—then called the Common Market—set out to create a single European market by reducing barriers to the free flow of products, services, finances, and labor among member countries and developing policies on trade with nonmember nations. Today, the European Union represents one of the world's single largest markets. Its 15 member countries contain more than 374 million consumers and account for 20 percent of the world's exports. During the next decade, as more European nations gain admission, the EU could contain as many as 450 million people in 28 countries.[6]

> **Economic community**
> A group of nations organized to work toward common goals in the regulation of international trade.

European unification offers tremendous trade opportunities for U.S. and other non-European firms. However, it also poses threats. As a result of increased unification, European companies will grow bigger and more competitive. Perhaps an even bigger concern, however, is that lower barriers *inside* Europe will create only thicker *outside* walls. Some observers envision a "Fortress Europe" that heaps favors on firms from EU countries but hinders outsiders by imposing obstacles such as stiffer import quotas, local content requirements, and other nontariff barriers.

Progress toward European unification has been slow—many doubt that complete unification will ever be achieved. However, on January 1, 1999, 11 of the 15 member nations took a significant step toward unification by adopting the Euro as a common currency. In January 2001, Greece became the twelfth member nation to adopt the Euro. Currencies of the individual countries will be phased out gradually until January 1, 2002, when the Euro will become the only currency. Adoption of the Euro will decrease much of the currency risk associated with doing business in Europe, making member countries with previously weak currencies more attractive markets. In addition, by removing currency conversion hurdles, the switch will likely increase cross-border trade and highlight differences in pricing and marketing from country to country.[7]

Even with the adoption of the Euro as a standard currency, from a marketing viewpoint, creating an economic community will not create a homogenous market. As one

Wal-Mart and other companies are expanding rapidly in Mexico and Canada to take advantage of the many opportunities presented by NAFTA. The trade agreement establishes a single market of 360 million people in Mexico, Canada, and the United States.

international analyst suggests, "Even though you have fiscal harmonization, you can't go against 2,000 years of tradition." [8] With 14 different languages and distinctive national customs, it is unlikely that the EU will ever become the "United States of Europe." Although economic and political boundaries may fall, social and cultural differences will remain, and companies marketing in Europe will face a daunting mass of local rules. Still, even if only partly successful, European unification will make a more efficient and competitive Europe a global force with which to reckon. [9]

In North America, the United States and Canada phased out trade barriers in 1989. In January 1994, the North American Free Trade Agreement (NAFTA) established a free trade zone among the United States, Mexico, and Canada. The agreement created a single market of 360 million people who produce and consume $6.7 trillion worth of goods and services. As it is implemented over a 15-year period, NAFTA will eliminate all trade barriers and investment restrictions among the three countries. Prior to NAFTA, tariffs on American products entering Mexico averaged 13 percent, whereas U.S. tariffs on Mexican goods averaged 6 percent.

Thus far, the agreement has allowed trade between the countries to flourish. Each day the United States exchanges more than $1 billion in goods and services with Canada, its largest trading partner. Since the agreement was signed in 1993, U.S. merchandise exports to Mexico are up 170 percent, while Mexican exports to the United States grew some 241 percent. In 1998, Mexico passed Japan to become America's second largest trading partner. Given the apparent success of NAFTA, talks are now underway to investigate establishing a Free Trade Area of the Americas (FTAA). This mammoth free trade zone would include 30 countries stretching from the Bering Strait to Cape Horn, with a population of 800 million and a combined gross domestic product of more than $11 trillion. [10]

Other free trade areas have formed in Latin America and South America. For example, MERCOSUR now links six members, including full members Argentina, Brazil, Paraguay, and Uruguay and associate members Bolivia and Chile. With a population of more than 200 million and a combined economy of more than $1 trillion a year, these countries make up the largest trading bloc after NAFTA and the European Union. There is talk of a free trade agreement between the EU and MERCOSUR. [11]

Although the recent trend toward free trade zones has caused great excitement and new market opportunities, this trend also raises some concerns. For example, in the United States, unions fear that NAFTA will lead to the further exodus of manufacturing jobs to Mexico where wage rates are much lower. Environmentalists worry that companies that are unwilling to play by the strict rules of the U.S. Environmental Protection Agency will relocate in Mexico, where pollution regulation has been lax.

Each nation has unique features that must be understood. A nation's readiness for different products and services and its attractiveness as a market to foreign firms depend on its economic, political–legal, and cultural environments.

Economic Environment

The international marketer must study each country's economy. Two economic factors reflect the country's attractiveness as a market: the country's industrial structure and its income distribution.

The country's *industrial structure* shapes its product and service needs, income levels, and employment levels. The four types of industrial structures are as follows:

◆ *Subsistence economies:* In a subsistence economy, the vast majority of people engage in simple agriculture. They consume most of their output and barter the rest for simple goods and services. They offer few market opportunities.

◆ *Raw material exporting economies:* These economies are rich in one or more natural resources but poor in other ways. Much of their revenue comes from exporting these resources. Examples are Chile (tin and copper), Zaire (copper, cobalt, and coffee), and Saudi Arabia (oil). These countries are good markets for large equipment, tools and supplies, and trucks. If there are many foreign residents and a wealthy upper class, they are also a market for luxury goods.

◆ *Industrializing economies:* In an industrializing economy, manufacturing accounts for 10 to 20 percent of the country's economy. Examples include Egypt, the Philippines, India, and Brazil. As manufacturing increases, the country needs more imports of raw textile materials, steel, and heavy machinery, and fewer imports of finished textiles, paper products, and automobiles. Industrialization typically creates a new rich class and a small but growing middle class, both demanding new types of imported goods.

◆ *Industrial economies:* Industrial economies are major exporters of manufactured goods and investment funds. They trade goods among themselves and also export them to other types of economies for raw materials and semifinished goods. The varied manufacturing activities of these industrial nations and their large middle class make them rich markets for all sorts of goods.

The second economic factor is the country's *income distribution.* Countries with subsistence economies may consist mostly of households with very low family incomes. In contrast, industrialized nations may have low-, medium-, and high-income households. Still other countries may have households with only either very low or very high incomes. However, in many cases, poorer countries may have small but wealthy segments of upper-income consumers. Also, even in low-income and developing economies, people may find ways to buy products that are important to them:

Philosophy professor Nina Gladziuk thinks carefully before shelling out her hard-earned zlotys for Poland's dazzling array of consumer goods. But spend she certainly does. Although she earns just $550 a month from two academic jobs, Gladziuk, 41, enjoys making purchases: They are changing her lifestyle after years of

Developing economies: In Central Europe, companies are catering to the new class of buyers with dreams of the good life and buying habits to match who are eager to snap up everything from western consumer goods to high fashions and the latest cell phones.

deprivation under communism. In the past year, she has furnished a new apartment in a popular neighborhood near Warsaw's Kabaty Forest, splurged on foreign-made beauty products, and spent a weekend in Paris before attending a seminar financed by her university. . . . Meet Central Europe's fast-rising consumer class. From white-collar workers like Gladziuk to factory workers in Budapest to hip young professionals in Prague, incomes are rising and confidence surging as a result of four years of economic growth. In the region's leading economies—the Czech Republic, Hungary, and Poland—the new class of buyers is growing not only in numbers but also in sophistication. . . . In Hungary, ad agency Young & Rubicam labels 11 percent of the country as "aspirers," with dreams of the good life and buying habits to match. Nearly one-third of all Czechs, Hungarians, and Poles—some 17 million people—are under 30 years old, eager to snap up everything from the latest fashions to compact disks.[12]

Thus, international marketers face many challenges in understanding how the economic environment will affect decisions about which global markets to enter and how.

Political–Legal Environment

Nations differ greatly in their political–legal environments. At least four political–legal factors should be considered in deciding whether to do business in a given country: attitudes toward international buying, government bureaucracy, political stability, and monetary regulations.

In their *attitudes toward international buying,* some nations are quite receptive to foreign firms and others are quite hostile. For example, India has bothered foreign businesses with import quotas, currency restrictions, and limits on the percentage of the management team that can be nonnationals. As a result, many U.S. companies left India. In contrast, neighboring Asian countries such as Singapore, Thailand, Malaysia, and the Philippines court foreign investors and shower them with incentives and favorable operating conditions.[13]

A second factor is *government bureaucracy*—the extent to which the host government runs an efficient system for helping foreign companies: efficient customs handling, good market information, and other factors that aid in doing business. A common shock to Americans is how quickly barriers to trade disappear in some countries if a suitable payment (bribe) is made to some official.

Political stability is another issue. Governments change hands, sometimes violently. Even without a change, a government may decide to respond to new popular feelings. The foreign company's property may be taken, its currency holdings may be blocked, or import quotas or new duties may be set. International marketers may find it profitable to do business in an unstable country, but the unstable situation will affect how they handle business and financial matters.

Finally, companies must also consider a country's *monetary regulations.* Sellers want to take their profits in a currency of value to them. Ideally, the buyer can pay in the seller's currency or in other world currencies. Short of this, sellers might accept a blocked currency—one whose removal from the country is restricted by the buyer's government—if they can buy other goods in that country that they need themselves or can sell elsewhere for a needed currency. Besides currency limits, a changing exchange rate also creates high risks for the seller.

Most international trade involves cash transactions. Yet many nations have too little hard currency to pay for their purchases from other countries. They may want to pay with other items instead of cash, which has led to a growing practice called **countertrade.** Countertrade makes up an estimated 20 percent of all world trade.[14] It takes several forms: *Barter* involves the direct exchange of goods or services, as when Australian cattlemen swapped beef on the hoof for Indonesian goods including beer, palm oil, and cement. Another form is *compensation* (or *buyback*), whereby the seller sells a plant, equipment, or technology to another country and agrees to take payment in the resulting products. Thus, Goodyear provided China with materials and training for a printing plant in exchange for finished labels. Another form is *counterpurchase,* in which the seller receives full payment in cash but agrees to spend some portion of the money in the other country within a stated time period. For example, Pepsi sells its cola syrup to Russia for rubles and agrees to buy Russian-made Stolichnaya vodka for sale in the United States.

Countertrade deals can be very complex. For example, a few years back, Daimler-Chrysler agreed to sell 30 trucks to Romania in exchange for 150 Romanian jeeps, which it then sold to Ecuador for bananas, which were in turn sold to a German supermarket chain for German currency. Through this roundabout process, DaimlerChrysler finally obtained payment in German money. In another case, when Occidental Petroleum Company wanted to sell oil to Yugoslavia, it hired a trading firm, SGD International, to arrange a countertrade. SGD arranged for a New York City automobile dealer-distributor, Global Motors Inc., to import more than $400 million worth of Yugoslavian Yugo automobiles, paid for by Occidental oil. Global then paid Occidental in cash. SGD, however, was paid in Yugos, which it peddled piecemeal by trading them for everything from cash to Caribbean resort hotel rooms, which it in turn sold to tour packagers and travel agencies for cash.[15]

Countertrade
International trade involving the direct or indirect exchange of goods for other goods instead of cash. Forms include barter, compensation (buyback), and counterpurchase.

Cultural Environment

Each country has its own folkways, norms, and taboos. The seller must examine the ways consumers in different countries think about and use certain products before planning a marketing program. There are often surprises. For example, the average French man uses almost twice as many cosmetics and beauty aids as his wife. The Germans and the French eat more packaged, branded spaghetti than do Italians. Italian children like to eat chocolate bars between slices of bread as a snack. Women in Tanzania will not give their children eggs for fear of making them bald or impotent.

Companies that ignore such differences can make some very expensive and embarrassing mistakes. Here's an example:

McDonald's and Coca-Cola managed to offend the entire Muslim world by putting the Saudi Arabian flag on their packaging. The flag's design includes

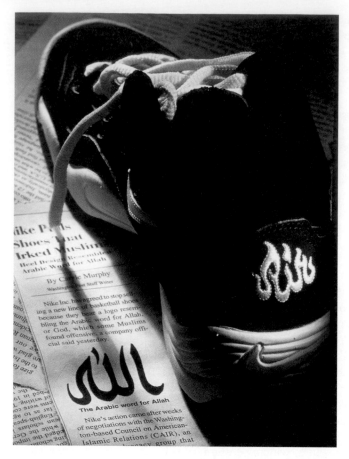

Overlooking cultural differences can result in embarrassing mistakes. When Nike learned that this stylized "Air" logo resembled "Allah" in Arabic script, it apologized and pulled the shoes from distribution.

a passage from the Koran (the sacred text of Islam), and Muslims feel very strongly that their Holy Writ should never be wadded up and tossed in the garbage. Nike faced a similar situation in Arab countries when Muslims objected to a stylized "Air" logo on its shoes, which resembled "Allah" in Arabic script. Nike apologized for the mistake and pulled the shoes from distribution.[16]

Business norms and behavior also vary from country to country. American business executives need to be briefed on these factors before conducting business in another country. Here are some examples of different global business behavior:[17]

◆ South Americans like to sit or stand very close to each other when they talk business—in fact, almost nose-to-nose. The American business executive tends to keep backing away as the South American moves closer. Both may end up being offended.

◆ Fast and tough bargaining, which works well in other parts of the world, is often inappropriate in Japan and other Asian countries. Moreover, in face-to-face communications, Japanese business executives rarely say no. Thus, Americans tend to become impatient with having to spend time in polite conversation about the weather or other such topics before getting down to business. And they become frustrated when they don't know where they stand. However, when Americans come to the point quickly, Japanese business executives may find this behavior offensive.

◆ In France, wholesalers don't want to promote a product. They ask their retailers what they want and deliver it. If an American company builds its strategy around the French wholesaler's cooperation in promotions, it is likely to fail.

◆ When American executives exchange business cards, each usually gives the other's card a cursory glance and stuffs it in a pocket for later reference. In Japan, however, executives dutifully study each other's cards during a greeting, carefully noting company affiliation and rank. They show a business card the same respect they show a person. Also, they hand their card to the most important person first.

By the same token, companies that understand cultural nuances can use them to advantage when positioning products internationally. For example, consider French cosmetics giant L'Oréal:

> It's a sunny afternoon outside Parkson's department store in Shanghai, and a marketing battle is raging for the attention of Chinese women. Tall, pouty models in beige skirts and sheer tops pass out flyers promoting Revlon's new spring colors. But their effort is drowned out by L'Oréal's eye-catching show for its Maybelline brand. To a pulsing rhythm, two gangly models in shimmering Lycra tops dance on a podium before a large backdrop depicting the New York City skyline. The music stops, and a makeup artist transforms a model's face while a Chinese saleswoman delivers the punch line. "This brand comes from America. It's very trendy," she shouts into her microphone. "If you want to be fashionable, just choose Maybelline." Few of the women in the crowd realize that the trendy "New York" Maybelline brand belongs to French cosmetics giant L'Oréal. . . . Blink an eye and L'Oréal has just sold 85 products around the world, from Redken hair care and Ralph Lauren perfumes to Helena Rubinstein cosmetics. In the battle for global beauty markets, L'Oréal has developed a winning formula: . . . conveying the allure of different cultures through its many products. Whether it's selling Italian elegance, New York street smarts, or French beauty through its brands, L'Oréal is reaching out to a vast range of people across incomes and cultures.[18]

Thus, understanding cultural traditions, preferences, and behaviors can help companies to avoid embarrassing mistakes and to take advantage of cross-cultural opportunities.

Deciding Whether to Go International

Not all companies need to venture into international markets to survive. For example, most local businesses need to market well only in the local marketplace. Operating domestically is easier and safer. Managers need not learn another country's language and laws, deal with volatile currencies, face political and legal uncertainties, or redesign their products to suit different customer needs and expectations. However, companies that operate in global industries, where their strategic positions in specific markets are affected strongly by their overall global positions, must compete on a worldwide basis to succeed.

Any of several factors might draw a company into the international arena. Global competitors might attack the company's domestic market by offering better products or lower prices. The company might want to counterattack these competitors in their home markets to tie up their resources. Or the company might discover foreign markets that present higher profit opportunities than the domestic market does. The company's domestic market might be stagnant or shrinking, or the company might need an enlarged customer base in order to achieve economies of scale. The company might want to reduce its dependence on any one market so as to reduce its risk. Finally, the company's customers might be expanding abroad and require international servicing.

Before going abroad, the company must weigh several risks and answer many questions about its ability to operate globally. Can the company learn to understand the preferences and buyer behavior of consumers in other countries? Can it offer competitively attractive products? Will it be able to adapt to other countries' business cultures and deal effectively with foreign nationals? Do the company's managers have the necessary international experience? Has management considered the impact of regulations and the political environments of other countries?

Because of the risks and difficulties of entering international markets, most companies do not act until some situation or event thrusts them into the global arena. Someone—a domestic exporter, a foreign importer, a foreign government—may ask the company to sell abroad. Or the company may be saddled with overcapacity and must find additional markets for its goods.

Deciding Which Markets to Enter

Before going abroad, the company should try to define its international *marketing objectives and policies*. It should decide what *volume* of foreign sales it wants. Most companies start small when they go abroad. Some plan to stay small, seeing international sales as a small part of their business. Other companies have bigger plans, seeing international business as equal to or even more important than their domestic business.

The company must also choose *how many* countries it wants to market in. Companies must be careful not to spread themselves too thin or to expand beyond their capabilities by operating in too many countries too soon. For example, although consumer products company Amway is now breaking into markets at a furious pace, it is doing so only after decades of gradually building up its overseas presence. Known for its neighbor-to-neighbor direct-selling networks, Amway expanded into Australia in 1971, a country far away but similar to the U.S. market. In the 1980s, Amway expanded into 10 more countries, and the pace increased rapidly from then on. By 1994 Amway was firmly established in 60 countries, including Hungary, Poland, and the Czech Republic. Following substantial success in Japan, China, and other Asian countries, the company entered India in 1998. Today, Amway sells its products in 80 countries and international proceeds contribute more than 70 percent of the company's overall revenues.[19]

Next, the company needs to decide on the *types* of countries to enter. A country's attractiveness depends on the product, geographical factors, income and population, political climate, and other factors. The seller may prefer certain country groups or parts of the world. In recent years, many major new markets have emerged, offering both substantial opportunities and daunting challenges (see Marketing at Work 15-2).

After listing possible international markets, the company must screen and rank each one. Consider the following example:

Many mass marketers dream of selling to China's more than 1.3 billion people. For example, Colgate is waging a pitched battle in China, seeking control of the world's largest toothpaste market. Yet, this country of infrequent brushers offers great potential. Only 20 percent of China's rural dwellers brush daily, so Colgate and its competitors are aggressively pursuing promotional and educational programs, from massive ad campaigns to visits to local schools to sponsoring oral care research. Through such efforts, in this $350 million market dominated by local brands, Colgate has expanded its market share from 7 percent in 1995 to 24 percent today.[20]

Marketing at Work 15-2

Emerging Markets: China and Russia

As Eastern Europe and Asia reform their markets, and as the United States continues to dismantle its trade barriers, U.S. companies are eagerly anticipating the profits that await them. Here are "snapshots" of the opportunities and challenges that marketers face in two emerging markets: China and Russia.

China: 1.3 Billion Consumers

In Guangdong province, Chinese "yuppies" walk department store aisles to buy $95 Nike or Reebok sneakers or think nothing of spending $4 on a jar of Skippy peanut butter in the supermarket section. Although the average annual income amounts to only $360 per person, China's ever-growing pool of elite consumers still has plenty of spending money because of subsidized housing and health care and lots of savings under the mattress.

The prevalence of wide-screen televisions, fancy stereos, and home-karaoke machines in Shanghai apartments suggests that this new upper-middle class has more money than it admits to. . . . Among urban households, fewer than one in five households had a color television in 1985; today the average such home has more than one. Then, 7 percent had a refrigerator; now 73 percent do. Cameras are four times more common. Among richer urban households, more than half now have a VCR, a pager, air conditioner, and a shower, and nearly a third of households also own a mobile phone.

In Shenzhen, Guangdong's second-largest city, consumers have the highest disposable income in all of China—$3,900 annually. With purchasing power like this, a population of 1.3 billion, and the

fastest-growing economy in the world, China is encouraging companies from around the planet to set up shop there. Instead of the communist propaganda of yore, modern Chinese billboards exclaim, "Give China a chance."

Yet for all the market potential, there are many hurdles to clear in establishing businesses in China and marketing to the Chinese. For one, China is not one market but many, and regional governments may discriminate against certain goods. Distribution channels are undeveloped, consisting of thousands of tiny mom-and-pop stores that can afford to stock only a few bottles or packages at a time. And China's dismal infrastructure can turn a rail shipment traveling from Guanzhou to Beijing into a month-long odyssey. Smart firms, such as Allied Signal and Kodak, try to jump these hurdles by partnering with Chinese government bodies or acquiring Chinese business partners who can help penetrate distribution channels and hire experienced personnel.

A major concern to some U.S. businesses has been China's distressing human rights record. Levi Strauss has turned its back on China's vast market for blue jeans because of such concerns. But other U.S. firms counter that industry can be part of the solution. "Supporting the business sector will result in economic and political freedoms for the Chinese people," says a 3M spokesperson.

Russia: Many Opportunities, Many Pitfalls

Contemporary Russia certainly looks like a nifty place for American marketers: 145 million people; gross domestic product (GDP) growth of 7.2 percent last year; a young, well-

educated, cultured population; a booming, younger middle class, many members of which are starting their own businesses.

Irina Lyakhnovskaya is a go-getter. Her hometown of Samara in central Russia straddles the Volga River and is surrounded by miles of fertile grassland and the Zhigulevskiye Mountains. Five years ago, she started a tourist company, with seed capital supplied by herself and three friends, that specializes in arranging hunting and fishing trips for visitors from Finland and Norway. She drives a Russian-made Lada that she purchased new for $3,500 two years ago, and she spends weekends at a country dacha that has an apple orchard she harvests to make her own wine. Last year she took vacations in Hungary and Romania, and this year she plans to get to Britain. In a country where the average factory worker is lucky to make $150 a month, she makes as much as $500. Lyakhnovskaya, 38, embodies a major shift in Russia's economic landscape. Boosted by a resurgent national economy and by its own bootstraps, a middle class is taking root in the former land of the proletariat. Analysts estimate 12 million to 30 million Russians, some 8 percent to 20 percent of the nation's 145 million population, qualify as middle class.

On the one hand, demographics and the economy—on the rebound from the 1998 crash—are converging to make Russia one of the more attractive emerging markets on the globe. Between 1997 and 2000, Russia's GDP grew an estimated 38 percent to $623.1 billion, compared with a 20 percent increase to $10 billion in U.S. GDP during that same period. Compared to other emerging markets, the population is more literate. It's a population that embraces technology, too: Television penetration is high in Russia, and although industries such as two-way telecommunications are in their infancy, that's changing quickly.

Still, Russia is not all sunshine and roses for American marketers. This fast-growing market also presents rampant corruption, a widespread lack of basic business controls, a barely liquid currency, and a business culture that, while increasingly capitalist, is definitely not American. Moreover, the newfound middle class is still fragile, fearing the prospect of a fresh national economic calamity. It's happened before. A fledgling middle class began to grow during the chaotic reign of Boris Yeltsin, only to see their fortunes wiped out by the economic crisis of 1998. "One new crisis, everything I have will be wiped out," says Lyakhnovskaya. All of this makes Russia an attractive but still tricky market in which to do business.

Food companies have done especially well in Russia. McDonald's opened its first Russian restaurant in 1990 and now has 58 outlets there—the McDonald's in Moscow's Pushkin Square is the world's busiest. Companies in other industries are also making a push into this promising but chancy market. The world's auto companies see huge potential. By 2005, some analysts expect, Russia will become one of the world's largest automotive markets. Indeed, between 1991 and 1998, with the growth of the country's middle class, Russian auto sales skyrocketed 60 percent.

Leisure pursuits, once considered a luxury, have also trickled down to the middle class. Gold's Gym, which operates 560 gyms worldwide, opened one in Moscow in 1993 that now is one of the chain's solid performers. The Moscow facility has about 3,000 members, matching the company's average worldwide. The Moscow gym looks much like those in the United States, except that the signs are in Cyrillic. "If I were to show you a video of the Moscow gym, you'd think it was New York or Los Angeles," says a Gold's executive. "The women are gorgeous, and people are in good shape."

Although U.S. businesspeople may feel more at home in Russia now than at any time in that country's history, they still face the typical challenges of an emerging market. Beyond corruption and difficult currency, differences in culture and social habits can affect how business is done. For instance, Russians place much more value on hospitality than Americans. "They tend to be touchy-feely; there's lots of hugging," says a Russian trade expert. Eating and drinking with business prospects is also important, although Americans can sometimes get into trouble trying to match Russians drink for drink. (The solution? "Say up front that you can't drink for medical reasons," advises the trade expert.)

Sources: Portions of the Russian example adapted from Lisa Bertagnoli, "To Russia with . . . Reservations," *Marketing News,* April 9, 2001, pp. 1, 11. Quotes and other information in both examples from "Business: Not Quite a Billion," *The Economist,* January 2, 1999, p. 56; and Paul Starobin, "Russia's Middle Class," *Business Week,* October 16, 2000, pp. 78–85.

Emerging markets: Contemporary Russia—with its young, well-educated, cultured population and a booming, younger middle class—looks like a nifty place for American marketers. However, the newfound middle class is still fragile, fearing the next national economic calamity.

Table 15-1 Indicators of Market Potential

1. Demographic Characteristics	4. Technological Factors
Size of population Rate of population growth Degree of urbanization Population density Age structures and composition of the population	Level of technological skills Existing production technology Existing consumption technology Education levels
2. Geographic Characteristics	5. Sociocultural Factors
Physical size of a country Topographical characteristics Climate conditions	Dominant values Lifestyle patterns Ethnic groups Linguistic fragmentation
3. Economic Factors	6. National Goals and Plans
GDP per capita Income distribution Rate of growth of GNP Ratio of investment to GNP	Industry priorities Infrastructure investment plans

Sources: Susan P. Douglas, C. Samuel Craig, and Warren Keegan, "Approaches to Assessing International Marketing Opportunities for Small and Medium-Sized Businesses," *Columbia Journal of World Business,* Fall 1982, pp. 26–32. Copyright 1982, 1999. *Columbia Journal of World Business.* Reprint with permission. Also see Tamer S. Cavusil, "Measuring the Potential of Emerging Markets: An Indexing Approach," *Business Horizons,* January–February 1977, pp. 87–91.

Colgate's decision to enter the Chinese market seems fairly simple and straightforward: China is a huge market without established competition. Given the low rate of brushing, this already huge market can grow even larger. Yet we still can question whether market size *alone* is reason enough for selecting China. Colgate also must consider other factors: Will the Chinese government remain stable and supportive? Does China provide for the production and distribution technologies needed to produce and market Colgate's products profitably? Will Colgate be able to overcome cultural barriers and convince Chinese consumers to brush their teeth regularly? Can Colgate compete effectively with dozens of local competitors? Colgate's current success in China suggests that it could answer yes to all of these questions. Still, the company's future in China is filled with uncertainties.

Possible global markets should be ranked on several factors, including market size, market growth, cost of doing business, competitive advantage, and risk level. The goal is to determine the potential of each market, using indicators such as those shown in Table 15-1. Then the marketer must decide which markets offer the greatest long-run return on investment.

General Electric's appliance division sells more than 12 million appliances each year in 150 world markets under the GE Profile, GE, Hotpoint, and RCA brand names. This experienced global marketer uses what it calls a "smart bomb" strategy for selecting global markets to enter. GE Appliances' executives examine each potential country microscopically, measuring factors such as strength of local competitors, market growth potential, and availability of skilled labor. Then they target only markets in which they can earn more than 20 percent on their investment. The goal: "To generate the best returns possible on the smallest investment possible." Once targets are selected, GE Appliances zeros in with marketing smart bombs—products and programs tailored to yield the best performance in each market. As a result of this strategy, GE is trouncing competitors Whirlpool and Maytag in Asian markets.[21]

Linking the Concepts

Slow down, stretch your legs, and think for a minute about the difficulties of assessing and selecting international markets.

◆ Assess China as a market for McDonald's. What factors make it attractive? What factors make it less attractive?

◆ Assess Canada as a market for McDonald's. In what ways is Canada more attractive than China? In what ways is it less attractive?

◆ If McDonald's could operate in only one of these countries, which one would you choose and why?

Deciding How to Enter the Market

Once a company has decided to sell in a foreign country, it must determine the best mode of entry. Its choices are *exporting, joint venturing,* and *direct investment.* Figure 15-2 shows three market entry strategies, along with the options each one offers. As the figure shows, each succeeding strategy involves more commitment and risk, but also more control and potential profits.

Exporting

Exporting
Entering a foreign market by selling goods produced in the company's home country, often with little modification.

The simplest way to enter a foreign market is through **exporting.** The company may passively export its surpluses from time to time, or it may make an active commitment to expand exports to a particular market. In either case, the company produces all its goods in its home country. It may or may not modify them for the export market. Exporting involves the least change in the company's product lines, organization, investments, or mission.

Companies typically start with *indirect exporting,* working through independent international marketing intermediaries. Indirect exporting involves less investment because the firm does not require an overseas sales force or set of contacts. It also involves less risk. International marketing intermediaries—domestic-based export merchants or agents, cooperative organizations, and export-management companies— bring know-how and services to the relationship, so the seller normally makes fewer mistakes.

Sellers may eventually move into *direct exporting,* whereby they handle their own exports. The investment and risk are somewhat greater in this strategy, but so is the potential return. A company can conduct direct exporting in several ways: It can set up a domestic export department that carries out export activities. It can set up an overseas sales

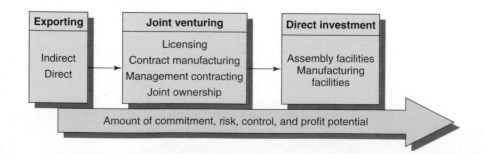

Figure 15-2
Market-entry strategies

branch that handles sales, distribution, and perhaps promotion. The sales branch gives the seller more presence and program control in the foreign market and often serves as a display center and customer service center. The company can also send home-based salespeople abroad at certain times in order to find business. Finally, the company can do its exporting either through foreign-based distributors who buy and own the goods or through foreign-based agents who sell the goods on behalf of the company.

Joint Venturing

A second method of entering a foreign market is **joint venturing**—joining with foreign companies to produce or market products or services. Joint venturing differs from exporting in that the company joins with a host country partner to sell or market abroad. It differs from direct investment in that an association is formed with someone in the foreign country. There are four types of joint ventures: licensing, contract manufacturing, management contracting, and joint ownership.

Joint venturing
Entering foreign markets by joining with foreign companies to produce or market a product or service.

Licensing **Licensing** is a simple way for a manufacturer to enter international marketing. The company enters into an agreement with a licensee in the foreign market. For a fee or royalty, the licensee buys the right to use the company's manufacturing process, trademark, patent, trade secret, or other item of value. The company thus gains entry into the market at little risk; the licensee gains production expertise or a well-known product or name without having to start from scratch.

Coca-Cola markets internationally by licensing bottlers around the world and supplying them with the syrup needed to produce the product. In Japan, Budweiser beer flows from Kirin breweries, Lady Borden ice cream is churned out at Meiji Milk Products dairies, and Marlboro cigarettes roll off production lines at Japan Tobacco, Inc. Online brokerage E*Trade has set up E*Trade-branded Web sites under licensing agreements in Canada, Australia/New Zealand, and France. And Tokyo Disneyland is owned and operated by Oriental Land Company under license from the Walt Disney Company. The 45-year license gives Disney licensing fees plus 10 percent of admissions and 5 percent of food and merchandise sales.[22]

Licensing
A method of entering a foreign market in which the company enters into an agreement with a licensee in the foreign market, offering the right to use a manufacturing process, trademark, patent, trade secret, or other item of value for a fee or royalty.

Licensing: Tokyo Disneyland is owned and operated by the Oriental Land Co., Ltd. (a Japanese development company), under license from Walt Disney Company.

Licensing has potential disadvantages, however. The firm has less control over the licensee than it would over its own production facilities. Furthermore, if the licensee is very successful, the firm has given up these profits, and if and when the contract ends, it may find it has created a competitor.

Contract manufacturing
A joint venture in which a company contracts with manufacturers in a foreign market to produce the product or provide its service.

Contract Manufacturing Another option is **contract manufacturing**—the company contracts with manufacturers in the foreign market to produce its product or provide its service. Sears used this method in opening up department stores in Mexico and Spain, where it found qualified local manufacturers to produce many of the products it sells. The drawbacks of contract manufacturing are decreased control over the manufacturing process and loss of potential profits on manufacturing. The benefits are the chance to start faster, with less risk, and the later opportunity either to form a partnership with or to buy out the local manufacturer.

Management contracting
A joint venture in which the domestic firm supplies the management know-how to a foreign company that supplies the capital; the domestic firm exports management services rather than products.

Management Contracting Under **management contracting,** the domestic firm supplies management know-how to a foreign company that supplies the capital. The domestic firm exports management services rather than products. Hilton uses this arrangement in managing hotels around the world.

Management contracting is a low-risk method of getting into a foreign market, and it yields income from the beginning. The arrangement is even more attractive if the contracting firm has an option to buy some share in the managed company later on. The arrangement is not sensible, however, if the company can put its scarce management talent to better uses or if it can make greater profits by undertaking the whole venture. Management contracting also prevents the company from setting up its own operations for a period of time.

Joint ownership
A joint venture in which a company joins investors in a foreign market to create a local business in which the company shares joint ownership and control.

Joint Ownership **Joint ownership** ventures consist of one company joining forces with foreign investors to create a local business in which they share joint ownership and control. A company may buy an interest in a local firm, or the two parties may form a new business venture. Joint ownership may be needed for economic or political reasons. The firm may lack the financial, physical, or managerial resources to undertake the venture alone. Or a foreign government may require joint ownership as a condition for entry.

KFC entered Japan through a joint ownership venture with Japanese conglomerate Mitsubishi. KFC sought a good way to enter the large but difficult Japanese fast-food market. In turn, Mitsubishi, one of Japan's largest poultry producers, understood the Japanese culture and had money to invest. Together, they helped KFC succeed in the

Joint ownership: KFC entered Japan through a joint ownership venture with Japanese conglomerate Matsushita.

semiclosed Japanese market. Surprisingly, with Mitsubishi guidance, KFC developed decidedly un-Japanese positioning for its Japanese restaurants:

> While its initial reception in Japan was great, KFC still had a number of obstacles to overcome. The Japanese were uncomfortable with the idea of fast food and franchising. They saw fast food as artificial, made by mechanical means, and unhealthy. KFC Japan knew that it had to build trust in the KFC brand and flew to Kentucky to do it. There it filmed the most authentic version of Colonel Sanders's beginnings possible. To show the philosophy of KFC—the southern hospitality, old American tradition, and authentic home cooking—the agency first created the quintessential southern mother. With "My Old Kentucky Home" by Stephen Foster playing in the background, the commercial showed Colonel Sanders's mother making and feeding her grandchildren KFC chicken made with 11 secret spices. It conjured up scenes of good home cookin' from the American South, positioning KFC as wholesome, aristocratic food. In the end, the Japanese people could not get enough of this special American chicken. The campaign was hugely successful, and in less than 8 years KFC expanded its presence from 400 locations to more than 1,000. Most Japanese now know "My Old Kentucky Home" by heart.[23]

Joint ownership has certain drawbacks. The partners may disagree over investment, marketing, or other policies. Whereas many U.S. firms like to reinvest earnings for growth, local firms often prefer to take out these earnings; and whereas U.S. firms emphasize the role of marketing, local investors may rely on selling.

Direct Investment

The biggest involvement in a foreign market comes through **direct investment**—the development of foreign-based assembly or manufacturing facilities. If a company has gained experience in exporting and if the foreign market is large enough, foreign production facilities offer many advantages. The firm may have lower costs in the form of cheaper labor or raw materials, foreign government investment incentives, and freight savings. The firm may improve its image in the host country because it creates jobs. Generally, a firm develops a deeper relationship with government, customers, local suppliers, and distributors, allowing it to adapt its products to the local market better. Finally, the firm keeps full control over the investment and therefore can develop manufacturing and marketing policies that serve its long-term international objectives.

Direct investment
Entering a foreign market by developing foreign-based assembly or manufacturing facilities.

The main disadvantage of direct investment is that the firm faces many risks, such as restricted or devalued currencies, falling markets, or government changes. In some cases, a firm has no choice but to accept these risks if it wants to operate in the host country.

Deciding on the Global Marketing Program

Companies that operate in one or more foreign markets must decide how much, if at all, to adapt their marketing mixes to local conditions. At one extreme are global companies that use a **standardized marketing mix,** selling largely the same products and using the same marketing approaches worldwide. At the other extreme is an **adapted marketing mix.** In this case, the producer adjusts the marketing mix elements to each target market, bearing more costs but hoping for a larger market share and return.

Standardized marketing mix
An international marketing strategy for using basically the same product, advertising, distribution channels, and other elements of the marketing mix in all the company's international markets.

The question of whether to adapt or standardize the marketing mix has been much debated in recent years. The marketing concept holds that marketing programs will be more effective if tailored to the unique needs of each targeted customer group. If this

Adapted marketing mix
An international marketing strategy for adjusting the marketing-mix elements to each international target market, bearing more costs but hoping for a larger market share and return.

concept applies within a country, it should apply even more in international markets. Consumers in different countries have widely varied cultural backgrounds, needs and wants, spending power, product preferences, and shopping patterns. Because these differences are hard to change, most marketers adapt their products, prices, channels, and promotions to fit consumer desires in each country.

The question of whether to adapt or standardize the marketing mix has been much debated in recent years. However, global standardization is not an all-or-nothing proposition but rather a matter of degree. Companies should look for ways to standardize to help keep down costs and prices and to build greater global brand power. But they must not replace long-run marketing thinking with short-run financial thinking. Although standardization saves money, marketers must make certain that they offer what consumers in each country want.[24]

Many possibilities exist between the extremes of standardization and complete adaptation. For example, although Whirlpool ovens, refrigerators, clothes washers, and other major appliances share the same interiors worldwide, their outer styling and features are designed to meet the preferences of consumers in different countries. Coca-Cola sells virtually the same Coca-Cola Classic beverage worldwide, positioned to have broad cross-cultural appeal. However, Coca-Cola is less sweet or less carbonated in certain countries. The company also sells a wide variety of other beverages created specifically for local markets and modifies its distribution channels according to local conditions.

Similarly, McDonald's uses the same basic operating formula in its restaurants around the world but adapts its menu to local tastes. For example, it uses chili sauce instead of ketchup on its hamburgers in Mexico. In India, where cows are considered sacred, McDonald's serves chicken, fish, vegetable burgers, and the Maharaja Mac—two all-mutton patties, special sauce, lettuce, cheese, pickles, onions on a sesame-seed bun. In Vienna, its restaurants include "McCafes," which offer coffee blended to local tastes, and in Korea, it sells roast pork on a bun with a garlicky soy sauce.[25]

Some international marketers suggest that companies should "think globally but act locally." They advocate a "glocal" strategy in which the firm standardizes certain core marketing elements and localizes others. The corporate level gives strategic direction; local units focus on the individual consumer differences. They conclude: global marketing, yes; global standardization, not necessarily.

Product

Five strategies allow for adapting product and promotion to a global market (see Figure 15-3).[26] We first discuss the three product strategies and then turn to the two promotion strategies.

Straight product extension
Marketing a product in a foreign market without any change.

Straight product extension means marketing a product in a foreign market without any change. Top management tells its marketing people: "Take the product as is and find customers for it." The first step, however, should be to find out whether foreign consumers use that product and what form they prefer.

Figure 15-3
Five global product and promotion strategies

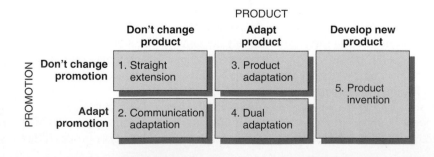

Straight extension has been successful in some cases and disastrous in others. Kellogg cereals, Gillette razors, IBM computer services, Heineken beer, and Black & Decker tools are all sold successfully in about the same form around the world. But General Foods introduced its standard powdered Jell-O in the British market only to find that British consumers prefer a solid wafer or cake form. Likewise, Philips began to make a profit in Japan only after it reduced the size of its coffeemakers to fit into smaller Japanese kitchens and its shavers to fit smaller Japanese hands. Straight extension is tempting because it involves no additional product development costs, manufacturing changes, or new promotion. But it can be costly in the long run if products fail to satisfy foreign consumers.

Product adaptation involves changing the product to meet local conditions or wants. For example, Procter & Gamble's Vidal Sassoon shampoos contain a single fragrance worldwide but the amount of scent varies by country: less in Japan, where subtle scents are preferred, and more in Europe. General Foods blends different coffees for the British (who drink their coffee with milk), the French (who drink their coffee black), and Latin Americans (who prefer a chicory taste). Gerber serves the Japanese baby food fare that might turn the stomachs of many Western consumers—local favorites include flounder and spinach stew, cod roe spaghetti, mugwort casserole, and sardines ground up in white radish sauce. Finnish cellular phone superstar Nokia customized its 6100 series phone for every major market. Developers built in rudimentary voice recognition for Asia where keyboards are a problem and raised the ring volume so the phone could be heard on crowded Asian streets. Even MTV, with its largely global programming, has retrenched along more local lines:

> Pummeled by dozens of local music channels in Europe, such as Germany's *Viva,* Holland's *The Music Factory,* and Scandinavia's *ZTV,* MTV Europe has had to drop its pan-European programming, which featured a large amount of American and British pop along with local European favorites. In its place, the division created regional channels broadcast by four separate MTV stations—MTV: U.K. & Ireland, MTV: Northern Europe, MTV: Central Europe, and MTV: Southern Europe. Each of the four channels shows programs tailored to music tastes of its local market, along with more traditional pan-European pop selections. Within

Product adaptation
Adapting a product to meet local conditions or wants in foreign markets.

Marketing mix adaptation: In India, McDonald's serves chicken, fish, and vegetable burgers, and the Maharaja Mac—two all-mutton patties, special sauce, lettuce, cheese, pickles, onions, on a sesame-seed bun.

each region, MTV further subdivides its programming. For example, within the U.K., MTV offers sister stations M2 and VH-1, along with three new digital channels: MTV Extra, MTV Base, and VH-1 Classic. Says the head of MTV Europe, "We hope to offer every MTV fan something he or she will like to watch any time of the day."[27]

In some instances, products must also be adapted to local customs or spiritual beliefs. In Asia, the spiritual world often relates directly to sales. Hyatt Hotels' experience with the concept of *feng shui* is a good example:

> A practice widely followed in China, Hong Kong, and Singapore (and which has spread to Japan, Vietnam, and Korea), *feng shui* means "wind and water." Practitioners of *feng shui,* or geomancers, will recommend the most favorable conditions for any venture, particularly the placement of office buildings and the arrangement of desks, doors, and other items within. To have good *feng shui,* a building should face the water and be flanked by mountains. However, it should not block the view of the mountain spirits. The Hyatt Hotel in Singapore was designed without *feng shui* in mind, and as a result had to be redesigned to boost business. Originally the front desk was parallel to the doors and road, and this was thought to lead to wealth flowing out. Furthermore, the doors were facing northwest, which easily let undesirable spirits in. The geomancer recommended design alterations so that wealth could be retained and undesirable spirits kept out. Western businesses, from hotel chains, restaurants, and grocery retailers to Las Vegas casinos that serve many Asian visitors, are now incorporating *feng shui* principles into their facilities designs.[28]

Product invention
Creating new products or services for foreign markets.

Product invention consists of creating something new for the foreign market. This strategy can take two forms. It might mean reintroducing earlier product forms that happen to be well adapted to the needs of a given country. The National Cash Register Company reintroduced its crank-operated cash register at half the price of a modern cash register and sold large numbers in Asia, Latin America, and Spain. Or a company might create a new product to meet a need in another country. For example, an enormous need exists for low-cost, high-protein foods in less developed countries. Companies such as Quaker Oats, Swift, Monsanto, and Archer Daniels Midland are researching the nutrition needs of these countries, creating new foods, and developing advertising campaigns to gain product trial and acceptance. Product invention can be costly but the payoffs are worthwhile.

Promotion

Companies can either adopt the same promotion strategy they used in the home market or change it for each local market. Consider advertising messages. Some global companies use a standardized advertising theme around the world. For example, to help communicate its global reach, IBM Global Services ran virtually identical "People Who Think. People Who Do. People Who Get It" ads in dozens of countries around the world. Of course, even in highly standardized promotion campaigns, some small changes might be required to adjust for language and minor cultural differences. For instance, when Heinz Pet Food introduced its 9 Lives cat food in Russia, it used its standardized advertising featuring Morris the Cat. It turns out, however, that Morris needed a makeover. Russian consumers prefer a fatter-looking spokeskitty (it's considered healthier), so Heinz put a beefier Morris on the package.[29]

Colors also are changed sometimes to avoid taboos in other countries. Purple is associated with death in most of Latin America; white is a mourning color in Japan; and green

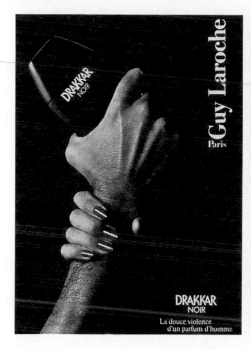
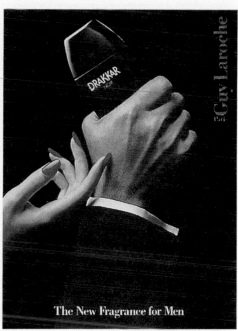

Some companies standardize their advertising around the world, adapting only to meet cultural differences. Guy Laroche uses similar ads in Europe (left) and Arab countries (right), but tones down the sensuality in the Arab version—the man is clothed and the woman barely touches him.

is associated with jungle sickness in Malaysia. Even names must be changed. In Sweden, Helene Curtis changed the name of its Every Night Shampoo to Every Day because Swedes usually wash their hair in the morning. Kellogg also had to rename Bran Buds cereal in Sweden, where the name roughly translates as "burned farmer." (See Marketing at Work 15-3 for more on language blunders in international marketing.)

Other companies follow a strategy of **communication adaptation,** fully adapting their advertising messages to local markets. Kellogg ads in the United States promote the taste and nutrition of Kellogg's cereals versus competitors' brands. In France, where consumers drink little milk and eat little for breakfast, Kellogg's ads must convince consumers that cereals are a tasty and healthful breakfast. In India, where many consumers eat heavy, fried breakfasts, Kellogg's advertising convinces buyers to switch to a lighter, more nutritious breakfast diet. Similarly, Coca-Cola sells its low-calorie beverage as Diet Coke in North America, the United Kingdom, and the Middle and Far East but as Light elsewhere. In Spanish-speaking countries, Coke Light spots position the soft drink as an object of desire, rather than as a way to feel good about yourself, as in is positioned in the United States. According to Diet Coke's global brand manager, this "desire positioning" plays off research showing that "Coca-Cola Light is seen in other parts of world as a vibrant brand that exudes a sexy confidence."[30]

Media also need to be adapted internationally because media availability varies from country to country. TV advertising time is very limited in Europe, for instance, ranging from four hours a day in France to none in Scandinavian countries. Advertisers must buy time months in advance, and they have little control over airtimes. Magazines also vary in effectiveness. For example, magazines are a major medium in Italy and a minor one in Austria. Newspapers are national in the United Kingdom but are only local in Spain.

Communication adaptation
A global communication strategy of fully adapting advertising messages to local markets.

Watch Your Language!

Many global companies have had difficulty crossing the language barrier, with results ranging from mild embarrassment to outright failure. Seemingly innocuous brand names and advertising phrases can take on unintended or hidden meanings when translated into other languages. Careless translations can make a marketer look downright foolish to foreign consumers.

We've all run across examples when buying products from other countries. Here's one from a firm in Taiwan attempting to instruct children on how to install a ramp on a garage for toy cars: "Before you play with, fix waiting plate by yourself as per below diagram. But after you once fixed it, you can play with as is and no necessary to fix off again." Many U.S. firms are guilty of such atrocities when marketing abroad.

The classic language blunders involve standardized brand names that do not translate well. When Coca-Cola first marketed Coke in China in the 1920s, it developed a group of Chinese characters that, when pronounced, sounded like the product name. Unfortunately, the characters actually translated to mean "bite the wax tadpole." Now, the characters on Chinese Coke bottles translate as "happiness in the mouth."

Several U.S. car makers have had similar problems when their brand names crashed into the language barrier. Chevy's Nova translated into Spanish as no va—"it doesn't go." GM changed the name to Caribe and sales increased. Ford introduced its Fiera truck only to discover that the name means "ugly old woman" in Spanish. And Rolls-Royce avoided the name Silver Mist in German markets, where mist means "manure." Sunbeam, however, entered the German market with its Mist Stick hair curling iron. As should have been expected, the Germans had little use for a "manure wand." A similar fate awaited Colgate when it introduced a toothpaste in France called Cue, the name of a notorious porno magazine.

One well-intentioned firm sold its shampoo in Brazil under the name Evitol. It soon realized it was claiming to sell a "dandruff contraceptive." An American company reportedly had trouble marketing Pet milk in French-speaking areas. It seems that the word pet in French means, among other things, "to break wind." Hunt-Wesson introduced its Big John products in Quebec as Gros Jos before learning that it means "big breasts" in French. This gaffe had no apparent effect on sales. Interbrand of London, the firm that created household names such as Prozac and Acura, recently developed a brand-name "hall of shame" list, which contained these and other foreign brand names you're never likely to see inside the local A&P: Krapp toilet paper (Denmark), Crapsy Fruit cereal (France), Happy End toilet paper (Germany), Mukk yogurt (Italy), Zit lemonade (Germany), Poo curry powder (Argentina), and Pschitt lemonade (France).

Travelers often encounter well-intentioned advice from service firms that takes on meanings very different from those intended. The menu in one Swiss restaurant proudly stated: "Our wines leave you nothing to hope for." Signs in a Japanese hotel pronounced: "You are invited to take advantage of the chambermaid." At a laundry in Rome, it was: "Ladies, leave your clothes here and spend the afternoon having a good time." The brochure at a Tokyo car rental offered this sage advice: "When passenger of foot heave in sight, tootle the horn. Trumpet him melodiously at first, but if he still obstacles your passage, tootle him with vigor."

Advertising themes often lose—or gain—something in the translation. The Coors beer slogan "get loose with Coors" in Spanish came out as "get the runs with Coors." Coca-Cola's "Coke adds life" theme in Japanese translated into "Coke brings your ancestors back from the dead." The milk industry learned too late that its American advertising question "Got Milk?" translated in Mexico as a more provocative "Are you lactating?" In Chinese, the KFC slogan "finger-lickin' good" came out as "eat your fingers off." And Frank Perdue's classic line, "It takes a tough man to make a tender chicken," took on added meaning in Spanish: "It takes an aroused man to make a chicken affectionate." Even when the language is the same, word usage may differ from country to country. Thus, the British ad line for Electrolux vacuum cleaners—"Nothing sucks like an Electrolux"—would capture few customers in the United States.

Sources: See David A. Ricks, "Perspectives: Translation Blunders in International Business," Journal of Language for International Business, 7, no. 2, 1996, pp. 50–55; David W. Helin, "When Slogans Go Wrong," American Demographics, February 1992, p. 14; "But Will It Sell in Tulsa?" Newsweek, March 17, 1997, p. 8; "What You Didn't Learn in Marketing 101," Sales and Marketing Management, May 1997, p. 20; Ken Friedenreich, "The Lingua Too France," World Trade, April 1998, p. 98; Richard P. Carpenter, "What They Meant to Say Was . . .," Boston Globe, August 2, 1998, p. M6; and Thomas T. Sermon, "Cutting Corners in Language Risky Business," Marketing News, April 23, 2001, p. 9.

Price

Companies also face many problems in setting their international prices. For example, how might Black & Decker price its power tools globally? It could set a uniform price all around the world, but this amount would be too high a price in poor countries and not high enough in rich ones. It could charge what consumers in each country would bear, but this strategy ignores differences in the actual costs from country to country. Finally, the company could use a standard markup of its costs everywhere, but this approach might price Black & Decker out of the market in some countries where costs are high.

Regardless of how companies go about pricing their products, their foreign prices probably will be higher than their domestic prices. A Gucci handbag may sell for $60 in Italy and $240 in the United States. Why? Gucci faces a *price escalation* problem. It must add the cost of transportation, tariffs, importer margin, wholesaler margin, and retailer margin to its factory price. Depending on these added costs, the product may have to sell for two to five times as much in another country to make the same profit. For example, a pair of Levi's jeans that sells for $30 in the United States typically fetches $63 in Tokyo and $88 in Paris. A computer that sells for $1,000 in New York may cost £1,000 in the United Kingdom. A DaimlerChrysler automobile priced at $10,000 in the United States sells for more than $47,000 in South Korea.

Another problem involves setting a price for goods that a company ships to its foreign subsidiaries. If the company charges a foreign subsidiary too much, it may end up paying higher tariff duties even while paying lower income taxes in that country. If the company charges its subsidiary too little, it can be charged with *dumping*. Dumping occurs when a company either charges less than its costs or less than it charges in its home market. Thus, Harley-Davidson accused Honda and Kawasaki of dumping motorcycles on the U.S. market. The U.S. International Trade Commission agreed and responded with a special five-year tariff on Japanese heavy motorcycles, starting at 45 percent in 1983 and gradually dropping to 10 percent by 1988. Various governments are always watching for dumping abuses, and they often force companies to set the price charged by other competitors for the same or similar products.[31]

Recent economic and technological forces have had an impact on global pricing. For example, in the European Union, the transition to a single currency will certainly reduce the amount of price differentiation. Once consumers recognize price differentiation by country, companies will be forced to harmonize prices throughout the countries that have adopted the single currency. Companies and marketers that offer the most unique or necessary products or services will be least affected by such "price transparency." For instance, Mail Boxes, Etc., which has 350 stores in Europe, believes that customers who need to send faxes won't refuse to do so because it costs more in Paris than in Italy.[32]

The Internet will also make global price differences more obvious. When firms sell their wares over the Internet, customers can to see how much products sell for in different countries. They might even be able to order a given product directly from the company location or dealer offering the lowest price. This will force companies toward more standardized international pricing.[33]

Distribution Channels

The international company must take a **whole-channel view** of the problem of distributing products to final consumers. Figure 15-4 shows the three major links between the seller and the final buyer. The first link, the *seller's headquarters organization*, supervises the channels and is part of the channel itself. The second link, *channels between nations*, moves the products to the borders of the foreign nations. The third link,

Whole-channel view
Designing international channels that take into account all of the necessary links in distributing the seller's products to final buyers, including the seller's headquarters organization, channels among nations, and channels within nations.

Figure 15-4
Whole-channel
concept for inter-
national marketing

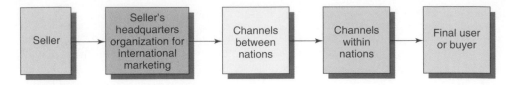

| Seller | → | Seller's headquarters organization for international marketing | → | Channels between nations | → | Channels within nations | → | Final user or buyer |

channels within nations, moves the products from their foreign entry point to the final consumers. Some U.S. manufacturers may think their job is done once the product leaves their hands, but they would do well to pay more attention to its handling within foreign countries.

Channels of distribution within countries vary greatly from nation to nation. First, there are the large differences in the *numbers and types of intermediaries* serving each foreign market. For example, a U.S. company marketing in China must operate through a frustrating maze of state-controlled wholesalers and retailers. Chinese distributors often carry competitors' products and frequently refuse to share even basic sales and marketing information with their suppliers. Hustling for sales is an alien concept to Chinese distributors, who are used to selling all they can obtain. Working with or getting around this system sometimes requires substantial time and investment.

When Coke first entered China, for example, customers bicycled up to bottling plants to get their soft drinks. Many shopkeepers still don't have enough electricity to run soft drink coolers. Now, Coca-Cola is setting up direct-distribution channels, investing heavily in refrigerators and trucks, and upgrading wiring so that more retailers can install coolers.[34] Moreover, it's always on the lookout for innovative distribution approaches:

Stroll through any residential area in a Chinese city and sooner or later you'll encounter a senior citizen with a red arm band eyeing strangers suspiciously. These are the pensioners who staff the neighborhood committees, which act as street-level watchdogs for the ruling Communist Party. In Shanghai, however, some of these socialist guardians have been signed up by the ultimate symbol of American capitalism, Coca-Cola. As part of its strategy to get the

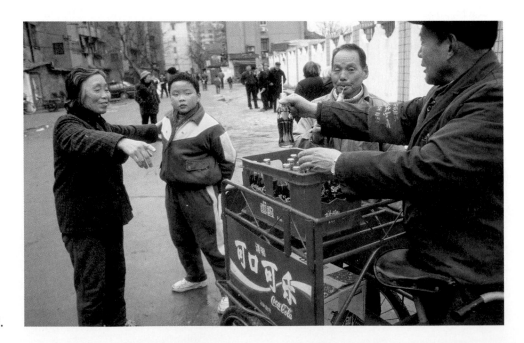

A "neighborhood committee" member sells Coke in Shanghai.

product to the customer, Coke approached 14 neighborhood committees . . . with a proposal. The head of Coke's Shanghai division outlines the deal: "We told them, 'You have some old people who aren't doing much. Why don't we stock our product in your office? Then you can sell it, earn some commission, and raise a bit of cash.' " Done. So . . . how are the party snoops adapting to the market? Not badly, reports the manager. "We use the neighborhood committees as a sales force," he says. Sales aren't spectacular, but because the committees supervise housing projects with up to 200 families, they have proved to be useful vehicles for building brand awareness.[35]

Another difference lies in the *size and character of retail units* abroad. Whereas large-scale retail chains dominate the U.S. scene, much retailing in other countries is done by many small, independent retailers. In India, millions of retailers operate tiny shops or sell in open markets. Their markups are high, but the actual price is lowered through haggling. Supermarkets could offer lower prices, but supermarkets are difficult to build and open because of many economic and cultural barriers. Incomes are low, and people prefer to shop daily for small amounts rather than weekly for large amounts. They also lack storage and refrigeration to keep food for several days. Packaging is not well developed because it would add too much to the cost. These factors have kept large-scale retailing from spreading rapidly in developing countries.

Linking the Concepts

Slow down here and think again about McDonald's global marketing issues.

◆ To what extent can McDonald's standardize for the Chinese market? What marketing strategy and program elements can be similar to those used in the United States and other parts of the Western world? Which ones must be adapted? Be specific.

◆ To what extent can McDonald's standardize its products and programs for the Canadian market? What elements can be standardized and which must be adapted?

Deciding on the Global Marketing Organization

Companies manage their international marketing activities in at least three different ways: Most companies first organize an export department, then create an international division, and finally become a global organization.

A firm normally gets into international marketing by simply shipping out its goods. If its international sales expand, the company organizes an *export department* with a sales manager and a few assistants. As sales increase, the export department can expand to include various marketing services so that it can actively go after business. If the firm moves into joint ventures or direct investment, the export department will no longer be adequate.

Many companies get involved in several international markets and ventures. A company may export to one country, license to another, have a joint ownership venture in a third, and own a subsidiary in a fourth. Sooner or later it will create an *international division* or subsidiary to handle all its international activity.

International divisions are organized in a variety of ways. The international division's corporate staff consists of marketing, manufacturing, research, finance, planning, and personnel specialists. They plan for and provide services to various operating units, which can be organized in one of three ways. They can be *geographical organizations,* with country managers who are responsible for salespeople, sales branches, distributors, and licensees in their respective countries. Or the operating units can be *world product groups,* each responsible for worldwide sales of different product groups. Finally, operating units can be *international subsidiaries,* each responsible for its own sales and profits.

Several firms have passed beyond the international division stage and become truly *global organizations.* They stop thinking of themselves as national marketers who sell abroad and start thinking of themselves as global marketers. The top corporate management and staff plan worldwide manufacturing facilities, marketing policies, financial flows, and logistical systems. The global operating units report directly to the chief executive or executive committee of the organization, not to the head of an international division. Executives are trained in worldwide operations, not just domestic *or* international. The company recruits management from many countries, buys components and supplies where they cost the least, and invests where the expected returns are greatest.

Proctor & Gamble recently took a big step in this direction by undertaking a global reorganization called Organization 2005. P&G is replacing its old geography-based organization with seven global business units organized by categories such as baby care, beauty care, and fabric-and-home care. Each unit is located in a different country. The reorganization is intended to streamline product development processes and quickly bring innovative products to the global market. These units will develop and sell their products on a worldwide basis.[36]

Moving into the twenty-first century, major companies must become more global if they hope to compete. As foreign companies successfully invade their domestic markets, companies must move more aggressively into foreign markets. They will have to change from companies that treat their international operations as secondary, to companies that view the entire world as a single borderless market.

STOP *Rest Stop: Reviewing the Concepts*

It's time to stop and think back about the global marketing concepts you've covered in this chapter. In the past, U.S. companies paid little attention to international trade. If they could pick up some extra sales through exporting, that was fine. But the big market was at home, and it teemed with opportunities. Companies today can no longer afford to pay attention only to their domestic market, regardless of its size. Many industries are global industries, and firms that operate globally achieve lower costs and higher brand awareness. At the same time, *global marketing* is risky because of variable exchange rates, unstable governments, protectionist tariffs and trade barriers, and several other factors. Given the potential gains and risks of international marketing, companies need a systematic way to make their global marketing decisions.

1. **Discuss how the international trade system, economic, political–legal, and cultural environments affect a company's international marketing decisions.**

A company must understand the *global marketing environment,* especially the international trade system. It must

assess each foreign market's *economic, political–legal,* and *cultural characteristics.* The company must then decide whether it wants to go abroad and consider the potential risks and benefits. It must decide on the volume of international sales it wants, how many countries it wants to market in, and which specific markets it wants to enter. This decision calls for weighing the probable rate of return on investment against the level of risk.

2. **Describe three key approaches to entering international markets.**

The company must decide how to enter each chosen market—whether through *exporting, joint venturing,* or *direct investment.* Many companies start as exporters, move to joint ventures, and finally make a direct investment in foreign markets. In *exporting,* the company enters a foreign market by sending and selling products through international marketing intermediaries (indirect exporting) or the company's own department, branch, or sales representative or agents (direct exporting). When establishing a *joint venture,* a company enters foreign markets by joining with foreign companies to produce or market a product or service. In *licensing,* the company enters a foreign market by contracting with a licensee in the foreign market, offering the right to use a manufacturing process, trademark, patent, trade secret, or other item of value for a fee or royalty.

3. Explain how companies adapt their marketing mixes for international markets.

Companies must also decide how much their products, promotion, price, and channels should be adapted for each foreign market. At one extreme, global companies use a *standardized marketing mix* worldwide. Others use an *adapted marketing mix,* in which they adjust the marketing mix to each target market, bearing more costs but hoping for a larger market share and return.

4. Identify the three major forms of international marketing organization.

The company must develop an effective organization for international marketing. Most firms start with an *export department* and graduate to an *international division.* A few become *global organizations,* with worldwide marketing planned and managed by the top officers of the company. Global organizations view the entire world as a single, borderless market.

Navigating the Key Terms

For a detailed analysis of the meaning and importance of each of the following key terms, visit our Web page at www.prenhall.com/kotler.

Adapted marketing mix
Communication adaptation
Contract manufacturing
Countertrade

Direct investment
Economic community
Embargo
Exchange controls
Exporting
Global firm
Joint ownership
Joint venturing
Licensing

Management contracting
Nontariff trade barriers
Product adaptation
Product invention
Quota
Standardized marketing mix
Straight product extension
Tariff
Whole-channel view

Travel Log

The following concept checks and discussion questions will help you to keep track of and apply the concepts you've studied in this chapter.

Concept Checks

Fill in the blanks, then look for the correct answers.

1. A _____ is one that, by operating in more than one country, gains marketing, production, R&D, and financial advantages that are not available to purely domestic competitors. This type of firm sees the world as one market.

2. The most common trade restriction is the _____ , which is a tax levied by a foreign government against certain imported products.

3. The purpose of a _____ , as a form of trade restriction, is to conserve on foreign exchange and to protect local industry and employment.

4. The _____ treaty is a 50-year old treaty designed to promote world trade by reducing tariffs and other international trade barriers. The most recent meeting was the Uruguay Round.

5. The _____ , as a form of an economic community, represents one of the world's single largest markets with 15 member countries, more than 374 million consumers, and 20 percent of the world's exports.

6. The four types of industrial structures are as follows: _____ , _____ , _____ , and industrial economies.

7. When a nation seeking to trade is cash-poor, it may choose to pay with other items instead of cash. This is called _____.

8. Once a company has decided to sell in a foreign country, it must decide the best mode of entry. Its choices are _____ , _____ , and _____.

9. When a company pays a fee or royalty in order to use another company's manufacturing process, trademark, patent, trade secret, or other item of value, the

company is using _____ as a means to enter an international market.

10. Coca-Cola uses the same product, pricing, communication, and distribution system world-wide. This is called a _____ marketing mix.

11. _____ involves changing the product to meet local conditions or wants.

12. Problems often occur in international marketing when a company ships to its foreign subsidiaries. _____ occurs when a company either charges less than its costs or less than it charges in its home market.

Concept Checks Answers: 1. global firm; 2. tariff; 3. quota; 4. General Agreement on Tariffs and Trade (GATT); 5. European Union; 6. subsistence economies, raw material exporting economies, industrializing economies; 7. countertrade; 8. exporting, joint venturing, direct investment; 9. licensing; 10. standardized; 11. Product adaptation; 12. Dumping.

Discussing the Issues

1. When exporting goods to a foreign country, a marketer may face various trade restrictions. Discuss the effects that each of these restrictions might have on an exporter's marketing mix: (a) tariffs, (b) quotas, and (c) embargoes.

2. A country's industrial structure shapes its product and service needs, income levels, and employment levels. Discuss examples of countries exhibiting each of the major types of industrial structures.

3. Once a company has decided to sell in a foreign country, it must determine the best mode of entry. Assume that you are the marketing manager for Mountain Dew and must devise a plan for marketing your product in China. Pick a mode of entry, explain your marketing strategy, and comment on possible difficulties you might encounter.

4. "Dumping" leads to price savings to the consumer. Determine why governments make dumping illegal. What are the *disadvantages* to the consumer of dumping by foreign firms?

5. Which type of international marketing organization would you suggest for the following companies: (a) a new division of Beanie Babies sold by Ty (www.ty.com) that intends to sell the stuffed animals exclusively online worldwide, (b) a European perfume firm that plans to expand into the United States, and (c) DaimlerChrysler planning to sell its full line of products in the Middle East.

Mastering Marketing

After examining the expansion strategies of CanGo, devise a plan where the company could expand into the international marketplace beyond any existing efforts. Choose at least one foreign market that would be a good candidate for your expansion strategy. Pick a mode of entry into that market. Discuss any difficulties that might be present in an attempt to enter this market. Evaluate your chances of success.

Traveling the Net

Point of Interest: Studying Merging Global Cultures and Markets on the World Wide Web

What area of the United States has the highest concentration of tuberculosis? What area produces population increases at twice the national average? Where is the largest Wal-Mart in the United States located? The answer to all these questions: along the border between the United States and Mexico. This huge and often desolate part of America stretches from San Diego, California, in the West to Brownsville, Texas, in the East. It is a complicated maze of contradictions: poverty, a high incidence of drug traf-

ficking, and an immigration problem of staggering proportions on one hand; merging cultures, wealth, and great manufacturing and trade opportunities on the other. Although the passage of NAFTA did little to fix the problems, it did increase the likelihood that opportunities will be realized once the two countries figure out how to work together in harmony. Understanding the facts can produce great opportunities. Wal-Mart read the border facts correctly and built its largest domestic store in Laredo, Texas, where both U.S. and Mexican consumers trade not only in profitable harmony. Facts and a desire to capitalize on opportunities led to the construction of The Trade Bridge in Laredo where the NAFTA trade river begins as it flows across America to Canada and beyond. Marketers have found that moving goods and services across the border in both directions can be highly profitable and beneficial to both economies. Good jobs, cheap labor, quality products, affordable products, and an Amexica spirit are all issues that will be discussed by the two countries' leaders in trade talks which occur on an increasingly frequent basis. To learn more about the challenges of the "border market," examine the following Web sites: (a) Center for International Business Education and Research—Michigan State University (http://ciber.bus.msu.edu/busres.htm), (b) International Trade Association (www.ita.doc.gov), (c) The 1998 World Fact Book—CIA publication (www.odci.gov/cia/publications/factbook/index.html), (d) The World Bank (www.worldbank.org), (e) the World Trade Organization (www.wto.org), and (f) Cyberatlas (www.cyberatlas.internet.com).

For Discussion

1. How could a manager seeking information on the Mexico/United States international market use the above reference sites to find needed data?

2. Does the Internet seem to be a better source of information than traditional sources?
3. What were the most interesting facts you learned about the Mexico/United States border market?
4. How could these facts be converted into opportunities for market expansion?
5. What problems occur when you use the sources cited in the above illustration? Can you think of alternatives for overcoming these problems?

Application Thinking

After considering the material found on the Web sites, put together a fact profile for a manager seeking to distribute a new $50 digital watch in Mexico. Make the following decisions based on your fact profile: (a) Based on your facts, which parts of Mexico seem to hold the most promise for your product? (b) How did you determine this? (c) What would be the best method of distribution for your new product? What mode of entry would be best? (d) What critical factors are missing from your fact profile? Where might you find this information? (e) Evaluate your Internet information search process. What did you learn? If you were starting again, what would you do differently?

MAP—Marketing Applications

MAP Stop 15

Nowhere is international competition more apparent than in the digital camera market. Overnight, the advent of digital cameras changed the way photographers view their equipment. Digital cameras offer opportunities for reproduction and Internet viewing unmatched by traditional models. However, the market is uncharted, chaotic, and increasingly crowded with more than 20 manufacturers worldwide. The latest entrant is film giant Fuji (www.fujifilm.com). As the world's number-two producer, Fuji now plans to meet or beat Kodak (www.kodak.com), Sony (www.sony.com), Olympus (www.olympus.com), and Konica (www.konica.com) in digital camera products. Fuji introduced its first digital camera in its own backyard—Japan—which is also a Sony stronghold. One factor motivating the move into digital cameras was Fuji's inability to crack Kodak's

worldwide share of the film market. If the wave of the future turns out to be digital, Fuji plans to ride the wave's crest for as long as it can.

Thinking Like a Marketing Manager

1. Analyze Fuji's strategy of entering the digital camera market. What challenges will Fuji most likely face? How might Fuji's traditional strengths in film aid its efforts in the new digital camera market?
2. What world markets should Fuji consider after Japan? Explain.
3. If you were the marketing manager of Fuji, what advertising strategy would you suggest for Fuji's new product venture? What distribution strategy? What role will price play in the success of the strategy?
4. What actions might Kodak, Olympus, Konica, and Sony take to counter Fuji's entry?

chapter 16

Marketing and Society: Social Responsibility and Marketing Ethics

ROAD MAP:
Previewing the Concepts

You've almost completed your introductory marketing travels. In this final chapter, we'll focus on marketing as a social institution. First, we'll look at some common criticisms of marketing as it impacts individual consumers, other businesses, and society as a whole. Then, we'll examine consumerism, environmentalism, and other citizen and public actions to keep marketing in check. Finally, we'll see how companies themselves can benefit from proactively pursuing socially responsible and ethical practices. You'll see that social responsibility and ethical actions are more than just the right thing to do; they're also good for business.

▶ After studying this chapter, you should be able to

1. identify the major social criticisms of marketing
2. define *consumerism* and *environmentalism* and explain how they affect marketing strategies
3. describe the principles of socially responsible marketing
4. explain the role of ethics in marketing

Before traveling on, let's visit the concept of social responsibility in business. Over the past 25 years, companies such as Ben & Jerry's and The Body Shop have pioneered the idea of "values-led business" or "caring capitalism"—putting "principles ahead of profits." But *can* a company dedicated to doing good still do well? *Can* it successfully serve a "double bottom line"—values *and* profits?

Chances are, when you hear the term *socially responsible business,* a handful of companies—and their founders—leap to mind, companies such as Ben & Jerry's Home-made (Ben Cohen, Jerry Greenfield) and The Body Shop International (Anita Roddick). Such social revolutionaries pioneered the concept of "values-led business" or "caring capitalism." Their mission: Use business to make the world a better place.

Ben Cohen and Jerry Greenfield founded Ben & Jerry's Homemade in 1978 as a company that cared deeply about its social and environmental responsibilities. It bought only hormone-free milk and cream and used only organic fruits and nuts to make its ice cream, which it sold in environmentally friendly containers. It went to great lengths to buy from minority and disadvantaged suppliers. From the start, Ben & Jerry's donated a whopping 7.5 percent of pretax profits to support projects that exhibited "creative problem solving and hopefulness . . . relating to children and families, disadvantaged groups, and the environment." By the mid-1990s, Ben & Jerry's had become the nation's number-two superpremium ice cream brand.

Anita Roddick opened The Body Shop in 1976 with a similar mission: "to dedicate our business to the pursuit of social and environmental change." The company manufactured and retailed natural-ingredient-based cosmetics in simple and appealing recyclable

packaging. All products were formulated without any animal testing and supplies were often sourced from developing countries. Roddick became a vocal advocate for putting "passion before profits," and The Body Shop, which now operates nearly 1,850 stores in 47 countries, donates a percentage of profits each year to animal-rights groups, homeless shelters, Amnesty International, Save the Rain Forest, and other social causes.

Both companies set up shop in the late 1970s and grew fast and furiously through the 1980s and early 1990s. However, as competitors not shackled by their "principles before profits" missions invaded their markets, growth and profits flattened. In recent years, both Ben & Jerry's and The Body Shop have struggled. In 2000, after several years of less than stellar financial returns, Ben & Jerry's was acquired by giant food producer Unilever. And Anita Roddick recently handed over The Body Shop's reins to a more business-savvy turnaround team.

What happened to the founders' lofty ideals of caring capitalism? Looking back, both companies may have focused on social issues at the expense of sound business management. Neither Ben Cohen nor Anita Roddick really wanted to be businesspeople. In fact, according to one analyst, Cohen and Roddick "saw businesspeople as tools of the military-industrial complex and profits as a dirty word." Cohen once commented, "There came a time [when I had to admit] 'I'm a businessman.' And I had a hard time mouthing those words." Likewise, Roddick admitted, "a lot of us would have slit our wrists if we ever thought we'd be part of corporate America or England. Big business was alien to me."

Having a "double bottom line" of values and profits is no easy proposition. In the words of one especially harsh critic, "Ben and Jerry want to use ice cream to solve the world's problems. They call it running a values-led business; I call it a mess. Operating a business is tough enough. Once you add social goals to the demands of serving customers, making a profit, and returning value to shareholders, you tie yourself up in knots." For sure, it's often difficult to take good intentions to the bank.

The experiences of the 1980s revolutionaries taught the socially responsible business movement some hard lessons. The result is a new generation of activist entrepreneurs— not social activists with big hearts who hate capitalism, but well-trained business managers and company builders with a passion for a cause. According to a recent *Inc.* article, here are some of the lessons:

◆ *What you sell is important:* The product or service, not just the mission, must be socially responsible. Hence, Honest Tea Inc. markets barely sweetened iced tea and totally biodegradable tea bags; WorldWise Inc. offers garden, home, and pet products made from recycled or organic materials; Sustainable Harvest Inc. sells organic, shade-grown coffee with a guaranteed base price for growers; CitySoft Inc. does Web development using urban workers; Wild Planet Toys Inc. creates nonsexist, nonviolent toys; and Village Real Estate Services revitalizes communities and neighborhoods.

◆ *Be proud to be in business:* Unlike the 1980s revolutionaries, the new young founders are businesspeople—and proud of it—and all appreciate solid business training. Honest Tea founder Seth Goldman won a business-plan competition as a student at the Yale School of Management and later started the company with one of his professors. WildPlanet CEO Daniel Grossman has an MBA from the Stanford Business School. Sustainable Harvest's David Griswold hires business school graduates because he believes that success "really depends on competing, using the rules of business. Good deeds alone don't work."

◆ *Make a solid commitment to change:* Cohen and Greenfield stumbled into making ice cream to make ends meet; Roddick owned a small hotel in England before opening her first store. By contrast the new social entrepreneurs' companies are a natural outgrowth of their long-held values. For example, WildPlanet's Grossman served for eight years in the U.S. Foreign Service. David Griswold cofounded and ran Aztec Harvest, a sales-and-marketing outfit for farmer-owned Mexican coffee cooperatives. And CitySoft CEO Nick Gleason was a community and labor organizer in Oakland, California, and ran his own urban-development consulting company, serving nonprofits, foundations, school districts, and governments.

◆ *Focus on two bottom lines:* Today's social entrepreneurs are just as dedicated to building a viable, profitable business as to shaping a mission. WorldWise's Lamstein comments, "You can't be successful if you can't do both." Lamstein's strategy for getting WorldWise up and running, built around the concept of environmentally responsible products, illustrates such double-bottom-line thinking. "Our whole concept was that our products had to work as well as or better than others, look as good or finer, cost the same or less, and be better for the environment," says Lamstein. Honest Tea's Goldman agrees: "A commitment to socially responsible business cannot be used as an excuse to make poor business decisions. If we were to accept lower margins, then we'd be doing the . . . socially responsible business movement a disservice, because we wouldn't be as competitive or as attractive to investors."

◆ *Forget the hype:* For these socially responsible companies, it's not about marketing and image. They go about doing their good deeds quietly. Village Real Estate Services concentrates primarily on marketing its services, not on publicizing the company's Village Fund, which funds the revitalization of urban neighborhoods. Honest Tea buys the peppermint leaves for its First Nation tea from I'tchik Herbal Tea, a small woman-owned company on the Crow Reservation in Montana. I'tchik gets royalties from the sales of the tea, as does a Native American organization called Pretty Shield Foundation, which includes foster care among its activities. However, "when we first brought out our peppermint tea, our label didn't mention that we were sharing the revenues with the Crow Nation," says Goldman. "We didn't want people to think that was a gimmick."

It remains to be seen how these new socially responsible companies will fare down the road. Many are less than five years old and post sales from $2 million to $10 million. Ben & Jerry's, by contrast, has sales of some $150 million (down from more than $350 million at its peak), and cash registers in Body Shop stores rang up nearly $1 billion in sales last year. Still, this much is clear: Social responsibility for the recent crop of company founders—at least at this early date—seems to be not about them nor even about their companies. It's about the mission.[1]

• •

Responsible marketers discover what consumers want and respond with the right products, priced to give good value to buyers and profit to the producer. The *marketing concept* is a philosophy of customer satisfaction and mutual gain. Its practice leads the economy by an invisible hand to satisfy the many and changing needs of millions of consumers.

Not all marketers follow the marketing concept, however. In fact, some companies use questionable marketing practices, and some marketing actions that seem innocent in themselves strongly affect the larger society. Consider the sale of cigarettes. On the face of it, companies should be free to sell cigarettes and smokers should be free to buy them. But this transaction affects the public interest. First, the smoker is harming his or her health and may be shortening his or her own life. Second, smoking places a financial burden on the smoker's family and on society at large. Third, other people around the smoker may suffer discomfort and harm from secondhand smoke. Finally, marketing cigarettes to adults might also influence young people to begin smoking. Thus, the marketing of tobacco products has sparked substantial debate and negotiation in recent years.[2] This example shows that private transactions may involve larger questions of public policy.

This chapter examines the social effects of private marketing practices. We examine several questions: What are the most frequent social criticisms of marketing? What steps have private citizens taken to curb marketing ills? What steps have legislators and government agencies taken to curb marketing ills? What steps have enlightened companies taken to carry out socially responsible and ethical marketing? We examine how marketing affects and is affected by each of these issues.

Social Criticisms of Marketing

Marketing receives much criticism. Some of this criticism is justified; much is not. Social critics claim that certain marketing practices hurt individual consumers, society as a whole, and other business firms.

Marketing's Impact on Individual Consumers

Consumers have many concerns about how well the American marketing system serves their interests. Surveys usually show that consumers hold mixed or even slightly unfavorable attitudes toward marketing practices. Consumers, consumer advocates, government agencies, and other critics have accused marketing of harming consumers through high prices, deceptive practices, high-pressure selling, shoddy or unsafe products, planned obsolescence, and poor service to disadvantaged consumers.

High Prices   Many critics charge that the American marketing system causes prices to be higher than they would be under more "sensible" systems. They point to three factors—*high costs of distribution, high advertising and promotion costs,* and *excessive markups.*

HIGH COSTS OF DISTRIBUTION.   A long-standing charge is that greedy intermediaries mark up prices beyond the value of their services. Critics charge that there are too many intermediaries, that intermediaries are inefficient and poorly run, or that they provide unnecessary or duplicate services. As a result, distribution costs too much, and consumers pay for these excessive costs in the form of higher prices.

How do resellers answer these charges? They argue that intermediaries do work that would otherwise have to be done by manufacturers or consumers. Markups reflect services that consumers themselves want—more convenience, larger stores and assortment, longer store hours, return privileges, and others. Moreover, the costs of operating stores keep rising, forcing retailers to raise their prices. In fact, they argue, retail competition is so intense that margins are actually quite low. For example, after taxes, supermarket chains are typically left with barely 1 percent profit on their sales. If some resellers try to charge too much relative to the value they add, other resellers will step in with lower prices. Low-price stores such as Wal-Mart, Best Buy, and other discounters pressure their competitors to operate efficiently and keep their prices down.

HIGH ADVERTISING AND PROMOTION COSTS.   Modern marketing is also accused of pushing up prices to finance heavy advertising and sales promotion. For example, a dozen tablets of a heavily promoted brand of aspirin sell for the same price as 100 tablets of less promoted brands. Differentiated products—cosmetics, detergents, toiletries—include promotion and packaging costs that can amount to 40 percent or more of the manufacturer's price to the retailer. Critics charge that much of the packaging and promotion adds only psychological value to the product rather than functional value. Retailers use additional promotion—advertising, displays, and sweepstakes—that adds several cents more to retail prices.

Marketers respond that consumers can usually buy functional versions of products at lower prices. However, they *want* and are willing to pay more for products that also provide psychological benefits—that make them feel wealthy, attractive, or special. Brand name products may cost more, but branding gives buyers assurances of consistent quality. Heavy advertising adds to product costs but adds value by informing millions of potential buyers of the availability and merits of a brand. If consumers want to know what is available on the market, they must expect manufacturers to spend large sums of money on advertising. Also, heavy advertising and promotion may be necessary for a firm to match competitors' efforts—the business would lose "share of mind" if it did not match competitive spending. At the same time, companies are cost-conscious about promotion and try to spend their money wisely.

A heavily promoted brand of antacid sells for much more than a virtually identical nonbranded or storebranded product. Critics charge that promotion adds only psychological value to the product rather than functional value.

EXCESSIVE MARKUPS. Critics also charge that some companies mark up goods excessively. They point to the drug industry, where a pill costing 5 cents to make may cost the consumer $2 to buy. They point to the pricing tactics of funeral homes that prey on the confused emotions of bereaved relatives and to the high charges for television repair and auto repair.

Marketers respond that most businesses try to deal fairly with consumers because they want repeat business. Most consumer abuses are unintentional. When shady marketers do take advantage of consumers, they should be reported to Better Business Bureaus and to state and federal agencies. Marketers also respond that consumers often don't understand the reasons for high markups. For example, pharmaceutical markups must cover the costs of purchasing, promoting, and distributing existing medicines plus the high research and development costs of formulating and testing new medicines.

Deceptive Practices Marketers are sometimes accused of deceptive practices that lead consumers to believe they will get more value than they actually do. Deceptive practices fall into three groups: deceptive pricing, promotion, and packaging. *Deceptive pricing* includes practices such as falsely advertising "factory" or "wholesale" prices or a large price reduction from a phony high retail list price. *Deceptive promotion* includes practices such as overstating the product's features or performance, luring the customer to the store for a bargain that is out of stock, or running rigged contests. *Deceptive packaging* includes exaggerating package contents through subtle design, not filling the package to the top, using misleading labeling, or describing size in misleading terms.

To be sure, questionable marketing practices do occur. For example, at one time or another, we've all gotten an envelope in the mail screaming something like "You have won $10,000,000!" In recent years, sweepstakes companies have come under the gun for their deceptive communication practices. Sweepstakes promoter Publishers Clearing House recently paid heavily to settle claims that its high-pressure tactics had misled consumers into believing that they had won prizes when they hadn't. The Wisconsin Attorney General asserts that "there are older consumers who send [sweepstakes companies] checks and

Questionable marketing practices: Sweepstakes promoter Publishers Clearing House recently paid heavily to settle claims that its high-pressure tactics had misled consumers into believing that they had won prizes when they hadn't.

money orders on a weekly basis with a note that says they were very upset that the prize patrol did not come."[3]

Deceptive practices have led to legislation and other consumer protection actions. For example, in 1938 Congress reacted to such blatant deceptions as Fleischmann's Yeast's claim to straighten crooked teeth by enacting the Wheeler-Lea Act giving the Federal Trade Commission (FTC) power to regulate "unfair or deceptive acts or practices." The FTC has published several guidelines listing deceptive practices. The toughest problem is defining what is "deceptive." For example, some years ago, Shell Oil advertised that Super Shell gasoline with platformate gave better mileage than did the same gasoline without platformate. Now this was true, but what Shell did not say is that almost *all* gasoline includes platformate. Its defense was that it had never claimed that platformate was found only in Shell gasoline. But even though the message was literally true, the FTC felt that the ad's *intent* was to deceive.

Marketers argue that most companies avoid deceptive practices because such practices harm their business in the long run. If consumers do not get what they expect, they will switch to more reliable products. In addition, consumers usually protect themselves from deception. Most consumers recognize a marketer's selling intent and are careful when they buy, sometimes to the point of not believing completely true product claims. One noted marketing thinker, Theodore Levitt, claims that some advertising puffery is bound to occur—and that it may even be desirable: "There is hardly a company that would not go down in ruin if it refused to provide fluff, because nobody will buy pure functionality. . . . Worse, it denies . . . people's honest needs and values. Without distortion, embellishment, and elaboration, life would be drab, dull, anguished, and at its existential worst."[4]

High-Pressure Selling Salespeople are sometimes accused of high-pressure selling that persuades people to buy goods they had no thought of buying. It is often said that insurance, real estate, cars, and jewelry are *sold,* not *bought.* Salespeople are trained to deliver smooth, canned talks to entice purchase. They sell hard because sales contests promise big prizes to those who sell the most.

Marketers know that buyers often can be talked into buying unwanted or unneeded things. Laws require door-to-door and telephone salespeople to announce that they are selling a product. Buyers also have a "three-day cooling-off period" in which they can cancel a contract after rethinking it. In addition, consumers can complain to Better Business Bureaus or to state consumer protection agencies when they feel that undue selling pressure has been applied. But in most cases, marketers have little to gain from high-pressure selling. Such tactics may work in the short run but will damage the marketer's long-run relationships with customers.

Shoddy or Unsafe Products Another criticism is that products lack the quality they should have. One complaint is that many products are not made well and services not performed well. A second complaint is that many products deliver little benefit. For example, some consumers are surprised to learn that many of the "healthy" foods being marketed today, such as cholesterol-free salad dressings, low-fat frozen dinners, and high-fiber bran cereals, may have little nutritional value. In fact, they may even be harmful.

[Despite] sincere efforts on the part of most marketers to provide healthier products,...many promises emblazoned on packages and used as ad slogans continue to confuse nutritionally uninformed consumers and...may actually be harmful to that group....[Many consumers] incorrectly assume the product is "safe" and eat greater amounts than are good for them....For example, General Foods USA's new Entenmann's "low-cholesterol, low-calorie" cherry coffee cake...may confuse some consumers who shouldn't eat much of it. While each serving is only 90 calories, not everyone realizes that the suggested serving is tiny [one-thirteenth of the small cake]. Although eating half an Entenmann's cake may be better than eating half a dozen Dunkin' Donuts, . . . neither should be eaten in great amounts by people on restrictive diets.[5]

A third complaint concerns product safety. Product safety has been a problem for several reasons, including manufacturer indifference, increased production complexity, poorly trained labor, and poor quality control. For years, Consumers Union—the non-profit testing and information organization that publishes *Consumer Reports*—has reported various hazards in tested products: electrical dangers in appliances, carbon monoxide poisoning from room heaters, injury risks from lawn mowers, and faulty auto-mobile design, among many others. The organization's testing and other activities have helped consumers make better buying decisions and encouraged businesses to eliminate product flaws (see Marketing at Work 16-1).

However, most manufacturers *want* to produce quality goods. The way a company deals with product quality and safety problems can damage or help its reputation. Compa-nies selling poor-quality or unsafe products risk damaging conflicts with consumer groups and regulators. Moreover, unsafe products can result in product liability suits and large awards for damages. More fundamentally, consumers who are unhappy with a firm's prod-ucts may avoid future purchases and talk other consumers into doing the same. Consider what happened to Bridgestone/Firestone following its recent recall of 6.5 million flawed Firestone tires. Product liability and safety concerns have driven the company to the edge of bankruptcy:

> Profits have disappeared, and both customers and tire dealers alike are fleeing the Firestone make. Ford, the tire maker's biggest customer, recently announced plans to replace another 13 million Firestone tires that it believes are unsafe. "You have a serious risk of the Firestone brand imploding," warns an industry analyst. How bad will the financial hit get? Cutting ties with Ford will cost the company 4 percent of its $7.5 billion in revenues—about 40 percent of its sales to car compa-nies. Mounting damages awards from rollover suits and legal bills could easily top the company's $463 million legal reserve. And if the National Highway Traffic & Safety Administration supports Ford's latest recall, Firestone could find itself liable for much of the $3 billion cost.[6]

Thus, quality missteps can have severe consequences. Today's marketers know that customer-driven quality results in customer satisfaction, which in turn creates profitable customer relationships.

Planned Obsolescence Critics also have charged that some producers follow a program of planned obsolescence, causing their products to become obsolete before they actually should need replacement. For example, critics charge that some producers contin-ually change consumer concepts of acceptable styles to encourage more and earlier buy-ing. An obvious example is constantly changing clothing fashions. Other producers are accused of holding back attractive functional features, then introducing them later to make older models obsolete. Critics claim that this occurs in the consumer electronics and com-puter industries. For example, Intel and Microsoft have been accused in recent years of holding back their next-generation computer chips or software until demand is exhausted for the current generation. Still other producers are accused of using materials and compo-nents that will break, wear, rust, or rot sooner than they should. One writer put it this way: "The marvels of modern technology include the development of a soda can which, when discarded, will last forever—and a . . . car, which, when properly cared for, will rust out in two or three years."[7]

Marketers respond that consumers *like* style changes; they get tired of the old goods and want a new look in fashion or a new design in cars. No one has to buy the new look, and if too

When *Consumer Reports* Talks, Buyers Listen

For more than 65 years, *Consumer Reports* has given buyers the low-down on everything from sports cars to luggage to lawn sprinklers. Published by Consumers Union, the nonprofit product-testing organization, the magazine's mission can be summed up by CU's motto: Test, Inform, Protect. With more than 4 million subscribers and several times that many borrowers, as dog-eared library copies will attest, *Consumer Reports* is one of the nation's most-read magazines. Its companion Consumer Reports Online site (www.consumerreports.org), established in 1997, is the Web's largest paid-subscriber site with 350,000 users.

Beyond being one of the most read publications, *Consumer Reports* is also one of the most influential. In 1988, when its car testers rated Suzuki's topple-prone Samurai as "not acceptable"—meaning don't even take one as a gift—sales

plunged 70 percent the following month. More recently, when it raved about Saucony's Jazz 3000 sneaker, sales doubled, leading to nation-wide shortages.

Although nonreaders may view *Consumer Reports* as a deadly dull shopper's guide to major household appliances, the magazine does a lot more than rate cars and refrigerators. In recent issues, it has looked at mutual funds, prostate surgery, home mortgages, retirement communities, public health policies, and consumer Web sites. In the 1930s, Consumers Union was one of the first organizations to urge a boycott of products imported from Nazi Germany, and it's been calling for nationalized health care since 1937. In the 1950s, it warned the nation that fallout from nuclear tests was contaminating milk supplies. In the 1960s and 1970s, it prodded car makers to install seat belts, then air bags.

Yet the magazine is rarely harsh or loud. Instead, it's usually under-stated, and it can even be funny. The very first issue in 1936 noted that Lifebuoy soap was itself so smelly that it simply overwhelmed your B.O. with L.O. And what reader didn't delight to find in a 1990 survey of soaps that the most expensive bar, Eau de Gucci at 31 cents per hand-washing, wound up dead last in a blind test.

Consumer Reports readers clearly appreciate CU and its magazine. It is unlikely that any other magazine in the world could have raised $17 million toward a new building simply by asking readers for donations. To avoid even the appearance of bias, CU has a strict no-ads, no-freebies policy. It buys all of its product samples on the open market and anonymously. CU's steadfast editorial independence has made *Consumer Reports* the bible of consumerism. "We're very

Consumers Union carries out its testing mission: Suitcases bang into one another inside the huge "Mechanical Gorilla," and a staffer coats the interior of self-cleaning ovens with a crusty concoction called "Monster Mash."

single-minded about who we serve," says Rhoda Karpatkin, CU's recently retired president. "We serve the consumer."

A visit to CU's maze of labs confirms the thoroughness with which CU's testers carry out their mission. A chemist performs a cholesterol extraction test on a small white blob in a beaker: a ground-up piece of turkey enchilada, you are told. Elsewhere you find the remains of a piston-driven machine called Fingers that added 1+1 on pocket calculators hundreds of thousands of times or until the calculators failed, whichever came first. You watch suitcases bang into one another inside a huge contraption—affectionately dubbed the "Mechanical Gorilla"—that looks like an eight-foot-wide clothes dryer.

Down the hall in the appliance department, a pair of "food soilers" will soon load 20 dishwashers with identical sets of dirty dishes. A sample dinner plate is marked off with scientific precision into eight wedge-shaped sections, each with something different caked to it— dried spaghetti, spinach, chipped beef, or something else equally difficult to clean. Next door, self-

cleaning ovens are being tested, their interiors coated with a crusty substance—called "Monster Mash" by staffers—that suggests month-old chili sauce. The recipe includes tapioca, cheese, lard, grape jelly, tomato sauce, and cherry pie filling—mixed well and baked one hour at 425 degrees. If an oven's self-cleaning cycle doesn't render the resulting residue into harmless-looking ash, 4 million readers will be so informed.

Some of the tests that CU runs are standard tests, but many are not. Several years ago, in a triumph of low-tech creativity, CU's engineers stretched paper towels across embroidery hoops, moistened the center of each with exactly ten drops of water, then poured lead shot into the middle. The winner held seven pounds of shot; the loser, less than one. Who could argue with that? There is an obvious logic to such tests, and the results are plainly quantifiable.

From the start, Consumers Union has generated controversy. The second issue dismissed the Good Housekeeping Seal of Approval as nothing more than a fraudulent ploy by publisher William Randolph Hearst to

reward loyal advertisers. *Good Housekeeping* responded by accusing CU of prolonging the Depression. To the business community, *Consumer Reports* was at first viewed as a clear threat to the American way of doing business. During its early years, more than 60 advertising-dependent publications, including the *New York Times, Newsweek,* and the *New Yorker,* refused to accept CU's subscription ads.

In 1939, in a move that would seem ludicrous today, Congress' new House UnAmerican Activities Committee (then known as the Dies Committee) branded CU a subversive organization. However, controversy has more often helped than hurt subscriptions. And through the years, only 13 makers of panned products have filed suit against CU challenging findings unfavorable to their products. To this day Consumers Union has never lost or settled a libel suit.

Sources: Portions adapted from Doug Stewart, "To Buy or Not to Buy, That Is the Question at *Consumer Reports*," *Smithsonian,* September 1993, pp. 34–43. Other quotes and information from Robin Finn, "Still Top Dog, Consumers' Pitt Bull to Retire," *New York Times,* October 5, 2000, p. B2; and the Consumers Union Web site at www.consumersunion.org and the Consumer Reports Online site at www.consumerreports.org, December 2001.

few people like it, it will simply fail. Companies frequently withhold new features when they are not fully tested, when they add more cost to the product than consumers are willing to pay, and for other good reasons. But they do so at the risk that a competitor will introduce the new feature and steal the market. These days, if Intel waits to introduce the latest computer chip innovation, it will likely find itself losing the technology race to competitor AMD.

Moreover, companies often put in new materials to lower their costs and prices. They do not design their products to break down earlier, because they do not want to lose customers to other brands. Instead, they implement total quality programs to ensure that products will consistently meet or exceed customer expectations. Thus, much of so-called planned obsolescence is the working of the competitive and technological forces in a free society—forces that lead to ever-improving goods and services.

Poor Service to Disadvantaged Consumers Finally, the American marketing system has been accused of poorly serving disadvantaged consumers. For example, critics claim that the urban poor often have to shop in smaller stores that carry inferior goods and charge higher prices. A Consumers Union study compared the food-shopping habits of

**Product safety:
Following its recall
of 6.5 million flawed
Firestone tires, product
liability and safety
concerns have driven
Bridgestone/Firestone
to the brink of
bankruptcy.**

low-income consumers and the prices they pay relative to middle-income consumers in the
same city. The study found that the poor do pay more for inferior goods. The results suggested that the presence of large national chain stores in low-income neighborhoods made
a big difference in keeping prices down. However, the study also found evidence of
"redlining," a type of economic discrimination in which major chain retailers avoid placing
stores in disadvantaged neighborhoods. Similar redlining charges have been leveled at the
home insurance, consumer lending, and banking industries.[8]

More recently, lenders and other businesses have been accused of "Weblining," the
Information Age version of redlining:

> As never before, the Internet lets companies identify (or "profile") high- and
> low-value customers, so firms can decide which product deals, prices, and services it
> will offer. For the most valued customers, this can mean better information and dis-
> counts. Low-value customers may pay the most for the least and sometimes get left
> behind. In lending, old-style redlining is unacceptable because it is based on geo-
> graphic stereotypes, not concrete evidence that specific individuals are poor credit
> risks. Webliners may claim to have more evidence against the people they snub. But
> their classifications could also be based on irrelevant profiling data that marketing
> companies and others collect on the Web. How important to your mortgage status,
> say, is your taste in paperbacks, political discussion groups, or clothing? Yet all these
> far-flung threads are getting sewn into online profiles, where they are increasingly
> intertwined with data on your health, your education loans, and your credit history.[9]

Clearly, better marketing systems must be built to service disadvantaged consumers.
One hope is to get large retailers to open outlets in low-income areas. Moreover, disadvantaged consumers clearly need consumer protection. The FTC has taken action against
merchants who advertise false values, sell old merchandise as new, or charge too much
for credit. The commission is also trying to make it harder for merchants to win court
judgments against low-income people who were wheedled into buying something.

Linking the Concepts

Hit the brakes for a moment and cool down. Few marketers *want* to abuse or anger consumers—it's simply not good business. Instead, as you know well by now, most marketers work to build long-term relationships with customers based on real value and caring. Yet, some marketing abuses do occur.

◆ Think back over the past three months or so and list the instances in which you've suffered a marketing abuse such as those just discussed. Analyze your list: What kinds of companies were involved? Were the abuses intentional? What did the situations have in common?

◆ Pick one of the instances you listed and describe it in detail. How might you go about righting this wrong? Write out an action plan, then do something to remedy the abuse. If we all took such actions when wronged, there would be far fewer wrongs to right!

Marketing's Impact on Society as a Whole

The American marketing system has been accused of adding to several "evils" in American society at large. Advertising has been a special target—so much so that the American Association of Advertising Agencies launched a campaign to defend advertising against what it felt to be common but untrue criticisms.

False Wants and Too Much Materialism

Critics have charged that the marketing system urges too much interest in material possessions. People are judged by what they *own* rather than by who they *are*. To be considered

The American Marketing Association runs ads to counter common advertising criticisms.

successful, people must own a large home, two cars, and the latest high-tech gadgets. This drive for wealth and possessions hit new highs in the 1980s, when phrases such as "greed is good" and "shop 'til you drop" seemed to characterize the times.

In the new millennium, even though many social scientists have noted a reaction against the opulence and waste of the previous decades and a return to more basic values and social commitment, our infatuation with material things continues.

It's hard to escape the notion that what Americans really value is stuff. Since 1987, we've had more shopping malls than high schools. We average six hours a week shopping and only forty minutes playing with our children. Our rate of saving is 2 percent—only a quarter of what it was in the 1950s, when we earned less than half as much in real dollars. In each of the past three years, more U.S. citizens have declared personal bankruptcy than have graduated from college. All this acquisition isn't making us happier; the number of Americans calling themselves "very happy" peaked in 1957.[10]

Nearly two-thirds of adults agree that wearing "only the best designer clothing" conveys status. Even more feel this way about owning expensive jewelry. Big homes are back in vogue, which means Americans have more space to fulfill their acquisitive fantasies, from master bathrooms doubling as spas and gyms to fully wired home entertainment centers.[11]

The critics do not view this interest in material things as a natural state of mind but rather as a matter of false wants created by marketing. Businesses hire Madison Avenue to stimulate people's desires for goods, and Madison Avenue uses the mass media to create materialistic models of the good life. People work harder to earn the necessary money. Their purchases increase the output of American industry, and industry in turn uses Madison Avenue to stimulate more desire for the industrial output. Thus, marketing is seen as creating false wants that benefit industry more than they benefit consumers.

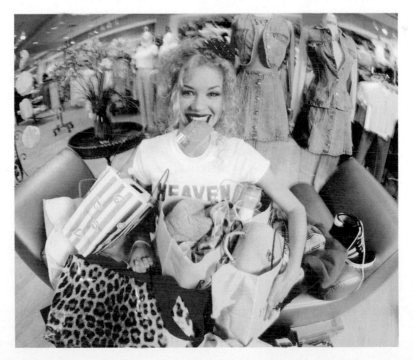

Too much materialism: Our infatuation with material things continues. It's hard to escape the notion that what Americans really value is stuff.

These criticisms overstate the power of business to create needs, however. People have strong defenses against advertising and other marketing tools. Marketers are most effective when they appeal to existing wants rather than when they attempt to create new ones. Furthermore, people seek information when making important purchases and often do not rely on single sources. Even minor purchases that may be affected by advertising messages lead to repeat purchases only if the product performs as promised. Finally, the high failure rate of new products shows that companies are not able to control demand.

On a deeper level, our wants and values are influenced not only by marketers but also by family, peer groups, religion, ethnic background, and education. If Americans are highly materialistic, these values arose out of basic socialization processes that go much deeper than business and mass media could produce alone. Moreover, some social critics even see materialism as a positive and rewarding force:

> . . . When we purchase an object, what we really buy is meaning. Commercialism is the water we swim in, the air we breathe, our sunlight and our shade. . . . Materialism is a vital source of meaning and happiness in the modern world. . . . We have not just asked to go this way, we have demanded. Now most of the world is lining up, pushing and shoving, eager to elbow into the mall. Getting and spending has become the most passionate, and often the most imaginative, endeavor of modern life. While this is dreary and depressing to some, as doubtless it should be, it is liberating and democratic to many more.[12]

Too Few Social Goods Business has been accused of overselling private goods at the expense of public goods. As private goods increase, they require more public services that are usually not forthcoming. For example, an increase in automobile ownership (private good) requires more highways, traffic control, parking spaces, and police services (public goods). The overselling of private goods results in "social costs." For cars, the social costs include traffic congestion, air pollution, and deaths and injuries from car accidents.

A way must be found to restore a balance between private and public goods. One option is to make producers bear the full social costs of their operations. The government could require automobile manufacturers to build cars with even more safety features and better pollution control systems. Automakers would then raise their prices to cover extra costs. If buyers found the price of some cars too high, however, the producers of these cars would disappear, and demand would move to those producers that could support the sum of the private and social costs.

A second option is to make consumers pay the social costs. A number of highway authorities around the world are starting to charge "congestion tolls" in an effort to reduce traffic congestion:

> Already, in Southern California, drivers are being charged premiums to travel in underused car pool lanes; Singapore, Norway, and France are managing traffic with varying tolls; peak surcharges are being studied for roads around New York, San Francisco, Los Angeles, and other cities. [Economists] point out that traffic jams are caused when drivers are not charged the costs they impose on others, such as delays. The solution: Make 'em pay.[13]

Interestingly, in San Diego, regular drivers can use the HOV (high-occupancy vehicle) lanes, but they must pay a price based on traffic usage at the time. The toll ranges from $.50 off-peak to $4.00 during rush hour.[14] If the costs of driving rise high enough, consumers will travel at nonpeak times or find alternative transportation modes.

Cultural Pollution Critics charge the marketing system with creating *cultural pollution.* Our senses are being constantly assaulted by advertising. Commercials interrupt serious programs; pages of ads obscure printed matter; billboards mar beautiful scenery.

Making consumers pay the social costs: On this private highway in California, consumers pay "congestion tolls" to drive in the fast—and unclogged—lane.

These interruptions continually pollute people's minds with messages of materialism, sex, power, or status. Although most people do not find advertising overly annoying (some even think it is the best part of television programming), some critics call for sweeping changes.

Marketers answer the charges of "commercial noise" with these arguments: First, they hope that their ads reach primarily the target audience. But because of mass-communication channels, some ads are bound to reach people who have no interest in the product and are therefore bored or annoyed. People who buy magazines addressed to their interests—such as *Vogue* or *Fortune*—rarely complain about the ads because the magazines advertise products of interest. Second, ads make much of television and radio free to users and keep down the costs of magazines and newspapers. Many people think commercials are a small price to pay for these benefits. Finally, today's consumers have alternatives. For example, they can zip and zap TV commercials or avoid them altogether on many cable or satellite channels. Thus, advertisers are making their ads more entertaining and informative.

Too Much Political Power Another criticism is that business wields too much political power. "Oil," "tobacco," "auto," and "pharmaceuticals" senators support an industry's interests against the public interest. Advertisers are accused of holding too much power over the mass media, limiting their freedom to report independently and objectively. One critic has asked: "How can [most magazines] afford to tell the truth about the scandalously low nutritional value of most packaged foods. . . . when these magazines are being subsidized by such advertisers as General Foods, Kellogg's, Nabisco, and General Mills? . . . The answer is *they cannot and do not.*"[15]

American industries do promote and protect their own interests. They have a right to representation in Congress and the mass media, although their influence can become too great. Fortunately, many powerful business interests once thought to be untouchable have been tamed in the public interest. For example, Standard Oil was broken up in 1911, and the meatpacking industry was disciplined in the early 1900s after exposures by Upton Sinclair. Ralph Nader caused legislation that forced the automobile industry to build more safety into its cars, and the Surgeon General's Report resulted in cigarette companies putting health warnings on their packages. More recently, giants such as AT&T, Intel, R.J. Reynolds, and Microsoft have felt the impact of regulators seeking to balance the interests of big business against those of the public. Moreover, because the media receive advertising revenues from many different advertisers, it is easier to resist the influence of one or a few of them. Too much business power tends to result in counterforces that check and offset these powerful interests.

Marketing's Impact on Other Businesses

Critics also charge that a company's marketing practices can harm other companies and reduce competition. Three problems are involved: acquisitions of competitors, marketing practices that create barriers to entry, and unfair competitive marketing practices.

Critics claim that firms are harmed and competition reduced when companies expand by acquiring competitors rather than by developing their own new products. The large number of acquisitions and rapid pace of industry consolidation over the past two decades have caused concern that vigorous young competitors will be absorbed and that competition will be reduced. In virtually every major industry—financial services, utilities, transportation, automobiles, telecommunications, health care, entertainment—the number of major competitors is shrinking.[16]

Acquisition is a complex subject. Acquisitions can sometimes be good for society. The acquiring company may gain economies of scale that lead to lower costs and lower prices. A well-managed company may take over a poorly managed company and improve its efficiency. An industry that was not very competitive might become more competitive after the acquisition. But acquisitions can also be harmful and, therefore, are closely regulated by the government.

Critics have also charged that marketing practices bar new companies from entering an industry. Large marketing companies can use patents and heavy promotion spending, and can tie up suppliers or dealers to keep out or drive out competitors. Those concerned with antitrust regulation recognize that some barriers are the natural result of the economic advantages of doing business on a large scale. Other barriers could be challenged by existing and new laws. For example, some critics have proposed a progressive tax on advertising spending to reduce the role of selling costs as a major barrier to entry.

Finally, some firms have in fact used unfair competitive marketing practices with the intention of hurting or destroying other firms. They may set their prices below costs, threaten to cut off business with suppliers, or discourage the buying of a competitor's products. Various laws work to prevent such predatory competition. It is difficult, however, to prove that the intent or action was really predatory. In recent years, Wal-Mart, American Airlines, Intel, and Microsoft have all been accused of various predatory practices. Take Microsoft, for example:

> Microsoft's. . . . reach extends beyond the PC into everything from computerized toys and TV set-top boxes to selling cars and airline tickets over the Internet. In its zeal to become a leader not just in operating systems but on the Internet, the company bundled its Internet Explorer browser into its Windows software. This move sparked an antitrust suit by the government, much to the delight of Microsoft's rivals. After all, Web-browsing innovator Netscape has seen its market share plummet as it tries to sell what Microsoft gives away for free.[17]

Although competitors and the government charge that Microsoft's actions are predatory, the question is whether this is unfair competition or the healthy competition of a more efficient company against the less efficient.

Citizen and Public Actions to Regulate Marketing

Because some people view business as the cause of many economic and social ills, grass-roots movements have arisen from time to time to keep business in line. The two major movements have been *consumerism* and *environmentalism*.

Consumerism

American business firms have been the target of organized consumer movements on three occasions. The first consumer movement took place in the early 1900s. It was fueled by rising prices, Upton Sinclair's writings on conditions in the meat industry, and scandals in the drug industry. The second consumer movement, in the mid-1930s, was sparked by an upturn in consumer prices during the Great Depression and another drug scandal.

The third movement began in the 1960s. Consumers had become better educated, products had become more complex and potentially hazardous, and people were unhappy with American institutions. Ralph Nader appeared on the scene to force many issues, and other well-known writers accused big business of wasteful and unethical practices. President John F. Kennedy declared that consumers had the right to safety and to be informed, to choose, and to be heard. Congress investigated certain industries and proposed consumer-protection legislation. Since then, many consumer groups have been organized and several consumer laws have been passed. The consumer movement has spread internationally and has become very strong in Europe. [18]

But what is the consumer movement? **Consumerism** is an organized movement of citizens and government agencies to improve the rights and power of buyers in relation to sellers. Traditional *sellers' rights* include:

Consumerism
An organized movement of citizens and government agencies to improve the rights and power of buyers in relation to sellers.

- ◆ The right to introduce any product in any size and style, provided it is not hazardous to personal health or safety; or, if it is, to include proper warnings and controls.
- ◆ The right to charge any price for the product, provided no discrimination exists among similar kinds of buyers.
- ◆ The right to spend any amount to promote the product, provided it is not defined as unfair competition.
- ◆ The right to use any product message, provided it is not misleading or dishonest in content or execution.
- ◆ The right to use any buying incentive schemes, provided they are not unfair or misleading.

Traditional *buyers' rights* include:

- ◆ The right not to buy a product that is offered for sale.
- ◆ The right to expect the product to be safe.
- ◆ The right to expect the product to perform as claimed.

Comparing these rights, many believe that the balance of power lies on the sellers' side. True, the buyer can refuse to buy. But critics feel that the buyer has too little information, education, and protection to make wise decisions when facing sophisticated sellers. Consumer advocates call for the following additional consumer rights:

- ◆ The right to be well informed about important aspects of the product.
- ◆ The right to be protected against questionable products and marketing practices.
- ◆ The right to influence products and marketing practices in ways that will improve the "quality of life."

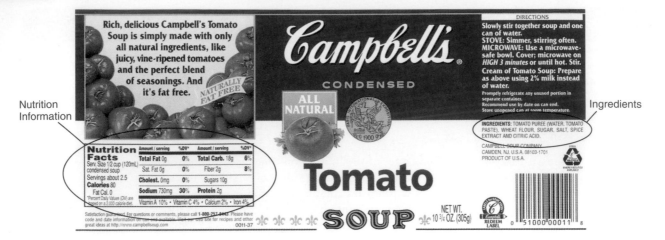

Nutrition Information

Ingredients

Consumer desire for more information led to putting ingredients, nutrition, and dating information on product labels.

Each proposed right has led to more specific proposals by consumerists. The right to be informed includes the right to know the true interest on a loan (truth in lending), the true cost per unit of a brand (unit pricing), the ingredients in a product (ingredient labeling), the nutritional value of foods (nutritional labeling), product freshness (open dating), and the true benefits of a product (truth in advertising). Proposals related to consumer protection include strengthening consumer rights in cases of business fraud, requiring greater product safety, and giving more power to government agencies. Proposals relating to quality of life include controlling the ingredients that go into certain products and packaging, reducing the level of advertising "noise," and putting consumer representatives on company boards to protect consumer interests.

Consumers have not only the *right* but also the *responsibility* to protect themselves instead of leaving this function to someone else. Consumers who believe they got a bad deal have several remedies available, including contacting the company or the media; contacting federal, state, or local agencies; and going to small-claims courts.

Environmentalism

Environmentalism
An organized movement of concerned citizens and government agencies to protect and improve people's living environment.

Whereas consumerists consider whether the marketing system is efficiently serving consumer wants, environmentalists are concerned with marketing's effects on the environment and with the costs of serving consumer needs and wants. **Environmentalism** is an organized movement of concerned citizens, businesses, and government agencies to protect and improve people's living environment. Environmentalists are not against marketing and consumption; they simply want people and organizations to operate with more care for the environment. The marketing system's goal, they assert, should not be to maximize consumption, consumer choice, or consumer satisfaction, but rather to maximize life quality. And "life quality" means not only the quantity and quality of consumer goods and services, but also the quality of the environment. Environmentalists want environmental costs included in both producer and consumer decision making.

The first wave of modern environmentalism in the United States was driven by environmental groups and concerned consumers in the 1960s and 1970s. They were concerned with damage to the ecosystem caused by strip mining, forest depletion, acid rain, loss of the atmosphere's ozone layer, toxic wastes, and litter. They also were concerned with the loss of recreational areas and with the increase in health problems caused by bad air, polluted water, and chemically treated food.

The second environmentalism wave was driven by government, which passed laws and regulations during the 1970s and 1980s governing industrial practices impacting the environment. This wave hit some industries hard. Steel companies and utilities had to invest billions of dollars in pollution control equipment and costlier fuels. The auto industry had to introduce expensive emission controls in cars. The packaging industry had to find ways to reduce litter. These industries and others have often resented and resisted environmental regulations, especially when they have been imposed too rapidly to allow companies to make proper adjustments. Many of these companies claim they have had to absorb large costs that have made them less competitive.

The first two environmentalism waves are now merging into a third and stronger wave in which companies are accepting responsibility for doing no harm to the environment. They are shifting from protest to prevention, and from regulation to responsibility. More and more companies are adopting policies of **environmental sustainability**—developing strategies that both sustain the environment and produce profits for the company. According to one strategist, "The challenge is to develop a *sustainable global economy:* an economy that the planet is capable of supporting indefinitely. . . . [It's] an enormous challenge—and an enormous opportunity."[19]

Sustainability is a crucial but difficult goal. John Browne, chairman of giant oil company BP, recently asked this question: "Is genuine progress still possible? Is development sustainable? Or is one strand of progress—industrialization—now doing such damage to the environment that the next generation won't have a world worth living in?"[20] Browne sees the situation as an opportunity. Five years ago, BP broke ranks with the oil industry on environmental issues. "There are good commercial reasons to do right by the environment," says Browne. Under his leadership, BP has become active in public forums on global climate issues and has worked to reduce emissions in exploration and production. It has begun marketing cleaner fuels and invested significantly in exploring alternative energy sources, such as photovoltaic power and hydrogen. All the while, company profits have reached all-time highs.

Figure 16-1 shows a grid that companies can use to gauge their progress toward environmental sustainability. At the most basic level, a company can practice *pollution prevention.* This involves more than pollution control—cleaning up waste after it has been created. Pollution prevention means eliminating or minimizing waste before it is created. Companies emphasizing prevention have responded with "green marketing" programs—developing ecologically safer products, recyclable and biodegradable packaging, better pollution controls, and more energy-efficient operations (see Marketing at Work 16-2). They are finding that they can be both green *and* competitive. Consider how the Dutch flower industry has responded to its environmental problems:

> Intense cultivation of flowers in small areas was contaminating the soil and groundwater with pesticides, herbicides, and fertilizers. Facing increasingly strict regulation, . . . the Dutch understood that the only effective way to address the problem would be to develop a closed-loop system. In advanced Dutch greenhouses, flowers now grow in water and rock wool, not in soil. This lowers the risk of infestation, reducing the need for fertilizers and pesticides, which are delivered in water that circulates and is reused. The . . . closed-loop system also reduces variation in growing conditions, thus improving product quality. Handling costs have gone down because the flowers are cultivated on specially designed platforms. . . . The net result is not only dramatically lower environmental impact but also lower costs, better product quality, and enhanced global competitiveness.[21]

Environmental sustainability
A management approach that involves developing strategies that both sustain the environment and produce profits for the company.

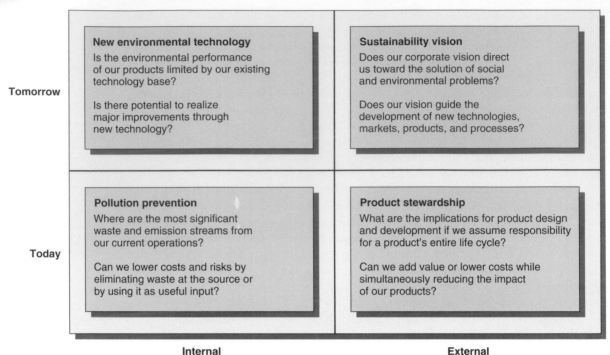

Figure 16-1
The environmental sustainability grid

Source: Reprinted by permission of *Harvard Business Review.* From "Beyond Greening: Strategies for a Sustainable World," by Stuart L. Hart, January–February 1997, p. 74. Copyright © 1997 by the President and Fellows of Harvard College; all rights reserved.

At the next level, companies can practice *product stewardship* — minimizing not just pollution from production but all environmental impacts throughout the full product life cycle. Many companies are adopting *design for environment (DFE)* practices, which involve thinking ahead in the design stage to create products that are easier to recover, reuse, or recycle. DFE not only helps to sustain the environment, it can be highly profitable:

> Consider Xerox Corporation's Asset Recycle Management (ARM) program, which uses leased Xerox copiers as sources of high-quality, low-cost parts and components for new machines. A well-developed [process] for taking back leased copiers combined with a sophisticated remanufacturing process allows . . . components to be reconditioned, tested, and then reassembled into "new" machines. Xerox estimates that ARM savings in raw materials, labor, and waste disposal in 1995 alone were in the $300-million to $400-million range. . . . By redefining product-in-use as part of the company's asset base, Xerox has discovered a way to add value and lower costs. It can continually provide lease customers with the latest product upgrades, giving them state-of-the-art functionality with minimum environmental impact.[22]

At the third level of environmental sustainability, companies look to the future and plan for *new environmental technologies.* Many organizations that have made good headway in pollution prevention and product stewardship are still limited by existing technologies. To develop fully sustainable strategies, they will need to develop new technologies. Monsanto is doing this by shifting its agricultural technology base from bulk chemicals to biotechnology. By controlling plant growth and pest resistance through

Environmental Farsightedness Today Pays Off Tomorrow

On Earth Day 1970, a newly emerging environmentalism movement made its first large-scale effort to educate people about the dangers of pollution. This was a tough task: At the time, most folks weren't all that interested in environmental problems. These days, however, environmentalism has broad public support. People hear and read daily about a growing list of environmental problems—global warming, acid rain, depletion of the ozone layer, air and water pollution, hazardous waste disposal, the buildup of solid wastes—and they are calling for solutions.

The new environmentalism has caused many consumers to rethink what products they buy and from whom. Nearly 87 percent of Americans are concerned about the environment. Roper Starch calls the core group of environmentally conscious consumers "greenback greens," noting that they are more likely to support environmental causes with their pocketbooks than to roll up their sleeves to volunteer. Such consumer attitudes have sparked a major marketing thrust—*green marketing*—the movement by companies to develop and market environmentally responsible products and themselves practice the three Rs of waste management: reducing, reusing, and recycling waste.

McDonald's provides a good example. It used to purchase Coca-Cola syrup in plastic bags encased in cardboard, but now the syrup is delivered as gasoline is, pumped directly from tank trucks into storage vats at restaurants. The change saved 68 million pounds of packaging a year. All napkins, bags, and tray liners in McDonald's restaurants are made from recycled paper, as are its carry-out drink trays and even the stationery used at head-

Corporate environmentalism: Enlightened companies are taking action not because someone is forcing them to, but because it is the right thing to do.

quarters. For a company the size of McDonald's, even small changes can make a big difference. For example, just making its drinking straws 20 percent lighter saved the company 1 million pounds of waste per year.

In an effort to reduce energy use, McDonald's even invited folks from outside the business, including several people from the Environmental Defense Fund (EDF), to suggest ways that the chain could make its restaurants more energy efficient. As a result, McDonald's built five "TEEM" restaurants (The Energy-Efficient McDonald's) as models of energy efficiency. One such restaurant in Detroit can draw heat from 50 feet below ground level to keep customers warm through the winter. Beyond simply conserving resources, each store saves up to four thousand dollars each year on energy bills.

Producers in other industries are also responding to environmental concerns. For example, 3M runs a *Pollution Prevention Pays* program, which has led to substantial reductions in pollution and costs. Xerox now remanufactures its copy machines and markets them as "proven workhorses" under names such as "Eco-series," "Renaissance," and "Green Line." Herman Miller, the large office-furniture manufacturer, set a trend in the furniture industry when it began using tropical woods from sustainably managed sources, altering even its classic furniture lines. But it went even further by reusing packaging, recapturing solvents used in staining, and burning fabric scraps and sawdust to generate energy for its manufacturing plant. These moves not only help the environment, they also save Herman Miller $750,000 per year on energy and landfill costs.

Service providers are going green, too. Studies indicate that 85 percent of travelers are willing to pay as much as 8 percent more to stay in an environmentally friendly hotel. Sheraton Hotels recently opened its first environmentally smart hotel in the United States—the Sheraton Rittenhouse Hotel in Philadelphia—using only materials and fabrics that are produced without toxic bleaches or dyes. All of the hotel's furniture is made of wood harvested from managed forests, and all of the carpets, draperies, paint, and wallpaper are free of toxic chemicals. A six-story central atrium houses bamboo trees, which grow at a rate of one meter each day and produce oxygen at a rate 35 percent higher than most other plants. The walls of the atrium are fashioned from *Wall Street Journal* rejects and soybeans, while the floor is made from engineered bamboo.

Even retailers are jumping onto the green bandwagon. For example, Grow Biz International has developed a $100 million business selling used equipment through retail chains such as Play It Again, Once Upon a Child, Computer Renaissance, Music Go Round, and Disk Go Round. And Wal-Mart is opening "eco-friendly" stores in which the air-conditioning systems use non-ozone-depleting refrigerant, rainwater is collected from parking lots and rooftops for landscaping, skylights supplement fluorescent lighting adjusted by photo sensors, and the road sign is solar powered.

The growth of the Internet has given the green movement a real boost. "The Internet has armed the busy, yet environmentally-conscious consumer with a new method of environmental activism: shopping," notes one analyst.

••••••••••••••••••••••••••••••

Online charity malls like GreaterGood.com, ShopForChange, and iGive, allow consumers to buy goods and have a small percentage of their purchase go to a charity of their choice, green or otherwise. Then there are click-to-donate sites, like The Rain Forest Site (www.therainforestsite.com), where clicking on a button automatically sends a donation to The Nature Conservancy, courtesy of merchants who pay for banner ads on the site. Other mall-like sites, such as EthicalShopper.com, GreenHome.com, and EcoMall.com, offer environmentally-friendly products, from chamomile shampoo to non-chlorine bleach. Also sprouting up are individual vendors, like DolphinBlue.com, which sells recycled paper and office supplies, and EcoBaby.com, which sells envirosafe baby products.

••••••••••••••••••••••••••••••

"Whether they buy from the expanding number of dot-coms specializing in enviro-friendly products, or frequent mainstream merchants through charity mall sites that donate a portion of sales to green causes," says the analyst, "e-commerce is expanding the opportunity to 'do the right thing' for Mother Earth."

During the early phase of the new environmentalism, environmentalists and regulators became concerned that companies were going overboard with their use of terms such as *recyclable,* *degradable, compostable,* and *environmentally responsible.* Perhaps of equal concern was that, as more and more marketers used green marketing claims, more and more consumers would view them as little more than gimmicks. Now, environmentalism appears to be moving into a more mature phase—broader, deeper, and more sophisticated. Gone are the hastily prepared environmental pitches and products designed to capitalize on or exploit growing public concern. "Dressing up ads with pictures of eagles and trees will no longer woo an environmentally sophisticated audience," says an environmentalist. "People want to know that companies are incorporating environmental values into their manufacturing processes, products, packaging, and the very fabric of their corporate cultures."

Some companies have responded to consumer environmental concerns by doing only what is required to avert new regulations or to keep environmentalists quiet. Enlightened companies are taking action not because someone is forcing them to, or to reap short-run profits, but because it is the right thing to do. They believe that environmental farsightedness today will pay off tomorrow—for both the customer and the company.

Sources: Quotes from Robert Rehak, "Green Marketing Awash in Third Wave," *Advertising Age,* November 22, 1993, p. 22; Lisa E. Phillips, "Green Attitude," *American Demographics,* April 1999, pp. 46–47; and Rebecca Gardyn, "Saving the Earth, One Click at a Time," *American Demographics,* January 2001, pp. 30–33. Also see Michael Malley, "Turning Green Practices into Greenbacks," *Hotel and Motel Management,* May 17, 1999, p. 8; and Amy Zuber, "Go, T.E.E.M.! New McDonald's Units Conserve Energy, Save Money," *Nation's Restaurant News,* March 13, 2000, p. 30.

bioengineering rather than through the application of pesticides or fertilizers, Monsanto hopes to fulfill its promise of environmentally sustainable agriculture.[23]

Finally, companies can develop a *sustainability vision,* which serves as a guide to the future. It shows how the company's products and services, processes, and policies must evolve and what new technologies must be developed to get there. This vision of sustainability provides a framework for pollution control, product stewardship, and environmental technology.

Most companies today focus on the lower-left quadrant of the grid in Figure 16-1, investing most heavily in pollution prevention. Some forward-looking companies practice product stewardship and are developing new environmental technologies. Few companies have well-defined sustainability visions. Emphasizing only one or a few cells in the environmental sustainability grid in Figure 16-1 can be shortsighted. For example, investing only in the bottom half of the grid puts a company in a good position today but leaves it vulnerable in the future. In contrast, a heavy emphasis on the top half suggests that a company has good environmental vision but lacks the skills needed to implement it. Thus, companies should work at developing all four dimensions of environmental sustainability. Hewlett-Packard is doing just that:

> Hewlett-Packard has evolved through three distinct phases of environmental sustainability over the past two decades. In the 1980s, the environmental concerns were primarily pollution control and prevention, with a focus on reducing emissions from existing manufacturing processes. . . . In the 1990s, the focus shifted to . . . a product stewardship function, which focused on developing global processes for tracking and managing regulatory compliance issues, customer inquiry response systems, information management, public policy shaping, product take-back programs, green packaging, and integrating "design for the environment" and life cycle analysis into product development processes. Today, sustainability is about developing technologies that actually contribute a positive impact to environmental challenges. [However,] HP has recognized that pollution prevention and product stewardship have become baseline market expectations. To be an environmental leader in the 21st century, HP needs to integrate environmental sustainability into its fundamental business [vision and] strategy.[24]

Environmentalism creates some special challenges for global marketers. As international trade barriers come down and global markets expand, environmental issues are having an ever-greater impact on international trade. Countries in North America, Western Europe, and other developed regions are developing stringent environmental standards. In the United States, for example, more than two dozen major pieces of environmental legislation have been enacted since 1970, and recent events suggest that more regulation is on the way. A side accord to the North American Free Trade Agreement (NAFTA) set up a commission for resolving environmental matters. And the European Union's Eco-Management and Audit Regulation provides guidelines for environmental self-regulation.[25]

However, environmental policies still vary widely from country to country, and uniform worldwide standards are not expected for many years. Although countries such as Denmark, Germany, Japan, and the United States have fully developed environmental policies and high public expectations, major countries such as China, India, Brazil, and Russia are in only the early stages of developing such policies. Moreover, environmental factors that motivate consumers in one country may have no impact on consumers in another. For example, PVC soft drink bottles cannot be used in Switzerland or Germany. However, they are preferred in France, which has an extensive recycling process for them. Thus, international companies are finding it difficult to develop standard environmental practices that work around the world. Instead, they are creating general policies and then translating these policies into tailored programs that meet local regulations and expectations.

Public Actions to Regulate Marketing

Citizen concerns about marketing practices will usually lead to public attention and legislative proposals. New bills will be debated—many will be defeated, others will be modified, and a few will become workable laws.

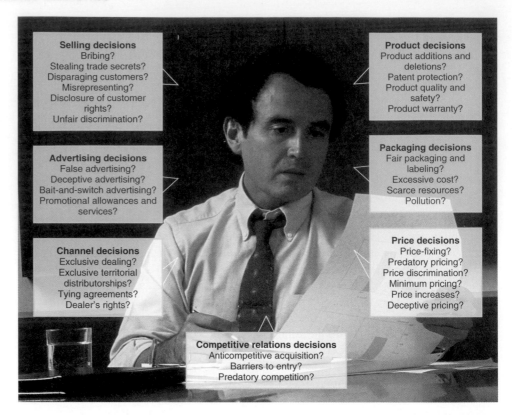

Selling decisions
Bribing?
Stealing trade secrets?
Disparaging customers?
Misrepresenting?
Disclosure of customer rights?
Unfair discrimination?

Advertising decisions
False advertising?
Deceptive advertising?
Bait-and-switch advertising?
Promotional allowances and services?

Channel decisions
Exclusive dealing?
Exclusive territorial distributorships?
Tying agreements?
Dealer's rights?

Product decisions
Product additions and deletions?
Patent protection?
Product quality and safety?
Product warranty?

Packaging decisions
Fair packaging and labeling?
Excessive cost?
Scarce resources?
Pollution?

Price decisions
Price-fixing?
Predatory pricing?
Price discrimination?
Minimum pricing?
Price increases?
Deceptive pricing?

Competitive relations decisions
Anticompetitive acquisition?
Barriers to entry?
Predatory competition?

Figure 16-2
Major marketing decision areas that may be called into question under the law

Many of the laws that affect marketing are listed in Chapter 4. The task is to translate these laws into the language that marketing executives understand as they make decisions about competitive relations, products, price, promotion, and channels of distribution. Figure 16-2 illustrates the major legal issues facing marketing management.

Business Actions Toward Socially Responsible Marketing

Enlightened marketing
A marketing philosophy holding that a company's marketing should support the best long-run performance of the marketing system; its five principles include consumer-oriented marketing, innovative marketing, value marketing, sense-of-mission marketing, and societal marketing.

Consumer-oriented marketing
The philosophy of enlightened marketing that holds that the company should view and organize its marketing activities from the consumer's point of view.

At first, many companies opposed consumerism and environmentalism. They thought the criticisms were either unfair or unimportant. But by now, most companies have grown to accept the new consumer rights, at least in principle. They might oppose certain pieces of legislation as inappropriate ways to solve specific consumer problems, but they recognize the consumer's right to information and protection. Many of these companies have responded positively to consumerism and environmentalism in order to serve consumer needs better.

Enlightened Marketing

The philosophy of **enlightened marketing** holds that a company's marketing should support the best long-run performance of the marketing system. Enlightened marketing consists of five principles: *consumer-oriented marketing, innovative marketing, value marketing, sense-of-mission marketing,* and *societal marketing.*

Consumer-Oriented Marketing **Consumer-oriented marketing** means that the company should view and organize its marketing activities from the consumer's point of view. It should work hard to sense, serve, and satisfy the needs of a defined group of customers.

Every good marketing company that we've discussed in this text has had this in common: an all-consuming passion for delivering superior value to carefully chosen customers. Only by seeing the world through its customers' eyes can the company build lasting and profitable customer relationships.

Innovative Marketing The principle of **innovative marketing** requires that the company continuously seek real product and marketing improvements. The company that overlooks new and better ways to do things will eventually lose customers to another company that has found a better way. An excellent example of an innovative marketer is Colgate-Palmolive:

> Colgate has become somewhat of a new-product machine in recent years. Worldwide, new products contribute 35 percent of Colgate's revenues, up from 26 percent five years earlier. In the United States, new products account for 58 percent of sales, up from 27 percent. The American Marketing Association (AMA) recently named Colgate-Palmolive its new-product marketer of the year. Colgate took the honors by launching an abundance of innovative and highly successful new consumer products, including Colgate Total toothpaste. Total is perhaps the best example of the company's passion for continuous improvement. Marketing research showed shifts in consumer demographics and concerns — a growing population of aging, health-conscious, and better-educated consumers. For these consumers, Total became a breakout brand that provides a combination of benefits, including cavity prevention, tartar control, fresh breath, and long-lasting effects. The company also launched an innovative marketing program for the new product, which included advertising in health magazines targeting educated consumers who have high involvement in the health of their mouth and teeth. Consumers responded by making Colgate-Palmolive the toothpaste market leader for the first time since 1962, with a 32 percent share versus Procter & Gamble's 25 percent.[26]

Innovative marketing
A principle of enlightened marketing that requires that a company seek real product and marketing improvements.

Value Marketing According to the principle of **value marketing,** the company should put most of its resources into value-building marketing investments. Many things marketers do — one-shot sales promotions, minor packaging changes, advertising puffery — may raise sales in the short run but add less *value* than would actual improvements in the product's quality, features, or convenience. Enlightened marketing calls for building long-run consumer loyalty by continually improving the value consumers receive from the firm's marketing offer.

Value marketing
A principle of enlightened marketing that holds that a company should put most of its resources into value-building marketing investments.

Sense-of-Mission Marketing **Sense-of-mission marketing** means that the company should define its mission in broad *social* terms rather than narrow *product* terms. When a company defines a social mission, employees feel better about their work and have a clearer sense of direction. For example, defined in narrow product terms, Ben & Jerry's mission might be "to sell ice cream and frozen yogurt." However, the company states its mission more broadly as one of "linked prosperity," including product, economic, and social missions (see www.benjerrys.com/mission.html). Reshaping the basic task of selling consumer products into the larger mission of serving the interests of consumers, employees, and others in the company's various "communities" gives Ben & Jerry's a vital sense of purpose. Like Ben & Jerry's, many companies today are undertaking socially responsible actions and building concern for their communities into their underlying cultures (see Marketing at Work 16-3).

Sense-of-mission marketing
A principle of enlightened marketing that holds that a company should define its mission in broad social terms rather than narrow product terms.

Societal Marketing Following the principle of **societal marketing,** an enlightened company makes marketing decisions by considering consumers' wants and interests, the

Societal marketing
A principle of enlightened marketing that holds that a company should make marketing decisions by considering consumers' wants, the company's requirements, consumers' long-run interests, and society's long-run interests.

Mission: Social Responsibility

In a recent poll, 92 percent of consumers said they believe it's important for companies to be good corporate citizens. More than three-quarters responded that they would switch brands and retailers when price and quality are equal for a product associated with a good cause. Companies have responded to this call for social responsibility with actions ranging from supporting worthwhile causes to writing social responsibility and good corporate citizenship into the underlying mission statements. Cause-related marketing by companies has increased more than 500 percent during the past decade.

Today, acts of good corporate citizenship abound. For example, American Express's Charge Against Hunger program—through which the company donated 3 cents from every transaction made during the traditional holiday season—raised more than $21 million for hunger relief in the United States. Maxwell House, a division of Kraft Foods, created a partnership with Habitat for Humanity to build 100 homes in as many days, while working to raise awareness for the organization. Post Cereal celebrated its 100th anniversary in unique fashion by donating to Second Harvest—the nation's largest network of hunger-relief charities—enough cereal to feed more than 1 million people. In addition, Post partnered with grocery retailers to sponsor a 100-day food drive across the United States, supported by national and local ads to increase hunger awareness and to encourage consumer participation in the drive.

It seems that almost every company has a pet cause. Alarm company ADT gives away personal-security systems to battered women. Avon Products helps fund the fight

against breast cancer—since 1993, it has raised more than $110 million for this cause. Dow donates employees' time and home construction materials to Habitat for Humanity. Coca-Cola sponsors local Boys and Girls Clubs, and Barnes & Noble promotes literacy.

Beyond aligning with good causes, socially responsible companies care about and serve the communities in which they operate. Take Saturn Corporation, for example:

• •

From its inception, Saturn has worked to distinguish itself as a unique car company. As its slogan states, Saturn is "A different kind of company. A different kind of car." The company claims to focus more on its employees, customers, and communities than on revenues and bottom lines. Saturn's president and CEO, Don Hudler, notes that "a part of Saturn's business philosophy is to meet the needs of

our neighbors." An example of this philosophy in action is Saturn Playgrounds, a company program for employee involvement and community betterment. The goal of the program is to provide young children in poor communities with a safe, fun environment during nonschool hours as an alternative to gangs, drugs, and crime. Backed by Saturn retail facility dollars, local Saturn employees and customers join with community members to build a community playground in a single day. So far, the Saturn Playgrounds project has built over 150 playgrounds and two Little League parks across the country. Joe Rypkowski, president of a local United Auto Workers union, commented that "the Saturn Playgrounds project is a perfect example of the partnership we've built at Saturn. Working together can bring powerful results, not just in our jobs, but in our communities."

• •

Social responsibility: Beyond aligning with good causes, socially responsible companies care about and serve the communities in which they operate. Here, backed by local retailers, Saturn retail team members and Saturn owners join with community members to build a community playground in a single day.

Each year, *Business Ethics* magazine selects its 100 Best Corporate Citizens, companies that excel at serving their various local, national, and global communities as well as shareholders and customers. Here are examples of companies heading up recent *Business Ethics* best 100 lists:

· ·

Procter & Gamble. The top company for 2001 was Procter and Gamble. The consumer-products giant scored especially high in service to its international communities. P&G markets 300 brands to nearly 5 billion consumers in 140 countries, with some 50 percent of revenues coming from overseas. It operates 93 manufacturing facilities in 44 countries outside the United States and has been generous in international grants and gifts in these communities, including earthquake relief in Turkey, community building projects in Japan, plus contributions for schools in China, school computers in Romania, special education in Malaysia, and shore protection in France. P&G contributes more than $75 million worldwide each year to support such causes.

The St. Paul Companies. The St. Paul, the $7.5 billion Minnesota-based insurer, gained *Business Ethics*' top score for "community," based on its commitment to development of its home communities of St. Paul and Minneapolis. Its Leadership Initiatives in Neighborhoods program, now in its sixteenth year, provides grants to current and emerging leaders to develop their leadership potential. Since 1998, The St. Paul has pledged more than $2.2 million to increase the number of teachers of color in Twin Cities urban schools, enhance the retention of talented educators, and better prepare teachers for urban classrooms. St. Paul employee committees are empowered to award grants in the communities where

they live and work. And The St. Paul's arts and diversity committee collaborates with United Arts, a local nonprofit organization, on local arts programming related to various cultures, perspectives, and diversity issues. "Increasingly, companies and employees are caring about their communities and want to be part of a greater cause," says Douglas Leatherdale, St. Paul's chairman and CEO. "They want to do the right thing . . . to take positive actions that make life better for everyone."

Pitney Bowes. This business equipment maker, headquartered in Stamford, Connecticut, also invests in local economic development as a part of its corporate culture. For example, it decided to keep its headquarters in a deteriorating section of Stamford's South End, and to work with grassroots organizations to improve the community. The company donated property near its headquarters for an affordable housing complex and has participated in a down-payment assistance program for home ownership. Pitney Bowes also supports the grassroots South End Neighborhood Revitalization Zone Initiative, which empowers community residents to make decisions about the neighborhood. "Because a lot of the people who live here are low-income," says Polly O'Brien, director of community affairs, "it's not always easy for them to complain about property owners who don't keep places clean or up to code." The program gives these people voice. "To us, it's very easy to sit and write a check, but it doesn't have the same impact for self-sufficiency as if you partner with people," said O'Brien. "It's really their success."

Gillette. Gillette earned the highest environment score for its proactive approach to environmental restoration. In 2000, the company extended its environmen-

tal commitment beyond its own facilities by setting up the Corporate Wetlands Restoration Partnership (CWRP), an innovative public-private program to restore America's valuable wetlands. Gillette founded the CWRP in Massachusetts, in partnership with state and federal agencies, to help restore vital wetlands damaged by development and pollution. To date, more than 20 companies have contributed over $1 million in funds and services to the Massachusetts partnership, which has nearly completed the restoration of the Sagamore Salt Marsh. The partnership is now expanding nationwide for greater impact, with Gillette as national corporate chair. The company also participates in the pilot EPA Environmental Leadership Program, another sign of going beyond its own impact in addressing environmental problems.

· ·

Social responsibility is no longer viewed as the enemy of good business. Instead, it's at the forefront of sound business practice. "The term 'corporate citizenship' is coming into broader use these days," says the editor of *Business Ethics,* "as awareness grows that business has responsibilities beyond profits." Moreover, doing what's good for a company's communities can also be good for the company. "We view corporate social responsibility as an asset we continue to nurture and grow," says The St. Paul's Leatherdale. "In the long term, it will benefit the company and its shareholders."

Sources: "Saturn Dealers Build Six New Playgrounds in One Weekend," *PR Newswire,* June 4, 1997; "Saturn Fact Facts: Community Partnerships," accessed online at http://media.gm.com, August 2001; Tom Klusmann, "The 100 Best Corporate Citizens in 2000," *Business Ethics,* March–April 2000; Philip Johansson, "The 100 Best Corporate Citizens for 2001," *Business Ethics,* March–April 2001; and Cynthia Wagner, "Economics: Evaluating Good Corporate Citizenship," *The Futurist,* July–August 2001, p. 16. For more information and examples, see the *Business Ethics* Web site at www.business-ethics.com.

IMMEDIATE SATISFACTION

	Low	High
High	Salutary products	Desirable products
Low	Deficient products	Pleasing products

LONG-RUN CONSUMER BENEFIT

Figure 16-3
Societal classification
of products

Deficient products
Products that have neither immediate appeal nor long-run benefits.

Pleasing products
Products that give high immediate satisfaction but may hurt consumers in the long run.

Salutary products
Products that have low appeal but may benefit consumers in the long run.

Desirable products
Products that give both high immediate satisfaction and high long-run benefits.

company's requirements, and society's long-run interests. The company is aware that neglecting consumer and societal long-run interests is a disservice to consumers and society. Alert companies view societal problems as opportunities.

A societally oriented marketer wants to design products that are not only pleasing but also beneficial. The difference is shown in Figure 16-3. Products can be classified according to their degree of immediate consumer satisfaction and long-run consumer benefit. **Deficient products,** such as bad-tasting and ineffective medicine, have neither immediate appeal nor long-run benefits. **Pleasing products** give high immediate satisfaction but may hurt consumers in the long run. An example is cigarettes. **Salutary products** have low appeal but may benefit consumers in the long run; for instance, seat belts and air bags. **Desirable products** give both high immediate satisfaction and high long-run benefits—a tasty *and* nutritious breakfast food.

An example of a desirable product is Herman Miller's Avian office chair, which is not only attractive and functional but also environmentally responsible:

Herman Miller, one of the world's largest office furniture makers, has received numerous awards for environmentally responsible products and business practices. In 1994 the company formed an Earth Friendly Design Task Force

Herman Miller's Earth Friendly Design Task Force infuses the company's design process with its environmental values. For example, the Avian chair is designed for the lowest possible ecological impact and 100 percent recyclability.

responsible for infusing the company's design process with its environmental values. The task force carries out life cycle analyses on the company's products, including everything from how much of a product can be made from recycled materials to how much of the product itself can be recycled at the end of its useful life. For example, the company's Avian chair is designed for the lowest possible ecological impact and 100 percent recyclability. Herman Miller reduced material used in the chair by using gas-assist injection molding for the frame, which resulted in hollow frame members (like the bones of birds, hence the chair's name). The frame needs no paint nor other finish. All materials are recyclable. No ozone-depleting materials are used. The chair is shipped partially assembled, thus reducing the packaging and energy needed to ship it. Finally, a materials schematic is imbedded in the bottom of the seat to help recycle the chair at the end of its life. This is truly a desirable product—it's won awards for design and function *and* for environmental responsibility.[27]

Companies should try to turn all of their products into desirable products. The challenge posed by pleasing products is that they sell very well but may end up hurting the consumer. The product opportunity, therefore, is to add long-run benefits without reducing the product's pleasing qualities. For example, Sears developed a phosphate-free laundry detergent that was also very effective. The challenge posed by salutary products is to add some pleasing qualities so that they will become more desirable in the consumers' minds. For example, synthetic fats and fat substitutes, such as NutraSweet's Simplesse and Procter & Gamble's Olestra, have improved the appeal of more healthful low-calorie and low-fat foods.

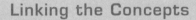

Linking the Concepts

Pause here, hold your place with your finger, and go way back and take another look at the Societal Marketing Concept section in Chapter 1.

◆ How does Figure 1-4 apply to the Enlightened Marketing section in this chapter?
◆ Use the five principles to assess the actions of a company that you believe exemplifies socially responsible marketing. (If you can't think of one, use Johnson & Johnson, Ben & Jerry's, or one of the companies discussed in Marketing at Work 16-3.)
◆ Use the principles of enlightened marketing to assess the actions of a company that you believe falls short of socially responsible marketing.

Marketing Ethics

Conscientious marketers face many moral dilemmas. The best thing to do is often unclear. Because not all managers have fine moral sensitivity, companies need to develop *corporate marketing ethics policies*—broad guidelines that everyone in the organization must follow. These policies should cover distributor relations, advertising standards, customer service, pricing, product development, and general ethical standards.

The finest guidelines cannot resolve all the difficult ethical situations the marketer faces. Table 16-1 lists some difficult ethical situations marketers could face during their careers. If marketers choose immediate sales-producing actions in all these cases, their marketing behavior might well be described as immoral or even amoral. If they refuse to go along with *any* of the actions, they might be ineffective as marketing managers and unhappy because of the constant moral tension. Managers need a set of principles that will

Table 16-1   Some Morally Difficult Situations in Marketing

1. You work for a cigarette company and up until now have not been convinced that cigarettes cause cancer. However, recent public policy debates now leave no doubt in your mind about the link between smoking and cancer. What would you do?

2. Your R&D department has changed one of your products slightly. It is not really "new and improved," but you know that putting this statement on the package and in advertising will increase sales. What would you do?

3. You have been asked to add a stripped-down model to your line that could be advertised to pull customers into the store. The product won't be very good, but salespeople will be able to switch buyers up to higher-priced units. You are asked to give the green light for the stripped-down version. What would you do?

4. You are thinking of hiring a product manager who has just left a competitor's company. She would be more than happy to tell you all the competitor's plans for the coming year. What would you do?

5. One of your top dealers in an important territory recently has had family troubles, and his sales have slipped. It looks like it will take him a while to straighten out his family trouble. Meanwhile you are losing many sales. Legally, you can terminate the dealer's franchise and replace him. What would you do?

6. You have a chance to win a big account that will mean a lot to you and your company. The purchasing agent hints that a "gift" would influence the decision. Your assistant recommends sending a fine color television set to the buyer's home. What would you do?

7. You have heard that a competitor has a new product feature that will make a big difference in sales. The competitor will demonstrate the feature in a private dealer meeting at the annual trade show. You can easily send a snooper to this meeting to learn about the new feature. What would you do?

8. You have to choose between three ad campaigns outlined by your agency. The first (a) is soft-sell, honest information campaign. The second (b) uses sex-loaded emotional appeals and exaggerates the product's benefits. The third (c) involves a noisy, irritating commercial that is sure to gain audience attention. Pretests show that the campaigns are effective in the following order: c, b, and a. What would you do?

9. You are interviewing a capable female applicant for a job as salesperson. She is better qualified than the men just interviewed. Nevertheless, you know that some of your important customers prefer dealing with men, and you will lose some sales if you hire her. What would you do?

help them figure out the moral importance of each situation and decide how far they can go in good conscience.

But *what* principle should guide companies and marketing managers on issues of ethics and social responsibility? One philosophy is that such issues are decided by the free market and legal system. Under this principle, companies and their managers are not responsible for making moral judgments. Companies can in good conscience do whatever the system allows.

A second philosophy puts responsibility not in the system but in the hands of individual companies and managers. This more enlightened philosophy suggests that a company should have a "social conscience." Companies and managers should apply high standards of ethics and morality when making corporate decisions, regardless of "what the system allows." History provides an endless list of examples of company actions that were legal and allowed but were highly irresponsible. Consider the following example:

> Prior to the Pure Food and Drug Act, the advertising for a diet pill promised that a person taking this pill could eat virtually anything at any time and still lose weight. Too good to be true? Actually the claim was quite true; the product lived up to its billing with frightening efficiency. It seems that the primary active ingredient in this "diet supplement" was tapeworm larvae. These larvae would develop in the intestinal tract and, of course, be well fed; the pill taker would in time, quite literally, starve to death.[28]

Each company and marketing manager must work out a philosophy of socially responsible and ethical behavior. Under the societal marketing concept, each manager must look beyond what is legal and allowed and develop standards based on personal integrity, corporate conscience, and long-run consumer welfare. A clear and responsible philosophy will help the company deal with knotty issues such as the one faced recently by 3M:

In late 1997, a powerful new research technique for scanning blood kept turning up the same odd result: Tiny amounts of a chemical 3M had made for nearly 40 years were showing up in blood drawn from people living all across the country. If the results held up, it meant that virtually all Americans may be carrying some minuscule amount of the chemical, called perfluorooctane sulfonate (PFOS), in their systems. Even though they had yet to come up with definitive answers—and they insisted that there's no evidence of danger to humans—the company reached a drastic decision. In mid-2000, although under no mandate to act, 3M decided to phase out products containing PFOS and related chemicals, including its popular Scotchgard fabric protector. This was no easy decision. Since there was as yet no replacement chemical, it meant a potential loss of $500 million in annual sales. 3M's voluntary actions drew praise from regulators. "3M deserves great credit for identifying the problem and coming forward," says an Environmental Protection Agency administrator. "It took guts," comments another government scientist. "The fact is that most companies...go into anger, denial, and the rest of that stuff. [We're used to seeing] decades-long arguments about whether a chemical is really toxic." For 3M, however, it shouldn't have been all that difficult a decision—it was simply the right thing to do.[29]

As with environmentalism, the issue of ethics provides special challenges for international marketers. Business standards and practices vary a great deal from one country to the next. For example, whereas bribes and kickbacks are illegal for U.S. firms, they are standard business practice in many South American countries. The question arises as to whether a company must lower its ethical standards to compete effectively in countries with lower standards. In one study, two researchers posed this question to chief executives of large international companies and got a unanimous response: No.[30] For the sake of all of the company's stakeholders—customers, suppliers, employees, shareholders, and the public—it is important to make a commitment to a common set of shared standards worldwide.

For example, John Hancock Mutual Life Insurance Company operates successfully in Southeast Asia, an area that by Western standards has widespread questionable business and government practices. Despite warnings from locals that Hancock would have to bend its rules to succeed, the company set out strict guidelines. "We told our people that we had the same ethical standards, same procedures, same policies in these countries that we have in the United States, and we do," says Hancock Chairman Stephen Brown. "We just felt that things like payoffs were wrong—and if we had to do business that way, we'd rather not do business." Hancock employees feel good about the consistent levels of ethics. "There may be countries where you have to do that kind of thing," says Brown. "We haven't found that country yet, and if we do, we won't do business there."[31]

Many industrial and professional associations have suggested codes of ethics, and many companies are now adopting their own codes. For example, the American Marketing Association, an international association of marketing managers and scholars, developed the code of ethics shown in Table 16-2. Companies are also developing programs to teach managers about important ethics issues and help them find the proper responses. They hold ethics workshops and seminars and set up ethics committees.

Table 16-2 American Marketing Association Code of Ethics

Members of the American Marketing Association are committed to ethical, professional conduct. They have joined together in subscribing to this Code of Ethics embracing the following topics:

Responsibilities of the Marketer

Marketers must accept responsibility for the consequences of their activities and make every effort to ensure that their decisions, recommendations, and actions function to identify, serve, and satisfy all relevant publics: customers, organizations, and society.

Marketers' professional conduct must be guided by:

1. The basic rule of professional ethics: not knowingly to do harm.
2. The adherence to all applicable laws and regulations.
3. The accurate representation of their education, training, and experience.
4. The active support, practice, and promotion of this Code of Ethics.

Honesty and Fairness

Marketers shall uphold and advance the integrity, honor, and dignity of the marketing profession by:

1. Being honest in serving consumers, clients, employees, suppliers, distributors, and the public.
2. Not knowingly participating in conflict of interest without prior notice to all parties involved.
3. Establishing equitable fee schedules including the payment or receipt of usual, customary, and/or legal compensation for marketing exchanges.

Rights and Duties of Parties in the Marketing Exchange Process

Participants in the marketing exchange process should be able to expect that:

1. Products and services offered are safe and fit for their intended uses.
2. Communications about offered products and services are not deceptive.
3. All parties intend to discharge their obligations, financial and otherwise, in good faith.
4. Appropriate internal methods exist for equitable adjustment and/or redress of grievances concerning purchases.

It is understood that the above would include, but are not limited to, the following responsibilities of the marketer:

◆ Disclosure of all substantial risks associated with product or service usage.
◆ Identification of any product component substitution that might materially change the product or impact on the buyer's purchase decision.
◆ Identification of extra cost-added features.

In the area of promotions,

◆ Avoidance of false and misleading advertising.
◆ Rejection of high-pressure manipulations, or misleading sales tactics.
◆ Avoidance of sales promotions that use deception or manipulation.

In the area of distribution,

◆ Not manipulating the availability of a product for purpose of exploitation.
◆ Not using coercion in the marketing channel.
◆ Not exerting undue influence over the reseller's choice to handle a product.

In the area of pricing,

◆ Not engaging in price fixing.
◆ Not practicing predatory pricing.
◆ Disclosing the full price associated with any purchase.

In the area of marketing research,

◆ Prohibiting selling or fundraising under the guise of conducting research.
◆ Maintaining research integrity by avoiding misrepresentation and omission of pertinent research data.
◆ Treating outside clients and suppliers fairly.

Table 16-2   **American Marketing Association Code of Ethics** *(contd.)*

Organizational Relationships

Marketers should be aware of how their behavior may influence or impact on the behavior of others in organizational relationships. They should not demand, encourage, or apply coercion to obtain unethical behavior in their relationships with others, such as employees, suppliers, or customers.

1. Apply confidentiality and anonymity in professional relationships with regard to privileged information.
2. Meet their obligations and responsibilities in contracts and mutual agreements in a timely manner.
3. Avoid taking the work of others, in whole, or in part, and representing this work as their own or directly benefitting from it without compensation or consent of the originator or owner.
4. Avoid manipulations to take advantage of situations to maximize personal welfare in a way that unfairly deprives or damages the organization of others.

Any AMA member found to be in violation of any provision of this Code of Ethics may have his or her Association membership suspended or revoked.

Further, more than 200 major U.S. companies have appointed high-level ethics officers to champion ethics issues and to help resolve ethics problems and concerns facing employees. For example, in 1991 Nynex created a new position of vice president of ethics, supported by a dozen full-time staff and a million-dollar budget. Since then, the new department has trained some 95,000 Nynex employees. Such training includes sending 22,000 managers to full-day workshops that include case studies on ethical actions in marketing, finance, and other business functions. One workshop deals with the use of improperly obtained competitive data, which managers are instructed is not permitted.[32]

Many companies have developed innovative ways to educate employees about ethics:

Citicorp has developed an ethics board game, which teams of employees use to solve hypothetical quandaries. General Electric employees can tap into specially designed software on their personal computers to get answers to ethical questions. At Texas Instruments, employees are treated to a weekly column on ethics over an electronic news service. One popular feature: a kind of Dear Abby mailbag, answers provided by the company's ethics officer, . . . that deals with the troublesome issues employees face most often.[33]

Still, written codes and ethics programs do not ensure ethical behavior. Ethics and social responsibility require a total corporate commitment. They must be a component of the overall corporate culture. According to David R. Whitman, chairman of the board of Whirlpool Corporation, "In the final analysis, 'ethical behavior' must be an integral part of the organization, a way of life that is deeply ingrained in the collective corporate body. . . . In any business enterprise, ethical behavior must be a tradition, a way of conducting one's affairs that is passed from generation to generation of employees at all levels of the organization. It is the responsibility of management, starting at the very top, to both set the example by personal conduct and create an environment that not only encourages and rewards ethical behavior, but which also makes anything less totally unacceptable."[34]

The future holds many challenges and opportunities for marketing managers as they move into the new millennium. Technological advances in every area, from telecommunications, information technology, and the Internet to health care and entertainment, provide abundant marketing opportunities. However, forces in the socioeconomic, cultural, and natural environments increase the limits under which marketing can be carried out. Companies that are able to create new customer value in a socially responsible way will have a world to conquer.

STOP Rest Stop: Reviewing the Concepts

Well—here you are at the end of your introductory marketing travels! In this chapter, we've closed with many important concepts involving marketing's sweeping impact on individual consumers, other businesses, and society as a whole. You learned that responsible marketers discover what consumers want and respond with the right products, priced to give good value to buyers and profit to the producer. A marketing system should sense, serve, and satisfy consumer needs and improve the quality of consumers' lives. In working to meet consumer needs, marketers may take some actions that are not to everyone's liking or benefit. Marketing managers should be aware of the main *criticisms of marketing*.

1. Identify the major social criticisms of marketing.

Marketing's *impact on individual consumer welfare* has been criticized for its high prices, deceptive practices, high-pressure selling, shoddy or unsafe products, planned obsolescence, and poor service to disadvantaged consumers. Marketing's *impact on society* has been criticized for creating false wants and too much materialism, too few social goods, cultural pollution, and too much political power. Critics have also criticized marketing's *impact on other businesses* for harming competitors and reducing competition through acquisitions, practices that create barriers to entry, and unfair competitive marketing practices.

2. Define *consumerism* and *environmentalism* and explain how they affect marketing strategies.

Concerns about the marketing system have led to *citizen action movements*. *Consumerism* is an organized social movement intended to strengthen the rights and power of consumers relative to sellers. Alert marketers view it as an opportunity to serve consumers better by providing more consumer information, education, and protection. *Environmentalism* is an organized social movement seeking to minimize the harm done to the environment and quality of life by marketing practices. The first wave of modern environmentalism was driven by environmental groups and concerned consumers, whereas the second wave was driven by government, which passed laws and regulations governing industrial practices impacting the environment. Moving into the twenty-first century,

the first two environmentalism waves are merging into a third and stronger wave in which companies are accepting responsibility for doing no environmental harm. Companies now are adopting policies of *environmental sustainability*—developing strategies that both sustain the environment and produce profits for the company.

3. Describe the principles of socially responsible marketing.

Many companies originally opposed these social movements and laws, but most of them now recognize a need for positive consumer information, education, and protection. Some companies have followed a policy of *enlightened marketing*, which holds that a company's marketing should support the best long-run performance of the marketing system. Enlightened marketing consists of five principles: *consumer-oriented marketing, innovative marketing, value marketing, sense-of-mission marketing,* and *societal marketing.*

4. Explain the role of ethics in marketing.

Increasingly, companies are responding to the need to provide company policies and guidelines to help their managers deal with questions of *marketing ethics*. Of course even the best guidelines cannot resolve all the difficult ethical decisions that individuals and firms must make. But there are some principles that marketers can choose among. One principle states that such issues should be decided by the free market and legal system. A second, and more enlightened, principle puts responsibility not in the system but in the hands of individual companies and managers. Each firm and marketing manager must work out a philosophy of socially responsible and ethical behavior. Under the societal marketing concept, managers must look beyond what is legal and allowable and develop standards based on personal integrity, corporate conscience, and long-term consumer welfare.

Because business standards and practices vary from country to country, the issue of ethics poses special challenges for international marketers. The growing consensus among today's marketers is that it is important to make a commitment to a common set of shared standards worldwide.

Navigating the Key Terms

For a detailed analysis of the meaning and importance of each of the following key terms, visit our Web page at **www.prenhall.com/kotler**.

Consumerism
Consumer-oriented marketing

Deficient products
Desirable products
Enlightened marketing
Environmentalism
Environmental sustainability
Innovative marketing
Pleasing products

Salutary products
Sense-of-mission marketing
Societal marketing
Value marketing

Travel Log

The following concept checks and discussion questions will help you to keep track of and apply the concepts you've studied in this chapter.

Concept Checks

Fill in the blanks, then look for the correct answers.

1. Consumers, consumer advocates, government agencies, and other critics have accused marketing of harming consumers through high prices, deceptive practices, _____ , _____ , _____ , and poor service to disadvantaged consumers.

2. Many critics charge that the American marketing system causes prices to be higher than they would be under more "sensible" systems. Three factors contribute to the high price perception: _____ , _____ , and _____.

3. The _____ Act gave the Federal Trade Commission (FTC) the power to regulate "unfair or deceptive acts or practices."

4. Critics have charged that some producers follow a program of _____ , causing their products to become obsolete before they actually should need replacement.

5. Common criticisms against modern advertising practice includes indictments that advertising has, creates, or contributes to: _____ , _____ , _____ , and too much political power.

6. _____ is an organized movement of citizens and government agencies to improve the rights and power of buyers in relation to sellers.

7. Traditional *buyer's rights* include: the right to not buy a product that is offered for sale; the right to expect _____ ; the right to expect _____.

8. _____ is an organized movement of concerned citizens, businesses, and government agencies to protect and improve people's living environment.

9. The environmental sustainability grid consists of four cells: new environmental technology, _____, _____, and _____.

10. Enlightened marketing consists of five principles: consumer-oriented marketing, _____, _____, _____, and societal marketing.

11. _____ marketing means that the company should define its mission in broad social terms rather than narrow product terms.

12. Products can be classified according to their degree of immediate consumer satisfaction and long-run consumer benefit. _____ products such as seat belts and air bags have low appeal but benefit consumers in the long run.

Concept Checks Answers: 1. high-pressure selling, shoddy or unsafe products, planned obsolescence; 2. high costs of distribution, high advertising and promotion costs, excessive markups; 3. Wheeler-Lea; 4. planned obsolescence; 5. false wants and too much materialism, too few social goods, cultural pollution; 6. Consumerism; 7. the product to be safe; the product to perform as claimed; 8. Environmentalism; 9. pollution prevention, sustainability vision, product stewardship; 10. innovative marketing, value marketing, sense-of-mission marketing; 11. Sense-of-mission; 12. salutary.

Discussing the Issues

1. You have been invited to appear along with an economist on a panel assessing marketing practices in the soft-drink beverage industry. You are somewhat surprised when the economist opens the discussion with a long list of criticisms, especially focusing on unnecessarily high marketing costs and deceptive promotional practices. Abandoning your prepared comments, you feel the need to defend marketing in general and in the beverage industry in particular. How would you respond to the economist's attack?

2. Comment on the state of consumers' rights on the Internet and in e-commerce. Design a "Bill of Rights" that would protect consumers while they shop for products and services on the Internet. Consider such issues as government regulation, ease and convenience of use, solicitation, privacy, and cost-efficient commerce.

3. Considering the comments made about Ben & Jerry's Ice Cream in the introduction to the chapter, comment on how a modern firm can establish and implement a strategy of environmental sustainability. Using a corporate example of your own choosing, match your example to Figure 16-1. How would your organization pay for such a program?

4. Compare the marketing concept with the principle of societal marketing. Should all marketers adopt the societal marketing concept? Why or why not?

5. You are the marketing manager for a small kitchen appliance firm. While conducting field tests, you discover a design flaw in one of your most popular appliances that could potentially be harmful to a small number of customers. However, a product recall would likely bankrupt your company and cause all of the employees (including yourself) to lose their jobs. What would you do? Explain.

Mastering Marketing

After examining the marketing strategies and practices of CanGo, evaluate those strategies and practices against the ethical guidelines proposed by the American Marketing Association in Table 16-2. Comment on strategies or practices that seem to be out-of-alignment. How would you remedy the situation(s)?

Traveling the Net

Point of Interest: Marketing and the Law

As business and marketing become more complicated, judging what is fair and honest becomes more difficult for consumer and marketer alike. In some industries and areas of practice, rules and regulations governing marketing are reasonably well established and understood. However, this is not the case with respect to marketing on the Internet, where there appears to be little or no established regulation. The wide-open spaces of the Internet have been characterized as the "old West" of the 1990s, where self-rule seems to abound. This will all change, but when and to what extent remains uncertain. However, understanding current laws and regulations pertaining to Internet practices, and anticipating future regulatory issues and actions, are extremely important for today's modern marketing manager. Take a look at the following Web sites: (a) Federal Trade Commission (www.ftc.gov), (b) Federal Communications Commission (www.fcc.gov), (c) FedWorld Information Network (www.fedworld.gov), (d) Consumer Information Center (www.pueblo.gsa.gov), and (e) National Archives and Records Administration (www.nara.gov).

For Discussion

1. How easy is it to find information about laws and regulations relating to marketing on the Internet? (a) If you were an entrepreneur wishing to set up a Web marketing site, where could you go to find out what laws govern what you could put on your Web site? (b) Based on your visits to the preceding sites, give illustrations of things you could not do on your Web site. (c) Describe the problems you encountered during your search for information.

2. Find at least one other Web site that provides information useful for establishing a Web site. Explain the site to your class.

3. The Internet offers consumers great opportunities but also potential difficulties, frustrations, and dangers. Offsetting its wonders, the World Wide Web is flooded with less-desirable elements such as spam

mail (unsolicited and often unwanted e-mail distributed indiscriminately in bulk), pornography, and unscrupulous offers and schemes. As a marketing manager of a firm that sells via the Internet, you want to interact with your consumers in a positive and uncluttered environment. (a) What organizations should be involved in regulating Internet usage and commerce? (b) What types of regulations would you propose? (c) What difficulties do you see in attempting to implement such regulations?

Application Thinking

The "greening of America" has much more to do with lifestyles than with forestry. Customers adopting a "green" lifestyle demand products and services that are more environmentally responsible. As consumers turn greener, companies respond with environmentally responsible products and programs. McDonald's, Wal-Mart, and Procter & Gamble are just a few of the companies that now cater to a more "green" way of consuming. See the "Community" section of the McDonald's Web site (www.mcdonalds.com) and the Internet Green Marketplace Web site (www.envirolink.org). Assume that you are a marketing manager for Crayola Crayons (www.crayola.com) and formulate a "green policy" that will make your product both environmentally responsible and competitive. As you formulate this policy, consider the product itself, packaging, distribution, promotion, and merchandising with distributors.

 MAP—Marketing Applications

MAP Stop 16

Are you fed up with products and services that do not work in the promised way? What can you do about it? Will complaining do any good? If you were to complain, to whom would you complain? You could go straight to a store manager or to the offending company to air your gripes. However, you may find that you are just one consumer trying to take on the "establishment." Now, a new day has dawned for the disgruntled consumer. The Internet is changing the way consumers can complain. Because of the Internet, your complaint is joined by thousands of others. Many, many consumers now have the chance to see your complaint via chat rooms, Web boards, and complaint Web sites. When thousands of people see something wrong, that something often gets fixed. Visit the following Web sites: **www.planetfeedback .com; www.ecomplaint.com; and, www.bbbonline .org.**

Thinking Like a Marketing Manager

1. As a consumer, think about problems you have had in the past with products or services. Make a complaint online to one of the Web sites mentioned.
2. What response did you receive to your complaint? Did anyone contact you? Did you get further information? Did you find others that had a similar complaint?
3. Critique the future of complaint Web sites. Will these sites effectively police the Internet? Are these sites a good alternative to federal or state regulation?
4. How can complaint Web sites be misused and/or harm honest merchants? Find one example in which you think this has happened.
5. Assume that you are the marketing manager for a newly established Internet company. Design a complaint policy that will ensure quick response, accuracy of complaint reporting, accountability, fairness, and genuine concern for the consumer. How would you promote this policy?

Marketing Arithmetic

One aspect of marketing not discussed within the text is marketing arithmetic. The calculation of sales, costs, and certain ratios is important for many marketing decisions. This appendix describes three major areas of marketing arithmetic: the *operating statement, analytic ratios,* and *markups and markdowns.*

Operating Statement

The operating statement and the balance sheet are the two main financial statements used by companies. The **balance sheet** shows the assets, liabilities, and net worth of a company at a given time. The **operating statement** (also called **profit-and-loss statement** or **income statement**) is the more important of the two for marketing information. It shows company sales, cost of goods sold, and expenses during a specified time period. By comparing the operating statement from one time period to the next, the firm can spot favorable or unfavorable trends and take appropriate action.

Table A1-1 shows the 2001 operating statement for Dale Parsons Men's Wear, a specialty store in the Midwest. This statement is for a retailer; the operating statement for a manufacturer would be somewhat different. Specifically, the section on purchases within the "cost of goods sold" area would be replaced by "cost of goods manufactured."

The outline of the operating statement follows a logical series of steps to arrive at the firm's $25,000 net profit figure:

Net sales	$300,000
Cost of goods sold	−175,000
Gross margin	$125,000
Expenses	−100,000
Net profit	$25,000

The first part details the amount that Parsons received for the goods sold during the year. The sales figures consist of three items: *gross sales, returns and allowances,* and *net sales.* **Gross sales** is the total amount charged to customers during the year for merchandise purchased in Parsons's store. As expected, some customers returned merchandise because of damage or a change of mind. If the customer gets a full refund or full credit on another purchase, we call this a *return.* Or the customer may decide to keep the item if Parsons will reduce the price. This is called an *allowance.* By subtracting returns and allowances from gross sales, we arrive at net sales—what Parsons earned in revenue from a year of selling merchandise:

Gross sales	$325,000
Returns and allowances	−25,000
Net sales	$300,000

The second major part of the operating statement calculates the amount of sales revenue Dale Parsons retains after paying the costs of the merchandise. We start with the inventory in the store at the beginning of the year. During the year, Parsons bought $165,000 worth of suits, slacks, shirts, ties, jeans, and other goods. Suppliers gave the store discounts totaling $15,000, so that net purchases were $150,000. Because the store is located away from regular shipping routes, Parsons had to pay an additional $10,000 to get the products delivered, giving the firm a net cost of $160,000. Adding the beginning inventory, the cost of goods available for sale amounted to $220,000. The $45,000 ending inventory of clothes in the store on December 31 is then subtracted to come up with the $175,000 **cost of goods sold.** Here again we have followed a logical series of steps to figure out the cost of goods sold:

Amount Parsons started with (beginning inventory)	$ 60,000
Net amount purchased	+150,000
Any added costs to obtain these purchases	+10,000
Total cost of goods Parsons had available for sale during year	$220,000
Amount Parsons had left over (ending inventory)	−45,000
Cost of goods actually sold	$175,000

The difference between what Parsons paid for the merchandise ($175,000) and what he sold it for ($300,000) is called the **gross margin** ($125,000).

In order to show the profit Parsons "cleared" at the end of the year, we must subtract from the gross margin the *expenses* incurred while doing business. *Selling expenses* included two sales employees, local newspaper and radio advertising, and the cost of delivering merchandise to customers after alterations. Selling expenses totaled $50,000 for the year. *Administrative expenses* included the salary for an office manager, office supplies such as stationery and business cards, and miscellaneous expenses including an administrative audit conducted by an outside consultant. Administrative expenses totaled $30,000 in 2001. Finally, the general expenses of rent, utilities, insurance, and

Table A1-1   Operating Statement: Dale Parsons Men's Wear Year Ending December 31, 2001

Gross Sales			$325,000
Less: Sales returns and allowances			25,000
Net sales			$300,000
Cost of goods sold			
Beginning inventory, January 1, at cost		$ 60,000	
Gross purchases	$165,000		
Less: Purchase discounts	15,000		
Net Purchases	$150,000		
Plus: Freight-in	10,000		
Net cost of delivered purchases		$160,000	
Cost of goods available for sale		$220,000	
Less: Ending inventory, December 31, at cost		$ 45,000	
Cost of goods sold			$175,000
Gross margin			$125,000
Expenses			
Selling expenses			
Sales, salaries, and commissions	$ 40,000		
Advertising	5,000		
Delivery	5,000		
Total selling expenses		$ 50,000	
Administrative expenses			
Office salaries	$ 20,000		
Office supplies	5,000		
Miscellaneous (outside consultant)	5,000		
Total administrative expenses		$ 30,000	
General expenses			
Rent	$ 10,000		
Heat, light, telephone	5,000		
Miscellaneous (insurance, depreciation)	5,000		
Total general expenses		$ 20,000	
Total expenses			$100,000
Net profit			$ 25,000

depreciation came to $20,000. Total expenses were therefore $100,000 for the year. By subtracting expenses ($100,000) from the gross margin ($125,000), we arrive at the net profit of $25,000 for Parsons during 2001.

Analytic Ratios

The operating statement provides the figures needed to compute some crucial ratios. Typically these ratios are called **operating ratios**—the ratio of selected operating statement items to net sales. They let marketers compare the firm's performance in one year to that in previous years (or with industry standards and competitors in the same year). The most commonly used operating ratios are the *gross margin percentage*, the *net profit percentage*, the *operating expense percentage*, and the *returns and allowances percentage*.

Another useful ratio is the *stockturn rate* (also called *inventory turnover rate*). The stockturn rate is the number of

Ratio	Formula	Computation From Table A1-1
Gross margin percentage	$= \dfrac{\text{gross margin}}{\text{net sales}}$	$= \dfrac{\$125,000}{\$300,000} = 42\%$
Net profit percentage	$= \dfrac{\text{net profit}}{\text{net sales}}$	$= \dfrac{\$25,000}{\$300,000} = 8\%$

Ratio		Formula		Computation From Table A1-1	
Operating expense percentage	=	$\dfrac{\text{total expenses}}{\text{net sales}}$	=	$\dfrac{\$100,000}{\$300,000}$	= 33%
Returns and allowances percentage	=	$\dfrac{\text{returns and allowances}}{\text{net sales}}$	=	$\dfrac{\$25,000}{\$300,000}$	= 8%

times an inventory turns over or is sold during a specified time period (often one year). It may be computed on a cost, selling price, or units basis. Thus the formula can be:

$$\text{Stockturn rate} = \frac{\text{cost of goods sold}}{\text{average inventory at cost}}$$

or

$$\text{Stockturn rate} = \frac{\text{selling price of goods sold}}{\text{average selling price of inventory}}$$

or

$$\text{Stockturn rate} = \frac{\text{sales in units}}{\text{average inventory in units}}$$

We will use the first formula to calculate the stockturn rate for Dale Parsons Men's Wear:

$$\frac{\$175,000}{(\$60,000 + \$45,000)/2} = \frac{\$175,000}{\$52,500} = 3.3$$

That is, Parsons's inventory turned over 3.3 times in 2001. Normally, the higher the stockturn rate, the higher the management efficiency and company profitability.

Return on investment (ROI) is frequently used to measure managerial effectiveness. It uses figures from the firm's operating statement and balance sheet. A commonly used formula for computing ROI is:

$$\text{ROI} = \frac{\text{net profit}}{\text{sales}} \times \frac{\text{sales}}{\text{investment}}$$

You may have two questions about this formula: Why use a two-step process when ROI could be computed simply as net profit divided by investment? And what exactly is "investment"?

To answer these questions, let's look at how each component of the formula can affect the ROI. Suppose Dale Parsons Men's Wear has a total investment of $150,000. Then ROI can be computed as follows:

$$\text{ROI} = \frac{\$25,000(\text{net profit})}{\$300,000(\text{sales})} \times \frac{\$300,000(\text{sales})}{\$150,000(\text{investment})}$$
$$= 8.3\% \times 2 = 16.6\%$$

Now suppose that Parsons had worked to increase his share of market. He could have had the same ROI if his sales had doubled while dollar profit and investment stayed the same (accepting a lower profit ratio to get higher turnover and market share):

$$\text{ROI} = \frac{\$25,000(\text{net profit})}{\$600,000(\text{sales})} \times \frac{\$600,000(\text{sales})}{\$150,000(\text{investment})}$$
$$= 4.16\% \times 4 = 16.6\%$$

Parsons might have increased its ROI by increasing net profit through more cost cutting and more efficient marketing:

$$\text{ROI} = \frac{\$50,000(\text{net profit})}{\$300,000(\text{sales})} \times \frac{\$300,000(\text{sales})}{\$150,000(\text{investment})}$$
$$= 16.6\% \times 2 = 33.2\%$$

Another way to increase ROI is to find some way to get the same levels of sales and profits while decreasing investment (perhaps by cutting the size of Parsons's average inventory):

$$\text{ROI} = \frac{\$25,000(\text{net profit})}{\$300,000(\text{sales})} \times \frac{\$300,000(\text{sales})}{\$75,000(\text{investment})}$$
$$= 8.3\% \times 4 = 33.2\%$$

What is "investment" in the ROI formula? *Investment* is often defined as the total assets of the firm. But many analysts now use other measures of return to assess performance. These measures include *return on net assets (RONA)*, *return on stockholders' equity (ROE)*, or *return on assets managed (ROAM)*. Because investment is measured at a point in time, we usually compute ROI as the average investment between two time periods (say, January 1 and December 31 of the same year). We can also compute ROI as an "internal rate of return" by using discounted cash flow analysis (see any finance textbook for more on this technique). The objective in using any of these measures is to determine how well the company has been using its resources. As inflation, competitive pressures, and cost of capital increase, such measures become increasingly important indicators of marketing and company performance.

Markups and Markdowns

Retailers and wholesalers must understand the concepts of **markups** and **markdowns.** They must make a profit to stay in business, and the markup percentage affects profits. Markups and markdowns are expressed as percentages.

There are two different ways to compute markups—on *cost* or on *selling price:*

$$\text{Markup percentage on cost} = \frac{\text{dollar markup}}{\text{cost}}$$

$$\text{Markup percentage on selling price} = \frac{\text{dollar markup}}{\text{selling price}}$$

Dale Parsons must decide which formula to use. If Parsons bought shirts for $15 and wanted to mark them up $10 to a price of $25, his markup percentage on cost would be $10/$15 = 67.7%. If Parsons based markup on selling price, the percentage would be $10/$25 = 40%. In figuring markup percentage, most retailers use the selling price rather than the cost.

Suppose Parsons knew his cost ($12) and desired markup on price (25%) for a man's tie, and wanted to compute the selling price. The formula is:

$$\text{Selling price} = \frac{\text{cost}}{1 - \text{markup}}$$

$$\text{Selling price} = \frac{\$12}{.75} = \$16$$

As a product moves through the channel of distribution, each channel member adds a markup before selling the product to the next member. This "markup chain" is shown for a suit purchased by a Parsons customer for $200:

		$ Amount	% of Selling Price
Manufacturer	Cost	$108	90%
	Markup	12	10
	Selling price	120	100
Wholesaler	Cost	120	80
	Markup	30	20
	Selling price	150	100
Retailer	Cost	150	75
	Markup	50	25
	Selling price	200	100

The retailer whose markup is 25 percent does not necessarily enjoy more profit than a manufacturer whose markup is 10 percent. Profit also depends on how many items with that profit margin can be sold (stockturn rate) and on operating efficiency (expenses).

Sometimes a retailer wants to convert markups based on selling price to markups based on cost, and vice versa. The formulas are:

$$\text{Markup percentage on selling price} =$$
$$\frac{\text{markup percentage on cost}}{100\% + \text{markup percentage on selling cost}}$$

$$\text{Markup percentage on cost} =$$
$$\frac{\text{markup percentage on selling price}}{100\% - \text{markup percentage on selling price}}$$

Suppose Parsons found that his competitor was using a markup of 30 percent based on cost and wanted to know what this would be as a percentage of selling price. The calculation would be:

$$\frac{30\%}{100\% + 30\%} = \frac{30\%}{130\%} = 23\%$$

Because Parsons was using a 25 percent markup on the selling price for suits, he felt that his markup was suitable compared with that of the competitor.

Near the end of the summer Parsons still had an inventory of summer slacks in stock. Therefore, he decided to use a *markdown,* a reduction from the original selling price. Before the summer he had purchased 20 pairs at $10 each, and he had since sold 10 pairs at $20 each. He marked down the other pairs to $15 and sold 5 pairs. We compute his *markdown ratio* as follows:

$$\text{Markdown percentage} = \frac{\text{dollar markdown}}{\text{total net sales in dollars}}$$

The dollar markdown is $25 (5 pairs at $5 each) and total net sales are $275 (10 pairs at $20 + 5 pairs at $15). The ratio, then, is $25/$275 = 9%.

Larger retailers usually compute markdown ratios for each department rather than for individual items. The ratios provide a measure of relative marketing performance for each department and can be calculated and compared over time. Markdown ratios can also be used to compare the performance of different buyers and salespeople in a store's various departments.

Key Terms

Balance sheet	Markdown	Operating statement
Cost of goods sold	Markup	(or profit-and-loss statement
Gross margin	Operating ratios	or income statement)
Gross sales		Return on investment (ROI)

Careers in Marketing

Now that you have completed this course in marketing, you have a good idea of what the field entails. You may have decided you want to pursue a marketing career because it offers constant challenge, stimulating problems, the opportunity to work with people, and excellent advancement opportunities. But you still may not know which part of marketing best suits you—marketing is a very broad field offering a wide variety of career options. This appendix helps you discover what types of marketing jobs best match your special skills and interests, shows you how to conduct the kind of job search that will get you the position you want in the company of your choice, describes marketing career paths open to you, and suggests other information resources.

Marketing Careers Today

The field of marketing is booming in the twenty-first century, with nearly a third of all Americans now employed in marketing-related positions. Marketing salaries may vary by company, position, and region, and salary figures change constantly. In general, entry-level marketing salaries usually are only slightly below those for engineering and chemistry but equal or exceed starting salaries in economics, finance, accounting, general business, and the liberal arts. Moreover, if you succeed in an entry-level marketing position, it's likely that you will be promoted quickly to higher levels of responsibility and salary. In addition, because of the consumer and product knowledge you will gain in these jobs, marketing positions provide excellent training for the highest levels in an organization. A recent study by an executive recruiting firm found that more top executives come out of marketing than any other functional group.

Overall Marketing Facts and Trends

In conducting your job search, consider the following facts and trends that are changing the world of marketing.

Technology: Technology is changing the way marketers work. For example, price coding allows instantaneous retail inventorying. Software for marketing training, forecasting, and other functions is changing the ways we market. And the Internet is creating new jobs and new recruiting rules. Consider the explosive growth in new media marketing. Whereas advertising firms have traditionally recruited "generalists" in account management, "generalist" has now taken on a whole new meaning — advertising account executives must now have both broad and specialized knowledge.

Diversity: The number of women and minorities in marketing continues to rise. Traditionally, women were mainly in retailing. Now, women and minorities are rapidly moving into all industries. They also are rising rapidly into marketing management. For example, women now outnumber men by nearly two to one as advertising account executives. As marketing becomes more global, the need for diversity in marketing positions will continue to increase, opening new opportunities.

Global: Companies such as Coca-Cola, McDonald's, IBM, MTV, and Procter & Gamble have become multinational, with offices and manufacturing operations in hundreds of countries. Indeed, such companies often make more profit from sales outside the United States than from within. And it's not just the big companies that are involved in international marketing. Organizations of all sizes have moved into the global arena. Many new marketing opportunities and careers will be directly linked to the expanding global marketplace. The globalization of business also means that you will need more cultural, language, and people skills in the marketing world of the twenty-first century.

Nonprofit organizations: Increasingly, colleges, arts organizations, libraries, hospitals, and other nonprofit organizations are recognizing the need for effectively marketing their "products" and services to various publics. This awareness has led to new marketing positions—with these organizations hiring their own marketing directors and marketing vice presidents or using outside marketing specialists.

Looking for a Job in Today's Marketing World

To choose and find the right job, you will need to apply the marketing skills you've learned in this course, especially marketing analysis and planning. Follow these nine steps for marketing yourself: (1) Conduct a self-assessment and seek career counseling; (2) examine job descriptions; (3) develop job search objectives; (4) explore the job market and assess opportunities; (5) develop search strategies; (6) prepare résumés; (7) write cover letter and assemble supporting documents; (8) interview for jobs; and (9) follow up.

Conduct a Self-Assessment and Seek Career Counseling

If you're having difficulty deciding what kind of marketing position is the best fit for you, start out by doing some self-testing or get some career counseling. Self-assessments require that you honestly and thoroughly evaluate your interests, strengths, and weaknesses. What do you do well (your best and favorite skills) and not so well? What are your favorite interests? What are your career goals? What makes you stand out from other job seekers? The answers to such questions may suggest which marketing careers you should seek or avoid. For help in making an effective self-assessment, look at the following books in your local bookstore: Richard Bolles, *What Color Is Your Parachute?* (Berkeley, CA: Ten Speed Press, published annually); Barbara Sher, *I Could Do Anything If I Only Knew What It Was: How to Discover What You Really Want and How to Get It* (New York: Bantam/Doubleday/Dell, 1995); and Nicholas Lore, *The Pathfinder: How to Choose or Change Your Career for a Lifetime of Satisfaction and Success* (New York: Simon & Schuster, 1998).

For help in finding a career counselor to guide you in making a career assessment, Richard Bolles's, *What Color Is Your Parachute?* contains a useful state-by-state sampling. (Some counselors can help you in your actual job search, too.) You can also consult the career counseling, testing, and placement services at your college or university.

Career Counseling on the Internet   Today an increasing number of colleges, universities, and commercial career counselors offer career guidance on the Internet. In general, college and university sites are by far the best. But one useful commercial site you might look at is JobSmart (www.jobsmart.org/tools/résumé/index.htm).

Examine Job Descriptions

After you have identified your skills, interests, and desires, you need to see which marketing positions are the best match for them. Two U.S. Labor Department publications in your local library, the *Occupation Outlook Handbook* and the *Dictionary of Occupational Titles,* describe the duties involved in various occupations, the specific training and education needed, the availability of jobs in each field, possibilities for advancement, and probable earnings.

Your initial career shopping list should be broad and flexible. Look for different ways to achieve your objectives. For example, if you want a career in marketing management, consider the public as well as the private sector, and regional as well as national firms. Be open initially to exploring many options, then focus on specific industries and jobs, listing your basic goals as a way to guide your choices. Your list might include "a job in a start-up company, near a big city, on the West Coast, doing new product planning, with a computer software firm."

Explore the Job Market and Assess Opportunities

At this stage, you need to look at the market and see what positions are actually available. You do not have to do this alone. Any of the following may assist you.

College Placement Centers   Your college placement center is an excellent place to start. Besides posting specific job openings, placement centers have the current edition of the *College Placement Annual,* which lists job openings in hundreds of companies seeking college graduates for entry-level positions, as well as openings for people with experience or advanced degrees. More and more, schools are also going on the Internet. For example, the Web site of the career center of Emory University in Atlanta, Georgia, has a list of career links (www.emory.edu/CAREER/Main/CareerLinks.html).

In addition, find out everything you can about the companies that interest you by consulting business magazines, annual reports, business reference books, faculty, career counselors, and others. Try to analyze the industry's and the company's future growth and profit potential, advancement opportunities, salary levels, entry positions, travel time, and other factors of significance to you.

Job Fairs   College placement offices often work with corporate recruiters to organize on-campus job fairs.

You might also use the Internet to check on upcoming career fairs in your region. For example, visit www.job web.com/employ/fairs/public_fairs.cfm.

Networking and the Yellow Pages   Networking, or asking for job leads from friends, family, people in your community, and career centers, is one of the best ways to find a marketing job. An estimated 33 percent of jobs are found through networking. The idea is to spread your net wide, contacting anybody and everybody.

The phone book's yellow pages are another effective way to job search. Check out employers in your field of interest in whatever region you want to work, then call and ask if they are hiring for the position of your choice.

Summer Jobs and Internships   In some parts of the country one in seven students gets a job where he or she interned. On the Internet, many sites have separate internship areas. For examples, look at Wetfeet (www.wetfeet.internshipprograms.com), the Monster Board (www.monster.com), and Idealist (www.idealist.org). If you know a company for which you wish to work, go to that company's corporate Web site, enter the personnel area, and check for internships. If there are none listed, try e-mailing the personnel department, asking if internships are offered.

The Internet   A constantly increasing number of sites on the Internet deal with job hunting. You can also use the Internet to make contacts with people who can help you gain information on companies and research companies that interest you. The Riley Guide offers a great introduction to what jobs are available (www.rileyguide.com). Other helpful sites are Employment Opportunities for People with Disabilities (www.dol.gov/dol/odep/public/joblinks_2.htm) and HireDiversity (www.hirediversity.com/), which contains information on opportunities for African Americans, Hispanic Americans, Asian Americans, and Native Americans.

Most companies have their own Web sites upon which they post job listings. This may be helpful if you have a specific and fairly limited number of companies that you are keeping your eye on for job opportunities. But if this is not the case, remember that to find out what interesting marketing jobs the companies themselves are posting, you may have to visit hundreds of corporate sites.

Develop Search Strategies

Once you've decided which companies you are interested in, you need to contact them. One of the best ways is through on-campus interviews. But not every company you are interested in will visit your school. In such instances, you can write (this includes e-mail) or phone the company directly or ask marketing professors or school alumni for contacts.

Prepare Résumés

A résumé is a concise yet comprehensive written summary of your qualifications, including your academic, personal, and professional achievements, that showcases why you are the best candidate for the job. Many organizations use résumés to decide which candidates to interview.

In preparing your résumé, remember that all information on it must be accurate and complete. Résumés typically begin with the applicant's full name, telephone and fax numbers, and traditional mail and e-mail addresses. A simple and direct statement of career objectives generally appears next, followed by work history and academic data (including awards and internships), and then by personal activities and experiences applicable to the job sought. The résumé usually ends with a list of references the employer may contact. If your work or internship experience is limited, nonexistent, or irrelevant, then it is a good idea to emphasize your academic and nonacademic achievements, showing skills related to those required for excellent job performance.

There are three types of résumés. *Chronological* résumés, which emphasize career growth, are organized in reverse chronological order, starting with your most recent job. They focus on job titles within organizations, describing the responsibilities required for each job. *Functional* résumés focus less on job titles and work history and more on assets and achievements. This format works best if your job history is scanty or discontinuous. *Mixed,* or *combined,* résumés take from each of the other two formats. First, the skills used for a specific job are listed, then the job title is stated. This format works best for applicants whose past jobs are in other fields or seemingly unrelated to the position.

Your local bookstore or library has many books that can assist you in developing your résumé. Popular guides are Tom Jackson, with Ellen Jackson, *The New Perfect Résumé* (Garden City, NY: Anchor Press/Doubleday, revised, 1996); Yana Parker, *The Damn Good Résumé Guide* (Berkeley, CA: Ten Speed Press, 1996); and Arthur Rosenberg and David Hizer, *The Résumé Handbook* (Adams Media Corporation, 1996). Computer software programs such as *WinWay Résumé,* provides hundreds of sample résumés and ready-to-use phrases while guiding you through the résumé preparation process.

Online Résumés   Today more and more job seekers are posting their résumés on the Internet. Preparing an electronic résumé is somewhat different from preparing a traditional résumé. For example, you need to know the relevant rules about scanning (including that your computer will be unable to scan the attractive fonts you used in your original résumé) and keywords. Moreover, if you decide to post your résumé in a public area such as a Web site, then for security purposes you might not want to include your street or business address or the names of previous employers or references. (This information can be mailed later to employers after you have been contacted by them.) Job Smart (jobsmart.org/tools/resume/index.htm) might assist you in writing your online résumé. In addition, placement centers usually assist you in developing a résumé. (Placement centers can also help with your cover letter and provide job interview workshops.)

After you have written your résumé, you need to post it. The following sites may be good locations to start: Monster.com (www.monster.com) and Yahoo! Résumé Services, a listing narrowed to business and economy companies (www.yahoo.com/Business_and_Economy/Companies/Employment/resume_services/).

Résumé Tips

◆ Communicate your worth to potential employers in a concrete manner, citing examples whenever possible.
◆ Be concise and direct.
◆ Use active verbs to show you are a doer.
◆ Do not skimp on quality or use gimmicks. Spare no expense in presenting a professional résumé.
◆ Have someone critique your work. A single typo can eliminate you from being considered.
◆ Customize your résumé for specific employers. Emphasize your strengths as they pertain to your targeted job.
◆ Keep your résumé compact, usually one page.
◆ Format the text to be attractive, professional, and readable. Avoid too much "design" or gimmicky flourishes.

Write Cover Letter and Assemble Supporting Documents

Cover Letter   You should include a cover letter informing the employer that a résumé is enclosed. But a cover letter does more than this. It also serves to summarize in one or two paragraphs the contents of the résumé and explains why you think you are the right person for the position. The goal is to persuade the employer to look at the more detailed résumé. A typical cover letter is organized as follows: (1) the name and position of the person you are contacting; (2) a statement identifying the position you are applying for, how you heard of the vacancy, and the reasons for your interest; (3) a summary of your qualifications for the job; (4) a description of what follow-ups you intend to make, such as phoning in two weeks to see if the résumé has been received; (5) an expression of gratitude for the opportunity of being a candidate for the job.

Letters of Recommendation and Other Supporting Documents
Letters of recommendation are written references by professors, former and current employers, and others that testify to your character, skills, and abilities. A good reference letter tells why you would be an excellent candidate for the position. In choosing someone to write a letter of recommendation, be confident that the person will give you a good reference. In addition, do not assume the person knows everything about you or the position you are seeking. Rather, provide the person with your résumé and other relevant data. As a courtesy, allow the reference writer at least a month to complete the letter and enclose a stamped, addressed envelope with your materials.

In the packet containing your résumé, cover letter, and letters of recommendation, you may also want to attach other relevant documents that support your candidacy, such as academic transcripts, graphics, portfolios, and samples of writing.

Interview for Jobs
As the old saying goes, "The résumé gets you the interview; the interview gets you the job." The job interview offers you an opportunity to gather more information about the organization, while at the same time allowing the organization to gather more information about you. You'll want to present your best self. The interview process consists of three parts: before the interview, the interview itself, and after the interview. If you successfully pass through these stages, you will be called back for the follow-up interview.

Before the Interview
In preparing for your interview, do the following:

1. Understand that interviewers have diverse styles, including the "chitchat," let's-get-to-know-each-other style; the interrogation style of question after question; and the tough-probing "why, why, why" style, among others. So be ready for anything.
2. With a friend, practice being interviewed and then ask for a critique. Or, videotape yourself in a practice interview so that you can critique your own performance. Your college placement service may also offer "mock" interviews to help you.
3. Prepare at least five good questions whose answers are not easily found in the company literature, such as "What is the future direction of the firm?" "How does the firm differentiate itself from competitors?" "Do you have a new-media division?"
4. Anticipate possible interview questions, such as "Why do you want to work for this company?" or "Why should we hire you?" Prepare solid answers before the interview. Have a clear idea of why you are interested in joining the company and the industry to which it belongs.

5. Avoid back-to-back interviews—they can be exhausting and it is unpredictable how long they will last.
6. Dress conservatively and professionally. Be neat and clean.
7. Arrive 10 minutes early to collect your thoughts and review the major points you intend to cover. Check your name on the interview schedule, noting the name of the interviewer and the room number. Be courteous and polite to office staff.
8. Approach the interview enthusiastically. Let your personality shine through.

During the Interview
During the interview, do the following:

1. Shake hands firmly in greeting the interviewer. Introduce yourself, using the same form of address the interviewer uses. Focus on creating a good initial impression.
2. Keep your poise. Relax, smile when appropriate, be upbeat throughout.
3. Maintain eye contact, good posture, and speak distinctly. Don't clasp your hands or fiddle with jewelry, hair, or clothing. Sit comfortably in your chair. Do not smoke, even if asked.
4. Carry extra copies of your résumé with you. Bring samples of your academic or professional work along.
5. Have your story down pat. Present your selling points. Answer questions directly. Avoid one-word or too-wordy answers.
6. Let the interviewer take the initiative but don't be passive. Find an opportunity to direct the conversation to things about yourself that you want the interviewer to hear.
7. To end on a high note, make your most important point or ask your most pertinent question during the last part of the interview.
8. Don't hesitate to "close." You might say, "I'm very interested in the position, and I have enjoyed this interview."
9. Obtain the interviewer's business card or address and phone number so that you can follow up later.

A tip for acing the interview: Before you open your mouth, find out *what it's like* to be a brand manager, sales representative, market researcher, advertising account executive, or other position for which you're interviewing.

After the Interview
After the interview, do the following:

1. After leaving the interview, record the key points that arose. Be sure to note who is to follow up and when a decision can be expected.
2. Analyze the interview objectively, including the questions asked, the answers to them, your overall interview presentation, and the interviewer's responses to specific points.
3. Immediately send a thank-you letter, mentioning any additional items and your willingness to supply further information.
4. If you do not hear within the specified time, write or call the interviewer to determine your status.

Follow Up

If you are successful, you will be invited to visit the organization. The in-company interview will probably run from several hours to an entire day. The organization will examine your interest, maturity, enthusiasm, assertiveness, logic, and company and functional knowledge. You should ask questions about issues of importance to you. Find out about the working environment, job role, responsibilities, opportunity for advancement, current industrial issues, and the company's personality. The company wants to discover if you are the right person for the job, whereas you want to find out if it is the right job for you. The key is to determine if the right fit exists between you and the company.

Marketing Jobs

This section describes some of the key marketing positions.

Advertising

Advertising is one of today's hottest fields in marketing. In fact, *Money* magazine lists a position in advertising as among the 50 best jobs in America.

Job Descriptions   Key advertising positions include copywriter, art director, production manager, account executive, and media planner/buyer. *Copywriters* write advertising copy and help find the concepts behind the written words and visual images of advertisements. *Art directors,* the other part of the creative team, help translate the copywriters' ideas into dramatic visuals called "layouts." Agency artists develop print layouts, package designs, television layouts (called "storyboards"), corporate logotypes, trademarks, and symbols. *Production managers* are responsible for physically creating ads, in-house or by contracting through outside production houses. *Account development executives* research and understand clients' markets and customers and help develop marketing and advertising strategies to impact them. *Account executives* serve as liaisons between clients and agencies. They coordinate the planning, creation, production, and implementation of an advertising campaign for the account. *Media planners* determine the best mix of television, radio, newspaper, magazine, and other media for the advertising campaign.

Skills Needed, Career Paths, and Typical Salaries
Work in advertising requires strong people skills in order to interact closely with an often difficult and demanding client base. In addition, advertising attracts people with high skills in planning, problem solving, creativity, communication, initiative, leadership, and presentation. Advertising involves working under high levels of stress and pressure created by unrelenting deadlines. Advertisers frequently have to work long hours to meet deadlines for a presentation. But work achievements are very apparent, with the results of creative strategies observed by thousands or even millions of people.

Because they are so sought after, positions in advertising sometimes require an MBA. But there are many jobs open for business, graphics arts, and liberal arts undergraduates. Advertising positions often serve as gateways to higher-level management. Moreover, with large advertising agencies opening offices all over the world, there is the possibility of eventually working on global campaigns.

Starting advertising salaries are relatively low compared to some other marketing jobs because of strong competition for entry-level advertising jobs. You may even want to consider working for free to break in. Compensation will increase quickly as you move into account executive or other management positions. For more facts and figures, see the Web pages of *Advertising Age,* a key ad industry publication (www.adage.com, click on the Job Bank button), and the American Association of Advertising Agencies (www.aaaa.org).

Brand and Product Management

Brand and product managers plan, direct, and control business and marketing efforts for their products. They are involved with research and development, packaging, manufacturing, sales and distribution, advertising, promotion, market research, and business analysis and forecasting.

Job Descriptions   A company's brand management team consists of people in several positions. The *brand manager* guides the development of marketing strategies for a specific brand. The *assistant brand manager* is responsible for certain strategic components of the brand. The *product manager* oversees several brands within a product line or product group. The *product category manager* directs multiple product lines in the product category. The *market analyst* researches the market and provides important strategic information to the project managers. The *project director* is responsible for collecting market information on a marketing or product project. The *research director* oversees the planning, gathering, and analyzing of all organizational research.

Skills Needed, Career Paths, and Typical Salaries
Brand and product management requires high problem-solving, analytical, presentation, communication, and leadership skills, as well as the ability to work well in a team. Product management requires long hours and involves the high pressure of running large projects. In consumer goods companies, the newcomer—who usually needs an MBA—joins a brand team as an assistant and learns the ropes by doing numerical analyses and watching senior brand people. This person eventually heads the team and later moves on to manage a larger brand, then several brands. Many industrial goods companies also have product managers. Product management is one of the best training grounds for future corporate officers. Product management also offers good opportunities to move into international marketing. Product managers command relatively high salaries. Because this job category encourages or requires a master's degree, starting pay tends to be higher than in other marketing categories such as advertising or retailing.

Sales, Sales Management

Sales and sales management opportunities exist in a wide range of profit and nonprofit organizations and in product and service organizations, including financial, insurance, consulting, and government organizations.

Job Descriptions Key jobs include consumer sales, industrial sales, national account manager, service support, sales trainers, sales management, and teleseller. *Consumer sales* involves selling consumer products and services through retailers. *Industrial sales* includes selling products and services to other businesses. *National account managers (NAM)* oversee a few very large accounts. *Service support* personnel support salespeople during and after the sale of a product. *Sales trainers* train new hires and provide refresher training for all sales personnel. *Sales management* includes a sequence of positions ranging from district manager to vice president of sales. The *teleseller* (not to be confused with the home consumer telemarketer) offers service and support to field salespeople.

Salespeople enjoy active professional lives, working outside the office and interacting with others. They manage their own time and activities. Competition for top jobs can be intense. Every sales job is different, but some positions involve extensive travel, long workdays, and working under pressure, which can negatively impact personal life. You can also expect to be transferred more than once between company headquarters and regional offices.

Skills Needed, Career Paths, and Typical Salaries Selling is a people profession in which you will work with people every day, all day long. Besides people skills, sales professionals need sales and communication skills. Most sales positions also require high problem-solving, analytical, presentation, and leadership ability as well as creativity and initiative. Teamwork skills are increasingly important.

Career paths lead from salesperson to district, regional, and higher levels of sales management and, in many cases, to the top management of the firm. Today, most entry-level sales management positions require a college degree. Increasingly, people seeking selling jobs are acquiring sales experience in an internship capacity or from a part-time job before graduating. Although there is a high turnover rate (one in four people leave their jobs in a year), sales positions are great springboards to leadership positions, with more CEOs starting in sales than in any other entry-level position. Possibly this explains why competition for top sales jobs is intense.

Starting base salaries in sales may be moderate, but compensation is often supplemented by significant commission, bonus, or other incentive plans. In addition, many sales jobs include a company car or car allowance. Successful salespeople are among most companies' highest paid employees.

Other Marketing Jobs

Retailing Retailing provides an early opportunity to assume marketing responsibilities. Key jobs include store manager, regional manager, buyer, department manager, and salesperson. *Store managers* direct the management and operation of an individual store. *Regional managers* manage groups of stores across several states and report performance to headquarters. *Buyers* select and buy the merchandise that the store carries. The *department manager* acts as store manager of a department, such as clothing, but on the department level. The *salesperson* sells merchandise to retail customers. Retailing can involve relocation, but generally there is little travel, unless you are a buyer. Retailing requires high people and sales skills because retailers are constantly in contact with customers. Enthusiasm, willingness, and communication skills are very helpful for retailers, too.

Retailers work long hours, but their daily activities are often more structured than some types of marketing positions. Starting salaries in retailing tend to be low, but pay increases as you move into management or some retailing specialty job.

Marketing Research Marketing researchers interact with managers to define problems and identify the information needed to resolve them. They design research projects, prepare questionnaires and samples, analyze data, prepare reports, and present their findings and recommendations to management. They must understand statistics, consumer behavior, psychology, and sociology. A master's degree helps. Career opportunities exist with manufacturers, retailers, some wholesalers, trade and industry associations, marketing research firms, advertising agencies, and governmental and private nonprofit agencies.

New-Product Planning People interested in new-product planning can find opportunities in many types of organizations. They usually need a good background in marketing, marketing research, and sales forecasting; they need organizational skills to motivate and coordinate others; and they may need a technical background. Usually, these people work first in other marketing positions before joining the new-product department.

Marketing Logistics (Physical Distribution)

Marketing logistics, or physical distribution, is a large and dynamic field, with many career opportunities. Major transportation carriers, manufacturers, wholesalers, and retailers all employ logistics specialists. Increasingly, marketing teams include logistics specialists, and marketing managers' career paths include marketing logistics assignments. Coursework in quantitative methods, finance, accounting, and marketing will provide you with the necessary skills for entering the field.

Public Relations Most organizations have a public relations staff to anticipate problems with various publics, handle complaints, deal with media, and build the corporate image. People interested in public relations should be able to speak and write clearly and persuasively, and they should have a background in journalism, communications, or the liberal arts. The challenges in this job are highly varied and very people oriented.

Nonprofit Services   The key jobs in nonprofits include marketing director, director of development, event coordinator, publication specialist, and intern/volunteers. The *marketing director* is in charge of all marketing activities for the organization. The *director of development* organizes, manages, and directs the fund-raising campaigns that keep a nonprofit in existence. An *event coordinator* directs all aspects of fund-raising events, from initial planning through implementation. The *publication specialist* oversees publications designed to promote awareness of the organization. Although typically an unpaid position, the *intern/volunteer* performs various marketing functions, and this work can be an important step to gaining a full-time position. The non-profit sector is typically not for someone who is money driven. Rather, most nonprofits look for people with a strong sense of community spirit and the desire to help others. So starting pay is usually lower than in other marketing fields. However, the bigger the nonprofit, the better your chance of rapidly increasing your income when moving into upper management.

Other Resources

Professional marketing associations and organizations are another source of information about careers. Marketers belong to many such societies. You may want to contact some of the following in your job search:

American Advertising Federation, 1101 Vermont Avenue, NW, Suite 500, Washington, DC 2005. (202) 898-0089 (www.aaf.org)

American Marketing Association, 250 South Wacker Drive, Suite 200, Chicago, IL 60606. (312) 648-0536 (www.ama.org)

Council of Sales Promotion Agencies, 750 Summer Street, Stamford,CT 06901. (203) 325-3911

Market Research Association, 2189 Silas Deane Highway, Suite 5, Rocky Hill, CT 06067. (860) 257-4008 (www.mra-net.org)

National Council of Salesmen's Organization, 389 Fifth Avenue, Room 1010, New York, NY 10016. (718) 835-4591

National Management Association, 2210 Arbor Boulevard, Dayton, OH 45439. (513) 294-0421

National Retail Federation, 701 Pennsylvania Avenue NW, Suite 710, Washington, DC 20004. (202) 783-7971 (www.nrf.com)

Product Development and Management Association, 401 North Michigan Avenue, Chicago, IL 60611. (312) 527-6644 (www.pdma.org)

Public Relations Society of America, 33 Irving Place, Third Floor, New York, NY 10003. (212) 995-2230 (www.prsa.org)

Sales and Marketing Executives International, Statler Office Tower, Number 977, Cleveland, OH 44115. (216) 771-6650 (www.smei.org)

Women Executives in Public Relations, P.O. Box 609, Westport, CT, 06881. (203) 226-4947 (www.wepr.org)

Women in Advertising and Marketing, 4200 Wisconsin Avenue NW, Suite 106–238, Washington, DC 20016. (301) 369-7400 (www.mamdc.org)

Notes

Chapter 1

1. See Stewart Alsop, "I'm Betting on Amazon," *Fortune,* April 30, 2001, p. 48; Robert D. Hof, "Amazon.com: The Wild World of E-Commerce," *Business Week*, December 14, 1998, p. 106; Kathleen Doler, "Interview: Jeff Bezos, Founder and CEO of Amazon.com Inc.," *Upside,* September 1998, pp. 76-80; Susan Stellin, "Internet Companies Learn How to Personalize Service," *New York Times,* August 28, 2000, p. C8; Geoffrey Colvin, "Shaking Hands on the Web," *Fortune,* May 14, 2001, p. 54; "Amazon.com May Link with Wal-Mart," *Chain Store Age,* April 2001, p. 74; and "About Amazon.com," accessed online at www.amazon.com, June 2001.

2. Here are some other definitions: "*Marketing* is the performance of business activities that direct the flow goods and services from producer to consumer or user." "*Marketing* is getting the right goods to the right people at the right place at the time at the right price with the right communication and promotion." "*Marketing* is the creation and of a standard of living." The American Marketing Association offers this definition: "*Marketing* is the process of planning and executing the conception, pricing, promotion, and distributing of ideas, goods, and services to create exchanges that satisfy individual and organizational objectives."

3. Erika Rasmusson, "Marketing More than a Product," *Sales and Marketing Management,* February 2000, p. 99.

4. See B. Joseph Pine II and James Gilmore, "Welcome to the Experience Economy," *Harvard Business Review*, July–August 1998, p. 99; and Jane E. Zarem, *Folio,* "Experience Marketing," Fall 2000, pp. 28–32.

5. See Theodore Levitt's classic article, "Marketing Myopia," *Harvard Business Review,* July–August 1960, pp. 45–56. For more recent discussions, see Dhananjayan Kashyap, "Marketing Myopia Revisited: "A Look through the 'Colored Glass of a Client,'" *Marketing and Research Today,* August 1996, pp. 197–201; Colin Grant, "Theodore Levitt's Marketing Myopia," *Journal of Business Ethics,* February 1999, pp. 397–406; Jeffrey M. O'Brien, "Drums in the Jungle," *MC Technology Marketing Intelligence,* March 1999, pp. 22–30; and Hershell Sarbin, "Overcoming Marketing Myopia," *Folio*, May 2000, pp. 55–56.

6. See Brian O'Reilly, "They've Got Mail!," *Fortune,* February 7, 2000, pp. 101–112.

7. For more on customer satisfaction, see Regina Fazio Marcuna, "Mapping the World of Customer Satisfaction, *Harvard Business Review*, May–June 2000, p. 30; David M. Szymanski, "Customer Satisfaction: A Meta-Analysis of the Empirical Evidence," *Academy of Marketing Science Journal,* Winter 2001, pp. 16–35; and Vikas Mittal and Wagner Kamakura, "Satisfaction, Repurchase Intent, and Repurchase Behavior: Investigating the Moderating Effect of Customer Characteristics," *Journal of Marketing Research,* February 2001, pp. 131–142.

8. For more on this measure and for recent customer satisfaction scores, see Claes Fornell, Michael D. Johnson, Eugene W. Anderson, Jaesung Cha, and Barbara Everitt Bryant, "The American Customer Satisfaction Index: Nature, Purpose, and Findings," *Journal of Marketing,* October 1996, pp. 7–18; and Eugene W. Anderson and Claes Fornell, "Foundations of the American Customer Satisfaction Index," *Total Quality Management,* September 2000, pp. S869–S882. Cited facts accessed online at the ACSI Web site at www.bus.umich.edu/research/nqrc/acsi.html, June 2001.

9. Lois Therrien, "Motorola and NEC: Going for Glory," *Business Week*, special issue on quality, 1991, pp. 60–61. For more on quality, see Roland T. Rust, Anthony J. Zahorik, and Timothy L. Keiningham, "Return on Quality (ROQ): Making Service Quality Financially Accountable," *Journal of Marketing*, April 1995, pp. 58–70; John Dalrymple and Eileen Drew, "Quality: On the Threshold or the Brink?" *Total Quality Management,* July 2000, pp. S697–S703; and Thomas J. Douglas and William Q. Judge, "Total Quality Management Implementation and Competitive Advantage," *Academy of Management Journal,* February 2001, pp. 158–169.

10. Accessed online at www.asq.org, June 2001.

11. Edwin McDowell, "Ritz-Carlton's Keys to Good Service," *New York Times*, March 31, 1993, p. 1; Don Peppers, "Digitizing Desire," *Forbes*, April 10, 1995, p. 76; Ginger Conlon, "True Romance," *Sales and Marketing Management,* May 1996, pp. 85–89; and Patricia Sheehan, "Back to Bed: Selling the Perfect Night's Sleep," *Lodging Hospitality*, March 15, 2001, pp. 22–24.

12. Andy Cohen, "It's Party Time for Saturn," *Sales and Marketing Management*, June 1994, p. 19; Michelle Krebs, "Another Hoedown at Saturn Ranch," *New York Times*, March 14, 1999; and information accessed online at www.saturn.com/homecoming, June 2001.

13. Tom Smith, "Dell Ties E-Storefront to Buyer Processes," *Internetweek*, May 17, 1999, p. PG6; and Michael Dell, "21st Century Commerce," *Executive Excellence*, December 1999, pp. 3–4.

14. For more discussion on demand states, see Philip Kotler, *Marketing Management: Analysis, Planning, Implementation, and Control,* 11th ed. (Upper Saddle River, NJ: Prentice Hall, 2003), Chap. 1.

15. See Kevin J. Clancy and Robert S. Shulman, "Breaking the Mold," *Sales and Marketing Management*, January 1994, pp. 82–84; James R. Rosenfield, "Plugging the Leaky Bucket," *Sales and Marketing Management*, October 1994, pp. 34–36; Susan Fournier, Susan Dobscha, and David Glen Mick, "Preventing the Premature Death of Relationship Marketing," *Harvard Business Review*, January–February 1998, pp. 42–50; and Erika Rasmusson, "Complaints Can Build Relationships," *Sales and Marketing Management*, September 1999, p. 89.

16. For more on assessing customer value, see Roland T. Rust, Valerie A. Zeithaml, and Katherine N. Lemon, *Driving Customer Equity: How Lifetime Customer Value Is Reshaping Corporate Strategy* (New York: Free Press, 2000); Joseph A. Ness, Michael J. Schrobeck, Rick A. Letendre, and Willmar J. Douglas, "The Role of ABM in Measuring Customer Value," *Strategic Finance*, March 2001, pp. 32–37; and Ness, Schrobeck, Letendre, and Douglas, "The Role of ABM in Measuring Customer Value—Part 2," *Strategic Finance*, April 2001, pp. 44–49.

17. Sam Hill and Glenn Rifkin, *Radical Marketing* (New York: HarperBusiness, 1999).

18. Ralph Waldo Emerson offered this advice: "If a man . . . makes a better mousetrap . . . the world will beat a path to his door." Several companies, however, have built better mousetraps yet failed. One was a laser mousetrap costing $1,500. Contrary to popular assumptions, people do not automatically learn about new products, believe product claims, or are willing to pay higher prices.

19. See Barry Farber and Joyce Wycoff, "Customer Service: Evolution and Revolution," *Sales and Marketing Management*, May 1991, p. 47; and Kevin Lawrence, "How to Profit from Customer Complaints," *The Canadian Manager*, Fall 2000, pp. 25, 29.

20. Gary Hamel and C. K. Prahalad, "Seeing the Future First," *Fortune*, September 5, 1994, pp. 64–70; and Philip Kotler, *Kotler on Marketing* (New York: Free Press, 1999), pp. 20–24.

21. See "Leaders of the Most Admired," *Fortune*, January 29, 1990, pp. 40–54; and Thomas A. Stewart, "America's Most Admired Companies," *Fortune*, March 2, 1998, pp. 70–82.

22. "Leaders of the Most Admired," p. 54.

23. Michael J. Weiss, "Online America," *American Demographics*, March 2001, pp. 53–60; and information accessed online at cyberatlas.internet.com, June 2001.

24. Robert D. Hof, "The 'Click Here' Economy," *Business Week*, June 22, 1998, pp. 122–128.

25. Robert D. Hof, "Survive and Prosper," *Business Week*, May 14, 2001, p. EB60.

26. Steve Hamm, "E-Biz: Down but Hardly Out," *Business Week*, March 26, 2001, pp. 126–130.

27. Kotler, *Kotler on Marketing*, p. 20.

28. Betsey McKay and Nikhil Deogun, "Is Coke Getting as Good as It Gives in P&G Partnership?" *Wall Street Journal*, February 22, 2001, p. B4; and Catherine Robinson and Greg W. Prince, "Coke's Got Company," *Beverage World*, March 15, 2001, p. 12.

29. Thor Valdmanis, "Alliances Gain Favor over Risky Mergers," *USA Today*, February 4, 1999, p. 3B. Also see Gabor Gari, "Leveraging the Rewards of Strategic Alliances," *Journal of Business Strategy*, April 1999, pp. 40–43; Rosabeth Moss Kanter, "Why Collaborate?" *Executive Excellence*, April 1999, p. 8; and Matthew Schifrin, "Partner or Perish," *Forbes*, May 21, 2001, pp. 26–28.

30. See Ben & Jerry's full mission statement online at www.benjerry.com. For more reading on environmentalism, see Stuart L. Hart, "Beyond Greening: Strategies for a Sustainable World," *Harvard Business Review*, January–February 1997, pp. 67–76; and Peter M. Senge, Goran Carstedt, and Patrick L. Porter, "Innovating Our Way to the Next Industrial Revolution," *MIT Sloan Management Review*, Winter 2001, pp. 24–38. For more marketing and social responsibility, see "Can Doing Good Be Good for Business?" *Fortune*, February 2, 1998, pp. 148G–148J; Sankar Sen and C. B. Bhattacharya, "Does Doing Good Always Lead to Doing Better? Consumer Reactions to Corporate Social Responsibility," *Journal of Marketing Research*, May 2001, pp. 225–243; Thea Singer, "Can Business Still Save the World?" *Inc.*, April 30, 2001, pp. 58–71; and Lois A. Mohr, Deborah J. Webb, and Katherine E. Harris, "Do Consumers Expect Companies to Be Socially Responsible? The Impact of Corporate Social Responsibility on Buying Behavior," *The Journal of Consumer Affairs*, Summer 2001, pp. 45–72.

31. Thomas G. Widmer and C. David Shepherd, "Developing a Hospital Web Site as a Marketing Tool: A Case Study," *Marketing Health Services*, Spring 1999, pp. 32–33.

32. Richard Cimino and Don Lattin, "Choosing My Religion," *American Demographics*, April 1999, pp. 60–65.

33. For other examples, and for a good review of nonprofit marketing, see Philip Kotler and Alan R. Andreasen, *Strategic Marketing for Nonprofit Organizations*, 5th ed. (Upper Saddle River, NJ: Prentice Hall, 1996); Philip Kotler and Karen Fox, *Strategic Marketing for Educational Institutions* (Upper Saddle River, NJ: Prentice Hall, 1995); Norman Shawchuck, Philip Kotler, Bruce Wren, and Gustave Rath, *Marketing for Congregations: Choosing to Serve People More Effectively* (Nashville, TN: Abingdon Press, 1993); William P. Ryan, "The New Landscape for Nonprofits," *Harvard Business Review*, January-February 1999, pp. 127-136; Don Akchin, "Nonprofit Marketing: Just How Far Has It Come?" *Nonprofit World*, January–February 2001, pp. 33–35.

34. Ira Teinowitz, "Postal Service Tries Image of Innovation," *Advertising Age*, October 1998, p. 6.

Chapter 2

1. See Andy Reinhardt, "The New Intel," *Business Week*, March 13, 2000, pp. 110–124; Paul McDougall and Brian Riggs, "Inside Intel," *Informationweek*, January 17, 2000, pp. 38–48; Andy Reinhardt, "Intel Inside Out," *Business Week*, December 4, 2000, pp. 116–120; Gordon Moore, Andrew Grove, and Craig Barrett, "Inside Intel," *Executive Excellence*, February 2000, p. 10; and Cliff Edwards, "Intel Inside the War Room," *Business Week*, April 30, 2001, p. 40.

2. See Philip Kotler, *Kotler on Marketing* (New York: Free Press, 1999), pp. 165–166.

3. For a more detailed discussion of corporate- and business-level strategic planning as they apply to marketing, see Philip Kotler, *Marketing Management: Analysis, Planning, Implementation, and Control*, 11th ed. (Upper Saddle River, NJ: Prentice Hall, 2003), Chap. 3.

4. For these and other examples, see Romauld A. Stone, "Mission Statements Revisited," *SAM Advanced Management Journal*, Winter 1996, pp. 31–37; Orit Gadiesh and James L. Gilbert, "Frontline Action," *Harvard Business Review*, May 2001; and "eBay Community," accessed online at www.ebay.com/community/aboutebay/community/index.html, June 2001.

5. Digby Anderson, "Is This the Perfect Mission Statement?" *Across the Board*, May–June 2001, p. 16.

6. Stone, "Mission Statements Revisited," p. 33.

7. See Gilbert Fuchsberg, "'Visioning' Mission Becomes Its Own Mission," *Wall Street Journal*, January 7, 1994, pp. B1, B3; and Sal Marino, "Where There Is No Visionary, Companies Falter," *Industry Week*, March 15, 1999, p. 20. For more on mission statements, see Thomas A. Stewart, "A Refreshing Change: Vision Statements That Make Sense," *Fortune*, September 30, 1996, pp. 195–196; Christopher K. Bart, "Making Mission Statements Count," *CA Magazine*, March 1999, pp. 37–38; Barbara Bartkus, Myron Glassman, and R. Bruce McAfee, "Mission Statements: Are They Smoke and Mirrors?" *Business Horizons*, November–December 2000, pp. 23–28; and George S. Day, "Define Your Business," *Executive Excellence*, February 2001, p. 12.

8. See Gary Hamel, "Reinvent Your Company," *Fortune*, June 20, 2000, pp. 98–112; and "Fortune 500," *Fortune*, April 16, 2001, pp. F1–F2.

9. For more on strategic planning, see John A. Byrne, "Strategic Planning," *Business Week*, August 26, 1996, pp. 46–51; Pete Bogda, "Fifteen Years Later, the Return of 'Strategy,'" *Brandweek*, February 1997, p. 18; Ian Wilson, "Strategic Planning for the Millennium: Resolving the Dilemma," *Long Range Planning*, August 1998, pp. 507–513; Robert W. Bradford, J. Peter Duncan, Peter Duncan, and Brian Tarcy, *Simplified Strategic Planning: A No-Nonsense Guide for Busy People Who Want Results Fast!* (Worcester, MA: Chandler House Press, 1999); Tom Devane, "Ten Cardinal Sins of Strategic Planning," *Executive Excellence*, October 2000, p. 15; and Dave Lefkowith, "Effective Strategic Planning," *Management Quarterly*, Spring 2001, pp. 7–11.

10. H. Igor Ansoff, "Strategies for Diversification," *Harvard Business Review*, September–October 1957, pp. 113–124. Also see Philip Kotler, *Kotler on Marketing* (New York: Free Press, 1999), pp. 46–48.

11. Nelson D. Schwartz, "Still Perking After All These Years," *Fortune*, May 24, 1999, pp. 203–210; Louise Lee, "Now Starbucks Uses Its Bean," *Business Week*, February 14, 2000, pp. 92–94; and Stephane Fitch, "Latte Grande, Extra Froth," *Forbes*, March 19, 2001, p. 58.

12. Michael E. Porter, *Competitive Advantage: Creating and Sustaining Superior Performance* (New York: Free Press, 1985); and Michel E. Porter, "What Is Strategy?" *Harvard Business Review*, November–December 1996, pp. 61–78. Also see Jim Webb and Chas Gile, "Reversing the Value Chain," *Journal of Business Strategy*, March–April 2001, pp. 13–17.

13. John C. Narver and Stanley F. Slater, "The Effect of a Market Orientation on Business Profitability," *Journal of Marketing*, October 1990, pp. 20–35. Also see Susan Foreman, "Interdepartmental Dynamics and Market Orientation," *Manager Update*, Winter 1997, pp. 10–19; and Kotler, *Kotler on Marketing*, p. 20.

14. Kotler, *Kotler on Marketing*, pp. 20–22.

15. Myron Magnet, "The New Golden Rule of Business," *Fortune*, February 21, 1994, pp. 60–63. Also see Tom Stallkamp, "Should Suppliers Be Partners?" *Business Week*, June 4, 2001, p. 30B; and Robert Mirani, "Emerging Technologies for Enhancing Supplier–Reseller Partnerships," *Industrial Marketing Management*, February 2001, p. 101.

16. Leslie Brokaw, "The Secrets of Great Planning," *Inc.*, October 1992, p. 152; and Philip Kotler, *Marketing Management: Analysis, Planning, Implementation, and Control*, 10th ed. (Upper Saddle River, NJ: Prentice Hall, 2000), Chap. 3.

17. Bradford McKee, "Think Ahead, Set Goals, and Get Out of the Office," *Nation's Business*, May 1993, p. 10. For more on small business strategic planning, see Wendy M. Beech, "In It for the Long Haul," *Black Enterprise*, March 1998, p. 25; and Nancy Upton, Elisabeth J. Teal, and Joe T. Felan, "Strategic and Business Planning Practices of Fast Growth Family Firms," *Journal of Small Business Management*, January 2001, pp. 60–72.

18. The four Ps classification was first suggested by E. Jerome McCarthy, *Basic Marketing: A Managerial Approach* (Homewood, IL: Irwin, 1960). For more discussion of this classification scheme, see Walter van Waterschoot and Christophe Van den Bulte, "The 4P Classification of the Marketing Mix Revisited," *Journal of Marketing*, October 1992, pp. 83–93; Michael G. Harvey, Robert F. Lusch, and Branko Cavarkapo, "A Marketing Mix for the 21st Century," *Journal of Marketing Theory and Practice*, Fall 1996, pp. 1–15; and Don E. Schultz, "Marketers: Bid Farewell to Strategy Based on Old 4Ps," *Marketing News*, February 12, 2001, p. 7.

19. Accessed online at Ad Age Dataplace, www.adage.com/dataplace, June 15, 2001.

20. Robert Lauterborn, "New Marketing Litany: 4P's Passé; C-Words Take Over," *Advertising Age*, October 1, 1990, p. 26. Also see Kotler, *Marketing Management: Analysis, Planning, Implementation, and Control,* 11th ed., Chap. 1.

21. For a good discussion of gaining advantage through implementation effectiveness versus strategic differentiation, see Michael E. Porter, "What Is Strategy," *Harvard Business Review*, November–December 1996, pp. 61–78. Also see Charles H. Noble and Michael P. Mokwa, "Implementing Marketing Strategies: Developing and Testing a Managerial Theory," *Journal of Marketing*, October 1999, pp. 57–73.

22. Brian Dumaine, "Why Great Companies Last," *Business Week*, January 16, 1995, p. 129. See James C. Collins and Jerry I. Porras, *Built to Last: Successful Habits of Visionary Companies* (New York: HarperBusiness, 1995); Geoffrey Brewer, "Firing Line: What Separates Visionary Companies from All the Rest?" *Performance*, June 1995, pp. 12–17; and Rob Goffee and Gareth Jones, *The Character of a Corporation: How Your Company's Culture Can Make or Break Your Business* (New York: HarperBusiness, 1998).

23. Joseph Winski, "One Brand, One Manager," *Advertising Age*, August 20, 1987, p. 86. Also see Jack Neff, "P&G Redefines the Brand Manager," *Advertising Age,* October 13, 1997, pp. 1, 18; Alan J. Bergstrom, "Brand Management Poised for Change," *Marketing News,* July 7, 1997, p. 5; and James Bell, "Brand Management for the Next Millennium," *Journal of Business Strategy,* March–April 1998, p. 7.

24. See Roland T. Rust, Valarie A. Zeithaml, and Katherine N. Lemon, *Driving Customer Equity: How Lifetime Customer Value Is Reshaping Corporate Strategy* (New York: Free Press, 2000).

25. For details, see Kotler, *Marketing Management: Analysis, Planning, Implementation, and Control*, 11th edition.

Chapter 3

1. Erick Schonfeld, "Schwab Puts It All Online," *Fortune*, December 7, 1998, pp. 94–100; Glenn Coleman, "The Battle for Your Money," *Money*, December 1999, pp. 134–140; Louise Lee, "David S. Pottruck," *Business Week*, September 27, 1999, p. EB51; Clinton Wilder, "Leaders of the Net Era," *Informationweek*, November 27, 2000, pp. 44–56; Elizabeth Corcoran, "The E Gang," *Forbes*, July 24, 2000, pp. 145–172; Adam Morgan, "Ten Ways to Knock Down a Giant," *Marketing*, January 11, 2001, p. 19; John Gorham, "Charles Schwab, Version 4.0," *Forbes*, January 8, 2001, pp. 88–95; and Mercedes M. Cardona, "Online Brokers Shift Gears to Retention, Not Trading," *Advertising Age*, April 16, 2001, p. 6.

2. Jerry Wind and Arvid Rangaswamy, "Customerization: The Next Revolution in Mass Customization," *Journal of Interactive Marketing*, Winter 2001, pp. 13–32.

3. John A. Byrne, "Management by the Web," *Business Week*, August 28, 2000, pp. 84–96.

4. Alan Mitchell, "Internet Zoo Spawns New Business Models," *Marketing Week*, January 21, 1999, pp. 24–25.

5. Paola Hjelt, "Flying on the Web in a Turbulent Economy," *Business Week*, April 30, 2001, pp. 142–148.

6. Information accessed online at www.gegxs.com/gxs/aboutus, May 23, 2001.

7. Gary Hamel and Jeff Sampler, "The E-Corporation: More than Just Web-Based, It's Building a New Industrial Order," *Fortune*, December 7, 1998, p. 82.

8. Frederick F. Reichheld and Phil Schefter, "E-Loyalty: Your Secret Weapon on the Web," *Harvard Business Review*, July–August 2000, pp. 105–113.

9. "E-commerce Trudges Through Current Slowdown," accessed online at www.cyberatlas.com, May 22, 2001.

10. "Blue Collar Occupations Moving Online," accessed online at www.cyberatlas.internet.com, April 12, 2001.

11. Roger O. Crockett, "A Web That Looks Like the World," *Business Week*, March 22, 1999, p. EB46–EB47. Also see "True Colors," *American Demographics*, April 2001, pp. 14–15.

12. See Joanne Cleaver, "Surfing for Seniors," *Marketing News*, July 19, 1999, pp. 1, 7; Sara Teasdale Montgomery, "Senior Surfers Grab Web Attention," *Advertising Age*, July 10, 2000, p. S4; and Hassan Fattah, "Hollywood, the Internet, & Kids," *American Demographics*, May 2001, pp. 51–56.

13. Michael J. Weiss, "Online America," *American Demographics*, March 2001, pp. 53–60.

14. Information accessed online at www.quickenloans.quicken.com, May 23, 2001.

15. Steve Hamm, "E-Biz: Down but Hardly Out," *Business Week*, March 26, 2001, pp. 126–130.

16. See Erin Strout, "Enron Builds an Electronic Empire," *Sales and Marketing Management*, January 2001, p. 39; and EnronOnline at www.enrononline.com.

17. Darnell Little, "Let's Keep This Exchange to Ourselves," *Business Week*, December 4, 2000, p. 48.

18. Cathy Bowen, "Behind the Spree in Payments for C2C," *Credit Card Management*, April 2000, pp. 28–34.

19. Heather Green, "How to Reach John Q. Public," *Business Week*, March 26, 2001, pp. 132–134.

20. Bradley Johnson, "Out-of-Sight Spending Collides with Reality," *Advertising Age*, August 7, 2000, pp. S4–S8.

21. Gary Hamel, "Is This All You Can Build with the Net? Think Bigger," *Fortune*, April 30, 2001, pp. 134–138.

22. See Ann Weintraub, "For Online Pet Stores, It's Dog-Eat-Dog," *Business Week*, March 6, 2000, pp. 78–80; "Death of a Spokes-pup," *Adweek*, December 11, 2000, pp. 44–46, and Jacques R. Chevron, "Name Least of Pet.com's Woes," *Advertising Age*, January 22, 2001, p. 24.

23. Hamm, "E-Biz: Down but Hardly Out," p. 127.

24. See Chuck Martin, *Net Future* (New York: McGraw-Hill, 1999), p. 33.

25. "E-commerce Trudges Through Current Slowdown," accessed online at www.cyberatlas.internet.com, May 22, 2001.

26. Laurie Freeman, "Why Internet Brands Take Offline Avenues," *Marketing News*, July 1999, p. 4; and Paul C. Judge, "The Name's the Thing," *Business Week*, November 15, 1999, pp. 35–39.

27. John Deighton, "The Future of Interactive Marketing," *Harvard Business Review*, November–December 1996, p. 154.

28. Adapted from information found in Don Peppers and Martha Rogers, "Opening the Door to Consumers," *Sales and Marketing Management*, October 1998, pp. 22–29; and Mike Beirne, "Marketers of the NextGeneration: Silvio Bonvini," *Brandweek*, November 8, 1999, p. 64.

29. Jeffrey F. Rayport and Bernard J. Jaworski, *e-Commerce* (New York: McGraw Hill, 2001), p. 116.

30. Lisa Bertagnoli, "Getting Satisfaction," *Marketing News*, May 7, 2001, p. 11.

31. Eilene Zimmerman, "Catch the Bug," *Sales and Marketing Management*, February 2001, pp. 78–82. Also see Ellen Neuborne, "Viral Marketing Alert," *Business Week*, March 19, 2001, p. EB8.

32. Devin Leonard, "Madison Ave. Fights Back," *Fortune*, February 5, 2001, pp. 150–154.

33. Rob Norton, "The Bright Future of Web Advertising," *Ecompany Now*, June 2001, pp. 50–60.

34. Dennis Callaghan, "Brands to Watch: Paul Allen: MyFamily.com," *MC Technology Marketing Intelligence*, February 2000, pp. 44–46; and "MyFamily.com Fact Sheet," accessed online at www.MyFamily.com, May 30, 2001.

35. See Thane Peterson, "E-I-E-I-E-Farming," *Business Week*, May 1, 2000, p. 202; and www.@griculture.com.

36. Arlene Weintraub, "When E-Mail Ads Aren't Spam," *Business Week*, October 16, 2000, pp. 112–113.

37. Erika Rasmusson, "Tracking Down Sales," *Sales and Marketing Management*, June 1998, p. 19.

38. See Robert Sales, "IFN Launches Infogate, Targets Online Equities Market Data Users," *Wall Street and Technology*, May 2000, p. 84.

39. Amy Cortese, "It's Called Webcasting, and It Promises to Deliver the Info You Want, Straight to Your PC," *Business Week*, February 24, 1997, pp. 95–104. Also see Amy Borrus, "Angry About Junk E-Mail? Congress Is Listening," *Business Week*, April 23, 2001, p. 53.

40. Elizabeth Corcoran, "The E Gang," *Fortune*, July 24, 2000, p. 145.

41. Michael Porter, "Strategy and the Internet," *Harvard Business Review*, March 2001, pp. 63–78.

42. See "Digital Divide Persists in the U.S.," accessed online at www.cyberatlas.com, July 8, 1999; Heather Green, Mike France, Narcia Stepanck, and Amy Borrus, "It's Time for Rules in Wonderland," *Business Week*, March 20, 2000, pp. 83–94; and Steve Jarvis, "Maybe This Year," *Marketing News*, April 23, 2001, pp. 1, 13.

Chapter 4

1. Quotes from James R. Rosenfield, "Millennial Fever," *American Demographics*, December 1997, pp. 47–51; Keith Naughton and Bill Vlasic, "The Nostalgia Boom: Why the Old Is New Again," *Business Week*, March 23, 1998, pp. 58–64; "New Beetles: Drivers Wanted," accessed online at www.vw.com/cars/newbeetle/main.html, August 11, 1998; and Keith Naughton, "VW Rides a Hot Streak," *Newsweek*, May 22, 2000, pp. 48–50. Also see James R. Rosenfield, "Millenial Fever Revisited," *Direct Marketing*, June 2000, pp. 44–47; "Volkswagen Is Awarded Two Best Car Picks from *Money Magazine*," VW press release, accessed online at www.vw.com, April 4, 2001; Susannah Meadows, Bret Begun, and Katherine Stroup, "Now Playing: 'Dude, Where's My Microbus?'" *Newsweek*, January 22, 2001, p. 9; and Jeff Green, "Heavy Traffic on Memory Lane," *Business Week*, January 15, 2001, p. 40.

2. Jennifer Lach, "Dateline America: May 1, 2025," *American Demographics*, May 1999, pp. 19–20. Also see Tom Weir, "Staying Stuck on the Web," *Supermarket Business*, February 15, 2001, pp. 15–16.

3. World POPClock, U.S. Census Bureau, accessed online at www.census.gov, June 2001. This Web site provides continuously updated projections of the U.S. and world populations.

4. Sally D. Goll, "Marketing: China's (Only) Children Get the Royal Treatment," *Wall Street Journal*, February 8, 1995, pp. B1, B3; and James L. Watson, "China's Big Mac Attack," *Foreign Affairs*, May–June 2000, pp. 120–134.

5. U.S. Census Bureau projections and POPClock Projection, U.S. Census Bureau, accessed online at www.census.gov, July 2001.

6. Lach, "Dateline America: May 1, 2025," p. 19.

7. See Joan Raymond, "The Joy of Empty Nesting," *American Demographics*, May 2000, pp. 49–54; and David Rakoff, "The Be Generation," *Adweek*, March 5, 2001, pp. SR18–SR22.

8. See Margot Hornblower, "Great X," *Time*, June 9, 1997, pp. 58–69; Janus Dietz, "When Gen X Meets Aging Baby Boomers," *Marketing News*, May 10, 1999, p. 17; Tammy Joyner, "Gen X-ers Focus on Life Outside the Job Fulfillment," *The Secured Lender*, May–June 2000, pp. 64–68; and Judi E. Loomis, "Generation X," *Rough Notes*, September 2000, pp. 52–54.

9. See Ken Gronback, "Marketing to Generation Y," *DSN Retailing Today*, July 24, 2000, p. 14.

10. See James U. McNeal, "Tapping the Three Kids' Markets," *American Demographics*, April 1998, pp. 37–40; and Carolyn M. Edy, "Babies Mean Business," *American Demographics*, May 1999, pp. 46–47.

11. Accessed online at www.growingupdigital.com/FLecho.html, October 1999. Also see Douglas Tapscott, *Growing Up Digital: The Rise of the Net Generation* (New York: McGraw-Hill, 1999); and Christine Y. Chen, "Chasing the Net Generation," *Fortune*, September 4, 2000, pp. 295–298.

12. See Gronback, "Marketing to Generation Y," p. 14; "Study Compares Gen Y to Boomers," *Home Textiles Today*, September

11, 2000, p. 14; and Rebecca Gardyn, "Grandaughters of Feminism," *American Demographics*, April 2001, pp. 43–47.

13. See J. Walker Smith and Ann Clurman, *Rocking the Ages* (New York: HarperBusiness, 1998); Mercedes M. Cardona, "Hilfiger's New Apparel Lines Getting Individual Efforts," *Advertising Age*, February 8, 1999, p. 24; and Alison Stein Wellner, "Generational Divide," *American Demographics*, October 2000, pp. 53–58.

14. See Rebecca Gardyn, "Unmarried Bliss," *American Demographics*, December 2000, pp. 56–61; and information accessed online at www.census.gov/population/projections/nation/hh-fam/table5n.txt, June 2001.

15. "How Far Have We Come? Fast Facts on Women and Work," accessed online at www.iVillage.com, June 21, 2001.

16. For these and other examples, see Kelly Shermach, "Niche Malls: Innovation for an Industry in Decline," *Marketing News*, February 26, 1996, p. 1; and Sue Shellenbarger, "'Child-Care Cams': Are They Good News for Working Parents?" *Wall Street Journal*, August 19, 1998, p. B1.

17. U.S. Census Bureau, "Geographical Mobility: Population Characteristics," accessed online at www.census.gov/population/socdemo/migration, May 2001.

18. See Kevin Heubusch, "Small Is Beautiful," *American Demographics*, January 1998, pp. 43–49; Brad Edmondson, "A New Era for Rural Americans," *American Demographics*, September 1997, pp. 30–31; Kenneth M. Johnson and Calvin L. Beale, "The Rural Rebound," *The Wilson Quarterly*, Spring 1998, pp. 16–27; and Alison Stein Wellner, "Size Doesn't Matter," *American Demographics*, May 2001, pp. 23–24.

19. Lauri J. Flynn, "Not Just a Copy Shop Any Longer, Kinko's Pushes Its Computer Services," *New York Times*, July 6, 1998, p. D1. Also see Carol Leonetti Dannhauser, "Who's in the Home Office," *American Demographics*, June 1999, pp. 50–56.

20. U.S. Census Bureau, "Educational Attainment in the United States (Update)," accessed online at www.census.gov/population/www/socdemo/educ-attn.html, December 2000.

21. See Fabian Linden, "In the Rearview Mirror," *American Demographics*, April 1984, pp. 4–5; Peter Francese, "America at Mid-Decade," *American Demographics*, February 1995, pp. 23–29; Rebecca Piirto Heath, "The New Working Class," *American Demographics*, January 1998, pp. 51–55; and *Digest of Education Statistics 1997*, National Center for Education Statistics, January 1998, at http://nces01.ed.gov/pubs/digest97.

22. The statistics in this paragraph were obtained from U.S. Census Bureau reports accessed online at www.census.gov, June 2001; and Chuck Paustian, "Anybody Can Do It," *Marketing News*, March 26, 2001, p. 23.

23. Laurie Freeman, "Cereal Marketers Find Sweet Tooth," *Advertising Age*, November 20, 2000, p. S4.

24. For these and other examples, see Laura Koss-Feder, "Out and About," *Marketing News*, May 25, 1998, pp. 1, 20; Jennifer Gilbert, "Ad Spending Booming for Gay-Oriented Sites," *Advertising Age*, December 6, 1999, p. 58; John Fetto, "In Broad Daylight," *American Demographics*, February 2001, pp. 16, 20; and Robert Sharoff, "Diversity in the Mainstream," *Marketing News*, May 21, 2001, pp. 1, 13.

25. Dan Frost, "The Fun Factor: Marketing Recreation to the Disabled," *American Demographics*, February 1998, pp. 54–58; and Michelle Wirth Fellman, "Selling IT Goods to Disabled End-Users," *Marketing News*, March 15, 1999, pp. 1, 17.

26. James W. Hughes, "Understanding the Squeezed Consumer," *American Demographics*, July 1991, pp. 44–50. For more on con-

sumer spending trends, see Cheryl Russell, "The New Consumer Paradigm," *American Demographics*, April 1999, pp. 50–58.

27. See Alison Stein Wellner, "The Money in the Middle," *American Demographics*, April 2000, pp. 56–64.

28. Debra Goldman, "Paradox of Pleasure," *American Demographics*, May 1999, pp. 50–53. Also see Kate Fitzgerald, "Luxury Marketing," *Advertising Age*, August 14, 2000, pp. S1, S6.

29. David Leonhardt, "Two-Tier Marketing," *Business Week*, March 17, 1997, pp. 82–90.

30. For more discussion, see the "Environmentalism" section in Chap. 20. Also see Michael E. Porter and Claas van der Linde, "Green *and* Competitive: Ending the Stalemate," *Harvard Business Review*, September–October 1995, pp. 120–134; Stuart L. Hart, "Beyond Greening: Strategies for a Sustainable World," *Harvard Business Review*, January–February 1997, pp. 67–76; Forest L. Reinhardt, "Bringing the Environment Down to Earth," *Harvard Business Review*, July–August 1999, pp. 149–157; and "Earth in the Balance," *American Demographics*, January 2001, p. 24.

31. See Karen Taylor, "Industry Helps Fuel R&D Funding Upswing," *Research Technology Management*, March–April 2001, pp. 7–8.

32. Also see V. Kasturi Rangan, Sohel Karim, and Sheryl K. Sandberg, "Do Better at Doing Good," *Harvard Business Review*, May–June 1996, pp. 42–54; Julie Garrett and Lisa Rochlin, "Cause Marketers Must Learn to Play by Rules," *Marketing News*, May 12, 1997, p. 4; and Sarah Lorge, "Is Cause-Related Marketing Worth It?" *Sales and Marketing Management*, June 1998, p. 72.

33. "13-Year-Old Bids over $3M for Items in eBay Auctions," *USA Today*, April 30, 1999, p. 10B.

34. See Cyndee Miller, "Trendspotters: 'Dark Ages' Ending; So Is Cocooning," *Marketing News*, February 3, 1997, pp. 1, 16.

35. See Bill McDowell, "New DDB Needham Report: Consumers Want It All," *Advertising Age*, November 1996, pp. 32–33; Norman Podhoretz, "Patriotism and Its Enemies," *Wall Street Journal*, July 3, 2000, p. A12; and John Fetto, "Patriot Games," *American Demographics*, July 2000, p. 48.

36. See Debbie Howell, "Health Food, Like Bell Bottoms, Puts Mojo Back in Mass," *DSN Retailing Today*, April 16, 2001, pp. 21–22.

37. Myra Stark, "Celestial Season," *Brandweek*, November 16, 1998, pp. 25–26. Also see Jennifer Harrison, "Advertising Joins the Journal of the Soul," *American Demographics*, June 1997, pp. 22–28; David B. Wolfe, "The Psychological Center of Gravity," *American Demographics*, April 1998, pp. 16–19; and Richard Cimino and Don Lattin, "Choosing My Religion," *American Demographics*, April 1999, pp. 60–65.

38. Philip Kotler, *Kotler on Marketing* (New York: Free Press, 1999), p. 3.

39. See Carl P. Zeithaml and Valerie A. Zeithaml, "Environmental Management: Revising the Marketing Perspective," *Journal of Marketing*, Spring 1984, pp. 46–53.

40. Howard E. Butz Jr. and Leonard D. Goodstein, "Measuring Customer Value: Gaining the Strategic Advantage," *Organizational Dynamics*, Winter 1996, pp. 66–67.

Chapter 5

1. See "Coke 'Family' Sales Fly as New Coke Stumbles," *Advertising Age*, January 17, 1986, p. 1; Jack Honomichl, "Missing Ingredients in 'New' Coke's Research," *Advertising Age*, July 22, 1985, p. 1; Leah Rickard, "Remembering New Coke," *Advertising Age*, April 17, 1995, p. 6; Rick Wise, "Why Things Go Better with Coke," *The Journal of Business Strategy*, January–February 1999, pp. 15–19; and Sean Mehegan, "Soft Drinks," *Adweek*, April 23, 2001, p. SR24.

2. See Philip Kotler, *Kotler on Marketing* (New York: Free Press, 1999), p. 73.

3. Christina Le Beau, "Mountains to Mine," *American Demographics,* August 2000, pp. 40–44. Also see Joseph M. Winski, "Gentle Rain Turns into Torrent," *Advertising Age,* June 3, 1991, p. 34; David Shenk, *Data Smog: Surviving the Information Glut* (San Francisco: HarperSanFrancisco, 1997); Diane Trommer, "Information Overload—Study Finds Intranet Users Overwhelmed with Data," *Electronic Buyers' News,* April 20, 1998, p. 98; and Stewart Deck, "Data Storm Ahead," *CIO,* April 15, 2001, p. 97.

4. Alice LaPlante, "Still Drowning!" *Computer World,* March 10, 1997, pp. 69–70.

5. See Geoffrey Brewer, "The Customer Stops Here," *Sales & Marketing Management,* March 1998, pp. 31–36; and Andy Patrizio, "Home-Grown CRM," *Insurance &Technology,* February 2001, pp. 49–50.

6. Stan Crock, "They Snoop to Conquer," *Business Week,* October 28, 1996, p. 172.

7. See Suzie Amer, "Masters of Intelligence," *Forbes,* April 5, 1999, p. 18.

8. Bruce Hager, "Dumpster Raids? That's Not Very Ladylike, Avon," *Business Week,* April 1, 1991, p. 32.

9. "Company Sleuth Uncovers Business Info for Free," *Link-Up,* January–February 1999, pp. 1, 8.

10. For more on marketing and competitive intelligence, see David B. Montgomery and Charles Weinberg, "Toward Strategic Intelligence Systems," *Marketing Management,* Winter 1998, pp. 44–52; Morris C. Attaway Sr., "A Review of Issues Related to Gathering and Assessing Competitive Intelligence," *American Business Review,* January 1998, pp. 25–35; and Conor Vibert, "Secrets of Online Sleuthing," *Journal of Business Strategy,* May–June 2001, pp. 39–42.

11. For more on research firms that supply marketing information, see Jack Honomichl, "Honomichl 50," special section, *Marketing News,* June 4, 2001, pp. H3–H37.

12. Justin Martin, "Ignore Your Customer," *Fortune,* May 1, 1995, pp. 121–126; and "Even Executives Are Losing Their Offices," *HR Magazine,* March 1998, p. 77. Also see William B. Helmreich, "Louder Than Words: On-Site Observational Research," *Marketing News,* March 1, 1999, p. 16; Kenneth Labich, "Attention Shoppers: This Man Is Watching You," *Fortune,* July 19, 1999, pp. 131–134; and Gerry Khermouch, "Consumers in the Mist," *Business Week,* February 26, 2001, p. 92.

13. Rebecca Piirto Heather, "Future Focus Groups," *American Demographics,* January 1994, p. 6. For more on focus groups, see Holly Edmunds, *The Focus Group Research Handbook* (Lincolnwood, IL: NTC Business Books, 1999).

14. Sarah Schafer, "Communications: Getting a Line on Customers," *Inc. Technology,* 1996, p. 102. Also see Judith Langer, "15 Myths of Qualitative Research: It's Conventional, but Is It Wisdom," *Marketing News,* March 1, 1999, pp. 13–14; and Alison Stein Wellner, "I've Asked You Here Because...," *Business Week,* August 14, 2000, p. F14.

15. For these and other examples, see "What've You Done for Us Lately?" *Business Week,* September 14, 1998, pp. 142–148; Sara Sellar, "Dust Off That Data," *Sales and Marketing Management,* May 1999, pp. 71–72; Kotler, *Kotler on Marketing,* p. 29; and Marc L. Songini, "Fedex Expects CRM System to Deliver," *Computerworld,* November 6, 2000, p. 10.

16. Kevin Fogarty, "Is CRM a Faint Hope?" *Computerworld,* June 4, 2001, p. 50.

17. Robert McLuhan, "How to Reap the Benefits of CRM," *Marketing,* May 24, 2001, p. 35.

18. Sellar, "Dust Off That Data," p. 72; and Stewart Deck, "Data Mining," *Computerworld,* March 29, 1999, p. 76. Also see Steven Isaac and Richard N. Tooker, "The Many Faces of CRM," *LIMRA's MarketFacts Quarterly,* Spring 2001, pp. 84–88; and Don Peppers and Martha Rogers, *One to One: Customer Strategies for the Business to Business World* (New York: Doubleday, 2001).

19. Ravi Kalakota and Marcia Robinson, *E-Business: Roadmap for Success* (Reading, MA: Addison-Wesley 1999).

20. "Business Bulletin: Studying the Competition," *Wall Street Journal,* March 19, 1995, pp. A1, A5.

21. See Nancy Levenburg and Tom Dandridge, "Can't Afford Research? Try Miniresearch," *Marketing News,* March 31, 1997, p.19; and Nancy Levenburg, "Research Resources Exist for Small Businesses," *Marketing News,* January 4, 1999, p. 19.

22. Jack Honomichl, "Honomichl Global 25," special section, *Marketing News,* August 16, 1999, pp. H1–H23; Rachel Miller, "Research Goes Global," *Campaign,* September 22, 2000, p. 36; and the AC Nielsen Web page accessed online at www.acnielsen.com, July 2001.

23. Many of the examples in this section, along with others, are found in Subhash C. Jain, *International Marketing Management,* 3rd ed. (Boston: PWS-Kent, 1990), pp. 334–339. Also see Jack Honomichl, "Research Cultures Are Different in Mexico, Canada," *Marketing News,* May 5, 1993, pp. 12–13; Naghi Namakforoosh, "Data Collection Methods Hold Key to Research in Mexico," *Marketing News,* August 29, 1994, p. 28; Ken Gotton, "Going Global with Research," *Marketing,* April 15, 1999, p. 35; and Jack Edmonston, "U.S., Overseas Differences Abound," *Advertising Age's Business Marketing,* January 1998, p. 32.

24. Jain, *International Marketing Management,* p. 338.

25. Clare Saliba, "U.S. Ends DoubleClick Privacy Probe," *E-Commerce Times,* January 23, 2001, accessed online at www. ecommercetimes.com/perl/story/?id=6917; "Getting to Know You.com," *U.S. News* and *World Report,* November 15, 1999, pp. 102–110; Heather Green, "Privacy: Outrage on the Web," *Business Week,* February 14, 2000, pp. 38–40; and Stuart Luman, "Online Privacy: US About To Come in from the Cold?" *Wired,* February 2001, p. 74.

26. See "MRA Study Shows Refusal Rates Are Highest at Start of Process," *Marketing News,* August 16, 1993, p. A15; "Private Eyes," *Marketing Tools,* January–February 1996, pp. 31–32; William O. Bearden, Charles S. Madden, and Kelly Uscategui, "The Pool Is Drying Up," *Marketing Research,* Spring 1998, pp. 26–33; and "Survey Results Show Consumers Want Privacy," *Direct Marketing,* March 1999, p. 10.

27. John Schwartz, "Chief Privacy Officers Forge Evolving Corporate Roles," *New York Times,* February 12, 2001, p. C1.

28. Ibid., p. C1. Also see Stephen F. Ambrose Jr. and Joseph W. Gelb, "Consumer Privacy Regulation and Litigation," *The Business Lawyer,* May 2001, pp. 1157–1178.

29. Cynthia Crossen, "Studies Galore Support Products and Positions, but Are They Reliable?" *Wall Street Journal,* November 14, 1991, pp. A1, A9. Also see Betsy Spethmann, "Cautious Consumers Have Surveyers Wary," *Advertising Age,* June 10, 1991, p. 34.

30. For example, see Betsy Peterson, "Ethics Revisited," *Marketing Research,* Winter 1996, pp. 47–48; and O. C. Ferrell, Michael D. Hartline, and Stephen W. McDaniel, "Codes of Ethics Among Corporate Research Departments, Marketing Research Firms, and Data Subcontractors: An Examination of a Three-Communities Metaphor," *Journal of Business Ethics,* April 1998, pp. 503–516. For discussion of a framework for ethical marketing research, see

Naresh K. Malhotra and Gina L. Miller, "An Integrated Model of Ethical Decisions in Marketing Research," *Journal of Business Ethics,* February 1998, pp. 263–280; and Kumar C. Rallapalli, "A Paradigm for Development and Promulgation of a Global Code of Marketing Ethics," *Journal of Business Ethics,* January 1999, pp. 125-137.

Chapter 6

1. Richard A. Melcher, "Tune-Up Time for Harley," *Business Week,* April 8, 1997, pp. 90–94; Ian P. Murphy, "Aided by Research, Harley Goes Whole Hog," *Marketing News,* December 2, 1996, pp. 16, 17; Dyan Machan, "Is the Hog Going Soft?" *Forbes,* March 10, 1997, pp. 114–119; Linda Sandler, "Workspaces: Harley Shop," *Wall Street Journal,* April 21, 1999, p. B20; Robert Francis, "Leaders of the Pack," *Brandweek,* June 26, 2000, pp. 28–38; and the Harley-Davidson Web site at, www.Harley-Davidson.com, July 2001. Also see Rich Teerlink, "Harley's Leadership U-Turn," *Harvard Business Review,* July–August 2000, pp. 43–48; Joan Raymond, "The Joy of Empty Nesting," *American Demographics,* May 2000, pp. 49–54, and "Harley-Davidson Profit Up," *New York Times,* April 11, 2001, p. C8.

2. World POPClock, U.S. Census Bureau, accessed online at www.census.gov, July 2001. This Web site provides continuously updated projections of the U.S. and world populations.

3. Statistics drawn from U.S. Census Bureau reports accessed online at www.census.gov, June 2001.

4. Roberta Bernstein, "Food for Thought," *American Demographics,* May 2000, pp. 39–42; and Jack Neff, "Suavitel Generates Waft of Success," *Advertising Age,* February 21, 2000, p. S4. For more examples, see Jeffery D. Zbar, "Marketing to Hispanics," *Advertising Age,* September 18, 2000, pp. S1–S23.

5. Calmetta Y. Coleman, "Attention Shoppers: Target Makes a Play for Minority Group Sears Has Cultivated," *Wall Street Journal,* April 12, 1999, p. A1; and Robert Sharoff, "Diversity in the Mainstream," *Marketing News,* May 21, 2001, pp. 1, 13.

6. Nancy Coltun Webster, "Multicultural," *Advertising Age,* November 17, 1997, pp. S1–S2.

7. See "L'eggs Joins New Approach in Marketing to African-American Women," *Supermarket Business,* June 1998, p. 81; Beth Belton, "Black Buying Power Soaring," *USA Today,* July 30, 1998, p. 1B; and Dana Canedy, "The Courtship of Black Consumers," *New York Times,* August 11, 1998, pp. D1, D2.

8. See David Kiley, "Black Surfing," *Brandweek,* November 17, 1997, p. 36; Kim Cleland, "Narrow-Marketing Efforts Winning the Internet Savvy," *Advertising Age,* November 16, 1998, p. S26; Chuck Ross, "BET Cries Foul, Hits Lack of Ad Commitment," *Advertising Age,* April 12, 1999, pp. S1, S16; and Larry Tucket, "Digital Divide," *Adweek,* November 15, 1999, pp. S34–S35.

9. Drawn from U.S. Census Bureau reports accessed online at www.census.gov, July 2001. Also see Bernstein, "Food for Thought," p. 40.

10. Louise Lee, "Speaking the Customer's Language—Literally," *Business Week,* September 25, 2000, p. 178.

11. See Christy Fisher, "Marketers Straddle Asian-America Curtain," *Advertising Age,* November 7, 1994; Lis A. Yorgey, "Asian Americans," *Target Marketing,* July 1999, pp. 75, 80; and Larry Moskowitz, "Missed Opportunity," *Pharmaceutical Executive,* April 2001, pp. 168–172.

12. See Kendra Parker, "Reaping What They've Sown," *American Demographics,* December 1999, pp. 34–38; and Ilana Polyak, "The Center of Attention," *American Demographics,* November 2000, pp. 30–32.

13. See Rick Adler, "Stereotypes Won't Work with Seniors Anymore," *Advertising Age,* November 11, 1996, p. 32; Richard Lee, "The Youth Bias in Advertising," *American Demographics,* January 1997, pp. 47–50; D. Allen Kerr, "Where There's Gray, There's Green," *Marketing News,* May 25, 1998, p. 2; Heather Chaplin, "Centrum's Self-Inflicted Silver Bullet," *American Demographics,* March 1999, pp. 68–69; and "Fewer Seniors in the 1990s but Their Ranks Are Set to Explode," *Business Week,* May 28, 2001, p. 30.

14. For more on social class, see Leon G. Schiffman and Leslie L. Kanuk, *Consumer Behavior,* 6th ed. (Upper Saddle River, NJ: Prentice Hall, 1997), Chap. 13; Rebecca Piirto Heath, "The New Working Class," *American Demographics,* January 1998, pp. 51–55; and Linda P. Morton, "Segmenting Publics by Social Class," *Public Relations Quarterly,* Summer 1999, pp. 45–46.

15. See Darla Dernovsek, "Marketing to Women," *Credit Union Magazine,* October 2000, pp. 90–96; and Sharon Goldman Edry, "No Longer Just Fun and Games," *American Demographics,* May 2001, pp. 36–38.

16. David Leonhardt, "Hey Kids, Buy This," *Business Week,* June 30, 1997, pp. 62–67. Also see Chankon Kim and Hanjoon Lee, "Development of Family Triadic Measures for Children's Purchase Influence," *Journal of Marketing Research,* August 1997, pp. 307–321; Judann Pollack, "Food Targeting Children Aren't Just Child's Play," *Advertising Age,* March 1, 1999, p. 16; Carolyn M. Edy, "Babies Mean Business," *American Demographics,* May 1999, pp. 46–47; and Paul Sensbach, "Don't Kid Around with Kid Packaging," *Marketing News,* November 20, 2000, p. 14.

17. This and other examples of companies using VALS 2 can be found in Rebecca Piirto, "Measuring Minds in the 1990s," *American Demographics,* December 1990, pp. 35–39; and Rebecca Piirto, "VALS the Second Time," *American Demographics,* July 1991, p. 6. For good discussions of other lifestyle topics, see Basil G. Englis and Michael Solomon, "To Be or Not to Be: Lifestyle Imagery, Reference Groups, and the Clustering of America," *Journal of Advertising,* March 1995, p. 13; and Tom Miller, "Global Segments from 'Strivers' to 'Creatives,'" *Marketing News,* July 20, 1998, p. 11.

18. See Paul C. Judge, "Are Tech Buyers Different?" *Business Week,* January 26, 1998, pp. 64–65, 68; Josh Bernoff, Shelley Morrisette, and Kenneth Clemmer, "The Forrester Report," Forrester Research, Inc., 1998; and the Forrester Web site at www.forrester.com, July 2001.

19. Myron Magnet, "Let's Go for Growth," *Fortune,* March 7, 1994, p. 70. Also see Timothy R. Graeff, "Consumption Situations and the Effects of Brand Image on Consumers' Brand Evaluations," *Psychology and Marketing,* January 1997, pp. 49–70; Dun Gifford Jr., "Moving Beyond Loyalty," *Harvard Business Review,* March–April 1997, pp. 9–10; Jennifer L. Aaker, "The Malleable Self: The Role of Self-Expression in Persuasion," *Journal of Marketing Research,* February 1999, pp. 45–57; and Swee Hoon Ang, "Personality Influences on Consumption: Insights from the Asian Economic Crisis," *Journal of International Consumer Marketing,* 2001, pp. 5–20.

20. Jill Venter, "Milk Mustache Campaign Is a Hit with Teens," *St. Louis Post-Dispatch,* April 1, 1998, p. E1; Dave Fusaro, "The Milk Mustache," *Dairy Foods,* April 1997, p. 75; Judann Pollack, "Milk: Kurt Graetzer," *Advertising Age,* June 30, 1997, p. S1; Verne, Gay, "Milk, the Magazine," *American Demographics,* February 2000, pp. 32–33; Rebecca Flass, "California Processors Vote to Continue 'Got Milk,'" *Adweek,* March 26, 2001, p. 5; and the Milk: Where's Your Mustache Web site at www.whymilk.com, July 2001.

21. See Leon Festinger, *A Theory of Cognitive Dissonance* (Stanford, CA: Stanford University Press, 1957); Schiffman and Kanuk,

Consumer Behavior, pp. 271–272; Jeff Stone, "A Radical New look at Cognitive Dissonance," *American Journal of Psychology*, Summer 1998, pp. 319–326; Thomas R. Schultz, Elene Leveille, and Mark R. Lepper, "Free Choice and Cognitive Dissonance Revisited: Choosing 'Lesser Evils' versus 'Greater Goods,'" *Personality and Social Psychology Bulletin*, January 1999, pp. 40–48; and Jillian C. Sweeney, Douglas Hausknecht, and Geoffrey N. Soutar, "Cognitive Dissonance After Purchase: A Multidimensional Scale," *Psychology and Marketing*, May 2000, pp. 369–385.

22. See Frank Rose, "Now Quality Means Service Too," *Fortune*, April 22, 1991, pp. 97–108; Chip Walker, "Word of Mouth," *American Demographics*, July 1995, p. 40; Thomas O. Jones and W. Earl Sasser Jr., "Why Satisfied Customers Defect," *Harvard Business Review*, November–December 1995, pp. 88–99; and Roger Sant, "Did He Jump or Was He Pushed?" *Marketing News*, May 12, 1997, pp. 2, 21.

23. The following discussion draws heavily from Everett M. Rogers, *Diffusion of Innovations*, 3rd ed. (New York: Free Press, 1983). Also see Hubert Gatignon and Thomas S. Robertson, "A Propositional Inventory for New Diffusion Research," *Journal of Consumer Research*, March 1985, pp. 849–867; Rogers, *Diffusion of Innovations*, 4th ed. (New York: Free Press, 1995); and Marnik G. Dekiple, Philip M. Parker, and Milos Sarvary, "Global Diffusion of Technological Innovations: A Coupled-Hazard Approach," *Journal of Marketing Research*, February 2000, pp. 47–59.

24. Sarah Lorge, "Purchasing Power," *Sales and Marketing Management,* June 1998, pp. 43–46.

25. Patrick J. Robinson, Charles W. Faris, and Yoram Wind, *Industrial Buying Behavior and Creative Marketing* (Boston: Allyn & Bacon, 1967). Also see Erin Anderson, Weyien Chu, and Barton Weitz, "Industrial Purchasing: An Empirical Exploration of the Buyclass Framework," *Journal of Marketing*, July 1987, pp. 71–86; Cynthia Webster, "Buying Involvement in Purchasing Success," *Industrial Marketing Management,* August 1993, p. 199; and Edward G. Brierty, Robert W. Eckles, and Robert R. Reeder, *Business Marketing*, 3rd ed. (Upper Saddle River, NJ: Prentice Hall, 1998), pp. 74–82.

26. Sarah Lorge, "Enron," *Sales and Marketing Management*, July 1999, pp. 48–52.

27. See John Huey, "The Absolute Best Way to Fly," *Fortune*, May 30, 1994, pp. 121–128; "My First Gulfstream," *Vanity Fair*, October 1998, pp. 236–258; and Steven Lipin and Andy Pasztor, "Defense Firm Set to Acquire Gulfstream," *Wall Street Journal*, May 17, 1999, p. A3. For more on influence strategies within buying centers, see R. Venkatesh, Ajay K. Kohli, and Gerald Zaltman, "Influence Strategies in Buying Centers," *Journal of Marketing*, October 1995, pp. 71–82; Philip L. Dawes, Don Y. Lee, and Grahame R. Dowling, "Information Control and Influence in Emergent Buying Centers," *Journal of Marketing*, July 1998, pp. 55–68; and Geok-Theng Lau, Mark Goh, and Shan Lei Phua, "Purchase-Related Factors and Buying Center Structure: An Empirical Assessment," *Industrial Marketing Management*, November 1999, pp. 573–587.

28. Frederick E. Webster Jr. and Yoram Wind, *Organizational Buying Behavior* (Upper Saddle River, NJ: Prentice Hall, 1972), pp. 33–37. Also see Brierty, Eckles, and Reeder, *Business Marketing,* Chap. 3.

29. Thomas V. Bonoma, "Major Sales: Who Really Does the Buying," *Harvard Business Review*, May–June 1982, p. 114. Also see Ajay Kohli, "Determinants of Influence in Organizational Buying: A Contingency Approach," *Journal of Marketing*, July 1989, pp. 50–65; and Jeffrey E. Lewin, "The Effects of Downsizing on Organizational Buying Behavior: An Empirical Investigation," *Academy of Marketing Science*, Spring 2001, pp. 151–164.

30. Robinson, Faris, and Wind, *Industrial Buying Behavior*, p. 14.

31. John H. Sheridan, "Buying Globally Made Easier," *Industry Week*, February 2, 1998, pp. 63–64; information accessed online at www.wiznet.net, September 1999; and John Evan Frook, "Catalog Management Race Begins," *B to B*, March 19, 2001, p. 20.

32. See Andy Reinhardt "Extranets: Log On, Link Up, Save Big," *Business Week*, June 22, 1998, p. 134; "To Byte the Hand That Feeds," *The Economist*, January 17, 1998, pp. 61–62; Ken Brack, "Source of the Future," *Industrial Distribution*, October 1998, pp. 76–80; James Carbone, "Internet Buying on the Rise," *Purchasing*, March 25, 1999, pp. 51–56; and "E-procurement: Certain Value in Changing Times," *Fortune,* April 30, 2001, pp. S2–S3.

Chapter 7

1. See Steve Jarvis, "P&G's Challenge," Marketing News, August 28, 2000, pp. 1, 13; Robert Berner, "Can P&G Clean Up Its Act?" Business Week, March 12, 20 01, pp. 80–83; and information accessed online at www.pg.com and www.tide.com, July 2001.

2. Arlene Weintraub, "Chairman of the Board," Business Week, May 28, 2001, p. 94.

3. Nelson D. Schwartz, "What's in the Cards for AmEx?" Fortune, January 22, 2001, pp. 58–70.

4. Laurel Cutler, quoted in "Stars of the 1980s Cast Their Light," Fortune, July 3, 1989, p. 76; and Robert E. Linneman and John L. Stanton Jr., Making Niche Marketing Work: How to Grow Bigger by Acting Smaller (New York: McGraw-Hill, 1991). Also see Arlene Weibtraub, "Little Niches That Grew," Business Week, June 18, 2001, p. 100.

5. For a collection of articles on one-to-one marketing and mass customization, see James H. Gilmore and B. Joseph Pine, Markets of One: Creating Customer-Unique Value through Mass Customization (Boston: Harvard Business School Press, 2001).

6. See Philip Kotler, Kotler on Marketing (New York: Free Press, 1999), pp. 149–150.

7. These and other examples found in Nelson D. Schwartz, "Still Perking After All These Years," Fortune, May 24, 1999, pp. 203–210; and www.usaopoly.com, July 2001.

8. See Bruce Hager, "Podunk Is Beckoning," Business Week, December 2, 1991, p. 76; David Greisling, "The Boonies Are Booming," Business Week, October 9, 1995, pp. 104–110; Leah Nathans Spiro, "Saks Tries on a Petite," Business Week, October 7, 1997, p. 8; Stephanie Anderson Forest, "Look Who's Thinking Small," Business Week, May 17, 1999, pp. 68–70; and Debbie Howell, "Villager's Hardware: The Convenience Version of Big-Box Do-It-Yourself," DSN Retailing Today, May 8, 2000, pp. 109–110.

9. Accessed online at www.olay.com/facecare/fcbodytips.htm, July 2001.

10. "Sega to Target Adults with Brand Extensions," Marketing Week, March 12, 1998, p. 9.

11. Pat Sloan and Jack Neff, "With Aging Baby Boomers in Mind, P&G, Den-Mat Plan Launches," Advertising Age, April 13, 1998, pp. 3, 38.

12. Alice Z. Cuneo, "Advertisers Target Women, but Market Remains Elusive," Advertising Age, November 10, 1997, pp. 1, 24; and Laura Q. Hughes and Alice Z. Cuneo, "Lowes Retools Image in Push Toward Women," Advertising Age, February 26, 2001, pp. 3, 51.

13. See "Automakers Learn Better Roads to Women's Market," *Marketing News*, October 12, 1992, p. 2; Alan Alder, "Purchasing Power Women's Buying Muscle Shops Up in Car Design, Marketing," *Chicago Tribune*, September 29, 1996, p. 21A; Jean Halliday, "GM Taps Harris to Help Lure Women," *Advertising Age*, February 17, 1997, pp. 1, 37; and Mary Louis Quinlin, "Women: We've Come a Long Way, Maybe," *Advertising Age*, February 13, 1999, p. 46.

14. "A Focus on Women at iVillage.com," *New York Times*, August 3, 1998, p. D6; Helene Stapinski, "Online Markets: You GO, Girls," *Sales and Marketing Management*, January 1999, pp. 47–48; Jennifer Gilbert, "Sites Play to Women's Specialized Interests," *Advertising Age*, May 1, 2000, pp. 56, 62; Sharon Goldman Edry, "No Longer Just Fun and Games," *American Demographics*, May 2001, pp. 36–38; and information accessed online at www.iVillage.com and www.girlson.com, July 2001.

15. Amanda Beeler, "Heady Rewards for Loyalty," *Advertising Age*, August 14, 2000, p. S8.

16. Brian Bremner, "Looking Downscale without Looking Down," *Business Week*, October 8, 1990, pp. 62–67; Anne Faircloth, "Value Retailers Go Dollar for Dollar," *Fortune*, July 6, 1998, pp. 164–166; Debbie Howell, "Dollar General: The Leader in the Realm of Deep Discount," *DSN Retailing Today*, May 8, 2000, pp. 59–62; and Jack Neff, "The Buck Stops Here," *Advertising Age*, November 6, 2000, pp. 3, 100.

17. "Lifestyle Marketing," *Progressive Grocer*, August 1997, pp. 107–110; and Philip Kotler, *Marketing Management: Analysis, Planning, Implementation, and Control*, 10th ed. (Upper Saddle River, NJ: Prentice Hall, 2000), pp. 266–267.

18. See Laurie Freeman and Cleveland Horton, "Spree: Honda's Scooters Ride the Cutting Edge," *Advertising Age*, September 5, 1985, pp. 3, 35; "Scooter Wars," *Cycle World*, February 1998, p. 26; Honda's Web site at www.hondamotorcycle.com/scooter; and Jonathon Welsh, "Transport: The Summer of the Scooter; Boomers Get a New Retro Toy," *Wall Street Journal*, April 13, 2001, p. W1.

19. See Mark Maremont, "The Hottest Thing Since the Flashbulb," *Business Week*, September 7, 1992; Bruce Nussbaum, "A Camera in a Wet Suit," *Business Week*, June 2, 1997, p. 109; Dan Richards, "The Smartest Disposable Cameras," *Travel Holiday*, December 1998, p. 20; "Point and Click," *Golf Magazine*, February 1999, p. 102; and Todd Wasserman, "Kodak Rages in Favor of the Machines," *Brandweek*, February 26, 2001, p. 6.

20. Stowe Shoemaker, "Segmenting the U.S. Travel Market According to Benefits Realized," *Journal of Travel Research*, Winter 1994, pp. 8–21.

21. See Warren Thayer, "Target Heavy Buyers!" *Frozen Food Age*, March 1998, pp. 22–24; Jennifer Ordonez, "Cash Cows: Hamburger Joints Call Them 'Heavy Users,'" *Wall Street Journal*, January 12, 2000, p. A1; and Brian Wonsink and Sea Bum Park, "Methods and Measures that Profile Heavy Users," *Journal of Advertising Research*, July–August 2000, pp. 61–72.

22. Kendra Parker, "How Do You Like Your Beef?" *American Demographics*, January 2000, pp. 35–37.

23. Daniel S. Levine, "Justice Served," *Sales and Marketing Management*, May 1995, pp. 53–61.

24. For more on segmenting business markets, see John Berrigan and Carl Finkbeiner, *Segmentation Marketing: New Methods for Capturing Business* (New York: HarperBusiness, 1992); Rodney L. Griffith and Louis G. Pol, "Segmenting Industrial Markets," *Industrial Marketing Management*, no. 23, 1994, pp. 39–46; Stavros P. Kalafatis and Vicki Cheston, "Normative Models and Practical Applications of Segmentation in Business Markets," *Industrial Marketing Management*, November 1997, pp. 519–530; and James C. Anderson and James A. Narus, *Business Market Management* (Upper Saddle River, NJ: Prentice Hall, 1999), pp. 44–47.

25. Cyndee Miller, "Teens Seen as the First Truly Global Consumers," *Advertising Age*, March 27, 1995, p. 9.

26. Shawn Tully, "Teens: The Most Global Market of All," *Fortune*, May 16, 1994, pp. 90–97; "MTV Hits 100 Million in Asia," *New Media Markets*, January 28, 1999, p. 12; and Brett Pulley and Andrew Tanzer, "Sumner's Gemstone," *Forbes*, February 21, 2000, pp. 106–111. For more on international segmentation, see V. Kumar and Anish Nagpal, "Segmenting Global Markets: Look Before You Leap," *Marketing Research*, Spring 2001, pp. 8–13.

27. See Michael Porter, *Competitive Advantage* (New York: Free Press, 1985), pp. 4–8. 234–236.

28. Nina Munk, "Why Women Find Lauder Mesmerizing," *Fortune*, May 25, 1998, pp. 97–106.

29. Paul Davidson, "Entrepreneurs Reap Riches from Net Niches," *USA Today*, April 20, 1998, p. B3; and information accessed online at www.ostrichesonline.com, July 2001.

30. Ira Teinowitz, "FTC Issues Critical Report on Violence," *Advertising Age*, September 2000, pp. 1, 70.

31. See "PowerMaster," *Fortune*, January 13, 1992, p. 82; Herbert Rotfeld, "The FTC and Marketing Abuse," *Marketing News*, March 17, 1997, p. 4; and George G. Brenkert, "Marketing to Inner-City Blacks: PowerMaster and Moral Responsibility," *Business Ethics Quarterly*, January 1998, pp. 1–18.

32. Joseph Turow, "Breaking Up America: The Dark Side of Target Marketing," *American Demographics*, November 1997, pp. 51–54.

33. For an interesting discussion of finding ways to differentiate marketing offers, see Ian C. MacMillan and Rita Gunther McGrath, "Discovering New Points of Differentiation," *Harvard Business Review*, July–August 1997, pp. 133–145.

34. See Kotler, *Kotler on Marketing*, pp. 59–63.

Chapter 8

1. Excerpt adapted from Penelope Green, "Spiritual Cosmetics. No Kidding," *New York Times*, January 10, 1999, p. 1. Also see Elizabeth Wellington, "The Success of Smell," *The News and Observer*, June 11, 2001, p. E1; and Mary Tannen, "Cult Cosmetics," *New York Times Magazine*, Spring 2001, p. 96.

2. See B. Joseph Pine and James H. Gilmore, *The Experience Economy* (New York: Free Press, 1999); Jane E. Zarem, "Experience Marketing," *Folio: The Magazine for Magazine Management*, Fall 2000, pp. 28–32; and Scott Mac Stravic, "Make Impressions Last: Focus on Value," *Marketing News*, October 23, 2000, pp. 44–45.

3. Mark Hyman, "The Yin and Yang of the Tiger Effect," *Business Week*, October 16, 2000, p. 110; and "Finance and Economics: A Tiger Economy," *The Economist*, April 14, 2001, p. 70.

4. Check out the tourism Web pages of these states at www.TravelTex.com, www.michigan.org, and www.iloveny.state.ny.us.

5. See Philip Kotler, Irving J. Rein, and Donald Haider, *Marketing Places: Attracting Investment, Industry, and Tourism to Cities, States, and Nations* (New York: Free Press, 1993), pp. 202, 273. Additional information accessed online at www.ireland.travel.ie and www.ida.ie, August 2001.

6. Accessed online at www.social-marketing.org/aboutus.html, August 2001.

7. Alan R. Andreasen, Rob Gould, and Karen Gutierrez, "Social Marketing Has a New Champion," *Marketing News*, February 7,

2000, p. 38; and information accessed online at www.social-marketing.org, August 2001.

8. See Lois Therrien, "Motorola and NEC: Going for Glory," *Business Week*, special issue on quality, 1991, pp. 60–61. For more on quality, see Roland T. Rust, Anthony J. Zahorik, and Timothy L. Keiningham, "Return on Quality (ROQ): Making Service Quality Financially Accountable," *Journal of Marketing*, April 1995, pp. 58–70; John Dalrymple and Eileen Drew, "Quality: On the Threshold or the Brink?" *Total Quality Management,* July 2000, pp. S697–S703; and Thomas J. Douglas and William Q. Judge, "Total Quality Management Implementation and Competitive Advantage," *Academy of Management Journal,* February 2001, pp. 158–169.

9. Philip Kotler, *Kotler on Marketing* (New York: Free Press, 1999), p. 17.

10. See "Hot R.I.P.: The Floppy Disk," *Rolling Stone*, August 20, 1998, p. 86; Owen Edwards, "Beauty and the Box," *Forbes*, October 5, 1998, p. 131; Bob Woods, "iMac Drives Apple's Q2 Results," *Computer Dealer News*, April 30, 1999, p. 39; and Pui-Wing Tam, "Designing Duo Helps Shape Apple's Fortunes," *Wall Street Journal,* July 18, 2001, p. B1.

11. Gerry Khermouch, "The Best Global Brands," *Business Week,* August 6, 2001, pp. 50–64.

12. Andrew Pierce and Eric Almquist, "Brand Building May Face a Test," *Advertising Age,* April 9, 2001, p. 22.

13. See Roland T. Rust, Katherine N. Lemon, and Valerie A. Zeithaml, *Driving Customer Equity: How Lifetime Customer Value Is Reshaping Corporate Strategy.* (New York: Free Press, 2000); and Katherine N. Lemon, Roland T. Rust, and Valerie A. Zeithaml, "What Drives Customer Equity," *Marketing Management,* Spring 2001, pp. 20–25.

14. See Paul N. Bloom, Gregory T. Gundlach, and Joseph P. Cannon, "Slotting Allowances and Fees: School of Thought and the Views of Practicing Managers," *Journal of Marketing,* April 2000, pp. 92–108; and Ira Teionwitz, "FTC Pinpoints Slotting Fees," *Advertising Age,* February 26, 2001, p. 52.

15. Warren Thayer, "Loblaws Exec Predicts: Private Labels to Surge," *Frozen Food Age,* May 1996, p. 1; "President's Choice Continues Brisk Pace," *Frozen Food Age,* March 1998, pp. 17–18; David Dunne and Chakravarthi Narasimhan, "The New Appeal of Private Labels," *Harvard Business Review,* May–June 1999, pp. 41–52; www.sendpc.com; and "New Private Label Alternatives Bring Changes to Supercenters, Clubs," *Dsn Retailing Today,* February 5, 2001, p. 66.

16. See Patrick Oster, "The Eurosion of Brand Loyalty," *Business Week,* July 19, 1993, p. 22; Marcia Mogelonsky, "When Stores Become Brands," *American Demographics*, February 1995, pp. 32–38; Stephanie Thompson, "Private Label Marketers Getting Savvier to Consumption Trends," *Brandweek,* November 24, 1997, p. 9; and David Dunne and Chakravarthi Narasimham, "The New Appeal of Private Labels," *Harvard Business Review,* May–June 1999, pp. 41–52; and Kusum L. Ailawadi, Scott Neslin, and Karen Gedenk, "Pursuing the Value-Conscious Consumer: Store Brands versus National Promotions," *Journal of Marketing,* January 2001, pp. 71–89.

17. See Doug Desjardins, "Popularized Entertainment Icons Continue to Dominate Licensing," *Dsn Retailing Today,* July 9, 2001, p. 4; and Emily Scardino, "Entertainment Licensing: Adding Equity Sells Apparel Programs," *Dsn Retailing Today,* June 4, 2001, pp. A10–A12.

18. David D. Kirkpatrick, "Snack Foods Become Stars of Books for Children," *New York Times*, September 22, 2000, p. A1.

19. See Silvia Sansoni, "Gucci, Armani, and … John Paul II?" *Business Week,* May 13, 1996, p. 61; Bart A. Lazar, "Licensing Gives Known Brands New Life," *Advertising Age,* February 16, 1998, p. 8; Laura Petrecca, "'Corporate Brands' Put Licensing in the Spotlight," *Advertising Age*, June 14, 1999, p. 1; and Rachel Miller, "How Licensing Can Invigorate Brands," *Marketing*, March 22, 2001, pp. 29–30.

20. Terry Lefton, "Warner Brothers' Not Very Looney Path to Licensing Gold," *Brandweek,* February 14, 1994, pp. 36–37; Robert Scally, "Warner Builds Brand Presence, Strengthens 'Tunes' Franchise," *Discount Store News,* April 6, 1998, p. 33; and "Looney Tunes Launched on East Coast," *Dairy Foods,* April 2001, p. 9.

21. Phil Carpenter, "Some Cobranding Caveats to Obey," *Marketing News,* November 7, 1994, p. 4; and Gabrielle Solomon, "Co-Branding Alliances: Arranged Marriages Made by Marketers," *Fortune,* October 12, 1998, p. 188.

22. See David Aaker, "Should You Take Your Brand to Where the Action Is?" *Harvard Business Review,* September–October 1997, pp. 135–145; Zeynep Gurhan-Canli and Durairaj Maheswaran, "The Effects of Extensions on Brand Name Dilution and Enhancement," *Journal of Marketing*, November 1998, pp. 464–473; and Lauren Goldstein, "Barbie's Secret Plan for World Domination," *Fortune,* November 23, 1998, pp. 38–39.

23. For more on the use of line and brand extensions and consumer attitudes toward them, see Deborah Roedder John, Barbara Loken, and Christopher Joiner, "The Negative Impact of Extensions: Can Flagship Brands Be Eroded?" *Journal of Marketing,* January 1998, pp. 19–32; Zeynep Gurrhan-Canli and Durairaj Maheswaran, "The Effects of Extensions on Brand Name Dilution and Enchancement," *Journal of Marketing,* November 1998, pp. 464–473; Daniel A. Sheinin, "The Effects of Experience with Brand Extensions on Parent Brand Knowledge," *Journal of Business Research,* July 2000, pp. 47–55; and Chung K. Kim, Anne M. Lavack, and Margo Smith, "Consumer Evaluation of Vertical Extensions and Core Brands," *Journal of Business Research,* June 2001, pp. 211–222.

24. See Joan Holleran, "Packaging Speaks Volumes," *Beverage Industry,* February 1998, p. 30; and "Packaging—A Silent Salesman," *Retail World,* August 28–September 8, 2000, p. 23.

25. Robert M. McMath, "Chock Full of (Pea)nuts," *American Demographics,* April 1997, p. 60.

26. Bro Uttal, "Companies That Serve You Best," *Fortune*, December 7, 1987, p. 116. For an excellent discussion of support services, see James C. Anderson and James A. Narus, "Capturing the Value of Supplementary Services," *Harvard Business Review*, January–February 1995, pp. 75–83.

27. See Heather Green, "A Cyber Revolt in Health Care," *Business Week,* October 19, 1998, pp. 154–156; Robert D. Hof, "Now It's Your Web," *Business Week,* October 5, 1998, pp. 164–176; Adrian Slywotzky, "Serving the Activist Consumer," *Sales and Marketing Management,* November 2000, pp. 39–40; and Bob Wallace and George V. Hulme, "The Modern Call Center," *Informationweek,* April 9, 2001, pp. 38–46.

28. See Paula Mergenbagen, "Product Liability: Who Sues?" *American Demographics*, June 1995, p. 48; "A Primer on Product Liability Laws," *Purchasing,* May 6, 1999, pp. 32–34; Pamela L. Moore, "The Litigation Machine," *Business Week,* January 29, 2001, pp. 115–123; and "Jury Awards in Product Liability Cases Increasing in Recent Years," *Chemical Market Reporter,* February 12, 2001, p. 5.

29. Ann Marie Kerwin, "Brands Pursue Old, New Money," *Advertising Age,* June 11, 2001, pp. S1, S11.

30. See David A. Aaker, "Should You Take Your Brand to Where the Action Is?" *Harvard Business Review*, September–October 1997, pp. 135–143.

31. Information accessed online at www.marriott.com, August 2001.

32. See Ronald Henkoff, "Service Is Everybody's Business," *Fortune*, June 27, 1994, pp. 48–60; Valerie Zeithaml and Mary Jo Bitner, *Services Marketing* (New York: McGraw-Hill, 1999), pp. 8–9; Allen Sinai, "Services in the U.S. Economy," accessed on line at http:// usinfor.state.gov/journals/ites/0496/ijee/ej10.htm; and "Gross Domestic Product," news release, U.S. Bureau of Economic Analysis, June 29, 2001, accessed on line at www.bea.gov/bea/newsrel/gdp101f.htm.

33. See James L. Heskett, Thomas O. Jones, Gary W. Loveman, W. Earl Sasser Jr., and Leonard A. Schlesinger, "Putting the Service–Profit Chain to Work," *Harvard Business Review*, March–April, 1994, pp. 164–174; and James L. Heskett, W. Earl Sasser Jr., and Leonard A. Schlesinger, *The Service Profit Chain: How Leading Companies Link Profit and Growth to Loyalty, Satisfaction, and Value* (New York: Free Press, 1997). Also see Anthony J. Rucci, Steven P. Kirn, and Richard T. Quinn, "The Employee–Customer–Profit Chain at Sears," *Harvard Business Review,* January–February 1998, pp. 83–97; and Eugene W. Anderson and Vikas Mittal, "Strengthening the Satisfaction–Profit Chain," *Journal of Service Research,* November 2000, pp. 107–120.

34. For excellent discussions of service quality, see A. Parasuraman, Valerie A. Zeithaml, and Leonard L. Berry, "A Conceptual Model of Service Quality and Its Implications for Future Research," *Journal of Marketing*, Fall 1985, pp. 41–50; Parasuraman, Zeithaml, and Berry, "Reassessment of Expectations as a Comparison Standard in Measuring Service Quality: Implications for Further Research," *Journal of Marketing*, January 1994, pp. 111–124; Zeithaml, Berry, and Parasuraman, "The Behavioral Consequences of Service Quality," *Journal of Marketing,* April 1996, pp. 31–46; and Valerie Zeithaml, "Service Quality, Profitability, and the Economic Worth of Customers: What We Know and What We Need to Learn," *Academy of Marketing Science Journal,* Winter 2000, pp. 67–85.

35. See Erika Rasmusson, "Winning Back Angry Customers," *Sales and Marketing Management,* October 1997, p. 131; and Stephen S. Tax, Stephen W. Brown, and Murali Chandrashekaran, "Customer Evaluations of Service Complaint Experiences: Implications for Relationship Marketing," *Journal of Marketing,* April 1998, pp. 60–76; and Stephen W. Brown, "Practicing Best-in-Class Service Recovery," *Marketing Management*, Summer 2000, pp. 8–9.

36. See James L. Heskett, W. Earl Sasser Jr., and Christopher W. L. Hart, *Service Breakthroughs* (New York: Free Press, 1990).

37. See Philip Cateora, *International Marketing*, 8th ed. (Homewood, IL: Irwin, 1993), p. 270.

38. See Carla Rapoport, "Retailers Go Global," *Fortune*, February 20, 1995, pp. 102–108; "Top 200 Global Retailers," *Stores,* January 1998, pp. S5–S12; Jeffery Adler, "The Americanization of Global Retailing," *Discount Merchandiser,* February 1998, p. 102; and Mike Troy, "The World's Largest Retailer," *Chain Store Age,* June 2001, pp. 47–49.

39. Lee Smith, "What's at Stake in the Trade Talks," *Fortune*, August 27, 1990, pp. 76–77.

Chapter 9

1. Quotes, extracts, and other information from Jay Greene, "Microsoft: How It Became Stronger Than Ever," *Business Week*, June 4, 2001, pp. 74–85; and Brent Schlender, "Microsoft: The Beast Is Back," *Fortune*, June 11, 2001, pp. 74–86.

2. For these and other examples, see Cliff Edwards, "Where Have All the Edsels Gone?" *Greensboro News Record*, May 24, 1999, p. B6.

3. See Philip Kotler, *Kotler on Marketing* (New York: Free Press, 1999), p. 51; Martha Wirth Fellman, "Number of New Products Keeps Rising," *Marketing News*, March 29, 1999, p. 3; Sarah Theodore, "Heads or Tails?" *Beverage Industry,* September 2000, p. NP4; and Eric Berggreb and Thomas Nacher, "Why Good Ideas Go Bust," *Management Review,* February 2000, pp. 32–36.

4. Gary Hamel, "Innovation's New Math," *Fortune*, July 9, 2001, pp. 130–131.

5. See Tim Stevens, "Idea Dollars," *Industry Week,* February 16, 1998, pp. 47–49; and William E. Coyne, "How 3M Innovates for Long-Term Growth," *Research Technology Management,* March–April 2001, pp. 21–24.

6. Paul Lukas, "Marketing: The Color of Money and Ketchup," *Fortune,* September 18, 2000, p. 38.

7. Pam Weisz, "Avon's Skin-So-Soft Bugs Out," *Brandweek*, June 6, 1994, p. 4; and information accessed online at www.avon.com, August 2001.

8. Kotler, *Kotler on Marketing*, pp. 43–44. For more on developing new-product ideas, see Andrew Hargadon and Robert I. Sutton, "Building an Innovation Factory," *Harvard Business Review,* May–June 2000, pp. 157–166.

9. Brian O'Reilly, "New Ideas, New Products," *Fortune,* March 3, 1997, pp. 61–64. Also see "Michael Schrage, "Getting Beyond the Innovation Fetish," *Fortune,* November 13, 2000, pp. 225–232.

10. See John McCormick, "The Future Is Not Quite Now," *Automotive Manufacturing and Production,* August 2000, pp. 22–24; "DaimlerChrysler Unveils NECAR 5 Methanol-Powered Fuel Cell Vehicle," *Chemical Market Reporter*, November 13, 2000, p. 5; Dale Buss, "Green Cars," *American Demographics,* January 2001, pp. 57–61; and Catherine Greenman, "Fuel Cells: Clean, Reliable (and Pricey) Electricity," *New York Times,* May 10, 2001, p. G8.

11. See Raymond R. Burke, "Virtual Reality Shopping: Breakthrough in Marketing Research," *Harvard Business Review,* March–April 1996, pp. 120–131; Mike Hoffman, "Virtual Shopping," *Inc.*, July 1998, p. 88; and Christopher Ryan, "Virtual Reality in Marketing," *Direct Marketing,* April 2001, pp. 57–62.

12. Adrienne Ward Fawcett, "Oreo Cones Make Top Grade in Poll," *Advertising Age*, June 14, 1993, p. 30; Becky Ebenkamp, "The New Gold Standards," *Brandweek*, April 19, 1999, p. 34; Ebencamp, "It's Like Cheers and Jeers, Only for Brands," *Brandweek*, March 19, 2001; and Ebenkamp, "The Focus Group Has Spoken," *Brandweek,* April 23, 2001, p. 24.

13. See Faye Rice, "Secrets of Product Testing," *Fortune*, November 28, 1994, pp. 172–174.

14. Judann Pollack, "Baked Lays," *Advertising Age,* June 24, 1996, p. S2; and Jack Neff and Suzanne Bidlake, "P&G, Unilever Aim to Take Consumers to the Cleaners," *Advertising Age,* February 12, 2001, pp. 1, 2.

15. See Robert McMath, "To Test or Not to Test," *Advertising Age,* June 1998, p. 64.

16. Emily Nelson, "Colgate's Net Rose 10% in Period, New Products Helped Boost Sales," *Wall Street Journal,* February 2, 2001, p. B6.

17. For a good review of research on new-product development, see Rajesh Sethi, "New Product Quality and Product Development Teams," *Journal of Marketing,* April 2000, pp. 1–14; Rajesh Sethi, Daniel C. Smith, and C. Whan Park, "Cross-Functional Product Development Teams, Creativity, and the Innovativeness of New Consumer Products," *Journal of Marketing Research,* February 2001, pp. 73–85; Shikhar Sarin and Vijay Mahajan, "The Effect of Reward Structures on the Performance of Cross-Functional

Product Development Teams," *Journal of Marketing,* April 2001, pp. 35–54; and Avan R. Jassawalla and Hemant C. Sashittal, "The Role of Senior Management and Team Leaders in Building Collaborative New Product Teams," *Engineering Management Journal,* June 2001, pp. 33–39.

18. Laurie Freeman, "Study: Leading Brands Aren't Always Enduring," *Advertising Age,* February 28, 2000, p. 26.

19. See David Stipp, "The Theory of Fads," *Fortune,* October 14, 1996, pp. 49–52; "Fads vs. Trends," *The Futurist,* March–April 2000, p. 67; Irma Zandl, "How to Separate Trends from Fads," *Brandweek,* October 23, 2000, pp. 30–33; and "Scooter Fad Fades, as Warehouses Fill and Profits Fall," *Wall Street Journal,* June 14, 2001, p. B4.

20. For an interesting discussion of how brand performance is affected by the product life-cycle stage at which the brand enters the market, see Venkatesh Shankar, Gregory S. Carpenter, and Lekshman Krishnamurthi, "The Advantages of Entry in the Growth Stage of the Product Life Cycle: An Empirical Analysis," *Journal of Marketing Research,* May 1999, pp. 269–276.

21. Mark McMaster, "Putting a New Spin on Old Products," *Sales and Marketing Management,* April 2001, p. 20.

22. Michael Hartnett, "Cracker Jack : Chris Neugent," *Advertising Age,* June 26, 2000, p. S22.

23. For a more comprehensive discussion of marketing strategies over the course of the product life cycle, see Philip Kotler, *Marketing Management,* 11th ed. (Upper Saddle River, NJ: Prentice Hall, 2003), Chap. 10.

Chapter 10

1. Thomas T. Nagle and Reed K. Holden, *The Strategy and Tactics of Pricing,* 2nd ed. (Upper Saddle River, NJ: Prentice Hall, 1995), p. 1. Also see Philip Kotler, *Kotler on Marketing* (New York: Free Press, 1999), pp. 142–148.

2. See John Greenwald, "Cereal Showdown," *Time,* April 29, 1996, p. 60; "Cereal Thriller," *The Economist,* June 15, 1996, p. 59; Gretchen Morgenson, "Denial in Battle Creek," *Forbes,* October 7, 1996, p. 44; Judann Pollack, "Post's Price Play Rocked Category, but Did It Work?" *Advertising Age,* December 1, 1997, p. 24; Carleen Hawn, "General Mills Tests Limits," *Forbes,* April 6, 1998, p. 48; Judann Pollack, "Price Cuts Unsettling to Cereal Business," *Advertising Age,* September 28, 1998, p. S10; Rekha Balu, and Susan Pulliam, "Kellogg, Long Treated as Stale by Wall Street, Shows Signs of Putting Some Snap in Its Walk," *Wall Street Journal,* February 16, 1999, pp. C2, C3; Terril Yue Jones, "Outside the Box," *Forbes,* June 14, 1999, pp. 52–53; and "Kellogg Concedes Top Spot to General Mills," *New York Times,* February 22, 2001, p. C4.

3. See Amy E. Cortese, "Good-Bye to Fixed Pricing?" *Business Week,* May 4, 1998, pp. 71–84; Robert D. Hof, "The Buyer Always Wins," *Business Week,* March 22, 1999, pp. EB26–EB28; Robert D. Hof, "Going, Going, Gone," *Business Week,* April 12, 1999, pp. 30–32; and Michael Vizard, Ed Scannell, and Dan Neel, "Suppliers Toy with Dynamic Pricing," *InfoWorld,* May 14, 2001, p. 28.

4. For an excellent discussion of factors affecting pricing decisions, see Nagle and Holden, *The Strategy and Tactics of Pricing,* Chap. 1.

5. See Steve Gelsi, "Spin-Cycle Doctor," *Brandweek,* March 10, 1997, pp. 38–40. Tim Stevens, "From Reliable to 'Wow,'" *Industry Week,* June 22, 1998, pp. 22–26; and William C. Symonds, "'Build a Better Mousetrap' Is No Claptrap," *Business Week,* February 1, 1999, p. 47.

6. See Timothy M. Laseter, "Supply Chain Management: The Ins and Outs of Target Costing," *Purchasing,* March 12, 1998, pp. 22–25,

and John K. Shank and Joseph Fisher, "Case Study: Target Costing as a Strategic Tool," *Sloan Management Review,* Fall 1999, pp. 73–82. Also check out the Swatch Web page at www.swatch.com.

7. Brian Dumaine, "Closing the Innovation Gap," *Fortune,* December 2, 1991, pp. 56–62.

8. Joshua Rosenbaum, "Guitar Maker Looks for a New Key," *Wall Street Journal,* February 11, 1998, p. B1; and information accessed online at www.gibson.com, September, 1999.

9. See Nagle and Holden, *The Strategy and Tactics of Pricing,* Chap. 4.

10. Kevin J. Clancy, "At What Profit Price?" *Brandweek,* June 23, 1997, pp. 24–28; and information accessed online at www.gmpvt.com, July 2001.

11. Melissa Campanelli, "The Price to Pay," *Sales* and *Marketing Management,* September 1994, pp. 96–102. Also see Corinna C. Petry, "The State of the Plate," October 2000, pp. 28–38; and "Nucor Ranks No. 1 with Customers," *Purchasing,* September 2, 1999, p. 32B26.

12. See Kotler, *Kotler on Marketing,* p. 54.

13. See Darren McDermott, "Cost-Consciousness Beats 'Pricing Power,'" *Wall Street Journal,* May 3, 1999, p. A1. Also see Thomas J. Winninger, "Competing on Value," *Executive Excellence,* September 2000, p. 13; and Robert B. Tucker, "Adding Value Profitably," *The American Salesman,* April 2000, pp. 17–20.

14. See John Bell, "Sam Walton (1918–1992): Everyday Low Prices Pay Off," *Journal of Business Strategy,* September–October 1999, pp. 36–38.

15. For a comprehensive discussion of pricing strategies, see Nagle and Holden, *The Strategy and Dynamics of Pricing,* Also see Robert J. Dolan and Hermann Simon, *Power Pricing: How Managing Price Transforms the Bottom Line* (New York: Free Press, 1997).

16. See Edward F. Moltzen, "Intel Cuts Chip Pricing, Again," *CRN,* June 4, 2001, p. 12.

17. Seanna Browder, "Nintendo: At the Top of Its Game," *Business Week,* June 9, 1997, pp. 72–73; Orit Gadiesh and James L. Gilbert, "Profit Pools: A Fresh Look at Strategy," *Harvard Business Review,* May–June 1999, p. 140; and N'Gai Croal, "Game Wars 5.0," *Newsweek,* May 28, 2001, pp. 65–66.

18. Susan Krafft, "Love, Love Me Doo," *American Demographics,* June 1994, pp. 15–16; Damon Darlin, "Zoo Doo," *Forbes,* May 22, 1995, p. 92; and the Zoo Doo Web site, www.zoodoo.com, July 2001.

19. See Nagle and Holden, *The Strategy and Tactics of Pricing,* pp. 225–228; and Manjit S. Yadav and Kent B. Monroe, "How Buyers Perceive Savings in a Bundle Price: An Examination of a Bundle's Transaction Value," *Journal of Marketing Research,* August 1993, pp. 350–358.

20. For more reading on reference prices and psychological pricing, see Richard A. Briesch, Lakshman Krishnamurthi, Tridib Mazumdar, and S. P. Raj, "A Comparative Analysis of Reference Price Models," *Journal of Consumer Research,* September 1997, pp. 202–214; John Huston and Nipoli Kamdar, "$9.99: Can 'Just-Below' Pricing Be Reconciled with Rationality?" *Eastern Economic Journal,* Spring 1996, pp. 137–145; Robert M. Schindler and Patrick N. Kirby, "Patterns of Right-Most Digits Used in Advertised Prices: Implications for Nine-Ending Effects," *Journal of Consumer Research,* September 1997, pp. 192–201; Dhruv Grewal, Kent B. Monroe, Chris Janiszewski, and Donald R. Lichtenstein, "A Range Theory of Price Perception," *Journal of Consumer Research,* March 1999, pp. 353–368; Tridib Mazumdar and Purushottam Papatla, "An Investigation of Reference Price Segments," *Journal of Marketing Research,* May 2000, pp. 246–258; and Indrajit Sinha and Michael Smith, "Consumers' Perceptions of Promotional Framing of Price," *Psychology* and *Marketing,* March 2000, pp. 257–271.

21. Tim Ambler, "Kicking Price Promotion Habit Is Like Getting Off Heroin—Hard," *Marketing*, May 27, 1999, p. 24.

22. Jack Trout, "Prices: Simple Guidelines to Get Them Right," *Journal of Business Strategy*, November–December 1998, pp. 13–16.

23. Philip R. Cateora, *International Marketing*, 7th ed. (Homewood, IL: Irwin, 1990), p. 540. Also see S. Tamer Cavusgil, "Pricing for Global Markets," *Columbia Journal of World Business*, Winter 1996, pp. 66–78; and Barbara Stottinger, "Strategic Export Pricing: A Long and Winding Road," *Journal of International Marketing*, 2001, pp. 40–63.

24. For an interesting discussion of buyer perceptions of price increases, see Margaret C. Campbell, "Perceptions of Price Unfairness: Antecedents and Consequences," *Journal of Marketing Research*, May 1999, pp. 187–199.

25. Jeff Ansell, "Luvs," *Advertising Age*, June 30, 1997, p. S16; and Jack Neff, "Kimberly-Clark Looses 'Bounty Killer,'" *Advertising Age*, April 2, 2001, p. 34.

26. For an excellent discussion of these issues, see Dhruv Grewel and Larry D. Compeau, "Pricing and Public Policy: A Research Agenda and Overview of Special Issue," *Journal of Marketing and Public Policy*, Spring 1999, pp. 3–10.

27. David Barboza, "Archer Daniels Executive Said to Tell of Price-Fixing Talks with Cargill Counterpart," *New York Times*, June 17, 1999, p. 6; and Stephen Labaton, "World Gets Tough on Fixing Prices," *New York Times*, June 3, 2001, p. C1.

28. Holman W. Jenkins Jr., "Business World: Flying the 'Angry' Skies," *Wall Street Journal*, April 29, 1998, p. A23.

29. Dan Carney, "Predatory Pricing: Cleared for Takeoff," *Business Week*, May 14, 2001, p. 50.

30. Mike France, "Does Predatory Pricing Make Microsoft a Predator?" *Business Week*, November 23, 1998, pp. 130–132.

31. Grewel and Compeau, "Pricing and Public Policy: A Research Agenda and Overview of Special Issue," p. 8.

32. For more on public policy and pricing, see Louis W. Stern and Thomas L. Eovaldi, *Legal Aspects of Marketing Strategy* (Upper Saddle River, NJ: Prentice Hall, 1984), Chap 5; Robert J. Posch, *The Complete Guide to Marketing and the Law* (Upper Saddle River, NJ: Prentice Hall, 1988), Chap. 28; Nagle and Holden, *The Strategy and Tactics of Pricing*, Chap. 14; Joseph P. Guiltinan and Gregory Gunlach, "Aggressive and Predatory Pricing: A Framework for Analysis," *Journal of Marketing*, July 1996, pp. 87–102; Bruce Upbin, "Vindication," *Forbes*, November 17, 1997, pp. 52–56; and Grewel and Compeau, "Pricing and Public Policy: A Research Agenda and Overview of Special Issue," pp. 3–10.

Chapter 11

1. Quotes and other information from Donald V. Fites, "Make Your Dealers Your Partners," *Harvard Business Review*, March–April 1996, pp. 84–95; and De 'Ann Weimer, "A New Cat on the Hot Seat," *Business Week*, March 1998, pp. 56–62; Mark Tatge, "Caterpillar Reports 26% Jump in Net Despite Weak Sales," *Wall Street Journal*, April 19, 2000, p. A8; Joseph T. Hallinan, "Caterpillar Beats Estimates, Says 2001 Will Hurt," *Wall Street Journal*, January 19, 2001, p. B6; and information accessed online at www.cat.com, October 2001.

2. For definitions and a complete discussion of distribution channel topics, see Anne T. Coughlin, Erin Anderson, Louis W. Stern, and Adel El-Ansary, *Marketing Channels*, 6th ed. (Upper Saddle River, NJ: Prentice Hall, 2001), pp. 2–3.

3. Rochelle Garner, "Mad as Hell," *Sales and Marketing Management*, June 1999, pp. 55–161; and Chuck Moozakis, "Herman Miller Builds Three-Pronged Strategy—Furniture Company Tailors Web Efforts to Size of Customer," *Internetweek*, June 11, 2001, pp. PG61–PG62.

4. Andy Cohen, "When Channel Conflict Is Good," *Sales and Marketing Management*, April 2000, p. 13.

5. "Business Floating on Air," *The Economist*, May 19, 2001, pp. 56–57; Richard Heller, "Galician Beauty," *Forbes*, May 28, 2001, p. 98; and Carlta Vitzthum, "Just-in-Time Fashion—Spanish Retailer Zara Makes Low-Cost Lines in Weeks by Running Its Own Show," *Wall Street Journal*, May 18, 2001, p. B1.

6. See Ilan Alon, "The Use of Franchising by U.S.-Based Retailers," *Journal of Small Business Management*, April 2001, pp. 111–122; and James H. Amos Jr., "Franchising, More Than Any Act of Government, Will Strengthen the Global Economy," *Franchising World*, May–June 2001, p. 8.

7. See Allan J. Magrath, "Collaborative Marketing Comes of Age—Again," *Sales and Marketing Management*, September 1991, pp. 61–64; Andrew E. Serwer, "What Price Loyalty?" *Fortune*, January 10, 1995, pp. 103–104; and Judann Pollack and Louise Kramer, "Coca-Cola and Pringles Eye Global Brand Linkup," *Advertising Age*, June 15, 1998, pp. 1, 73.

8. See Garner, "Mad as Hell," pp. 55–61.

9. Subhash C. Jain, *International Marketing Management*, 3rd ed. (Boston: PWS-Kent Publishing, 1990), pp. 489–491. Also see "Ever-Shorter Channels—Wholesale Industry Restructures," *Focus Japan*, July–August 1997, pp. 3–4; and Michael R. Czinkota and Masaaki Kotabe, "Entering the Japanese Market: A Reassessment of Foreign Firms' Entry and Distribution Strategies," *Industrial Marketing Management*, November 2000, pp. 483–491.

10. For examples, see Philip Cateora, *International Marketing*, 7th ed. (Homewood, IL: Irwin, 1990), pp. 570–571; Dexter Roberts, "Blazing Away at Foreign Brands," *Business Week*, May 12, 1997, p. 58; and "Taking On Distribution," *Business China*, June 5, 2000, p. 2.

11. For more on channel relationships, see James A. Narus and James C. Anderson, "Rethinking Distribution," *Harvard Business Review*, July–August 1996, pp. 112–120; James C. Anderson and James A. Narus, *Business Market Management* (Upper Saddle River, NJ: Prentice Hall, 1999), pp. 276–288; and Jonathon D. Hibbard, Nirmalya Kumar, and Louis W. Stern, "Examining the Impact of Destructive Acts in Marketing Channel Relationships," *Journal of Marketing Research*, February 2001, pp. 45–61.

12. Pat Curry, "Channel Changes," *Industry Week*, April 2, 2001, pp. 45–48.

13. For a full discussion of laws affecting marketing channels, see Coughlin, Anderson, Stern, and El-Ansary, *Marketing Channels*, Chap. 12.

14. James R. Stock, "The 7 Deadly Sins of Reverse Logistics," *Material Handling Management*, March 2001, pp. MHS5–MHS11; and Martin Piszczalksi, "Logistics: A Difference Between Winning and Losing," *Automotive Manufacturing and Production*, May 2001, pp. 16–18.

15. Shlomo Maital, "The Last Frontier of Cost Reduction," *Across the Board*, February 1994, pp. 51–52; and Suzanne Koudsi, "Attention Kmart Bashers," *Fortune*, November 13, 2000, pp. 213–222.

16. See Robert E. Danielson, "CPFR: Improving Your Business without Being Limited by Technology," *Apparel Industry Magazine*, February 2000, pp. 56–57; and Ben A. Chaouch, "Stock Levels and Delivery Rates in Vendor-Managed Inventory Programs," *Production and Operations Management*, Spring 2001, pp. 31–44.

17. John Huey, "Wal-Mart: Will It Take Over the World?" *Fortune*, January 30, 1989, pp. 52–64; and Mike Troy, "Wal-Mart: Behind the Scenes Efficiency Keeps Growth Curve on Course," *Dsn Retailing Today*, June 4, 2001, pp. 80, 91.

18. J. William Gurley, "Why Dell's War Isn't Dumb," *Fortune,* July 9, 2001, pp. 134–136.

19. For statistics on freight shipments, see *United States 1997 Economic Census: Transportation,* U.S. Department of Transportation, issued December 1999, accessed online at www.bts.gov.

20. See Lara L. Sowinski, "Supply Chain Management and Logistics Software," *World Trade,* February 2001, pp. 34–36; Keith Schultz, "Supply Chain Management Tools," *Internetweek,* June 25, 2001, pp. PG25–PG34; and Karen Lundegaard, "E-Commerce (A Special Report)—Bumpy Ride: Supply-Chain Management Sounds Beautiful in Theory; In Real Life, It's a Daunting Task," *Wall Street Journal,* May 21, 2001, p. R21.

21. See Sandra J. Skrovan, "Partnering with Vendors: The Ties that Bind," *Chain Store Age Executive,* January 1994, pp. 6MH–9MH; Robert D. Buzzell and Gwen Ortmeyer, "Channel Partnerships Streamline Distribution," *Sloan Management Review*, March 22, 1995, p. 85; and Ken Cottrill, "Reforging the Supply Chain," *Journal of Business Strategy,* November–December 1997, pp. 35–39.

22. Skrovan, "Partnering with Vendors," p. 6MH; and Susan Caminiti, "After You Win, the Fun Begins," *Fortune*, May 2, 1994, p. 76.

23. Tom Stein and Jeff Sweat, "Killer Supply Chains—Six Companies Are Using Supply Chains to Transform the Way They Do Business," *Information Week,* November 11, 1998, p. 36; and Susan Reda, "Internet-EDI Initiatives Show Potential to Reinvent Supply Chain Management," *Stores,* January 1999, pp. 26–27.

24. "Is Third Party Logistics in Your Future?" *Modern Materials Handling,* December 2000, pp. S3–S15.

25. Ibid., p. S3.

Chapter 12

1. Quotes and information in this Home Depot tale are from Patricia Sellers, "Companies That Serve You Best," *Fortune,* May 31, 1993, pp. 74–88; Patricia Sellers, "Can Home Depot Fix Its Sagging Stock?" *Fortune,* March 4, 1996, pp. 139–146; Thomas H. Nodine, "Home Depot's Leading Indicators of Value," *Harvard Business Review,* March–April 1999, p. 100; Bernie Marcus, Arthur Blank, and Bob Andelman, *Built from Scratch. How a Couple of Regular Guys Grew the Home Depot from Nothing to $30 Billion* (New York: Random House, 1999); "Retailer of the Year Awards: The Home Depot—Best Trained Sales Staff," *Home Textiles Today,* March 26, 2001, p. SS4; and "The Home Depot Reports Record First Quarter 2001 Earnings," Home Depot press realease, May 15, 2001, accessed online at www.homedepot.com.

2. For more on the convenience store industry, see "2001 SOI Highlights," National Association of Convenience Stores, accessed online at www.cstorecentral.com, August 2001.

3. Andrew W. Franklin, "The Impact of Wal-Mart Supercenters on Supermarket Concentration in U.S. Metropolitan Areas," *Agribusiness,* Winter 2001, pp. 105–114; Richard Turcsik and Jenny Summerour, "David vs. Goliath," *Progressive Grocer,* March 2001, p. 7; and Laura Heller, "Wal-Mart Outprices Atlanta Competition," *Dsn Retailing,* June 18, 2001, pp. 1, 42.

4. See Ray A. Smith, "Outlet Centers Go Upmarket with Amenities," *Wall Street Journal,* June 6, 2001, p. B12.

5. Wendy Zellner, "Warehouse Clubs: When the Going Gets Tough . . . ," *Business Week,* July 16, 2001, p. 60.

6. "The Limited Inc. Annual Report 2000," accessed online at www.limited.com/annual.

7. Quotes from on Shelly Branch, "How Target Got Hot," *Fortune,* May 24, 1999, pp. 169–174; and "Target Works Its Market Magic," *Dsn Retailing Today,* April 2, 2001, pp. 43, 64.

8. Myron Magnet, "Let's Go for Growth," *Fortune,* March 7, 1994, pp. 60–72. Also see Dierdre Donahue, "Bookstores: A Haven for the Intellect," *USA Today,* July 10, 1997, pp. D1, D2; and Christina Nifong, "Beyond Browsing," *Raleigh News and Observer*, May 25, 1999, p. E1.

9. "It's Not Just a Mall. It's Mallville, U.S.A.," *New York Times Magazine,* February 8, 1998, p. 19; Kristen Ostendorf, "Not Wed to Tradition," Gannett News Service, January 5, 1998; and "The History of Mall of America," accessed on line at www.mallofamerica.com, December 1999.

10. Andrea Bermudez, "Bijan Dresses the Wealthy for Success," *Apparel News.Net,* December 1–7, 2000, accessed online at www.apparelnews.net/Archieve/120100/News/newsfeat.htm.

11. Steven Bergsman, "Slow Times at Sherman Oaks: What's Ailing the Big Malls of America?" *Barron's,* May 17, 1999, p. 39.

12. Ibid., p. 39.

13. Dean Starkman, "The Mall, Without the Haul—'Lifestyle Centers' Slip Quietly into Upscale Areas, Mixing Cachet and 'Curb Appeal,'" *Wall Street Journal,* July 25, 2001, p. B1.

14. Amy Barrett, "A Retailing Pacesetter Pulls Up Lame," *Business Week,* July 12, 1993, pp. 122–123.

15. See Malcolm P. McNair and Eleanor G. May, "The Next Revolution of the Retailing Wheel," *Harvard Business Review,* September–October 1978, pp. 81–91; Stephen Brown, "The Wheel of Retailing: Past and Future," *Journal of Retailing,* Summer 1990, pp. 143–147; Stephen Brown, "Variations on a Marketing Enigma: The Wheel of Retailing Theory," *Journal of Marketing Management,* 7, no. 2, 1991, pp. 131–155; Stanley C. Hollander, "The Wheel of Retailing," reprinted in *Marketing Management,* Summer 1996, pp. 63–66; and Jennifer Negley, "Retrenching, Reinventing and Remaining Relevant," *Discount Store News*, April 5, 1999, p. 11.

16. Diane Crispell, "Retailing's Next Decade," *American Demographics,* May 1997, p. 9. Also see Barbara Martinez, "REIT Interest: Will the Internet Kill All the Shopping Centers?" *Wall Street Journal,* February 17, 1999, p. B12.

17. Charles Haddad, "Office Depot's E-Diva," *Business Week,* August 6, 2001, pp. EB22–EB24.

18. Stephanie Anderson Forest and Keith Naughton, "I'll Take That and That and That and . . . ," *Business Week,* June 22, 1998, p. 38; and Chip E. Miller, James Reardon, and Denny E. McCorkle, "The Effects of Competition on Retail Structure: An Examination of Intratype, Intertype, and Intercategory Competition," *Journal of Marketing,* October 1999, pp. 107–120.

19. See "The Fortune 500," *Fortune,* April 16, 2001, p. F1.

20. Regina Fazio Maruca, "Retailing: Confronting the Challenges that Face Bricks-and-Mortar Stores," *Harvard Business Review,* July–August 1999, pp. 159–168. Also see Marshall L. Fisher, Ananth Raman, and Anna Sheen McClelland, "Rocket Science Retailing Is Almost Here: Are You Ready?" *Harvard Business Review,* July–August 2000, pp. 115–124.

21. James Cox, "Red-Letter Day as East Meets West in the Aisles," *USA Today,* September 11, 1996, p. B1; "Wal-Mart Around the World," Wal-Mart 2001 Annual Report, accessed online at www.Wal-Mart.com/corporate/annual_2001/p8.html.

22. Carla Rapoport, "Retailers Go Global," *Fortune,* February 20, 1995, pp. 102–108; Joseph H. Ellis, "Global Retailing's Winners and Losers," *Chain Store Age,* December 1997, pp. 27–29; "Global Retailing in the Connected Economy," *Chain Store Age,* December 1999, pp. 69–82; and "Top 200 Global Retailers," *Stores,* October 2000, pp. G6–G15.

23. Tim Craig, "Carrefour: At the Intersection of Global," *Dsn Retailing Today,* September 18, 2000, p. 16. Also see Richard Tomlinson, "Who's Afraid of Wal-Mart?" *Fortune,* June 26, 2000, pp. 186–196.

24. Nifong, "Beyond Browsing," p. E1.

25. Kathleen Cholewka, "Standing Out Online: The 5 Best E-Marketing Campaigns," *Sales and Marketing Management,* January 2001, pp. 51–58.

26. "McKesson: Online Annual Report 2001," accessed online at www.mckesson.com/wt/ar_2001.php, August 2001.

27. Facts accessed online at www.supervalu.com, August 2001.

Chapter 13

1. The first four of these definitions are adapted from Peter D. Bennett, *Dictionary of Marketing Terms* (Chicago: American Marketing Association, 1995).

2. See Don E. Schultz, Stanley I. Tannenbaum, and Robert F. Lauterborn, *Integrated Marketing Communication* (Chicago, IL: NTC, 1992), Chap. 3 and 4. Also see James R. Ogdan, *Developing a Creative and Innovative Integrated Marketing Communications Plan* (Upper Saddle River, NJ: Prentice Hall, 1998); and David Picton and Amanda Broderick, *Integrated Marketing Communications* (New York: Financial Times Management, 1999).

3. P. Griffith Lindell, "You Need Integrated Attitude to Develop IMC," *Marketing News,* May 26, 1997, p. 6. For more discussion of integrated marketing communications, see J. P. Cornelissen and Andrew L. Lock, "Theoretical Concept of Management Fashion? Examining the Significance of IMC," *Journal of Advertising Research,* September–October 2000, pp. 7–15; Stephen J. Gould, "The State of IMC Research and Applications," *Journal of Advertising Research,* September–October 2000, pp. 22–23; and Kim Bartel Sheehan and Caitlin Doherty, "Re-Weaving the Web: Integrating Print and Online Communications," *Journal of Interactive Marketing,* Spring 2001, pp. 47–59.

4. Stuart Elliott, "Fewer Viewers, More Commercials," *New York Times,* June 8, 1999, p. 1; Bill Carter, "After Super Bowl, 'Survivor' Is the Season's Top Hit on TV," *New York Times,* January 30, 2001, p. C8; and Joe Flint, "Oscar Ratings Fall, but the Program Finishes on Time," *Wall Street Journal,* March 27, 2001, p. B8.

5. Michele Marchetti, "What a Sales Call Costs," *Sales and Marketing Management,* September 2000, p. 80.

6. Information on advertising spending accessed online at the Ad Age Dataplace, www.adage.com, July 2001. Also see "Worldwide Ad Spending," *Advertising Age,* January 1, 2001, p. 10.

7. For more on advertising budgets, see Andrew Ehrenberg, Neil Barnard, and John Scriven, "Justifying Our Advertising Budgets," *Marketing and Research Today,* February 1997, pp. 38–44; Dana W. Hayman and Don E. Schultz, "How Much Should You Spend on Advertising?" *Advertising Age,* April 26, 1999, p. 32; and Laura Q. Hughes, "Measuring Up," *Advertising Age,* February 5, 2001, pp. 1, 34.

8. Information from Gary Levin, "'Meddling' in Creative More Welcome," *Advertising Age,* April 9, 1990, pp. S4, S8; Eleftheria Parpis, "TBWA: Absolut," *Adweek,* November 9, 1998, p. 172; Sarah Theodore, "Absolut Secrets," *Beverage Industry,* July 2000, p. 50; and the Q & A section at www.absolut.com, July 2001.

9. "Swimming the Channels," *American Demographics,* June 1998, p. 37; and information accessed online at www.magazine.org, July 2001.

10. Joe Mandese, "'ER' Tops Price Charts," *Advertising Age,* October 2, 2000, pp. 1 +.

11. Larry Armstrong, "Smart TV Get Even Smarter," *Business Week,* April 16, 2001, pp. 132–134; and Jeff Howe, "Total Control," *American Demographics*, July 2001, pp. 28–32.

12. Edward A. Robinson, "Frogs, Bears, and Orgasms: Think Zany if You Want to Reach Today's Consumers," *Fortune,* June 9, 1997, pp. 153–156. Also see Chuck Ross, "MBC Blasts Beyond the 15-Minute Barrier," *Advertising Age,* August 7, 2000, p. 3.

13. For current magazines rates and circulations, see www.mediastart.com.

14. See *AAAA's TV Commercial Production Survey Shows Largest Cost Increase in 13 Years,* news release, American Association of Advertising Agencies, November 16, 2000, accessed online at www.aaaa.org.

15. See Gary Schroeder, "Behavioral Optimization," *American Demographics,* August 1998, pp. 34–36; Erwin Ephron, "Ad World Was Ripe for Its Conversion to Optimizers," *Advertising Age,* February 22, 1999, p. S16; and Steven J. Stark, "A New and Improved Tool," *Broadcasting and Cable,* February 28, 2000, pp. 30–32.

16. Information on advertising agency income and billings accessed online at http://adage.com/dataplace/archieves/dp514.html, July 2001.

17. Patti Bond, "Today's Topic: From Russia with Fizz, Coke Imports Ads," *Atlanta Journal and Constitution*, April 4, 1998, pp. E2.

18. See "U.K. Tobacco Ad Ban Will Include Sports Sponsorship," *AdAgeInternational.com,* May 1997; "Coca-Cola Rapped for Running Competition in India," *AdAgeInternational.com,* February 1997; Naveen Donthu, "A Cross Country Investigation of Recall of and Attitude Toward Comparative Advertising," *Journal of Advertising,* 27, June 22, 1998, pp. 111; and John Shannon, "Comparative Ads Call for Prudence," *Marketing Week,* May 6, 1999, p. 32.

19. "Promotion Practices Condensed," *Potentials,* November 1998, p. 6. Also see Jack Neff, "Trade Promotion Rises," *Advertising Age,* April 3, 2000, p. 24.

20. Debra Aho Williamson, "P&G's Reformulated Pert Plus Builds Consumer Relationships," *Advertising Age,* June 28, 1999, p. 52.

21. "DSN Charts: Coupons," *Discount Store News,* May 3, 1999, p. 4.

22. See "Electronic Coupon Clipping," *USA Today,* May 11, 1999, p. 1B; Cara Beardi, "Catalina Expands in Cyberworld," *Advertising Age,* January 22, 2001, p. 19; and Roger O. Crockett, "Penny-Pinchers Paradise," *Business Week,* January 22, 2001, p. EB12.

23. See Kate Bertrand, "Premiums Prime the Market," *Advertising Age's Business Marketing,* May 1998, p. S6; and Paul Nolan, "Promotions Come Alive with the Sound of Music," *Potentials,* April 1999, p. 10.

24. See "Power to the Key Ring and T-Shirt," *Sales and Marketing Management,* December 1989, p. 14; and Chad Kaydo, "Your Logo Here," *Sales and Marketing Management,* April 1998, pp. 65–70.

25. See Richard Szathmary, "Trade Shows," *Sales and Marketing Management,* May 1992, pp. 83–84; Srinath Gopalakrishna, Gary L. Lilien, Jerome D. Williams, and Ian Sequeira, "Do Trade Shows Pay Off?" *Journal of Marketing,* July 1995, pp. 75–83; Peter Jenkins, "Making the Most of Trade Shows," *Nation's Business,* June 1999, p. 8; and Ben Chapman, "The Trade Show Must Go On," *Sales and Marketing Management,* June 2001, p. 22.

26. Adapted from Scott Cutlip, Allen Center, and Glen Broom, *Effective Public Relations,* 8th ed. (Upper Saddle River, NJ: Prentice Hall, 1999), Chap. 1.

27. Diane Brady, "Wizard of Marketing," *Business Week*, July 24, 2000, pp. 84–87.

28. Al Ries and Laura Ries, "First Do Some Publicity," *Advertising Age*, February 8, 1999, p. 42.

29. See Mark Gleason, "Edelman Sees Niche in Web Public Relations," *Advertising Age,* January 20, 1997, p. 30; Michael Krauss, "Good PR Critical to Growth on the Net," *Marketing News,* January 18, 1999, p. 8; Steve Jarvis, "How the Internet Is Changing Fundamentals of Publicity," *Marketing News,* July 17, 2000, p. 6; and Don Middleberg, *Winning PR in the Wired World: Powerful Communications Strategies or the Noisy Digital Space* (New York: McGraw-Hill Professional Publishing, 2000).

Chapter 14

1. Quotes from Andy Cohen, "Top of the Charts: Lear Corporation," *Sales and Marketing Management,* July 1998, p. 40. Also see "Lear Corporation," *Sales and Marketing Management*, July 1999, p. 62; Fara Warner, "Lear Won't Take a Back Seat," *Fast Company,* June 2001, pp. 178–185; and "This Is Lear," accessed online at www.lear.com, July 2001.

2. See Bill Kelley, "How to Sell Airplanes, Boeing-Style," *Sales and Marketing Management,* December 9, 1985, pp. 32–34; Andy Cohen, "Boeing," *Sales and Marketing Management,* October 1997, p. 68; and Stanley Holmes, "Rumble Over Tokyo," *Business Week,* April 2, 2001, pp. 80–81.

3. Geoffrey Brewer, "Love the Ones You're With," *Sales and Marketing Management,* February 1997, pp. 38–45.

4. Michele Marchetti, "What a Sales Call Costs," *Sales and Marketing Management*, September 2000, p. 80.

5. See Martin Everett, "Selling by Telephone," *Sales and Marketing Management,* December 1993, pp. 75–79.

6. Geoffrey Brewer, "Lou Gerstner Has His Hands Full," *Sales and Marketing Management*, May 8, 1998, pp. 36–41; and Michelle Cioci, "Marketing to Small Businesses," *Sales & Marketing Management,* December 2000, pp. 94–100.

7. See "A Phone Is Better Than a Face," *Sales and Marketing Management,* October 1987, p. 29. Also see Brett A. Boyle, "The Importance of the Industrial Inside Sales Force: A Case Study," *Industrial Marketing Management,* September 1996, pp. 339–348; Victoria Fraza, "Upgrading Inside Sales," *Industrial Distribution,* December 1997, pp. 44–49; and Michele Marchetti, "Look Who's Calling," *Sales and Marketing Management,* May 1998, pp. 43–46.

8. Rick Mullin, "From Lone Wolves to Team Players," *Chemical Week,* January 14, 1998, pp. 33–34; and James P. Morgan, "Cross-Functional Buying: Why Teams Are Hot," *Purchasing,* April 5, 2001, pp. 27–32.

9. Robert Hiebeler, Thomas B. Kelly, and Charles Ketteman, *Best Practices: Building Your Business with Customer-Focused Solutions* (New York: Arthur Andersen/Simon & Schuster, 1998), pp. 122–124. Also see Mark A. Moon and Susan Forquer Gupta, "Examining the Formation of Selling Centers: A Conceptual Framework," *Journal of Personal Selling and Sales Management,* Spring 1997, pp. 31–41; and Donald W. Jackson Jr., Scott M. Widmier, Ralph Giacobbe, Janet E. Keith, "Examining the Use of Team Selling by Manufacturers' Representatives: A Situational Approach," *Industrial Marketing Management,* March 1999, pp. 155–164; and Henry Canaday, "Flyaway Sales," *Selling Power,* October 2000, pp. 104–113.

10. See George H. Lucas Jr., A. Parasuraman, Robert A. Davis, and Ben M. Enis, "An Empirical Study of Sales Force Turnover," *Journal of Marketing,* July 1987, pp. 34–59; Thomas R. Wotruba and Pradeep K. Tyagi, "Met Expectations and Turnover in Direct Selling," *Journal of Marketing,* July 1991, pp. 24–35; Chad Kaydo, "Overturning Turnover," *Sales and Marketing Management,* November 1997, pp. 50–60, and Marchetti, "What a Sales Call Costs," p. 80.

11. See Geoffrey Brewer, "Mind Reading: What Drives Top Salespeople to Greatness?" *Sales and Marketing Management,* May 1994, pp. 82–88; Barry J. Farber, "Success Stories for Salespeople," *Sales and Marketing Management,* May 1995, pp. 30–31; Roberta Maynard, "Finding the Essence of Good Salespeople," *Nation's Business,* February 1998, p. 10; and Jeanie Casison, "Closest Thing to Cloning," *Incentive,* June 1999, p. 7.

12. See "To Test or Not to Test," *Sales and Marketing Management,* May 1994, p. 86; and Elena Harris, "Reduce Recruiting Risks," *Sales and Marketing Management,* May 2000, p. 18.

13. Sarah Lorge, "Getting into Their Heads," *Sales and Marketing Management,* February 1998, pp. 58–67.

14. Robert Klein, "Nabisco Sales Soar After Sales Training," *Marketing News,* January 6, 1997, p. 23. Also see Malcolm Fleschner, "Training: How to Find the Best Training Solutions for Your Sales Team," *Selling Power,* June 2001, pp. 93–97.

15. Kevin Dobbs, "Training on the Fly," *Sales and Marketing Management*, November 2000, pp. 93–98. Also see Malcolm Fleschner, "Training: Easy Does It," *Selling Power,* March 2001, pp. 118–122.

16. Christen P. Heide, "All Levels of Sales Reps Post Impressive Earnings," press release, www.dartnell.com, May 5, 1997; and *Dartnell's 30th Sales Force Compensation Survey,* Dartnell Corporation, August 1998.

17. Geoffrey Brewer, "Brain Power," *Sales and Marketing Management,* May 1997, pp. 39–48; Don Peppers and Martha Rogers, "The Price of Customer Service," *Sales and Marketing Management,* April 1999, pp. 20–21; and Michelle Marchetti, "Pay Changes Are on the Way," *Sales and Marketing Management,* August 2000, p. 101.

18. David Prater, "The Third Time's the Charm," *Sales and Marketing Management,* September 2000, pp. 101–104.

19. Melinda Ligos, "Point, Click, and Sell," *Sales and Marketing Management,* May 1999, pp. 51–56; Tim Wilson, "Salespeople Leverage the Net," *Internetweek,* June 4, 2001, pp. PG11, PG13; and Amy J. Morgan and Scott A. Inks, "Technology and the Sales Force: Increasing Acceptance of Sales Force Automation," *Industrial Marketing Management,* July 2001, pp. 463–472.

20. Bob Donath, "Delivering Value Starts with Proper Prospecting," *Marketing News,* November 10, 1997, p. 5. Also see Sarah Lorge, "The Best Way to Prospect," *Sales and Marketing Management,* January 1998, p. 80; and "Skills Workshop: Prospecting," *Selling Power,* October 2000, pp. 54–56.

21. David Stamps, "Training for a New Sales Game," *Training,* July 1997, pp. 46–52; and Erin Stout, "Throwing the Right Pitch," *Sales and Marketing Management,* April 2001, pp. 61–63.

22. Betsey Cummings, "Do Customers Hate Salespeople?" *Sales and Marketing Management,* June 2001, pp. 44–51; and Don Chambers, "Draw Them In," *Selling Power,* March 2001, pp. 51–52.

23. "Briefcase Full of Views: Johnson & Johnson Uses Virtual Reality to Give Prospects an Inside Look at Its Products," *American Demographics,* April 1997.

24. Gary Hamel and Jeff Sampler, "The E-Corporation: More Than Just Web-Based, It's Building a New Industrial Order," *Fortune,* December 7, 1998, pp. 80–92.

25. For these and other direct-marketing statistics in this section, see *Economic Impact: U.S. Direct Marketing Today Expenditure Survey,* Direct Marketing Association, accessed online at www.the-dma.org/library/publications/libres-ecoimpact2.sht, July 2001.

26. Carol Krol, "Pizza Hut's Database Makes Its Couponing More Efficient," *Advertising Age*, November 30, 1998, p. 27; and Dana Blakenhorn, "Marketers Hone Targeting," *Advertising Age*, June 18, 2001, p. T16.

27. For these and other examples, see Jonathan Berry, "A Potent New Tool for Selling: Database Marketing," *Business Week*, September 4, 1994, pp. 56–62; Weld F. Royal, "Do Databases Really Work?" *Sales and Marketing Management*, October 1995, pp. 66–74; Daniel Hill, "Love My Brand," *Brandweek*, January 19, 1998, pp. 26–29; "FedEx Taps into Data Warehousing," *Advertising Age's Business Marketing*, January 1999, p. 25; and Harriet Marsh, "Dig Deeper into the Database Goldmine," *Marketing*, January 11, 2001, pp. 29–30.

28. Betsy Spethmann, "Can We Talk?" *American Demographics*, March 1999, pp. 42–44. Also see Tricia Campbell, "Database Marketing for the Little Guys," *Sales and Marketing Management*, June 1999, p. 69.

29. *Economic Impact: U.S. Direct Marketing Today Executive Summary*, Direct Marketing Association, 2001.

30. Matthew L. Wald, "Third Area Code Is Added in the Land of the Toll-Free," *New York Times*, April 4, 1998, p. 10.

31. Kevin R. Hopkins, "Dialing in to the Future," *Business Week*, July 28, 1997, p. 90; and Holly McCord, "1-900-CALL-AN-RD," *Prevention*, August 1997, p. 54.

32. See James Heckman, "How Telemarketers Are Coping with the Rising Tide of State Regs," *Marketing News*, April 12, 1999, p. 4; Catherine Siskos, "Pulling the Plug on Telemarketers," *Kiplinger's Personal Finance Magazine*, July 1999, pp. 18–20; "'Don't Call Us List Takes Effect Today," *New York Times*, April 1, 2001, p. A31; and Gerda Gallop-Goodman, "Please Don't Hang Up," *American Demographics*, May 2001, p. 28.

33. *Economic Impact: U.S. Direct Marketing Today Executive survey*, Direct Marketing Association, 2001.

34. Hallie Mummert, "The Year's Best Bells and Whistles," *Target Marketing*, November 2000, pp. TM3–TM5; and Susan Reda, "Software Package Seeks to Revive CD-ROMs as Consumer Marketing Technology," *Stores*, November 2000, pp. 66–70.

35. Kruti Trivedi, "Telemarketers Don't Want You, Just Your Answering Machine," *Wall Street Journal*, August 6, 1999, p. B1; Karen E. Nussel, "Voice Mail Offers Opportunities," *Advertising Age's Business Marketing*, August 1999, p. 16; and Stuart Elliot, "ABC Backs Away from Using Voice Mail to Promote Lineup," *New York Times*, July 22, 2000. p. B1.

36. *Economic Impact: U.S. Direct Marketing Today Executive Summary*, Direct Marketing Association, 2001.

37. "Catalog Study Now Available," *Business Forms, Labels, and Systems*, June 20, 2001, p. 24; and Richard S. Hodgson, "It's Still the Catalog Age," *Catalog Age*, June 2001, p. 156.

38. "Lillian Vernon Announces New Catalog Title," *Direct Marketing*, April 1998, pp. 15–16.

39. Molly Prior, "Lands' End Crosses Threshold of Internet Retailing Excellence," *Dsn Retailing Today*, November 6, 2000, pp. 6, 52; and Carol Sliwa, "Clothing Retailer Finds Worldwide Business on the Web," *Computerworld*, April 30, 2001, p. 40.

40. Example adapted in part from Moira Pascale, "Archie's Online Boom," *Catalog Age*, August 1999, p. 10.

41. Ron Donoho, "One-Man Show," *Sales and Marketing Management*, June 2001, pp. 36–42.

42. Erika Brown, "Ooh! Aah!" *Forbes*, March 8, 1999, p. 56; and Shirley Leung, "Grill Sales Slow but Big Payouts Flow to Foreman," *Wall Street Journal*, February 2, 2001, p. B1.

43. See Jacqueline M. Graves, "The Fortune 500 Opt for Infomercials," *Fortune*, March 6, 1995, p. 20; "Infomercials," *Advertising Age*,

September 8, 1997, pp. A1–A2; Carol Krol, "Navy Infomercial Aims at Prospective Recruits," *Advertising Age*, May 31, 1999, p. 12; Dave Guilford, "Cadillac Takes New Route for Sevill STS: Infomercial," *Advertising Age*, August 23, 1999, p. 8; Jean Halliday, "Volvo Ready to Act on Leads After Infomercial Success," *Advertising Age*, January 25, 1999, p. 61; and Alison Stein Wellner, "Hot Wheels," *American Demographics*, August 2000, pp. 48–49.

44. See Steve Sullivan, "Shopping Channels: Less Hard Sell," *Broadcasting and Cable*, November 27, 2000, pp. 86–90; and Bob Tedeschi, "Television Shopping Channels May Become the Big Winners in the Competition for Online Sales," *New York Times*, April 16, 2001, p. C4.

45. "Lining Up for Interactive Kiosks," *Nation's Business*, February 1998, p. 46; Warren S. Hersch, "Kiosks Poised to Be a Huge Growth Market," *Computer Reseller News*, May 18, 1998, p. 163; Catherine Yang, "No Web Site Is an Island," *Business Week*, March 22, 1999, p. EB38; "Kiosk: Disney Store," *Chain Store Age*, December 2000, p. 14A; and Larry Beck, "The Kiosk's Ship Has Come In," *Dsn Retailing Today*, February 19, 2001, p. 14.

46. "Interactive: Ad Age Names Finalists," *Advertising Age*, February 27, 1995, pp. 12–14.

47. Yang, "No Web Site Is an Island," p. EB38.

48. "Sweepstakes Groups Settles with States," *New York Times*, June 27, 2001, p. A14; and "Business Brief—Publishers Clearing House: Payment of $34 Million Set to Settle with 26 States," *Wall Street Journal*, June 27, 2001, p. B8.

49. John Hagel III and Jeffrey F. Rayport, "The Coming Battle for Customer Information," *Harvard Business Review*, January–February 1997, pp. 53–65; Bruce Horovitz, "AmEx Kills Database Deal After Privacy Outrage," *USA Today*, July 15, 1998, p. B1; and Carol Krol, "Consumers Reach the Boiling Point," *Advertising Age*, March 29, 1999, p. 22.

50. Melanie Rigney, "Too Close for Comfort, Execs Warn," *Advertising Age*, January 13, 1992, p. 31. Also see "Summary of '1992 Harris-Equifax Consumer Privacy Survey,'" *Marketing News*, August 16, 1993, p. A18; Jennifer Lach, "The New Gatekeepers," *American Demographics*, June 1999, pp. 41–42; and Stephen F. Ambrose Jr. and Joseph W. Gelb, "Consumer Privacy Regulation and Litigation," *The Business Lawyer*, May 2001, pp. 1157–1178.

Chapter 15

1. Mark L. Clifford and Nicole Harris, "Coke Pours into Asia," *Business Week*, October 28, 1996, pp. 72–77; Mark Gleason, "Sprite Is Riding Global Ad Effort to No. 4 Status," *Advertising Age*, November 18, 1996, p. 30; Lauren R. Rublin, "Chipping Away," *Barron's*, June 12, 2000, pp. 31–34; Betsy McKay, "Coca-Cola Restructuring Effort Has Yet to Prove Effective," *Asian Wall Street Journal*, March 2, 2001; Hillary Chura and Richard Linnett, "Coca-Cola Readies Global Assault," *Advertising Age*, April 2, 2001, pp. 1, 34; Sean Mehegan, "Soft Drinks," *Adweek*, April 23, 2001, p. SR24; and "The Story of Coca-Cola," accessed online at www.coca-cola.com, August 2001.

2. John Alden, "What in the World Drives UPS?" *International Business*, April 1998, pp. 6–7; Karen Pennar, "Two Steps Forward, One Step Back," *Business Week*, August 31, 1998, p. 116; Michelle Wirth Fellman, "A New World for Marketers," *Marketing News*, May 10, 1999, p. 13; and Alan Greenspan, "International Trade: Globalization vs. Protectionism," *Vital Speeches of the Day*, April 15, 2001, pp. 386–388.

3. Gail Edmondson, "See the World, Erase Its Borders," *Business Week*, August 28, 2000, pp. 113–114.

4. "The Unique Japanese," *Fortune*, November 24, 1986, p. 8; and James D. Southwick, "Addressing Market Access Barriers in Japan Through the WTO," *Law and Policy in International Business,* Spring 2000, pp. 923-976. For more on nontariff and other barriers, see Warren J. Keegan and Mark C. Green, *Principles of Global Marketing* (Upper Saddle River, NJ: Prentice Hall, 2000), Chap 8.

5. Douglas Harbrecht and Owen Ullmann, "Finally GATT May Fly," *Business Week*, December 29, 1993, pp. 36-37; and Ping Deng, "Impact of GATT Uruguay Round on Various Industries," *American Business Review*, June 1998, pp. 22-29. Also see Helene Cooper, "U.S. Seeks a New Rounds of WTO Talks," *Wall Street Journal*, July 18, 2001, p. A12; and the WTO Web site at www.wto.org.

6. Information about the European Union accessed online at http://europa.eu.int, August 2001.

7. Stanley Reed, "We Have Liftoff! The Strong Launch of the Euro Is Hailed Around the World," *Business Week*, January 18, 1999, pp. 34-37; and Allyson L. Stewart-Allen, "Changeover to Euro Has Hidden Expenses," *Marketing News,* July 30, 2001, p. 6.

8. James Welsh, "Enter the Euro," *World Trade*, January 1999, pp. 34-38.

9. For more on the European Union, see "Around Europe in 40 Years," *The Economist,* May 31, 1997, p. S4; "European Union to Begin Expansion," *New York Times,* March 30, 1998, p. A5; Joan Warner, "Mix Us Culturally? It's Impossible," *Business Week,* April 27, 1998, p. 108; and Paul J. Deveney, "World Watch," *Wall Street Journal*, May 20, 1999, p. A12.

10. Charles J. Whalen, "NAFTA's Scorecard: So Far, So Good," *Business Week*, July 9, 2001, pp. 54-56; Geri Smith, "Betting on Free Trade: Will the Americas Be One Big Market?" *Business Week,* April 23, 2001, pp. 60-62; and Ernesto Zedillo, "Commentary: Free Trade Is the Best Diplomacy," *Forbes*, July 23, 2001, p. 49.

11. Larry Rohter, "Latin America and Europe to Talk Trade," *New York Times*, June 26, 1999, p. 2.

12. David Woodruff, "Ready to Shop Until They Drop," *Business Week*; June 22, 1998, pp. 104-108.

13. Virginia Postrel, "The Wealth of Nations Depends on How Open They Are to International Trade," *New York Times,* May 17, 2001, p. C2.

14. Dan West, "Countertrade," *Business Credit*, April 2001, pp. 64-67.

15. For these and other examples, see Louis Kraar, "How to Sell to Cashless Buyers," *Fortune*, November 7, 1988, pp. 147-154; Nathaniel Gilbert, "The Case for Countertrade," *Across the Board*, May 1992, pp. 43-45; Darren McDermott and S. Karen Witcher, "Bartering Gains Currency," *Wall Street Journal,* April 6, 1998, p. A10; and Anne Millen Porter, "Global Economic Meltdown Boosts Barter Business," *Purchasing*, February 11, 1999, pp. 21-25; and S. Jayasankaran, "Fire-Fighting," *Far Eastern Economic Review,* May 31, 2001, p. 52.

16. Rebecca Piirto Heath, "Think Globally," *Marketing Tools,* October 1996, pp. 49-54; and "The Power of Writing," *National Geographic*, August 1999, p. 128-129.

17. For other examples, see *Dun & Bradstreet's Guide to Doing Business Around the World* (Upper Saddle River, NJ: Prentice Hall, 2000); Betsy Cummings, "Selling Around the World," *Sales and Marketing Management,* May 2001, p. 70; and Philip Kotler, *Marketing Management: Analysis, Planning, Implementation, and Control*, 11th ed. (Upper Saddle River, NJ: Prentice Hall, 2003), Chap. 7.

18. Gail Edmondson, "The Beauty of Global Branding," *Business Week*, June 28, 1999, pp.70-75. Also see Don Davis, "L'Oreal Continues Acquisition Binge," *Global Cosmetic Industry,* June 2000, p. 15.

19. Charles A. Coulombe, "Global Expansion: The Unstoppable Crusade," *Success*, September 1994, pp. 18-20; "Amway Hopes to Set Up Sales Network in India," *Wall Street Journal*, February 17, 1998, p. B8; Gerald S. Couzens, "Dick Devos," *Success*, November 1998, pp. 52-57; and information accessed online at www.amway.com/OurStory/o-hist.asp, August 2001.

20. See "Crest, Colgate Bare Teeth in Competition for China," *Advertising Age International,* November 1996, p. I3; Mark L. Clifford, "How You Can Win in China," *Business Week,* May 26, 1997, pp. 66-68; and Ben Davies, "The Biggest Market Retains Its Luster," *Asia Money*, January 1998, pp. 47-49.

21. Linda Grant, "GE's 'Smart Bomb' Strategy," *Fortune*, July 21, 1997, pp. 109-110; Richard J. Babyak, "GE Appliances: The Polar Approach," *Appliance Manufacturer*, February 1997, p. G22; Joe Jancsurak, "Asia to Drive World Appliance Growth," *Appliance Manufacturer*, February 1999, pp. G3-G6; and Jim Rohwer, "GE Digs into Asia," *Fortune,* October 2, 2000, pp. 165-178.

22. Robert Neff, "In Japan, They're Goofy about Disney," *Business Week*, March 12, 1990, p. 64; and "In Brief: E*Trade Licensing Deal Gives It an Israeli Link," *American Banker,* May 11, 1998; John Engen, "Going Going Global," *USBanker,* February 2000, pp. 22S-25S; and "Cowboys and Samuri: The Japanizing of Universal," *Wall Street Journal*, March 22, 2001, p. B1.

23. See Cynthia Kemper, "KFC Tradition Sold Japan on Chicken," *Denver Post*, June 7, 1998, p. J4.

24. See Theodore Levitt, "The Globalization of Markets," *Harvard Business Review*, May-June 1983, pp. 92-102; David M. Szymanski, Sundar G. Bharadwaj, and Rajan Varadarajan, "Standardization versus Adaptation of International Marketing Strategy: An Empirical Investigation," *Journal of Marketing*, October 1993, pp. 1-17; Ashish Banerjee, "Global Campaigns Don't Work; Multinationals Do," *Advertising Age*, April 18, 1994, p. 23; Cyndee Miller, "Chasing Global Dream," *Marketing News,* December 2, 1996, pp. 1, 2; and Jeryl Whitelock and Carole Pimblett, "The Standardization Debate in International Marketing," *Journal of Global Marketing,* 1997, p. 22.

25. See "In India, Beef-Free Mickie D," *Business Week*, April 7, 1995, p. 52; Jeff Walters, "Have Brand Will Travel," *Brandweek,* October 6, 1997, pp. 22-26; and David Barboza, "From Abroad, McDonald's Finds Value in Local Control," *New York Times*, February 12, 1999, p. 1; and Nanette Byrnes, "Brands in a Bind," *Business Week,* August 28, 2000, pp. 234-238.

26. For more, see Warren J. Keegan, *Global Marketing Management*, 7th ed. (Upper Saddle River, NJ: Prentice Hall, 2002), pp. 346-351.

27. Lawrence Donegan, "Heavy Job Rotation MTV Europe Sacks 80 Employees in the Name of 'Regionalisation,'" *The Guardian*, November 21, 1997, p. 19; "MTV Hits 100 Million in Asia," *New Media Markets,* January 28, 1999, p. 12; Brett Pulley and Andrew Tanzer, "Sumner's Gemstone," *Forbes*, February 21, 2000, pp. 106-111, and Sally Beatty and Carol Hymowitz, "Boss Talk: How MTV Stays Tuned into Teens," *Wall Street Journal*, March 21, 2000, p. B1.

28. Bernd H. Schmitt and Yigang Pan, "In Asia, the Supernatural Means Sales," *New York Times*, February 19, 1995, 3, 11; Sally Taylor, "Tackling the Curse of Bad Feng Shui," *Publishers Weekly,* April 27, 1998, p. 24; Michael Schrage, "Sorry About the Profits, Boss. My Feng Shui Is Off," *Fortune,* November 27, 2000, p. 306; and Barry Janoff, "East Meets West," *Progressive Grocer,* January 2001, pp. 47-49.

29. Erika Rasmusson, "Global Warning," *Sales and Marketing Management*, November 1998, p. 17; and Bradley Johnson, "IBM

Talks Global Clout, in Foreign Languages," *Advertising Age*, June 7, 1999, p. 10.

30. Kate MacArthur, "Coca-Cola Light Employs Local Edge," *Advertising Age,* August 21, 2000, pp. 18–19.

31. See Michael Oneal, "Harley-Davidson: Ready to Hit the Road Again," *Business Week*, July 21, 1986, p. 70; and "EU Proposes Dumping Change," *East European Markets,* February 14, 1997, pp 2–3.

32. Maricris G. Briones, "The Euro Starts Here," *Marketing News*, July 20, 1998, pp. 1, 39.

33. Ram Charan, "The Rules Have Changed," *Fortune,* March 16, 1998, pp. 159–162.

34. See Maria Shao, "Laying the Foundation for the Great Mall of China," *Business Week*, January 25, 1988, pp. 68–69; Mark L. Clifford and Nicole Harris, "Coke Pours into China," *Business Week,* October 28, 1996, p. 73; and Patrick Powers, "Distribution in China: The End of the Beginning," *China Business Review,* July–August, 2001, pp. 8–12.

35. Richard Tomlinson, "The China Card," *Fortune,* May 25, 1998, p. 82; and Paul Mooney, "Deals on Wheels," *Far East Economic Review*, May 20, 1999, p. 53.

36. Peter Galuszka and Ellen Neuborne, "P&G's Hottest New Product: P&G," *Business Week*, October 5, 1998, p. 96; and Christine Bittar, "Cosmetic Changes," *Brandweek,* June 18, 2001, p. 2.

Chapter 16

1. Portions adapted from Thea Singer, "Can Business Still Save the World?" *Inc.,* April 30, 2001, pp. 58–71. Other information from Harriot Marsh, "Has the Body Shop Lost Its Direction for Good?" *Marketing,* May 10, 2001, p. 19; Mike Hoffman, "Ben Cohen: Ben & Jerry's Homemade, Established in 1978," *Inc.* April 30, 2001, p. 68; and Sarah Ellison, "Body Shop Hopes for New Image with an Omnilife Deal—Possible Takeover Could Spruce Up Brand That Has Lost Its Appeal over the Years," *Wall Street Journal,* June 8, 2001, p. B4.

2. See Lois Biener and Michael Siegel, "Tobacco Marketing and Adolescent Smoking: More Support for a Causal Inference," *American Journal of Public Health,* March 2000, pp. 407–411; and Greg Winter, "Tobacco Producers Are Willing to Talk with Justice Department," *New York Times,* June 22, 2001, p. C1.

3. James Heckman, "Don't Shoot the Messenger: More and More Often, Marketing Is the Regulators' Target," *Marketing News,* May 24, 1999, pp. 1, 9; "Sweepstakes Groups Settles with States," *New York Times,* June 27, 2001, p. A.14; and "Business Brief—Publishers Clearing House: Payment of $34 Million Set to Settle with 26 States," *Wall Street Journal,* June 27, 2001, p. B8.

4. Theodore Levitt, "The Morality(?) of Advertising," *Harvard Business Review*, July–August 1970, pp. 84–92. For counterpoints, see Heckman, "Don't Shoot the Messenger" pp. 1, 9.

5. Sandra Pesmen, "How Low Is Low? How Free Is Free?" *Advertising Age*, May 7, 1990, p. S10; and Karolyn Schuster, "The Dark Side of Nutrition," *Food Management*, June 1999, pp. 34–39.

6. David Welch, "Firestone: Is This Brand Beyond Repair?" *Business Week,* June 11, 2001, p. 48.

7. Cliff Edwards, "Where Have All the Edsels Gone?" *Greensboro News Record*, May 24, 1999, p. B6. For a thought-provoking short case involving planned obsolescence, see James A. Heely and Roy L. Nersesian, "The Case of Planned Obsolescence," *Management Accounting*, February 1994, p. 67. Also see Joel Dryfuss, "Planned Obsolescence Is Alive and Well," *Fortune*, February 15, 1999,

p. 192; and Atsuo Utaka, "Planned Obsolescence and Marketing Strategy," *Managerial and Decision Economics,* December 2000, pp. 339–344.

8. See Judith Bell and Bonnie Maria Burlin, "In Urban Areas: Many More Still Pay More for Food," *Journal of Public Policy and Marketing*, Fall 1993, pp. 268–270; Tony Attrino, "Nationwide Settles Redlining Suit in Ohio," *National Underwriter,* April 27, 1998, p. 4; Kathryn Graddy and Diana C. Robertson, "Fairness of Pricing Decisions," *Business Ethics Quarterly*, April 1999, pp. 225–243; Gordon Matthews, "Does Everyone Have the Right to Credit?" *USBanker,* April 2001, pp. 44–48.

9. Marcia Stepanek, "Weblining," *Business Week,* April 3, 2000, pp. EB26–EB43. Also see Karin Helperin, "Wells Fargo Online Service Accused of Redlining," *Bank Systems and Technology,* September 2000, p. 19.

10. John De Graaf, "The Overspent American/Luxury Fever," *The Amicus Journal,* Summer 1999, pp. 41–43.

11. Carolyn Setlow, "Profiting from America's New Materialism," *Discount Store News,* April 17, 2000, p. 16.

12. James Twitchell, "Two Cheers for Materialism," *The Wilson Quarterly*, Spring 1999, pp. 16–26; and Twitchell, *Lead Us into Temptation: The Triumph of American Materialism* (New York: Columbia University Press, 1999).

13. Kim Clark, "Real-World-O-Nomics: How to Make Traffic Jams a Thing of the Past," *Fortune,* March 31, 1997, p. 34.

14. Lee Hultgreen and Kim Kawada, "San Diego's Interstate 15 High-Occupancy/Toll Lane Facility Using Value Pricing," *ITE Journal*, June 1999, pp. 22–27.

15. From an advertisement for *Fact* magazine, which does not carry advertisements.

16. See Shawn Tully, "It's Time for Merger Mania II," *Fortune*, June 7, 1999, pp. 231–232; and "Americas: Merger Mania," *Futures,* February 2000, p. 14.

17. Steve Hamm, "Microsoft's Future," *Business Week*, January 19, 1998, pp. 58–68; and Ronald. A. Cass, "Microsoft, Running Scared," *New York Times*, June 28, 1999, p. 17.

18. For more on the evolution of consumerism, see Paul N. Bloom and Stephen A. Greyser, "The Maturing of Consumerism," *Harvard Business Review*, November–December 1981, pp. 130–139, Robert J. Samualson, "The Aging of Ralph Nader," *Newsweek*, December 16, 1985, p. 57; Douglas A. Harbrecht, "The Second Coming of Ralph Nader," *Business Week*, March 6, 1989, p. 28; George S. Day and David A. Aaker, "A Guide to Consumerism," *Marketing Management,* Spring 1997, pp. 44–48; Benet Middleton, "Consumerism: A Pragmatic Ideology," *Consumer Policy Review,* November–December, 1998, pp. 213–217; and Penelope Green, "Consumerism and Its Malcontents," *New York Times,* December 17, 2000, p. 9.

19. Stuart L. Hart, "Beyond Greening: Strategies for a Sustainable World," *Harvard Business Review,* January–February 1997, pp. 66–76. Also see Jacquelyn Ottman, "What Sustainability Means to Marketers," *Marketing News,* July 21, 1997, p. 4; and James L. Kolar, "Environmental Sustainability: Balancing Pollution Control with Economic Growth," *Environmental Quality Management*, Spring 1999, pp. 1–10.

20. Peter M. Senge, Goran Carstedt, and Patrick L. Porter, "Innovating Our Way to the Next Industrial Revolution," *MIT Sloan Management Review,* Winter 2001, pp. 24–38.

21. Michael E. Porter and Claas van der Linde, "Green *and* Competitive: Ending the Stalemate," *Harvard Business Review*, September–October 1995, pp. 120–134.

22. Hart, "Beyond Greening," p. 72. For other examples, see Jacquelyn Ottman, "Environmental Winners Show Sustainable Strategies," *Marketing News,* April 27, 1998, p. 6. Also see "Environment, Health, and Safety 2000 Progress Report," Xerox Corporation, accessed online at http://www2.xerox.com/downloads/ehs2000pdf.

23. Hart, "Beyond Greening," p. 73; Carl Pope, "Billboards of the Garden Wall," *Sierra,* January–February 1999, pp. 12–13; and Hendrik A. Verfaille, "A New Pledge for a New Company," *Executive Speeches,* February–March 2001, pp. 10–13.

24. Lynelle Preston, "Sustainability at Hewlett-Packard: From Theory to Practice," *California Management Review,* Spring 2001, pp. 26–36.

25. See John Audley, *Green Politics and Global Trade: NAFTA and the Future of Environmental Politics* (Georgetown University Press, 1997); Lars K. Hallstrom, "Industry Versus Ecology: Environment in the New Europe," *Futures,* February 1999, pp. 25–38; Joe McKinney, "NAFTA: Four Years Down the Road," *Baylor Business Review,* Spring 1999, pp. 22–23; Andreas Diekmann and Axel Franzen, "The Wealth of Nations and Environmental Concern," *Environment and Behavior,* July 1999, pp. 540–549.

26. Michelle Wirth Fellman, "New Product Marketer of 1997," *Marketing News,* March 30, 1998, pp. E2, E12; Mercedes M. Cardona, "Colgate Boosts Budget to Further 5-Year Plan," *Advertising Age,* May 15, 2000, p. 6; and Emily Nelson, "Colgate's Net Rose 10 percent in Period, New Products Helped Boost Sales," *Wall Street Journal,* February 2, 2001, p. B6.

27. Information accessed online at www.HermanMiller.com, October 2001.

28. Dan R. Dalton and Richard A. Cosier, "The Four Faces of Social Responsibility," *Business Horizons,* May–June 1982, pp. 19–27.

29. Joseph Webber, "3M's Big Cleanup," *Business Week,* June 5, 2000, pp. 96–98.

30. John F. Magee and P. Ranganath Nayak, "Leaders' Perspectives on Business Ethics," *Prizm,* Arthur D. Little, Inc., Cambridge, MA, first quarter, 1994, pp. 65–77. Also see Kumar C. Rallapalli, "A Paradigm for Development and Promulgation of a Global Code of Marketing Ethics," *Journal of Business Ethics,* January 1999, pp. 125–137.

31. John F. Magee and P. Ranganath Nayak, "Leaders Perspectives on Business Ethics," pp. 71–72. Also see Thomas Donaldson, "Values in Tension: Ethics away from Home," *Harvard Business Review,* September–October 1996, pp. 48–62; Patrick E. Murphy, "Character and Virtue Ethics in International Marketing: An Agenda for Managers, Researchers, and Educators," *Journal of Business Ethics,* January 1999, pp. 107–124; and Gopalkrishnan, "International Exchanges as the Basis for Conceptualizing Ethics in International Business," *Journal of Business Ethics,* February 2001, pp. 3–25.

32. Mark Hendricks, "Ethics in Action," *Management Review,* January 1995, pp. 53–55.

33. Kenneth Labich, "The New Crisis in Business Management," *Fortune,* April 20, 1992, pp. 167–176, here p. 176.

34. From "Ethics as a Practical Matter," a message from David R. Whitman, chairman of the board of Whirlpool Corporation, as reprinted in Ricky E. Griffin and Ronald J. Ebert, *Business* (Upper Saddle River, NJ: Prentice Hall, 1989), pp. 578–579. For more on marketing ethics, see Lynn Sharp Paine, "Managing for Organizational Integrity," *Harvard Business Review,* March–April 1994, pp. 106–117; Tom McInerney, "Double Trouble: Combining Business and Ethics," *Business Ethics Quarterly,* January 1998, pp. 187–189; John F. Gaski, "Does Marketing Ethics Really Have Anything to Say?" *Journal of Business Ethics,* February 1999, pp. 315–334; and Thomas W. Dunfee, N. Craig Smith, and William T. Ross, "Social Contracts and Marketing Ethics," *Journal of Marketing,* July 1999, pp. 14–32.

Video Cases

Video Case 1

The Journal News: How You Know
Newspapers and Customers

"Unlike many other products, newspapers have the ability to create a relationship with their customers every single day. Each day we deliver a completely new product to *all* of our customers," said John Green, vice president of marketing for *The Journal News*. "If customers want to read sports first, they pull that out of the paper; if they want business, they go there first. They can participate in the newspaper in a way that's comfortable for them. That's building a relationship with the reader."

What attracts customers to a newspaper like *The Journal News* to begin the relationship-building process? "We deliver a person's local world," said John. *The Journal News* sells in Westchester, Rockland, and Putnam counties outside New York City so that it's a proverbial stone's throw from one of the leading U.S. newspapers, *The New York Times*. To get those households in Westchester, Rockland, and Putnam counties to take two newspapers requires that *The Journal News* be absolutely the best local newspaper that it can be. The paper must give customers a lot of unbiased and up-to-date news so that they will know what is going on. That's the basis for the paper's slogan: How you know.

Gannett and The Journal News

In 1960, there were eleven newspapers in those three counties: *The Reporter Dispatch, The Herald Statesman, The Daily Argos, The Standard Star, The Daily Item, The Daily Times, The Tarrytown Daily News, The Citizen Register, The Star, The Putnam Reporter Dispatch,* and *The Rockland Journal News.* Then, in the 1960s, Gannett, the largest newspaper publishing company in the United States, began buying the papers. In addition to its 99 daily newspapers, Gannett publishes USA *Today* and 15 newspapers in the United Kingdom. It has 22 television stations scattered across 43 states of the United States and the United Kingdom.

With all these ventures, why would it be interested in so many relatively small local papers? The answer lay in the demographics of those three counties. They covered approximately 820 square miles with 1.3 million people, or half a million households. That was a very large market in a small area. Furthermore, these were the bedroom communities for New York City. Incomes were high and consumers well educated for the most part—just the kind of households that are likely to read the newspaper.

Gannett began a process of conversion from eleven local papers to one local paper, covering the entire geographic area.

Management chose the name *The Journal News,* taken from *The Rockland Journal News.* By dropping the word *Rockland,* the newspaper ceased to be identified with just one geographic area. If it had chosen *The Tarrytown Daily News,* residents of places such as Yonkers and White Plains could have used the name to claim "That's not our paper." Because Rockland County is on the other side of the Hudson River from Westchester and Putnam counties, customers in those counties were less familiar with the name and didn't associate it with a specific geographic area.

The Journal News comes in four editions: the northern, central, and southern editions for Westchester and Putnam counties and a Rockland edition for Rockland County. With each edition, the staff is able to localize the news to that particular region. Of course, sections such as business and lifestyle and even classifieds can stay the same across all editions. Thus, having four editions provides the opportunity to increase locationalization while maintaining some of the advantages of consolidation of the original eleven newspapers.

Having the old titles has also provided the opportunity to relaunch some of those as weekly papers. As John commented, "Each week, each day, we have far more local news than we can use; so we have re-launched five of our old brands. That enables us to cash in on the brand equity we already had in those old brands and it enables us to provide much more depth to coverage of local events. We call them little celebrations of life—things such as the PTA, the high schools, the grade and middle schools. The weeklies cover everything that isn't in the daily paper."

There are other offerings in *The Journal News* product assortment. The company has a custom publishing division, which can print material in a variety of formats such as playbills for Broadway. In addition, there are in-house magazines for the local market—a horse magazine, a golf magazine, and a bridal magazine. The company does travel publications for the counties and other printed products as well. In short, *The Journal News* is willing to maximize use of its printing capabilities to meet local needs.

What is the relationship with Gannett? According to John, "Gannett runs their newspapers autonomously. They offer a tremendous amount of support and a tremendous amount of backing, yet they allow each newspaper group to run their own newspaper." That means that *The Journal News* is free to provide coverage of events in a manner best suited to its markets.

Marketing the New Paper

Marketing the new paper was not always easy. Although the company was fortunate to have a readily usable name, it still had to concentrate on promoting the new paper. It knew that it would encounter a lot of resistance—that folks would think,

"That's not *my Tarrytown Daily News*" — the paper that they had read for years.

The staff took to the streets, so to speak. They went into all distribution locations and talked to the owners and customers. They did a lot of point-of-purchase advertising, radio, television, cable, and outdoor bus sign advertising. "We were buying everything we could possibly buy, because we wanted people to feel comfortable with this newspaper change," said John.

The point-of-purchase advertising was particularly important for this paper as it has a heavy percentage of single copy buyers. That means customers go to a deli, 7-11, or café to get a cup of coffee, maybe a bagel, and a newspaper. That's part of their lifestyle. All the other newspapers are going to be represented there, so *The Journal News* has to have a point-of-purchase presence — something that makes it stand out to attract readers the first time. *If* readers like the paper, they'll be back the next morning or the next time that they purchase a paper. Of course, John and his staff would like customers to be so enamored of the paper that they would pick up the telephone and order a seven-day subscription, but changing lifestyles is hard to do.

Another means of promoting the paper is its Web site at www.thejournalnews.com. More extensive information is provided at the Web site, and it is updated during the day so that customers have a reason to look at it several times a day. Old information can be archived at the site if someone wants to conduct research into happenings in the past. The Web site also reaches customers who have moved away from the area but want to keep up with what is going on there. If they subscribe to the newspaper, it arrives several days late, so the Web site enables them to stay current with what is happening.

Price is not much of an issue in selling newspapers. As John commented, "Purchase normally has nothing to do with price unlike other products. Newspapers are just not an expensive product." Usually the prices are about the same anyway, so customers can rarely make a decision based on price.

Distribution requires extensive coverage of the market. In many cities and towns, newspapers can rely on home delivery, but not *The Journal News* because of consumer lifestyles. So, it has to be everywhere that a customer might buy a paper — at gas stations, at restaurants, in boxes on the corner, at bookstores, at drugstores, and so on. A few boxes placed at major intersections will not be sufficient.

What News?

The major issue each day with a newspaper is what news story should get the front page. Many times, it's a foregone conclusion. At most newspapers, if the President makes a big announcement, that will go on the front page. But at *The Journal News,* answering the front page question is a little trickier. The lead story could be either national or local. Determining which takes precedence is quite difficult as no matter which one is chosen, it will probably disappoint or irritate someone. But the staff and John know that people love to hate their local newspaper, which means that newspaper people have to develop thick skins.

Sometimes the decision is easy. The day of and days following the World Trade Center disaster, it was easy to know that that should be the lead news. After all, many of the people in *The Journal News'* market area had friends, relatives, or loved ones who had worked in the World Trade Towers. National and local news converged then.

Personality of the Paper

How newspapers cover stories can impact the personality of the paper as well as satisfy the information needs of readers. While many of the newspaper's stories are serious, others provide great opportunity for building a lighter image and personality. An example is *The Journal News* coverage of the 2000 World Series. The paper began printing fan cards and selling newspapers with the fan cards in them. As a result, Yankee Stadium was full of the fan cards. The day of the last game, the staff went to Yankee Stadium with newspapers emblazoned with the headline "Yankees Win." They knew that fans leaving the game would want some memento of the occasion and a newspaper with the right headline was just the ticket. All told, the staff had a lot of fun with the series, sold a lot of papers, and got free publicity for the paper.

Of course, Mets fans may not have been so happy about it, but, remember, someone is always going to "hate" the local paper. At least the Yankee fans could "love" it, and that will go a long way toward building a relationship with them. Even the non-Yankee fans could take pride that *their* paper scooped the *Times.* So the last day of the series, the staff at *The Journal News* actually made up the news for that day's product. Were they ever glad that the Yankees won!

Questions for Discussion

1. What is the mission of the Gannett newspaper empire? What is the mission of *The Journal News?* Why do these work well together?
2. Use the Boston Consulting Group growth share matrix to classify all of *The Journal News* products and services. Is this a desirable portfolio of offerings?
3. Gannett also has a product portfolio. What are its components? How do those "products" support each other?
4. Has *The Journal News* segmented the market? If so, how?
5. What is its marketing mix? Describe each P.
6. What is its competition? How do or can they respond to the competition?

Sources: Interviews at *The Journal News* and *The Journal News* Web site.

Video Case 2

Berlin Redevelopment Corporation: "The New Berlin"

Suppose you worked for a U.S. firm selling industrial components that wanted to access the growing industrial base of Eastern Europe. Where would you locate your base of operations? Prague? Budapest? Warsaw? Berlin? Whatever city you choose, it has to be attractive to your U.S. managers and their families; should have an infrastructure of business services such as communication and distribution networks, transportation facilities, media, and so forth; has to be accessible to markets; and needs to have a qualified workforce.

If someone suggested Berlin, what would you think of? Scenes of World War II bombing destruction? People fleeing East German guards? Dancing on the former Wall? Print articles detailing the difficulties of reunification? Those negative impressions tarnished Berlin's image by the early nineties. Buildings were crumbling—even the Reichstag, seat of the German government for decades. Businesses were fleeing because of the lack of an adequate business infrastructure, with a resulting loss of 250,000 jobs.

However, decay was only part of the story. Visitors to the city did find signs of growth. Streets and sidewalks were closed because of construction; traffic was snarled due to detours and closed lanes; and cranes dominated the city skyline. And there were signs of life as well. Jazz poured from underground cafés, smartly dressed folk attended concerts, and lively schoolchildren toured the zoo.

Groups such as the Berlin Economic Development Corporation (EDC founded in 1979) and the Partnership for Berlin (founded in 1994) are responsible for much of this development. Whereas the EDC focuses on bringing business and industry to Berlin, the Partnership is the marketer, charged with presenting the new city to the world.

When beginning its work, the EDC inventoried Berlin's strengths. These included a number of universities (Humboldt, Technical University of Berlin, Free University of Berlin, and 13 other technical colleges); medical research facilities (four university hospitals, the Biomedical Research Campus Berlin-Buch, the Max Delbruck Center for Molecular Medicine, the Robert Rossle Cancer Clinic, and the Franz Volhard Cardiovascular Clinic); over 240 other research institutes—lingering evidence of East Berlin's position as the scientific hub of communist Eastern Europe and Berlin's unique geographical location. Because it's approximately halfway between Paris and Moscow, and Stockholm and Rome, both the east–west and north–south routes cross in Berlin, making it the most eastern city of Western Europe and the most western city of Central Europe. Having had feet in both the free and communist worlds qualifies it to bring the East and West together. Today over 200,000 Russians live in Berlin along with citizens of 179 other countries, confirming the city's role as one of the most international cities in Europe.

The EDC built on the scientific and technology base by expanding the facilities at Adlershof (a scientific center since the 1930s). By 2010, the WISTA Science and Business Center—the most modern research and technology center in Europe—will be open. At WISTA and the medical research facilities, the emphasis is on application as well as research because that enables firms to get new products, services, and procedures to market more quickly and will, thereby, attract more firms. The Fachhochshcule of Technology and Business created a Business Start-up center.

The city fully digitized communications by installing nearly 40,000 miles of fiber optic cable so that today Berlin contains 50 percent of the fiber optic cable in Europe. Twelve billion dollars is going into the renovation of underground stations and lines and the construction of a new train station that will accommodate 250,000 travelers per day. Berlin's three airports (two in the West, one in the East) will be combined to create one of the biggest international airports in Europe, serving 20 million passengers annually.

The Partnership for Berlin raised the city's visibility through advertisements in *Time, Newsweek, Der Spiegel*, and other international magazines. It led walking, biking, and riding tours through the construction sites to highlight the city's growth and publicized events such as Berlin's fiftieth international film festival, Museum Night (when all museums are open throughout the evening), the Berlin Speech given by prestigious figures such as the U.N. Secretary General, and the relocation of the federal government from Bonn in 1999. It continually stresses the size of consumer markets—over 5 million locally and hundreds of millions of consumers regionally and in Eastern Europe.

These efforts successfully tempted firms such as DaimlerChrysler, Newsweek International/Newsweek Services, British Petroleum, Sony, IBM, and Time to locate in Berlin. In addition, 400 trade fairs and congresses are held there each year. Examples are the International World of Consumer Electronics, the International Tourism Exchange, and the International Aerospace Exhibition.

Accompanying the growth of industry is an explosion of young people. Nearly half of Berlin's 3.5 million inhabitants are under the age of 35—most of whom are well educated. While attracted by the lure of 170,000 new jobs, they stay because they are charmed by a city that is almost 50 percent green with parks and forests and nearly 125 miles of navigable waterways. They like the cultural opportunities. Berlin has 8 symphony orchestras, 167 museums, and 150 theaters. There's an ambitious art scene such as the Art Forum Berlin, the Biennial Art Festival, and other festivals such as the Love Parade with a million ravers, the Christopher Street Day Parade, the Berlin Marathon, plus golfing and riding tournaments.

Would you locate your firm there? What more would you need to know in order to choose Berlin?

Questions for Discussion

1. Write a mission statement for the Berlin EDC.
2. What is Berlin's competitive advantage? Do the strategy efforts of the EDC exploit this competitive advantage? Has this been a well-thought-out strategy?
3. What is the mission of the Partnership?
4. Describe its marketing strategy in terms of the four Ps.
5. The Partnership's slogan is *Das Neue Berlin*, which is translated as "The New Berlin." Is this a good slogan? Why or why not?
6. What microenvironmental and macroenvironmental influences have hindered or helped the creation of a positive image for Berlin?

Sources: Materials provided by the Partnership for Berlin, personal interviews with EDC and Partnership personnel, and the Web site www.Berlin.de/partner.

Video Case 3

Sputnik: Insights from the Streets

If Levi-Strauss & Company wants to know what jeans 17-year-olds want, it calls a big market research firm and does a survey. Right? Wrong. Levi's calls Sputnik in New York, and Sputnik sends its teenage and twenty-something correspondents to the streets, clubs, coffeehouses, parks, cafés — any hangout — to videotape the trendsetters themselves — today's alternative youth. Why? Because the mainstream may be right behind them.

These are not the usual depth interviews or focus groups. The founders of Sputnik, Janine Lopiano-Misdom and Joanne De Luca, disdain such efforts because they don't get at the reality of consumers in their natural environment having a conversation with the interviewer. Lopiano-Misdom and De Luca, in their new book, *Street Trends: How Today's Alternative Youth Cultures Are Creating Tomorrow's Mainstream Markets,* recommend that target marketers deliberately bypass focus groups "to get down with the streets, to be in the trenches every day."

So Sputnik correspondents, video equipment on hand, strive for intimacy to uncover the personal quirks, desires, and interests of the individual, his or her circle of friends, and the influences around them. They go after the trendsetters, not the followers, and to reach them, Sputnik's interviewers go to the trendsetters' latest enclaves, wherever that might be, not to labs or rented focus group rooms. Followers can tell you what's happening now, but for the future, you have to find the trendsetters — and find out about the music they listen to (the most direct link to young people, according to Lopiano-Misdom), the products they buy, and the clothes they choose to wear.

Sputnik videotapes the conversations to pick up the body language as well as to record what respondents are saying about their likes and dislikes. So, a Sputnik report includes not only a written document but also an edited videotape — because seeing and hearing, in this case, is believing. To really understand some of teens and twenty somethings' styles, fashions, fads, colors, and the way they view the world, these tapes have to be seen. Because many of these trendsetters are heavy viewers of videos, Sputnik is actually videotaping the video watchers.

How do you know the youth on camera are trendsetters? Through their peers. How can you get to the trendsetters? By entering their "scene." Obviously, this is not going to work for the housewife looking for some part-time work conducting interviews. It takes someone who understands the alternative culture, who respects the people he or she is talking with, and who can connect with them in order to have intimate conversations and reveal on videotape deeper insights than are found in surveys, magazines, and TV shows. In short, it takes another member of the culture, but one with a journalistic bent — someone who is able to probe responses and get at the "story." That's why Sputnik's interviewers are called correspondents. They are exploring respondents' lifestyles to determine how they are plugged into the product.

Where does Sputnik find its correspondents? Usually through a snowballing technique. Once Sputnik finds one good correspondent, he or she frequently suggests other possible correspondents. Upon being hired, correspondents are given a brief training session in which they are shown a sample of a tape and given pointers about what was done well and what poorly. Because correspondents are freelancers often working on other, non-Sputnik projects, Sputnik usually contacts them by telephone about new assignments. Once briefed about the client's general problem, they are turned loose.

The company can find respondents anywhere that's appropriate. For example, Sputnik might go to a skateboard exhibition to film interviews for an athletic shoe manufacturer or go to hear a band play at the local coffee place to check out makeup for a cosmetics manufacturer. For fashion brands, it might locate respondents in groups near high schools or at clubs. The respondents and interviewing locations are determined by the type of product being investigated. Do Sputnik interviewers have problems with club owners? Not usually as long as they typically get permission in advance and the respondents are happy with the interview.

Most Sputnik interviews occur in big cities such as New York, Atlanta, Miami, and Chicago and cities with large student populations such as Austin, Texas, and San Diego because that's where the trendsetters are. For some clients, Sputnik will conduct interviews outside the United States in locations such as London, Berlin, Paris, Tokyo, and Sao Paulo. Going outside the United States poses language problems, however, so Sputnik prefers to stay in the United States. Otherwise the videotapes have to be translated if done in a foreign language or be translated simultaneously with the interview. Because the videotapes are Sputnik's "data," translation efforts may impair the quality of the insights attainable in the interviews.

The quality of correspondents' work is ascertainable on the videotapes that they turn in. By watching the videos, Sputnik's principals, De Luca and Lopiano-Misdom, can tell whether correspondents are interviewing the right type of respondents, asking the right questions, and working in the right environment. New correspondents are given extensive feedback about their performance in order to help them improve. If respondents on tape give a series of yes–no answers, appear uncomfortable, or the interview is short, the correspondent is not doing a good job. According to Lopiano-Misdom, correspondents must relentlessly ask, Why? Why? Why? Knowing what, when, and where does not uncover motivations and needs. To get at that, one must continually ask why.

Given the length of most videotapes (a whole evening in a club), Sputnik samples tend to be much smaller than those used with surveys. The company makes a trade-off between sample size and depth of information.

The videotapes are important not only for their story but also as a quality control measure. They reveal the quality of the interviewer's work, which is frequently not ascertainable from interviewer's written comments. Environments and the appearance and type of respondent cannot be checked in written reports or audiotapes. Additionally, the videotapes give the full story. Comments are not condensed according to what the interviewer thinks is important. Remember, one would rarely tell interviewers exactly what problem the firm is trying to solve. Doing so would unduly constrain their questioning. Instead, correspondents are given general problem areas that they must explore on their own.

Sputnik was founded in 1994 by Janine Lopiano-Misdom and Joanne De Luca—both of whom had 14 years each working in research and marketing. Realizing that surveys and focus groups were not the answer to understanding youth, they wanted to start a "grassroots" marketing research firm that would use today's tools to search out tomorrow's trends.

To understand trends, they maintain, you have to understand the culture that produces the trend and why it emerged. To understand the culture, you have to get into it, experience it, and be able to think like members of the culture. Then, you might be able to analyze where fashion or food is going with this group. This is a bubble-up theory of fashion and style rather than the trickle-down approach. "Now we're watching kids, whereas we used to watch designers," says Ruth A. Davis, a product director at Reebok International Limited and a Sputnik client.

Every research project produces reams of videotape that Lopiano-Misdom, De Luca, and staff pore over, looking for commonalities, themes, or ideas across interviews. Once these are identified, Lopiano-Misdom and De Luca use them to point clients in the right direction. An example is product development research done for Burlington Industries in which club kids said they would like to have plastic jeans. (After all, this is a group that likes reflective materials and shiny things.) Would people really want plastic jeans? Probably not, but Sputnik suggested that Burlington use materials that resemble plastic. The result? Laminated jeans popular among high schoolers.

Sputnik does more than product development, however. It can help clients create brand images and messages and adopt marketing strategies geared toward creating insider brands that remain relevant to youthful consumers. Through assessments of videotapes, Sputnik staff can explain to a firm how the youth market sees it and where it should be headed. PepsiCo's Mountain Dew used Sputnik research to develop promotions. Finding that pagers were still considered cool, Mountain Dew developed a successful promotion for a low-priced pager if consumers did enough Dew.

Is research based on small samples of alternative youth valid? Should corporations pour millions into product development or promotion based on the results? Reebok's Ms. Davis cautions that cutting-edge trends are useful to follow but shouldn't be relied on totally. According to Christopher Ireland, a principal in Cheskin + Maasten/Imagenet, alternative kids may experiment with ten trends, only one of which crosses over to the mainstream culture. The trick is to identify which is *the one* trend.

Does this bother Lopiano-Misdom and De Luca? Not at all. They are too busy producing their new biannual videotape, which aggregates video data for purchase by the general public, and keeping up with the demand for research from firms such as Reebok; Burlington; PepsiCo; Asics Tiger; PRO-Keds, Ked Corporation; BOSS; AVIA Group; Sam & Libby; Gap, Inc; and Converse.

Questions for Discussion

1. What type of research does Sputnik conduct? Causal, descriptive, or exploratory?
2. What are the advantages and disadvantages of the research techniques used by Sputnik?
3. For each of the following, compare the Sputnik approach with the standard marketing approach.
   a. sample selection
   b. selection and training of interviewers
   c. data collection
   d. data analysis
   e. report writing
4. Suppose you worked for a toiletries company making products such as shampoo, conditioner, or hair spray. Would it make sense for your firm to hire Sputnik to research product areas such as hair color?
5. Suppose you worked for a cellular telephone company such as Nokia. Would it make sense for your firm to hire Sputnik?

Video Case 4

Sony Ericsson: Supply Chain Management

In 2001 telecommunications leader Ericsson and the Sony Corporation joined forces to establish Sony Ericsson Mobile Communications. Their combined mobile phone business had sales of over $7 billion in the year 2000. The company offers a range of mobile communications products that go far beyond simple mobile phone technology.

The slender and stylish T28 World can be used to access GSM (Global System for Mobile Communications) services in Europe, Asia, the Pacific, Africa, and North and South America. At the most advanced end of the technology scale, the newly introduced T68 mimics a Windows Pocket PC device, offering mobile e-mail (with the ability to insert pictures and sounds), along with the ability to surf the Internet, update your calendar, organize your notes, and synchronize and share your information with a PDA or laptop.

The T28 World is the smallest GSM mobile telephone ever developed by Ericsson, measuring 3.9 by 2 by 0.6 inches, or 97 by 50 by 15 millimeters, and weighing between 89 and 114 grams, depending upon the battery selected. Even so, it still contains 300 components. This complicated piece of technology is designed by Ericsson engineers, and produced through the R&D efforts of Ericsson and numerous suppliers closely working together with aligned technologies, measurement, and testing systems.

The outer sheath and flip-up mouthpiece are not just pieces of plastic. They are made with magnesium to become shatterproof if you drop your phone. In addition, these features provide protection for the chips, circuits, and batteries inside and prevent heat buildup so that you can use that telephone 24 hours per day, 7 days a week. Finally, the sheathing has to be molded in a fashion that is appealing to consumers, fits easily into the hand, and looks good. Given the specs for one non-high-tech component, just consider what is involved in the technology inside.

Considering the demands for the sheathing, it's obvious that Ericsson must select suppliers carefully with an eye to a long-run relationship. It has four factors in mind when choosing suppliers: (1) the supplier's technical knowledge and performance abilities; (2) the supplier's commercial performance in terms of patents and intellectual property rights; (3) the supplier's capabilities in terms of capital, personnel, facilities, and knowledge (e.g., can the firm ramp up to the level of production Ericsson requires?); and (4) timing (can the supplier develop the component and produce it in time for the product launch?). All of these factors are important because each firm is relying on the other. The supplier relies on Ericsson for sales revenue and profits to justify the expense, time, and effort expended in developing parts and production for Ericsson. Ericsson, on the other hand, must have a long-term, stable supply of components in order to support its global marketing efforts. The lifetime of technology in this industry is exceedingly short—as little as a year sometimes. Thus, Ericsson's customers (network operators and distributors) cannot wait—even a week—for Ericsson to deliver those T28s throughout their life-cycle.

Components are extremely important to Ericsson as it is an assembler of components and not a manufacturer. To make chips requires a different technology than does the molding of sheathings and flip pieces, which again is different from batteries. There are so many technologies in the average mobile telephone that, at present, no one company could make all the parts. Therefore, Ericsson keeps a "basket" of suppliers—each of which makes parts for multiple Ericsson products. In turn, Ericsson has multiple, but few, suppliers for each component. This arrangement reduces the business risk for all firms involved. So, company X that makes the sheathing for the T28 sells other products to Ericsson. If the T28 bombs, then everyone is protected as no one is overly dependent on any one Ericsson product.

Over time, this means that the personnel at Ericsson and the supplier get to know each other very well. They visit each other's facilities; they are involved in R&D on various components; and Ericsson keeps the supplier apprised of what its needs are likely to be in the future. Each of these interactions—whether by phone, by e-mail, or in person—is important to reassure each partner that the other is performing as promised, to make sure that the technologies are aligned and that a consistent message is sent and received between the layers of personnel in the firms involved. Eventually, people on both sides get to know each other quite well, so that the relationship can become personal as well as business, but it is always a professional relationship.

Because of this close association, Ericsson uses a highly structured approach to forecasting supplier selection. It begins by determining how the current supplier base is likely to evolve over the next five to seven years so that it understands what that will look like in the future. Second, it determines what the patent portfolio of suppliers will look like and how rapidly they are developing their own special technologies. This enables Ericsson to know if it needs to field suppliers for a new technology or can find a supplier in its current base. Ericsson also keeps current suppliers up-to-date on what it will need in the future and what it should be developing.

Once chosen, suppliers tend to stay in the Ericsson basket for a long time. The supplier of that sheathing for the T28 has been with Ericsson for over 10 years. Given the importance of the supplier to Ericsson and vice versa, it only makes sense to have a carefully maintained deep and long relationship with one another. Once in the supplier basket, firms know that Ericsson will stick with them through several problem periods before dissolving the relationship. This is consistent with the time and effort that Ericsson puts into selecting suppliers and consistent with building trust in them. Constant shifting of suppliers would engender distrust, cause difficulties in assembly operations, and make it difficult for Ericsson to satisfy market demand. Both parties would lose in that situation, and that is not allowable in this fast-paced business. If Ericsson stumbles, Nokia, Motorola, or Qualcom will jump into the breech to get ahead.

Questions for Discussion

1. What type of buy is the sheathing for the T28?
2. What environmental factors affect the relationship between Ericsson and its suppliers?
3. What are the organizational factors?
4. What are the major drivers that determine the nature of the relationship between Ericsson and its suppliers?
5. Visit your local "retailer" of mobile phones to examine the latest models to find out (a) what features are available, (b) how long models of telephones stay on the market, (c) what types of frequencies telephones in the United States use, and (d) whether you can buy telephones that will work around the globe. How important is it to have a global mobile standard today? In the future?

Sources: Materials found at the Sony Ericsson Web site and personal interviews with Ericsson personnel.

Video Case 5

House of Blues: Singing the Blues?

When Isaac Tigrett founded the House of Blues in 1992, he was on a mission to "create a profitable, principled, global entertainment company that would encourage racial and spiritual harmony." Born in the South and immersed in the fertile southern and African American culture of the region, Tigrett wanted to expose Americans to the rich cultural heritage of the blues. He believed he could use both the blues and folk art as a bridge to racial harmony in our increasingly multi-cultural environment.

The first step in this process was establishing the initial House of Blues restaurant in Cambridge, Massachusetts. This was quickly followed by Houses of Blues in New Orleans, Los Angeles, Orlando, Myrtle Beach, Chicago, Las Vegas, and the newest House of Blues in Anaheim, California. While each of these themed restaurants features such southern specialties as crispy catfish nuggets for appetizers, the Elwood—a blackened chicken sandwich—and white chocolate banana bread pudding with whipped cream, each is also free to adapt its menu to local tastes. For example, the Los Angeles House of Blues offers tempura chicken tenders, a spicy swordfish sandwich, and seared ahi tuna with a shiso leaf dressing, while the Cambridge House of Blues offers a roasted portobello mushroom sandwich served with a watercress-jicama salad. The Myrtle Beach House of Blues features New Orleans–style seafood gumbo, pizza, and southern pecan pie. The House of Blues Anaheim features jambalaya, southern-smoked BBQ chicken, and cheese grits for its Sunday Gospel Brunches and offers assorted fruit salad and Caesar salad with "wood oven croutons." The croutons in Myrtle Beach are "oven baked," and that Atlantic Coast favorite, key lime pie, is added to the dessert list for its version of the Gospel Lunch experience.

Each restaurant also has a different decor and facilities. The Orlando House of Blues is covered with corrugated Mississippi tin and nestled in a voodoo garden and Louisiana-style bayou. It boasts a state-of-the-art, 2,000-person concert hall complete with a 30-foot-tall hydraulic stage. The plaster and clay ceiling of its 500-seat restaurant displays such traditional blues greats as B. B. King and Robert Johnson. The House of Blues restaurant in Chicago is smaller—only 300 seats—but is divided into two rooms. One hall contains bas-reliefs of Chicago blues legends and the other boasts Delta blues legends. Each of these is decorated with pieces from Tigrett's extensive folk art collection. Tigrett claims to have created a "juke-joint" opera house to showcase blues and blues-influenced music, which, he claims, is America's authentic "Opera."

The Chicago HOB is part of the Marina City renovation complex. Marina City was designed in the mid-1960s as one of the first urban high-rise residential developments. It was described as a city within a city because it contained both apartments and commercial buildings. Tigrett renovated 55,000 square feet of the commercial property to house television production, multimedia, and radio broadcast facilities along with a 1,500-person concert venue that includes a multimedia restaurant, a classically designed music hall, and a bilevel Foundation room enhanced with Opera sky boxes—all this plus a Loew's House of Blues hotel with 400 rooms and 30 guest suites.

Houses of Blues also attempt to nurture local music groups. Jim Mallonee, who books acts at the Myrtle Beach HOB, comments, "If we can give a local band an opportunity to showcase themselves—if they've got a buzz that's beneficial for both sides—then why not make it work on occasion? Any good promoter would do that." By booking acts into the Myrtle Beach HOB, which attracts large tourist crowds, Mallonee is also fulfilling HOB's goal of supporting new music groups. At a tourist location, the band may be seen by people from many states who would not normally be exposed to the group. "So the band is not only appealing to the local crowd they help to draw, but they are also exposing themselves to people from 10 states in one fell swoop," says Mallonee.

The House of Blues markets itself to business firms as well as individual restaurant and concert goers. In Chicago, corporations can rent the Opera sky boxes, which enable their guests to watch shows at the restaurant. In Myrtle Beach, corporate executives can use the multimedia and Internet connections found in all rooms and booths of the House of Blues to participate more cost and time effectively in business presentations, executive conferences, and trade shows.

To continue its growth and spread the word about the blues culture, House of Blues has entered a number of other ventures, some of them successful and some of them not. According to Tigrett, "The House of Blues is a brand that is into new media, books, CDs, records, television and concerts. It's not about restaurants anymore. It's about zones of entertainment." From specialty themed restaurants, the jump to selling recordings and books about the blues in HOB facilities was obvious. An online catalog selling the recordings, books, videos, T-shirts, dinnerware, and so on with the HOB logo would naturally follow.

Less obvious have been the House of Blues' ventures with radio, TV, and the Internet. "Music and art transcend all cultural barriers," said Tigrett, "and now the World Wide Web and the Internet are providing the means to bridge any communication gap that may separate us." HOB teamed with Sun MicroSystems to create the HOB Web site (www.hob.com) and HOB New Media, an interactive entertainment and electronic publishing division. New Media under the direction of Marc Schiller developed LiveConcerts.com—an Internet site specifically dedicated to live concerts. "Usually the people that were putting up concerts—including ourselves—weren't doing it on a regular basis," Schiller comments. "It would be once every couple of months, and if you didn't happen to log on, you'd miss the concert. So we decided that we were going to create a destination on the Internet specifically for live concerts." And New Media has been busy with other projects—cybercasting rock concerts, creating a Web site for the Olympics, and teaming up with Sun Microsystems on a Super Bowl project.

Providing music access on the Internet has become a major part of what House of Blues does, and in March 2000 House of Blues Entertainment, Incorporated, announced a two-year alliance with MTV. Events produced and hosted by House of Blues will be co-branded with MTV and offered through live pay-for-view events through MTV.com. HOB Media Properties President Lou Mann, who is "absolutely thrilled to be a partner with MTVi," sees no conflict between media giant MTV and the HOB's original goals of promoting diverse talent and new unrecognized talent. He believes the alliance "underlines our commitment in the record industry to supporting the promotion of established and emerging artists."

Despite all this activity, the HOB has been criticized for ignoring its roots—and not moving fast enough in opening new restaurants, which are the personal, up-close sales center of the firm. One reason that HOB does not franchise its restaurants is because it is a privately held corporation. Opening a new HOB, however, takes a lot of money, as the Chicago restaurant cost $20 million. Part of that is due to the unique designs of each restaurant and the use of expensive art. Costs could be lowered through a standardized decor used in multiple sites. To date, however, the HOB has resisted efforts to "package" its restaurants.

Tigrett stated that he wasn't interested in attracting massive audiences to HOB venues. "Eventually, if we are successful, we're going to have bus loads of grandparents and kids and families flocking to our places," he says. "But now that is not the demographic I want. I want the hip and the cool, and the more I can hold back that family demographic, the greater will be our ability to leverage the [HOB] brand in the future."

But Tigrett's time at HOB ran out. In spite of his close association with Dan Aykroyd, another board member, Tigrett was ousted as CEO of HOB. The board wanted to rein in his spending habits and maybe bring the family demographic closer to the present than Tigrett planned. Due to excessive spending on the Atlanta Olympics site, other publicity stunts, and aggressive diversification efforts, HOB was losing money, and the corporate investors want a house on a much more solid footing.

To help HOB's restaurant business grow, it is broadening its music appeal. Chris Stevenson, vice president of marketing at HOB, says the blues part of the brand's name has hindered the company's efforts to be recognized as a broad-based music brand. "It's a complex brand. House of Blues is about a whole portfolio of music, not just blues. That's what we need to communicate to consumers," he says. This echoes Tigrett's contention that the blues is the basis for most other American musical forms. But widening the appeal seems to be at odds with the name House of Blues and the mission to spread the southern culture of the blues.

Questions for Discussion

1. How did Tigrett's vision of the House of Blues represent segmentation of the music market?
2. What kind of segmentation does the local adaptation of each House of Blues represent?
3. How does House of Blues segment its market?
4. Should House of Blues franchise its operation? Why or why not?
5. Does broadening the types of music promoted by House of Blues blur the meaning of the brand?
6. How might HOB's Internet business activities impact the brand?

Sources: "Diversity, not Airplay, the Key for House of Blues' Booker Mallonee," *Amusement Business,* March 24, 1997, p. 6; Business Editors, "The MTVi Group and House of Blues Announce Strategic Internet Alliance," *Businesswire.com,* March 2, 2000; Jeff Jensen, "House of Blues Ventures Woo a Broader Musical Base," *Advertising Age,* December 15, 1996,

p. 16; Jill Krueger, "Striking a Different Chord: Blues Man Meets House," *Orlando Business Journal,* August 29, 1997, 14, no. 13, p. 12; Kathleen Morris, "Oh Yeah, They Also Serve Food," *Business Week,* February 24, 1997, p. 60; Kathleen Morris, "For Its Founder, House of Blues Indeed," *Business Week,* October 13, 1997, p. 6; and numerous press releases from the House of Blues Web site.

Video Case 6

Exclusively Weddings: Courting the Bride-to-Be

Responding to the Market

In a typical year, 2,400,000 couples tie the knot, which makes for a lot of weddings. Furthermore, they spend over $20,000 on average for a wedding and that's without the honeymoon. The average engagement period is about one year because it frequently takes that long to plan today's average wedding—unless one has a lot of help.

All of this means that millions of young women all across the United States are poring over bridal magazines, searching the Internet, shopping in dozens of stores, and discussing their wedding plans endlessly with their friends, relatives, groom, and most anyone else who wants to listen. They see lots of fabulous dresses, gifts, and wedding ideas in magazines such as *Elegant Bride, Brides, Modern Bride,* and *Martha Stewart Weddings*.

Suppose, however, that the bride-to-be finds a gift idea or wedding accessory that she likes in a magazine; where does she go to buy it? If she lives in a small town, her choices are limited. Even in larger cities, it can be exhausting to shop continuously for all the things one wants for a wedding.

Recognizing this need in the market and the lack of competition from other catalogers, Pace Communications of Greensboro, North Carolina, launched *Exclusively Weddings* in 1992. First catalog had only 16 pages, but it quickly grew to 48, then, 52, 56, and finally 96 pages. As it lengthened, so did the breadth and depth of the product assortment. Initially, the catalog did not sell invitations or favors for guests—all categories that have become "hot sellers" for *Exclusively Weddings.* In the first catalog, most product categories had only one or two entries, but if products in the category sold well, management deepened the assortment. For example, there were only two pairs of toasting flutes for the bride and groom, but now the catalog features over five pages of toasting flutes and the fall 2001 catalog featured a pair of flutes on the cover. Today, one can find an amazing array of products in categories such as baskets, bouquet holders, CDs and videos, gifts, jewelry, luminaries, napkins, photo albums and frames, ring pillows, and unity candles and accessories. It seems that whatever you want, *Exclusively Weddings* has it.

Exclusively Weddings' success is no accident. It reflects a strong focus on the target market, which is first-time brides-to-be with more upscale tastes. It also reflects a strong commitment to quality in products and service. Sher Silver, executive vice president of *Exclusively Weddings,* commented:

> One of the most important aspects of our catalog is that our items are very high quality. One of the difficulties that we have is conveying to customers through photography the high quality of the items that we sell. Other catalogs might show an inexpensive, or cheaply made item which can be made to look good in a photograph. Whereas an expensive item will look good, but it may not look that different in a photograph. It's a big challenge trying to get across to our customer that our items are crafted of the finest materials and workmanship.

Quality service means many things. From polite telephone operators to speedy delivery of goods, a bride-to-be receives top-quality treatment at *Exclusively Weddings.* For many brides-to-be, wedding decisions are among the most important decisions that they have made. Thus, telephone operators need to be especially well informed to answer questions and be helpful, encouraging, and reassuring. Realizing that many times brides are ordering at the last minute, *Exclusively Weddings* aims to turn orders around in 48 hours, unless the items need personalization.

Quality service extends beyond the order process. Engraving and printing are major services offered by *Exclusively Weddings.* Many silver items can be engraved with the couple's names and wedding dates; fabric items can be embroidered with the same information or customized messages; invitations, place cards, and thank-you notes can be printed and embossed. The bride can use standard wording or her own customized message. To make it easier to transmit her customized message, the bride can easily input it on the Internet order form rather than dictate it over the telephone.

The focus on quality is evident on the eweddings Web site. In the About Us section, *Exclusively Weddings* proudly states that it employs over 50 people dedicated to providing brides with the very best in products and services. These people work in a variety of departments such as the phone center, warehousing, shipping, quality control, printing, engraving, and purchasing. Actually quality control is two groups—incoming and outgoing. Incoming quality control checks the goods from vendors, and outgoing makes sure that the engraving, printing, and the like are well done and accurate.

The Product Line

The focus on quality has endeared *Exclusively Weddings* to its vendors so that it carries goods from some of the most prestigious companies in the industry such as Sherry et Cie, Paddy Gordon Designs, and Bernardaud.

Over the years, the folks at *Exclusively Weddings* began to develop their own ideas for products. For example, they had a silver picture frame with two openings. They suggested that brides-to-be give that to their fathers with a picture of the daughter as a child on one side and as a bride on the other. They call it the Daddy's Girl® frame and engrave the dates of the pictures on the frame for free. To promote this frame, they had a

little verse which went: "To My Father: The man of my dreams is so special because he shares your finest qualities, and even though I will be a married woman soon, I will always be Daddy's Girl." Brides were so taken with that verse that the folks at *Exclusively Weddings* designed a frame with an opening for the bride's picture on one side and the verse engraved on the frame on the other side. This has become a very popular item. Another popular item that it developed is the Mother's Hanky, which you can look up on its Web site.

Coming up with new product ideas and perceptions requires a lot of creativity. For example, several years ago, *Exclusively Weddings* had a new product for its catalog, which was a dome votive candleholder. Once the candle was lit, a wedding scene, carved into the porcelain dome, appeared. While this was a stunning product, Sher realized that it needed meaning for customers. She came up with the idea of a Honeymoon Candle that the couple would light on the first night (and hopefully succeeding nights) of their honeymoon. So, *Exclusively Weddings* featured it as the Honeymoon Candle and it sold very well. It sold so well that other vendors have copied it and called theirs a Honeymoon Candle, too, even though that positioning was purely a creation of Sher's!

While there are a lot of products that sell well year after year, there are also fads as brides and grooms are constantly looking for unique ideas for their weddings. A good place to look for unique ideas is in a catalog, so *Exclusively Weddings* has to be constantly looking for new ideas from vendors. It was the first to introduce wedding luminaries (lighted bags perforated with wedding designs that can be used to outline sidewalks and steps in the dark), and it was among the first to introduce bubbles for the bride and groom, disposable cameras, and bells. The bubbles are blown at the bride and groom as they leave the wedding and are sold in containers that have gotten increasingly fancy over the years. Guests find disposable cameras on each table at the reception or dinner to take pictures with. They leave the cameras and the couple has the pictures developed. Finally, the bells are favors given to the guests to ring when they feel like it. When the couple hears the bells ringing, they are supposed to kiss. These and other goodies such as truffles and other favors for guests were first featured on the pages of *Exclusively Weddings.*

Fads not only grow; they also decline. While the bubbles have started to decline, other fads are still growing. For example, guests for years threw rice at couples as they departed; then there was a shift to birdseed. Today, *Exclusively Weddings* has a product named Designer Wedding Rice. This is a rice product that is heart shaped and dissolves in water and crushes under foot—environmentally correct rice! Leaves no mess behind. *Exclusively Weddings* is the only catalog to carry streamers that can be thrown at the bride and groom. Who knows what the next fad will be?

Going on the Internet

In 2000, *Exclusively Weddings* launched its Web site—www.eweddings.com, where it offers much of the same merchandise. Pace worked with Beacon Technologies to develop the design and functionality of the site. Putting a catalog on the

Internet turned out to be quite a difficult proposition— so difficult that it took over six months to get the Web site up and running. Part of the difficulty was the sheer volume of information that had to go on the Web site—product descriptions as well as stock numbers, prices, and personalization codes. For products such as invitations, a great deal of information must be given in the form of standard messages and opportunities created for customers to write their own message.

For the Future

What sorts of new ventures is *Exclusively Weddings* thinking of? "One thing that we're doing to increase business during a normally very slow time for us is a holiday catalog. We have picture frames, key rings, flasks and money clips and many other items that would make great gifts. Further, during the holiday season, we have a special holiday gifts department on our Web site," says Sher. In addition to promotion on the Web site, each bride will receive a little holiday catalog with her other purchases.

Other ideas include putting the catalog on heavier paper and changing the logo. Heavier paper might connote a higher-quality image, but it would increase postage and printing costs dramatically. Because this catalog is aimed at an upscale market and recipients who have requested it, it is sent first class. The U.S. Postal Service increases charges for every tenth of an ounce; so at present, the staff evaluates a lot of decisions by how they will affect postage charges. The question is whether the image will benefit enough from the heavier paper to be worth the cost.

With regard to the logo, some observers think that the cursive script of the logo is dated, while others think that it connotes elegance and the upscale quality of the catalog. Who is right? Whose opinion should *Exclusively Weddings* seek to answer that question?

Another possibility would be to have a live button on the Web site that one could click on to connect to a "live computer chat" with a customer service representative. Then, consumers could get immediate answers to their questions. Sher believes that it's possible to lose customers if they can't get answers to questions quickly and that many customers don't want to wait for e-mail answers to their questions. But is she right? Would the button keep those consumers from leaving? If not, then it would not be worth the expense.

All of these are hard questions to answer, but they must all be dealt with to maintain the competitive position of the catalog.

Questions for Discussion

1. What is the positioning of *Exclusively Weddings*? How has it attempted to create this positioning? (Hint: To answer this question, carefully consider who the target market is.)
2. How can it maintain its positioning given the increase in competition? Should it lower its sights?
3. Is the holiday catalog a good idea? Would it appeal to the same target market or to others? How could it be promoted?
4. Should *Exclusively Weddings* use heavier paper? In your opinion, will that have much impact on consumers' perceptions?

5. Should it change the logo? (To see the logo, go to its Web site. The logo is shown in the top left corner of each page. It's the cursive spelling-out of *Exclusively Weddings*.)
6. Is the button on the computer screen that is linked to a customer service representative a good idea? Why or why not?

Sources: Interviews with personnel at *Exclusively Weddings* and materials furnished by the company.

Video Case 7

Nivea: Softening and Standardizing Global Markets

Just as healthy skin requires the proper pH balance to flourish, a strong global brand must find the right balance between marketing efforts that build consistency in the overall brand's worldwide positioning and the need to appeal to specific geographical and cultural markets. Beiersdorf (BDF), the German manufacturer of Nivea skin care products, seems to have mastered that balancing act with all the skill of an Olympic gymnast.

Introduced in 1912, Nivea Creme was a unique water-in-oil emulsion, a formulation that set it apart from the fat-only creams available at the time. The snow-white color of the cream led to its name, Nivea—derived from the Latin word *nives,* which means "snow". The brand's positioning also made it distinct from other products on the market: It was a multipurpose cream sold at a price that made it attainable to the masses, rather than to only upper-class women who comprised the competition's target market.

Over the years, Nivea's positioning strategy has remained as simple and steadfast as the now-familiar blue-and-white package. Despite all the technological developments the company has introduced in skin care products, and all the markets it has sold in, Nivea's marketing always focuses on key brand benefits—high quality, reasonable price, straightforward approach, and mild skin care.

This commitment to the mainstream market and focus on multipurpose applications means that every product introduced under the Nivea name has to conform to guidelines established to ensure that everyone working on the brand around the world would know what it stands for. Nivea's marketing strategy is well stated by Rolf Kunish, chairman of the Beiersdorf Group: "The strategy of concentration on exploiting market potentials and regional growth opportunities is to be continued. The same applies to moves into new market segments and to increased investment in research and development."

Exploiting market potentials (the global market for cosmetics and toiletries was valued at $175.4 billion in the year 2000) means constantly introducing new products that meet the current market's needs and the needs of newly targeted market segments. One example of this strategy from the past is Nivea's emphasis on the health and active lifestyles of women as more women went to work in the 1920s. Others include the introduction of sunscreen, skin protection, and tanning products to match the more active, outdoor lifestyles in vogue from the 1960s to today; and products for every skin type and need, consistent with the multiplicity of product choices available in most products today. To meet the needs of new market segments, Nivea expanded its lines of products for children and men. All of these new products were guided by the constant Nivea standards that each product must meet a basic need, be simple and uncomplicated, refrain from offering to solve only one specific problem, be a quality leader, and be priced such that consumers perceive a balanced cost–benefit relationship.

BDF's new-product strategy was honed in the 1970s when competitive challenges prompted the company to take steps to revitalize the brand using a two-pronged approach. First, to counteract perceptions that Nivea had an older, less dynamic image than other brands, the company for the first time described specific product benefits in its advertising, instead of focusing on the variety of settings in which each product could be used. Second, BDF introduced additional products that would leverage the recognition and reputation of the Nivea name in growing segments of the market. These are subbrands, such as Nivea Shower and Bath, Nivea for Men, Nivea Sun, Nivea Hair Care, Nivea Body, Nivea Visage, and the recently introduced Nivea Baby.

During the 1980s, new products were supported by separate ad campaigns that helped build individual personalities and associations for each subbrand, while linking them to each other and to Nivea Creme through the use of the word care in all headlines. The subbrands helped establish Nivea as a broad skin and personal care brand, but their success was both pleasing and problematic for BDF. The company worried that the proliferation of products bearing the Nivea name might leave consumers confused about what the brand represented and that the image of Nivea Creme, the heart of the brand, might be weakened or diluted.

A recent example of this was the introduction of Nivea Visage Anti-Wrinkle Cream Q10 in 1998. This new treatment contains a restructuring coenzyme, Q10, that functions as an antioxidant and stimulates cell renewal, thereby leaving skin toned and smooth. Tests indicate that it will reduce signs of aging by 43 percent in 10 weeks when used regularly. Given the aging of markets around the world, a wrinkle-reducing cream posed enormous market share and revenue potential. Although Q10 was discovered by a U.S. scientist, Beiersdorf holds the exclusive world patent to use it in beauty fields. Naturally, the company had to exploit this opportunity.

But where should it be positioned in the company's product mix? It has a very different formula than the original Nivea creme, and its specific consumer benefits are quite different. Therefore, marketing management decided to include it in the Visage subbrand line. Visage is a more upscale product aimed at mostly urban consumers between the ages of 18 and 54. In these age ranges, wrinkle reduction is more likely to be effective, and the appeal of the product would be greatest. Although Visage is a more upscale product for Beiersdorf, the price of the anti-wrinkle cream is still under $10, which gives it strong appeal for the mass market.

By the 1990s, Beiersdorf had developed a global positioning strategy for its product mix. All ads for the core brand,

Nivea Creme, had to incorporate its underlying values of timelessness and agelessness, motherhood and a happy family, honesty and trustworthiness, and the product benefits of mildness and quality. Ads for the subbrands had to reflect elements of these values as well as those that were uniquely their own. This strategy was supported by the creation of a worldwide name for each product category and common packaging on a global basis. Moreover, all ads, regardless of the country in which they ran, had to evoke common emotion, use the same typeface, incorporate aspirational people, and employ a uniform Nivea logo.

The result is a highly standardized approach to global marketing. Rather than focusing on the individual differences in peoples around the globe, the firm focuses on the similarities. After all, as one company official notes, all people have skin and many people have the same needs and ideas.

When a firm operates in as many markets as BDF does, consistency, simplicity, and focus on the same benefits not only create a universal brand image, they also reduce headaches because fewer decisions have to be made. Standardized advertising campaigns need be adapted only slightly by translation into the local language. Because the costs can be spread around the globe, it's much less expensive to run a single global campaign, and marketing control is much simpler and easier. Packaging costs are reduced and product recognition is very high when people encounter the product in other countries.

The second element of the BDF strategy, exploiting regional growth opportunities, may necessitate some tempering of the standardized global approach. Because Nivea Creme is a European product, its appeal and marketing approach can be very similar in many parts of the globe such as the United States, Canada, Latin America, and South America, which were settled primarily by Europeans. The result is commonality in cultural backgrounds and light skin types, so that many products developed for the German market can be sold in these markets with little or no product or marketing adaptation. The appeal of skin care products in these markets is the same—a healthy, glowing skin.

As Nivea moves away from this common European cultural base, its products may be less well suited to the market. This is particularly true in African nations, where a majority of people have much darker skin and may require different sorts of moisturizers and sunscreen products. In between the European and African markets are the Asian markets, which are characterized by yellow and frequently more pale complexions. Although Nivea sells well in some Asian markets, such as Indonesia and Thailand, it sells less well in Japan. The difference in sales is attributable to both market and cultural conditions.

In the past, Japanese markets were strongly protected with relatively little competition from nondomestic manufacturers. Unfortunately for Japanese merchants, the resulting high prices lured foreign producers, and BDF was no exception. As more companies entered the Japanese market, competition increased, price maintenance was abolished, and prices have fallen. As a result, BDF has reduced the number of products sold there, focusing on the more profitable ones.

Besides differences in market conditions, there are cultural differences between European, U.S., and Japanese markets. Europe and the United States are "low-context countries," which means that ads should explicitly state what the product will do. Japan, in contrast, is a "high-context" country in which product claims do not need to be explicitly stated. Instead Japanese consumers want to know about the company and form a relationship with it. Once satisfied about the company, then they will buy the company's products. Thus, Japanese and German advertising are quite different—an advertising campaign prepared for Germany requires more than just a little tweaking in order to promote products successfully in Japan.

All of these differences might argue for more adaptation of Nivea products and marketing outside Germany and the European market. However, as economies develop, they tend to acquire many of the same tastes as do developed economies. An example is Russia, where men—especially younger men—are beginning to spend more on cosmetics. They are buying many of the same brands as their Western European counterparts— Gillette, Nivea for Men, Old Spice, and a few designer brands such as Christian Dior, Armani, Aramis, Guy Laroche, Gucci, and Paco Rabanne. Price is not the only crucial variable in the purchase decision. These men are interested in product characteristics such as fragrance. The bottom line in selling to these markets seems to be the increasing homogenization of markets, which favors the standardized global approach.

Taking this into account, Beiersdorf decided in 1997 to expand its product line for men—particularly with skin care products. "Men are becoming more aware of looking after their skin," says Thomas Ingelfinger, a marketing director for Nivea, but he admits that it will take some time to educate men. "There is a significant inertia which won't go in one or two years," he comments.

Nonetheless, *Euromonitor* observes that the male grooming market grew by about 28 percent from 1993 through 1997. It predicts that the fastest growth in the growing cosmetics and toiletries market will be coming from men's products.

The quest to convince men of the need to take better care of their skin has led Nivea into some interesting comarketing ventures. One is its alliance with Norelco to produce the new battery-operated Advantage Razor. To use it, one presses the side buttons to squeeze a moisturizing lotion onto one's face. While you might think this would cause a goopy mess, amazingly enough, it doesn't. Although the shave isn't much closer, your skin feels softer, and you don't have to wash your face. For men with a five o'clock shadow, a quick, no-water shave could be a real plus as they rush out of the office to meet a date or attend a social function. Of course, the razor costs between $119.95 and $134.95, with clip-on trimmer, but that contains five lotion inserts and a choice of lotion or gel, each of which lasts about eight shaves. A refill of five inserts costs about $8.00.

Questions for Discussion

1. How do economic, legal, and cultural factors affect the worldwide marketing of Nivea products?
2. Describe Beiersdorf's product and promotion strategies for Nivea. Is BDF engaging in product adaptation, dual adaption, or something else? What are the arguments for and against this strategy?
3. Would you say that Beiersdorf engages in global rather than international marketing? Explain your answer.
4. Find a Nivea ad and try to adapt it for the Japanese market.
5. How would you market the new line of men's skin products from Nivea? Would you use a standardized or customized approach? Why?
6. From a marketing viewpoint, is the homogenization of global markets good or bad? From a nationalism viewpoint, is this homogenization good or bad?
7. Should Beiersdorf continue with its fairly rigid standardized marketing strategy?

Sources: "Nivea Launches Anti-Wrinkle Cream in Italy," *Drug and Cosmetic Industry,* May 1998, p. 22; "Nivea to Test UK Men," *Marketing,* May 15, 1997, p. 9; "Men in the Mirror," *Cosmetics International,* October 1998, pp. 8–9; "Men's Lines Grow in Russia," *Cosmetics International,* March 25, 1997, p. 2; "Beiersdorf Beauty Sales Get a Boost from Nivea," *Women's Wear Daily,* March 1, 1996, p. 11; "Sales Indicate Global Direction of Beiersdorf," *Cosmetics International,* July 10, 1997, p. 12; "Beiersdorf Increases Profits as Nivea Sees Continued Success," *Cosmetics International,* June 25, 1996, pp. 12–14; Melissa Drier, "Beiersdorf's Growth Bolstered by Nivea," *Women's Wear Daily,* February 28, 1997, p. 11; Ron Geraci, "The Electric Glide," *Men's Health,* May 1998, p. 70; Imogen Matthews, "Global Trends in Personal Care," *Euromonitor,* 38, no. 6, p. 56; and information from the Nivea Web site (www.nivea.com).

Video Case 8

NASCAR: Racing for Sponsorships

With pedal-to-the-metal growth, stock car racing has roared out of the dirt tracks in the Southeast to second place among American sports. Although football is currently more popular, NASCAR racing is growing faster. Annual revenues for NASCAR are over $2 billion; more than 6 million fans attend races each year with another 123 million watching on TV, and attendance at Winston Cup races (the top level of NASCAR racing) are rising at a phenomenal 65.5 percent. Each of the three Winston Cup races held at the Texas Motor Speedway drew almost 200,000 fans. For the region in which a track is located, hosting a Winston Cup race is roughly equivalent to hosting the Super Bowl, and there are 38 Winston Cup races annually. Sales of NASCAR licensed products alone have grown from $80 million in 1990 to over $900 million.

Why is stock car racing so popular? There are lots of answers to this question, but one of the most frequently given is that it's family oriented. At any race, you will find whole families in the stands or camped out in the infield where they can get close to the action. Stock car racing has cleaned up its act tremendously from the early days of dusty, dirty tracks; stands with primitive facilities, and beer-drinking, tobacco-spitting, brawling fans. Today's tracks are clean and comfortable; they feature air-conditioned suites with gourmet meals and hospitality tents with linen-covered tables and waiters anxious to deliver the requested food. It's a suitable environment for any family, anywhere. The venerable Indianapolis Motor Speedway has held NASCAR races since 1994. In the past five years, new state-of-the-art speedways have opened near Los Angeles, Dallas–Fort Worth, Miami, Las Vegas, and St. Louis, and the newly opened Chicagoland Speedway has met with resounding success. Rumor even has it that Donald Trump may be supporting efforts to build a track near The Big Apple.

The stars of stock car racing are also a different breed. In NASCAR racing, there are no strikes, the drivers and crews are well-behaved, and, more importantly, they are responsive to fans. At every race, you will find smiling drivers patiently autographing programs. Fans can come to qualifying trials and camp in the infield before a race with the result that they can mingle with the drivers and pit crews—in no other sport can they do that. When a balloon and letter released to bolster the American spirit shortly after the events of September 11, 2001, landed in a tree on his Trinity, North Carolina, farm, Kyle Petty invited the two young girls who released it and their family to visit him. Few other athletic stars would do that. And NASCAR intends to keep the image of drivers clean and the sport fan-friendly. It will fine any driver, no matter how popular, found violating the rules, and it encourages interaction between fans and drivers.

People can relate to the racing vehicles. The cars you see on the track start out like the cars you could buy in a dealership. They are standard American cars, not exotic sports or formula-one models. The engines are standard V8s with a maximum displacement of 358 cubic inches. Every feature of the car—cylinder compression, carburetor, height, weight, aerodynamic design—is regulated by NASCAR with the result that many cars are not that much different.

To determine winners, NASCAR uses a point system that ensures close racing. Points are allocated so that a steady driver who finishes in the top five consistently throughout the season will garner more points than one who wins a dozen races, but doesn't finish a dozen other races. To be a grand champion, drivers must enter all the major races in their circuit and they must finish. This means that whether you go to Talledega, Darlington, Phoenix, or Watkins Glen, you will get to see the top drivers.

One major difference between stock car racing and other sports is that driving teams are not sponsored by cities, but by corporations. Every driver's car and uniform are covered with decals denoting various sponsors; after winning a race, the driver and pit crew engage in the "hat" dance of changing hats for photos so that *all* of their sponsors will be pictured in the winners' circle. Any spot on a car except the roof and the doors where the team's number is located can be used for advertising. Teams can sell the hood, trunk, and bumpers for $250,000 to several million dollars. Corporations with smaller budgets can buy 26-inch decals for a mere $62,000. Says Bill France Jr., on the board of directors of NASCAR, "We have the biggest uniform in professional sports." And the uniform isn't just seen by fans at the track—TV time means the message is broadcast to many, if not all, of the country's largest markets. "What's NASCAR about?"

According to former Winston Cup Series champ Rusty Wallace, "It's about 200,000 people on a four-acre facility watching kick-butt racing televised all over the world."

Sponsorship does not stop with the driving teams. Individual races such as the Mountain Dew Southern 500, racing circuits such as the Winston Cup Series, and awards such as the Anheuser-Busch Pole Award can be sponsored. In addition, firms can advertise at a race or become an official NASCAR sponsor. For example, Coca-Cola is the official soft drink of NASCAR (Gatorade is the official sports beverage), and Planters is the official snack food.

Sponsorship is necessary precisely because stock car racing is expensive—$8 million a year for teams running in the middle of the pack and up to $15 million a year for the leading stock car teams, according to Don Coble, sportswriter for the *Jacksonville Times-Union*. Purchase of a standard American car is just the beginning. It takes drivers, pit crews, mechanics, and increasing technology to adjust, maintain, and refine cars within NASCAR standards and teams frequently need several cars. To recoup these costs, team owners obtain winnings—but those cannot be counted on—and sponsorships. In addition, racetracks are expensive. The new Texas Motor Speedway near Dallas cost $160 million, and the construction tab for a brand-new state-of-the-art raceway can run up to $200 million. Again, a lot of sponsors are needed to foot the bill.

But why would 250 corporations, over 70 of which are Fortune 500 companies, want to pour millions of dollars into stock car sponsorships? The answer is the nature of the fans. As already indicated, families attend races, which means that corporate sponsors can reach both women and children in addition to the men at races. Over 38 percent of stock car racing fans are women, which is why you see all those P&G detergents advertised on race cars. Over 29 percent of fans have incomes over $50,000 per year, so this is a relatively affluent crowd. Stock car racing appeals to the 25 to 44 age group, which most advertisers and corporations are trying to reach.

Most importantly, NASCAR fans are brand loyal. When Kodak surveyed fans, it found that 95 percent of them buy Kodak film (the official film of NASCAR). According to Performance Research, a marketing research firm in Newport, Rhode Island, over 70 percent of NASCAR fans consciously choose NASCAR sponsors' products over other brands, whereas only half of tennis fans and golf fans have that same kind of loyalty, and only one in three fans of football, baseball, and basketball buy sponsors' products. More astonishingly, over 40 percent of NASCAR fans said they purposely switched to the sponsors' brand. Finally, fans know that drivers are supported by sponsors and that without the sponsors, there would be no racing. According to Ardy Arani, director at Championship Group/Atlanta, "when you see Joe Montana holding a candy bar, you know he has been paid to do a commercial. When you see Bill Elliott, you know McDonald's has paid for him to race. So you better go to McDonald's or Elliott might not race."

For corporations, association with the fast, tough, exciting, innovative, and aggressive sport of stock car racing carries over to their corporate image. Somehow being a NASCAR sponsor breathes new life into old products such as cereal brands

(Kellogg is the official cereal of NASCAR) and makes them more exciting to today's customers.

But a sponsorship is only as good as the use that the firm makes of it. To leverage their investment in a sponsorship, corporations need to devise promotional tie-ins that enable them to deepen their relationship with NASCAR fans or reach a broader audience.

Examples of successful sponsorship efforts abound. Heilig-Meyers, a Charlotte, North Carolina, furniture retailer offered a 10 percent discount on purchases to customers who brought in a ticket stub from a Charlotte race. Thorn Apple Valley meats ran a "mega meat sale" at a Super Kmart in Canton, Michigan, which featured five NASCAR show cars in the store's parking lot, a live on-location broadcast by a popular hard-rock radio station, ticket giveaways for the circuit race nearby and a sweepstakes for a go-car replica of the company's NASCAR vehicle. The Coca-Cola company featured nine members of the Coca-Cola Racing Family on eight-ounce classic bottles along with Coca-Cola Racing Family graphics and drivers' images on six-pack carriers for the bottles. McDonald's gave away different die-cast NASCAR cars in Happy Meals. McDonald's and Service Merchandise cosponsored a promotion. Service Merchandise offered a set of racing models plus stand that included a food offer from McDonald's, while McDonald's bags promoted the exclusive collection available at Service Merchandise and included a $3 coupon toward purchase of the set. RJ Reynolds has a Winston Cup fan club in which members get reduced-cost Winston merchandise such as calendars, baseball caps, and T-shirts along with the latest news on drivers, races, and NASCAR for a small entry fee. The result is a large database that Reynolds can use to promote its other products as well as cigarettes.

George Pyne, NASCAR senior vice president, has the major responsibility to develop sponsorships tied to NASCAR itself, and right now, he would like to find a hotel or motel chain(s) to be a NASCAR sponsor(s). After all, NASCAR fans travel on average over 200 miles to get to a race and once there, they spend $126 per person per race on ticket, food, lodging, and souvenirs. For a family of four, that's $604 on the average. Some families will spend more, and the statistics indicate that there are many affluent NASCAR fans who would stay in more upscale lodgings. Of course, there are also less affluent families who would opt for more budget-priced motels or hotels. Thus many hotel or motel chains should be glad to become NASCAR sponsors.

According to George, "it is important for any sponsor to have a clear-cut set of goals for their sponsorship. They should think about whether they want to sponsor a car or event. Sponsoring a car will get them media exposure at the track and can be used for retail events; whereas sponsoring an event will generate regional appeal, provide them with signage at the event and provide them an opportunity for hospitality at the event." In addition, George stresses that NASCAR wants sponsors that will leverage their sponsorships in interesting ways to broaden the appeal of NASCAR to potential fans in order to maintain the growth of stock car racing and NASCAR.

Questions for Discussion

1. If you were George Pyne, what types of hotels or motels would you want to sign a deal with? List the criteria that each should have and relate those to characteristics of the NASCAR market.
2. What type of sponsorship should a hotel or motel chain agree to? Why?
3. What types of promotional tie-ins could a hotel or motel chain create to exploit their NASCAR sponsorship?

Sources: "Driving NASCAR," *Discount Store News*, May 15, 1995, 34, no. 10 p. A46; "NASCAR Bottled Up," *Beverage World*, September 15, 1998, p. 34; "Number Reflect NASCAR's Growth," *Knight-Ridder/Tribune Business News*, April 6, 1998, p. 406B; "Service Merchandise, McDonald's Celebrate NASCAR's 50th," *Discount Store News*, 37, no. 17, p. 2; Dale Buss, "Retailers, Start Your Engines," *Supermarket News*, September. 14, 1998, 48, no. 37, p. 80; Holly Cain, "NASCAR Boom Leaves Track-Poor Northwest Behind," *Seattle Post-Intelligencer Reporter*, February 15, 2000; *Don Coble*, "Economy Drives NASCAR Sponsors Away," *Jacksonville Times Union Online*, July 19, 2001; Adam Cohen, "Blowing the Wheels Off Bubba," *Time*, February. 26, 1996, 147, no. 9, p. 56–57; Robert G. Hagstrom, *The NASCAR Way* (New York: John Wiley, 1998;) Suzanne Oliver, "A Fan-Friendly Sport," *Forbes*, July 3, 1995, 156, no. 1, p. 10 ff Donna Seiling, "West Mifflin Firm Seeks Sweet Taste of Success with NASCAR Candy Bar," *Pittsburgh Business Times*, June 5, 1998, 17, no. 46, p. 5; plus interview with George Pyne at NASCAR.

Video Case 9

The New Products Showcase: A Museum of Losers

Eighty percent of all new products fail. How can a company ensure that *its* new product is among the 20 percent that succeed? "Research, research, research," according to Bob McMath of the New Products Showcase in Ithaca, New York. And one way that you might do research is to visit his museum of new-product losers (and occasional winners).

Fascinated with new products, Bob has been collecting examples of new-product flops for 30 years—ever since he left Colgate-Palmolive, where he learned one of his first lessons about managing new products. Not all failures result from marketplace factors. After shepherding a deodorant through a new-packaging design process, Bob saw it shot down by a boss who simply didn't like the color blue—anywhere—including on Bob's new deodorant packaging. "He was a brown suit kind of guy," muses Bob.

In the New Products Showcase, Bob and his staff have collected over 60,000 once-new consumer products, some of which are 30 years old. There are products in five categories: foods, beverages, health and beauty care, household, and pet items. They are neatly arranged on shelves and wall units in a 6,500-square-foot warehouse, where you can wander around inspecting items at your leisure. Bob and his staff entertain a continuous flow of representatives from prestigious companies who come to

Showcase to search for new-product and packaging ideas, review what's been done in the past, track trends, and evaluate current product development projects. Bob preaches that most companies have a kind of "corporate Alzheimer's." Most don't know much about past new-product activities—their own, let alone those of competitors. They need to browse his showcase to avoid repeating past mistakes.

Bob and his staff hold workshops for company new-product groups to help stimulate creativity in generating new-product ideas and to critique the proposed new-product positioning plans. They can often point out mistakes in a new product's name, packaging, proposed positioning, or labeling that might save millions of dollars in development costs as well as possible embarrassment over a new-product flop. For example, if Gillette had first checked with Bob several years ago, it might not have marketed its new shampoo under the name For Oily Hair Only. Although the product was sound, Bob predicted that the name would create problems. What consumer wants to advertise to other shoppers, checkout clerks, and whoever else might be looking on that he or she is plagued by oily hair?

To date, firms such as Bausch & Lomb, General Mills, Kellogg, Sara Lee, Kimberly-Clark, Scott Paper, Kraft General Foods, Nabisco, Procter & Gamble, and Mitsubishi Corporation have stopped by Bob's place in Ithaca to inspect the results of over $12 billion in product development costs—mostly spent by other firms. While there, they can listen to Bob expound on "Why Products Fail: Principles for Success"; listen to Marilyn Raymond, staff consumer behaviorist and home economist, talk about "Preparing for 2000 and Beyond: Emerging Trends and Consumer Hot Buttons"; or participate in "Shop the Showcase," a series of directed exercises using the products on display as stimuli for new-product, -packaging, and -positioning ideas.

Those who can't make it to Ithaca can read Bob's book, *What Were They Thinking?*, in which he discusses many of the reasons that new products fail. One major reason is that a new product doesn't offer the consumer a clear benefit. Rather than focusing on *benefits*, or what consumers want, the company focuses on *features*, what the lab people like to talk about. However, successful new-product marketers know that features are not nearly as powerful as benefits in selling products. As an example, Bob points out that year in and year out Coca-Cola offers consumers refreshment through a series of ever-changing advertisements. "Suppose," Bob contends, "that Coke's advertising slogan had been 'The pause that's cold and wet' rather than 'The pause that refreshes.'"

Miller and Pepsi could have learned from Coca-Cola. For example, when Miller introduced Clear Beer from Miller, what benefits was it offering the consumer? None, really. The new product tasted about the same as previous products but looked like water, suggesting that it might be watered down. Needless to say, the product flopped. Pepsi had the same problems with Clear Pepsi. Not only did these products fail, they damaged each company's flagship brand by cannibalizing sales of regular Miller beer and Pepsi and by tarnishing the equity of the main brands. As Bob asks in his book, "What were they thinking?"

Sometimes, new-product developers fail to adequately consider how consumers use and think about products. For example,

Nabisco brought us Oreo Little Fudgies, which were Oreos with a chocolate coating. But this line extension simply didn't fit consumers' fancies. For decades, cookie munchers have been pulling their Oreos apart and going for the good stuff inside. When they tried pulling apart the little fudgies, all they got was a big mess.

Another product that violated consumer behavior and familiarity patterns was Sweater Fresh, a sweater freshener and deodorizer. Instead of sending a dirty sweater to the dry cleaners or putting it in the laundry, consumers could simply spray it with Sweater Fresh and put it in the dryer for a few minutes. It all sounds great, but the idea didn't wash with consumers. According to Bob, consumers associate odor with dirt. Although Sweater Fresh did eliminate odors, consumers still viewed the sweaters as too dirty to wear.

Bob also warns that companies can't trust consumers to read labels. His classic example involves Heublein's Wine and Dine, a kind of upscale Hamburger Helper. This new product was attractively packaged in a box that showed a bottle of chianti on one side of the box and pasta on the other. How did typical consumers use this product? Most cooked up the pasta, chilled the wine, and sat down to dine in style. Unfortunately, this behavior brought an unexpected and unpleasant result. It turns out that the wine was for cooking, not for drinking— it was laced with salt and herbs. "Yuck, phooey" might be a good way to describe a consumer's response to the first sip. Of course, *if* consumers stopped to read the label, they learned that the wine was to be used to spice up the pasta. But few consumers—mostly harried working women anxious to get dinner on the table—bother to read the details on a box.

Bob also believes that you can't fool the customer. Take cause-related marketing, for example. A firm such as Ben & Jerry's has been very successful in selling its Rain Forest Crunch and donating part of the proceeds to save the Brazilian rain forest. The product tastes good and it's made with plenty of nuts from the rain forest. However, when Wegman's supermarkets tried selling a private label rain forest snack line, consumers weren't buying it, literally. The product flopped when consumers realized that it contained too few rain forest products to be credible.

Other products that failed to fool consumers include those gourmet TV dinners you once saw in your grocer's freezer section. On the assumption that Americans were tiring of the standard TV dinner fare of mashed potatoes and green beans with fried chicken or salisbury steak, producers tried to jazz up their dinners with ingredients such as grilled eggplant and ratatouille. Unfortunately, many consumers—especially children—didn't like these more exotic sides. As a result, 25 percent to 33 percent of the average gourmet TV dinner ended up in the trash. People quit buying them because they didn't like paying more for something they didn't eat. Bob notes that you simply can't fool consumers' taste buds. "If you've ever tasted sugar-free Jell-O Pudding," he concludes, "you know that the proof of the pudding is in the eating. It's awful. That's not just my opinion. Most people agree, which is why sales are so poor."

With these examples in mind, what questions do Bob, his staff, and the thousands of failed products at the New Products Showcase suggest? To be certain that their new products are truly innovative and likely to succeed, companies should ask the following questions:

1. Is the new product positioned to create new users or new usage?
2. Is there new packaging that provides a consumer benefit?
3. Is value added through a new formulation?
4. Is there a technological introduction?
5. Does the product open up a new market for the category?

Companies that stop to ask such questions may avoid the dubious distinction of having their new products one day appear in Bob McMath's museum of losers.

Questions for Discussion

1. How do Bob McMath's "don'ts," as discussed in the case, mesh with the new-product development process outlined in the text?
2. Explain why the five questions at the end of the case are important in determining the success of new products.
3. How would Bob's guidelines for new products explain the success of Mentadent, cell phones, and Snackwell cookies?
4. How would you explain the failure of these products: rabbit jerky, Gerber's baby food for adults, and Dr. Care toothpaste (a toothpaste for kids that came in an aerosol can)?

Sources: "Shelf Centered," *People*, March 23, 1998, p. 166; Michael J. McCarthy, "Food Companies Hunt for a Next Big Thing but Few Can Find One," *Wall Street Journal*, May 6, 1997, pp. A1, A6; Robert M. McMath and Thom Forbes, *What Were They Thinking?* (New York: Times Business Press, Random House, 1998); Heather Pauly, "Flipping Over Flops," *Chicago Sun-Times*, June 29, 1998, pp. 1, 45; and materials from the New Products Showcase.

Video Case 10

Clarins: Beating Industry Standards
On The Virtues of Being Anonymous

While most of us are looking for positive feedback and reinforcement at work, Marc Rosenblum, senior vice president, finance and operations for Clarins U.S.A. in Orangeburg, New York, and Scott Cohen, senior manager of distribution, are looking for exactly the opposite. "We strive to be anonymous because that means we're doing a good job," Marc comments. Scott chimes in: "Yeah, if no one knows we're here, it means there are no problems in distribution and we're the good guys."

Being one of the "unnoticeable good guys in distribution" has become increasingly important in the last decade. As retailers attempt to manage their supply chain better, the importance of distribution increases as the size of retailer inventories goes down. After all, retailers who have fewer goods in inventory need replenishment in a hurry, and that's what Marc and Scott are responsible for.

Changes in Retailing

In the last decade, retailers have increasingly taken control over the ordering of their goods. To do that, they have computerized their inventory and sales systems, which meant that they could continuously know exactly what they sold and how much of it. This led to the installation of computer-generated replenishment ordering systems to replace systems operated by humans, in order to speed up ordering and reduce costs. The result was that stores knew exactly what they needed and could forecast how quickly they needed it. When they ordered goods, they expected that order to arrive within a certain time frame and to become active, meaning ready for sale, very, very quickly upon receipt. By installing these systems, retailers exerted great pressure on their suppliers to improve *their* distribution and logistics systems.

Clarins U.S.A. Takes Up the Distribution and Logistics Challenge

What has this meant for Clarins U.S.A.? In the United States, Clarins is a marketing and distribution operation as all production is done in France. When goods arrive at the receiving department in the Orangeburg, New York, warehouse, containers are broken down by contents, and the container ID information is read into a computerized receiving program. That program knows what should be in the container so that when workers break the container down, they are able to put the contents onto pallets of body lotion or a fragrance such as Chrome for men by Clarins. The computer creates a license plate (a rectangular label) that goes on the pallet and tells what is on the pallet by type of product and number of boxes.

Once goods are palletized, they are stored on exceptionally high shelves. Given a shortage of warehouse square footage, Scott and his team have chosen to go up with higher shelves and to employ narrow aisle technology. Narrow aisle means just that—the aisles are narrower, which means more storage space in the same amount of warehouse square footage. But narrow aisle requires "skinnier" forklift trucks to move the pallets on and off the shelves.

When needed, goods are moved toward the pick line, which is where orders are assembled and prepared for shipping. The term *pick* comes from having workers who pick the goods off shelves and put them into shipping containers that move continuously down a conveyor line. To begin the picking and packing process, workers receive a computerized shipping label, which contains a purchase order number and indicates where the goods are being sent. Accompanying the shipping label is a pick ticket that tells operators which items should go into a carton. Once filled, the cartons pass over a weigh station that is part of the computer system. Because the computerized scales know what should be in each carton, the computer can predict the weight of the carton. If the carton is within ±1.4 percent of the correct weight, the computer passes the carton down the conveyor line. The assumption is that it contains the appropriate goods. If the carton's weight falls outside these limits, it is rejected and must be checked by a worker to verify that the contents are correct.

Once goods pass the weigh station, they approach sortation lanes where the cartons are diverted into different lanes according to where they're going. When all the cartons going to—for example, Saks Fifth Avenue in Atlanta—are collected in the sortation lane, they are palletized and then wrapped in film with the license plate attached. Finally, they are stored near the loading dock for the retailer to collect. Once the retailer sends a trucker to the loading dock and the pallets are loaded, they are no longer the responsibility of Clarins U.S.A.

The Importance of Information Systems

The backbone of the logistics system at the warehouse is clearly the information system. Everything is computerized. Operators have RF guns (radio frequency "guns") with which they can read license plates and determine what is in a container. These are tied into the computer system and help to check the contents of all containers.

To improve distribution when Clarins sales grew in the United States, Marc and his team faced a major decision. Should they buy or build their own information system? They chose to build their own because of the inflexibilities of some off-the-shelf systems. As Marc explained, "Some of the packaged software that has been developed by very large companies had been designed to solve or to meet the challenges of several industries. As a result, sometimes with the peculiarities of the cosmetic wholesale business, there were unique challenges. For example, I know that with some of the brands that we distribute for other companies, their software limited them to being able to only fill orders for one fragrance at a time. Thus, if a store sent them an order for three different brands of fragrance, they had to create three different orders. They had to go so far as to instruct their sales force not to solicit or accept orders that were not set up that way." What a problem! So, Marc chose to increase the information systems department at Clarins U.S.A. and build its own system. Doing so, he estimates, did not cost any more than buying software from another company and having it modified for its company's use. Having its own information systems department is much more convenient and provides better control over information handling.

Having a lot of information in the right form readily available at one's fingertips has gotten to be very important because retailers have instituted something called a charge back system. If there is something wrong with a shipment that they receive, they charge that against the invoice from the distributor. So, if the wrong goods are sent or even if goods arrive a day late, the retailer can charge that against the invoice and reduce payment to the distributing firm. To dispute such charge backs, Clarins U.S.A. is able to extract large quantities of information for each order from its system and can usually refute the retailer's claim. In the few instances in which retailers remain unconvinced, the Clarins U.S.A. credit department sets up meetings with retailers. At those meetings, "we will go through line by line, page by page and we will prove every single claim is erroneous," says Heather Marzano, director of credit and retail services for Clarins U.S.A.. The outcome? Clarins U.S.A. pays very few charge backs.

Conclusion

It's amazing how hard Marc, Scott, Heather, and the rest of the folks at Clarins U.S.A. have worked to remain anonymous.

While the industry standard for inventory replenishment models is five days, Clarins U.S.A. is able to get 95 percent of the orders it receives on the shipping dock either the day or the day after the order is received. That puts the company three to four days ahead of the industry standard, and that's going to be tough for other cosmetics companies and other retail suppliers to meet or beat.

Perhaps this proves that with the help of technology, the good guys can come in first!

Questions for Discussion

1. What kind of vertical marketing system does the Clarins case exemplify?
2. How do customer service needs affect the distribution and logistics system at Clarins?
3. How does the distribution and logistics system at Clarins help it build relationships with its customers?
4. What are the goals of the Clarins logistics system? Why are these important?
5. How does Clarins implement each of the major logistics functions discussed in the text? Are there any that Clarins is not responsible for?
6. In your opinion, what could Clarins do to improve its distribution and logistics system?

Sources: Interviews with Clarins personnel and materials provided by the company.

Video Case 11

Forum Shops: Entertainment Retailing

Why do you think people go to Las Vegas? Gambling? No. Most people today go to Las Vegas to shop. A study by Plog Research of Reseda, California, of 8,000 leisure travelers to Las Vegas revealed that 67 percent listed shopping as their major activity, whereas only 18 percent listed gambling.

It is not ordinary retailing that's attracting folks to Vegas to shop. It's entertainment retailing that's causing this big change, and the Forum Shops at Caesar's is leading the way.

While the Forum Shops at Caesar's began rather modestly—only 250,000 square feet initially—it is certainly one of the most dramatic centers in the United States, and it's a prime example of themed shopping centers that are cropping up across this country. Based on the Forum in Rome, the entire shopping center attempts to recreate the vias, marketplaces, and piazzas that might have been found in ancient Rome. These also are good for just strolling or window shopping 24 hours a day or sitting at a table enjoying a cappucino and maybe thinking how unfortunate that the real Romans of yesteryear hadn't discovered coffee.

At the intersections of major shopping streets, there are fountains and statues of Roman gods and goddesses. Prime among these is the Festival Fountain, featuring a seven-minute special effects fantasy spectacular. During that time, Bacchus, the god of merriment and wine, wakes up and decides to throw a party for himself, and the Forum shoppers gather in his domed rotunda. Apollo, the god of music, provides the music with his lyre and entices an appearance of Venus, the goddess of love. Plutus, the god of wealth, provides the decor by bringing the fountain to life with cascades of jewel-like effects in the waters. Through music, sound effects, animatronics, computer-controlled waterscape effects, and theatrical lighting and special scenic projections on the dome, these marble gods come to life, talk, laugh, sing, and at the end invite shoppers to enjoy the pleasures of the Forum Shops at Las Vegas. Just imagine the impact of this on a first-time visitor who just stepped out of the Nevada sun into the neoclassical world of a latter-day Rome!

Following the main thoroughfare of quarried stone from Festival Fountain, one passes two-story shops with burnt orange façades entered through carved and grilled doorways and topped with statues of actual Roman senators. At the main piazza is the Fountain of the Gods, which features a rushing-waters fountain, the Temple of Neptune, beneath a 52-foot-high dome. Eventually one passes the 25-foot statue of Fortuna to enter the Caesar's Palace gaming casino. The entire shopping center is under a curved ceiling painted to represent a Mediterranean sky. Through special effects, the lighting of the ceiling changes every 20 minutes from a rosy dawn to a bright afternoon, a glorious golden sunset, and a darkened evening sky complete with stars.

"The Forum Shops is entertainment," says Terry Dougall of Dougall Design, which did the interior of Forum Shops. "It transports the visitor into something totally unique." He is referring to a "journey" through ancient Rome, spanning the period from 300 B.C. to A.D. 1700. The streetscape traverses time through architecture and replication of materials, textures, and design details of each period.

More than that, Dougall contends that "merchandise is secondary. It's not the product but the environment that has to be on display," he says. "You have to do something inside to get people in front of the product." Christopher Barriscale of a New York firm of architects says, "The design of a retail store is of the utmost importance. There's a lot of competition out there. The lifestyle retailers are targeting beyond product to the environment it's displayed in." These comments reinforce the idea that outside of location, the proper tenant lineup is the second most important factor in retailing. Michael P. McCarty, senior vice president and director of market research for the Simon DeBartolo Group, which developed the Forum Shops, adds, "Entertainment cannot overcome a poor tenant mix in the balance of a mall."

"Every weekend here is like Christmas at other malls," comments general manager Thomas A. Roberts. When it first opened, management anticipated that 10 million visitors would annually wander the streets of this Rome, but their estimates were off as more than 20 million visitors came in 1998. To support this extravagant shopping experience, the rents are high at the Forum Shops—in excess of $250 and $300 per square foot. That means that the 4,000-square-foot Bernini unit at Forum Shops would pay more than a million dollars rent a year. Does that make business sense? It does when the Bernini unit at Forum (the top-grossing unit of Bernini) rings up

$1,700 in sales per square foot a year. President Manny Mashouf of Bebe comments that his shop at Forum is also his top-grossing unit and brings in around $1,500 per square foot in sales annually. Not all shops at the Forum do as well, but average sales per square foot is a little over $1,300, which compares very favorably with a national average of $350 per square foot. All of which goes to show that entertainment retailing works.

Shopping while on vacation is entirely different. Shoppers are relaxed, have much more time to examine goods, be entertained, or spend time chatting or drinking a cup of coffee or just browsing and window shopping. The result is a often a major shopping spree even though the tourist is going to the same stores and buying the same goods that are available at home. It's the experience that matters. Comments one tired Forum Shops visitor, "It's just a better experience to shop when I'm away. I'm more focused on shopping."

From the retailer's point of view, tourists are wonderful customers. They spend four to ten times more than local shoppers do and rarely return anything. Frequently, shops carry only the higher ends of their lines at the Forum because as CEO Larry Hansel says, "Price is no object in this center."

Indeed the Forum is known for its upscale tenants, which include Christian Dior, Gucci, Fendi, Bulgari, Salvatore Ferragamo, Stuart Weitzman, Hugo Boss, DKNY, Emporio Armani, The Polo Store/Ralph Lauren, FAO Schwartz, and Lalique. But there are more everyday stores there as well, such as Banana Republic, Gap, Victoria's Secret, The Disney Store, Swatch, Brookstone, and Footworks. But even the Disney Store at the Forum Shops is different. Here a "Goofy" Zeus sends down bolts of lighting from a perch high atop a store column, causing fiber optics in the floor to swirl around Mickey's head and run along a path to a giant torch, lighting its flame. By the way, Mickey is a bronze-gilded sculpture in keeping with the Romanesque theme. Entertainment doesn't end when one leaves the street to enter a shop.

To capitalize on its success, the Forum Shops expanded in 1997 by adding another 283,000 square feet. The centerpiece of the new addition is the Roman Great Hall, which is 160 feet in diameter and 85 feet high. The major attraction is "Atlantis"—an enormous fountain that "comes to life" every hour from 10 A.M. to 11 P.M. The wrath of the gods is unleashed on the city of Atlantis. Fire, water, smoke, and special effects combine in an extravaganza as animatronic characters Atlas, Gadrius, and Alia struggle to rule Atlantis. Surrounded by a 50,000-gallon saltwater aquarium, the mythical sunken continent rises and falls before spectators' eyes.

In 1998 the Forum Shops announced the re-creation of the Pantheon, one of the greatest architectural masterpieces in Roman history. The Pantheon added 240,000 more square feet of multilevel specialty retail, restaurant, and entertainment space connecting to the existing Forum Shops.

And it seems that people visiting Las Vegas can't get enough—construction on the Pantheon had no sooner ended in May of 2000 when Forum Shops announced it would begin its third phase of expansion in the fall—adding 200,000 square feet of leasable space.

Recalling the comments of McCarty, it's important for the Forum Shops to begin considering what stores it would like to have in the new space. For example, the current Forum Shops has only one bookstore. What about adding a larger Barnes & Noble type of store? What about a candy store—a Godiva or Brach's specialty store? While there are many upscale shoes, what about a moderate-priced shoe store such as a Nine West or a woman's specialty shop such as the Limited to go with the designer shops? Or possibly an Imposters store, which makes copies of Bulgari-type jewelry. With regard to new tenants, Rick Sokolov, president and chief operating officer of Simon DeBartolo, says, "Obviously, it's [the Forum Shops] so successful that we can bring in who we want. It's a who's who." The question of the right "who's who" tenants will occupy management at the Forum Shops for the next couple of years.

Questions for Discussion

1. Compare a local mall to the description of the Forum Shops in the case in terms of
   a. use of a theme for the shopping center
   b. entertainment value of the shopping center
   c. types of retail tenants
   d. types of shoppers
2. Do you think that a Forum Shops type of mall would do well in a city of 1 million people that is not a tourist destination? Why or why not?
3. Why do you think retail sales are so high per square foot at the Forum Shops?
4. Would the same Roman theme and series of fountains and gods be as enticing to shoppers in other cities as it is in Las Vegas? Why or why not?
5. If you were going to add a bookstore, which would you add—a large Barnes & Noble store or a smaller specialty store?
6. If you were going to add a candy store, would you add a Godiva or a Brach's store?
7. Would you add the Nine West Store? the Imposters Store?

Sources: Teena Hammond, "Las Vegas Retailing on a Roll," *WWD*, April 29, 1997, 173, no. 82, p. 15; Teena Hammond, "Second Expansion Set for Las Vegas Forum Shops," *WWD*, May 26, 2998, 175, no 104, p. 3; Sarah Hoban, "Retail Entertainment," *Commercial Investment Real Estate Journal*, March–April 1997, pp. 24–9; Laurie MacDonald, "Under Renovation," *Footwear News*, August 5, 1995, 52, no. 35, p. 8; Michael Marlow, "Caesars' Forum Shops Conquers New Territory," *Daily News Record*, September 5, 1997, 27, no. 107, p. 17; Hubble Smith, "Forum Shops Set to Expand Again," *Las Vegas Review-Journal*, May 22, 2000; Dean Starkman, "Mall Developers Envision Shopping Paradise, and It's Called Las Vegas", *Wall Street Journal*, July 11, 2001, pp. B1, B10; Marianne Wilson, "Disney's One-Two Punch," *Chain Store Age Executive with Shopping Center Age*, July 1995, 71, no. 7, p. 92; and numerous materials supplied by the Forum Shops.

Video Case 12

U.S. Military Academy: Heavy Duty Promotion

How tough would your promotion job be if people didn't know your product and acceptance of it could mean death in battle? Sound tough? It's the job of Colonel Michael L. Jones of the U.S. Military Academy (USMA) in West Point, New York, and he wouldn't trade it for any other job. Why? Stirring words such as *honor, duty*, and *courage*. Since its founding in 1802, its mission has been "To educate, train, and inspire the Corps of Cadets so that each graduate is a commissioned leader of character committed to the values of Duty, Honor, Country: professional growth throughout a career as an officer in the United States Army; and a lifetime of selfless service to the nation." Some of the biggest names in U.S. history are graduates of West Point: Lee, Sherman, Grant, MacArthur, Eisenhower, Schwarzkopf, and astronauts Frank Borman and Buzz Aldrin. It's said that "At West Point, much of the history we teach was made by people we taught."

Ranked in the top tier of U.S. universities, it's an impressive academic institution and a molder of leadership and character. To be accepted at West Point, you must pass the "Whole Candidate Score," which means have well-above-average academic credentials, high SAT and ACT scores, leadership abilities, and physical aptitude—usually demonstrated through participation in athletics—and, oh, be nominated by someone like the vice president of the United States or a member of Congress. You can't just apply; you have to be nominated.

Finding the right young people for the USMA demands identifying them as early as the eighth grade. USMA field force members search for students who completed algebra, first-year high school English, and foreign language in the eighth grade because that's evidence of college aspirations. Potential applicants are also identified through searches bought from the Educational Testing Service and ACT. Then, they are sent direct-mail pieces. If they respond, they will receive a series of nurturing mailings until the second semester of their junior year in high school. If they have not opened a file by then, the process ends.

Potential applicants receive the West Point Catalog, ViewBook, videos geared to their interests, other specialized mailings, and are directed to the USMA Web site where they can apply electronically using the nine-step admissions process. They can also download video clips, pictures, maps, and other information about the USMA.

The Web site is a major recruiting tool. Beginning in 1999, applicants received passwords that allowed them to check the status of their application at all times. By 2000, they were able to identify and communicate with cadets from their hometown or zip code. The Web site (www.usma.edu) also contains press releases, information about parents' clubs, speakers, the visitors' center, and has the option of downloading a map directing you to West Point.

Besides print and electronic media, the academy uses personal contact. Colonel Jones has a field force of 400 Reserve officers who work for him plus another 1,600 volunteers. These people relentlessly canvas high schools—speaking in public forums, identifying and contacting prospects, and helping them select a high school academic curriculum. Academy cadets also volunteer to recruit candidates and visit their home areas, speaking to groups, talking to prospects, visiting schools, and even making appearances on local radio and TV if the opportunity arises.

The clincher, Colonel Jones thinks, is a trip to West Point for a daily tour or overnight visit. The applicant is squired around by a volunteer cadet (one-on-one) so that he or she learns what life is like at the academy and that cadets are regular people. Meanwhile, parents go on walking tours with other cadets.

Because parents are important in recruiting cadets, there are 130 parents' clubs across the United States in which parents provide support for one another, set up visits to the academy, and are kept abreast of what is happening with their child's application or cadet career.

The theme of all promotions for the USMA is simple and brutal. "You must be willing to stand up and die for your country leading people in time of war." That's an easy message to convey to youth, but a hard one to convey to mothers. Hence, the heavy emphasis on "selling to parents" as well as youth. The theme is conveyed in all promotional materials, which use the same font and colors for the words *West Point*. The goal is a consistent message and appearance to candidates and the public.

While the USMA has no funds for media such as radio and television, it does get some coverage there. The Army–Navy game is broadcast at Thanksgiving, but frequently viewers think these are enlisted men playing—again underscoring how little most citizens know about the academy. More recently, *Rolling Stone* and *Parade* carried features on West Point. Given the complimentary nature of the articles and reach of these periodicals, they should prove valuable in helping Colonel Jones explain what and who the Academy is.

What would Colonel Jones like to do in the future? Go totally digital to improve the print quality of the catalog, prospectus, and brochures. He also wants more video clips so that any potential applicant can find a clip of whatever he or she is interested in at West Point.

Questions for Discussion

1. How are promotions integrated at the U.S. Military Academy?
2. Describe how the promotions program at USMA moves potential candidates from awareness to purchase (decision to go to the USMA).
3. What types of appeals are used in USMA promotions? Why are these likely to be effective? (Visit the Web site and pick one promotional message.)
4. Visit the USMA Web site. List all the types of information at the Web site (history, etc.) For each type of information, describe the intended audience. Decide why the information was included, and why it would be effective in the USMA's recruiting.
5. How can the USMA collect feedback from its Web site and other promotions such as the catalog and brochures?

Sources: Printed and Web materials from West Point and personal interview with Colonel Jones.

Video Case 13

American Standard: Selling and Distribution

What's changing in America's homes? The answer is bathrooms. They have become a major fashion statement. They've gotten bigger and more luxurious. Practicality and functionality have given way to style and elegance. Bathrooms are for relaxing in whirlpools and listening to piped-in music as Americans seek to dissipate their cares in warm water and send them down the drain with the bath water. That may be why one of the largest manufacturers of bathroom fixtures and ceramics, American Standard, has the slogan, "Made for the Soul."

Who buys all these fancy fixtures and appointments? Only a few homeowners actually buy these products and even then it's usually as replacements. Instead, plumbing contractors make most bathroom fixture purchases. Others who might influence the purchase are builders, contractors, and architects.

How can a company like American Standard reach and sell to all these multiple targets? How can it cater to Americans' current obsession with luxury bathrooms when those folks don't buy their own sinks? How can it maintain sales in less luxury-oriented environments such as public buildings, churches, schools, hospitals, tract housing, and apartment complexes?

Channels of Distribution

To understand selling at American Standard, one has to understand the channels of distribution. There are two distinct channels of distribution for ceramic bathroom products and each channel is quite different from the other. But selling in both channels is dominated by the nature of each channel's market.

First channel is the retail channel, the one most of us knows best. It consists mainly of big box stores such as Lowe's or Home Depot and its market is the home renovator and a few builders and plumbing professionals. Customers pick out the product, buy it (one sink, not two or more) or two items (a sink and a tub), pay cash, and usually install the product(s) themselves at home or occasionally they hire a plumber to handle the installation. The product mix in these stores is limited to a few, more popular models and inventory turn is relatively quick. There are also a few small retailers in this category who sell a more exclusive line of products and are willing to order product for the customer. Prices at the smaller stores are usually higher, but so is the level of service. What is constant is the market and single item purchases—home renovators buying one sink for the most part.

In this retail channel, American Standard is in a pull mode. It advertises products in magazines and through its Web site. The emphasis is making sure that product is in the store and has favorable placement, good displays, and that the American Standard's point-of-purchase materials are displayed because customers frequently make decisions in the store. Most sales are made at the executive level and are chain or region-wide. Salespeople calling on local stores focus on managing displays and maintaining sufficient inventory.

The second channel is the wholesale channel. This channel consists of distributors who use their showrooms to sell to contractors, builders, plumbing companies, and architects. These buyers purchase products for installation in homes, apartments, schools, and hotels that they are building for or selling to someone else. This channel is characterized by multiple decision-making, multiple purchasing (large numbers of sinks) and sometimes customized items (for a hotel, for example).

Push dominates the wholesale channel. Selling is the primary promotional tool and it is aimed at not only the distributor, but also those who influence the purchase process. Salespeople engage in creative selling where they sometimes have to identify potential purchasers (a new hotel or apartment complex in the planning stage) and keep in touch with them for months or even years before the purchase is made.

In the wholesale channel, there are approximately 4,000 distributive outlets in the United States owned by roughly 1300 companies or individuals. That necessitates many more sales calls and each call covers an individual or only a few stores. The workload of the sales person is much greater as they are trying to get placement of the product, set up displays, and affect gatekeepers and other influencers who are involved in the purchase decision.

The difference between the two channels is illustrated in the introduction of new products. If American Standard wants to introduce a new product in the retail channel, this can be done at the national level. The new product is shown to Lowe's or Home Depot executive buyers who decide to carry it in dozens of stores. In the wholesale channel, to introduce a new product requires sales reps calling on dozens of distributors, explaining the new product and helping them display it to good advantage in their stores. One successful sale in the retail channel may get the product in a 100 stores; whereas a successful sale in the wholesale channel may take longer and get the product in only one store or just a few.

Today, the market for plumbing fixtures is about $5.5 billion, split 55 percent in wholesale and 45 percent in retail. The retail channel, however, is growing faster so that within three years the split may be 50-50 between wholesale and retail.

Types of Sales Representatives

What's it like to sell in these two channels of distribution? Would the same person be equally suited to each channel? Given the differences in selling, the answer to that question has to be no.

In the wholesale channel, the sales rep has to be more flexible and able to interact with a wider range of people—from plumbers to architects. According to David Lipkin, Vice President of Sales, "they almost have to be chameleon-like in their approach to the marketplace. On any given day, they're with a plumber. They're with a builder. They've got to be flexible. They've got to be a lot more inquisitive to know where decisions are being made."

David divides the traits that a successful sales person should have into two categories: "Can Do" traits and "Will Do"

traits. "Can Do" traits are education, experience, and being presentable/appearance and manners. "Will Do" traits are related to the personality of the person. Can they get along with others? Are they a team player? Can they stand on their own two feet? Do they have the ability to make decisions without having to call someone every time? Are they stable? When in school, did they play sports, sing in the choir, or hold student government offices?

One characteristic that David thinks is very telling about sales candidates is the handling of blame. He asks "Do they blame others for failure or do they take credit for failure themselves? We all fail. The question is who do you blame for it? We can manage our successes and we can manage our failures." If job candidates tend to slough the blame for grades or performance off on others, they also tend not to get the job.

David's description of the wholesale sales rep indicates why the "Will Do" traits are so important. "This is you working out of your home, or out of a regional office, but being in there very infrequently. This is being able to get up every morning, get out into the field, be a self-starter and get the job done, and being able to work long hours." He asks "What are the things that you can tell me about your ability to get out there? Do you know when a plumbing contractor buys? 6:30 to 7:30 or 8:00 in the morning because the rest of the time he's getting $45 an hour. Every time he's standing there talking to you, he's not making $45 an hour or $65 in some markets or even $70."

In a job interview with David, he asks about habits and interests. He wants to know about "stick-to-it-iveness". The applicant should understand that he or she is selling the moment he or she walks in the door and they have to sell David on themselves before he will hire them.

The Ladder of Success for Sales Reps

Given the differences in selling, opportunities for advancement and compensation vary between the two channels. In the retail channel, there are the route-type sales reps who are managed by regional and national sales managers. As one moves from the sales rep to sales manager positions, the nature of the job changes. The sales manager is responsible for supervising his sales reps and for managing regional buys for retail managers at higher levels. That's a matter of regional sales managers working with regional store managers. Given that the sales rep is mostly concerned with adequate inventory and display, the sales managers actually do more selling to store managers than do the reps.

Sales managers sometimes come from the ranks of retail sales reps but frequently they are recruited from among sales reps in the wholesale channel because those reps have a stronger sense of how to manage a business, are accustomed to dealing with higher level managers and have stronger selling skills. On the other hand, promising retail sales reps may be shifted to the wholesale channel to build their selling skills. Thus, sales reps and sales managers can move from one channel of distribution to another, but usually that movement is at a higher rung on the ladder.

Incentives are greater in the wholesale channel where the rep has more opportunity to sell. Retail sales reps are more likely to be paid a salary whereas the wholesale sales reps are on commission and the result is higher income among wholesale sales reps.

A Third Type of Sales Rep

American Standard also hires some missionary salespeople called architectural engineer specification people and builder sales reps. The architectural engineer specification person has a much more detailed knowledge of the product and how it is used in buildings coupled with a greater knowledge of architecture and construction. They can help sell by providing in-depth information, and they frequently are used to train other sales reps in the features, benefits, and advantages of American Standard products compared to the competition.

The builder sales rep is responsible for managing the relationships of pull-through by insuring that builders are aware of American Standard products and work to move decision makers away from competitive products. The major function of both of these reps is to support the regular sales staff with more detailed knowledge of the needs of each buyer and more information about American Standard products.

Sales Territories

Sales territories are affected by work load which, in turn, is affected by the number of new constructions. In some old markets such as the Boston area, there's relatively little new construction. A builder might only do 30 to 50 homes a year. On the other hand, in Colorado, a builder may be building hundreds of new houses a year. Thus, the size of the territory is very much determined by the amount and type of building activity in it.

The company has to continually monitor construction within each territory to find high-use forms of construction such as hotels, schools, public buildings and apartments that could use American Standard products. To some extent, that's the sales rep's job. He or she may find that a new hotel is going up and is responsible for calling on the architect designing the hotel to begin the influence process early on. But the company can also find high growth opportunities in sources such as the McGraw-Hill Dodge reports.

The Problems of moving from selling to managing

What's the biggest problem for someone like David when he moves from selling to managing? "Giving up control and turning it over to someone else. I had to give up control of the everyday decisions that influence the successes and the failures of my business and turn that responsibility over to others. . . I felt out of control as my teams developed and, in fact, my skills as a manager were developed over the years I became much more comfortable with allowing others to make the kinds of decisions that are necessary to move our business forward." That's one reason why many sales reps do **not** want to move into management.

These comments place a heavy emphasis on developing teams and management skills. At American Standard, there are processes in place to help with this. Each manager is responsible for identifying three people who work under him or her

who could rise to the top of the organization. To do that, however, they would have to take over David's position, which also means that part of managing is looking for one's replacement.

Truly selling and sales management are in constant motion with twists and turns in career paths that are not always foreseeable. Maybe a sense of adventure should be added to the traits sales people need.

Questions for Discussion

1. Explain the relationship between the type of selling, promotional opportunities, incentives, and sales territories with the type of channel of distribution. How does the customer at the end of the channel affect each of these sales management decisions?

2. How does David's list of "Can Do" and "Will Do" traits stack up with the ones provided in the textbook? How could you explain any differences in the two lists?

3. Would you agree with David that how people handle blame is important in selecting sales reps? Why or why not? Explain your answer in terms of the requirements of sales reps.

4. Where should sales territories be larger? In Boston or Colorado? How could the size of the territory affect compensation?

5. American Standard has purchased an European manufacturer of very high end, luxury bathroom fixtures — the Porcher company. Which channel of distribution do you think these fixtures will be sold through? What type of selling is involved? How does the customer affect the sales of these luxury fixtures? Should American Standard use their regular sales reps to sell this line or should they have a separate sales staff?

Sources: Interviews with American Standard personnel, the American Standard Web site; Michael Pollick, "What's New?", *Sarasota Herald Tribune*, July 16, 2001, p. 3; Pamela Sebastian Ridge, "American Standard Polishes Its Brands for Future Growth — New Management Team Aims to Raise Productivity, Profits and Performance," *Wall Street Journal*, August 28, 2001, p. B6; Jeffrey L. Rodengen, *The History of American Standard,* Write Stuff Enterprises, Inc., 1999.

Video Case 14

Maxim Direct: Maximizing Direct-Marketing Returns
The Situation

Will Spivey, Ross Schlemmer, and Debbie Rudolph, managers at Maxim Direct, were meeting to determine follow-up program(s) for their previous year's very successful campaign for Schult Homes, a producer of manufactured housing. That promotional campaign had resulted in a database of over 150,000 households that were "real" prospects for purchase of a manufactured home. Now, the issue was creation and implementation of another direct-response campaign to turn those prospects into new owners of a manufactured home built by their client.

The Company

Maxim Direct is a full-service direct-marketing agency that provides clients with services in the four key areas of direct marketing: consulting (client services and account management), creative (developing and communicating campaigns), implementation (printing, production, teleservices), and analytics (data analysis). Founded in 1999, it is relatively new to the direct-marketing scene, but in those few short years, it has successfully differentiated itself from many similar firms. What distinguishes Maxim Direct is its focus on strategy rather than on just communication (developing creative campaigns) or analytics (mining large data banks). Instead, Maxim Direct develops a strategy to solve the client's problem and then implements that strategy and analyzes the results. A good example of its approach to client problems is its campaign for Schult Homes.

The Client

Schult Homes is a leader in the manufactured housing industry. Founded in 1934, Schult has a strong heritage of quality and craftsmanship resulting in an excellent product. Over the years, Schult incorporated many new features in its homes such as "uni-strength" construction (for a stronger product), maintenance-free features, and energy-conserving designs. While early homes emphasized practical features such as sofa beds and portable water tanks, today's homes are loaded with the latest in convenient, luxurious appointments including walk-in closets, cathedral ceilings, whirlpool tubs, and natural wood cabinetry. Over the years, the market has responded to Schult quality: In the 1940s, the king of Egypt ordered a Schult home, and the U.S. government bought Schult homes for workers during and after World War II.

Product quality is the start of Schult's market strategy; thorough follow-up service is the finishing touch. High standards of service are possible because of its strong network of franchises. These retail partners serve a dual purpose: While they are customers of Schult, they, in turn, are part of Schult as they provide much of the service that final consumers receive. Thus, any marketing effort undertaken by Schult must take the needs of these important partners into consideration.

The Problem

At the start of the new millennium, sales were off throughout Schult's 220 franchises, and inventories were stacking up when prospects failed to materialize on the selling lot. Why? The economy was strong and people were moving to site-built homes rather than manufactured housing. In addition, the manufactured housing category was overbuilt, and there were lots of liquidators and wholesalers cutting price at the bottom end of the market. All of which put pressure on full-price providers such as Schult.

Although direct marketing seemed to be an ideal solution to generate more parking lot traffic, there was a major problem in implementing a direct-marketing campaign for Schult. Mass-marketing data banks did not have the data variables needed to identify potential purchasers of manufactured housing. As Will put it: "there are no easily identifiable segmentation drivers for

who . . . would be interested in manufactured housing. Research has shown that if you know someone who lives in manufactured housing and if you're related to someone who lives in manufactured housing, you think it's a perfectly acceptable housing alternative. If you don't, you have a natural bias against the category. We had to build a program that would let people raise their hand, if you will, and say, 'I am interested in this category. Talk to me about your product.'"

But the problem didn't end there. Once consumers raised their hands, they had to go to a dealer and those dealers had to be sold on the direct-marketing campaign. According to Ross: "we had to sell them [dealers] into it [the direct-response campaign]. It was an investment for them." Franchisers had to spend part of their promotional budget supporting the direct-response campaign. Therefore, it was important that Maxim Direct develop a campaign that would appeal to dealers, be easy to implement, be highly visible, generate excitement, and really drive up the number of prospects in their lots.

The Campaign

Maxim Direct's solution: the Gold Key Home Giveaway. It started primarily with a direct-response television ad informing consumers to call a 1-800 number to register to win a free home. Recognizing that not all potential respondents might see the TV ad, Maxim Direct also created door hangers that were placed on doorknobs of apartment units across the country. Emblazoned on each hanger was the phrase: "Where's the key?" along with a telephone number for recipients to call. Dealers also received newspaper slicks and radio scripts that they could use to advertise the campaign on local media—again asking individuals to call to register.

When recipients called, they gave their names and contact information—that registered them to enter the contest. Once registered, each respondent received a Gold Key package in the mail containing, among other materials, a tin key. The respondent was supposed to take the key to the Schult retailer identified in the mailer to see if he or she were a finalist to win a free home. If the number on the respondent's key matched a number on the list at the retailer, that person was a finalist. There could be as many as 20 finalists at each participating retailer.

The promotion ended on Finalist Day in mid-May when the finalists returned and tried to open a home with a real key given to them in a sealed envelope. Earlier, each retailer had received a lock, which retailers installed in a manufactured home on their lots. Only one lucky respondent among all the finalists nationwide had a door-opening key with which to win a house. Thus, until the end of the promotional campaign, no one knew who would win the free home!

The Results

After the fun and excitement of designing and implementing a campaign comes the analytic stage. How well did the campaign work? How could one evaluate such a campaign? One tool for evaluation might be the increase in retail traffic. In this case, the increase can be directly measured by the number of respondents who took their keys to a Schult dealer. On average,

1,000 respondents showed up at each participating dealer. Of those 1,000 respondents, 20 became finalists, but the other 980 became leads—individuals who might buy a manufactured house. Furthermore, they were in a dealership where the dealer's salespeople could offer them incentives to purchase even though they hadn't won.

The generation of leads provides another measure of the success of a direct-mail campaign: cost per lead. Maxim Direct calculated that it reduced the cost per lead through this campaign by more than 90 percent based on Schult's history.

Through the campaign, Maxim Direct had built a database of over 150,000 households who were leads for future sales or, to use Will's terminology, households that had "raised their hands" to show that they were interested in a manufactured home. All of that data could be further analyzed to determine —for example—what sections of the country were most responsive (the Midwest).

To break even on the campaign, Schult had to sell a couple of hundred homes across the country. Sales during the campaign exceeded the break-even point by a factor of five. As a result, the client's rate of return on its investment in direct marketing rose by over 500 percent.

The Next Step

Now, it's a year later and the team is trying to come up with its next step. What could it do with these 150,000 household names and addresses? Should it run another full-fledged direct-response campaign? If so, what form of direct marketing should the firm use? What sort of creative—theme—should it use?

Questions for Discussion

1. How does the Gold Key campaign illustrate the benefits of direct marketing (as opposed to mass marketing)?
2. What forms of direct marketing did Maxim Direct use in this campaign? How did each form contribute to the success of the campaign?
3. How could Maxim Direct determine the success of the campaign among dealers?
4. What should Will, Ross, and Debbie do in the next step? Help them design a new campaign aimed at the households in their data set. Determine what form(s) of direct-response marketing you would use and a theme for the campaign. Outline the steps in your campaign, and be sure to remember planning for analysis of the campaign!

Sources: Shult Homes Web site and materials provided by Maxim Direct.

Video Case 15

George C. Moore: Becoming Easier to Do Business Through the Internet

George C. Moore, manufacturer of woven and knit narrow elastic products, was the first firm in its industry to take the plunge into Internet marketing by establishing a business-to-business Internet site. Although the company had hoped to sell products over the site, that wasn't really the primary reason for the decision. According to Goran Elovsson, executive vice president at George C. Moore, the primary reasons were customer service and response to increased global competition.

> We're starting the web site primarily to become easier to do business with. We believe right now with competition being extremely fierce all over the globe we have a very difficult time competing on price—especially with foreign imports.

> We need to add value to our customers in other ways than just by price or product. There's opportunities to that by streamlining the supply chain which enables us to reduce lead times, to be a lot more flexible and quicker to respond than we would otherwise be. Technology gives us that opportunity.

The Benefits of a Business-to-Business Web Site

How does technology make it possible for George C. Moore to achieve its goals? First of all, the Internet is a 24-hour, 360+-days-a-year service center. Customers anywhere on the globe can browse Moore's online catalog, look for specials on overstocked items, look for new products pictured through high-resolution photography on the site, send orders, check their inventory, and previous orders from Moore, and track current orders to discover their location and shipping status. Thus, the Internet effectively eliminates the impact of time differences around the globe. No more waiting in India until 8 A.M. when someone will be in Moore's offices to place an order. On top of the time and flexibility advantages, the Internet is cheaper than telephone, fax, or snail-mail ordering. Customers can further reduce the time necessary to send and track orders by doing that for themselves. All of this makes it easier to do business with George C. Moore.

But the benefits of the Web site don't end there. The company can also sell new items more easily. Instead of putting together packets containing new samples and mailing them to prospective buyers, the company can picture the new items on its Web site and send e-mail notices about the new items to prospects around the globe. This process reduces the waste of unread mail packages that wound up in the wastebasket. *And* it's also easier, faster, cheaper, and has greater reach than the old method. Because of the lower cost, the company can "afford" to alert buyers around the globe to new offerings and can target special messages to selected high-potential prospects. The Web site also offers the same advantages in selling overstocked items with the additional benefit of being able to reach smaller buyers that the company would not normally be able to sell to.

A final advantage of the Web site is that it enables George C. Moore to greatly enhance its relationship with customers by linking information systems. If the customer purchases the same items repeatedly, the computer can be programmed to reorder when inventories drop. Thus, George C. Moore begins to manage its customer's inventory. By relieving the customer of inventory management effort, George C. Moore increases its value to the customer and effectively streamlines the supply chain for the customer.

Building the Web Site

The Web site grew out of discussions about the George C. Moore information Web site and the possibilities of e-business. In the spring of 2000, the company surveyed customers and found that they were interested in such a service. So, the company formed a committee that was a blend of marketing and technical people. The committee consisted of Goran Elovsson; Rodger Allinson, director of information systems; his program manager, Marcia Ball Greenhalgh; Andrew Dreher, director of sales and marketing; Cheryl DeBartolo, customer service manager; and Hugh Pepper, George C. Moore system analyst. The committee charged Rodger with finding a professional Web developer, and he eventually hired E-One of Omaha, Nebraska, because E-one had an existing commerce program that would work well to meet the company's needs.

E-One, Rodger, and his people worked until the fall of 2000 on the Web site. In building the Web site, they tried to use navigation guides and other devices familiar to Internet users. They did run into a major problem, however, with stock numbers. Each manufacturer has different stock numbers for items that they want to order, and those numbers are different from the ones used by George C. Moore. Thus, the developers had to build cross-reference files so that the customer could order by the manufacturer's number or by Moore's number.

Once they had a prototype site built, they invited two key customers to help them test the site. To demonstrate the site, they used the customer's information in order to show how easy it would be to use the site. Feedback from these sessions was used in further refining the Web site.

But that is not the end of the feedback process. There are statistical programs built into the software to collect data with which to analyze the functioning of the Web site over time. Rodger and his employees will be able to determine the number of hits, how long customers were at the site, what features they used at the site, how quickly information was processed, and the accuracy of information. Plus the company will actively seek feedback from users in the future.

The Web Site as Part of the Promotional Mix

The Web site has important implications for the promotional mix at George C. Moore. It will replace many print communications with electronic ones. Although the communication medium changes, the message does not; it remains the same. In fact, putting the catalog online allows the company to continuously update the catalog—something not possible with the old, printed catalogs. Samples, which are a form of sales promotion will still be sent to customers, but only after the customer requests them.

The major change will involve personal promotions. Salespeople can spend less time on order taking and processing—especially routine order taking—and be able to spend more time with customers discussing the customers' needs and wants. Thus, the Web site is intended to enhance, not detract from, the customer service representative's performance.

Design of the Web Site

The Web site has two domains—a public one that anyone can access and a private one that only registered customers can access. The public domain allows for browsing by anyone, and the private domain allows customers to feel safe about placing their orders online. They know that no one other than them and George C. Moore can access their order and inventory information.

But seeing is believing! To try out the Web site, go to www.georgecmoore.com and check it out for yourself.

Customer Response to the Site

During the test stage for the Web site, several companies had an opportunity to observe and "try out" the site. What did they think? "George C. Moore's Web-based initiative should require less directed follow-up by the buyers and allow them to spend more time in supplier development and other true sourcing activities," said John Levicki of *Vanity Fair*. He also added, "Companies in our industry must remember that they are supplying more than just a material or a product. They have to supply a complete package of products and services that exceeds that of their competition. George C. Moore is doing the 'right thing' by developing this website."

Angie Gray of Scott Healthcare believes that the site will provide both customers and suppliers with greater efficiency, easier processes, access to vital historical data, and reduced inventory carrying costs. She commented, "This new technology will allow George C. Moore a value-added advantage over other competitors that may offer lower quality products at a lower price."

Those comments sound like George C. Moore has in fact achieved all it set out to do with its Web site. But what do you think? Did you find it easy to use? Could you find new product offerings? Overstocked items? You can be part of the customer feedback monitoring system. Send your comments and suggestions for improvement to Rodger Allinson at rallinson@themooreco.com.

Questions for Discussion

1. Make a table of all the benefits that the Web site can provide to George C. Moore and a separate table of benefits provided to customers. Are most of the entries the same?
2. Explain how the Web site streamlines the supply chain.
3. Evaluate the process the company used to develop the Web site. What did it do well? What could have been improved?
4. For which types of buying situations (straight or modified rebuy, new buy) is the Web site likely to be used for initially? What factors would increase the likelihood that customers will use it for all buying situations?
5. Visit the Web site and evaluate it.

Sources: Interviews at George C. Moore, its Web site, and press releases.

Video Case 16

Yahoo: Calling to the World!

Yahoo—oo-oo!!! Sweet sound of victory—Or? Are you one of those millions of daily-Yahoo!-viewing Internet users who have made it the most popular and first-to-be-profitable portal on the Internet? If you aren't, you are a target for Yahoo! and its many competitors such as Google, NBCi, Excite, and archrival AOL that are scrambling to become the Internet portal-of-choice of the United States and maybe the world.

Yahoo! records more than 1.2 billion (that's billion) page views per day. More than 200 million unique users take advantage of the Yahoo! global network worldwide. There are over 71 million registered users who have given the company personal data in order to use the wide range of services Yahoo! offers. It's the number-one portal for users at work and many home users dial up through AOL, but then shift to Yahoo! In a recent Web survey by sparkpeople.com, Yahoo! was identified as the favorite portal by 47 percent (4,709) of the respondents, with Google in second place, trailing behind at 21.5 percent (2,151). More conventional Nielsen ratings for 2001 place Yahoo! at number one for users, reach, and time on the site spent worldwide.

Why Yahoo!? While many observers would attribute Yahoo!'s success to its wide array of services—providing Internet access service that is fun, easy to use, and friendly. Yahoo! encourages users by delivering content that is informative, fun, and highly customizable. The idea is to present the Internet in an easy-to-use package while bringing together both users-to-users and users-to-business. But a lot of Internet service providers do this now—so what sets Yahoo! apart?

The people at Yahoo! would tell you it is its brand image—fun, easy to use, "the place you would go first." Why is it fun? Well, the name is kinda' funky and cool—definitely different—not some technospeak such as InfoSeek or technobabble such as Lycos. It suggests something to the user. "It reinforces the idea that when I go to Yahoo, I'll be so pleased that I'll be Yahooing afterwards," says Owen Shapiro, senior analyst at Leo J. Shapiro and Associates. So, the name, which is an acronym for Yet Another Hierarchical Officious Oracle, connotes pleasure and happiness, having had a good time. Is that what customers want? Do they want to have fun exploring the Internet; find unusual services (a hamster camp?); spot unusual sites that zero in on their interests? It would be hard to believe that the answer would be no.

How does Yahoo! reinforce the name? Its distinctive Yahoo! logo is bright red, which is an unusual start, its TV ads are a little off-the-wall, and it advertises in unlikely places such as tins of breath mints, Slinkys, parachutes, skateboards, sailboats, yo-yos, and kazoos. If advertising media tell us something about the audience and the company, what do some of the media listed above tell us about Yahoo! and it's audience? The audience is young, active, interested in the unusual, and likes to have a good

time. Where will we see Yahoo! next? On shoes, music CDs, movies, and product placements on shows such as *Ally McBeal*.

The real value or appeal of the fun image may be that it eliminates an intimidating technological image. Yahoo!'s service is perceived to be easy-to-use (not simple) and entertaining. As companies try to build and maintain market share, they will have to attract and retain more and more households that are older or less computer literate and—that will be a harder sell than attracting young people or office workers who conquered their computer and Internet fears long ago at work.

In the Internet services industry, innovation is critical. How can employees be motivated to keep up the pace? How can a firm keep the entrepreneurial spirit that launched it and made it a success? The management must create the right environment. At Yahoo!, the company motto is "Do what's crazy, but not stupid." Lots of work is done at the coffee shop or around the coffee table, and employees preserve the casual atmosphere in dress—not many places where you can wear your baseball cap backward at work—and office antics such as bouncing balloons over the walls of cubicles. Executives meet in rooms named Decent and Consistent, just so people will be forced to say, "Oh, they're in Decent" or "They're in Consistent." Keeps you thinking and on your toes, but doesn't intimidate. People are relaxed and able to let the ideas flow. Eliminates stress from watching computer screens and hunching over terminals.

And lots of ideas are needed to create the many services that Yahoo! provides. Just look at its home page for the long list of subjects one can search on the Net. In addition to all the other sites that Yahoo! can take you to (that's why it's called a portal—go through the Yahoo! door to other sites), there are a lot of Yahoo! services. There are links to travel services, career services, yellow pages, maps, and auto guides. It has a great news service because of links to sources such as Reuters, Associated Press, and *Hollywood Reporter*. There's shopping in stores such as the Gap, and there are auctions if you want to bid on a painting, a set of dishes, or some computer parts. It can even help you find a house *and* a mortgage online.

Why so many services from Yahoo!? The company needs to convert surfers and browsers to loyal Yahoo! customers. The company earns advertising revenue from other firms, but Yahoo! has to be more than just the doorway to other firms. It needs to build its own revenue stream. Especially now, when advertising revenues are unpredictable, the economy is uncertain, and some well-financed competition is nipping at its heels.

To generate loyal customers, the company needs to know who they are and what they want in order to delight and entertain them. Through programs such as My Yahoo!, the company learns about the customers—who they are, where they live, what they do, and what their interests are. Yahoo! can profile customers and send them suggestions as to items that they might want to buy, sites they might want to visit, information that they might be interested in, trips they might like, or events they might like to catch such as the World Series. It's a major opportunity for Yahoo! to build a strong relationship that will translate into loyalty.

Competition is becoming fierce, as newcomers add many of the same services offered by Yahoo! to their own mix, and others, such as Expedia and Travelocity, compete directly with particular ones. Take a look at the InfoSeek Web site if you want a good look at some competition for Yahoo! Decide for yourself—how does it compare? Will Yahoo! be able to compete with the magic of Disney? Yahoo!'s strong relationships will need to continue to translate into loyalty—and loyalty which, in turn, means spending more time (and money) with Yahoo! than with the competition.

Online sales to customers are growing and in the future they will have to generate a bigger share of Yahoo!'s revenue. Why is that so important? Because Internet advertising revenues may well decline. Fallout from the dot-com industry and recent economic conditions have all ready had some impact. And some advertisers aren't convinced that Internet advertising is worth shifting their traditional media budgets because much Internet advertising is limited to "banners," "pop-ups," and promotions that many marketers feel is much more limited than a 30-second television spot. For many customers, advertisements online are like billboards by the highway—often passed too fast to be read, distracting, and downright annoying much of the time.

There are those well-financed competitors on the cyberspace horizon, too. Many of Yahoo!'s competitors have incorporated some Yahoo! features. NBC's Web site, featuring the colorful NBA peacock logo, allows convenient links in categories including Web searches, shopping on the Web, and quick access to business information, among other things; AOL's Web site is lively and offers instant messaging; and the InfoSeek Disney Web site is as lively as they come, featuring promotions for Disney's latest film ventures.

And the competition is not limited to big companies with portals. PC makers, in an attempt to raise their margins and create loyalty to their computers, are creating their own Internet portals. These firms are tired of being distributors for Intel and Microsoft; they want to recapture their relationship with the final consumer. Portals offer the bigger PC makers such as Compaq, Dell, and Gateway a greater revenue stream as they steer users to their Internet products.

Thinking of competition from large and small firms around the globe. . . . Et vous Yahoo!? Another way that Yahoo! has expanded is internationally. Currently it is available in 20 countries in their languages as well as English, including, for starters, Australia and New Zealand, Canada, Taiwan, Denmark, France, Germany, Italy, Japan, Korea, Norway, Spain, Sweden, the United Kingdom, and Ireland. Is it the same Yahoo!? Not exactly. It is localized for things such as weather, travel, news, fashion, and so on. But much of it is the same. Some subjects can be used anywhere in the world with many of the same sites attached. And Yahoo! tries to create the same fun, friendly, human, and accessible image, which isn't always easy. Not everyone has the same idea of what is fun and what is human. Even so, Yahoo! has been quite successful internationally, including such places as Australia, Canada, France, South Africa, and the United Kingdom.

This question of standardizing the Yahoo! image globally or making it a multiple local brand is not unique to Yahoo! Even Coca-Cola is adapted to local markets. The formula and packaging is changed slightly to appeal to local tastes, and the label-

ing is in a foreign language. Often marketing is very localized. On the other hand, Disney is marketed the same worldwide, and the products are not adapted locally. Mickey Mouse is the same everywhere. While books and movies might be translated and dubbed into foreign languages, the scenes, characters and settings are the same. The question is whether Yahoo!'s image lends itself to a standard global identity.

While it has been successful in Europe and the Far East, what about nondomestic markets closer to home, such as Latin and South American countries? This is a very large block of consumers (over 700 million) who almost all speak some form of Spanish (the exception is Brazilians who speak Portuguese) along with Indian dialects. This could be a large market with a similar language. Of course, income and education levels are lower than in Europe and many parts of the Far East, and there are a number of countries smaller than Germany, France, and Japan for which Yahoo! might have to localize its format. A good start is Yahoo! en Espanol, but even that would have to change as the spanish spoken in different Latin and South American countries is not the same.

But the major markets will be the United States and Europe and some affluent Asian countries in the near future. What is Yahoo! doing to appeal to users here? It is trying to make Yahoo! accessible in as many outlets as possible—to telephones, televisions, pagers, handheld organizers, and the like. "We want to build the biggest company we can," says Tim Koogle, vice chairman of the Yahoo! board of directors. "We've taken the lid off."

But does everyone want Yahoo! everywhere? Will older users be comfortable with all this technology? Will young users remain loyal? Is accessing Web sites a good experience on the small screen of a palm pilot or cell phone—on which, in my case at least, the screen doesn't come in color? Will small screens affect readability? Will they force the quantity of information to be reduced? These are just some of the questions that face the clever dudes at Yahoo! as they enter the twenty-first century.

Co-branding offers Yahoo! a means of responding to the many threats it faces. For example, it has concluded a deal with AT&T Worldnet Service that both sides are very enthusiastic about. "This agreement with AT&T adds outstanding connectivity to the Yahoo! experience, giving new Yahoo! Online users an integrated, simple way of getting online and taking advantage of everything Yahoo! and the Internet have to offer, " says Jeff Mallett, chief operating officer at Yahoo! From the AT&T side, "This combination provides Yahoo! Online users with what they would expect from two Internet leaders—rapid, easy access to the best of the Net," Dan Schulman, president of AT&T WorldNet Service. "Now, Yahoo!'s members can get connected to a wide array of AT&T communications from one Web location."

Yahoo! has also signed a deal with Amazon.com in which Amazon becomes the premier book merchant throughout many of Yahoo!'s World sites including its international ones. This expands Yahoo!'s offerings and Amazon's markets, and the good brand image of both companies serves to reinforce each other's image. It seems to be working. In 2001 Yahoo! announced new relationships with American Airlines, The Dockers? Brand, Hallmark Inc., McDonald's, Pizza Hut, and Sears.

Not all of these deals are just about profits. In combination with Oracle, Yahoo! created the Yahoo! Club, a virtual community in which thousands of teachers, students, and parents can interact. This is made possible through Oracle's Promise, a $100 million philanthropic initiative of Oracle Corporation. According to David Filo, one of Yahoo!'s founders, "The Yahoo! Oracle's Promise Club is a virtual community where educators and parents across the nation can discuss and foster education in one central location. By creating this private, dedicated forum, we are extending our vision to ensure equal access to the Internet (in low-income schools) and the valuable education resources it offers."

While all of these efforts are aimed at final consumers, Yahoo! is not overlooking the business market. Its Yahoo! Small Business site is a comprehensive online resource to help small business professionals and entrepreneurs compete in business. The site provides news and small business information about products and services such as those provided by Airborne Express, FedEx, and UPS and industry news. Small business leaders can meet at this site to share ideas, discuss business issues, and improve their communication skills.

However you look at it, Yahoo! seems to have cast its net wide to capture as many Internet users as possible. Even with all of the competition, "Yahoo has the potential to emerge as the first pure Internet giant," says analyst Paul Noglows of Hambrecht and Quist Inc. President of the E*Trade Group, Christos M. Cotsakos, comments that banking on Yahoo is a no-brainer. "It's like playing Double Jeopardy," he says. "You place your biggest bets on the squares that will give you the best return. And Yahoo! is the Double Jeopardy Square on the Internet."

Questions for Discussion

1. Explain how Yahoo! creates its image of fun, friendliness, humanness, and accessibility.
2. What does Yahoo! sell—a product or a service?
3. How does Yahoo! add value to its marketing offering?
4. Should Yahoo! be standardized or localized in various global markets?
5. Would Latin and South America make a good market for Yahoo!? Why or why not?
6. How has Yahoo! segmented its markets? What products has it aimed at each segment?
7. How can Yahoo! serve both older and younger markets?
8. Evaluate the handheld devices, televisions, and pages as potential access devices for Yahoo!
9. What are Yahoo!'s best means of responding to the competition?
10. Compare the Yahoo! and InfoSeek pages in terms of excitement, interest, attractiveness, ease of use, and communication of brand image. Which do you think is better?

Sources: Amy Cortese, "Portals: A Golden Door for PC Makers," *Business Week*, October 12, 1998, p. 90; Steve Hamm, "Yahoo! The Company, the Strategy, the Stock," *Business Week*, September 7, 1998, pp. 66–76; Kara Swisher, "Yahoo's Profit Beats Forecasts as Traffic Swells," *Wall Street Journal*, April 9, 1998, p. B6; survey results from the sparkpeople! Web site, November 3, 2001; numerous press releases from the Yahoo!

Web site; and an interview with Karen Edwards, formerly vice president of brand marketing at Yahoo!

Video Case 17

Syngenta: Standardization or Customization of Marketing Strategy?

In the United States

Richard Herrin sat at his desk and thought how much easier his life would be if markets were the same throughout North America. As NAFTA manager for Syngenta, he was responsible for marketing products such as Agri-mek, a leading insecticide from Syngenta, in Canada, the United States, and Mexico. Because Canada accounted for very few sales, most Agri-mek sales were in the United States and Mexico. Sales of insecticides and warmer temperatures just seemed to go together naturally , but the similarities apparently ended there.

The market for Agri-mek was quite different in Mexico, which had led to implementing different strategies in the two countries in the past. For a while, that had worked, but now Syngenta corporate headquarters wanted to find synergies in marketing products across countries to save marketing costs and efforts. It would also present a more consistent image of products across national boundaries. The result would be a standardized marketing strategy. "Marketing would be so much easier if the markets were just the same . . . ," he mused.

In Mexico

Francisco Rios, director of marketing, and Raul Castro, customer service manager, were also thinking about the marketing of Agri-mec (spelled differently in the two countries), but their deliberations were quite different. Generic competitive products were their main concern, and they wished that those products would somehow disappear. But as Raul commented, "they are here to stay and they're going to take market share because of lower price."

"I know, I know," responded Francisco. "We can't wish them away, so we will have to be very aggressive in defending our market share by creating ways to overcome the lower price of generics using the quality of our products and the resources of Syngenta."

Syngenta

Syngenta was a "new" corporation resulting from the merger of Novartis Crop Protection and Astra-Zeneca. As a result, it was the world's leading agribusiness corporation. Worldwide headquarters were in Basle, Switzerland, with regional headquarters in other parts of the world. The North American NAFTA headquarters were in Greensboro, North Carolina.

Before the merger, Novartis Crop Protection in the United States was the number-two company in the industry and Zeneca was number five. After the merger, they were one of the top two U.S. companies. In Mexico, however, Novartis Crop Protection was number one and Zeneca number two, so that Syngenta clearly became the number-one company there.

Syngenta strategy had two major components: (1) to capitalize on the strengths of its global crop protection and seeds businesses and (2) to actively manage the product portfolio, focusing on grower's needs and expectations and the demands of the entire food and feed chain, delivering increasingly tailored local solutions. Whatever strategy Richard, Francisco, and Raul chose, it had to fit within these overall aims of corporate strategy.

Market leadership or market follower status could dramatically affect a company's marketing strategy. Strategy was also impacted by the fluctuation of market position across product categories. In general, Syngenta was the market leader in Mexico and therefore would employ a defensive strategy to maintain its position. In the United States, where Syngenta's market position fluctuated according to product category, it had to utilize an offensive strategy where it was a market follower.

The position of Agri-mek (U.S.)/Agri-mec (Mexico) illustrated how strategies might differ across markets. Agri-mec was by far the market leader in Mexico, accounting for most of Syngenta's 16 percent share of the insecticide market. No other company had more than 10 percent of that market. In the United States, Syngenta's share of the insecticide market was a little over 10 percent, and Agri-mec's share was less than 7 percent, with the result that it was third in insecticide sales.

Market share statistics did not tell the whole story. Sales of insecticides were a little over $1 billion, with about 85 percent of sales in the United States and 15 percent in Mexico. Thus, dollar sales were much higher in the United States, and that also affected marketing strategy.

Marketing Strategy in the United States

In developing marketing strategy, one would normally begin with the target market. In the United States, the final customers were growers and the immediate target market would be distributors. Because of consolidation and centralization among distributors, it took relatively few distributors to reach the grower market; ten distributors could sell to 85 percent of the market.

Given the size of the market in dollar sales, Syngenta sold a variety of branded products made from abamectin (the active ingredient in Agri-mek), which fits well with Syngenta's desire for active portfolio management. The brands were Agri-mek, Avid, Clink, Varsity, and Zephr—each aimed at different types of growers. For example, Avid was aimed at the turf and ornamental market while Agri-mek was aimed at citrus and vegetable growers. Agri-mek was the largest selling brand.

In terms of promotional activities, Syngenta had an active advertising program aimed primarily at distributors. Advertising consisted of print ads, direct mailings, public relations events, and sales meetings tailored to individual brands. Salespeople in the United States focused their efforts on selling the individual brands in the portfolio. They were able to devote considerable time to determining individual distributor's needs and then to develop a program of products and services to meet those needs. In turn, they relied on distributors—along with some advertising support from Syngenta—to sell to growers.

Marketing in Mexico

Francisco and Raul dealt with a very different market situation. Most distributors in Mexico were much smaller. It took about 85 distributors in Mexico to reach 80 percent of the market. In addition, distributors frequently placed inventory in facilities that did not belong to them, such as buildings owned by farmers' associations. Sometimes, they even used houses instead of commercial facilities. While doing so relieved distributors of the need to invest in larger warehouses, it also meant that competing products were often stored in the same building. Thus, distributors had difficulty controlling their inventories.

Not only were distributors smaller, but most growers were smaller as well. They bought in smaller quantity and frequently needed credit to pay for their purchases. To respond to these needs, Syngenta sells Agri-mec in smaller containers in Mexico.

Given the credit needs of growers, the role of the salesperson was different in Mexico. The distributor must give growers credit in order to sell goods. Frequently, growers paid distributors after they sold their crops. But that meant that Syngenta needed to give distributors credit so that they, in turn, could give growers credit. Salespeople then became the main means of payment collection. Therefore, they spent relatively little time determining distributor's needs and developing solutions to meet those needs and more time collecting payments.

Because the market was smaller in dollar terms, Syngenta sold only one abamectin-based brand, which was Agri-mec. That one product was aimed at growers of a wide range of products.

Prices were actually higher in Mexico because they were set in Basle, Switzerland, based on market conditions and margin contribution. Thus, Agri-mec's leading position resulted in a higher price. Offsetting that was the effect of taxes. Agrichemicals were exempt from sales taxes in order to promote farming, because it represented 20 percent of the Mexican economy, whereas growers in the United States had to pay sales taxes. This effectively eliminated most of the price differential between the two countries.

Given the fragmentation of the market in Mexico, advertising could not be as targeted as in the United States. However, the company did advertise in trade magazines, television, and sales brochures. Direct marketing was not used because of difficulties with the Mexican postal system. Advertising in Mexico focused more on the Syngenta product portfolio than on individual products and brands.

The Threat of Generics

Although their markets differed, the three managers had a common enemy—generic forms of abamectin-based insecticides. The enemy was already available in Mexico where patent protection was more difficult, but patent protection would expire in the United States. in 2001. At that point, all of them would have to contend with the threat of generics.

Generics were mostly made in China and sold for about 15 percent less than Syngenta's Agri-mek/Agri-mec. The higher price of Agri-mec in Mexico coupled with the growers' need for credit made the Mexican market much more likely to lose sales to generics. Once generics were available in the United States., branded sales of these insecticides might drop as much as 30 percent across the two countries.

Countering the threat of generics would not be easy as the factors that increased sales of generics in the two countries were different. What worked in one country might not be as effective in the other.

There were a number of tactics that Syngenta could employ—price reductions, offering unbranded product alternatives (Syngenta's own generic products), changes in advertising messages, and incentives to the distribution chain. Advertising could be refocused to stress the inferiority of generic formulations, packaging, and customer support. To appeal to distribution channel members, the company was considering bundling products and services for distributors. Under this scheme, Syngenta would be a one-stop supplier for all of the distributors' agricultural needs. This would require refocusing sales efforts from selling products to the selling of a service in which Syngenta would provide everything—diagnostics, products, and technical support required for the complete crop growing cycle. Instead of purchasing individual products, the distributor would contract for a service package with the company. By creating this level of convenience and by contracting with distributors, the company hoped to block sales of generics by competitors. But again, there was the problem of standardizing strategies. Should Syngenta use the same strategy in Mexico as in the United States? If they decided to employ different strategies, how could Richard, Francisco and Raul convince top management that different strategies were necessary?

Questions for Discussion

1. Make a table summarizing the differences and similarities of the marketing mixes in the United States and Mexico. Be sure to include the target market(s).
2. Should Syngenta use a standardized or customized market strategy for selling Agri-mek/Agri-mec across the United States and Mexico? Why or why not?
3. Evaluate each of the proposed tactics to deal with the threat of generics in terms of the impact on the marketing mix in each country, Syngenta's position as a leader/follower and Syngenta's overall corporate strategy:
   a. price reductions
   b. introduction of unbranded Syngenta products
   c. refocusing of advertising
   d. incentives to the distribution channel
4. If you were Richard, which of these tactics would you want to use in the United States? How could you support the selection of that strategy?
5. If you were Francisco and Raul, which of these tactics would you want to use in Mexico? How could you support the selection of that strategy?
6. Which of these tactics should Syngenta employ in your opinion if the strategy must be standardized? Be prepared to defend your answer.

Sources: Interviews with Syngenta personnel, the Syngenta Web site, and company materials such as advertising.

Video Case 18

WNBA: We do more!

When Senda Berenson Abbott adapted James Naismith's basketball rules for women to play at Smith College, she had no idea what she was starting. Within a decade, women across the United States were playing basketball at Tulane, the University of California at Berkeley, Stanford, the North Carolina College for Women, and Ivy League schools for women such as Smith and Mt. Holyoke. The rules kept changing, making the game more like men's basketball until Dr. Anna Norris published the *Official Basket Ball Guide for Women*. In 1924, the International Women's Sports Federation was formed and hosted its own version of the Olympics, which included basketball for women, who were excluded from the men's Olympics. Women's basketball continued to grow at the high school and college level with sporadic attempts to take it to the professional level until 1996, when the American Basketball League was formed. The WNBA (Women's National Basketball Association) followed in 1997.

As is obvious from the name, the WNBA is affiliated with the NBA. Partly because of this affiliation and partly to avoid competing in the crowded winter sports schedule, the WNBA chose to play a shorter season of 30 games in the summer of 1997. Initially there were 8 teams, which quickly expanded to 10 for the 1998 season. The addition of 4 new teams during the last brings the latest total to 16 teams. The WNBA consists of two conferences of 8 teams each. The Eastern Conference consists of the Charlotte Sting, the Cleveland Rockers, the Detroit Shock, the Indiana Fever, the Miami Sol, the New York Liberty, the Orlando Miracle, and the Washington Mystics. The Western Conference consists of the Houston Comets, the Los Angeles Sparks, the Minnesota Lynx, the Phoenix Mercury, the Portland Fire, the Sacramento Monarchs, the Seattle Storm, and the Utah Starzz.

The WNBA also adopted a different set of rules to control league play. Its three point line is 19 feet 9 inches instead of the NBA's 22 feet. Lane size is 12 feet wide compared to the NBA's 16 foot wide lanes. Although the WNBA ball is smaller (28.5 inches instead of 29.5 inches), it is the same size as that used in high school and college. Games last for two 20-minute halves, and the league uses a 30-second shot clock instead of the NBA's 24-second shot clock.

In its first season, the WNBA averaged more than 9,500 attendance at games—far more than hoped for—and scored a respectable rating of 2 on NBC. Because each rating point is equal to 980,000 TV households, this means that nearly 2 million people watched WNBA games. The WNBA's clout was evident in its ability to sign TV deals not only with NBC but also with ESPN and Lifetime, giving the league hefty exposure. The WNBA also attracted a slew of prestigious sponsors including the likes of American Express, Anheuser-Busch, Champion, Coca-Cola, General Motors, Kellogg Company, Lady Foot Locker, Lee Jeans, McDonald's, Nike, Sears, and Spalding. Licensees include Accessory Network (duffel bags), Aminco (jewelry), Bulova, ESPN Video, HarperCollins, Huffy (backboards), Mattel (WNBA Barbie), Hunter Manufacturing (mugs, ceramics), Pinnacle (trading cards), and Wincraft (fan packs, bumper strips), The licensed merchandise has been flying off the shelves at games, making it difficult for vendors to keep adequate merchandise supplies.

Although it took a long time to establish professional women's basketball in the United States, it seems to be on secure footing. The WNBA honored its ten millionth fan at the second game of the 2001 Championship Series. According to some sports pundits, the WNBA has more to offer than even the NBA. First is affordability. Tickets average $16 instead of the NBA's much higher prices. The Charlotte Sting offers a "Buzz Package for groups," offering a $16 ticket, a $5 food coupon, and a Sting T-shirt, for each member of your group. Even Rosie O'Donnell pays only $62.50 for a courtside seat in Madison Square Garden to see the Liberty—a seat that costs Spike Lee $1,000 to watch the Knicks.

The second is the level of competition. According to UCLA's legendary coach John Wooden, women's basketball is more watchable than men's basketball. It's more structured and team oriented than the helter-skelter men's games. A third attraction is accessibility. After the loss to New York, Sting star Vicky Bullett signed everything put in front of her and then asked, "Have I missed anyone?" Have any of you gotten close to Allen Iverson or Michael Jordan lately for an autograph?

Although less obvious, but equally important, the WNBA also has a strong sense of giveback. It has adopted two causes that all teams in the league support. The first is a commitment to breast cancer awareness. Because breast cancer affects one in every nine women in this country, it is an issue for all women, according to Val Ackerman, president of the WNBA. She continues, "We are pleased that the WNBA, our players, our partners and our fans have formed a team to make an impact in the fight against breast cancer."

In 1997, the WNBA produced two breast cancer awareness public service announcements that featured Cynthia Cooper of the Houston Comets and Pam McGee of the Sacramento Monarchs. WNBA marketing partner General Motors donated 50 cents for every fan who attended a WNBA game to the National Alliance of Breast Cancer Organizations (NABCO), and GM's Buick Division also contributed $32,000 to NABCO ($1,000 for every Buick Regal Player of the Game on nationally televised WNBA games). GM's total contribution came to $575,000. Lee Jeans also got into the act with its "Shoot for the Cure" program. At halftime, a randomly selected fan was invited onto the court to "shoot for the cure" by making as many baskets as possible—each worth certain dollar amounts—during a 30-second time period. Champion (maker of WNBA uniforms) contributed $25,000 from the sales of its licensed merchandise.

In the fight against breast cancer, the WNBA began sponsoring in-arena breast Health Awareness Nights at games early on. In conjunction with Sears, the program has been expanded, and last year a 50-cent donation was made to for every fan who attended one. Sears and the WNBA have raised funds for the National Alliance of Breast Cancer Organizations (NABCO) by making donations on behalf of 16 Breast Health Heroes and through the Sears–WNBA Breast Health Awareness Auction. In October 2001, the National Alliance of Breast Cancer Organizations was presented with a check for $377,872 from Sears and the WNBA.

In addition to the breast awareness program, the WNBA and Nike sponsor a program aimed at children called "Be Active." This program, designed in conjunction with the President's Council on Fitness, attempts to teach youngsters aged 11 to 15 how to get fit and stay in shape through proper nutrition, eating habits, and exercise. The program travels to all WNBA cities plus Philadelphia and San Jose. At a "Be Active" clinic, local WNBA stars talk to the children and their mothers about fitness, the importance of exercise, and how to eat right. This is reinforced through a series of drills, that is, think exercises. Participants may be selected in any number of ways. They may simply be asked to sign up, or they may be selected from housing areas near the WNBA playing site. The focus of the program is to reduce the growing obesity among American children. It has been promoted through public service announcements featuring Ruthie Bolton-Holifield, the Sacramento Monarchs all-WNBA guard. This year the program offers a sweepstakes (entry is based on submitting a Six-Week "Be Active" Progress Log) with the grand prize a trip for two to Portland, Oregon, to visit Nike's campus and work out with Jackie Stiles.

Not all of the giveback is planned at the league level, however. Washington Mystics' forward Heidi Burge developed "Heidi's Hoops for Hope"—a nonprofit organization that includes clinics and camps emphasizing life skills as well as basketball skills. According to Heidi, "I did this thing in inner city D.C. because I know there are parts where the basketball is really good, but they don't have the resources." This includes raising money for uniforms and equipment as well as camps and clinics. Perhaps if young people are busy playing basketball and learning life skills, they are off the streets.

Through efforts such as these, the WNBA has attracted a very loyal following of fans and families. One of the most vocal is Rosie O'Donnell, who says, "But one of the great things about the WNBA is that it has allowed women to be dreamers. I caught the fever big. . . ." That goes for all those mothers and fathers taking their daughters to games as well as for the girls not only who can dream of being basketball players but also can learn valuable lessons about responsibility to the community and society.

Questions for Discussion

1. How does the WNBA's support of breast cancer awareness illustrate social responsibility in marketing?
2. Why would the WNBA select breast cancer awareness and physical fitness for children as causes that the league would support? Do these causes mesh with the image, aims, and goals of the WNBA?
3. What other national causes could the WNBA support?
4. Should the WNBA support more than its current two causes?
5. What sort of local causes should WNBA teams support? Think of the WNBA team nearest you, and outline a plan

for creating community support for the WNBA through involvement with a community issue.

6. Is it a good idea for individual players to form foundations such as Heidi Burge has done? Do these efforts reduce support for the WNBA-supported causes?

Sources: Marianne Bhonslay, "Born to be Rivals," *Sporting Goods Business*, July 10, 1998, 31, no.11, pp. 40–42; Dan Crawford, "Rival Women's Basketball Leagues Slug It Out for Supremacy On and Off Court," *Business First-Columbus*, October 31, 1997, 14, no.10, pp. 1–2; Kimberly Davis, "At the Top of Their Game," *Ebony*, June 2001, pp. 70–74; Steve Wulf, "The N.B.A.'s Sister Act," *Time*, August 4, 1997, 150, no. 5, pp. 41–44; interview with Mark Pray of the WNBA; and numerous press releases from the WNBA Web site.

Glossary

Adapted marketing mix An international marketing strategy for adjusting the marketing-mix elements to each international target market, bearing more costs but hoping for a larger market share and return.

Administered VMS A vertical marketing system that coordinates successive stages of production and distribution, not through common ownership or contractual ties, but through the size and power of one of the parties.

Adoption process The mental process through which an individual passes from first hearing about an innovation to final adoption.

Advertising Any paid form of non-personal presentation and promotion of ideas, goods, or services by an identified sponsor.

Advertising agency A marketing services firm that assists companies in planning, preparing, implementing, and evaluating all or portions of their advertising programs.

Advertising objective A specific communication *task* to be accomplished with a specific *target* audience during a specific period of *time*.

Affordable method Setting the promotion budget at the level management thinks the company can afford.

Age and life-cycle segmentation Dividing a market into different age and life-cycle groups.

Agent A wholesaler who represents buyers or sellers on a relatively permanent basis, performs only a few functions, and does not take title to goods.

Allowance Promotional money paid by manufacturers to retailers in return for an agreement to feature the manufacturer's products in some way.

Approach The step in the selling process in which the salesperson meets the customer for the first time.

Attitude A person's consistently favorable or unfavorable evaluations, feelings, and tendencies toward an object or idea.

B2B (business-to-business) e-commerce Using B2B trading networks, auction sites, spot exchanges, online product catalogs, barter sites, and other online resources to reach new customers, serve current customers more effectively, and obtain buying efficiencies and better prices.

B2C (business-to-consumer) e-commerce The online selling of goods and services to final consumers.

Baby boom The major increase in the annual birthrate following World War II and lasting until the early 1960s. The "baby boomers," now moving into middle age, are a prime target for marketers.

Behavioral segmentation Dividing a market into groups based on consumer knowledge, attitude, use, or response to a product.

Belief A descriptive thought that a person holds about something.

Benefit segmentation Dividing the market into groups according to the different benefits that consumers seek from the product.

Brand A name, term, sign, symbol, design, or combination of these, intended to identify the goods or services of one seller or group of sellers and to differentiate them from those of competitors.

Brand equity The value of a brand, based on the extent to which it has high brand loyalty, name awareness, perceived quality, strong brand associations, and other assets such as patents, trademarks, and channel relationships.

Brand extension Using a successful brand name to launch a new or modified product in a new category.

Break-even pricing (target profit pricing) Setting price to break even on the costs of making and marketing a product; or setting price to make a target profit.

Broker A wholesaler who does not take title to goods and whose function is to bring buyers and sellers together and assist in negotiation.

Business analysis A review of the sales, costs, and profit projections for a new product to find out whether these factors satisfy the company's objectives.

Business buyer behavior The buying behavior of organizations that buy goods and services for use in the production of other products and services that are sold, rented, or supplied to others.

Business portfolio The collection of businesses and products that make up the company.

Buying center All the individuals and units that participate in the business buying-decision process.

By-product pricing Setting a price for by-products in order to make the main product's price more competitive.

C2B (consumer-to-business) e-commerce Online exchanges in which consumers search out sellers, learn about their offers, and initiate purchases, sometimes even driving transaction terms.

C2C (consumer-to-consumer) e-commerce Online exchanges of goods and information between final consumers.

Captive-product pricing Setting a price for products that must be used along with a main product, such as blades for a razor and film for a camera.

Catalog marketing Direct marketing through print, video, or electronic catalogs that are mailed to a select customers, made available in stores, or presented online.

Category killer Giant specialty store that carries a very deep assortment of a particular line and is staffed by knowledgeable employees.

Causal research Marketing research to test hypotheses about cause-and-effect relationships.

Chain stores Two or more outlets that are owned and controlled in common, have central buying and merchandising, and sell similar lines of merchandise.

Channel conflict Disagreement among marketing channel members on goals and roles—who should do what and for what rewards.

Channel level A layer of intermediaries that performs some work in bringing the product and its ownership closer to the final buyer.

Click-and-mortar companies Traditional brick-and-mortar companies that have added e-marketing to their operations.

Click-only companies The so-called dot-coms, which operate only online without any brick-and-mortar market presence.

Closing   The step in the selling process in which the salesperson asks the customer for an order.

Co-branding   The practice of using the established brand names of two different companies on the same product.

Cognitive dissonance   Buyer discomfort caused by postpurchase conflict.

Commercialization   Introducing a new product into the market.

Communication adaptation   A global communication strategy of fully adapting advertising messages to local markets.

Competition-based pricing   Setting prices based on the prices that competitors charge for similar products.

Competitive advantage   An advantage over competitors gained by offering consumers greater value, either through lower prices or by providing more benefits that justify higher prices.

Competitive-parity method   Setting the promotion budget to match competitors' outlays.

Concentrated marketing   A market-coverage strategy in which a firm goes after a large share of one or a few submarkets.

Concept testing   Testing new-product concepts with a group of target consumers to find out if the concepts have strong consumer appeal.

Consumer buyer behavior   The buying behavior of final consumers—individuals and households who buy goods and services for personal consumption.

Consumer market   All the individuals and households who buy or acquire goods and services for personal consumption.

Consumer product   Product bought by final consumer for personal consumption.

Consumerism   An organized movement of citizens and government agencies to improve the rights and power of buyers in relation to sellers.

Consumer-oriented marketing   The philosophy of enlightened marketing that holds that the company should view and organize its marketing activities from the consumer's point of view.

Contract manufacturing   A joint venture in which a company contracts with manufacturers in a foreign market to produce the product or provide its service.

Contractual VMS   A vertical marketing system in which independent firms at different levels of production and distribution join together through contracts to obtain more economies or sales impact than they could achieve alone.

Convenience product   Consumer product that the customer usually buys frequently, immediately, and with a minimum of comparison and buying effort.

Convenience store   A small store, located near a residential area, that is open long hours seven days a week and carries a limited number of high-turnover convenience goods.

Conventional distribution channel   A channel consisting of one or more independent producers, wholesalers, and retailers, each a separate business seeking to maximize its own profits even at the expense of profits for the system as a whole.

Corporate VMS   A vertical marketing system that combines successive stages of production and distribution under single ownership—channel leadership is established through common ownership.

Corporate Web site   A Web site designed to build customer goodwill and to supplement other sales channels, rather than to sell the company's products directly.

Cost-plus pricing   Adding a standard markup to the cost of the product.

Countertrade   International trade involving the direct or indirect exchange of goods for other goods instead of cash. Forms include barter, compensation (buyback), and counterpurchase.

Cultural environment   Institutions and other forces that affect society's basic values, perceptions, preferences, and behaviors.

Culture   The set of basic values, perceptions, wants, and behaviors learned by a member of society from family and other important institutions.

Customer database   An organized collection of comprehensive data about individual customers or prospects, including geographic, demographic, psychographic, and behavioral data.

Customer relationship management   Special software and analysis techniques for integrating and applying the individual customer data contained in databases.

Customer sales force structure   A sales force organization under which salespeople specialize in selling only to certain customers or industries.

Customer satisfaction   The extent to which a product's perceived performance in delivering value matches a buyer's expectations.

Customer value   The difference between the values the customer gains from owning and using a product and the costs of obtaining the product.

Customerization   Leaving it to individual customers to design the marketing offering—allowing customers to be *prosumers* rather than only consumers.

Decline stage   The product life-cycle stage in which a product's sales decline.

Deficient products   Products that have neither immediate appeal nor long-run benefits.

Demand curve   A curve that shows the number of units the market will buy in a given time period, at different prices that might be charged.

Demands   Human wants that are backed by buying power.

Demarketing   Marketing to reduce demand temporarily or permanently—the aim is not to destroy demand but only to reduce or shift it.

Demographic segmentation   Dividing the market into groups based on demographic variables such as age, sex, family size, family life-cycle, income, occupation, education, religion, race, and nationality.

Demography   The study of human populations in terms of size, density, location, age, gender, race, occupation, and other statistics.

Department store   A retail organization that carries a wide variety of product lines—typically clothing, home furnishings, and household goods; each line is operated as a separate department managed by specialist buyers or merchandisers.

Derived demand   Business demand that ultimately comes from (derives from) the demand for consumer goods.

Descriptive research   Marketing research to better describe marketing problems, situations, or markets, such as the market potential for a product or the demographics and attitudes of consumers.

Desirable products   Products that give both high immediate satisfaction and high long-run benefits.

Differentiated marketing   A market-coverage strategy in which a firm decides to target several market segments and designs separate offers for each.

Direct investment   Entering a foreign market by developing foreign-based assembly or manufacturing facilities.

Direct marketing   Direct communications with carefully targeted individual consumers to obtain an immediate response.

Direct marketing channel   A marketing channel that has no intermediary levels.

Direct-mail marketing   Direct marketing through single mailings that include letters, ads, samples, foldouts, and other "salespeople with wings" sent to prospects on mailing lists.

Direct-response television marketing Direct marketing via television, including *direct-response television advertising* or *infomercials* and *home shopping channels*.

Discount A straight reduction in price on purchases during a stated period of time.

Discount store A retail institution that sells standard merchandise at lower prices by accepting lower margins and selling at higher volume.

Disintermediation The displacement of traditional resellers from a marketing channel by radical new types of intermediaries.

Distribution center A large, highly automated warehouse designed to receive goods from various plants and suppliers, take orders, fill them efficiently, and deliver goods to customers as quickly as possible.

Distribution channel A set of interdependent organizations involved in the process of making a product or service available for use or consumption by the consumer or business user.

Diversification A strategy for company growth through starting up or acquiring businesses outside the company's current products and markets.

Dynamic pricing The practice of charging different prices depending on individual customers and situations.

E-business The use of electronic platforms—intranets, extranets, and the Internet—to conduct a company's business.

E-commerce Buying and selling processes supported by electronic means, primarily the Internet.

Economic community A group of nations organized to work toward common goals in the regulation of international trade.

Economic environment Factors that affect consumer buying power and spending patterns.

E-marketing The "e-selling" side of e-commerce—company efforts to communicate about, promote, and sell products and services over the Internet.

Embargo A ban on the import of a certain product.

Engel's laws Differences noted over a century ago by Ernst Engel in how people shift their spending across food, housing, transportation, health care, and other goods and services categories as family income rises.

Enlightened marketing A marketing philosophy holding that a company's marketing should support the best long-run performance of the marketing system; its five principles include consumer-oriented marketing, innovative marketing, value marketing, sense-of-mission marketing, and societal marketing.

Environmental management perspective A management perspective in which the firm takes aggressive actions to affect the publics and forces in its marketing environment rather than simply watching and reacting to them.

Environmental sustainability A management approach that involves developing strategies that both sustain the environment and produce profits for the company.

Environmentalism An organized movement of concerned citizens and government agencies to protect and improve people's living environment.

Exchange The act of obtaining a desired object from someone by offering something in return.

Exchange controls Government limits on the amount of foreign exchange with other countries and on the exchange rate against other currencies.

Exclusive distribution Giving a limited number of dealers the exclusive right to distribute the company's products in their territories.

Experimental research The gathering of primary data by selecting matched groups of subjects, giving them different treatments, controlling related factors, and checking for differences in group responses.

Exploratory research Marketing research to gather preliminary information that will help define problems and suggest hypotheses.

Exporting Entering a foreign market by selling goods produced in the company's home country, often with little modification.

Extranet Electronic collections of information obtained from data sources within the company.

Factory outlet Off-price retailing operation that is owned and operated by a manufacturer and that normally carries the manufacturer's surplus, discontinued, or irregular goods.

Fads Fashions that enter quickly, are adopted with great zeal, peak early, and decline very quickly.

Fashion A currently accepted or popular style in a given field.

Focus group interviewing Personal interviewing that involves inviting six to ten people to gather for a few hours with a trained interviewer to talk about a product, service, or organization. The interviewer "focuses" the group discussion on important issues.

Follow-up The last step in the selling process in which the salesperson follows up after the sale to ensure customer satisfaction and repeat business.

Franchise A contractual association between a manufacturer, wholesaler, or service organization (a franchiser) and independent businesspeople (franchisees) who buy the right to own and operate one or more units in the franchise system.

Franchise organization A contractual vertical marketing system in which a channel member, called a franchiser, links several stages in the production-distribution process.

Gender segmentation Dividing a market into different groups based on sex.

Generation X The group of people born between 1965 and 1976 during the "birth dearth."

Generation Y (echo boom) The 72 million children of the baby boomers, born between 1977 and 1994.

Geographic segmentation Dividing a market into different geographical units such as nations, states, regions, counties, cities, or neighborhoods.

Global firm A firm that, by operating in more than one country, gains R&D, production, marketing, and financial advantages in its costs and reputation that are not available to purely domestic competitors.

Group Two or more people who interact to accomplish individual or mutual goals.

Growth stage The product life-cycle stage in which a product's sales start climbing quickly.

Growth-share matrix A portfolio-planning method that evaluates a company's strategic business units in terms of their market growth rate and relative market share. SBUs are classified as stars, cash cows, question marks, or dogs.

Handling objections The step in the selling process in which the salesperson seeks out, clarifies, and overcomes customer objections to buying.

Horizontal marketing system A channel arrangement in which two or more companies at one level join together to follow a new marketing opportunity.

Hybrid marketing channel Multi-channel distribution system in which a single firm sets up two or more marketing channels to reach one or more customer segments.

Idea generation The systematic search for new-product ideas.

Idea screening Screening new-product ideas in order to spot good ideas and drop poor ones as soon as possible.

Income segmentation Dividing a market into different income groups.

Independent off-price retailer Off-price retailer that is either owned and run by entrepreneurs or is division of larger retail corporation.

Indirect marketing channel Channel containing one or more intermediary levels.

Individual marketing Tailoring products and marketing programs to the needs and preferences of individual customers.

Industrial product Product bought by individuals and organizations for further processing or for use in conducting a business.

Innovative marketing A principle of enlightened marketing that requires that a company seek real product and marketing improvements.

Inside sales force Inside salespeople who conduct business from their offices via telephone or visits from prospective buyers.

Integrated direct marketing Direct-marketing campaigns that use multiple vehicles and multiple stages to improve response rates and profits.

Integrated marketing communications (IMC) The concept under which a company carefully integrates and coordinates its many communications channels to deliver a clear, consistent, and compelling message about the organization and its products.

Integrated supply chain management The logistics concept that emphasizes teamwork, both inside the company and among all the marketing channel organizations, to maximize the performance of the entire distribution system.

Intensive distribution Stocking the product in as many outlets as possible.

Interactive marketing Marketing by a service firm that recognizes that perceived service quality depends heavily on the quality of buyer-seller interaction.

Intermarket segmentation Forming segments of consumers who have similar needs and buying behavior even though they are located in different countries.

Intermodal transportation Combining two or more modes of transportation.

Internal databases Electronic collections of information obtained from data sources within the company.

Internal marketing Marketing by a service firm to train and effectively motivate its customer-contact employees and all the supporting service people to work as a team to provide customer satisfaction.

Internet A vast public web of computer networks that connects users of all types all around the world to each other and to an amazingly large "information repository." The Internet makes up one big "information highway" that can dispatch bits at incredible speeds from one location to another.

Intranet A network that connects people within a company to each other and to the company network.

Introduction stage The product life-cycle stage in which the new product is first distributed and made available for purchase.

Joint ownership A joint venture in which a company joins investors in a foreign market to create a local business in which the company shares joint ownership and control.

Joint venturing Entering foreign markets by joining with foreign companies to produce or market a product or service.

Learning Changes in an individual's behavior arising from experience.

Licensing A method of entering a foreign market in which the company enters into an agreement with a licensee in the foreign market, offering the right to use a manufacturing process, trademark, patent, trade secret, or other item of value for a fee or royalty.

Lifestyle A person's pattern of living as expressed in his or her activities, interests, and opinions.

Line extension Using a successful brand name to introduce additional items in a given product category under the same brand name, such as new flavors, forms, colors, added ingredients, or package sizes.

Local marketing Tailoring brands and promotions to the needs and wants of local customer groups—cities, neighborhoods, and even specific stores.

Macroenvironment The larger societal forces that affect the microenvironment—demographic, economic, natural, technological, political, and cultural forces.

Management contracting A joint venture in which the domestic firm supplies the management know-how to a foreign company that supplies the capital; the domestic firm exports management services rather than products.

Manufacturers' sales branches and offices Wholesaling by sellers or buyers themselves rather than through independent wholesalers.

Market The set of all actual and potential buyers of a product or service.

Market development A strategy for company growth by identifying and developing new market segments for current company products.

Market penetration A strategy for company growth by increasing sales of current products to current market segments without changing the product.

Market positioning Arranging for a product to occupy a clear, distinctive, and desirable place relative to competing products in the minds of target consumers.

Market segment A group of consumers who respond in a similar way to a given set of marketing efforts.

Market segmentation Dividing a market into smaller groups of buyers with distinct needs, characteristics, or behaviors who might require separate products or marketing mixes.

Market targeting The process of evaluating each market segment's attractiveness and selecting one or more segments to enter.

Marketing A social and managerial process by which individuals and groups obtain what they need and want through creating and exchanging products and values with others.

Marketing audit A comprehensive, systematic, independent, and periodic examination of a company's environment, objectives, strategies, and activities to determine problem areas and opportunities and to recommend a plan of action to improve the company's marketing performance.

Marketing communications mix (promotion mix) The specific mix of advertising, personal selling, sales promotion, and public relations a company uses to pursue its advertising and marketing objectives.

Marketing concept The marketing management philosophy that holds that achieving organizational goals depends on determining the needs and wants of target markets and delivering the desired satisfactions more effectively and efficiently than competitors do.

Marketing control The process of measuring and evaluating the results of marketing strategies and plans, and taking corrective action to ensure that objectives are achieved.

Marketing environment The actors and forces outside marketing that affect marketing management's ability to develop and maintain successful transactions with its target customers.

Marketing implementation The process that turns marketing strategies and plans into marketing actions in order to accomplish strategic marketing objectives.

Marketing information system (MIS) People, equipment, and procedures to gather, sort, analyze, evaluate, and distribute needed, timely, and accurate information to marketing decision makers.

Marketing intelligence The systematic collection and analysis of publicly available information about competitors and developments in the marketing environment.

Marketing intermediaries Firms that help the company to promote, sell, and distribute its goods to final buyers; they include resellers, physical distribution firms, marketing service agencies, and financial intermediaries.

Marketing logistics (physical distribution) The tasks involved in planning, implementing, and controlling the physical flow of materials, final goods, and related information from points of origin to points of consumption to meet customer requirements at a profit.

Marketing management The analysis, planning, implementation, and control of programs designed to create, build, and maintain beneficial exchanges with target buyers for the purpose of achieving organizational objectives.

Marketing mix The set of controllable tactical marketing tools—product, price, place, and promotion—that the firm blends to produce the response it wants in the target market.

Marketing process The process of (1) analyzing marketing opportunities; (2) selecting target markets; (3) developing the marketing mix; and (4) managing the marketing effort.

Marketing research The systematic design, collection, analysis, and reporting of data relevant to a specific marketing situation facing an organization.

Marketing strategy The marketing logic by which the business unit hopes to achieve its marketing objectives.

Marketing strategy development Designing an initial marketing strategy for a new product based on the product concept.

Marketing Web site A Web site that engages consumers in interactions that will move them closer to a direct purchase or other marketing outcome.

Market-penetration pricing Setting a low price for a new product in order to attract a large number of buyers and a large market share.

Market-skimming pricing Setting a high price for a new product to skim maximum revenues layer by layer from the segments willing to pay the high price; the company makes fewer but more profitable sales.

Maturity stage The stage in the product life-cycle in which sales growth slows or levels off.

Merchant wholesaler Independently owned business that takes title to the merchandise it handles.

Microenvironment The forces close to the company that affect its ability to serve its customers—the company, suppliers, marketing channel firms, customer markets, competitors, and publics.

Micromarketing The practice of tailoring products and marketing programs to the needs and wants of specific individuals and local customer groups—includes *local marketing* and *individual marketing.*

Mission statement A statement of the organization's purpose—what it wants to accomplish in the larger environment.

Modified rebuy A business buying situation in which the buyer wants to modify product specifications, prices, terms, or suppliers.

Motive (drive) A need that is sufficiently pressing to direct the person to seek satisfaction of the need.

Natural environment Natural resources that are needed as inputs by marketers or that are affected by marketing activities.

Need A state of felt deprivation.

New product A good, service, or idea that is perceived by some potential customers as new.

New task A business buying situation in which the buyer purchases a product or service for the first time.

New-product development The development of original products, product improvements, product modifications, and new brands through the firm's own R&D efforts.

Niche marketing Focusing on subsegments or niches with distinctive traits that may seek a special combination of benefits.

Nontariff trade barriers Nonmonetary barriers to foreign products, such as biases against a foreign company's bids, or product standards that go against a foreign company's product features.

Objective-and-task method Developing the promotion budget by (1) defining specific objectives; (2) determining the tasks that must be performed to achieve these objectives; and (3) estimating the costs of performing these tasks. The sum of these costs is the proposed promotion budget.

Observational research The gathering of primary data by observing relevant people, actions, and situations.

Occasion segmentation Dividing the market into groups according to occasions when buyers get the idea to buy, actually make their purchase, or use the purchased item.

Off-price retailer Retailer that buys at less-than-regular wholesale prices and sells at less than retail. Examples are factory outlets, independents, and warehouse clubs.

Online (Internet) marketing research Collecting primary data through Internet surveys and online focus groups.

Online advertising Advertising that appears while consumers are surfing the Web, including banner and ticker ads, interstitials, skyscrapers, and other forms.

Online databases Computerized collections of information available from online commercial sources or via the Internet.

Open trading networks Huge e-marketspaces in which B2B buyers and sellers find each other online, share information, and complete transactions efficiently.

Opinion leader Person within a reference group who, because of special skills, knowledge, personality, or other characteristics, exerts influence on others.

Optional-product pricing The pricing of optional or accessory products along with a main product.

Outside sales force (or field sales force) Outside salespeople who travel to call on customers.

Packaging The activities of designing and producing the container or wrapper for a product.

Percentage-of-sales method Setting the promotion budget at a certain percentage of current or forecasted sales or as a percentage of the unit sales price.

Perception The process by which people select, organize, and interpret information to form a meaningful picture of the world.

Personal selling Personal presentation by the firm's sales force for the purpose of making sales and building customer relationships.

Pleasing products Products that give high immediate satisfaction but may hurt consumers in the long run.

Political environment Laws, government agencies, and pressure groups that influence and limit various organizations and individuals in a given society.

Portfolio analysis A tool by which management identifies and evaluates the various businesses making up the company.

Preapproach The step in the selling process in which the salesperson learns as much as possible about a prospective customer before making a sales call.

Presentation The step in the selling process in which the salesperson tells the "product story" to the buyer, highlighting customer benefits.

Price The amount of money charged for a product or service, or the sum of the values that consumers exchange for the benefits of having or using the product or service.

Price elasticity A measure of the sensitivity of demand to changes in price.

Primary data Information collected for the specific purpose at hand.

Private brand (or store brand) A brand created and owned by a reseller of a product or service.

Private trading networks (PTNs) B2B trading networks that link a particular seller with its own trading partners.

Product Anything that can be offered to a market for attention, acquisition, use, or consumption that might satisfy a want or need. It includes physical objects, services, persons, places, organizations, and ideas.

Product adaptation Adapting a product to meet local conditions or wants in foreign markets.

Product bundle pricing Combining several products and offering the bundle at a reduced price.

Product concept The idea that consumers will favor products that offer the most quality, performance, and features and that the organization should therefore devote its energy to making continuous product improvements. A detailed version of the new-product idea stated in meaningful consumer terms.

Product development A strategy for company growth by offering modified or new products to current market segments. Developing the product concept into a physical product in order to ensure that the product idea can be turned into a workable product.

Product invention Creating new products or services for foreign markets.

Product life-cycle (PLC) The course of a product's sales and profits over its lifetime. It involves five distinct stages: product development, introduction, growth, maturity, and decline.

Product line A group of products that are closely related because they function in a similar manner, are sold to the same customer groups, are marketed through the same types of outlets, or fall within given price ranges.

Product line pricing Setting the price steps between various products in a product line based on cost differences between the products, customer evaluations of different features, and competitors' prices.

Product mix (or product assortment) The set of all product lines and items that a particular seller offers for sale.

Product position The way the product is defined by consumers on important attributes—the place the product occupies in consumers' minds relative to competing products.

Product quality The ability of a product to perform its functions; it includes the product's overall durability, reliability, precision, ease of operation and repair, and other valued attributes.

Product sales force structure A sales force organization under which salespeople specialize in selling only a portion of the company's products or lines.

Product/market expansion grid A portfolio-planning tool for identifying company growth opportunities through market penetration, market development, product development, or diversification.

Production concept The philosophy that consumers will favor products that are available and highly affordable and that management should therefore focus on improving production and distribution efficiency.

Promotional pricing Temporarily pricing products below the list price, and sometimes even below cost, to increase short-run sales.

Prospecting The step in the selling process in which the salesperson identifies qualified potential customers.

Psychographic segmentation Dividing a market into different groups based on social class, lifestyle, or personality characteristics.

Psychological pricing A pricing approach that considers the psychology of prices and not simply the economics; the price is used to say something about the product.

Public Any group that has an actual or potential interest in or impact on an organization's ability to achieve its objectives.

Public relations Building good relations with the company's various publics by obtaining favorable publicity, building up a good corporate image, and handling or heading off unfavorable rumors, stories, and events. Major PR tools include press relations, product publicity, corporate communications, lobbying, and public service.

Pull strategy A promotion strategy that calls for spending a lot on advertising and consumer promotion to build up consumer demand. If the strategy is successful, consumers will ask their retailers for the product, the retailers will ask the wholesalers, and the wholesalers will ask the producers.

Push strategy A promotion strategy that calls for using the sales force and trade promotion to push the product through channels. The producer promotes the product to wholesalers, the wholesalers promote to retailers, and the retailers promote to consumers.

Quota A limit on the amount of goods that an importing country will accept in certain product categories; it is designed to conserve on foreign exchange and to protect local industry and employment.

Reference prices Prices that buyers carry in their minds and refer to when they look at a given product.

Relationship marketing The process of creating, maintaining, and enhancing strong, value-laden relationships with customers and other stakeholders.

Retailer Business whose sales come *primarily* from retailing.

Retailing All activities involved in selling goods or services directly to final consumers for their personal, nonbusiness use.

Sales force management The analysis, planning, implementation, and control of sales force activities. It includes setting and designing sales force strategy; and recruiting, selecting, training, supervising, compensating, and evaluating the firm's salespeople.

Sales promotion Short-term incentives to encourage the purchase or sale of a product or service.

Sales quota A standard that states the amount a salesperson should sell and how sales should be divided among the company's products.

Salesperson An individual acting for a company by performing one or more of the following activities: prospecting, communicating, servicing, and information gathering.

Salutary products   Products that have low appeal but may benefit consumers in the long run.

Sample   A segment of the population selected for marketing research to represent the population as a whole.

Secondary data   Information that already exists somewhere, having been collected for another purpose.

Segment marketing   Isolating broad segments that make up a market and adapting the marketing offer to match the needs of one or more segments.

Segmented pricing   Selling a product or service at two or more prices, where the difference in prices is not based on differences in costs.

Selective distribution   The use of more than one, but fewer than all, of the intermediaries who are willing to carry the company's products.

Selling concept   The idea that consumers will not buy enough of the organization's products unless the organization undertakes a large-scale selling and promotion effort.

Selling process   The steps that the salesperson follows when selling, which include prospecting and qualifying, preapproach, approach, presentation and demonstration, handling objections, closing, and follow-up.

Sense-of-mission marketing   A principle of enlightened marketing that holds that a company should define its mission in broad social terms rather than narrow product terms.

Sequential product development   A new-product development approach in which one company department works to complete its stage of the process before passing the new product along to the next department and stage.

Service   Any activity or benefit that one party can offer to another that is essentially intangible and does not result in the ownership of anything.

Service inseparability   A major characteristic of services—they are produced and consumed at the same time and cannot be separated from their providers, whether the providers are people or machines.

Service intangibility   A major characteristic of services—they cannot be seen, tasted, felt, heard, or smelled before they are bought.

Service perishability   A major characteristic of services—they cannot be stored for later sale or use.

Service variability   A major characteristic of services—their quality may vary greatly, depending on who provides them and when, where, and how.

Service–profit chain   The chain that links service firm profits with employee and customer satisfaction.

Shopping center   A group of retail businesses planned, developed, owned, and managed as a unit.

Shopping product   Consumer good that the customer, in the process of selection and purchase, characteristically compares on such bases as suitability, quality, price, and style.

Simultaneous (or team-based) product development   An approach to developing new products in which various company departments work closely together, overlapping the steps in the product-development process to save time and increase effectiveness.

Single-source data systems   Electronic monitoring systems that link consumers' exposure to television advertising and promotion (measured using television meters) with what they buy in stores (measured using store checkout scanners).

Slotting fees   Payments demanded by retailers before they will accept new products and place them on shelves.

Social classes   Relatively permanent and ordered divisions in a society whose members share similar values, interests, and behaviors.

Social marketing   The design, implementation, and control of programs seeking to increase the acceptability of a social idea, cause, or practice among a target group.

Societal marketing   A principle of enlightened marketing that holds that a company should make marketing decisions by considering consumers' wants, the company's requirements, consumers' long-run interests, and society's long-run interests.

Societal marketing concept   The idea that the organization should determine the needs, wants, and interests of target markets and deliver the desired satisfactions more effectively and efficiently than do competitors in a way that maintains or improves the consumer's and society's well-being.

Specialty product   Consumer product with unique characteristics or brand identification for which a significant group of buyers is willing to make a special purchase effort.

Specialty store   A retail store that carries a narrow product line with a deep assortment within that line.

Standardized marketing mix   An international marketing strategy for using basically the same product, advertising, distribution channels, and other elements of the marketing mix in all the company's international markets.

Straight product extension   Marketing a product in a foreign market without any change.

Straight rebuy   A business buying situation in which the buyer routinely reorders something without any modifications.

Strategic business unit (SBU)   A unit of the company that has a separate mission and objectives and that can be planned independently from other company businesses.

Strategic planning   The process of developing and maintaining a strategic fit between the organization's goals and capabilities and its changing marketing opportunities. It involves defining a clear company mission, setting supporting objectives, designing a sound business portfolio, and coordinating functional strategies.

Style   A basic and distinctive mode of expression.

Subculture   A group of people with shared value systems based on common life experiences and situations.

Supermarket   Large, low-cost, low-margin, high-volume, self-service store that carries a wide variety of food, laundry, and household products.

Superstore   A store much larger than a regular supermarket that carries a large assortment of routinely purchased food and nonfood items and offers services such as dry cleaning, post offices, photo finishing, check cashing, bill paying, lunch counters, car care, and pet care.

Supply chain management   Managing value-added flows of materials, final goods, and related information between suppliers, the company, resellers, and final users.

Survey research   The gathering of primary data by asking people questions about their knowledge, attitudes, preferences, and buying behavior.

Systems selling   Buying a packaged solution to a problem from a single seller, thus avoiding all the separate decisions involved in a complex buying situation.

Target costing   Pricing that starts with an ideal selling price, then targets costs that will ensure that the price is met.

Target market   A set of buyers sharing common needs or characteristics that the company decides to serve.

Tariff A tax levied by a government against certain imported products. Tariffs are designed to raise revenue or to protect domestic firms.

Team selling Using teams of people from sales, marketing, engineering, finance, technical support, and even upper management to service large, complex accounts.

Technological environment Forces that create new technologies, in turn creating new product and market opportunities.

Telephone marketing Using the telephone to sell directly to customers.

Territorial sales force structure A sales force organization that assigns each salesperson to an exclusive geographic territory in which that salesperson sells the company's full line.

Test marketing The stage of new-product development in which the product and marketing program are tested in more realistic market settings.

Third-party logistics (3PL) provider An independent logistics provider that performs any or all of the functions required to get their clients' product to market.

Transaction A trade between two parties that involves at least two things of value, agreed-upon conditions, a time of agreement, and a place of agreement.

Undifferentiated marketing A market-coverage strategy in which a firm decides to ignore market segment differences and go after the whole market with one offer.

Unsought product Consumer product that the consumer either does not know about or knows about but does not normally think of buying.

Value analysis An approach to cost reduction in which components are studied carefully to determine if they can be redesigned, standardized, or made by less costly methods of production.

Value chain The series of departments which carry out value-creating activities to design, produce, market, deliver, and support a firm's products.

Value delivery network The network made up of the company, suppliers, distributors, and ultimately customers who "partner" with each other to improve the performance of the entire system.

Value marketing A principle of enlightened marketing that holds that a company should put most of its resources into value-building marketing investments.

Value pricing Offering just the right combination of quality and good service at a fair price.

Value proposition The full positioning of a brand—the full mix of benefits upon which it is positioned.

Value-based pricing Setting price based on buyers' perceptions of value rather than on the seller's cost.

Vertical marketing system (VMS) A distribution channel structure in which producers, wholesalers, and retailers act as a unified system. One channel member owns the others, has contracts with them, or has so much power that they all cooperate.

Viral marketing The Internet version of word-of-mouth marketing—e-mail messages or other marketing events that are so infectious that customers will want to pass them along to friends.

Want The form taken by a human need as shaped by culture and individual personality.

Warehouse club Off-price retailer that sells a limited selection of brand name grocery items, appliances, clothing, and a hodgepodge of other goods at deep discounts to members who pay annual membership fees.

Web communities Web sites upon which members can congregate online and exchange views on issues of common interest.

Webcasting The automatic downloading of customized information of interest to recipients' PCs, affording an attractive channel for delivering Internet advertising or other information content.

Wheel of retailing concept A concept of retailing that states that new types of retailers usually begin as low-margin, low-price, low-status operations but later evolve into higher-priced, higher-service operations, eventually becoming like the conventional retailers they replaced.

Whole-channel view Designing international channels that take into account all the necessary links in distributing the seller's products to final buyers, including the seller's headquarters organization, channels among nations, and channels within nations.

Wholesaler A firm engaged *primarily* in wholesaling activity.

Wholesaling All activities involved in selling goods and services to those buying for resale or business use.

Credits

Chapter 1

2 Courtesy of Aaron Goodman; **7** Reprinted with permission of State of Health Products; **9** © David Young-Wolff, PhotoEdit; **13** © General Motors Media Archives; **16** © Commuter Connections, used with permission; **18** Courtesy of Gage Rob, Getty Images, Inc.; **22** Courtesy of Toby Talbot, AP/Wide World Photos; **24** Courtesy of Johnson & Johnson; **25** Courtesy of George Diebold, Corbis/Stock Market; **28** Reprinted with permission of Bank One Corporation; **31** © Lands' End, Inc., used with permission; **32** © 2001 Dell Computer Corporation and Microsoft Corporation. All rights reserved. Used with permission; **35** Courtesy of the U.S. Postal Service.

Chapter 2

42 Courtesy of Intel Corporation; **45** Courtesy of International Business Machines Corporation. Unauthorized use not permitted; **46** © 3M. All rights reserved. Reprinted with permission; **50** Courtesy of Pharmacia Corporation; **51** Courtesy of General Electric Corporation; **54** Reprinted with permission of Michael Newman/PhotoEdit; **58** Courtesy of Wal-Mart, Inc./Bill Cornett Photography; **62** Courtesy of Rolls Royce & Bentley Motor Cars, Inc., © Toyota Corporation. All rights reserved; **65** Courtesy of Bruce Ayres/Getty Images Inc.

Chapter 3

76 © Charles Schwab; **81** (Both) Courtesy of Reflect.com; **83** © Anton Vengo/SuperStock, Inc, **86** © David Young-Wolff, PhotoEdit, © Michael Newman/PhotoEdit, © SuperStock, Inc.; **88** Courtesy of Pfizer; **90** (Both) Copyright © 2001 Sun Microsystems, Inc. All rights reserved. Used by permission; **91** These materials have been reproduced with the permission of eBay, Inc. Copyright © eBay, Inc. All rights reserved; **94** © Getty Images, Inc.; **96** A. Ramey/PhotoEdit; **98** © Sony; **100** © Burpee; **103** © 2001 Mypoints.com, Inc. Used with permission; **104** © iVillage.com.

Chapter 4

116 © Volkswagen of America, Inc.; **121** Courtesy of Wal Mart; **124** © Index Stock Imagery, Inc.; **126** Courtesy of Nautica, Inc. Photograph by Mike Toth; **128** © Index Stock Imagery, Inc.; **129** Courtesy of Dan Lamont Photography; **132** Reprinted with permission of Volkswagen of America, Inc.; **135** Reprinted with permission of Business Week; **136** © Dixon Ticonderoga; **137** Courtesy of Sally Wiener Grotta/Corbis/Stock Market; **142** Courtesy of Avon Products, Inc.; **147** Courtesy of David McLain/Aurora & Quanta Productions.

Chapter 5

154 Courtesy of Roger Ressmeyer/Corbis; **155** © Tom, DeeAnn McCarthy/Corbis/Stock Market; **163** © The Dialog Corporation. Used with permission; **164** © Stern Associates; **165** © Getty Images, Inc/PhotoDisc, Inc.; **169** © 2001 Active Group. Used with permission; **170** © Greenfield Online, 2001. Used with permission; **174** Twin Vision Productions, Inc.; **175** Courtesy of SPSS Smarter CRM; **179** Courtesy of SBA; **180** © Roper Starch Worldwide Inc.

Chapter 6

190 © Harley-Davidson Motor Company. Reprinted with permission; **194** © General Mills; **195** © Charles Schwab; **198** © Warner Bros. Courtesy of Chevrolet and Warner Bros.; **200** Jeep® is a registered trademark of DaimlerChrysler Corporation; **201** © Bachmann/PhotoEdit; **203** © McCann Erickson Worldwide, Inc.; **206** Courtesy of Bozell Worldwide on behalf of the National Fluid Milk Processor Promotion Board. All rights reserved; **208** Courtesy of Bell Sports; **211** Screen Shot courtesy of 1-800-FLOWERS.com ®; **216** Courtesy of Intel Corporation; **218** © Allegiance Healthcare Corporation; © **220** 1998 Volvo Trucks North America, Inc. © RIPSAW, Inc.; **222** © L.D. Gordon/Getty Images Inc.; **226** © General Electric.

Chapter 7

234 © The Proctor & Gamble Company. Used by permission; **238** © 2001 Vans, Inc. Used with permission; **240** © Levi's, Inc.; **242** © AP/Wide World Photos; **245** Used by permission of Lowe's Companies Inc.; **246** © Neiman Marcus; **248** Courtesy of Leo Burnett; **251** © Claritas, Inc.; **253** © MTV, a division of Viacom; **257** © Oshkosh Truck; **259** © Zenobia Holiday; **261** © Volvo Corporation; **265** Courtesy of Pillsbury Europe; **267** © Mark Hanauer/ONYX, Southwest Airlines; **268** © Midwest Express Airlines, Inc.

Chapter 8

276 © Philosophy, Inc. Used with permission; **279** © Sony Corp.; **281** Metreon is a registered trademark of LTMA Inc., a business unit of Sony Corporation of America © Sony Corp.; **284** Reprinted with permission of ServiceMaster; **286** Courtesy of Save the Children; **288** © 2001 Apple, Inc. Used with permission; **289** © James Worrell Photographs/James Worrell Photography; **290** © Aaron Goodman; **292** Loblaw Brands Limited; **293** Reprinted with permission of Little Simon, an imprint of Simon & Schuster Children's Publishing Division from The Cheerios Play Book by Lee Wade; **296** © Maratha Stanitz Photography; **299** Courtesy of Gary Armstrong; **301** Trademark by H.J. Heinz Company. Reproduced with permission; **304** Rolex Watch U.S.A., Inc.; **308** © 1992 The Ritz Carlton Hotel Company. All rights reserved. Reprinted with the permission of The Ritz Carlton Hotel Company, L.L.C.; **311** © AllState Insurance Company; **313** © Mushi Ahmed Photography.

Chapter 9

320 © Corbis; **324** Robert Haller/New Products Showcase and Learning Center; **326** © 3M Corporation; **327** © Avon Corporation; **329** © Liason Agency, Inc., DaimlerChrysler Corporation; **332** Shaw Industries, Inc.; **334** Reproduced with permission of Elumens Corporation; **338** Courtesy of Hershey'®s; **341** © The Terry Wild Studio, Inc.; **344** © (Left) AP/Wide World Photos, (Right) FritoLay, Inc.

Chapter 10

352 © The Terry Wild Studio, Inc.; **355** Reprinted with permission from CNET, Inc. © Copyright 1995-2001. www.cnet.com; **357** © Four

Seasons Hotel; **358** © Swatch; **361** © Kinko's Inc.; **363** © 2001, Gibson Guitar Corp. All Rights Reserved; **368** Reprinted courtesy of Caterpillar, Inc.; **370** Courtesy of Parker Pen Company and McCann Erickson Worldwide; **372** © Dell Computer Corporation; **374** Images courtesy of Nintendo of America, Inc.; **377** Blair Seitz/Photo Researchers, Inc.; **379** © D. Young-Wolff/PhotoEdit; **382** Charles Gupton/Stock Boston; **384** Courtesy of Jean Patou, Inc.; **387** Courtesy of the Kimberly-Clark Corporation.

Chapter 11

396 Reprinted Courtesy of Caterpillar Inc.; **405** (Left) © Jan Staller/TimePix, (Right) © AP/Wide World Photos; **406** © Cereal Partners UK; **407** Reproduced with permission by International Business Machine Corporation; **412** (Left) ©Lee Lockwood/Black Star, (Right) © Michael Rizza/Stock Boston; **413** Courtesy of Bentley Motors Ltd.; **415** Charles Gupton/Stock Boston; **417** Courtesy of General Electric Corporation; **423** Courtesy of Roadway Express, Inc.; **425** © Churchill & Klehr Photography; **426** © Ryder Systems, Inc.

Chapter 12

434 Courtesy Home Depot; **440** (Left) © Bonnie Kamin/PhotoEdit, (Right) © Churchill & Klehr Photography; **442** (Left) © Bill Horsman/Stock Boston, (Right) © LearnRight Corporation; **445** © (Top) A. Ramey/PhotoEdit, (Bottom) Katherine Lambert; **448** © Peter Brandt/Getty Images, Inc.; **450** Courtesy Mall of America; **452** (Top) © Office Depot, Inc., (Bottom) © Travelocity.com; **456** © Playstation.com; **460** (Both) Courtesy of Flemming Companies, Inc.; **462** Courtesy of McKesson Corporation.

Chapter 13

468 (Both) Courtesy of American Standard; **471** (All) Courtesy of Hachette Filipacchi Magazines; **474** © Dell Computer Corporation; **477** © Jon Feingersh/Stock Boston; **481** © McNeil Consumer & Specialty Pharmaceuticals; **483** (left) Fross Zelnick Lehrman & Zissu, P.C., © 1985 V&S Vin & Sprit AB. Used by permission.,(right) Fross Zelnick Lehrman & Zissu, P.C., © 1990 V&S Vin & Sprit AB. Used by permission.; **485** (Both) Courtesy of Leo Burnett; **488** Used with permission of Volkswagen of America; **491** Michael J. Treola/AP/Wide World Photos; **494** Jeep® is a trademark of DaimlerChrysler Corporation. Web site pages are used with permission from DaimlerChrysler

Corporation; **497** Lladro Collectors Society; **498** Courtesy of Catalina Marketing; **500** © Jeff Scheid/Gamma-Liason, Inc.; **503** © John Storey Photography; **504** © Butterball a division of ConAgra Foods.

Chapter 14

512 © Lear Corporation; **514** (Left) © John Henley/Stock Market, (Right) © Gabe Palmer/Stock Market; **518** Courtesy of DuPont & Company; **519** Courtesy of Procter & Gamble; **520** © Dan Bosler/Getty Images Inc.; **523** © AP/Wide World Photos; **525** © John Coletti/Stock Boston; **528** © Rob Nelson/Black Star; **529** © American Express Incentive Services; **532** Courtesy of Advanced Sterilizations Products, a division of Ethum, Inc.; **535** © Dell Computer Corporation; **538** Courtesy of Fingerhut Companies, Inc.; **540** ©McDonald's Corporation; **542** © Frank LaBua, Inc.; **545** © Karen Leitza/Karin Leitza; **549** Courtesy of the DMA.

Chapter 15

556 © Mark Henley/Impact Photos Ltd.; **558** (Left) © Jeffrey Aaronson/Network Aspen, (Right) © Pablo Bartholomew/Getty Images, Inc.; **560** (Both) © Dell Computer Corporation; **564** ©Wesley Bocxe/The Image Works, **566** © Joseph Polleross/Regina Maria Anzenberger; **568** © Cary S Wolinsky/Cary Sol Wolinsky/Trillium Studios ; **572** © Peter Blakely/Corbis/SABA Press Photos, Inc.; **575** © Walt Disney Attractions Japan, Ltd.; **576** (Left) © Donald Dietz/Stock Boston, (Right) © D. Bartruff/The Image Works; **579** © Douglas E. Curran/Agence France-Presse; **581** (Both) © Prestige & Collections; **584** © Fritz Hoffmann/Fritz Hoffmann.

Chapter 16

592 Used with permission of Wild Planet Inc., used with permission of Honest Tea, used with permission of Village Real Estate Services, and used with permission of Worldwise; **595** © Churchill & Klehr Photography; **596** © AP/Wide World Photo; **599** (Both) © Enrico Ferorelli; **601** © AP/Wide World Photos; **602** (Both) Courtesy of the American Association of Advertising Agencies, **603** © Susan Werner/Getty Images Inc.; **605** Courtesy of the California Private Transportation Company; **608** © Campbell's Soup Company; **611** (Top) Reprinted with permission of Church & Dwight Co., Inc., (Bottom) Reprinted with permission of McDonald's Corporation; **616** Copyright 2003 General Motors Corp. Used with permission of GM Media Archives; **618** © Herman Miller, Inc.

Index

Company, Brand, and Organization Index

Note: Locators in *italics* indicate additional display material

System Requirements

PC

Pentium®-based PC or compatible processor
At least 32 MB of RAM
(64 MB for Windows® NT)
Windows® 95 or higher;
Windows®2000; Windows® ME;
Windows® NT 4.0 or higher
Sound Blaster or compatible sound card with speakers or headphones
4x or faster CD-ROM drive
Internet connection
QuickTime 4 or higher
Netscape 4.7 or Microsoft Internet
Explorer 4.01sp2 or later versions
Monitor with 800x600 resolution

Macintosh

PowerPC Processor-based Macintosh
At least 32 MB of RAM
Mac OS 7.6 or later
4x or faster CD-ROM drive
Internet connection
QuickTime 4 or higher
Netscape 4.7 or Microsoft Internet
Explorer 5 or later versions
Monitor with 800x600 resolution

Setup Instructions

FOR WINDOWS® USERS:
1. Start your computer.
2. Insert the Mastering Marketing CD into the CD-ROM drive.
3. If Mastering Marketing does not automatically start, double click the My Computer icon on your desktop.
4. Double click on the CD-ROM drive.
5. Double click the MasteringMarketing.html file.
6. Follow the instructions on the screen.
7. If you encounter any problems, see the readme file on the CD-ROM.

FOR MAC USERS:
1. Start your computer.
2. Insert the Mastering Marketing CD into the CD-ROM drive.
3. Double click on the Mastering Marketing icon on the desktop.
4. Double click the MasteringMarketing.html file.
5. Follow the instructions on the screen.
6. If you encounter any problems, see the readme file on the CD-ROM.

END-USER LICENSE AGREEMENT FOR PRENTICE HALL SOFTWARE